Effective Instruction for Students with Learning Difficulties

PATRICIA THOMAS CEGELKA

San Diego State University

WILLIAM H. BERDINE

University of Kentucky

ALLYN AND BACON

Boston   London   Toronto   Sydney   Tokyo   Singapore

We dedicate this book to our children, from whom we
have learned so much so effectively, and who have
enriched our lives so immeasurably:

Bill Cegelka
Lara Berdine
Michael Berdine

Series Editor: Ray Short
Editorial Assistant: Christine M. Shaw
Marketing Manager: Ellen Mann
Editorial-Production Service: Colophon

Composition Buyer: Linda Cox
Manufacturing Buyer: Megan Cochran
Cover Administrator: Linda Knowles
Cover Designer: Suzanne Harbison

Copyright © 1995 by Allyn and Bacon
A Simon & Schuster Company
Needham Heights, MA 02194

This textbook is printed on
recycled, acid-free paper.

Library of Congress Cataloging-in-Publication Data
Cegelka, Patricia Thomas.
    Effective instruction for students with learning difficulties /
Patricia Thomas Cegelka, William H. Berdine.
        p. cm.
    Includes bibliographical references and index.
    ISBN 0-205-16268-1
    1. Learning disabled youth—Education.   2. Teaching.
3. Behavioral assessment.   4. Learning disabled youth—Behavior
modification.. I. Berdine, William H.   II. Title.
LC4704.C44   1995
371.91—dc20   94-25105
                                                          CIP

Printed in the United States of America
10 9 8 7 6 5 4 3 2 1   00 99 98 97 96 95

Photo Credits: Chapters 1, 5, 7: Will Faller; Chapters 2, 8, 9, 12: Stephen Marks; Chapters 3, 4, 6, 10, 14: Jim Pickerell; Chapter 11: Robert Harbison; Chapter 13: Brian Smith.

Contents

PREFACE

This book is designed to help teachers work effectively with students who experience academic achievement difficulties. Today, it is estimated that these students constitute as many as 40% of the kindergarten–12 population. The reasons for their academic difficulties may be known, unknown, or hypothesized. Some of the students who fail to profit from traditional instruction come from low-income families, families headed by single parents, migrant as well as homeless families, or refugee and/or migrant backgrounds, or they have in their histories a variety of other factors that may be associated with low academic achievement. They may receive educational support from such programs as Chapter 1, Migrant Education, or others. Many students from this group may have identifiable disabilities that qualify them for special education services. The majority, however, do not.

Regardless of the factors that contribute to their students' achievement difficulties, and regardless of the categorical labels that might be attached to these students in order to qualify them for needed educational services, decades of research demonstrate that the learning challenges they present are essentially similar. This teacher effectiveness research has proved equally applicable to these students regardless of categorical or etiological considerations. Recent developments in such areas as learning strategies, integrated service delivery, and peer-mediated instruction provide new approaches for promoting the academic achievement of this population of students. What we know incontestably is that schools and teachers can make a difference. By accepting responsibility for student learning; by structuring their classrooms into positive, safe, and efficient environments; by using instructional approaches of demonstrated efficacy; and by frequently and directly measuring students' performance, teachers can make a difference. They can facilitate the learning of all students.

This textbook is designed for use in college courses on the instruction of students who are "at risk" for academic failure, both those identified for special education and those who are not but who experience similar learning challenges. The chapters are authored by leading experts in various aspects of instruction, and emphasize both the conceptual underpinnings and the pragmatic "best practices" of effective instruction for these students. The book's approach is preventative, not remedial. Its focus is on how to teach students effectively regardless of the label that might be applied to them or the setting to which they might be assigned. Included are teacher-directed and peer-mediated practices drawn from the effective teaching research literature: designing, presenting, and evaluating of lessons; instructional pacing and feedback; cooperative learning and peer tutoring; learning strategies; and metacognition. All incorporate frequent opportunities for students to respond to instruction that is efficient and effective, and that leads to attaining valid educational objectives. All are designed to elicit high task engagement by students, and to lead to mastery and fluency of that which is taught. All are presented within the context of integrated, collaborative service delivery that focuses on the achievements of all students.

Contributors

Anita L. Archer   Dr. Archer serves as an educational consultant to school districts on effective instruction, classroom management, and study skills instruction. She has taught low-performing elementary and middle school students, and has received six Outstanding Educator awards. She has been a faculty member at San Diego State University, the University of Washington, and the University of Oregon. Dr. Archer is nationally known for her presentations and publications on instructional procedures and design. Recently, she co-authored *Skills for School Success,* a study skills program for elementary and middle school students with Dr. Mary M. Gleason.

William H. Berdine   A former classroom teacher of students with moderate to severe mental retardation, Dr. Berdine is currently Chair and Director of Graduate Studies in the Department of Special Education at the University of Kentucky. In his capacity as a teacher trainer, Dr. Berdine has participated in developing and implementing a nationally recognized outcomes-based teacher training model for special education teachers in the mild learning and behavior disabilities and moderate/severe intellectual disabilities areas. His current research interests include the full inclusion of individuals with intellectual disabilities with their age mates in regular education school settings, and education reform at the state, local, and university preservice levels.

Nadine S. Bezuk   A former elementary and high school mathematics teacher, Nadine S. Bezuk is currently the Associate Director of the School of Teacher Education at San Diego State University, where she is also an associate professor of mathematics education. Dr. Bezuk is especially interested in helping all children excel in mathematics, as well as helping parents help their children learn mathematics. Her current research interests focus on preparing teachers to meet the needs of all children in mathematics.

Janis A. Bulgren   Dr. Bulgren is an Assistant Research Scientist at the University of Kansas Center for Research on Learning and the Institute for Research in Learning Disabilities. She is also Courtesy Assistant Professor in the Department of Special Education. Her research has focused on the development and use of teaching routines designed for secondary level mainstream content teachers. A former classroom teacher, Dr. Bulgren has been involved in the development of learning strategies to help students recall critical content information and content enhancement routines for teachers to use in planning and delivering instruction that is sensitive to the needs of a wide range of students' abilities. In these studies, she has worked with teachers to enhance student understanding through an in-depth analysis of a single concept, through the use of analogy, and through comparison of selected concepts. Her current research interest is in exploring ways that teachers can help students respond to reasoning tasks inherent in content class demands.

Patricia Thomas Cegelka   A former special education teacher, school psychologist, and methods and materials consultant, Dr. Cegelka has been a teacher trainer for over 25 years. A Professor of Special Education at San Diego State University, she has made the design and delivery of quality personnel preparation programs the focus of her career. Dr. Cegelka has developed several innovative model programs, each of which has as its cornerstone the empirically sound preparation of teachers to deliver effective instruction. She has written extensively in the areas of teacher preparation, career education, mental retardation, parent-professional partnerships, and ethnolinguistic diversity in special education.

Carol Sue Englert   A former resource and consulting teacher in the area of learning disabilities, Carol Sue Englert is currently a Professor of Education at Michigan State University in the Department of Counseling, Educational Psychology and Special Education. She has conducted several studies that focus on the development and enhancement of special education students' strategies in producing and comprehending expository discourse. Her more recent work involves a collaborative research project with special education teachers to design and implement an integrated literacy curriculum emphasizing the role of oral and written language in a discourse community. She teaches courses on literacy instruction and assessment in special education.

Katharine S. Furney   A former special education teacher, Katharine S. Furney is currently involved in teaching and supervising graduate students in the University of Vermont's Consulting Teacher/Learning Specialist Program, and conducting research on the effectiveness of transition policies and services. She has spent 3 years co-coordinating a model demonstration project designed to promote effective practices in transition assessment, planning, and services. Ms. Furney has developed and field-tested curricula for secondary level students with and without disabilities, in the areas of career awareness, job-seeking skills, and self-advocacy.

Mary M. Gleason   Dr. Gleason is an Associate Professor at the University of Oregon where she trains teachers of children and youth with disabilities. Dr. Gleason formerly taught elementary and middle school students in both regular and special needs classrooms. Based on her years of teaching experience and the current professional literature, she trains special education personnel in the skills of solving instructional problems in classrooms using effective instruction, well-designed curriculum materials, and good organizational skills. Dr. Gleason has conducted research and curriculum development in mathematics, reading, writing, study skills, and computer use.

Susan Brody Hasazi   A former special education teacher and administrator, Dr. Hasazi has been preparing secondary level special educators at the University of Vermont for over 15 years. As a professor at the University of Vermont, Dr. Hasazi has directed a variety of teacher preparation, model demonstration, and research projects focused on improving the transition of young adults from school to the adult community. She has written in the areas of collaborative consultation, transition policy, and secondary and vocational curriculum for students with disabilities.

Marc Hull   In his roles as the State Director of Special and Compensatory Education, Associate Professor at the University of Vermont and Texas A & M University, and special education teacher, Dr. Hull has been a leader in special education for over 20 years. To his current role as superintendent of schools in Danville, Vermont, he brings a rich background and knowledge of education administration, personnel preparation, and promising practices in transition planning and community-based instruction. Dr. Hull has collaborated with research efforts at the University of Vermont to develop, implement, and analyze statewide follow-up studies on the employment, residential, and community options available to students with disabilities. He has also written extensively in areas associated with vocational curriculum and programs.

Stephen Isaacson   Dr. Isaacson is an Associate Professor of Special Education at Western Oregon State College (Monmouth). He received his Ph.D. degree in 1985 from Arizona State University. Prior to becoming a teacher educator, Dr. Isaacson worked for several years in the public schools as both a teacher and a program specialist. He serves as a consultant to the Council for Exceptional Children's Academy for Effective Instruction and gives workshops on effective classroom instruction throughout the United States. His research interests include teacher effectiveness and written language.

B. Keith Lenz   Dr. Lenz is an Associate Research Scientist at the University of Kansas Center for Research on Learning and the Institute for Research in Learning Disabilities. He is also Courtesy Associate Professor in the Department of Special Education. Dr. Lenz directs a variety of research, development, and training projects related to adolescents and young adults with disabilities, as well as individuals judged to be at risk for school failure in the traditional school setting. Recent research has focused on how regular classroom teachers plan for individualization and inclusion, the development of planning and teaching routines for promoting student success in secondary regular classroom settings, and the development of effective learning and social strategy interventions for the *Strategies Intervention Model.* He is currently leading a project targeted at reform in how secondary teacher education efforts are organized and delivered.

Sharon Rowe Stewart   Dr. Stewart, an Associate Professor in Communication Disorders at the University of Kentucky, is a certified speech-language pathologist with a doctorate in special education. She has worked for 20 years with children with language-learning disabilities, including 4 years as a language resource teacher in the public schools. As a speech-language pathologist with training in both speech-language pathology and special education, she has been actively involved in teaching, researching, and writing, focusing on both oral and written language.

CHAPTER 1

An Overview of Effective Education for Students with Learning Problems

PATRICIA THOMAS CEGELKA

CHAPTER OBJECTIVES

At the conclusion of this chapter, the reader will be able to:
1. Identify variables associated with increasing numbers of students who are "at risk" for academic failure.
2. Describe the basic service delivery models for Chapter 1 and special education students with learning handicaps.
3. Discuss the factors that are leading to a more integrated model of service delivery.
4. Identify schoolwide variables associated with effective education.
5. Identify instructional principles associated with effective education of students who are low achieving.
6. Describe an evaluation model for determining program quality.

This book is about effective instruction for students who experience learning difficulties. Included in this group are special education students who have mild cognitive and/or behavioral disabilities as well as students who are not in special education but who have similar educational needs. It is estimated that 25%–40% of all students are experiencing significant academic difficulties. This book presents instructional approaches that have been empirically validated as effective with these students.

There are four underlying premises to this textbook. First, all children are capable of learning, and the vast majority can master the basic curricula of the schools. Second, the major mission of schools is to maximize the learning of all students, preparing them to become independent, participating and contributing citizens of our society. The third premise holds that student failure is a result of the schools' failure to adequately address student needs. This failure occurs because of deficiencies in the educational program, in the school structure, in the curriculum, and/or in the delivery of instruction. The fourth premise is that effective education can be provided to all students. Schools can be structured to effectively educate all students, including those who present special challenges, and teachers can learn empiri-

cally based instructional approaches that promote their learning and achievement.

In recent years, the educational system has encountered significant difficulties in accomplishing its mission to effectively educate all students. The fact that so many school children can be considered **at risk** for academic failure is a situation that has been attributed to a variety of societal factors. Risk factors are not causal in effect; rather, they can be viewed as probability estimates or predictors of performance of the students in which they are found. A student is considered at risk when she shares with others certain characteristics for which there is a known probability of academic difficulties and/or failure.

The majority of these at risk students are from low socioeconomic backgrounds and single-parent households. They may have parents who are unemployed or hold low-paying, transient jobs, and who themselves have minimal educational backgrounds. Approximately three-fourths of the mothers of school-age children are now in the work force, and one-fourth of all families are single-parent families. Of these, half live below the poverty level. Between one-fourth and one-third of all school-age children are latchkey children, and approximately one-fourth of the students currently enrolled in grades kindergarten through 12 will fail to complete high school (*Education Week,* 1986).

Each year, significant numbers of children arrive at school having not learned many of the behaviors and concepts associated with educational success, a situation that impedes their subsequent academic performance. Many, but not all, students who experience academic difficulties are from nonmainstream backgrounds. The National Assessment of Educational Progress (1985) found that more than 10% of students from *advantaged* backgrounds also lack the ability to read popular magazines, and 50% cannot read most newspaper stories or popular novels. Overall, school dropout rates are estimated to be from 25%–35%, with over half of all all dropouts being functionally illiterate. Among 17 year olds still in school, 13% were determined to be functionally illiterate and 44% were marginally illiterate (Reeves, 1988).

The number of children less than age 18 who come from high-risk environments will continue to increase through the early years of the 21st century (Reynolds & Lakin, 1987). This means that a growing proportion of the population may fail to acquire basic literacy skills at a time when the demands of our increasingly scientific and technological age require higher levels of abstract thinking. The potential economic costs to the nation, as well as the costs in terms of the personal self-efficacy of individuals, are enormous. In addition to the costs associated with welfare, crime prevention, unemployment, and lost tax revenues, the low skill levels of large numbers of our populace portends a decrease in national economic productivity, with adverse implications for our nation's leadership position in the community of nations.

As we prepare for the 21st century, we must provide effective education for all students, particularly those who are the most challenging. This chapter identifies the population of students who tend to have achievement difficulties, and describes current and evolving program models. It discusses administrative and instructional features of effective schools and provides an overview of the instructional skills and educational concepts pre-

sented in the following chapters of this textbook. Finally, it describes an evaluation model for quality practices in educating students with learning problems.

STUDENTS AT RISK FOR ACADEMIC FAILURE

Attempts to address these challenges have resulted in the creation of various categorical programs that target services to specific groups of students. Special education, Chapter 1, bilingual education, and migrant education are examples of such categorical programs. Each stems from federal legislation, is addressed in state legislation, and includes criteria for student eligibility and formulas for program funding. Each is grounded in a concern for groups of students who have special needs that must be addressed if they are to achieve their full potential in school as well as in the greater community.

These categorical programs were initiated beginning in the 1960s, a social action period characterized by the War on Poverty and the Great Society. Federal legislation stipulated eligibility and service delivery requirements, and set aside monies that could be used only in designated ways for students identified for the categorical services. During the following three decades, these programs grew dramatically in response to concerns over the challenges that identifiable groups of students faced.

The purposes of these special programs have been to address the conditions leading to low achievement. In many instances, the programs were compensatory or remedial in nature. This has been particularly true of special education programs for students with identifiable disabilities. Other categorical programs (bilingual education, Chapter 1, or migrant education) have been designed to address unique learning needs associated with limited English proficiency, poverty status, or migrant family lifestyles.

Many students who experience learning difficulties are identified and assigned to these categorical programs on the basis of extensive testing and assessment, consideration of family variables (e.g., income level), and teacher recommendations. However, other students who also have significant learning difficulties that lead to school failure may not meet the qualification requirements for any of the categorical programs. They continue in the regular classroom, dependent on the skills of their teacher and any additional support programs that their schools may provide.

Compensatory Education Programs

The 1960s were characterized by broad sociopolitical movements (e.g., civil rights and the War on Poverty) that focused on the entitlement of individuals to full access to opportunities within the nation. It was widely recognized that poverty, unemployment, general lack of opportunity, and similar life circumstances foreclosed many citizens from opportunities to participate fully in the American Dream. The prevailing political wisdom deemed these problems be addressed through federally designed programs designed to extend equality of opportunity to individuals who were considered environmentally "disadvantaged." The intent of these programs was to improve the probability of educational success of students from low-income families by compensating for these environmental disadvantages. Project Head Start targeted young children from low-income families, providing preschool programs to improve their mental processes and skills. Subsequent Follow Through programs were funded in an effort to build upon the gains made through Head Start programs, extending the educational support to these children through Grade 3. Extensive research on the efficacy of Follow Through constituted some of the earliest efforts to document what today are generally referred to as effective educational practices, the instructional approaches and methodologies emphasized throughout this text.

Title 1 provisions of the 1965 Elementary and Secondary Education Act provided fiscal support to school districts heavily impacted by high numbers of students from low-income homes. **Title 1 programs** attempted to compensate for presumed environmental deficits associated with poverty and to help educationally deprived students catch up with their peers. In 1981, these programs were restructured under the Education and Consolidation and Improvement Act, and Title 1 became known as Chapter 1. At the same time, steps were taken to ensure that only students who were both low achieving from low-income homes received services and that these services were clearly supplemental to those already provided in the regular classroom (Stein, Leinhardt, & Bickel, 1989). The majority of students who have received Chapter 1 services have been in grades kindergarten through 8, poor, and from either African-American or Hispanic families (Slavin, 1989)

Under federal program regulations, five models of Chapter 1 service delivery emerged: (1) pull-out, (2) in-class, (3) add-on, (4) replacement, and (5) schoolwide (Slavin, 1989). Each of these is summarized as follows:

1. **Pull-out programs.** Students are "pulled out" of their regular classrooms to receive 20–40 minutes of remedial instruction in identified academic area(s). This instruction typically is provided by a designated Chapter 1 teacher in a Chapter 1 classroom setting of eight or fewer students.
2. **In-class programs.** In this model, the Chapter 1 teacher, or an instructional aide directed by that teacher, works directly with eligible students in the classroom setting to which the students are regularly assigned.
3. **Add-on programs.** Additional services outside of the regular school program are provided. Examples include summer school programs, after-school programs, and pre-kindergarten or extended day kindergarten programs.
4. **Replacement programs.** In this model, eligible students are served in self-contained Chapter 1 classrooms. District funds support the basic costs of these classrooms, with Chapter 1 monies supporting the excess costs.

5. **Schoolwide programs.** This option is available to schools in which at least 75% of the population qualify for Chapter 1 services due to the extreme poverty and underachievement of the student body.

The most typical model of Chapter 1 service delivery has been the pull-out program. This model clearly meets the "supplement, not supplant" requirement that Chapter 1 monies not be used to fund programs that are provided to non-Chapter 1 students out of district funding. As depicted in Figure 1.1, most pull-out services have been in the areas of reading, mathematics, and/or language development.

Special Education Programs

The 1960s also saw a phenomenal growth in special education programs for students with identifiable disabilities. While prior to this time the majority of special education programs had been designed for students with mild mental retardation, during this decade, program provisions expanded to offer classes to students with more severe levels of mental retardation as well as to students with learning disabilities. However, serving students with disabilities was discretionary on the part of the schools, and frequently these students were excluded from the public schools or were admitted but not provided with any special services.

PL 94-142, the Education for All Handicapped Children Act, enacted in 1975, revolutionized educational services for students with disabilities. Special education services became an entitlement for these populations of students. In addition to mandating free, appropriate education for all children with handicapping conditions, this law addressed the importance of nonbiased assessment, broad-based assessment and team planning, parental participation in the education decision-making process, and placement in the least restrictive environment consistent with the educational needs of the student. The development of individualized educational programs for students was mandated

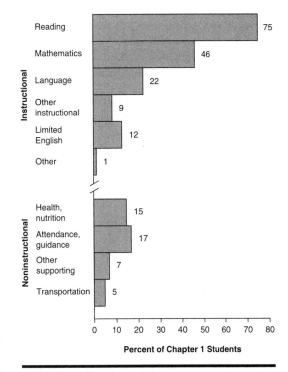

FIGURE 1.1 Services Received by Chapter 1 Students: Percentages for Each Service
Source: Kennedy et al. (1986).

as were periodic reviews of student progress and eligibility. Provision also was made for including needed related services, for example, counseling, occupational therapy, adapted physical education, speech pathology, physical therapy, and social work. The implementation of this law greatly expanded the availability and improved the quality of educational services to students with disabilities.

In 1990, PL 94-142 was amended by the Individuals with Disabilities Education Act, PL 101-476, commonly referred to as **IDEA.** These amendments placed a strong emphasis on preparing students for transition into adulthood and on meeting the needs of special education students from diverse ethnolinguistic backgrounds. Further, IDEA added two categories to the previous list of eleven that may qualify students for special education.

Categories of Disability

There are now twelve categories of disability that may qualify a student for special education services. These are depicted as follows:

1. Specific learning disabilities
2. Speech or language impairments
3. Mental retardation
4. Serious emotional disturbance
5. Multiple disabilities
6. Hearing impairments
7. Orthopedic impairments
8. Other health impairments
9. Visual impairments
10. Deaf-blindness
11. Autism
12. Tramautic brain injury

Eligibility for special education services requires that a given student be formally classified as having one of these disabilities. The final determination for special education eligibility is based on the extent to which the identified disability interferes with the student's educational progress. Both criteria must be met: disability classification and special educational needs.

The learning problems are relatively mild for the vast majority of students identified for special education. These students qualify for special education due to mild mental retardation, learning disabilities, or behavior disorders. *Mild mental retardation* refers to intellectual functioning that is approximately 2 standard deviations below the mean of an individual, standardized test of intelligence and that is accompanied by deficits in adaptive behavior (Grossman, 1983). To be considered as *learning disabled,* a student typically is of average or above-average intelligence, and has a discrepancy between potential and academic achievement that is educationally significant and is not the result of environmental, cultural, or economic factors, or any other form of disability. A student who is labeled as having serious *emotional disturbances* or behavioral disorders is one who chronically and signifi-

cantly exhibits behaviors that are socially unacceptable and/or personally unsatisfying (Kauffman, 1981).

Although these are considered to be separate conditions, many educators have come to question the utility of attempting to differentiate students into these separate categories (Ysseldyke, 1987). The students appear to be essentially similar in regard to such factors as etiology and learning characteristics, and to benefit from its same educational and related intervention approaches. While federal and many state regulations still require the categorical identification of these students, increasingly less categorical terminology and service delivery systems have evolved. Terms such as *mild handicapping conditions,* or *learning and behavior disorders,* or *learning handicapped* are now used to identify students who have mild mental retardation, behavior disorders, and/or learning disabilities. In this text, the more generic terms of learning difficulties, learning problems, learning handicaps, and mild cognitive disabilities are used interchangeably. In some specific instances, the term *learning disabilities* also is used. This is done to mirror the language of a given research study being discussed. If such a study was done with a particular categorical grouping of students, the categorical designation used in the study is also used in this text. However, we propose that the preponderance of research demonstrating the efficacy of instructional programs and approaches with one category of disability is generalizable to other categories of mild cognitive disabilities as well as to the broader group of academically at risk or low-achieving students.

Service Delivery Models

Special education, by law, provides a full continuum of services, ranging from fully segregated to fully-integrated with resource support to the regular class teacher. Since the passage of PL 94-142, the field has been moving steadily away from the more segregated settings of special schools and special day classes, particularly for students with mild disabilities. Increasingly, these students have come to be served in resource room pull-out programs. Typically, these programs have been remedial or tutorial at the elementary level, with secondary programs either continuing to provide remedial and tutorial support or offering separate academic classes for students with learning handicaps. In recent years, the efficacy of this approach has been questioned. Criticisms of the pull-out approach, applicable to both special education and compensatory education approaches, can be summarized into six categories of concern: (1) instructional fragmentation, (2) time erosion, (3) oversight responsibility for the individual teacher, (4) ownership of educational services, (5) procedural requirements, and (6) student outcomes (Stein et al., 1989).

Instructional fragmentation can be a problem with the pull-out approach. Due to scheduling difficulties and lack of coordination between the two teachers, students may receive duplicate instruction in some areas of the curriculum and no instruction in others. For example, students may be pulled out for assistance in reading during math, social studies, or science class. This can mean that an entire curriculum area is omitted or shortchanged. Further, students may receive remedial instruction that is inconsistent with and unrelated to the instruction of the regular classroom. This makes generalization of skills acquired in the remedial setting to the regular curriculum improbable, particularly if the two teachers do not communicate about what each is doing with the student.

Time erosion occurs because of the amount of time that students spend in transition from one activity and one classroom to another. Not only do students spend time physically moving from setting to setting, but they also lose time closing down one task and then settling in to work in the next. Further erosion of time occurs if the pace of instruction in the remedial setting is slow or if the

teacher focuses on lower-level skills, two characteristics that have been documented for many remedial settings.

Within a given class, multiple children may be pulled out to receive specialized services several times a day. This can be a managerial headache for the teacher, who may be unable to devise a class schedule that accommodates all students. Just keeping track of who is coming and going can be a challenge. This may result in a *diluted sense of responsibility* for a given student on the part of the regular class teacher. Not only will no one teacher "be on top of" the program the student is receiving or the progress he is making, but the child may fail to identify with a single, caring adult (Slavin, 1987) and may feel limited identification with the homeroom class. The departmentalized nature of the special services, which typically are administered out of the central office of the school district, can reduce the school principal's sense of program ownership and responsibility. As Stein et al. (1989) pointed out, this disempowerment is ironic given recent research evidence on the importance of the leadership provided by site principals. The special program may be viewed as a "stepchild" within the school, receiving little attention from the principal or consideration in schoolwide resource planning and scheduling. Furthermore, the *procedural regulations* and stipulations regarding how monies must be used, and the types of forms and reports that must be filed can strain relationships between regular class and remedial teachers and between site administrators and district program directors.

While the foregoing considerations are of relevance, the primary issue relates to the extent to which the pull-out model positively impacts on student achievement. Research into the efficacy of special education (Madden & Slavin, 1989) and of Chapter 1 (Carter, 1984) has failed to support meaningful differential effects of these models.

Collaborative consultation models evolved in response to many of these concerns. In this service delivery model, students remain in the regular classroom, with the special services personnel providing support to the classroom teacher. Resource teachers serve as consultants to the regular class teachers, helping them to devise instructional strategies and programs, identify materials, and so forth. Additionally, the special education teacher or aide may provide individual or small-group instruction to special needs students in the regular classroom. This team teaching or side-by-side teaching serves to increase the instructional resources available in the classroom.

Another new direction has been to focus the role of the special education teacher, particularly at the secondary school level, on teaching students learning strategies that they can apply across content areas. Lower-achieving students typically are less spontaneous in generating and/or using such strategies. By directly teaching students strategies on how to learn new material and approach classroom assignments, special education teachers strive to enhance knowledge and skill acquisition, while at the same time maintaining them in the regular school curriculum.

These new directions have developed in large part due to dissatisfaction with the outcomes of self-contained, segregated special education services. Decades of research data have failed to unequivocally support the efficacy of either special day classes or pull-out programs. Further, both philosophical and legal considerations call for educating students with disabilities in the least restrictive environment and providing them with full access to the core curriculum of the schools. Finally, few educationally relevant differences appear between students who have mild cognitive disabilities, and therefore are eligible for special education, and other students who are similarly low-achieving, but who are not identified for special education. Ysseldyke (1987, p. 264) observed that educators have a difficult time "of differentiating low-achieving and mildly handicapped students, of sorting from all those students who are experiencing difficulties in school

those to be labeled handicapped and given special education services."

In addition, the instructional practices found to be effective with one subgroup of students are essentially identical to those effective with other students who encounter learning difficulties. Characteristics of effective educational programs for students who experience learning difficulties, regardless of categorical grouping, include accommodation of instruction to individual needs, high levels of teacher-directed instruction, articulated instructional goals, and a brisk instructional pace with frequent opportunities for student responses. Ultimately, good teaching and a high regard for the potential of individual students typify effective educational practices.

The focus of evolving models for integrated or more inclusive service delivery is on improving the capacity of schools to more effectively provide for all students. Current innovations in program structure are experimenting with collapsing categorical barriers to providing support services to students who need them—special education students, Chapter 1 students, bilingual education students, and so forth. Chapter 2 describes these less categorical approaches to delivering effective education. Included is an overview of collaborative consultation, coordinated service delivery, and prereferral intervention. The thrust of each of these innovations is to design school programs that are viable and effective for all students.

ACHIEVING EFFECTIVE SCHOOLS

A plethora of recommendations for improving schools and increasing student achievement have been proposed by various educational reform groups. These recommendations tend to fall into one of the following three categories: (1) school-wide practices; (2) changes in the scope, structure, and focus of the curriculum; and (3) the identification and implementation of more powerful and effective instructional strategies. In the paragraphs that follow, each of these categories of educational change is outlined.

Schoolwide Considerations

Administrative considerations have focused on the structure and climate of the schools, and on increased professionalism for educators. Slavin (1989) and Ogden and Germinario (1988) summarized schoolwide factors characteristic of effective education to include the following:

- **Positive learning climate.** Orderly classrooms; high expectations for student achievement and behavior; a pleasant physical environment; well-established rules; emphasis on maximizing instructional time.
- **An academic emphasis with clear goals and objectives.** Emphasis on basic skills and an academic curriculum; input from parents and staff; clearly articulated and publicly communicated goals; objectives and assessment procedures aligned to the curriculum.
- **Strong leadership.** Strong instructional leadership by principal with top priority on student learning; focuses on school goals; motivates staff.
- **Systematic staff development and training.** A well-conceptualized program of professional development which focuses on research-based effective practices and involves meaningful opportunities, follow-up, and incentives.
- **Formative evaluation of programs.** Ongoing systematic monitoring of student achievement by principal and teachers; evaluation of program processes and outcomes; use of evaluation results to modify and improve programs.

These recommendations strongly endorse the potential of a positive learning climate in successful schools. An additional element of such a climate is respect and accommodation for the cultural and linguistic diversity of students (Edmonds, 1986). This is a critical consideration for the effective education of students with learning problems, given the high proportion of these students who are from diverse cultural, racial, and/or linguistic backgrounds.

School Curriculum

Educational reform efforts targeted at school curriculum have emphasized the identification of a common core of knowledge and skills, and the specification of higher standards of student performance within the curriculum. Responding to concerns about a fragmented, incoherent, and limited curriculum, efforts have been made to identify the core of

> . . . ideas, experiences, and traditions common to all of us by virtue of our membership in the human family at a particular moment in history. These shared experiences include our use of symbols, our sense of history, our membership in groups and institutions, our relationship to nature, our need for well-being, and our growing dependence on technology. (Boyer, 1983, p. 95).

This culturally unifying body of knowledge is viewed as revolving around a common set of concepts of history, literature, science, mathematics, civics, and drama that serve to broaden our sense of shared tradition and heritage. By specifying curriculum content and setting performance or proficiency standards, state and local educational agencies have standardized much of the curriculum across schools and districts. At the same time, requirements for graduation for secondary schools have increased, both in terms of the total number of courses required and the number of "difficult" academic courses that a student must complete. While these changes undoubtedly have resulted in increased academic attainment for some, critics have expressed concern that these higher standards, particularly where there may be little change in the instructional approaches used or the support systems employed, may have unintended effects of increasing the failure rate of the lower quartile or so of the student population.

Another concern is that the core may exclude important curriculum arenas that, if included, could decrease the potential for failure for at risk students. Examples are life skills curricula in the areas of personal growth and social skills (communication, social interaction, decision-making skills), sex education, drug education, and physical education (Ogden and Germinario, 1988). Well-developed curricula in these areas have the potential of enhancing overall student efficacy in both school and community arenas.

Attention also has been paid to reducing failure for students through the process of analyzing given curricula and selecting for instruction only the most salient and critical skill and knowledge components. By selecting for instruction only those aspects of a curriculum that are of relevance to future instruction and to the future success of the student, teachers can increase the amount of instructional focus on these components, thereby increasing student success. In other words, teachers should strive to eliminate the idiosyncratic and nonessential bits of skills and knowledge that encroach on instructional time and dilute instructional focus.

More recently, curriculum change has been addressed from an additional perspective. A sound conceptual understanding of underlying principles and relationships is necessary if students are to develop the kinds of abstract thinking skills needed to address the complex issues of a technological society. Educators have been designing conceptually based discovery approaches to shift the focus of instruction away from rote learning of segmented bits of information. Curricular content areas are being analyzed with an emphasis on how particular topics can be organized, represented and adapted to the diverse interests and abilities of individual learners, and presented for instruction (Shulman, 1987). This marriage of pedagogical reasoning to the structure of content, referred to as *pedagogical content knowledge,* is a promising direction for enhancing overall instructional efficacy within a framework that is responsive to individual diversity. It also presents special challenges for students who are low achieving. Research has shown that students who are low achieving and/or from lower socioeconomic classes require more structure from their teachers, more teacher-directed instruction; and more redundancy (Brophy, 1984). These students also need more explanation of the lesson content in order to generate the meanings necessary for understanding (Presseisen, 1988).

Effective Instructional Strategies

Systematic research and analysis have led to identifying an impressive array of classroom variables that are associated with effective educational programs. As a result, much is now known about instructional strategies that work with all students, including those who are difficult to teach. In a review of programs specifically designed for students at risk for academic failure, Slavin and Madden (1989, p. 45) found that "Consistently effective classroom programs accommodate instruction to individual needs while maximizing direct instruction, and they frequently assess student progress through a structured hierarchy of skills." They went on to emphasize that accommodating individual student needs within the context of teacher-directed instruction is of particular importance for students who are at risk for academic failure. They identified within-class ability grouping as an efficient strategy for such accommodation in that it provides teachers the opportunity to work with three to four small groups of students, presenting lessons at different levels of instructional difficulty appropriate to the students' needs. Specifying a structured hierarchy of skills for students to master was another common feature of effective programs. Using cooperative learning groups also was associated with program efficacy. It is important to note that such groups do not provide initial instruction (the teacher does), but the groups do provide expanded opportunities for students to be actively engaged in learning, to discuss and explain concepts, to help one another, and to work toward common goals and rewards. Finally, frequent assessment of student progress for the purposes of planning and modifying instruction was an attribute of effective educational programs for students at risk for academic failure.

Much of what has been documented through teacher effectiveness research is basically common sense. For example, it is not surprising that research has documented that classroom teachers play a critical role in the academic achievement of their students. No matter how well conceptualized and packaged, curriculum materials in and of themselves are insufficient. The key variable is the teacher. Specific types of teacher behaviors are associated with effective educational outcomes across categorical programs. One of the most critical attributes of effective teachers is the high level of expectations that they hold for their students. They communicate these expectations through their emphasis on academic instruction, their verbal and nonverbal communications with students, and the extent to which they structure their classroom to promote on-task behavior and efficient learning on the part of students.

Instructional features of effective programs for students who are low achieving include teacher-directed instruction that is delivered in small, homogeneous groups and is responsive to individual student differences, clear instructional objectives, and constant assessment of students' progress and needs accompanied by specific procedures to remediate any small problems before they grow into large ones (Stein et al., 1989). Lloyd (1987) identified a similar set of underlying features common to effective instruction with students who have learning disabilities. He suggests that the following features become the basic technology of academic interventions with students with learning difficulties:

1. Maximizing instructional time through utilization of small groups.
2. Previewing prior learning.
3. Establishing and communicating a clear goal for instruction.
4. A brisk instructional pace and high rate of progress through carefully sequencing concepts and skills.
5. Active student responding, with mastery of each step before proceeding to the next.
6. Introducing lessons by gaining the students' attention and communicating the instruction goal.

7. Explicit modeling or demonstration of the targeted behaviors.
8. Pointing out distinctive features and giving examples as well as nonexamples.
9. Providing for high levels of successful practice, defined by accuracy levels of 80% or higher.
10. Careful monitoring of performance.
11. Providing immediate teacher feedback and correction.
12. Closing the lesson by reviewing the skills/concepts covered, previewing the next day's lesson, and/or assigning independent seatwork or homework if the students can work independently on the particular skills at a 90% or higher accuracy level.
13. Implementing brief, smooth transitions between lessons.
14. Maintaining continuous records of student performance.

A significant aspect of these instructional features is that "they tend not to vary across programs or settings, and features which are found to be effective are effective in both compensatory and special education contexts [and] do not seem to be tied to specific types of low-achieving children or to specific settings. . . . "(Stein, et al, 1989, p. 160).

Research continues to support the efficacy of teacher-directed instruction in teaching basic academic skills, school skills, and content. Direct instructional techniques appear to focus the instruction, ensuring that teachers are teaching what is supposed to be taught. They teach component skills sequentially and elicit high levels of active responding from their students. These are all practices found to be particularly effective with students who have achievement problems.

In recent years, there has been a trend toward employing nondirective discovery-based approaches to instruction as a means of encouraging higher-order thinking skills. These discovery approaches are termed **constructivist**, implying that they help the learners to construct knowledge through the self-regulated transformation of old knowledge to new knowledge (Poplin, 1988). In this way, they are thought to elicit "true understanding" of a type not available through more teacher-directed instruction.

The research on constructivist approaches has not addressed the unique needs of students with learning difficulties, however. Indeed, as Harris and Pressley (1991) have pointed out, even with more capable learners, true discovery is rare, inefficient, and time consuming. There is insufficient time for all students to discover all that they need to know, discovery may contain many errors, and in any given class, only a small proportion of students may make most of the discoveries (Resnick, 1987).

There may be less of a dichotomy between the two theoretical approaches than some purport. Harris and Pressley (1991, p. 393) concluded that " . . . educators need not choose between constructed and instructed knowledge, but, rather, recognize that active mental construction is a part of all human learning and instruction . . . " The explicit, direct instruction of procedures by which students can access knowledge provides for efficient, effective, and meaningful knowledge acquisition. Among these procedures are cognitive learning strategies that can empower students to regulate their own learning. Throughout the text, learning strategies are described as tools that promote both the academic attainment and learning independence of students. Learning strategies are described separately and in some detail in Chapters 9 and 13, while the chapters that deal with teaching reading and spelling (Chapter 10), teaching written expression (Chapter 11), and teaching mathematics (Chapter 12) each incorporate aspects of learning strategy instruction. In these chapters, teacher-direct instruction is used to teach both lower-order skills and learning strategies. The latter provide the processes and concepts by which students can acquire the higher cognitive understandings (Isaacson, 1989).

OVERVIEW OF TEXT

As indicated by its title, this text focuses on instructional strategies demonstrated to be effective with low-achieving students. The text describes empirically based approaches to identifying, assessing, and managing student behavior; to designing and delivering instruction; to teaching learning strategies, basic skills, and content area subjects; and to preparing students for transition into adult life. These powerful instructional strategies that can facilitate the academic and personal development of students who experience achievement difficulties in both regular or special education classrooms. The context for delivering much of this instruction is within a collaborative environment in which various educational programs and personnel work together to promote student learning. Chapter 2 describes this context.

The teaching strategies described in this text are those that research has demonstrated to be effective with both sets of students as well as with the more typical or "average" students who do succeed well academically. While all students benefit from powerful, effective instructional strategies, students with learning problems *must* receive such instruction if they are to succeed in school. Each of the following thirteen chapters deals with an important component of effective instructional practices. Objectives at the beginning of each chapter describe the skills and knowledge that the reader should have attained after reading the chapter. Mastery content questions at the end of each chapter reflect the chapter objectives.

Chapter Previews

There are several recurring themes interwoven throughout the chapters. One unifying theme is the collaboration of professional staff across classes and programs. Another is an emphasis on observable school behaviors and active, teacher-directed instruction. The importance of prior planning and preparation by classroom teachers is a consistent value, as is delivery of instruction in small groups. Constantly assessing student progress is a recurring strand that focuses on using individual student performance data as the basis for modifying instructional efforts. As described previously, learning strategy instruction is another common theme. The instructional goals underlying all of the chapters include improved student outcomes, generalization of skills to other environments, and increased competence and independence.

Chapter 2 describes the integrated context in which the instruction of students with learning difficulties can occur. It emphasizes collaborative consultation and prereferral intervention approaches. Chapter 3 presents the technical tools required for observing and analyzing behavior, developing behavioral objectives, and recording behavioral data. Chapter 4 overviews approaches to assessing student behavior for the purpose of making educationally relevant decisions. It emphasizes the use of individual student data derived from curriculum-based assessment (CBA) for making important decisions about student instruction.

Building on the technical skills developed in Chapters 3 and 4, Chapter 5 describes techniques and procedures for systematically analyzing and changing behavior. These are built upon the principles of applied analysis of behavior that have evolved over decades of research on the relationship of behavior to the stimuli that surround it. Chapter 6 focuses on developing classroom structures that promote the social and academic learning of all students.

Chapter 7 describes effective approaches for structuring and presenting lessons. This chapter expands on the principles involved in establishing effective learning environments by highlighting strategies to increase the task engagement and content mastery of students. Chapter 8 describes various approaches to accommodating individual differences. Chapter 9 focuses on the variety of skills that students must acquire in order to be successful in school. This chapter identifies these behaviors as those relating to: (1) organizing materials for class, for example, bringing pencils and paper, and remembering to hand in homework; (2) organizing and managing time, for example, keeping track of due dates and exam dates; and (3) organizing content of assignments, for example, format or structure of content, and neatness of finished paper. Chapter 9 emphasizes the strategic approaches for achieving success and independence as a student.

Chapters 10–12 focus on teaching basic skills: reading and spelling, written expression, and mathematics. They emphasize instruction of the component skills, strategies for becoming self-directed learners, underlying comprehension and motivation, as well as ultimately becoming independent learners. Chapter 13 presents approaches for enhancing student learning in content classes at the secondary school level. This chapter reviews the strategies intervention model curriculum specifically designed for older students and presents approaches that teachers can use to make content more accessible to students. Chapter 14 discusses aspects of transition from secondary schools to adulthood.

DETERMINING EFFECTIVENESS OF EDUCATIONAL PRACTICES

Improving educational practice is an important educational goal at all levels—national, state, district, school, and individual student. Over the past 15-plus years, educational researchers across the nation have made great strides in identifying effective practices. The most salient of these are presented in this textbook. However, our notions about effective practices is not static. It is, instead, dynamic, changing in response to new innovations and new environmental demands. Our goal as educators must be to constantly search out, test, and utilize effective strategies and procedures.

Quality educational programs are those in which the teachers, administrators, and related staff continually evaluate the efficacy of the practices they use. Careful monitoring of educational outcomes provides information upon which to consider changing educational practices, and/or adopting new practices and innovations. The potential changes could involve minor tinkering with specific aspects of instruction, or major innovations and reforms. The key question that should guide us as educators is always, "Are we achieving the outcomes targeted?"

The Model for Program Quality, developed by the California Task Force on Program Effectiveness, is one approach to implementing continuous cycles of evaluation. Presented in Figure 1.2 (Cegelka et al., 1988), this model views effective education not as something to be *accomplished,* but rather as a continuous state of *achieving.* Its focus is on the continuous evaluation of student outcomes, for example, the extent to which students are acquiring the targeted knowledge and skills. Unlike the univariate, "one-shot" models of evaluation (e.g., standardized achievement tests) that provide infrequent, generalized indices of student performance at a single point in time, the program quality model provides for frequent, criterion-specific and curriculum-specific indices of effectiveness.

Outcome data are collected using procedures consistent with the curriculum-based assessment methods described in Chapter 4. The outcome data are then cycled back to the planning stage, where the educator makes decisions about the potential need for change. As presented, the model limits its consideration to those three areas most directly and closely related to student instruction: (1) instructional settings, (2) the curriculum, and (3) the instructional processes or strategies. Class-

room teachers also have the most direct influence over these variables.

Should the outcome data suggest that program changes are in order, either because current approaches are not working or because new ones might work more effectively and efficiently, then alternatives are designed at the planning stage. These are implemented through program delivery, with new evaluation data once again being cycled back to the planning stage as the basis for determining future program directions. These cycles should occur relative to the planning and delivery of programs at the individual student level, the classroom level, the school-site level, and the district level, as well as state and national levels.

Although Figure 1.2 depicts only a single planning and evaluation cycle, educators should think in terms of multiple, overlapping cycles. At the individual student level, for example, planning and evaluation includes, but is not limited to, the annual individualized educational program (IEP) cycle. Certain goals require weekly or even daily planning and evaluation cycles. Similarly, at the school-site level, goals having to do with

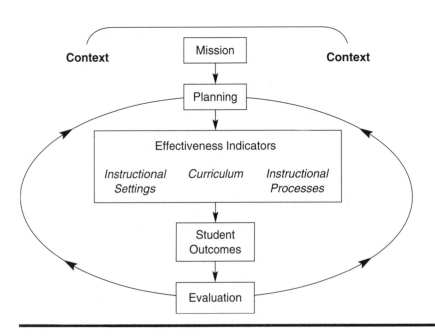

FIGURE 1.2   Conceptual Model for Quality Special Education

school climate could be incorporated, again with student outcome data as the dependent variable. Because goals such as this are not likely to be appropriately implemented if they are reviewed only annually, more frequent (e.g., monthly) cycles of evaluation should address these concerns. In other words, planning and evaluation should be a central feature of all educational endeavors, with the duration of the planning and evaluation cycles being appropriate to the questions being addressed.

Whenever program evaluation data reveal that programs are not attaining targeted student outcomes, or are not doing so within a reasonable time period, educators should search out new practices that can be tailored to the specific setting or situation. Ongoing evaluation of student outcomes provides a basis for determining how long these new practices should be continued. By approaching education from an experimental frame of mind, always asking "How well does this work?" educators can identify the most effective practices for teaching all students, including those who may experience low academic achievement due to learning handicaps or other challenges.

SUMMARY

This book is designed to assist teachers in working effectively with students who are low-achieving. It describes educational practices that are known to be effective with students identified for special education services as well as other students who evidence similar learning difficulties. Increasingly, educators have come to recognize the similarities of these students and to embrace the notion that an identifiable set of instructional practices is effective regardless of the categorical label that may or may not be applied to the student.

The methods and strategies presented in the remaining chapters of this textbook have been empirically documented through research across a broad array of student groups. This "effective instruction research" emphasizes the importance of teacher-directed instruction that is systematic in design and delivery, and that takes place within an environment that is well structured and positive in tone. The instruction must actively engage the student; elicit frequent responses from all students; and provide modeling, corrective feedback, guided practice, and frequent reviews. The importance of data collection based on actual student performance is emphasized throughout this book. Such data can be used to plan day-to-day instruction, assess student progress over time, and evaluate the effectiveness of the program provided.

This instruction is best delivered within a framework that is collaborative in nature. Across classrooms and categorical programs, teachers are most effective if they can work together, sharing their expertise to provide programs that are highly qualitative in design and consistent across settings. Increasingly, mandates for full inclusion of students within the least restrictive school environment are promoting cooperation among teachers and programs. Chapter 2 extends the discussion of collaborative service delivery, describing a collaborative consultation framework within which teachers can work together, with other professionals, and with the parents and families of their students, to better provide optimal educational opportunities for all students.

CONTENT MASTERY QUESTIONS _____

1. Identify societal factors that are contributing to the increasing numbers of students considered to be "at risk" for academic failure.

2. What have been common features and problems of special education and compensatory education programs?

3. Describe four categories of schoolwide practices that are associated with effective schools.

4. In what ways has the movement toward upgrading the core curriculum affected students with learning problems? What are possible effects of higher standards and the omission of less academic subjects (e.g., life skills, social skills)?

5. Identify six instructional practices that have been empirically validated for students with learning difficulties.

6. What is the purpose of continually monitoring both pupil progress and program effectiveness?

REFERENCES

Boyer, L. L. (1983). *High school: A report on secondary education in America.* New York: Harper & Row, Publishers.

Brophy, J. (1984). *Research linking teacher behavior to student achievement.* East Lansing, MI: Institute for Research on Teaching.

Carter, L. F. (1984). The sustaining effects of compensatory and elementary education. *Educational Researcher, 13*(7), 4–13.

Cegelka, P. T., Traupmann, K., Grisafe, J., et al. (1988). *Model for program quality in special education: The program effectiveness in special education task force report.* Sacramento, CA: Resources in Special Education.

Demographics and the at-risk population. *Education Week, 5,* 14–16, 18–21.

Eaton, W. (1981). Demographic and social-ecologic risk factors for mental disorders. In D. Regier & A. Gordon (Eds.), *Risk factor research in the major mental disorders.* Washington, D.C.: U.S. Department of Health and Human Services (ADM 81-1086).

Edmonds, R. (1986). Characteristics of effective schools. In U. Neisser (Ed.), *The school achievement of minority children: New perspectives.* (pp. 93–104). Hillsdale, NJ: Lawrence Erlbaum.

Grossman, H. J. (Ed.) (1983). *Classification in mental retardation.* Washington, DC: American Association on Mental Deficiency.

Harris, K. R., & Pressley, M. (1991). The nature of cognitive strategy instruction: Interactive strategy construction. *Exceptional Children, 57*(5), 392–404.

Isaacson, S. (1989). Confused dichotomies: A response to DuCharme, Earl and Populin. *Learning Disability Quarterly 12,* 243–247.

Kauffman, J. M. (1981). *Characteristics of children's behavior disorders.* (2nd Ed.). Columbus, OH: Merrill.

Kennedy, M. M., Birman, B. F., & Demaline, E. E. (1986). The effectiveness of Chapter 1 services. Washington, D.C.: Office of Educational Research and Improvement, U.S. Department of Education, p. 2.

Lloyd, K. W. (1987). Direct academic interventions in learning disabilities. In R. E. Slavin, N. L. Karweit, & N. A. Madden (Eds.). *Effective programs for students at risk.* (pp. 52–71). Boston, MA: Allyn & Bacon.

National Assessment of Educational Progress (1985). *The reading reportcard: Progress toward excellence in our schools: trends in reading over four national assessments, 1971–1984.* Princeton, NJ: NAEP.

Ogden, E. H., & Germinario, V. (1988). *The at-risk student: Answers for educators.* Lancaster, PA: Technomic.

Poplin, M. S. (1988). Holistic/constructivist principles of the teaching/learning process: Implications for the field of learning disabilities. *Journal of Learning Disabilities, 21*(7), 401–416.

Presseisen, B. S. (1988). Teaching thinking and at-risk students: Defining the population. In B. S. Presseisen (Ed.), *At-risk students and thinking: Perspectives from research.* Washington, D.C.: National Education Association and Research for Better Schools.

Reeves, M. S. (1988). Self-interest and the common weal: Focusing on the bottom half. *Education Week,* pp. 14–16, 18–21.

Resnick, L. B. (1987). Constructing knowledge in school. In L. S. Liben (Ed.). *Development and learning: Conflict or congruence?* (pp. 19–50). Hillsdale, NJ: Lawrence Erlbaum.

Reynolds, M. C., & Lakin, K. C. (1987). Noncategorical special education: Models for research and practice. In M. C. Wang, M. C. Reynolds, and H. J. Walberg (Eds.), *Handbook of special education: Research and practice. Vol. 1.* (pp. 331–356). Oxford, England: Pergamon Press.

Shulman, L. S. (1987). Knowledge and teaching: Foundations of the new reform. *Harvard Educational Review* (Special Issue: Teaching in the Eighties: A need to change), 1–22.

Slavin, R. E. (1987). Grouping for instruction in elementary school. *Educational Psychologist, 22,* 109–127.

Slavin, R. E. (1989). Students at risk of school failure: The problem and its dimensions. In R. E. Slavin, N. L. Karweit, & N. A. Madden (Eds.), *Effective programs for students at risk.* (pp. 3–22). Boston, MA: Allyn & Bacon.

Slavin, R. E. & Madden, N. A., (1989). Effective pull-out programs for students at risk. In R. E. Slavin, N. L. Karweit, & N. A. Madden (Eds.). *Effective programs for students at risk.* (pp. 52–71). Boston, MA: Allyn & Bacon.

Stein, M. K., Leinhardt, G., & Bickel W. (1989). Instructional issues for teaching students at risk. In R. E. Slavin, N. L. Karweit, & N. A. Madden (Eds.), *Programs for students at risk.* (pp. 145–194). Needham, MA: Allyn & Bacon.

Ysseldyke, J. E. (1987) Classification of handicapped students. In M. C. Wang, M. C. Reynolds, and H. J. Walberg (Eds.)., *Handbook of special education: Research and practice. Vol. 1* (pp. 253–272). Oxford, England: Pergamon Press.

CHAPTER 2

Collaborative Consultation:
A Key to Effective
Educational Delivery

WILLIAM H. BERDINE
PATRICIA THOMAS CEGELKA

CHAPTER OBJECTIVES

At the conclusion of this chapter, the reader will be able to do the following:

1. Describe the educational rationale for collaborative consultation and prereferral intervention.
2. Describe the similarities, differences, and definitions among the conceptual frameworks of collaborative consultation.
3. Identify the people, process, and procedural implementation variables involved in the implementation of collaborative consultation.
4. Describe the concepts of "at risk" and prevention within the framework of prereferral intervention.
5. List the necessary stage for implementation of prereferral intervention.
6. Describe collaboration strategies for working with other agencies, parents, and families.
7. Discuss key considerations in planning for and conducting a parent-teacher conference.

A major challenge to educators is identifying instructional and programmatic practices that promote the optimal learning of students who differ significantly in terms of learning, linguistic, socioeconomic, and cultural characteristics. The remaining chapters of this textbook describe approaches of proven effectiveness for students with learning difficulties. These approaches are applicable to such educational settings as special education classes; regular classes; and Chapter 1, bilingual, or related types of programs. They have been empirically documented as effective for low achieving students.

This chapter is designed to provide a context in which these approaches can be most efficiently and effectively delivered. This context is one of collaboration: collaboration among teachers and other school-site personnel, collaboration with professionals in other agencies, and collaboration with parents. Faced with the complexities of contemporary society and the increasing diversity of students, teachers can no longer afford to follow the traditional practice of flying solo behind the closed doors of their classrooms. Today, they are

expected to provide instruction that is age appropriate, culturally/linguistically sensitive, and conceptually grounded. Teachers are to do this within the context of the least restrictive environment for students who present a wide range of learning and behavioral challenges.

To meet these challenges, educators are developing new programmatic structures and service delivery systems. The self-contained classroom in which individual teachers assume singular responsibility for a group of students is giving way to collaborative approaches that involve teams of professionals working with the students and their families. Collaboration of this sort among teachers in general education, special education, Chapter 1, and other categorical programs is increasingly viewed as essential to providing appropriate education to all students who may be "at risk" for academic difficulties and school failure.

In addition to collaboration among teachers, collaboration with other educational personnel as well as across service delivery agencies is increasingly commonplace. For example, teachers now work closely with school psychologists and counselors, vocational education, and rehabilitation personnel (see Chapter 14 for discussion), as well as local family support, mental health, and child care agencies. Finally, the importance of developing and maintaining a productive collaboration with the parents and families of students with learning difficulties cannot be overestimated.

This chapter documents the evolution of collaborative consultation approaches. It overviews the development of school-based models for collaboration, and delineates critical features and implementation variables of school-based collaboration. This chapter then highlights using prereferral teacher assistance as a key strategy for meeting unique learning needs in the mainstream classroom. In a final section, this chapter overviews transdisciplinary collaboration and presents strategies for working effectively with parents and families.

In presenting these options for educational service delivery, the chapter seeks to sensitize readers to the need to reach out and touch a colleague. To teach most effectively, teachers must learn to both give and receive collaborative assistance in meeting the educational needs of all pupils.

HISTORICAL BACKGROUND

Although the concept of consultation has its roots in medieval Europe (Gallessich, 1982), it was not until 1959 that the term *consultation* was first included in *Psychological Abstracts*. The fact that it caught on rapidly from that point was, in large part, due to the dramatic expansion in the number of children being identified for special education. As described in Chapter 1 of this book, the prevailing service delivery model for students with special needs has involved segregated, categorical programming. The identification, classification, and placement of children into specialized programs has been funded by categorical monies set aside for these purposes. Special education, gifted education, Chapter 1, Head Start, bilingual education, and migrant education have all developed as categorical programs within the school system.

Since the early 1980s, many educators have questioned the efficacy of this approach. They were concerned about the effectiveness of segregated and/or pull-out programs in terms of both the academic and social development of students with mild handicapping conditions. An increasing emphasis on the general education classroom as the least restrictive environment (LRE) and most appropriate environment for many of these students has prompted a shift to more integrated service delivery models characterized by collaborative consultation among teachers (Friend, 1988). Contemporary reform initiatives in education have called for the breaking down of categorical barriers in order to provide better educational services to all students who present special learning challenges.

The roots of this movement are at least 25 years old (Lilly, 1988). Since the early 1960's it has become clear that any effort to "reform" education must involve renewed efforts to systematically collaborate and consult with colleagues across all curricular domains and all student services. Today, school-based consultation has become a dynamic feature in the continued evolution of educational services for students with learning challenges.

COLLABORATION MODELS

Several models of school-based consultation that were developed during the 1980s continue to influence the field today (Cipani, 1985; Idol-Maestas, 1983; Knight, Meyers, Paolucci-Whitcomb, Hasazi, & Nevin, 1981; Lilly & Givens-Ogle, 1981; Paolucci-Whitcomb & Nevin, 1985; Stainback & Stainback, 1984). Despite specific differences, these models are more similar than dissimilar. They all reject orientations that rely primarily on the skills of teachers segregated in their isolated classrooms, assisted occasionally by outside "experts," and to favor collaborative orientations.

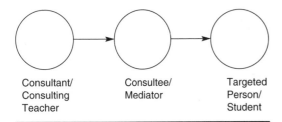

Consultant/	Consultee/	Targeted
Consulting	Mediator	Person/
Teacher		Student

FIGURE 2.1   Triadic Model for Educational Application

Source: Adapted from Tharp and Wetzel (1969)

Tharp & Wetzel's (1969) triadic model of consultation (Figure 2.1) has been the dominant influence on the development of the consultative process in education. In this indirect model of service delivery, a **consultant** (consulting teacher) directly interacts with a **mediator** (teacher or other service delivery person), who, in turn, interacts directly with the **targeted person** (student). The consultant does not directly provide services to students with learning difficulties, but instead works with the teacher or other service delivery professional responsible for providing the services.

The consultant comes into the setting as the result of a request from a mediator (e.g., the classroom teacher) for "expert" advice about some identified situation or situations. In order for this type of consultation to be effective, the mediator must be able to acknowledge the "need" for an expert without any loss of professional or personal confidence.

Despite the simplicity of the model's design, actual implementation efforts have revealed several drawbacks. The hierarchical or linear conceptualization of the triadic model may interfere with developing true collaboration among the consultant and the classroom teacher. Further, without consistent or systematic *direct* interaction with the target student, the consulting teacher may either become disassociated with the immediate problems of classroom management or instruction, or be viewed as such by the classroom teacher. These factors may strain relationships among consulting teachers and classroom teach-

ers (Pugach and Raths, 1983) and impede implementation of the consultant's advice (Reisberg & Wolf, 1986).

When consultation involves crossing over between special education and general education, the problem of professional credibility may arise (Gans, 1985; Johnson, Pugach & Hammitte, 1988; Pugach & Johnson, 1989; Leyser & Abrams, 1984; West & Brown, 1987). The special educator may be viewed as too specialized and as having too little experience in meeting the "real-world" demands of large, **heterogeneous classrooms.** Further, the individualized, more behavioral orientation of special educators may be at odds with the more normative, cognitive approaches of general education. Special education professionals may not be well prepared to cope with the congregate settings, large numbers of students, or the heterogeneity of the regular classroom.

Difficulties may stem from the selection of professionals selected to serve as consultants. Many individuals who are excellent classroom teachers lack the training and skills needed in working effectively with other adults. Consultants not only must have considerable instructional expertise themselves, but they also must be able to interact with colleagues in a manner that is supportive and nondemeaning. Issues revolving around the skills and credibility of the consultants tend to be persistent problems that impede the development of cooperative interactions that can result in desirable changes in student behavior and performance.

The perception of credibility or its lack thereof is closely tied to the question of ownership of the problem. In other words, who will be chiefly responsible for doing something about the problem? Is the problem "owned" by the classroom teacher who is experiencing difficulty with the situation? Or does ownership of the problem reside with the consultant who is called in to assist the teacher? Or is the problem owned by the student(s) whose academic or social behavior is cause for concern?

Idol, Paolucci-Whitcomb, and Nevin (1986) describe a collaborative triadic model that expressly inhibits either the consultant or the classroom teacher from sole ownership of the problem or as solely responsible for the process of intervention and resolution. Idol et al. (1986, p. 5) clearly state that "collaborative consultation requires team ownership of the identified problem." In their model, a relationship of parity exists between the consulting teacher and the classroom teacher or mediator. The consultant does not serve as a supervisor of instruction or as an "interested" but not directly involved observer. Successful resolution of the educational challenge presented by the student depends on the combined skills and talents of the two professional educators.

Idol et al. (1986, p. 1) define **collaborative consultations** as:

> "Collaborative consultation *is an* interactive process *that enables* teams of people with diverse expertise *to generate* creative solutions to mutually defined problems. *The outcome is enhanced and altered from the original solutions that any team member would produce independently.*

The actual roles and functions of the consulting teacher and the classroom teacher within the collaborative consultation process will vary with each target student or situation. However, collaborative consultation is most effective when both individuals have received reciprocal training in the process of collaborative consultation. All educational personnel, including school staff (e.g., school building administrators) and ancillary staff (e.g., school counselors, social workers, physical therapists, and occupational therapists), that may have direct involvement with managing students should receive training in collaborative consultation.

IMPLEMENTING COLLABORATIVE CONSULTATION

Three levels of school context variables continually interact within the collaborative consultation framework. These are the persons, the processes, and the procedures involved both directly and indirectly in the consultation effort. Figure 2.2 depicts variables of importance to designing and implementing collaborative consultation. A brief discussion of each of these eleven variables and their importance to effective consultation follows. A more in-depth discussion of the model can be found in Tindal, Shinn, & Rodden-Nord (1990).

People Variables

Some of the most complex variables that impact on collaborative consultation are *"people variables,"* found in the persons that participate. The background and skills of the consultant, the consultee (or teacher), and the client (student) all impact on the process. In addition, the administrative support for the process impacts both the processes and the outcomes. Each of these is elaborated on in the following paragraphs.

Consultant Background and Skills. The consultant's role is complex, requiring a broad array of competencies, including knowledge of instructional methodology, communication techniques, student assessment, data collection, and data analysis. The skills consultants bring to the collaborative consultation as well as the formal training they receive are of utmost importance. Generally speaking, consultants will need skills that permit them to work effectively across a wide variety of teacher-certification areas and across various educationally related disciplines. Consultants need to possess the following (Idol-Maestas & Ritter, 1985):

- Skills in assessing the behavior and the study of students
- Group interaction skills for participating in staff conferences
- Skills in developing written individual education plans (IEPs)
- Skills in decelerating inappropriate social behaviors

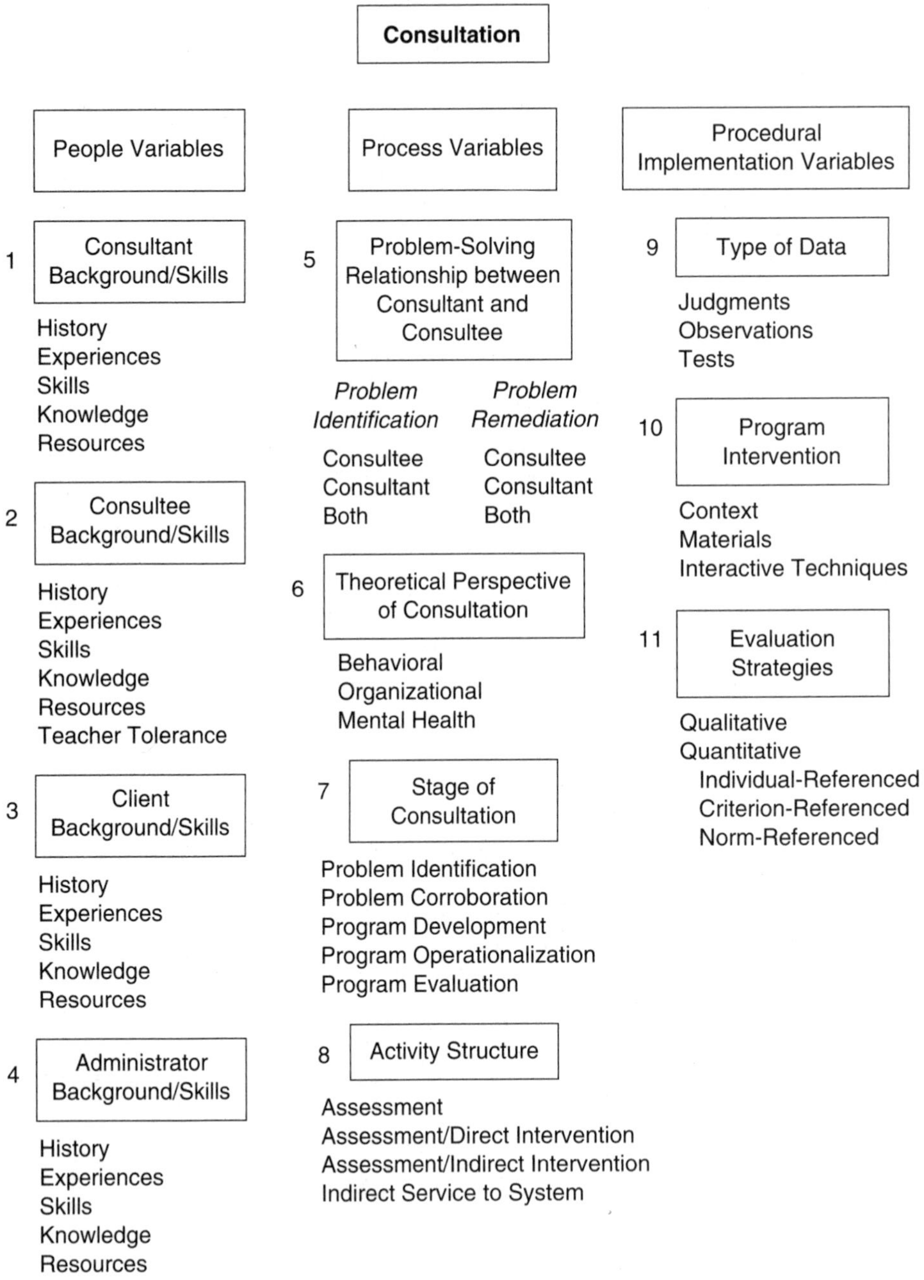

```
                              ┌─────────────────┐
                              │  Consultation   │
                              └─────────────────┘
```

People Variables	Process Variables	Procedural Implementation Variables

1 Consultant Background/Skills

History
Experiences
Skills
Knowledge
Resources

2 Consultee Background/Skills

History
Experiences
Skills
Knowledge
Resources
Teacher Tolerance

3 Client Background/Skills

History
Experiences
Skills
Knowledge
Resources

4 Administrator Background/Skills

History
Experiences
Skills
Knowledge
Resources

5 Problem-Solving Relationship between Consultant and Consultee

Problem Identification	Problem Remediation
Consultee	Consultee
Consultant	Consultant
Both	Both

6 Theoretical Perspective of Consultation

Behavioral
Organizational
Mental Health

7 Stage of Consultation

Problem Identification
Problem Corroboration
Program Development
Program Operationalization
Program Evaluation

8 Activity Structure

Assessment
Assessment/Direct Intervention
Assessment/Indirect Intervention
Indirect Service to System

9 Type of Data

Judgments
Observations
Tests

10 Program Intervention

Context
Materials
Interactive Techniques

11 Evaluation Strategies

Qualitative
Quantitative
　Individual-Referenced
　Criterion-Referenced
　Norm-Referenced

FIGURE 2.2 Consultation Model

Source: From "Contextually based school consultation: Influential variables" by G. Tindal, M.R. Shinn, and K. Rodden-Nord, *Exceptional Children,* 56(4), 1990, p. 326. Copyright 1990 by The Council for Exceptional Children. Reprinted with permission.

- Skills in locating appropriate instructional materials
- Skills in generating activities for specified objectives

In an extensive review of the research, Reisberg and Wolf (1988) extracted three general areas of importance to effective consultation in special education. These include: (1) careful and cooperative project development, including effective systems change strategies (Huefner, 1988; Reisberg & Wolf, 1986; Wang, 1987); (2) effective communication and problem-solving skills (Conoley & Conoley, 1982; DeBoer, 1986; Rosenfield, 1987); and (3) appropriate assessment and use of instructional strategies in mainstream settings (Heron & Harris, 1987; Idol et al., 1986; Rosenfield, 1987). According to Phillips & McCullough (1990) successful school consultation should be characterized by:

- An indirect service approach (such as provided in the triadic model)
- Development of collaborative professional relationships (which includes the notion of co-ownership of the problem)
- Mutual recognition of the consultee's (teacher) right to not accept the consultation (e.g., consultation is voluntary) and respect for the confidentiality of any contact made regarding both teachers and students
- A problem-solving orientation
- Attention to the twofold goal of immediate problem resolution and increased consultee skill/knowledge that can be applied to independent resolutions of similar problems in the future

Consultee Background and Skills. Successful consultation depends on the background, skills, attitudes, and expectations of the individual(s) receiving the consultation, as well as those providing the consultation. Consultee variables that can contribute to the failure of consultation efforts include a lack of knowledge, inadequate skills or confidence, and lack of objectivity (Gutkin, 1981). This suggests that systematic training may be an important prerequisite to successful participation in the consultation process.

In some instances, the act of identifying the consultee or consultees is complicated. For example, the problem presented may not directly involve a student, but may be focused on other aspects of the school setting. There may be problems in dealing with ancillary or support personnel (i.e., a teacher aide or a speech therapist), or perhaps with an administrative function. Each of these may or may not directly involve a teacher as the consultee. However, the teacher most frequently plays a critical role whenever the "target of change" or presenting problem involves interaction with a student(s).

In many instances, more than one consultee may be involved. For example in a mainstreaming situation, both the regular and special education teacher may require consultant assistance. In other instances, the parents and a teacher(s) may be involved in addressing a student-related problem. The active involvement of more than three persons modifies the triadic model to some degree. However, including additional mediators (i.e., teachers, parents, and administrators) may actually facilitate a successful consultation conclusion. The number of persons involved is of much less importance than is the readiness on the part of the consultee(s) for consultation. Consultee characteristics having the greatest impact on the success of consultation include the following:

- Expectations and tolerance, the standards of acceptable classroom behavior that they demand and the degree to which they are willing to tolerate certain behaviors (Kerr & Zigmond, 1986; Walker & Rankin, 1983)
- Understanding the consultation process and their cooperation with consultants (Sandoval, Lambert, & Davis, 1977)
- Acceptance of specific treatments, or perceptions of treatments that will be effective in their classrooms, particularly in reference to the perceived degree of effectiveness of the proposed interventions and the amount of

time/resources required to implement the treatment (Witt & Elliott, 1986)

- Acceptance of the consultant's beliefs and theoretical orientation (Medway & Forman, 1980; Rosenfield, 1985)

Client Background and Skills. The client (in most cases, the student) is the only participant in the collaborative consultation process with a predetermined role. *A priori* assessment of the targeted client's past experiences, history of school achievement, involvement in special education services and the existence of an IEP, and the availability of additional human resources (e.g., including family and community) provides vital background knowledge for the consultant and consultee. They must know whether the targeted problem involves skill deficits (the individual can or cannot do something) or performance deficits (the individual will or will not do something for which the skills are present). This information is needed prior to beginning the consultation process. This background information helps the consultant and consultee collaborate in designing intervention programs that involve the targeted student as an active participant with co-ownership of the problem.

Administrator. Collaborative consultation, by the very nature of involving multiple persons, cannot operate within an administrative vacuum. The support of the school building principal may be one of the most critical variables for consultation success (Idol & West, 1987). Recent research on the role of the site principal as instructional leader (Deal, 1987) highlights the importance of involving the principal to the fullest extent possible. The very nature of the due process requirements in special education (identification, classification, diagnosis, and IEP development) lends additional impetus to the active involvement of school administrators. Typically, the first steps toward collaboration have begun with the special education assessment, identification, and placement committee. By federal mandate, this committee includes the referring regular class teacher, the receiving special education teacher, the school building administration, the student and parent or guardian, and any other school staff that may have a role in the student's IEP. A shift toward developing prereferral intervention teams, described later in this chapter, is extending the collaborative consultation ethic to the broader school community. Prereferral intervention assistance involves teams of teachers who focus on specific problems prior to, and frequently in lieu of, referral to special education.

Process Variables

Although the triadic model depicts the involvement of three sets of individuals (consultant, consultee, and student with the targeted problem), the two individuals principally responsible for establishing the process and putting it into operation are the consultant and the consultee/mediator. The problem-solving relationships as well as the theoretical perspectives of these two individuals are of significance to the consultation processes and outcomes.

Problem-Solving Relationships. A critical variable in the consultation process is the ability of the consultant and the consultee to efficiently and effectively identify who will do what, to whom, when, where, and how often. How this will be monitored or evaluated is essential for the consultation to succeed. Tindal et al. (1990) have described three common relationships that emerge in the triadic model: (1) the consultee problem identification–consultant remediation relationship; (2) the consultant identification of the problem and the consultee teacher's remediation of the problem relationship, and (3) the consultant and consultee problem identification and remediation relationship. There is little empirical evidence to support the efficacy of any of these relationship types over the others.

The first relationship, **consultee problem identification–consultant remediation,** has typified the consultant relationships between regular and special educators. In this situation, a teacher identifies a problem that he cannot manage effectively and requests assistance from a designated consulting teacher or consultant. Neel (1981) notes that this relationship may be effective for both initial intervention and short-term or crisis intervention. However, it is not generally effective over time. A major shortcoming is its failure to develop the skills, characteristics, or competencies the consultee teacher needs in order to manage similar problems without consultative assistance in the future.

The second consultative relationship involves the **consultant identification of the problem and the consultee teacher's remediation of the problem.** This type of relationship is often found with experienced teachers who have a broad array of intervention skills and methodologies, but who are experiencing difficulties in identifying or assessing the particular problem at hand. This may be the scenario in mainstream settings where an experienced regular classroom teacher is confronted with providing instruction for a student with a unique learning or behavioral problem. In this case, the special education consultant assists in identifying the problem so that an intervention procedure can be implemented. As mainstreaming and full inclusion of special education students becomes more widespread, this type of consultant-consultee relationship may become more common. This relationship highlights the need for the consultant to have highly polished communication skills and problem identification skills, as well as knowledge of available resources. This situation requires that the consultee have a willingness to accept the consultant's advice and implement the plan cooperatively. Problems may occur when (1) the consultee provides an inaccurate description of the presenting problem or withholds pertinent information, resulting in an intervention plan that may be inadequate or implemented prematurely; (2) the consultee is reluctant to implement the consultant's intervention alone or in the absence of administrative support; (3) the consultant performs

poor or nonexistent follow-up and evaluation of effectiveness; and/or (4) ineffective intervention programs are implemented and not changed or terminated (Tindal et al., 1990).

A third relationship, the **consultant and consultee problem identification and remediation,** best promotes consensus decision making, joint ownership of the problem, and equity in regard to designing and implementing interventions. This type of relationship is most probable in those situations when all of the consultant and consultee background and skills described previously are present. The student with the targeted problem benefits from the expertise, skills, and active involvement of the consultee and consultant. However, problems can also occur with this relationship. Because the relationship requires active involvement of both members of the dyad, it may not always be time efficient (Tindal et al., 1990). Also, problems may occur if there is disagreement over any aspect of the consensus process for identifying, implementing, altering, or terminating an intervention plan.

Theoretical Perspectives of Consultation. The manner in which a teacher approaches instruction, the way she perceives the student's behavior to originate, the way she collects and evaluates data, the interventions she uses, and the consequences she employs all significantly impact the success of the collaborative consultation. Both the consultant and consultee must be aware of their respective theoretical training and perspectives. While neither the consultant nor the consultee will, especially during the initial interactions, be inclined to change positions, having a working knowledge of other perspectives may be helpful. The three most common theoretical approaches to consultation are described as follows:

1. **Behavioral consultation** focuses on assisting the consultee in introducing specific changes in the students environment to modify the targeted observable and/or measurable problem(s) in a predictable direction (i.e., accelerate, decelerate, or maintain status quo)

2. **Mental health consultation** is generally directed toward changing the clients' feelings so the targeted problems are eliminated or changed in a desired direction. Gibbins (1978) notes that in this consultation model, observable behaviors are regarded as important only to the extent that they affect the targeted persons' feelings or emotional being.
3. **Organizational developmental consultation,** as described by Schmuck (1982), targets improved client functioning within a complex social system. This model emphasizes assisting targeted persons to better understand the complex social system in which they live, thereby helping them become more effective at functioning within that system.

While all three models have relevance to collaborative consultation in school-based settings, the behavioral model has the greatest application when working with students with learning or behavioral problems.

Stages of Consultation

In Figure 2.2, Variable 7, stage of consultation of the process variables, five stages of consultation are described. Each of the these stages has evolved out of earlier research on consultation stages (Alpert, 1977; Bergan, 1977; Dustin & Ehly, 1984; Idol & West, 1987). The **problem identification stage** entails using collaborative efforts between the consultant and consultee to identify and prioritize the student's problem(s) as well as to establish methodology to confirm the problem(s) existence and its parameters. **Problem corroboration** involves collecting data in a systematic manner to validate the problem that either the consultant or the consultee identified earlier. For reasons of reliability or accuracy of data collection, typically one or the other member of the consulting dyad will perform this function. **Program development** entails the highest levels of direct contact between consultant and consultee, and is a prerequisite to actually implementing any intervention or plan of action.

The main focus of the next stage, **program operationalization,** encompasses the actual implementation of the intervention(s) designed to change the targeted problem in a predictable direction. Depending on the problem-solving relationship described previously, this stage will involve varying levels of collaborative efforts. The final stage, **program evaluation,** typically is characterized by the collection and analysis of data upon which to judge the success of the intervention effort.

The ability to identify the stage of the consultation process at any given time permits the consultee and consultant to better make the transition from one level to another. This facilitates movement into one of the four levels of activity described next.

Activity Structure

The **activity structure** of collaborative consultation focuses specifically on *what* is done and by *whom,* and includes identification of all consultation participants and their specific roles in the process. There are four levels of activity fitted around two functions: data collection for assessment, and identification of intervention strategies (see Variable 8, activity structure, in Figure 2.2). In the first activity level, *assessment or consultant assessment,* the consultation process is primarily one of assessment for purposes of determining the existence, the characteristics, and the qualities of a problem. Recommendations may be made for intervention but actual intervention at this level is not typical. Ysseldyke, Reynolds, and Weinberg (1984) note this is the level of consultation activity often associated with school psychologists, and their role in assessing students and making recommendations. The second level of activity, *consultant assessment and direct program implementation,* is most often seen in the traditional role of the special education resource room teacher. This level does not involve a great deal of direct consultative activity other than that which occurs as a result of students' returning to their regular class teacher with specific remedial assignments from the resource room teacher. As eligibility for special services has already been determined, at this level of activity the emphasis is on getting programs in place and operational, not on directly consulting with referring teachers. The third level of activity, *consultant assessment and indirect program implementation,* best fits the triadic model and collaborative consultation. At this level, the consultant works directly with the consultee, who in turn directly works with the student. The consultant works only indirectly with the student through contact with the consultee. The fourth level of activity, *indirect service to system,* refers to consultative services that are outside the classroom but involve contact with potential consultees such as through in-service workshops on collaborative consultation on instructional strategies and interventions. The purpose here is to upgrade or sharpen the consultee background and skills.

The third and final variable outlined in Figure 2.2 deals with aspects of procedural implementation of school-based consultation and will be discussed in the next section of this chapter.

Procedural Implementation Variables

The actual implementation of a consultation plan includes data collection, intervention, and evaluation. **Data collection** documents the process of a consultative activity. Of interest is the kind of data to be collected, who is to collect it, and when it is to be collected. The data collection procedure used should be systematic and well codified. Approaches involving student self-reports, anecdotal records, or logs should be avoided because these are difficult to corroborate. Using predetermined questions provides a structure for corroboration to such informal data collection procedures such as parent, student, or teacher interviews. Systematic strategies for data collection have been classified into three dimensions.

1. **Category systems** are appropriate for large response classes with multiple forms or behaviors. Such response classes might include

skill development in interpersonal interaction or communication arenas. The Flanders Interaction Analysis (Amidon & Hough, 1967) is an example of formal instrumentation that reflect category systems' data collection needs.

2. **Sign strategies** are used to collect specific or discrete events or behaviors that lend themselves well to time-sampling procedures. Time-sampling procedures such as momentary time sampling or interval time sampling (described in Chapter 3) might be employed here.

3. **Multiple coding systems** are designed to collect data from settings where some elements of both category and sign systems data may be prevalent. These settings would include large response classes that have specific discrete characteristics. Such consultation situations would include both the quality or type of instruction provided and the consequent student responding. The Code for Instructional Structure and Student Academic Response (CISSAR) (Stanley & Greenwood, 1980) is an example of a multiple coding system that might be used.

Within these data collection systems a wide variety of data may be collected. Included are quantitative or nonquantitative systems, systematic or nonsystematic data, formal (CISSARs noted previously) or informal (structured or guided interview as described earlier) systems, and current or historical data systems for use in situations involving temporal considerations.

Intervention. Once a decision is made on the type of data collection procedure to be used, the consultation effort is then prepared to enter into the intervention phase, Variable 10 in the model depicted in Figure 2.2. The process of collaborative consultation should result in more than the efficient and effective resolution of a targeted problem. It also should result in enhancing of the consultant's and consultee's skills in managing problems relevant to the classroom. The choice of an intervention strategy should be based on the considerations of what is known about effective

- **Collaborative Standard**
  The format should maximize the following:
  1. Pooling of staff talents/resources.
  2. Multidisciplinary involvement in "think-tank" environment.
  3. Evolution of problem-solving and effective intervention skills.
  4. Joint responsibility and accountability.
  5. The creation of a collaborative ethic in the school.

- **Ecological Relevance Standard**
  The format should be feasible in terms of the following:
  1. Logistics of operation.
  2. Cost.
  3. Side effects.
  4. Organizational structure.
  5. Training and staff development.

- **Efficacy Standard**
  The format should be validated or demonstrated effective by the following:
  1. Empirical research studies.
  2. Social validity measures.
  3. Data regarding probability of generalized benefits (i.e., extent to which "domino effect" will involve multiple staff and students).
  4. Data available regarding implementation efforts in similar settings.

FIGURE 2.3 Standards for Informal Evaluation of the Potential Merit of Relevance of Consultation-Based Program Formats

Source: From "Consultation-based programming: Instituting the collaborative ethic in schools" by V. Phillips and L. McCullough, *Exceptional Children,* 56(4), 1990, p. 296. Copyright 1990 by The Council for Exceptional Children. Reprinted with permission.

teaching and the best practices in managing classroom behaviors. Figure 2.3 depicts informal standards that can be used in determining the relative merits of any given consultation format. Additional selection considerations include the feasibility of the various interventions given the available resources, theoretical orientations, and time availability of professionals critical to the intervention. A design format for dealing with feasibility issues is provided in Figure 2.4.

Closely related to selecting a specific intervention format is identifying evaluation procedures to document the relative effectiveness of the consultative activities.

Evaluation.   Evaluation is Variable 11, the final variable of the model for collaborative consult-

ation in school-based settings. Evaluating the effect of consultation should be specific to the process outcome between the consultant and consultee, or between the consultee and the targeted person, or, indirectly, between the consultant and the targeted person with the problem. Tindal et al. (1990) noted that the effects or success of an intervention can be evaluated using qualitative approaches or one of three quantitative approaches: (1) individually referenced, (2) criterion referenced, or (3) norm referenced.

An example of a qualitative approach to data collection involves using such non-normed instrumentation as the **The Instructional Environment Scale (TIES)** (Ysseldyke & Christenson, 1987). This scale consists of three components: (1) a classroom observation, (2) a structured stu-

1. Degree of disruption to school and classroom procedures and/or teacher routines.

2. Side effects on significant persons:
   - The student (e.g., social ostracism, academic failure).
   - Peers.
   - Home/family.
   - Faculty/staff.

3. Degree of support services required:
   - Availability.
   - Procedures for accessing.
   - Funding considerations.

4. Prerequisite competencies for delivery of intervention:
   - Skills of teacher or intervention:
     —Experienced in the specific intervention.
     —Not experienced in the intervention, but has access to the necessary staff development.
     —Not experienced in the intervention and does not have access to the necessary staff development.
   - Philosophical bias of teacher or intervening personnel:
     —Agrees with selected intervention.
     —Disagrees with selected intervention.

5. Probability of intervention being successful in achieving the student goal (including the degree to which the intervention personnel can control necessary variables).

6. Immediacy of results:
   - Will selected intervention effect change in student performance immediately?
   - Will selected intervention require a more lengthy period of implementation before significant changes in student behavior occur?

7. Consequences of nonintervention (short- and long-term prognosis for student if behaviors are left uncorrected).

8. Potential of intervention for transition:
   - Into student self-regulation and goal realization.
   - Into additional student support networks (current and future).

FIGURE 2.4 Feasability Considerations of Intervention Design

Source: From "Consultation-based programming: Instituting the collaborative ethic in schools" by V. Phillips and L. McCullough, *Exceptional Children,* 56(4), 1990, p. 299. Copyright 1990 by The Council for Exceptional Children. Reprinted with permission.

dent interview, and (3) a structured teacher interview. Data from these components are used to develop an Instructional Rating Profile that describes twelve factors that are critical for student learning. These factors are: (1) instructional presentation, (2) classroom environment, (3) teacher expectations, (4) cognitive emphasis, (5) motivational strategies, (6) relevant practices, (7) academic engaged time, (8) informal feedback, (9) adaptive instruction, (10) progress evaluation, (11) instructional planning, and (12) student understanding. (The reader will note that these are factors emphasized throughout this text).

Individually referenced strategies are probably the most commonly used quantitative evaluation technique used in consultative activities (Idol-Maestas, 1983). They focus on measuring a relative change in the targeted problem area(s) over time, and in comparing past and predicted levels of performance. Direct observation of behavior and curriculum-based assessment, both of which are described in detail in Chapters 3 and 4, are two approaches to such data collection. **Criterion-referenced techniques** are generally useful when the targeted student's behavior or targeted change can be compared to either meeting or approaching a predetermined level (i.e., criterion). **Norm-referenced techniques** are useful when a valid normative comparison group is available to compare to the targeted student's performance. Each of these approaches also is more fully described in Chapter 4.

Circumventing Barriers

A conceptual framework such as the one described here increases the probability of successful collaborative efforts. This framework addresses the importance of the following factors (Phillips & McCullough, 1990):

- The development and maintenance of administrative support and systems-level coordination
- Systematic program development that includes multilevel participatory planning and decision making
- Ownership that engenders the motivation as well as expectations of meaningful results
- Attention to the feasibility of the intervention strategies selected
- Lowering resistance to collaboration through the provision of staff development activities that are practical and specific

In these ways potential barriers to person-to-person collaborative consultation can be significantly reduced. Another promising consultation approach employs computer software programs that provide "expert systems" of consultation to teachers faced with student challenges. Fuchs, Fuchs, Hamlett, and Stecker (1991) reported the success of one such program they developed in mathematics instruction. This program developed graphic displays of student data, assisted teachers in formulating interventions based on this data, and evaluated the effects of these interventions.

In conclusion, note that successfully resolving the targeted problem by itself, does not necessarily indicate successful consultation. The overall success of the collaborative consultation is ensured when the consultee demonstrates the ability to deal capably with similar situations in the future without the direct assistance of the consultant. Collaborative consultants in education need to learn to cope with a "Maytag Syndrome" in which their products (e.g., the results of their consultative efforts) are so well developed and durable that they rarely need servicing!

PREREFERRAL INTERVENTION

There is widespread concern among educators and others that many of the students identified for special education do not, in actual fact, possess a disability that qualifies them for these categorical services. Because economic cutbacks have led to dramatic reductions of remedial and support services to students within the educational system generally, school personnel often view special education as one of the few remaining avenues for addressing individual student problems. Therefore, considerable pressure exists at the school-site level for identifying and classifying students for special education services.

The act of referring students to special education typically represents the most critical point in the special education decision-making process. Without systematic prereferral intervention, 92% of the total number of students referred to special education each year are evaluated, and 55%–78% of these students are declared eligible for and subsequently receive such services (Fuchs, Fuchs, Bahr, Fernstrom, & Stecker, 1990).

In an effort to stem this tide, and to provide appropriate assistance within the general classroom, schools are moving toward preventative approaches to resolving academic and behavioral problems. Pianta (1990) notes that three forms of preventive service delivery have been documented as successful in schools (e.g., Catterall, 1987; Cowen, 1980; Forman and Linney, 1988; Paget, 1988; Shapiro, 1988; Fuchs et al., 1990). These include primary prevention, secondary prevention, and tertiary prevention or remediation. **Primary prevention** refers procedures or processes that are made available to the general student population that will either reduce the rate of occurrence of a particular problem or make its occurrence less likely to happen among students who currently are believed to be at risk *but who do not as yet* manifest the problem. Strategies for implementing primary prevention that have empirical documentation for their effectiveness include: education about a targeted problem, community organization, competency promotion, natural caregiving, and consultation and collaboration (Zins, Coyne & Ponti, 1988). **Secondary prevention** targets a selected student population that is known to exhibit risk factors whose outcomes are not desirable. The focus of secondary prevention efforts are typically twofold. First, to reduce the impact of the known negative outcome for students at risk *and currently exhibiting* problems or difficulties in school as a result. Second, to establish intervention programs to ameliorate or reduce the known risk factors so that students found in the risk group, but not exhibiting any problems to date, will not show problems in the future. Secondary prevention efforts are well known to educators and include programs aimed at dropout prevention; substance abuse prevention; tutorial programs for students failing; and probably largest of all, prereferral intervention programs aimed at maintaining students in the LRE and avoiding special education eligibility determination. **Tertiary prevention** or remediation programs attempt to deal with student problems after they have been found to exist. In other words, the risk factors have been attained and are being exhibited by the student. Remedial programs or tertiary prevention efforts attempt to not only prevent a problem from becoming worse, but also to positively impact on the immediate aspects of the problem as they relate to school. Tertiary prevention programs are typically the most common form of prevention effort in schools. Much of what is called special education is tertiary in that it is remedial and rehabilitative. Pianta (1990) states that the emphasis on disabilities, identifying individuals, assessment, and labeling are all hallmarks of remedial interventions. Special education programs exist as the result of the documentation that a student has failed and the regular school setting cannot provide effective services.

The conceptual framework of prereferral intervention is clearly affixed to notions of preventing persons who are at risk for being inappropriately or prematurely removed from their current educational setting. In addition to making use of primary and secondary intervention strategies, prereferral intervention emphasizes the importance of making use of available resources to focus more time on instruction and less on diagnostic (e.g., eligibility) processes.

Developing prereferral intervention programs has represented a promising response to the pressures to better accommodate students with learning problems in the mainstream classrooms without referral to special education. In schools where there is systematic prereferral intervention, the actual referrals to special education have declined by 50% or more (Cegelka, McDonald, & Gaeta, 1987).

Key Features

Prereferral intervention is a form of indirect consultation in that resources are directed at assisting the teacher to deal with the students having difficulty within the general education classroom setting. The essential features include (Graden, Casey, & Christenson, 1985):

- Collaborative efforts among teachers to assist one another in addressing special challenges presented by individual students
- A program of in-service preparation and staff development that provides skills needed to meet the educational needs of increasingly diverse groups of students
- Addressing student problems with the context or ecology of the student, school, and community
- Providing indirect services to students with problems through direct contact with their teachers

Different districts use different terminology for prereferral intervention teams. Such teams may be referred to as school study teams (SSTs), child study teams, teacher assistance teams (TATs), mainstream assistance teams, and similar names. The term used in this text is *teacher assistance team (TAT)*. Regardless of the nomenclature selected, these teams involve classroom teachers who serve as a consultative resource to their peers. In some schools, this process is, by definition, a regular education process and does not involve special education personnel. Other schools choose to include special education teachers, but only as resource personnel, not as team leaders. The staff at these schools believe that general education teachers will assume more responsibility for and ownership of educational challenges of students in their classrooms if they assume leadership for this process, instead of deferring to the "specialists." In addition to classroom teachers, parents of the students in question are frequently included in the team meetings, as are school nurses, psychologists, and speech therapists. In schools with students from diverse cultural and linguistic backgrounds, it is important that professional staff from these backgrounds be included on the TATs to the extent possible. When this is not

possible, community members from backgrounds similar to that of the student in question can assist the team in determining the potential roles that this diversity may play in the situation as well as in recommending appropriate interventions.

Teachers have the option of bringing to the team a particular problem or situation involving an individual student or group of students. Many schools have established procedures that require initial review and consideration by their TATs prior to formal referral of a student for special education assessment. The TAT may have developed a list of research-supported interventions that can be successful with many problem situations. Teachers may be required to document their use of three or four of these interventions prior to presenting a case to the team.

After reviewing the situation and the interventions attempted, the team may recommend that the teacher attempt additional interventions on the school list, provide in-class observation and consultation, tailor new interventions, or the team may recommend additional services and/or special education consideration. Teacher contracts with the target student(s) as well as systematic self-monitoring, charting, and evaluation on the part of the teachers tend to strengthen the design and implementation phases of this process (Fuchs, Fuchs, Bahr, Reeder, Gilman, Fernstrom, & Roberts, 1990). Contracting and data collection approaches are described in Chapters 3, 4, and 5.

Components of Prereferral Intervention

Figure 2.5 illustrates one model for preferral intervention. Graden et al. (1985) developed this six-stage model. The initial three stages involve one-to-one consultation from a consultant to the consultee, with the fourth stage involving input from a more broad-based committee or team. Stages 5 and 6 involve referral, disability diagnosis, and determination of eligibility for special education. The model conceptualizes a process wherein an individual consultant works with the

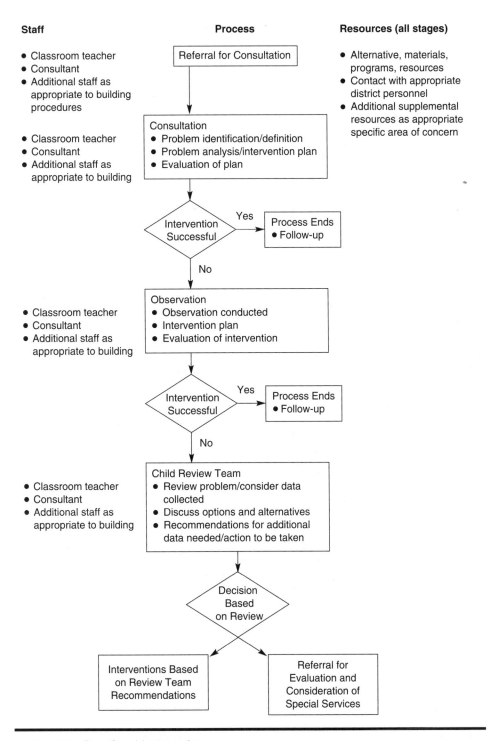

Staff

- Classroom teacher
- Consultant
- Additional staff as appropriate to building procedures

- Classroom teacher
- Consultant
- Additional staff as appropriate to building

- Classroom teacher
- Consultant
- Additional staff as appropriate to building

- Classroom teacher
- Consultant
- Additional staff as appropriate to building

Process

Referral for Consultation

Consultation
- Problem identification/definition
- Problem analysis/intervention plan
- Evaluation of plan

Intervention Successful → Yes → Process Ends
- Follow-up

No

Observation
- Observation conducted
- Intervention plan
- Evaluation of intervention

Intervention Successful → Yes → Process Ends
- Follow-up

No

Child Review Team
- Review problem/consider data collected
- Discuss options and alternatives
- Recommendations for additional data needed/action to be taken

Decision Based on Review

Interventions Based on Review Team Recommendations

Referral for Evaluation and Consideration of Special Services

Resources (all stages)

- Alternative, materials, programs, resources
- Contact with appropriate district personnel
- Additional supplemental resources as appropriate specific area of concern

FIGURE 2.5 Prereferral Intervention

Source: From "Implementing a prereferral intervention system: Part I. The model" by J. L. Graden, A. Casey, and S. L. Christenson, *Exceptional Children,* 51(5), 1985, p. 380. Copyright 1985 by The Council for Exceptional Children. Reprinted with permission.

referring teacher through the first three stages service provision, involving the TAT only at Stage 4. A variation on this involves the school-site team, instead of an individual consultant, working with the teacher from the beginning of the process. In either of these configurations a "consultant" can be considered to be operating. A thorough understanding of these stages can facilitate using the instructional and curricular applications advocated in subsequent chapters of this book.

Stage 1: Request for Consultation.   The process of prereferral intervention begins when a teacher perceives a problem relative to a student's performance or behavior (or both) for which the teacher has been unable to design and implement effective interventions. The classroom teacher typically initiates the prereferral intervention process by either formally or informally requesting assistance with a student's performance and/or behavior problem. Some prereferral intervention systems provide an initial informal forum in which teachers can seek assistance. Others require a more formal procedure, involving filling out a brief referral form and perhaps documenting specific interventions already attempted.

Stage 2: Consultation.   The actual consultation process involves (1) problem identification and definition to establish its parameters, (2) problem analysis to establish intervention plans, and (3) implementation of the plan and evaluation of its effectiveness. Graden et al. (1985) recommend the following behavioral consultation steps:

- Establishing a positive, collaborative, shared problem-solving relationship between the consultant(s) and the consultee.
- Assisting the referring teacher or school personnel in specifying the reason(s) for referral in objective, specific, measurable, and behavioral terms.

- Setting priorities for intervention. Within these priorities are considerations for assessing the discrepancy between the student's current performance and the teacher's expectations, as well as any classroom/school variable that may be affecting the student's performance.
- Collaboratively designing intervention strategies in which both the consultant and referring school personnel hold ownership. Additionally, other school personnel, family or other students may be included, as appropriate, to the problem being targeted. ,
- Implementing the intervention plan with an evaluation procedure in place to determine successful resolution of the problem, need for changes in intervention, need for additional follow-up, or additional assessment and a new intervention plan. Additional data collection, assessment, or the development of a new intervention plan requires implementing Stage 3 of the model (i.e., observation).

The active involvement of the consultant is terminated when the referral problem is successfully resolved, although follow-up and possible scheduled monitoring may occur. Termination should occur, however, only if the referring teacher is satisfied with the outcome.

Stage 3: Observation.   The referring classroom teacher and the consultant must jointly come to an agreement about the success of the intervention. Sometimes, despite careful planning and implementation, an intervention plan may not resolve the targeted problem. In this event, additional observation on the consultant's part, as well as data collection and assessment on the teacher's part, may be needed. Stage 3 activities have the significant advantage that they permit the examination of the targeted problem retrospectively under systematic data collection circumstances. Subsequent observations, assessments, and intervention plans developed at this time permit comparative analysis of behavioral intervention and instructional techniques. If these collaborative efforts are effective, the process moves to Stage 4, which brings additional expertise to bear on the situation.

Stage 4: Conference.   This stage of prereferral intervention formally involves additional school building or system personnel. If an individual consultant has been working with the teacher, then a specialized team may be formed to provide more specific input. Or, if the teacher already has been working with an assistance time, this may be the point at which an expert (from the team, school, or district) may be called in to give one-to-one assistance in analyzing and designing strategies. In either instance, additional resources are needed and a broader range of individuals, including individuals with more specific expertise, is accessed. The involvement of special education personnel at this time is informal or collegial in nature and does not constitute formal special education service delivery. The additional personnel review previous attempts at intervention, recommend modification of existing plans, attempt additional interventions, and/or refer the student for formal diagnostic and evaluation procedures with special education identification and services as one of several possible outcomes. Formal referral to special education constitutes Stage 5 of the model.

Stage 5: Formal Referral.   The use of the term *formal referral* clearly differentiates this level from earlier stages in which the student may not have been a part of the school system's formal evaluation or psycho-educational services. At Stage 5, the processes of additional data collection and intervention are required to meet all local, state, and federal due-process guidelines. Parental permission and involvement at this point becomes mandatory. Data collected in previous stages are reviewed and additional data are collected using psychoeducational assessments, criterion- and norm-referenced instrumentation. Curriculum-based assessment (described in Chapter 4) may also be included.

Stage 6: Formal Program Meeting.   Two types of decisions may be made in Stage 6: (1) to plan and implement further interventions within the context of the student's current placement or (2) to deem the student eligible for special education services. If the decision is made to continue the student within the current classroom setting, then the behavioral consultation and intervention procedures are continued in that setting. If the student is found eligible for special education services, due-process requirements must be met and a school-based admissions and release committee must be scheduled to develop the student's individual education program (IEP). Identifying the student for special education services does not automatically remove the regular class teacher from the picture. In all likelihood, the student will continue in the current classroom placement for a significant portion, if not all, of the school day. At this juncture, the regular class teacher and consultant, with their extensive experiences with the student, become collaborative partners with special education personnel.

WORKING WITH FAMILIES AND OTHERS

Developing partnerships beyond the confines of the school site can be of major importance in designing and delivering a full range of effective services for students with learning difficulties. Just as it is important for teachers to learn to collaborate with each other, so must they also learn to work collaboratively with the parents and families of their students, as well as with professionals in other agencies who come in contact with these same students. Professionals working in all areas of education and related service delivery need to develop collaboration skills.

They must understand the parent's perspective, learn collaboration approaches, and identify service delivery options that maximize appropriate services for individuals with disabilities. Barriers to collaboration may arise from differences in the skills, attitudes, and perceptions of parents and professionals, as well as from structural differences among various agencies that provide services for students with significant challenges.

Working with Other Agencies

In addition to the schools, agencies that may come into direct contact with students with learning difficulties and related special needs can include developmental services, health services, rehabilitation, medicaid, child protective services, and welfare and social services. Parents may have only limited knowledge about the availability of nonschool services for their children, while professionals tend to be knowledgeable about only their specific system or some portion of that system.

The capacity to share information across agency boundaries appears to be at a primitive state of development (Johnson, Bruininks, & Thrulow, 1987). Structural differences in organizations, conflicting policy goals, differences in application procedures and eligibility criteria, variations in funding cycles and fiscal years, discontinuity in geographic areas covered, and inconsistent national policy are all barriers to effective service planning and delivery for individual children eligible for such services (Edgar, Horton, & Maddox, 1984; Johnson et al., 1987). A Rand Corporation report (Brewer & Kakalik, 1979) concluded that the service system is fragmented, uncoordinated, and not particularly responsive to the total needs of the individual.

Several strategies that promote greater interagency collaboration and planning have been proposed. Promising approaches involve collaborating with parents, educators, and health field personnel in managing children with special education needs using integrated case management systems have been proposed (Wray & Wieck, 1985) wherein all agencies interacting with a family or child would work together using a common client file. A key innovative strategy that has evolved in recent years is the creation of paid positions as "parent facilitators" of parents who have confronted similar challenges to work with other parents and to assist agencies in coordinating their services in a manner that is accessible and beneficial to families. These programs not only provide other parents with an approachable and knowledgeable advocate or guide, they also promote the spirit of collaboration within and between agencies.

Collaborating with Families

Over the past several years, the concept of parent-professional collaboration has gained increased credibility and support among parents and professionals. Acceptance of this philosophy of shared responsibility can enhance the effectiveness of classroom instruction. More frequent contacts between parents and professionals have been shown to result in significant improvements in the reading performance of low-achieving students (Iverson, Brownlee, & Walberg, 1981). In addition, studies have shown that planned training can prepare parents to foster the language development, motor, and cognitive skills of their children (Lombardino & Mangan, 1983; Macy, Solomon, Schoen & Galey, 1983; Sandler, Coren & Thurman, 1983), as well as to intervene to improve the academic and classroom behaviors of their children (Chapman & Heward, 1982; Imber, Imber, & Rostein, 1979).

Despite the numerous advantages of and reasons for parental involvement, there is convincing evidence that we are nowhere close to achieving equal partnerships among parents and professionals (Turnbull & Leonard, 1980; Turnbull & Turnbull, 1990). A plethora of studies indicate that parents of special education students have been excluded from meaningful participation in IEP team meetings (Hoff, Fenton, Yoshida, & Kaufman, 1978; Gilliam 1979; Goldstein, Strickland,

Turnbull & Curry, 1980). Over half of the time, IEPs are completed before the meetings and without parental participation (Turnbull & Leonard, 1980), with one study revealing that 50% of the time the parents could not identify the type of placement recommended for their child during the staffing (Hoff et al., 1978). The average IEP meeting has been documented as lasting only 36 minutes and consisting primarily of teachers presenting the IEP to the parents (Goldstein et al., 1980). This lack of meaningful parent participation is true within special education generally, as well as specifically with disabled children from minority group backgrounds (Lynch & Stein, 1982, 1983). Parents tend to view professionals as uncaring and arrogant (Turnbull, 1983), while professionals frequently see parents as adversarial, angry, pushy, and denying (Sonnenschein, 1981).

Interestingly, communication between families and professions appears to be a major source of stress for both parties (Bensky et al., 1980; Turnbull, 1983). In many cases, parents are uncomfortable with schools and teachers. Perhaps they come from diverse cultural and linguistic backgrounds and feel out-of-place or awkward in the schools. They may view schools with a certain reverence that inhibits their behaving in ways that their cultural backgrounds would view as interfering. Parents who themselves experienced academic difficulties and school failures also may avoid schools. Finally, parents may find it almost impossible to visit schools during the day because they work outside of the home, have preschool children that they must care for, or are economically disadvantaged and have difficulties finding transportation to the school.

The growing cultural and linguistic diversities of our population present new challenges for both professionals (most of whom are Anglo) and parents of children with disabilities (Lynch & Lewis, 1982; Lynch & Stein, 1982, 1983). A specialized base of information and skills is required to achieve active participation and meaningful partnerships with these diverse groups in planning and delivering programs for children with dis-

abilities. Home-school collaboration is most effective when both the professionals and the parents exhibit respect for one another and openness in working together. Table 2.1 lists characteristics of parents and professionals that facilitate effective collaboration. In many cases, the responsibility for initiating and guiding the collaboration process rests primarily with the professional personnel.

Approaches developed to increase parental involvement with the schools involve training teachers to communicate effectively (Sawyer & Sawyer, 1980), scheduling meetings and events during evening hours, providing child care and possibly even transportation (Lynch & Stein, 1982; 1983), and involving parents as colearners or tutors (Shapero & Forbes, 1981) in the classroom.

Informal Strategies. The schools' systematic sharing of information can have positive effects. Research has shown that most parents prefer informal and frequent communication about their children's progress over procedures that require specific formal and active participation (Turnbull & Turnbull, 1990). Examples are sending notes or newsletters (either that the school administrators or the students in the classroom have developed) home or using recorded telephone messages (both in the primary language of the family)

Individual teachers can promote positive home-school relationships by seeking out ways of interacting with parents about their students in a positive way. One strategy is to set up a system whereby students can earn "Good Student Reports" that they can take to their parents each week. Another strategy that some teachers use with great success it to set aside no more than 5 or 10 minutes a day to phone two to three parents to tell them that it is a joy to work with their child. In many cases, this will be the first time that the parents have ever heard good news about their student from the schools. Teachers can introduce the call simply by identifying themselves, and saying: "I have only a couple of minutes, but I want you to know how much I am enjoying having Randy in my room this year." The teacher

TABLE 2.1   Effective Parent-Professional Collaboration

For parents
- Believe that parents are equal partners with professionals and accept responsibility for solving problems and planning.
- View the professional as a person who is working for the well-being of the child.
- Target mutual understanding of a problem as the goal for interactions with professionals.
- Maintain a file of important documents and correspondence of services provided.
- Express the needs of the family to the professional in an assertive manner.
- Accept that a professional has responsibilities for working with many children and their families.
- When notable situations or significant changes occur, communicate the information quickly with relevant professionals.
- Communicate with other parents.
- Encourage communication among all professionals working with the child.
- Maintain realistic expectations, recognizing that because definitive answers are difficult to obtain, collaboration must be a continuing process.

For professionals
- Be empathetic with parents; mentally reverse roles to consider how they feel.
- Maintain an awareness of the child as multidimensional, with varied roles and skills.
- Keep in mind that the child is a part of a family with its own distinct roles, values, and expectations.
- Remember that, with rare exception, parents are motivated by love and commitment to their child.
- Respect the role of parents as one of equality in the collaboration process; they are the experts on their child.
- Value the comments and insights of parents and make use of their knowledge.
- Communicate with the parents about the progress of the child.
- Distinguish between fact and opinions when discussing problems and potentials.
- Steer the parents toward solutions and resources, providing written and oral evaluations about potential services, supportive options, and relevant agencies.
- Target mutual understanding of a problem as the goal for interactions with parents.
- Involve parents in developing action plans and in reviewing and evaluating the effectiveness of these plans.
- Make appointments and hold conferences at convenient times.
- Obtain and share information from other appropriate professionals to ensure that necessary information is communicated and that parents do not expend unnecessary energy searching for assistance.
- Avoid sharing unnecessary information or gossiping about the families of students with other professionals.

Source: Adapted from Volser-Hunter and Exo (1987)

should then relay one specific positive anecdote or observation, thank the parent for his time, and encourage the parent to visit the classroom or call the teacher in the future. By beginning early in the school year and calling in the early evenings so as to catch parents who work outside the home, teachers can establish a positive link between the classroom and the family. It is good to try to call all parents within the first 2 or 3 weeks of school. After that, a similar call every 5 or 6 weeks on the average should maintain the relationship.

Formal Strategies.   Formal strategies can include home-school contracts (described in Chapters 4 and 5) and parent/family-school conferences. Family contacts through such mechanisms as newsletters, notes, and telephone calls can smooth the way for parent-teacher conferences later in the year. Informational group meetings early in the school year for all parents of students in your class can further smooth the way for later individual family conferences. Such meetings provide parents with an opportunity to visit the physical class, learn about its program, and to meet the teacher under low-stress conditions.

Setting Up a Conference. When asking a parent to come to the school for a conference about a specific student, the teachers should notify parents both in writing and by phone. Care must be taken to schedule the meeting at a time that is convenient for the parents and the parents should be provided with written information about the date, time, place, and topics to be discussed. Other family members invited and other professionals who will attend should also be specified. A follow-up phone call provides parents with an opportunity to gather more information about the nature and purpose of the meeting, and to add topics they want to discuss. Research has shown that when parents are sent a preconference awareness packet (containing information about the conference and suggestions for preparing for it), they are more likely to attend (Kinlock, 1986).

Preparing for a Conference. The teacher should have in mind a clear objective or set of objectives for the conference. The teacher should review the student's work, gather samples that reflect student progress, summarize key information, and develop an agenda that outlines key questions to be asked and concerns to be probed. Teachers should think about the roles of the other participants, and plan for their involvement and mentally rehearse the conference. It is important that the teacher give prior thought to the tone of the conference. It is almost always unfair, inaccurate, and counterproductive to say or do anything during a conference that appears to blame the par-

ents or the family situation for the student's difficulties. Parents, even sophisticated, highly educated ones, tend to be apprehensive about being requested to meet with the teacher of a child having difficulties in school. They may be overly sensitive to any suggestion, no matter how oblique, that they are at fault. When a particularly delicate situation must be discussed (e.g., suspected child abuse or change in the student's educational placement), even greater care should be taken in planning the discussion that is to occur. Finally, the environment should be arranged so as to enhance communication and minimize interruptions. For example, it is preferable that all adults should sit in equal-size chairs rather than having the teacher in an adult chair and the parents in student chairs. Remember that a major responsibility is putting the parents at ease and establishing rapport with them.

Conducting a Conference. During a conference, the teacher will first want to establish rapport among all participants, and then gather and give information, elicit a mutually agreed upon plan of action, and then summarize the conference (Stephens & Wolf, 1980). Turnbull and Turnbull (1990) have recommended guidelines for conducting a parent-teacher conference. They recommend that at the beginning of the conference, a few minutes should be allowed for participants to relax and get to know each other. They should be introduced to one another and their various roles in the conference explained. The teacher should then begin by specifically commenting on positive attributes of the student prior to introducing problem areas or concerns. Problem areas should be described with anecdotes and, where appropriate, examples of work reflecting the problem in question. The teacher should remain sensitive to the impact that the discussion is having on the parents and provide opportunities for parents to interject information and to ask questions. To the extent possible, a give-and-take atmosphere should be established. The teacher should propose possible resolutions to the problem, keeping in mind that the parents may or may not be open to taking an active instructional or partnership role in any proposed interventions. A consensus should be reached and responsibilities of the the conference participants specified. Options for follow-up activities should be clearly stated and the dates of any subsequent meetings set at this time. Teachers should take special care in ending the meeting on a positive note, and to thank the parents and other participants for their contributions.

SUMMARY

Collaborative consultation is the key to addressing many student challenges within the classroom and school, among agencies, or between the home and school, or home-agency-school. The processes of collaborative consultation and prereferral intervention provide educators with alternatives for meeting the challenges of providing students with services within appropriate learning environments. As classroom teachers are asked to educate increasingly heterogeneous groupings of students, the need for collaborative consultation grows.

Current concepts of collaborative consultation emphasize the goal, common to both regular and special education, of providing effective education for all children. Collaborative consultation provides a process that facilitates access to the multitude of resources available to promote that goal.

This chapter has discussed barriers to collaboration, and described the importance of mutual ownership of problem situations and parity among those who work together to resolve them. It delineates several models of collaborative consultation and describes the variables critical to the success of these models. Using collaborative consultation as a prereferral intervention strategy is promoted as a means for dealing with learning problems before they develop into disabling conditions. Developing productive relationships with other agencies that provide services (mental health, welfare, protective) to students at risk for academic failure can serve to more effectively marshall additional resources to benefit the student. Finally, working collaboratively with the parents and families of students from a diversity of backgrounds can enhance the effectiveness of educational efforts. Both informal and formal strategies can be utilized to involve parents and families in more productive relationships with the schools.

Collaborative consultation provides a context in which teachers can extend their effectiveness with students. This context provides a facilitative environment in which teachers can employ the instructional skills and strategies described in the remaining chapters of this textbook.

CONTENT MASTERY QUESTIONS _____

1. What educational, social, and legislative factors have led to the current emphasis on attention collaborative consultation and prereferral intervention?
2. Outline the history of school-based consultation from medieval Europe to the 1980s.
3. Describe the three components of the triadic model.
4. Contrast "expert" and collaborative models of collaboration.
5. In the triadic model, where does problem ownership reside? Explain.
6. Define "collaborative consultation."
7. What are key people variables that impact upon collaborative consultation?

8. Describe the three problem-solving relationships that determine who mediates a problem.

9. What are the three theoretical models for consultation?

10. List the five stages of consultation.

11. Describe the four levels of activity involved in collaborative consultation.

12. Describe and discuss the three procedural implementation variables.

13. Discuss the two concepts that are at the core of the prereferral intervention framework.

14. Describe the six stages of prereferral intervention.

15. Describe two informal strategies that teachers can use to communicate with parents.

16. List and briefly discuss steps that teachers should take to ensure the success of parent-teacher conferences.

REFERENCES

Alpert, J. L. (1977). Some guidelines for school consultants. *Journal of School Psychology, 15*(4), 308–319.

Amidon, E. J., & Hough, J. B. (1967). *Interaction analysis: Theory, research and application.* Reading, MA: Addison-Wesley.

Bensky, J. M., Shaw, S. F., Gouse, A. S., Batens, N., Dixon, B., & Beane, W. E. (1980). Public Law 94-142 and stress: A problem of educators. *Exceptional Children, 47*(1), 24–29.

Bergan, J. R. (1977). *Behavioral consultation.* Columbus, OH: Charles E. Merrill.

Brewer, H. A., & Kakalik, J. S. (1979). *Handicapped children: Strategies for improving services.* New York: McGraw-Hill.

Catterall, J. S. (1987). An intensive group counseling dropout prevention intervention: Some cautions on isolating at-risk adolescents within high school. *American Educational Research Journal, 24*(4), 521–540.

Cegelka, P. T., MacDonald, M., & Gaeta, R. (1987). Promising programs: Bilingual special education. *Teaching Exceptional Children, 20,* 48–50.

Chapman, J. E., & Heward, W. C. (1982). Improving parent-teacher communication through recorded telephone messages. *Exceptional Children, 49,* 79–82.

Cipani, E. (1985). The three phases of behavioral consultation: Objectives, intervention, and quality assurance. *Teacher Education & Special Education, 8,* 144–152.

Conoley, J. C., & Conoley, C. W. (1982). *School consultation: A guide in practice and training.* New York: Pergamon Press.

Cowen, E. L. (1980). The primary mental health project: Yesterday, today, and tomorrow. *Journal of Special Education, 14*(2), 143–154.

Deal, T. E. (1987). Effective school principals: Counselors, engineers, pawnbrokers, poets . . . or instructional leaders. In W. Greenfield (Ed.), *Instructional leadership* (p. 88). Boston: Allyn & Bacon.

DeBoer, A. L. (1986). *The art of consulting.* Chicago: Arcturus Books.

Dustin, D., & Ehly, S. (1984). Skills for effective consultation. *School Counselor, 32*(1), 23–29.

Edgar, E., Horton, B., & Maddox, M. (1984). Post-school placements: Planning for public school students with developmental disabilities. *Journal for Vocational Special Needs Education, 6*(2), 15–18, 26.

Forman, S., & Linney, J. (1988). School-based prevention of adolescent substance abuse: Programs, implementation and future direction. *School Psychology Review, 17,* 550–558.

Friend, M. (1988). Putting consultation into context: Historical and contemporary perspectives. *Remedial and Special Education, 9*(6), 7–13.

Fuchs, D., Fuchs, L. S., Bahr, M. W., Fernstrom, P., & Stecker, P. M. (1990). Prereferral intervention: A prescriptive approach. *Exceptional Children, 56*(6), 493–513.

Fuchs, D., Fuchs, L. S., Bahr, M. W., Reeder, P., Gilman, S., Fernstrom, P., & Roberts, H. (1990). Preferral intervention to increase attention and work productivity among difficult-to-teach pupils. *Focus on Exceptional Children, 22,* 1–8.

Fuchs, L. S., Fuchs, D., Hamlett, C. L., & Stecker, P. M. (1991). Effects of curriculum-based measurement and consultation on teacher planning and achievement in mathematics operations. *American Educational Research Journal, 28*(3), 617–641.

Gallessich, J. (1982). *The profession and practice of consultation.* San Francisco: Jossey-Bass.

Gans, K. D. (1985). Regular and special educators. *Teacher Education and Special Education, 8*(4), 188–189.

Gibbins, S. (1978). Public Law 94–142: An impetus for consultation. *School Psychology Digest, 7,* 18–25.

Gilliam, J. E. (1979). Contributions and status rankings of educational planning committee participants. *Exceptional Children, 45,* 466–468.

Goldstein, G., Strickland, B., Turnbull, A. P., & Curry, L. (1980). An observational analysis of the I.E.P. conference. *Exceptional Children, 46,* 278–286.

Graden, J. L., Casey, A., & Christenson, S. L. (1985). Implementing a prereferral intervention system: Part I. The model. *Exceptional Children, 51*(5), 377–384.

Gutkin, T. B. (1981). Relative frequency of consultee lack of knowledge, skills, confidence, and objectivity in school settings. *Journal of School Psychology, 19*(1), 57–61.

Heron, T. E., & Harris, K. D. (1987). *The education consultant: Helping professionals, parents, and mainstreamed students,* (2nd Ed.). Boston: Allyn & Bacon.

Hoff, M. K., Fenton, K. S., Yoshida, R. K., & Kaufman, M. J. (1978). Notice and Consent: The school's responsibility to inform parents. *Journal of School Psychology, 16,* 265–273.

Huefner, Dixie Snow. (1988). The consulting teacher model: Risks and opportunities. *Exceptional Children, 54*(5), 403–414.

Idol, L., Paolucci-Whitcomb, P., & Nevin, A. (1986). *Collaborative consultation.* Rockville, MD: Aspen.

Idol, L., & West, J. F. (1987). Consultation in special education (Part II): Training and practice. *Journal of Learning Disabilities, 20*(8), 474–493.

Idol-Maestas, L. (1983). *Special educator's consultation handbook.* Rockville, MD: Aspen.

Idol-Maestas, L., & Ritter, S. (1985). A follow-up study of resource/consulting teachers: Factors that facilitate and inhibit teacher consultation. *Teacher Education and Special Education, 8,* 121–131.

Imber, S. D., Imber, R. B., & Rostein, C. (1979). Modifying independent work habits: An effective teacher-parent communication program. *Exceptional Children, 46,* 218–221.

Iverson, B. K., Brownlee, G. D., & Walberg, H. J. (1981). Parent-teacher contracts and student learning. *Journal of Educational Research, 74,* 394–396.

Johnson, D. R., Bruininks, R. H., & Thrulow, M. L. (1987). Meeting the challenge of transition planning through improved interagency cooperation. *Exceptional Children, 53,* 522–530.

Johnson, L. J., Pugach, M. C., & Hammitte, D. J. (1988). Barriers to effective special education consultation. *Remedial and Special Education, 9*(6), 41–47.

Kerr, M. M., & Zigmond, N. (1986). What do high school teachers want? A study of expectations and standards. *Education and Treatment of Children, 9,* 239–249.

Kinlock, D. (1986). *An investigation into the impact of a preparation strategy on teachers' perceptions of parent participation in the IEP review conference of learning disabled and educable mentally retarded students.* Unpublished doctoral dissertation. University of Missouri, Columbia

Knight, M. F., Meyers, H. W., Paolucci-Whitcomb, P, Hasazi, S. E., & Nevin, A. (1981). A four year evaluation of consulting teacher service. *Behavioral Disorders, 6,* 92–100.

Leyser, Y., & Abrams, P. D. (1984). Changing attitudes of classroom teachers toward mainstreaming through inservice training. *Clearing House, 57,* 250–255.

Lilly, M. S. (1988). The regular education initiative: A force for change in general and special education. *Education and Training in Mental Retardation, 23*(4), 253–260.

Lilly, M. S., & Givens-Ogle, L. (1981). Teacher consultation: Present, past, and future. *Behavioral Disorders, 6,* 73–77.

Lombardino, L., & Mangan, N. (1983). Parents as language trainers: Language programming with developmentally delayed children. *Exceptional Children, 49,* 358–361.

Lynch, E. W., & Lewis, R. B. (1982). Multicultural considerations in assessments and treatments of learning disabilities. *Learning Disabilities: An Interdisciplinary Journal, 1*(8), 93–103.

Lynch, E. W., & Stein, R. (1983). *Cultural Diversity and P.L. 94-142. A comparative study of parent participation across Hispanic, Black and Anglo families.* San Diego: San Diego State University.

Lynch, E. W., & Stein, R. (1982). Perspectives on parent participation in special education. *Exceptional Education Quarterly, 3*(2), 616–623.

Macy, D. J., Solomon, G. S., Schoen, M., & Galey, G. S. (1983). The DEBT project: Early intervention for handicapped children and their parents. *Exceptional Children, 49,* 447–448.

Medway, F. J., & Forman, S. G. (1980). Psychologist's and teacher's reactions to mental health and behavioral school consultation. *Journal of School Psychology, 18*(4), 338–348.

Neel, R. S. (1981). How to put the consultant to work in consulting teachers. *Behavioral Disorders, 6,* 78–81.

Paget, K. (1988). Adolescent pregnancy: Implications for prevention strategies in educational settings. *School Psychology Review, 17,* 570–580.

Paolucci-Whitcomb P., & Nevin, A. (1985). Preparing consulting teachers through a collaborative approach between university faculty and field-based consulting teachers. *Teacher Education and Special Education, 8,* 132–143.

Phillips, V., & McCullough, L. (1990). Consultation-based programming: Instituting the collaborative ethic in schools. *Exceptional Children, 56*(4), 291–304.

Pianta, R. C. (1990). Widening the debate on educational reform: Prevention as a viable alternative. *Exceptional Children, 56*(4), 306–313.

Pugach, M., & Johnson, L. J. (1989). Prereferral interventions: Progress, problems, and challenges. *Exceptional Children, 56*(3), 217–226.

Pugach, M., & Raths, J. D. (1983). Testing teachers: Analysis and recommendations. *Journal of Teacher Education, 34*(1), 37–43.

Reisberg, L., & Wolf, R. (1986). Developing a consulting program in special education: Implementation and interventions. *Focus on Exceptional Children, 19*(3), 1–14.

Reisberg, L., & Wolf, R. (1988). Instructional strategies for special education consultants. *Remedial Education and Special Education, 9*(6), 29–40.

Rosenfield, S. (1987). *Instructional consultation.* Hillsdale, NJ: Lawrence Erlbaum.

Rosenfield, S. (1985). Teacher acceptance of behavioral principles: An issue of values. *Teacher Education and Special Education, 8*(3), 153–158.

Sandler, A., Coren, A., & Thurman, S. K. (1983). A training program for parents of handicapped preschool children: Effects upon mother, father, and child. *Exceptional Children, 47,* 355–358.

Sandoval, J., Lambert, N. M., & Davis, J. M. (1977). Consultation from the consultee's perspective. *Journal of School Psychology, 15*(4), 334–341.

Sawyer, H. W., & Sawyer, S. H. (1980). A teacher-parent communication training approach. *Exceptional Children, 47,* 305–306.

Schmuck, R. A. (1982). Organization development in the schools. In C. R. Reynolds and T. Gutkin (Eds.), *Handbook of school psychology* (pp. 829–857). New York: John Wiley & Sons.

Shapero, S., & Forbes, S. H. (1981). A review of involvement program for parents of learning disabled children. *Journal of Learning Disabilities, 14,* 499–504.

Shapiro, E. S. (1988). Preventing academic failure. *School Psychology Review, 17,* 601–613.

Sonnenschein, P. (1981). Parents and professionals: An uneasy relationship. *Teaching Exceptional Children, 14*(2), 62–65.

Stainback, W., & Stainback, S. (1984). A rationale for the merger of regular and special education. *Exceptional Children, 51,* 102–111.

Stanley, S. O., & Greenwood, C. R. (1980). *CISSAR: Code for instructional structure and student academic response: Observers manual.* Kansas City, KS: Juniper Gardens Children's, Bureau of Child Research, University of Kansas.

Stephens, T. M., & Wolf, J. S. (1980). *Effective skills in parent/teacher conferencing.* Columbus: Ohio State University, National Center for Educational Materials and Media for the Handicapped.

Tharp, R., & Wetzel, R. (1969). *Behavior modification in the natural environment.* New York: Academic Press.

Tindal, G., Shinn, M. R., & Rodden-Nord, K. (1990). Contextually based school consultation: Influential variables. *Exceptional Children, 56*(4), 324–336.

Turnbull, A. P. (1983) Parent-professional interactions. In M. E. Snell (Ed.), *Systematic instruction of the moderately and severely handicapped* (2nd ed.) (pp. 45–73). Columbus, OH: Charles E. Merrill.

Turnbull, A. P., & Leonard, J. (1980). Parent involvement in special education: Emerging advocacy roles. *School Psychology Review, 10,* 37–44.

Turnbull, A. P., & Turnbull, J. A. (1990). *Families, professionals, and exceptionality: A special partnership.* Columbus, OH: Merrill.

Walker, H. M., & Rankin, R. (1983). Assessing the behavioral expectations and demands of less restrictive settings. *School Psychology Review, 12,* 272–284.

Wang, M. C. (1987). Toward achieving educational excellence for all students: Program design and student outcomes. *Remedial and Special Education, 8,* 25–34.

West, J. F., & Brown, P. A. (1987). State departments of education policies on consultation in special education: The state of the art. *Remedial and Special Education, 8*(3), 45–51.

Witt, J. C., & Elliott, S. N. (1986). Acceptability of classroom intervention strategies. In T. R. Kratochwill (Ed.), *Advances in school psychology,* Vol. 4 (pp. 251–288). Hillsdale, NJ: Lawrence Erlbaum.

Wray, L., & Wieck, C. (1985). Moving persons with developmental disabilities toward less restrictive environments through case management. In K. C. Lakin & R. H. Bruininks (Eds.), *Strategies for achieving community integration of developmentally disabled citizens* (pp. 219–230). Baltimore: Paul H. Brookes.

Ysseldyke, J., & Christenson, S. (1987). *The instructional environmental scale.* Austin, TX: Pro-Ed Publishing Co.

Ysseldyke, J., Reynolds, M., & Weinberg, R. A. (1984). *School psychology: A blueprint for training and practice.* Minneapolis: National School Psychology Inservice Training Network, University of Minnesota.

Zins, J. E., Coyne, R. K., & Ponti, C. R. (1988). Primary prevention: Expanding the impact of psychological services in the schools. *School Psychology Review, 17,* 542–549.

CHAPTER 3

Identifying and Measuring Behavior

PATRICIA THOMAS CEGELKA

CHAPTER OBJECTIVES

At the conclusion of this chapter, the student will be able to:
1. Pinpoint and describe behavior in observable terms.
2. Define operant and respondent classes of behavior and provide examples of each class.
3. Write behavioral objectives for both academic and social behaviors.
4. Identify the key steps of task analysis.
5. Identify and describe considerations for selecting a data collection approach.
6. Describe the five approaches to data collection.
7. List seven guidelines for data collection.
8. Compute interrater reliability.
9. Develop and interpret simple line performance data graphs.

The primary role of teachers is to bring about changes in the academic and social behaviors of students. They accomplish this by organizing the environment and designing instruction in ways that facilitate learner acquisition of new knowledge and skills. Instructional effectiveness is increased when teachers are specific about the knowledge and skill objectives they are attempting to teach, and when they measure students' progress relative to these objectives. This requires proficiency in several technical skills relating to identifying, describing, analyzing, and measuring behaviors. Once a target behavior is precisely defined, data can be collected on the behavior to determine its current state and whether changes occur over time. In addition to collecting data on their students, teachers may collect data on their own behaviors (e.g., the ratio of positive to negative verbal comments the teacher makes) as a means of evaluating and improving their interactions with students. Many teachers teach their students to keep data on their own individual behaviors. Not only does this take some of the burden off the teacher, but it helps to shift responsibility for behavior management to the students themselves.

The first half of this chapter describes how to pinpoint, define, and observe behaviors; how to formulate behavior objectives; how to task analyze behaviors; and how to measure behavior changes. The second half of the chapter describes approaches to the frequent and direct measurement of student behavior. It contrasts these approaches to more traditional approaches. Throughout the chapter the emphasis is on the application of empirical methods to measuring student outcomes and thereby evaluating the effectiveness of instruction.

FOCUSING ON OBSERVABLE BEHAVIORS

Identifying classroom objectives in terms of *observable* student behaviors provides focus and precision to instruction. Verbs such as *identify, draw, hold,* and *list* more precisely specify the target behaviors than do such frequently used terms such as *learn, understand,* or *appreciate.* Using verbs that denote observable behaviors helps to specify what students are expected to do and to determine when students have accomplished these outcomes. We cannot directly observe the internal processes of knowledge acquisition (e.g., *learning*) or the possession of positive self-concepts;

we can only infer that knowledge has been acquired or particular self-concepts have been formed through the individual's observable behavior. For example, one can infer that Juan has *learned* simple addition facts or *understands* place value, when he attains a score of 90%, or better, on a test of these math facts. One similarly might infer that Peter possesses a positive self-concept when he initiates appropriate social interactions with others, responds positively to interactions that others initiate, attends school cheerfully, plays cooperatively on the playground, smiles, achieves well academically, and so forth. In other words, the cognitive knowledge or affective state is inferred from the observable behavior of the student.

Another advantage of focusing on observable behaviors is that behavioral occurrences can be described and recorded. One can count the behavior and determine how frequently it occurs. Two or more people can agree on the dimensions of the specific behavior and whether the behavior is increasing or decreasing. Such interobserver reliability adds confidence to data and permits a more accurate evaluation of the outcomes of intervention efforts. Instructional objectives can be developed based on data about current behaviors of students, and information can be communicated about current and desired levels of skill development to parents and others. Finally, day-to-day instructional decisions can be made based on observable student progress.

Interpreting Behaviors

Focusing on observable aspects of behavior provides teachers with a direct and objective approach to decision making. It reduces the vague or subjective interpretations of student behaviors that may be invalid and unreliable, and that do not provide specific direction for instructional efforts. Such interpretative statements label behaviors (often erroneously) but are of little instructional value.

As an example, consider the student who reads with several hesitations and a high rate of errors. Based on their personal orientations and skill levels, four different teachers could provide four different descriptions of the student's behavior:

"Nicole is very anxious when she reads."
"Nicole is dyslexic."
"Nicole is learning disabled."
"Nicole read fifteen words with eight errors."

The first three statements represent various interpretations of the reading behavior. Because they do not refer to anything directly observable, there is no way to verify the accuracy of these interpretations. There would be little agreement among observers on the frequency or strength that such internal states were manifest. Furthermore, these statements are of little educational relevance in that they do not suggest an instructional direction to the teacher. The fourth statement, "Nicole read fifteen words with eight errors," represents an observation that multiple observers can document and agree upon. It suggests that some form of intervention is needed (e.g., give Nicole easier materials to read, teach word recognition skills, reinforce appropriate responding). The description of the behavior provides a basis for interpreting the behavior, implementing interventions, and evaluating these interventions.

Another illustration of a behavior that is open to varying interpretations involves a child crying in class. Different observers might state:

"Eric feels insecure."
"Eric is spoiled."
"Eric cried after falling and scraping his knee."
"Eric cried for one minute after the teacher told him to return to his seat."

As with the previous example, the first two statements represent interpretations of Eric's behavior; they refer to unobservable and hypothetical conditions. "Feeling insecure" or being "spoiled" do not reference objective, observable events that can be directly recorded and measured. The third statement, "Eric cried after falling and scraping his knee" includes three observable events: crying, falling, and scraping. The fourth statement also includes directly observable events: Eric's crying and the teacher talking. Further, it provides more specificity by delineating how long the crying lasted.

Specific behavioral observations such as these provide a basis for determining whether or not interventions are needed, for planning the interventions, and for evaluating whether or not these interventions result in desired changes in the target behavior. The target behaviors (reading, crying) can be observed, counted, and displayed on a graph. Over time, it can be determined whether Nicole is making fewer reading errors and whether Eric is crying either less frequently or for shorter periods of time, for example, for 0.5 minute instead of 1 minute.

Classes of Behavior

Teachers are primarily interested in student behaviors that are observable and that are under the voluntary control of the individual. These are referred to as **operant** behaviors, meaning that they are controlled by their consequences. Most behaviors are operant. Only a few behaviors are actually **respondent** in nature, meaning that they are involuntary or reflexive responses. Examples include salivation when food is placed in one's mouth, rapid eye blinks in a dust storm, or knee jerks when the patellar tendon is tapped. The relationship between respondent behaviors and their preceding or antecedent stimuli is essentially invariable.

Operant behaviors, in contrast, are closely tied to their consequences. They occur as a function of these consequences. Behaviors that result in consequences that are pleasurable or satisfying to the individual are strengthened, meaning that they are likely to be emitted again in the future, while behaviors that do not result in satisfying consequences are unlikely to be emitted in the future. For example, if reading results in failure experiences for Nicole (and possibly

teacher scolding or classmate ridicule as well), it is unlikely that Nicole will want to spend much time reading. She may avoid reading through absences from school, misbehavior, or sullen refusal. She may become a class clown during reading periods, masking her reading failure with her misbehavior.

In the case of Eric's falling and scraping his knee, the crying could be a respondent behavior elicited by the pain, or it could be an operant behavior developed through past experiences of receiving attention whenever he cried after falling. In order to decide whether the crying is operant or respondent, voluntary or involuntary, more information is needed about the past consequences of the behavior. Has falling been paired with increased adult attention in the past? Through observation, one can determine the extent to which Eric's behavior is related to the behaviors others emit when he cries. If his crying appears to be related to the amount of attention he receives, then the crying is probably at least partially operant. This means that the crying can be eliminated or decreased by changing the responses that others give when Eric cries.

On the other hand, it is highly improbable that Eric's crying when he is reprimanded in class is anything other than an operant behavior. Examining the past consequences to crying would no doubt reveal a history of pleasurable consequences (e.g., attention from peers or adults, hugs, and getting his own way). In other words, Eric cries because crying has proven effective in the past in getting what he wants in a specific situation. It has resulted in pleasurable consequences.

IDENTIFYING BEHAVIORAL GOALS

A teacher is responsible for assisting students to develop new behaviors and/or to change aspects of existing behaviors. The behaviors targeted should be relevant to the well-being and progress of individual students or to the progress and general well-being of their classmates. The behavior could be either academic or social, and can involve such disparate activities as paying attention and being "on task," completing assignments, talking out in class, or fighting on the playground. The behavior selected for change is known as a *target behavior.* To be considered targets for behavioral change, behaviors must meet the following three criteria:

1. The behavior must be *observable.* It must have physical properties that enable it to be clearly described in precise behavioral terms.
2. The behavior must be *operant,* that is, under the voluntary control of the individual. It is unlikely that a teacher would want to—or could—change a respondent behavior, such as the rate of eye blinking or the student's pulse.
3. The behavior must be *specific.* For example, teachers generally want to decelerate disruptive behavior. While this may be a general starting point, it does not specify exactly what constitutes the disruptive behavior. Whenever a statement of a target behavior (e.g., "Murray's behavior is disruptive.") is open to more than one interpretation, more specificity is needed. Murray may be tapping loudly with his pencil, pulling the hair of the child at the next desk, singing to himself, or throwing books around the room. All of these are specific, observable behaviors that are subject to change through the application of behavioral techniques.

An additional consideration in describing a target behavior is to specify the **movement cycle** of the behavior. In other words, to pinpoint when the behavior begins and when it ends. This is not as self-evident as it may seem. Take, for example, out-of-seat behavior. The manner in which the movement cycle is defined will greatly affect how the results of the behavior change effort are interpreted. Consider the following three definitions of *out-of-seat behavior:*

1. Out-of-seat behavior begins when the child's body loses all contact with the chair on which he is sitting . . . and ends when any part of his body retouches the chair (Moyer & Nelson, 1973, p. 12).
2. Out-of-seat behavior begins when the seat of the child loses contact with the seat of the chair and ends when the seat of the child regains contact with the seat of the chair.
3. Out-of-seat behavior begins any time the seat of the child loses contact with the seat of the chair for 3 seconds and continues until the seat of the child regains contact with the seat of the chair.

In the first example, the target behavior occurs each time the child loses complete contact with the chair. Standing on the chair, standing by the chair while holding onto it, or raising up on his knees in the chair would not be recorded as out-of-seat behaviors. In the second instance, in which out-of-seat behavior is defined more precisely (e.g., the seat of the child losing contact with the seat of the chair), out-of-seat behavior would have occurred in each of the examples given. Standing by or on the chair, kneeling on the chair, and similar behaviors would count as being out-of-seat. The third definition is even more precise: Every 3 seconds that the child's seat is out of contact with the seat of the chair is counted as a separate occurrence of the target behavior. Should the child leave her chair and wander about the room for 15 seconds, the observer would count five instances of out-of-seat behavior.

In the first two definitions of the movement cycle, time was not a consideration; being out-of-seat for 5 seconds or 5 minutes would both count as only one occurrence of the behavior. The teacher must determine when the length of time of the behavior is an important consideration. The ability to keep this type of data influences how precisely a movement cycle is defined. The presence of a teacher's aide increases the feasibility of measuring the behavior in terms of duration.

One final consideration in describing target behaviors is specifying the situation in which the behavior occurs. There are few universal target behaviors (self-mutilation being one such behavior). Typically, a behavior is appropriate in some situations and inappropriate in others. The goal is to help students to discriminate between these situations. Running, being out-of-seat, talking without permission, and shouting are all behaviors that are desirable in some situations and undesirable in other situations. All of these behaviors may be appropriate on the playground, and some of them (talking without permission or being out-of-seat) may be appropriate in some classroom situations, such as a small group project involving cooperative learning activities.

DEVELOPING BEHAVIORAL OBJECTIVES

Once the observable student behaviors have been identified, then instructional objectives can be developed for teaching new behaviors or changing existing ones. *Behavioral objectives* are written statements of specific observable behaviors that have been identified as desirable outcomes for an individual student or a group of students. They serve to clarify the goals of the instructional programs or interventions in both the social and academic arenas. An instructional objective must be behavioral, meaning that it must be stated in terms of directly observable behaviors. As noted in the preceding section of this chapter, some verbs denote clearly observable behaviors, while others do not. For example, words such as *know, understand, believe, enjoy,* and *appreciate* do not describe behaviors that can be objectively observed and measured; they can only be inferred. On the other hand, words such as *write, state, recite, list,* and *identify* do describe behaviors that are both observable and measurable. Table 3.1 differentiates among three types of action verbs: (1) those that can be directly observed, (2) those that are more ambiguous, and (3) those that cannot be directly observed. By using directly observable and unambiguous action verbs in writing instructional objectives, one can identify the target behavior, consistently observe it to determine the extent to which it currently exists, implement a program to change that behavior, and evaluate

the results of that program in terms of actual student behavior changes. Precisely identifying the target behavior informs the students of the expected outcome, facilitates communication between the teacher and others, and permits continuity of instruction when people other than the teacher are involved (Alberto & Troutman, 1990).

When initially developing instructional objectives, it can be helpful to think in terms of broader education goals, such as learning the alphabet, mastering addition facts at the first-grade level, increasing appropriate interactions in a group setting. Each of these goals can then be made more specific by targeting observable behaviors that are indicative of these goals. For example, while one can only infer what a student has learned, it is possible to directly observe and measure what the student *does*. Hence, a teacher can infer that the student has attained the goal of learning the alphabet when she *recites* the alphabet, *writes* the alphabet, *identifies* letters out of sequence, or *alphabetizes* a list of words. Similarly, completing twenty single-digit addition problems at 90% accuracy on a worksheet is one measure of mastering addition facts at the first-grade level. Appropriate social interactions might involve a small group instructional situation in which the students respond correctly to teachers questions, respond only when called on, and keep their hands to themselves.

Stating the target behavior in observable terms is the primary attribute of a correctly written behavioral objective. In addition, the behavioral objective also should include a statement of the conditions under which the behavior should occur (e.g., "When asked to recite the alphabet,. . . ." or "When given a list of twenty names, ...") as well as a statement of the criterion for acceptable performance. For example, an objective that states "When asked by the teacher, the student shall recite the alphabet," may include as its criterion *"with only one error"* or *"with no errors and only two hesitations of 1 second or more."*

TABLE 3.1   Levels of Action Verbs

Action Verbs That Are Directly Observable

To cover with a card	To draw	To place
To mark	To lever press	To cross out
To underline	To point to	To circle
To repeat orally	To walk	To say
To write	To count orally	To read orally
To shade	To put on	To name
To fill in	To number	To state
To remove	To label	To tell what

Ambiguous Action Verbs

To identify in writing	To check	To construct
To match	To take away	To make
To arrange	To finish	To read
To play	To locate	To connect
To give	To reject	To select
To choose	To subtract	To change
To use	To divide	To perform
To total	To add	To order
To measure	To regroup	To supply
To demonstrate	To grooup	To multiply
To round off	To average	To complete
To inquire	To utilize	To summarize
To acknowledge	To find	To borrow
To see	To convert	To identify

Action Verbs That Are Not Directly Observable

To distinguish	To be curious	To solve
To conclude	To apply	To deduce
To develop	To feel	To test
To concentrate	To determine	To perceive
To generate	To think	To create
To think critically	To discriminate	To learn
To recognize	To appreciate	To discover
To be aware	To become competent	To know
To infer	To wonder	To like
To realize fully	To analyze	To understand

Source: Alberto, P.A., and Troutman, A.C. (1990) *Applied Behavioral Analysis for Teachers: Influencing Student Performance.* Columbus, OH: Merrill Publishing Co., p. 67. Reprinted with permission from Research for Better Schools, Inc.

Mager and Pipe (1984) have delineated guidelines for writing behavioral objectives. These three components of correctly stated behavioral objectives are listed as follows:

1. **Observability.** The objective or goal should be stated in terms of behaviors that classroom personnel can easily observe and measure. The objective should clearly delineate

the behavior that the student will be able to demonstrate when the teaching procedure is completed.

EXAMPLE   *Albert will orally identify numerals 1 through 5.*

2. **Conditions for occurrence.** The behaviorally stated objective must include a context or conditional statement regarding when or under what conditions the skill or objective should be observable. The observer should have a definite idea as to when to expect the targeted behavior to occur and when the observer should be able to verify the occurrence of the behavior.

EXAMPLE: Albert will orally identify numerals 1 through 5 *when presented with the appropriate number symbols.*

3. **Criteria of performance.** The criteria for mastery must be clearly specified. This mastery statement indicates that the student has obtained sufficient skill to perform the task satisfactorily and/or that the student has obtained a level of skill such that he is ready to progress to the next instructional level.

EXAMPLE   Albert will orally identify numerals 1 through 5 when presented with the appropriate number symbols *without any misses, ten out of ten times.*

To summarize, a behavioral objective identifies the instructional goal in terms of observable behaviors. It states the conditions under which the target goal is to be demonstrated and it specifies the criteria for acceptable performance. Behavioral objectives assist the teacher in clarifying what to teach a student, they inform the student of the expected outcome, and they provide a basis for monitoring and evaluating student progress.

TASK ANALYSIS

Sometimes an educational goal or objective may be too far removed from the student's current level of functioning to be meaningful instructionally. For example, a long-term goal of education is to develop children into productive adult citizens. Typically, this encompasses a range of expectations, from not littering the streets, to paying taxes, to political participation. However, to be meaningful instructionally, this goal must be broken down into more manageable components that specify behaviors for varying ages or competency levels of individuals. At the first-grade level, good citizenship might involve following classroom rules, cleaning up after oneself, sharing, and completing assigned tasks, while at the secondary level it might involve participating in student government and accepting responsibilities in various clubs. In a more academic vein, alphabetizing a set of thirty library index cards is a fairly distant goal for someone who cannot identify letters of the alphabet or recite the alphabet. Clearly, subskills must first be taught; proficiency in them is a prerequisite to the larger alphabetizing task.

Task analysis is the process of dividing a target behavior into a skill sequence that comprises its essential components or substeps. Breaking the target behavior into its component parts and developing behavioral objectives for each of these steps permits the teacher to identify the precise point at which the student is experiencing difficulty and to develop instructional sequences for these substeps. Task analysis can be used to identify critical topographic features (e.g., the physical features of the task such as grasping a pencil or the pattern of moving one's eyes across a printed page), it may focus on the conceptual aspects of a task, or it may encompass both components. It is not necessary, nor is there sufficient time, to task analyze all instructional tasks in the classroom. Typically, teachers analyze a task when one or more students experience difficulty with it.

Four approaches to developing task analyses are outlined in Table 3.2. While each of the four approaches utilizes somewhat different procedures to effect a task analysis, they all use the same essential processes as follows:

TABLE 3.2   Approaches to Developing Task Analyses

Watch a master
This approach involves watching a person who is proficient in the performance of the task and writing down a complete sequence of each of the steps that this "master" performs. Particularly well suited to the analysis of motor tasks, this approach also can be used to analyze cognitive and affective tasks, such as using appropriate verbal salutations or engaging in an interpersonal interaction.

Self-monitoring
In this approach, you serve as your own master, performing the task or skill and recording the essential components as they are performed. You may want to use a tape recorder to avoid interrupting your performance to record each step. When completed, you should perform the task a second time, following the steps you have identified; you can add, delete, or modify steps as necessary.

Brainstorming
This approach is particularly useful for analyzing complex tasks that do not conform easily to a strict temporal sequence. You begin by identifying the terminal objective or goal, and then writing down all of the subtasks involved in the goal. Arrange these tasks in as logical an order as possible, and then review the listing for completeness as well as sequence.

Goal analysis
Particularly well suited for identifying behaviors that signal the attainment of a complex, nonobservable behavior (such as self-concept and social acceptance), this approach focuses on identifying those behaviors that signal the attainment of the goal. For each behavior on your list, you should determine how frequently or how well the criterion behavior must be performed.

1. Identifying the sequence of subtasks involved in the performance of a targeted behavior and designing incremental instructional programs based on each subtask.
2. Writing a behavioral objective for each of these steps, thereby permitting the teacher to limit the scope of instruction at any given moment to a discrete performance, not an entire performance domain.
3. Determining the performance entry level for the targeted task and specifying the prerequisite skills (e.g., the point at which that particular task analysis begins).

Tasks can be analyzed in terms of their temporal order, developmental sequence, or by difficulty level (McLoughlin & Lewis, 1990). *Temporal order* refers to the sequence in which the substeps must be performed (e.g., one must pull on a pair of jeans before zipping them up). A *developmental sequence* involves a gradual progress through a hierarchy of subskills which build upon previously acquired skills (e.g., in math, addition comes before subtraction, which comes before multiplication, which comes before division). Analysis of a task *by difficulty level* focuses on teaching easier skills before progressing to more difficult ones. For example, manuscript writing of lowercase letters might proceed from straight-line letters (i, t, i), to straight-line and slant letters (v, x, w, y, z), to circle and curve letters (o, c, s), to circle and line letters (a, b, e, p, g, d, q), to curve and line letters (j, h, m, k, n, f, r, u) (Affleck, Lowenbraun, & Archer, 1980).

To complete a temporal task analysis, break a task down into the appropriate number of substeps and ask "What skills are required to accomplish this step?" Continue asking this question until the task is sufficiently analyzed to be useful instructionally with a particular student or group of students. Once a task analysis has been completed, the teacher can check its adequacy by performing the steps outlined, and adding or deleting steps as necessary. If a given student still experiences difficulty at one substep, repeat the task analysis process, breaking that substep down into smaller substeps. The subskills are the prerequisites for each step or substep in the task analysis. Each of these subskills must be mastered as the student progresses toward the target behavior. Examples of two task-analyzed skills are presented in Tables 3.3 and 3.4.

In completing a task analysis, it is important that the focus be on the task itself, not the individual student. This encourages a more objective analysis of the task and produces a task analysis that can be used with other students in other situations. A completed task analysis can be used an endless number of times in instructional programming.

Task analysis is an essential part of good teaching. It brings into sharper focus any particular learning difficulty a student may have, thereby increasing teacher efficiency. It serves as a tool for assessing attained skills and as a basis for individualizing instruction (Alavosius & Sulzer-Azaroff, 1990; Zencius, Davis, & Cuvo, 1990). At the same time, it provides a vehicle for monitoring and recording pupil achievement.

Utilizing Task Analysis

Breaking large, global tasks into small, discrete steps permits one to focus instruction on specific steps instead of an entire domain. Once a task analysis has been completed, the teacher can assess the student's performance to determine which steps in the sequence the student already has mastered and at what step the student encounters difficulty. It is important to keep in mind that for each learning task, there are prerequisite skills that a student must possess prior to being taught a particular instructional sequence. **Prerequisite skills** are those component skills essential to the performance of a new task. For example, prior to writing the alphabet, the student must demonstrate particular motor skills (e.g., holding the pencil appropriately) as well as particular knowledge skills (e.g., identifying each of the letters separately, reciting the alphabet).

Instruction should begin at the point in the skill sequence at which a student first begins to experience difficulty but still functions with some degree of success. The task analysis provides the teacher with the sequence of skills leading to the target behavior. Each of the subsequent task-analyzed steps of this sequence becomes an instructional objective. Instruction of these steps can be individualized by modifying the presentation of the task, providing for different response modes, or even by further analyzing a given step into smaller substeps. Knowledge of prerequisite skills, coupled with a careful analysis of

---

TABLE 3.3   Example of Task Analysis for Zipping a Jacket

TASK SEQUENCE

1. Pull opposite sides of jacket together.
2. Align zipper tab with zipper end.
3. Insert zipper end into zipper tab while holding side of jacket with zipper base.
4. Hold opposite side of jacket.
5. Grasp zipper tab between thumb and fore/middle finger.
6. Pull zipper tab to top of jacket.
7. Push zipper tab down flat against zipper
8. Release zipper tab and jacket.

TABLE 3.4 Example of Task Analysis for Drinking from a Glass

Task Sequence	Passed Pretest	Date Completed
1. Move arm to glass	+	1/12
2. Grasp glass with hand	+	1/12
3. Lift glass	+	1/14
4. Move glass to mouth	+	1/15
5. Tilt/raise glass and tilt neck	+	1/17
6. Swallow	+	1/20
7. Lower arm to table	+	1/25
8. Release glass		

subsequent task steps, assists the teacher in designing instructional programs that ensure student success at the entry point of each new instructional activity. This initial success tends to make the learning experience positive, efficient and effective.

Task analysis also assists in tracking improvements in individual student performance, permitting the identification of progress that may be too subtle to pick up when thinking only in terms of larger terminal objectives. A checklist that includes all components of the task is useful for tracking progress. With a space to record the date on which the child achieves each subtask, a checklist such as presented in Table 3.5 specifies what a child can do, and provides information about the child's rate of progress along a particular skill continuum.

Task analysis helps to break educational goals and objectives into manageable instructional objectives that can be taught sequentially. Attaining these objectives, however, should be viewed as a necessary, but not sufficient, criterion of performance. The ultimate instructional goal transcends the simple performance of each subskill. Ultimately, the teacher will want the student to perform the total task with fluency. True mastery involves speed and automaticity, and the ability to generalize the task skills to new situations. Analyzing a task into teachable subskills can be a key step to this mastery. After each separate substep is learned and proficiency

TABLE 3.5 Task Analysis Checklist for Writing Behavioral Objectives

	Pretest		Posttest	
SUBTASKS	YES	NO	YES	DATE ACCOMPLISHED
1. Names person to complete action (e.g., Vanessa)	×			
2. Writes objective using observable verbs (e.g., will say the word)		×	×	3/14
3. Writes criterion (e.g., nine of ten times)		×	×	3/25
4. Writes conditions (e.g., when presented with ten cards)		×	×	4/1
5. Writes behavior objectives as part of instructional planning		×		

on the task is demonstrated, new instructional objectives should target fluency of performance.

MEASURING BEHAVIOR

Once teachers have learned to describe behaviors in precise, observable terms and to task-analyze behaviors into meaningful components or substeps, they then are ready to collect data on behavior. Data collection encompasses a plethora of approaches, from simple checklists (such as those described for marking progress within the subtasks of a task analysis) to criterion-referenced tests; curriculum-based measures; and commercially developed, standardized tests. For purposes of planning, monitoring, and adjusting instruction, data based on the direct observation of student behavior is the most useful. Observational data on academic and social behaviors help the teacher to identify problem areas, develop intervention programs, and evaluate the effects of interventions as they are implemented. This monitoring permits the teacher to alter instruction in response to student behavior, thereby avoiding false assumptions about student progress.

Data that are collected before any efforts have been made to change a behavior is referred to as **baseline data.** A key advantage of collecting baseline data is that it permits an objective assessment of a given situation. Individual student data can be compared with data from other students to determine the extent to which a behavior is discrepant. A teacher initially may describe a problem with a student in terms of a specific behavior only to find out through data collection that the student emits that behavior no more or less frequently than is typical in the classroom. What was assumed to be the problem is actually not the problem after all. This tells the teacher to look further and, possibly, to do a self-check for potential bias. For example, it may be that Melissa is not talking out more than other students, but that the pitch or tone of her voice is of an irritating quality such that any talking out seems excessive to the teacher. Comparing data across children will confirm whether the impression that a teacher has of a situation is accurate.

Another example involves a teacher's concern with Martha's math performance. Ms. Tingent wondered if Martha's low rate of completing math problems correctly might be a function of inattentiveness during large group instruction. She had her aide collect momentary time sample data on Martha's on-task behavior each day for a week during the 20-minute large group instructional period. In addition, the aide collected data on the behavior of two "good students" who were achieving slightly above grade level, who caused few, if any, problems in the classroom, and who completed assignments accurately and on time. Data from these two students provided a comparison point for interpreting the data on Martha's behavior. The aide divided the 20-minute instructional period into ten intervals of 2 minutes each. Using a stopwatch, every 2 minutes she would observe the three students in a predetermined order—first Martha, then Sue, and then John—making a tally for each if she observed on-task behavior. The data she collected is presented in Table 3.6. She converted this data into daily percentages for each student and depicted it on a simple graph, as shown in Figure 3.1. Both the graph and a visual inspection summary of the data indicate that Martha's on-task behavior is considerably less than that of her two classmates.

In addition to helping to pinpoint possible problem areas, baseline data also provides a basis for evaluating the effectiveness of intervention efforts. By comparing data collected after an intervention was initiated with data collected before any efforts were made to change the behavior, teachers can determine the effects of the intervention employed. They can determine exactly how much a behavior has changed in the desired direction and do not have to rely on subjective impressions of the success of efforts. Whaley and Mallott (1971) developed an amusing anecdote about a kindergarten teacher and one of her students, Jimmy-the-Pincher, that underscores the importance of taking both baseline and interven-

TABLE 3.6   Momentary Time Sampling for Martha's On-Task Behavior

	MARTHA	*SUE*	*JOHN*
Day 1	⑷	⑷ III	⑷ III
Day 2	IIII	⑷ IIII	⑷ II
Day 3	⑷ I	⑷ ⑷	⑷ IIII
Day 4	III	⑷ IIII	⑷ I
Mean	4.5	9.0	7.5

tion data as an antidote to the vagaries of subjective evaluation.

It seems that whenever Jimmy got close to his kindergarten teacher, he pinched her. Being a bright, behaviorally oriented teacher, she quickly pinpointed pinching as a target behavior to be decelerated. She devised a behavioral change plan that featured the acceleration of an incompatible behavior. (An incompatible behavior *is one that cannot coexist with another behavior, e.g., sitting down and standing up, being in-seat and out-of-seat, working quietly and fighting with another child). The teacher reasoned that reinforcement of the incompatible behavior (in this case, patting the teacher) should accelerate that behavior, re-*

sulting in the deceleration of the pinching. Thereafter, each time Jimmy approached her, the teacher said, "Pat, Jimmy. Don't pinch." After only a few days, the teacher happily reported that pinching was no longer a problem. A colleague's independent observations revealed, however, that the frequency of Jimmy's teacher-pinching had not changed. Although Jimmy now patted the teacher more, he pinched her just as frequently as ever. The only thing that had changed was the teacher's impression of Jimmy. In actuality, the intervention strategy had no effect on the target behavior. Comparisons of the data collected during baseline and after intervention provided an objective basis for judging the success of the intervention strategy.

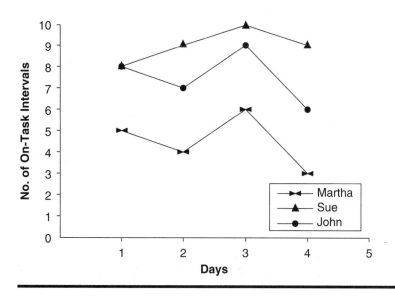

FIGURE 3.1   Comparison Graph of Martha's On-Task Behavior

Dimensions of Behavior

Data can be collected on a variety of dimensions of a behavior. Typically, there is some particular aspect of the behavior that a teacher pinpoints as needing to change. A student may be unable to perform specific tasks such as drinking from a glass, holding a pencil when writing, sharpening a pencil, or swinging a baseball bat. These are all topographical features of a response. Other features of interest may have to do with where the behavior occurs (locus), how often a behavior occurs or how accurately it is emitted (frequency and accuracy), how long it takes a student to respond after being given directions (latency), the length of time during which the behavior continues (duration), and the amount of strength used in making the response (force or magnitude). The following list highlights the key features of each of these dimensions:

- **Topography.** The form and content of a response; the observable features of a response.

  EXAMPLES   Lifting a fork to mouth; switching on the light; picking up a pencil; walking across the room; raising a hand; shaking hands; looking at a book; zipping a jacket.

- **Locus.** The object toward which the behavior is directed.

  EXAMPLES   In social interactions—peers, parents; in self-help tasks—clothes, bed, food; in academic tasks—books, computer, worksheet; in vocational tasks—boss, co-workers, equipment.

- **Frequency.** The number of times a specific behavior occurs. **Rate** is the number of times per minute (or hour, week, month). **Percentage** is the ratio of number completed to total number possible.

  EXAMPLES   Number of math problems correct; number of math problems completed per minute; percentage of correct answers.

- **Duration.** The period of time in which a response continues.

  EXAMPLES   Winning times in sports events; length of on-task behavior; time spent cleaning a desk; getting dressed; walking around a room.

- **Latency.** The time elapsed between the stimulus and the response; or the interval between ending one response and beginning another.

  EXAMPLES   Teacher says, "Put away materials" and 5 seconds later, students begin cleaning up. John finishes one math problem and begins the next 2 seconds later.

- **Force or magnitude.** The intensity of response or the force involved.

  EXAMPLES   Pushing on a door; hitting or patting a friend; whispering or shouting; the noise level in a room; the strength of a handshake; keyboarding on a manual typewriter as opposed to a computer.

The first step in selecting a measurement strategy is determining which dimensions of a behavior are of concern. The next consideration is the nature of the change targeted for that behavior. If the goal is to increase responses, simple frequency tallies will suffice, or percentages of correct responses can be calculated. If the goal is to increase or decrease the amount of time that a student is engaged in a task, then duration should be measured. Other factors that influence the type of data collected include: (1) the need for precision in data recording, (2) the number of students in the classroom, (3) the availability of an aide or other observer, and (4) the capability of the students to record their own behaviors.

Data Collection Approaches

A simple checklist or tally sheet is all that is required to record most behaviors. This tally record can be kept on a clipboard, or some teachers will cut an index card in two and tape half around their wrists for recording convenience. Other teachers will wear a "golfer's pal" to record the behaviors of one or two students. The number and types of behavior being recorded, convenience, and teacher preference will dictate the type of recording devise selected. Sample tally sheets are presented in Figure 3.2. An index card taped to a student's desk is convenient if the teacher is keeping interval or time-sampling data, or if the student is recording his own data. For example, the teacher could periodically mark a tally for on-task behavior, or students could keep their own records of such behaviors as working for 15 minutes, talking out, completing assignments, and so forth. Machines can also collect data. Various hardware, such as digital counters, bar code wands, and personal computers can be useful in counting and tracking behaviors.

Data collection procedures can be devised for each of the behavioral dimensions described previously. These include event recording, duration recording, interval and time-sampling recording, latency recording, and magnitude or force recording. Recording data in terms of permanent products is another approach.

Event recording of discrete instances of behavior is the simplest and most frequently used observational recording system. Event data can be represented as simple frequency counts, or as percentages or rate of occurrence of the target behavior.

Many teachers prefer **frequency data** because it is easy to collect. All that is required is to tally the occurrence or nonoccurrence of a target behavior. Such behaviors might include talking out, completion of assignments, or out-of-seat behavior. Teachers can use simple tally marks for each occurrence of the behavior and then depict them graphically. Figure 3.3 depicts the number of times each day Cora raised her hand to ask a question. The reader should note that the data implies no value judgment as to whether or not hand raising is considered a desirable or an undesirable behavior.

Frequency data also can be used for comparative analyses of student behaviors. For example, Socorro's teacher also might be interested in the frequency with which Socorro speaks out in class without raising her hand. Figure 3.4 illustrates a comparative data sample for Socorro's appropriate and inappropriate question-asking behavior. A vertical phase line separates the baseline data from the intervention data.

Shirley's Talk Outs
Continuous Frequency Record

No. of Talk Outs

Monday, September 5	ⅢⅢⅢ Ⅲ
Tuesday, September 6	ⅢⅢⅢ ⅢⅢⅢ Ⅰ
Wednesday, September 7	ⅢⅢⅢ ⅢⅢⅢ
Thursday, September 8	ⅢⅢⅢ ⅢⅢⅢ
Friday, September 9	ⅢⅢⅢ Ⅱ

Time Interval Data

Date: September 12					
Time:	10:00	11:00	12:00	1:00	2:00
Talk Outs	Ⅱ	ⅢⅠ	Ⅱ	ⅢⅠ	ⅢⅠ

FIGURE 3.2   Sample Tally Sheets

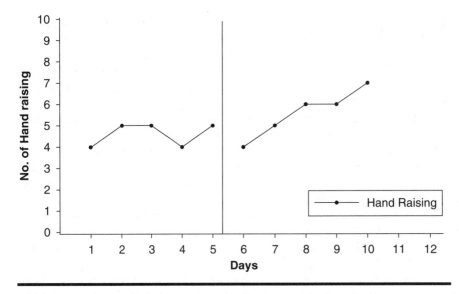

FIGURE 3.3   Frequency of Socorro's Hand Raising to Ask Questions

Frequency data requires observation periods of equal length. In Figures 3.2 and 3.3, the observation periods were the the morning half of the day. However, if Socorro had been absent for part of the morning on Wednesday, then data from that day could not be compared with data from the other days. In a similar fashion, the time period for smaller recording times should be constant for comparison purposes (e.g., all 20-minute observation periods).

Percentage and **rate data** are more informative than simple frequency data whenever the time intervals for the behavior vary or when the number of opportunities to respond differ. Accu-

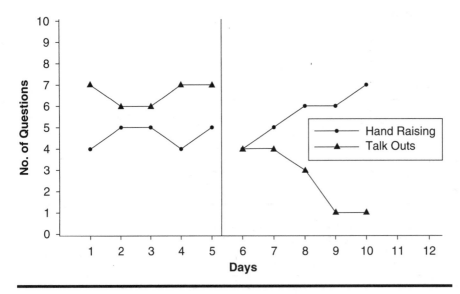

FIGURE 3.4   Comparative Data on Socorro's Hand Raising

racy may be expressed as percentage data or rate data. Examples include the percentage correct on a math assignment, or the percentage of words read correctly. Percentage data may be calculated in the following ways:

$$\frac{\text{No. correct}}{\text{Total number}} = \text{Percentage correct}$$

or

$$\frac{\text{No. incorrect}}{\text{Total number}} = \text{Percentage incorrect}$$

By using percentage data, the teacher can compare a student's performance over 5 days when the math assignments included twenty, twenty-two, eighteen, twenty-four, and twenty-six problems (of which Dick completed fifteen, twenty-one, fourteen, twenty-one, and twenty-four successfully), or over 4 weeks during which the number of homework assignments required varied from five to eight to three to ten (of which Dick turned in three, six, three, and nine).

For Dick, the percentages of math problems successfully completed over the week were 86% overall (95/110), with daily percentages being 75, 95, 78, 88, and 92% correct. He also handed in 81% of all homework assignments (21/26), or for each of the 4 weeks, he completed 60, 75, 100, and 90% of the homework assignments. Both of these are illustrated as follows:

Dick's Math Problems Correct

Monday	15/20	=	75%
Tuesday	21/22	=	95%
Wednesday	14/18	=	78%
Thursday	21/24	=	88%
Friday	24/26	=	92%
Total	95/110	=	86%

Dick's Homework Completion

Week 1	3/5	=	60%
Week 2	6/8	=	75%
Week 3	3/3	=	100%
Week 4	9/10	=	90%
Total	21/26	=	81%

Rate data can provide a useful measure of fluency and relative learning speed. The latter suggests whether or not the instruction is efficient. In other words, is it setting the conditions under which the student can acquire skills at optimal speed? Two instructional strategies or programs may teach the same skills effectively, but if one teaches a student five new skills in 1 hour and the other teaches these same five skills in 4 hours, then the former is obviously more desirable. Many teachers use rate data in making daily or weekly instructional decisions. Rate data can be computed by dividing the number of responses by the amount of time elapsed.

For example, if during a 5-minute session, Sammie gave twenty responses, of which fifteen were correct, his total rate of responding would be four per minute, while his rate of correct responses would be three per minute. By using the percentage data formula discussed earlier in this section, we see that Sammie's overall accuracy would be 75%.

$$\frac{\text{No. of responses}}{\text{No. of time units (minutes or hours)}} = \text{Rate}$$

$$\frac{20 \text{ Total responses}}{5 \text{ minutes}} = 4 \text{ Correct per minute}$$

$$\frac{15 \text{ total correct responses}}{5 \text{ Minutes}} = 3 \text{ Correct per minute}$$

Duration data is based on time and is appropriate for depicting behaviors when the length of the occurrence is important. Typically, these behaviors occur infrequently but last for a relatively long period of time. Earlier in this chapter we described different movement cycles for out-of-seat behavior. This is an instance when the duration of the behavior may be significant. While it may be of some interest to know that Juan was out of his seat twice on Monday, it is even more informative to know that each of these occurrences lasted more than 90 minutes! Because estimating time is highly unreliable, the teacher should use a stopwatch or a wristwatch with a second hand for recording duration. The forms illustrated in Figure

3.5 are useful in recording data procedures when duration is a key consideration.

Interval data can be collected for behaviors that can be difficult to record on every occurrence. With this intermittent sampling method, the observer records whether or not the behavior occurred during a fairly brief prescribed time period. For example, a teacher might record whether or not a behavior occurs on a 15-second interval for 5 minutes. Every 15 seconds the teacher records whether a behavior did occur (+) or did not occur (−) during that time. A positive (+) mark indicates that the behavior occurred at least once; it does not indicate how many times the behavior may have occurred during the 15 seconds. Generally, it is most useful to transform raw interval

Date of Observation	Length of Observation	Length of Behavior	Percent of Total Time

Student: _____ Date: _____ Observer: _____

Activity: _____ Location: _____

A. Total Observation Period: _____ hr _____ min
 A.1. Total Minutes: _____

B. Duration of Event:
 B.1. Time Started: _____
 B.2. Time Ended: _____
 B.3. Length of Session: _____

C. Percent of Time: _____
 (Divide A.1. by B.3.)

FIGURE 3.5   Two Examples of Duration Data Recording Forms

data into percentage-of-time data by dividing the number of intervals in which the behavior occurred by the total number of observation intervals. For example, in the behavior data recorded in Figure 3.6 there were twenty separate observations (four times a minute for 5 minutes) during which fourteen observations of the behavior were recorded. The percentage of occurrence is $14 \div 20 \times 100$, or 70%.

Interval recording has several advantages over continuous recording. Most importantly, it is sensitive to both frequency and duration, and is applicable to most continuous performance situations. This last factor is of particular relevance to the classroom teacher, who may need to take data on one or more students while at the same time managing the ongoing instruction of the entire class. By probing at prespecified time periods on a systematic basis, the teacher can obtain reliable classroom data without neglecting the rest of the classroom.

Variations of time-interval sampling include **partial interval time samples** and **whole interval time samples.** In partial interval time samples, the behavior must occur at some time during the time interval, not necessarily at the beginning or end. Whole interval samples require that the behavior take place for the entire duration of the time-sample interval.

Momentary time sampling is another form of interval data collection. In this procedure, the teacher records whether or not a behavior is occurring at the beginning or end of a specified interval of time. For example, a teacher might record on-task behavior during a 40-minute seatwork period by observing a student every 5 minutes. This would provide eight observations during the 40-minute period. At the beginning of each 5-minute interval, the teacher would mark down whether the student was on-task or off-task. Figure 3.7 depicts such data that Ms. Tingent collected on Anita's on-task behavior. The chart reveals that Anita was attending to task during four observations and not attending to task for four observations.

Time sampling is a relatively simple data collection procedure that does not impede ongo-

	15 Seconds	30 Seconds	45 Seconds	60 Seconds
Minutes				
1	+	+	−	+
2	+	+	+	−
3	−	+	−	+
4	+	+	+	+
5	+	−	+	+

Occurrence of Target Behavior (+) = 14
Nonoccurrence of Target Behavior (−) = 6
Percent of Occurrence (+/ 20) = 70%

FIGURE 3.6   Example of Interval Recording Form

Minutes	5	10	15	20	25	30	35	40
On-Task (+)	+	+			+		+	
Off-Task (−)			−	−		−		−

Occurrence of On-Task (+) = 4   Percent of On-Task = 50%
Occurrence of Off-Task (−) = 4   Percent of Off-Task = 50%

FIGURE 3.7   Momentary Time Sampling for Anita's On-Task Behavior

ing instruction. Although some precision may be lost by not recording every instance of a behavior, over a period of several days this procedure can provide data useful in instructional decision making.

Permanent products that result from behavior constitute another form of data collection. By measuring the tangible products of task engagement, teachers do not have to directly observe student engagement in the task. Examples such as written assignments that the student has completed in math, language arts, social studies, and the like can provide a record of progress over time. Other target behaviors and their products include the following:

Target Behavior	**Tangible Product**
Straightening the desk	Neat desk
Going to the library	Books checked out
Cleaning the room	Bed made; clothes put away
Mowing the yard	Trimmed grass

Videotapes and audiotapes of the student's performance are additional tangible products. Videos of physical performances, from sports events to domestic chores, permit teachers to carefully analyze the components of the behavior. In a similar fashion, an audiotape of a student reading a passage or playing a piece of music also facilitates the teacher's careful analysis of the student's behavior at a later time. Machine recordings such as printouts of percentage correct or total amount of time at work are other permanent products that can be analyzed independent of teacher direct observation of behavior.

Data Collection Guidelines

Whenever data is collected, it is important that it be both valid and reliable. **Validity** relates to the extent to which data measures what they are intend to measure and **reliability** refers to the consistency of measurement. An old adage suggests that one must be careful to compare apples to apples and oranges to oranges. Utilizing the same precise definition of the specific observable behavior and its movement cycle every time data is collected is essential. It is impossible to tell what is going on if the definition shifts from day to day. For example, if on Monday the observer records instances of out-of-seat behavior whenever the seat of the child loses contact with the seat of the chair, but on Tuesday only when the student leaves his chair and walks around the room, there will be no information about the relative occurrence of the behavior. It would be impossible to tell if the out-of-seat behavior is increasing, decreasing, or remaining the same. Sometimes the teacher's definition gradually and unintentionally shifts. Gradual changes in the definition for the target behavior over time is known as *observer drift*. Such shifts in definition affect the validity of performance data and make it impossible to evaluate the effectiveness of the intervention or instructional procedures. Occasional reliability checks with other observers can eliminate this tendency.

To ensure validity, data also should be collected during similar time periods. This is particularly true when considering frequency data. For example, it would not be meaningful to compare raw data from a 15-minute observation with data from a 35-minute period. Only when the data is converted to percentages can one compare data collected at unequal time intervals. The time of day that the data is collected also is an important consideration. The conditions under which the behavior is observed also should remain constant. It would not be meaningful to compare talking behavior during a math test with talking on the playground. The extent to which a student exhibits a given behavior, such as being on-task, may vary with the subject or the time of day. A student may typically pay more attention to math than to silent reading and/or may be more attentive during the morning than immediately after lunch. Because students are more likely to be fresh and attentive early in the day, comparisons of behaviors that occur at 8:30 A.M. and 1:15 P.M. may be specious.

The length of the observation period must be appropriate for the behavior being observed. Some behaviors can be adequately observed in fairly brief periods of time, while others require more extended observation periods. For example, a 10-minute tutorial session might be an appropriate period to observe and record letter-sound recognition responses, while the entire school day would be a more appropriate period for observing and recording fighting behavior.

Objectivity is another important consideration in collecting data. Recorder bias can lead to inconsistency in data collection attitudes. The race, ethnicity, primary language, social economic status, attractiveness, and a myriad of other student characteristics can interfere with observer objectivity. Similarly, knowledge about the giftedness of a student's siblings, the awards she has previously won, or the reputation of the student as a troublemaker can result in biased observations. Finally, observers who have a vested interest in the child, such as parents or friends, may be overly generous in their interpretations of what they see. The latter can be a particular problem if the observer is someone like a parent who has a vested interest in the child.

Kerr and Nelson (1989) have recommended guidelines for collecting data that are valid and reliable, as well as sensitive and precise. These guidelines specify the following:

1. **Select a direct and sensitive measurement strategy.** Direct measures provide precise data on the effects of instruction or interventions and are sensitive to the effects of changes in the instruction or intervention program. Products or results of behavior change efforts such as grades and weight change can be inaccurate reflections of changes in behavior.

2. **Observe and record daily for as long as possible.** The observation sample must be long enough to encompass a representative sample of the behavior. The longer the observation and recording periods, the more accurate the samples of behavior. Continuous recording is necessary for infrequent behaviors in order to obtain an adequate sample. A high frequency of recording serves to detect changes when establishing a new behavior. Probes can be used to obtain periodic data on maintenance of behaviors.

3. **Observe and record behavior where it occurs.** For valid data, the behavior must be observed where it occurs, for example, if fighting in the lunchroom is a problem, collect data when the student is in the lunchroom, not when he is waiting at the bus stop.

4. **Keep observation time relatively constant.** Record in the same time period for the same length of time whenever possible. If this is not possible, then convert to rate or percentage data to adjust for differences in observation length.

5. **Once a behavior is defined, observe and record only responses meeting that definition.** Carefully define all critical aspects of the behavior; work with a partner to establish reliability prior to beginning data collection and do periodic reliability checks to detect observer drift.

6. **Monitor only as many behaviors in as many settings as you can manage.** Monitor behaviors that are most important and most discrepant from target behaviors. The more severe the problems a student or group of students have, the more behaviors there are to monitor. Teachers should begin by observing one or two behaviors in a single student and gradually expand observations to include the same behavior in other students. To the extent possible, use others (aides or the students themselves) to collect data.

7. **Remain as unobtrusive as possible while collecting data.** Data collectors can intrude on a setting, affecting the nature of the interactions that occur. Students may show off; become self-conscious; or, if they know that data are being collected, in other ways alter their behavior. To avoid these pitfalls, the observer should remain as inconspicuous as possible when entering or leaving the room and while collecting data. Eye contact or other interactions with the students should be avoided and data collection should be delayed until the students have become accustomed to the presence of the data collector.

Interrater Reliability

It is important that the data recorded be accurate and reliable. The most desirable way of maintaining data collection consistency is to work with a partner who is trained in the recording procedures used. A teacher's aide or another teacher can serve occasionally as the independent observer to provide a reliability check for the teacher's observations. Interrater reliability can be computed either as the total reliability or as point-by-point reli-

ability. The total reliability procedure simply consists of the two observers (e.g., teacher and teacher's aide) comparing the data that each recorded on the same behavior. It is particularly applicable for data involving simple frequency or numerical counts. It involves dividing the smallest number of observations by the largest number of observations and multiplying by 100:

$$\text{Total reliability} = \frac{\text{Smallest total}}{\text{Largest total}} \times 100$$

The teacher decides that 7-year-old Nick is talking out in class without permission more than is acceptable. Her baseline data reveals twenty-five instances of talk outs during the first 30 minutes of the school day. During the same time period, the aide observes twenty instances of Nick's talking out. The interrater reliability is:

$$\frac{20}{25} = 0.8 \times 100 = 80\%$$

Point-by-point reliability is more appropriate for time-based observations such as time-interval sampling. Comparisons are made between the two observers for each observation interval. The total number of agreements is divided by the number of agreements plus the number of disagreements and multiplied by 100 to obtain a percentage.

$$\frac{\text{No. of agreements}}{\text{No. of agreements} + \text{no. of disagreements}} \times 100 = \text{Reliability}$$

An example of point-by-point reliability would be observations of on-task behavior taken at 15-second time intervals for 30 minutes. There are four observation periods per minute or one hundred twenty total periods. The teacher observed seventy-five instances of off-task behavior and the aide observed seventy, of which sixty-five were in the same time intervals that the teacher observed and five were not. There was a total of ten disagreements: the aide observed five instances that the teacher did not observe and the teacher observed five instances of off-task behavior that the aide did not observe. The computation of point-by-point reliability would be:

$$\frac{65}{65 + 10} \times 100 = 0.866 \times 100 = 87\%$$

Acceptable limits of interobserver reliability vary with the nature of the behavior being observed, the purposes for which the observation data will be used, and with teacher preference. If the behavior is extreme and totally unacceptable, the interobserver reliability figures may not be as important as intervening to change the behavior, thus lower limits of reliability will be acceptable. Further, the magnitude of the decision being made affects the level of reliability desired. If the data are being used for less critical purposes, such as general screening, the teacher can tolerate lower-reliability values. If a major change in curriculum or program placement depends on the observation data, high levels of interobserver reliability are necessary. Typically, interobserver reliability in the 80–90% range is desirable. Interobserver reliability of less than 70% has implications for the validity of the data. The target behavior may not have been defined well to begin with, or observer drift may have occurred over time, or the teacher and/or aide may not be adequately trained to collect the data.

It is a good idea to do an observer reliability check at least once during each behavior change project. This helps to ensure that the target behavior, as initially defined, is still being focused upon and that the actual results of the intervention or instructional procedures used are being evaluated. To improve interobserver reliability, be sure that the behavior is clearly defined in observable terms and that the procedures for observing and coding the behavior have been delineated. It is also helpful to practice recording data with other observers. The teacher should be sure to record the data immediately as the behavior occurs, not at some later time according to memory. Using stopwatches, tape recorders, golfer's pals, and the like can help to ensure accuracy.

INTERPRETING DATA

Analyzing the direct observation data of student behavior can greatly assist in planning and evaluating instruction. Simple, straightforward data for individual students, or small numbers of individual students, can be analyzed through visual inspection summaries. However, in most instances, graphic displays typically are preferred as tools for communicating information about student progress. It has been demonstrated that when teachers graph data, student achievement increases (Fuchs & Fuchs, 1986). Not only do graphic displays facilitate teachers in monitoring student performance and adjusting instructional programs, they also provide important feedback to students on their performance. By efficiently communicating information about student performance, graphic displays of performance data lead to improved student attainment. Many teachers find it helpful to give graphic displays of performance data to parents, teacher colleagues, and others.

Simple line graphs of behavioral data can be plotted on standard equal-interval graph paper. Typically, the performance data is plotted on the vertical axis or y axis, with the horizontal axis or x axis indicating the time units (e.g., minutes, sessions, hours, days, weeks). Graphs should be clearly labeled to indicate the student and behavior being observed. The time units of the observation and the frequency of the observation can then be marked off in equal increments. The intersection of the x and y axis represents zero, with the first instance of the behavior marked on the y axis and the first observation period marked on the x axis. Figure 3.8 illustrates sample graphs for frequency, percent, and rate data. Once the basic graph is developed, then for each observation period, the data can be plotted and lines drawn to connect the various observation periods. This provides a clear visual representation of the data.

Collecting and plotting baseline data provides a starting point for planning and implementing behavioral and instructional interventions. As a rule of thumb, three to five sessions of baseline

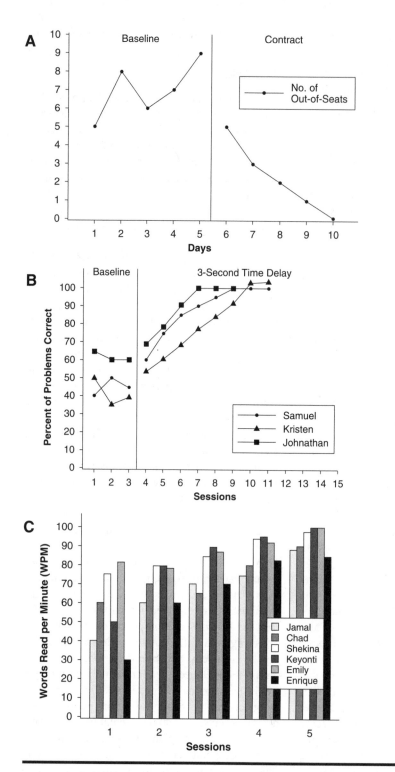

FIGURE 3.8 (A) Frequency Data for Maria's Out-of-Seat Behavior, (B) Percent Data for Multiplication Problems, (C) Rate Data for Words Read per Minute

data are needed for academic behaviors, with five to seven sessions required to establish a baseline for social behaviors. Whenever three or more data points are plotted, it is possible to determine directionality or trend of the behavior. The graph may show inconsistent response data with no directionality, stable data with little to no change, or increasing or decreasing response data.

Teachers are interested in the mean level of the data, the central tendency or trend, and the variability of the performance data. The mean level, or average performance, can be computed mathematically and depicted either numerically or graphically by drawing a horizontal line at the mean level. **Central tendency lines** are horizontal lines drawn through the mean data point for each phase or condition. They visually represent the average levels of the behavior. These lines can be used to evaluate the amount of relative change in the data within and between conditions. Figure 3.9 depicts a central tendency line for one set of data.

Data on percentage of math seatwork problems completed correctly have been analyzed through a visual summary chart in Table 3.7 as well as displayed graphically (see Figure 3.10). The mean completion rate is 77.7%. There is little

variability between the student's best and worst performances; thus, the performance is stable.

In some instances where there is no actual data trend, there still could be high variability in the behavior. *Variability* refers to the range of performance from the highest to the lowest levels. Generally, the greater the variability of a student's performance, the more unstable it is considered. This variability or instability indicates that the behavior is not under the control of the intervention procedures. Stable behavior indicated by low variability is a goal of behavior change efforts. Figure 3.11 depicts no-trend data with both low and high variability.

Trend or progress lines depict the general path of the performance within each phase, making it possible to predict the direction of the performance in future sessions. In addition to showing no trend, as in Figure 3.11, behavioral data could have either accelerating or decelerating trend lines, as depicted in Figure 3.12.

Trend lines can be drawn free-hand or developed more precisely through the use of "split middle" and "quickie split middle" techniques (White, 1974). These procedures are described in the discussion of curriculum-based assessment in Chapter 4.

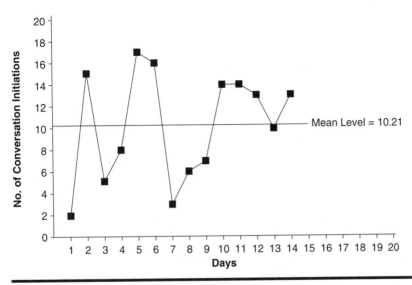

FIGURE 3.9   Central Tendency Lines

TABLE 3.7   Visual Summary Chart for Martha's Math Performance Data

DAY	PERCENTAGE	DAY	PERCENTAGE
January 13	68%	January 27	85%
January 14	70%	January 28	71%
January 15	80%	January 29	70%
January 16	70%	January 30	70%
January 17	70%	January 31	63%
January 20	86%	February 3	75%
January 21	88%	February 4	80%
January 22	90%	February 5	82%
January 23	85%	February 6	83%
January 24	83%	February 7	85%

Mean performance level from January 13 through February 7 = 77.7%

Depicting Behavior under Different Conditions

Baseline data provides a starting point for identifying target behaviors and planning academic instruction or social interventions. The baseline phase also provides a comparison point for evaluating the effectiveness of the behavior change efforts. Each time a new condition is introduced, this should be indicated by drawing a vertical line on the graph. This line marks the change in condition from baseline to intervention, or from one intervention to another. The graphic presentation of data should communicate the sequence of baseline and intervention conditions, the time spent in each condition, the independent and dependent variables, and the relationship among these variables (Tawney and Gast, 1984). Figure 3.13 depicts baseline data and two interventions. Notice that the behavior accelerated modestly with the first intervention, but a new strategy resulted in more a dramatic behavior increase.

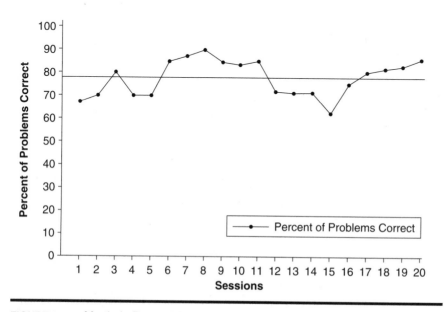

FIGURE 3.10   Martha's Percent Correct on Subtraction Problems

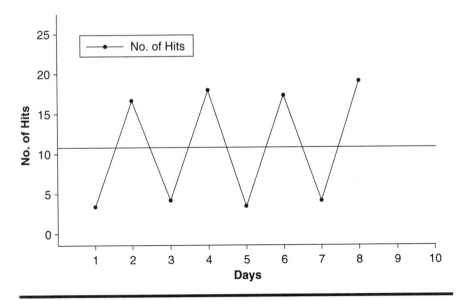

FIGURE 3.11   No. Trend Data with Variability

Graphing performance data in this way assists teachers in modifying their programs in attempts to improve student progress.

Other Graphic Representations of Data

The simple graphs described in the previous paragraphs are the most commonly used form of graph in applied behavioral analysis. Three additional methods for displaying data graphically include cumulative graphs, ratio graphs, and bar graphs. In a *cumulative graph,* the data points plotted represent the total number of responses over time, not just that day's responses. This presents an additive view of the behavior across time. For example, if a student must read a total of twenty books to earn admission to a special showing of a movie, then each new data point would represent one book added to the sum of all previously read books Figure 3.14 depicts Molly's progress over a 10-week summer vacation. During the first 4 weeks, she read two, one, three, and three books. However, in Week 5 she read five books, which moved her rapidly up the chart. She then returned to reading two books per week. With a cumulative graph, the slope is always either flat or upward, for each data point de-

picts performance that incorporates previous accomplishment or skill acquisition. A plateau or straight line indicates no responding or no progress, a steep slope indicates rapid progress, and a gradual slope indicates slow progress or slow responding.

Ratio graphing is an approach depicting behavioral data that are associated with precision teaching. Ratio data depict proportional changes associated with varying rates of behavior. Data for ratio graphing are converted to rate-per-minute and are plotted much the same way as line graph data. The primary difference is in the form of the graph or chart. The form of the special equal ratio chart paper permits plotting behaviors that occur only once a day (or 0.000695 times per minute) or as frequently as 1,000 times per minute. This facilitates the comparison of data collected at different times, in different activities, and for different response opportunities. Figure 3.15 shows an example of the Standard 'Celeration Chart paper. This equal-ratio chart paper permits teachers to quickly interpret the plotted data for purposes of making instructional decisions based on student's rate of performance.

Another means of depicting data is with a *bar graph.* This type of graph depicts progress toward

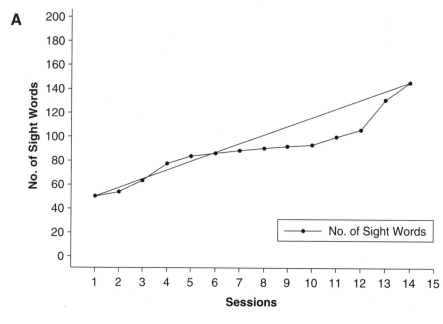

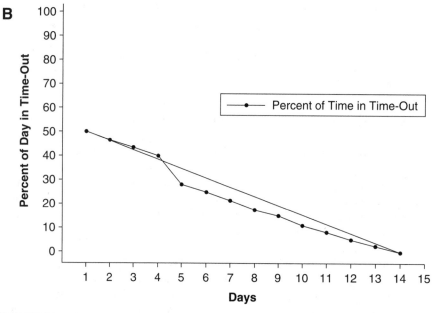

FIGURE 3.12 (A) Accelerating Trend Line and (B) Decelerating Trend Line

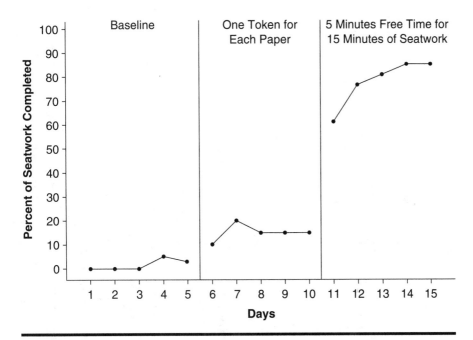

FIGURE 3.13   Baseline Data with Two Intervention Phases

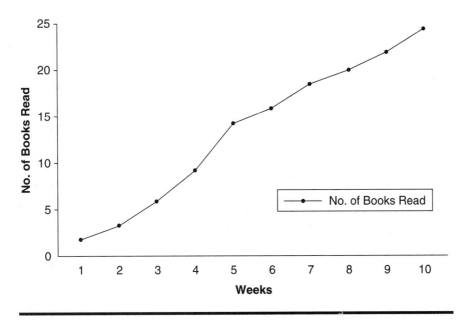

FIGURE 3.14   Cumulative Graph for Molly's Summer Reading

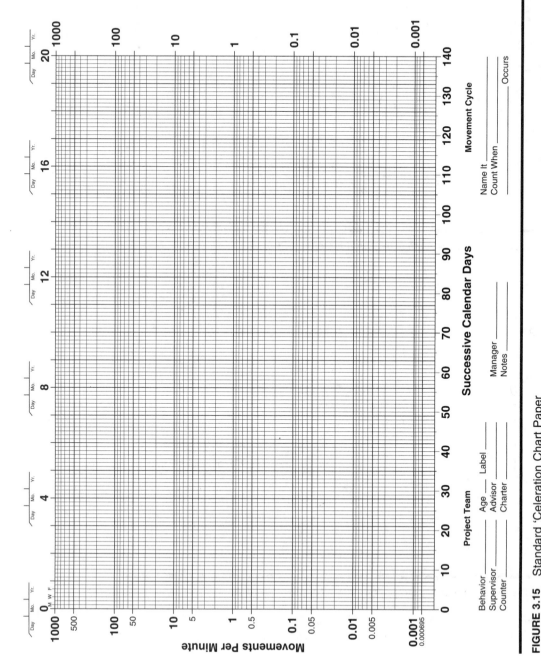

FIGURE 3.15 Standard 'Celeration Chart Paper

Source: Developed by O.R. Lindsley in 1965–1967. Available from Behavior Research Co., P.O. Box 3351, Kansas City, KS 66103. Used with permission.

a goal, and is easy for students to use and understand. Bar graphs also can be useful in communicating information on student progress to parents. When students keep their own bar graphs, they sometimes find the act of filling them in each day to be reinforcing in and of itself. Bar graphs can depict a single student's progress on a single behavior, or data from multiple students or behaviors can be depicted. Figure 3.16 illustrates these uses.

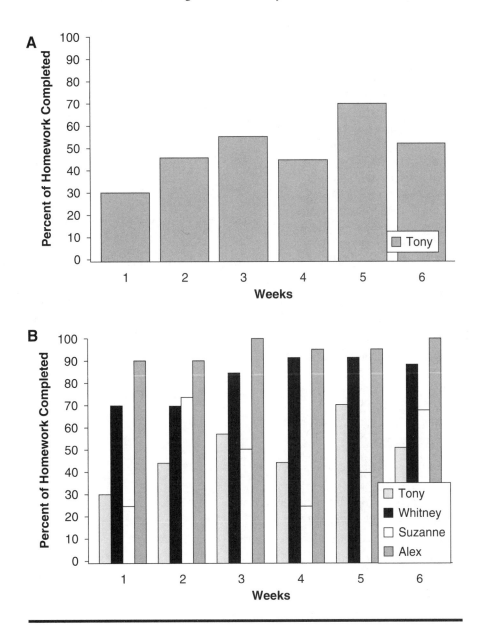

FIGURE 3.16 Bar Graph for (A) Tony's Homework Completion and (B) Students' Homework Completion

SUMMARY

The frequent collection of direct observation data on student performance is an essential aspect of effective teaching. It provides a basis for comparing an individual student's performance against that of others as well as against the individual student's own instructional target. This information assists the teacher in determining whether or not special intervention efforts should be made.

In order to systematically record data on behavior, teachers must be able to define it in precise and observable terms. Further, teachers need to articulate target behaviors in unambiguous behavioral objectives. Proficiency in task analysis permits teachers to analyze the target behavior into a hierarchy of its component parts. By pinpointing where in this hierarchy a student experiences trouble, teachers can determine the point at which instruction should begin. At the same time, the task analysis can be used to sequence instruction through each substep leading to the target objective.

The collection of direct observation data on student performance can assist teachers in planning and evaluating instructions. Data can be collected on various dimensions of a behavior, such as its topography, locus, frequency, duration, latency, and force or magnitude. There are several potential pitfalls in collecting data that are valid, reliable, and sensitive. Following general guidelines for collecting data can help teachers to avoid these pitfalls.

The data collected will tell whether or not the individual's behavior is discrepant from the behavior of peers and whether or not it is changing in the desired direction at a rate that is sufficient. By graphing baseline and intervention data, the teacher can evaluate the effectiveness and efficiency of the interventions. Frequent graphing of student academic behavior has been shown to increase student achievement. This chapter presents many graphing alternatives, including simple line graphs of the frequency, percentages, or rate of a behavior, as well as various types of bar data. By observing the slope of the data, teachers can determine whether the behavior is changing in the direction desired and if the rate of change is acceptable.

Chapter 4 builds on the behavior observation and data recording skills introduced in this chapter. It describes more traditional approaches to assessing academic and other school-related behaviors, and compares these to direct observation procedures. A fairly new approach involving the collection of direct data on the actual skills and objectives of a specific curriculum is presented as a recently developed approach to instructional decision making. Curriculum-based assessment approaches represent an extension of the direct observation skills presented in this chapter.

CONTENT MASTERY QUESTIONS

1. List three reasons for describing behaviors in observable terms. Describe a behavior observably.

2. What is the difference between operant behaviors and respondent behaviors? Provide an illustration for each class of behavior.

3. List and briefly describe the five considerations for describing a target behavior.

4. List the three components of a behavioral objective. Write a behavioral objective for a student learning Dolch sight words.

5. What are the three processes essential to performing a task analysis?

6. Discuss and describe the process for performing a task analysis. Write a task analysis adding two two-digit numbers with carrying.

7. Discuss three reasons for collecting baseline data prior to implementing an intervention.

8. Define the six dimensions of behavior and provide an example of each.

9. Discuss the six considerations involved in selecting a measurement strategy.

10. List and briefly discuss the five types of data collection methods.

11. List and briefly discuss the seven guidelines for collecting data.

12. What is interrater reliability? Write the two formulas for computing interrater reliability.

13. Define the following parts of a performance data graph:

   a. The vertical axis
   b. The horizontal axis
   c. Data points
   d. Phase lines
   e. Central tendency line
   f. Trend line

14. What are three methods for graphically displaying data other than a simple line graph.

REFERENCES

Affleck, J. Q., Lowenbraun, S., & Archer, A. (1980). *Teaching the mildly handicapped in the regular classroom* (2nd. Ed.). Columbus, OH: Merrill.

Alavosius, M. P., & Sulzer-Alazoff, B. (1990). Acquisition and maintenance of health care routines as a function of feedback density. *Journal of Applied Behavior Analysis, 23,* 151–162.

Alberto, P. A., & Troutman, A. C. (1990) *Applied behavioral analysis for teachers: Influencing student performance.* Columbus, OH: Merrill.

Fuchs, L., & Fuchs, D. (1986). Effects of systematic formulative evaluation: A meta-analysis. *Exceptional Children, 53,* 199–208.

Kerr, M. M., & Nelson, C. M. (1989). *Strategies for managing behavior problems in the classroom.* 2nd Ed. Columbus, OH: Merrill.

Mager, R. F., & Pipe, P. (1984). *Analyzing performance problems.* Belmont, CA: Fearon Press.

McLoughlin, J. A., & Lewis R. B. (1994) *Assessing special students.* (3rd Ed.). Columbus, OH: Merrill.

Moyer, J., & Nelson, C. M. (1973). *Behavior modification for the classroom.* Unpublished module, Joint Methods Course, Department of Special Education. Lexington: University of Kentucky.

Tawney, J. W., & Gast, D. M. (1984). *Single subject research in special education.* Columbus, OH: Merrill.

Whaley, O. R., & Mallott, R. W. *Elementary principles of behavior.* New York: Appleton-Century-Crofts.

White, O. R. (1974). *The "split-middle"—a "quickie" method of trend estimation.* Seattle: Experimental Education Unit, Child Development and Mental Retardation Center, University of Washington.

Zincius, A. H., Davis, P. K., & Cuvo, A. S. (1990). A personalized system of instruction for teaching checking account skills to adults with mild disabilities. *Journal of Applied Behavior Analysis, 23,* 245–252.

CHAPTER 4

Assessing School Behaviors

WILLIAM H. BERDINE
PATRICIA THOMAS CEGELKA

CHAPTER OBJECTIVES

At the conclusion of this chapter, the reader will be able to:

1. Describe the purposes of assessment and the types of assessment procedures.
2. Discuss traditional assessment forms (i.e., standardized, norm-referenced tests, and criterion-referenced tests).
3. Describe the salient features of curriculum-based assessment (CBA).
4. Discuss concept-based CBA and fluency-based measures.
5. Describe decision-making rules for CBA.
6. List and discuss uses of CBA on individual, schoolwide, and system-wide bases.

ASSESSING STUDENT BEHAVIOR

Assessing student behavior provides a basis for making decisions about eligibility and placement into special programs, the selection of instructional approaches, and the effectiveness of various programs and interventions. It involves collecting varying forms of data on behaviors of interest. This data is obtained from formal and informal measures of behavior including standardized tests of aptitude and achievement, teacher-made progress tests, criterion-referenced tests (either commercially developed or teacher made), and direct observations of student behavior. Collecting and interpreting direct observation data has been described in Chapter 3. **Curriculum-based assessment (CBA)** is an extension of these direct observation approaches that encompasses frequent, structured probes of student performance. Measures of personality preference, motivation, sociometric status, and career aptitudes and interests are additional forms of assessment that can shed additional light on student characteristics and needs.

This chapter provides an overview of the purposes of and issues surrounding student assessment. It briefly overviews assessment for purposes of determining eligibility for special education programs and making placement decisions. Measures of aptitude, achievement, classroom performance, and personal and social attributes are potential sources of information for determining program eligibility and placement. Although a range of data sources are considered, these eligibility and placement decisions rely primarily on standardized, norm-referenced test data. This type of data typically provide little direction to teachers in developing instructional programs for their students. For them, data collected on the day-to-day performance of students are considerably more meaningful. For this reason, this chapter focuses on assessment for purposes of planning, monitoring, and evaluating instruction. Included here is a discussion of the emerging trend toward CBA and measuring student achievement.

Assessment Purposes

Assessment involves a systematic process of asking educationally relevant questions about a student's learning needs in order to make decisions about instructing and placing that individual (Wallace and McLoughlin, 1988). It includes: "Any process of gathering intrapersonal or interpersonal performance data on a pupil's current behavior, language, or motor skills in any environment that involves a part of the student's current or planned educational program." (Berdine & Meyers, 1987, p. 4)

School assessment domains include academic, language, and social skills. Domains relating to early childhood development (e.g., motor, social, and cognitive skills) and to young adulthood (e.g., independent living, occupational interests and aptitudes, and social and community adjustment skills) are also relevant educationally. Assessing environmental factors in the classroom, home, or community/occupational situation can shed further light on instructional decision making.

Basic assessment questions that might be asked cover the following: (1) determining that a school performance problem exists, (2) specifying possible causes of that problem, (3) planning instructional programs that are responsive to the characteristics and needs of the student(s), and (4) evaluating the effectiveness of these instructional programs. These four basic questions include the following:

- **Is there a school performance problem?** Is the student's achievement below grade level?
- **What underlying causative factor(s) relates to the performance problems)?** Does the student have a handicapping condition that qualifies her for special education services? Is the student's primary language other than English? Is the learning problem a function of inadequate educational opportunity (e.g., lack of schooling, poor teaching, or failure to cover specific skills/content) or has the student failed to learn for some other, unknown reason (such as lack of motivation or unique individual learning needs)?
- **What are the student's educational needs?** What are the student's academic and social skill strengths and weaknesses? What cognitive and learning strategies does the student evidence? What goals and objectives are appropriate and what services (e.g., bilingual, special, and/or general education) are required?
- **How effective is the educational program that the student receives as a function of this assessment and planning process?** Does the student make adequate progress toward the instructional goals and objectives, both long term and short term? Are the targeted outcomes being attained?

Types of Assessment

Three types of assessment are relevant educationally. One typically involves formal, standardized assessment procedures involving specially qualified personnel, such as school psychologists. This level focuses primarily on screening students for special educational services, determining their eligibility, and selecting the most appropriate program placements for them. The latter two decision-making processess involve an interdisciplinary team of educational personnel, professionals, and parents, such as the child study team or Individual Education Program (IEP) team. The second type of assessment is considerably more interesting to classroom teachers; it involves planning, delivering, and evaluating day-to-day instruction of students. A third assessment level measures the effectiveness of educational efforts and programs.

These three assessment levels are overlapping in that teacher assessment of school difficulties is a critical step in the screening and referral process: Further, classroom performance data is an important consideration in determining whether or not the student qualifies for special services. Finally, student outcome data has implications for both future eligibility and placement decisions, as well as for ongoing instructional planning.

Some assessment procedures are primarily formative in nature, constituting an integral part of the teaching process. These procedures evaluate outcomes as the instruction is taking place, thereby providing data that can be useful in guiding day-to-day decision making. Others are **summative evaluations,** meaning that they are periodic evaluations (e.g., weekly exams or yearly achievement tests) that indicate the status of the individual relative to the variables measured, for example, math skills mastered and general grade-level achievement.

Examples of summative evaluations include intelligence tests as well as standardized achievement tests, such as the Comprehensive Basic Test of Skills (given to students approximately every 3 years as they progress through school), minimum competency tests, teacher-made achievement or unit tests are forms of traditional summative evaluations. Formative evaluation approaches encompass criterion-referenced assessments, teacher-made probes, direct observation data, and CBA.

Assessment Considerations

In selecting or devising approaches to assessing student performance, a variety of factors must be considered. These include:

1. What areas of performance are of concern?
2. What is the purpose of the assessment?
3. What assessment resources are available, or needed?
4. How appropriate are the procedures or instrument selected?

Specifying the performance areas of concern is a critical first step. The selection of procedures and instruments will vary, depending on whether there are concerns about general cognitive functioning, language or motoric development, classroom behavior, personal-social interactions, career choices, or academic achievement (e.g., reading, math, or written language). Next, the purpose of the assessment must be considered. Is the purpose for initial screening only, determining program eligibility, or selecting a program placement? Or is the primary purpose for developing and delivering appropriate instruction? Or is instructional/programmatic evaluation the focus of assessment interest?

Another consideration is whether the resources needed to carry out the assessment are necessary or available. There is little to be gained from considering time consuming and costly individual assessment procedures if there are no qualified personnel available to administer them or if the monetary resources cannot support such assessment. A final, critical consideration has to do with the appropriateness of the assessment procedures/instruments selected. Their technical quality in terms of reliability and validity are of interest. **Reliability** refers to the stability of the score, or the consistency with which a device or procedure measures a trait or set of behaviors over time. **Validity** relates to the extent to which the device or procedure accurately measures what it is designed to measure. An important consideration regarding validity is the extent to which the device is being used for the purposes for which it was developed.

TRADITIONAL ASSESSMENT PRACTICES

Educational assessment has traditionally taken two basic forms: (1) standardized, norm-referenced assessment and (2) criterion-referenced assessment. Both types of tests are commercially available for most school subjects and are available for either group or individual administration. Standardized, norm-referenced tests have been developed for measuring aptitudes, achievement, interests, and social and emotional factors. Criterion-referenced tests sample proficiency within a continuum of skills, providing explicit information on what the individual can or cannot do. Additional informal methods of educational assessment include questionnaires, interviews, checklists, and rating scales, all measures that provide indirect data about the student, frequently about nonobservables such as values, opinions, and past events (McLoughlin and Lewis, 1990).

Standardized, Norm-Referenced Tests

Tests are standardized when they carefully specify the test materials, administration procedures, scoring procedures, and interpretation. These standardized features permit teachers to compare the performance of one student with that of others. Norm-referenced tests are those that have been administered using the standardized procedures to a large group of individuals who, in total, are assumed to represent a specific population (e.g., all third graders, all 12 year olds, or all college students). These measures examine a student's performance in relation to the normative group on which the instrument was standardized. This reference group, assumed to be an "average" or "normal" group relative to the characteristics being measured, is selected to include representative proportions of the general population in terms of age, sex, geography, and sociocultural factors (e.g., 10-year-old females and males, distributed across geographic regions and ethnic, racial, and cultural subgroups). Technically sound instruments have been developed with population samples that are large, heterogeneous, and well selected to adequately reflect the full range of children's characteristics (Oakland, 1980).

The results of these measures can be considered valid to the extent that the student being assessed is similar to those students included in the standardization sample and the extent to which standardized administration/scoring/interpreting procedures are followed. This former consideration has been the focus of concern about assessment practices involving students from racial, ethnic, and linguistic minority groups. For instance, test norms established with primarily white, middle-class students have questionable applicability to students from diverse backgrounds.

Norm-referenced tests most typically of educational interest include aptitude tests and achievement tests. The result is a variety of score types, such as intelligence quotients (IQs), age scores, grade-equivalent scores, percentile scores, stanine scores, and standard scores. Each of these scores provides an index of the individual's performance relative to the comparison group on which the instrument was normed.

A critical assumption in norm-referenced testing is that the traits being measured are normally distributed within the population. This means that they are symmetrically distributed about the mean, as represented by a bell-shaped, or so-called normal curve. Figure 4.1 displays a normal distribution curve representing a theoretical distribution of scores plotted from a mathematical equation (Hopkins & Antes, 1979). The curve is bell-shaped and symmetrical, with the preponderance of scores clustering around the midpoint. Within a normal distribution, half of the scores fall below the mean and half of them fall above the mean score. Approximately two-thirds (67%–68%) of the scores fall within 1 standard deviation of the mean, while only 4% of the scores are greater than 2 standard deviations from the mean.

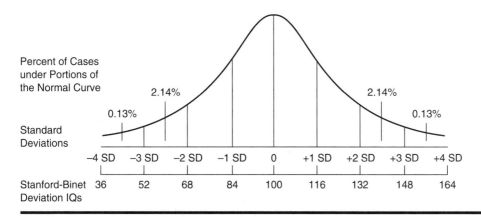

FIGURE 4.1   Normal Distribution Curve

(**Standard deviation** is a measure of central tendency for a group of scores, providing an indication of how far from the mean score, or midpoint, a particular score falls).

Examples of frequently used standardized, norm-referenced tests are listed in Table 4.1. Examples of both group and individually administered tests are included.

Criterion-Referenced Tests

Criterion-referenced tests provide an alternate form of testing procedures that indicate the level of a student's performance within a particular curriculum area. These tests compare a student's score to a specified level of mastery rather than to other students' performances. They provide information on where on a continuum of skills (e.g., adding simple math facts) a student currently is performing. This performance measure is specific to the identified task or domain, and is independent of other individuals' performances. As criterion-referenced measures provide more explicit information about what a student can and cannot do, they are generally more useful than norm-referenced tests in planning instruction for an individual student. Commercially available criterion-referenced tests may include standardized materials, directions, and scoring procedures. They include a series of probes into a curriculum domain, and may or may not reflect the particular curriculum being taught in a given school or classroom. Examples of commercially available criterion-referenced instruments are presented in Table 4.2.

Concerns with Traditional Assessment Practices

Both of these more traditional assessment categories have serious technical and practical limitations. Norm-referenced procedures have come under the greatest criticism for their potential bias against minority group individuals. Frequently, the sample populations upon which these tests are normed do not include adequate numbers of minority group individuals and/or individuals from low socioeconomic backgrounds. The disproportional representation in special education of students from diverse racial and cultural-linguistic backgrounds on the basis of aptitude (e.g., IQ) scores obtained on such tests has been the focal point of considerable litigation during the past 20 years. This has been a major source of controversy in special education and has led many authorities to call for a moratorium on the use of standardized, norm-referenced tests.

While discrimination against many minority group students has been a major criticism, it is not the only concern surrounding the use of norm-referenced tests. These instruments have been criticized as being costly and time consuming to administer. For these reasons, they cannot provide frequent measures of student progress. Also, they may be technically inadequate relative to validity (e.g., does the instrument measure what it says it measures) and reliability (e.g., the consistency of a student's scores on repeated occasions of taking the test). Further, poorly trained examiners may select inappropriate tests and/or use test in ways in which they were not intended. Examiners may also administer and score tests inaccurately, or fail to properly follow the standardized procedures specified. They may then misinterpret and/or misuse the results, leading to recommendations for placement and instruction of students that have little to do with the testing outcomes.

In addition, the tests themselves may contain content that is of limited relevance to a particular setting. Achievement tests may focus on types of content or skills not greatly emphasized by a particular curriculum or a given school district. Because norm-referenced achievement tests attempt to include many curricula, they may truly represent none. For this reason, their scores may have little generalizability to a particular school or curriculum. Further, individual students may fail to perform as well as they could, due to transitory illnesses or motivational factors. Finally, norm-referenced standardized tests are of little value in formulating instruction. Their scores do not trans-

TABLE 4.1 Standardized, Norm-Referenced Tests

Aptitude and Ability Tests
- Cognitive Abilities Test (Thorndike & Hagen, 1993)[1]
- Wechsler Intelligence Scale for Children—Revised (Wechsler, 1991)
- Stanford-Binet Intelligence Scale (4th ed.) (Thorndike, Hagen, & Sattler, 1986)
- Kaufman Assessment Battery for Children (Kaufman & Kaufman, 1983)[2]
- Otis-Lennon School Ability Test (Otis & Kennon, 1989)[1]
- Woodcock-Johnson Psycho-Educational Battery—Revised: Tests of Cognitive Ability (Woodcock & Johnson, 1989)[2]
- Slossen Intelligence Test (Nicolson & Hibpshman, 1990)

Achievement Tests
- California Achievement Tests (1992)[1]
- Comprehensive Tests of Basic Skills (1990)[1]
- Iowa Tests of Basic Skills (1993)[1]
- Peabody Individual Achievement Test—Revised (Markward, 1989)
- Wide Range Achievement Test—Revised (1984)
- Kaufman Test of Educational Achievement (Kaufman & Kaufman, 1985)
- Woodcock-Johnson Psycho-Educational Battery—Revised: Tests of Cognitive Ability (Woodcock & Johnson, 1989)[2]

Behavior Rating Scales
- AAMR Adaptive Behavior Scale-School (2nd ed.)(Lambert, Nihira, & Leland, 1993)
- Adaptive Behavior Inventory for Children (Mercer & Lewis, 1977)
- Behavior Rating Profile (Brown & Hammill, 1983)
- Perfile de Evaluacion del Comportamientl (Brown & Hammill, 1983) (a Spanish language version of the Behavior Rating Scale)
- Walker Problem Behavior Identification Checklist (Walker, 1983)

Self-Concept and Attitude Tests
- Piers-Harris Children's Self-Concept Scale (Piers & Harris, 1984)
- Coopersmith Self Esteem Inventories (Coopersmith, 1981)
- Survey of School Attitudes (Hogan, 1973)
- Peers' Attitudes Toward the Handicapped Scale (Bagley & Green, 1981)

[1]Group test.
[2]These tests also contain academic achievement measures.

late into useful information for teachers to use in formulating day-to-day instruction. They provide only general scores and yield no information regarding proficiency on the specific critical skills emphasized in a given curriculum. Further, because these tests are designed to be administered infrequently, once or twice a year at most, they provide virtually no feedback that can be used to guide day-to-day instruction.

Concerns over the inherent problems of norm-referenced testing led to the development of **criterion-referenced** measures. These measures, which may be obtained either commercially or teacher developed, provide information on the mastery of specific skills at certain levels of proficiency. Teacher-made tests are useful instructionally, but they may suffer from technical difficulties (e.g., validity and reliability) due to the teacher's lack of formalized training in test construction. Both developing and administrating a series of criterion-referenced measures can be cumbersome and time consuming: It is un-

TABLE 4.2   Selected Criterion-Referenced Tests

Academic Achievement
- BRIGANCE Diagnostic Inventories
  —Comprehensive Inventory of Basic Skills (1983)
  —Inventory of Essential Skills (1981)
- Criterion-Referenced Test of Basic Skills (Lundell, Brown, & Evans, 1976)
- Hudson Educational Skills Inventory (Hudson, Colson, Welch, Banikowski, and Mehring, 1989)
- KeyMath Diagnostic Arithmetic Test (Connolly, 1988)[1]
- Multilevel Academic Skills Inventory (Howard, Zucker, & Morehead, 1982)

Social Skills and Study Skills
- Instructional Based Appraisal System (Meyen, Gault, & Howard, 1976) (for students with mild and/or severe handicapping conditions; also includes career education, prevocational skills, physical education, and science)
- System FORE (Bagai & Bagai, 1979)

[1]Also has normative, standardization data.

likely that a teacher can develop or obtain commercially sufficient numbers of measures for retesting after additional instruction of students who fail to meet criterion. Criterion-referenced measures, like norm-referenced ones, provide "single shot" views of student performance and do not provide a picture of student performance over time. Further, criterion-referenced tests sample a skill area, using test items thought to be representative of the broader skill domain. They may not be sufficiently limited in focus, reflective of the particular curriculum being used, or contain enough test items within each skill domain to actually guide the day-to-day instructional decision-making process. Table 4.3 summarizes the salient features of these traditional forms of educational assessment.

In recent years, many special education leaders have called for a moratorium on standardized, norm-referenced testing. They cite concerns over such factors as assessment bias and the disproportionate placement of minority group students into special education programs; the difficulties in using assessment data to differentiate among low achievers, Chapter one students, students with learning disabilities, and those with mild mental retardation; the irrelevance of most eligibility as-

sessments to specific instructional planning; and the enormous fiscal cost of the assessment identification processes.

New Directions in Educational Assessment

Criterion-referenced tests are of greater **formative evaluation** utility for teachers. Instead of measuring individual performance against that of a normative population, they compare a student's performance on identified instructional skills to a specified mastery level. Because criterion-referenced tests focus on specific skills of the individual and outline the extent of mastery for each skill, they can be fairly useful in planning instruction and monitoring progress. However, these tests do not mirror the exact curriculum being taught, nor do they pinpoint the specific nature of that difficulty nor prescribe instructional strategies. Furthermore, they typically are designed to be used only once or twice a year.

More useful approaches to formative evaluation involve the frequent and direct observation of student behavior within a specified set of learning tasks. This type of measure assesses the student's actual performance in the environment in which he functions and/or the curriculum in

TABLE 4.3 Salient Features of Norm-Referenced and Criterion-Referenced Tests

Standardized, Norm-Referenced Tests
Including both aptitude and achievement tests, these measures compare one individual's performance with that of a broader representative group considered to be "average" or "normal" in regard to the characteristics being measured. They have been criticized for possible bias against individuals from minority and low-income groups. Sometimes they are technically inadequate in terms of validity and reliability. They tend to be expensive and time consuming to administer. Further, they tend to be broadly focused and, consequently, to have limited relevance to any particular educational setting or curriculum, and to be of little value in formulating instruction.

Criterion-Referenced Tests
Developed in response to the concerns over normative testing, criterion-referenced tests measure the performance of a student within a particular curriculum area. They provide information on the level within a continuum of skills (e.g., adding simple math facts) that a student is currently performing. This performance measure is specific to the identified curricular area and does not compare the performance of one individual to that of others. As criterion-referenced measures provide more explicit information on what a student can and cannot do, they are generally more useful than norm-referenced tests in planning instruction for an individual student. These tests may also suffer from technical difficulties, particularly when they are teacher-made. Besides the probability of validity and reliability difficulties, teacher-made tests are time consuming and difficult to construct. Whether commercially developed, or "homemade," they can be used only once or twice a year and therefore do not provide a picture of student performance over time. Further, they may not contain a sufficient number of items in a skill area to get a true picture of student performance, or they may not be sufficiently aligned with the actual curriculum of a given classroom.

which he is being instructed. Further, because the direct observation data is taken as the instruction is taking place and as the skills are being developed, it provides information on the current performance of the student that can be used for educational programming on a day-to-day or week-to-week basis. Task analysis checklists, described in Chapter 2, provide direct observation means of tracking student progress through an instructional sequence composed of the task-analyzed substeps of a particular skill.

Direct observation procedures can be used to collect data on any academic or social behavior of interest. This data indicates the extent to which one student's behavior is discrepant from that of his peers, an important consideration in deciding whether or not the behavior should be changed. It can indicate where to begin instruction, and it provides feedback on the success of these efforts. CBA procedures incorporating these features are described in the following section.

Curriculum-Based Assessment (CBA)

CBA provides a means of "obtaining direct and frequent measures of a student's performance on a series of sequentially arranged objectives derived from the curriculum used in the classroom." (Blankenship & Lilly, 1981). It pinpoints where a student is functioning within a curriculum, providing information that can be used to develop individual instructional programs (Tucker, 1985).

Unlike more traditional normative or criterion-referenced assessment practices, CBA directly links assessment to the *specific* curriculum being used in a particular setting with a particular student. Data from frequent measures of individual students progress within a particular curriculum can be used in making day-to-day or week-to-week adjustments in instruction.

CBA can be as informal as classroom quizzes, administered to assess whether or not students have mastered targeted skills or content. Informal CBA inventories may be used prior to instruction as pretests to determine whether there is a need for instruction in a given area (McLoughlin & Lewis, 1990). More formalized models of CBA that have evolved in recent years include the accuracy-based model, the criterion-referenced model, and the fluency-based measurement model.

The accuracy-based approach and criterion-referenced approach are both primarily instructional models. The former focuses on the percentage of correct student responses. By pinpointing where the student is experiencing difficulty, they provide a starting point for instruction and for monitoring student progress. The criterion-referenced model analyzes the sequence of skills to be taught, establishes objectives for each, and tests student mastery of these objectives (Blankenship, 1985; Idol-Maestas, 1983). Useful for content instruction as well as basic skill development, this CBA model is designed primarily for continuous assessment of short-term goals. Both the accuracy-based and criterion-referenced models of CBA utilize primarily production-type responses, although some selection-type responses (e.g., underlining) may also be used.

The third CBA approach is the fluency-based model, often referred to as curriculum-based measurement (CBM). In this model, rate of progress is the key consideration. Using a time series analysis, the focus is on the graph of the student's performance: Does the slope of the graph of student behavior over time indicate an acceptable rate of improvement? Deno and Mirkin (1977) originally developed this model at the University of Minnesota. Its purpose was to create and test a formative evaluation model that teachers could use to evaluate the effectiveness of their interventions and improve the success of students who had academic handicaps. High validity and reliability of CBMs have been found for reading fluency (Fuchs & Deno, 1992), spelling, written expression, and math, (Salvia & Hughes, 1990). In recent years it also has been used effectively in additional areas such as social skill development.

CBMs have the following five instructional applications (Deno, 1985):

1. Screen, assess, refer, and identify those students in need of additional services.
2. Set appropriate educational goals.
3. Place students within a curriculum.
4. Guide teachers in day-to-day assessment of student progress.
5. Adjust instructional methods and programs before students experience significant failures.

Advantages of CBA

A straightforward approach to the assess-teach-assess instructional cycle, CBA has several advantages over traditional assessment approaches. First and foremost, it utilizes the curriculum in which the student is being taught. Such direct measurement of student responses requires no inferences on the part of the teacher. In a very real sense, *what you see is what you get.* As the assessment procedures utilize the curriculum being studied by the student, the **content validity** of the assessment procedure is maximized. There is little room for doubt about the relevance of the assessment to the curriculum of the particular school district. Further, **test-retest reliability** is strengthened since CBA uses the same curriculum materials, although different content selections, each time for assessing the student. The problems of selecting representative **normative** samples are essentially eliminated since the student's performance is compared only against her own performance or, in some instances, to that of classmates who are being instructed in the same curriculum.

Another important advantage is that CBA may be used frequently, two to three times a week, or even daily, without diminishing its effectiveness. Frequent measurement data are preferable because they provide more detailed information on a student as well as regular feedback for instructional planning. Since traditional achievement tests are designed to be given only infrequently, they do not provide teachers with immediate information on instructional effectiveness. By directly measuring a student's performance on a particular skill, either daily, or two or three times a week, discrepancies between an individual student's performance and expected performance can be identified. This provides teachers with a basis for adjusting instruction, and, in turn, for evaluating the effectiveness of the new instructional strategies selected. Due to the continuous collection of individual learning data, the child becomes a guide to both curriculum and instruction.

Frequent measurement is not a difficult task when the teacher uses brief probes (1–3 minutes in length) taken directly from the curriculum materials being used each day. It is relatively simple to design the CBA probes and little time is required to administer them. This "homemade" quality also means that this is an inexpensive form of assessment.

CBA is useful instructionally because it provides data on the extent to which individual students are benefiting from instruction. This performance data can serve as a basis for adjusting instruction to the individual student's needs. "The key to using this CBA strategy is the ability to identify and control task difficulty across various curricular assignments relative to each student's need" (Glickling & Thompson, 1985, p. 211). Production data based on the direct and observable responses of the student are sensitive to growth in student performance over relatively short periods of time. Further, directly observing student performance can provide clues as to what processes the student uses to derive an answer and where he is having difficulty. These data provide a vehicle for continuously monitoring and changing instructional delivery as needed for the purpose of maximizing student learning.

Developing CBAs

There are various approaches to developing and implementing CBAs. Each begins with the actual curriculum that is being taught to the student. Using a primarily criterion-referenced or accuracy-based model, the CBAs might take the form of fairly lengthy placement or progress tests. For purposes of monitoring and guiding instruction, frequent and direct measures of student behavior within specific curricula can be obtained with one to two minute "probes". The accuracy of student performance can be transformed into **percentage data** or **rate data,** and charted on a graph that also depicts the target goal for the student's performance. The graph of student performance can then be compared with the target goal to determine if the student is making adequate progress toward that goal. If this graph indicates that progress is not leading toward attainment of that goal within a reasonable period of time, then modifications in the instructional program are required.

CBAs can be developed for the instruction of concepts (e.g., social skills, science, and social studies) as well as for basic tool skills (e.g., reading, spelling, and math) through the use of task analysis. By analyzing the skills or concepts of a curriculum into its subskills or subconcepts, a hierarchical sequence can be developed for assessment and instruction purposes. The key steps to developing a CBA are to: (1) determine the specific questions about student performance that are of interest and (2) write performance objectives that delineate these behaviors (Howell, Kaplan, & O'Connell, 1979). A task-analytic approach for developing and using CBAs, presented in Table 4.4, can be used with both basic tool skills and content subject areas.

In a content curriculum area such as social studies or science, developing a criterion-referenced CBA involves analyzing the information or concepts the instruction targets. Figure 4.2 is a

TABLE 4.4   Task Analytic Model for Developing and Using CBAs

1. List the skills presented in the curriculum material or area selected.
2. Examine this list to determine that all important skills are included; add any that are not.
3. Make sure that the edited list has all skills in the correct order.
4. Write a behavioral objective for each skill on the list.
5. Prepare testing material for each objective developed.
6. Plan procedures for administering the CBA.
7. Give the CBA immediately prior to beginning instruction on a topic.
8. Study the results to determine which students:
   a. Have already mastered the targeted skills and should receive instruction in higher skill or content levels of curriculum
   b. Have mastered the prerequisite skills to begin receiving instruction in the targeted area
   c. Do not have the prerequisite skills and are therefore not ready for instruction in the targeted skill area, but should receive instruction in the prerequisite skill or content areas
9. Re-administer the CBA after instruction on the skills and study the results to determine which students:
   a. Have met criterion and are ready to move on to the next skill or content within the curriculum
   b. Are making progress
   c. Are making inadequate progress toward mastery
10. Periodically re-administer the CBA to assess long-term retention of the targeted skills.

sample of a partial CBA of a life sciences curriculum adapted from a workbook that Idol, Nevin and Paolucci-Whitcomb (1986) developed.

In a content area such as this, the teacher may be using chapters from a textbook or developing her own instructional units from various sources. In either instance, she should pay special attention that the concepts and skills are organized into an appropriate sequence of subconcepts and subskills. Failure to analyze and sequence difficult or complex concepts appropriately can make it impossible to construct a CBA that is useful for placing a student into the curriculum.

Commercially developed curricular materials are designed such that both the lessons within a text and the series of texts across the grades become progressively more difficult. Nonetheless, the teacher should examine this sequence to be sure that it is the most appropriate one for students' instruction. It is possible that a somewhat different sequence would be better for a particular purpose or with a particular group of students.

In the basic skill areas, somewhat different forms of CBAs might be developed, depending on their proposed uses. The CBAs might target initial placement of a student into a curriculum from an accuracy or criterion-referenced perspective, or they might focus on the frequent monitoring of student progress in that curriculum, thereby focusing on the rate of accurate responses.

If the goal is to initially place students into the appropriate level of a reading series, three or more sets of CBAs should be developed for each separate level of the reading series. By administering these sets of CBAs over a period of several days, the teacher reduces the possibility of measurement error. A reading series typically

Life Science CBA

Student: _____

(Mark: + when mastered and − when not)

Skills   Evaluation Dates

1. Classify organisms in various environments/habitats.

Habitats	**Organisms**
Pond	Adult salamander
Field	Grasshoppers
Forest	Dandelions
Sea	Swordfish
Village	Whale
	Waterstrider
	Algae
	Dog
	Human
	Chipmunk

2. Describe the interdependence among organisms.
   a. Identify how each organism gets food.
   b. Describe environmental factors that could keep organism from reproducing.
   c. Describe how each organism obtains water.
   d. Identify ways in which different organisms respond to various stimuli.
   e. Describe how various organisms adapt to moving in the environment.

3. Make recommendations about solutions to various environmental problems.
   a. Describe key aspects of problems such as litter, sewage disposal, water pollution, air pollution, soil conservation, and population size.
   b. Outline proposals that others have made for addressing these problems.
   c. Propose three recommendations and describe their potential impact.

4. Relate structures of organisms to their functions (insert specific organism).

Structures (Diagrams)	**Functions**
Human body	Transport water to cells
Crayfish	Transport food to cells
Insect	Get rid of waste
Single-cell organism	Breath
Plant	Respond to environment
Tree	Move
	Reproduce

FIGURE 4.2   Partial CBA of a Life Sciences Curriculum

Source: From L. Idol, A. Nevin, and P. Paolucci-Whitcomb (1986). *Models of Curriculum-Based Assessment.* Rockville, MD: Aspen Publishers, pp. 75–76. Adapted with permission from PRO-ED, Austin, TX.

includes five books at the first-grade level (three preprimers, a primer, and a first-level textbook); two each for the second- and third-grade levels; and one each for the fourth-, fifth- and sixth-grade levels. Idol et al. (1986) have outlined guidelines for developing and administering criterion-referenced CBAs for reading. They include the following:

1. Randomly select one hundred-word passages from the first quarter of all reading texts in the series.
2. Using the actual textbook pages, or copies of them, insert an arrow ($\rightarrow$) to mark the beginning of the passage and a bracket (]) to mark off the end. The teacher's version also should include a slash (/) to indicate the actual one hundredth word. (The teacher may need to have a student read beyond the one hundredth word to complete a paragraph in order to answer comprehension questions. However, figure the reading rate based only on the one hundred words.)
3. Instruct the student to read as well as possible, but not to worry if some of the words are hard. Indicate where to begin and stop reading. Administer the sample neutrally without praising, instructing, or encouraging the student.
4. For initial curricular placement, begin one textbook level below where the student is estimated to be fluent and continue through the last text for the grade level of the student (e.g., 3.2 for third grade). Give passages at all levels on Day 1. On subsequent 2 days, again give the selection of passages at all levels.

    Either have a copy of the CBA for each student on which errors can be marked, or use clear acetate to cover a single copy and mark the student's reading errors as they occur.
5. Use a stopwatch to time the student's reading, recording in seconds the time it takes to complete the passage.
6. Mark as one error each time the student does the following:

- Pauses and is unable to say a word within 5 seconds
- Omits a word or says the wrong word
- Adds a word or words not in the sample
- Mispronounces a proper name (e.g., "Tim" for "Tom") the first time. (Accept the same mispronunciation subsequently without marking it as an error)
- Omits an entire line (attempt to redirect the student to the line, but its omission is only one error, not one error for each word omitted). (In the case of an omitted line, reduce the total words scored accordingly, for example, from one hundred to ninety-four).

7. Do *not* score the following as errors:

- Repetitions
- Self-corrected errors
- The deletion of suffixes (e.g., -ed or -s) in speech patterns

8. Determine accuracy by subtracting from the total number of words read the number of errors and dividing that by the total number of words.

- For a one hundred-word passage, with nine errors:

  $100 - 9 = 91$ words read correct

  $$\frac{91}{100} = 91\%$$

- For a one hundred-word passage where a six-word line was omitted and nine errors were made:

  $100 - 6 = 94$ total words read

  $94 - 9 = 85$ words read correct

  $$\frac{85}{96} = 90.4\%$$

- For a primer passage of fifty words, with five errors:

  (50×2) minus $(5 \times 2) = 90$

  $$\frac{90}{100} = 90\%$$

9. Figure correct words per minute (cwpm) by dividing the number of correct words for each passage by the number of seconds it took to read the passage and multiplying that dividend by 60.

- For a one hundred-word passage with twelve errors read in 2 minutes and 20 seconds with 12 errors:

2 minute, 20 seconds = 140 seconds

$$100 - 12 = 88 \text{ correct}$$

$$\frac{88 \text{ correct}}{140 \text{ seconds}} = 0.629 \text{ correct words/second}$$

$$629 \times 60 = 37.71 \text{ cwpm}$$

Teachers should develop five or six questions per passage, writing both the questions and acceptable answers out before testing. According to Idol et al. (1986), these questions should adhere to the wording of the passage as nearly as possible and should include two text explicit questions (TE) (e.g., explicitly drawn from the passage and/or pictures), two that are text implicit (TI) (e.g., based on details of the passage and/or pictures, and two that are script implicit (SI) (requiring the integration of prior knowledge with the passage and/or pictures). These three types of questions are illustrated in the sample reading CBA in Table 4.5. These were developed for a Level 6 reading passage from the Ginn (1982) series.

Teachers should administer the CBAs over 3 days, recording the student performance data on a form such as shown in Figure 4.3. For each book, the teacher circles the median or middle scores for accuracy (correct/100), rate (correct words per minute, or cwpm), and comprehension. The middle score for each of these variables at each grade level text should be identified across the 3 days of testing. Students should be placed in the highest book level at which they meet the criteria. Idol et al. (1986) recommends the following criteria:

Reading accuracy: 95% or better
Reading comprehension: 83% or better
Correct words/minute: 25+ at preprimer level
30+ in Grades 1–3
50+ in Grades 4–6

Math CBAs for initial placement into a curriculum can be developed in a similar fashion. The teacher will need to examine the instructional program in math to identify the concepts and skills included, as well as their scope and sequence. The CBA developed should reflect the actual scope and sequence the teacher identifies, not just that reflected in the commercial material. The teacher also will want to determine whether the concepts and skills are task analyzed appropriately for instructional purposes. The placement tests provided with the math series may be expanded by developing several items for each of the math subskills. In this way samples can be obtained over 3 days instead of just 1 day. The placement CBAs might be from 20–30 minutes in length to determine mastery at specific criterion levels or the teacher could focus more strictly on rate of correct responding (fluency), as described in the following section. In scoring a math CBA, the number of correct responses possible reflects the total number of math operations, not the total number of problems. For example, the answer to a problem that involved adding 24 plus 15, would be scored in terms of the two digits in the answer, the 3 and the 9, as

$$\begin{array}{r} 24 \\ + 15 \\ \hline 39 \end{array}$$

two separate responses, making the problem worth 2 points. The resulting performance data provide a basis for determining both basic mastery and fluency.

Fluency-Based CBMs

Monitoring students' progress within a curriculum requires frequent measures of performance, meaning that the CBAs should be short and easy

TABLE 4.5   Comprehension Questions for Reading CBA

Across the Fence *Level 6; pp 32–33*
"Hello again," Dad said. "I have something that you may want to do. I made up
some clues for you to read. First, you read the clues, then you go where the clues
tell you to go. You will find another clue there. Go from clue to clue. The last clue
will take you to something you will like."
   "Can we read the clues by ourselves?" I asked.
   "Yes, you can," said Dad.
   Dad gave me the first clue. It said: I'm very tall. Some of me is up in the air. A
bird can come home to me. What/$_{100}$ am I?

Comprehension Questions
(TE) 1. What did Dad make up?
         (Some clues)
(TI) 2. How will the children find the clues?
         (Read the clues, go where they say, and find another clue)
(TE) 3. What will the last clue take them to?
         (Something they will like)
(TI) 4. Why did they think the clue was telling about a tree?
         (Because that is where a bird would go, or an answer from any other part
         of the clue, for example, tall, in the air)
(SI) 5. What is the answer to the clue?
         (A tree or a tall pole)
(SI) 6. Why do you think Dad made up the clues for them to read?
         (He wanted to give them something to do; he wanted them to have some
         fun; he wanted them to look for what he was going to give them—the
         "something you will like")

Source: From L. Idol, A. Nevin, and P. Paolucci-Whitcomb (1986). *Models of Curriculum-
Based Assessment.* Rockville, MD: Aspen Publishers, p. 11. Reproduced with permission from
PRO-ED, Austin, TX.

to administer. Rate or fluency is the primary consideration in determining mastery. CBMs of student
achievement in reading, writing, and spelling
may be developed using the following four approaches (Marston, 1989):

1. In reading, counting the number of words a
   student reads correctly from either a basal
   reader or word list in a 1-minute interval.
2. In the area of written expression, counting
   the number of words or letters written during
   a 3-minute interval, given either a story
   starter or topic sentence.
3. In spelling, counting the number of correct letter sequences (White & Haring, 1980)
   or words spelled correctly during a 2-min-

ute interval, given words dictated every 7
seconds.
4. In math, counting the number of correctly
   written digits during a 1–2 minute interval
   from grade-level computational problems.

   Carbone (1987) has summarized the following four steps for developing and administering
fluency-based CBMs:

1. **Conduct initial assessment of a student in
   a given performance area.** Assessing a student begins with direct and repeated measures of the rate of behavior within a given
   skill area. An initial reading assessment
   could involve several 1-minute samples of

CBA Perfomance Recording Form

Student's Name_____ Age _____ Grade _____ Teacher _____
Examiner _____ CBA Curriculum _____ Classroom Curriculum _____

	Book No.																			
Day 1 Date	Words																			
	Error Tally																			
	Correct/100																			
	Seconds																			
	Correct Words/Min																			
	% Comprehension																			
Day 2 Date	Words																			
	Error Tally																			
	Correct/100																			
	Seconds																			
	Correct Words/Min																			
	% Comprehension																			
Day 3 Date	Words																			
	Error Tally																			
	Correct/100																			
	Seconds																			
	Correct Words/Min																			
	% Comprehension																			

FIGURE 4.3 CBA Data Recording Form

Source: From L. Idol-Maestas (1983). *Special Educator's Consultation Handbook.* Rockville, MD: Aspen Publishers, p. 202. Reproduced with permission from PRO-ED, Austin, TX.

oral reading from a basal reader series over several days. By recording the rate of correct and incorrect words read, the teacher would obtain a measure of reading fluency. To measure math fluency, students can be given 1-minute timed samples from worksheets taken from the math text. Repeated measures of rate of behavior over several days would indicate level of mastery of these facts.

2. **Chart data on a rate graph.** For each skill area, chart the rate data on a graph. This depicts baseline performance and provides a means of analyzing patterns of responding in the skill area.

3. **Design an instructional program.** Based upon the baseline performance data, a teacher can design an instructional program that includes a long-term goal (several weeks) and a short-term goal (a few days) within that skill area. These goals should be stated in terms of performance rate to be achieved and the instructional methods to be implemented.

4. **Frequently assess student progress toward achieving the goals established.** Additional brief probes of student performance can be administered on a daily or weekly basis in conjunction with ongoing instruction. A couple of probes each week provide reliable data

on student progress within a given skill. A graph depicting each of these data points provides a picture of the progress that the student is making toward attaining the short-term and long-term goals. With the graphic display the teacher can easily observe the strength and direction of a student's performance, and make predictions for future performance. If progress does not match these expected goals, adjustments can be made in the instruction to obtain higher rates of performance increments.

Plotting CBM Data

When measuring rate of progress within a curriculum, the primary consideration is whether or not the student is going to attain the instructional goal in a timely fashion. Data trend lines, described in a preceding section of this chapter, are useful in depicting such progress toward a goal because they provide a summary and a guide for making predictions about future performance. A goal or aim line can be established by drawing a line from the median performance level at baseline to the specified goal level on a standard data graph form, with the y or vertical axis indicating the dependent variable of rate and the x or horizontal axis representing time. This line represents the slope of progress that the student must achieve to attain the goal within the specified time period. By then charting the student's actual performance, the teacher can compare the trend line's incline in relation to the aim line, estimate the actual rate of movement toward the curriculum goal, and determine whether changes need to be made in the instruction.

The trend line can be drawn free-hand, marking a straight line from the first nonbaseline entry through the midpoint of the data entries for a specified period. A more reliable technique is the "split-middle" method of trend analysis, or the faster "quickie" split-middle technique (White, 1974). To draw a trend line using the quickie split-middle method, the total number of data

points, is divided in half with a vertical line. If there are an odd number of data points, the vertical line is drawn through the middle or mid-data point. With even numbers of data points, the vertical line is drawn half way between the two central data points, dividing the graph into two halves. Next, the middle data points for each half are marked with vertical lines and the median rate is indicated by drawing a horizontal line that divides each set of data points in half. A quarter-intersection line connecting the two points of intersection is called the **split-middle trend line.** This line describes the actual trend of student performance. Table 4.6 provides a task analysis of the procedures for determining split-middle trend lines. Figure 4.4 represents graphic illustrations of the procedure for the quickie split-middle trend line.

Goal or **Aim lines** describe the progress required to reach a predetermined criterion. They are particularly useful for CBA where specific goals have been derived from the curriculum being taught and daily or weekly student performance is used to guide instruction toward achieving those goals. They depict the progress rate required to attain the target behavior within a prescribed time period. Table 4.7 provides a task analysis for the process of plotting or drawing aim lines. Figure 4.5 presents graphic illustrations of aim lines.

Once the aim line is drawn, a **line of progress** can be drawn using the split-middle technique. Because this line depicts the actual progress of the student, it can be compared with the aim line for predicting whether or not the student will reach the criterion indicated in a behavioral objective (White & Haring, 1980; Wolery, Bailey, & Sugai, 1988). When the student's performance falls outside the aim line for a period of 3 or more consecutive days, the intervention procedures need to be reexamined. Figure 4.6 illustrates the relationship of aim lines and trend lines during two phases of an instructional program. Here, the teacher collected performance data twice each week for 5 weeks. After the initial 5 weeks of intervention, the slope of the progress was below that of the aim line, insufficient to

TABLE 4.6   Task Analysis of Drawing a Line of Progress Using the Quickie Split-Middle Technique

To draw a split middle trend line through a given set of student performance data, the following steps should be used:

1.0 Count the number of data points.
2.0 Draw a slash (/) mark to divide the number of data points in half.
    2.1 If there are an *EVEN* number of data points, draw the slash exactly between the two halves.
    2.2 If there are an *ODD* number of data points, draw the slash through the data point which divides the points into two equal halves.
3.0 Draw a vertical line through the mid-date (middle date) for each half.
    3.1 Count the number of days in half the data points.
    3.2 Draw a vertical line through the mid-date.
        3.2.1 If there are an *EVEN* number of data points, draw the vertical line through the date that divides the points into two equal parts.
        3.2.2 If there are an *ODD* number of data points, draw the vertical line through the date that divides the points into two equal halves.
4.0 Draw a horizontal line through the midrate (middle rate).
    4.1 Count the number of rate data points.
    4.2 Draw a horizontal line that divides the data in half
        4.2.1 If there are an *EVEN* number of data points, draw a horizontal line exactly between the two middle data points.
        4.2.2 IF there are an *ODD* number of data points, draw the horizontal line through the rate that divides the points into two equal halves.
5.0 Draw a line between the points of intersection of the midrate and mid-date lines for each half.
6.0 Draw a second line by shifting up or down (parallel to the line drawn in 5.0 so that the same number of data points fall above and below this line.
7.0 Write a label for this line that is referred to as the split-middle trend line.

reach the established goal. Phase A data clearly indicated that the student would not accomplish the goal within the specified time period. Accordingly, the teacher changed the instructional program, instituting new teaching strategies. Five weeks of data for the changed program, again collected twice a week, were charted as Phase B of the graph. Analysis of this trend or progress line reveals a slope greater than that of the aim line. This means that the rate of progress is greater than required, suggesting that the student will accomplish the target goal sooner than projected. Based on this, the teacher may want to increase the level of targeted behavior identified.

Using CBA Data

The empirical evidence overwhelming supports the effectiveness of frequent data collection and subsequent instructional program modification (Fuchs, Deno, & Mirkin, 1983; Fuchs & Fuchs, 1986; White & Haring, 1980). The frequent collection of performance data improves instruction. Graphing this data is even more effective. A plethora of research studies have shown that teachers who graph student performance data facilitate higher student achievement than those who only collect the data (Fuchs & Fuchs, 1986). Graphs assist teachers in monitoring student performance more accurately, permit comparison of performance across different conditions, and provide feedback that can be used for decision mak-

1. Divide the Data Points in Half

2. Divide Each Half into Halves

3. Find the Median Value (Middle Rate)

4. Draw a Line Connecting the Two Intersections

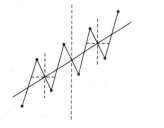

FIGURE 4.4 Quickie Split-Middle Trend Line Procedures

ing. Further, graphs can provide effective feedback to students, therein affecting subsequent performance.

Software programs can be employed to automatically graph students' scores. Initial experimentation indicates that when this software is specifically programmed as an expert system in a given skill area, it can formulate advice that experts might provide. Fuchs, Fuchs, Hamlett, and Stecker (1991) reported on a study in which CBM coupled with a computerized expert system led to higher student gains than did CBM alone. The development and use of such a system is a promising future direction.

Although the existing research indicates that frequent data collection has a greater impact on student performance than occasional data collection, no specific rules for the rate of data collection, kind of data, or other procedural guidelines are given. There are some indications that data can be more effective relative to instructional decision making if it is used at least every 7–10 days (Fuchs et al., 1983; Howell & McCollum-Gahley, 1986). However, as Salvia and Hughes (1991) point out, common sense may often dictate more frequent decision making in regard to instructional programs that are progressing at a rate or in a direction that the teacher did not intend. The point is, teachers, unlike automobile mechanics, cannot be given absolute "mile markers" at which point they ought to make certain decisions. Rather, classroom teachers, those working with students with mild learning difficulties as well as all others, need to rely on some rather general "rules of the road," fairly well documented, but certainly not proven, regarding making decisions about ongoing instructional programming.

Salvia and Hughes (1990) have capsulated the essential rules for making decisions about formative data into four basic teacher performance areas: (1) maintaining an existing instructional program, (2) modifying an existing instructional program, (3) initiating instruction at a new level of the existing instructional objective, and (4) initiating a new instructional program for a new in-

TABLE 4.7 Task Analysis for Drawing Aim Lines

1.0 Draw start mark.
    1.1 Determine the mid-date (middle date of the last 3 days of baseline).
    1.2 Determine the midrate (middle rate of the last 3 days of baseline).
2.0 Draw aim star.
    2.1 Determine target behavior aim rate.
    2.2 Determine target behavior aim date.
    2.3 Draw aim star at the intersection of the aim rate and aim date.
3.0 Draw aim line.
    3.1 Connect aim star and start mark with a straight line.

Source: Used with permission of the author, G.M. Sugai (1989) Department of Special Education, University of Oregon, Eugene.

structional objective. The remainder of this section will elaborate on each of these four rules of the road for instructional program decision making.

1. Maintaining an existing instructional program. The decision to maintain an existing program without change can be difficult for a teacher to make. The data display procedures described in this chapter provide the teacher with a quantitative and visual display technique for making this decision. The data trend line depicted in the visual data display can provide a basis for making a decision to maintain or alter instruction

2. Modifying an existing instructional program. The decision to change an existing instructional program can be equally difficult. The availability of a data base can make this decision considerably easier. The basic point is to decide whether or not the student's rate of progress is sufficient to achieve the criterion goal within a projected time period. Salvia and Hughes (1990) note that at least six instructional program changes may be indicated by analyzing aim line data. Those decisions are as follows:

- Increasing the slope of the aim line by setting an earlier-than-expected date for attaining criterion.
- Increasing the criterion or performance goal.
- Decreasing the slope of the aim line by extending the expected date for reaching criterion.

- Teaching a smaller "slice" of the instructional objective.
- Moving back to a prerequisite (i.e., earlier) objective in the instructional program.
- Changing instructional procedures in regard to both how and under what conditions the instructional program should be presented.

Teachers need to become sensitive to patterns within student performance data that may indicate further need for change in programming. The following data patterns may indicate the need for further instructional program modification:

- Correct responses exceeding anticipated rate of student progress.
- Few or no correct students' responses.
- Correct responding occurring, but with a high rate of response errors.
- Correct responding occurring but at an unacceptably low rate.
- Rate of correct responding flattening (slowing down) or decreasing (falling below) aim line.

3. Initiating instruction at a new level of the existing instructional objective. There are roughly three stages or levels of skill development. These include basic acquisition of the skill, developing fluency with the skill, and generalizing the skill to other appropriate/relevant settings and stimulus conditions. Each of these stages should be completed before proceeding to a new

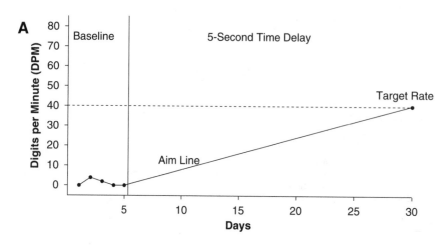

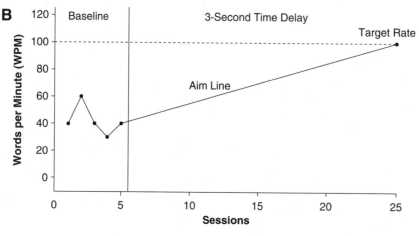

FIGURE 4.5   Drawing Aim Line for Goal of (A) 40 WPM by Day 30 and (B) 100 WPM by Session 25

objective. Criterion performance may vary from student to student but generally the criterion of 90% accuracy is considered minimal prior to moving from one stage of skill development to the next. Failure to adequately acquire the basic components of a new skill may mean that fluency and generalization stages are never reached.

4. Initiating a new instructional program for a new instructional objective.   As a general rule of the road student performance at or above criterion for at least 2 consecutive days is sufficient to in-

itiate instruction on a new objective. The teacher may begin to phase in instructional programming for a new objective while at the same time initiating a maintenance program for the objective on which the student has just met the criteria. Skills that are sequential in nature may be maintained as integral parts of curricula through repeated application at the next levels of the program. In curricular areas where the instructional objectives may not be sequential, teachers will need to build in opportunities for students to review, practice,

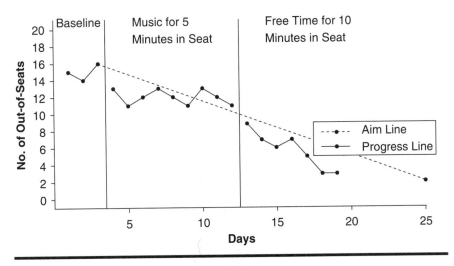

FIGURE 4.6   Graphing Aim and Progress Lines

and maintain previously accomplished objectives..The old adage, "if you don't use it, you lose it," is applicable.

Classroom Efficiency and CBA

A major instructional issue is the efficiency with which students are able to successfully progress through curricula. In addition to promoting effective decision-making relative to instruction, CBA also promotes instructional efficiency. Bott (1991, p. 270), in her thorough analysis of issues involved in teachers applying CBA, noted that "CBA in the classroom is efficient when teachers invest some time in planning and preparation, use assessment routines that are quick and accurate, involve other persons as assistants, and make optimal use of the available time, technology, and resources." Bott's eight-step model for CBA implementation summarizes steps in implementing CBA that are applicable across subject areas. Figure 4.7 presents this model.

USES OF CBAs

CBAs have been described in terms of their usefulness in placing individual students in a given curriculum and in monitoring student progress toward an instructional goal. CBA data provide information on the rate of progress and, by implication, the efficiency of instruction. It also provides a basis for analyzing the specific types of errors being made. Both of these sets of information can guide decisions about potential changes in subsequent instruction.

In addition to these individual student instructional uses, CBM also has been instituted on schoolwide and systemwide bases. Data on all students within a class, a school, or a school system can provide a reference point from which to make decisions about the relative progress of individual students. The accumulated data also can provide a norm for establishing criteria by which to identify students for special services (Shinn, 1989; Marston, Deno, & Tindal, 1984; Tindal, Wesson, Deno, Germann, & Mirkin, 1985). CBMs have been demonstrated to reliably differentiate between regular education and special education students (Marston & Magnusson, 1985; Peterson, Heistad, Peterson, & Reynolds, 1985). By having data on the mean performance of all students within a curriculum, discrepancy from that mean can be utilized to screen students for special services as well as to place them into

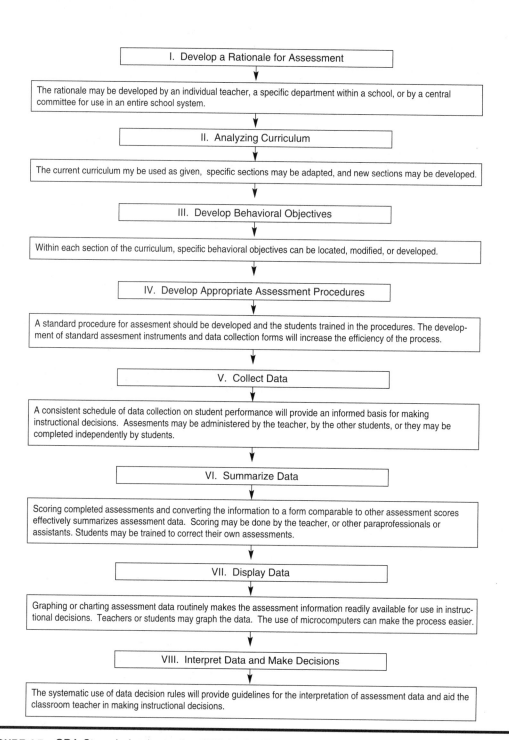

I. Develop a Rationale for Assessment

The rationale may be developed by an individual teacher, a specific department within a school, or by a central committee for use in an entire school system.

II. Analyzing Curriculum

The current curriculum my be used as given, specific sections may be adapted, and new sections may be developed.

III. Develop Behavioral Objectives

Within each section of the curriculum, specific behavioral objectives can be located, modified, or developed.

IV. Develop Appropriate Assessment Procedures

A standard procedure for assesment should be developed and the students trained in the procedures. The development of standard assesment instruments and data collection forms will increase the efficiency of the process.

V. Collect Data

A consistent schedule of data collection on student performance will provide an informed basis for making instructional decisions. Assesments may be administered by the teacher, by the other students, or they may be completed independently by students.

VI. Summarize Data

Scoring completed assessments and converting the information to a form comparable to other assessment scores effectively summarizes assessment data. Scoring may be done by the teacher, or other paraprofessionals or assistants. Students may be trained to correct their own assessments.

VII. Display Data

Graphing or charting assessment data routinely makes the assessment information readily available for use in instructional decisions. Teachers or students may graph the data. The use of microcomputers can make the process easier.

VIII. Interpret Data and Make Decisions

The systematic use of data decision rules will provide guidelines for the interpretation of assessment data and aid the classroom teacher in making instructional decisions.

FIGURE 4.7   CBA Steps in Implementing CBA in the Classroom

Source: Reprinted with the permission of Macmillan Publishing Company, Inc. from *Curriculum-Based Assessment: Testing What Is Taught* by John Salvia and Charles Hughes. Copyright © 1990 by Macmillan Publishing Company.

special educational programs. Students who deviate considerably from the local norms, falling perhaps within the bottom 10% within a given curriculum, might be identified to receive special education assistance. Data from traditional approaches of evaluating students for eligibility for special services have been criticized as having little relevance to the actual educational intervention the student needs. By using the exact curriculum that will comprise the student's educational program, this shortcoming is neutralized. Another major criticism of most standardized, normative tests has been their potential bias against students from minority ethnic, racial, and linguistic backgrounds. CBAs circumvent this shortcoming as well, at least insofar as the curriculum being utilized also is nonbiased.

One regional special education system developed a set of CBA procedures for across-the-board use. The Total Special Education System (TSES) focuses on discrepancies between student performance and specific environmental demands in academics, social skills, vocational skills, and mainstreamed placement skills (Germann & Tindal, 1985). This systems utilizes direct observation of students in natural environments to identify discrepancies in their behavior and skill levels. Established criteria are used to identify the degree of discrepancy between an individual student's behavior and the established median in the environment in which the student is functioning. This information is then used to determine eligibility for services and the range of services needed, to establish program goals, and to define mastery criteria.

Increasingly, CBA is being used for pre-referral intervention. For example, the state of Louisiana now requires that a CBA be performed prior to formal referral to special education of any student suspected of having a mild handicapping condition. These data are analyzed to determine whether the problems exhibited are related to a disability or to the curriculum (Tucker, 1985).

SUMMARY

This chapter has provided an overview of the variety of approaches that can be used to evaluate and assess a child's needs in an educational setting. The assessment process begins with identifying a problem area, followed by collecting data for delineating the nature of the problems, and developing appropriate interventions. Traditionally, school assessment has relied on standardized, norm-referenced tests and on commercially available criterion-referenced measures. These data have been used to screen students for specific problems, to assess individual abilities, to determine eligibility for specialized programs, to monitor individual progress, and to evaluate programs by measuring the achievement of individuals or groups. Many of these approaches have been criticized as having a variety of shortcomings, ranging from their technical soundness, the extent to which they reflect meaningful performance, the one-shot picture of performance that they provide, and their potential for bias relative to students from nonmajority ethnolinguistic groups.

Less traditional informal approaches to assessment have emerged in recent years as a major source of assessment information. Examples include direct observation of classroom behavior, teacher-made criterion-referenced tests, and CBA. These approaches are of a more formative evaluation nature in that they provide a basis for day-to-day instructional planning. They establish the student's instructional needs on the basis of ongoing performance within a given curriculum and setting. CBA data permit teachers to determine not only if the student is making progress, but if the progress is rapid enough relative to realizing long-term objectives. The frequent and direct measure of student progress is the key to effective and efficient instruction in the curricular skill areas of reading, spelling, writing, and math, as well as in content subjects and in career/vocational preparation. Each of these areas is described in later chapters of this textbook.

CONTENT MASTERY QUESTIONS

1. List and briefly discuss the four basic questions for student assessment.

2. Discuss the three levels of assessment and provide an example of each level.

3. Discuss and describe the four considerations for assessment development and/or selection.

4. List and discuss the two traditional forms of student assessment regarding method, content/information, validity assumptions, and concerns.

5. List and discuss the three approaches to curriculum-based assessment (CBA). How can CBAs be applied instructionally?

6. What are four applications of and five advantages to using CBAs?

7. Discuss development of CBAs in terms of content curriculum areas and basic skill areas. How does CBA development differ within these two areas?

8. Describe the four steps for developing and administering a fluency-based curriculum-based measure (CBM).

9. Describe the process for determining the split-middle trend line, aim line, and progress line. Why are these lines of importance in plotting CBA data?

10. List and briefly discuss the four decision-making rules for CBA.

11. What are the eight steps necessary to implement CBA in the classroom effectively?

12. Discuss the uses of CBAs on individual, schoolwide, and systemwide bases.

REFERENCES

Berdine, W. H., & Meyer, S. A. (1987). *Assessment in special education.* Boston: Allyn & Bacon.

Blankenship, C. S. (1985). Using curriculum-based assessment data to make instructional decisions. *Exceptional Children, 52,* 233–238.

Blankenship, C., & Lilly, S. (1981). *Mainstreaming students with learning and behavior problems.* New York: Holt, Rinehart, & Winston.

Bott, D. A. (1991). Managing CBA in the classroom. In J. Salvia & C. Hughes (Eds.), *Curriculum-based assessment: Testing what is taught.* New York: Macmillan.

Carbone, V. J. (1987). *Curriculum-based assessment: More than an educational fad.* Des Moines, IA: Mountain Plains Regional Resource Center.

Deno, S. L. (1985) Curriculum-based measurement: The emerging alternative. *Exceptional Children, 52,* 219–252.

Deno, S., & Mirkin, P. K. (1977). *Data-based program modification: A manual.* Reston, VA: Council for Exceptional Children.

Fuchs, L. S., & Deno, S. L. (1992). Effects of curriculum within curriculum-based measurement. *Exceptional Children, 53*(3), 232–243.

Fuchs L., Deno, S., & Mirkin, P. (1983). Data-based program modification: A continuous evaluation system with computer technology to facilitate implementation. *Journal of Special Education Technology, 6*(2), 50–57.

Fuchs, L., & Fuchs, D. (1986). Effects of systematic formulative evaluation: A meta-analysis. *Exceptional Children, 53,* 199–208.

Fuchs, L. S., Fuchs, D., Hamlett, C. L., & Stecker, P. M. (1991). Effects of curriculum-based measurement and consultation on teacher planning and student achievement in mathematics operations.

American Educational Research Journal, 28(3), 617–641.

Germann, G., & Tindal, G. (1985). An application of curriculum-based assessment: The use of direct and repeated measurement. *Exceptional Children, 52,* 244–265.

Glickling, E. E., & Thompson, V. P. (1985). A personal view of curriculum-based assessment. *Exceptional Children, 52,* 205–218.

Hopkins, C. D., & Antes, R. (1979). *Classroom testing: Administration, scoring and score interpretation.* Istasca, IL: Peacock Publishing Co., Inc.

Howell, K. W., Kaplan, J. S., & O'Connell, C. Y. (1979). *Evaluating exceptional children.* Columbus, OH: Merrill.

Howell, K. W., & McCollum-Gahley, J. (1986). Monitoring instruction. *Teaching Exceptional Children, 19,* 47–49.

Idol, L., Nevin, A., & Paolucci-Whitcomb, P. (1986). *Models of curriculum-based assessment.* Rockville, MD: Aspen Publishers.

Idol-Maestas, L. (1983). *Special educator's consultation handbook.* Rockville, MD: Aspen Publishers, Inc.

Marston, D. B. (1989). A curriculum-based measurement approach to assessing academic performance: What it is and why do it. In M. R. Shinn (Ed.). *Curriculum-based measurement: Assessing special children.* New York: The Guilford Press.

Marston, D., Deno, S. L., & Tindal, G. (1984). Eligibility for learning disabilities services: A direct and repeated measurement approach. *Exceptional Children, 50,* 544–555.

Marston, D., & Magnusson, D. (1985). Implementing curriculum-based measurement in special and regular education settings. *Exceptional Children, 52,* 266—276.

McLoughlin, J. A., & Lewis, R. B. (1990) *Assessing special students* (3rd Ed.). Columbus, OH: Merrill.

Oakland, T. (1980). Nonbiased assessment of minority group children. *Exceptional Educational Quarterly, 1*(3), 31–46.

Peterson, M., Heistad, D., Peterson, D., & Reynolds, M. (1985). Montevideo individualized prescriptive instructional management system. *Exceptional Children, 52,* 239–243.

Salvia, J., & Hughes, C. (1991). *Curriculum-based assessment: Testing what is taught.* New York: Macmillan.

Shinn, M. R. (1989). Identifying and defining academic problems: CMB screening and eligibility procedures. In M. R. Shinn (Ed.), *Curriculum-based measurement: Assessing special children* (pp. 90–129). New York: Guilford Press.

Tindal, G., Wesson, C., Deno, S. L., Germann, G., & Mirkin, P. K. (1985). The Pine County model for special education delivery: A data-based system. In T. Kratochwill (Ed.), *Advances in school psychology, Vol IV* (pp. 223–250). Hillsdale, NJ: Lawrence Erlbaum Associates.

Tucker, J. A. (1985). Curriculum-based assessment: An introduction. *Exceptional Children, 52,* 199–204.

Wallace, G., & McLoughlin, J. (1988). *Learning disabilities* (3rd Ed.). Columbus, OH: Merrill.

White, O. R. (1974). *The "split-middle"—a "quickie" method of trend estimation.* Seattle, WA: Experimental Education Unit, Child Development and Mental Retardation Center, University of Washington.

White, O. R., & Haring, N. G. (1980). *Exceptional teaching* (2nd Ed.). Columbus, OH: Merrill.

Wolery, M., Bailey, D. B., & Sugai, G. M. (1989). *Effective teaching: Principles of applied behavior analysis with exceptional students.* Boston, MA: Allyn & Bacon.

CHAPTER 5

Managing Student Behavior

PATRICIA THOMAS CEGELKA

CHAPTER OBJECTIVES

At the conclusion of this chapter, the reader will be able to:

1. Identify and describe setting events/antecedent stimuli and define stimulus control.
2. Define and discuss various types of consequences.
3. Discuss the definition, categories, axioms for usage, and schedules for use of reinforcers.
4. Identify procedures for establishing and maintaining behaviors.
5. Describe positive and negative strategies for decreasing behavior.
6. Compare and contrast the AB design with the ABAB design.

BEHAVIORAL PRINCIPLES AND PROCEDURES

The previous chapters dealt with important technical skills relating to pinpointing and describing observable behaviors, developing behavioral objectives, and measuring academic and social behavior. This chapter builds on these skills to develop techniques for modifying or changing student behaviors. The principles and procedures described here have developed through decades of empirical research.

As described in Chapter 3, there are two classes of behavior: operant and respondent. The vast majority of behaviors are **operant behaviors,** meaning that they are learned or acquired as a function of their consequences. Behaviors that result in consequences that are necessary or pleasurable to the individual are strengthened, meaning that they are more likely to occur in the future. Conversely, systematically removing positive consequences can lead to the extinction of a behavior. Those few reflexive behaviors over which individuals have no voluntary control, such as the patellar knee jerk response or eyes tearing in the presence of onions, are called **respondent behaviors.** These behaviors are more or less automatic and are considered part of the individual's physiology. They are controlled by

their eliciting stimuli or antecedents, in contrast to operant behaviors that are controlled by their consequences.

This chapter presents the relationship of behaviors to the stimuli that precede them (antecedents) and the stimuli that follow them (consequences). The chapter details methods for identifying the varying effects of consequences (positive, negative, and neutral; accelerating and decelerating) and for selecting the consequences to use. Finally, it describes skills for systematically applying behavioral principles to change behavior as well as for measuring the effectiveness of behavior change efforts.

The Roles of Antecedents and Consequences

A first step in analyzing a target behavior is to identify the relationships of that behavior to the antecedent and consequent stimuli. Antecedents are events that occur just prior to the behavior, while consequences are the events that occur after the behavior. When a student is not displaying the desired behavior, an analysis of the target behavior in relation to its antecedents and consequences helps to pinpoint the nature of the difficulty. It may be that the curriculum, instruction, or other environmental variables are leading to learning difficulties, or it may be that the consequences are not affecting the behavior in the manner desired.

Antecedents.   **Antecedents** are those environmental stimuli or conditions that occur just prior to a behavior. They are aspects of the environment that provide cues for individual and group behavior. Referred to as *setting events,* they set the stage for the behaviors.

Within a classroom, the antecedents include the curriculum, the design of instruction, and the teaching behaviors. The conceptual soundness of the curriculum (e.g., its scope, sequence, and accuracy) is a key consideration. Curriculum objectives should be clear and comprehensible, and the content should be sensitive to cultural differences and pluralistic in orientation. Curriculum should be motivating and appropriate to the age and ability of the students, and should be well designed in terms of both conceptual and instructional features. The quality of the instructional materials themselves is an important consideration, as is the extent to which students have their own copies of the materials or must share them.

The way in which the curriculum is delivered is also a critical antecedent event. A wide variety of instructional delivery variables can affect the extent to which students become actively involved in the lesson, as opposed to engaging in less productive classroom behaviors. For example, the nature of the lesson (e.g., cooperative learning versus an individual activity) can affect student motivation, as can the mastery of critical prerequisite skills. Teacher presentation also is a critical consideration. Does the teacher demonstrate effective teaching behaviors in structuring and presenting the lessons? Can all students see and hear the teacher? Are the directions given clearly: "Louis, spell 'theater.'" "Margaret, please sit down?" Is the tone of voice friendly or angry, firm or uncertain, sarcastic or solicitous? Does the teacher turn away from the class or move closer to a particular student? Is the teacher smiling, frowning, or grimacing? Does he com-

municate humor and support? Is his manner brisk and peppy?

In addition to these antecedents that relate directly to the design and delivery of instruction, a host of other antecedent stimuli can affect the students' behavior and learning. The temperature and crowdedness of the room, the seating arrangements, various extraneous noises, and the behaviors of their classmates all influence students. When some students are chatting with neighbors, wandering around the room, or resting their heads of their desks, other students may begin to behave in a similar manner. On the other hand, if the class is generally on-task, with all classmates working at their desks, a different setting event exists, one that encourages task-oriented behavior on the part of all students.

Successful students are those who have learned to respond differentially to different antecedent stimuli. For example, the playground and the movie theater are antecedent stimuli for what are typically very different behaviors. The antecedent stimulus of teacher instruction also provides a setting event for particular types of student responses. When these responses are reinforced, they are more likely to occur again in the presence of the specific antecedent stimulus. **Stimulus control** is achieved when the desired response occurs predictably in the presence of a given stimulus but not in the presence of other stimuli. Whenever that stimulus is presented (such as verbal directions from the teacher to get ready for working), students respond in a specific manner (placing their papers and pencils on the desk, folding their hands, and looking at the teacher) because this response is associated with desirable consequences. The students have learned that there is a predictable relationship between the antecedent stimulus, their behavior, and the consequences. When they behave predictably in the face of those antecedent stimuli, their behavior is considered to be under stimulus control.

In an effective classroom, the curriculum is sound, the instructional design is of high quality, and the instructional delivery is systematic and effective. Within this context of appropriate antecedent stimuli, applying behavioral principles to shape and reinforce desired behaviors serves to optimize student learning.

Consequences.   **Consequences** are those events or stimuli that occur just after a behavior. They may be functionally related to the behavior, serving to either increase or decrease it, or they may be neutral, having no effect on the behavior whatsoever. By systematically recording data on a given behavior, the teacher can determine if a consequence serves to increase the behavior, decrease the behavior, or has no effect. Consequences that strengthen the responses that they follow are known as **reinforcers.** Because they result in consequences that the individual desires or needs, reinforcers increase the probability that the behavior will occur in the future. They strengthen that behavior. For example, when Juan is praised each time he completes an assignment, his rate of assignment completion increases. The praise is a positive reinforcer. Positive reinforcers can include social reinforcers (praise and approval), tangible reinforcers (tokens, objects, and food) and activity reinforcers (privileges and special assignments).

Negative reinforcers also are consequences that increase the probability of a behavior occurring in the future. However, the behavior is reinforced or strengthened because of the *contingent removal* of the stimulus. The behavior is associated with the removal of an aversive stimulus present in the environment. For example, in the case in which an uncomfortable breeze is blowing in the room, the behavior of shutting the window is negatively reinforced by the removal of the breeze. When a child completes her homework in order to avoid parental nagging, negative reinforcement also has occurred. Because the use of negative reinforcement by teachers involves aversive stimuli and can have adverse and unintended effects, it is NOT a recommended teaching strategy. Negative reinforcement is best thought of as an explanatory concept in that it explains the relationship between stimuli and behavior. All consequences that increase the future probability of a

behavior are reinforcers: some because of their addition (positive reinforcement) and some because of their removal (negative reinforcement).

In addition to reinforcing behaviors, consequences also may punish the behavior. *Punishment* decreases the probability of the behavior occurring in the future. It can do so through either adding a consequence (e.g., spanking, time out, or time after school) or removing one (e.g., loss of a privilege, earned points or tokens, or recess time). Punishment occurs when a consequence that follows a behavior decreases the likelihood of the behavior occurring in the future.

An example of punishment might be a teacher's yelling at students who are talking loudly in the lunchroom. The cessation of their talking indicates that punishment has occurred. At the same time, an unintended effect may be that the probability of the teacher's yelling in the future is increased. His yelling is negatively reinforced by the removal of the aversive stimulus, student talking. The yelling serves to punish the loud talking behavior (the students cease talking); the students' response then serves to reinforce the yelling. Typically, the cessation of a behavior associated with punishment may be fairly short term. One student stops talking, but a few minutes later another one begins to talk. A vicious cycle can develop when student talks, teacher yells, student stops, another student talks, teacher yells, and so on.

Differentiating between punishment and negative reinforcement can be tricky for the neophyte learner. Like negative reinforcement, punishment involves using aversives, but the aversives are used to control the behavior that they follow. The key consideration is to analyze the behavior sequence of stimuli and responses to determine what the effect of any given consequence is: Does it stop the behavior (punishment) or increase the behavior (reinforcement)? If it increases the behavior, does it do so by removing an aversive stimuli (negative reinforcement) or adding a stimuli (positive reinforcement)?

As illustrated previously, punishing consequences can involve adding aversives, such as spanking and scolding. Punishment can involve removing positive consequences as well. This is referred to as response cost, meaning that the inappropriate behavior of the student results in losing something desirable. Consider, for example, Abraham who bullies younger children. If the principal paddles Abraham whenever he picks on younger children, then a stimulus is added. However, if he loses free time or tokens as a consequence of his behavior, then response cost has been applied.

Punishment can have unplanned adverse results (discussed later in this chapter) and therefore should be used sparingly, if at all. Positive reinforcement encompasses a much more applicable set of strategies for teachers to use in developing desired behaviors. Positive reinforcement should be used to establish and strengthen desired student behaviors from the beginning of the school year. For example, during the second day of the school term, Ms. Tingent, a third grade teacher, was working with her class to establish classroom rules and procedures. She explained to her students that when they wanted her attention, they should raise a hand and wait for her to acknowledge the signal. During a class discussion the next day, Ms. Tingent commented to the class as a whole, as well as to individual students, that she really appreciated the way they raised their hands when they wanted to make a comment or ask a question. She continued to do so during each class discussion that week. Because positive attention from the teacher is generally prized (particularly in the elementary grades), these comments served to establish the practice of students raising their hands for permission to talk during group discussion times.

There is an important distinction between using positive reinforcement and establishing a generally positive classroom environment, although both are desirable. The latter refers to the overall tenor of a classroom, one that supports student development and learning. The former involves the scientific application of behavioral principles in shaping and maintaining behavior. This means that the reinforcement must be contingent on the target behavior, applied in a precise manner to that behavior, and must specifically link the behavior with the reinforcer. It requires systematical and consistent application of behavioral principles and procedures.

CATEGORIES OF REINFORCERS

We already have seen that consequences can have varying functional effects on behavior. They can be positive, negative, or neutral. They may reinforce (accelerate) or punish (decelerate) a behavior. Consequences that increase or strengthen the behavior are referred to as *reinforcers*. Unconditioned or primary reinforcers are those that do not rely on previous learning to acquire reinforcing value. Examples include food, water, warmth, shelter, air, and sex. Conditioned or secondary reinforcers are those that have acquired their reinforcing value because they have been paired with already-established reinforcers. Some of these conditioned reinforcers are those that are more or less normative within a given cultural environment. Grades, praise or social acceptance, and salaries are examples of natural reinforcers for many students. Frequently, teachers use more arbitrary reinforcers that are not typically associated with a behavior in order to gain initial control of the behavior. Examples are tokens, checkmarks, candy, points, earning special privileges, and the like. When students do not exhibit desired target behaviors, this suggests that this behavior may not have been reinforced in the past. The natural or normative contingency relationship is not functioning. The typical consequences may be either neutral or punishing for these students, or the reinforcement schedule has been too weak to shape and/or maintain the behavior. In these instances, arbitrary reinforcers come into play.

When selecting reinforcers, it is important to recognize that students differ in their reinforcer preferences and histories. No given reinforcer or schedule of reinforcers will work equally well with all students. Further, over time reinforcers can lose their values. Therefore, it is important to identify a wide selection of reinforcers that are appropriate in terms of the ages, genders, backgrounds, and preferences of students. Fortunately, the array of potential reinforcers is almost endless. Reinforcers can be grouped into categories such as social reinforcers, activity reinforcers, tangible reinforcers, and token reinforcers. These categories are described in the following paragraphs.

Social Reinforcers

Social reinforcers are typically a natural part of human interchange, are readily available, and entail no monetary cost. Included are interactions that come from other individuals, such as words, gestures, attention, or physical contact. Teacher praise, pats on the back, or smiles frequently function as social reinforcers, strengthening the behaviors that they follow. Table 5.1 lists examples of verbal and physical expressions of social reinforcement.

Social reinforcement is the most commonly used form of reinforcement in general society. This makes it particularly appropriate for use with children. However, the fact that social reinforcers are so natural, readily available, and easy to use is both a plus and a minus. It is relatively easy to establish a generally positive and approving environment. However, it is considerably more difficult to use social reinforcers in a precise and contingent manner; frequently they are applied in a manner only loosely related to the target behavior. Random, noncontingent reinforcement is not only ineffective, but it may also confuse students and/or reinforce inappropriate or undesired behaviors. Sometimes teachers praise frequently, but do so in a noncontingent manner such that no "if-then" or "behavior-consequence" connection is made (Anderson, Evertson, & Emmer, 1980; Brophy, 1981). According to Brophy (1981, p 15.), such praise has little effect because it "is not systematically contingent on desirable behavior, lacks specification of the behavioral elements to be reinforced, and/or lacks credibility." Instead of simply stating "That's good, John," teachers should be specific about the behavior that is being praised, for example, "I like the way John is sitting and working quietly." To be effective, praise should (1) be genuine, warm, and spontaneous; (2) specifically describe the desirable student behavior; (3) be used with all pupils, even those with large repertoires of undesirable behaviors; (4) avoid disrupting appropriate pupil behavior; and (5) be varied in delivery and not overused to the point of becoming meaningless (Wolery, Bailey, & Sugai, 1988).

TABLE 5.1   Examples of Social Reinforcers

VERBAL EXPRESSIONS	PHYSICAL EXPRESSIONS
Excellent!	Nodding
Good job!	Winking
Nice try	Smiling
That's right!	Clapping
Correct	Laughing
Nice Work	Standing by student
Thanks for coming when called.	Sitting beside student
Good listening.	Signaling "OK"
I appreciate you trying that problem.	Patting back
May I use your paper as an example for the class?	Putting hand on shoulder
	Rubbing neck
You worked hard on that paper. I can really tell.	Patting head
	Elbowing
	Hugging

Activity Reinforcers

Inexpensive activity reinforcers are abundantly available in the school setting. Examples include extra recess, special chores (e.g., taking attendance or serving as line monitor), free time, extra art time, and almost any other activity that is available within the school that students engage in voluntarily. Through a process of contracting with the students and their families, home activities (e.g., television time or a special outing) also can be utilized. Table 5.2 lists potential activity reinforcers. Because it is difficult to immediately reinforce a student with an activity, activity reinforcers are frequently used in conjunction with a token or point system. This permits students to receive the immediate reinforcement of tokens or points that can be used later to purchase activity reinforcers.

Tangible Reinforcers

Tangible reinforcers include any object that is used to reinforce a target behavior. Grades and salaries are examples of natural tangible reinforcers. More arbitrary tangible reinforcers include such things as toys, games, marbles, grooming items, and art supplies. Although children tend to respond well to them, tangibles can be problematic in that students may come to expect tangible rewards for everything that they do. Another

negative aspect is that tangibles may become expensive for the teacher. For these reasons, tangibles are best used only in situations where social and activity reinforcers are not effective. Students who have had aversive experiences in school such that they do not respond to teacher praise or to activity reinforcers may need the strong, immediate reinforcement that only tangibles can provide. The teacher should always pair the use of tangibles with praise or other more intrinsic reinforcers, so that in time the student will begin to respond to social reinforcement and the arbitrary tangibles can be faded. The goal of any reinforcement strategy is eventually to move the student to a point where she is responsive to the same types of reinforcement that maintain the behaviors of her peers. Table 5.3 includes a list of tangible reinforcers that students may either purchase outright or purchase the right to use.

While edibles sometimes are viewed as a separate and distinct reinforcer category, they are included here as a subset of tangible reinforcers. Edibles are frequently used with young children or with individuals with severely limited behavioral repertoires. With older children, treats such as candy or popcorn sometimes are included among the tangible reinforcers that teachers use to reinforce appropriate classroom behavior. Several concerns have arisen about the use of edibles as reinforcers in school classrooms. These in-

TABLE 5.2 Examples of Activity Reinforcers

5 Minutes in free-time area	10 Minutes of extra recess
Being first in line	10 Minutes of extra physical education
Passing out papers	15 Minutes of music
Collecting papers	Running an errand
Being read a story	Playing game with peer
Grading papers	10 Minutes of drawing
Helping in the office	Visit to counselor
Petting class pet	Visit to principal
Feeding class pet	5 Minutes talking with teacher
5 Minutes talking with peer	Working with peer
Selecting own work area	Skip assignment
10 Minutes of computer time	Taking a walk
Watching television	Getting a book from the library

TABLE 5.3 Examples of Tangible Reinforcers

Coloring book	Balloon
Colored pencils/	Toy jewelry
markers	Pet
Stickers	Bicycle mirror
Grab bag	Construction paper
Poster	Computer banner
Cassette tape	Notebook/folder
Home note	Glitter
Pencil	Fingernail polish/lipstick
Toy car	Calendar
Card	Computer
Puzzle	game/cartridge
Videotape	Stuffed animal/doll

clude nutritional considerations as well as concerns over the ethics of withholding food from children. On the practical side, it is sometimes difficult for teachers to exercise enough control over the student's environment to ensure the effectiveness of edible consequences. For example, with students who have ample access to candy at home, or who bring it to school with them, teachers probably will find that candies or sweets are not effective classroom reinforcers. Other criticisms are that they are messy, can be expensive over time, and children tend to satiate on them rather quickly.

Tokens and Points

Tokens and points can be reinforcing because they can accrue and be exchanged for other reinforcers. Teachers can dispense tokens immediately, without interrupting ongoing instruction or disrupting the class, and provide opportunities later for students to "purchase" backup reinforcers. Tokens and points can be used with individual students or as the basis for a whole-class management system. Token economies have been widely used in special education classes, as well as with other students who are low achieving, as a means of encouraging on-task academic and social behaviors for which natural reinforcers are not yet functional. For many students who begin their formal schooling with little prior preparation, the natural reinforcers of grades, learning opportunities, or an increased sense of self-competence are not operable. Tokens or points, backed up by strong reinforcers, can assist these students in acquiring appropriate school behaviors, including on-task learning behaviors that lead to the development of academic competence. Tokens can teach students to delay gratification, "save" for more expensive items, and to make choices. Just as money is a reinforcer on which society in general never tires, so students almost never satiate on tokens. The key to effectively using tokens is having an attractive array of items and activities for which the tokens can be exchanged. This requires considerable time and vigilance on the part of the teacher, who must periodically change and update these activities, "price" them appropriately, maintain appropriate student records or "accounts," and ensure that the backup reinforcers are not available to the students noncontingently (i.e., independent of the token economy).

IDENTIFYING REINFORCERS TO USE

Once an array of reinforcers have been identified, the teacher must decide how to use these reinforcers to shape and maintain desired student behaviors. There are four important axioms to remember in using reinforcers. They are: (1) reinforcers are not universal, (2) the effect of specific reinforcers changes over time, (3) reinforcers should be as unobtrusive as possible, and (4) data collection is critical to determining the effect of reinforcers.

Reinforcers are not universal. Teachers sometimes make the mistake of assuming that the consequences selected will be reinforcing for all students in their classroom. This is not a safe assumption because students come to the classroom with different preferences based on their individual histories and experiential backgrounds. Some students already are responsive to grades and teacher approval; a good grade, a smile, or praise from the teacher will motivate them to do well.

However, these are not the students who typically experience significant learning difficulties. Frequently, students with learning problems have had little prior success in school. They find school aversive and feel that there is little that they can do to improve their school performance. For these students, teachers may need to identify other reinforcers, such as special privileges or free time, special recognition for progress, or tangible items for desired behavior.

A good source for information about reinforcer preferences are the students themselves. The teacher can directly ask what the students like to do best, ask significant others (e.g., parents, friends, and other teachers), and observe students during periods in which they are free to do anything they like. From these sources, a list of potential reinforcers can be developed and then prioritized into a reinforcement hierarchy for use with that particular student.

In developing reinforcement hierarchies, it is helpful to remember that some types of consequences are more typical or common to students at different ages. Wolery et al. (1988) have pointed out that young children tend to respond to social consequences such as smiles, overt enthusiasm, tickles, pats, toys, and play, while older students are more responsive to social reinforcers such as "high fives" or "giving five," verbal praise (e.g., "all right" and "rad"), subtle smiles and eye contact, and even being left alone. The only way that a teacher can determine which consequences are actually reinforcing for a given student is to try them out with that student.

The effect of specific reinforcers changes over time. It is unlikely that a given reinforcer will work equally well with a student all the time. The effect of a reinforcer is related to the individual's state of deprivation or satiation with regard to it. For instance, an edible, such as a cookie, will be more reinforcing if there is a relative state of deprivation (e.g., cookies are not widely available to the student) instead of satiation (where the student has just eaten six with lunch). Edible treats probably would be more reinforcing at midmorning than just after lunch. In the same vein, extra

free time probably will be less reinforcing on the afternoon following a morning field trip. Many reinforcers will lose their values over time; satiation occurs. The novelty may wear off, changes may occur in the child's environment that make the reinforcer more readily available in out-of-school settings, or the child may have matured or progressed to the point where a particular consequence has lost its reinforcing strength. A teacher must be sensitive to changes such as these and remain flexible in selecting new reinforcing consequences from the student's reinforcement hierarchy listing.

Reinforcers should be as unobtrusive as possible. Teachers should utilize reinforcers that are as naturally related to the behavior and as unobtrusive in the environment as possible. Arbitrary reinforcers should be used only when natural reinforcers are not sufficiently powerful to accomplish the behavioral change goal. Remember that the long-term goal is to maintain established behaviors through their natural consequences. If the teacher does not know the reinforcement preferences and history of a given student or group of students, he might utilize reinforcers that are more arbitrary than necessary. For example, while token economies have proven effective in countless situations, they are not always appropriate. Consider a third grade class in an upper middle-class neighborhood in which most parents are professionals. It is likely that these students already are highly motivated to achieve in school; that they have histories of school achievement; and that grades, praise, approval, and the acquisition of new knowledge and skills will continue to motivate them to excel academically. For these students, a token economy is superfluous; it represents a giant step backward from the goal of internalizing natural reinforcers for desirable behavior. However, in a classroom of students who are low achieving, who have experienced considerable school failure, and for whom academic achievement has no intrinsic motivation, a token economy may serve to motivate the students to learn the targeted skills.

Data collection is critical to determining the effect of reinforcers. The only way to know if a particular consequence is reinforcing or if a behavior change strategy is having the desired effects is to collect data on the occurrence of the behavior. Baseline data provide a starting point for changing a behavior. It tells how frequently the behavior is occurring, the extent to which it differs from the behavior of other students in the class, and whether the behavior should be accelerated or decelerated. Further, it provides a comparison point for determining the success of intervention procedures. By collecting pre- and post-data, the teacher can determine exactly how much a behavior has changed in the desired direction without having to rely on subjective impressions.

Schedules of Reinforcement

A **continuous reinforcement** schedule works most effectively in the initial building or developing of a response. A student who receives reinforcement every time she emits a target behavior is on a continuous reinforcement schedule. This type of schedule teaches the student the relationship between the behavior and the contingent reinforcement. **Intermittent reinforcement** schedules are those where reinforcement occurs for only some, but not all, instances of the target behavior. The following examples identify four types of intermittent schedules of reinforcement and suggest methods for thinning reinforcement by altering each of them:

1. **Fixed rate schedule.** Reinforce every so many occurrences of the behavior (e.g., for every third time Johnny raises his hand, an FR3 schedule).
2. **Fixed interval schedule.** Reinforce the response the first time it occurs after a preset period of time (e.g., the first time that Cora raises her hand after each 10-minute interval, an FI10 schedule).
3. **Variable rate schedule.** Reinforce at predetermined average rate, such as an average of every five times the response is emitted

(FR5). The student might receive praise for completing three math problems, then six, then four, and then seven problems.
4. **Variable interval schedule.** Reinforce behavior after a predetermined variable passage of time, say on the average of every 10 minutes (VI10). (e.g., the teacher might praise Cora the first time she holds up her hand after 5 minutes, then after 15 minutes, then 10 minutes, and so forth).

In everyday life, most consequences are presented on an intermittent schedule of reinforcement. Not only do intermittent schedules approximate real life, but they are also easier for the teacher to implement. Furthermore, while behaviors that receive continuous reinforcement extinguish rapidly once the reinforcers are withheld, intermittent schedules maintain a behavior almost indefinitely.

Consider the example of parents of a baby who cries for long periods of time after being put to bed each evening. They decide to extinguish the behavior by ignoring the crying. After checking to make sure that the infant is okay physically, they refrain from going into the nursery and picking up the baby. The probable response of the baby will be to cry even longer and harder. Typically, after one or two nights of no reinforcement, the bedtime crying will cease. However, if the parents tough it out for several hours and then give in, picking up the infant, cuddling her, and carrying her around the house, just the opposite will occur. The crying will be reinforced and strengthened, for now the baby has learned that if she just cries long enough, reinforcement will be forthcoming.

When establishing a desired behavior, such as completing assignments, hand raising, or being on-task, a continuous schedule of reinforcement will work best. Once the targeted behavior is established, it is desirable to shift to a schedule that will maintain and promote generalization of it to more naturalistic settings, under different stimulus conditions, and with a variety of persons. By shifting to an intermittent schedule of reinforcement, particularly a variable rate or variable interval schedule, the behavior will be maintained almost indefinitely.

This process can involve shifting from continuous to variable schedules of reinforcement, thinning the schedules of reinforcement, and shifting from arbitrary to natural or intrinsic reinforcers. These shifts, if executed properly, will serve to reduce the expectation for reinforcement; result in higher, steadier rates of responding; and maintain the behavior over a long period of time. It is necessary to proceed slowly, carefully monitoring each shift to ensure that the behavior is not weakened in the process. By collecting data for each change in the reinforcement schedule, a teacher can make sure that the behavior is maintained at the desired level. If he moves too quickly to reduce the frequency of reinforcement or to shift from artificial to more natural reinforcers, the behavior may decrease.

ESTABLISHING AND MAINTAINING BEHAVIORS

Teachers can systematically apply reinforcement to establish new behaviors, increase behaviors, and maintain existing behaviors. While behavioral change techniques can be applied to any operant behavior, it is important that the behaviors pinpointed for change be socially important. The behavior change effort should have social validity, meaning that the behaviors selected are relevant to the individual's everyday functioning. Further, the outcomes should be of sufficient magnitude to effect that behavior in a significant way within the social community of which the individual is a part (Wolfe, 1978; Kazdin & Matson, 1981). Behaviors selected for change also should be ones that are likely to increase the probability of the student receiving reinforcement from the natural environment (Bailey & Lessen, 1984).

Strengthening a Behavior

Any behavior that is already within the repertoire of an individual can be strengthened and modified through the application of contingent rein-

forcement. After pinpointing the target behavior, the teacher should initiate a generous reinforcement schedule. With behaviors that are weak (or nonexistent), continuous reinforcement schedules are recommended. The reinforcers used may need to be arbitrary as well. Ongoing data collection will indicate the relative success of the reinforcers and schedules selected. Once a behavior has been established at its desired strength, it is preferable to shift to more natural reinforcers and to more normative reinforcement schedules. Data collection will serve to evaluate and guide behavior change efforts. Procedures for using positive reinforcement to increase behavior include the following:

1. **Specify clear target behaviors.** Pinpoint a target behavior and describe it precisely in behavioral terms. Develop a behavioral objective for the target behavior.
2. **Reinforce successive approximations.** When the student does not currently display the target behavior at the desired strength, reinforce gradual approximations of that behavior. This step-by-step procedure of making reinforcement contingent on behaviors that increasingly resemble the goal is necessary because the discrepancy between current and desired levels of behavior may be too great for a student to overcome immediately. Gradual approximation serves to shape target behaviors that are weak or absent at baseline.
3. **Reinforce contingently.** A contingent relationship exists when the emission of a particular behavior results in a particular consequence. In establishing or changing a behavior, the teacher must make sure that the reinforcer is only available on a contingent basis, in other words, only after the student has performed the target behavior. Noncontingent reinforcement weakens the relationship between the behavior and the reinforcer, making it more difficult to shape the behavior.
4. **Reinforce immediately and continuously.** When working on a new behavior, the reinforcement should be continuous and immedi-

ate. This means that the reinforcement should be delivered after every instance of the behavior and as immediately as feasible. This procedure will strengthen the relationship between the behavior and the contingent reinforcer.

5. **Reinforce consistently.** When reinforcement of specific behaviors is consistent, students learn more quickly the relationships between behaviors and their consequences. Further, consistent reinforcement application serves to increase the likelihood that particular situations will cue certain behaviors, thereby establishing stimulus control over the target behaviors.

The systematic application of these procedures is an effective approach for changing individual behavior. They can result in modifying the full range of academic and social behaviors.

Prompting a Behavior

Sometimes a student has acquired a behavior but needs assistance in exhibiting it at appropriate times. For example, students may know how to apply the spelling rule about adding *ing* to a consonant-vowel-consonant word but the teacher needs to prompt them to "Remember the *ing* rule with words that end in consonants." In teaching regrouping in arithmetic, the teacher may want to prompt the students by asking questions such as "What number are we starting with in the ones column?" and "Must we rename?"

A *prompt* is a stimulus given before a behavior to assist the student in performing that behavior. Prompts can be verbal, gestural, pictorial, or physical. Verbal prompts are statements that remind students how to do a task (as opposed to verbal directions to perform the task). They can be in the form of hints, explicit directions, or reminders of rules that apply. The teacher's bodily movements can serve as gestural prompts to communicate specific information about what to do. They include such actions as pointing to an object, using a hand movement to indicate that a stu-

dent should approach or the class should wait before responding, or signaling. Written information or pictures can also serve to prompt appropriate behavior. Displaying the alphabet across the top of the chalkboard can prompt students in dictionary tasks, sample problems on the board can prompt correct arithmetic work, and pictures of task steps can prompt the appropriate sequence of behavior. Physical prompts involve physically guiding the student through the response. In teaching a student to hold a pencil correctly, to swing a bat, or to perform other physical tasks that the student is having difficulty performing, physical guidance may be required. Prompting can be fairly intrusive and time consuming. As soon as feasible, a teacher will want to fade the use of prompts to increase instructional efficiency and to ensure broader stimulus control.

Shaping New Behaviors

When students do not exhibit a target behavior, it may be necessary to teach that behavior. This can be accomplished through a gradual process of reinforcing approximations. **Shaping,** one of the most effective procedures for teaching a new behavior, develops a new behavior through differentially reinforcing successive approximations of that behavior. It requires reinforcing the behavior of the student that is closest to the target behavior, then gradually shifting reinforcement to minor improvements or approximations toward the target behavior. Shaping procedures for an academic behavior are described in the following example.

> *Each day students in the math group are given independent worksheets containing ten problems of the type that has been presented, practiced, and reviewed during small group instruction. Margie never completes more than one or two of the problems on her worksheet. To shape completion of the entire worksheet, the teacher begins by reinforcing Margie for completing two problems each day in order to earn free-time tokens. Next, Margie is required to complete three problems. This shift is made by reinforcing Margie for com-*

pleting the third problem by copying down the an-swer during instruction. She then is required to complete four problems on her own, and so on until she receives free-time tokens only when she completes the entire math assignment.

In shaping a behavior, it is important to ex-plicitly define the target behavior to be estab-lished as well as the sequence of responses that will be reinforced as shaping occurs. The educa-tor should task analyze the target behavior to identify the substeps that compose it and then as-sess to determine where in that sequence the student currently is performing. She should differentially reinforce the child for each successive step to-ward that goal. Differential reinforcement should be used to reinforce only those responses that move the behavior closer to the terminal goal. This means that once a student has established a response at one step of the sequence, reinforce-ment will be contingent on the student responding appropriately at the next level of skill acquisition. In this way, the teacher contingently reinforces gradual approximations to the target behavior. She continues to reinforce each instance of the target behavior until it is well established within the student's behavioral repertoire. Once the stu-dent is emitting the behavior at a high level, the teacher should shift to an intermittent reinforce-ment schedule.

While shaping is effective in teaching a be-havior, and can be used in conjunction with other procedures, it also can be a time-consuming pro-cedure that may require an extended training pe-riod. It should be used only when more efficient procedures such as intermittent reinforcement and prompting are ineffective.

Modeling

Another important technique for developing new behaviors is **modeling.** This involves a person who is an expert in that behavior demonstrating it. Beginning in earliest life, we learn to imitate the behaviors of others. From smiling and playing peek-a-boo as infants to acting, public speaking,

and swinging a golf club as adolescents or adults, modeling plays a key role in developing new be-haviors. Modeling can be particularly useful in teaching complex behaviors such as social skills (Gelfand & Hartmann, 1984).

As discussed in later chapters of this book, the teacher's modeling of skills is a critical step in delivering instruction in all academic areas. When modeling a target skill as part of instruc-tion, the teacher should demonstrate each step in the skill in a slow, deliberate manner, exaggerat-ing the steps in the behavior so that students can attend to the critical features. Also, verbally label actions as they are performed.

Examples of modeling to teach a spelling les-son involving suffixes and an arithmetic lesson involving regrouping are illustrated as follows:

SPELLING RULE When we add a suffix be-ginning with a vowel to a word that ends in a vowel-consonant-vowel, we double the final consonant and add the suffix.

The teacher points to *trap* and *ing* written on the chalkboard, stating: "Look at this exam-ple. I want to write the word *trapping*. Trap ends with a consonant-vowel-consonant" (The teacher points to letters.) "The ending *ing* begins with a vowel letter (point to the *i*). So I will double the final consonant and write *ing*." (She writes *trapping* as she talks.)

ARITHMETIC RULE When we take away more than we start with, we must borrow 10 and rename.

The teacher points to a problem written on the chalkboard:

$$\begin{array}{r} 86 \\ -59 \\ \hline \end{array}$$

She states: "We are starting with 6 in the ones column and taking away 9. We have to rename because we are taking away more than we started with: 9 is more than 6. We borrow 10 from the next column and rename: 16. We take 9 away from 16.

In these examples, modeling was accompanied by verbal prompts. This is because modeling is most effective when paired with verbalizations that both focus the student on the critical behaviors and prompt the student to respond. In addition to teachers or parents, peers also serve as behavioral models. Sometimes they are more effective models than adults, especially when the peer model is a prestigious peer (i.e., a class leader or star athlete). Other commonalties that can affect the model's influence include such characteristics as sex, age, ethnicity, and shared interests or traits.

Modeling can teach both desirable or undesirable behaviors, serving to either accelerate or decelerate them. For instance, a student may learn to show off or act out by observing the positive attention that classmates receive from their peers when they behave in this manner. On the other hand, observing the contingent relationship between certain behaviors and their consequences (such as removal from the group, loss of tokens, or teacher disapproval) can serve to decrease the probability of other students exhibiting those behaviors. Models also can provide examples of appropriate classroom and social interaction behaviors, such as being prepared for instruction, following class rules, asking the teacher for assistance, and ignoring disruptive peer behavior. Systematic reinforcement of appropriate behavior in peers creates an opportunity for other students to observe the pleasurable consequences of such behavior.

Contingency Contracting

Contracts are increasingly a part of everyday life. We enter into marriage contracts, home purchasing contracts, employment contracts, consumer credit contracts, and insurance contracts. A **contract,** in its simplest form, is a formal, written agreement that specifies the relationship of the behaviors of the participating parties. It describes an "if—then" situation. For example, if you meet health prerequisites and pay set premiums at specified times, then, in the event of your death, the contracting insurance company will pay a specified amount of money to your designated beneficiaries.

A teacher can use contingency contracts (also referred to as behavior contracts) to effectively modify behaviors of those individual students who have proven resistant to less intrusive modification attempts. He can contract with students to complete and/or hand in more assignments, to complete their work with a higher degree of accuracy, to arrive at school more promptly, or to perform a host of other behaviors. Contingency contracts also can be developed between the teacher and the student's parents; between the parents and their child; or among the teacher, the parent, and the student. This is particularly useful in situations where all or most of the important reinforcers for the child occur outside the school. By making home consequences (e.g., play time, special excursions, and television) contingent on specified school behaviors, the probability of desired school behaviors increase. Contracting has the additional advantages of enhancing the contacts between the teacher and the student and/or the teacher and the parent. Sitting down together and negotiating in good faith is a positive behavior that communicates concern, respect, and trust. At the same time, the contracting process makes children more aware of their behavior and puts them in a position of exercising a greater degree of self-management. Examples of contingency contracts are presented in Figure 5.1.

Contingency contracts should be individually negotiated between the student and all involved parties (the teacher, other teachers, the parents, and so forth) who have a role in the contract. Remember that the student's active participation in setting the contract terms is essential to the success of the contract.

A contingency contract pinpoints the behavior to be increased or decreased, the consequences that will be delivered contingent on that behavior, and the criteria that will be used for determining if the terms of the contract have been met (Rutherford & Polsgrove, 1981). The target behaviors should be clearly observable and pre-

A. | Date: Monday, May 10

Behavior: During morning seatwork time, Bobby Atkinson will not leave his desk without permission from Ms. Lewis.

Criteria: 3 out of 5 days

Consequence: Feed the gerbils on Friday afternoon

_____   _____
            Teacher   Student

B. | Date: Tuesday, January 8

Task: Read pages 110–116 in science text
         Complete the 12 items on the assigned worksheet

Consequence: If Andrea gets a 75% or higher on the worksheet, she gets 5 points towards Friday Special. If she gets lower than 75%, she will correct the missed items with teacher assistance.

_____   _____
            Teacher   Student

C. | Date: _____

I, Alicia Garcia, agree to the following conditions for Mr. Samuel's class:
    I will work quietly during study time
    I will complete my in-class assignments
    I will turn in my math homework on time

I, Mr. Samuel, agree to give Alicia the following points:
    Working quietly during study time = 5 points each day
    Completing in-class assignments = 5 points each day
    Turning in math homework = 10 points each day

    Total possible = 20 points each day

I, Mrs. Garcia, agree to let Alicia exchange points as follows:
    30 minutes of television = 20 points
    One videotape = 80 points
    Dinner out = 100 points

_____   _____   _____
     Student   Teacher   Parent

FIGURE 5.1   (A) Weekly School Contract for Bobby's In-Seat Behavior, (B) Daily School Contract for Andrea's Science Worksheet, and (C) Home-School Contract for Alicia's Math Performance

cisely defined so that there can be virtually no question as to whether or not they have occurred. In pinpointing the target behaviors, remember that initially it may be necessary to specify ap-proximations to the ultimate goal desired. For example, if a student currently is handing in only one out of five math homework assignments each week, a teacher might begin by contracting for two or three assignments per week. Once the student meets this intermediate criterion, she can renegotiate the contract to specify greater accomplishment for the reinforcer: "Bobby will hand in all math homework assignments this week, with only one miss." It generally is a good idea to provide for some margin of error, particularly with a fairly long-term contract. Otherwise, early in the day or week, the student may lose all opportunities to successfully meet the terms of the contract and therefore have little motivation to expend further effort on the desired behavior. Another option is to have a sliding scale of reinforcement, for example, "If Bobby completes four math homework assignments this week, he will receive two picks from the activity list. If he completes three assignments, he will receive one pick from the activity list." A bonus clause might specify that should he hand in all five homework assignments, the teacher would send a "good student" letter home to his parents.

In developing contracts, it is important to be sure that the target behavior is at an appropriate difficulty level for the individual student. For example, if Bobby is just mastering the multiplication tables, a contract specifying that he complete even one advanced algebra homework assignment for the week would be ludicrous. At the same time, the contingency relationship must be appropriate. A TransAm automobile would be an excessive reinforcer for handing in a week's worth of math homework, while two extra minutes of free time on Friday probably would be too small of a consequence.

Discuss with the student (and other parties, if applicable) which activities, items, or privileges might be earned. These might include reinforcers available at school or at home. If the latter is included, be sure to include the parents in the negotiations. Parents can indicate special home privileges or events (a trip to the ice cream store or a Saturday outing for the student and a parent) that they are willing to provide. Write down all desired options. Permit the student to choose the reward, specifying the behavior required for the award and delivery conditions. The reward can be

either directly given to the student, or the student might accumulate tokens or points toward the reward. Write the amount of the reward and delivery conditions into the contract; if parents or others are involved, specify their responsibilities as part of the written contract.

Implicit in contracts are penalties for failure to perform. This might include cancelling the contract's potential reinforcers, or imposing a response cost or fine for specified behaviors (e.g., loss of points for aggressive behavior). Any penalties should be appropriate to the behavior and not so punitive as to make the contracting process undesirable to the student. Ten considerations for developing contingency contracts are as follows:

1. Involve student in developing the contract.
2. Clearly specify observable behaviors that the student is capable of performing.
3. Reinforce students for performing behaviors, not merely extinguishing or suppressing behaviors.
4. Reinforce accomplishment, not obedience.
5. Contract for approximations of the desired goal behaviors.
6. Provide immediate and frequent behaviors.
7. Provide reasonable reinforcement for the behavior.
8. Collect data on the contracted behavior to determine if conditions are met.
9. Teach the student to evaluate his own performance, thereby encouraging him to assume greater responsibility for and to exercise more self-control over behavior.
10. Implement the contract honestly; do not violate the conditions of the contract.

POSITIVE STRATEGIES FOR DECREASING BEHAVIORS

In addition to establishing and strengthening desired behaviors, behavior management strategies can be used to reduce or decelerate the frequency of undesired responses. Procedures for decreasing the occurrence of such behaviors include both positive and negative approaches. Positive strategies for decreasing behaviors include the differential reinforcement of other behaviors, extinction, and time-out from positive reinforcement. Negative strategies include various forms of punishment, such as response cost, verbal reprimands, and physical punishment. These procedures are discussed in the following paragraphs.

Differential Reinforcement of Other Behaviors

One useful approach to decreasing undesirable behaviors is to differentially reinforce incompatible or alternative responses. In this context, *incompatible* refers to the physical impossibility of the two behaviors occurring at the same time. By strengthening the incompatible behavior, the undesired behavior is weakened. For example, a student can not sit at a desk and walk around the room at the same time. Therefore, reinforcing desk sitting results in decreased room walking. Along the same vein, a student cannot daydream and be on-task, or study and be disruptive, simultaneously. In choosing an incompatible behavior to reinforce, a teacher can select from almost anything that the student does.

She also may choose to reinforce a behavior that *could* co-occur with the inappropriate behavior. Typically, this alternative behavior serves to functionally reduce the occurrence of the undesired behavior by providing the student with a behavioral strategy that increases the probability of task success and reinforcement. For example, a teacher might teach the student a learning strategy that can be employed for successfully completing an assignment or as an alternative to disruptive behavior.

Extinction

Extinction refers to the behavioral procedure of withholding reinforcement from a response that previously was reinforced. This results in decreasing the occurrence of and eventually elimi-

nating a behavior. As stated earlier in the chapter, extinction occurs most rapidly when the targeted behavior has been under a continuous reinforcement schedule. The most difficult responses to extinguish are those maintained on intermittent reinforcement schedules. Because not every response has been reinforced in the past, withdrawing reinforcement has no immediate effect. Students have learned to delay gratification; they simply learn to emit more instances of the behavior as they wait for the teacher to respond.

For example, with disruptive students, teacher reprimands frequently have an effect opposite than that intended: the reprimands increase rather than decrease the probability of the behavior occurring in the future. Apparently, teacher attention, even critical attention, can act as a positive consequence. This may be particularly true for students who, because of poor academic performance and/or a lack of general school success, have found no other way to obtain teacher attention. Because teachers seldom attend to every instance of acting out behavior, but respond only some of the time, the first few times the teacher purposely ignores the disruptions have little effect on the frequency of the behavior. After several instances of ignoring, however, the students increase the frequency, duration, and/or intensity of their acting out behavior. Having come to expect teacher scolding or reprimands, the students try harder to achieve that expected consequence. When using extinction, a teacher must expect that the target behaviors will increase before they decrease.

The worst thing that a teacher can do at this time is to give in to the increased disruptiveness and attend to the target behavior. If the teacher finds the increased disruptiveness so annoying or aversive as to once again scold the instigators, the students will have only learned that increased amounts of misbehavior are required to attain the desired consequence of teacher attention. Not only will the attempt at extinction have failed, but in all likelihood, the strength of the target response has increased and extinction will be even more difficult to achieve in the future. Once the target behavior has been extinguished through withdrawal of reinforcement, the inadvertent subsequent reinforcement of that behavior may result in the behavior being reestablished at its original rate of occurrence.

When using extinction procedures, it is necessary to identify the consequences that are reinforcing the behavior and gain control over these reinforcers. This can be fairly difficult in some cases. Peer approval, a strong reinforcer for most adolescents, is one over which teachers exercise little control. Further, peer approval may be dispensed outside the classroom, after school in the neighborhood—an environment where a teacher may have little influence. Within the class, a teacher can devise a classwide strategy in which peers are reinforced for ignoring the inappropriate behavior.

Simply ignoring the inappropriate behavior results in fairly gradual reductions in the behavior. It is more effective to pair the ignoring with reinforcing appropriate behavior. Teachers are more successful when they pair consistent reinforcement of the desired behavior with withholding reinforcement for the undesired behavior. They can praise the disruptive students as well as peer models for sitting quietly, raising their hands, and working hard.

Time-Out from Positive Reinforcement

Removing a student from a situation or setting in which reinforcers are available is known as a **time-out.** Time-out procedures can range from such nonexclusionary practices as planned ignoring (e.g., withdrawal of adult attention), to exclusion from reinforcement opportunities, to seclusion in a time-out room. **Seclusion,** or physical isolation of a student, is the most restrictive and most controversial time-out procedure. It can be an effective intervention with behaviors that are seriously and chronically disruptive, (i.e., such as fighting, cursing, and spitting). However, it is an exacting procedure that requires a specific plan for a given student to be developed in consultation with other staff, approved by the school administration, and specified on the Individual

Education Program (IEP) of students in special education. This plan must specify the behaviors upon which seclusion is contingent, the length of time and location of the seclusion, how the seclusion will be monitored, and how the effectiveness of the seclusion procedures will be evaluated. Seclusion is a frequently misunderstood and oversimplified procedure, leading to abuses that are ineffective, unprofessional, unethical, and possibly illegal.

Nonseclusionary time-out procedures are preferable for most classroom applications. These procedures involve removing the reinforcing consequences from the student. One form of nonseclusionary time-out is **planned ignoring,** in which the teacher ignores the student for a brief time contingent upon the student emitting a specific target behavior. In a one-to-one instructional situation, the teacher can simply turn his face away from the student for several seconds, responding positively to the student when appropriate behavior is again displayed. The student's classmates also may be instructed to ignore the student for a period of time when specific behaviors occur. *In-seat time-out,* another procedure for withdrawing reinforcers, requires the student to sit at her desk with head on arms or to work for a set period of time without earning points or tokens. Students also may be required to turn away from the group (facing a wall or the corner) for several minutes, or to stand or sit on the sidelines at recess or during an activity. Another time-out procedure includes removing instructional materials from the student's environment, making it impossible for the student either to continue a reinforcing activity or to earn points and tokens for task completion. These procedures should be used in combination with positive reinforcement for appropriate behavior.

AVERSIVE BEHAVIOR REDUCTION STRATEGIES

Strategies for decreasing behaviors, discussed previously, all involve some type of punishment. *Punishment* is the contingent presentation of aversive consequences following a behavior and resulting in a decrease in that behavior. The aversive consequences are categorized as response response cost, verbal reprimands, and physical punishment. Virtually everyone has had some experience with punishment, which tends to be one of society's most widely used behavioral control approaches.

Response Cost

The removal or withdrawal of reinforcers contingent on a behavior is known as **response cost.** This strategy, which can be effective in quickly reducing unwanted behaviors, is a form of punishment that can be used in an acceptable fashion. It is a good procedure for decreasing behaviors that have been resistant to other decelerating strategies. It is particularly applicable to behaviors in which extinction is not possible because the maintaining reinforcers either are unknown or are not under the teacher's control (e.g., peer approval).

Response cost should be used only to reduce unwanted behavior, not to punish inaccurate responses (although it might be used to punish sloppy or careless work). When a student emits a target response, reinforcers (e.g, recess, tokens, or privileges) already acquired are contingently removed. Prior to implementing a response cost procedure, the teacher should precisely pinpoint the target behavior and specify the amount of reinforcer to be removed. Fighting could result in a response cost of five tokens or one recess period, or the privilege of attending a class party. Parents might "fine" their offspring by removing car driving privileges for one grading period when grades are unacceptably low. In implementing response cost procedures, it should be clear that the consequences removed actually are positive reinforcers of some importance to the student.

Response cost procedures are fairly easy to administer and typically do not result in the negative side effects associated with aversive consequences or other types of punishment. There is no response cost when the disruptive behavior re-sults in removing a neutral consequence. Demonstrated to be effective with a broad range of behaviors, response cost most typically is used in conjunction with a token economy or contingency contracting where quantitative data can be kept.

Verbal Reprimands

Verbal reprimands may include disapproval, scoldings, threats, nagging, and just saying "no." When used infrequently and within the context of a highly reinforcing environment, they can be effectively and appropriately employed in the classroom setting. However, verbal reprimands may be used at such a high rate, or they may be so loud and abusive that students either ignore them or avoid interacting with the teacher. It is never appropriate to utilize verbal reprimands that constitute severe attacks on the individual's sense of self-worth and dignity. Furthermore, teachers should be vigilant about the amount of verbal criticism used so as not to fall into the "the criticism trap." Many teachers use far too much verbal criticism, frequently with little awareness that they are doing so.

Verbal reprimands may not have the intended outcome of weakening behavior. Instead they may reinforce the behavior that they are intended to weaken. When a teacher yells at a student to "Return to your seat and stay there." the student may comply immediately. The student's compliance serves as a reinforcer that strengthens the teacher's reprimanding behavior. It is likely that the student soon will be out of the seat again, with the teacher once more responding by yelling. Soon, a good deal of the time is spent yelling, a situation that increases everyone's frustration, has limited long-range positive behavioral outcomes, and wastes instructional time. In situations such as this, teachers have become "trapped" into behavioral patterns that are counterproductive to their long-term goals (Jensen, Sloane, & Young, 1988).

To be effective, verbal reprimands should be used carefully, precisely, consistently, and infrequently. Verbal reprimands are most effective in classroom environments that otherwise are highly reinforcing. Apparently, even gentle verbal reprimands are perceived as aversive within a context typified by high rates of positive reinforcement. Jensen et al. (1988) have suggested the following guidelines for using verbal reprimands:

1. Before giving a reprimand, the teacher should first state the pupil's name and then wait until he stops what he is doing and pays attention to the teacher. When reprimands are given in a half-hearted way to a half-hearted listener, they not only tend to be ineffective, but they also teach the student not to listen when a reprimand is given.

2. When giving a reprimand, the teacher's facial expressions and tone of voice should be neutral.

3. The reprimand should be brief. It should communicate clearly what the undesired behavior is.

4. When responding to a student's undesired behavior, the teacher should not explain why it is undesirable. A simple statement such as "Jean, smacking kids in my class is unacceptable. Don't do it again." is enough.

5. The teacher should not threaten, but should make the reprimand once. Nothing is gained by threatening or warning, except more time to misbehave. Instead of using verbal threats with reprimands, the teacher should follow a reprimand with a positive consequence. This will teach pupils to listen and follow a request the first time with or without threats.

6. Once the teacher has stated the reprimand, she should watch for a desired behavior from the offender that can be praised or otherwise attended to positively.

7. Reprimands should be used infrequently. Frequent reprimands establish a generally negative and aversive atmosphere in the class and are not effective in decreasing undesired behaviors. Reprimands are most effective when they are used sparingly in a highly positive environment.

Reprimands, when used infrequently and appropriately, can be effective in teaching students to discriminate acceptable from unacceptable behavior. This is especially true when they provide specific feedback about an unacceptable behavior in a particular situation, when they are followed by reinforcement of appropriate behavior, and when the teacher's delivery of them provides a model of the desired behavior.

Physical Punishment

Physical punishment is never acceptable within the context of the regular school setting. The use of corporal punishment (spanking, hitting, and slapping) has serious ethical and potential legal implications. It tends to have long-term negative effects, including an increased probability that the student will use physical punishment as an adult. For these reasons, its application is not discussed in detail in this chapter.

Drawbacks to Punishment

While punishment can result in immediate observable results in terms of behavior changes, it should be used sparingly and precisely, if at all. With the exception of carefully structured response cost programs and the use of mild verbal reprimands (always followed by positive reinforcement of desired responses), the disadvantages to using punishment outweigh the advantages. As noted by Bushell (1973), punishment suppresses a behavior only while the punishment is present; it does not replace the inappropriate behavior with an alternative behavior; it encourages escape/avoidance; it can lead to aggressive behaviors; and it does not generalize to other settings.

The frequent use of punishment tends to reduce the potential reinforcing value of teacher attention, thereby reducing opportunities for effective instruction in the future. It is extremely difficult for the teacher to be viewed as a source of positive consequences when past interactions have been aversive. As indicated earlier, the immediate success of aversive consequences in terms of student compliance can increase the likelihood that the teacher will use punishment in the future. This, in turn, can lead to creating an environment that is generally aversive and punitive. All aspects of the learning environment—the teacher, the building, and the curriculum—may become aversive to the student.

Punishment tends to be used inconsistently, a function more of a teacher's feelings of stress at a given moment than of students' behaviors. As a result, students may have difficulty predicting a teacher's responses. They may not know whether to expect a pat or a slap. General avoidance behaviors such as truancy or frequent crying can result. Further, frequent punishment can lead to higher levels of aggressive behavior on the part of the students, both now and when they become adults. Other potential possible emotional responses include generalized suppressions of responding (withdrawal).

Even when punishment results in the intended effect, this effect is generally temporary, particularly when alternative positive behaviors are not reinforced. Students may not have a repertoire of alternative behaviors and/or they may not know when to demonstrate these behaviors. Finally, efforts to punish may have unintended effects in that negative teacher attention and/or the resulting peer attention can be so reinforcing that the aversive consequence has little effect.

EVALUATING BEHAVIOR CHANGE EFFORTS

The continuous collection of performance data improves instruction. Graphing this data is even more effective. A plethora of research studies have shown that teachers who graph student performance data facilitate higher student achievement than those who only collect the data (Fuchs & Fuchs, 1986). Graphs assist teachers in monitoring student performance more accurately, permit comparison of performance across different conditions, and provide feedback that can be used

for decision making. Further, graphs can provide effective feedback to students, therein affecting subsequent performance.

Systematic efforts to change behavior using applied behavioral analysis constitute a form of research. Hypotheses are made about changes in the behavior given specific interventions, and data are collected and compared to test these hypotheses. More traditional research forms compare the behaviors of groups of students to one another. Frequently, one group is the experimental group, meaning that some specific intervention occurs with them. Their performance is compared with that of a control group to whom no new intervention is added. This provides a measure of the effect of the intervention or treatment, isolating that effect from those that would normally occur regardless of the intervention (e.g., with the passage of time, students' reading will improve with any method, or they will mature and their behavior will change for reasons unrelated to the intervention).

Individual behavior change research, typically referred to as single-subject research, focuses on the behavior of only one individual, not that of a large group of individuals. The target behavior is measured before and after intervention to determine whether or not the intervention was effective. For example, one of Ms. Tingent's students is out-of-seat several times per day. She pinpoints this behavior, carefully describes its parameters, plans an intervention, and collects data on the frequency of occurrence before and after the intervention is implemented. The student serves as his own control; data on his behavior following intervention is compared with data on his behavior prior to the intervention to determine the effectiveness of the intervention. The CBA procedures described in Chapter 4 are additional applications of single-subject research. Here, data is collected as instructional procedures change to ensure that students are making the progress desired.

Wolery et al. (1988) identified the following two distinctive characteristics of single-subject research designs:

1. Repeated measures are collected over time on the target behavior under standard conditions.
2. The performance of the individual under one experimental condition (e.g., intervention) is compared with his or her past performance under a different condition.

The simplest single-subject design for modifying a behavior is an AB design. The two phases of this design are baseline (A) and intervention (B). Chapter 3 described procedures for collecting and graphing behavioral data. Remember, for each phase of the intervention project, data on several instances of the behavior should be collected. Three to five instances of the behavior should be collected for academic behaviors and five to seven instances for social behavior. Within each successive phase of the behavior change project, there should be a fairly stable rate of performance before a new phase is introduced. This demonstrates that the behavior is under environmental control and makes it possible to measure the effects of a new treatment condition.

Figure 5.2 illustrates a behavior change project using the AB design. Ms. Tingent, the teacher, was concerned about the frequency of Linda's talking out in class, particularly during the mornings when much of the academic instruction occurred. Baseline data for 1 week identified a total of forty-four talk outs, or an average of 8.8 per morning. She decided to establish daily goals with Linda and to reward her with 5 minutes of extra lunch recess for every morning that she achieved these goals. Ms. Tingent and Linda agreed upon the intervention goal of not more than five talk outs per morning for the first week. During intervention phase (i.e., the contingency contract phase), Linda's talk outs fell to a total of nineteen or 3.8 per day. Visual examination of Figure 5.2 indicates that the intervention was successful.

While the AB design serves to demonstrate the change in performance following a modification of the contingencies, it does not actually prove that the contingency (5 minutes of recess during lunch period for reduced talking) controlled the behavior. There may be some competing explanation. To prove the effectiveness of the contingency, a teacher would need to withdraw the intervention and observe whether or not the behavior returns to baseline. Once the behavior had returned to baseline, the intervention condi-

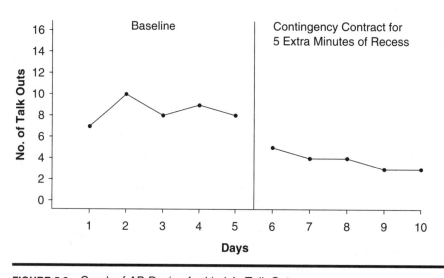

FIGURE 5.2 Graph of AB Design for Linda's Talk Outs

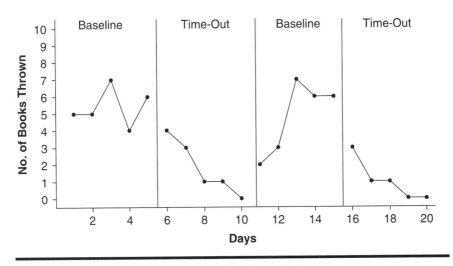

FIGURE 5.3   Graph of ABAB Design for Vera's Book Throws

tion should be reinstated to once again return the behavior to the desired strength. This more sophisticated design is known as an **A B A B design** because it involves the following four steps:

(A) Collect baseline data
(B) Institute the intervention and measure the behavior change
(C) Withdraw the intervention, returning to baseline
(D) Reinstate the intervention

This type of design provides research control and serves to validate the interventions. Figure 5.3 of Vera's book throwing behavior depicts an ABAB design. This visual presentation of data illustrates that the opportunity of earning time-outs did modify the behavior. Causality has been established. For most classroom interventions, the teacher's overriding concern is not on proving experimental control, but on changing student behavior. In these instances, the simple AB design is sufficient. However, she occasionally will want to include the reversal and reinstatement phases as a check on her teaching effectiveness and efficiency.

SUMMARY

This chapter has presented concepts and procedures that encompass a technology of behavior management that can be utilized to change almost any behavior. These strategies, developed over decades of empirical study, constitute behavior change tools that are both effective and powerful. It is the professional's responsibility to employ these tools to attain worthy and important goals, keeping in mind that the ultimate goal is the self-efficacy of the student.

The relationship of behaviors to their antecedents and consequences was emphasized. The focus has been on operant behaviors because these are the behaviors that are under the control of their consequences. These consequences can be reinforcing, either positively or negatively, meaning that they tend to increase the probability of the behavior occurring. Consequences also can be punishing, meaning that they result in decreases in the behavior. The chapter has stressed positive approaches to changing behavior, including positive reinforcement for strengthening desired behaviors as well as positive approaches to decreasing undesirable behaviors.

Categories of positive reinforcers were described, including social, tangible, and activity reinforcers. Continuous and intermittent schedules of reinforcers were described and differentiated relative to their varied use in establishing new behaviors and maintaining existing one. Using positive reinforcers with token economies and contingency contracts were presented as ways to shape and encourage students' self-control and self-management.

New behaviors can be shaped through using differential reinforcement of gradual approximations. In establishing a new behavior, it is important that every instance of that behavior be reinforced initially. Once a behavior is established, intermittent reinforcement will maintain it almost indefinitely.

The strategies described here can be used to improve the academic and social functioning of students in any classroom at any age level. They can be used to reinforce or punish behaviors, increase or decrease behaviors, to develop new behaviors, and to change existing behaviors. They can be applied to individuals or to groups of students.

These procedures should be used as precisely as possible. For this reason, a teacher should occasionally monitor his efforts through interrater reliability checks. At the same time, he should strive for upmost precision whenever important decisions are being made based on the data. The single-subject research design implicit in behavior change efforts permits comparing an individual's performance before and after intervention efforts. By taking repeated measures over time, the teacher can obtain a meaningful picture of the behavior in question and can determine the extent to which it is occurring in a desirable fashion.

Simple baseline/intervention (AB) designs and reversal (ABAB) designs have been described. More sophisticated designs are available but are beyond the scope of this chapter. Using precise tools for interpreting graphic displays of single-subject data, such as central tendency lines, trend or progress lines, and/or aim lines, were delineated in Chapter 3.

Systematically and carefully applying behavioral concepts and procedures can assist in improving instruction and raising student achievement. They also provide a basis for arranging and structuring a classroom to encourage appropriate student behavior and self-responsibility. Through preventative discipline measures involving the physical arrangement of the classroom, developing and enforcing classroom rules, communicating clear expectations to students, and reinforcing desired behaviors, teachers can develop a classroom environment that is effective for both low-achieving and high-achieving students. Chapter 6 describes specific approaches to developing such an instructional environment.

CONTENT MASTERY QUESTIONS

1. Discuss and describe three types of setting events within a classroom. How can one determine if stimulus control has been achieved? Provide an example of stimulus control.

2. Define and provide two examples of the three forms of consequences.

3. Define a reinforcer and discuss the four categories of reinforcers. Provide two examples of each category of reinforcers.

4. Discuss and describe the four axioms for reinforcer usage.

5. What are the two types of reinforcement schedules? Which schedule is best for teaching a new behavior? Describe how one maintains behavior using reinforcement schedules.

6. Describe the five procedures for using positive reinforcement to increase behavior.

7. What is a prompt? List and provide an example of the four types of prompts.

8. Define shaping and discuss the process for shaping a target behavior.

9. Describe and discuss the process for modeling a target skill; include factors affecting the model and possible uses for modeling.

10. List the steps for developing a contingency contract.

11. Define differential reinforcement of other behaviors and describe the implementation of this procedure.

12. Define extinction and discuss the two factors that can affect the effectiveness of the extinction procedure.

13. Define time-out and list the four time-out procedures.

14. Define response cost and describe the implementation of this procedure.

15. Describe the seven guidelines for using verbal reprimands effectively.

16. Define physical punishment and discuss the five drawbacks to applying a punishment procedure.

17. Compare and contrast the AB design with the ABAB design.

REFERENCES

Anderson, L. M., Evertson, C. M., & Emmer, E. T. (1980). Dimensions in classroom management derived from research. *Journal of Curriculum Studies, 12*(4), 343–356.

Bailey, S. L., & Lessen, E. I. (1984). An analysis of target behaviors in education: Applied but how useful? In W. L. Heward, T. E. Heron, D. S. Hill, & J. Tap-Porter (Eds.), *Focus on behavior analysis in education* (pp. 162–176). Columbus, OH: Charles E. Merrill.

Brophy, J. E. (1981). Teacher praise: A functional analysis. *Review of Educational Research, 51,* 5–32.

Bushell, S., Jr. (1973). *Classroom behavior: A little book for teachers.* Englewood Cliffs, NJ: Prentice-Hall.

Fuchs, L., & Fuchs, D. (1986). Effects of systematic formulative evaluation: A meta-analysis. *Exceptional Children, 53,* 199–208.

Gelfand, D. M., & Hartmann, D. P. (1984). *Child behavior analysis and therapy* (2nd ed.). New York: Pergamon.

Jensen, W. R., Sloane, H. N., & Young, K. R. (1988). *Applied behavioral analysis in education.* Englewood Cliffs, NJ: Prentice-Hall.

Kazdin, A. E., & Matson, J. L. (1981). Social validation in mental retardation. *Applied Research in Mental Retardation, 2,* 39–54.

Rutherford, R. B., Jr., & Polsgrove, L. (1981). Behavioral contracting with behaviorally disordered and delinquent children and youth: An analysis of the clinical and experimental literature. In R. B. Rutherford, Jr., & A. G. Prieto (Eds.), *Severe behavior disorders of children and youth* (Vol. 4) (pp. 49–69). Reston, VA: Council for Children with Behavior Disorders.

Wolery, M., Bailey, D. B., & Sugai, G. M. (1988). *Effective teaching: Principles of applied behavior analysis with exceptional students.* Boston, MA: Allyn and Bacon.

Wolfe, M. M. (1978). Social validity: The case for subjective measurement, or how applied behavioral analysis is finding its heart. *Journal of Applied Behavior Analysis, 11,* 203–214.

CHAPTER 6

Structuring the Classroom for Effective Instruction

PATRICIA THOMAS CEGELKA

CHAPTER OBJECTIVES

At the conclusion of this chapter, the reader will be able to:

1. Describe the activities (i.e., getting acquainted with the school, arranging the classroom, and establishing routines and rules) that a new teacher should engage in prior to the beginning of the school term.
2. Discuss how to structure the first day(s) of school to maximize effectiveness.
3. Describe how to establish rules and routines within the classroom to maintain control.
4. Discuss procedures for effectively managing the instructional schedule.
5. Describe the procedures for monitoring student behavior within the classroom.
6. Discuss strategies for responding to appropriate and inappropriate behavior.
7. Discuss the importance of evaluating the learning environment and possible methods to evaluate the environment.

STRUCTURING THE CLASSROOM FOR EFFECTIVE INSTRUCTION

Good classroom management is an essential aspect of effective instruction. By maximizing the amount of time that teachers engage in direct teaching and that students engage in active learning, it sets the stage for effective education. The research on effective instruction consistently has demonstrated that effective teachers allocate more time to instruction and that their students are actively engaged in instruction for a higher percentage of that time (Stallings, 1980; Fisher and Berliner, 1985). While good classroom management is a critical variable for all students, it is a particularly important consideration for students who have difficulties paying attention and/or achieving academically. These are the students who are least likely to focus on the relevant concepts and tasks without assistance. A well-structured learning environment provides the framework that increases the amount of time that

students spend mastering the academic and social curriculum of the school.

The two most important areas of classroom management are management of instructional time and management of student behavior (White, Wyne, Stuck, & Coop, 1983; Doyle, 1986). When instructional time is well managed, and instruction is effectively structured and presented, behavior problems are minimized. In other words, good instruction prevents most behavior problems from occurring. Effective teachers are prepared to initiate instruction at the beginning of the class period, make full use of the time allocated for instruction, and maintain a high level of on-task behavior. They establish clear classroom rules and routines, and explicitly teach these to the students. They carefully monitor student behavior, consistently implementing these rules and procedures, and intervening promptly and consistently when inappropriate behavior occurs.

The teachers' major responsibility is to create a calm, orderly classroom environment in which routines, procedures, and expectations are clearly established for all students. According to Rieth and Evertson (1988, p.1), these preinstructional factors "provide the essential staging area from which effective instruction is launched." Developing such an environment requires careful advanced preparation and planning prior to the first day of school. The weeks immediately preceding and following the opening of the school term are the most critical times of the entire school year. During this time, effective teachers devote their energies to structuring their classrooms into attractive, efficient learning environments. Well before the first day of school, they become acquainted with the school facility and its staff, they organize the physical space of their classrooms, and they carefully plan the basic rules and routines that will make their classrooms operate efficiently. During the first several days of the school year, the major focus of instruction is on explicitly teaching these rules and routines. Students are taught systematic lessons on the rules and procedures. Throughout the school year, the teachers periodically review these lessons, they consistently monitor and respond to student behavior, and they evaluate the classroom structure to identify those aspects that require attention and revision.

This chapter describes activities in which effective teachers engage before the beginning of the school term, approaches to structuring the physical space of the classroom to facilitate learning, procedures for establishing and teaching classroom rules and routines, and strategies for maintaining classroom discipline. It draws from the growing body of teacher effectiveness research in both general education (Brophy & Good, 1986) and special education (Bickel & Bickel, 1986; Englert, 1983).

BEFORE THE SCHOOL TERM BEGINS

Getting to Know the School

As quickly as possible, new teachers should become acquainted with the school itself. A teacher will want to become familiar with the physical layout of the school and its facilities and resources. She will want to learn the location of the library, computer lab, playground, bus areas, lunchroom, faculty workrooms, playgrounds, and other school facilities. Additional areas of great importance are the offices for the school nurse, principal, counselor, custodian, and other support staff.

New teachers need to become familiar with the school calendar, philosophy, rules, and policies, as well as the structure of the school programs. They should learn about the support personnel and services available to students. Are there special education resource consultants? Bilingual education consultants and programs? Reading specialists? A guidance counselor? A school psychologist? Will the teacher have one or more teacher's aides and, if so, for how long each day? Do volunteers work in the school? What kind of schoolwide parent outreach or parent participation program is there?

It also is important to meet the other staff members in the school. The central administrative and clerical staff are important resources. The school secretary, for example, can be a fountain of information on school procedures. The new teacher should become acquainted with the other teachers and support staff in the school, particularly those who may interact directly with the students in his class. It is important to ascertain the extent to which the school is structured to encourage cooperation among staff. For example, is there a school-based teacher assistance team to aid teachers working with students experiencing difficulties in the classroom? If so, who serves on it and how often does it meet? Does the school philosophy and scheduling encourage inclusion of students with disabilities in the regular education classroom, team teaching, or other forms of collaboration? Are there other teachers who would be receptive to collaborating for a part of each day or week? Are there support personnel with whom the teacher can collaborate in handling unique situations? Understanding all of these aspects of the school makes it possible for the teacher to plan a sound instructional program and to design procedures for accessing the available resources and activities.

Arranging the Classroom Environment

The physical arrangement of the classroom significantly influences student behavior and student learning. It can increase or decrease the amount of time students spend in active learning, the extent to which they pay attention, and the amount of disruptive behavior they emit. Teachers should structure the physical space of the classroom so as to minimize the amount of time diverted from active learning. The ability of students and teachers to move easily about the room without interrupting ongoing activities, the accessibility of instructional materials and aids, and the visibility of students to the teacher and the teacher to students all combine to dramatically decrease the amount of nonproductive time in the classroom. The most effective classrooms are those where only 5–13% of the total instructional day is spent on activities such as setting up equipment and materials.

A first step to organizing classroom space is to identify the types of activities in which students will be engaged. Students participate in a variety of activities within different areas of the classroom each day. There tends to be a greater variety of activities at the elementary level than at the secondary level (Rounds, Ward, Mergendoller, & Tickunoff, 1982). Studies of elementary classrooms have identified between eleven and fifty-three different types of activities (Berliner, 1983). An abbreviated listing includes: teacher lectures, whole-class discussions, seatwork, reading circles, small group instruction, cooperative learning activities, checking work, sharing periods, transitions (entering and leaving), housekeeping (attendance, clean up, and pencil sharpening), films/videos, games, contests, art projects, science projects and teachers' instructions.

The room arrangement can facilitate these activities and promote orderly movement of students. It can minimize distractions and noise, im-

prove the quality of student interactions, and increase the percentage of time students spend on their academic tasks (Rieth & Evertson, 1988). The room arrangement can also affect the teacher's ability to monitor student work and behavior, an important aspect of effective instruction (Good & Brophy, 1987; Evertson, Emmer, Clements, & Worsham, 1994).

Careful thought should be given to how various arrangements of the furniture and equipment can facilitate the types of activities planned for the classroom. Will there be individual and small group instruction as well as whole-class activities? Will students work independently some of the time and in small cooperative groups at other times? Will there be peer tutoring? Will an aide or volunteer work with some students while the teacher works with others? What about special interest areas and learning centers, a reading corner, individual study carrels, and time-out or quiet areas for students? Once a teacher has decided on these features, she than can make an inventory of the available equipment and supplies. Are the storage units movable? Are there study carrels for individual students' use? Are the tables, chairs, student desks, bookshelves, storage closets, and classroom partitions movable?

The equipment and instructional materials available in the classroom also are important considerations in arranging the furniture and instructional areas. The teacher should know whether each student receives individual copies of the textbooks, or if there are supplemental texts and resources available. Is there an in-class library of free-reading materials? Does the classroom have its own computers? What about an overhead projector, a built-in screen, a pull-down map, chalkboards, and bulletin boards?

Once the teacher has identified types of instructional opportunities and has a list of the furniture, equipment, and supplies available, he is ready to design the physical space of the classroom. The room arrangement should ensure that materials and equipment are readily accessible, and that the teacher can easily see all students. Evertson, Emmer, Clements, and Worsham (1994) developed suggestions for organizing and storing instructional supplies and materials, as depicted in Table 6.1.

In structuring the room arrangement, the teacher should remember that there is a close relationship between teacher proximity, mobility, and classroom discipline: According to Jones (1987), the easier it is for the teacher to get to each student, the better will be the classroom discipline. An open room arrangement facilitates timely movement from one area of the room to another, ensuring that the teacher can quickly respond to student needs as well as to potential behavior problems.

The way in which the physical space in the classroom is organized signals important information to students about how they are expected to interact with the teacher and with each other, and the manner in which they are expected to accomplish classroom tasks (Rosenfield, Lambert, & Black, 1985). For example, the traditional "custodian" arrangement of classrooms into neat rows of student desks all facing the teacher's desk and front chalkboard is convenient for the school janitor but can impede the teacher's ability to move quickly to assist a student whose desk is several rows away. In a more open arrangement, the teacher can move directly to the student without disrupting the entire class. Further, the custodial room arrangement suggests a mode of interaction and instruction that is characterized by whole-class instruction, limited student-student interaction, and regimentation, while other arrangements are more conducive to small group instruction, cooperative learning activities, and individualization (see Figures 6.1 and 6.2). While many different student desk arrangements are possible, it is important to arrange them so that all students can see the whole-group instruction area without having to leave their seats. At the same time, the

TABLE 6.1 Suggestions for Organizing and Storing Instructional Supplies

Textbooks and Other Instructional Materials
The textbooks and other instructional materials available to each individual student may be kept in the students' desks, in individual student bins, or similar places. Materials and supplies that must be shared with other students should be arranged on easily accessible bookshelves and cabinets.

Frequently Used Classroom Materials
Materials and supplies such as pencils, erasers, rulers, water-soluble markers, chalk for art projects, masking tape, staplers, glue, and so forth should be kept in a readily accessible cabinet or shelf.

Teacher's Supplies
There are many items that a teacher will use regularly that should be kept in his desk. These include smaller items such as utility pencils, pens, paper, chalk and erasers, overhead transparency sheets, scissors, transparent tape, ruler, stapler, paper clips, and thumbtacks. In addition, larger items such as a flip chart, lesson plan books, and teachers' editions of textbooks should be located either on the desk or close to it.

Other Materials
Other items that are important for the room include a large clock, a calendar, a desk bell or a timer to use to signal the start or stop of some activities, and extra lunch money. Facial tissues, paper towels, soap, bandages, and a few small tools (hammer, pliers, and screw driver) also should be kept in an accessible place.

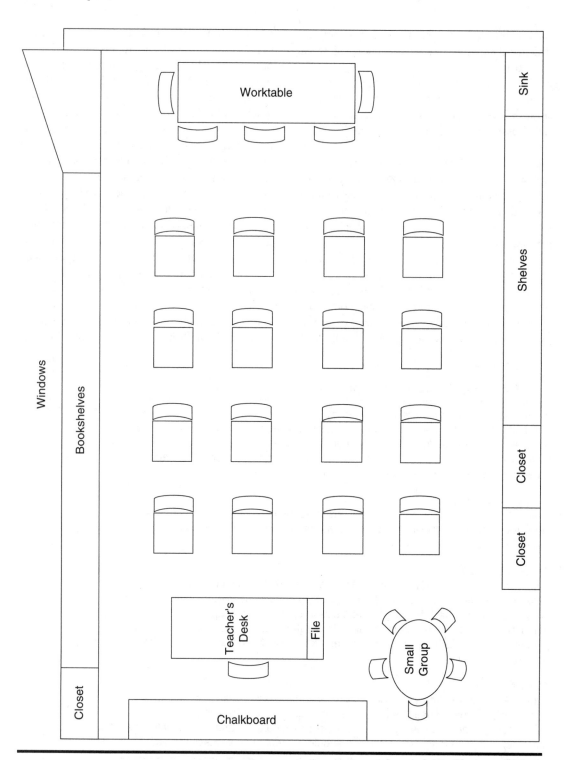

FIGURE 6.1   Custodian Arrangement

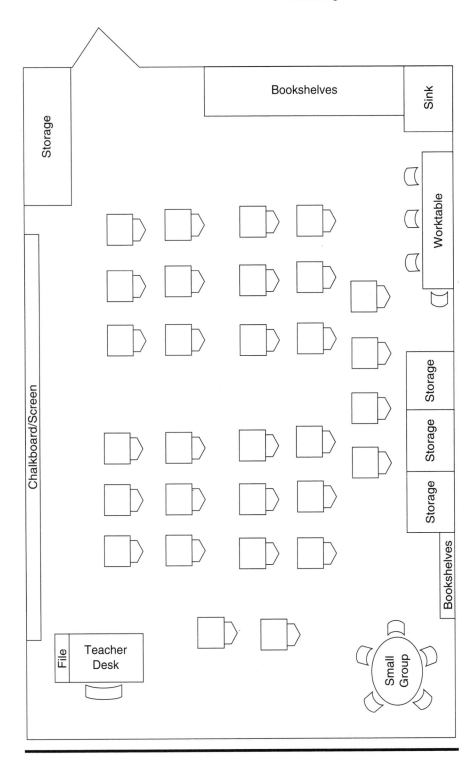

FIGURE 6.2   Classroom Design with Greater Student Access

desk arrangement should avoid having students face potential sources of distraction, such as small group work areas, activity areas, doors, or windows.

Evertson, Emmer, Clements, and Worsham (1994)[1] identified four keys to good room arrangement. They are:

1. **Keep high-traffic areas free of congestion.** High-traffic areas include group work areas, the space around the pencil sharpener and trash can, doorways, certain bookshelves and supply areas, students' desks, and the teacher's desk. High-traffic areas should be kept away from each other, have plenty of space, and be easily accessible.

2. **Be sure that the teacher can easily see the students.** Careful monitoring of students is a major management task. If the teacher cannot see students, it will be difficult to prevent task avoidance or disruption. Therefore, clear lines of sight must be maintained between areas of the room that the teacher will frequent and student work areas.

3. **Keep frequently used teaching materials and student supplies readily accessible.** Easy access to and efficient storage of such materials and supplies will aid classroom management by allowing activities to begin and end promptly, and by minimizing time spent getting ready and cleaning up.

4. **Be certain students can easily see instructional presentations and displays.** Seating arrangements should allow students to see the overhead projector screen or chalkboard without moving their chairs, turning their desks around, or craning their necks. The instructional area should not be located away from a substantial number of students. Such conditions encourage students to pay attention and they make it easier for students to take notes or copy material.

---

[1]*Source:* Adapted with permission from C. M. Everston, E. T. Emmer, B. S. Clements, and M. E. Worsham (1994). *Classroom Management for Elementary Teachers.* Englewood Cliffs, NJ: Prentice-Hall.

Establishing Routines and Rules

Organizing the physical space of the classroom is only the first step toward effective classroom management. The teacher also must develop plans for managing student behavior within that physical structure. Before the first student arrives in the classroom, the teacher should identify rules and procedures that will provide the necessary structure for a safe and productive learning environment.

Classroom rules should be clear, concise, and few in number. The classroom rules selected to govern classroom behavior must be broad enough to cover all possible situations, but precise enough so that the teacher can easily identify when a student is or is not complying with the rule. They also should be stated in positive, behavioral terms and they must be easily enforceable. It generally works best to identify a fairly brief list of four to six rules for general classroom behavior. In addition, the teacher should identify the school rules that students must follow.

Classroom procedures are needed for such activities as entering and leaving the classroom, getting the teacher's attention, fire drills, going to the restroom, using the water fountain, moving from one area of the room to another, getting ready to work, handing in assignments, what to do when in-class assignments are completed, making transitions between assignments, sharpening pencils, and similar "going-to-school" behaviors. Before the beginning of the school term the teacher should identify those that are critical to the smooth functioning of the classroom and plan to teach these procedures within the first few days of the school term.

STRUCTURING THE FIRST DAYS OF THE SCHOOL YEAR

Effective teachers know that the first few days of school are critical to developing a successful learning environment. Research has shown that what teachers do the first day of school can set the pattern for the entire school year (Evertson &

Emmer, 1982). Teachers cannot assume that students enter the classroom already understanding the types of school behaviors that are acceptable. Many have little idea as to what is expected of them at school, either generally or within a classroom specifically. The students have not learned what behaviors are considered appropriate or desirable. Teaching appropriate school and classroom behaviors constitute the initial instructional lessons of the year.

When rules and routines are not specifically identified and taught, teacher expectations appear vague and students do not receive enough information to guide their behavior. Left to their own resources, children are inclined to seek information, amusement, and diversion from each other. They tend to wander about the classroom, chat, whisper, daydream, and engage in other nonpurposeful behaviors. Such behavior disrupts the classroom and makes it difficult for the teacher to regain the students' attention and to teach effectively. However, if the teacher gives careful instructional attention to these procedures during the first several days of the school year, she can establish routines that will increase the probability that students will comply with the classroom rules and decrease the amount of time she spends each day giving directions, passing out materials, and controlling students. This, in turn, increases the number of minutes per day available for actual instruction, which, in turn, increases students' learning opportunities.

The teacher should underscore the importance of classroom rules and routines by introducing them early in the morning on the first day of school. As soon as a majority of the students are assembled, the teacher should introduce the rules and the basic routines that will govern the classroom behavior for the remainder of the school year. While students should be explicitly taught what they need to know about using the room, they should not be overloaded with information. Only the key procedures should be introduced on the first day. Additional procedures can be added as they are needed. Repeatedly during the initial weeks of school, the teacher should continue to focus on these basic procedures through discussions, reviews, and rehearsals.

Because the way in which the first day of the school year is handled critically influences how well students will learn throughout the term, teachers should give a great deal of prior thought and detailed planning to this day. Every minute should be carefully planned. The teacher should prepare a blueprint that carefully orchestrates all the activities that will take place in the classroom. Considerations to be addressed include how to greet the children and their parents, how to direct them to their seats, and what activities should be prepared so that students can work independently while their classmates are arriving. Will the teacher be at the door when the students arrive? Will there be name tags? How much time will the teacher spend talking to parents? How will he ensure an orderly first hour while communicating to students that this is a safe and happy environment in which they can learn and grow without fear?

In planning for a smooth beginning, teachers should make sure that all of the needed materials have been collected and organized so that it will not be necessary to leave the classroom to obtain them from a central storage room or duplication area. This sort of detailed planning increases the likelihood that the teachers will be able to stay in close proximity to the students throughout the day. Maintaining this contact is an important step toward establishing control as the teacher and the leader in the classroom.

Early on that first day, the teacher should discuss the layout of the room and school. Remember that many students will never have been in the school building before that first day of school. They will need to know the location of the bathroom, lunchroom, library, and key offices, as well as where to line up for after-school buses.

The academic activities introduced on the first day of school should be simple, enjoyable ones that involve the entire class. The teacher should not attempt to group students at this time, but should focus on getting to know them, making sure that they feel comfortable in the classroom, and ensuring that they learn the classroom behaviors important for their success throughout the school year. For both academic and nonacademic activities, the teacher should give clear, precise directions and closely monitor the classroom. Specific assignments should be prepared and ready to give the class whenever the teacher must attend to clerical tasks in the room, deal with minor emergencies, or work individually with a student. A booklet or folder of work that students can do independently (e.g., mazes, math problems, coloring, and crossword puzzles) can help keep the students on-task during these times.

It is helpful to learn each student's name on the first day. A readily available photocopy of the names or a seating chart are helpful. The teacher should have the students help her learn how to pronounce their names and indicate what name or nickname they prefer. If there are two or more students with the same given names, ask what each prefers to be called or devise a system to differentiate among them (i.e., "Mark B." and "Mark W.").

ESTABLISHING CONTROL IN THE CLASSROOM

The teacher should establish control in the classroom immediately. Being at the door to greet the students communicates to them that the teacher is in charge. Minute-by-minute planning serves to prevent the types of disruptiveness that occurs when students are at loose ends or do not know what to do. Rules for the school and for the room should be discussed early in the day. From the first minute, the teacher should monitor student behavior closely and stop misbehavior *promptly* in a firm and positive manner. At the same time, the teacher also should reinforce students who are behaving appropriately and following the classroom rules.

Developing Class Rules

In establishing classroom rules, the teacher can identify the key rules and present them to the class, using a wall chart. Some teachers choose to involve students in the rule development process.

This involvement may increase the students' sense of "ownership" over the rules as well as their understanding of the rules. The teacher can engineer this involvement by leading the class in a group discussion of the importance of rules, identifying for them those situations that rules should govern, and encouraging them to generate possible rules. By writing down on the chalkboard all the suggested rules and leading a discussion of them, the teacher can guide the students to a final list of classroom rules. Typically, the final list will be similar to the one the teacher would have developed independently. Frequently, teachers are amazed at the students' apparent enthusiasm for law and order. Students may lobby for long listings of complicated, detailed, and restrictive rules. The teacher's job is to tactfully guide the students to condense their listing to a limited number of rules that are desirable and enforceable. As a final step, the rules probably will need to be edited to make sure that they are worded simply and stated in positive behavioral terms.

The following are several important considerations in developing classroom rules:

1. Rules should be few in number.
2. Rules should be explicit.
3. Rules should be worded positively, telling the students what to do rather than what not to do.
4. Rules should be posted in the classroom.
5. Rules should be followed consistently.
6. Rules should be simple and direct, and easy to follow.
7. Rules must be taught to students.

The following list of rules from one classroom illustrates these principles:

1. Bring your books and materials to class.
2. Be in your seat when the bell rings.
3. Follow directions.
4. Work quietly and raise your hand before talking.
5. Touch other student's belongings only with their permission.

Because these rules specify observable behaviors, it is easy to decide whether or not they are being followed. For example, the student and the teacher (or anyone else) can easily determine if the student is seated when the bell rings, raises his hand for permission to talk, or follows directions. This would not be the case with a more global or generic rule such as "Be courteous." This more generic statement does not communicate precisely what is expected and is open to many different ideas and interpretations. Individual students might interpret the rule differently from the teacher. These differences could be idiosyncratic, a function of age and/or sex differences, or culturally based. When the teacher states classroom rules in behavioral terms, the teacher, the students, and other observers can agree as to whether or not a student is complying with that rule. Rules such as "Work quietly," "Raise your hand," and "Touch other student's belongings only with their permission" specify precise behaviors that can be objectively observed and enforced.

In addition to referring to precise, observable behaviors, it is preferable for rules to be stated in positive terms that focus on what students should do, instead of on what they should *not* do. For example, rules such as "Keep your hands to yourself" or "Raise your hand for permission to talk" are much better than negative statements such as "Do not hit your classmates" or "Do not talk out in class." It is preferable that rules pass what some educators have humorously referred to as the "Dead Man's Test" (Homme, Csanyi, Gonzales, & Rechs, 1970). This means there should be no rules that describe behaviors that are so passive that a dead person could comply with them. Instead, each rule established should describe an observable behavior that a student must actively perform. Finally, the classroom rules should be enforceable and they should be designed to teach students to become responsible for their own behaviors.

Once the teacher has established rules, she should write them down on a large piece of tagboard with thick, felt-tip pens. The tagboard can then be prominently posted in the classroom as a reminder of the rules. This display also can be used in teaching and reviewing the rules.

Teaching Rules

Identifying and displaying classroom rules are important first steps. However, these steps will be relatively ineffective in and of themselves. Classroom rules also must be *taught* directly to the students just as reading, arithmetic, and content subjects are taught. In a real sense, these rules are an essential part of the overall curriculum. What differentiates effective from ineffective teachers is the extent to which the rules and procedures are directly taught to the students, how well students are monitored, and how consistently the teachers follow through on the rules (Englert, 1984; Emmer et al., 1984). A teacher should utilize the same effective instructional strategies used in teaching academic skills and knowledge.

One of the first steps in teaching the rules is to review each rule after it is posted. State the rule and lead the class in a discussion of the purpose and importance of the rule. For example, the "raise your hand" rule is important because "if everyone talked at the same time, we would not be able to hear each other." A scripted minilesson format can be used for teaching all the rules, with slight modifications made in the script for each separate rule. The sample script presented in Table 6.2 introduces a set of classroom rules specifically developed for instructional periods. The three rules here are:

1. Watch the teacher and watch your work.
2. Keep your hands and feet to yourself.
3. Talk only on your turn.

The sample lesson can easily be modified to teach any rule or set of rules established. It serves to focus student attention on each rule, requires student participation through vocalization of each rule, and provides practice and reinforcement. The latter is particularly important. By praising students for demonstrating each rule, teachers can hasten the acquisition of rule-following behavior.

TABLE 6.2   Script for Introducing a Set of Classroom Rules

TEACHER	STUDENT
"Today we're going to talk about the rules we developed for our classroom. First we'll talk about what rules we follow when I am teaching a lesson to you." (Point to each rule as you say it.)	
"The first rule for lesson time is, Watch the teacher and watch you work. What is the first rule?" (Hand signal)	
	"Watch the teacher and watch your work."
"Right. That means that when I am teaching a lesson, you should be either watching me, or watching the chalkboard, my book, or your workbook, depending on what I ask you to look at. Here's the second rule for lesson times: Keep your hands and feet to yourself. What's the second rule?" (Hand signal)	
	"Keep your hands and feet to yourself."
"That's right. That means that during lessons you should keep your hands and feet under control so that you don't accidentally bother anyone else."	
"Here's the third rule for lesson times: Talk only on your turn. What's the rule?" (Hand signal)	
	"Talk only on your turn."
"That means that you should talk only when I call on you or when I ask everyone to answer, but at no other time."	
"Now. . . . by yourselves." (pause) "Get ready" (Point to each rule as students say it.) (Hand signal)	
	"Watch the teacher and watch your work. Keep your hands and feet to yourself. Talk only on your turn."
"Very nice. Now let's practice doing what the rules say. I'm going to begin teaching a lesson. I want you to concentrate on following the rules during this practice time, and I'll see who I can catch following each rule we talked about." (Place the rules poster right next to you so that students can see it easily without diverting their attention from you.)	

(continued)

TABLE 6.2   continued

Teacher	*Student*
(Begin teaching one or two pages from a sample lesson you have selected for this purpose. After every few seconds, praise two or three students for following one of the rules. At first, use the wording of the rules to praise the students: "Good, Jean and Jason, you're watching the teacher. That's the way to pay attention." Or, "Mark and Juanita, you're keeping your hands and feet to yourselves—way to work." Call on different students each time you praise and refer to different rules. Continue 2 or 3 minutes, then begin your regularly scheduled lesson. Continue to praise rule following but at a lesser rate).	
(Repeat this introduction, substituting the appropriate rules immediately before each of the activities for which you and your students have developed rules. Follow the introduction with 2 or 3 minutes of appropriate practice such as seatwork practice and transition practice)	

Source: From *Structuring Your Classroom for Academic Success* (pp. 59–61) by S.C. Paine, J. Radicchi, L.C. Rosellini, L. Deutchman, and C.B. Darch, 1983, Champaign, IL: Research Press. Copyright 1983 by the authors. Reprinted by permission.

This is another example of catching students being good—reward students who are following the rules with praise, a smile, a nod, or some other form of positive attention. Even after all of the students have demonstrated their ability to follow the rules, the teacher should still praise students occasionally for appropriate behavior. Recall from Chapter 5 that intermittent reinforcement is powerful—it will maintain a behavior indefinitely.

Classroom rules should be reviewed every day for the first 4 or 5 days after they are initially introduced to the students. After that, they should be reviewed at the beginning of every week for 1 or 2 months; then on the first Monday of every month as well as the first day back from a vacation period of more than 2 days. Review lessons should also be taught whenever a new student joins the class, as well as whenever else it seems necessary. The review lesson, depicted in Table 6.3, is similar to the script for introducing a new rule.

Establishing Routines

An important aspect of effective classroom management is establishing procedures for a myriad of day-to-day routines that comprise the school day. These include routines for beginning the school day, making transitions between lessons, and entering and leaving the room. Routines can be developed for such behaviors as sharpening pencils, asking the teacher for assistance, and lining up for recess, just to mention a few. Evertson et al. (1984) have identified procedures for the following categories of activity: (1) procedures for using the classroom facilities/materials, (2) procedures for using other school areas; (3) procedures for beginning/ending the day; (4) procedures for whole-class seatwork and teacher-led activities, (5) procedures for small group activities, and (6) general procedures. In each of these categories, expectations should be established. In some instances, schoolwide rules will be in effect and must be considered in establishing your individual classroom routines and procedures. Issues to be considered for each of these six procedural categories are listed in the following sections.

Procedures for Using the Classroom Facilities/Materials

- What routines will assist students in keeping their personal desks and storage areas neat and clean?
- How will students access learning centers, enter and leave them, behave in them, and care for the learning center materials?
- How will students access and use shared materials, bookshelves, cabinets, and drawers, and so forth?
- Are the teacher's desk and storage areas to be off limits for students?
- When and how can classroom drinking fountains, sinks, pencil sharpeners, and bathrooms be used?

Procedures for Using Other School Areas

- Will the teacher have hall passes (perhaps tagboard on strings to be worn around student necks) for accessing out-of-class drinking fountains and bathroom, and for going to other areas such as the administrative office, library, or special services room?
- How will students line up for entering and leaving the classroom as a group?
- What seating arrangements, table manners, noise levels, and entering and leaving procedures will be established for the lunchroom?
- What procedures for going to and returning from the playground are needed? Will students be permitted to return to the school individually or only as a group? What safety rules will apply? How will the teacher get the students' attention when playtime is over?

Procedures for Beginning/Ending the School Day

- What school rules govern student entry into the building at the beginning of the day? When students arrive at the classroom, will the teacher meet them at the door?
- Are students expected to be in their seats, to have their materials on their desks or put away inside their desks, or to be sitting quietly or engaging in an activity (e.g., silent reading or journal writing)?
- Will there be a brief opening class routine (i.e., Pledge of Allegiance, roll call, sharing, a riddle for the day, or a discussion of the lunch menu)?
- Are there "classroom nuggets" written on the board for early arrivers or for students to work on between assignments during the day?
- How will administrative matters (taking role, reporting absences, collecting permission slips, and so forth) be handled?
- Will there be specific routines for concluding the school day (i.e., straightening school desks, a brief lesson review, gathering materials, or lining up)?

Procedures for Whole-Class Seatwork and Teacher-Led Activities

- How and when shall instructional materials and supplies be distributed (e.g., by an aide before school or during recess)?
- Will students be required to raise their hands during class discussions? Are there rules governing listening to others?
- How are assignments communicated to students (i.e., written on the board for students to copy in their notebooks)?
- Will students raise their hands or use another signal for help during seatwork? Under what circumstances can students come to the teacher's desk for assistance?
- What rules govern out-of-seat behavior and talking during seatwork times?
- How will assignments be handed in, checked, and returned?

- What kinds of activities (extra credit, nuggets, and free reading) should students engage in after they complete their seatwork?

Procedures for Small Group Activities

- How will transitions into and out of groups be structured to ensure brief, nondisruptive transitions (i.e., a hand signal or a bell)?
- How will students know what materials to bring to small group?
- What behaviors are expected of students in the small group?
- What behaviors are expected of students not in the small group?

General Procedures

- What are the school procedures for fire, storm, or earthquake drills?
- Are there specific school procedures for the lunchroom, playground, and assemblies?
- How are students to behave when the teacher is interrupted while delivering instruction (e.g., sit quietly, continue to work, or do "filler" activities)?
- Will the teacher designate helpers or monitors to assist in housekeeping chores and to teach responsibilities?

Much the same approach can be used in teaching classroom routines and procedures as used in teaching classroom rules. These procedures should be taught explicitly through structured minilessons. The sample lessons for teaching rules, presented in Tables 6.2 and 6.3, can be adapted for teaching and practicing classroom routines. If these behaviors are to become automatic, practice and rehearsal are essential. It is helpful to use specific signals (i.e., a bell or an arm movement) to get the children's attention and/or to signal the time for a particular behavior or routine. A short phrase (e.g., "Eyes on me") or the teacher lifting an arm overhead can signal to the students that they should stop whatever they are doing and attend.

MANAGING THE INSTRUCTIONAL SCHEDULE

Just as a blueprint for the sequence of activities is important to guide the first day of school, so a daily schedule of instructional activities should provide a structure for the remainder of the school year. A carefully thought out schedule helps to ensure that all targeted instructional objectives are addressed. A consistent schedule helps to establish an efficient instructional pace. Further, it adds to the predictability of the day. Routine has its benefits for students as well, particularly those who are young, who are distractible, who are new to the schooling process in this country, and who are insecure or easily excitable. A predictable schedule incorporates a variety of signals that inform students of the behaviors expected. For example, a standard opening activity at the beginning of the day helps signal that the school day has begun.

Much of the class schedule may already have been determined. The time that the school day begins and ends, and the schedules for recess, lunch, and special instructional periods (e.g., physical education, music, art, and computer lab) are aspects of the day over which the teacher typically has little control. The instructional activities of the class must fit around these time-certain aspects of the schedule. The teacher should efficiently schedule curriculum activities to ensure that she includes content and skill objectives, social and affective considerations, and time for large and small groups as well as individual students. The teacher also should specifically schedule transition activities such as lining up for recess and straightening up desks at the end of the day.

If the teacher is in a full-day, self-contained classroom such as typically found at the elementary level, more options exist for scheduling instructional time. Fewer options are available with the blocked-periods schedule of middle schools, or the 50-minute schedule of secondary schools. In the self-contained settings, the teacher has the option of scheduling the more difficult "brain-

TABLE 6.3 Script for Reviewing a Set of Classroom Rules

TEACHER	STUDENT
"Today we're going to review the rules in effect when I am teaching a lesson to you." (Point to the chart)	
"What is the first rule?" (Hand signal) (Repeat until firm: after the first response, answer with the students, if necessary.)	
	"Watch the teacher and watch your work."
"What does that mean?" (Call on a single student to describe briefly what the rule means.)	
	(Student responds in own words.)
"What is the first rule? (Hand signal)"	
	"Watch the teacher and watch your work."
"What is the second rule?" (Hand signal)	
	"Keep your hands and feet to yourself."
"What does that mean?" (Call on a single student to describe briefly what the rule means.)	
	(Student responds in own words.)
"Everybody, What is the second rule?" (Hand signal)	
	"Keep your hands and feet to yourself."
"What is the third rule?" (Hand signal)	
	"Talk only on your turn."
"What does it mean?" (Call on a third student.)	
	(Student responds in own words.)
"Everybody, what is the third rule?" (Hand signal)	
	"Talk only on your turn."
"Good. Let's practice the rules during our lessons, and I'll see who I can catch following them."	
(Begin the regularly scheduled lesson. Occasionally praise students who are following various rules.)	

Source: From *Structuring Your Classroom for Academic Success* (pp. 61–62) by S. C. Paine, J. Radicchi, L. C. Rosellini, L. Deutchman, and C. B. Darch, 1983, Champaign, IL: Research Press. Copyright 1983 by the authors. Reprinted by permission.

intensive" subjects in the first part of the morning, followed by discussion subjects like social studies or health. The afternoons can then be left free for high-interest, low-pressure work (i.e., art, music, and free reading).

The Premack Principle can be applied in sequencing the day's activities. This principle states that when a low-probability behavior is followed by a high-probability or preferred behavior, the likelihood of the low-probability behavior occurring again in the future is increased (Premack, 1959). This principle has also been referred to as Grandma's Law, in reference to the types of contingency arrangements that grandmothers have made since time immemorial: "First you eat your vegetables and then you may have your dessert." Just as the promise of dessert can spur children to eat their vegetables, so can the juxtaposition of a less preferred activity before one that is more preferred serve to motivate students to finish the former. This could mean scheduling less preferred instruction (i.e., math) just before recess or lunchtime, or it could mean having a high-priority activity (i.e., language development) scheduled after math period each day.

In developing the classroom schedule, a teacher needs to remember that some individual students may be pulled out of class for special activities and instruction, like band practice, speech therapy, remedial reading, or counseling. To the extent possible, the teacher should attempt to schedule instruction and coordinate with the other teachers so that students are not absent during critical instructional periods on a regular basis. The teacher should pencil into the daily schedule those times when individual students are absent from the classroom.

MAINTAINING CLASSROOM DISCIPLINE

The authority that a teacher exhibits and the manner in which he interacts with students can greatly affect the orderliness of the classroom environment. Careful planning of the first several days of school can go a long way toward establishing the teacher as the leader of the classroom. Effective structuring of the classroom's physical space, identifying and teaching classroom rules, and establishing instructional routines and schedules also are essential components to effective classroom management. All of these are *preventative* steps designed to prevent classroom disruptions by promoting a calm and orderly learning environment. The following is a listing of preventative discipline measures:

1. Create an effective design for the physical space of the classroom, with seating patterns arranged to facilitate monitoring of student behavior, physical access to all students, and efficient use of instructional materials.
2. Carefully plan daily schedules and instructional activities.
3. Develop and teach classroom rules and procedures.
4. Continually monitor and enforce rules and procedures.
5. Visually scan the classroom frequently so that it is possible to respond to potential problems or minor disruptions before they develop into larger problems.
6. Reinforce appropriate behavior: "Catch them being good."
7. When disruptive behavior occurs, respond immediately and firmly.

Monitoring Behavior

Explicitly stated classroom rules and routines define the basic parameters of acceptable behavior for the classroom. In and of themselves, however, they are not sufficient. In addition, the teacher must constantly monitor student behavior to make sure that it is consistent with the established rules and procedures. This is particularly important during the initial acquisition stage. Evertson et al. (1994) developed procedures for classroom monitoring, which are described as follows.

During large group instruction, the teacher should position herself in a location to visually scan the room frequently. A teacher may focus too much on the chalkboard where she is writing information or on displays that they are sharing with the class. Teachers may pay more attention to students seated in the front and middle sections of the classroom than to those seated on the periphery of the class. Further, teachers tend to call on and pay more positive attention to students who are bright, well behaved, and responsive in class. (This may be because student responses and learning are reinforcing to teachers!) To better monitor all students, the teacher should move around during the lesson and scan the room frequently.

When working with a small group of students while the rest are engaged in individual seatwork, the teacher should locate his chair to ensure an unobstructed view of the entire classroom. While working with the small group, teachers should look up frequently and be alert for problems, intervening immediately when off-task or disruptive behavior occurs. After completing the small group instruction, the teacher should circulate around the room and provide individual assistance to students before entering into another small group activity.

When all students are involved in seatwork, the teacher should be moving about the room to check on student progress and to respond to individual needs. If a student needs assistance that will take more than 1 or 2 minutes, the teacher should have the student come to the teacher's desk for help. This way the teacher can remain in position to monitor other students while working with an individual student. Finally, the teacher may want to establish a rule that no more than two students can come to the teacher's desk for help at one time or implement a procedure for calling students who need help to the teacher's desk individually. This way students are not milling around, obstructing the teacher's view of the classroom, and engaging in off-task behavior.

Responding to Appropriate Behavior

Frequently reinforcing appropriate behavior early in the school term will help to shape and strengthen such behavior. The teacher should make a point with students to "catch them being good." In other words, students should be intermittently reinforced for appropriate behavior. At the beginning of the day, the individual students, or the entire class, can be complemented for being in their seats ready to begin instruction. The teacher could say: "I like the way you are working quietly at your desks." Or, if only some of the children are ready when the bell rings, they can be singled out for recognition: "Julie, Theresa, and Ricardo have their books on the their desks and are ready to begin. Thank you." This both reinforces their behavior and identifies these three individuals as models for other students to follow. As others follow the rules, the teacher can comment positively on their compliance: "I see that Jose is ready. And Ann. Thank you." Simple praise and acknowledgement such as this provides feedback and direction to students, and it shapes and develops desired classroom behaviors.

The teacher should use "I" messages to both reinforce and encourage appropriate behavior. Examples include:

> "I've noticed how neatly you have been doing your assignments lately, Scott. Keep up the good work."
> "I appreciate the fact that you were all so quiet when I was called out of the classroom. It shows me how responsible you are."
> "I am impressed with how hard you have worked on this."

Other forms of positive reinforcement include Happy Faces, stickers, positive notes or phone calls to parents, good grades, and bonus points or tokens. The points or tokens could be exchanged for extra minutes of recess, special privileges or duties, free-choice time at the end of the day (e.g., minutes on the computer, playing an instructional game, or watching a video), a special weekly event or party, or specific tangible rewards (snacks, combs, or art supplies) that can be purchased at a class store. These reinforcers are referred to as *backup reinforcers,* meaning that they *back up* the tokens, thereby imparting value to them.

Token Economies

If a large number of students demonstrate difficulty conforming to class rules and routines, a classwide token economy can be helpful. **Token economies** are a contingency management system wherein students can earn tokens for specific appropriate behavior and can exchange these tokens at a later time for backup reinforcers.

Token economies serve a variety of purposes. They can make classroom management easier and they can promote greater effort on the part of students who are making little academic progress. Students for whom token economies are particularly effective are those who experience significant difficulty in social, behavioral or academic skill areas; those who are particularly challenged by mental and behavioral deficits; and children who have little motivation to achieve in school or to comply with school rules.

Token economies sound quite simple, but actually they are quite intricate and involved to establish and manage. Table 6.4 provides guidelines for establishing and operating a token economy. The types of tokens to be used and the range of backup reinforcers must be identified. Specific rules must be articulated for earning tokens, losing tokens (e.g., response cost for specific inappropriate behaviors), and exchanging tokens. Basic operational guidelines for receiving and spending tokens are needed, as well as clear procedures for dealing with inappropriate behaviors of students within the economy. In addition, there must be rules and procedures for fading the use of the tokens. This can be done through systematically coupling more natural or generally available reinforcers (e.g., grades, praise, and Happy Faces) with the tokens. This pairing of reinforcers facilitates the movement toward dispensing fewer tokens and/or dispensing them on a more intermittent basis.

Continuous collection and evaluation of student performance data are critical to measure if satiation has occurred, if new backup reinforcers are effective, or if shifts in reinforcement schedules are having the desired effects. The primary purpose is to determine whether the desired changes in student behavior are occurring. Typically, these data are not difficult to keep. Teachers can tape 3×5-inch cards to the students' desks and enter check marks for each token earned. Students also can keep their own records, graphing the number of tokens earned.

Responding to Inappropriate Behavior

Inappropriate behavior can occur for several reasons. The rules and routines for the class may be vaguely stated or students may not have sufficiently learned them. Students may be frustrated by assignments that they do not understand, they could be bored or distracted, they may be seeking attention, or they may be simply testing the limits. Sometimes inappropriate behavior is best ignored. This is true for minor occurrences of short duration (e.g., calling out an answer during discussion, brief whispering to a neighbor, or periods of inattentiveness). In these instances the behaviors are not disruptive and they do not greatly affect student involvement in learning. Responding would consume too much teacher energy and interrupt the lesson (Evertson et al., 1994).

Disruptive behavior, on the other hand, should be dealt with promptly. This is particularly important at the beginning of the school term when teachers should respond to every deviation from the stated rules and procedures. Calm, matter-of-fact, responses to disruptive behavior can have what Jones and Jones (1990) describe as the "positive ripple effect." This means that in addition to altering the behavior of the targeted student, it results in behavioral improvements among the other students in the classroom as well. Teachers should never respond in a manner that creates greater disruption than that to which they are responding. Further, harsh or angry responses are counterproductive. They have a "negative ripple effect," tending to make students anxious and more disruptive, and frequently undermining any positive control that the teacher may have.

Teacher responses to inappropriate behavior should cause little disruption to the class and should focus on the student correcting her own

TABLE 6.4   Guidelines for Establishing and Operating a Token Economy

Characteristics of useful tokens
1. Portable, that is, easily transported
2. Resistant to satiation.
3. Can be given immediately.
4. Practical to setting.
5. Teacher controlled.
6. Compatible with educational or treatment program.
7. Easily dispensed.

Planning and implementation steps
1. Select and define target behaviors.
2. Identify possible backup reinforcers.
3. Select possible object or symbol for token.
4. Build token as conditioned reinforcer.
5. Establish exchange system and relative value of backup reinforcers.
6. Inform students of rules for token economy.
7. Develop plan for fading use of token system.
8. Establish clear recordkeeping plan.

Basic operation guidelines
1. Deliver tokens and backup reinforcers consistently.
2. Control for token inflation.
3. Focus on increasing desirable behaviors and skills.

4. Specify rules and procedures in specific and observable terms.
5. Obtain as many free, inexpensive, and student-selected backups as possible.
6. Engage in marketing and merchandising.
7. Incorporate instructional opportunities into token economy, for example, saving, checking, and deposits.
8. Pair token and backup reinforcers with social praise and other natural reinforcers.
9. Obtain approval and informed consent from administrators and parents.
10. Establish clear procedures for student noncompliance and teacher misuse.

Fading a token economy
1. Move from artificial to natural token and backup reinforcers.
2. Delay the presentation of reinforcement.
3. Move from continuous and predictable to more intermittent and unpredictable schedules of reinforcement.
4. Transfer stimulus control from artificial to more natural setting stimuli.
5. Teach students to self-manage the token economy.

Source: From Mark Wolery, Donald B. Bailey, Jr., & George M. Sugai, *Effective Teaching: Principles and Procedures of Applied Behavior Analysis with Exceptional Students* (p. 485). Copyright © 1988 by Allyn & Bacon. Reprinted by permission.

behavior. The following lists the principles for responding to inappropriate behavior (Kerr & Nelson, 1989)[2]:

1. Immediate, calm responses are most effective in stopping inappropriate behavior and in preventing such behavior from "spreading" to other students.
2. Responses that are calm and focus on the *behavior,* not the student as an individual, emphasize the dignity and worth of the student.

3. The teacher's physical proximity and eye contact are important first steps in responding to disruptive behavior.
4. The teacher's intervention should not have a more disruptive influence than that of the behavior it is intended to reduce.
5. Teacher responses that are inappropriately angry add to the disruptiveness of the classroom, create tension, and increase student disobedience.
6. Teacher responses should not simply stop inappropriate behavior, but should provide students with opportunities to respond in an acceptable manner.
7. Effective communication skills can be effective in resolving conflicts.

[2]*Source:* Reprinted with the permission of Merrill, an imprint of Macmillan Publishing Company from *Strategies for Managing Behavior Problems in the Classroom,* 2nd ed. by Mary Margaret Kerr and C. Michael Nelson. Copyright © 1989 by Merrill Publishing Company.

8. Consistency in responding to behavior is critical: maintain the same expectations in an activity at all times for all students.
9. Flexibility permits teachers to adapt to individual needs (e.g., student illness), unexpected situations, and emergencies.

It is important to respond promptly and calmly to stop the inappropriate behavior and to redirect the student to more acceptable and productive ways of behaving. In many instances, teachers can accomplish this with a glance or facial expression, by moving close to the student, or by asking the student for an on-task response. Established cues, either verbal or nonverbal, can signal students to stop what they are doing and look at the teacher. Examples include using a raised index finger with an individual or a raised arm for the entire class, or having a single phrase, such as "Eyes on me," that signals students that they should give their undivided attention to the teacher.

In responding to inappropriate behavior, the teacher should focus on the *behavior,* not on the student as an individual. Nothing should be said or done to denigrate the student; rather the dignity and worth of the student should be acknowledged. Angry responses by the teacher can escalate the disruptiveness and tension in the classroom. Instead, the teacher should focus on resolving the conflict by providing the student(s) with opportunities to behave appropriately. Good communication skills on the teacher's part, coupled with calm, consistent responses to student behavior, go a long way toward resolving problem situations that may arise in the classroom.

Another approach for responding to disruptive behavior of an individual student is to state the student's name, establish eye contact, then follow up with a specific verbal interaction at a closer distance. If a frustrated student exclaims that the work is dumb, the teacher might agree that the work is difficult and ask if the student would like some help with it. If a student is not following a specific rule or procedure (i.e., talking out or being out of seat), a teacher could ask her to state what this rule is and then to demonstrate it. If several students or the entire class are disruptive or noncompliant, the teacher could ask them to state the rule and/or describe the behaviors associated with the procedure or rule. They also should then demonstrate the appropriate behavior, with the teacher reinforcing them. When a student is off-task and not working on the given assignment, the teacher can simply redirect his attention to that task. For example, "Martha, you should be writing now." or "Chau, you need to complete all of the addition problems on that page."

Should a student take something from another's desk, the teacher should state the student's name and remind her that the behavior is not allowed. The teacher might say, "Kay, look at me. Taking things from other students' desks without permission is not allowed in this classroom. If you need something, raise your hand." After maintaining eye contact for a couple of seconds, the teacher should tell the student to "Please continue with your writing paper."

Using "I" messages also can be effective. If a student is whispering with a neighbor, the teacher might say, "Anita, I have a hard time talking to the class when you whisper. Would you please pay attention." Again, the teacher should pause for a moment or two, maintain eye contact, and then have the student go on with the lesson.

There are seemingly endless ways that teachers can intervene through positive verbal statements to provide feedback to students that they should stop their inappropriate behavior and exhibit more productive responses. Once the student has altered the behavior in the desired direction, the teacher should resume the previous tasks. However, it is important to check frequently to make sure that the undesired behavior has not recurred. When a simple, direct verbal direction does not have the desired effect, then more intrusive approaches must be considered. Table 6.5 lists strategies for controlling disruptive behavior.

Although most inappropriate student behavior can be dealt with through direct verbal inter-

TABLE 6.5   Strategies to Manage Disruptive Behavior

Teacher-mediated interventions
1. Public posting of student(s) performance on a target behavior.
2. Differential reinforcement of other behaviors or low rates of the target behavior.
3. Contingency contracts.
4. Brief (2–3 seconds) time-out from reinforcement.
5. Group contingencies on either an individual student's or the entire class's performance of the target behavior.

Peer-mediated interventions
1. Group goal setting and feedback on target behavior(s).
2. Peer monitoring of student performance on target behavior.

Self-mediated interventions
1. Self-recording by the student on her performance of the target behavior.
2. Self-evaluation by the student on his performance of the target behavior.
3. Self-instruction by the student on steps to accomplish a target task.

Source: Reprinted with the permission of Merrill, an imprint of Macmillan Publishing Company from *Strategies for Managing Behavior Problems in the Classroom,* Second Edition by Mary Margaret Kerr and C. Michael Nelson. Copyright © 1989 by Merrill Publishing Company.

vention, a system of penalties should be in place for major rule violations. (See the discussion of response cost in Chapter 3.) These penalties might include loss of activity points; detention; time-out in a restricted area away from classmates; demerits; or denying or withholding privileges such as recess time, free-choice periods, or being designated as a classroom helper. The purpose of penalties is to reduce the likelihood that the student will emit the inappropriate or disruptive behavior in the future. Potential sanctions should be specified in advance and should not come as a surprise to the students. When assessing penalties, the teacher should always inform the student(s) what specific behavior is resulting in the penalty. At the same time, the student(s) should be reminded of the desired behavior and its positive consequences. There must be a reasonable relationship between the size of the penalty and the importance of the behavior. For example, it would be unfair and counterproductive to exclude a student from a class trip for a single incident of whispering in class. Inflated penalties are likely to result in resentment and anger, and possibly in behavior that is even more

disruptive. If the activity that the student stands to lose is highly valued and infrequently available, there should be incremental steps before loss of the activity or privilege. It can be counterproductive to remove an important reinforcer for a single instance of undesired behavior. It is better to give a specified number of demerits, or assess students specified numbers of points or tokens for specific misbehaviors, before students lose a particular privilege. This approach has the benefit of providing the student with warnings before the loss is incurred.

Finally, teachers should evaluate the effectiveness of the penalty system. They should collect data on the target behavior both before (baseline) and after a penalty is imposed. Penalties should only be used when it is clear that they result in improved behavior.

Student Contracts

When students experience ongoing behavioral difficulty, the teacher might want to consider individual contracts. A *contract* is a clearly stated agreement written to specify the exact behavior that the student will emit as well as the contingencies associated with that behavior. The explicit focus of a contract serves to crystallize for students the expectations of the environment, and to emphasize the relationship between student behavior and consequences. Individual or class contracts specify the rewards and penalties that are in the teacher's direct control. Home-school contracts incorporate consequences under the parent's jurisdiction. Chapter 5 described specific considerations in developing and implementing contracts.

EVALUATING THE LEARNING ENVIRONMENT

Student performance does not exist in a vacuum, but is affected by a variety of classroom variables. Increasingly, when students experience learning difficulties, the educational evaluation process includes examination of situational factors in the learning environment that may be shaping or maintaining the behaviors of concern. Many view a valid assessment of the learning environment to be as critical as a valid assessment of the individual (Heller, Holtzman, & Messick, 1982; McLoughlin & Lewis, 1994). Ysseldyke & Christenson (1987a) have proposed that educators not categorize or label a student without considering the role that instructional factors play in the learning difficulties that the student manifests. The variables relating to structuring the learning environment, that have been described in this chapter all influence the quality of the learning environment, and interact reciprocally with student characteristics and academic outcomes. The extent to which the learning environment is conducive to student task engagement and is tolerant of different behaviors that students manifest is contextually related to student outcomes.

Aspects of the learning environment can be evaluated by developing direct observation systems and checklists on variables of interest or by using and/or modifying one of the available systems. The quantity and quality of teacher-student interactions can be assessed using the Brophy-Good Teacher-Child Dyadic Interaction System

(Brophy and Good, 1969) or the Flanders Interaction Analysis Categories (Flanders, 1970). Ysseldyke and Christenson (1987b) developed a vehicle for systematically describing qualitative aspects of the learning environment. The Instructional Environment Scale (TIES) includes three components: (1) a classroom observation, (2) structured student interview, and (3) structured teacher interview. Factors included in these three categories include instructional presentation, classroom environment, teacher expectations, cognitive emphasis, motivational strategies, relevant practice, academic engaged time, informal feedback, adaptive instruction, progress evaluation, instructional planning, and student understanding. While not a normed measure, TIES data provide a starting point for designing instructional interventions for students, including possible modifications in the learning environment itself.

SUMMARY

This chapter has described considerations for structuring the classroom into an effective learning environment. Teachers should begin planning for these procedures prior to the beginning of the school term and they should become acquainted with the school site, identify the key resources and programmatic features of the school, and become acquainted with the school faculty and staff.

Teachers must then turn their attention to designing an effective physical arrangement for the classroom. This arrangement should facilitate the instructional groupings and activities that the teacher plans, and promote efficient transitions between activities and quiet movement within the classroom. Four key considerations in arranging the classroom are: (1) keeping high-traffic areas free of congestion, (2) making sure that the teacher can easily see all students, (3) making frequently used teaching materials and student supplies readily accessible, and (4) ensuring that students can easily see instructional presentations and displays. An underlying axiom to space arrangement is that when the arrangement of desks and other furniture make it easy for the teacher to move directly to any student, fewer classroom discipline problems will occur.

Before the first student arrives at school, the teacher needs to devote considerable thought and planning determining which rules and procedures will promote an efficient and effective learning environment. These rules should be few in number, positively stated, and behavioral in nature. Routines should be established for entering and leaving the classroom; using instructional materials and spaces; beginning the day; whole-class, small group, and individual instruction; and a variety of general procedures. Much of the instructional emphasis during the early weeks of the school term should focus on establishing and teaching these rules and procedures, as one step toward developing an effective discipline program. This instruction should be carefully planned and delivered using effective presentation techniques.

This chapter delineates considerations for structuring the first day of school and approaches for responding to both appropriate and inappropriate student behavior. The teacher's use of "I" messages and positive reinforcement that is specific to student behavior are described. Some inappropriate behavior is best ignored, while disruptive behavior should be responded to promptly, firmly, and calmly. Individual student contracts and token economies can be effective.

Careful, systematic planning and continuously monitoring the learning environment can teach students to behave in productive and socially appropriate ways, and minimize the distractions, interruptions, and confusions that detract from learning. This means that the teacher can be ready to start instruction at the beginning of the school day, utilize a maximum portion of the school day for instructional activities, and increase the amount of time that students are on-task and learning. The thought given to structuring the instructional setting and planning the instructional lessons, coupled with the consistent and positive application of consequences, can serve to motivate students to learn both the academic and social curricula of the school at the same time that they develop into independent and self-regulating students.

CONTENT MASTERY QUESTIONS _____

1. With what areas of the school should a new teacher be acquainted? What personnel?

2. Discuss briefly the factors that a new teacher must consider in arranging the classroom.

3. List and detail the four keys to a good room arrangement.

4. During the first days of the school year, the teacher establishes the structure for the entire year. Discuss five ways that a teacher can facilitate a successful learning environment.

5. Discuss and describe the seven guidelines for developing classroom rules.

6. Prepare a set of rules suitable for a middle school classroom.

7. Take one rule and discuss how to teach it to students.

8. List the six categories of classroom procedures and provide two issues to be considered for each category.

9. List five classroom procedures and describe how they might be taught.

10. What is the Premack Principle? Give an example of this principle used within an instructional schedule.

11. Describe how a teacher monitors students during large group instruction, small group instruction, and seatwork.

12. Discuss and describe a teacher "catching them being good," and list five possible reinforcers for appropriate behavior.

13. List the guidelines for establishing a token economy.

14. Identify four strategies for dealing with disruptive behavior.

15. Discuss the five essential elements of a classroom contract. Provide a sample contract for in-seat behavior.

16. Discuss the importance of evaluating the learning environment and possible methods for completing this evaluation.

REFERENCES

Berliner, D. C. (1983). Developing conceptions of classroom environments: Some light on the classroom studies of ATI. *Educational Psychologist, 18,* 1–13.

Bickel, W. E., & Bickel, D. D. (1986). Effective schools, classroom, and instruction: Implications for special education. *Exceptional Children, 52,* 489–500.

Brophy, J. E., & Good, T. L. (1986). Teacher behavior and student achievement. In M. C. Wittrock (Ed.), *Handbook of research on teaching* (3rd Ed.) (pp. 328–375). New York: Macmillan.

Brophy, J. E., & Good, T. L. (1969). *Teacher-child dyadic interaction: A manual for coding classroom behavior* (Report Series NO 127). Austin, TX: Research & Development Center for Teacher Education, University of Texas.

Doyle, W. (1986). Classroom organization and management. In M. C. Wittrock (Ed.), *Handbook of research on teaching* (3rd Ed.) (pp. 392–431). New York: Macmillan, Inc.

Emmer, E. T., Everson, C. M., Sanford, J. P., Clements, B. S., & Worsham, M. E. (1984). *Classroom management for secondary teachers.* Englewood Cliffs, NJ: Prentice-Hall.

Englert, C. S. (1983). Measuring special education teacher effectiveness. *Exceptional Children, 50,* 247–254.

Englert, C. S. (1984). Measuring teacher effectiveness from the teacher's point of view. *Focus on Exceptional Children, 17*(2), 1–16.

Evertson, C. M., & Emmer, E. T. (1982). Effective management at the beginning of the school year in junior high classes. *Journal of Educational Psychology, 74*(4), 485–498.

Evertson, C. M., Emmer, E. T., Clements, B. S., & Worsham, M. E. (1994). *Classroom management for elementary teachers.* Boston, MA: Allyn and Bacon.

Evertson, C. M., Evertson, E. T., Sanford, J. P., & Clements, B. S. (1983). Improving classroom management: An experiment in elementary classrooms. *Elementary School Journal, 84*(2), 173–188.

Fisher, C. W., & Berliner, D. C. (Eds.). (1985). *Perspective on instructional time.* New York: Longman.

Flanders, M. (1970). *Analyzing teacher behavior.* Menlo Park, CA: Addison-Wesley.

Good, T. L., & Brophy, J. E. (1987). *Looking in classrooms* (4th Ed.). New York: Harper & Row.

Heller, K. A., Holtzman, W. H., & Messick, S. (Eds.). (1982). *Placing children in special education: A strategy for equity.* Washington, DC: National Academy Press.

Homme, L., Csanyi, A. P., Gonzales, M. A., & Rechs, J. R. (1970). *How to use contingency contracting in the classroom.* Champaign, IL: Research Press.

Jones, F. H. (1987). *Positive classroom discipline.* New York: McGraw-Hill.

Jones, V. F., & Jones, L. S. (1990). *Comprehensive classroom management.* Boston: Allyn & Bacon.

Kerr, M. M., & Nelson, C. M. (1989). *Strategies for managing behavior problems in the classroom* (2nd Ed.). Columbus, OH: Merrill.

McLoughlin, J., & Lewis, R. B. (1994). *Assessing special students* (3rd Ed.). Columbus, OH: Merrill.

Paine, S., Radicchi, J., Rosellini, L. C., Deutchman, L., & Darch, C. B. (1983). *Structuring your classroom for academic success.* Champaign, IL: Research Press Co.

Premack, D. (1959). Toward empirical behavior laws: I. Positive reinforcement. *Psychological Review, 66,* 219–233.

Reith, H., & Evertson, C. (1988). Variables related to the effective instruction of difficult-to-teach children. *Focus on exceptional children, 10*(5), 1–8.

Reynolds, M. C., & Birch J. W. (1977). *Teaching exceptional children in all of America's schools.* Reston, VA: Council for Exceptional Children.

Rosenfield, P., Lambert, N., & Black, A. (1985). Desk arrangement effects on pupil classroom behavior. *Journal of Educational Psychology, 77,* 101–108.

Rounds, T. S., Ward, B. A., Mergendoller, J. R., & Tickunoff, W. J. (1982). *Junior high school transition study, Vol. 2, Organization of instruction,* (Rep No. EPSXSP-82-3). San Francisco: Far West Laboratory.

Smith, R. M., Neisworth, J. T., & Greer, J. B. (1979). *Evaluating educational environments.* Columbus, OH: Merrill.

Stallings, J. A. (1980). Allocated academic learning time revisited, or beyond time on task. *Educational Researcher, 9,* 11–16.

White, K. P., Wyne, M. D., Stuck, G. B., & Coop, R. H. (1983). *Teaching effectiveness evaluation project* (Final report). Chapel Hill, NC: School of Education, University of North Carolina at Chapel Hill.

Wolery, M., Bailey, D. B., Jr., & Sugai, G. M. (1988). *Effective teaching: Principles and procedures of applied behavior analysis with exceptional students.* Boston: Allyn & Bacon.

Ysseldyke, J. E., & Christenson, S. L. (1987a). Evaluating students' instructional environments. *Remedial and Special Education, 8,* 17–24.

Ysseldyke, J. E., & Christenson, S. L. (1987b). *The Teacher Evaluation Rating Scales.* Austin, TX: PRO-ED.

CHAPTER 7

Effective Instructional Delivery

Anita L. Archer
Mary M. Gleason
Stephen Isaacson

CHAPTER OBJECTIVES

At the conclusion of this chapter, the reader will be able to:

1. Define allocated time and describe a number of procedures that increase allocated instructional time.
2. Define student task engagement and describe teacher practices that can be used to promote on-task behavior.
3. Outline guidelines for selecting content for instruction.
4. Outline the components that would be found in the opening, body, and close of an instructional lesson.
5. Design lessons in a systematic manner.
6. Describe procedures that teachers can use to gain frequent responses from all students within an instructional lesson.
7. Discuss additional lesson delivery strategies including maintaining a brisk pace, providing thinking time, ensuring high levels of accuracy, monitoring responses, providing feedback, and maintaining attention.

Recent research in general and special education has extended the knowledge base on how classrooms should be organized for instruction, and what teachers should say and do to promote student achievement. The next two chapters focus on the major components of instruction: teacher-directed instruction and independent work. This chapter addresses teacher-directed instruction beginning with a discussion of time management, both the time teachers allocate for instruction and the practices that enhance student task engagement, and selection of appropriate content for instruction. Next, the chapter discusses two critical aspects of teacher-directed instruction, the design of instructional lessons and the delivery of those lessons including procedures for eliciting responses, maintaining an appropriate pace, monitoring student responses, and providing feedback to students. In Chapter 8, the selection and management of independent work and interventions to facilitate individual student growth will be discussed.

TIME MANAGEMENT

Time is one of the most precious commodities in classrooms. Because there is a limited amount of time in the school day, teachers make continual tradeoffs as they make decisions about how they allocate time to instructional and noninstructional activities. These decisions are crucial because the more time that students spend actively engaged in teacher-directed instruction, the more opportunities they have to learn (Borg, 1980; Greenwood, Delquadri, Stanley, Saso, Whorton, & Schulte, 1981). The effective management of time during the school day has a critical impact on the achievement of all students.

There are two components of instructional time: (1) allocated time and (2) engaged time. **Allocated time** is the time allotted in the classroom to instructional activities. **Engaged time** is the time in which students are actually engaged in the instructional activity. It is possible for students to spend much less time engaged in instruction than the teacher allocates. Effective teaching practices help to ensure that students are, in fact, engaged in instruction for the same amount of time allocated for instruction. These two components are elaborated on in the following sections.

Allocated Time

Allocated instructional time includes the time set aside or scheduled for academic instruction (such as reading, mathematics, writing, and social studies) as well as for other areas of instruction (music, art, social skills, and physical education). Much of the school day is spent in noninstructional rather than instructional activities. In summarizing reports of classroom studies, Good (1983) concluded that only 50–60% of the typical school day is spent in the actual instruction of students. The rest of the day is consumed in noninstructional activities such as student socializing, students waiting for lessons to begin, time between lessons and in other transitions (e.g., lining up and passing out instructional materials), and/or nonacademic activities (e.g., lunch count and office announcements).

Thurlow, Ysseldyke, Graden and Algozzine (1983) reported that some students with learning disabilities averaged only 9 minutes per day in active reading practice. Further, only one-fourth of the 1.5 hours allocated for reading instruction involved active or overt academic responding (e.g., reading, writing, and speaking). Similarly, Hall, Delquadri, Greenwood, and Thurston (1982) reported that in a 6-hour school day, special education students might read silently 11 minutes, read aloud 4 minutes, and write for 1 hour.

Even small changes in managing instructional time can have a significant impact on student achievement. Leinhardt, Zigmond, and Cooley (1981) reported a study in which students with learning disabilities spent only an additional 5 minutes per day in silent reading practice. This translated into an additional 15 hours of practice each year and an average gain of 1 month on an end-of-year achievement test. Although time in a school day is finite, teachers can increase the total instructional time significantly by merely saving seconds and minutes from time normally lost in noninstructional activities, for example, between lessons or waiting for the lesson to begin. By diminishing the time students spend in these less essential activities, teachers can increase the time allocated for more important academic activities. To increase the amount of time allocated for instruction, teachers can: (1) develop daily and weekly instructional schedules, (2) adhere to these lesson schedules, (3) monitor the transitions between activities, (4) maintain lesson smoothness, and (5) group students for instruction.

Scheduling More Time for Academics. A basic strategy to increase allocated time is to set aside generous amounts of time for academic subjects. In developing instructional schedules, teachers should aim for a fifty-fifty split between teacher-directed instruction and independent work time (Sindelar, Wilson, & Gartland, 1984; Wilson & Wesson, 1986). This split can be achieved in several ways. The students' time spent in noninstructional and task management activities can be decreased through implementing more efficient procedures. For example, teaching routines for recurring tasks to students, and the teachers arranging and managing instructional materials can result in significantly less time spent on noninstructional activities (see Chapter 6 for a discussion of these approaches). The number of independent, seatwork tasks also can be decreased while simultaneously increasing the time students spend in teacher-directed instruction.

Students in classrooms with more discussion and review make greater academic gains than do students in classrooms that emphasize task management and independent written assignments. This is true for students with average achievement as well as for students with learning difficulties. Unfortunately, discussion and review is frequently shortchanged in the instructional delivery process. In one study, Stallings (1980) reported that students in remedial secondary classrooms averaged only 5% of the class time in discussion and review activities.

The way in which instruction is scheduled also can affect the quality of the instructional time. For example, in one classroom the teacher read a story to her students immediately after recess each day. Observations revealed that 30% of her students were off-task during story time. However, when the teacher built into the schedule a brief "rest period" before the story, visual attention to the teacher and the story increased, and off-task behavior decreased to only 10%. Scheduling more preferred activities or lessons after ones that are less preferred also can be beneficial. Students frequently will work more diligently on a less preferred subject when they know that a more favored one follows. Sensitivity to student needs and preferences when developing the instructional schedule can improve the degree of on-task behavior, directly impacting the quality and efficiency of the instruction provided.

Adhering to the Lesson Schedule.   Carefully adhering to a lesson schedule is a second time management procedure. It is not uncommon for a teacher to call a group for a lesson and allow 10 minutes to elapse before beginning the lesson (Gaskins, 1988). These delays may be due to time students spend putting away their seatwork or chatting and conversing on the way to the instructional area. Teacher delays in beginning instruction or the teacher interrupting the lesson for managerial or disciplinary actions are additional causes of time delays (Gaskins, 1988). To compensate, teachers then may let the lesson run over schedule by several minutes, which means that the next small group also gets a late start. Continual encroachments on the daily schedule can result in reduced instructional time for the current lesson as well as for subjects scheduled later in the day.

Beginning lessons on time means more than simply assembling students at the appointed hour. Teachers also must ensure that lessons begin quickly. Little time should be lost gaining the students' attention or monitoring to see whether they

have brought the proper learning materials. A procedure for starting lessons efficiently is to teach students a signal that indicates when they should give full attention to the teacher. Such a signal can assist students in shifting their attention from the old task to the new one and help to orient students to an impending change before it is implemented (Anderson, 1985). Using signals is described more fully later in this chapter.

Strategies for gaining and/or redirecting student attention can help to ensure that lessons begin and conclude quickly and smoothly, and that the lesson schedule is followed. This results in a cumulative saving of considerable instructional time each day.

Monitoring Transitions.   The careful planning and monitoring of transition times between lessons is another important time management technique. By making sure that the transitions or amount of time between instructional activities is short, teachers increase the time available for instruction. The most frequent transitions during the school day involve stopping and starting activities, passing out and collecting instructional materials and papers, and moving from one location to another. Individual transitions may average as much as 8 minutes each and account for 20%, or 80 total minutes, or more of the instructional day (Paine, Radicchi, Rosellini, Duetchman, & Darch, 1983). Efficient transitions should take no more than 2 minutes between lessons that involve a change of activity and location, and 30 seconds between lessons that only involve a change of activity (Engelmann, 1982). Altogether, teachers should strive to ensure that no more than 40 minutes per day are spent in transition activities.

Teachers who are well prepared, and who have all materials ready and accessible at the beginning of the school day, spend less time making transitions. Effective teachers write transition times into their daily schedules and plan for them to occur at logical places. They also teach students procedures for making smooth transitions. Less effective teachers tend to call for transitions suddenly, without warning, when many students are still in the middle of a task. They provide little time for task completion, review, or consolidation prior to redirecting the students' attention and they leave much of the transition process to chance.

A first step toward teaching students procedures for making brisk, quiet transitions is to develop and post rules or guidelines for transition times. According to Paine, et al. (1983), four such guidelines might be:

1. Move quietly.
2. Put your books away and get what you need for the next activity. (The teacher may need to state what the activity will be and what specific materials are needed.)
3. Move your chairs quietly. (For those instances when students carry their desk chairs to small group).
4. Keep your hands and feet to yourself. (Paine et al., 1983).

Teachers should describe and model these desired transition behaviors to their students. They should establish a signal for transition times and provide students with practice in following the transition procedures. As students learn these procedures, teachers should continue to monitor transitions, providing review and rehearsal when performance does not meet criterion levels. The following lists five procedures for developing effective transitions between activities (Engelmann, 1982; Paine et al., 1983):

1. Discuss appropriate transition behavior with students (e.g., how to behave, what to do with lesson materials, and how to move through the transition quickly).
2. Model how to make an appropriate transition by presenting examples and nonexamples of each transition behavior (e.g., how to behave and not to behave, what to do with materials and what not to do).
3. Provide a signal and have students rehearse making a transition.

4. Monitor students' performance during the rehearsal and provide feedback on their performances.
5. Schedule additional practice until students meet the criterion goals.

Maintaining Lesson Smoothness.   Maintaining lesson smoothness by minimizing intrusions into the lesson is another management technique that can preserve instructional time. Effective teachers use several techniques to insulate the lesson from distractions within and outside the instructional group.

Intrusions may result from student confusion about what to do. When students do not fully understand what is expected of them, they may gaze about the room looking for cues, whisper to their neighbor, "mill around," or begin an unrelated task. The first step to decreasing distractions is for teachers to present directions carefully and clearly. Students should be told exactly what is expected of them. If the task involves two simultaneous activities or multiple steps, directions for the separate components or steps should be spaced, not presented at the same time. This way, the attention of the entire group is focused on the same step and individual students do not become confused by attempting to follow multiple directions about which they are not yet clear.

Student-instigated distractions, such as opening books, borrowing pencils, or chatting with classmates, can interrupt the teacher while giving directions. Teaching a simple rule that directs students to keep books closed and pencils on their desks enhances their attention to and understanding of task directions.

Sometimes, teachers actually interrupt their own lesson momentum by engaging in counterproductive behaviors. They start an activity, then drop it abruptly before it is completed. Or, they flip-flop between two activities, starting one activity and then returning to a prior activity to give further directions. These behaviors often are associated with failure to develop a carefully thought out lesson schedule as well as failure to efficiently organize instructional materials prior to the lesson. Failing to provide students with their own individual learning materials is another counterproductive teacher behavior. In addition, teachers should model or rehearse the finished product of the lesson. This can involve the teacher's completing a math problem correctly on the board and/or providing guidance and direction to students in completing a sample problem. This form of modeling or rehearsal can prompt students to stay on task by providing visual cues about what to do (Kounin & Doyle, 1975). The teacher's careful advance preparation and planning can preclude many of these interruptions. Greater clarity in the teacher's presentation and increased student task engagement make for a more efficient use of instructional time.

Grouping Students for Instruction. Greater time efficiency is achieved when teachers group students for instruction. Research has shown that greater academic gains are made when students spend a large portion of the day receiving instruction from an instructor (Borg, 1980; Greenwood, Delquadri, Stanley, Sasso, Whorton & Schulte, 1981; Leinhardt, Zigmond, & Cooley, 1981). A good rule of thumb is that 50% of the student's day should be spent in teacher-directed instruction. The classroom teacher, a consultant or team teacher, a paraprofessional, a parent volunteer, or a peer tutor can provide this instruction.

While special education practices traditionally emphasized one-to-one individual instruction, this form of individualization frequently is neither efficient nor efficacious. In fact, some research suggests that the time teachers spend working with one or two students is negatively related to student gains in achievement, while the time spent working with groups is positively related to achievement gains (Soar, 1973; Stallings & Kaskowitz, 1974). Group instruction tends to be as effective as one-to-one instruction in terms of student learning, and in some instances is more effective (Polloway, Cronin, & Patton, 1986; Rosenshine, 1980; Soar, 1973; Stallings & Kaskowitz, 1974). Furthermore, by grouping students, the teacher can provide more teacher-directed in-

struction with more opportunities for active student engagement. This means that students will learn more in a given period of time. For example, a special education teacher might work with twelve children during an hour. If the teacher was to provide individual tutoring, each student would receive 5 minutes of instruction followed by 55 minutes of independent work time. Even if a paraprofessional worked individually with the students for an additional 5 minutes each, they still would receive only 10 minutes of active instruction apiece. However, if the teacher were to group the students into two or three groups, each student would receive 20–30 minutes of instruction from the teacher. Backup instruction by the paraprofessional would increase the total amount of teacher-directed instruction to between 40 and 60 minutes for the hour.

The range of academic diversity of students in a classroom makes it virtually impossible to perfectly match the students in each instructional group. For some students in the group, this means that the initial instruction is below their instructional level and that they are reviewing prior learning. Nonetheless, small group instruction translates into more instructional time and significantly more active learning opportunities for all students, typically resulting in increased achievement for each individual. The following excerpt describes the experience of a special education teacher who instituted small group instruction in her high school special education math class. It illustrates the benefits of small group instruction in terms of increased allocated time and improved student learning. It further demonstrates that individual student's needs can be met effectively in small group learning arrangements.

Mary Morgan is an example of a secondary teacher who had implemented individualized programs in her special education math classes. Each student in her class had individual packets containing worksheets with the math problems they were learning. Mary, however, found herself running between the ten students in her class. She provided 5 minutes of instruction to one student and then ran to help the next student. By the time she assisted the second student, a third student was stuck on a different problem. Mary quickly became frustrated because her students were not receiving large blocks of time for instruction and practice.

That summer, Mary attended a workshop on effective instruction. Although she had reservations about meeting individual needs in a small group situation, she was ready to try almost anything to improve her math class. The following fall she identified one small group for instruction. Initially, she instructed only her lower-achieving students while she gave the higher-achieving students enrichment activities until she could narrow the gap between their performance levels. Soon she had a group of students for whom she scheduled 20–40 minutes of teacher directed instruction, and 15 minutes of seatwork. The results were phenomenal. Within 2 years, her students were mainstreamed into the regular mathematics curriculum and they actually surpassed their regular-class peers.

The increased amount of teacher-directed instruction available through small group arrangements is a particularly important consideration for students who have learning difficulties. These students are less likely than their more academically successful peers to discover new skills, strategies, relationships, or knowledge independently. Because they are less likely to independently impose structure on a task presented to them, they prosper from the structure and direction the teacher provides. Further, they tend to be more focused and attend to a task more diligently during teacher-directed instruction than in independent work.

Flexible grouping arrangements can be helpful in introducing concepts and strategies to larger groups of students. With flexible groupings, teachers may teach a single skill or strategy to an entire class of students, and then break the class into subgroups for more intensive instruction and practice. As an illustration, teachers in one district decided to use flexible grouping arrangements to teach their students a specific learning strategy for comprehending story narra-

tives. The strategy involved identifying the underlying story structure and involved teaching students to approach story narratives with five story questions in mind. These were:

1. "What is the setting?"
2. "What is the problem confronting the main character?"
3. "How does the main character respond?"
4. "What is the outcome of the response?"
5. "What is the story conclusion?"

Figure 7.1 represents this learning strategy, adapted from a story frame that Idol (1987) used.

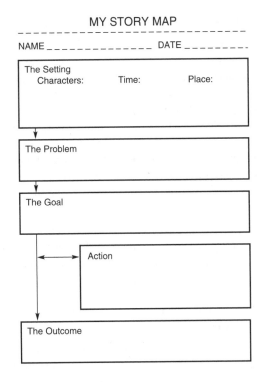

FIGURE 7.1   Components of the Story Map

Source: From "Group story mapping: A comprehension strategy for both skilled and unskilled readers" by L. Idol, 1987, *Journal of Learning Disabilities, 20(4),* p. 199. Copyright 1987 by PRO-ED, Inc. Reprinted by permission.

Using flexible grouping, the teachers introduced the comprehension strategy to the entire class. They taught the students about the elements of story structure and the questions that guide readers in comprehending narrative text. Later, when it was time to assign practice tasks, teachers individualized by providing individuals or subgroups with additional instruction and different practice materials. In this way, teachers formed a large group for direct instruction in and demonstration of the targeted strategy, but individualized for guided instruction and independent practice. Flexible grouping increased the learning time available to all students while responding to the learning potential of individual students.

Analyzing Time Management Practices

One of the first things teachers can do to increase the amount of time allocated to active instruction is to analyze their own time management practices. An example of a simple data collection form and rating scale is provided in Figure 7.2.

Teachers can analyze their current daily schedules as a first step to evaluating their use of time in the school day. The first portion of Figure 7.2 depicts one daily schedule. The use of instructional time can be calculated by adhering to the following steps:

1. List the number of students in each lesson conducted in a specific period of time.
2. List the number of students in the classroom.
3. Calculate the total time spent in direct instruction in each lesson.
4. Note how many lessons per hour are conducted.

Using these values, the percent of students participating in teacher-directed lessons per hour and the percent of time spent in direct instruction can be calculated by using the formulas provided in the Analysis Section of Figure 7.1. Teachers then should rate themselves on teaching practices associated with effectively managing allocated time. A rating scale for this purpose is shown in Figure 7.3.

Once teachers have completed this self-evaluation process, they decide if and how they should reallocate instructional time. Such reallocation could involve revising instructional schedules, adhering to schedules, altering instructional practices, monitoring transitions, maintaining lesson smoothness and continuity, or grouping students for instruction.

STUDENT ENGAGED TIME

Engaged time refers to the proportion of time that students are actually **on-task** or engaged with the instructional activity. To progress through the curriculum, students must attend to and interact with the instructional content in a meaningful way for a sustained period of time. Student task engagement is critical during teacher-directed instruction as well as independent seatwork.

Many students with achievement difficulties often exhibit short attention spans, a situation that makes inadequate student attention to task a serious problem. If a teacher provides 1 hour for math instruction, for example, but the student is on-task only 50% of the time, he receives 30 minutes of actual instruction. For students with learning problems, this level of off-task behavior only increases the learning gap that exists between them and their classroom peers. They tend to fall further and further behind their classmates with each passing school year. Teachers can enhance the amount of task engagement on the part of students by: (1) increasing students' response opportunities, (2) maintaining a brisk pace, and (3) monitoring students' responses. These and other practices are described later in this chapter.

Analyzing Student Task Engagement

The level of student task engagement in a given classroom can be measured using a self-analysis approach similar to the one described previously for examining teacher management of allocated time. Englert and Thomas (1982) described a system for measuring levels of student task involvement. Using this system, the teacher can collect

---

Teacher: _____   School: _____

Grade: _____   Subjects: _____

Time Allocated for Instruction

No. of Students in Lesson: Lesson No. 1 _____ 2 _____ 3 _____ 4 _____

No. of Students Not in Lesson
    but in Room: Lesson No. 1 _____ 2 _____ 3 _____ 4 _____

Number of Minutes of Instruction:
    Lesson 1
    Lesson 2
    Lesson 3
    Lesson 4
    Lesson 5

No. of Lessons per Hour: _____

Analysis Section

a. *Percentage of Students in Instruction per Hour:*
   Divide the number of students in lessons by the total number of students
   in the room to determine the percentage of students you involve in
   direct instruction per hour.   _____%

b. *Percentage of Different Students in Instruction per Hour:*
   Repeat previous computation but only count the number of different students
   included in direct instruction during the observation students (e.g., count
   each student only once even if the student is in two lessons). Divide this
   number by the total number of students in the room during the
   observation period.   _____%

c. *Percentage of Observation Period Spent in Direct Instruction:*
   Divide the total number of minutes of instruction for the observation
   period by the total observation time in minutes.   _____%

d. *Time Spent in Transitions or Nonacademic Subjects:*
   Subtract the ending time from one lesson from the beginning time of the
   next lesson (e.g., 2:45 P.M. subtracted from 3:00 P.M.). Repeat this
   procedure for all lessons during the observation period and sum the
   transition time between lessons. Divide that number by the total
   observation time in minutes.   _____%

FIGURE 7.2   Time Management: Data Collection Form for Measuring
Allocated Time

---

time-on-task data every 10–15 seconds on students engaged in seatwork activities. During teacher presentation to the whole class or to small groups, an aide or colleague can collect these data. At the end of the specified interval, the recorder simply looks at each student in the classroom in a prespecified order and makes a decision about whether the student is on-task (+) or off-task (–). Figure 7.4 shows an example of an observation form that can be used for this purpose. This form enables the teacher to record task engagement for an entire classroom by: (1) count-

Respond to each item in terms of the extent to which it describes yourself:

(1) Not at all descriptive
(2) Descriptive to a small extent
(3) Descriptive to a moderate extent

(4) Descriptive to a large extent
(5) Descriptive to an extremely large extent

Management Behaviors	Performance Evaluation				
1. Starts lesson on time	1	2	3	4	5
2. Adheres to lesson schedule	1	2	3	4	5
3. Time allocations to objectives reflect students' instructional needs	1	2	3	4	5
4. Uses attention signals to begin and end lesson	1	2	3	4	5
5. Gains all students' attention before giving instructions	1	2	3	4	5
6. Maintains a brisk transition	1	2	3	4	5
7. Directions for transition to next activity provided	1	2	3	4	5
8. Follows up on transitions by monitoring behavior	1	2	3	4	5
9. Starts new lesson or activity quickly	1	2	3	4	5
10. Uses small group instructional arrangements and flexible grouping arrangements whenever possible	1	2	3	4	5

FIGURE 7.3   Practices for Effective Management of Allocated Time

ing the number of students on-task during each interval, (2) counting the number of students off-task during each interval, (3) summing the number of students on-task across all intervals, and (4) dividing the total number of students on-task from Step 3 by the total number of student on-task and off-task (e.g., the sum of the numbers obtained in Steps 1 and 2). Next the teacher can use the self-evaluation form found in Figure 7.5 to evaluate those teacher behaviors that maximize student engaged time.

CONTENT SELECTION AND COVERAGE

One of the most critical considerations in using instructional time wisely is to carefully select and plan the delivery of curriculum content. In many locales, state or district guidelines specify the curriculum. Curriculum frameworks, goals and objectives, and sequences are mandated for varying grade levels. Nonetheless, individual teachers exercise considerable discretion over the curricula within their classrooms. They decide which in-

structional content is most relevant and important for students to learn, and what instruction it is at the appropriate level of difficulty for individual students. They decide how much emphasis to give various curriculum components and they make decisions about the design of the instructional lessons that they present. The content actually taught to students is likely to be a compromise between officially adopted curriculum and a variety of interacting factors. These factors include teacher expertise and enjoyment of a subject, time constraints, the students' needs as teachers see them, and the degree of external monitoring such as district achievement testing (Brophy, 1982).

Curricular decisions are of particular importance for students who have learning difficulties because these students have little time to lose if they are to be successful in school. This means that the instruction provided to them must, by necessity, be efficient. It should stress the skills/knowledge that: (1) are salient for their future schooling and/or adult lifes, (2) are unknown to

Teacher: _____   Date: _____

Subject: _____

Number of Students in Lesson: _____

Number of Students in Room: _____

Beginning Time of Observation: _____   Ending Time: _____

Observation/Lesson No.   1   2   3   4   5

Recording On-Task Behavior of Seatwork Students

Before the observation begins, decide in advance how often you plan to scan the room and count the number of seatwork students who are on-task and off-task. A reasonable amount of time that you might allow between the times you scan is every ten or fifteen minutes. Once you have decided how often you plan to scan the room, you are ready to begin. At the end of the selected time interval, look up and scan the room (be sure to consistently scan in the same order). Count the number of students who are off-task and record on the form below. At the end of the lesson, calculate the percentage of seatwork students who are engaged. A reasonable goal in a small class of students is 75% or higher. The same observation form could be used with students in direct instruction, although the on-task goal for such students is 90%

	1	2	3	4	5	6	7	8	9	10	11	12	13
No. of Students Engaged													
No. of Students Not Engaged													

Percentage of Students Engaged: _____

Percent Formula: Divide the number of students engaged by the total number of students (e.g., the sum of the number of students engaged plus the number of students not engaged).

FIGURE 7.4   Observation Form for Task Engagement

them but not beyond their entry behaviors, and (3) are as widely generalizable as possible. Teachers must make informed choices about what constitutes the most relevant concepts and skills, and they must eliminate "curriculum fluff" if they are to use instructional time efficiently with low-achieving students. Carefully selecting and designing curriculum can reduce the achievement discrepancies within a classroom, while instruction that is inefficient, ineffective, or trivial means that precious learning time and effort is wasted.

For students who are unable to master all the knowledge and skill competencies within a curriculum, the teacher must decide which are truly *important* to the student. Teachers should ask themselves if the skills and knowledge are critical to future study in the content area, are needed for successful functioning in the school environment, or are necessary for successful adult functioning.

Respond to each item in terms of the extent to which it describes yourself:

(1) Not at all descriptive   (4) Descriptive to a large extent
(2) Descriptive to a small extent   (5) Descriptive to an extremely large extent
(3) Descriptive to a moderate extent

Management Behaviors	Performance Evaluation				
1. Positions self to allow clear view of all students	1	2	3	4	5
2. Scans room *frequently*	1	2	3	4	5
3. Circulates between lessons to monitor and assist students	1	2	3	4	5
4. Maintains high level of student time on-task (e.g., 80%)	1	2	3	4	5
5. Maintains high success rates in seatwork (e.g., 90%)	1	2	3	4	5
6. Prepares students for seatwork tasks	1	2	3	4	5
7. Models how to perform seatwork tasks	1	2	3	4	5
8. Tells rationale for seatwork (e.g., tells what, how, when, and why)	1	2	3	4	5
9. Asks questions to provide rehearsal and verify understanding of seatwork task	1	2	3	4	5
10. Provides active forms of seatwork practice (e.g., requires an active rather than a passive response)	1	2	3	4	5
11. Sets standards for assignments (e.g., neatness, accuracy, timeliness)	1	2	3	4	5
12. Establishes procedures for early finishers, students needing help	1	2	3	4	5
13. Requires students to correct work, or make up missed or unfinished work	1	2	3	4	5
14. Uses tutoring (e.g., peer, volunteers, aides) and other specialized instructional technology to increase the opportunities for active response during seatwork	1	2	3	4	5

FIGURE 7.5   Self-Evaluation: Effective Management of Task Engagement

If the skills and information are not salient to future study, school success, or adult functioning, they should be deleted from the curriculum for low-achieving students.

For example, a language arts textbook may introduce several categories of composition: different types of sentences, expository paragraphs, narrative paragraphs, opinion paragraphs, poems, similes, metaphors, friendly letters, and business letters. Of these, the most important probably are those relating to writing complete sentences and coherent paragraphs. These are critical skills because they are required in other school subjects, are important to school success, and have implications for adult adjustment. Writing various types of personal and business letters meets these same criteria, and are especially relevant for successful adult functioning. Hence, for students with achievement difficulties, the teacher would focus instruction on the two broad areas of writing sentences and paragraphs, and writing personal and business letters. The composition units on poetry, similes, and metaphors might be de-emphasized, not because of lack of teacher or student interest, but in the interest of using the limited instructional time more efficiently. In the same manner, math instruction might delete considerations of alternative base systems and Roman numerals from the curriculum in favor of emphasizing skills more critical to school success and adult functioning such as basic operations, using the calculator, solving word problems, and telling time.

Teachers should also omit nonessential bits of information that represent vaguely interesting digressions from the instructional focus. Similarly, teachers should delete new terms or skills that will be used only within the immediate lesson and that have little future applicability. The teacher needs to identify these bits of curricular fluff and eliminate them from the instructional lessons.

In addition to being salient, the skills selected for inclusion also should reflect the student's current level of functioning. Students should receive direct instruction only on skills and knowledge *unknown* to them and for which they have the prerequisites for entry behaviors. Sometimes teachers proceed through a curriculum sequence in a lock-step manner, regardless of whether or not the student already has mastered some of the skills being covered. They put all their third-grade students, for instance, through the entire third-grade math curriculum even though some students can demonstrate mastery on the total curriculum, or components of it, at the beginning of the school year. It is inefficient to use instructional time reteaching skills that students already have mastered. It also conveys a lack of respect for students and can bore them.

On the other hand, some students will not be ready for the curriculum designated for a particular grade level. If they have not acquired the prerequisites, then instruction should be postponed until these preskills are mastered. For example, for instruction on writing friendly letters, students should already have mastered writing complete sentences and coherent paragraphs. Curriculum-based assessment, presented in Chapter 4, is an avenue for pinpointing where instruction should be introduced. It can indicate which skills the student already has mastered and which are unknown, but still not beyond her entry behaviors.

Finally, instruction should be focused on skills that are **generalizable.** Teaching strategies that have the widest possible generalization maximizes the efficiency of instruction (Engelmann & Carnine, 1982). For example, it would be inefficient to teach students each of the one hundred addition facts separately. Instead, they can be taught a finger strategy for solving addition facts (e.g., "Put up fingers for the smaller addend. Say the second addend. Then, touch each finger as you count. Say the sum."). When a strategy such as this is taught, the students emerge with a procedure that is generalizable to a larger set of skills or information (in this instance, all of the addition facts). They learn more in less time and they have enhanced retention (e.g., it is easier to remember one strategy than one hundred facts).

Another example involves teachers reading narrative passages with students. Questions about the passage content frequently include such text-specific inquiries as "Where is Sam going? What do you think Sam will do next? Why did Sam stop at the grocery store?" While these questions may assist students in understanding the current passage, they are unlikely to effect comprehension of future stories. A more generalizable approach would be to use questions based on a story-grammar structure (e.g., "Who is the main character? What is the main character's problem? What did the main character do to try to solve the problem? What happened in the end? How did the character feel? How did you feel?") Consistently using such questions teach a generalizable approach to analyzing and understanding not only the current story, but any future stories that the students might read.

Wisely selecting content is one way of maximizing the use of instructional time. Additional considerations include scheduling a large portion of each day for content instruction and covering as much content as possible each day. Research suggests that an extensive content coverage is related to higher student achievement. Content coverage can be measured in terms of the number of objectives mastered in a specific amount of time, the number of specific facts (e.g., sight words) taught and learned per day, the number of pages covered per day, and/or the number of questions or concepts presented per lesson.

DESIGNING INSTRUCTIONAL LESSONS

All students benefit from the presentation of well-designed lessons. This is a particularly important consideration for students with academic challenges. The lesson design model that the Council for Exceptional Children's *Academy on Effective Instruction* developed (Archer, Isaacson, Adams, Ellis, Morehead, & Schiller, 1989) is particularly

well adapted to the needs of students who experience achievement difficulties. This model, depicted in Table 7.1, divides the lesson into three separate components: the *opening,* the *body,* and the *close.* The efficacy of this conceptualization has been supported by a wide variety of empirical research (Anderson, Evertson, & Brophy, 1982; Carnine, Silbert, & Kameenui, 1990; Englert, 1983; Emmer, Evertson, Sanford, Clements, & Worsham, 1982; Hunter & Russell, 1981; Rosenshine, 1983; Rosenshine & Stevens, 1986).

The Lesson Opening

Before beginning a lesson, the teacher should gain every student's attention. He should then review the necessary preskills and concepts and preview the instruction that is about to take place. The goals and objectives of the current lesson should be clearly stated and the concepts and skills asso-

TABLE 7.1 Lesson Design Model

DESCRIPTION OF COMPONENT		EXAMPLE WORDING
	Opening	
Attention	Gain the students' attention.	"Thank you. We are going to begin."
Review	Review prior knowledge necessary for today's lesson.	"In our last lesson, we . . . "
Goal	State the goals of today's lesson.	"Today, you will learn. . . . "
	Body	
Model (I do it.)	Demonstrate the skill or strategy for your students.	"Watch as I . . ."
Prompt (We do it.)	Assist students in performing the skill or strategy by performing the skill simultaneously or verbally prompting the students.	"Let's . . . together."
Check (You do it.)	Carefully observe your students as they perform the skill or strategy.	"Your turn to . . ."
	Close	
Review	Review the skill, strategy, or information presented in the lesson.	"Today, we learned . . ."
Preview	Preview the content of the next lesson.	"Tomorrow, we will . . ."
Independent work	Assign homework or seatwork.	"Today, I would like you to . . ."

ciated with the lesson should be identified. This serves to activate background knowledge and provide information concerning the significance of what is being taught. While teachers may vary the time or emphasis they give to these activities, each of these elements is essential.

Gaining Attention. The first step in any lesson is to gain the students' attention. Teachers can do this by giving a signal that already has been established as a cue for students to pay attention. The variety of signals that can be used is almost endless. Teachers can use a verbal cue such as: "May I have your attention, please?" "Eyes and ears up here." "Listen." "Class, look here." Or they can use nonverbal or visual signals such as holding up a reading book or raising an arm.

To be effective, a verbal prompt should be followed by silence and individual student eye contact until students attend. If the initial cue is not successful, the teacher can repeat the cue, praise students who are attending, move closer to students having difficulty attending, and/or prompt an individual student ("Mathew, we are going to begin now."). This type of teacher follow-through plays an important role in gaining and maintaining the students' attention.

Throughout the day there are numerous occasions when teachers must start lessons, or within lessons, redirect students' attention from an old activity to a new one. Consistent differences have been found among teachers in gaining and monitoring students' attention at both the beginning and close of lessons (Arlin, 1979). Successful teachers clearly announce the beginning of the lesson (e.g., "Pencils down; eyes on me.") and allow ample "wait time" (pausing until attention was obtained) to permit follow-through. Less successful teachers announce the transition, but tend to pause only momentarily without waiting until all students are ready before presenting the directions for the next activity.

Reviewing Prior Learning. Once teachers have gained the attention of every student, they then should precede to a lesson review. A review of

prior knowledge that is related to the current instruction is an important first step to introducing a lesson. A review not only activates student attention, but it can provide teachers with critical information about students' readiness for a given lesson. When teachers fail to provide a review of concepts from previous lessons, or to actively test and monitor students' recall and understanding of prior learning, they may be wasting valuable time by presenting instruction about which the students have confused or incomplete prior knowledge or skills.

The form of the review can be varied, but it should involve more than statements such as, "Remember what we did yesterday?" Instead, teachers should check students' performance at the start of the lesson by requiring them to verbalize the meaning of concepts and to apply those concepts to problems (Englert, 1984). For instance, a teacher might ask students to explain the meaning of a key concept taught in the previous day's lesson and apply it directly to a problem situation. A teacher might also choose to systematically review selected preskills. For example, if the teacher is introducing two-digit division, a review of the steps in one-digit division (divide, multiply, subtract, and bring down) would be useful. If the teacher is introducing telling time to 5 minutes, a review of counting by fives would be appropriate.

The important feature of the review is that all students are actively engaged in answering verbal questions, writing responses, or doing some task to demonstrate their prior knowledge and skills (Englert, 1984). If the review indicates that students have not firmly developed the preskills, then these skills must be taught before preceding with the scheduled lesson.

The Lesson Preview. Following the review, effective teachers provide a **preview** of the content and skill objectives for the current lesson. Low-achieving students learn best when teachers make frequent reference to what is being learned, why it is important, and how it relates to other learning (Anderson, 1984; Roehler & Duffy, 1984).

The teacher begins by stating the goal of the lesson clearly and directly so that students understand what they are to attend to during the lesson. For example, the teacher might state: "Today, we are going to learn how to record assignments on a calendar." "In this lesson, you will learn how to write a paragraph that includes a topic sentence and related details." The goal of the lesson draws the students' attention to the critical information during the lesson, giving them a "set" for learning. Stating the goal is useful to the teacher as well as the students for it focuses the teacher's attention on the lesson outcome and assists the teacher in staying on the topic.

In many cases, the goal should be accompanied with an explanation about the relevance of the skill or strategy. This can address *why* the skill is important, *when* the skill can be used, and *where* it might be used. When introducing a strategy for proofreading, for example, the teacher might state the goal and relevance in the following manner:

> *Today you are going to learn a strategy for proofreading your papers. When you proofread, you find and fix up your mistakes. If you carefully find and fix up all of your mistakes, the writer will better understand what you are saying. You will also get higher grades on assignments if you correct the errors. You can use this strategy when you complete assignments in school, when you write a letter or even a note to someone. Tell me some of things that you write that you should proofread.— You can use this strategy in this class, in your other classes, at home, and in the future on a job. Think of places where you write things that should be proofread.*

The statement of relevance not only increases students' motivation and their subsequent attention to the content of the lesson, but it increases the probability that they will generalize the new skill to other situations. Promoting generalization is particularly important when teaching learning strategies, organizational skills, social skills, and vocational skills.

In addition to simply stating what will be covered and its relevance, teachers can link the current lesson to prior learning beyond that provided during the review. Studies have shown that students learn better when new information is linked with what they already know (Anderson, 1984; Roehler & Duffy, 1984), and that low achievers fail to spontaneously activate background knowledge (Bransford et al., 1982; Wong, 1980). This can adversely affect their ability to comprehend, make inferences, and predict events. To overcome this barrier, explicit teacher-directed discussion can link background knowledge with the current lesson. Teachers can ask students questions that require them to discuss related experiences, predict information or events on the basis of background knowledge, and critically evaluate information on the basis of their own experiences.

Table 7.2 presents an example lesson. Carefully examine the opening of the lesson. Did this teacher gain attention? Review prior knowledge? State the lesson's goal? Tell students a rationale for the skill being taught? Link the current lesson with relevant background information?

The Lesson Body

Teaching a new skill requires that teachers do more than identify the instructional goal, establish a rationale, describe the skill, and link it to prior learning. In addition, they should actively teach the skill or concept by demonstrating and modeling strategies related to it and by providing students with guided practice opportunities. This structure of lesson presentation is sometimes referred to as the *model, prompt, check* approach. Each of these components is described in the following paragraphs.

Modeling the Target Behavior. Effective teachers provide instructional **models** of the new skill or strategy (Browder, Shoen, & Lentz, 1986–1987; Englert, 1984; Rivera & Smith, 1988). Viewing a *systematic, dynamic model* can increase the efficiency and effectiveness with which the student learns. This is true for simple

TABLE 7.2 Example Lesson[1]

COMPONENT	Strategy:	Determining the factors of a number.
	Preskills:	Division facts.

DIALOG

Opening

Attention

T: Let's Begin. (Pauses and gains eye contact with students.)

S: (Attend to teacher.)

Goal

T: Today we are going to learn how to figure out the factors of a number. Listen, a factor is a number that divides evenly into another number. A factor is a number that divides . . .

S: Evenly into another number.

T: So, if a number is a factor, will there be a remainder?

S: No.

T: We need to learn how to figure out the factors of a number so that we can continue our work in fractions. When you can figure out the factors of a number, you can add, subtract, multiply, and divide fractions with unlike denominators. You can also use factors to reduce fractions.

Review

T: Before we begin our work with factors, let's review some difficult division facts. (Points to problems on the board.) Write these problems and the answer on your paper.

S: (Write and solve division facts.)

T: (Monitors and examines answers.)

T: (When majority of students are done, regains attention.) Let's check these problems together. 81 divided by 9 is . . .

S: 9

T: 42 divided by 7 is . . .

S: 6

T: (Continues with other problems based on students' prior errors: $56 \div 8$; $72 \div 8$; $49 \div 7$; $32 \div 8$; $63 \div 7$; $64 \div 8$.)

Body

Model

T: (Writes 12 on the board.) Watch carefully as I figure out the factors of the number 12. Remember, a factor is a number that divides into another number evenly.

T: First, the number 1 is a factor of any number, because one divides evenly into every number. What number is a factor of every number?

S: 1.

T: What number would be a factor of 45?

S: 1.

T: What number would be a factor of 608?

S: 1.

T: Yes, one would be a factor of every number. The first factor you will always write down will be one.
(Writes 12
           1.)

(continued)

TABLE 7.2 continued

| **COMPONENT** | Strategy: | Determining the factors of a number. |
| | Preskills: | Division facts. |

Body

T: Listen carefully to this second hint. The number itself is always a factor of the number. So, 12 is a factor of 12 because it divides evenly into 12. So, what other number is a factor of 12.

S: 12.

T: So, what two numbers could be factors of 82?

S: 1 and 82.

T: So, what two numbers would be factors of 756?

S: 1 and 756.

T: Watch where I write the number 12.
(Writes   12
            1   12.)

T: Now, I need to figure out the rest of the factors. I have tried one. The next number is 2. Does 2 divide evenly into 12?

S: Yes.

T: So, is 2 a factor of 12?

S: Yes.

T: (Writes   12
              1, 2   12.)

T: How many times does 2 divide into 12?

S: 6.

T: Six also divides evenly into 12. So, is 6 a factor of 12?

S: Yes

T: Watch where I write the 6.
(Writes   12
            1, 2   6, 12.)

T: I tried 1 and 2, what number is next?

S: 3.

T: Does 3 divide evenly into 12?

S: Yes.

T: So, is 3 a factor of 12?

S: Yes.

T: (Writes   12
              1, 2, 3   6, 12.)

T: How many times does 3 divide into 12?

S: 4.

T: So, is 4 a factor of 12?

S: Yes.

T: Watch where I write the 4.
(Writes   12
            1, 2, 3   4, 6, 12.)

T: I tried 1, 2, and 3. What number is next?

S: 4.

TABLE 7.2 continued

COMPONENT	Strategy:	Determining the factors of a number.
	Preskills:	Division facts.

Body

T: (Points to 4.) But look we already know that four is a factor of 12. When we come to a factor that we already have, we STOP. Now, we have all of the factors of the number.

T: Read the factors of 12.

S: 1, 2, 3, 4, 6, 12.

T: These are all of the numbers that divide evenly into 12.

Prompt

T: Let's figure the factors of 15 together. On your paper, write 15. Put your pencils down and look up when you are done. (Monitors.)

S: (Write 15.)

T: What is the first number that we know is a factor of 15?

S: 1.

T: What other number do you know is a factor of 15?

S: 15.

T: Good. Write those number under 15. When you are done, look up.

T: (Monitors and then writes the following on the board:)

    15
    1   15.)

T: Be sure you have written your numbers in the same place.

T: After we try 1, what number should we try next?

S: 2.

T: Does 2 divide evenly into 15?

S: No.

T: So, is 2 a factor of 15?

S: No.

T: We have tried 1 and 2. What number should we try next?

S: 3.

T: Does 3 divide evenly into 15?

S: Yes.

T: So, is 3 a factor of 15?

S: Yes.

T: How many times does 3 divide into 15?

S: 5.

T: So, is 5 a factor of 15?

S: Yes.

T: Write down 3 and 5. Look up when you are done.

T: (Monitors and then writes:)

       15
   1, 3   5, 15.)

T: We have tried 1, 2, and 3. When number would we try next?

S: 4.

(continued)

TABLE 7.2   continued

COMPONENT	Strategy:	Determining the factors of a number.
	Preskills:	Division facts.

Body

T: Does 4 divide evenly into five?
S: No.
T: So, is 4 a factor of 15?
S: No.
T: What number would we try next?
S: 5.
T: But we already have 5, so what do we do?
S: STOP.
T: Yes, we would stop because we have all of the factors of 15.
T: Read the factors of 15.
S: 1, 3, 5, 15.
T: Excellent. Now, let's figure out the factors of 18.
(The teacher prompts the students using the same wording. Prompting continues until the students demonstrate a high level of accuracy on this strategy.)

Check

T: Now, it's your turn. Figure out the factors of 14. Look up when you are done.
S: (Write factors of 14.)
T: (Monitors and then writes:
14
1, 2, 7, 14.)
T: Check your answer with me.
S: (Check answer with answer on board.)
T: Find the factors of 20.
S: (Write factors of 20.)
T: (Monitors and then writes:
20
1, 2, 4,   5, 10, 20.)
T: Check you answer with mine.
S: (Check answers with answer on board.)
T: (Repeats check step with additional numbers ensuring a number of consecutive accurate responses.)

Close

Review

T: You did an excellent job learning how to figure out the factors of a number. Everyone, what is a factor?
S: A number that divides evenly into another number.
T: If there is a remainder, is the number a factor?
S: No.

Preview

T: Tomorrow, we will review the strategy for determining factors and will use our knowledge of factors to reduce fractions.

TABLE 7.2   continued

COMPONENT	Strategy: Preskills:	Determining the factors of a number. Division facts.

Close

Independent work

T: Turn to page 76 in your math book.
S: (Turn to page 76.)
T: Put your finger on Exercise A.
S: (Touch exercise A.)
T: In this exercise, you are to find the factors for each number. Do all of the items in Exercise A. Don't forget to check the odd items with the answers in the back of the book.
      Begin working.
S: (Do exercise.)
T: (Monitors and provides feedback.)

[1]T = teacher; S = students.

skills (such as saying a word, spelling a word, writing a cursive letter, or using a strategy to solve an addition fact) as well as for more complex ones (such as writing a paragraph, starting a conversation, or applying a learning strategy to reading a textbook).

It may be necessary to preteach critical steps or vocabulary terms before a concept or strategy can be modeled. For example, teaching narrative structure might require teaching concepts such as *problem, setting, response, outcome,* and *conclusion.* To establish these as meaningful vocabulary for the students, teachers need to define and model the terms. The teacher should provide two to three examples of the concept in order to underscore its critical dimensions. To ensure mastery, carefully selected nonexamples also should be provided. Each time the teacher presents an example or nonexample, she should show the students what features are used in making the discrimination and how to regulate or monitor the use of the skill through self-questions (e.g., "This is a setting. How do I know? Because it tells me *where* and *when.*"). Finally, teachers should provide discrimination practice that actively involves students in saying whether particular instances are examples or nonexamples, and justifying their answers. This forces students to verbalize the concept in making decisions and allows teachers to check student understanding.

When modeling the new strategy, the teacher should proceed step by step, showing and telling students about each step in the strategy or skill (Brophy, 1982). If the step in the strategy is covert, the teacher should make that step overt by orally describing what he is thinking. Each step introduced is accompanied by an explanation of what the teacher will be doing next, followed by a demonstration that labels the actions being performed. This procedure helps students to not only learn the steps of the strategy, but to gain insight into the thinking that directs the process. The pairing of the explanation with the demonstration not only labels the actions being performed, but describes the inner thinking that helps one make decisions, direct performance, recover from bottlenecks, and monitor the results of one's actions. With simpler basic skills the model provides a straightforward example of the behavior involved. With complex skills or strategies, the focus is on the thinking and problem-solving processes used rather than the correct answer. Too often, less effective teachers simply "test" knowledge by asking questions (Durkin, 1978–1979), or model procedures for completing tasks. They fail to explain the mental processes used to perform a task or answer a question (Duffy, Roehler, & Herrmann, 1988). When effective teachers provide mental modeling of learning tasks throughout the day, they teach their students the cognitive strategies needed for independent learning.

When demonstrating a strategy or skill, the wording should be clear and consistent. By eliciting frequent responses, teachers can increase the attentiveness and verify the understanding of their students. This can be done by having students answer questions based on their prior knowledge or by asking students to repeat information that has just been presented. If a strategy is particularly difficult, the demonstration can be repeated.

The model portion of the factoring lesson in Table 7.2 illustrates these steps. Did the teacher demonstrate the strategy? Did the teacher proceed step by step? Did the teacher describe the strategy as it was modeled? Did the teacher use clear, consistent language in the model? Did the teacher elicit responses from students during the model?

Providing Guided Practice. Following modeling, and prior to introducing independent practice, teachers should provide **guided practice** of the skill or strategy (Coker, Lorentz, & Coker, 1980; Englert, 1984; Stevens & Rosenshine, 1981). This ensures that students are learning the skill correctly and keeps them from practicing errors during independent work. Guided practice can be thought of as involving two stages: **prompt** and **check,** sometimes referred to as *lead* and *test* (Carnine, Silbert, & Kameenui, 1990).

The **prompt** stage provides an opportunity for the teacher to assist students in performing the skill or strategy. This ensures that initial practice is successful. In some cases, the prompt can be accomplished by the teacher performing the skill at the same time as the students (e.g., "Say the word with me. Against." "Spell the word *'through'* with me. t-h-r-o-u-g-h."). Simultaneous

prompting can be done in those instances where the teacher and students can both perform the skill *and* observe each other. If the students cannot observe the teacher while performing the skill, the teacher should provide verbal prompts (e.g., "Your turn to write a cursive p. Up, down, up, around, and finish." "Let's proofread the next sentence together. What do we check first? Sense. *Touch each word and say it with me. The boys was going to the store. Does that sentence make sense?* No. *What did the writer mean to say?* The boys were going to the store. *Good, cross out 'was' and write 'were' above it.* ") With either prompting procedure, the teacher should employ the same instructional language as introduced in the model, should carefully monitor students' responses, and should continue prompting until students are performing the skill accurately.

The prompt segment of the example lesson in Table 7.2 illustrates the basic features of prompting students. Did the teacher assist students in applying the strategy? Did the teacher prompt students by performing the strategy at the same time or by prompting verbally? Did the teacher use the same instructional language as used in the model?

After students demonstrate proficiency with prompts, the teacher then should **check** for understanding by having them perform the skill without prompts or other assistance (e.g., *"Say the word by yourselves." "Continue to make the letter s." "Proofread the next sentence. Correct any errors."*) The purpose of the check is to verify that the students can perform the skill without prompts, hints, or cues, and to be sure that they are ready for independent practice (seatwork or homework). During the check, the teacher continues to carefully monitor all responses, providing corrections as needed and positive feedback. Several successful guided practice trials on the skill or strategy are needed to review key concepts and strategies to consolidate student knowledge.

Examine the check segment of the factoring lesson found in Table 7.2. Did the students factor numbers without the aid of the teacher? Were responses required from all students? Did the teacher monitor their responses? Did the teacher provide feedback to students?

While **model, prompt,** and **check** can occur in quick succession (e.g., *"This word is against."* *"Say the word with me. Against." "What word?"* "Against.") for more complex strategies, these steps might extend over a number of days. For example, when teaching a long division strategy, the teacher might model and prompt on the first day. On the second day, the model might be repeated with many additional items prompted. On the third day, the model could be faded, with items prompted and checked. On the fourth day, the number of prompted items might be reduced and the number of items checked increased. The timing of this sequence would, of course, depend on student performance each day.

The Lesson Closing

During the formal close of a lesson, the skills and concepts learned are summarized and linkages are made to future learning. The lesson close can include a review, a preview, and independent work. The **review** is a summary of the critical information presented in the lesson. Where appropriate, it includes one final practice. For example, a teacher could close a lesson in the following way:

> *Today you learned a strategy for proofreading your written work. First, you check for* _____ *sense. Next, you check for* _____ *capitals. Next, you check for* _____ *punctuation. Next, you check for* _____ *spelling. Why is it important to proofread all written products that someone else will need to read? —When can you use this strategy?*

It is also wise to include a preview of the next lesson (e.g., *"Tomorrow, we are going to practice locating and correcting spelling errors."*). The *preview* provides students and teachers with a road map to future instruction. It indicates where the instruction is going and that a logical path is being followed. Finally, the teacher may introduce independent seatwork to be completed in

class or as homework. The purpose of independent work is to provide successful practice with at least 90% accuracy (Rosenshine & Stevens, 1986). This means that independent work should be given only when students have demonstrated a high level of accuracy during group instruction. Strategies for structuring seatwork effectively are described in Chapter 8.

Examine the close of the factoring lesson found in Table 7.2. Did the teacher review the lesson's content? Did the teacher preview the content of the next lesson? Did the teacher assign independent work?

DELIVERY OF INSTRUCTION

While the design of the lesson is critical, it is also important that the teacher use delivery or presentation skills that increase students' attention and the accuracy of their responses. During the lesson, the teacher should: 1) maintain a brisk instructional pace, 2) elicit frequent responses from all of the learners, 3) provide adequate thinking time when responses are requested, 4) maintain student attention, 5) ensure high levels of accuracy and 6) monitor student responses and provide feedback. When these teacher practices are used, the attention, success, and on-task behaviors of the students will be enhanced and the amount of content that can be covered will be increased.

Eliciting Frequent Responses

The most important lesson, delivery skill, active participation, involves eliciting frequent responses from all students during the lesson. A faster presentation rate, with frequent student responses, leads to greater amounts of on-task behavior and higher student achievement (Brophy & Good, 1986; Coker, Lorentz, & Coker, 1980; Englert, 1983; Greenwood, Delquadri, & Hall, 1984; Gall, 1984; Rosenshine, 1983; Rosenshine & Stevens, 1986; West & Sloane, 1986). Active student participation provides critical feedback to the teacher. In addition, students are more attentive when responses are consistently elicited, and active responding provides them with more opportunities to practice the critical information.

Frequently checking student progress permits the teacher to make adjustments as she presents the lesson. When students appear to be mastering the concept or skill, the teacher can move on to new information and examples. However, if students seem to be confused or unsure, the teacher can adjust instruction by repeating information, presenting additional examples, or otherwise clarifying the presentation.

True active participation goes beyond occasional students' responses during the lesson. The number of responses to be elicited depends on the type of response (e.g., written responses will take longer) and the complexity of the responses (e.g., more time is required for answering an inferential comprehension question than for answering a literal comprehension question). Generally, teachers should ask students to say, write, or do something several times during each minute of the lesson. A pattern of input-response-input-response-input-response should be adopted during teacher-directed instruction.

While the amount of active participation is more critical than the type of response gained, there are a number of response types that can be elicited. Students can be required to *say* something orally, *write* something, or *do* something of an action nature.

Oral Responses. The teacher can ask students to *say* responses as a group, to a partner, or individually. Group oral responses can be used when the response is short and the wording is the same across learners. For example:

TEACHER: Which branch of the government makes the laws?
STUDENTS: The legislative branch.

or

TEACHER: What are the four steps in our memorization strategy?
STUDENTS: Read, Cover, Recite, Check.

A cue or signal by the teacher will help ensure that students have adequate thinking time and don't simply mimic other students' responses. For example, the teacher might ask a question, raise his hand to indicate thinking time, and then lower his hand to signal student response. If signals are carefully taught and consistently used, quick responses can be elicited from students of all ages. Group oral responses as well as other unison responses are likely to promote more attention and on-task behavior than individual responses (McKenzie, 1979; Sindelar, Bursuch, & Halle, 1986).

The teacher also can ask students to tell a partner a response. Partner responding is most effective if the teacher carefully selects the partners, matching lower-performing students with middle-performing students, and assigns the partners numbers (one and two) so directives can be given to specific members of the partnership (e.g., "Ones, tell your partner the definition of natural resources and two examples of a natural resource." "Twos, tell your partner the definition for renewable resources and two examples of renewable resources."). Teachers should carefully monitor partner responding to ensure on-task behavior. It also is helpful for students to look up at the teacher to indicate when they have finished the responses. When all students have responded, the teacher should provide feedback on the correct response. While partner responding can be used with all groups of learners, it is particularly powerful when working with middle school and high school students.

The teacher may choose to call on individual students for an oral response. This is particularly appropriate when the response wording is long or different across learners, making group oral responses impossible, or when the teacher wishes to verify individual learning. The most common practice when asking for individual oral responses is to call a student's name, pose the question, listen to the answer, and then to give feedback on the response. However, if this practice is used, the other students are unlikely to attend after a student's name is called. Instead, the teacher should: (1) first pose the question, (2) raise her hand as a signal to inhibit blurting, (3) provide thinking time for all students, (4) make eye contact with students as they formulate answers, (5) call on one student, (6) listen to his/her response, and (7) provide feedback. If this procedure is used, all students are more likely to attend to the question, formulate an answer, and pay attention to their peer's answer as well as the teacher's feedback. As a result, an individual response can be changed into a group response with all students participating.

Written Responses. Students can also be asked to *write* responses. Some content areas (e.g., spelling, mathematics, handwriting, and written expression) necessitate written responses during teacher-directed instruction. Other content areas can be adapted to accommodate written responses. For example, in social studies students could be directed to: "Write the three branches of the federal government on your concept map." In science, they could be instructed to: "Write the definition for natural resources on your paper." The major difficulty when using written responses is the differential response time across students. Some students will be fast in writing their answers and some will take considerable time. To reduce waiting time, the written responses required during teacher-directed instruction should be short, never more than one item. Students should be given a verbal signal to indicate completion (e.g., "Put your pencils down and look up when you are done."). While responses usually are written on paper, slates and similar materials can display the responses in a manner that makes teacher monitoring easier.

Action Responses. Students can also be asked to *do* something during the lesson. They can respond by using hand signals (e.g., "Put one finger up for executive branch, two fingers for legislative branch, and three fingers for judicial branch.") or by displaying a response card (e.g., "Listen to this story problem. Then, hold up the card that shows the correct operation."). Students

can be asked to place their fingers or pencils on a specific part of the instructional stimulus (e.g., *"Put your finger on the title of the story." "Touch the directions." "Put your pencil next to Box A on the concept map."*). In addition to indicating student comprehension or mastery, touching or pointing responses can be used to bring students' attention to critical stimuli. This makes it easy for teachers to monitor that students' attention is on the correct stimuli.

To summarize, active participation is perhaps the most powerful variable in effective lesson delivery. When teachers elicit responses throughout the lesson, not only is there greater student attention to instruction and rehearsal of the lesson information, but the structure of the lesson improves and teaching can be adjusted based on student performance. Review Table 7.3 for a summary of best practices for eliciting students' responses.

Maintaining a Brisk Instructional Pace

Establishing a brisk pace when presenting information helps to maintain students' attention during the lesson (Evertson, Anderson, Anderson, & Brophy, 1980; Englert, 1984). A brisk instructional pace permits teachers to teach more in less time and to move students through the curriculum rapidly. After one question is presented and a student responds correctly, the teacher should present the next question without delay. By shortening the time between the student's answer and the presentation of the next question, teachers move more briskly through the lesson, increase the number of correct responses that students produce, and maintain higher levels of students' attention to task. At the same time, they cover more content (Carnine, 1981).

Providing Thinking Time

The importance of maintaining a brisk instructional pace cannot be overemphasized. However, although a brisk pace is important, well-intentioned efforts to preserve the lesson pace should

TABLE 7.3 Best Practices for Eliciting Responses[1]

Type of Response	Teaching Procedure
Oral Response as a Group	If students are looking at the teacher:
(Response is short and the wording is the same across students.)	**T:** Asks a question. **T:** Raises her hand to signal thinking time. **S:** Think of answer. **T:** Says "Everyone" and lowers hand. **S:** Say answer.
	If students are looking at a stimulus on the board, chart, or overhead: **T:** Points to stimulus. **T:** Asks a question. **T:** Gives thinking time. **S:** Think of answer. **T:** Taps. **T:** Say answer.
	If students are looking at their own books or worksheets: **T:** Asks question or gives a directive. **T:** Gives thinking time. **S:** Think of answer. **T:** Signals auditorily (e.g., a tap or voice signal). **S:** Respond.
Oral Response to a Partner	The teacher assigns students response partners and the number 1 or 2. **T:** Asks a question or gives a directive. **T:** Tells one partner to respond. (Ones, tell your partner. . . .) **T:** Tells students to look up when they are done. **S:** Tell answer to partner. **T:** Monitors. **T:** Gives feedback to the group.
Oral Response as an Individual	**T:** Asks a question. **T:** Raises his hands to signal thinking time. Gives eye contact to all students to encourage formulation of an answer. **S:** Think of answer. **T:** Calls on one student. **S:** Give answer.
Written Responses	**T:** Gives a directive or asks a question. Tells students to put their pencils down and to look up when they are done. **S:** Write response. **T:** Monitors. **T:** Gives feedback to students.
	If slate is used: **T:** Gives directive or asks a question. **S:** Write response.

TABLE 7.3 continued

Type of Response	Teaching Procedure	
	T:	Says "Show me."
	S:	Display answer on slates.
	T:	Monitors responses.
	T:	Gives feedback.
Action Responses		
Touch	**T:**	Gives directive.
	S:	Touch stimuli.
	T:	Monitors.
Action Responses		
Student hand signals	**T:**	Introduces the hand signals (e.g., 1 = legislative, 2 = executive, 3 = judicial) and writes on board.
	T:	Gives "content-free" directive (e.g., "Show me executive.")
	S:	Show hand signal.
	T:	Asks a question.
	S:	Indicate answer with hand signal.
	T:	Monitors hand signals.
	T:	Gives feedback.

T = teacher; S = student.

not interfere with providing adequate thinking time for all students. Teachers may allow low achievers less **thinking-time** between teacher question and student response. Because teachers do not wish to embarrass the low-achieving students who may not know the answers, they quickly insert the correct answer for them. The purpose of thinking time is to permit students time to recall and reflect. Diminished thinking-time increases the probability that students with learning difficulties will not learn to think deeply or strategically when called upon. In the long run, the cumulative effects of this teaching-learning pattern can be devastating. The students who volunteer and respond in class attain higher learning and achievement outcomes. If low-achieving and special education students are to ever catch up with their peers, they need to have more, not fewer, response opportunities.

Developing higher-level thinking skills is facilitated when teachers allow lengthier thinking-times following the presentation of questions. Typically, teachers wait less than 1 second before intervening and providing the answer. By extending this time to 3–5 seconds, teachers can increase not only the target student's response accuracy, but promote greater thinking involvement of the the entire class. The following teacher/pupil effects are associated with lengthier thinking-times: (1) longer student responses; (2) increased numbers of unsolicited appropriate responses, with corresponding decreases in non-responses; (3) increased numbers of student questions; (4) a greater variety and type of student responses; and (5) improvements in the quality and level of student discourse.

Ensuring High Levels of Accuracy

Maintaining high levels of student accuracy is another important instructional consideration. Effective teachers monitor students' understanding of lesson content and make judgments about the pacing of the lesson for the ability levels of the students. The accuracy of student responses is the primary criterion for judging the adequacy of the lesson. It is acceptable for high-achieving students to perform at somewhat lower accuracy levels (e.g., 70%) during lesson presentation, for as independent learners, they can self-correct and impose needed structure during independent work. However, students with learning problems should perform at an 80% accuracy level during direct instruction. This means that approximately 80% of teachers' questions should be answered correctly (Block, 1980).

Several instructional techniques can be employed to ensure high student accuracy. First, the instructional task can be broken into smaller steps (Rosenshine & Stevens, 1986). The discussion of task analysis in Chapter 3 outlines approaches for breaking down an instructional task. For example, in one instructional episode, students may be required to perform only the initial steps of a multistep procedure. Then, additional steps can be introduced on subsequent days until the entire sequence is mastered.

Second, teachers should introduce new skills in unmixed presentations before mixing them with previously learned skills. For example, if a student is learning a new sound (e.g., short *i*), words with that sound should be practiced alone before they are mixed with words containing previously learned sounds (e.g., short *a*) or presented in sentences. Third, teachers can maintain errorless lessons by increasing the amount of teacher modeling and by providing additional cues to students before they respond. Fourth, teachers can intersperse their demonstration with frequent questions to maintain student attention and to check their understanding (Rosenshine & Stevens, 1986).

Monitoring Responses and Providing Feedback

A high percentage of correct student answers during instruction is positively related to achieve-ment gain (Block, 1980; Borg, 1980; Fisher, Berliner, Filby, Marliave, Cohen, & Deshaw, 1980; Rosenshine, 1983; Stevens & Rosenshine, 1981). For this reason, careful monitoring is an essential teacher presentation skill. During the lesson presentation, teachers must be constantly aware of students' responses. They must listen carefully to students' oral responses, especially when group oral responses are used, and they must carefully monitor written and action responses so that correct responses can be acknowledged and errors corrected.

When a student or group of students makes a correct response on an easy or a previously mastered item, the teacher should give limited praise (e.g., a short verbal statement, a nod of the head, or a smile) and quickly move to the next student or question. Extensive praise on these items can slow the pace of the lesson as well as detract from the value of teacher praise. However, hesitancy in responding may indicate that the student and her classmates are not firm on the concept or skill. Therefore, if the student makes a correct but hesitant response, the teacher should provide praise, acknowledging the correct response and the effort of the student, and then quickly reteach the information.

The ways in which teachers handle incorrect responses has implications for academic progress as well as the self-esteem of students. Teachers should immediately correct the error with the student(s) who makes it, rather than "fish" for the answer from other students. After all, the student(s) who made the error is the one who needs practice on the response. The correction should be done in a businesslike manner that is neither too threatening, which will reduce the desire to respond in the future, or too reinforcing, which might encourage carelessness. Finally, the correction should always result in the student making the correct response.

The actual correction procedure would depend on whether the teacher believes the error is a result of carelessness or a lack of knowledge (Rosenshine & Stevens, 1986). If the error is due to carelessness, the teacher should repeat the question, emphasizing the salient words within the question, and have the student respond. If the error is due to lack of knowledge, the teacher should either tell the student the answer or prompt him in using the appropriate strategy from which to derive the answer. In all cases, the end result must be an accurate response from the student. To strengthen the correction procedure, the teacher should later return to the item or a similar item and recheck the student. Table 7.4 presents a summary of best practices in response to correct and incorrect responses.

Error Drill and Fluency-Building Drills

It is useful for teachers to provide **error drills** on all troublesome concepts. This involves providing repeated practice until students are confident and firm in making the learned response. Items to which students respond incorrectly should be presented again on alternating trials with other items until students are responding fluently.

An ideal time to develop fluency on the targeted skill is during the final stages of the presentation. Although many teachers think that fluency is a natural by-product of the lesson, lessons do not automatically lead to fluency. For example, students with learning difficulties may laboriously generate answers as they are led through a workbook page in reading or mathematics. Once they complete a correct performance, they should be required to reread the targeted words or rework some of the math problems for acquiring and demonstrating fluency. This type of **fluency-building activity** does not require inordinate amounts of time, but it does require a continuing concern for developing automaticity in the learner.

TABLE 7.4 Best Practices When Responding to Correct and Incorrect Responses

Type of Student Response	Teacher's Response
Correct responses	
Correct and immediate	1. Briefly acknowledge the response.
	2. Move to additional input or another question.
Correct and hesitant	1. Praise the student for her effort.
	2. Reteach the information to all students.
Incorrect responses	
General guidelines	1. Correct the error with the student who made the incorrect response or with the entire group. Don't "fish" for the correct answer.
	2. Correct the error in a neutral, businesslike manner.
	3. Have the student(s) make the correct response.
	4. Firm up the response by checking with another example or returning to the same item later in the lesson.
Incorrect response due to carelessness	1. Repeat the question or directive.
	2. Have student make the correct response.
Incorrect response due to lack of knowledge.	1. Tell the student the answer or guide the student to the correct response through prompting.
	or
	2. Have the student give the correct response.

Maintaining Attention

Some students have considerably more difficulty paying attention than others. Nonetheless, all students must attend to the teacher and, in many instances, to their peers as well if they are to gain from the instructional lesson. Teachers can increase the attention to task by using specific teaching procedures. For example, they can model alertness and enthusiasm through body language and voice. A brisk instructional pace and a peppy presentation style that elicits frequent students' responses help to maintain students' attention. In addition, close physical proximity of the teacher to the students increases attention to task. Chapter 6 describes ways of structuring physical space that facilitate the teacher's movement to students' desks for purposes of regaining students' attention, interrupting nonattentive or disruptive behavior, or working with an individual student.

When attention begins to wane, teachers need to adjust their instruction. They can determine what adjustments are needed by asking themselves the following questions: "Am I eliciting enough responses?" "Is the pace of the lesson brisk?" "Am I close enough to my students?" "Am I modeling alertness?" "Should I move closer to Dawn's desk?"

SUMMARY

Consistently, research has shown that what teachers say and do in classrooms has a profound effect on student performance. Before the teacher can present instructional lessons or provide independent or cooperative practice activities, the teacher must carefully organize the instructional time and select the content. When addressing time management, the teacher must consider the amount of time allocated to instructional activities and procedures for increasing students engagement during teacher-directed instruction and independent work. Teachers can increase the amount of time allocated to instruction by: 1) carefully scheduling more time for instructional activities with a

fifty-fifty split between teacher-directed instruction and independent activities; 2) adhering to the lesson schedule; 3) monitoring transitions between activities and teaching students transition guidelines; 4) maintaining the momentum or smoothness of the lesson by reducing intrusions; and 5) grouping students to increase the amount of time they spend in teacher-directed instruction. In addition to allocating more time for instructional activities, teachers must use practices that promote more student task engagement during teacher-directed instruction and independent work. Eliciting continual responses from students, monitoring student performance, and maintaining a brisk pace are some of the practices that increase task engagement. Systems for self-evaluation of time allocation and for evaluation of student task engagement are described as means of gathering information that can be used to restructure instructional practices when necessary.

Not only do teachers need to carefully orchestrate the use of time in the classroom, they must carefully select the content that will be taught and practiced. When teaching students with learning difficulties, it is particularly important to select content that: 1) is salient for future schooling and/or adult lifes, 2) is unknown to students and for which they have the necessary preskills, and 3) focuses on generalizable strategies.

The chapter also describes procedures for designing and delivering efficient and effective teacher-directed lessons. When a lesson is carefully structured, student learning is enhanced. Well-designed lessons include an opening, a body, and a close. During the opening of the lesson, the teacher gains students' attention, reviews prior knowledge particularly necessary preskills germane to today's lesson, and communicates the goal and rationale of the lesson. During the body of the lesson, the teacher **models** or demonstrates the new skill or strategy being careful to proceed step-by-step, to describe what he is doing, and to share the thinking that would occur as the strategy was performed. Next, the teacher **prompts** or guides students in performing the skill or strategy, and finally **checks** students' understanding by having them perform the skill or strategy independently. In the close of the lesson, the teacher reviews the content of today's lesson, previews the next lesson, and assigns independent work, either seatwork or homework, to provide additional practice.

While carefully structuring lessons is critical, the delivery or presentation of the lesson is equally important especially when teaching students with academic and behavioral challenges. The teacher must actively engage the students in the lesson by having them say, write, and do things. A variety of active participation strategies can be utilized to ensure that all students are participating. Students could: say answers as an entire group when the answer is short and the wording of the answer would be the same across students; say answers to their assigned partners; say answers as individuals after sharing answers with their partners; write down answers; put their finger or pencil on the desired stimuli; or indicate the answer using student hand signals. Across all

of these response procedures, adequate thinking time must be given so that answers will be accurate and complete. In addition to maximizing student active participation and adequate thinking time, the teacher must: 1) maintain a brisk instructional pace by moving quickly to new activities, questions or responses; 2) ensure high levels of student accuracy by carefully modeling skills and strategies, breaking content into small steps, and carefully selecting initial examples; 3) monitoring responses and providing feedback on correct and incorrect responses; and 4) maintaining the attention of students.

Chapter 8 extends this discussion of effective teaching practices. It presents considerations for selecting and organizing independent work whether seatwork or homework. In addition, approaches for modifying both aspects of instruction, teacher-directed instruction and independent work, so that individual students are more successful are introduced. The importance of systematic review of content and of maintaining student progress records is underscored.

CONTENT MASTERY QUESTIONS

1. Define allocated time and describe a number of procedures that increase allocated instructional time.

2. Define student task engagement and describe teacher practices that can be used to promote on-task behavior.

3. How can a teacher analyze her time-management practices? Describe the self-evaluation process.

4. Describe the self-analysis of student engaged time within the classroom.

5. Outline guidelines for selecting content for instruction.

6. List the three components of a lesson.

7. Discuss what you would include in the opening of a lesson.

8. Describe the three components of the body of a lesson; model, prompt, and check.

9. Describe three ways to end a lesson.

10. Design a lesson to teach one of the following skills: telling time to five minutes, determining the meaning of a pronoun within context, or changing a fraction to an equivalent fraction.

11. Describe procedures that teachers can use to gain frequent responses from all students within an instructional lesson.

12. Tell the importance of maintaining a brisk instructional pace.

13. Describe procedures that a teacher could use following: 1) an immediate, correct response, 2) a hesitant, correct response, 3) an incorrect response due to carelessness, and 4) an incorrect response due to lack of knowledge.

14. Outline a number of procedures that teachers could use to increase the attentiveness of students during the teacher-directed lesson.

REFERENCES

Anderson, L. M., Evertson, C. M., & Brophy, J. E. (1982). *Principles of small group instruction in elementary reading.* East Lansing, MI. Institute for Research on Teaching, Michigan State University.

Anderson, L. M. (1984). The environment of instruction: The function of seatwork in a commercially developed curriculum. In G. G. Duffy, L. R. Roehler, & J. Mason (Eds.), *Comprehension Instruction: Perspectives and Suggestions* (pp. 93–103). New York: Longman.

Anderson, L. W. (1985). Time and learning. In C. W. Fisher & D. C. Berliner (Eds.), *Perspectives on instructional time* (pp.157–185). New York: Longman.

Archer, A., Isaacson, S., Adams, A., Ellis, E., Morehead, J. K., & Schiller, E. P. (1989). *Academy for effective instruction: Working with mildly handicapped students.* Reston, VA: The Council for Exceptional Children.

Arlin, M. (1979). Teacher transitions can disrupt time flow in classrooms. *American Educational Journal, 16,* 42–56.

Block, J. H. (1980). Success rate. In C. Denham & A. Lieberman (Eds.), *Time to learn* (pp. 95–106). Washington, DC: National Institute of Education.

Blumenfeld, P. C., & Meece, J. L. (1988). Task factors, teacher behavior, and students' involvement and use of learning strategies in science. *Elementary School Journal, 88,* 235–250.

Borg, W. R. (1980). Time and school learning. In C. Denham & A. Lieberman (Eds.), *Time to Learn* (pp. 27–72). Washington, DC: National Institute of Education.

Bransford, J. D., Stein, B. S., Nye, M. J., Franks, J. F., Auble, P. M., Mezynski, K. J., & Perfetto, G. A. (1982). Differences in approach to learning: An overview. *Journal of Experimental Psychology: General, 3,* 390–398.

Brophy, J. E. (1982). How teachers influence what is taught and learned in classrooms. *Elementary School Journal, 83,* 1–13.

Brophy, J., & Good, T. L. (1986). Teacher behavior and student achievement. In M. C. Wittrock (Ed.), *Handbook of research on teaching* (3rd., pp. 328–374). New York: Macmillan.

Browder, D. M., Shoen, S. F., & Lentz, F. E. (1986–1987). Learning to learn through observation. *Journal of Special Education, 20,* 447–459.

Carnine, D. W. (1981). High and low implementation of direct instruction teaching techniques. *Education and Treatment of Children, 4,* 43–51.

Carnine, D., Silbert, J., & Kameenui, E. J. (1990) *Direct instruction reading.* Columbus, OH: Merrill Publishing Co.

Coker, H., Lorentz, C. W., & Coker, J. (1980). *Teacher behavior and student outcomes in the Georgia study.* Paper presented to the American Educational Research Association Annual Meeting. Boston.

Duffy, G. G., Roehler, L. R., & Herrmann, B. A. (1988). Modeling mental processes helps poor readers become strategic readers. *The Reading Teacher, 41,* 762–767.

Durkin, D. (1978–79). What classroom observations reveal about comprehension instruction. *Reading Research Quarterly, 14,* 481–533.

Emmer, E. T., Evertson, C., Sanford, J., Clements, B., & Worsham, M. (1982). *Organizing and managing the junior high classroom.* Austin, TX: Research and Development Center for Teacher Education, University of Texas.

Emmer, E. T., Evertson, C. M., Sanford, J. P., Clements, B. S., & Worsham, M. E. (1984). *Class-*

room management for secondary teachers. Englewood Cliffs, NJ: Prentice-Hall.

Engelmann, S. (1982). Dear Ziggy. *Direct Instruction News, 1,* (3), 9.

Englert, C. S. (1983). Measuring special education teacher effectiveness, *Exceptional Children, 50,* 247–254.

Englert, C. S. (1984). Examining effective direct instruction practices in special education settings. *Remedial and Special Education, 5,* 38–47.

Englert, C. S., & Thomas, C. C. (1982). Management of task involvement in special education *Teacher Education and Special Education, 5,* 3–10.

Evertson, C., Anderson, C., Anderson, I., & Brophy, J. (1980). Relationships between classroom behaviors and student outcomes in junior high mathematics and English classes. *American Educational Research Journal, 17,* 43–60.

Fisher, C. W., Berliner, D. C., Filby, N. N., Marliave, R., Cahen, L. S., & Dishaw, M. M. (1980). Teaching behaviors, academic learning time, and student achievement: An overview. In C. Denham & A. Lieberman (Eds.). *Time to learn* (pp. 7–32.) Washington, DC: National Institute of Education.

Gall, M. (1984). Synthesis of research on teachers' questioning. *Educational Leadership, 42*(3), 40–47.

Gaskins, R. W. (1988). The missing ingredients: Time on task, direct instruction, and writing. *The Reading Teachers, 41,* 740–755.

Good, T. L. (1983). Classroom research: A decade of progress. *Educational Psychologist, 18,* 127–144.

Greenwood, C. R., Delquadri, J., & Hall. R. V. (1984). Opportunity to respond and student academic performance. In W. Heward et al. (eds.), *Focus on behavior analysis in education.* Columbus, OH: Charles E. Merrill.

Greenwood, C. R., Delquadri, J., Stanley, S., Sasso, G., Whorton, D., & Schulte, D. (1981). Allocating opportunities to respond as a basis for academic remediation: A developing model for teaching. In R. B. Rutherford, A. g. Prieto, & J. E. McGlothlin (Eds.), *Severe behavior disorders of children and youth, monograph in behavior disorders* (pp. 22–33.) Reston, VA: Council for Children with Behavioral Disorders.

Hall, R. V., Delquadri, J., Greenwood, C. R., & Thurston, L. (1982). The importance of opportunity to respond in children's academic success. In E. B. Edgar, N. G. Haring, J. R. Jenkins, & C. G. Pious

(Eds.), *Mentally handicapped children: Education and training* (pp. 107–140).

Hunter, M., & Russell, D. (1981). Planning for effective instruction: Lesson design. In *Increasing your teaching effectiveness.* Palo Alto, CA: The Learning Institute.

Idol, L. (1987). Group story mapping: A comprehension strategy for both skilled and unskilled readers. *Journal of Learning Disabilities, 20,* 196–205.

Kounin, J. (1970). *Discipline and group management in classrooms.* New York: Holt, Rinehart & Winston.

Kounin, J. S., & Doyle, P. H. (1975). Degree of continuity of a lesson's signal system and the task involvement of children. *Journal of Educational Psychology, 67,* 159–164.

Leinhardt, G., Zigmond, N., & Cooley, W. W. (1981). Reading instruction and its effects. *American Educational Research Journal, 18,* 343–361.

McKenzie, G. (1979). Effects of questions and testlike events on achievement and on-task behavior in a classroom concept learning presentation. *Journal of Educational Research, 72,* 348–350.

Paine, S. G., Radicchi, J., Rosellini, L. C., Deutchman, L., & Darch, C. B. (1983). *Structuring your classroom for academic success.* Champaign, IL: Research Press Co.

Polloway, E. A., Cronin, M. E., & Patton, J. R. (1986). The efficacy of group versus one-to-one instruction: A review. *Remedial and Special Education, 7,* 22–30.

Rivera, D., & Smith, D. D. (1988). Using a demonstration strategy to teach midschool students with learning disabilities how to compute long division. *Journal of Learning Disabilities, 21,* 77–81.

Roehler, L. R., & Duffy, G. G. (1984). Direct explanation of comprehension processes. In G. G. Duffy, L. R. Roehler, & J. Mason (Eds.), *Comprehension instruction: Perspectives and suggestions,* pp. 265–280. New York: Longman.

Rosenshine, B. (1980). How time is spent in elementary classrooms. In C. Denham & A. Lieberman (Eds.), *Time to learn* (pp. 107–126). Washington, DC: National Institute of Education.

Rosenshine, B. (1983). Teaching functions in instructional programs. *Elementary School Journal, 83,* 335–352.

Rosenshine, B., & Stevens, R. (1986). Teaching functions. In M. C. Wittrock (Ed.), *Handbook of re-*

search on teaching (3rd Edition, pp. 376–391). New York: Macmillan.

Sindelar, P. T., Bursuch, W. D., & Halle, J. W. (1986). The effects of two variations of teacher questioning on student performance. *Education and Treatment of Children* 9(1), 56–66.

Sindelar, P., Wilson, R., & Gartland, D. (1984). The effects of lesson format on the acquisition of mathematical concepts by fourth graders. *Journal of Educational Research, 78,* 40–44.

Soar, R. S. (1973). *Follow through classroom process measurement and pupil growth* (1970–1971). Gainesville: University of Florida, Institute for the Development of Human Resources (ERIC Document Reproduction Service No. ED 106 297)

Stallings, J. (1980). Allocated academic learning time revisited, or beyond time on task. *Educational Researcher, 9*(10), 11–16.

Stallings, J., & Kaskowitz, D. (1974). *Follow through classroom observation evaluation,* 1972–73. Menlo Park, CA: Stanford Research Institutes.

Stevens, R., & Rosenshine, B. (1981). Advances in research on teaching. *Exceptional Education Quarterly, 2,* 1–9.

Thurlow, M. L., Ysseldyke, J. E., Graden, J., & Algozzine, B. (1983). Instructional ecology for students in resource and regular classrooms. *Teacher Education and Special Education, 6,* 248–254.

West, R. P., & Sloane, H. N. (1986). Teacher presentation rate and point delivery rate: Effects of classroom disruption, performance accuracy, and response rate. *Behavior Modification, 10*(3), 267–286.

Wilson, R., & Wesson, C. (1986). Making every minute count: Academic learning time in LD classrooms. *Learning Disabilities Focus, 2,* 13–19.

Wong, B. Y.L. (1980). Activating the inactive learner: Use of question/prompts to enhance comprehension and retention of implied information in disabled children. *Learning Disability Quarterly, 3,* 29–37.

CHAPTER 8

Meeting Individual Instructional Needs

ANITA L. ARCHER
MARY M. GLEASON
CAROL SUE ENGLERT
STEPHEN ISAACSON

CHAPTER OBJECTIVES

At the conclusion of this chapter, the reader will be able to:

1. Discuss and describe the factors involved in the effective selection and coverage of content.
2. Discuss and describe possible modifications of effective instructional practices for students with learning difficulties.
3. Discuss and describe cooperative learning, peer tutoring, and computer-assisted instruction in terms of development, implementation, effectiveness, and considerations.
4. Discuss and implement the procedure for selecting an appropriate instructional modification.
5. Discuss and describe the guidelines for selecting appropriate seatwork and the process for preparing seatwork so that it is meaningful for students with learning difficulties.
6. Discuss and describe effective instructional strategies to increase task engagement during seatwork.
7. Discuss and describe the importance of systematic content review and of maintaining continuous records of student academic progress.

INDIVIDUALIZING INSTRUCTION

Effective instruction requires thoughtful advance planning, systematically designing and delivering lessons, and implementing a variety of instructional practices that maximize instructional time and student learning. This chapter builds on the procedures developed in the preceding chapters. One approach to maximizing individual achievement is through increased content coverage. Another is to implement instructional modifications designed to meet the specific needs of individual students. A final consideration is to increase instructional efficiency through effectively managing independent seatwork. Each of these considerations is delineated in this chapter.

A brisk pace of instruction increases the amount of content covered. In any given day, week, semester, or school year, effective teachers teach more in less time by maintaining a brisk pace and by moving students through the curriculum rapidly. One way of accomplishing this is to probe student learning through a series of rapid questions. After one question is presented and a student responds correctly, effective teachers quickly present the next question, minimizing the time delay between the student responses and the subsequent question. As a result, they not only move more briskly through the lesson, but they maintain high levels of student attention to task while increasing the number of correct responses that students produce.

Examining the actual instructional practices of two teachers illustrates the importance of teacher pacing and content coverage. John and Peggy, who teach in fifth- and sixth-grade upper elementary classrooms, are actively involved in teaching students a similar lesson on using the narrative story structure. However, significant differences are evident in their pacing and their provision of practice opportunities. This is illustrated in the following description:

John stands in the middle of the classroom and starts his lesson with a review of the previous lesson. He reviews and reteaches what happened the day before, testing and monitoring student recall as he does so. He begins by asking students to state the type of questions the story structure answered. When students hesitate, he has them look at a handout that he distributed in the last class. He allows them one minute of study, and then, directing them to cover up the handout, he begins to orally test their recall of the story questions. He tells students in advance that each may tell him only one answer, therefore enabling a greater number of students to respond. As students respond, John checks their answers against the form to monitor their performance.

John promotes active responding by a system of taking class votes. For example, he asks students if they agree that the story structure can help them know what questions to answer in their reading and writing. He then displays a story part on the overhead projector, pauses a moment, and asks them to vote on which element of the story structure it is: the story setting, problem, response, or outcome. He directs students to give a "thumbs up" if they agree or a "thumbs down" if they disagree. Throughout the presentation, he intersperses discussion of text structure with frequent questions. In the process, he maintains a brisk pace while involving students as active participants in the learning process. At least eight students make individual responses, while the whole class responds at least six times during the lesson.

John develops students' conceptual understanding of the lesson by telling them when they can use the procedure (e.g., to help them comprehend social studies passages). He reminds them that the social studies selection they just completed presented the three elements of story structure: a problem, a historical figure's response, and the outcome of the response. He promotes generalization by pointing out that knowledge of story structure can enhance their memory of stories, can improve their ability to compose stories, and can be applied in reading a variety of content area texts when they find a section of the text that presents a problem and a response.

He closes instruction by having students summarize the lesson and rehearse the story structure questions. This provides one last review of the main ideas of the lesson and helps the students to internalize the story structure questions.

Peggy has a different instructional style. While presenting essentially the same content, she sits behind her desk and does not circulate among the students. She provides a handout of the story structure questions and immediately begins to lecture on the new content. Her lecture presentation means that the students are passive recipients of the information that she presents. Her presentation style is slow and she interrupts herself several times to deal with individual behavior problems and to remind students of unrelated assignments and school events.

Her content questions are similar to those of John's, such as "What questions does the story structure answer?" However, Peggy permits her students to read the text structure questions right off the handout. They are not required to internalize or memorize the questions. Furthermore, since a single student reads off an entire set of questions, only one student (rather than entire class) identifies the story structure elements, and there are fewer response opportunities. In her entire lesson, only six students get an opportunity to respond orally, while the remaining eighteen students sit passively.

Peggy presents no examples of text from which students can practice identifying text structure. She makes no reference to occasions when the strategy can be used, nor does she tell students how it can help them. Her overall style is slow paced and laid back. At the lesson's conclusion, Peggy provides no summary of the lesson. Nor does she remind students to use the strategy. In fact, the end-of-period bell signals the end of instruction, with Peggy rushing to hand out a dittoed assignment sheet that she has not previously presented or reviewed with the students.

The two teachers differed considerably in both their presentation styles and in the ways in which they structured the lesson. John maintained higher levels of active task engagement on the part of students by providing four times as many practice opportunities as did Peggy. He also provided more carefully structured lesson phases. He began with a review of text structure questions, he had students practice applying the information to recognize elements of the story structure in passages, and he concluded the lesson with a final practice and review of the key concepts. The lesson phases are less distinct in Peggy's lesson. She did not communicate the lesson objective to students, she did not provide either a review of prior learning or active practice on the key concepts, she did not maintain a brisk pace, and she failed to summarize the key points at the close of the lesson. Overall, her instruction was both less efficient and less effective than John's, meaning that the instructional time was not used well.

MODIFYING INSTRUCTIONAL PRESENTATION

Attributes of effective instruction already discussed in this chapter and Chapter 6 include allocating lots of time for teacher-directed instruction, adhering to the lesson schedule, teaching small groups of students, providing well-designed and structured lessons, eliciting frequent responses, maintaining a brisk instructional pace, maintaining student attention and task engagement, ensuring high response accuracy, maintaining lesson smoothness, and monitoring responses and providing feedback. This chapter describes considerations for modifying these instructional procedures in ways that are responsive to students with learning difficulties.

Feedback Following Question Presentation

During the guided practice and review stages of lesson presentation, students are asked to make frequent responses. Teachers must then provide feedback to those responses. Rosenshine and Stevens (1986) have described the types of teacher responses appropriate in various situations.

First, when students quickly respond with correct answers, teachers should simply ask a new question in order to preserve the momentum of the lesson. This is important when teachers are trying to promote greater automaticity and flu-

ency. Second, when students are correct, but hesitant, teachers should provide statements of affirmative feedback (e.g., "correct" or "good"). Finally, when students are incorrect due to lack of knowledge, teachers should provide prompts or hints that lead students to the correct answer. This is preferable to telling the student the correct answer or calling on another student. Errors provide teachers with "teachable moments" when they can teach students additional problem-solving information or strategies. Attempts to prompt students should be relatively brief. If it takes an inordinately long time to guide students to the correct answer, or if students make frequent errors, another demonstration of the skill may be needed. Teachers can reteach the material to the entire class, to the instructional group, or during independent seatwork or peer tutoring sessions to specific individuals within the group.

Small Group Follow-Up Instruction

When the majority of the students demonstrated mastery during lesson presentation, but a few still are not performing the criterion, the teacher needs to move on with instruction in order to maintain the attention of the higher-performing students. This does not mean that the teacher accepts that some students will not master some skills or content. Instead, teachers must devise safety nets to ensure the success of all students. One viable option is to work with students still experiencing difficulty in a separate small group while the remaining students work independently or with a cooperative partner or team. An open invitation ("Please join me at the table if you are going to have any difficulty on these items.") coupled with private invitations extended at break ("Jason I know that you can learn this math. All you need is a little extra explanation. Tomorrow, when I invite students to a small group, I want you to be at the table.") can ensure that the students needing assistance receive it.

At the same time, the actual small group work must be rewarding so that students will continue to participate. First, it is best to do *exactly* the same work that students at their desks are doing. In this manner, students will be finishing their independent work and will be completing it accurately, both of which are reinforcing. During the small group instruction, the teacher might wish to model the skill again, but more frequently the emphasis will be on providing increased amounts of prompting. Once students demonstrate proficiency, they should be dismissed from the group to complete the work independently. A paraprofessional can provide this type of small group follow-up instruction while the teacher works with a different group or monitors seatwork. In these instances, it is important that the paraprofessional has carefully observed the initial lesson, and is prepared to employ similar instructional language and strategies.

Cooperative Learning

Cooperative learning is another way to support low-performing students as they complete independent work (Johnson & Johnson, 1987). Cooperative learning, when students work on carefully designed tasks with a single partner or a number of students on a team, takes advantage of the natural desire of students, particularly secondary students, to interact with their peers and has the potential of enhancing academic as well as nonacademic, social and communication skills.

Cooperative learning will be more powerful if it is an *adjunct to teacher-directed instruction* rather than a substitute for teacher-directed instruction. When direct instruction precedes the cooperative learning activity, students have a body of common knowledge and a common instructional language that promotes participation of all students. For example, if a two-student cooperative team is working on a math assignment and the lower-achieving student has difficulty, the higher performing student can explain the operation using language similar to that which the teacher used. With social studies projects, prior directed instruction means that all students, including those with achievement problems, bring a common knowledge base to the interaction.

The teacher must determine which types of learning goals are best facilitated by what type of structural arrangement such as small groups, learning pairs, and/or individual assignments. A combination of both individual and peer-assisted groupings can be the best choice. In general, **peer-assisted instruction** can be accomplished through small groups of students working together, pairs of students working together, or some combination of these two types of groupings.

Many cooperative learning structures involve teams of four or five students. For example, students might be assigned to heterogeneous groups to collectively complete a single worksheet or lesson. Students who have difficulty in completing assignments are matched with students who do not have difficulty completing assignments. The relative content knowledge of the students, their interests, and interpersonal compatibility are additional considerations in structuring the groups. Groups may need to stay together for some time in order for the members to build productive working relationships. However, if competition between groups is included as part of the activity structure, it may become important to change the composition of groups so that one group does not always win.

Within the group, students may be instructed to assist each other until all students have learned the material. The "Jigsaw" structure (Aronson, Blaney, Stephan, Sikes, & Snapp, 1978) breaks the academic material into segments and each segment is assigned to one group member. All the students are assigned the same segment study and discuss the material together. They return to their original teams and teach the material to the other team members. In all of these examples, roles are carefully delineated, ensuring that all members of the class are actively participating in the activity.

The quality of implementation is key to the success of cooperative learning activities. For example, if the teacher simply said, "Complete this math worksheet with your partner," it is probable that the higher-performing student in the partnership would complete the work with the lower-performing student learning little. Instead, the activities must be carefully structured so that each student has a specific role. If students were working with partners to complete a math assignment, the following structure might be delineated:

1. Both partners solve the first problem.
2. Partners check their answers with an answer key.
3. If either partner makes an error, the other partner demonstrates and explains how to complete the problem.
4. If both partners miss the problem, they consult with the teacher.

In the same manner, the following roles might be assigned for joint reading of a science or social studies textbook:

1. The first partner reads a paragraph as the second partner follows along.
2. Both partners cover the paragraph.
3. The second partner recites the topic of the paragraph and at least two important details.
4. The first partner adds to or corrects the recitation.
5. Both partners lift their hands and check the paragraph.
6. The roles are reversed on the next paragraph.

To be successful, the teacher must carefully plan the cooperative learning activities. To ensure success, teachers need to develop detailed procedures and materials that carefully delineate using space, time, materials, and student pairings or groupings. It is useful if routines for working with a cooperative team or partner are established and utilized over time. Valuable instructional time is always lost when the teacher must explain classroom procedures. However, if the teacher introduces a cooperative routine and is subsequently able to give a simple directive (e.g., "Do Exercise C on page 77. Use our partner math routine." "Open your book to page 273. Find the heading 'sedimentary rock.' Read this section with your partner. Don't forget to read, cover, recite, and check."), class time can be dedicated to teacher-directed instruction or the cooperative activity. Table 8.1 presents considerations for planning

and structuring cooperative learning activities, which are explained in the following paragraphs.

Certain prerequisite skills appear to be necessary in order for a student to respond appropriately within a cooperative goal structure. Students must be aware that they are members of a group and that each member has a role in the group. They must be able to identify and respond to the actions and performances of the other members. Skills such as active listening, working collaboratively, managing conflicts, and acknowledging the efforts and contributions of others are important. Students must know how to accept criticism, interrupt appropriately, ask questions, answer questions, ask for help, and negotiate, to name a few. These skills may not be in the repertoires of some students, including students with disabilities as well as others. When this is the case, specific social skill instruction should be provided.

Another type of prerequisite skill relates to the level of content knowledge that students possess. To a certain degree, more knowledgeable peers can address and compensate for insufficient knowledge and skills of other members of the group. Peers may not easily address wide gaps in knowledge or skills, and the teacher should deal with these gaps. The teacher, not the peers, is responsible for presenting necessary background information as well as all content that is new. If the teacher thinks that the students may not have the knowledge to successfully complete the task in an efficient manner, then additional content instruction should be provided prior to giving peer group assignments.

If care is not taken, cooperative learning groups can deteriorate into socialization times with emergent behavioral problems. As in all classroom activities, the teacher must vigilantly monitor the cooperative teams. The level of on-task behavior and the quality of the academic interaction increase with monitoring. Individual as well as group accountability is necessary to promote cooperation and academic growth. All members of the cooperative group should be held accountable for a definite outcome such as com-

TABLE 8.1   Steps for Implementing Cooperative Learning Groups

Step	Description
1. **Determine appropriateness of using a cooperative learning structure.**	Decide whether goals can best be reached by students working individually, in pairs, or in small groups.
2. **Assess prerequisite skills.**	Determine whether or not the students have the necessary social skills and content knowledge background to work in cooperative groups.
3. **Provide an advance organizer.**	Review the goals and purposes of the peer-assisted structure and state expectations for performance. Emphasize the need for cooperation, adherence to procedures, and attainment of specific learning goals.
4. **Explain the peer-assisted structure and procedures.**	Organize the peer-assisted groupings, and present the procedures and materials that developed to facilitate the peer-assisted process.
5. **Model appropriate peer-assisted interaction and provide guided practice.**	Demonstrate how the assignment should be initiated as a cooperative effort, guiding the students through the first part of the assignment. Allow students who understand the assignment and completion process to re-explain the process to those students who do not understand.
6. **Monitor peer-assistance and provide appropriate feedback.**	Circulating group to group, monitor progress toward completing the assignment and following the peer-assisted assignment completion procedures. Intervene briefly where necessary, making notes of observed difficulties as the basis for providing more detailed feedback later and to use in future instructional planning.
7. **Provide a postorganizer.**	At the end of the cooperative learning time, quickly review the purpose of the task. Survey students on what they learned about both the content and the peer-assisted process. Provide general feedback to students on behaviors that were observed during assignment completion and identify the general areas that students need to improve. If this type of activity will be used again, write these areas of needed improvement on the chalkboard as a reminder.
8. **Evaluate learning and the peer-assistance process.**	After the class is over, review the evaluation data and permanent products, such as written assignments, diagrams, drawings, and audiotape recordings. Evaluate content learning and peer-assisted participation for both the group and for the individual.
9. **Inform students of performance and set goals for improved performance.**	Meet with each group and provide feedback on overall group performance on both content learning and group processes. Work with the group as well as individual members to develop goals for improving performance. Depending on the nature of the task and the skills of the group, the individual goals and plans may or may not be included as part of a group activity.
10. **Continue to implement, evaluate, and inform.**	The teacher should continue to provide evaluative feedback to students. As the peer-assisted assignment completion process becomes routinized, students will become more skillful in participating in cooperative learning groups and less teacher direction will be required.

pleting the math assignment, writing a paragraph, mapping the story content, reading the science or social studies textbook, or learning social studies information. Generally, a single grade for the task is given to all group members. However, if this were the only accountability, some students might not participate at the desired level, relying on their classmates to carry the burden. As a result, students must be held accountable for their individual performance as well. For example, a social studies test might be given to determine individual student knowledge, or students might independently complete the second half of a math assignment.

Peer Tutoring

Peer tutoring arrangements are one form of cooperative learning that can increase students' task engagement and enhance the number of active responses students make during seatwork time. It is one of the most powerful and inexpensive interventions for students with achievement difficulties. It can promote the academic achievement and the interpersonal/social skills of both tutors and tutees (Jenkins & Jenkins, 1985, 1987). It has been reported that peer tutors increased spelling practice from one practice per week for six of eighteen words to ten practices per week for all eighteen words. Classwide peer tutoring with mainstreamed students with mild learning problems has been shown to increase tutee performance by significantly improving on both math quizzes and social studies tests. Successful tutoring programs depend on teachers planning, carefully preparing and training tutors, and a data management system for monitoring student progress (Jenkins and Jenkins, 1985). Teachers must plan procedures for the following components:

1. Assigning students to tutoring pairs or teams (e.g., randomly or by ability levels)
2. Instructional procedures (e.g., tutor dictates word and question and tutee must "say or write" the response)

3. Error correction procedure (e.g., tutee writes correct answer three times)
4. Assigning points for correct responses and error corrections (e.g., 2 points for correct responses and 1 point for corrected answers)
5. Assigning points for appropriate tutoring behaviors (e.g., clear and succinct presentations, use of error correction procedures, and appropriate use of points)
6. Data management system (e.g., weekly tests and total team points posted and announced).

The tutors should be selected from those students who complete classroom work without prompting, take initiative in solving problems, have higher academic skills than the tutee, and maintain commitments. The tutors should also be empathetic, cooperative students who can provide positive role models to the tutees. Before beginning work with the tutees, the tutors should receive training in the teaching formats, the error correction procedures, and on data collection. Both the tutors and the tutees should receive training on critical interpersonal skills such as active listening, ignoring distractions, giving compliments, receiving compliments, being supportive, and maintaining confidentiality.

Once a tutoring program is under way, the teacher's active supervision is critical. The teacher should monitor the tutoring sessions, provide encouragement and feedback to both the tutors and tutees, provide technical assistance to the tutors as needed, and ensure that the time is used productively. In addition, the teacher supervisor will need to communicate progress to the parents and other classroom teachers, and make adjustments in the program as needed.

There are three reasons why peer tutoring programs work. First, peer tutoring increases the total number of responses students make in a practice session, resulting in greater student rehearsal. Second, as students work with peers, they make active or overt responses rather than passive responses. Active responding, combined with immediate feedback for correct and incorrect responses, results in greater academic achievement. Third, peer-tutoring programs are beneficial because they require active rehearsal of the criterion academic behavior. For example, peer-tutoring programs in spelling require that students spell words to dictation, the a condition that matches the test conditions and test criterion exactly. In contrast, spelling workbooks often require students to simply copy words from spelling lists in sentences and puzzles. Copying tasks do not match the test condition (e.g., dictation) and

the test criteria (e.g., memory). Thus, practice tasks must be scrutinized to determine whether they match the *critical* goal. When there is a poor match, teachers need to redesign the seat-work tasks to provide practice that matches the criterion and that provides more active forms of practice.

Cross-age tutors can successfully use tutoring formats such as those depicted in Table 8.2. They are adaptable to most classroom curricula,

TABLE 8.2   Example Formats for Peer Tutoring in Reading

Passage Words Format

Tutor materials	For each story, there are two groups of words: (1) necessary words and (2) challenge words. The groups have been divided into lists of ten words each.
Tutor format	This activity will take 5 minutes each day. The teacher will indicate when students should begin and end the activity.
Necessary words	1. (Point to the first word.) **This word is _____ . Say it with me. _____ What word?** 2. (Repeat for each word in the list.) 3. (Go back to the top of the list.) **Now read the words again.** 4. (Have the tutee read the list until he reads the words quickly and accurately.) 5. (Repeat these procedures with all of the lists of necessary words.)
Correction of errors	1. (Point to the word.) **This word is _____ . What word?**

If the tutee can read the necessary words quickly and accurately, use the same format to practice the challenge words.

Passage Reading Format

Tutor materials	Passage in the student's reading book.
Tutor format	Twenty minutes will be spent on this activity. The teacher will indicate the beginning and ending of the reading session. 1. (Point to the title of the story.) **Read the title of the story.** 2. **Now, read the story to me.** 3. (Follow along carefully as the tutee reads.)
Correction of errors	If the tutee makes an error, point to the word and say: **This word is _____ .** **What word?** **Read the sentence again.** If you finish reading the story before the end of the time period, read the story again.

allow for preteaching content, and can be utilized during each tutoring session.

Utilizing Computers

Computer software programs are another means for individualizing instruction for students with learning problems. The primary use of micro-computers for both special education and general education teachers is to provide practice on skills already developed through teacher-directed instruction (Semmel & Lieber, 1986). Special education teachers use microcomputers more frequently for remedial purposes than do general education teachers. Microcomputers also are used in classrooms for recreational purposes, for teaching new skills, and as word processing tools. Teachers use microcomputer software to develop or modify instructional programs for students as well as to develop or "author" their own. Software programs also are available to assist in grading, to score standardized tests, to prepare Individual Education Programs (IEPs), and to maintain records of student progress and manage classroom records.

The availability of software has mushroomed in recent years to the point that there are literally thousands of programs with potential educational applications. The quality of the software varies greatly, and care must be taken to select software that is appropriate to the learning task as well as to the characteristics of the learners. Care should be taken to select software that is well designed and that can accomplish the purposes for which it is used. The software evaluation worksheet presented in Figure 8.1 provides a useful guide for evaluating software.

Typical software programs for students with learning problems tend to be of either the drill-and-practice or the tutorial variety. Instructional game programs can provide additional, highly motivating practice or serve as recreation or reinforcement. Software programs also have been developed to provide simulations of real-life or imaginary situations; these can be used to teach problem solving, decision making, and critical thinking skills

The majority of the current software programs are **drill-and-practice programs,** designed as a follow-up of teacher-directed instruction. They can be used to build fluency or automaticity of lower-order skills such as math facts, word decoding, or sight word recognition (Semmel & Lieber, 1986; Torgesen & Young, 1983). Drill-and-practice programs can provide effective practice for increasing the skills of students, particularly low-performing students (Kulik, Kulik, & Bangert-Drowns, 1985; Roth & Beck, 1984). Their primary purpose is to build high rates of correct responding to already learned material (Semmel & Lieber, 1986), not to develop new skills and concepts. The most appropriate time to use drill-and-practice programs is after basic concepts or behaviors related to the skill have been taught, when students have demonstrated reasonably high accuracy rates, and before applying those skills to higher levels of the curriculum hierarchy (Hofmeister, 1984). Teachers have difficulty scheduling sufficient time to provide the amount of organized practice needed to develop rapid response rates, overlearning, and automaticity. Microcomputer software can provide this level of practice. Because high accuracy is needed, students with learning difficulties may need greater amounts of teacher-directed instruction prior to using a microcomputer for practice opportunities (Woodward, Carnine, Gersten, Gleason, Johnson, & Collins, 1986).

When selecting drill-and-practice programs, several considerations are germane. The directions for the student should be clear and concise and the program should provide completed examples to assist the student. The practice tasks should require the student to perform the desired outcome behaviors and not require other skills (e.g., keyboarding skills and reading skills) beyond the student's abilities. In addition, the software program should utilize good correction procedures. If the program simply reports that an error has occurred, tells the correct answer, and moves on, little learning will occur. Instead, the

Directions: Complete this worksheet as you review the instructional program and its documentation. Fill in the identifying information, complete the description of the program, and then evaluate its usefulness for your special population.

A. Identifying Information

Name of Instructional Program: _____

Publisher: _____ Cost: _____

Back-up Copy Provided? _____ Available? _____ Cost: _____

Computer: _____ Other Equipment: _____

Your Special Population: _____

Ages of Your Population: _____

Grade or Skill Levels of Your Population: _____

B. Descriptive Information

1. What is the purpose of the instructional program, as stated by its publisher?

2. What curriculum area or areas does it address?

3. What type of instructional program is it? _____ Tutorial

   _____ Simulation _____ Drill and practice _____ Arcade-type drill

   _____ Problem solving _____ Educational game _____ Teacher Utility

   _____ Other (specify) _____

4. For what type of learner was the program designed?

   Age Level _____ Grade Level: _____

   Ability Level _____

   Interest Level _____

5. Are the objectives of the program stated? _____ Yes _____ No

   If they are stated, what skills or information does the program attempt to teach or review? (State briefly)

6. How does the program present information? (Check all that apply)

   _____ Text _____ Graphics _____ Animation _____ Color

   _____ Music _____ Sound effects _____ Speech

7. Is the information presented clearly? Is text legible and readable? Are graphics comprehensible? Are sounds audible and intelligible?

   _____ Yes _____ No If no, explain:

8. Are directions for using the program clearly stated and understandable?

   _____ Yes _____ No

   Do directions appear: _____ Within the program _____ In the program's documentation or manual

9. Is the program under user control? That is, can the user control the program's movement from screen to screen? Review directions at any time? Exit the program at any time?

   _____ Yes _____ No If no, explain:

10. What **computer use demands** are placed on the learner?

    _____ Insert disk and turn on the computer _____ Select from menu

    _____ Other (specify: _____)

(continued)

FIGURE 8.1   **continued**

11. What **academic demands** are placed on the learner?

_____ Reading (level: _____) _____ Spelling (level: _____)

_____ Other (specify _____ level: _____)

_____ Other (specify _____ level: _____)

12. What **physical demands** are placed on the learner?

_____ Keyboard must be used to enter responses

     _____ Press any key

     _____ Press a key from one-half or one-quadrant of keyboard

     _____ Press one specific key

     _____ Press several keys in order

_____ Other device(s) used to enter responses (specify: _____

_____)

13. What **speed demands** are placed on the learner?

_____ Presentation of information controlled by program

     (_____ Moderate _____ Fast _____ Slow)

_____ Presentation of information is under user control

_____ Unlimited response time

_____ Response time set by program

     (_____ Moderate _____ Fast _____ Slow)

_____ Response time can be varied by user

14. What **accuracy demands** are placed on the learner?

_____ User can correct typing errors

_____ Program does not allow correction of typing errors

_____ Program traps common errors

_____ Program requires correct spelling of all responses

_____ Program allows only one correct response for most questions

15. Is feedback about response accuracy provided to learners appropriately?

a. Knowledge of results provided after each response? _____ Yes _____ No

b. Correct responses confirmed? _____ Yes _____ No

c. Learner informed if response incorrect? _____ Yes _____ No

d. Another trial provided if response incorrect? _____ Yes _____ No

e. No. of trials provided: _____

f. Correct response demonstrated if learner fails to answer correctly? _____ Yes _____ No

g. Learner allowed opportunity to respond after demonstration of correct response?
   _____ Yes _____ No

16. Does the program use any branching procedures besides differential treatment of correct and incorrect responses? _____ Yes _____ No   If yes, explain:

17. What techniques are used for reinforcement and motivation? (Check all that apply)

_____ Knowledge of results and confirmation of correct responses

_____ Summary information about learner performance

_____ Text message of praise for correct responses

_____ Graphics display and/or sound for correct responses

_____ Competitive game in which correct responses earn points

_____ Other (specify: _____)

Reinforcement is: _____ Continuous _____ Intermittent

18. What user options are available to students and teachers?

    a. Students can select: _____ Activity from menu _____ Difficulty

    _____ No. of questions   _____ Type of questions

    Other (explain: _____)

    b. Teachers can select: _____ Sound on or off _____ Difficulty

    _____ No. of questions   _____ Type of questions

    _____ Sequence of instruction   _____ No. of trials

    _____ Speed of presentation   _____ Speed demands for responses

    Other (explain _____)

    c. Teachers can: _____ Enter own content into program

    _____ Review student records

    _____ Other (explain: _____)

19. Is the program's documentation adequate?

    a. All program features fully and clearly explained? _____ Yes _____ No

    b. Rationale for program, purpose, and objectives, and field test data included?

    _____ Yes _____ No

    c. Print materials provided for students? _____ Yes _____ No

    If available, are they appropriate? _____ Yes _____ No

    d. Documentation suggests additional learning activities? _____ Yes _____ No

20. Other comments about the instructional program:

C. Overall Evaluation

Rate the appropriateness of the instructional program for your population in each of the following areas using this scale:

Excellent	Adequate	Inadequate
1	2	3

	Excellent	Adequate	Inadequate
a. Curricular content (program addresses functional skills)	1	2	3
b. Interest level (program is age-appropriate)	1	2	3
c. Ease of use for learners	1	2	3
d. Demands upon learner (computer use, academic, speed, accuracy, physical)			
e. Instructional procedures	1	2	3
f. Motivational value	1	2	3
g. Appropriate use of the medium	1	2	3
h. Important instructional variables under teacher control	1	2	3
i. Other (specify: _____)	1	2	3

In summary, what is your overall evaluation of the instructional program for your population? Would you recommend its use? If you would, for what purpose or purposes? Are there aspects of the program about which you would like to caution other special educators?

FIGURE 8.1 Worksheet for Software Evaluation

Source: From *Worksheet for Software Evaluation* by R. B. Lewis, 1983, San Diego, CA: San Diego State University. Copyright 1983 by Rena Lewis. Reprinted by permission.

program should use the same correction procedures of a skillful teacher. It should indicate the error, tell the student the correct answer or guide the student to the answer, have the student make the correct response, and provide additional practice using parallel items. Finally, the program should have a data collection system that allows the teacher to monitor the student's progress in the program and make decisions concerning the ongoing use of the program. Many drill-and-practice programs incorporate game elements (e.g., video arcade style graphics, audio affects, and varied presentation paces) designed to motivate the student. Recent research has suggested that these features may exacerbate attention difficulties of some students with learning problems. The gaming elements of a program may compete for student attention, distracting students from the instructional elements of the program (Semmel & Lieber, 1986).

Tutorial programs are the second most frequently used type of software programs used with special education students. These programs introduce new skills and concepts, and provide practice relating to the material covered. Much of the available tutorial software has been criticized as only marginally helpful in acquiring new skills and knowledge (Carlson & Silverman, 1986). However, when the design of the program pairs small clusters of new information with about twice as much previously mastered information, software programs can effectively teach new content as well (Ellis & Sabornie, 1986).

As in teacher-directed instruction, the quality of tutorial programs is related to the extent to which the program utilizes optimum instructional design (Torgesen, 1986). Programs should be based on mastery learning, with well-defined objectives, carefully sequenced and integrated instruction, and sound decision-making features. The new skills should be modeled using clear examples, proceed step by step, and elicit frequent student responses. After the skill has been modeled, students should be prompted on the use of the skill and finally checked for their understanding. In other words, the computer

program, like the skillful teacher, should utilize a model, prompt, and check lesson format. During the instructional portion of the program all errors should be corrected and students should be required to redo incorrect responses.

Acquiring word processing proficiency on the microcomputer holds considerable promise for students with learning difficulties. While word processing does not in and of itself teach composition skills, it can be a valuable adjunct to the teacher's instruction. It circumvents the problems of slow production due to handwriting that is messy and slow. Once basic cursor and keyboarding skills are learned, microcomputer composition can be faster than handwriting, resulting in neater papers and possibly less hand cramping. Finally, word processing makes revisions easier. Misspelled words are easily corrected, and grammatical and syntactical errors can be fixed with facility, and sentences and paragraphs can be moved around with alacrity. Built-in checking programs for spelling, punctuation, and capitalization can improve the mechanical aspects of writing and leave students free to concentrate on the conceptual aspects of the task. Computerized thesauruses help students to select more powerful and precise terms to include in their compositions. The finished product can have a polished look that is almost impossible for many students to attain through handwritten efforts. Producing finished looking papers appears to be motivating for students, increasing their sense of "authorship" and their willingness to work on compositions over longer periods of time (Neuman, 1985).

Proficiency at word processing requires mastering several prerequisite skills. The teacher should directly teach these skills to the students, using software programs as ancillary aids when appropriate. Proficiency in typing is highly related to the length, quality, and story structure of compositions (MacArthur, Graham & Skarvold, 1986). Delivering and monitoring keyboarding instruction involving 5–10 minutes per day of computer time can lead to acceptable levels of keyboarding proficiency (Neuman & Morroco, 1986). Moving the cursor within the text is a related skill area that can cause students problems. Inefficiently moving the cursor can make it difficult for students to position it at the desired space. Naive learners tend to delete unintended letters or words and to insert spacing errors in the prose lines. Related prerequisites include using editing features of the program, saving and then accessing files, and printing drafts and finished papers. Systematic instruction can address these needs and make word processing a functional skills for students with learning difficulties.

Additional Instructional Modifications

In this chapter the focus has been on effective and efficient interventions for meeting the needs of individual students within the context of group instruction. When teachers maximize the amount of teacher-directed instruction; present systematic lessons; maximize active participation; respond appropriately to correct and incorrect responses; carefully orchestrate independent work; and expand instruction using cooperative learning, computer-assisted instruction, and peer tutoring, the majority of at-risk students will be successful. However, additional modifications for individual students may still be necessary. These modifications must be carefully designed so that they can be implemented in the classroom. The principles presented in the following paragraphs can guide selecting appropriate modifications.

First, *the intervention should not demand a great deal of additional time from the teacher.* A teacher's career is demanding. Tasks include preparing for instruction, managing students, presenting lessons, developing materials, collaborating with other professionals, and attending meetings. As a result, a time-consuming intervention is unlikely to be maintained. For example, audiotaping all the chapters in a social studies book to assist a nonreader in fifth grade might be a successful intervention but totally nonpragmatic. On the other hand, using partners for reading during social studies would take little

additional preparation and would meet the same goal, that is, supporting the nonreader in the classroom.

Second, *the intervention should be one that can be implemented on a continuous basis.* If the intervention must be modified on a daily basis, the probability of ongoing implementation is low. For example, if Jason has difficulty reading the directions in his assignments, then the teacher could rewrite the directions daily on his paper. This intervention would be difficult for the teacher to maintain. On the other hand, the teacher might train Jason's peer partner to read the directions to Jason and have Jason circle the "action words" (e.g., write, underline, or circle) in the directions. This simple intervention could be used every day in all Jason's subjects with little additional effort.

Third, *the modification should still result in the student's successful learning.* Too often the lowest-performing student is given tasks during class that do not enhance her own learning such as coloring pictures, copying words, and completing dot-to-dots. While these activities occupy the student, they do not enhance learning. In all cases, the modification should be one that engages the students and promotes academic success. In one classroom, Mark, a low-performing student, used the spelling instructional time to make classroom posters, color pictures, and complete puzzles. These activities did not promote spelling growth. To accommodate Mark, a better alternative was needed. For example, Mark could use the time to study a "personal spelling list" using a strategy such as: copy, cover, write, check. At the end of each period, a peer could administer a spelling test to Mark and his spelling list could be adjusted for the next day.

Fourth, when possible, *the instructional modification should be beneficial to more than one student in the classroom.* Teachers are much more likely to utilize an intervention if they see its benefit to all or many of their students. For example, if Harry is having difficulty remembering his homework assignments, the teacher might introduce using an assignment calendar to the whole class. If Martha is having difficulty reading her science textbook, the teacher might utilize partner reading with all the students. If Jason has difficulty taking notes in his middle school classes, the teacher might assign a class notetaker who would be responsible for taking notes, and making a copy for Jason and for the class notebook, available to all students.

Read each of the examples in Table 8.3. Ask yourself: Would this intervention take relatively little teacher time? Could it be used over time? Would it promote student learning? Would it benefit more than one student in the classroom? Next, try to think of an alternative intervention for each example that matches these guidelines.

SEATWORK MANAGEMENT STRATEGIES

Students spend anywhere from 50 to 70% of the school day in independent activities. Yet research has shown that the more time that students spend in independent activities, the lower their levels of task engagement and academic achievement (Rosenshine, 1980). This suggests that teachers must be particularly skillful in selecting and managing seatwork if students are to be actively and meaningfully engaged with the lesson. Criteria that teachers should strive for is 80% engagement during seatwork, and 90% engagement during direct instruction (Emmer, Evertson, & Anderson, 1980; Morsink, 1982). The procedures for analyzing student task engagement during seatwork, described in Chapter 7, are useful in determining the extent to which this criterion is being met.

Independent work, both seatwork and homework, must be carefully planned and orchestrated (Anderson, Brubaker, Alleman-Brooks, & Duffy, 1985; Brophy & Good, 1986; Walberg, Paschal, & Weinstein, 1985). Research shows that if students with achievement difficulties are to derive maximum benefit from such assignments, the independent activities must be fairly easy. The purpose of independent activities is to develop fluency and reinforce a skill taught earlier rather than to teach a new skill. To ensure success on

independent work, variables that should be considered include:

- Selecting appropriate assignments
- Introducing unfamiliar tasks
- Establishing routines for completing assignments
- Monitoring the independent work
- Providing feedback on the independent work

Selecting Appropriate Assignments

Independent work should be fairly easy and should always be a follow-up of teacher-directed instruction. Guided practice during lesson presentation provides opportunities for teachers to determine if the students are sufficiently proficient to work on the skill or concept independently. If students have not demonstrated 90% accuracy in group instruction, then independent work should be delayed.

The purpose of independent activities is to develop fluency and reinforce a skill taught earlier rather than to teach a new skill. Teachers who program success rates of 90–100% on independent academic assignments produce more learning than teachers who tolerate lower success rates (Berliner, 1984; Rosenshine, 1983). Conversely, tasks that are too procedurally or cognitively complex may distract students from the cognitive components of the task. They spend more time seeking help or figuring out procedures, and less time using high-level cognitive strategies.

While teachers sometimes assume that students with learning difficulties are to blame for their failure to progress academically, these problems may be symptomatic of larger instructional issues involving the match between students and the learning material. Strategies that teachers can use to ensure that seatwork is meaningful include carefully preparing the students for seatwork assignments, communicating work standards and expectations, promoting on-task behavior, and holding students accountable for their seatwork performance.

TABLE 8.3 Examples of Individual Modifications

STUDENT'S CHALLENGE	SELECTED MODIFICATION
Jason has difficulty reading the word problems in the third-grade math book.	During independent math practice time, all students will work with a peer book partner. Jason's partner will read the problems for Jason.
Marie has a great deal of difficulty writing numbers and letters. As a result, it takes Marie an inordinate amount of time to complete independent work assignments.	The teacher will meet with Marie and establish a special agreement concerning seatwork and homework. Marie will do the odd items on any assignment first. She will be held accountable for those items. If she finishes those items before the end of the work session, she will then do the even items.
Because of spelling difficulties, Marcus cannot take adequate notes in his high school science or civics classes.	A class notetaker will be selected in each class. The notetaker will make three sets of notes using carbon paper: a personal set, a class set for students who have been absent, and a set for Marcus.
Charles cannot read the science text being used in fifth grade.	During class, all students will read with a partner using a strategy (read, cover, recite, and check). Charles's partner will read a paragraph, both students will cover the paragraph, Charles will recite the critical information, and both students will check the paragraph for accuracy.
James is a slow reader and has difficulty picking out the critical parts of textbook material.	James will receive one of the special highlighted textbooks. Before the school year began, the social studies teacher previewed and highlighted the textbook to emphasize important information. A paraprofessional then duplicated the highlighting in five books for students with special needs to use.
Mary has not yet developed advanced writing skills. However, she must write four reports for her social studies class.	All students are given an outline for each report. The students research the topic, complete the outline, and write the paper. Mary will work with a paraprofessional to research the topic. She will then complete the report outline. Using the outline, Mary will verbally report the information to her teacher.
Jose cannot read the science tests given in middle school.	On test days, Jose will meet with the school librarian who will verbally administer the test.
Andrew is having difficulty passing the tests in civics because of the amount information.	Prior to each test, the teacher will tell students the information needed to receive a passing grade on the test. The first items on the test will be the critical items. Andrew and other students can focus their study on that information and their test session on the parallel items.
Paula has difficulty following class directions. As a result, she often does not have necessary materials out, is looking at the wrong part of her worksheet, or is on the wrong page in the book.	Each student in the class is assigned a peer partner. After the teacher gives a directive ("Take out your math book and open to page 77."), she will say "Check your partner." Partners will ensure that the directions have been followed.
Jeff does not finish his homework.	All members of the class record their assignments on a monthly calendar. At the end of the day, the teacher will check Jeff's calendar, initial it if all assignments are recorded, and verify that Jeff has all necessary materials. At the end of home study period, Jeff's mother will check all assignments for completion and sign the calendar.

Despite the importance of high success rates, students who are in the greatest need of being assigned high-success materials may be less likely to be assigned such materials. In one study, it was found that 44 and 50% of the tasks assigned to low-achieving students in language arts and mathematics, respectively, reflected an overestimate of students' ability to perform the task. As a result, students tended to concentrate on the production aspects of the work, had high error rates, and spent considerable time waiting for help. Even when they manage to complete the tasks correctly, post-task interviews may reveal limited understanding of the problem-solving processes themselves. The problem is exacerbated when teachers emphasize procedural aspects of tasks (e.g., layout, neatness, and writing the date) rather than the processes used to perform the task. This suggests to students that if they follow the task requirements and procedures, their performance will be acceptable regardless of the actual learning taking place.

Seatwork should be focused, requiring students to perform the desired outcome behavior, not some ancillary behavior. If the desired outcome is for students to decode consonant-vowel-consonant words, the assignment should require actually reading words, not just filling in missing letters or circling pictures of objects with certain vowel sounds. In the same vein, if students are learning to spell words following a certain rule (e.g., When a word ends in a consonant and an *e*, drop the *e* before adding an ending that begins with a vowel.), tasks that actually require spelling words (e.g., writing words dictated by a partner or writing words dictated by a Language Master) are more appropriate than copying tasks (e.g., writing sentences using spelling words or filling in a blank with the correct spelling word) that do not actually require spelling the words.

Not only should the task require the desired outcome behavior, but it should also require thinking! While this may seem obvious, many assignments do not actually require students to think about the critical information. For example, if the problems in a subtraction assignment all require regrouping, the student does not have to make the most critical discrimination, to regroup or not to regroup. After students have mastered the regrouping process, a better assignment would mix regrouping and nonregrouping problems. Similarly, an English mechanics assignment that required students to copy a series of sentences adding capitals at the beginning and question marks at the end would require no contemplation of the skill being practiced. If on the other hand, the assignment required students to add all missing capitals and punctuation, careful thinking would result.

Not only should the task require students to perform the outcome behavior, to really think about the knowledge or skills being practiced, and not require inordinate teacher instructional time, the *format* should also promote student success. The assignment should have a limited number of discrete tasks or sets of directions. Assignments that include examples of completed items also are desirable. Finally, the assignment should not require other skills (e.g., reading skills or writing skills) beyond the students' abilities. The sample lesson format in Table 8.4 illustrates these features.

These guidelines can be used to select in-class assignments to be completed independently or cooperatively with a team or partner and when selecting homework assignments. When assigning homework, teachers need to keep in mind that students do not have the same resource persons available for assistance (e.g., the teacher, paraprofessional and peers) as he has during school hours. Homework is advantageous in that it increases the amount of "time-on-task" for students and affects subsequent learning, particularly when the homework is presented at the correct difficulty level and the teacher grades or comments on it (Walberg, Paschal, & Weinstein, 1985).

Preparing for Seatwork

The teacher's advance preparation significantly affects the value students derive from seatwork.

TABLE 8.4   Guidelines for Selecting Independent Work (Seatwork and Homework)[1]

Skill	1.	Has the skill been introduced during teacher-directed instruction?
	2.	Have students demonstrated a level of accuracy during teacher-directed instruction on the skill?
Task	1.	Does the task require students to perform the desired outcome behavior?
	2.	Does the task require that the students actually think about the skill as they complete the assignment?
	3.	Would the task itself require little additional instruction?
Format	1.	Are the directions clear and concise?
	2.	Does the assignment provide completed examples to assist students?
	3.	Does the assignment not require other skills (e.g., reading or writing) beyond the students' abilities?

[1]When selecting assignments, consider the skill being practiced, the assignment's task, and the assignment's format.

Many teachers fail to provide adequate rationale for seatwork or to give adequate procedural directions (Anderson, Brubaker, Alleman-Brooks, & Duffy, 1984). This can lead students to believe that the goal is seatwork completion, not increased task proficiency. In fact, many teachers may inadvertently reinforce this belief by requiring students who do not finish their seatwork to forfeit recess. This can encourage students, particularly those at the low end of the achievement spectrum, to resort to using assignment completion strategies that circumvent or defeat the purpose of the assignment (e.g., learning). To enhance the probability that students are correctly focused while they do an assignment, the teacher should tell them what is being practiced and how it relates to other learning. Knowledge of the goal

has a major effect on the amount that low-achievement students learn (Wong, Wong, & Le-Mare, 1982). When teachers communicate what the skill is, how to perform the skill, when to use the skill, and what its long-term value is, students are more likely to focus on achieving task proficiency instead of on the short-term goal of producing a product, resulting in higher achievement.

If the assignment involves novel or unfamiliar tasks, the teacher needs to decide if these components are relevant enough to merit their inclusion. Novel tasks take a great deal of time to introduce, time that could be better spent in teaching critical skills and information. However, if the novel or unfamiliar task is essential to the skill or concept being developed and/or is required later in the curriculum, then the teacher should provide instruction on how to perform the task. This instruction should follow the same systematic model as with other lessons. After reading the directions with the students, the teacher should model performance by completing one item, prompt students on one or more additional items, and then check their understanding of the assignment's task by observing their performance on an additional item. When the independent assignment appears to involve no unfamiliar tasks, instruction may not be necessary, or a brief intervention such as observing students completing one item may be appropriate.

Increasing On-Task Behavior

Task engagement during seatwork can be increased in several ways. First, students with learning problems should not be given seatwork that involves learning new material. Instead, seatwork should always be a follow-up to teacher-directed instruction and should involve only those skills on which students have demonstrated a level of accuracy. Students need to understand the relevance of the assignments as well as what they must do to complete the seatwork satisfactorily. Clear, concise teacher directions communicate expectations for assignment com-

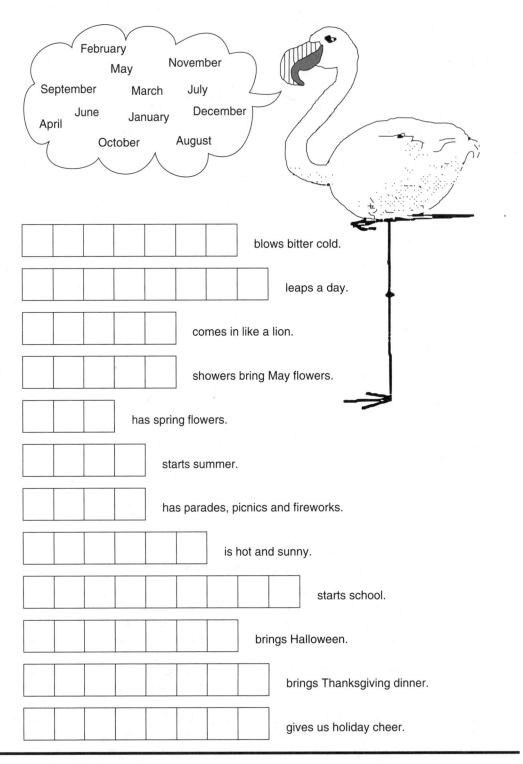

February
May
November
September
March
July
June
December
April
January
October
August

[ ][ ][ ][ ][ ][ ][ ] blows bitter cold.

[ ][ ][ ][ ][ ][ ][ ][ ] leaps a day.

[ ][ ][ ][ ][ ] comes in like a lion.

[ ][ ][ ][ ][ ] showers bring May flowers.

[ ][ ] has spring flowers.

[ ][ ][ ][ ] starts summer.

[ ][ ][ ][ ] has parades, picnics and fireworks.

[ ][ ][ ][ ][ ][ ] is hot and sunny.

[ ][ ][ ][ ][ ][ ][ ][ ][ ] starts school.

[ ][ ][ ][ ][ ][ ][ ] brings Halloween.

[ ][ ][ ][ ][ ][ ][ ][ ] brings Thanksgiving dinner.

[ ][ ][ ][ ][ ][ ][ ][ ] gives us holiday cheer.

FIGURE 8.2 Monthly Puzzle Fun

Directions: Circle the word in each pair with the long vowel sound.

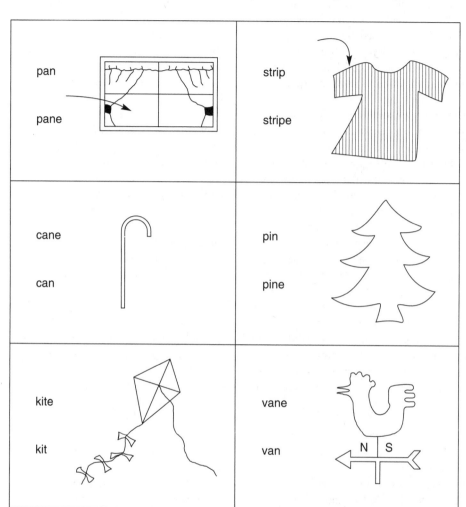

FIGURE 8.3   Long Vowel Exercise

pletion. On-task behavior will be greater when routines for seeking assistance on seatwork, and completing and handing in the assignments have been established so that students know what is expected of them. See Chapter 6 for a discussion of the importance of teaching classroom routines to students.

Children learn best and their task engagement is higher when they are making active or overt responses. During both teacher-directed instruction and seatwork, overt responding can be measured in terms of the number of questions a student answers, the number of seconds a pupil reads, and so forth. Opportunities for students to demonstrate products of their seatwork include such behaviors as handing in assignments, reading word lists or passages to the teacher or a peer, and completing task cards.

Unfortunately, active responding is not the norm in most general and special education classrooms. It has been estimated that while students in special education classrooms spend nearly 1,000 hours per school year in the school building, they may receive only 10 hours per year of practice in reading aloud. It has been reported that while 75% of the special education school day is used in academic instruction, only 25% of that time involves students actively responding. As an example of this, a student may spend 2 hours in reading practice but be engaged in making active reading responses (reading aloud or silently) only 9 minutes of that time. Over the course of the school year, such students spend only 26 hours in reading practice, while 109 hours of reading time is spent engaged in task management behavior.

The problem is further compounded when the reading materials for content area subjects are too difficult for students with learning difficulties. This results in fewer sustained reading opportunities and can lead to situations where the only active reading practice some students receive each day is the 5–10 minutes of directed reading practice provided in pull-out settings such as in the special education resource room, the remedial reading lab, or the Chapter 1 program. During the rest of the day, the difficulty level of the material they are provided curtails students from reading practice, making for poor use of the school day.

The design of the seatwork activities can affect the extent to which active and meaningful responding is required of students. The activities presented in many dittos and workbooks frequently constitute little more than busywork to keep students occupied while the teacher works with other students. Two examples of such workbook activities are shown in Figures 8.2 and 8.3. Like many other workbook activities, they require only passive responses from students who are instructed to circle, write, or copy words. These exercises do not require students to orally produce responses, comprehend, or generate ideas of their own. In fact, the write-the-month activity in Figure 8.2 requires no reading practice

since students simply have to count the number of letters and boxes to accurately complete the worksheet. Similarly, the long vowel exercise in Figure 8.3 requires no active reading response insofar as students merely need to discriminate and circle words that contain the final *e*.

With simple modifications, teachers can provide students with more active practice. For example, instead of simply requiring students to circle words on a workbook page, teachers can ask students to orally pronounce the words they circle. After completing the page, they can read the words orally to a teacher or peer who checks their reading accuracy or fluency.

Instead of relying upon dittos or workbooks for practice, teachers should give students sustained practice in targeted skills. Too often, the focus of workbooks is on small response units (e.g., letters, words, or sentences) that are presented in isolation from their natural or real-world contexts. To provide sustained practice, students need applied activities that require using the skill in natural contexts. For example, assignments involving reading connected text increases response opportunities, and develops critical fluency and comprehension skills. Students should read silently or orally with a peer on a regular basis.

As a part of writing instruction, students should similarly engage in sustained writing opportunities. Some research suggests that although 43% of observed class time at the high school level was devoted to paper-and-pencil tasks, less than 3% involved writing that was a paragraph in length or longer. If students with learning problems are to learn to think beyond simple letter, word, and paragraph units, they must receive sustained practice writing connected text. This can be easily accomplished if teachers schedule sustained and meaningful writing opportunities as part of the daily work.

Teacher interactions with students during seatwork is highly related to student task engagement. Moreover, studies by Rieth and his colleagues suggest that students with mild handicaps are seven times more likely to be on-task when they are assigned teacher-supervised activities rather than independent seatwork. Teacher-supervised activities are those in which teachers circulate frequently to monitor performance, provide encouragement and feedback, and reteach misunderstood concepts.

Teachers can increase student task engagement during seatwork by varying the activities of students. For example, with students who have short attention spans, teachers can space out the independent work rather than giving long seatwork assignments. One teacher chose to meet with students for group instruction and then dismiss them to work at a listening center where a tape-recorded story prompted on-task reading behavior. After finishing, the students worked at their seats for a short time, with the teacher checking their work. Next, the students worked together in a peer-tutoring arrangement for 15 minutes. Finally, they were assigned to either the classroom computers or the Language Master. In this way, the teacher demonstrated sensitivity to the attention spans of her students. She scheduled activities that broke up the time students spent working on their own and ensured that they made active responses throughout the period.

Another effective practice is breaking seatwork into smaller instructional segments. The instructional format for this procedure is of the demonstration-practice-demonstration-practice variety. For example, teachers may demonstrate how to perform part of a problem or strategy (e.g., writing narratives) and then have students practice that step. Next, they provide an explanation for the next part of the problem, again supervising as students work on that component. This instructional format keeps students focused on smaller units of learning, thereby promoting high success and attention-to-task while diminishing the likelihood that student confusion and questions will interrupt seatwork practice.

Actively monitoring seatwork performance also can ensure that students are continually engaged. Teachers can circulate frequently and position themselves at all times so that they can continually scan students to prompt on-task behavior and to intervene quickly when students need assistance. In addition, effective teachers establish routines for seatwork that convey to students what they are to do when they are finished early (e.g., turn over my "needs help" card and continue working). These routines serve as important guides for behavior during those times when students are most likely to interrupt themselves or others (Rieth & Evertson, 1988). The routines also promote on-task behavior that leads to the targeted student outcomes.

Monitoring Independent Work

Finally, during seatwork time, teachers should monitor students while they work on assignments. They should make sure that the students understand the task goal and are able to do the work. When not teaching a group of students, the teacher should move around the classroom, examine students' responses, and provide feedback on their work. Frequent monitoring also is essential, albeit more difficult, when the teacher is teaching a small group and other students are working independently. To accomplish this, the teacher should position himself in the small group so that all students working at their desks are in view. For this reason, it is better to stand than to sit when teaching a group. Second, the teacher should continually scan the students at their desks to ensure that they are completing their assignments, and praise the students for their efforts (e.g., "You are really working." "Thank you for completing your assignments.") Finally, when the opportunity arises during instruction (e.g., students are completing problems or students are reading silently), the teacher moves to students' desks and examines their work. A paraprofessional or an adult volunteer can help to monitor students' work completion while the teacher works with a small group.

When students make many mistakes on their assignments, this is evidence that they are unprepared for the independent practice. At this point, the best option is to have students terminate their work on the assignments and to immediately reteach the skill or to reteach the skill on the following day. It is important to remember that it is not simply practice that leads to perfection. Only "perfect practice" (or nearly perfect practice) benefits students. Practicing errors will create frustration and adversely affect students' views of themselves as learners.

Providing Feedback

Just as students need consistent feedback on their responses during teacher-directed instruction, feedback on their independent assignments increases individual accountability and student learning (Evertson, Emmer, Sanford & Clements, 1983; Rieth & Evertson, 1988; Rieth, Polsgrove & Semmel, 1981). This feedback should be as immediate as possible (e.g., the same day or the next day) and should result in increased learning by bringing the student's attention to her mistakes and, when feasible, requiring the student to redo missed items (Evertson & Emmer, 1982).

Several correction procedures can be used, including self-correction with keys, self-correction during group, and teacher corrections. In a special education classroom, keys for independent assignments might be kept in a special "correcting" area. Students compare their answers to the key, circle any mistakes with a special correcting pen, and return to their desks to redo missed items. Self-correction during the instructional group time is also a viable procedure. Here, the teacher reads the answers, students circle missed items, and the teacher reteaches items that many students missed. If time permits, students then redo missed items. When teachers choose to collect and correct a set of assignments, students should be given a special time to review teacher's feedback and to correct missed items. If this time is not given, students are likely to glance at the grade and "stuff" the papers into their desks, backpacks, or notebooks without benefiting from the written comments and corrections.

Communicating Work Standards and Expectations

Effective teachers hold students **accountable** for their seatwork performance and maintain high task engagement by communicating their work standards and expectations. Emmer, Evertson, Sanford, Clements, and Worsham (1984) list the following practices associated with clarity in communicating work standards to students:

1. Stress is placed on the necessity for completing all assignments.
2. Emphasis is placed on making up missed, incomplete, or unsatisfactory work.
3. Due dates are emphasized, and due dates are not extended in order that efficient work habits are reinforced.
4. Work requirements, including policies regarding neatness, format, and completion, are spelled out.
5. Students' full attention is required when lesson assignments are presented.
6. Emphasis is placed on understanding and learning, such that individual students were asked whether they understood or not.
7. Systems are utilized for keeping track of student progress, including mastery learning systems.

Establishing Routines for Completing Assignments

Student success on independent work is greater when teachers establish routines for communicating assignments, distributing materials for assignments, gaining help on assignments, and completing assignments (Evertson & Emmer, 1982; Reith & Evertson, 1988). The routines selected should be used consistently over time, promote on-task behavior, and optimize student independence rather than dependence. For example, students might be taught the following routine for gaining assistance during class: "Ask your partner for assistance. If your partner cannot assist you, put up your 'Help Wanted' sign. Continue working until the teacher can assist you." This routine could be used on a daily basis whenever the student needed assistance, it promotes on-task behavior whereas raising her hand for assistance would lead to off-task behavior, and the routine would encourage independence in that it requires the student to continue working on meaningful tasks while waiting for the assistance. Routines for independent work is another example of preventative behavior management procedures that can contribute to a smoothly running classroom. Example routines for completing seatwork are presented in Table 8.5.

PROVIDING SYSTEMATIC REVIEW

In order to ensure that the students maintain the skills and knowledge introduced and initially mastered, **systematic review** is important. Often in pursuit of instruction on new skills and the desire to move forward in the curriculum, previously taught skills are neglected. This is problematic, especially low-performing students. If the teacher forgets the skills, the students will often also forget the skills.

Given the challenge of maintaining student's skills and knowledge, a systematic plan should be adopted for cumulative review. For example, in math the teacher might utilize the following plan:

1. Begin each day with warm-up review problems.
2. On Mondays review all of the major concepts taught during the previous 2 weeks.
3. Every 3 weeks, review the major concepts taught to date in math.
4. Incorporate review problems into daily independent assignments.

In science, a teacher might use the following plan:

1. Twice a week, review the major concepts taught in a previous chapter using the concept map introduced during initial instruction.

2. Prior to each chapter test, review major concepts from prior bodies of knowledge.
3. Include major concepts from prior chapters on each subsequent test.
4. When appropriate, review previously taught concepts as they relate to new concepts.

In a beginning reading program, the teacher might adopt this review plan:

1. Incorporate previously taught phoneme-grapheme associations into daily sound drill.
2. Incorporate previously taught decodable word patterns as discrimination words in daily decoding exercises.
3. Review sight words taught in the past five selections each day.

Each of these teachers has developed a plan that will enhance the probability of retention.

Systematic review contributes to overall achievement as illustrated in the following real-life parable. One teacher at Pine Valley Elementary School taught the one hundred science concepts in the science textbook with passion. She was careful to teach each of the concepts to a high level of mastery, but she did not review the concepts throughout the year. At the end of the year, the mean score on a test of these concepts was 40. Next door, a second teacher taught science with equal passion. Because of his desire to spend time on review, he was more selective, teaching only eighty concepts in science. However, each week, he dedicated one of his science classes to review previously introduced bodies of knowledge. At the end of the year, the students took a test and their mean score on the eighty concepts was 70. So, the moral of this story is "Less, when reviewed systematically, can be more."

MAINTAINING PROGRESS RECORDS

Teachers need to administer frequent tests, either daily or semiweekly, to measure and record progress. This frequent recording of progress serves several important functions. These tasks are use-

TABLE 8.5   Example Routines for Independent Work Completion

ACTIVITY	EXAMPLE ROUTINES

Communicating assignments	In-class assignments
	    1. Verbally state the directions.
	    2. Write the assignment on the board.
	
	Homework assignments
	    1. Have students open their calendars.
	    2. Verbally state the directions.
	    3. Have students record the assignment on calendars.
	    4. Record the assignment on the class calendar.
	    5. Monitor as students record calendar entries.

Distributing materials for assignments	Basic materials (pencils and paper)
	    1. Distribute paper and pencils on Mondays when notebooks are cleaned out.
	    2. If student fails to bring notebook to class, less desirable materials will be utilized (e.g., newsprint and kindergarten pencils).
	
	Small group assignments
	    1. Textbooks will be kept in desks.
	    2. Additional materials will be passed out in group.
	
	Large group assignment
	    1. Textbooks will be kept in desks.
	    2. First person in each row will distribute other materials.

Gaining help on assignments	When working independently or in a cooperative group
	    1. Ask peer for assistance.
	    2. If peer cannot assist, display "Help Wanted" sign on desk.
	    3. Continue working. Do other items on the assignment, work on another assignment, or read.
	    4. When the teacher is available, ask for help by clearly stating your question.

Completing assignments	In-class assignments
	    1. Complete assignments at your desk.
	    2. Work by yourself unless assigned to a partner or cooperative team.
	    3. Place completed assignments in the "Done" box.
	    4. If you finish early, do one of the following "buffer" activities:
	      • Read a book
	      • Write in your journal
	      • Complete other assignments

ful in communicating with other professionals, parents, and with the students themselves. They document the instructional actions of teachers and the effects of these actions on students.

The collection of daily performance measures are themselves an instructional intervention that affects teachers and students. For teachers, daily or biweekly monitoring of objectives using curriculum-based assessment can produce more significant effects on student achievement than employing more conventional norm-referenced tests that are administered in developing the program but are rarely used in monitoring student progress. By systematically evaluating the effects of their instructional decisions on the basis of measurable changes in student performance, they are in a better position to continually evaluate teaching effects and to alter instruction to meet individual needs. For students, the collection of daily measures can increase their involvement and control of their own academic progress. As they see the effects of their efforts to learn on their performance, they develop more confidence, an enhanced internal locus of control, and a greater sense of their ability to self-regulate.

PERSONAL ATTRIBUTES ASSOCIATED WITH EFFECTIVE TEACHING

One final set of effective teacher characteristics merits discussion. Throughout this text, effective and efficient teaching behaviors that promote student achievement with students are described. These represent state-of-the-art best practices. In addition to exhibiting these characteristics, teachers who are most successful in enhancing the academic growth, social behaviors, and self-esteem of students, exhibit additional less quantifiable characteristics as well. These are attitudinal characteristics that they demonstrate in their day-to-day approaches to instruction and to students. They seem to have a passion and a commitment for teaching students with learning difficulties. Their behaviors communicate a strong belief that all students can learn and can manage their own behaviors. They have high expectations for their students. These expectations are not vague words, but are matched by teacher practices. They expect students to learn, to be on-task, and to complete their work. Effective teachers are willing to engage in the planning and preparation, lesson delivery, and self-evaluative practices that ensure that these outcomes are realized. Effective teach-

ers truly understand the motto "What you expect equals what you get."

In addition, these teachers exhibit an urgency. They understand that time is of the essence with low-achieving students. They protect instructional time, being careful not to waste time that could be spent on academic pursuits. They are goal oriented and orchestrate their time accordingly. Finally, these teachers understand and truly believe that they make a difference. They see their actions as directly related to the outcomes of their students. Thus, when achievement is waning, they look to instructional practices that will propel students forward. When student behavior is inappropriate, they examine their classroom practices to find a new solution. They accept responsibility for their classroom and students. They approach their profession with a commitment and a passion that is evident in their every behavior.

SUMMARY

Strategies for selecting and covering curriculum content can result in more meaningful uses of instructional time and greater student learning. Teachers need to make careful, informed decisions about what curriculum to include and what to emphasize in teaching students with learning problems. They should choose content and skills that are the most salient to future school and life demands that the students will face. The curriculum should be at an appropriate level of difficulty and it should be as broadly generalizable to other situations as possible. By carefully choosing the curriculum, maintaining a brisk pace in presenting it, with lots of questions to students, teachers can maximize the amount of curriculum they cover, and the amount of information and skills that students learn.

To enhance the students' success, effective teachers implement a variety of procedures that are responsive to the individual student's needs, effective in promoting the academic success of the student, and efficient in promoting academic achievement. They elicit responses from all students, provide adequate wait time for the responses, regroup students for additional follow-up instruction, provide cooperative learning and peer-tutoring delivery when appropriate, utilize instructional computers and software, and engage in other modifications that are responsive to individual differences. These modifications do not require a great deal of additional teacher preparation time, can be implemented on a continuous basis, result in successful learning, and are potential to benefit many students in the classroom.

Effective teachers also orchestrate independent work (seatwork or homework assignments) by carefully selecting independent work, introducing unfamiliar tasks, establishing routines for completing assignments, monitoring work completion, and providing feedback. They schedule systematic reviews of prior instruction and learning, and maintain meaningful records of student performance.

The procedures detailed in this chapter, as well as Chapter 6, focus on instruction that facilitates the success of students with learning difficulties. However, many are equally applicable when teaching normally progressing or gifted students. It appears that good instruction is good instruction.

CONTENT MASTERY QUESTIONS

1. Describe the process for selecting relevant curriculum content for students with learning difficulties.

2. Discuss the importance of teacher pacing for increasing content coverage.

3. Describe the instructional practices of a teacher displaying brisk pacing.

4. Describe the process for providing feedback and correcting errors.

5. Describe the development and implementation of cooperative learning including both considerations and prerequisite skills.

6. Design a peer-tutoring program to teach mathematics skills. (Be sure to include all six components).

7. Discuss computer-assisted instruction in terms of types of programs, prerequisite skills, and possible outcomes.

8. Discuss the principles involved in selecting appropriate instructional modifications. Select two instructional strategies and evaluate them based on these principles.

9. Delineate guidelines in the selection process of appropriate seatwork.

10. Describe the procedure a teacher should follow to prepare for seatwork.

11. Discuss the importance of active responding during seatwork and describe four simple modifications for increasing on-task behavior.

12. Discuss the three-step process required to monitor students during independent work.

13. Describe three error correction procedures and provide an illustration of each.

14. Discuss the importance of communicating work standards and expectations as well as the importance of establishing routines.

15. Discuss the importance of systematic review and provide an illustration of its use.

16. Discuss the importance of maintaining records of student academic progress.

REFERENCES

Anderson, L. M. (1984). The environment of instruction: The function of seatwork in a commercially developed curriculum. In G. G. Duffy, L. R. Roehler, & J. Mason (Eds.), *Comprehension instruction: Perspectives and suggestions* (pp. 93–103). New York: Longman.

Anderson, L. M., Brubaker, N. L., Alleman-Brooks, J., & Duffy, G. G. (1985). A qualitative study of seat work in first grade classrooms. *The Elementary School Journal, 86,* 123–140.

Anderson, L. M., Evertson, C. M., & Brophy, J. E. (1979). An experimental study of effective teaching in first grade reading groups. *The Elementary School Journal, 79,* 193–223.

Anderson, L. M., Evertson, C. M., & Brophy, J. E. (1982). *Principles of small group instruction in elementary reading.* East Lansing, MI: Institute for Research on Teaching, Michigan State University.

Archer, A., Isaacson, S., Adams, A., Ellis, E., Morehead, J. K., & Schiller, E. (1989). *Academy for effective instruction: Working with mildly handicapped students.* Reston, VA: The Council for Exceptional Children.

Aronson, E., Blaney, N., Stephan, C., Sikes, J., & Snapp, M. (1978). *The jigsaw classroom.* Beverly Hills, CA: Sage.

Becker, W. C. (1977), Teaching reading and language to the disadvantaged—What we have learned from field research. *Harvard Educational Review, 47,* 518–543.

Berliner, D. C. (1979). Tempus educare. In P. L. Peterson & H. J. Walberg (Eds.) *Research on Teaching: Concepts, findings and implications,* pp. 120–135, Berkeley: McCutchan.

Block, J. H. (1980). Success rate. In C. Denham & A. Lieberman (Eds.), *Time to learn* (pp. 95–106). Washington, D.C.: National Institute of Education.

Borg, W. R. (1980). Time and school learning. In C. Denham & A. Lieberman (Eds.), *Time to learn* (pp. 27–72). Washington, D.C.: National Institute of Education.

Brophy, J. E. (1982). How teachers influence what is taught and learned in classrooms. *Elementary School Journal, 83,* 1–13.

Brophy, J. E., & Evertson, C. M. (1976). *Learning from teaching: A developmental perspective.* Boston: Allyn & Bacon.

Brophy, J., & Evertson, C. (1977). Teacher behavior and student learning in the second and third grade. In G. D. Borich (Ed.), *The appraisal of teaching: Concepts and process* (pp. 79–95). New York: Addison-Wesley.

Brophy, J., & Good, T. L. (1986). Teacher behavior and student achievement. In M. C. Wittrock (Ed.), *Handbook of research on teaching* (3rd., pp. 328–374). New York: Macmillan.

Browder, D. M., Shoen, S. F., & Lentz, F. E. (1986–87). Learning to learn through observation. *Journal of Special Education, 20,* 447–459.

Carlson, S. A., & Silverman, R. (1986). Microcomputers and computer-assisted instruction in special classrooms: Do we need the teacher? *Learning Disability Quarterly, 9*(2), 105–110.

Carnine, D., Silbert, J., & Kameenui, E. J. (1990). *Direct instruction reading.* Columbus, OH: Merrill Publishing Co.

Coker, H., Lorentz, C. W., & Coker, J. (1980). *Teacher behavior and student outcomes in the Georgia study.* Paper presented to the American Educational Research Association Annual Meeting. Boston, MA.

Ellis, E. S., & Sabornie, E. J. (1986). Efective instruction with microcomputers: Promises, practices, and preliminary findings. *Focus on Exceptional Children, 19,* 1–16.

Emmer, E. T., Evertson, C., Sansford, J., Clements, B., & Worsham, M. (1982). *Organizing and managing the junior high classroom.* Austin, TX: Research and Development Center for Teacher Education, University of Texas.

Englemann, S., & Carnine, D. (1982). *Theory of instruction: Principles and applications.* New York: Irvington.

Englert, C. S. (1983). Measuring special education teacher effectiveness, *Exceptional Children, 50,* 247–254.

Englert, C. S. (1984). Examining effective direct instruction practices in special education settings. *Remedial and Special Education, 5,* 38–47.

Englert, C. S. (1984). Measuring teacher effectiveness from a teacher's point of view. *Focus on Exceptional Children, 2,* 15.

Englert, C. S., & Thomas, C. C. (1982). Management of task involvement in special education classrooms. *Teacher Education and Special Education, 5,* 3–10.

Evertson, C., & Emmer, E. (1982). Effective manage-ment at the beginning of the school year in junior high classes. *Journal of Educational Psychology, 74,* 485–498.

Evertson, C., Emmer, E., Sanford, J., & Clements, B. (1983). Improving classroom management: An experiment in elementary school classrooms. *Elementary School Journal, 84,* 173–188.

Evertson, C., Emmer, E., Clements, B., Sanford, J., Worsham, M., & Williams, E. (1981). *Organizing and managing the elementary school class-room.* Austin, TX: Research and Development Center for Teacher Education, University of Texas.

Fisher, C. W., Berliner, D. C., Filby, N. N., Marliave, R., Cohen, L. S., & Deshaw, M. M. (1980). Teaching behaviors, academic learning time, and student achievement: An overview. In C. Denham & A. Lieberman (Eds.), *Time to learn.* Washing-ton, D.C.: National Institute of Education.

Gall, M. (1984). Synthesis of research on teachers' questioning. *Educational Leadership, 42*(3), 40–47.

Good, T. L., & Grouws, D. (1979). The Missouri mathematics effectiveness project: An experi-mental study in fourth-grade classrooms. *Journal of Educational Psychology, 71,* 355–362.

Good, T. L., Grouws, D. A., & Ebmeier, H. (1983). *Active mathematics teaching,* New York: Longman.

Greenwood, C. R., Delquadri, J., Stanley, S., Sasso, G., Whorton, D., & Schulte, D. (1981). Allocating opportunities to respond as a basis for academic remediation: A developing model for teaching. In R. B. Rutherford, A. G. Prieto, & J. E. McGlothin (Eds.), *Severe behavior disorders of children and youth, monograph in behavior disorders* (pp. 22–23). Reston, VA: Council for Children with Be-havior Disorders.

Hofmeister, A. M. (1984). The special educator in the information age. *Peabody Journal of Education, 62*(1), 5–21.

Hunter, M., & Russell, D. (1981). Planning for effec-tive instruction: Lesson Design. In *Increasing your teaching effectiveness.* Palo Alto, CA: The Learning Institute.

Jenkins, J., & Jenkins, L. (1985). Peer tutoring in ele-mentary and secondary program. *Focus on Excep-tional Children, 17,* 1–12.

Jenkins, J., & Jenkins, L. (1987). Making peer tutoring work. *Educational Leadership, 44,* 64–69.

Kulik, J. A., Kulik, C. C., & Bangert-Drowns, R. L. (1985). Effectiveness of computerbased educa-tion in elementary schools. *Computers and Hu-man Behavior, 1,* 59–72.

Leinhardt, G., Zigmond, N., & Cooley, W. W. (1981). Reading instruction and its effects. *American Educational Research Journal, 18,* 343–361.

Mercer, C. D., & Snell, M. E. (1977). *Learning theory research in mental retardation: Implications for teaching.* Columbus, OH: Charles E. Merrill.

McKenzie, G. (1979). Effects of questions and testlike events on achievement and on-task behavior in a classroom concept learning presentation. *Journal of Educational Research, 72,* 348–350.

McKenzie, G. R, & Henry, M. (1979). Effects of testlike events on on-task behavior, test anxiety, and achievement in a classroom rule-learning task. *Journal of Educational Research 71,* 370–374.

Neuman, S. B., & Morroco, C. C. (1986). Two hands is hard for me: Keyboarding and learning disabled children. Newton, MA: University of Lowell, Education Development Center.

Neuman, S. B., Morroco, C. C. Bullock, M., Cushman, H., Neale, M., Packard, D., & Traversi, D. (1985). *A model teaching environment for using word processors with LD children. The writing project* (Tech. Re. No. 2). Newton, MA: Education De-velopment Center.

Niedermeyer, F. C. (1970). Effects of training on the instructional behaviors of student tutors. *The Journal of Educational Research, 64,* 119–123.

MacArthur, C. A., Graham, S., & Skarvold, J. (1986). *Learning disabled students' composing with three methods: Handwriting, dictations, and word processing.* (Research Report #109). College Park: University of Maryland, Institute for the Study of Exceptional Children and Youth.

Osborn, J. (1982). The purpose, uses, and contents of workbooks and some guidelines for teachers and publishers. In R. C. Anderson, J. Osborn, & R. J. Tierney (Eds.), *Learning to read in American schools: Basal readers and content texts.* Hillside, NJ: Lawrence Erlbaum.

Polloway, E. A., Cronin, M. E., & Patton, J. R. (1986). The efficacy of group versus one-to-one instruc-tion: A review. *Remedial and Special Education, 7,* 22–30.

Phye, G. D. (1979). The processing of informative feedback about multiple-choice test performance.

Contemporary Educational Psychology, 4, 381–394.

Rieth, H., & Evertson, C. (1988). Variables related to the effective instruction of difficult-to-teach children. *Focus on Exceptional Children, 20,* 1–8.

Rieth, H., Polsgrove, L., McLeskey, J., Payne, K., & Anderson, R. (1978). The use of self-recording to increase the arithmetic performance of severely behaviorally disordered students. *Monographs in Behavioral Disorders, 2,* 50–58.

Rieth, H., Polsgrove, L., & Semmel, M. (1981). Instructional variables that make a difference: Attention to tasks and beyond. *Exceptional Education Quarterly, 2,* 61–82.

Rivera, D., & Smith, D. D. (1988). Using a demonstration strategy to teach midschool students with learning disabilities how to compute long division. *Journal of Learning Disabilities, 21,* 77–81.

Roehler, L. R., & Duffy, G. G. (1984). Direct explanation of comprehension processes. In G. G. Duffy, L. R. Roehler, & J. Mason (Eds.), *Comprehension instruction: Perspectives and suggestions,* pp. 265–280. New York: Longman.

Rosenshine, B. (1980). How time is spent in elementary classrooms. In C. Denham & A. Lieberman (Eds.), *Time to learn* (pp. 107–126). Washington, DC: National Institute of Education.

Rosenshine, B. (1983). Teaching functions in instructional programs. *Elementary School Journal, 83,* 335–352.

Rosenshine, B., & Stevens, R. (1986). Teaching functions. In M. C. Wittrock (Ed.), *Handbook of research on teaching* (3rd ed., pp. 376–391). New York: Macmillan.

Roth, S. F., & Beck, I. L. (1984). *Research and instructional issues related to the enhancement of children's decoding skills through a microcomputer program.* Paper presented at the annual meeting of the American Educational Research Association, New Orleans.

Semel, M. I., & Lieber, J. A. (1986). Computer applications in instruction. *Focus on Exceptional Children 18*(4), 1–12.

Sindelar, P. T., Bursuch, W. D., & Halle, J. W. (1986). The effects of two variations of teacher questioning on student performance. *Education and Treatment of Children, 9*(1), 56–66.

Smith, D. D., & Lovitt, T. C. (1975). The differential effects of reinforcement contingencies on arithmetic performance. *Journal of Learning Disabilities, 9,* 21–29.

Soar, R. S. (1973). *Follow through classroom process measurement and pupil growth* (1970–71). Gainsville: University of Florida, Institute for the Development of Human Resources.

Stallings, J., Needles, M., & Stayrock, N. (1979). *How to change the process of teaching basic reading skills in secondary schools.* Menlo Park, CA: SRI International.

Stallings, J., & Kaskowitz, D. (1974). *Following through classroom observation evaluation, 1972–73,* Menlo Park, CA: Stanford Research Institute.

Stevens, R., & Rosenshine, B. (1981). Advances in research on teaching, *Exceptional Education Quarterly, 2,* 1–9.

Torgesen, J. K. (1986). Using computers to help learning disabled children practice reading: A research-based perspective. *Learning Disabilities Focus, 1,* 72–81.

Torgesen, J. K., & Young, K. (1983). Priorities for the use of microcomputers with learning disabled children. *Journal of Learning Disabilities, 16,* 234–237.

Wilkenson, A. C. (1983). Learning to read in real time. In A. C. Wilkenson, (Ed.), *Classroom computers and cognitive science.* New York: Academic Press.

Walberg, H. J., Pashal, R. A., & Weinstein, T. (1985). Homework's powerful effects on learning. *Educational Leadership, 42*(7), 76–129.

Wong, B. Y. L., Wong, R., & LeMare, L. (1982). The effects of knowledge of criterion task on comprehension and recall in normally achieving and learning disabled children. *Journal of Educational Research, 76,* 119–126.

Woodward, J., Carnine, D., Gerston, R., Gleason, M., Johnson, G., & Collins, M. (1986). Applying instructional designing principles to CAI for mildly handicapped students: Four recently conducted studies. *Journal of Special Education Technology, 8,* 12–26.

CHAPTER 9

Skills for School Success

ANITA L. ARCHER
MARY M. GLEASON

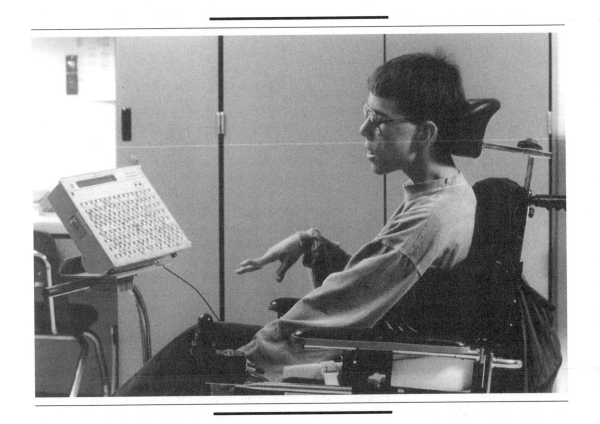

CHAPTER OBJECTIVES

At the conclusion of this chapter, the reader will be able to:

1. Design a lesson plan to effectively teach school behaviors.
2. Discuss criteria for selecting organizational skills to be directly taught and describe strategies for teaching them.
3. Describe the characteristics of learning strategies and provide illustrations of strategies from learning strategies curricula.
4. Delineate instructional procedures for teaching learning strategies.
5. Describe strategies for maintaining and generalizing school behaviors, organizational skills, and learning strategies prior to, during, and after instruction.

Students with learning problems universally have difficulty in one or more of the basic skill areas. They require additional systematic instruction in reading, writing, spelling, handwriting, and/or mathematics. However, such assistance in and of itself may not be sufficient to ameliorate the academic deficits. In addition, the underlying skills needed for success in all classrooms must be addressed. Even if a student's reading, writing, and mathematics skills improve, school success is not guaranteed. If the student continues to arrive late to class, fails to bring class materials, cannot locate homework at the beginning of class, forgets when a report is due, has no approach to reading the classroom textbook, and randomly circles *a, b,* or *c* on a multiple choice test, school achievement difficulties will continue.

This chapter focuses on how teachers can assist students to establish new behaviors that would help them achieve more success in school. The following three areas of skill fundamental to classroom success are addressed: (1) critical school behaviors, (2) organizational skills, and (3) learning strategies. These are depicted in Figure 9.1. For each of these areas, the selection of appropriate skills is discussed, example skills and strategies are presented, and instructional procedures are suggested. The chapter closes with a discussion of the critical topic of the maintenance and generalization of these skills across settings, materials, and time.

SCHOOL BEHAVIORS

To be successful in the classroom, students must exhibit certain school behaviors that allow the teacher to teach and students to learn. Students need to exhibit these behaviors *before class* (e.g., arrive on time, enter in a pleasant manner, bring class materials, and get ready for learning by clearing off her desk), *during class* (e.g, follow the classroom rules, listen to the teacher and classmates, work at appropriate times, follow teacher directives, ask for assistance in a pleasing manner, and move quickly from activity to activity), and *after class* (e.g., take materials home, complete homework, and bring homework back to school) (Archer & Gleason, 1989). Many students with learning and achievement difficulties do not consistently exhibit these behaviors within special education settings or within mainstream classes. In fact, the failure to exhibit these behaviors often leads to initial special education referrals and to ongoing difficulties in school.

Success in classes is highly related to students' school behaviors, organization skills, and learning strategies.

Success in Elementary and Secondary Classes

Basic Skill Classes	Content Area Classes
Reading	Science
Mathematics	Social Studies
Language Arts	Health
English	Art
	Physical Education
	Performing Arts
	Vocational Education

School Behaviors

Before Class	During Class	After Class
Arrive on time	Follow classroom rules	Take materials home
Enter in a pleasant manner	Listen carefully	Complete homework
Bring materials to class	Work during class	Bring homework back
Get ready for learning	Follow teacher directives	
	Ask for assistance	
	Move quickly to new activity	

Organization Skills

Organization of materials (e.g., use of notebook or folders)
Organization of time (e.g., use of calendar, scheduling work)
Organization of content on paper (e.g., heading, margins)

Learning Strategies

Gaining Information
Strategies for: Reading expository material
Reading narrative material
Gaining information from verbal presentations
(lectures, demonstrations)

Demonstrating Knowledge of Skills
Strategies for: Completing daily assignments
Answering written questions
Writing narrative and expository products
Preparing for and taking tests

FIGURE 9.1   Skills for School Success

Source: Reprinted from *Skills for School Success,* Archer and Gleason (1989), by permission of the authors and Curriculum Associates.

While many students learn these behaviors incidentally, others must be explicitly taught them, preferably at the beginning of the school year. More effective teachers systematically review the behavioral expectations at the beginning of the year, teach needed behaviors in organized lessons, periodically review them throughout the year, and provide students with systematic feedback on their behavior performance (Brophy, 1983; Evertson & Emmer, 1982).

While the lessons designed for the varying skill areas of school behaviors, organizational skills, and learning strategies would differ somewhat, certain key components would be common to each. These components mirror those of effective lesson design described in Chapter 7. They include:

1. **Introduce the behavior.** State or read the behavioral guideline. Have students repeat or read the behavioral guideline to ensure the students' attention.

2. **Provide a rationale for the behavior.** Explain the importance of the behavior in terms of the teacher's ability to teach, the student's ability to learn, and classmates' ability to learn.

3. **Provide examples and nonexamples of behavioral performance.** Present verbal vignettes to students that illustrate appropriate and inappropriate performance of the behavior. The examples and nonexamples will clarify the boundaries of the behavior for your students.

4. **Check students' understanding using examples and nonexamples.** Present verbal vignettes illustrating appropriate and inappropriate performance of the behavior. Have students determine if the school behavior is being illustrated.

5. **If appropriate, model performance of the behavior.** Whether teaching a classroom routine or a strategy for a behavior, it is important to provide a model of that behavior. For example, students might be taught the following steps for asking for help in a teacher-pleasing manner: (1) state your question clearly, (2) listen to the teacher, and (3) thank the teacher (Archer &

Gleason, 1989). If a multistep strategy is introduced, the behavior should be modeled with each step clearly demonstrated and described.

6. **When appropriate, provide positive practice on the behavior.** Positive teacher-directed practice can be useful in establishing critical school behaviors. For example, if the targeted school behavior is to "follow teacher directions," the teacher can provide immediate practice on the behavior ("Let's practice following directions. Take out a piece of paper and a pencil.") followed by teacher feedback ("Good. You took out a piece of paper and a pencil. You followed the direction quickly. As a result, I could teach and you could learn.")

While explicit instruction on critical school behaviors is essential, the actions of the teacher *after* initial instruction will be of even greater importance. Students should receive a great deal of feedback on their performance of the school behaviors throughout the initial weeks of the school term. Feedback can be directed to the individual as well as the class as a whole, and can consist of verbal feedback or using written checklists. Examples of checklists are provided in Figure 9.2. Written checklists for the behavior can assist students to monitor and evaluate their own use of school behaviors. In addition, positive consequences (e.g., praise, smiles, special privileges, and notes to parents) can strengthen the performance of critical school behaviors. Negative consequences (e.g., time owed, loss of privileges), though not as powerful as positive consequences, also can deter the exhibition of less desirable school behaviors, if administrated consistently and fairly.

In addition to directly teaching critical school behaviors, teachers also must *act* in a manner that communicates that they really do *expect* the behavior. When students have been instructed to arrive to class on time, then the teacher's actions must be in concert with this directive. For example, the teacher should be at the door or other designated place before the

Name _____

During-Class Checklist

I should:
1. Follow the classroom rules.
2. Listen carefully.
3. Work during class.
4. Ask for help when I need it.

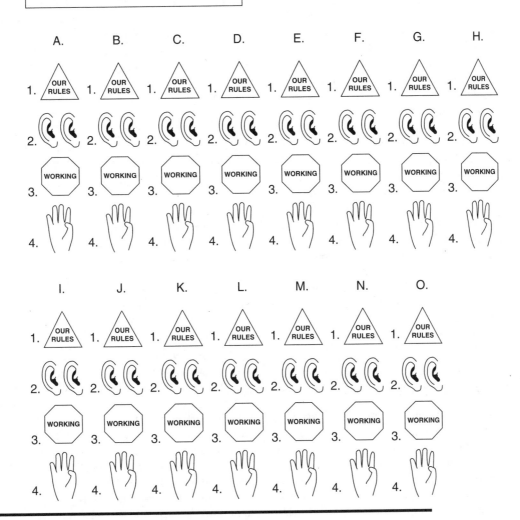

FIGURE 9.2 Feedback Checklist for During Class Behaviors.

Source: Reprinted from *Skills for School Success,* Archer & Gleason (1989), by permission of the authors and Curriculum Associates.

students arrive and he should greet them. Next, the teacher should begin teaching immediately to illustrate that being on time is essential. Similarly, if the teacher has requested that students bring materials to class each day, they must act as if that is a real expectation. If each time a student fails to bring a notebook or pencil to class, the teacher automatically provides the new pencils or a high-quality paper, then students learn that bringing materials to class is not really important. On the other hand, the teacher can convey the message that bringing materials to class is critical by restating the expectation, telling the student that her materials would be checked tomorrow, and then loaning the student less desirable supplies. Teachers should always remember that their actions really do speak louder than words.

In summary, critical school behaviors should be taught in the same manner as academic skills. Teachers must: (1) identify the target behavior, (2) explicitly teach the behavior, (3) review the behavior, (4) provide feedback to students on their performances, and (5) monitor behavior performance so that instruction can be adjusted. Because appropriate school behaviors are critical to the students' success, particularly those with learning difficulties, acquiring these behaviors cannot be left to chance. Teachers must teach them, expect them, and act in ways that reinforce those expectations.

ORGANIZATIONAL SKILLS

There is strong evidence that many students with mild learning difficulties do not exhibit the organizational skills necessary for school success (Heron & Harris, 1987; Shields & Heron, 1989). Students may not be able to locate their homework, may not come to class with necessary materials, and may not remember when assignments are due. These difficulties, which may be reflected in the poor achievement and low grades of the students, can be overcome through systematically teaching organizational skills.

Organizational skills selected for direct instruction should meet three criteria. First, the skill should *match the students' current needs and ages.* For example, teaching a first-grade student how to use a take-home folder would be appropriate, while teaching the student how to use a notebook would be inappropriate. Second, *the organizational skill should be generalizable* to other settings and future years. Students might be taught to organize their desks by being shown a model desk and having them organize their desks in exactly the same manner. This might even result in a room full of organized desks! However, the students would not be able to generalize this skill to desks in future classrooms or to organizing other materials. It would be far more desirable to teach them a generalizable strategy for organizing any set of material. For example, in the *Skills for School Success* program (Archer & Gleason, 1989), students are taught the following organizational strategies:

1. Get rid of anything that you do not need.
2. Put like things together.
3. Put like things in the same space.
4. Put small things in a container.

Students could apply this strategy to organizing their desks during the current year and in future years. In addition, they could organize any set of materials at home or school such as toys, records, books, and clothing.

Third, the organizational system should be one that the student can *utilize independently.* Teachers may attempt to help students be more successful at school by doing things for them, instead of having them assume responsibility for being organized. For example, instead of having students record assignments themselves, the teacher might write the assignments for them on individual calendars. The teacher might insert homework in each student's binder at the end of the day, placing a star on those assignments that need to be completed for the next day. Or, the teacher could write the headings on the student's paper rather than requiring that behavior from the students. This type of assistance promotes dependence, not independence. Students might become organized in the specific educational setting but would learn little to facilitate independent organization in the future. It is more beneficial to teach students to use an assignment calendar, to store their own materials in a notebook, and to write a heading on each assignment. The goal of instruction should always be to promote independence rather than dependence.

Skills for School Success (Archer & Gleason, 1989), a commercially available program developed for the elementary and middle school grades, is designed to teach organizational skills that reflect these criteria. They match the students' needs, are generalizable, and stress independent implementation. The program provides specific instruction on the skills described in the following discussions.

ORGANIZING MATERIALS

Many students have no system for organizing their materials. They are likely to arrive in class without a pencil or pen, to sort through their pockets and lunch bags in search of the elusive homework, or to borrow a piece of paper from their neighbor. Students of all ages should be taught an organizational system that helps them do the following things: (1) bring necessary materials to class, (2) transport materials between class and home, (3) store materials for later completion or study, and (4) retrieve necessary materials quickly.

In the primary grades, folders can be used to meet these goals. Students can be given an "In-Class" folder and a "Take-Home" folder. Both of these folders can be labeled on the front cover with the student's name and room number. The pockets of the In-Class folder can be labeled "WORK" for assignments to be completed during seatwork time and "PAPER" for paper to be used during teacher-directed instruction or for completing assignments. The pockets of the Take-Home folder can be labeled "LEAVE AT HOME"

and "BRING BACK TO SCHOOL." At the end of the day, returned papers and notices can be placed in the "LEAVE AT HOME" pocket, while homework assignments and notices needing a parent's response can be placed in the "BRING BACK TO SCHOOL" pocket.

In the upper grades, students can be taught to use a three-ring binder for organizing their school materials. They each will need a sturdy three-ring binder, a plastic pouch for pencils and pens, dividers for each class or subject, an additional divider labeled "paper," and notebook paper. The binder facilitates transporting materials to and from class, systematically organizing classroom materials, storing assignments and class handouts, and quickly retrieving of necessary materials.

While using notebooks and folders seem relatively simple, both require explicit teacher-directed instruction. First, the teacher should present an example folder or notebook, explain its use, and provide a rationale for its use. This rationale should underscore the benefits of the system over the students' current methods (e.g., in the upper grades—folded papers in books, spiral binders, and assorted folders). Second, the teacher should guide students in setting up the organizational system. In the upper grades, this would involve labeling the dividers and placing all materials in the binder (e.g, pouch, dividers, divider-labeled paper, and notebook paper). Third, the teacher should provide simulated exercises in using the folder or notebook. For example, the teacher might say, "Your English teacher gives you a homework assignment. Show me where you would put it." "In math, your teacher said, 'Take out your last quiz.' Show me where you would find it." Fourth, the teacher should clearly establish expectations for using the binder or folder.

While these systems are not difficult to introduce to students, they require a good deal of teacher vigilance to establish consistent use. The discussion on maintenance and generalization at the end of this chapter elaborates on this. Students need to be carefully monitored in using the notebook or folder, giving them feedback, positive consequences (e.g., a positive grade recorded in the grade book, a star on a chart, stickers, occasional certificates of accomplishment, access to special events, or academic awards) and negative consequences (e.g., using less desirable supplies when the binder is not brought to class, a negative grade recorded in the grade book, or loss of tokens or points), depending on the students' performances. In addition, special time will need to be set aside periodically for cleaning out and reorganizing the binder or folders.

TIME MANAGEMENT

As with organizing materials, many students have no system for organizing their time. They may forget when assignments are due, wait until the last moment to study for a test, or be unable to plan completing multiple assignments. Upper-grade students need to develop a time management system that: (1) results in a clear record of all classroom assignments and school events, (2) allows for planning of home study, and (3) promotes advance planning and completing long-term assignments. While teachers often use weekly assignment sheets, a monthly calendar has several advantages. A monthly calendar promotes advance planning and is a better tool for recording assignments and tests that may be assigned 1 or 2 weeks before the due date.

Using a monthly calendar effectively involves several critical preskills that should be directly taught to the students. Prior to introducing the monthly calendar, teachers should teach students the meaning of such terms as *due date* (many students inaccurately assume it is the day you "do" an assignment). Second, they must teach students how to locate due dates on calendars given the various types of directions. For example, students must be able to locate *tomorrow; day after tomorrow; this Tuesday, Wednesday, Thursday, or Friday; next Monday, Tuesday, Wednesday, Thursday, or Friday; on a specific date; in 1 week, 2 weeks, or 3 weeks* on their calendars. Third, students must be taught how to write brief, clear calendar entries. For example, they can be taught to write an abbreviation for a subject followed by a brief description of the assignment (e.g., Rdg.—Read pp. 72–78; Eng.—Exer. a & b, p. 106; S. S.—Test Ch. 4). Using symbols and abbreviations in the entries makes it possible to record numerous assignments for a single date. Fourth, these preskills should be combined in simulated practice in which students locate today's date, listen to the teacher's directions, locate the due date, and record an entry on the calendar (e.g., "Pretend that it is April 7. In math class, the teacher said, 'Complete pages 14 and 15 by the day after tomorrow.' Write an entry on your calendar.")

In addition to learning how to record assignments on a monthly calendar, students need to learn how to plan home study time using their calendars. They can be taught to examine their calendars and determine homework that is due tomorrow. Then they can examine the calendars for upcoming tests, projects, or assignments, and determine something that they could do in advance on that assignment. Students might be instructed to write an "Action List" or "To Do List" for evening study. In addition, they can learn to break large assignments into smaller tasks. For example, the assignment to complete a written report on a selected state could be broken down into the following task outline:

Task 1. Select state.
Task 2. Locate reference books.
Task 3. Take notes on material in reference books.
Task 4. Write an outline.
Task 5. Write first draft of report.
Task 6. Edit and write second draft of report.
Task 7. Write final draft of paper.

The student can then target intermediate due dates for each task and record these on the calendar, resulting in a time line to guide assignment completion.

As with using the binder or folder, the primary challenge is not teaching the skill; it is getting students to consistently *use* the skill. To promote using the calendar, the teacher can: (1) give clear directions that can be recorded on the calendars, (2) check entries on calendars, (3) remind students to record assignments on their calendars, (4) provide a homework planning time at the end of the day, and (5) provide students with feedback on using their calendars. As with the folders and binders, positive consequences can be given for consistent use of the calendar, as well as, adverse consequences for failure to record assignments on the calendar.

ORGANIZING CONTENT ON PAPERS

The appearance of completed assignments is important. Not only will appearance affect the grade the student receives, but it also may influence the teacher's overall attitude toward the student. If the assignment has a heading, is well organized, and is written neatly, the teacher is likely to think that the student put effort into it and wanted to do well, even if some answers are incorrect. As a result, the teacher may provide additional help to the student. Given the importance of work appearance, all students should be taught the attributes of an attractive paper. Figure 9.3 outlines one set of standards for papers that students might be taught.

When working with lower-achieving students, it is best to teach each set of attributes or standards separately. First, a teacher can present an example assignment containing all the attributes of a correct heading. Next, the teacher can present incorrect headings (nonexamples) and be asked to determine the attributes that are incorrect. Finally, students can be given practice writing and evaluating their own headings.

To ensure continuous use of standards, the teacher can use the following guidelines:

1. Remind students to use the HOW standards when completing assignments.

HOW Should Your Papers Look?

H = Heading
1. First and last name
2. Date
3. Subject
4. Page number if needed

O = Organized
1. On the front side of the paper
2. Left margin
3. Right margin
4. At least one blank line at the top
5. At least one blank line at the bottom
6. Good spacing

W = Written neatly
1. Words and numbers on the lines
2. Words and numbers written neatly
3. Neat erasing or crossing out

FIGURE 9.3 Standards for Student Papers: HOW Should Your Paper Look?

Source: Reprinted from *Skills for School Success,* Archer & Gleason (1989), by permission of the authors and Curriculum Associates.

2. Provide feedback to students on the appearance of their papers using a checklist for the HOW standards.
3. Guide students in self-evaluation of their own papers.
4. Provide positive feedback for legible, well-organized papers such as positive comments, stickers, stars, or bonus points.
5. Display excellent papers on a bulletin board.
6. Have students redo papers that do not reflect the standards.

Using a self-monitoring checklist is a particularly powerful procedure for promoting transfer of neat-paper skills to the regular classroom and other settings (Anderson-Inman, Paine, & Deutchman, 1984a). The continuous use of all organizational skills is based on *telling* students to use the skill, giving them *opportunities* to use the skill, *monitoring* their use of the skill, and providing them with *feedback* on skill use.

LEARNING STRATEGIES

In elementary and secondary classes, students are expected to perform a myriad of tasks. They read textbooks, listen to lectures, complete written reports, answer chapter questions, prepare for tests, and respond to other common classroom tasks. However, many students fail to spontaneously employ systematic strategies and approaches to these tasks. Other students utilize procedures that are not effective or are inordinately time consuming. Despite the fact that many students do not utilize systematic study procedures, teachers frequently assume that students will be able to do school tasks, and thus do not directly teach these skills and strategies. As a result, these skills are the "invisible curriculum" in the schools: seldom taught, often needed, frequently unknown (Dean, 1977).

The following paragraphs describe characteristics of learning strategies, provide examples of learning strategies, and present instructional procedures for introducing learning strategies. At the end of this chapter, the actual use and generalization of these strategies are delineated.

CHARACTERISTICS OF
LEARNING STRATEGIES

Learning strategies are task-specific techniques that students use in responding to classroom tasks. They are, in effect, the individual's approach to a task. They incorporate elements of cognitive and metacognitive training that enable the student to complete tasks independently (Ellis, Lenz, & Sabornie, 1987a; Schumaker & Deshler, 1984). For example, a student might be taught a step-by-step strategy for reading a textbook selection, answering chapter questions, writing a report, or proofreading written work. Learning strategies are designed to empower students and to increase their independence. As such, the evolving work in learning strategies represents a viable and exciting direction in educational research and practice.

While learning strategies differ greatly, there are some common characteristics that are useful to note.

1. Learning strategies are task specific rather than content specific. Learning strategies address common classroom tasks that can be applied to a variety of content areas. For example, a strategy for taking multiple-choice tests is applicable to multiple-choice tests in reading, mathematics, science, health, or social studies. In classrooms, students gain information for the most part by listening to the teacher or by reading text material. They demonstrate knowledge or skills by completing assignments, answering questions, writing reports, making oral presentations, and/or taking tests. These tasks require the student to initiate one or more strategies. When writing a report, for example, the student would need a strategy for taking notes on material in reference books, a strategy for organizing and writing the report, and a strategy for proofreading the written product.

2. Learning strategies should match the curriculum demands of the school setting and represent an area of skill deficiency. The curriculum demands the student faces should be a major determinant of the task-specific strategies that would be taught (Deshler & Schumaker, 1986; Schumaker & Deshler, 1984). For example, if the student attends three classes in which the teacher lectures, learning a strategy for taking notes would meet an immediate need. Likewise, learning a proofreading strategy would be seen as beneficial by the seventh grade student who is asked to write in many of his classes. Students should be taught strategies in those areas in which they demonstrate little or no skill. If students already are able to take well-organized notes, instruction on a new note-taking strategy would not be necessary. However, if students are unable to extract or recall critical information from reading expository textbooks, learning a textbook reading strategy would be beneficial.

3. Learning strategies generally involve a small number of ordered steps. Learning strategies generally involve applying specific steps in a prescribed, logical order. Strategies that contain a relatively small number of steps facilitate initial acquisition and later recall of the strategy steps.

4. Learning strategies are, by design, generalizable. Learning strategies are designed to generalize to the same type of task across subject areas, situations, and instructors. Thus, when using a learning strategy approach, students would be taught a strategy for reading all expository textbooks rather than a strategy that only applies to this year's science book. Likewise, a student would be taught a strategy that could be used to study or memorize any information (e.g., words and definitions, spelling words, math facts, lecture notes, chapter summaries, and lists of facts) rather than separate strategies for each type of content.

5. Learning strategies are designed to increase cognition and metacognition. *Cognition* is promoted when a strategy requires the active involvement of the student. For example, a text reading strategy can encourage careful reading by requiring a student to read a paragraph and then to verbally restate the information. Learning strategies can increase **metacognition,** or one's awareness, monitoring, and regulating of one's cognitive processes. (Haller, Child, & Walberg, 1988). The transfer and use of a strategy are greatly facilitated when students are taught how to employ the strategy; when and where to use it; and how to monitor, check, and evaluate strategy use (Pressley, Borkowski, & O'Sullivan, 1984). Students can continually evaluate their own learning ("Did I learn the most important points in this chapter?" "Did I recite the most important information?" "Do I understand my notes?") and the quality of their work ("Did I complete all of the items? Did I do the work accurately? Did I proofread my assignment?") Strategies that include steps that direct students to evaluate or monitor their own performances can enhance self-regulatory behaviors involved in planning, revising, monitoring, and evaluating. For exam-

ple, in a the Read-Cover-Recite-Check textbook reading strategy, students read a paragraph, cover the material, recite the critical content, and then check their recitation with the actual passage content. An assignment completion strategy might direct students to recheck their assignments upon completion (Are all items done? Are the answers accurate?). Similarly, a writing strategy might direct students to evaluate their papers as to audience, content, structure, and mechanics.

6. Learning strategies attempt to transform passive learners into active learners. Students with learning difficulties tend to be passive in their approach to learning tasks (Griffey, Zigmond, & Leinhardt, 1988; Paris & Oka, 1986; Torgesen, 1982). Often they do not become totally engaged in the learning task, do not attend to the critical content, or do not actively participate in the learning process. Instead, these students may focus on assignment completion rather than on the intended learning. Strategy steps that increase cognition or metacognition contribute to active involvement in learning. In addition, many strategies will include specific *overt behaviors* to increase task involvement. For example, students may be asked not only to read the directions, but to circle important words in the directions. Or, rather than relying on simply reading text material, they may be directed to take notes on the material as a study procedure. These overt behaviors compel the student to become less passive and more actively involved in the task. In addition, they allow the teacher to monitor actual use of the strategy: something that is not possible if all of the strategy behaviors are covert.

7. Learning strategies may be accompanied by a "remembering device." Strategies can be accompanied by a "remembering device," which may be a word or list of letters that corresponds to the strategy steps. **Mnemonics,** as they are known as, can facilitate associative memory, thereby helping students to recall the strategy steps (Mastropieri & Scruggs, 1989). They can be used to learn abstract as well as concrete information (Scruggs & Mastropieri, 1992). Such remembering devices can be useful in the acquisition and retention of discriminations, concepts, facts, rules or procedures (Mastropieri & Scruggs, in press). Nonetheless, remembering devices are not essential attributes of learning strategies. For example, they are unnecessary when the steps are simple and logical. Further, efforts to create remembering devices can be counterproductive when they complicate the learning strategy by adding additional steps or using less common wording. Neither of these are desirable. The strategy should have as few steps as possible and should always be stated as simply as possible.

SAMPLE STRATEGIES

There has been a great deal of work in developing learning strategies for use with regular and special education students. Some researchers have focused on developing strategies in response to a certain type of task, such as writing expository products or reading text material. Others have formulated sets of strategies into formal learning strategies curricula. The *Informed Strategies for Learning* (Paris, Cross, & Lipson 1984), the *Learning Strategies Curriculum* developed at the University of Kansas Institute for Research in Learning Disabilities (Deshler & Schumaker, 1986), and *Skills for School Success* (Archer & Gleason, 1989) are three examples of such curricula. Much of the discussion in this chapter is derived from the *Skills for School Success,* a program developed to teach learning strategies to elementary and middle school students. The *Learning Strategies Curriculum,* on the other hand, was specifically designed and empirically validated on students in middle schools and secondary schools. This curriculum is described in Chapter 13, which deals with enhancing content learning of students at the secondary school level.

A common feature of all strategies developed is that they address gaining information in classes (i.e., reading expository material, reading narrative material, and gaining information from verbal presentations) or demonstrating knowledge or skills (i.e., completing daily assignments, writing narrative products, writing expository products, and preparing for and taking tests). While the strategies presented in this section represent only a small subset of learning strategies, they provide a snapshot of the types of strategies available for student instruction.

Strategies for Reading Expository Material

In both elementary and secondary classes, students are expected to read **expository material,** material in science, social studies, history, health, and other content-area classes. Over the years, this difficult task has prompted the development of numerous strategies, all designed to increase students' reading comprehension. These strategies address two complementary aspects of expository reading: (1) previewing the content of the chapter, and (2) actively reading the material with increased understanding and recall of the information.

Previewing Strategies. Before reading a chapter in a content-area textbook, it is useful to preview or survey the information-laden sections of the chapter. The chapter title, the introductory section, the section headings and the subheadings, the summary, and the end-of-chapter questions help the reader to gain an understanding of the organization of the selection and an idea of the content covered in the chapter. This serves to develop a framework or schema for reading the selection.

When the content or organizational structure of the chapter is complex or the information presented in the chapter is beyond students' prior knowledge, the preview is best done as a teacher-directed activity. A preview strategy designed for use with elementary and middle school students is depicted in Figure 9.4. In this strategy, called *Warm-Up* (Archer & Gleason, 1989), the teacher guides students in examining salient aspects of the chapter before reading commences. First, the students read the title and the introduction to the chapter, and answer a rhetorical question, "What

Warm-up

Before you read a chapter in your science, social studies, or health book, **warm up.** Use these steps to find out what the chapter is about <u>before</u> you begin to read.

Step 1: Read the TITLE of the chapter and the INTRODUCTION.

Step 2: Read the HEADINGS and the SUBHEADINGS.

Step 3: Read the CHAPTER SUMMARY.

Step 4: Read the QUESTIONS at the end of the chapter.

Step 5: Say to yourself, "This chapter will talk about _____."

FIGURE 9.4   Strategy for Previewing the Content of an Expository Chapter: Warm-Up

Source: Reprinted from *Skills for School Success,* Archer & Gleason (1989), by permission of the authors and Curriculum Associates.

will this chapter be about?" Next, they identify the headings and the subheadings within the chapter as the teacher records these on the board or the overhead transparency, illustrating the chapter's organization. Finally, students read the summary and the questions at the end of the chapter. From this teacher-directed activity, students gain an overview of the chapter content and an understanding of the chapter's organization. In Chapter 13, another preview strategy, TRIMS, which has been specifically developed for use in secondary content-area classes, is introduced and illustrated.

Strategies for Reading Expository Material. Many expository reading strategies have been developed and studied with elementary and secondary students. All these strategies attempt to change passive reading behaviors of students to behaviors characterized by active engagement in the reading process. Instead of passively reading and rereading the chapter, students are directed to perform "active" behaviors such as formulating questions on the content, taking notes, underlining main ideas, or verbally paraphrasing the critical information. Second, these strategies direct the student's attention to the most important concepts, ideas, and details. Finally, the content area reading strategies universally engage students in some type of information rehearsal in which the students verbally recite or write down important information. Two types of expository learning strategies, those that utilize verbal rehearsal and those that utilize written rehearsal, are described in the following section.

Since Robinson's development of SQ3R (Survey, Question, Read, Recite, Review) in 1946, several strategies involving verbal rehearsal or recitation have been developed for use with elementary and secondary students. The *Paraphrasing Strategy* (Schumaker, Denton, & Deshler, 1984), also referred to as **RAP strategy,** consists of the following steps: (1) <u>R</u>ead a paragraph. (2) <u>A</u>sk yourself, "What were the main idea and details in this paragraph?" and (3) <u>P</u>ut the main idea and details in your own words (p. 58). Similarly, *Active Reading* (Archer & Gleason, 1989), a strategy appropriate for elementary students and lower-achieving secondary students because of its simplicity, utilizes verbal recitation. Using Active Reading, depicted in Figure 9.5, the student *reads* a single paragraph, *covers* the paragraph, *recites* the important information, and then *checks* his recitation of the critical information by reexamining the paragraph content. This process would continue through the entire selection.

Before the strategy is introduced, students should be taught to verbally retell the content they read. First, they learn to identify topics of paragraphs. Once, they can state a word or a phrase topic for a paragraph, they learn to identify critical details in the paragraph and to retell the topic and details in their own words. Once students can retell paragraph content, the teacher models the entire strategy and provides guided practice until proficiency is reached. Then students practice the strategy independently.

Active Reading

R = Read
Read a paragraph.
- Think about the topic.
- Think about the important details.

C = Cover
Cover the paragraph with your hand.

R = Recite
Tell yourself what you have read.
- Say the topic.
- Say the important details.
- Say it in your own words.

C = Check
Lift your hand and check.

If you forget something important, begin again.

FIGURE 9.5 Strategy for Reading an Expository Selection

Source: Reprinted from *Skills for School Success,* Archer & Gleason (1989), by permission of the authors and Curriculum Associates.

Another way to actively involve students in reading expository selections is through written rehearsal such as taking notes on the content or writing a summary of the content. Taking notes on written material is useful for several reasons. When students take notes, they have to attend closely to the author's message and evaluate what information is important, and thus what should be recorded. They then can use their notes when studying for a test, writing a paragraph summary of the content, answering chapter questions, or writing a report. Smith and Tompkins (1988) also believe that note-taking promotes deeper mental processing of the selection content.

When teaching note-taking strategies to students, care should be taken that the strategy does not remove attention from the content. Often teachers introduce formal outlining in which the relationships among ideas are shown through in-dentation, numbers (Roman and Arabic), and letters (uppercase and lowercase). While outlining might assist students in organizing their own ideas in preparing for a speech or writing a paper, it can be problematic for taking notes on written material since many students will be more concerned about the appropriate designation (e.g., "Should this be a Roman numeral I, a capital A, or a lowercase a?") than the author's message. Instead, a simple style of note-taking in which the subordination of ideas is illustrated through systematic indentation of topics and supporting details could be taught.

One simple system of note-taking, which Archer and Gleason (1989) developed, is particularly appropriate for students with learning difficulties since the notes follow the structure of the text material and use the paragraph as the unit of analysis. Figure 9.6 presents example notes. In this system, students record the heading or the subheading in the center of the paper, followed by the corresponding page number. Next, students take notes on each paragraph in the section. First, they record a topic for the paragraph, and then indent and record the important paragraph details. When the notes have been completed and checked for clarity, students go back and record questions in the left-hand margin for each of the paragraphs. Later, students use the questions to study their notes.

Another form of written rehearsal involves writing a summary of the passage content. This is an excellent activity for several reasons. Summarizing can help students understand the organization of the text material, and it provides practice in determining main ideas and critical concepts in the selection. Finally, the effort to identify critical content during the summarizing process can help students remember those ideas (Murrell & Surber, 1987).

Summarizing is a complex task and must be directly taught to students. It involves applying the following rules (Brown & Day, 1983):

1. Delete trivial information.
2. Delete redundant information.

Taking Notes on Written Material

1. Write down the heading or subheading and the page number.
2. Take notes on each paragraph.
   a. Write a word or phrase that tells about the whole paragraph.
   b. Indent and write the important details that you should remember from the paragraph.

Example Notes

Mammals (p. 156)

Characteristics of mammals

   —have backbones

   —nurse their young

   —have hair

   —are warm-blooded

   —have more well-developed brain than other animals

Where mammals live

   —most live on land and have four legs

   —some live in trees in forest or jungle

   —dolphins, whales, porpoises, and manatees live in water

   —gophers and moles live underground

What mammals eat

   —plants (herbivorous)

   —animal flesh (carnivorous)

   —insects (insectivorous)

The skeleton of mammals

   —provides framework for body and protects organs

   —is attached to muscles

   —contains more than 200 bones

Guidelines for Good Note-taking

1. Write your notes in your own words.
2. Make your notes brief.
3. Use abbreviations and symbols.
4. Be sure you understand your notes.

FIGURE 9.6 Indentation Style Notes Taken on an Expository Passage

Source: Reprinted from *Skills for School Success,* Archer & Gleason (1989), by permission of the authors and Curriculum Associates.

3. Substitute superordinate terms for lists of items.
4. Integrate a series of events with a superordinate action term.
5. Select a topic sentence.
6. Invent a topic sentence if there is none.

Applying these rules involves two types of thinking: (1) a selection process in which judgements are made about what information should be selected or rejected and (2) a reduction process in which ideas must be condensed by substituting general ideas for more detailed ones (Johnson, 1983).

Rinehart, Stahl, and Erickson (1986) taught sixth-grade students four rules for producing summaries:

1. Identify main information
2. Delete trivial information
3. Delete redundant information
4. Relate main and supporting information

In this instruction, teachers modeled each of the four summarization rules and students applied the rules to individual paragraphs. When summarization of paragraph content was mastered, students were taught three steps to use in summarizing multiple-paragraph selections:

1. Write summaries of each paragraph in the selection.
2. Create a summary of the paragraph summaries by amalgamating them into a single paragraph.
3. Apply the four summarization rules to this paragraph.

After students practiced this strategy, they were presented with selections to summarize without writing separate summaries for the individual paragraphs. Here, the students were taught to write the overall idea of the selection followed by the most important ideas of the selection in as few sentences as possible.

Several empirically validated summarization strategies have been developed (Pressley, Johnson, Symon, McGoldrick, & Kurita, 1989).

In some cases, students have been taught to write a single sentence to summarize a paragraph (Jenkins, Heliotis, Stein, & Haynes, 1987) or procedures for summarizing single paragraphs using the rules listed previously (Bean & Steenwyk, 1984). Other authors have taught students to use spatial displays (e.g., maps or diagrams) to assist in the summarization process.

Strategies for Reading Narrative Selections

All narrative stories have similar elements, including a setting introduced at the beginning of the story, a main character, other characters, a problem or challenge that the main character generally experiences, attempts to resolve the problem, a resolution of the problem, and the emotional response of the main character or other characters to the resolution. Because of the consistent structure of narrative passages, narrative reading strategies attempt to draw students' attention to these elements often referred to as *story grammar.* When students are taught to examine a story for these elements, their comprehension and recall of the story improves (Idol, 1987; Idol & Croll, 1987; Short & Ryan, 1984).

While story grammar training always focuses on the general structure of the story, the strategies themselves may vary. Short and Ryan (1984) taught fourth-grade students who were reading below grade level to ask themselves the following questions as they read a story: (1) Who is the main character? (2) Where and when did the story take place? (3) What did the main characters do? (4) How did the story end? (5) How did the main character feel? This story grammar strategy was taught and practiced over many sessions. After training, students in the strategy group remembered the story better than untrained students.

Griffey, Zigmond and Leinhardt (1988) found that teaching students with learning disabilities a story structure and self-questioning strategies increased passage comprehension. In the first part of their training, students learned the

CAPS strategy, which corresponds to the elements of a story: C = Characters, A = Aim, P = Problem, and S = Solution. After students had been introduced to the story elements, they were trained to ask themselves questions about the story elements corresponding to CAPS: Who are the characters? What is the aim of the story? What problem happens? How did the characters solve the problem? Applying these questions as they read stories resulted in increased scores on comprehension measures.

Strategies for Completing Daily Assignments

The two most common types of assignments in elementary and secondary schools involve: (1) completing an assignment with a set of directions and/or (2) answering written questions on expository or narrative material. A strategy that Archer and Gleason (1989) developed can be employed when a student has an assignment with a set of directions followed by a series of parallel items. This first type of assignment occurs in reading, language arts, mathematics, English, and spelling instructions. Students with learning problems may fail to read the directions, to carefully consider what they are supposed to do, to complete all items on the assignment, to check their work for accuracy, or to turn their assignments in. The strategy, outlined in Figure 9.7, involves four major steps:

1. Plan it.
2. Complete it.
3. Check it.
4. Turn it in.

These steps not only assist the student in completing assignments, but they also give the teacher, an aide, or a parent a systematic procedure for helping a student to complete an assignment. For example, Michael, who has been taught this strategy, is having difficulty with a language arts assignment and asks the teacher for assistance. The teacher might work with him in the following manner:

T: Michael, this assignment has a set of directions. What do you need to do first?
S: Plan it.
T: When you plan it, what do you do?
S: I read the directions carefully.
T: Good, read the directions out loud.
S: "Read each sentence below. Write a compound word in the box."
T: Now, what should you do?
S: Circle the words that tell me what to do.
T: What words would you circle?
S: Read and write.
T: Circle those words.
S: (Circles words.)
T: What should you do next?
S: Get out the materials that I need.
T: What materials are needed?
S: A pencil.
T: Now, what would you do?
S: Tell myself what to do.

Completing Assignments

Step 1: **Plan it.**
- Read the directions carefully.
- Circle the words that tell you what to do.
- Get out the materials you need.
- Tell yourself what to do.

Step 2. **Complete it.**
- Do all the items.
- If you can't do an item, ask for help or go ahead to the next item.
- Use **HOW.**

Step 3: **Check it.**
- Did you do everything?
- Did you get the right answers?
- Did you proofread?

Step 4: **Turn it in.**

FIGURE 9.7 A Strategy for Completing Daily Assignments

Source: Reprinted from *Skills for School Success,* Archer & Gleason (1989), by permission of the authors and Curriculum Associates.

T: Good, Michael. Tell me what you are supposed to do. Remember to touch the circled words.

S: I am supposed to read each sentence and write a compound word in the box.

T: After you plan your assignment, what should you do?

S: Complete it.

T: Good, Michael. Do the first item. (Teacher monitors and models item if necessary.) Now, finish this assignment.

Notice that the strategy has not only empowered the student, but also the teacher. Once a strategy has been taught, the teacher has a procedure that allows more systematic interaction with students so that independence rather than dependence is promoted. As illustrated here, the goals of learning strategy instruction are *strategic* students, *strategic* teachers, and a *strategic* classroom.

The second most common assignment given students is answering written questions on expository or narrative materials. Many students have difficulty with this task. They may not read the question carefully or may not have a procedure for locating the answer within the chapter. In addition, many students write incomplete sentence answers that do not incorporate wording from the question. To alleviate these problems, students can be taught a specific strategy for this task in which they first read the question; then change it into part of the answer; and, finally, write it down. This strategy, depicted in Figure 9.8, benefits students in several ways: it gives the students a way to get the task started, the subsequent answer will be a complete sentence, and it encourages the student to carefully contemplate the question before referring back to the chapter content. Next, students locate the section of the chapter that talks about the topic by examining the headings and the subheadings. Finally, students locate and complete the answer.

Daily assignments usually involve writing sentences or paragraphs. This requires proofreading, detecting and correcting sense, capitali-

---

Answering Chapter Questions

Use this strategy when you need to answer questions in your science, social studies, or health book. Remember, words from the question can be used in your answer.

Step 1:   Read the question carefully.

Step 2:   Change the question into part of the answer and write it down. With the question **Why?**, use part of the answer to the previous question in your answer.

Step 3:   Locate the section of the chapter that talks about the topic. Use the headings and subheadings to help you.

Step 4:   Read the section of the chapter until you find the answer.

Step 5:   Complete the answer.

FIGURE 9.8   A Strategy for Answering Written Questions on Expository Material That Has Already Been Read

Source: Reprinted from *Skills for School Success,* Archer & Gleason (1989), by permission of the authors and Curriculum Associates.

---

zation, punctuation, and spelling errors. The inability to detect and correct errors, especially spelling errors, characterizes the writing performance of students with learning problems. In response to this challenge, several proofreading or error-monitoring strategies have been developed. In the *Error Monitoring Strategy* that is a part of the *Learning Strategies Curriculum* (Schumaker, Nolan, & Deshler, 1985), students are taught to monitor written work for Capitalization, Overall appearance, Punctuation, and Spelling (**COPS strategy**). Similarly, the strategy that Archer and Gleason (1989) developed, depicted in Figure 9.9, directs students to proofread for sense, capitals, punctuation, and spelling. Given that detecting and correcting spelling errors is particularly challenging, students are taught a pragmatic routine for correcting spelling errors. Since many of the misspelled words appear in the assignment, students are first directed to look at the assignment. Next, they look for the unknown word in the text material and the glossary. If the word is not found in any of these sources, the student underlines the word and later asks a better speller how to spell the word. Obviously, these same proofreading strategies can be applied to longer written products. However, we must stress that proofreading should be used for any "public communication" such as daily assignments, reports, essays, stories, and letters.

Strategies for Writing Expository Products

Writing expository products is challenging for all students but particularly for students with academic achievement problems. These students often engage in little advance planning before writing, have difficulty generating content, produce products that are inordinately short, and pro-

---

Proofreading Your Assignments

Before you turn in an assignment, check each sentence by using these steps.

1. Check to be sure the sentence makes SENSE.
2. Check the CAPITALS.
3. Check the PUNCTUATION.
4. Check the SPELLING.

   If you don't know how to spell a word,
   - look in the assignment.
   - look in the textbook.
   - look in the glossary.

   If you can't find the word,
   - underline the word.
   - ask someone how to spell the word when you are done.

FIGURE 9.9   A Proofreading Strategy

Source: Reprinted from *Skills for School Success,* Archer & Gleason (1989), by permission of the authors and Curriculum Associates.

duce products that do not match the conventions and features of the type of written product under consideration (Graham, Harris & Sawyer, 1987; Graham & Harris, 1989). Despite these challenges, numerous highly effective strategies have been developed and researched with students who have specific learning disabilities. These strategies are designed to produce varying genre of written products such as essays, descriptions, factual reports, arguments, and explanations.

Graham and Harris (1989) taught students with learning disabilities a self-instructional strategy for writing essays when given such topics as "Do you think children should be allowed to have their own pets?" Before being introduced to the essay writing strategy, students were provided pretraining on the components of a good essay. Using the mnemonic **TREE strategy,** students were introduced to and practiced generating essay components: T = note Topic sentence. R = note Reasons. E = Examine reasons, and N = note Ending. These elements correspond to the general structure of an argument, including premise, reasons and data to support the premise, and conclusion. Students practiced the mnemonic and the meaning of each step until mastery was demonstrated. Following the pretraining, which involved an oral commitment by the students to learning the strategy, the teacher introduced a three-step composition strategy. The steps included: (1) Think, "Who will read this, and why am I writing it?" (2) Plan what to say using TREE. (3) Write and say more.

After the strategy was described, the teacher actively modeled it using a "thinking outloud" procedure. The teacher also modeled four types of self-instruction during the development and writing of the essay: (1) problem definition, (2) planning, (3) self-evaluation, and (4) self-reinforcement. Instruction continued with verbal rehearsal of the strategy steps, controlled practice in which the teacher and student jointly composed essays, and independent practice. As a result of the strategy training, subjects included more of the essay components in their compositions, the proportion of nonfunctional essay elements dropped, and the quality of the essays was judged superior.

Another program, *Cognitive Strategy Instruction for Writing* (Raphael, Kirshner, & Englert, 1986), utilizes specially designed "think sheets" to guide students in completing each step of the writing process: Planning, Organizing, Writing, Editing, and Revising (**POWER strategy**) (Englert, Raphael, Anderson, Anthony, Fear, & Gregg, 1988). This program is described more fully in the discussion of teaching written language expression in Chapter 11.

Strategies for Writing Narrative Products

Strategies for writing stories, like the strategies for reading stories, have been built around story grammar elements. In a study by Graham, Harris, and Sawyer (1987), fifth- and sixth-grade learning disabled students were taught a strategy for developing and writing narrative stories. This strategy included the following steps:

1. Look at the picture (stimulus item).
2. Let your mind be free.
3. Write down the story part reminder (W-W-W; What = 2; How = 2).
4. Write down story part ideas for each part.
5. Write your story—use good parts and make sense.

Before being introduced to the entire strategy, students received training on the mnemonic device in Step 3. The students were presented with a chart containing the mnemonic and were taught to generate the following story grammar questions: Who is the main character? Who else is in the story? When does the story take place? Where does the story take place? What does the main character do? What happens when she tries to do it? How does the story end? How does the main character feel? Students used the content generated from answering these questions as blueprints for their stories. As a result of training on this strategy, students were able to generate stories containing more of the story grammar elements.

The posttraining stories received significantly higher quality ratings than did pretraining stories.

Strategies for Preparing for and Taking Tests

In many classes, student acquisition of skills and knowledge is measured through test performance. This is particularly true in the secondary schools where scores on tests often compose the major portion of the grade. As a result, students must be given assistance in both preparing for and taking tests.

Test Preparation Strategies. Prior to taking tests in such subjects as science, social studies, and history, students need to review and study information found in their textbooks, class notes, handouts, study guides, and completed assignments. Many times students attempt to learn the information by simply reading and rereading the material. However, if they would use some aspect of verbal or written rehearsal, their recall of the information would increase. A simple verbal rehearsal strategy can be used to study many different types of materials. **RCRC strategy,** developed by Archer and Gleason (1989), utilizes the same steps as outlined for Active Reading: "R = Read. Read a little bit of material. Read it more than once. C = Cover. Cover the material with your hand. R = Recite. Tell yourself what you have read. C = Check. Lift your hand and check. If you forget something important, begin again." In the upper elementary grades, students are taught to couple verbal rehearsal (recite) with written rehearsal.

Often times students are required to learn lists of information such as food groups, continents, nutrients, or branches of earth science in preparation for a content-area test. To facilitate this task, students can be taught to devise personalized mnemonic devices to enhance recall of the information (Archer & Gleason, 1989; Nagel, Schumaker, & Deshler, 1986). The student might memorize the first letters in the word, create a word from the first letters, or construct a sentence in which the first letters of the sentence words correspond to the first letters of the list items. Immediately before taking a test, the student would write down all of the mnemonic devices that he had created and the corresponding information. This reference could then be used as the student completed items on the test.

Test-Taking Strategies.   Students are expected to take tests with a variety of formats including multiple-choice, true-false, short answer, and matching. There is a good deal of evidence that students with mild learning handicaps are deficient in test-taking strategies and systematic approaches to tests. They may fail to attend to the critical information within the directions, are often misled by irrelevant information in the test, dawdle, and may not be persistent in searching for the correct answer (C. A. Hughes, 1985, unpublished data). However, there is also good evidence that these students can learn test-taking skills that improve their scores. For example, Scruggs, Mastropieri, & Tolfa-Veit (1986) directly taught students test-taking skills to employ when taking standardized tests. The students were able to learn and to use these skills during the testing sessions, and thus improved their performance on these tests.

Strategies for taking tests fall into two categories: (1) general test-taking strategies and (2) format-specific strategies (e.g., multiple-choice, short answer, and true-false). Carman and Adams (1972) developed a strategy referred to as **SCORER.** This test-taking strategy includes the following steps: (1) Schedule time, (2) look for Clue words, (3) Omit difficult questions, (4) Read carefully, (5) Estimate answers, and (6) Review the work. When using this strategy, students plan their time by reviewing the entire test to determine easy and difficult items, varying point values for test items, and the number of test items. As students complete the test, they are directed to attend to such clue words as *always, never, sometimes,* or *usually,* to omit the more difficult items until the entire test has been completed, and to read the directions and items carefully. When an item requires a calculation,

students are encouraged to estimate the answer before performing the actual calculation so that obviously wrong answers can be eliminated and careless errors avoided. Finally, they are taught to review all answers on the test.

Other test-taking strategies focus on common test formats. For example, in the *Skills for School Success program* (Archer & Gleason, 1989), students are taught separate strategies for taking multiple-choice, true-false, and short answer tests. The strategy for taking multiple-choice tests involves several steps that parallel those in SCORER:

1. Read the item.
2. Read the choices. Watch for "all of the above" and "none of the above."
3. Cross out the choices that are obviously wrong.
4. Look at the remaining choices and pick the best answer.
5. If you cannot answer a question, put a mark next to it and come back to it later.
6. Check your test.
7. Change an answer only for a good reason. Usually your first answer is best.

TEACHING LEARNING STRATEGIES

Preskills and Difficult Steps

Preskills should be taught and mastered before introducing a new strategy (Lloyd, Saltzman, & Kauffman, 1981). For example, before a proofreading strategy could be introduced, students need some knowledge of basic capitalization and punctuation generalizations. Without this knowledge they cannot be expected to locate and correct errors. Likewise, before introducing a systematic strategy for decoding multisyllabic words, students need to be able to locate and pronounce the affixes, recognize and give the major sound for vowel graphemes, blend syllables into a word, and recognize correct and incorrect pronunciations of words (A. Archer, 1989, unpublished data). Similarly, strategies for reading and comprehending expository textbooks require that the student has mastered a level of decoding sufficient to access the written content. Thus, the teacher must examine the strategy that she intends to teach and determine the necessary foundation skills the strategy demands. These must be taught to a high level of mastery to better ensure ease of learning the strategy and reduction of errors. In many cases, preskill training will constitute the majority of time spent on strategy introduction.

Identifying difficult steps in the strategy and teaching these in advance can also facilitate learning strategy instruction. This can be done only when the steps are discrete and can be thus isolated for instruction. In the strategy for answering chapter questions, described previously, the step involving changing the question into part of the answer might prove to be particularly challenging. In order to facilitate strategy instruction, this step could be extracted and introduced unencumbered by the other steps. Students could be taught how to turn a variety of questions into part of the answer without being required to locate or complete the answer. Once this difficult step is mastered, the entire strategy can be introduced. In the strategy for proofreading assignments, the most difficult steps might be the first one ("Check to be sure the sentence makes sense.") and the final one, checking and correcting spelling errors. Once again, these steps can be taught separately before incorporating them into the entire strategy.

When students are carefully taught necessary preskills and difficult strategy steps in advance, strategy instruction can be relatively easy. As a result, students experience more success and the overall time given to explanations will be reduced.

Selecting Examples for Learning Strategy Instruction

Before teachers begin strategy instruction, they must carefully select examples that can be used during demonstration and student practice of the strategy. The following guidelines are helpful:

1. Select examples that clearly apply to the strategy. For instance, if teaching a textbook reading strategy such as paraphrasing (Schumaker, Denton, & Deshler, 1984), expository or factual passages rather than narrative passages would be selected. To teach proofreading, sentences should be devised that contain common errors (e.g., *sense errors*—deletion of words, inclusion of extra words, and wrong verb tense; *spelling errors*—phonetic spellings, spelling rule errors, and homonyms) to illustrate the strategy application.

2. Utilize a full range of examples. To promote **generalization** of the learning strategy to a variety of materials and settings, a range of examples will communicate the breadth of application to students (Deshler, Alley, Warner, & Schumaker, 1981). To teach a text reading strategy, newspaper articles; encyclopedia articles; or text from science, social studies, health, or civics books could be selected. This would help students see that this strategy is useful across subjects. Similarly, using a wide variety of samples (e.g., answers to questions, a friendly letter, a book report, a science experiment report, and a chapter summary) to teach a proofreading strategy would underscore the utility of this strategy for any written product that is meant to communicate to another person.

3. Order the examples from easy to more difficult. During initial instruction of a learning strategy, students need to focus on the steps in the strategy rather than on the content of the specific task. Hence, the initial examples should be relatively simple. For instance, a textbook reading strategy might first be applied to below-grade-level passages. As students become more familiar with the strategy, the difficulty of the materials could be increased. When teaching students the Plan it step for completing assignments, the initial practice assignments should have explicit directions (e.g., "Read the sentence. Underline the word that goes in the sentence.") The students could easily read the directions, circle the direction words, and retell what they are suppose to do. Later, the Plan it step could be applied to more complex assignment directions (e.g., "We have been learning how to use context to figure out the meaning of an unknown word. You are going to use this skill in this exercise. Read each sentence. Underline the word that goes in the sentence. The context will help you pick the word.")

Introducing New Learning Strategies

There are several effective models of learning strategy instruction (Deshler, Schumaker, & Lenz, 1984a; Deshler, D. D., Schumaker, J. B., Lenz, B. K. & Ellis, E., 1984b; Graham, Harris, & Sawyer, 1987; Roehler & Duffy, 1984; Paris, Cross, & Lipson, 1984; Pressley, Borkowski & O'Sullivan, 1984; Wong, 1985). The model presented here is an expansion of the instructional model presented in Chapter 7. Not surprising, the instructional procedures used to introduce learning strategies are similar to those employed when teaching other skills and academic strategies. These procedures include: (1) demonstrate or model the strategy, (2) prompt students in the use of the strategy, and (3) check students on their application of the strategy. These steps, model, prompt, and check, will be explained below as they apply to learning strategy instruction.

1. Model the strategy. When teaching learning strategies, the teacher should directly model application of the strategy. First, the teacher should clearly demonstrate each step in the strategy, exaggerating the critical features of the steps to ensure student attention. As the teacher demonstrates the step, he should describe exactly what he is doing using clear, easily understood language. Next, the teacher must make any covert strategy steps *overt* so that students can observe them. For example, when teaching read, cover, recite, and check (Archer & Gleason, 1989), the teacher would read the information out loud, recite the information out loud, and then verbally compare his recitation to the original information.

By telling students what they are "thinking," teachers model the covert thinking that occurs as they use the strategy.

Students can become actively involved in the demonstration by being required to *repeat critical information* or *answer questions about the new information* presented in the demonstration. For example:

T: The first step in the strategy is READ. What is the first step in the strategy?
S: *Read.*
T: Yes, first we read a small bit of information. If we were studying words and definitions, would you read one definition or many definitions?
S: *One definition.*

Questions that demand prior knowledge also can be asked. For example, when demonstrating the strategy for proofreading, the teacher could involve the students by asking such questions as:

T: Next, we proofread for capitals. What do we proofread for?
S: *Capitals.*
T: What should each sentence begin with?
S: *A capital.*
T: What are some other things that we should capitalize within a sentence?
S: *Names of people. Names of places. Months. Days of the week.*
T: Good. Watch me proofread this sentence for capitals.

Because student attention is highly related to the number of responses elicited during instruction, teachers should strive to continually elicit student responses, even during the demonstration stage. This can ensure attentiveness and subsequent learning.

2. Prompt students in use of the strategy. Once students have observed a demonstration of the learning strategy, they should be given an immediate opportunity to practice the strategy. To ensure that their initial practice is successful, the teacher should guide or prompt each step in the strategy. This can involve either telling students the strategy step, or asking them to say or read the strategy step, having them perform the step, and providing feedback to them. It is important that the language of instruction (the strategy step wording and directives) be held constant through each successive prompt.

3. Check students on their application of the strategy. After demonstrating proficiency on the strategy steps when prompted, students should practice the strategy without any assistance. This practice should be done during the instructional group so that the teacher is available to give corrective feedback. This instructional step should include several successful practice opportunities involving a range of examples.

In some cases, teachers may wish to describe the strategy steps and the rationale for each step prior to the actual demonstration. This can assist students in better understanding the teacher's demonstration. Another important component can be the verbal rehearsal of the strategy steps following modeling or prompting. Verbal rehearsal can be done in many different ways such as students can repeat the steps as a group, students can say the steps to a partner, an individual student can say the steps, or each successive student can say one of the strategy steps in order. While the verbal rehearsal procedures might vary, the outcome must be the same: students quickly say the steps in the strategy. These instructional procedures are illustrated in Figure 9.10.

Most learning strategies will take many days of instruction, depending on the complexity of the strategy and the learning ability of your students. During the initial acquisition phase, most of the instructional focus will be on modeling and prompting use of the strategy. However, the modeling should be faded fairly quickly so that students rely on their recall of the strategy steps. Once students have developed some accuracy on the strategy, proficiency is stressed. Now, the instruction is dominated by the prompt and check steps.

The example found in Figure 9.11 illustrates learning strategy instruction over time. Note how the modeling was faded after the second day of instruction, the amount of prompted practice was reduced, and the amount of unprompted practice was increased. Independent work (seatwork and homework demanding use of the strategy) was added when students demonstrated a high level of proficiency during the instructional group. Finally, the teacher scheduled systematic review of the strategy to ensure maintenance.

MAINTENANCE AND GENERALIZATION

The greatest challenge regarding school behaviors, organizational skills, and learning strategies is not initial instruction, but rather getting students to actually *use* the skills that they have been taught. Students with learning difficulties may not automatically transfer or generalize skills they learn to other environments, new materials, and novel situations (Alley, Deshler, Clark, Schumaker & Warner, 1983; Anderson-Inman, Walker & Purcell, 1984b; Ellis, Lenz & Sabornie, 1987a).

To ensure that a new skill or strategy is actually employed, teachers must systematically plan for generalization. They can do this by selecting and implementing interventions *before* demonstrating the strategy, *during* instruction on the new skill, and *after* skill instruction. The following section described several interventions that can increase the probability of generalization.

Before Instruction

There are many things that we can do *before* actual demonstration of a school behavior, organizational skill, or learning strategy that would increase the probability of actual use and generalization to other environments, materials, or situations.

1. Carefully select the skill or strategy that will be taught. Teachers should select skills that the student needs, can be applied in a variety of settings, have proven effectiveness, are relatively simple for the student to employ, and have a specific outcome that the teacher can observe. If the skill or strategy meets these criteria, students will be more likely to choose to use the skill.

Opening of the Lesson

1. Gain Students' Attention

T: Everyone, let's begin (Pause and monitor to ensure attention.)

2. Review Relevant Past Learning

(Note: There are no preskills or difficult steps that need to be reviewed for this lesson.)

3. State the Goal of the Lesson

T: Today you are going to learn a strategy for memorizing or studying information carefully. What will this strategy help you do?

S: Memorize or study information carefully.

Provide a Rationale for the Strategy

(Note: The rationale should address WHY the strategy would be beneficial, WHEN the strategy might be applied, and WHERE it could be used.)

T: In many of your classes, you must memorize or study information carefully so that you can remember the information for a class discussion, an assignment, or a test. Many times students do not remember information that they have studied. Raise your hand if you have ever forgotten information when you took a test?

S: (Raise hands.)

T: The strategy that you are going to learn will help you remember information. You will be able to use this strategy whenever you need to memorize something or study it carefully. For example, you could use this strategy to study spelling words, math facts, words and definitions, science facts, poems, or social studies facts. Tell me one thing that you have had to memorize or study carefully in the past.

S: Spelling words.

S: Multiplication facts.

S: States and capitals.

S: Poems.

S: Summaries in the science book.

T: All of you have had to memorize things in the past. This strategy will certainly help you in the future. You will be able to use it in this class, in your other classes, and when you study at home.

Body of the Lesson

4. Describe the Strategy

(Note: Stress the rationale for each strategy step. Actively involve students in the instruction.)

T: (Distributes copies of the strategy to students.)

RCRC

When you need to memorize something or study something carefully, use RCRC.

R = Read
   Read a little bit of material. Read it more than once.

C = Cover
   Cover the material with your hand.

R = Recite
   Tell yourself what you have read.

C = Check
   Lift your hand and check.
   If you forget something important, begin again.

(continued)

FIGURE 9.10 continued

T: Let's look at the steps in the strategy. The first step is READ. What does R stand for?

S: Read.

T: Read the next line.

S: Read a little bit of material. Read it more than once.

T: When you study information, it is best to study just a little information at a time. To help you really think about the information, you should read it more than one time. Should you read the information once or more than once?

S: More than once.

T: The next step is COVER. What does C stand for?

S: Cover.

T: Read the next line.

S: Cover the material with your hand.

T: Yes, after you read the information, you should cover it with your hand. When the information is covered, you will have to really think about what you read.

T: The next step is RECITE. What does R stand for?

S: Recite.

T: Read the next line.

S: Tell yourself what you have read.

T: Yes, recite means to tell yourself what you have read. When possible, you should say it in your own words. Reciting the information makes you think carefully about what you have read.

T: After you recite, you lift your hand and CHECK. What does C stand for?

S: Check.

T: Read the next line.

S: Lift your hand and check.

T: Yes, next you would lift your hand and check to be sure you said the most important information. Read the last line.

S: If you forget something important, begin again.

T: If you say the wrong information or leave something important out, you should begin again.

5. **Rehearse the Strategy Steps**
(Note: Continue until the students can say the steps in the strategy. Verbal rehearsal can be done after the model step of the lesson.

T: Let's review the steps in this strategy. When you need to memorize something or study something carefully, you can use Read, Cover, Recite, Check. Say those steps.

S: Read, Cover, Recite, Check.

T: Again.

S: Read, Cover, Recite, Check.

T: Ones, tell your partners the steps in the strategy.

S: Read, Cover, Recite, Check.

T: Twos, tell your partners the steps in the strategy.

S: Read, Cover, Recite, Check.

6. Model the Strategy

(Note: As you model the strategy, make the covert behaviors overt.)

T: (Distributes the study stimuli to students.)

Words and Definitions

1. Iris—The colored part of the eye
2. Cornea—A clear covering that protects the iris
3. Pupil—The opening in the iris that changes size to let more or less light into the eye
4. Retina—The inner lining of the back of the eyeball
5. Lens—The part of the eye that directs light to the retina
6. Optic nerve—The nerve that goes from the eyeball to the brain
7. Eyelashes—Hairs that help keep dirt out of the eye
8. Tears—A special liquid that cleans the eye

T: We are going to use RCRC to study these words and definitions. My turn first. I will study the definition. What is the first step in the strategy?

S: Read.

T: Yes, I will read it more than one time so I can really think about the definition. "Iris—The colored part of the eye." "Iris—The colored part of the eye."

T: After I read, what should I do?

S: Cover.

T: (Covers the definition with hand.) I cover up the definition so I can really think about it.

T: What should I do next?

S: Recite.

T: Listen to me recite the definition in my own words. Iris. That is the part of the eye that is colored.

T: What should I do after I recite?

S: Check.

T: Yes, I will lift my hand and check. (Lifts hand.) "Iris—The colored part of the eye." Good, I said the important information. If I had made a mistake or left out important information, I would need to begin again.

7. Prompt the Use of the Strategy

T: Now, it's your turn to do the strategy with me. What is the first step?

S: Read.

T: Read no. 2. Be sure to read it more than once.

S: (Read the word and definition.)

T: After you read, what should you do?

S: Cover.

T: Good, cover up the definition.

(continued)

FIGURE 9.10   continued

S: (Cover the word and definition.)

T: What should you do next?

S: Recite.

T: Tell yourself the word and definition. Try to use your own words.

S: (Recite quietly to themselves.)

T: Jeff, what did you say?

S: The cornea is a clear covering that protects the iris.

T: Great. After you recite, what should you do?

S: Check.

T: Lift your hand and check. Be sure you said the important information.

S: (Check their recitation with the word and definition.)

T: Raise your hand if you said the most important information.

S: (Raise hands.)

T: If you forgot any information, what would you do?

S: Begin again.

T: (Continue prompting on additional examples.)

8. **Check the Use of the Strategy**

   T: Now, it's your turn. Study no. 7 and no. 8 using RCRC. When you are done, go back and study all of the words and definitions. You will be taking a short quiz on these definitions to see how well you studied.

   S: (Study the words and definitions using Read, Cover, Recite, Check.)

   T: (Monitors carefully, observing the use of the overt behaviors in the strategy.)

   T: (Distributes quiz on definitions.)

   S: (Take the quiz.)

   T: (Gives feedback on the quiz items.)

   T and **S:** (Discuss the quiz results in relationship to use of the strategy.)

Close of the Lesson

9. **Review**

   T: Today, you learned a strategy for memorizing or studying information carefully. What are the steps in the strategy?

   S: Read, Cover, Recite, Check.

   T: What are some things that you could study using RCRC?

   S: (Provide examples.)

10. **Preview**

    T: Tomorrow, you will use RCRC to study questions and answers. Later, we will learn how to study chapter summaries, spelling words, and other class material.

11. **Independent Work**

    (Note: No seatwork or homework is given after this lesson.

FIGURE 9.10   Example of a Learning Strategy Lesson (T = Teacher, S = Student)

Learning Strategy Instruction

Initial Acquisition							Proficiency			
Day 1	Day 2	Day 3	Day 4	Day 5	Day 6	Day 7	Day 8	Day 9	Day 10	Day 11
M	M	P	P	P	P				R	
M	P	P	P	P	P					
P	P	P	P	C	C					
P	P	P	C	C	C					
P	P	C	C	C	C					
	P	C	C	C	C					
		C	C	C	C					

Teacher-Directed Instruction

			I	I	I	I	I	I	

Independent Work

M = Model using one example.
P = Prompt using one example.
C = Check using one example.
R = Review lesson.
I = Independent work using the strategy.

FIGURE 9.11 Strategy Instruction Over Time

Source: Reprinted from *Skills for School Success,* Archer & Gleason (1989), by permission of the authors and Curriculum Associates.

2. Provide a rationale for the skill or strategy instruction. Before a strategy is demonstrated, students need a global understanding of the strategy, a rationale for its use over other approaches to the same task, and an idea of the learning gains that might be expected if the strategy were to be used (Palincsar & Brown, 1987). In other words, students must be told *why* they will be learning the new skill or strategy. For example, when introducing the notebook organization system, the teacher can show students a notebook, pointing out its organization and explaining why it would be beneficial to the student (e.g., quick retrieval of class materials, transporting materials from class to class, and organizing materials for more efficient study). The notebook strategy can be contrasted to methods that students have used in the past that were less desirable (e.g., pockets, folders, and lunch boxes), the deficiencies in these systems, and why using the notebook would be superior.

3. Discuss when and where the strategy or skill can be employed. Not only should we discuss *why* the skill will be useful, but *when* and *where* the skill might be appropriately utilized. From the beginning, students must realize that their teacher expects them to use the skill and the range of application of the specific skill (Palincsar & Brown, 1987). In teaching a proofreading strategy, teachers could discuss the types of written products that could be proofread (e.g., daily assignments, written reports, letters, notes, and essay tests) and the environments in which the strategy could be used. Students also could be encouraged to suggest personal examples in which a proofreading strategy could be utilized.

4. Gain an informal or formal commitment to learning the strategy. Before demonstrating the strategy, it is often useful to gain a commitment to learn the strategy from students. In some cases, this might be done informally. For example, after describing the notebook and benefits of its use, students might be asked to raise their hands if they believe the notebook would assist them. In other situations, particularly if the training is more involved and the strategy is complex, a formal commitment might be sought. Students could be asked to sign a written contract stating their willingness to learn, practice, and use the strategy. They might also write personal goals stating the outcomes they wish from the training.

During Instruction

When teaching critical school behaviors, organizational skills, and learning strategies, the teacher can do a number of things to promote generalization. These include:

1. Ensure that students master the strategy or skill. During instruction, students must practice the strategy until they can perform it both accurately and fluently (Deshler & Schumaker, 1986). Only if the strategy steps can be carried out almost automatically is there capacity remaining for higher-order skills such as planning and monitoring strategy use (Shiffrin & Schneider, 1977).

2. Continue to discuss why the skill is being taught, when the skill can be used, and where the skill can be applied. On each day of instruction, some time should be devoted to discussing the rationale for learning the specific strategy or skill. A discussion of why, when, and where the strategy can be used increases student motivation for learning the skill and establishes a set for generalization: they understand that subsequent use of the strategy is expected. Students can be asked to suggest situations in which they will employ the strategy. These suggestions could be orally stated to the teacher, to a partner, or written down.

3. Discuss cues that students might encounter that would signal using the strategy. Because they are often not attracted to a specific environmental stimuli, critical school behaviors, organizational skills, and learning strategies are more difficult than many academic strategies to generalize. For this reason, it is important to teach students the characteristics of tasks when the strategy will help (Deshler & Schumaker, 1986; Gelzheiser, Shepherd, & Wozniak, 1986). For example, cues for taking notes include a teacher lecturing, writing important information on the board or overhead, or telling students that the information is important.

4. During instructional activities, use a variety of stimuli. To increase the probability of generalization, the stimuli should be varied across practice sessions (e.g., different text materials and assignments). For example, if a strategy for completing assignments is taught, it should be practiced with reading, spelling, language arts, science, social studies, and mathematics assignments. If the strategy is taught using only one type of assignment, such as language arts, students might believe that the strategy is not applicable to other subjects.

5. Provide feedback that illustrates the relationship between strategy use and outcome. During initial instruction, the teacher can stress the relationship between the student's performance and using the strategy, thereby promoting future generalization. For example, if a student locates and corrects all errors in a written assignment, the teacher can give feedback that stresses successfully using the strategy. "You used all of the steps in the proofreading strategy. As a result, you were able to find and fix up your errors. This assignment will be easy for a teacher to read and understand." In the same manner, feedback can be given when the outcome is less desirable and the strategy has not been employed. "I can tell that you proofread for sense, capitalization, and punctuation errors. However, you have left a number of spelling errors in your assignment, making it difficult for me to understand. What steps could you use to correct your spelling errors?"

6. Engage students in self-monitoring and self-evaluation activities. While receiving instruction on a skill or strategy, students can learn **self-management** skills such as self-questioning, self-monitoring of behaviors, self-evaluation (Gelzheiser, Shepherd, & Wozniak, 1986; Wong & Jones, 1982), or self-recording procedures such as graphing their daily progress (Harris & Graham, 1985). Later, they can use these procedures to monitor their own strategy performance. For example, students learning a proofreading strategy could be given a checklist to evaluate their application of each of the proofreading steps. When practicing a strategy for textbook reading, students could graph the percentage of topics and critical details that they recalled. Self-evaluation and self-monitoring can also be done on a more informal basis. For example, students could verbally report how they used the strategy and how it benefited their performance.

After Instruction

Generalization must be addressed not only before and during instruction, but *after* instruction as well. If the skill or strategy is no longer practiced or reviewed, it is likely to disappear from the student's repertoire. Instructional procedures that promote generalization are summarized in Figure 9.12. They include the following:

1. Tell students that they are expected to use the skill or strategy. This simple procedure of clearly stating teacher expectations will increase the probability of students employing the skill (Deshler, Alley, Warner, & Schumaker, 1981). "I expect you to take your notebook to every class. I also expect you to take it home every night and to bring it to school every day. I also expect you to keep your notebook neat and to put things away in the correct place within your notebook." If the expectations are not explicit, generalization and maintenance of the strategy or skill are likely to be minimal (Ellis, Lenz, & Sabornie, 1987a).

2. Remind students to use the skill or strategy. Students can be verbally reminded to use the strategy before a specific task in class (e.g., "Put your math paper in your NOTEBOOK." "Be sure that you proofread this assignment." "When you read Chapter 4, use Read, Cover, Recite, and Check."). Written prompts also can be used to encourage strategy use. For example, copies of the strategies can be given to students as references in their notebooks. Posters with strategy steps can be posted in the classroom as a reminder to the student and to the teacher. Copies of strategies can be kept in study areas at home or, in some cases, on the student's desk at school.

3. Review the strategy periodically. As with academic strategies, critical school behaviors, organizational skills, and learning strategies should be reviewed periodically within the context of well-organized lessons. During these lessons, the steps in the strategy can be reviewed and verbally rehearsed. The importance of the steps and the strategy can be re-emphasized and practice on the strategy can be provided. These "booster sessions" will probably be necessary for long-term maintenance of the strategy (Harris & Graham, 1985).

4. Provide opportunities to use and practice the skill or strategy. Students must be given opportunities to practice the strategies that they have been taught. If they have learned how to take notes on a lecture, the teacher must lecture and require that students take notes. If they have learned a strategy for reading expository textbooks, they must be required to read segments of expository textbooks. A strategy without the opportunity for application is useless. This would be analogous to learning to play golf in an area with no golf courses. Soon the skill would disappear.

5. Require the students to use the skill or strategy in other environments. Not only should students be given practice opportunities in the classroom in which they learn a strategy, but they should be required to use the strategy in other appropriate environments. When teaching a note-taking strategy, a teacher might require students to bring to class lecture notes taken in other courses. Likewise, they might be assigned the

Summary of Generalization Interventions

Before Instruction
1. Carefully select the skill or strategy that will be taught.
2. Provide a rationale for the skill or strategy instruction.
3. Discuss when and where the strategy or skill can be employed.
4. Gain an informal or formal commitment to learning the strategy.

During Instruction
1. Ensure that students master the strategy or skill.
2. Continue to discuss WHY the skill is being taught, WHEN the skill can be used, and WHERE the skill can be applied.
3. Discuss cues that students might encounter that would signal use of the strategy.
4. During instructional activities, use a variety of stimuli.
5. Provide feedback that illustrates the relationship between strategy use and outcome.
6. Engage students in self-monitoring and self-evaluation activities.

After Instruction
1. Tell students that you expect them to use the skill or strategy.
2. Remind students to use the skill or strategy.
3. Review the strategy periodically.
4. Provide opportunities to use and practice the skill or strategy.
5. Require the students to use the skill or strategy in other environments.
6. Continue to discuss WHY, WHEN, and WHERE the strategy could be applied and the environmental cues that tell students when to use the strategy.
7. Elicit a commitment to actually using the skill or strategy.
8. Provide feedback on performance and use of the strategy.
9. Engage students in self-evaluating and self-monitoring their strategy use.
10. Inform others about the skill or strategy that has been taught.

FIGURE 9.12   Summary of Generalization and Maintenance Interventions

Source: Reprinted from *Skills for School Success,* Archer & Gleason (1989), by permission of the authors and Curriculum Associates.

task of applying their proofreading strategies in one class and then reporting back on its use.

6. Continue to discuss why, when, and where the strategy could be applied and the environmental cues that tell the student when to use the strategy. Students' knowledge and beliefs about the how, when, why, and where of strategy use are important if students are to take control of their cognitive processing (Pressley, Snyder, & Cariglia-Bull, 1987; Swanson, 1989). For this reason, ongoing discussion concerning applying the strategy should be initiated. For example, af-

ter a note-taking strategy has been mastered, students can state why they intend to use the skill, when they plan to use it, and where they intend to use it. This information could be communicated verbally to the teacher, to the class, or to a peer partner. In addition, students benefit from ongoing discussion of environmental cues that signal using the strategy and how to adapt the strategy to varying classroom demands (Deshler & Schumaker, 1986).

7. Elicit a commitment to actually using the skill or strategy. Just as it was useful to gain a commitment to initially learning a skill or strategy, it is helpful to gain an informal or formal commitment to actually *using* the specific skill. In many cases, an informal commitment is adequate: "Raise your hand if you are going to bring your notebook to school each day. Raise your hand if you plan to take it to each class. Raise your hand if you plan to take your notebook home each night so that you can complete your homework." With more complex strategies that require use in many situations and settings, a formal contract stating the student's willingness to use the strategy and the situations in which she intends to use the strategy can be formulated between the teacher and the student.

8. Provide feedback on performance and use of the strategy. As stated previously, this feedback will be most useful if the relationship between the using the strategy and the outcome are stressed. "You have been doing an excellent job using your notebook and calendar. Your teachers report that you are turning in many more homework assignments." "Notice how well you did on the vocabulary test when you used the memorization strategy."

9. Engage students in self-evaluating and self-monitoring of their strategy use. Systematic implementation of skills will depend on the students' ability to self-monitor their performance (Gelzheiser, Sheperd, & Wozniak, 1986). On an informal level, students can simply report orally on their successful and less successful applications of the skill or strategy. On a more formal basis, they can use a checklist to indicate completing strategy steps or to evaluate a product for evidence of successful strategy application (e.g., a proofreading checklist).

10. Inform others about the skill or strategy that has been taught. While it is always more desirable to teach critical school behaviors, organizational skills, and learning strategies in the classroom of intended use, occasionally they will be taught in a separate setting (e.g., the resource room) with the hopes of generalizing them to another setting (e.g., regular classroom or home). The appropriate adults (teachers, parents) in the latter environment should be familiar with the strategy. They should be introduced to it, understand its rationale, and know the procedures that can be employed to promote use. Other teachers should be given a copy of the strategy and perhaps even a poster to display in their classrooms. This will serve as a reminder to prompt the student in using the strategy and may lead to whole classroom instruction on the strategy.

SUMMARY

To be successful in regular classes or special education programs, students need to learn school success skills that go beyond mastery of basic academic skills such as reading, language arts, and mathematics. They also must learn how to be students. Many will require explicit direct instruction on these skills.

Successful students exhibit critical school behaviors before, during, and after school. By arriving on time, and bringing their class materials and homework, they communicate that they are ready for instruction. During class, they adhere to classroom rules, listen carefully, follow directions, ask for assistance when needed, work diligently, and move quickly from one task to another. After class they take materials home, complete homework, and return to school with it.

Students also need to master basic organizational skills. They need to organize materials, work spaces, and time, as well as the content that they produce. Notebooks and folders represent two approaches to organizing school assignments, with monthly calendars assisting students in managing their time. Assignments can be organized by using headings, organizing contents, and writing neatly.

This chapter presents characteristic features of learning strategies and describes several sample strategies for use in reading expository and narrative materials, completing daily assignments, writing expository and narrative passages, and preparing for and taking tests. The importance of teaching critical preskills and difficult steps for each strategy are emphasized, as are selecting and using good examples.

When teaching critical school behaviors, school organizational skills, and learning strategies, the effective lesson design and presentation steps described throughout this text should be employed. The targeted skills should be previewed, tied to prior learning, and connected to desirable outcomes. Teachers should actively model them; provide guided practice, carefully monitoring and checking; and finally, provide independent practice and periodic prompts and reviews.

Critical school behaviors, organizational skills and learning strategies should be maintained and generalized to other settings. This occurs when the skills are carefully selected, and their importance and usefulness are clear to the students. Students need to commit to learning and using the strategies, they must identify cues for using the strategy, and they must achieve mastery in the strategy use.

Once learned, these skills and strategies facilitate student achievement in the academic and life skills described in the remaining chapters of this text. They empower students by decreasing their dependence on external sources, such as the teacher. This increases the likelihood that they will become truly independent learners in the future.

MASTERY CONTENT QUESTIONS

1. Describe the six key components for teaching school behaviors.

2. Design a lesson plan to teach students to arrive on time (be sure to include the components for instruction as well as the teacher actions following instruction).

3. List the criteria for selecting organizational skills to be directly taught.

4. Describe strategies for teaching primary and secondary students to organize materials, time, and paper content. Provide two advantages for implementing each strategy described.

5. List seven characteristics of learning strategies.

6. Describe one of the learning strategies that can be used to preview expository material.

7. Discuss three similarities among expository learning strategies and describe two of the expository learning strategies.

8. Describe the focus of narrative learning strategies.

9. Describe two strategies for teaching students to complete daily assignments.

10. Describe two strategies for teaching students to write expository products and one for narrative products.

11. Describe two test preparations and two test-taking learning strategies.

12. Discuss two teacher actions that should occur prior learning strategies instruction.

13. Describe the three guidelines for selecting examples for learning strategies instruction.

14. Discuss and describe the three instructional steps involved in teaching new learning strategies.

15. Discuss and describe instructional procedures prior to, during, and after direct instruction that increase maintenance and generalization of school behaviors, organizational skills, and learning strategies.

REFERENCES

Alley, G. R., Deshler, D. D., Clark, F. L., Schumaker, J. B., & Warner, M. M. (1983). Learning disabilities in adolescent and adult populations: Research implications (Part II). *Focus on Exceptional Children, 15*(9), 1–14.

Anderson-Inman, L., Paine, S. C., & Deutchman, L. (1984a). Neatness counts: Effects of direct instruction and self-monitoring on the transfer of neat-paper skills to nontraining setting. *Analysis and Intervention in Developmental Disabilities, 4,* 137–155.

Anderson-Inman, L., Walker, H. & Purcell, J. (1984b). Promoting the transfer of skills across handicapped students in the mainstream. In W. L. Heward, T. E. Heron, D. S. Hill, & J. Trap-Porter (Eds.) *Focus on behavior analysis in education.* Columbus, OH: Charles E. Merrill.

Archer, A., & Gleason, M. (1989). *Skills for school success.* North Billerica, MA: Curriculum Associates.

Bean, T. W., & Steenwyk, F. L. (1984). The effect of three forms of summarization instruction on sixth graders' summary writing and comprehension. *Journal of Reading Behavior, 16,* 297–306.

Brophy, J. E. (1983). Classroom organization and management. *Elementary School Journal, 83,* 254–285.

Brown, A. L., & Day, J. D. (1983). Macrorules for summarizing texts: The development of expertise. *Journal of Verbal Learning and Verbal Behavior, 22,* 1–14.

Carman, R. A., & Adams, W. R. (1972). *Study skills: A student's guide for survival.* New York: Wiley.

Dean, J. (1977). Study skills—learning how to learn. *Education, 5,* 9–11.

Deshler, D. D., Alley, G. R., Warner, M. M., & Schumaker, J. B. (1981). Instructional practices for promoting skill acquisition and generalization in severely learning disabled adolescents. *Learning Disability Quarterly, 4,* 415–421.

Deshler, D. D., & Schumaker, J. B. (1986). Learning strategies: An instructional alternative for low-achieving adolescents. *Exceptional Children, 52*(6), 583–590.

Deshler, D. D., Schumaker, J. B., & Lenz, B. K. (1984a). Academic and cognitive interventions for LD adolescents: Part I. *Journal of Learning Disabilities, 17,* 108–117.

Deshler, D. D., Schumaker, J. B., & Lenz, B. K. & Ellis, E. (1984b). Academic and cognitive interventions for LD adolescents: Part II. *Journal of Learning Disabilities, 17,* 170–179.

Ellis, E. S., Lenz, B. K., & Sabornie, E. J. (1987a). Generalization and adaptation of learning strategies to natural environments: Part 1: Critical agents. *Remedial and Special Education, 8*(1), 6–20.

Ellis, E. S., Lenz, B. K., & Sabornie, E. J. (1987b). Generalization and adaptation of learning strategies to natural environments: Part 2: Research into practice. *Remedial and Special Education, 8*(2), 6–23.

Englert, C. S., Raphael, T. E., Anderson, L. M. et al. (1988). A case for writing intervention: Strategies for writing informational text. *Learning Disabilities Focus, 3*(2), 98–113.

Evertson, C. M., & Emmer, E. T. (1982). Effective management at the beginning of the school year in junior high class. *Journal of Educational Psychology, 74,* 485–498.

Gelzheiser, L. M., Shepherd, M. J., & Wozniak, R. H. (1986). The development of instruction to induce skill transfer. *Exceptional Children, 53*(2), 125–129.

Graham, S., & Harris, K. R. (1989). Improving learning disabled student's skills at composing essays: Self instructional strategy training. *Exceptional Children, 56*(3), 201–214.

Graham, S., Harris, K. R., & Sawyer, R. (1987). Composition instruction with learning disabled students: Self-instructional strategy training. *Focus on Exceptional Children, 20*(4), 1–11.

Griffey, Q. L., Jr., Zigmond, N., & Leinhardt, G. (1988). The effects of self-questioning and story structure training on the reading comprehension of poor readers. *Learning Disabilities Research, 4*(1), 45–51.

Haller, E. P., Child, D. A., & Walberg, H. J. (1988). Can comprehension be taught? A quantitative synthesis of "metacognitive" studies. *Educational Researcher, 17*(9), 5–8.

Harris, K. R., & Graham, S. (1985). Improving learning disabled students' composition skills: Self-control strategy training. *Learning Disability Quarterly, 8,* 27–36.

Heron, T. E., & Harris, K. C. (1987). *The educational consultant: Helping professionals, parents, and mainstreamed students* (2nd ed.). Austin, TX: PRO ED.

Idol, L. (1987). Group story mapping: A comprehension strategy for both skilled and unskilled readers. *Journal of Learning Disabilities, 20,* 196–205.

Idol, L., & Croll, V. J. (1987). Story-mapping training as a means of improving reading comprehension. *Learning Disability Quarterly, 10,* 214–229.

Jenkins, J. R., Heliotis, J., Stein, M. L., & Hayes, M. (1987). Improving reading comprehension by using paragraph restatements. *Exceptional Children, 54,* 54–59.

Johnson, N. (1983). What do you do if you can't tell the whole story? The development of summarization skills. In K. E. Nelson (Ed.). *Children's Language,* Vol. 4. Hillsdale, NJ: Lawrence Erlbaum & Associates.

Lloyd, J., Saltzman, N. J., & Kauffman, J. M. (1981). Predictable generalization in academic learning as a result of preskills and strategy training. *Learning Disabilities Quarterly, 4,* 203–216.

Mastropieri, M. A. & Scruggs, T. E. (1989). Constructing more meaningful relationships: Mnemonic instruction for special purposes. *Educational Psychology Review, 1,* 83–111.

Murrell, P. C., Jr, & Surber, J. R. (1987). *The effect of generative summarization of the comprehension of main ideas from lengthy expository text.* Paper presented at the annual meeting of the American Educational Research Association, Washington, D.C.

Nagel, D. R., Schumaker, J. B., & Deshler, D. D. (1986). *The first-letter mnemonic strategy.* Lawrence, KS: Excel Enterprises.

Palincsar, A. S., & Brown, D. A. (1987). Enhancing instructional time through attention to metacognition. *Journal of Learning Disabilities, 20*(2), 66–75.

Paris, S. G., Cross, D. R., & Lipson, M. Y. (1984). Informed strategies for learning: A program to improve children's reading awareness and comprehension. *Journal of Educational Psychology, 76,* 1239–1252.

Paris, S. G., & Oka, E. R. (1986). Self-regulated learning among exceptional children. *Exceptional Children, 53,* 103–108.

Pressley, M., Borkowski, J. G., & O'Sullivan, J. T. (1984). Memory strategy instruction is made of this: Metamemory and durable strategy use. *Educational Psychologist, 19*(2), 94–107.

Pressley, M., Johnson, C. J., Symons, S., McGoldrick, J. A., & Kurita, J. A. (1989). Strategies that improve children's memory and comprehension of text. *The Elementary School Journal, 90*(1), 3–32.

Pressley, M., Snyder, B. L., & Cariglia-Bull, T. (1987) How can good strategy use be taught to children? Evaluation of six alternative approaches. In S. M. Cormier & J. D. Hagman (Eds.), *Transfer of learning: Contemporary research and applications* (pp. 81–120). Orlando, FL: Academic Press.

Raphael, T. E., Kirschner, B. W., & Englert, C. S. (1986). *Text structure instruction within process-writing classrooms: A manual for instruction.* Occasional Paper No. 104). East Lansing : Michigan State University, Institute for Research on Teaching.

Rinehart, S. D., Stahl, S. A., & Erickson, L. G. (1986). Some effects of summarization training on reading and studying. *Reading Research Quarterly, 21,* 422–438.

Robinson, F. P. (1946) *Effective study.* New York: Harper & Brothers Publishers.

Roehler, L. R., & Duffy, G. G. (1984). Direct explanation of comprehension processes. In G. G. Duffy, L. R. Roehler, & J. Mason (Eds), *Comprehension instruction: Perspectives and suggestions* (pp. 265–280). New York: Longman.

Schumaker, J. B., Denton, P. H., & Deshler, D. (1984). *Learning strategies curriculum: The paraphras-*

ing strategy. Lawrence, KS: University of Kansas.

Schumaker, J. B., & Deshler, D. D. (1984). Setting demand variables: A major factor in program planning for the LD adolescent. *Topics in Language Disorders Journal, 4*(2), 22–40.

Schumaker, J. B., Nolan, S. M., & Deshler, D. D. (1985). *Learning strategies curriculum: The error monitoring strategy.* Lawrence, KS: University of Kansas.

Scruggs, T. E., & Mastropieri, M. A. (1992). Classroom applications of mnemonic instruction: Acquisition, maintenance, and generalization. *Exceptional Children, 58,* 219–229.

Scruggs, T. E., Mastropieri, M. A., & Tolfa-Viet, D. (1986). The effects of coaching on the standardized test performance of learning disabled and behaviorally disordered students. *Remedial and Special Education, 7*(5), 37–41.

Shields, J. M., & Heron, T. E. (1989). Teaching organization skills to students with learning disabilities. *Teaching Exceptional Children, 21*(2), 8–13.

Shiffrin, R. M., & Schneider, W. (1977). Controlled and automatic human information processing: Perceptual learning, automatic attending, and a general theory. *Psychological Review, 84,* 127–190.

Short, E. J., & Ryan, E. B. (1984). Metacognitive differences between skilled and less skilled readers: Remediating deficits through story grammar and attribution training. *Journal of Educational Psychology, 76,* 225–235.

Smith, P. L., & Tompkins, G. E. (1988). Structured notetaking: A new strategy for content area readers. *Journal of Reading, 32*(1), 46–53.

Swanson, H. L. (1989). Strategy instruction: Overview of principles and procedures for effective use. *Learning Disability Quarterly, 12,* 3–14.

Torgesen, J. K. (1982). The learning disabled child as an interactive leader: Educational implications. *Topics in Learning and Learning Disabilities, 2,* 45–51.

Wong, B. Y. L. (1985). Self-questioning instructional research. *Review of Educational Research, 55,* 227–268.

Wong, B. Y. L., & Jones, W. (1982). Increasing metacomprehension in learning disabled and normally achieving students through self-questioning training. *Learning Disability Quarterly, 5*(2), 228–240.

CHAPTER 10

Teaching Reading and Spelling

Sharon Rowe Stewart
Patricia Thomas Cegelka

CHAPTER OBJECTIVES

At the conclusion of this chapter, the reader will be able to:

1. Describe readiness skills for reading and spelling.
2. Discuss the oral language development of preschoolers.
3. Describe the content and procedures characteristic of a literate classroom.
4. Describe effective instructional procedures for teaching reading and spelling.
5. Describe content and instructional procedures for teaching word attack skills in reading, including phonics, structural analysis, and contextual analysis.
6. Discuss methods for increasing reading fluency.
7. Describe strategies for teaching reading comprehension, including literal, inferential, organizational, and critical comprehension.
8. Describe strategies for promoting use of metacognitive strategies during reading.
9. Describe strategies for teaching spelling, including phonics, spelling rules and patterns, irregular words, use of outside sources, and proofreading.
10. Describe commonly used reading and spelling curricula.

Written language skills encompass reading and spelling (discussed in this chapter), as well as writing (described in the following chapter). Difficulties with written language are among the most pervasive and persistent areas of difficulty for students with mild handicaps as well as for other students who experience academic achievement difficulties (Gerber, 1984; Morsink, 1984; Reith, Polsgrove, & Eckert, 1984). Reading deficiencies are found in as many as 40% of all school-aged children in this country (Lipson & Wixson, 1985). Eighty percent of adults with learning disabilities have significant difficulties with spelling, difficulties that may continue even after an underlying reading problem has been overcome or, in many instances, where a reading problem never existed (Bookman, 1984; Gerber & Hall, 1987). Because reading and spelling are language-based activities, they can present unique challenges for students from ethnolinguistically diverse backgrounds who are being taught these skills in English.

Reading and spelling difficulties tend to limit student progress in nearly all academic areas. For example, poor readers have difficulty comprehending information found in textbooks, a primary source of knowledge necessary for academic progress. They also experience difficulty in locating and comprehending reading material necessary for completing assigned seatwork, homework, and independently written reports. Students who have not mastered independent reading skills tend to fall further and further behind their classmates in academic achievement as their progress through the grades.

Poor spelling also impedes students' academic performance in a variety of ways. Poor spelling reduces intelligibility and is distracting, resulting in lower grades for written work. Further, students who focus on lower-order skills such as spelling may fail to master important higher-level writing skills such as using appropriate text organization, writing with a purpose, and organizing and developing ideas (Hall, 1981). Finally, poor spelling can have far reaching effects because poor spellers are often considered to be careless in their work or less intelligent than other students (Graham & Miller, 1979).

This chapter focuses on effective approaches for teaching reading and spelling to students with academic achievement difficulties. It defines and provides a conceptual orientation to both sets of skills. It discusses these skill areas within the broader context of the language arts program and identifies readiness factors that affect the development of each skill area. The chapter then describes effective approaches for initially teaching reading, including word recognition and comprehension skills. Curriculum materials are discussed as well as procedures for remediating reading difficulties when they occur. The chapter continues with a discussion of effective procedures for spelling instruction. Specific methods for teaching rules and patterns, irregular words, proofreading, and using outside sources are presented. Commercially available programs and remediation procedures for students with achievement difficulties are also discussed.

READINESS FOR READING AND SPELLING

Most children engage in reading- and spelling-related activities at early ages. Even toddlers demonstrate knowledge of books by holding them upright, turning pages individually from front to back, and "reading" the pictures or telling a story they have heard many times. Later, they learn that reading occurs from left to right and top to bottom and that words, not pictures, are read (Chall, 1983). Three-year-old children often recognize common store signs, road signs, brand names of familiar food and drink items, and other words they encounter frequently in their homes and surrounding environments. At first, children may recognize these words only when they occur in context (e.g., when "Coca-Cola" appears on the can), but they gradually acquire the ability to identify many words without the contextual cues (Hiebert, 1978). By kindergarten age, many children already possess extensive knowledge of the reading process, including the advantages and purposes of reading, the organization and use of books and other reading materials, and some letter names and sounds. Some children are already engaged in real reading. Spelling knowledge begins as children learn to use various writing materials and begin to draw circles, squares, and triangles. They combine these shapes into designs and by age 3 begin to draw human figures, animals, houses, trees, and other items in their environment. They may tell stories about their drawings, dictate stories for adults to write, "write" their own captions or stories, and write their names on their artwork.

There are predictable stages in the spelling development of young children, during which they attempt to develop their own spelling strategies (Gentry, 1984). These developmental stages are presented in Table 10.1. In the first stage, **preliterate spelling,** children randomly string letters of the alphabet together without regard to letter-sound relationships. When they proceed to the second stage, **semiphonetic spelling,** children use letters that correctly represent some speech sounds heard in the word. At the third stage, **phonetic spelling,** words are spelled exactly like they sound, although spellings may be unconventional. The fourth level, **transitional spelling,** is characterized by using vowels in every syllable, occasional overgeneralization of spelling rules, and some conventional spelling resulting in close approximations of correct spellings. Correct spelling represents the final stage of development.

Students who enter school with lots of experience with print are prepared to respond more quickly to early reading instruction. They understand the purpose of reading and much of the initial phonics instruction constitutes a review of what they have already learned. In school, the reading- and spelling-related activities of the pre-

TABLE 10.1   Spelling Development Stages

Stage	Characteristics	Examples
Preliterate	Random ordering of letters and other symbols sometimes interspersed with "letter-like" marks	bBp = monster P3 = giant
	Implicit understanding: Speech can be recorded by means of graphic symbols	
Semiphonetic	One-, two-, and three-letter representations of discrete words. Letters used represent some sounds heard in the word.	MSR = monster P = pie DG = dog
	Implicit understanding: Speech consists of discrete words. Recorded speech consists of written words. Specific letters stand for specific speech sounds.	
Phonetic	Spellings include all sound features of words, as child hears and articulates them.	Transition PPL = people
	Implicit understanding: Every sound feature of a word is represented by a letter or combination of letters. The written form of a word contains every speech sound, recorded in the same sequence in which sounds are articulated when the word is spoken.	
Transitional	Vowels are included in every recorded syllable; familiar spelling patterns are used; standard spelling is interspersed with "incorrect" phonetic spelling.	tode = toad come = come highked = hiked
	Implicit understanding: It is necessary to spell words in such a way that others may read them easily. There are various ways to spell many of the same sounds. Every word has a conventional spelling that is used in print. Many words are not spelled entirely phonetically.	

Source: From "Learning to spell developmentally" by J.R. Gentry (1981) *The Reading Teacher, 34,* 378–381. Copyright 1981 by the International Reading Association. Adapted by permission.

school years are replaced by formal reading and spelling instruction.

Increasing numbers of children arrive at school without the pre-academic skills that are predictive of academic success. They may come from homes where there are limited experiences from which to construct meaning or where, due to language and cultural differences, they learn knowledge and values that are not reflected in the standard school curriculum.

Critical Preskills

The best predictors of beginning reading achievement are fluency of letter-name recognition and the ability to discriminate between phonemes.

Both of these skills appear to be closely related to the amount of exposure to print materials that children have during their preschool years. Fluent letter-name recognition is one indicator of extensive familiarity with print. In the same fashion, awareness of separate sounds also is correlated with extensive print experiences.

Phonemes are the small speech sounds that correspond roughly to individual letters or graphemic units and that make up syllables. Although most children can hear phoneme differences, low-readiness readers are not prepared to think consciously about them. These children will require explicit instruction in order to develop the phonemic awareness required for reading. A variety of games and activities can be employed for this purpose. These include nursery rhymes, rhymed stories, and rhyme production; the segmentations of sentences into individual words, investigations of word length, clapping, and dancing to syllabic rhythms; and solving puzzles, as well as isolating and identifying initial, final, and internal phonemes (Anderson, Heibert, Scott, & Wilkinson, 1985; Stahl, Osborne, & Lehr, 1990).

Sound blending and segmentation are two important auditory preskills that can be directly taught. Through teacher modeling and guided practice, students can be taught to hold each continuous sound for about 1 1/2 seconds, switching from sound to sound without pausing. For example, teachers can slowly pronounce a word and then have students say it the "fast way."

TEACHER: Get ready. "iiiiiffff" What word is that?
STUDENTS: If

Segmentation requires the student to analyze the sounds of a word as it is auditorily broken into phonemic segments. Such training has the advantage of emphasizing to students that words are made up of discrete sounds. This training is effective and efficient when articulation is invoked, pronunciation is slowed and overemphasized, and when irrelevant aspects of the problem are minimized.

Oral Language Development

Oral language development includes receptive and expressive communication. *Receptive language* is defined as the receiving and understanding of visual or auditory stimuli through a process referred to as *decoding*. *Expressive language* entails the transmission of information, either vocally or motorically (e.g., writing, acting out, drawing, and diagraming). The expressive transmission of information is known as *encoding*. Receptive language develops first, a fact that becomes apparent when one considers the ability of infants and toddlers to respond to oral communications before they can speak. This means that by the time children enter school at about age six and have academic demands placed on them, they have had almost 20,000 hours of receptive language experience. This becomes a particularly important consideration for young students whose native language is other than English. These students tend to go through a long "silent period" before they begin speaking English, a fact that teachers often mistake as an indication of low ability or unique learning difficulties. In actuality, the students are simply going through the same receptive period for their second language that all students progress through for their primary language. It is unrealistic to expect young students from linguistically diverse backgrounds to require significantly less receptive English language exposure prior to using English expressively, particularly as a tool for academic learning. While these students typically can develop conversational use of English at a basic interpersonal communication level within a couple of years, it takes considerably longer (up to 7 years) before they have mastered English sufficiently to use it as an abstract learning tool. It is for this reason that many authorities support the development of basic literacy skills in the students' primary language while the students are making the transition to English language proficiency.

By the time most children begin school, they can use language effectively for many different purposes. They can produce several types of complex sentences and use high-level grammar skills such as verb tenses, singular and plural noun and verb forms, the possessive *s,* and many irregular plural nouns and verbs. They may have a vocabulary of between 1,500–2,000 words. Many children learn that words are made of individual sounds that can be manipulated to make new words or to play rhyming games.

Because most reading and spelling programs assume that children who enter school are competent in oral language, those who lack oral language skills are at a distinct disadvantage in learning to read and spell. Children who have difficulty learning language or who come from culturally or linguistically different backgrounds will require special attention to the development of the specific oral English language skills associated with academic achievement. Table 10.2 identifies some of the important language skills that children are expected to have when they reach school age.

Concept Development

Meaningful reading and spelling requires that children have knowledge of the concepts underlying the specific vocabulary and general topic areas. Concept development occurs best when children have the freedom to interact with their environment, when they can see, hear, touch, taste, smell, and manipulate objects in their world. When children have few opportunities to explore the world, they will have restricted knowledge of concepts. Consequently, young children require multiple experiences with concrete materials. Furthermore, adults should model the appropriate language to match these experiences so that youngsters learn both the concepts and the words that represent them.

Teachers can expand the experiential base of students, and thus help them to acquire and use general knowledge through such activities as field trips, interest areas, films and videos, and access to books, as discussed later in this chapter. They also can systematically teach prior knowledge, provide necessary preinformation in introducing content, ensure that students know the meanings of specific reading and vocabulary words, and simplify the material to eliminate superfluous content.

CREATING A READING ENVIRONMENT

A classroom should be structured to provide a rich language environment that promotes literacy development. This is particularly important for children with learning difficulties and those who have limited interactions with print. The importance of literacy can be conveyed through class bulletin boards, library and reading areas, learning centers, and special interest areas. In addition, cooperative learning opportunities, field trips, sharing periods, hands-on displays, guest speakers, discussion periods, and filmstrips and videos all promote oral language development while enhancing the experiential base of students.

Through reading selected stories and books to students, the teacher can provide a model of reading fluency. Reading aloud to students has been identified as the single most important activity for building the knowledge and skills that predicate reading success. Some special educators (McNutt, 1984), have identified reading to students as a crucial practice, particularly for children from linguistically and culturally diverse environments, and poor readers who might otherwise observe the reading of only other poor readers. The vocabulary and syntax of the materials read should be slightly above the linguistic maturity level of the children for greatest gains. The model of reading fluency that the teacher provides may be the primary mechanism by which these students experience fluent reading and writing. Further, when reading aloud to children, teachers can actively engage students in the stories, make them aware of words as print units, and emphasize the value and enjoyment of reading. They can teach basic book knowledge by pointing out the front and back of the book, the table of contents, the illustrations, the title page, the pages, and the page numbers. Students learn the different purposes of reading and recognize the functional nature of

TABLE 10.2 Oral Language Skills Expected of Children Ready to Enter School

1. Intelligible speech, although sounds occasionally may be substituted or distorted

2. Fully developed complex sentences seven to eight words in length, incorporating words, and word endings such as:

   Articles (*a, the*)
   Prepositions
   Pronouns
   Auxiliary verbs (*is, are, was, were*)
   Plural noun endings (*s*)
   Verb endings (*ing, ed, s*)
   Irregular past tense verbs
   Copula verbs (forms of *to be* preceding another verb)
   Possessive (*'s*)

3. A variety of sentence types including:

   Negatives
   Imperatives
   Interrogatives
   Complex and compound

4. An expressive vocabulary of about 2,000 words with a much larger receptive vocabulary

5. Language, including slang, that matches the dialect of peers and adults in the family and neighborhood

6. Use of language:

   Ask permission
   Give excuses
   Question others
   Make polite requests
   Carry on meaningful conversations
   Tell stories
   Give instructions
   Provide descriptions about objects, experiences, and feelings
   Reason
   Imagine
   Discuss events removed in time and space

7. Metalinguistic abilities, including ability to:

   Separate sentences into words and, perhaps, words into syllables
   Monitor and correct own speech
   Begin to play with language (rhymes, riddles, and word substitutions)

written language by reading memos to the class, reading instructions for completing a task, looking up words in the dictionary, and reading recipes for cooking exercises. Displaying written work (e.g., poems, stories, and assignments) of students as well as others can serve to underscore the importance of reading. Making individual or class books is another activity to promote interest in reading.

Teachers can model different word attack and comprehension skills as they read aloud to their classes. When a difficult or unknown word appears, they can sound out the word or ask, "What word makes sense here?" Asking students such questions as, "What will happen next?" and "Does the story makes sense?" promotes comprehension.

When teachers write on the chalkboard or transparency, they can model spelling strategies for their students, using phonics or applying structural rules to predict spelling. They can then lead the class in examining the spelling to confirm accuracy or make corrections. In a similar fashion, teachers also can demonstrate use of the dictionary or a computer spell-check program. Teachers should provide multiple opportunities for real reading (Anderson et al., 1985) and spelling (Hillerich, 1982; Zutell, 1978). Students can record class activities; write notes to parents, teachers and others; publish a class newsletter; or keep a diary or journal to practice reading and spelling skills.

From 5–15 minutes should be set aside each day for sustained silent reading as well as for independent writing (e.g., individual journals). The latter has been found to be particularly effective with second-language learners who are encouraged to write about their experiences as a vehicle for developing English language proficiency (Goldman & Rueda, 1988). In these instances, teachers should avoid correcting spelling or syntax, but should focus on the meaning and purpose of the student's effort. By writing out responses to the content of students' writings, teachers can provide a model of correct writing and spelling, emphasize that the primary purpose of writing is to convey information, and thereby encourage the students' continued efforts.

INSTRUCTIONAL PRACTICES

The principles of effective instruction, as detailed elsewhere in this text, apply to teaching reading and spelling. These are generalizable principles that should be used in teaching reading and spelling, as well as other skill and content areas of the curriculum. After an extensive review of research on reading instruction for students with learning disabilities, Lewis (1983) recommended that teachers: (1) teach, (2) teach directly, (3) focus the learners on the task, (4) provide strategies for the task performance, and (5) teach for automaticity. Each of these is briefly described as follows:

1. **Teach.** While the recommendation to *teach* may seem simplistic, it is a critical one. Inefficient use of time has been shown to result in as little as 16 minutes of instructional contact per day between teachers and individual students with learning disabilities, with students engaged in reading activities less than a half-hour per day (Leinhardt, Zigmond, & Cooley, 1981; Zigmond, Vallacorsa, & Leinhardt, 1980). Increased teaching time increases the academic engaged time of students, and time spent actually reading is more highly correlated with achievement than any other teacher or student behavior (Carnine, Silbert, & Kameenui, 1990). Further, specialized reading instruction, or remedial reading, should supplement the regular reading program, not supplant it (Haynes & Jenkins, 1986). When students miss regular class instruction in reading to go to pull-out programs, their reading time progress will be attenuated. As little as 10–15 minutes per day of reading instruction can lead to greatly improved reading proficiency (Leinhardt, Zigmond, & Cooley, 1981).

2. **Teach skills directly**. Reading and spelling should be taught directly. While the readiness skills and language/literacy development approaches described previously are important foundations for developing and extending reading, research demonstrates that students with achievement difficulties progress more rapidly when discrete skills are directly taught to them. In direct teaching, the instructional goal is identified and the learning activities are designed to facilitate acquisition of this goal. When teachers use consistent instructional practices involving teacher demon-

stration, guided practice, and feedback to learners, the academic achievement of low-performing students increases (Rosenshine & Stevens, 1984).

3. **Focus students' attention.** Many students with achievement difficulties exhibit attention difficulties characterized by poor attention and distractibility. Teachers can assist students in focusing on the relevant features of the learning task. Students should be told to listen for certain types of information and be directed to attend to specific features such as the middle of words, prefixes, and suffixes. They also can be taught to monitor their own learning by self-recording accuracy data on recall questions.

4. **Teach strategies.** Direct training in using various strategies can improve reading performance (Wong, 1979; 1980; Wong & Jones, 1982) as well as spelling performance (Englert, Hiebert, & Stewart, 1985). A strategy involves applying a series of ordered steps to solve a particular problem or complete a task. Strategies not only provide a systematic approach to obtaining information or solving a learning problem, but also are generalizable across a large number of examples. Reading and spelling skills that require strategies include the following:

- Sounding out or spelling a single-syllable word.
- Sounding out or spelling a multisyllabic word.
- Selecting the main idea from a paragraph.
- Determining the meaning of words using context clues.
- Sequencing events in a passage.
- Reading an expository sentence.
- Using a dictionary.

5. **Teach for automaticity.** Students must learn to perform new skills quickly, accurately, and in a variety of settings. Automaticity can be developed through opportunities for guided practice, and generalization can be promoted through preteaching the compo-

nent parts of the strategy, providing prompts, identifying environmental cues for using a strategy, and providing guided and independent practice in a variety of settings. Extensive practice with guided and silent reading also can promote automaticity. When readers are able to identify words effortlessly and automatically, they can devote more of their cognitive energy to the tasks of comprehending and thinking about what they are reading.

TEACHING READING

There are two essential and interrelated processes in reading: (1) recognizing written symbols and (2) comprehending the meaning of these symbols. **Word recognition** involves acquiring sight words as well as **word attack** skills including phonics, structural analysis, and contextual analysis, for deciphering unknown words. Comprehension involves understanding the meaning of the words and sentences read.

There is a tendency to dichotomize reading instruction as meaning emphasis or code emphasis. However, virtually all instruction in reading has as its ultimate goal comprehending the meaning and includes instruction in word attack skills. The code-emphasis approach, as Chall (1983) described, is a developmental model that assumes that reading is made up of component skills, beginning with a focus on decoding tasks (i.e., letter-sound recognition) and, as this becomes more automatic, moving to a more holistic comprehension focus. By second or third grade, most readers attain sufficient decoding automaticity or fluency at the visual and phonological memory levels to shift to a more holistic approach. As decoding becomes more automatic, students no longer approach reading as a word-by-word task and shift to a semantic or meaning focus (Potter & Wamre, 1990).

Advocates of whole-language tend to view reading as basically a generative process based on the experiential meaning that the child brings to materials read. They eschew what they view as fragmented approaches of phonics instruction, and de-emphasize directly teaching word attack skills. During initial instruction, the stress is on recognizing the most frequently appearing sight words and using context to figure out new words. Introducing discrete word attack skills within a whole-language framework tends to be gradual and analytic (e.g., deriving letter-sound relationships from whole words, and emphasizing sounding out word parts, not each and every sound). Phonetic reading approaches, on the other hand, are synthetic, involving the intensive teaching in isolation of all main sound-symbol relationships from the start of formal reading instruction; the emphasis on meaning, while never absent, is less apparent during early instruction, but increases with the age and skill of the readers.

Research favors code-emphasis approaches over the meaning-emphasis or comprehension approaches, particularly for students with learning difficulties (Adams, 1991; Becker & Gersten, 1982; Chall, 1967, 1983; Gurren & Huges, 1983). Code-emphasis approaches have proved more efficacious with populations labeled "disadvantaged" (Stahl, 1990) and with special education populations (Biggins & Uhler, 1979; Williams, 1985). Lewis (1983) noted that decoding skills traditionally have been emphasized in teaching reading to students with mild handicapping conditions and that there is no substantive body of research that argues for an alternative approach. In summary, for students with achievement difficulties as well as those without achievement difficulties, programs that provide for direct and systematic instruction in phonics have produced results superior to meaning-emphasis approaches to reading in the early grades. Furthermore, teaching individual letter sounds prior to introducing their use in words (*synthetic phonics*) has been documented as preferable in beginning reading to introducing sounds in words and then teaching individual sounds (*analytic phonics*).

The code-emphasis approach also is a more efficient approach to learning to read. This is because code-emphasis strategies better facilitate generalization, with each letter-sound relationship applicable to a large number of new words. Thus, each and every word that a student learns does not have to be taught separately; rather, the sound-symbol relationships taught provide keys to unlocking an infinite number of words.

For thorough details on the direct instruction of reading using a phonics approach, see Carnine's et al. (1990) *Direct Instruction Reading* (2nd edition). Adam's (1991) seminal book, *Beginning to Read: Thinking and Learning About Print,* analyzes, evaluates, and integrates all the major research about learning to read.

Teaching Phonics as the Key to Reading

Phonics involves teaching letter-sound correspondences of the alphabetic system. It is the primary approach to sounding out new words. Phonics instruction begins with preskills, such as auditory blending and segmenting that assist students in associating sounds with words and in discriminating letter sounds. While there are twenty-six letters in the English alphabet, there are more than 200 letter-sound associations in the the one- and two-syllable words that typify most primary-grade materials. Instruction in letter-sound correspondence prepares students for sounding out new words. They must learn that individual letters have sounds associated with them, and that these are the key to translating letters and words into meaningful language. This means that for effective and efficient instruction, careful thought must be given to sequencing the introduction of these letter-sound associations Guidelines for teaching phonics skills are listed as follows and elaborated upon in the following paragraphs:

1. Use lowercase letters for initial instruction.
2. Introduce more frequently occurring and useful skills first.
3. Focus initial instruction on easy sounds and letters.
4. Maintain a reasonable pace for introducing new letter-sound associations.
5. Teach consonants (*C*) first, but introduce vowels (*V*) early.

6. Teach the most common sounds of letters first.
7. Teach continuous sounds before stop sounds.
8. Introduce sound blending early.
9. Begins sound-blending instructions with VC and CVC words that have continuous sounds.
10. Next, introduce CVC words that begin with stop sounds.
11. Teach words beginning with consonant blends next.
12. Specifically teach consonant digraphs.
13. Teach regular words before irregular ones.

Use lowercase letters for initial instruction. Since the majority of words that students will read are composed of lowercase letters, these should be taught first. When the uppercase and lowercase versions look exactly the same (e.g., *sS,* and *cC*), both cases can be introduced at the same time.

Introduce more frequently occurring and useful skills first. Letter sounds, words, and skills that students will encounter most frequently during initial reading should be taught early in the program. For example, the letter sounds /a/, /m/, /s/, and /i/ appear more frequently than /v/, /w/, /j/, and /x/. This means that vowel sounds should be taught first, along with the *b, c, d, f, g, h, k, m, n, p, r, s,* and *t* consonant sounds.

Focus initial instruction on easy sounds and letters. Easy sounds, such as /a/ and /m/ should be introduced before more difficult sounds such as /l/ and /e/. Letter-sound correspondences that occur more frequently (/a/, /m/, and /s/) should be taught before those that are less frequent (/v/,/w/, /j/, and /x/). Further, letters that are visually similar (*p, b,* and *d; p* and *q; m* and *n; v* and *w;* and *n* and *r*) should be separated for instruction as should letters that sound similar (/f/ and /v/; /b/, /d/, and /p/; /k/ and /g/; /m/ and /n/; /o/ and /u/; and /e/ and /i/). According to Carnine et al. (1990), the number of letters that should separate teaching similar letters depends on the extent of the similarity. Instruction of visually similar letters should be separated by instruction in at least one or two dissimilar letters, while instruction in auditorily similar letters should be separated by instruction in at least three letters with dissimilar sounds. When letters are similar both visually and auditorily, their teaching should be separated by at least six dissimilar sounds.

Maintain a reasonable pace for introducing new letter-sound associations. Carnine et al. (1990) have observed that the rate at which letter sounds are introduced is related to the skills students have when they enter school. With students who have little to no prior learning of letter-sound correspondences, a recommended rate is one new letter sound every 2 or 3 days as long as daily practice is provided. After students have mastered the initial five or six letter sounds, a new letter sound can be introduced even if they are experiencing difficulty with one of the previous correspondences. However, the new letters should be dissimilar from the one that is presenting difficulty. For example, a vowel could be introduced even though students are having difficulty with a consonant, but not if the students are having difficulty with a vowel, since all vowels are similar in sound.

Teach consonants first, but introduce vowels early. Because consonants tend to have a clear one-to-one letter-sound correspondence, they should be taught first. Irregular consonant sounds (such as *c* in *city* instead of *cat, g* in *giant* instead of *got, s* in *sure* instead of *sun,* and *h* as in *hour* instead of *hat*) can be taught later after the alphabetic principle has been established. Vowels tend to be highly irregular, only sometimes having a clear letter-sound correspondence. However, as they are the most useful sounds and highly important for decoding words, vowels should be introduced early in the program. Generally, children are able to articulate vowel sounds before 6 years of age, when formal reading instruction usually begins.

Teach the most common sounds of letters first. When teaching letter-sound correspondences, it is better to teach the most common sounds of letters before teaching the letter names. With vowels, the most common sound is the short sound as typically found in one-syllable words. Table 10.3 depicts the most common sounds for vowels and consonants.

Teach continuous sounds before stop sounds. All vowels and certain consonants are described as *continuous* sounds (sounds such as *s* that can be said for several seconds without distortion), while other consonants are listed as *stop* sounds (those than can be pronounced only momentarily without distortion). Because continuous sounds (e.g., /s/ and /m/) are considered easier to hear and may be easier to produce than certain stop sounds, they should be taught first. The less frequently used consonant sounds of *j, q, v, w, x, y,* and *z* should be taught later. Table 10.4 presents a sequence for introducing letters.

Introduce sound blending early. Sound-blending instruction can begin as soon as four or five sounds have been mastered. These letter sounds can be used to decode CVC trigrams such as *cat, big, bat,* and *tag.* Once students can blend sounds into words, word-list exercises involving regular words (i.e., those in which each letter represents its most common sound) can be intro-

TABLE 10.3 Vowel and Consonant Sounds

Continuous Sounds		Stop Sounds	
a	(fat)	b	(boy)
e	(bet)	c	(can)
f	(fill)	d	(did)
i	(sit)	g	(got)
l	(let)	h	(his)
m	(mad)	j	(jet)
n	(nut)	k	(kiss)
o	(not)	p	(pet)
r	(rat)	q	(quit)
s	(sell)	t	(top)
u	(cut)	x	(fox)
w	(wet)		
y	(yes)		
z	(zoo)		

Source: Reprinted with the permission of Macmillan Publishing Company from *Direct Instruction Reading,* Second Edition by Douglas Carnine, Jerry Silbert, and Edward J. Kameenui. Copyright © 1990 by Macmillan Publishing Company.

duced. These should include only letters that the students already have mastered and two-thirds of the words should be of a type (e.g., CVC) already familiar to the students. The ordering of the words should be unpredictable (e.g., the same letter should not be in the same position in more than two consecutive words). Considerable practice (perhaps 4–6 weeks) may be required for students to master these words. Using the student's performance as a guide, the teacher can gradually introduce new word types, practicing each to fluency before moving to a more difficult word type. Table 10.5 lists the word types in order of difficulty.

In teaching sound blending, teachers should begin with a statement of the lesson's purpose, review previous relevant learning, and then provide a teacher demonstration and guided practice for the students. For example, a teacher might state, "Today we are going to learn to use the letter sounds to make words." Then, pointing to each letter on the chalkboard or transparency, ask: "Everyone, what is this sound? (point) What is this sound (point)?" After reviewing each sound, the teacher then: (1) explains that these sounds can be blended together to form a word, (2) models this sound blending, and (3) instructs students to blend the sounds together. This procedure is repeated for each trigram. By calling on each student to sound out words, the teacher can check for comprehension and then provide appropriate independent practice using flash cards, worksheets, or the Language Master. These words should be reviewed each day, providing additional prompted practice as well as independent practice, until the students have demonstrated both accuracy and fluency.

Begin instruction with VC and CVC words that start with continuous sounds. Begin sound blending instruction with VC and CVC words that are short and frequently occurring. Provide lots of practice (e.g., twenty to thirty lessons) on these VC and CVC patterns, integrating all new letter-sound correspondences that students learn. After students can sound out four CVC words without error, begin to introduce CVCC words.

TABLE 10.4 Sequence for Letter Introduction

a	m	t	s	i	f	d	r	o	g	l	h	u	c	b	b	k	v	e	w	j	p	y
	T	L	M	F	D	I	N	A	R	C	H	G	B	x	q	z	J	E	O			

Source: Reprinted with the permission of Macmillan Publishing Company from *Direct Instruction Reading,* Second Edition by Douglas Carnine, Jerry Silbert, and Edward J. Kameenui. Copyright © 1990 by Macmillan Publishing Company.

Next, introduce CVC words that begin with stop sounds. Have the students say the sound of the word's second and third letters, then adding the stop sound at the beginning in order to sound out the entire word (e.g, *uutt* and then *c–uutt* and then *cut*). When signaling, teachers should touch briefly on the stop sound and then move quickly to the next letter, holding the signal slightly longer than usual at this second letter.

Teach words beginning with consonant blends next. *Consonant blends* are limited in number and are invariant in pronunciation. They occur whenever two or more consonants appear in succession and are each pronounced. Examples of consonant blends are *br, bl, sc, st, scr,* and *str.* Words with consonant blends in the initial position (e.g., *bright, bloom, screw,* and *stop*) should be introduced after the students have mastered CVC blending. Those with consonant blends that contain continuous sounds are easier than those that contain a stop sound.

Using modeling and prompted practice, the teacher should introduce consonant blends individually. Blends beginning with continuous sounds (*snap, sped,* and *spot*) are easier and should be introduced before initial consonant blend words beginning with stop sounds (*plan, glad,* and *drag*). Consonant blends in the final position also should be specifically taught, such as in the words mu*st*, fa*st*, a*sk*, we*nt*, se*nd*, ha*nd*, and si*nk*.

Specifically teach consonant digraphs. *Consonant digraphs* differ from consonant blends in that the successive consonants form a single sound instead of a sound where each letter is heard. They may occur in both initial and final positions and should be taught specifically.

Initial Position:	*ch*in, *ch*ick, *sh*ip, *sh*ut, *sh*all, *th*at, *th*e, *th*ey, *th*ank, *wh*en
Final Position:	mu*ch*, ri*ch*, wi*sh*, di*sh*, too*th* ba*th*, wi*th*, so*ng*, ri*ng*, and ba*ng*

Teach regular words before irregular ones. Initial instruction should be limited to so-called **regular** words that comply with phonics rules and are pronounced in terms of their most common sounds. Students should be provided with multiple applications of each phonics rule to assist them in applying the rules to sound out words as well as in generalizing them to future reading.

TABLE 10.5 Regular Word Types in Order of Difficulty

VC and CVC words that begin with continuous sounds (e.g., *at, sam*)
CVCC words that begin with continuous sounds (e.g., *runs, lamp, fish*)
CVC words that begin with stop sounds (e.g., *hot, cap*)
CCVC words that begin with continuous sounds (e.g., *slap, frog*)
CCVC words in which one of the initial sounds is a stop sound (e.g., *crib, stop*)
CCVCC words (e.g., *brand, clump*)
CCCVC and CCCVCC words (e.g., *split, sprint*)

Source: Reprinted with the permission of Macmillan Publishing Company from *Direct Instruction Reading,* Second Edition by Douglas Carnine, Jerry Silbert, and Edward J. Kameenui. Copyright © 1990 by Macmillan Publishing Company.

A listing of phonics rules is provided in Table 10.6.

A large number of words in the English language are **irregular words** in that the letter-sound correspondences are exceptions to the phonics rules and are unique to either that single word or to a small group of words. It is better to delay introducing irregular words until after the students can sight-read regular CVC words with proficiency. Irregular words that are used more frequently (e.g., *was* and *said)* should be introduced first. Table 10.7 contains a list of common **sight words** from which irregular words can be identified.

One approach is simply to teach irregular words as facts to be memorized, grouping irregular words that have the same letter-sound correspondence (e.g., *walk, talk,* and *chalk; to,* and *do*). Because of their difficulty level, teaching irregular words should be spaced out, with new words introduced only after previous words have been mastered. Only one new irregular word should be introduced every three or four lessons.

Develop sight word skills. Once a student has mastered sounding out a word list, instruction in sight reading of the word list can begin. Carnine et al. (1990) have outlined procedures for developing sight word vocabularies. Pointing to words written on the chalkboard, the teacher first models the subvocal sounding out of the words prior to saying them out loud at a normal rate. The vocal modeling is an important step because it provides the students with a strategy that is inconsistent with guessing behavior. After the students can sound out the words subvocally, the teacher instructs them to read the words "the fast way," pointing to each word as the students pronounce it.

When the students have demonstrated that they can read each word on the word list in less than 3 seconds, they can be prompted to sight-read the words the fast way. Moving their fingers under the sounds, they say the words to themselves and then, at the teacher's signal, say them aloud in unison. After approximately a week, the prompting of students to sound out each word can be dropped, and they simply can say the words in unison the fast way as the teacher points to them. Words produced in error can be written on the chalkboard and reviewed as sight words. When the students have demonstrated the ability to sight-read all of the word list, they are ready to practice reading the word list without the teacher's direction. Finally, individual students should be asked to read the words in sentences.

TABLE 10.6 Phonic Rules

1. When the letter *e* is followed by *e, i,* or *y,* its sound is usually /*s*/ (*city, cent, nice*).
2. When the letter *c* is followed by *a* or *o,* its sound is usually /*k*/ (*cot, cat, coat, incantation*).
3. When *c* and *h* are next to each other, they make only one sound (*church, chum, lunch*).
4. When *s* and *h* are next to each other, they make only one sound (*shot, shine, wish*).
5. When a word ends in the letter *e,* say the name (long vowel sound) of the vowel (*bake, make, like*).
6. When there are two vowels side by side, the word takes the sound of the first vowel (*coat, mean*).
7. When *y* is the final letter of a word, it usually has a vowel sound (*cry, litany*).
8. If there are two consonants that are the same in the middle of a word, say the sound (short sound) of the vowel (*tipped, mapping*).
9. When two consonants are side by side (double consonants), only one sound is heard (*fell*).
10. If there is one consonant in the middle of a word, say the name (long vowel) of the first vowel (*hiking, baked*).

TABLE 10.7   Sight Words as a Source of Irregular Words

Basic Sight Vocabulary List:
The 200 most-frequent words in the Kucera-Frances (1967) Corpus

Rank	Word	Rank	Word	Rank	Word	Rank	Word	Rank	Word
1	the	45	when	89	many	133	know	177	don't
2	of	46	who	90	before	134	while	178	does
3	and	47	will	91	must	135	last	179	got
4	to	48	more	92	through	136	might	180	united
5	a	49	no	93	back	137	us	181	left
6	in	50	if	94	years	138	great	182	number
7	that	51	out	95	where	139	old	183	course
8	is	52	so	96	much	140	year	184	war
9	was	53	said	97	your	141	off	185	until
10	he	54	what	98	may	142	come	186	always
11	for	55	up	99	well	143	since	187	away
12	it	56	its	100	down	144	against	188	something
13	with	57	about	101	should	145	go	189	fact
14	as	58	into	102	because	146	came	190	through
15	his	59	than	103	each	147	night	191	water
16	on	60	them	104	just	148	used	192	less
17	be	61	can	105	those	149	take	193	public
18	at	62	only	106	people	150	three	194	put
19	by	63	other	107	Mr.	151	states	195	thing
20	I	64	new	108	how	152	himself	196	almost
21	this	65	some	109	too	153	few	197	hand
22	had	66	could	110	little	154	house	198	enough
23	not	67	time	111	state	155	use	199	far
24	are	68	these	112	good	156	during	200	look
25	but	69	two	113	very	157	without	201	head
26	from	70	may	114	make	158	again	202	yet
27	of	71	then	115	would	159	place	203	government
28	have	72	do	116	still	160	American	204	system
29	an	73	first	117	own	161	around	205	better
30	they	74	any	118	see	162	however	206	set
31	which	75	my	119	men	163	home	207	told
32	one	76	now	120	work	164	small	208	nothing
33	you	77	such	121	long	165	found	209	night
34	were	78	like	122	get	166	Mrs.	210	end
35	her	79	our	123	here	167	thought	211	why
36	all	80	over	124	between	168	went	212	called
37	she	81	man	125	both	169	say	213	didn't
38	there	82	me	126	life	170	part	214	eyes
39	would	83	even	127	being	171	once	215	find
40	their	84	most	128	under	172	general	216	going
41	we	85	made	129	never	173	high	217	look
42	him	86	after	130	day	174	upon	218	asked
43	been	87	also	131	same	175	school	219	later
44	has	88	did	132	another	176	every	220	knew

Source: From D.D. Johnson, (1971). "The Dolch list reexamined." *The Reading Teacher 24,* 455–456. Reprinted with permission of the International Reading Association.

Introduce passage reading after students can sound out words. Passage reading can be introduced when students can sound out the words on a word list with relative ease. It is important to remember that sounding out passages is considerably more difficult than sounding out words. Passage reading involves less teacher structuring and more reader independence.

Once students can sight-read words with no more than a 3-second thinking pause for each word, sight word passage reading can be introduced. Initially, the teacher may want the students to sound out the passage and then sight-read one to two of the passages' sentences. Unison responding is useful here in that it increases students' attention and provides each student with several response opportunities. Students should continue to sound out passages prior to sight-reading them for several weeks to discourage guessing. As students gain in proficiency, teachers can gradually reduce the thinking time from 3 seconds per word, to 2 1/2 and then 2 seconds a word, and so on. First-grade students should receive extra practice in the form of a second 15–20-minute reading period each day. Slow

learning students also probably will need this extra practice throughout their primary school years, and even beyond. It is through such practice that reading fluency develops.

Structural Analysis

Structural analysis is another set of word decoding skills. It involves teaching students to use their knowledge of affixes, inflected endings, base words, contractions, and syllabication to analyze unknown words. Affixes and inflected endings should be introduced systematically, separating any instruction of similar word parts. Table 10.8 lists a possible sequence for beginning instruction in these word parts.

Carnine et al. (1990) recommend that words formed by adding affixes to a base word can be introduced when students are able to read one-syllable words at a rate of about 20 words per minute. Prefixes or suffixes should be introduced in isolation with the teacher modeling the sounds made by the affix and having students practice. The new affix should be practiced in isolation for several days and then introduced in a word-list

TABLE 10.8   Sample Sequence for Introducing Common Prefixes and Suffixes

Prefix/Suffix	Example	Rule
-er	batter	Inflected ending
-ing	jumping	Inflected ending
-ed	jumped	Inflected ending
-y	funny	Suffix
-un	unlock	Prefix
-est	biggest	Inflected ending
-le	handle	Suffix
a-	alive	Prefix
be-	belong	Prefix
re-	refill	Prefix
de-	demand	Prefix
-ic	picnic	Suffix
-ful	careful	Suffix
-ly	sadly	Suffix

Source: Reprinted with the permission of Macmillan Publishing Company from *Direct Instruction Reading*, Second Edition by Douglas Carnine, Jerry Silbert, and Edward J. Kameenui. Copyright © 1990 by Macmillan Publishing Company.

exercise, making sure to indicate how they affect word meaning. Finally, the affix should be included in stories using similar words. Suffixes and inflected endings should first be taught using base words ending with consonants and then with base words ending with vowels. The final step includes attaching affixes and inflected endings to multisyllabic words. A list of common affixes and inflected endings, their meanings, and examples are found in Table 10.9.

Students can also be taught to use their knowledge of base words to decode compound words. Various activities can be designed to emphasize the two base words, such as matching drills using two lists of words with pairs that can be combined to form real words or nonsense words, cloze procedures in which half of each compound word is left blank and students must fill it in with an appropriate word, and silly pictures that students can label using compound words (e.g, a stick of flying butter for *butterfly*). Instruction in compound words should include a discussion of how knowledge of individual base words can be used to determine the meaning of compound words.

Instruction should also be provided in contractions. Polloway and Smith (1992) suggest that students should be able to recognize pronoun-verb (e.g., *I'll, he's, I've,* and *they've*) and negative (e.g., *didn't, won't, can't,* and *haven't*) contracted forms of words and be able to substitute the equivalents. Examples of commonly used contractions are found in Table 10.10.

The average number of syllables in words students read will increase throughout the grade levels. As students encounter more multisyllabic words, they can use rules for dividing words into syllables and accenting syllables to assist in decoding and determining word meaning. Each rule should be taught individually and systematically by writing it on the board and demonstrating its use in several words.

Students should first practice applying the rule to known words and then practice on unknown words out of context. Finally, unknown words requiring use of the rule are presented in passage reading. Students' ability to apply the rule is assessed according to their ability to decode unknown words in context. A list of common rules for dividing words into syllables and accenting syllables is found in Table 10.11.

Contextual Analysis

Contextual analysis involves using surrounding information (e.g., word meaning, and sentence structure) and text structure to decode unknown or irregular words. To help students use contextual analysis, they must understand that a variety of cues can be used to decode words and that the words must make sense in the sentence. They also must attend to the orthographic structure (e.g., spelling) of the words.

Practice in using contextual analysis can include instructing students to identify words that "make sense" using the cloze procedure. An alternative approach is to provide part of the word instead of a blank so that students can select words that make sense and are consistent with phonic and structural clues. When reading aloud to students, teachers can supplement such instruction by pausing periodically so that students can predict appropriate words or phrases that complete the thought. Carnine et al. (1990) describe a procedure in which students are taught a strategy for pronouncing unknown words using phonic and structure rules as they ask themselves whether the word makes sense in the context. To use this procedure, first the students are taught that when they come to a word for which there is no phonic or structural cue for the vowel sound, they should first pronounce the word with the first vowel representing its long sound. If the word does not make sense in context, students pronounce the word with another vowel sound until they create a word that makes sense in context.

Fluent Decoding

Research indicates that better readers decode words both accurately and fluently and that fluent decoding is associated with improved compre-

TABLE 10.9 Common Affixes and Inflected Endings

Common Affix Forms	Meaning	Examples
Suffix		
-able	capable of being	agreeable, comfortable
-ance	stage of being	allowance, insurance
-ant	one who	accountant, expectant
-ent	being one who	violent, excellent
-er	relating to, like	harder, older
-ful	full of	joyful, thoughtful
-fy	to make	beautify, magnify
-ish	like	foolish, sheepish
-ist	one who	artist, geologist
-ive	relating to	active, creative
-less	unable to, without	careless, thoughtless
-ly	in a way	honestly, loudly
-ment	state of being	excitement, movement
-ness	state of being	blindness, faithfulness
-ous	full of	mysterious, victorious
-tion	act, state of being	confusion, protection
-ward	turning to	southward, forward
-ible	capable of, worthy	credible, edible
-age	state or act of	advantage, bondage
-ty	quality or state	equality, majesty
-some	like	handsome, lonesome
Prefix		
anti-	against	antiwar, antifreeze
abs-	from	abstain, absent
bi-	two	bicycle, bifocal
co-	with, together with	coworker, coeducation
de-	down, from, away	defrost, desegregate
dis-	opposite	disenchant, disinherit
en-	in, into, make	entrust, engrave
ex-	former, from	exclude, exclaim
im-	not, in	impatient, implant
in-	not, into	incredible, indefensible
inter-	between	interracial, interlude
ir-	not, into	irreversible, irrecoverable
mis-	wrong	misread, misbehave
non-	not	nondrinker, nonvoting
pre-	before	predict, preface
pro-	for, in front of	prolabor, proactivity
re-	back again	rediscover, redirect
semi-	half, partly	semiprofessional, semiannual
sub-	under, less than	subterranean, subtitle
super-	over, above	superhuman, superimposed
trans-	beyond, across	transceiver, transcription
un-	not	unlucky, unhealthy
Common Inflected Endings		
-ing	Present progressive	running, laughing
-ed	Past tense	called, studied, cracked
-s	Plural	shoes, cats
-'s	Possessive	John's, Joyce's
-er	Comparative	bigger, stronger
-est	Superlative	biggest, strongest

TABLE 10.10   Commonly Used Contractions

I've	doesn't	they're
we've	can't	we're
you've	hasn't	you're
they've	hadn't	I'm
	didn't	
I'll	wouldn't	it's
they'll	couldn't	who's
we'll	shouldn't	that's
you'll	weren't	he's
he'll	isn't	she's
she'll	aren't	let's
I'd	don't	here's
we'd	haven't	there's
you'd	hasn't	what's
they'd	wasn't	
he'd	won't	
she'd	mustn't	

hension (Ehri & Wilce, 1983). One way to promote fluency is for teachers and good readers to model fluent reading by reading aloud to students. Practice opportunities in fluent reading can be provided by using predictable materials that contain repetitive or familiar structures which enable students to predict the next word, line, or episode (Rhodes, 1981). To use this technique, the teacher selects a predictable book and reads it aloud to the class several times. As the story is read, students are invited to join in on any parts they know. A comprehensive list of predictable books is found in Rhodes and Dudley-Marling (1988).

The teacher can model fluent reading by reading passages aloud, explaining pauses and inflections, and discussing the need to continue reading if they do not know the word. Students read along orally with the teacher as much as possible. If they are hesitant, the reading may be repeated. Next, the students are timed for 1 minute as they read aloud independently. If they hesitate on any word, the teacher supplies it after a 3-second wait. At the end of the reading, the teacher reviews any missed words. Charting the reading rate (number of words per minute) of different

passages each day provides a visual picture of improvement in reading rate over time (Downs & Morin, 1990).

READING COMPREHENSION

Reading comprehension requires activating the readers' background knowledge and interpreting the printed text based on that knowledge. The types of background knowledge used include the readers' understanding of the general topic, specific vocabulary, and organization of the text. Mature readers remain active in the reading comprehension process by asking questions that allow them to make predictions and interpret the text. As part of this process, they continually evaluate the meaningfulness of what they have read. When readers encounter information that is inconsistent with their prediction or interpretation, they invoke correction strategies (e.g., using word recognition skills or modifying their interpretation until the inconsistency is resolved).

Comprehension is a complex behavior incorporating a variety of interwoven skills. It can be conceptualized as occurring at increasing levels of complexity, beginning at the literal level and progressing through the organizational, inferential, and critical levels (Lerner, 1985). **Literal comprehension** is the least complex comprehension level in which readers recognize and understand material stated directly in the text. For **organizational comprehension,** readers move beyond simply identifying stated facts to organizing facts according to order of importance and text structure organization. Readers at this level can identify main idea statements and subordinate supporting details. They also are able to organize and remember material based on the predictable structure of text and, later, according to various types of expository text structures. **Inferential comprehension** involves going beyond what is explicitly stated in the text to identify implied meanings. Readers at this level hypothesize or conjecture based on information, logic, and personal experiences. At the **critical comprehension** level, readers make judgments and evaluations

TABLE 10.11   Rules for Dividing and Accenting Syllables

Dividing Syllables
1. In a compound word, the syllabic division usually comes between the words of which it is composed.
2. Prefixes and suffices usually form separate syllables.
3. Polysyllabic words ending in a consonant and *le* usually form the last syllable with the consonant plus *le.*
4. If there is a single consonant between two vowels in a polysyllabic word, the consonant often begins the last syllable if the preceding vowel has a long sound and with the first vowel if the first vowel has a short sound.
5. When two vowel letters are separated by two consonants, the syllables will usually divide between the consonants.
6. Syllables usually do not break between digraphs or diphthongs.
7. Words do not divide between two vowels unless each vowel forms a separate syllable.
8. The suffix *ed* does not constitute a separate syllable unless the preceding syllable ends with a *t* or a *d.*

Accenting Syllables
1. When a word contains a prefix or suffix, the accent usually falls on or within the root word.
2. The accent most often falls on the first syllable of a two-syllable word if there is no other clue.
3. The accent usually falls on the first word of a compound word.
4. When a two-syllable word has a final syllable containing two vowel letters, that syllable usually is accented.
5. When a two-syllable word functions as either a noun or a verb, the accent is usually on the first syllable when the word is a noun and on the second syllable when the word functions as a verb.
6. When a multisyllabic word ends in *tion,* the accent falls on the preceding syllable.
7. When there is a double consonant within a word, the accent usually falls on the syllable ending with the first letter of the consonant pair.

---

based on their own experiences, knowledge, and values. At this level, readers discern between reality or fantasy and fact or opinion. In addition to making judgments about validity, they compare, analyze, and draw conclusions.

Teaching Comprehension

Reading comprehension requires that students have knowledge of the general topic, specific vocabulary, and text organization. Teachers can ensure that students are able to comprehend the reading material by either presenting them only with pas-

sages about which they have prior knowledge or by preteaching concepts and specific vocabulary prior to having students read the material. To the extent possible, teachers should build on the students' prior knowledge, using this as a base for introducing new background information. For example, if the students are to read stories about Daniel Boone, the teacher might ask students what they know about life on the frontier, fill in with additional information, and discuss specific vocabulary words. Whenever possible, necessary concepts should be presented using concrete examples and a variety of media instead of verbal descriptions. For example, a discussion of life on the frontier could include filmstrips and movies, other books containing pictures and stories of frontier life, class activities in which students replicate certain frontier activities (e.g., making candles, and eating dried fruits and meat), and perhaps even a field trip to a site where frontier life is demonstrated. Such experiences allow students to gain a broader understanding of concepts than can be learned through abstract words and assists them in establishing a purpose for reading. Such activities are particularly important for students who have language and general knowledge deficits.

Teachers can effectively develop reading comprehension by using systematic instruction. They can provide instruction on literal, organizational, inferential, and critical comprehension skills. They can develop comprehension through specific strategy instruction, story grammar and scaffolding approaches, and reciprocal teaching.

Teaching Literal Comprehension. Literal comprehension, or rote recall, is the simplest type of comprehension. In literal comprehension, answers to questions are explicitly stated in the text. Students can answer questions about stories that are read aloud to them or retell these stories. Literal comprehension also can be taught by having students answer questions about their readings (e.g., *who, what, when, where,* and *why*), assuming that they have sufficient decoding skills. The comprehension exercises should focus only on important facts in the passage. Requiring students to recall details that do not contribute to understanding the story may be detrimental since poor readers often have difficulty distinguishing important facts from trivial details.

Carnine et al. (1990) suggest a strategy for teaching students to improve literal comprehension. In the first step, students decode the passage until they can read it fluently. Fluent reading is then followed by question asking or some other activity to assess comprehension. Students who complete the task successfully proceed to the next section. If they do not succeed, they are directed to reread the passage until they come to the sentence that contains the answer.

Summary writing is another comprehension strategy that can be effective with older students. Summarizing has the advantages of focusing students' attention on the task, restating information in their own words, and making connections between their prior knowledge and new material. In essence, students retell the text. This approach has proved to be an effective instructional technique for enhancing overall comprehension (Gambell, Pfeiffer, & Wilson, 1985).

Organizational Comprehension. A goal of instruction at this more advanced level is to help students identify main ideas and supporting details. Begin the instruction by teaching students that the main idea can be found by using the following rules:

1. The main idea is the most general statement in the paragraph.
2. Most of the other sentences refer to it.
3. Most of the other sentences elaborate or qualify the statement.
4. Other sentences are not related without the main idea statement.

Using simple, self-made paragraphs, teachers first write the main idea sentence in the middle of a sheet of paper and box it in. Remaining sentences are written away from the box, circles are drawn around each, and arrows are drawn to the main idea sentence. The teacher explains how the circled sentences relate to the main idea sentence and then covers up the main idea sentence to illustrate that the remaining sentences lose their meaning without it. She repeats this procedure with other paragraphs in which the position of the main idea sentence is rotated. After students become adept at identifying the main idea sentence, they are taught to paraphrase the main idea and supporting details to make a summary of what they have read (Wong, Wong, Perry, & Sawatsky, 1986).

Other procedures for teaching main idea and detail include Statement PIE in which students find the main idea and subordinate Proof, Information, and Example statements (Englert & Lichter, 1982; Wallace & Bott, 1989) and the Paraphrasing Strategy in which students implement the RAP procedure of reading the paragraph, asking "What were the main ideas and details?," and putting the main idea and details into their own words (Schumaker, Denton, & Deshler, 1984).

The text structure can help students understand and remember what they have read. To identify the sequential text structure, students read a passage containing a sequence of events, underline the words that coincide with each event, and number the underlined events beginning with one. They then write the numbers in front of the appropriate items in the question (Carnine et al., 1990).

A more difficult task involves using the structure of stories to aid comprehension. Students with little knowledge of text structure or story grammar can benefit from direct instruction in text organization, particularly story grammar (Buss, Ratliff, & Iron, 1985). Thomas, Englert, and Morsink (1984) developed a simple story structure that includes a *setting,* which introduces the main characters and describes the date and location of the story; a *problem,* which confronts the main character; the main character's *response* to the problem, and the **outcome** of the problem, including the main character's response. A simple way to help students use story structure is to ask comprehension questions that focus on story parts. Students predict story parts, fill-in missing story parts in a cloze task, and unscramble stories according to story parts. As students begin reading in the content areas, instruction in the different expository text structures can also be provided (Meyer, 1975). Instruction in text structure is helpful to students with learning disabilities in that it provides a useful aid for approaching unfamiliar content (Palincsar & Brown, 1985). Additional discussion of methods for comprehending expository text are detailed in Chapter 13 on content-area instruction.

Inferential Comprehension. Making predictions about content not explicitly stated in the text is the focus of instruction in inferential comprehension. A widely used technique for improving comprehension at all levels is the Directed Reading-Thinking Activity (DRTA) (Stauffer, 1975). In the first step, students are directed to attend to the title, illustrations, or first part of the story. Students are then asked what the story might be about and all predictions are recorded on the chalkboard. Students read to a designated stopping point, at which time one student volunteers to summarize the reading and the group evaluates the predictions, discarding some and modifying or confirming others. The procedure is repeated throughout the story.

In another procedure for teaching students how to make inferences, materials in which relationships are specifically stated are used (Carnine et al., 1990). Using multiple passages in which the critical rule or relationship can be identified, teachers point out the rule, ask students to answer questions requiring use of the rule, and then ask students why they gave their answers. When students become proficient at this task, they are taught to make inferences when the relationship is unstated. Such passages require that students have prior knowledge, allowing them to understand the implied relationship. Consequently, the teacher may need to provide information necessary for comprehension so that students can identify relevant information in order to make inferences.

Critical Comprehension. At the critical comprehension level, students are encouraged to use their own experiences, emotional responses, and values to evaluate the text. One strategy for critical reading requires students to identify the author's conclusion, determine what evidence is presented (e.g., Is it evidence or opinion?), determine the trustworthiness of the author (e.g., Is the author qualified? Is the author biased?), and identify faulty arguments (e.g., Does the evidence warrant the conclusion?) (Carnine et al., 1990).

Metacognitive Strategies. Effective readers engage in **metacognitive strategies** before, during, and after reading to improve comprehension. Activating background knowledge is an important prereading strategy. Teachers can teach students to activate background knowledge through brainstorming activities. They can prepare students for the reading selection by stating the topic or title of the reading and instructing students to take 3 minutes to think of or jot down any words that the topic makes them think of. After 3 minutes, the teacher can write the longest list on the chalkboard. Words from other lists are added so that ideas from many students are represented. Students can then be encouraged to reflect on their ideas and associations. They can discuss why certain words or ideas were selected and, finally, identify new information that they have learned as a part of this prereading activity. Using such a procedure, students' responses gradually change from relating personal experiences to describing the relationships between pieces of knowledge.

Structured overviews provide an effective follow-up activity to brainstorming. First, the students identify the topics of the ideas generated during brainstorming. They then organize these ideas under the general topic areas. During this process, some ideas may be dismissed, rewritten, or reorganized. Brainstorming and structured overviews can be used repeatedly until students can use them independently.

Students can be taught to self-monitor their comprehension by asking themselves periodically whether what they are reading makes sense. If the answer is "yes," students should continue reading. If the answer is "no," they should implement correction procedures in which they locate the source of the confusion, implement an appropriate strategy for correcting the problem (e.g., use phonic, structural, or contextual strategies), and then reread to see if the passage makes sense. During instruction in self-monitoring, students state the steps of the comprehension monitoring process and then observe as the teacher models

the process. Using a "think-aloud" technique, the teacher describes the process while reading the text. Students then practice the strategy by "talking aloud" as they read with the teacher's feedback. Finally, they use the strategy silently.

Effective readers remember more if they ask themselves questions during reading. Wong and Jones (1982) describe a procedure for improving self-questioning in which students are taught to ask themselves why they are reading the material, find the main idea, think of questions about the content and search for answers, and then look back on both the questions and answers to decide how each provided more information about the content.

Reciprocal teaching (Palincsar & Brown, 1985) is an explicit comprehension approach that involves a great deal of teacher-student dialogue related to asking questions about the content being read. Teachers and students take turns generating summaries of the main content, developing potential test questions, clarifying difficult parts of the text, and predicting future content. At the outset, the teacher verbally models these steps by thinking aloud about the content: "Let's see. The major point on this page was that there are three branches to the federal government. These are the executive, legislative, and judicial. Now what test question might be asked about this?" As the students' proficiency increases, the teacher encourages them to take over each of these tasks, providing guidance and prompting. This helps students learn to develop questions and to paraphrase text in relatively sophisticated ways. This approach has been shown to be effective with at-risk students, whose reading comprehension skills improved from a baseline of 15% to 85% accuracy after ten sessions of reciprocal comprehension instruction (Palincsar & Brown, 1984). Gains of this magnitude appear to maintain long after the students receive instruction in this approach, with data demonstrating consistently high comprehension scores 6 weeks and 8 months after reciprocal teaching instruction (Pearson & Doyle, 1987).

READING CURRICULA

Various curriculum materials are available for teaching reading. These range from traditional basal reading series, to newer "whole-language" basal series, to highly structured phonics programs, to other corrective and remedial approaches. Empirical evidence of the effectiveness of reading curricula with students who are low-achieving is lacking. This section summarizes several approaches that are widely used with students with learning difficulties.

Although a variety of basal series are available, few of them utilize empirically validated instructional sequence and procedures. *Reading Mastery* is one of the few such series. Designed for students through third grade, it provides a highly structured program that explicitly teaches phonics rules and structural analysis. Students are instructed in small groups for 30–40 minutes daily using intensive, highly structured instruction procedures that provide extensive practice, corrective feedback, frequent monitoring, and reinforcement. The first level of the program emphasizes basic decoding skills, including sound-symbol identification, left-to-right sequence, and oral blending of sounds to make words. The focus at the second level is on important sound combinations and word discrimination, and various word attack skills. Literal and inferential comprehension are also taught. The third level stresses skills in word attack, vocabulary, literal comprehension, sequencing, cause and effect, fact and opinion, point of view, and motive interpretations. Information in the science, social studies, and language arts areas is also presented at this level. Students' behaviors and responses are carefully monitored, and skill development is regularly assessed using tests provided. Materials in this series include teacher's guides, lesson plans, reading books and workbooks, spelling books, take-home readers, tests, and cassettes with sound pronunciations.

The SRA *Corrective Reading Program* (Englemann, Becker, Hanner, & Johnson, 1980), which is based on direct instruction concepts, is available for students in Grades 4–12, and adults who have not mastered decoding and comprehension skills. The program is divided into separate decoding and comprehension strands, each containing 340 lessons and three levels of skill developments. Each daily lesson includes teacher-led work, independent study, and tests of students' progress. Materials in this program include a teacher's manual; placement tests; presentation materials; and student materials including stories, contracts, and charts.

A recent approach to preventing reading failures with at-risk students is the *Reading Recovery* program (Pinnell, 1990). The development of this approach was predicated on research indicating that poor readers lack many of the basic strategies for reading such as knowing that a sentence should be read from left to right, looking at pictures for clues to meaning, or rereading words. They may not even know that the text should make sense. Reading Recovery includes features of both whole language reading and phonics approaches. The program is designed primarily for the lower 20% of readers at each grade level and has as its purpose the provision of accelerated instruction. Its goal is to have students read independently after 16–20 weeks of daily half-hour lessons. The program begins with a diagnostic survey to determine student proficiency in letter recognition, comprehension, and writing skills. Following this, for the initial 2 weeks, instruction is provided on a one-to-one tutorial basis. Stories are introduced that contain mostly words that the student knows, with a new story or book being introduced each day. Each day, students reread previously learned material to refine word-recognition and comprehension skills and to enhance student confidence. There is some research indicating that students in this program tend to read three levels above similar groups of students who receive other compensatory help and maintain this advantage in subsequent years (Viadero, 1990). The program is available only to teachers who receive intensive preparation that may involve weekly after-school sessions for a full year. This large initial investment appears to be the program's biggest drawback.

Two approaches that are widely used in special education settings, despite relatively weak empirical evidence of their effectiveness, are the language experience approach and multisensory approaches. As both approaches can be useful in meeting students' needs, they are included in this review. The *language experience approach* (LEA) involves teaching reading through student-dictated stories. Used as both a developmental and remedial approach to reading instruction, it is especially useful for students who have language and/or experiential deficits. It takes advantage of students' individual language and experiential repertoire and tends to be highly motivating. The first step is to have students engage in a group activity or discussion that will serve as the basis for a story. Next, students discuss the experience under the guidance of the teacher, who writes key concepts and vocabulary from the discussion on the chalkboard. The teacher then assists students in sorting and organizing information so that a story can be written. Students then dictate the story as the teacher writes it on the chalkboard or overhead transparency. They review it and suggest revisions. After the final draft of the story is written, the teacher reads it aloud several times at a normal rate while running a hand under the print. Next, students are invited to read along in unison several times and then volunteers can read it aloud individually. Students may copy the story and illustrate it, with the stories preserved in book form and placed in the class library available for check-out.

Studies have shown that the LEA can be used successfully to teach irregular sight words (Bridge, Winograd, & Haley, 1983) and to promote reading fluency (Peterson, Scott, & Sroka, 1990). However, the major disadvantage of this approach when used as the sole method of reading instruction is the lack of a structured, systematic method of teaching word recognition and comprehension skills.

Visual-auditory-kinesthetic-tactile methods are based on the premise that students learn best through multisensory stimulation. The *Fernald method* (Fernald, 1943) stresses whole-word learning using language experience and tracing techniques. In the first stage, the teacher writes a word selected from student-dictated stories in large letters with a crayon on paper. Students trace the word with their fingers as they say each part of the word aloud. This process is repeated until students can write the word correctly without the sample. If students make errors when tracing or writing, they must start over so that the word is always written as a unit. Each correctly written word is placed alphabetically in a word bank, which students later use to write other stories. This approach can serve to initially motivate a student, and it does direct students' attention to the shapes of individual letters and words and can help them discriminate the differences to similar letter pairs (e.g., *b* and *d; p* and *q*).

Unlike the Fernald approach, the *Gillingham method* (Gillingham & Stillman, 1968) is a highly structured, phonetically oriented approach. In the first step, students learn the names and sounds of various letters, each of which the teacher introduces individually. The teacher presents a letter on a card and tells students the letter name and corresponding sound. Students repeat the sound and then trace over the letter that the teacher has written. After mastering the first ten letters, students learn to blend the letters to form CVC words and then to spell them. At the next stage, students apply their skills in various reading, writing, and spelling activities.

TEACHING SPELLING

Spelling is a complex skill essential for written communication. Graham and Miller (1979, p. 2) define spelling as "the ability to recognize, recall, reproduce, or obtain orally or in written form the correct sequence of letters in words" Skilled spellers have memorized the spellings of many words so that they are able to write fluently, giving little conscious attention to spelling. When they encounter words they do not know how to spell, they have two main resources upon which to draw. First, they may rely on intrinsic sources including their memory of phonic, structural, and spelling rules to generate possible spellings. As they make spelling attempts, they use their visual memory to check for correctness. If the word appears incorrect, spellers selectively try another spelling and continue to revise until they are satisfied that the spelling is correct. If such strategies are unsuccessful, spellers may refer to extrinsic sources, such as the dictionary or aid from a teacher or friend. Intrinsic and extrinsic sources may be used simultaneously.

Rules and Patterns

Knowledge of phonics, structure, and spelling rules are intrinsic sources that assist spellers in generating unknown words. Phonics rules involve applying predictable sound-symbol associations to generate spellings. Structure rules include knowledge of base words, affixes and inflected endings, compound words, contractions, and syllabication. Structure rules are especially useful for multisyllabic words in which students can separate words into units, recall the spellings associated with those units, and then combine the units to spell words. Spelling rules encompass the use of capitalization, periods, and apostrophes, as well as generalizable rules such as how to add suffixes when a word ends in *y*, whether a word should be spelled using *ie* or *er,* and so forth.

Whereas young spellers rely more on phonics rules to spell unknown words, mature spellers rely more on structure and spelling rules. As spellers gain experience in spelling, most words will become part of their sight vocabularies. Sight vocabularies also include irregular words that do not follow any generalizable rules or patterns.

Proofreading

Good spellers do not need to be able to recall the complete spelling of a word in order to recognize whether or not it is spelled correctly. Once a spelling attempt has been made, students may scan the word to see if it is spelled accurately. Although the procedure is not exact, it usually detects incorrect spellings. When an error is found, knowledge of rules and patterns or external sources may be used to determine whether or not the spelling is correct. Using external sources requires the ability to alphabetize, find the approximate location of a target word in the dictionary, and use guide words.

Phonemic versus Whole-Word Approach

Whether spelling instruction should focus on using generalizable phonic, structural, and spelling rules or on memorizing whole words is rooted in the controversy over the regularity of the English language. According to a review of the literature that Graham and Miller (1979) conducted, phonics-based instruction results in greater gains in spelling than nonphonics approaches. This appears to be particularly true for students who have spelling difficulties (Polloway & Smith, 1992).

Beginning Spelling Instruction with Phonics

Spelling instruction that emphasizes phonics, structural, and spelling rules stresses the application of these rules as a means of developing spelling skills. Rule instruction is supplemented by the memorizing of irregular words, proofreading, and using outside sources such as the dictionary. Graham and Miller (1979) propose systematic instruction that follows the scope and sequence shown in Table 10.12. Each level corresponds roughly to one grade level.

Segmentation. Specific procedures have been described elsewhere in this chapter for teaching phonics. Beginning with teaching letter-sound correspondence, instruction proceeds to sound-blending, applying phonics to regular words, mastering regular and irregular words, and structural analysis. These procedures can be applied to spelling instruction with some adaptations. For

TABLE 10.12 Spelling Instruction Scope and Sequence

	LEVEL 1	LEVEL 2	LEVEL 3	LEVEL 4	LEVEL 5	LEVELS 6–8
Spelling vocabulary	25 words	275 words	400 words	460 words	460 words	460 words each
Phonic skills	Consonants ———————→					
		Consonant clusters ———————→				
		Digraphs ———————→				
		Vowels ———————————————————→				
			Base words ———————————————→			
			Suffixes ———————————————————→			
			Prefixes ———————————————————→			
Spelling rules		Capitalization				
			Adding suffixes			
			Punctuation-abbreviation			
			Apostrophes			
			Words do not end in *v*			
			Letter *q* followed by *u*			
Proofreading			Spelling ———————————————————→			
Dictionary		Picture dictionary				
		Alphabetical order				
			Target word			
			Alphabetical guide			
			Independent dictionary work ———→			

Source: From "Spelling research and practice: A unified approach" by S. Graham and L. Miller, 1979, *Focus on Exceptional Children,* 12(2), p. 6. Copyright 1979 by the Love Publishing Company. Reprinted by permission.

example, presenting letters visually and having students produce corresponding sounds orally can be modified so that the sounds are presented orally with students stating or writing the letter(s) represented by the sound. In addition to the sound-blending exercises described in the reading section, students should practice segmenting words into sounds. The teacher can begin by modeling the procedure, saying a word containing letter-sound correspondences the students know and then segmenting it into its parts: "Listen. 'SAT' I can say it slowly. 'S-A-T'." The teacher should point out that each sound goes with a letter and that by putting the letters together, students can spell the word. After the teacher demonstrates the procedures, the students practice it orally and then, as they become more proficient, write the letter(s) representing the sounds in order to spell the word.

Applying Phonics to Regular Words. Once students can segment words and associate letters with spoken sounds, exercises involving regular words can be introduced. Guidelines presented in the reading section apply here as well. When students become proficient at spelling various types of regular words through segmentation, spelling in more extended writing (i.e., sentences and passages) can be introduced. Finally, students should memorize these words as spelling sight words.

Teaching Rules

Both structural rules and spelling rules are important features of the instructional program. Similar to instruction in structural analysis in reading, the focus in spelling is on using knowledge of compound words, contractions, prefixes, suffixes, and root words to spell. Procedures used to teach these skills in reading should be modified so that students use knowledge of these rules to spell words.

Students should be taught the most common spelling rules that apply to a large number of words. Instruction begins with the teacher stating a rule and providing multiple examples of its use. The students then state the rule and practice applying it to spelling words on a teacher-generated word list. Finally, students can be guided to use the rule in more extended writing. As students learn these rules, multiple examples using real words should be provided. Teachers may select spelling rules from the following list:

- When a rule ends in a VC *e* and you want to add an ending that begins with a vowel, drop the "*e*" (*baking, raced,* and *making*).
- When a word ends in a CVC, double the consonant before adding an ending that begins with a vowel letter (e.g., *running, tapped,* and *ripped*).
- When a word ends with C-*y* and you want to add any ending except *ing,* change the *y* to *i* (e.g., *tried,* and *cried*)
- If a word ends in a *s, z, ch, sh,* or *x,* add *es* to make the plural word.
- If a word ends in a consonant and *ys,* add *es* to make the plural word.

Spelling Irregular Words

Words that follow no identifiable rules or patterns must be memorized as sight words. It is suggested that these words be systematically and gradually introduced, beginning with those words that are easiest to spell and are most likely to be found in students' writings. One source of irregular words, or "spelling demons," is the list of the most fre-

quently misspelled words in the elementary grades, found in Table 10.13.

Just as students are taught to use patterns from known words to read unknown words, students can be shown how to use these patterns to spell unknown words. Teaching spelling words in groups called *word families* can help students remember spellings and understand how new words can be spelled from known words. Table 10.14 contains some common word families.

Explicit instruction in using spelling patterns from known words to spell new words can be provided. An effective strategy used with students exhibiting mild handicapping conditions involves teaching students that "when words rhyme, the last parts are often spelled the same." In the first step of this procedure, students are provided copies of words they spelled correctly on a pretest that they put in their spelling bank. The next step involves presenting students with a set of unknown words containing spelling patterns found in the known words. For each unknown word, students find the spelling bank word that rhymes with the new word, identify the portions in both words that rhyme and are spelled the same, and spell the new word using the rhyming elements of the spelling bank word. In the last step, students use the new words in a variety of tasks intended to teach generalization, such as using the words in cloze sentences (Englert, Hiebert, & Stewart, 1985).

The best words to use for illustrating various rules and patterns, and for instruction in irregular words, are those that students are likely to use. These may be words from their texts, words used most frequently in their own writing, and/or words that the students select. (Graham, 1983; Manning & Manning, 1986). Whatever the source of the spelling words, students should only study words they understand. If necessary, vocabulary development should be conducted prior to spelling instruction in unknown words (Hillerich, 1982). One possible source of words is the list of one hundred words most frequently used in children's written work found in Table 10.15.

TABLE 10.13   Spelling Demons

about	come	has	Mar.	said	think
address	coming	have	maybe	Santa Claus	thought
afternoon	couldn't	haven't	me	Saturday	through
again	cousin	having	Miss	saw	time
all right	daddy	he	morning	school	to
along	day	hear	mother	schoolhouse	today
already	Dec.	hello	Mr.	send	together
always	didn't	her	Mrs.	sent	tomorrow
am	dog	here	much	sincerely	tonight
an	don't	him	my	snow	too
and	down	his	name	snowman	toys
answer	Easter	home	nice	some	train
anything	every	hope	Nov.	something	truly
anyway	everybody	hospital	now	sometime	two
April	father	house	nowadays	sometimes	until
are	Feb.	how	o'clock	soon	vacation
arithmetic	fine	how's	Oct.	stationery	very
aunt	first	I	off	store	want
awhile	football	I'll	on	studying	was
baby	for	I'm	once	summer	we
balloon	fourth	in	one	Sunday	weather
basketball	Friday	isn't	our	suppose	well
because	friend	it	out	sure	went
been	friends	it's	outside	surely	were
before	from	I've	party	swimming	we're
birthday	fun	Jan.	people	teacher	when
bought	getting	just	play	teacher's	white
boy	goes	know	played	Thanksgiving	will
boys	going	lessons	plays	that's	with
brother	good	letter	please	the	won't
brought	good-by	like	pretty	their	would
can	got	likes	quit	them	write
cannot	grade	little	quite	then	writing
can't	guess	lots	receive	there	you
children	had	loving	received	there's	your
Christmas	Halloween	made	remember	they	you're
close	handkerchiefs	make	right	they're	yours

Source: From: Fitzgerald, James A. *A Basic Life Spelling Vocabulary*. Milwaukee: The Bruce Publishing Company, 1951 (pp. 140–150). Reprinted by permission of the Glencoe Press.

Poor spellers seem to benefit from procedures in which a limited number of words are introduced simultaneously accompanied by frequent testing (Bryant, Drabin, & Gettinger, 1981; Frank, Wacker, Keith, & Sagen, 1987; Gettinger, Bryant, & Fayne, 1982) and followed by the introduction of new words. For example, teachers might introduce five words missed on a pretest, have students practice them, and then test students at the end of the day. Words mastered are dropped from the list and replaced with new words so that a "flow" spelling list is maintained (Hansen, 1978).

TABLE 10.14   Word Families

ab	ead	i	oach	ub
ace	eak	ibe	oad	ube
ack	eal	ick	oak	ucb
act	eam	id	oal	ud
ad	ean	ide	oam	udf
ade	eap	ife	oan	uff
aft	ear	iff	oap	ug
ag	eat	ift	oast	ule
age	eck	ig	oat	ull
aid	ed	ike	ob	ult
ail	eed	ile	obe	um
aim	eel	ill	ock	ume
ain	eem	ilt	od	un
air	een	im	ode	une
ait	eep	ime	oft	unk
ake	ear	in	og	up
alk	eet	ince	oid	ur
all	eg	ind	oil	ure
alt	eil	ine	oke	urn
ame	elm	ink	ole	urt
amo	elp	int	oll	us
an	elt	ip	om	use
ance	em	ipe	ome	ush
and	en	ire	on	usk
ane	end	irt	one	uso
ang	ent	is	oof	ust
ank	ep	ise	ook	ut
ant	esk	ish	ool	utz
ap	ess	isk	oom	uzz
ape	esy	iss	oon	
ar	et	ist	oop	
arc	etch	it	oor	
ard	ew	itch	oot	
are		ite	op	
ark		ive	or	
arm		ix	orb	
arn		ize	ord	
arp		izz	ore	
art			ork	
ase			orn	
ash			ort	
ase			ot	
ask			otch	
at			ote	
atch			ow	
ate			owe	
ave			ox	
aw			oy	
ax				
av				

Another effective presentation method is to include both known and unknown words on spelling lists. Students appear to learn more new words when known words are included than when all the words are new (Frank et al., 1987; Neef, Iwata, & Page, 1980).

Effective instruction in mastering regular and irregular sight words requires teaching students a specific method for studying spelling words that they can use independently. The common practice of having students write a word several times does not ensure spelling retention (Graham, 1983). Students are also ineffective when told to "study" words without being provided a procedure. Table 10.16 presents several effective word study techniques that can be taught to students.

An important strategy for improving students' spelling performance is having them correct their own errors. An effective procedure is for students to copy the misspelled words as written, then write the word correctly on a card, look at the correctly spelled word and say it aloud, turn the card over, write the word, and then check it. An effective modification involves having students circle the errors and then verbalize to themselves that they need to remember the missed part prior to writing the word correctly (Gettinger, 1985).

Another procedure that has proven effective is for teachers to imitate student misspellings and then spell the word correctly (Kauffman, Hallahan, Haas, Brame, & Boren, 1978; Nulman & Gerber, 1984); however, this procedure demands more teacher time. To solve the problem of teacher time, Hasselbring (1982) developed a computer program for correcting spelling errors that takes the role of the teacher.

Error Monitoring

Good spellers monitor their writing for errors and implement correction procedures. Although error monitoring is developmentally acquired by most individuals, poor spellers often fail to monitor their own work. Teachers can instruct students in these procedures by thinking aloud as they identify and correct spelling errors in their own work.

TABLE 10.15 One Hundred Most Frequently Used Words in Written Work

Rank	Word	Rank	Word	Rank	Word	Rank	Word
1	the	26	school	51	would	76	now
2	I	27	me	52	our	77	has
3	and	28	with	53	were	78	down
4	to	29	am	54	little	79	if
5	a	30	all	55	how	80	write
6	you	31	one	56	he	81	after
7	we	32	so	57	do	82	play
8	in	33	your	58	about	83	came
9	it	34	got	59	from	84	put
10	of	35	there	60	her	85	two
11	is	36	went	61	them	86	house
12	was	37	not	62	as	87	us
13	have	38	at	63	his	88	because
14	my	39	like	64	mother	89	over
15	are	40	out	65	see	90	saw
16	he	41	go	66	friend	91	their
17	for	42	but	67	come	92	well
18	on	43	this	68	can	93	here
19	they	44	dear	69	day	94	by
20	that	45	some	70	good	95	just
21	had	46	then	71	what	96	make
22	she	47	going	72	said	97	back
23	very	48	up	73	him	98	an
24	will	49	time	74	home	99	could
25	when	50	get	75	did	100	or

Source: From "The case for basic written vocabulary" by S. Folger, 1946, *The Elementary School Journal, 47,* p. 17. Copyright 1946 by the University of Chicago Press. Reprinted by permission.

Published programs are also available for teaching error monitoring such as the *Error Monitoring Strategy* (Schumaker, Nolan, & Deshler, 1985). Using this program, students learn the **COPS** method of analyzing their writing for **C**apitals, **O**rganization, **P**unctuation, and **S**pelling errors.

Using External Sources

The purpose of instruction in this skill is for students to independently use outside sources to spell unknown words. A hierarchy of skills for teaching using the dictionary include the following (Cohen & Plaskon, 1980):

1. Alphabetizing
2. Using guide words
3. Locating words of uncertain spelling
4. Locating appropriate word meanings
5. Interpreting pronunciation marks (diacritical markings)

Instruction may begin with simple picture dictionaries and then progress to standard dictionaries. Poor spellers should also be informed of dictionaries for poor spellers including *The Bad Speller's Dictionary* (Kreivsky & Linfield, 1974). Finally, other alternatives can be made available such as computer spell-check programs

TABLE 10.16   Word Study Techniques

Fitzgerald Method (Fitzgerald, 1951)
1. Look at the word carefully.
2. Say the word.
3. With eyes closed, visualize the word.
4. Cover the word and then write it.
5. Check the spelling.
6. If the word is misspelled, repeat Steps 1–5.

Horn Method 1 (Horn, 1919)
1. Look at the word and say it yourself
2. Close your eyes and visualize the word.
3. Check to see if you were right. (If not, begin at Step 1).
4. Cover the word and write it.
5. Check to see if you were right. (If not, begin at Step 1).
6. Repeat Steps 4 and 5 two more times.

Horn Method 2 (Horn, 1954c)
1. Pronounce each word carefully.
2. Look carefully at each part of the word as you pronounce it.
3. Say the letters in sequence.
4. Attempt to recall how the word looks, then spell the word.
5. Check this attempt to recall.
6. Write the word.
7. Check this spelling attempt.
8. Repeat the previous step if necessary.

Visual-Vocal Method (Westerman, 1971)
1. Say the word.
2. Spell the word orally.
3. Say the word again.

4. Spell the word from memory four times correctly.

Gilstrap Method (Gilstrap, 1962)
1. Look at the word and say it softly. If it has more than one part, say it again, part by part, looking at each part as you say it.
2. Look at the letters and say each one. If the word has more than one part, say the letters part by part.
3. Write the word without looking at the book.

Fernald Method Modified
1. Make a model of the word with a crayon, grease pencil, or magic marker, saying the word as you write it.
2. Check the accuracy of the model.
3. Trace over the model with your index finger, saying the word at the same time.
4. Repeat Step 3 five times.
5. Copy the word three times correctly.
6. Copy the word three times from memory correctly.

Cover-and-Write Method
1. Look at the word. Say it.
2. Write word two times.
3. Cover and write one time.
4. Check your work.
5. Write word two times.
6. Cover and write one time.
7. Check your work.
8. Write the word three times.
9. Cover and write one time.
10. Check your work.

Source: From "Spelling research and practice: A unified approach" by S. Graham and L. Miller, 1979, *Focus on Exceptional Children, 12*(2), p. 11. Copyright 1979 by the Love Publishing Company. Adapted by permission.

that check for misspellings on computer generated text.

Curriculum Materials

Although teachers can develop their own spelling programs, most use published spelling series. Formal instruction in these programs usually begins at the end of first grade or the beginning of second grade. In most classrooms, spelling instruction is a whole-class activity that follows the same routine each week. Typically, students are introduced to twenty or twenty-five spelling words on Monday. A pretest or practice activity may be the focus of Tuesday's lesson. On Wednesday, students perform a practice activity such as using each spelling word in a sentence followed by additional activities and instruction in spelling rules on Thursday. A post-test of all the spelling words is administered on Friday. In most instances, there is no provision for reviewing words missed on the post-test; instead, all students move on to the next lesson the following week.

Although spelling series are convenient for teachers, they are pedagogically unsound in several ways. First, they fail to account for the wide range of spelling abilities among students in the classroom. Second, the target words may not reflect the vocabulary or words students may need to know for their own purposes. The failure to provide for meaningful practice, including using the words in real writing activities, is another weakness. In addition, many of the suggested activities may be irrelevant to learning to spell. For example, in some spelling series, less than 30% of the items in spelling workbooks are related to the spelling words assigned (Delquadri, Greenwood, Stratton, & Hall, 1983). Finally, published spelling programs fail to reflect the research base concerning the features of spelling instruction in such areas as specific study methods, error correction procedures, and distributed practice.

If commercial spelling programs are to be used, certain modifications can be made to individualize for students with mild handicaps. For example, students can be assigned only those spelling words that they missed on the pretest. Instead of assigning all words on Monday, a few words can be assigned, practiced, and tested daily until all words have been learned. Daily practice and testing should be made consistent and relevant. More individualized practice can be provided by having students take tests and complete assignments on the Language Master, tape recorder, or computer. Some teachers reorganize the spelling words for the year so that each lesson focuses on a particular rule (Hansen, 1978). Graham (1985) provided specific suggestions for evaluating spelling programs and materials. Programs should be selected to meet the needs of individual students.

Spelling Mastery. *Spelling Mastery* (Dixon, Englemann, & Olen, 1981) is a direct instruction basal spelling series with five levels intended for students at all ability levels in Grades 2–6. Entry-level skills for this series includes 1 year of reading and mastery of sound-blending and decoding skills. This series is designed to teach spelling using phonics (individual sounds and letters), morphographic (prefixes, suffixes, and root words), and whole-word methods. Students are instructed for 15–20 minutes at least every other day using effective instruction procedures, and progress is carefully monitored. Series materials include the teacher's book and a book for every student.

Corrective Spelling through Morphographs. *Corrective Spelling through Morphographs* (Dixon & Englemann, 1979) is an intensive 1-year program designed for use with remedial spellers in Grades 4–12. Content is taught in daily 20–30-minute lessons. The focus of this program is mastery of morphemic generalizations (e.g., affixes, base words, and inflected endings) rather than phonics rules. The content of Corrective Spelling is similar to the content of Levels C and D of the Spelling Mastery series, but the skills are taught in 1 year instead of 2 years.

Multisensory Approaches. Similar to programs available for remedial reading, several multisensory programs are available for spelling instruction. The Fernald (1943) approach discussed in the reading section also can be used to teach spelling. Using this approach, teachers write and say the word while students watch and listen; students trace the word while saying the word; copy the word as they say it slowly; write the word from memory; and finally, place the learned words in a file box, which are used in writing stories. Support for teaching new words is systematically faded until students learn words merely by looking at it.

The Gillingham method (Gillingham & Stillman, 1968) is another technique that can be used to teach spelling as well as reading. In this method, students learn sound-symbol correspondences and use them to read and spell words. Instruction in multisyllabic words and irregular words is carefully sequenced. The technique used in studying spelling words is called simultaneous oral spelling. When the teacher says a spelling word, the student repeats the word, names the letters, writes the letters as she says them, and then reads the word. Letter names rather than sounds are used so that the method can be applied to nonphonetic words. Sentence and story writing are introduced after students are able to write any three-letter, phonetically pure word.

SUMMARY

Few skills are as important to academic success and independent living as reading and spelling. They are complex tasks that many individuals begin to acquire through exposure and experimentation as preschoolers and continue to refine through direct instruction and continued practice into adulthood. Unfortunately, many low-achieving students never achieve competence in these essential skills. Youngsters from culturally or linguistically different backgrounds may lack the early reading and spelling related opportunities available to most children, thus placing them at a disadvantage when they enter school. Others may have specific linguistic, cognitive, and/or perceptual deficits that prevent them from benefiting from these early experiences and direct instruction. There are also those children who lack reading and spelling skills due to poor instruction.

This chapter described empirically validated procedures for reading and spelling instruction that are intended to address the particular needs of low-achieving students. The importance of creating an environment that promotes literacy and the necessity for establishing readiness skills were discussed. Information concerning generalizable effective instruction procedures that should provide a framework for all reading and spelling instruction was also provided. A discussion of an appropriate scope and sequence, and specific procedures for teaching reading and spelling followed. Curriculum materials and their modification and remedial procedures were also described.

MASTERY CONTENT QUESTIONS

1. Describe readiness skills for reading and spelling.

2. Identify the important oral language skills children are expected to have when they reach school age.

3. Describe the characteristics of a classroom designed to promote literacy.

4. Identify and discuss the five principles for effective instruction in reading and spelling.

5. Describe the content and procedures of instruction of word attack skills in reading, including phonics, structural analysis, and contextual analysis.

6. Identify methods for increasing reading fluency.

7. Discuss strategies for teaching, literal, inferential, organizational, and critical reading comprehension.

8. Describe techniques for promoting use of metacognitive strategies during reading.

9. Discuss approaches to spelling instruction, including phonics, spelling rules and patterns, using outside sources, and proofreading.

10. Describe commonly used reading and spelling curricula.

REFERENCES

Adams, M. J. (1991). *Beginning to read: Thinking and learning about print.* Cambridge, MA: The MIT Press.

Anderson, R. C., Hiebert, E. H., Scott, J. A., & Wilkinson, I. A. (1985). *Becoming a nation of readers: The report of the Commission on Reading.* Washington, DC: National Institute of Education.

Becker, W. C., & Gersten, R. (1982). A follow-up on Follow Through: The later effects of the direct instruction model on children in fifth and sixth grades. *American Education Research Journal, 19,* 78–92.

Biggins, C., & Uhler, S. (1979). Is there a wordable decoding system? *Reading Improvement, 16,* 47–55.

Bookman, M. O. (1984). Spelling as a cognitive-developmental linguistic process. *Academic Therapy, 20*(1), 21–32.

Bridge, C., Winograd, P., & Haley, D. (1983). Using predictable materials to teach beginning readers. *The Reading Teacher, 36,* 884–891.

Bryant, N. D., Drabin, I. R., & Gettinger, M. (1981). Effects of varying unit size on spelling achievement in learning disabled children. *Journal of Learning Disabilities, 14,* 200–203.

Buss, R. R., Ratliff, J. L., & Irion, J. C. (1985). Effects of instruction on the use of story starters in composition of narrative discourse. In J. A. Niles, & R. Lalik (Eds.), *Issues in literacy: A research perspective.* (pp. 55–126). Rochester, NY: National Reading Conference.

Carnine, D., Silbert, J., & Kameenui, E. J. (1990). *Direct instruction reading* (2nd ed.). Columbus, OH: Charles E. Merrill.

Chall, J. S. (1967). *Learning to read: The great debate.* New York: McGraw-Hill.

Chall, J. S. (1983). *Learning to read: The great debate* (2nd ed). New York: McGraw-Hill.

Cohen, S. B., & Plaskon, S. B. (1980). *Language arts for the mildly handicapped.* Columbus, OH: Charles E. Merrill.

Delquardi, J. C., Greenwood, C. R., Stretton, K., & Hall, R. V. (1983). The peer tutoring spelling game: A classroom procedure for increasing opportunity to respond and spelling performance. *Education and Treatment of Children, 6,* 225–239.

Dixon, R., & Englemann, S. (1979). *Corrective spelling through morphographs.* Palo Alto, CA: Science Research Associates.

Dixon, R., Englemann, S., & Olen, L. G. (1981). *Spelling mastery: A direct instruction series.* Chicago: Science Research Associates.

Downs, J., & Morin, S. (1990). Improving reading fluency with precision teaching. *Teaching Exceptional Children, 22*(3), 38–40.

Ehri, L. C., & Wilce, L. S. (1983). Cipher versus cue reading. *Journal of Educational Psychology, 75,* 3–13.

Englemann, S., Becker, W., Hanner, S., & Johnson, G. (1980). *Corrective reading program.* Chicago: Science Research Associates.

Englert, C. S., Hiebert, E. H., & Stewart, S. R. (1985). Spelling unfamiliar words by an analogy strategy. *Journal of Special Education, 19,* 291–306.

Englert, C. S., & Lichter, A. (1982). Using statement-pie to teach reading and writing skills. *Teaching Exceptional Children, 14,* 164–170.

Fernald, G. (1943). *Remedial techniques in basic school subjects.* New York: McGraw-Hill.

Fitzgerald, J. A. (1951). A basic life spelling vocabulary. Milwaukee: The Bruce Publishing Co.

Folger, S. (1946). The case for basic written vocabulary. *The Elementary School Journal, 47,* 14–17.

Frank, A. R. (1987). Directed spelling instruction. *Teaching Exceptional Children, 20,* 10–13.

Frank, A. R., Wacker, D. P., Keith, T. Z., & Sagen, T. K. (1987). Effectiveness of a spelling study package for learning disabled students. *Learning Disabilities Research, 2,* 110–118.

Gambell, L., Pfeiffer, W., & Wilson, R. (1985). The effects of retelling upon reading comprehension and recall of text information. *Journal of Educational Research, 78,* 216–220.

Gentry, J. R. (1981). Learning to spell developmentally. *The Reading Teacher, 34,* 378–381.

Gentry, J. R. (1984). Developmental aspects of learning to spell. *Academic Therapy, 20*(1), 11–19.

Gerber, M. M. (1984). Orthographic problem-solving ability of LD and normally achieving students. *Learning Disability Quarterly, 7,* 157–164.

Gerber, M. M., & Hall, R. J. (1987). Information processing approaches to studying spelling deficiencies. *Journal of Learning Disabilities, 20,* 34–42.

Gettinger, M. (1985). Effects of teacher-directed versus student-directed instruction and cues versus no cues for improving spelling performance.

Journal of Applied Behavior Analysis, 18, 167–171.

Gettinger, M., Bryant, N. D., & Fayne, H. R. (1982). Designing spelling instruction for learning-disabled children: An emphasis on unit size, distributed practice, and training for transfer. *The Journal of Special Education, 16,* 439–448.

Gilingham, A., & Stillman, B. (1968). *Remedial teaching for children with specific disability in reading, spelling, and penmanship.* Cambridge, MA: Educator's Publishing Service.

Goldman, S., & Rueda, R. (1988). Developing writing skills in bilingual exceptional children. *Exceptional Children, 54,* 543–551.

Graham, S. (1983). Effective spelling instructions. *The Elementary School Journal, 83,* 560–567.

Graham, S. (1985). Evaluating spelling programs, and materials. *Teaching Exceptional Children, 17*(4), 299–303.

Graham, S., & Miller, L. (1979). Spelling research and practice: A unified approach. *Focus on Exceptional Children, 12*(2), 1–16.

Hall, J. (1981). *Evaluating and improving written expression: A practical guide for teachers.* Boston, MA: Allyn and Bacon.

Hall, R. J. (1984). Orthographic problem-solving. *Academic Therapy, 20,* 67–76.

Hansen, C. L. (1978). Writing skills. In N. G. Haring, T. C. Lovitt, M. D. Eaton, and C. L. Hansen (Eds.). *The fourth R: Research in the classroom.* (pp. 93–126). Columbus, OH: Charles E. Merrill.

Hasselbring, T. S. (1982). Remediating spelling problems of learning-handicapped students through the use of microcomputers. *Educational Technology, 22,* 31–32.

Haynes, M. C., & Jenkins, J. R. (1986). Reading instruction in special education resource rooms. *American Educational Research Journal, 23*(2), 161–190.

Hiebert, E. H. (1978). Preschool children's understanding of written language. *Child Development, 49,* 1231–1234.

Hillerich, R. L. (1982). Spelling: What can be diagnosed? *The Elementary School Journal, 83,* 138–147.

Johnson, D. D. (1971). The Dolch list reexamined. *The Reading Teacher, 24,* 455–456.

Kauffman, J. M., Hallahan, D. P., Haas, K., Brame, T., & Boren, R. (1978). Imitating children's errors to improve their spelling performance. *Journal of Learning Disabilities, 11,* 217–222.

Kreivsky J., & Linfield, J. (1974). *Bad speller's dictionary.* New York: Random House.

Leinhardt, C., Zigmond, N., & Cooley, W. W. (1981). Reading instruction and its effect. *American Educational Research Journal, 18,* 343–361.

Lerner, J. (1989). *Learning disabilities: Theories, diagnosis, and teaching strategies* (5th ed). Boston: Houghton Mifflin.

Lewis, R. B. (1983). Learning disabilities and reading: Instructional recommendations from current research. *Exceptional Children, 50,* 230–240.

Lipson, M. Y., & Wixson, K. K. (1985). Reading disability research: An Interactionist perspective. Paper presented at the annual meeting of the American Educational Research Association, Chicago.

Maheady, L., Sacca, M. K. & Harper, G. F. (1991). Peer-mediated instruction. Review of potential applications for special education. *Reading, Writing, and Learning Disabilities, 7,* 75–102.

Manning, M. M., & Manning, G. L. (1986). *Improving spelling in the middle grades* (2nd ed.). Washington, DC: National Educational Association.

Mastropieri, M. A., & Scruggs, T. E. (1989). Constructing more meaningful relationships: Mnemonic instruction for special populations. *Educational Psychology Review, 1,* 83–111.

McNutt, G. (1984). A holistic approach to language arts instruction in the resource room. *Learning Disability Quarterly, 7*(4), 315–320.

Meyer, B. J. F. (1975). *The organization of prose and its effects on memory.* Amsterdam: North Holland.

Morsink, C. V. (1984). Learning disabilities. In W. H. Berdine and A. E. Blackhurst (Eds.). *An introduction to special education* (2nd ed.) (pp. 391–426). Boston: Little, Brown.

Neef, N. A., Iwata, B. A., & Page, T. J. (1980). The effects of interspersal training versus high-density reinforcement on spelling acquisition and retention. *Journal of Applied Behavior Analysis, 13,* 153–158.

Nulman, J. H., & Gerber, M. M. (1984). Improving spelling performance by imitating a child's errors. *Journal of Learning Disabilities, 17,* 328–333.

Palincsar, A. S., & Brown, A. L. (1984). The reciprocal teaching of comprehensions-fostering and comprehension-monitoring activities. *Cognition and Instruction, 1*(2), 117–175.

Palincsar, A. S., & Brown, A. L. (1985). Reciprocal teaching: A means to a meaningful end. In

J. Osborn, P. Wilson, & R. Anderson (Eds.). *Reading education: Foundation for a literate America* (pp. 299–309). Lexington, MA: D. C. Heath.

Pearson, P. D., & Doyle, J. (1987). Explicit comprehension instruction: A review of research and a new conceptualization of instruction. *The Elementary School Journal, 88*(2), 151–165.

Peterson, S. K., Scott, J., & Sroka, K. (1990). Using the language experience approach with precision. *Teaching Exceptional Children, 22*(3), 28–30.

Pinnell, G. S. (1990). Success for low achievers through Reading Recovery. *Educational Leadership, 48*(1), 17–21.

Polloway, E. A., & Smith, J. E. (1992). *Language instruction for students with disabilities (2nd ed.)* Denver: Love Pub. Co.

Potter, M. L., & Wamre, H. M. (1990). Curriculum-based measurement and developmental reading models: Opportunities for cross-validation. *Exceptional Children, 57*(1), 16–25.

Reith, H. J., Polsgrove, L., & Eckert, R. (1984). A computer-based spelling program. *Academic Therapy, 20,* 59–65.

Rhodes, L. K. (1981). I can read! Predictable books as resources for reading and writing instruction. *The Reading Teacher, 34,* 511–518.

Rhodes, L. K., & Dudley-Marling, C. (1988). *Readers and writers with a difference: A holistic approach to teaching learning disabled and remedial students.* Portsmouth, NH: Heinemann.

Rosenshine, B., & Stevens, R. (1984). Classroom instruction for reading. In P. D. Pearson (Ed.), *Handbook of reading research.* (pp. 745–798). New York: Longman.

Schumaker, J. B., Denton, P. H., & Deshler, D. D. (1984). The paraphrasing strategy. Lawrence, KS: University of Kansas.

Schumaker, J. B., Nolan, S. M., & Deshler, D. D. (1985). *The error monitoring strategy.* Lawrence, KS: University of Kansas.

Scruggs, T. E. & Mastropieri, M. A. (1992). Classroom applications of mnemonic instruction: Acquisition, maintenance, and generalization. *Exceptional Children, 58,* 219–229.

Stahl, S. A. (1990) Riding the pendulum: A rejoinder of Schickedanz and McGee and Lomax. *Review of Educational Research, 60*(1), 141–151.

Stauffer, R. G. (1975). *Directing the reading-thinking process.* New York: Harper & Row.

Thomas, C. C., Englert, C. S., & Morsink, C. V. (1984). Modifying the classroom program in language. In C. V. Morsink (Ed.), *Teaching special needs students in regular classrooms* (pp. 239–276). Boston: Little, Brown.

Viadero, D. (1990). New Zealand import: An effective, but costly, way to teach reading. *Education Week, 10*(10), pp. 1–4.

Wallace G., & Bott, D. (1989). Statement pie: A strategy to improve the paragraph writing skills of adolescents with learning disabilities. *Journal of Learning Disabilities, 22,* 541–553.

Williams, J. P. (1985). The case for explicit decoding instruction. In J. Osborn, P. Wilson, & R. Anderson (Eds.), *Reading education: Foundation for a literate America* (pp. 205–214). Lexington, MA: D. C. Heath.

Wong, B. (1979). Increasing retention of main ideas through questioning strategies. *Learning Disability Quarterly, 2,* 42–48.

Wong, B. (1980). Activating the inactive learner: Use of questions/prompts to enhance reading comprehension and retention of implied information in learning disabled children. *Learning Disability Quarterly, 5,* 228–240.

Wong, B. Y. L., & Jones, W. (1982). Increasing meta-comprehension in learning disabled and normally achieving students through self-questioning training. *Learning Disability Quarterly, 5,* 228–240.

Wong, B. Y. L., Wong R., Perry, N., & Sawatsky, D. (1986). The efficacy of a self-questioning summarization strategy for use by underachievers and learning disabled adolescents in social studies. *Learning Disabilities Focus, 2,* 20–35.

Zigmond, N., Vallecorsa, Z., & Leinhardt, G. (1980). Reading instructions for students with learning disabilities. *Topics in Language Disorders, 1,* 89–98.

Zutell, J. (1978). Some psycholinguistic perspectives on children's spelling. *Language Arts, 55,* 844–850.

CHAPTER 11

Teaching Written Language Skills

CAROL SUE ENGLERT

CHAPTER OBJECTIVES

At the conclusion of this chapter, the reader will be able to:

1. Describe the writing process and the writing problems of students with learning handicaps.
2. Identify the features of a writing environment that stresses the audience and purpose of writing.
3. Design and implement a lesson that focuses on modeling the subprocesses of written expression.
4. Design and implement a lesson that focuses on teaching text organization and structures to writers.
5. Assess students' knowledge of the writing process and text organization.

WRITTEN EXPRESSION

Written expression is one of the most demanding academic skills taught in school. It requires mastering multiple strands of complex cognitive operations and motoric skills, all of which must be executed spontaneously, simultaneously, and intelligently (Kameenui & Simmons, 1990). The complexity of the demands involved in written expression means that this basic skill should receive careful and systematic instructional attention. Traditionally, however, such instruction has not been available in most classrooms. As a result, many students with learning difficulties, as well as other naive writers, have writing deficiencies that threaten their adjustment both in school and as adults in vocational settings (Alley & Deshler, 1979; Cohen & Plaskon, 1980). This can be particularly true for those students with learning problems who also are bilingual or limited-English proficient. For these students, the cognitive demands associated with second-language processing complicates the already complex demands of written expression.

Factors contributing to students' writing difficulties include the following:

1. The absence of explicit instruction on written expression as a part of the school curriculum.
2. The small amount of time allocated to written expression during the school day.
3. Teachers who are inadequately prepared to teach writing; many have received no formal teaching preparation in this area.
4. Poorly developed student skills in decoding, reading, and spelling, as well as limited proficiency in the English language.
5. An overemphasis on the mechanics of writing at the expense of developing the underlying cognitive operations.
6. Inadequately developed thinking skills and writing strategies on the part of the students.

In the past, writing instruction has focused primarily on the mastery of mechanical and grammatical conventions. Correct spelling and punctuation, writing complete sentences, using capital letters, correct grammar, and overall neatness have been emphasized. As a result, students themselves may fail to view writing as a communication vehicle, seeing it instead as a collection of separate mechanical skills. When remediation efforts center on improving these types of skills, only the surface features of written expression are affected. For a significant and long-lasting impact, instructional programs in written expression need to address the underlying cognitive approaches and strategies of the students.

Effective instruction requires that teachers understand the writing process and the writing difficulties that many students with achievement problems experience. Further, they need to master an array of empirically validated instructional strategies. This chapter focuses on each of these areas, drawing upon current research on the writing process and related writing problems of students with learning difficulties and related problems. It describes the nature of the writing process, analyzes general types of writing problems, and presents instructional strategies for promoting the cognitive aspects of writing as well as for remediating mechanical difficulties.

THE WRITING PROCESS

Traditional approaches to teaching writing have focused on the *products* of the written expression, not the underlying *processes*. The product approach shaped the nature of writing instruction for much of the twentieth century. Because it viewed writing as an art rather than a set of skills that could be taught, instruction primarily emphasized writing mechanics, grammar, and spelling. In the face of such instruction, students often were mired in the practice of discrete skills rather than learning to communicate to a meaningful audience. More recently, the focus of instruction has begun to shift to conceptual and strategic aspects of writing.

The writing process can be viewed as involving three overlapping and recursive subprocesses or stages: (1) prewriting, (2) drafting, and (3) revising (Hayes & Flower, 1987). These are depicted in Table 11.1. Each of these subprocesses places demands on writers that require them to think about what they are writing, and to select and employ specific writing strategies. These subprocesses, the strategies related to them, self-questions that successful writers address as they engage in strategy use throughout the writing process, and the problems children with learning difficulties experience are discussed in the following sections.

TABLE 11.1 Writing Stages or Subprocesses

Prewriting stage	*Planning*	What is the purpose of the writing?
		Who is the audience?
		What background knowledge does the writer have about the topic?
Prewriting stage	*Organizing*	How can this knowledge be organized and categorized?
		What text structure should be used (e.g., narrative or expository)?
Drafting stage		How can these ideas be sequenced into an initial draft?
		Does this draft address the potential questions and needs of the audience?
		What words or phrases are tentative selections and should be revisited during editing?
Editing and revising stage		How can this writing better communicate meaning?
		Does each passage make sense? Is it complete? Are there inconsistencies?
		What information should be eliminated and what should be added?
		What key words should be included to signal relationships?
		Are the grammar, punctuation, and spelling correct?

The Prewriting Stage: Planning

During **prewriting,** the students collect, generate, and organize ideas into writing plans. They plan and organize their compositions. During planning, writers must consider three questions related to their purposes, their audiences, and their background knowledge. They need to ask themselves:

1. "Why am I writing this paper?"
2. "Who is going to read my paper?"
3. "What do I already know about the topic?"

During the planning stage, students must learn to consider the intended audiences and the purposes of the writings (e.g., to inform, to amuse, or to express a point of view) (Vallecorsa, Ledford, & Parnell, 1991). This consideration can influence both what they write and how they organize their compositions. They then must identify the background knowledge that they possess about the topics.

Purpose and Audience.   Too often, students perceive that the sole audience is the teacher and the sole purpose of the writing task is to write about a teacher-assigned topic for grades. Under these circumstances, they are less precise in specifying their purposes and in communicating information about their topics. They assume that their audiences already know the information and understand the purposes of the papers.

An example is Joe, a fourth-grade student with learning disabilities, who was asked to "Explain how to do something that you know a lot about. Explain it to someone who doesn't know much about your topic." Joe wrote the following about baseball (Englert, Raphael, Anderson, Fear & Greggs, 1988, p. 101): "Because it is a good sport. Because I can win a trophy. Because I like trophys. I would put them in my room. So my room would look nice."

In this composition, Joe treats writing as a way of answering the question, "Why do you like baseball?" His paper reflects two major problems

that can result from teacher-assigned topics. First, Joe does not explicitly state his purpose, assuming that since it was a teacher assigned topic, the reader already knows the purpose. Second, since the teacher is Joe's sole audience, he does not elaborate upon his ideas. Like many other students in this situation, Joe seems to assume that the teacher is already an expert on his topic. Consequently, he merely "mentions" ideas rather than explaining them. This approach attenuates the extent to which students inform their audiences about the topics and rehearse the advanced cognitive strategies necessary to communicate effectively.

Background Knowledge.   Writers also must consider what they know about their topics, accessing relevant ideas from their background knowledge. Poor writers typically spend less time than skilled writers in such planning activities as note-taking, idea generation, and rereading and revising. They spend little effort either improving their writing plans or gathering additional information (Hillocks, 1984).

Writers tend to produce better organized compositions and include more ideas when they write about familiar topics that they know well (Graves, 1983; Scardamalia & Bereiter, 1986). However, even when students know their topics well, some students have difficulties activating relevant ideas, engaging in sustained thinking, or searching their memories to produce more informative texts (Englert, Raphael, Fear & Anderson, 1988). Joe, for example, had difficulty retrieving the full set of knowledge he possesses about playing baseball.

The inability to access information and sustain the idea generation process has been referred to as the problem of **inert knowledge.** In other words, existing background knowledge is not activated in relevant situations (Bereiter & Scardamalia, 1982). Some students may lack strategies for systematic memory searches (e.g., **brainstorming**). Or, they may tell everything they know about topics in whatever order comes to mind. They also may have difficulties in producing multiple statements about familiar topics and restarting or sustaining the idea generation process after one line of productive thought has ended.

Mary, a fifth-grade student identified as learning disabled, does not seem to know what information to retrieve and has difficulties sustaining her thinking about a topic. When she was asked to explain a game she knew a lot about to someone who did not know how to play it, she wrote: "Now how to play Sorry. Do you want to know how to play Sorry? If you want to know." Yet when Mary was asked to orally explain how to play Sorry, she easily provided the information that was missing from her written text. She knew what materials were needed as well as the steps for playing the game. This suggested that Mary knew a great deal more about her topic than she represented in her text.

Mary's explanation illustrates the type of incomplete composing that many students with mild handicaps and related learning difficulties exhibit. Mary prematurely terminates the idea generation process before she has exhausted her fund of relevant ideas. Furthermore, she does not seem to be able to access the topical knowledge she does possess, nor does she know how to restart the idea generation process after she has produced an initial set of ideas. Many students who produce inadequate texts possess far more topic knowledge than their writings show (Englert, Raphael, Anderson et al., 1988). External prompting (either from teachers or more experienced peers) is required to prevent these less successful writers from ending the idea generation process prematurely.

The Prewriting Stage: Organizing

Writers organize ideas at two levels. First, they consider their brainstormed ideas, writing purposes, and the needs of their audiences. Based upon these sources of information, they structure their ideas into local groupings or categories of superordinate and subordinate ideas. Second, writers organize these grouped ideas into the

global text structures they plan to use. In doing so, they address two implicit questions:

1. "Which of my brainstormed ideas can be categorized or grouped together, and how can they be labeled?"
2. "How can I order these categorized ideas into a well-organized sequence?"

Generating Categories. As part of composition planning, students must be able to examine their brainstormed ideas and see which of their ideas can be grouped into categories. Difficulties in identifying and generating categories of information can impede their composing performances. For example, Joe might have grouped his brainstormed ideas into the following organizational categories:

1. Why I like baseball.
2. How to play baseball.
3. How teams win trophies.

His inability to plan his paper by organizing his ideas into categories is reflected in the paper's lack of clarity and coherence.

A simple way to determine students' skills in using categories is to interview the students. The teacher might begin the interview by describing a hypothetical student (e.g., Sylvia) who needs help identifying topics and generating ideas for an animal report, and then asking the student being interviewed to advise this fictional classmate on her writing (Englert, Raphael, Fear & Anderson, 1988). The teacher can guide the student by asking such questions as:

1. "What animal can she write about?"
2. "What information can she include in the report about this animal?"
3. "Which of these ideas go together?"
4. "What can we call those ideas?"

The interview provides the teacher with information about the success of students in generating categories (e.g., where it lives and what it eats) and categorizing brainstormed ideas under both teacher-prompted and unprompted conditions. At the same time, the interview provides a model for students to use in organizing the ideas that they brainstorm.

Selecting Text Structure. In addition to generating categories and labels, the writer also must construct an appropriate global structure in which to embed this information (Scardamalia & Bereiter, 1986). Text structure genre such as narration, explanation, comparison/contrast, and problem/solution can be thought of as "cognitive frames" that answer different sets of questions. This leads writers and readers to instantiate the frame with particular types of text information. For example, texts with a basic *narrative* structure address such questions having to do with setting, problem situation, response, outcome, and conclusion. These text structure questions are depicted in Table 11.2.

Unskilled writers frequently appear not to understand the story schema (e.g., setting, problem, response, and outcome) essential to both writing and comprehending stories (Nodine, Barenbaum & Newcomer, 1985). Knowledge of this narrative frame leads writers to produce the answers to the questions, resulting in coherent and well-formed stories.

Successfully organized *expository* texts are organized into different categories of information. These categories address different sets of questions. Depicted in Table 11.2, these focus attention on what is being explained and the steps or sequences of the explanation. Well-formed expository texts not only address specific types of questions, but they also are "reader friendly" in that they contain signals that help readers rapidly locate information. For example, the comprehensibility of the text is improved when signal or key words such as *first, second,* or *next* cue readers about the location of explanations or information.

Good writers use both the text structure questions and key words to produce well-formed and considerate texts. However, many students with learning problems have difficulty generating superordinate labels or categories for a given set of related details. Because of this, they may appear to possess limited knowledge of the broad conceptual categories that can facilitate idea generation and categorization (Englert & Raphael, 1988). In addition, they also may lack working knowledge of expository text frameworks (e.g., comparison/contrast, step-by-step explanation, and key words) that can help them to systematically retrieve and organize their ideas to produce coherent prose.

Billy, a fourth-grade student diagnosed as having mild mental retardation, was asked to write an explanation that told someone how to do something, such as how to play a game or make a certain type of food. He generated a string of associative ideas related to the various activities he likes. He wrote: "I like sports and swimming and I like Math games. And I like riding my bike. My mom takes me to the store."

TABLE 11.2 Text Structure Questions

Narrative text questions	1. What is the setting (i.e., main character, time, and place)?
	2. What is the problem confronting the main character?
	3. How does the main character respond?
	4. What is the outcome of the response?
	5. What is the story conclusion?
Expository text questions	1. What is being explained?
	2. What are the steps?
	3. What happens first? Second? Third?

This composition seems driven by a concern for "What can I say next?" rather than by a concern for how each idea ties back to his writing goal or purpose. Each new idea stimulates the construction of the next idea (e.g., sports, swimming, and math) without thought to its overall contribution to the topic. Consequently, Billy's paper takes a rambling "on and on" quality. This associative writing approach has been described as knowledge telling strategy (Scardamalia & Bereiter, 1986). Specifically, it is characterized by writers' attempts to tell all that they know about their topics in a "knowledge dump" with little to no attention paid to text structure, idea organization, or the complete development of ideas. Billy's composition, for example, fails to include information that answers the questions for the explanation text structure (e.g., What is being explained? What are the steps? What happens first, second, and third?). It does not include key words (e.g., *first, second,* and *third*) that would make it easier for the reader to locate the key ideas and it does not group or categorize Billy's ideas well. Some of his ideas have to do with sports, but others (e.g., going to the store) appear to be random, thereby causing his organizational pattern to fall apart. A better working knowledge of text structure frameworks could help him systematically retrieve and organize ideas into better compositions.

To summarize, prewriting is an important subprocess that instructional programs for written expression should use. A successful program to develop writing skills is characterized by the following:

1. Emphasizing the audiences and purposes for writing.
2. Developing students' abilities to retrieve topical information from background knowledge and engaging in sustained thinking about familiar topics.
3. Instructing in the processes related to text organization, including categorizing and labeling brainstormed ideas, and organizing ideas based upon text structures.

4. Developing text organizational strategies to replace the knowledge-telling writing strategies of poor writers.

The Drafting Stage

The second stage or component of the writing process is the **drafting** stage. Here, writers translate their evolving internal plans into print. During this "first pass," students focus on writing their ideas more fully and on elaborating the points they have outlined during the prewriting stage. They should not focus on the technical aspects of their compositions at this time (Vallecorsa, Ledford & Parnell, 1991).

Drafting tentative writing plans into formal prose requires a great deal of cognitive work (Hayes & Flower, 1987). Writers must explain briefly sketched ideas, interpret nonverbal material in verbal form, carry out mental instructions, arrange related ideas together, insert signals that convey relationships among them, and discover new ideas. In addition, throughout the drafting process, they must provide additional details and information to create an interesting and/or informative text for their targeted audience.

During oral communication, speakers receive continual cues from the listener relative to levels of understanding, agreement, confusion, and the need for additional information. With written communication, however, the audience is more distant and provides no immediate feedback. Writers must develop new communication skills in which they: (1) address remote and indeterminate audiences; (2) engage in cooperative discourse with distant audiences; and (3) monitor their messages for clarity, engaging in recursive and ongoing revisions (Rubin, 1987).

Many students with learning problems have difficulty distancing themselves from their texts and imagining the questions of their readers. The compositions of Joe and Mary, for example, contain several ambiguities. Joe fails to explain why he likes baseball. Mary does not explain how to play Sorry despite the fact that she leads her readers to expect the information (e.g., "Do you want to know how to play Sorry?"). For these students, their writing purposes and intended audiences do not constrain the information included in their texts. Essentially, they write in isolation, dumping their knowledge on the page without seeming to ask themselves questions such as, "Have I told my readers all that I know?" "Will they understand my paper?" "Does this paper make sense?"

Vallecorsa et al. (1991) noted that many students at the drafting stage evidence too much concern over the technical aspects of their writings and tend to dwell on presenting ideas perfectly the first time. By having students clearly label their work as "Draft No. 1," the first-pass nature of the drafting effort is emphasized. This creates the expectancy that subsequent efforts are to follow. In addition, it is preferable to have students write on every other line of their papers, leaving a lot of room for revisions.

Modeling appropriate thought processes can help to focus students on the tentative nature of the draft compositions. The teacher can lead students in completing a group draft of a paper (Vallecorsa et al., 1991). First, the teacher can guide the development of a prewriting plan for the composition. When converted into a transparency and displayed on an overhead projector, this plan can be used to guide students in generating a draft on the chalkboard. The procedure might be as follows (Vallecorsa et al., 1991, p. 54):

> The teacher asks questions of students about items on the planning guide ("What are we going to say about this?"), rapidly writing down students' comments. Throughout the activity, the teacher makes frequent statements such as "I'm not sure that's the best way to say it, but we'll look at it more closely later" or "There may be a better word we could use here, but we'll decide on that later." The teacher highlights the words or phrases in question as a reminder to return to them later.

The objective behind activities such as this is to let students know what it feels like to create imperfect drafts. Several other strategies can be used to assist students to compensate for specific learning difficulties that pose particular challenges. For example, if students have poor motor skills, they might "draft" their papers using tape recorders, which the teacher then transcribes. They also could dictate directly to the teacher or an aide, who simultaneously enters the information into a word processor. Some students find that drafting their own works onto computers increases their writing fluency; results in better organized, lengthier, more comprehensive drafts; and reduces mechanical production errors (Kerchner & Kistinger, 1984).

The Editing and Revising Stage

The third subprocess or stage of writing, **editing,** involves editing, revising, and readying the text for sharing with a real audience (Florio-Ruane & Dunn, 1985). These processes comprise much of what teachers traditionally have focused on during *initial* writing instruction. In this model, they are final steps to writing instruction, coming after students have developed communicative texts.

During editing, writers evaluate how well they have achieved their goals. They modify their drafts to better meet these goals and to better address the needs of their audiences. Writers may eliminate unnecessary information, add key words to signal relationships or organizational patterns, fill in gaps with additional details, or reorganize ideas to conform to text structures or conceptual categories. They address implicit questions such as "What parts are not clear to my audience?" "What more does my audience need to know?" "Did I accomplish my purpose and organizational plan?" and "What parts need to be changed?"

There are five requirements or stages of editing, each of which may inhibit a student's performance. These stages require that writers:

1. Focus on text structure problems first.
2. Distance themselves from their own writing, taking the role of the naive reader.
3. Take an active role in monitoring and fostering comprehension.

4. Self-regulate by checking composition against the writing goals.
5. Check for technical correctness (spelling, grammar, and punctuation).

A first editing requirement is to focus on global problems related to the meaning of the text. Less skilled writers tend to focus their attention on local problems related to mechanics (Faigley & Witte, 1983; Hayes, Flower, Schriver, Stratman, & Corey, 1985). While better writers attend to text structures and text-level problems, novices approach revisions as sentence-level or mechanical tasks (e.g., spelling and grammatical conventions) in which the goal is to improve individual words and phrases without really modifying the meaning of the texts.

A second editing requirement is to distance oneself from one's own writing (e.g., to read it through the eyes of a naive reader). Many unskilled writers have difficulty accomplishing this shift in perspective. Knowledge of one's own text makes it difficult to detect its faults. The writers may be better able to detect errors in the less familiar texts that their peers produced (Bartlett, 1981). Therefore, having students read papers of classmates or peer partners may better promote the development of editing skills.

A third editing requirement relates to monitoring and fostering comprehension. Editors must themselves possess adequate comprehension skills in order to detect violations to the meaning of texts, and to employ fix-up strategies when comprehension breakdowns are identified. Many students with learning difficulties approach the editing tasks as passive readers. They do not question the meaning of texts and may not employ appropriate correction strategies in response to communication breakdowns (Reid, 1988). Many students with learning disabilities, for example, do not consider it unusual for passages not to make sense. As a result, they do not automatically detect errors in texts, although they can be prompted to identify such errors if teachers tells them that the errors are present (Bos & Filip, 1984). Thus, teachers may need to directly teach

monitoring strategies and prompt students in their use.

A fourth requirement for the editing stage relates to the self-control and self-regulatory abilities of the students. In writers with learning problems, the ability to independently check performances by comparing the composition to the writing goals or purposes may be inadequately developed. Due to incomplete knowledge of text structure goals, they may rely on external or mechanic features rather than on internal criteria to make decisions about texts. For example, Englert, Raphael, Fear, & Anderson (1988) asked students with learning disabilities to read and edit a comparison/contrast paper that a hypothetical child named Pamela wrote. The following text shows the editorial changes produced by Alexia, a fourth grader who is identified as learning disabled. Pamela's original text is shown in regular type and the text revisions Alexia made are in italics.

> Some ways McDonalds and Ponderosa is alike. McDonalds has a playground it is fun. They go out and pick the flowers. *They are pretty and not to touch. Just to look at. McDonalds has a slide. They have these hamburger toys that you go under or on top of them or you can pretend you're on a trail and you can go through them.*

Alexia's changes suggest that she has an inadequate understanding of the comparison/contrast text structure. Although the directions emphasized that the composition should tell how McDonald's and Ponderosa were alike and different, Alexia failed to address both restaurants in her editing. She did not appear to understand the text structure goals. Her interview confirmed that she lacked awareness of the importance of including information about Ponderosa. When she was asked whether the paper was done, she replied "Well, how much was she supposed to write? One paragraph or a whole paper? In the thing [directions] you said she wanted a whole paper, so she ain't done." When her answer was probed with the question, "If you were Pamela, would you turn the paper in now?" she replied "If that's all I have to write, yeah." Alexia's comments were typical of students with learning disabilities. She used external criteria (e.g., paper length and what the teacher expects) rather than internal criteria (e.g., whether it makes sense) or text structure criteria (e.g., whether it addresses the comparison/contrast questions) to check the accuracy and completeness of the paper. Because their teachers may take for granted that they have mastered self-regulatory behaviors, a reliance upon external evaluation criteria can seriously handicap students with learning difficulties.

The fifth, and final, editing stage relates to what traditionally has been regarded as the writing curriculum such as correct spelling, and using appropriate grammar and punctuation. Joe, for example, does not have a clear concept of a complete sentence (e.g., "So my room would look nice."). Mary exhibits a similar problem. In these, and in other papers of students with learning difficulties, spelling errors are frequent. Teaching these students a specific strategy for evaluating their papers can improve their performance in this area. Using mnemonic devices can help guide students in evaluating their written works (Schumaker et al., 1982). As described more fully later in this chapter, COPS is a strategy using a mnemonic device that prompts students to check the following:

> **C**apitalization
> **O**rganization
> **P**unctuation
> **S**pelling

Teachers should extensively model self-evaluation strategies during group editing practice. As students gain proficiency, they can move to first editing their own drafts and then meeting with the teacher to review and extend their editing efforts. They next revise the draft, self-edit, and obtain teacher's input again, and then revise once more. This process can be repeated as many times as necessary until both the student and the teacher are satisfied with the final draft. With time, much of the teacher's role in conferencing can be shifted to peer partners.

It also is helpful to teach students to identify and used common transition words that signal order of importance, chronological order, and order of location (Vallecorsa et al., 1991). Extensive practice on this can be provided during reading instruction. In addition, students can generate lists of transition examples that they can refer to when evaluating and revising their compositions. A final strategy that Vallecorsa and her colleagues suggested is to have students read their compositions aloud to their classmates. This provides them with auditory feedback and assists them in identifying problems such as missing words, sentence fragments, and run-on sentences.

In summary, the literature on editing suggests that self-monitoring skills must be taught as part of the writing process. Successful programs to develop editing and revising skills are likely to pursue the following goals:

1. Improve the students' abilities to attend to text structures and text-level problems.
2. Develop the students' abilities to distance themselves from their own and others' texts.
3. Improve the students' abilities to monitor and identify text inconsistencies and correct confusions.
4. Enhance the students' abilities to independently check and regulate performance, and to use internal rather than external criteria to guide text generation, monitoring, and revision.
5. Improve spelling, punctuation, and grammar as the students work toward producing final drafts.

WRITING INSTRUCTION

Writing instruction involves establishing a safe environment where students can take risks as they write on a variety of topics. However, creating a writing environment alone does not guarantee developing critical writing abilities. This section focuses on the features of a good writing environment as well as those instructional practices that are necessary to develop and refine the writing knowledge and skills of students.

The Writing Environment

Regardless of the students' writing problems, teachers will want to emphasize audiences, purposes, and the subprocesses of writing (e.g., prewriting, drafting, and revising). For beginning writers and students with a great deal of anxiety about writing, teachers will need to provide risk-free environments in which the students can experiment with written language without fear of correction or criticism. For these students, a process approach to writing may be the most effective instructional intervention. This approach also can address difficulties such as those associated with an inability to engage in sustained thinking about a writing topic, difficulties in gaining distance from the text, and problems in monitoring or evaluating text for inconsistencies and confusion.

The process approach to writing is characterized by the following instructional features: (1) sustained writing opportunities and frequent opportunities to write, (2) child-selected topics, (3) immersion in the writing subprocesses, (4) creation of a writing community, and (5) emphasis on risk-taking behavior. These features are described in the following sections.

Frequent and Sustained Writing Opportunities.
Opportunities to compose written expression are rare for special education students. Students may compose texts once a week, or only before holidays when teachers can think of clever writing topics. One study found that students with learning disabilities averaged less than 10 minutes per day actually engaged in composing tasks. This makes writing practice too infrequent for students to systematically experiment with written language or to develop writing automaticity.

On a more frequent basis, writing instruction may focus upon acquiring mechanical skills through paper-and-pencil exercises. These exercises often involve worksheets intended to refine the student's abilities to correct or to compose sentences and paragraphs. However, when students concentrate only on isolated sentences or paragraphs, they may never learn to sustain their thinking about topics or to draw systematically upon their vast storage of background knowledge to produce compositions (Englert, Rafael, Anderson, et al., 1988). Furthermore, when students experience only short writing activities, such as answering questions or writing paragraphs on different topics in each class, they do not learn to invoke cognitive strategies that can be used for planning and revising. Further, they have little opportunity to learn the combination of cognitive processes related to text production (Roit & McKenzie, 1985; Walmsley, 1984).

Creating an environment in which students have time to think, reflect, write, and rework drafts is important to growth in writing (Bos, 1988). It has been recommended that students with learning problems work for a minimum of 45 minutes a day at least four times per week in order to acquire adequate expressive writing skills (Graham & Harris, 1988). By writing themselves during this time and then sharing their own writing strategies, teachers can provide role models that can motivate and guide their students.

Not only should teachers schedule lengthy periods of writing time several times a week, but they should provide for sustained opportunities for students to work on the same piece across writing sessions. This encourages students to develop their own internal criteria for determining the paper's completeness, and discourages them from relying on external criteria, such as the end of the writing period. Teachers may unwittingly reinforce the reliance on external criteria by insisting that students complete their day's writing by the end of the period. In reversing this instructional pattern, teachers accept the individuality of their students as writers. Some students may choose to complete their papers in a single period, while other students may wish to do additional research and work on the same paper for a week or more.

Topic Selection.   The relative use of teacher-selected versus child-selected writing topics remains a controversial issue (Graves, 1982; Lee, 1987). Both have a place in the writing program. Teacher-assigned topics are useful in extending the students' abilities to produce new types of writing or in refining their skills in new areas. For example, the teachers may specifically target the development of student proficiency with expository writing by modeling how to write a comparison/contrast text and by asking students to compose their own comparison/contrast papers. In this way, they can guide students to develop new skills or to extend existing skills.

Teachers should balance the instructional programs to include opportunities for children to write about their own selected topics as well as teacher-directed topics. Student-chosen topics maximize the knowledge students have to include in their writings and they minimize the cognitive load associated with content generation, thereby freeing resources to be used in other aspects of the writing process. Because writers are more familiar with topics that they generate, they produce longer and better-organized drafts. Students have less difficulty thinking of what to say because they more easily access background information. As a result, the amount written, the writing fluency, and its level of organization, as well as the students' interest in writing may increase.

Child-selected topics also can reinforce the informant role of writers. When students write about familiar topics, they are put in the position of being the expert who knows the topic best. This enhances their sense of self-competence, emphasizes their role as informants, and encourages their ownership of writing.

Journal writing has proved effective with many students who have learning difficulties. Rueda (1986) reported on the efficacy of interactive journal writing with special education students from Spanish-speaking backgrounds. Using specially created computer software programs, students wrote journal entries, to which their teachers then responded. Teachers tended to use conversational or personalized levels of responding, a strategy that resulted in more extended topic chains than did more "classroom-like" strategies such as asking for clarification and giving directives. It is possible that a personalized style of responding may be particularly important for linguistic-minority students who feel estranged from the cultural context of the classroom.

Over time, students who write about student-selected topics frequently move to experimenting with varying types of text structures and to writing about a broader range of subjects (Bos, 1988). When they share compositions with each other and see what other students are writing, students gain new insights into what to write about and how to write. These factors may motivate them to experiment with various writing forms and topics. Exposure to a variety of text structures during reading instruction and other parts of the curriculum provides additional models for students' experimentation with new text structures.

Teachers can assist students in selecting writing topics by brainstorming with the class lists of possible topics. These lists should be exhaustive and contain all contributing topics. Interest inventories also can help students identify favorite activities, games, sports, animals, places to visit, and so forth. The students can develop personal writing folders that contain the information from the interest inventory as well as the listings of brainstormed topics. These folders can be kept in their desks for easy access and revision . Teachers can refer students to their folders, or to classwide listings posted in the rooms, whenever students begin the topic selection process.

Occasionally, a teacher may find a student who writes repeatedly about the same topic or who employs the same type of text genre. While in some instances the teacher may want to expand the student's choices, this does not necessarily signal a need for intervention. For example, a student named Robert chose to write two papers about sports: the first paper was about football and the second paper was about ice hockey. The two stories he composed are shown in Figures

How to Play Football

I am going to explain how to play football. First, you need the people, like a coach, referee, players, fans and the quarterback. You need people to play football.

Then you need the equipment like a helmet, football, shoes, uniform with a number kneepads and shoulderpads.

Now you need a place. An indoor field or an outdoor field. Finally, you need the rules like facemask and holding.

To choose who gets the ball, one team chooses heads or tails. Then they flip the coin. One team kicks the ball and the other team catches the ball. They try to get 6 points. It's called a touchdown. To get a first down, you get 4 tries. Where the person gets the ball is where the ball is played. The team passes or runs the ball until they get past the end zone. They get six points for a touchdown. Then they can go for 2 points or 1 point. If you make a touchdown, you get 6 points and go for 1 point.

FIGURE 11.1   Robert's Football Story

How to Play Hockey

After school I went home and I turn on the TV. The teams are the Detroit Red Wings and Chicago Blackhawks. Before the game a man said "This is how to play hockey. To play each team needs materials. They need face guards, ice skates, jerseys, puck and players. The most important thing is the fans.

Next you ned to know how to play hockey. These are the steps. First the players come on the ice. The referee drops the puck. One of the two players in the circle have to hit the puck to their teammates. The teammates take the puck and try to score. To score you hit the puck in the net. At the end who ever has more points wins."

FIGURE 11.2   Robert's Hockey Story

11.1 and 11.2. The stories are similar and reflect Robert's enthusiasm for sports. At the same time, they provided Robert with the opportunity to practice specific skills that he transferred from one paper to the next. For instance, in each composition Robert wrote an explanation and a text structure that answers questions on the topic, clarifies steps, uses key words, and identifies things needed. Selecting topics within the single category of sports enabled Robert to better concentrate on mastering the new text structure genre. What he learned in writing one paper (e.g., the need to talk about game rules and points), he applied with greater automaticity in writing the second paper. Furthermore, he was able to improve in his ability to introduce his topic (e.g., introducing a narrator and naming the two opposing teams). Students may write about the same topics in order to concentrate on refining their skills, or because it offers them some sense of control over the writing process. In these circumstances, a

teacher should not intervene too quickly unless the student continues to narrowly select topics without demonstrating writing improvement.

Some researchers have expressed concern that while child-selected topics promote fluency and interest, their exclusive use will restrict the development of other important writing skills (Bereiter & Scardamalia, 1982). For example, students may engage primarily in expressive writing because it makes fewer demands on the higher-level processes; the familiarity of the topics means that they have to engage in less planning and framing. It is important that teachers closely monitor writing performance to ensure that students develop skills in dealing with the different types of writing problems.

Immersion in the Writing Subprocesses. Student writers need to experience the entire writing process of prewriting, drafting, and editing. This means that teachers should guide students in each of these writing stages. Because writers write and engage in the writing subprocesses with different purposes and goals, they may complete their papers at different times. Some writers may work exhaustively on their single papers until they are finished and then write their second papers more rapidly, with less revision and rewriting. The individual writers will make decisions about how long they spend in a single subprocess and when to proceed to the next subprocess.

Some critics of this process approach to writing have felt that story writing places an unfair burden on beginning or unskilled writers, particularly those with learning difficulties (Kameenui & Simmons, 1990). They note that expressive writing requires the application of a variety of complex skills that require deliberate demonstration, careful explanation, and direct teaching. They recommend that a scope and sequence of writing skills should guide instruction. Such scope and sequence might include steps involved in the mechanics of writing, writing simple sentences, writing paragraphs, and editing.

Hillocks (1984) has asserted that mere exposure to the processes of prewriting, drafting, and editing is insufficient to guarantee the improvement in written expression. He proposes that to facilitate student learning, teachers need to articulate clear objectives for each writing episode and actively model the various writing subprocesses. Since students cannot "see" the cognitions underlying planning, monitoring, or revising, teachers must provide windows into such cognitions through instructional dialogues that help students understand the thinking that produced the text.

Teacher dialogue can be used to model the writing strategies for each subprocess and the cognitions that help students regulate their uses of these strategies. For the planning aspect of the prewriting process, teachers can model activities such as: (1) selecting a topic, (2) identifying an audience and a purpose, and (3) brainstorming information. For the organizing aspect of prewriting, teachers can model how to: (1) select relevant information from the brainstormed list of ideas, (2) organize the brainstormed ideas into well-formed categories, and (3) use text structure questions to guide their retrieval and organization of information. For the editing and revising subprocesses, teachers can model several editing activities, such as: (1) monitoring the paper for meaning, (2) reading the paper from the reader's perspective, (3) checking the paper's adherence to the organizational plan or text structure questions, and (4) identifying whether the paper meets objectives related to audience and purpose.

Thinking aloud, teachers should model not only the various tasks, but the thinking that guides the process. For example, to teach planning, a teacher can model brainstorming techniques and discuss how she retrieves relevant ideas about a topic. A sample planning dialogue for writing an explanation paper is shown in Figure 11.3 (see Englert, 1990; Englert & Raphael, 1989; Raphael & Englert, 1990), depicts how the teacher can highlight the kinds of ideas writers include and why they include them, as well as the questions writers ask themselves during planning.

Creating a Writing Community.   A classroom environment that is conducive to writing development is one in which the teacher is accepting and encouraging, where high-interest activities and tasks are used, and where teacher praise and opportunities to share written work reinforce student efforts (Bos, 1988; Graham & Harris, 1988). A writing community can be established in the classroom by using such techniques as an "author's chair," peer partners and peer conferencing, teacher conferencing, and story publication.

In the first technique, the student writers can sit in the **author's chair** while they read their stories to the class. Their classmates then ask the writers questions about their papers (e.g., "What do turtles eat? Where did you get your turtle? Where would your turtle live in the wild?"). These questions serve to underscore the responsibility of writers to anticipate and answer readers' questions. If used before the written piece is completed, the author's chair can actually become a crucial instructional tool that influences the unfinished piece as writers look for answers to their peers' questions (Lee, 1987). Questions also help readers understand what it means to read for

T: I want to write a paper about something I know a lot about. What could I write about? Well, I know a lot about dog training and I have a new puppy I am trying to train. So, I could write about "How to train a dog." I also know something about sewing. I won a sewing contest two years in a row so I could talk about how to sew. I also know a little bit about taking care of horses. (Record three topics on overhead.)

T: All of these are good topics, but I think I'll write about taking care of horses. More people are interested in horses than in sewing. I'm also not sure I know enough about dog training to write about it for others, but I can always talk to my sister to get more ideas for my paper about taking care of horses.

T: Before I actually write my paper, I have to plan and organize my ideas. Today we're going to learn to plan our papers. Next, we'll learn how to organize our planned ideas. When we plan, we ask ourselves three important questions: Who am I writing for? Why am I writing this? What do I know? Each of these questions is very important in helping me write a composition that is interesting to my readers yet informative. (Record questions on an overhead.)

T: The "WHO" I am writing for is very important because I need to include different information for different audiences. How would writing a paper about taking care of horses be different if I was writing for a kindergartner than if I was writing for a sixth grader? (Elicit ideas and explain the importance of audience.)

T: For this paper, I think I'll write my paper for students your age—fifth graders. Fifth graders are usually interested in horses, and since you are fifth graders, I can write my paper for you. You can even help me write my paper. Who are other audiences you might write your papers for? (Elicit ideas, highlight the diversity of their audiences, and the information needs of different audiences.)

T: The third thing I ask myself in planning a paper is "WHAT DO I KNOW?" This is the fun part of planning because I brainstorm everything I know about taking care of horses. I record my ideas in any order and I don't worry about complete sentences or spelling words correctly. These are my notes to help me remember my ideas—they are not for the teacher or anyone else but me.

T: When I brainstorm, I simply record my ideas and words right out of my head. I'm going to use this blank overhead as my brainstorming sheet. For example, I'm thinking that shoeing horses is an important aspect of taking care of horses so I'll write down the words "shoeing horses." I know, too, that horses need to eat particular kinds of food so I'll write the phrase "Kinds of food horses eat." I'm going to write down the word "veterinarian" because I know my sister has the vet come out at least once a year to take care of the horses. I'm not sure how to spell veterinarian, but it doesn't really matter because the brainstorming sheet is just for me. I'm also going to write in the margin, "What does the veterinarian do?," because that's a question my readers will want me to answer. If I don't know the answer, I can find it or ask my sister.

T: What are some other ideas or questions that I can record on my brainstorming sheet? (Record ideas and some questions in the margins.)

T: I noticed several things while we brainstormed ideas. One thing I noticed is that, together, we came up with more ideas than if I had brainstormed alone.

(continued)

It's often a good idea to talk to others when you brainstorm ideas to see if you can come up with other ideas.

T: I also noticed that we used questions and one or two word phrases to help us plan our papers rather than write our ideas out completely. These are our personal notes to help us remember ideas and jog our memories so we don't forget ideas. You only need to write questions or words that you will understand and that help you remember.

T: When do you think you might plan a paper as we planned this one? (Discuss the occasions when students might use planning strategies.)

T: How could you go about planning your paper as we planned this one? (Review planning strategies, the questions writers ask themselves, and the planning steps.) Discuss with students that, when they plan a paper, they can brainstorm and record their ideas on a blank sheet of paper. Discuss the importance of planning strategies.

T: Tomorrow, we are going to learn to order and organize these ideas for our paper so it makes sense.

FIGURE 11.3 Script for Modeling How to Plan an Explanation Paper (T = teacher, S = student)

meaning and to ask questions in the comprehension process.

For students who have difficulty asking questions, teachers can model how to ask "Wh-" (what, when, where, why, who, and how) questions. A list of the Wh- questions should be displayed on a bulletin board for easy reference. One teacher found that her young students became quite successful in asking questions after only a week of guided instruction. The questions her students asked of a first-grade author in response to his story about a visit to the zoo are shown in Figure 11.4. Notice that students requested expository information of the author. As students become skilled in asking content questions, teachers may wish to expand their repertoires of questions by introducing students to specific types of text structures and text structure questions appropriate to each type.

Publication of stories is a second strategy that can have a substantial impact on both the motivation to write and awareness of audience. Through the publication of stories in class books, students learn that they are not just writing alone or for their teachers, but for an expanded audience that can include classmates, the entire school, and their parents and other family members. They become more aware of the purposes of writing and their participation in a writing community. Their enthusiasm for writing increases.

Publication formats can vary considerably. One teacher typed individual stories on separate pages, returned the stories to authors for illustrations, put the finished class stories in a manila folder, and bound the stories with brackets that were inserted through holes punched in the folder. The students published a story every other week and the publications were the most popular source of independent reading in her classroom. Another teacher produced three bound copies of each child's story with the author illustrating each page of text. One copy of the publication then was returned to the author, a second copy was kept in the classroom for other students to check out and read, and a third copy was placed in the school library.

Peer conferencing is a third technique that can reinforce students' awareness of their audience and promote high levels of interaction. In peer conferences, authors read their written drafts

Justin in the Zoo

Windy and a Brown Boy
and Ian and David and
Justin went to see the Zoo.
We saw Zebras.   They were

What do they eat?   How big are they?

eating,   We   saw Lions,

How do they roar?

They were roaring,   We

saw giraffes They were

What kind of leaves does your giraffe eat?

eating   leave   on the

FIGURE 11.4   Story about a Visit to the Zoo

to their peers, who ask questions and offer advice. Although peer conferencing is often scheduled in the editing phase of writing, authors can use peer conferencing for assistance during any writing phase, such as planning, organizing, or drafting.

For successful peer conferencing, teachers need to model the format and language of conferences, including how to give and receive feedback. The conference format can consist of the following: (1) the author begins by stating where he is in the writing process, (2) the author and the editor read the composition together, (3) the author asks the editor to retell the paper and respond to the content, and (4) the editor makes suggestions pertinent to original concerns of the author (Calkins, 1986). Figure 11.5 depicts a set of guidelines developed for authors and editors in giving and receiving feedback (Englert et al., 1989).

Teachers can model the editing and revising by putting compositions on overheads and leading classroom dialogues about the compositions and how to revise them. Through these dialogues, teachers model how to read for meaning, and how to add, discard, or move ideas in the texts. At first, teachers may wish to use students' papers from previous years with the students' names erased. However, students may soon volunteer their own papers for the classroom dialogues, especially if they are allowed to lead the classroom dialogues. Figure 11.6 shows a sample dialogue in which the teacher models editing and revising processes (see Englert, 1990; Raphael & Englert, 1990). Notice how the teacher only discusses editing conventions, but models how to record questions and ideas in the margins of the paper while de-emphasizing neatness and technical perfection.

Peer conferencing has several advantages that make it a critical component of a good writing program. First, peer conferencing places clear emphasis on the communicative function of writing, a function not always clear when students write alone or for their teachers. Second, peer editors serve as external monitors for what works and what does not. By carrying out dialogues with their readers, authors come to internalize this process and to carry on these dialogues with their own texts. Third, young writers learn to "decen-

ter" or "distance" themselves from what they have written by responding to someone else's writing first and then they apply the same meaning criteria to their own writings. Fourth, peer questions reinforce writers' roles as informants and their abilities to sustain their thinking about topics. To avoid negative and unhelpful peer feedback, students must be taught appropriate peer review approaches. Teachers can model positive and helpful feedback during sharing and can lead students in establishing rules for providing feedback.

Teacher conferencing can be used to create a writing community in which students are knowledgeable of writing strategies. Conferences can be used to guide students in identifying something to write about, to brainstorm ideas for papers, and to draft and edit texts. Strategy conferences in which teachers focus on the strategies students use to write need to be carefully conducted so that students still retain their "voices" and personalities in their papers, and are involved in making critical decisions about what happens to their papers (Calkins, 1986). Students are apt to become passive if teachers take too great a role in editing papers or assigning revision tasks to students. Teachers can inadvertently silence students' oral and written voices, and students' ultimate control of the writing process (Florio-Ruane & Lensmire, 1989).

To avoid this problem, teachers should ask questions that only the authors of the papers can answer (e.g., "Why did you pick this topic?" "Can you tell me more about _____ ?" "Why do you think the main character did that?" "What part of the story would you like to work on?"). By asking questions that require writers to act as informants—either by teaching teachers about their own writing strategies or about their stories—students' own writing awareness and cognitive abilities are enhanced, while teachers acquire valuable information about students' writing development. Furthermore, this type of questioning develops and refines students' writing voices rather than silencing them.

Emphasis on Risk-Taking Behavior. A final feature of an effective writing environment is the

Giving Feedback

1. *Give positive feedback, not negative feedback.*

Positive Feedback	Negative Feedback
• I liked your story because I learned interesting things about Hawaii.	• It wasn't interesting to me.
• Your story is very funny.	• Your story is really boring.
• I liked the part about how you and your friend invented a new word.	• I didn't like any of it.
• Your story is very descriptive.	• Your story isn't good.

2. *Give suggestions, not orders.*

Suggestion	Order
• It might sound nice if you explain . . .	• Write better.
• To make the ending clearer you could put . . .	• Change it.
• Why don't you try adding . . .	• Add more.
• If you put your sentences into paragraphs . . .	• Make it better.

3. *Make specific suggestions, don't be vague.*

Specific	Vague
• In the first paragraph, you could introduce the main character.	• Change the beginning.
• Correct the spelling for the words I underlined.	• Fix your spelling.
• In the second paragraph, it might be nice to add a description of the haunted house.	• Add more
• In the last sentence, you could write how the man felt when he returned home to his friends.	• Make it better.

Receiving Feedback

Step 1. Think about how hard your editor worked.
Step 2. Think about all the suggestions your editor made.
Step 3. What will you do?

Positive Actions	*Negative Actions*
• Thank my editor for all her work. Example: "Thanks for reading my story. Your ideas are very helpful."	• Get mad. Example: "You don't know what you are talking about."
• Pay attention to helpful suggestions. Example: "Your suggestion about adding a description of the setting seems like a good idea."	• Ignore my editor's suggestions. Example: "I won't do any of your suggestions."
• Select suggestions I want to follow. Example: I think I will use these three suggestions when I revise my paper."	• Argue with my editor. Example: "Why do I need to change anything? You are wrong."
• Begin to fix my work. Example: I'll start my final draft by adding two sentences about the main character to the first paragraph."	• Pout. Example: I don't have to do it if I don't want to."

FIGURE 11.5 Guidelines for Author and Editor to Use in Giving Feedback

Source: C. S. Englert, T. E. Raphael, and L. M. Anderson (1989). *Cognitive Strategy Instruction in Writing Project.* East Lansing, MI: Institute for Research on Teaching, Michigan State University. Reprinted with permission.

T: Here is a story written by a student. His teacher had asked him to write an explanation in which he explained how to do something. Let's read it. (Read aloud following story displayed on an overhead transparency.)

How to Play Dodge Ball

One day I was bored, I had nothing to do except walk around. About one hour later one of my friends came over. He told me he was bored so that is why he came over. He asked me what I want to do, I said, "How about playing Dodge Ball." Then he said how do you play Dodge Ball. So I had to show him. It took him a week till he got the hang of it. The end.

T: Who can tell me what this paper is mainly about?

S: (Being bored.)

T: Okay. I'm wondering if this author meant to write an explanation of what you do when you're bored, or if he meant to write an explanation of how to play dodge ball. I'm confused. What do you think?

S: (Well, it was obvious to me. Cause it says, "How to play dodge ball. I think the author . . .")

T: I wondered that, too, because titles are supposed to be what's in the paper. I don't think this is mainly about dodge ball. What could this author do? What does this author need to do to make this an explanation of how to play dodge ball?

S: (Tell his friend how to play dodge ball in writing. Add some information at the end of his paper about how to play.)

T: How should he tell his friend how to play dodge ball? What's missing?

S: (He should have said "This is how you play it." Then he should have listed some steps.)

T: You mean down here when the author wrote . . . (Record questions on the passage on the overhead, "How do you play dodge ball?" "What are the steps?")

T: Perhaps we can give some helpful hints to help the author. What kinds of things should he include when he explains how to play dodge ball?

S: (Equipment you need. How to make teams and the rules for playing dodge ball.)

T: Okay. I'm going to record some of your ideas in the margin to help the author. I'm going to write the words, "Equipment?" "Teams?" and "Rules?." When we write explanations about games, we often include information about equipment, teams, rules, and the steps for playing—what to do first, second, and third. Those are important ideas that our readers will need to know if they want to learn how to play the game.

T: Now, if I'm the author trying to insert this information in my paper, I can use these questions to improve my paper. I simply see what questions my reader has, and address those questions by using a caret (^) and arrows to show where the information goes. For example, where the reader asks, "What are the steps?," I put a caret and arrow, and insert the missing information in the margins or up above the print. "What are the steps for playing dodge ball?"

S: (First, you pick teams. You need at least four people on a team . . . You'll need to find a place to play, too. You have to play outside on a playground or in a gym where there is lots of room to throw a ball . . . Then you need to play the game. One team divides up its players who stand at opposite sides, while the other team stands in the middle . . .)

T: These are excellent ideas. I'm going to record these ideas next to the arrow like this. I've already got the first sentences, "First you pick the teams. You need at least four people on a team." Who can help me phrase the next part about where to play the game? (Continue to elicit information and record information on the passage until students have answered the questions about the steps, equipment, and rules.)

T: One of the things I really like about doing this paper is the introduction. It tells me that dodge ball is something I can do on a day that I don't have something else to do. It's a boring day, but it can be made fun by playing dodge ball. Are there other parts of the paper that you like?

T: Are there other parts of the paper that you have question about or would like to change? (Elicit ideas from students. Whenever appropriate, model how to record questions, as well as how to add, delete, and move information.)

T: I'm thinking that these changes would make a very good explanation. You have some excellent ideas about editing this paper. What are some of the things we did when we edited this paper?

S: (We asked questions . . . Thought of things that we like or didn't like about the paper . . . Asked ourselves whether the paper made sense and what the paper was about.)

T: What are some things we did when we revised this paper? (Discuss editing conventions.)

FIGURE 11.6 Classroom Dialogue about Editing and Revising (T = teacher, S = students)

Source: C. S. Englert, T. E. Raphael, and L. M. Anderson (1989). *Cognitive Strategy Instruction in Writing Project.* East Lansing, MI: Institute for Research on Teaching, Michigan State University. Reprinted with permission.

teachers' emphasis and acceptance of risk-taking behaviors. Teachers encourage students to take risks when they themselves participate in the writing community as writers. Teachers can share their writings with students, talk about their own writing problems, and describe how they solved them. This heightens students' awareness that writing is a problem-solving activity, and that all writers encounter challenging problems that must be solved in the writing process.

Teachers also can foster risk-taking behaviors by emphasizing that the purpose of writing is communication rather than producing a composition that is free of spelling or grammatical mistakes. It is difficult for many students to focus both on the meaning and the mechanical features of the texts at the same time. By responding to the content of texts rather than the mechanical errors, teachers can guide students to focus on meaning first. For example, with the student, Max, whose paper left many unanswered questions, his teacher could ask him questions about his baseball topic such as "Why do you like baseball?" "Do you play on a team?" "What equipment does a baseball team need?" By emphasizing the content of papers first and de-emphasizing mechanics until the papers are ready for their final drafts or publication, teachers can help students understand that the most important aspects of the written language process are the messages of the paper rather than their surface appearance.

Teachers should provide risk-free environments in which writers are willing to make mistakes and experiment with written language. Writers should be encouraged to invent spellings if they do not know the conventional spelling, and try out new writing methods—even when those methods may result in less than superior products. For example, Chris, a fifth grader with learning disabilities, wrote a paper that was an explanation of playing Car Wars. His first explanation was an introduction that rambled and contained irrelevant information as he attempted to create a context for his paper (Englert & Raphael, 1989, p. 144):

> One day I was in Frandor with my mom, brother, and my two sisters. And me and my brother went into the Hobby Hub. The problem was—he had money and I didn't. And he got the game Car Wards that he had wanted for a long time, and a book for the game that has weapons for the car. And now I will tell you how to play. Fist, you need to read the instruction book . . .

After reading his peers' papers, Chris decided to try a different approach. As he stated to Carla, another student in the class, "[For this paper,] I am going to get right to the point." Notice how Chris begins his second explanation, getting right to the point as he had explained to Carla (Englert & Raphael, 1989, p. 144):

> I'm going to get right to the point. I'm going to explain how to take care of a kitten or a cat. First, I'm going to tell you how to feed a kitten or cat. When you get your kitten, check if it has big or little teeth. If it has little teeth, give it soft cat food. if it has medium teeth, mix hard cat food and soft cat food. Then when it is a full grown cat, give it just hard cat food. Give it a cat food it likes . . .

Although Chris's second explanation begins abruptly and lacks context-setting statements, it is apparent that he is experimenting with written language and new writing patterns. By actively constructing different writing patterns and analyzing their effects, Chris may ultimately create introductions somewhere between his first and second attempts. Because experimentation is welcomed without censure, Chris and other students are encouraged to try new strategies and to imitate others. Because classroom dialogues focus on the "what" and "how" of writing papers, students feel comfortable trying new language patterns without fear of teachers' or students' criticism.

Instructional Practices to Refine Writing Skills

Continually refining writing skills is an important goal of any writing program. In addition to creating effective writing environments, teachers also need to directly teach critical writing skills. Research indicates that effective writing programs contain the following elements: (1) a clear statement of objectives; (2) the teacher presenting the information, with students working on tasks in small groups before proceeding to similar tasks independently; and (3) applying criteria to a writing sample not only in judging the piece, but in generating ideas to improve it (Hillocks, 1984).

Schema-building approaches are based on the assumption that writers have internalized maps and genre for specific text structures. Knowledge of such structures can aid writers because the text structures serve as prefabricated plans that can be used to structure and shape the compositions (Bereiter & Scardamalia, 1982). This plan can be used during prewriting to gather and organize information, during drafting to generate information, and during editing to monitor and revise the texts.

One of the easiest text structures to introduce to students is the narrative or story structure. Because of their preschool experiences with television, storyreading, and storytelling, children already have a broad understanding of story structure when they start school. Although this knowledge may be tacit, it can be formalized in the writing programs to improve storywriting skills.

Narrative Structure.   Several studies have demonstrated that instruction in **story structure** can improve students' written compositions. Students can be directly taught the structural elements representative of story grammars, for example, setting, initiating event or problem, internal response, overt attempts, outcome, and conclusion (Fitzgerald & Teasley, 1986). Students should be told that knowledge of the story grammar elements can assist them in understanding and writing stories. It is helpful for teachers to think aloud in presenting the story grammar elements. In this way teachers verbally model the thinking that is involved in using the story grammar to guide the composing process. The following instructional sequence can be effective in directly teaching story grammar:

1. Focus on one story constituent and its temporal relation to other story parts.
2. Describe the story element (e.g., setting), pointed out the element in a story (e.g., *Hansel and Gretel*), and give two or three examples of the element that would be appropriate for a story on a wall chart.
3. Elicit two or three other examples of the story element from learners;
4. Present nonexamples and explain why these were not good examples of the story element being studied (e.g., different story part or misplaced within a story).
5. Ask students to identify and/or predict missing story information from an incomplete story.
6. Provide scrambled stories.

Cognitive behavior modification is another approach to teaching story structure (Graham & Harris, 1988, 1989a). This approach teaches students to make self-statements to elicit genre-related elements, and to improve their control and regulation of the writing process. It instructs them to ask a series of questions that can guide practice in identifying these story grammar elements in stories. These questions include:

1. Who is the main character?
2. When does the story take place?
3. Where does the story take place?
4. What does the main character want to do?
5. What happens when the main character tries to do it?
6. How does the story end?
7. How does the main character feel?

After learning to identify story elements using these questions, the students can then practice generating them by looking at pictures. When students can define, identify, and generate all story elements, teachers can introduce the following five-step strategy to guide story writing:

1. Look at the picture.
2. Let your mind be free.
3. Write down the story part reminder.
4. Write down story ideas for each question.
5. Write your story, use good parts and make sense.

Posting classroom charts to list these strategies can be helpful, as can providing students with individual prompt cards. As students compose the stories, the teachers can model self-instructions involving problem definition (e.g., What is it I have to do?"), story planning using the five strategy steps, self-evaluation, and self-reinforcement. The instructors and students can compose stories together, after which the students can independently compose stories. Once students have learned the basic story structure elements, cognitive behavior modification can result in stories that contain a significantly larger number and variety of story elements, and that are of high quality (Graham & Harris, 1989a).

Sometimes, particularly by middle school, students have a greater knowledge of story structure than is apparent in their compositions. The cognitive burden of a writing task (e.g., choosing words, sentences, and information to include) makes it difficult for them to access this knowledge. Teachers can provide students with cue cards listing the story grammar elements (character, setting, problem, plan, and ending) and can direct students to use the cards to check each element during the planning and writing phases. This has been shown to significantly increase the number of story elements included, and to improve story organization and coherence. The simplicity of the strategy suggests its use for students who need reminders to apply skills already in their repertoires.

Using story frames can also direct students' attention to the key elements of narrative structure. There are several ways that story frames can be used as part of the teaching process. During prewriting, students can be asked to plan and organize their stories by generating narrative information that completes the story frames. During drafting, teachers can remind students to use their completed story frames to ensure that they consider their original plans in producing well-organized stories. Finally, during editing, students can monitor their writing performance by filling out story frames with information from their papers or by comparing their actual stories to their plans to see if their stories are complete. To prepare students for these steps, teachers should think aloud about the planning, drafting, and editing processes, showing students how to perform the processes, and modeling the decisions that writers make.

Cognitive Strategy Instruction in Writing. **Cognitive Strategy Instruction in Writing (CSIW)** (Englert, Raphael, Anderson et al., 1988; Englert, Raphael, Anderson, in progress) is an entire writing program that teaches students to produce well-formed expository text structures using schema building. The goal of the CSIW program is to internalize the writing subprocesses. It encompasses the clear statement of objectives, modeling strategies by using teacher think alouds, presenting information to students who work in small groups, and applying writing criteria in evaluating and revising sample texts. Further-

more, CSIW provides direct instruction in metacognitive processes—the thinking that produced the texts. It apprentices students in both the cognitive actions that produce texts, and the inner talk that directs students during the writing process.

In CSIW, students are first introduced to a specific type of expository text structure, and the questions and key words that characterize that text structure. The text structures introduced in CSIW include explanations, comparison/contrast texts, and "expert" papers that consist of categories of main ideas and related details.

The CSIW program cycles students through an instructional process that begins with the teachers modeling the text structure questions and key words for specific types of text structures. Using four writing samples, the teachers highlight the types of questions addressed by the writing samples, and the key words that signal the location of the information that answers the text structure questions. The four writing samples, selected to represent the range from very effective to poorly written papers, are placed on overhead transparencies and the quality of each paper is rated in terms of the degree to which it answers the relevant text structure questions (e.g., for an explanation paper, did the author tell what was being explained, who or what materials were needed, and the steps?). The teachers also have students rate the papers in terms of the degree to which key words are used to cue the important information, and the degree to which the paper captures and maintains readers' attention.

Initially, teachers think aloud about the relevant features found in writing samples, leading students to identify text structure features and features related to audiences and purposes. However, students soon are invited to identify text structure features, as well as the parts of the papers they particularly like or have questions about, and the parts that make the papers interesting to the readers. Once problems are identified, teachers and students are encouraged to hold classroom dialogues about writing strategies and solutions (Englert & Raphael, 1989; Raphael &

Englert, 1990). This provides students with a basis for internalizing a text structure schema they can later use as a guide in retrieving, organizing, signaling, and monitoring ideas.

Next, the teacher models how to plan, organize, write, edit, and revise papers using his or her knowledge of text structure questions, audiences, and purposes. The teachers do this by modeling and thinking aloud while engaging in each writing subprocess, from planning through final draft. Using teacher-guided dialogues, teachers and students jointly plan, organize, write, edit, and revise class papers (Englert, 1990). Next, students practice the dialogues and strategies, collaboratively and individually, as they develop their own papers using "think sheets" provided for that purpose. *Think sheets* (described in more detail later) are designed to cue and scaffold students' use of the newly modeled strategies. Student ownership of the writing experience is fostered by establishing a social context in which they write for real audiences (e.g., peers) and purposes (e.g., publication of their papers). The goal is for students eventually to control the writing process independently, no longer needing the support of the teachers or curriculum materials.

Think Sheets.   CSIW think sheets are designed to make writing processes and strategies explicit to students. The term, *think sheets,* was selected to underscore their differences from traditional worksheets, which typically focus only on isolated writing skills. Each think sheet elicits procedures correlated to strategies related to the writing subprocess, and directs students' attention to specific strategies and mental operations for performing the subprocess. Think sheets have been developed for planning, organizing, writing, and editing and revising processes.

The *plan* think sheets cue students to consider their writing purposes or goals, their intended audiences, and their background knowledge related to their selected topics. As depicted in Figure 11.7, the plan think sheet contains such self-questions as, "Who am I writing for?" (audience), "Why am I writing this?" (purpose), and "What do I know?" (activation of background knowledge). These questions are used to prompt students to perform specific planning activities while emphasizing the development of self-instructional statements and questions important to the activation and control of planning strategies.

The *organize* think sheets consist of a set of pattern guides that cue students to consider organizational groups and the relationships among ideas as they develop their writing plans. Essentially, this subprocess makes text structures more visible to students. For example, the *organize* think sheet for explanations prompts students to order their groups of ideas into categories related to: "What is being explained?" "What are the materials?" "What are the steps?" "What happens first? last?" (see Figure 11.8). The *organize* think sheet for writing comparison/contrast papers represent a different visual pattern with questions specific to comparing and contrasting (see Figure 11.9).

Furthermore, since "pure" structures may rarely occur in students' textbooks or in library resources (Schallert & Tierney, 1981), another *organize* think sheet may be used to demonstrate that text structures do not always conform to the well-organized explanation or comparison/contrast text structures. Instead, they incorporate multiple text structures into a single passage. For example, when an author writes about a country, she may write about its climate, topography, resources, and culture. While these categories may lead the author to explain the steps in mining resources, or compare/contrast one country with another, the categories of information rather than the explanation or comparison/contrast text structure drive the composing process. To communicate to students the idea that texts have shifting text structures, students are introduced to a form of writing called "expert writing," which is centered upon categories of information (e.g., superordinate and related details). For this structure, the *Expert Organize* think sheet prompts students to group the ideas they brainstormed during planning into categories with appropriate superordi-

Name: _____   Date: _____

Topic: _____

WHO: Who am I writing for?

_____

_____

WHY: Why am I writing this?

_____

_____

WHAT: What do I know? (Brainstorm)

1. _____

2. _____

3. _____

4. _____

5. _____

6. _____

7. _____

8. _____

FIGURE 11.7   Plan Think Sheet

Source: C. S. Englert, T. E. Raphael, and L. M. Anderson (1989). *Cognitive Strategy Instruction in Writing Project.* East Lansing, MI: Institute for Research on Teaching, Michigan State University. Reprinted with permission.

nate labels, and to order their ideas in preparation for their first drafts. Figure 11.10 shows a completed expert organize think sheet for a composition about taking care of dogs.

The *write* think sheet prompts strategies for drafting papers. Colored paper, rather than white lined paper, is used to underscore the notion that a draft is not a final copy (i.e., neatly written on clean white paper). The emphasis on the draft nature of the writing is designed to signal students to focus on content and organization rather than on mechanics or grammatical conventions. In composing their first drafts, students translate their writing plans into formal prose using tactics

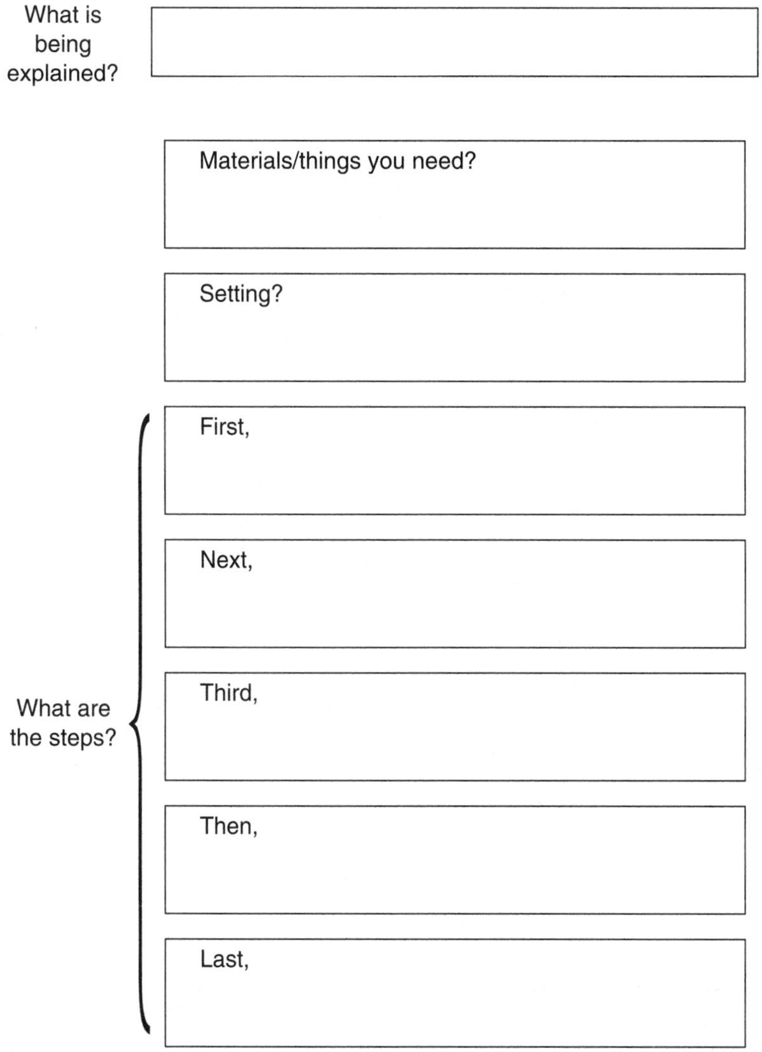

What is
being
explained?

Materials/things you need?

Setting?

First,

Next,

Third,

What are
the steps?

Then,

Last,

FIGURE 11.8 Explanation Organization Form

Source: C. S. Englert, T. E. Raphael, and L. M. Anderson (1989). *Cognitive Strategy Instruction in Writing Project.* East Lansing, MI: Institute for Research on Teaching, Michigan State University. Reprinted with permission.

to engage their readers through their introductions and conclusions. They use key words as signals to cue the location of specific types to text information; and flesh out their text to conform to their plans, audiences, and writing purposes. The *write* think sheets refer students to their pre-draft goals and organizational plans, thereby diminishing their reliance upon the knowledge-telling strategy.

The *edit* think sheet, displayed in Figure 11.11, guides students to reflect on their papers in terms of both the content and organization, and to

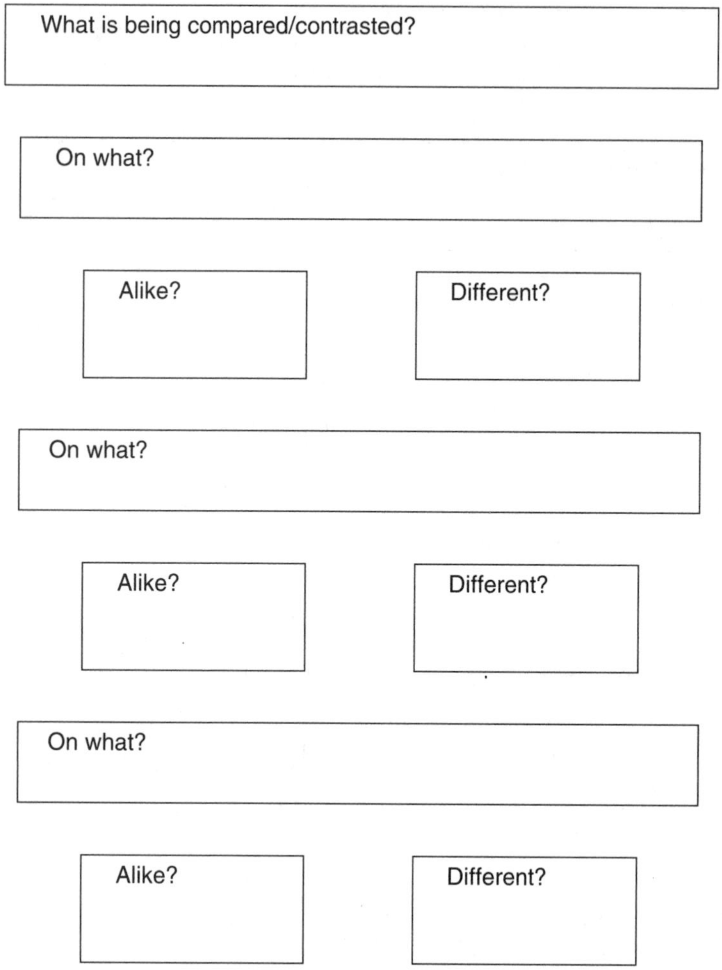

What is being compared/contrasted?

On what?

| Alike? | Different? |

On what?

| Alike? | Different? |

On what?

| Alike? | Different? |

FIGURE 11.9 Comparison/Contrast Organization Form

Source: From "Developing successful writers through cognitive strategy instruction" by C. S. Englert and T. E. Raphael, pp. 105–151. In J. E. Brophy (ed.), *Advances in Research on Teaching,* vol. 1. Copyright 1989. JAI Press Inc.

prepare for peer-editing sessions. The first set of prompts directs students to reread their papers, placing stars next to the parts they like and do not wish to change, and explaining why they like the parts indicated. They then put question marks by the parts that might be confusing to their readers or that require clarification, and they explain why these sections might cause confusion. In this way, students are encouraged to focus on the content of their papers from the perspective of their readers, and to interact directly with their first drafts in identifying their papers' strengths and weaknesses.

The second set of prompts on the *edit* think sheet focuses students' attention on the extent to which the paper conforms to the text structure used and potential interest to their audiences. Prompts for organization asks them to rate the ex-

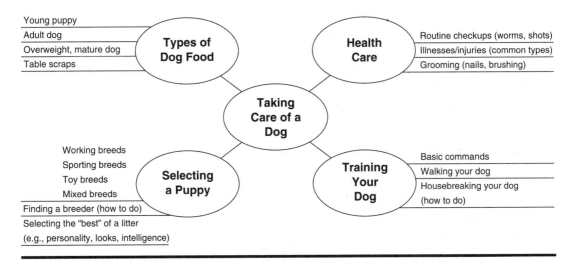

FIGURE 11.10   Completed Expert Think Sheet

Source: From "Developing successful writers through cognitive strategy instruction" by C. S. Englert and T. E. Raphael, pp. 105–151. In J. E. Brophy (ed.), *Advances in Research on Teaching,* vol. 1. Copyright 1989. JAI Press Inc.

tent to which they used the criterion text structure features in their papers (e.g., for explanation: Did you: Tell what was being explained? Tell what materials you need? Make the steps clear? Use key words?). These prompts change to match the questions of the particular text structure (e.g., narrative and explanation) being taught. For each of the prompts, students rate themselves according to three simple self-rating choices ("yes," "sort of," and "no"). Finally, students prepare for their peer-editing sessions by identifying problem areas (e.g., by reviewing their ratings and locating places in their paper that have been marked confusing or unclear), and by writing two or more questions to ask their peer editors.

In responding to each of these self-edit questions and locating the information in their own papers, students learn to perform the text analysis strategies that underlie successful writing. These strategies include:

- Using text cues to identify important information.
- Procedures related to monitoring the clarity and integrity of the meaning being constructed.

- Fix-up strategies to remedy communication breakdowns.

Learning the editing criteria and to ask specific questions that they can apply to their own or others' writings has a powerful effect on students' writings (Hillocks, 1984). Students begin to internalize the criteria and generate new material even when the criteria are not present.

Peer editors use the *editor* think sheets. They are identical to edit think sheets in the questions they ask, guiding peer editors to focus on both content and organization, and to make constructive suggestions. Authors and editors then meet to brainstorm ways to improve the papers, and collaborating on the revisions.

After students complete both the editing and peer editing processes, they consider how to finally revise their own texts. The *revision* think sheet aids in this task. This think sheet guides students to reflect on their first drafts by using their *edit* and *editor* think sheets. Students identify areas of concern and assume control over their papers by listing all the suggestions generated and received, and deciding on the changes to implement. Following this think sheet, students return

---

Edit

Name: _____   Date: _____

Read to Check Your Information. Reread my paper.

What do I like best? (Put a * by the parts I like best.)

What parts are not clear? (Put a ? by unclear parts.)

Question Yourself to Check Organization. Did I

Tell what was being explained?	Yes	Sort of	No
Tell what things you need?	Yes	Sort of	No
Make the steps clear?	Yes	Sort of	No
Use keywords (first, second)?	Yes	Sort of	No
Make it interesting?	Yes	Sort of	No

Plan Revision. (Look back)

What parts do I want to change?

1. _____

2. _____

Write two or more questions for my editor.

1. _____

2. _____

FIGURE 11.11   Self-Edit Think Sheet for Explanations

Source: C. S. Englert, T. E. Raphael, and L. M. Anderson (1989). *Cognitive Strategy Instruction in Writing Project.* East Lansing, MI: Institute for Research on Teaching, Michigan State University. Reprinted with permission.

to their drafts and implement their revision plans. They then move to the final copies using lined sheets of white paper. After final copies, the papers are copyedited in preparation for publication.

Internalization of the writing processes, the overall goal of the CSIW curriculum, is promoted by the self-questions of the think sheets. They provide vehicles for teachers to use in leading class discussions about which writing strategies to use, how to use them, and when to use them. The sample writing lessons constitute a second component of the CSIW curriculum that promotes internalization of the writing processes.

Sample Writing Lessons. Teachers can use the sample writing lessons to model the thinking, problem-solving, and self-regulatory processes that underlie the component process. For each writing subprocess, teachers present the think sheets on overheads as they model through personal examples of how to use the writing strategies associated with that subprocess. The teachers' dialogues help students gain control of their own writings as they hear the inner speech and reflective thought that directs the writing process.

In the planning stage, for example, teachers model self-talk as they make frequent references to their own problem-solving strategies (e.g., "I remember that . . . I can picture . . ."). These references to one's inner thinking include references to activating strategies (e.g., "I should ask myself the planning questions.), implementing strategies (e.g., "I'll brainstorm as many ideas as I can. I don't have to worry about using complete sentences or the order of my ideas."), monitoring strategies (e.g., "How am I doing? Have I thought of everything the reader needs to know?"), and task management (e.g., "It's okay if I haven't remembered everything. I can come up with more ideas when I organize or draft my ideas.").

Similarly, in modeling revising, teachers present compositions on overheads as they lead students in identifying text structure features (e.g., the set of questions the text structure was able to answer and the presence of key words, such as "Did I tell . . . What is being explained? What materials I need? What are the steps?"), as well as features of the papers that they particularly like ("I like this part best because the introduction really tells readers what the paper is about, e.g., taking care of cats."), have questions about ("I wonder if my readers will know what I mean when I say to buy the right kind of cat food?"), or that makes the papers interesting to their readers (e.g., "I think this part will be interesting to the reader because . . ."). When writing problems are identified, teachers and students hold classroom dialogues about writing strategies and solutions. They collaborate in generating problem-solving strategies and hypothesizing ways the authors can use writing alternatives to solve the problems. In this way, teachers model the inner thinking that guides editing and revising processes.

The third means by which CSIW fosters the internalization of writing strategies is its emphasis on the students' own mental activities.

Through gradually eliminating the think sheets and teacher think alouds, students gain control of the writing subprocesses. Once students understand planning activities, for example, teachers can phase out certain questions or eliminate the entire think sheets. Students can participate in modifying the think sheets for other purposes (e.g., for use in reading, note-taking, writing in content areas, or monitoring their performance). This helps them internalizeei the components of the program in ways that foster their later independence, self-regulation, and generalization to other curriculum areas.

Other Strategy Instruction Programs. In addition to the direct instruction in writing strategies that CSIW provides, a variety of similar strategies have been developed to prompt or remind students to use critical cognitive processes that they might not otherwise employ. Graham & Harris (1989b) describe a writing strategy that can be employed to teach essay writing skills. It utilizes a mnemonic (**TREE**) to provide four prompts:

1. **Topic.** Note the Topic sentence
2. **Reasons.** Note the Reasons
3. **Examine.** Examine the reasons, asking "Will my reader buy this?"
4. **Ending.** Note the Ending

The mnemonic and its prompts correspond to the general framework for producing arguments (e.g., premise, reasons or data to support the premise, and conclusion). A chart providing the mnemonic can be placed in front of the students, with the teacher modeling the use of the strategy by thinking out loud while writing the essay. The instructor models four additional types of self-instruction during the planning and writing of the essay: (1) problem definition, (2) planning, (3) self-evaluation, and (4) self-reinforcement. Following modeling, the instructor and students discuss the importance of "What we say to ourselves while we work." Students then generate and record on small charts their own examples of the four previously mentioned types of self-instruction during the essay planning and writing stages. Following modeling, the instructor and students discuss the importance of self-talk. Students than generate and record on small charts their own examples of the four types of self-instruction. This strategy can result in substantial improvements in the essay elements that students generate (Graham and Harris, 1989b).

Setting product goals for what a paper will accomplish and articulating process goals for achieving these goals is the focus of another strategy that has proved effective with students with learning disabilities (Graham, MacArthur, Schwartz & Voth, 1989). The mnemonic **PLANS strategy** represents four prompts for planning a paper:

1. **P**ick goals (goals related to length, structure, and purpose)
2. **L**ist ways to meet goals
3. **A**nd make
   Notes
4. **S**equence the notes

The mnemonic is embedded in a three-step executive writing strategy: (1) Do PLANS, (2) Write and say more, (3) Evaluate if you were successful in achieving your goals. Using this strategy, Graham et al. found that students can produce essays that are longer, more complete, and qualitatively better when compared with pretest essays. A single practice session can result in the desired generalization for all students.

Specific Writing Problems.   Programs such as those described previously address writing problems due to poor organizational skills, failure to employ text structures well, and lack of writing strategies. Two additional areas of concern relate to the mechanics of writing and writing productivity.

Writing Mechanics.   **Writing mechanics** encompass spelling, grammatical, and punctuation considerations. Writing problems related to these areas can stem from: (1) inadequate instruction in these areas and/or (2) inadequate emphasis on self-monitoring and self-control training. Suffi-

cient instructional time should be allocated for students who need assistance in mastering the mechanics of writing.

For spelling difficulties, it is helpful for teachers to directly instruct students on high-frequency spelling words using commercial sight word lists (e.g., Dolch sight word list) and selecting frequently misspelled words from students' compositions. When writing draft compositions, students can be encouraged to use invented spellings when they cannot remember the correct spellings of words. When teaching writing, teachers must be sensitive to the developmental spelling abilities of students (see Chapter 9 on the discussion of spelling).

For grammatical and punctuation difficulties, direct instruction in targeted skills should follow a teaching sequence similar to that used for introducing a new concept. Essentially, teachers should present concept rules for particular writing skills (e.g., for detecting sentence fragments); present examples and nonexamples of the concept; provide discrimination practices; and finally, provide practice in detecting (and correcting) the target concepts in sentences and passage contexts.

At times, students may learn new mechanical skills in isolation but fail to apply the skills in contexts. These students may not have learned sufficient self-monitoring and self-control skills. To foster students' abilities to self-monitor and apply mechanical skills in writing contexts, teachers may want to consider using the **COPS strategy** (Schumaker, Deshler, Alley, Warner, Clark, & Nolan, 1982), an instructional strategy that focuses on prompting students to self-monitor written drafts for mechanical errors. In the COPS strategy, students interrogate themselves and "COPS" a written draft by asking themselves the following self-questions:

- Have I **C**apitalized the first word and the proper nouns?
- (**O**)verall appearance—Have I made any handwriting, margin, messy, or spacing errors?

- Have I used <u>P</u>unctuation, commas, and semi-colons correctly?
- Do the words look like they are <u>S</u>pelled right? Can I sound them out or should I use the dictionary?

Schumaker et al. (1982) found that secondary students with learning disabilities trained in using the COPS strategy improved in their abilities to detect and correct mechanical errors in their own and others' writings. COPS is a useful strategy that can be used as part of self-editing or peer editing. Given the limited attention capacity of many students with learning disabilities, attention should not be unduly focused upon mechanical skills during drafting.

Mechanical skills should be considered as part of the editing and revising processes rather than the drafting subprocess of writing. If students concentrate on mechanical skills during drafting, they will have little attention remaining to focus upon more important content or text-level concerns. In addition, mechanical skills are best taught in the context of students' own writings rather than in isolation (Bos, 1988). This means that targeted mechanical skills should be selected based upon the types of problems observed in children's writings and students should be instructed within the context of their own written drafts.

Writing Productivity. **Writing productivity** refers to the number or quantity of words in students' papers. Better writers are able to write longer messages. Further, fluency is significantly correlated with other measures of writing skills. Students with learning problems typically produce written papers that contain significantly fewer words than the papers of their peers. One approach to addressing this shortcoming is to provide frequent practice, as described earlier in this chapter. Increased levels of direct instruction also may be required.

Teachers can count and graph the number of words or targeted word classes (e.g., adjectives) in students' papers. Once a baseline measure of performance has been graphed over several days, teachers can share the graphs with students and simply instruct them to increase either the number of words written or their use of particular word classes. By graphing performance over time and sharing the results with students, the quantity of students' written products is likely to increase. For greater impact on performance, students can be involved in the intervention program by self-assessing, self-recording, and self-reinforcing their own writing performance (Ballard & Glynn, 1975).

Self-instructional strategy training can increase the range of children's written vocabulary (Harris & Graham, 1985). A strategy for increasing students' use of verbs, for example, directs students to do the following:

1. Look at a picture and write down good action words.
2. Think of a good story idea to use my words in.
3. Write my story—make sense and use good action words.
4. Read my story and ask—"Did I write a good story?"
5. Fix my story—"Can I use more good action words?"

Self-instructional prompts such as these enhance students' abilities to brainstorm, define the problems (e.g., "What is it I have to do?"), self-evaluate, and self-reinforce. Once students become familiar with the strategy, self-regulation procedures can be introduced. These procedures require students to set specific goals related to the amount and types of vocabulary they can include in their compositions, to graph performance, to evaluate their success in achieving their goals, and to establish a new goal for their next stories.

This approach has been shown to result in substantial increases above baseline levels in the number of action verbs, adjectives, and total number of words (Harris & Graham, 1985). The research showed that not only were the postintervention stories rated qualitatively superior to those written during baseline, but that generalization from the training setting to another setting was obtained and maintained for up to 6 weeks. Clearly, self-instructional programs can be highly effective in increasing the diversity of students' written vocabulary and in generalizing their productivity to new contexts.

ASSESSMENT

The assessment of writing progress helps teachers adjust the writing programs to meet students' needs. In this section, two questions relating to teachers' evaluations of students' knowledge and performance are addressed: (1) What can teachers look for when examining students' writing samples? and (2) What can teachers talk to students about in interviews or observe when they ask students to write?

Writing Samples

To evaluate students' drafting strategies, teachers can ask students to generate different types of compositions to determine their sensitivity to different text structures, writing purposes, and audiences. For example, teachers can ask students to generate the following types of compositions: (1) story narrative (e.g., "You have read many different stories in your reader. Write a story that might appear in your reader. You can write it for students of any age."); (2) comparison/contrast (e.g., "Write a paper in which you compare and contrast two things—that is, tell how two things are alike and are different, such as two places, people, or things."); (3) explanation (e.g., "Write a paper in which you explain how to do something, such as how to play a game or make a certain type of food."); and (4) expert paper (e.g., "Everyone knows something about which they are an expert. For example, you may have a hobby, game, or a sport about which you know a great deal. Pick something you know well. Write a paper about it in which you teach someone about your topic."). Table 11.3 presents sample evaluation criteria for the explanation and the comparison/contrast genre.

To evaluate students' writings, teachers can calculate the percentage of the text structure features that are present in students' papers. Teachers can adapt the evaluation forms to different text structures by changing the text structure features in the section entitled "Primary Trait Score."

Interviewing Students. In addition to examining students' written products, teachers should talk to students about texts—their own and others' texts. To assess students' knowledge of the writing process, teachers can develop questions that tap students' declarative knowledge, that is, their abilities to describe strategies for planning, organizing, writing, editing, and revising texts. Englert, Raphael, Fear and Anderson (1988) developed an example of one such interview to evaluate children's knowledge about writing. This interview used hypothetical students with writing problems to elicit students' thinking about writing. Table 11.4 shows sample questions from the interview to evaluate students' knowledge about planning and editing.

As is evident in the interview, teachers can evaluate children's abilities to plan and organize their papers by asking questions such as: "What are the steps the writer can follow in writing this paper? Where can a writer get ideas for a paper like this? How can a writer organize her ideas before she begins to write?" Teachers also can assess children's abilities to activate information from background knowledge and organize that knowledge through a series of questions that have them brainstorm ideas about a particular topic (e.g., "What kinds of information would you include in a report about _____ ?"), and their abilities to look back at their brainstormed ideas and organize the ideas into categories (e.g., "Which of the ideas you have generated belong together? What can you call that group of ideas?").

To evaluate editing strategies, teachers can select written stories and ask the students to evaluate and edit them. Interview questions require that students respond to the passages, identify and describe the problems in the texts, and correct problems (see Table 11.2). The ease with which students can identify text-level problems

TABLE 11.3 Sample Evaluation Criteria for the Explanation and the Comparison/Contrast Genre

Comparison/Contrast Evaluation Criteria

Student's initials: _____   Examiner's name: _____

	Points			
	2	1	0	Score
1. Primary trait score (organization)				
Tell what was being explained?	Yes	Sort of	No	_____
Tell what things you need?	Yes	Sort of	No	_____
Name the steps clearly?	Yes	Sort of	No	_____
Use key words? (*first, second*)	Yes	Sort of	No	_____
Make it interesting?	Yes	Sort of	No	_____
Total				_____
Percentage				_____
2. Sense of expository text				
Does the author inform the reader rather than tell a story?	Yes	Sort of	No	_____
Is the paper "reader friendly" and "reader considerate?"	Yes	Sort of	No	_____
Total				_____
Percentage				_____
3. Holistic				
The overall rating this paper receives.	3	2	1	

Comparison/Contrast Evaluation Criteria

Student's initials: _____   Examiner's name: _____

	Points			
	2	1	0	Score
1. Primary trait score (organization)				
Tell what was being compared and contrasted?	Yes	Sort of	No	_____
Tell what they were being compared and contrasted on?	Yes	Sort of	No	_____
Tell how they were alike?	Yes	Sort of	No	_____
Tell how they were different?	Yes	Sort of	No	_____
Use key words? (*like, different*)	Yes	Sort of	No	_____
Make it interesting?	Yes	Sort of	No	_____
Total				_____
Percentage				_____
2. Sense of expository text				
Does the author inform the reader rather than tell a story?	Yes	Sort of	No	_____
Is the paper "reader friendly" and "reader considerate?"	Yes	Sort of	No	_____
Total				_____
3. Holistic				
The overall rating this paper receives.	3	2	1	

Source: C. S. Englert, T. E. Raphael, and L. M. Anderson (1989). *Cognitive Strategy Instruction in Writing Project.*
East Lansing, MI: Institute for Research on Teaching, Michigan State University. Reprinted with permission.

TABLE 11.4   Interview Questions for Planning

Here's the first student. Her name is Sally. She sent along a problem that she wants to ask you about. Her problem is this—she has a hard time getting her paper started. Yesterday, her teacher told the class to "Write about anything you want to write about." Sally said she just sat there. She didn't know what to say—or how to begin her paper.

1. *Planning: Sources of information*	What advice can you give Sally? What else can Sally do to think of ideas for her paper?
2. *Planning: Organizing ideas*	Before she starts writing, can Sally do anything to help organize her ideas?
3. *Planning: Steps in process*	I talked to Sally's teacher and she told me that next week everyone in class is going to pick a different wild animal and write a report about that wild animal. Can you tell Sally the steps she can follow in writing her report. (What can she do first? Second? Third?)
4. *Planning: Topic selection and idea generation*	Now let's give Sally even more specific advice. What animals can she write about? (List one or more animals and have students select an animal.) What kinds of information can Sally include in her report about this animal? (Record information on index cards).
5. *Planning: Predicting an organizing strategy*	Here's what you said Sally might talk about in her paper. (Review briefly.) I'm going to give these cards to Sally when I see her. How do you think she might use these cards? Anything else she can do with them?
6. *Planning: Grouping and categorizing ideas*	Look how you've ordered the cards. Do you see any ideas that can go together in a group? Put the cards that you think belong together in a small stack. If we were to put a blank card on top of the stack that has a word or phrase that tells Sally what all these ideas are about (what these ideas have in common), what would we write on it for Sally? (Record the information on the card. Report for each stack.)
7. *Planning: Knowledge of audience/purpose*	Look back over your cards. Would Sally use the exact same information in her paper if her teacher asked her to write a paper to convince her parents to let her keep this _____ as a pet? What would she include? Why would that information convince your parents? What wouldn't she include?
8. *Planning: Process report writing*	When I asked Sally's teacher what else you could do to help Sally improve her writing, the teacher said she really needed help writing reports. The teacher said next month each student has to write a report about two states. In the paper, students are to compare and contrast two states—they are supposed to tell how the states are alike and different. The teacher said Sally has family that live in Florida, and since she visits them often, it might be a good idea for Sally to write a report about how Florida and Michigan are alike and different. Can you suggest some things Sally might talk about in her paper? (Write down students' suggestions.)

Source: C. S. Englert, T. E. Raphael, and L. M. Anderson (1989). *Cognitive Strategy Instruction in Writing Project.* East Lansing, MI: Institute for Research on Teaching, Michigan State University. Reprinted with permission.

rather than mechanical problems is an important aspect of this part of the evaluation process. Of equal importance is students' abilities to describe and explain whether their papers are finished or not, and whether they invoke internal criteria (e.g., text structure and meaning) rather than external criteria (e.g., mechanics and length of papers) in describing the need for text changes.

Finally, students' observations and interviews with them as they plan, draft, and edit their own texts should be conducted to determine students' writing strategies and their sensitivity to audiences and purposes. Table 11.5 shows a sample checklist for evaluating observations and interviews. Essentially, observations and interviews with students should be conducted to help teachers corroborate students' awareness of the strategies for performing the writing process. For example, planning involves students' sensitivities to purposes, audiences, and background knowledge; drafting entails students' awarenesses of how to transcribe plans into texts and to distance themselves from their texts; and editing involves students' abilities to monitor their texts and employ fix-up strategies when communication breakdowns are detected.

To evaluate the effects of intervention strategies over time, teachers simply need to re-administer the writing measures, examining changes in students' applications of text structure features in their written drafts and their knowledge of planning, drafting, and editing strategies.

SUMMARY

In this chapter, attention has been focused on the writing processes and problems encountered by many students with learning difficulties. It presents instructional procedures and strategies that can teach written expression, assess writing progress, and remediate writing difficulties.

The first portion of the chapter describes the writing subprocesses related to planning, organizing, drafting, and editing. It stresses the roles of self-questions and self-regulation in activating relevant strategies to plan, monitor, and check performance. Students must learn important language skills and strategies related to planning, drafting, and editing. In addition, they must develop self-regulating mechanisms to determine the efficacy of chosen writing strategies. Finally, teachers must be sensitive to the writing problems of students in order to assess writing knowledge and skills, prescribe appropriate instructional strategies, and evaluate instructional effects.

The second portion of the chapter describes various approaches for teaching written expression. Until recently, writing programs have tended to focus on the mechanical difficulties of many students. Currently, evolving efforts focus on the cognitive complexities of the writing process. The focus is on immersing students in the writing process and teaching them the strategies that mature, self-regulating writers use to compose texts.

This instruction emphasizes teachers' modeling through classroom dialogues. Teacher think alouds can make the processes of writing visible to students by addressing the underlying thought processes that guide composing. Think alouds provide models of the composing processes and the structures that underlie the production of well-organized prose. Specific instruction in the organizational structures that underlie text increases students' control of those structures in planning, organizing, drafting, editing, and revising text. In some cases, additional direct instruction to improve students' mechanical skills or increase written productivity is necessary. The chapter delineates one curriculum specifically developed to teach strategic thinking for writing, the CSIW program. It also describes other similar strategies that can be used to prompt using cognitive processes. Two mnemonics are described, TREE and PLANS.

The chapter underscores the importance of classrooms as literacy environments in which students become aware of the questions and needs of their audiences. Peer writing partners can provide feedback about communication breakdowns and about the information needs of readers. When stu-

TABLE 11.5 Interview Questions for Editing

This is another student. Her name is Pamela. Pamela's teacher asked her to write a paper in which she compared and contrasted two places—like two restaurants, two cities, two streets, or two countries. Pamela was supposed to tell how the two places were alike and how they were different. She started to write her paper, but she wasn't sure she was doing it right. Let's read what she has written.

> Some ways McDonald's and Ponderosa Steak House is alike.
> McDonalds has a playgrownd it is fun. they go out and pick the flowers.

1. *Monitoring: Use of text structure in monitoring text*	Pamela was supposed to tell how two places are alike and how they are different. Look back at her paper. Is she doing the assignment right?
2. *Monitoring: Use of text structure to check finishing*	Is Pamela's paper finished? How do you know? What can she do now?
3. *Monitoring: Fixing-up stories*	Let's help Pamela by editing the part of the paper she has written. I'll read the story aloud while you read along. When we're finished, we'll see if anything needs to be changed. Is there anything that needs to be changed? (Why?) Let's fix those things that you think can be changed. What should we change first? How should we change it? (Examiner should make changes on story. Read changes back to student.) Pamela thought that it might help her if you would show her how to finish her paper. I'll repeat the assignment again so that you know what the paper is supposed to be about. Pamela's teacher asked her to compare and contrast two places. In other words, this paper is supposed to tell how two places are alike and how they are different. To help her, write the next part for her. You can either write it yourself, or dictate the next part to me, I'll write it for you.

Source: C. S. Englert, T. E. Raphael, and L. M. Anderson (1989). *Cognitive Strategy Instruction in Writing Project.* East Lansing, MI: Institute for Research on Teaching, Michigan State University. Reprinted with permission.

dents begin to internalize the questions of their partners, they can use these questions as guides to drafting when the partners are no longer present. This approach fosters a communicative context in which writers learn to anticipate and address the questions of a distant audience.

The final section of the chapter focuses on how teachers can monitor and measure writing progress to determine the efficacy of the writing curriculum. Teachers can assess students' competence in using different forms of text structures through observation of writing samples and through student interviews. The resulting data provide a basis for redirecting instructional attention to those processes and strategies that are insufficiently developed. In remedial instruction, as in initial developmental writing instruction, the focus should remain on writing as a thinking and problem-solving process.

CONTENT MASTERY QUESTIONS

1. Identify the two related subprocesses writers engage in during the prewriting stage of the writing process.

2. Describe the goals, skills, and activities of the drafting stage.

3. Discuss the implications of five editing challenges that unskilled writers face during the editing stage of the writing process.

4. List key features of an effective writing environment.

5. Identify advantages of and use of both teacher-selected and child-selected topics.

6. List the text structure questions for narrative and expository texts.

7. Describe key elements of a narrative story frame.

8. Describe ways in which teachers can model the cognitive processes and strategic thinking involved in writing.

9. Discuss the applications of think sheets of the CSIW program.

10. Identify uses of mnemonic strategies for teaching essay writing skills.

11. Describe instructional practices to remediate problems in writing mechanics and productivity.

12. Discuss and describe the two-step process for assessing the student's knowledge of the writing process and text organization.

REFERENCES

Alley, G., and Deshler, D. (1979). *Teaching the learning disabled adolescent: Strategies and methods.* Denver: Love.

Armbruster, B. B., & Anderson, T. H. (1984). *Producing considerate expository texts: Or easy reading is damned hard writing* (Reading Education Report No. 46). Urbana: University of Illinois, Center for the Study of Reading.

Ballard, K., & Glynn, T. (1975). Behavioral self-management in story writing with elementary school children. *Journal of Applied Behavior Analysis, 8,* 387–398.

Barenbaum, E. M. (1983). Writing in the special class. *Topics in Learning and Learning Disabilities, 3*(3), 12–20.

Bartlett, E. J. (1981). *Learning to write: Some cognitive and linguistic components.* Washington, DC: Center for Applied Linguistics.

Bereiter, C., & Scardamalia, M. (1982). From conversation to composition: The role of instruction in a developmental process. In R. Glaser (Ed.). *Advances instructional psychology* (Vol. 2, pp. 1–64). Hillsdale, NJ: Lawrence Erlbaum & Associates.

Bos, C. S. (1988). Process oriented writing with mildly handicapped students. *Exceptional Children, 54,* 521–527.

Bos, C. S., & Filip, D. (1984). Comprehension monitoring in learning disabled and average students. *Journal of Learning Disabilities, 17,* 229–233.

Calkins, L. M. (1986). *The art of teaching writing.* Portsmouth, NH: Heinemann.

Cohen, S. B., & Plaskon, S. P. (1980). *Language arts for the mildly handicapped.* Columbus, OH: Charles E. Merrill.

Englert, C. S. (1990). Unraveling the mysteries of writing through strategy instruction. In T. E. Scruggs and B. Y. L. Wong (Eds.), *Intervention research in learning disabilities* (pp. 186–223). NY: Springer–Verlag.

Englert, C. S., & Raphael, T. E. (1989). Developing successful writers through cognitive strategy instruction. In J. E. Brophy (Ed.), *Advances in research on teaching* (vol. 1. pp.105–151). Greenwich, CT: JAI Press.

Englert, C. S., & Raphael, T. E. (1988). Constructing well-formed prose: Process, structure, and metacognitive knowledge. *Exceptional Children, 54,* 513–520.

Englert, C. S., Raphael, T. E., & Anderson, L. M. (in progress). *Teaching cognitive strategies to mildly handicapped students: A classroom intervention study.* East Lansing, MI: Institute for Research on Teaching, Michigan State University.

Englert, C. S., Raphael, T. E., & Anderson, L. M. (1986, December). *Metacognitive knowledge and writing skills of upper elementary students and students with special needs: Extensions of text structure research.* Paper presented at the National Reading Conference, Austin, TX.

Englert, C. S., Raphael, T. E., Fear, K., & Anderson, L. M. (1988). Students' metacognitive knowledge about how to write informational texts. *Learning Disability Quarterly, 11,* 18–46.

Englert, C. S., Raphael, T. E., Anderson, L. M., Anthony, H., Fear, K., & Greggs, S. (1988). A case for writing intervention: Strategies for writing information text. *Learning Disabilities Focus, 3,* 98–113.

Englert, C. S., Stewart, S. R., & Hiebert, E. H. (1988). Young writers' use of text structure in expository text generation. *Journal of Educational Psychology, 80,* 143–151.

Faigley, L., & Witte, S. (1983). Analyzing revision. *College Composition and Communication, 32,* 400–414.

Fitzgerald, J., & Teasley, A. B. (1986). Effects of instruction in narrative structure on children's writing. *Journal of Educational Psychology, 78,* 424–432.

Florio-Ruane, S., & Dunn, S. (1985). *Teaching writing: Some perennial questions and some possible answers.* (Occasional Paper No. 85). East Lansing, MI: Michigan State University, Institute for Research on Teaching.

Florio-Ruane, S. and Lensmire, T. (1989). The role of instruction in learning to write. In J. E. Brophy (Ed.), *Advances in research on teaching* (Vol. 1, 73–104). Greenwich, CT: JAI Press.

Graham, S., & Harris, K. R. (1988). Instructional recommendations for teaching writing to exceptional students. *Exceptional Children, 54,* 506–512.

Graham, S., & Harris, K. R. (1989a). Components analysis of cognitive strategy instruction: Effects on learning disabled students' compositions and self-efficacy. *Journal of Educational Psychology, 81,* 353–361.

Graham, S., & Harris, K. R. (1989b). Improving learning disabled students' skills at composing essays: Self-instructional strategy training. *Exceptional Children, 56,* 201–214.

Graham, S., MacArthur, C., Schwartz, S., & Voth, T. (in press). Improving LD students' compositions using a strategy involving product and process goal-setting. *Exceptional Children.*

Graves, D. H. (1975). An examination of the writing processes of seven-year-old children. *Research in the Teaching of English, 9,* 227–241.

Graves, D. H. (1982). Break the welfare cycle: Let writers choose their topics. *Forum, 3,* 75–77.

Graves, D. H. (1983). *Writing: Teachers and children at work.* Portsmouth, NH: Heinemann.

Harris, K., & Graham, S. (1985). Improving learning disabled students' composition skills: Self-control strategy training. *Learning Disability Quarterly, 8,* 27–36.

Hayes, J. R., & Flower, L. S. (1987). On the structure of the writing process. *Topics in Learning Disorders, 7,* 19–30.

Hayes, J. R., Flower, L. S., Schriver, K., Stratman, J., & Carey, L. (1985). *Cognitive processes in revision* (Tech. Rep. No. 12). Pittsburgh, PA: Carnegie Mellon University, Communication Design Center.

Hayes, J. R., Schriver, K. A., Spilka, R., & Blaustein, A. (1986, March). *If it's clear to me, it must be clear to them.* Paper presented at the Conference on College Composition and Communication. National Council of Teachers of English, New Orleans.

Hillocks, G. (1984). What works in teaching composition: A meta-analysis of experimental treatment studies. *American Journal of Education, 93,* 133–170.

Idol, L. (1987). Group story mapping: A comprehension strategy for both skilled and unskilled readers. *Journal of Learning Disabilities, 20,* 196–205.

Kameenui, E. J., & Simmons, D. C. (1990). *Designing instructional strategies: The prevision of academic learning problems.* Columbus, OH: Merrill.

Kerchner, L. B., & Kistinger, B. J. (1984). Language processing/word processing: Written expression, computers, and learning disabled students. *Learning Disability Quarterly, 7,* 329–335.

Langer, J. A. (1984, December). *Reading and writing in school-age children.* Paper presented at the National Reading Conference, St. Petersburg, FL.

Lee, J. W. (1987). Topic selection in writing: A precarious but practical balancing act. *The Reading Teacher, 41,* 180–184.

Meyer, B. J. F. (1975). *The organization of prose and its effects on memory.* Amsterdam: North-Holland.

Nodine, B. F., Barenbaum, E., & Newcomer, P. (1985). Story composition by learning disabled, reading disabled and normal children. *Learning Disability Quarterly, 3,* 46–53.

Nystrand, M. (1990). Sharing words: The effects of readers on developing writers. *Written Communication, 70*(1), 3–24.

Raphael, T. E., & Englert, C. S. (1990). Writing and reading: Partners in constructing meaning. *The Reading Teacher, 43,* 388–400.

Reid, D. K. (1988). *Teaching the learning disabled: A cognitive developmental approach.* Boston: Allyn & Bacon.

Richgels, D. J., McGee, L. M., Lomax, R. G., & Sheard, C. (1987). Awareness of four text structures: Effects on recall of expository text. *Reading Research Quarterly, 22,* 177–196.

Roit, M. L., & McKenzie, R. G. (1985). Disorders of written communication: An instructional priority for LD students. *Journal of Learning Disabilities, 18,* 258–260.

Rubin, D. L. (1987). Divergence and convergence between oral and written language. *Topics in Language Disorders, 7,* 1–18.

Scardamalia, M., & Bereiter, C. (1986). Research on written composition. In M. C. Wittrock (Ed.), *Handbook of research on teaching* (3rd ed., pp.778–803). New York: Macmillan.

Schumaker, J., Deshler, D., Alley, G., Warner, M., Clark, F., & Nolan, S. (1982). Error monitoring: A learning strategy for improving adolescent performance. In W. M. Cruickshank and J. W. Lerner (Eds.), *Best of ACLD* (Vol. 3, pp. 170–183). Syracuse: Syracuse University Press.

Ulichny, P., & Watson-Gegeo, K. A. (1989). Interactions and authority: The dominant interpretive framework in writing conferences. *Discourse Processes, 12,* 309–328.

Vallecorsa, A. L., Ledford, R. R., & Parnell, G. G. (1991). Strategies for teaching composition skills to students with learning disabilities. *Teaching Exceptional Children, 23,* 52–55.

Walmsley, S. A. (1984). Helping the learning disabled child overcome writing disabilities in the classroom. *Topics in Learning and Learning Disabilities, 3*(4), 81–90.

Williams, J. P. (1986). Teaching children to identify the main idea of expository texts. *Exceptional Children, 53,* 163–168.

CHAPTER 12

Effective Mathematics Instruction for All Students

NADINE S. BEZUK
PATRICIA THOMAS CEGELKA

CHAPTER OBJECTIVES

At the conclusion of this chapter, the reader will be able to:

1. Describe the new direction for mathematics curricula for all students.
2. Discuss students' characteristics related to mathematics learning.
3. Delineate instructional guidelines for teaching mathematical concepts to all students.
4. Discuss effective teaching strategies for content within the mathematics skill sequence.
5. Describe activities and materials for effective mathematics teaching throughout the mathematics skill sequence.

One of the essential basic tool subjects, mathematics involves the mastery of specific vocabulary and concepts, as well as computational skills, procedures, problem-solving strategies, and various forms of higher mathematics. Despite the broad array of skills and concepts required for mastery, and the increasing importance of mathematical skills in this technological age, math is often a neglected area of the curriculum. As little as 20 minutes a day may be allocated to math instruction in elementary schools (Mastropieri & Scruggs, 1987), with only a fraction of this being teacher-led instruction. Instead, approximately 35% of the math time in first- and second-grade classes; and 55% of the time in third-, fourth-, and fifth-grade classrooms is devoted to independent seatwork (Baker & Zigmond, 1989). Most of the instruction focuses on rote learning of arithmetic facts, completing worksheets, and rote pacing through the textbook. As a result, many students will fail to master basic math facts and procedures, and even greater numbers will have difficulty applying mathematics knowledge to real- world situations or in solving non-routine problems. Students will leave schools without the mathematical proficiencies required for productive lives, unable to compete internationally in mathematical accomplishments and poorly prepared to sustain our technological-based society (National Research Council, 1989).

Analyses of the disparity between current achievement trends and societal needs for higher levels of math proficiency have led to a call to reconceptualize mathematics instruction. Proponents point out that in this age of science and technology (Mathematical Sciences Education Board, 1989, p.3), "The rudimentary skills that satisfied the needs of the workplace in the past no longer suffice. . . . Workers are less and less expected to carry out mindless, repetitive chores. Instead, they are engaged actively in team problem-solving, talking with their co-workers and seeking mutually acceptable solutions."

Reform recommendations encompass fundamental changes in the design of curriculum and delivery of instruction. Contemporary mathematics education currently is experimenting with theoretically grounded approaches for attaining new kinds and levels of math proficiency. By stressing the development of underlying comprehension over rote memorization and application, these approaches may result in increased overall math functioning for many students while at the same time precluding difficulties from developing in many students who otherwise might experience achievement problems in math.

This chapter overviews these reform efforts, describes math curricula, and reviews the skills necessary to succeed in these curricula and the related characteristics of many low-achieving students. It then recommends instructional procedures to assist students with learning difficulties to master these basic skills and concepts, and describes activities designed to promote competent, higher-order mathematics thinking.

THE CHANGING FOCUS OF MATHEMATICS INSTRUCTION

Criticisms of current math instruction have focused on the limited scope of mathematics typically included in elementary and secondary school programs. A major concern has been the relative emphasis given to efficient computation at the cost of promoting mathematical understanding, problem solving, and reasoning. The widespread use of calculators and computers make high levels of computation efficiency less necessary. At the same time they require that workers have more highly developed abstract reasoning and strategic thinking skills. To cope confidently with the demands of today's society, the individual must grasp the implications of the mathematical concepts (e.g., change, logic, and graphs) that permeate daily news and routine decisions.

The National Council of Teachers of Mathematics (NCTM) (1989) recommended that the elementary math curriculum be broadened beyond its traditional focus on arithmetic computation to include more emphasis on conceptual understanding as well as on current underrepresented mathematics domains such as geometry, measurement, and statistics. Recommendations for improved instruction include greater levels of active student involvement in such activities as abstracting, applying, convincing, classifying, inferring, organizing, representing, inventing, generalizing, specializing, comparing, explaining, patterning, validating, proving, conjecturing, analyzing, counting, measuring, synthesizing, and ordering.

NEW DIRECTIONS IN MATHEMATICS CURRICULA

The evolving focus of math instruction decreases the emphasis on manipulating symbols and memorizing rules, and devotes more attention to investigating and understanding variables, expressions, and equations. The NCTM has advocated conceptually oriented math curricula that actively involve children in doing mathematics, emphasizing the development of children's mathematical thinking and reasoning abilities. Students would no longer be predominantly passive learners of rote addition, subtraction, multiplication, and division facts. Instead, they would be actively engaged in developing conceptual understanding based on their experiences with math. A stronger problem-solving emphasis includes using word problems, everyday problems, strategies for solving problems, and open-ended problems. Often overlooked areas such as geometry, measurement, probability and statistics, patterns, relationships, and functions are targeted for increased attention. Ideally, these topics would be taught together as an integrated whole, not as isolated topics, and the connections between them would be a prominent feature of the curriculum. Further, the curriculum should include a broad range of content, and make appropriate and ongoing use of calculators and computers.

The NCTM's (1989) *Curriculum and Evaluation Standards for School Mathematics* developed standards at three levels: elementary (Grades Kindergarten–4), middle schools (Grades 5–8), and secondary schools (Grades 9–12). Each level contains general standards common to all grade levels as well as more specific content standards for the particular level. This is illustrated in the outline of the Standards for the first two levels in Table 12.1.

TABLE 12.1   Curriculum and Evaluation Standards

GRADES Kindergarten–4
1: Mathematics as problem solving
2: Mathematics as communication
3: Mathematics as reasoning
4: Mathematical connections
5: Estimation
6: Number sense and numeration
7: Concepts of whole number operations
8: Whole number computation
9: Geometry and spatial sense
10: Measurement
11: Statistics and probability
12: Fractions and decimals
13: Patterns and relationships

GRADES 5–8
1: Mathematics as problem solving
2: Mathematics as communication
3: Mathematics as reasoning
4: Mathematical connections
5: Number and number relations
6: Number systems and number theory
7: Computation and estimation
8: Patterns
9: Algebra
10: Statistics
11: Probability
12: Geometry
13: Measurement

Source: National Council of Teachers of Mathematics, 1989.

Proposed math curricula emphasize using language in mathematics, encouraging students to talk about and express their ideas orally and/or in writing during early conceptual development activities. Hands-on experiences and activities would help students to develop relational understanding of mathematics, including conceptual knowledge, procedural knowledge, and the connections between the two. Students would come to recognize that the rules and processes of procedural knowledge have a conceptual basis and meaningful rationale, and that mathematics symbols are just a way to record or represent ideas and concepts. This focus on the relationships among mathematical skills and concepts would lead students to understand not only *how* but also *why* skills are applied.

Many of these recommendations are just beginning to be reflected in curriculum materials and programs. The early stage of development of this reformation means that it is not yet known which types of approaches are most effective and with which types of learners they are effective. This chapter discusses some issues to be considered when designing effective mathematics instruction aligned with these recommendations for students with learning and achievement problems.

STUDENT CHARACTERISTICS RELATED TO MATHEMATICS LEARNING

Some students with learning difficulties may qualify for placement in special education primarily because of difficulties with mathematics. One study found problems in mathematics achievement to be of major concern. For that sample of students identified as having learning disabilities, one-fourth had been placed in special education primarily for that reason and two-thirds required special assistance with math learning (McLeod & Armstrong, 1982). As much as 33% of the instructional time in special education resource rooms is spent on mathematics (Carpenter, 1985).

Russell and Ginsburg (1984) noted that students with difficulties in math tended to be competent in several areas of mathematics. They may have knowledge of the basic mathematical concepts and nonalgorithmic procedures (e.g., one-to-one correspondence and relative size), can count by tens, and may use insightful solutions that reduce the need for calculations. Students have difficulties, however, due to incomplete knowledge of basic skills and facts (e.g., counting, writing numerals, and automatic recall of basic facts), poorly developed mental arithmetic skills, and inadequate self-monitoring in written work. They also may exhibit difficulties in dealing with large numbers and in solving story problems. Immaturities or "bugs" in addition and subtraction, such as subtracting the upper, smaller number from the bottom number in a subtraction problem, can impede their math performances. Additional areas of difficulty encompass learning basic associations, computation, measurement, and separating relevant from irrelevant numerical information in story problems (Derr, 1985; Peters, Lloyd, Hasselbring, Goin, Bransford, and Stein, 1986; Englert, Culatta & Horn, 1987).

These difficulties may be related to a variety of learner characteristics. Among those that Reisman and Kauffman (1980) described as having relevance for math instruction are a slower rate of learning; poor memory; inadequate verbal skills; and difficulties with symbol systems, arbitrary associations, and in attending to salient features and relationships. In addition, many students have inadequate problem-solving strategies and may not have learned to make inferences, draw conclusions, or deal with abstractions. While it is unlikely that any given individual student would exhibit all these difficulties, the existence of one, or several, of these problems should be considered in planning and delivering instruction.

Rate and Amount of Learning

All children, regardless of rate of intellectual development, tend to develop quantitative concepts in the same order. According to Piagetian developmental theory, most normally developing children can understand operations with concrete materials at the age of 7 or 8 years old, signaling that they are ready for formal instruction in math. However, it may be another 2, 3, or even more years before some students with mild cognitive impairments or other learning difficulties reach these milestones. Hands-on experiences that can assist students in developing concrete operation concepts and skills include working with Cuisenaire rods and various Montessori materials (e.g., cylinder blocks, a counting box with spindles, bead frames, metric number rods, and learning boards with pegs and skittles for computation) and similar manipulatives.

While as many as 90% of students aged 9–12 years have mastered the conservation concept, this is true of only about half of the students with learning disabilities (Derr, 1985). Mastering the conservation principle means that the individual recognizes the quantitative value of a given substance remains constant even when the physical arrangement is changed. For example, the student will understand that a pint of liquid is still a pint regardless of whether it is in a tall, narrow cylinder or poured into a wide, flat pan. Derr explains that the child is able to hold in his mind that which he saw before and compare it to what he now sees, concluding that since nothing was taken away or added, the amount remains the same. Because conservation underlies so many mathematics concepts and operations, students who have not mastered it lack the prerequisite skills for instruction in topics such as regrouping, money conversion, or measurement equivalencies. Hands-on experiences in pouring liquid into containers or manipulating an array of blocks and then reversing these processes can underscore the principle that matter can be conserved. Through such activities as this, students can construct the concepts that are essential for true mathematical understanding.

Memory and the Need for Repetition

Memory plays an important role in learning math. Difficulties with initial attending to stimuli, coupled with the distractibility that is characteristic of some students with learning difficulties, can interfere with the process of storing information into memory. Students must be able to retain learning and to access this stored data in order to apply math concepts and skills, and to acquire new ones. Examples of mathematics-related memory problems include recalling the configuration of the digits 0–9, remembering the sequence for performing math operations, and applying math strategies. One study, for example, found that sixth graders with learning difficulties relied on less efficient counting strategies than on memory-retrieval strategies to solve basic addition facts (Geary, Widaman, Little, & Cormier, 1987). The slow reaction time of low achievers relative to basic addition algorithms can result from difficulties in determining which addend is larger and from which numeral to start counting. Figure 12.1 depicts computation errors due to failure to remember the sequence of operations.

In addition to a need for a variety of conceptually oriented activities, many learners with memory difficulties will benefit from planned instructional repetition. Repetition and drill can consolidate learning by underscoring for the learner the salient features of a task. Repetition as it relates to developing automaticity of skills is discussed in more detail later in this chapter.

Verbal Skills

Several mathematical relationships are embedded in our day-to-day use of language. Quantitative, spatial, and temporal concepts represented in our spoken language include the use of singular and plural forms; discrimination and the use of words such as *in/on, over/under,* and *in/out;* and the use of comparatives (e.g., *shorter, taller, more,* and *greater than*) and superlatives (e.g., *tallest* and *most*) to denote relationships. The use of different tenses structures problem situations temporally (e.g., *have/had*). Inflectional endings can change the mathematical meaning (e.g., *short/ shorter*) of a concept.

Quite early in life, children tend to acquire basic mathematical knowledge as a function of their everyday experiences (Russell & Ginsburg, 1984). They become proficient with the informal concepts of relative magnitude and employ self-taught strategies for solving basic problems. This is true across socioeconomic classes and international cultures. This early and widespread development of informal mathematical knowledge suggests that most children with learning difficulties tend to have adequately developed informal concepts and skills.

Mathematical language in and of itself is a precise form of communication that is unique unto itself. Words and symbols associated with the language of mathematics include **denominator, addend, polygon, function,** and **factor.** These typically are not included in the students' other reading matter and life experiences, but are present only during mathematics instructional periods. This means that mathematics vocabulary should be introduced in much the same manner as new words are introduced in reading lessons. Students should hear, speak, read, and write the terms at least six times during introductory lessons and have approximately thirty subsequent exposures, in contexts, over the following weeks. Capps and Cox (1991) have suggested that failure to adequately teach mathematics terms and symbols is a major contributing factor to low achievement in mathematics.

Lack of verbal sophistication and memory difficulties can impede math performance in several ways. Students may have difficulty remembering information provided in complex problems or the sequence of steps required for solutions. By orally labeling the steps of math processes while performing them ("I am adding the tens. I will carry one to the hundreds column. . . ."), the students can circumvent short-term memory problems, concentrate more intensely on given exercises or problem situations, and rehearse the math processes. Semantic and syntactical structures in the wording of story problems can serve as barriers to students' performances. Students who are not reading at their grade levels in all likelihood will have difficulty solving word problems provided in the math texts for their grade levels. Orally presenting problems, rewriting problem situations to control for vocabulary, and small group or peer-assisted learning experiences can partially compensate for some of these language and reading difficulties that impede math performances.

Mastering those symbols or *logographs* (e.g., symbols representing one or more words) associated with addition, subtraction, multiplication, division, and the equal sign is an important

$$\begin{array}{r} 36 \\ \times\ 32 \\ \hline 72 \\ 108\ \ \\ \hline 1152 \end{array}$$

(Added "carried one" twice)

$$\begin{array}{r} 37 \\ \times\ 37 \\ \hline 93 \end{array}$$

(left-to-right computation)

$$\begin{array}{r} 602 \\ -\ 328 \\ \hline 326 \end{array}$$

("8 - 2 = 6" "2 - 0 = 2", "6 - 3 = 3")

$$\begin{array}{r} 35 \\ \times\ 24 \\ \hline 120 \end{array}$$

("4 × 5 = 20", "4 × 3 = 12")

$$\begin{array}{r} 36 \\ \times\ 3 \\ \hline 48 \end{array}$$

("3 × 6 = 18", "1 + 3 = 4")

$$\begin{array}{r} 723 \\ -\ 136 \\ \hline 659 \end{array}$$

("6 + 3 = 9", "3 + 2 = 5", "7 - 1 = 6")
(Change operation within algorithm)

FIGURE 12.1   Computation Errors

component of the math curriculum. These symbols are arbitrary abstractions that must be mastered as part of math learning. This abstract reasoning can pose problems for students who have not progressed beyond concrete levels of thinking. Abstraction difficulties, in concert with inadequate development of prior knowledge and procedures, can make it difficult for some students to "discover" conceptual linkages among processes and to intuitively grasp relationships that are not directly taught to them.

Quantitative Relationships and Generalizations

The most basic math relationship is **one-to-one correspondence.** Mastering this concept is a prerequisite to understanding the mathematical ideas of equality, more than, and less than. Sequencing and matching elements of one set to the elements of another set is an example of lower-order math relationships. Out of these ideas students develop the concepts of equivalent sets with the same cardinal number property, thereby developing, for instance, the concept of *threeness* (Reisman & Kauffman, 1980).

Attending to Salient Features

The ability to identify and attend to the most relevant aspects of a situation is critical to the processes of abstracting and classifying. Students must disregard extraneous cues (e.g., color, size, and shape) to focus on the critical elements of the math tasks. They must differentiate the essential from the nonessential or irrelevant attributes, skills that are inadequately developed in many students with learning difficulties (Blankenship & Lovitt, 1976; Englert, Culatta, & Horn, 1987). When given extraneous numerical information (e.g., "Rita had four dolls. Rita had three puzzles. Rita had five apples. How many toys did Rita have?"), some students with learning difficulties will add all numerical information to obtain an answer of "twelve." They fail to actively comprehend the problem situation and to discriminate between essential and nonessential information. They incorrectly and rotely used all numbers without identifying those associated with *toys* (Englert et al., 1987).

The difficulties in dealing with extraneous information appear to be specific to the type of information included. Problems in separating essential from nonessential information may occur when the numerical information in the object position (e.g., three puzzles, and five apples) rather than with extraneous subject information.

Approach to Problem Solving

The manner in which students approach mathematics problems can predict the success of their problem-solving efforts. The extent to which they systematically identify the major procedures or operations called for, their skills in selecting problem-solving strategies, and their efficiency in implementing the relevant strategies and procedures accurately are critical considerations. Additional important characteristics are student persistence or perseverance, reliance on external feedback and encouragement, and self-monitoring skills. The ability to make decisions and judgments among alternatives as well as the ability to infer and hypothesize are components of creative problem solving. These skills are necessary for handling abstract and complex information (Reisman & Kauffman, 1980).

Abstraction and Complexity

Dealing with abstract information and complex situations is another area in which many students with learning problems encounter considerable difficulties. Due to slower cognitive development, and possible short-term and long-term memory deficits, they have more difficulty than their age-peers in classifying objects or ideas, finding logical relationships and making logical deductions, using similes and metaphors, generating hypotheses, and choosing among alternatives. These difficulties suggest a need to make problems more concrete, to restrict their complexity, and to teach students strategies for problem solving.

Additional Factors Associated with Mathematics Difficulties

Many educators believe that specific perceptual disabilities are the cause of some mathematics achievement difficulties. When students lose their places in solving algorithms, they may incorrectly read multidigit numbers and/or interpret geometric shapes incorrectly. They may have difficulties in discriminating between numbers, operation symbols, coins, and decimal places. They may tend to reverse digits in numbers and they may make errors in writing ordinal numbers or fractions. Poor organizational skills may lead to inaccuracies in organizing numerals into the correct columns.

Motivational factors associated with low sense of self-efficacy and "learned helplessness" also can impede math achievement (Bartel, 1982; Grimes, 1981). As a result of past academic failures, students may lack of confidence in their ability to perform well. As a result, they may come to believe that success or failure is under the control of agents and events external to them and that there is little that they can do to affect their academic performances. This can affect their interests in the subject areas as well as their motivation to work hard at achieving mathematics proficiency.

The exact nature of the effect of the relationship between these factors on math learning has not been empirically determined. However, many experts believe that inadequate instruction is the most frequent cause of learner difficulties relative to math achievement (Bartel, 1982). Teachers tend to be inadequately prepared to provide effective math instruction, situations that result in their scheduling little time for math, providing only abbreviated teacher-led instruction, developing few meaningful exploration activities for students, and focusing on rote-learning with math worksheets as the primary instructional vehicle. This rote-learning may, in fact, tend to foster student passivity and learned helplessness as they wait for teachers' questions, attempting to avoid questions for which they may not have the correct answers (Parner & Cawley, 1991). Inadequate conceptual understanding on the part of teachers; inflexibility in following a prescribed math curriculum; failure to adapt instruction to address the cognitive characteristics of the learners; and providing limited strategy training and insufficient

opportunities to practice, with too much focus on rote learning, all can adversely affect higher-level math achievement. The results can be incomplete learning and failure to generalize. A stronger emphasis on conceptual development, with more of a focus on independent, productive thinking and less on getting the correct answer, and the use of learning goals for students have been recommended as alternative approaches (Kamii, 1982; Cawley, 1985a).

INSTRUCTIONAL GUIDELINES

Instructional reform in math education has emphasized both discovery-oriented and cognitively guided approaches to mathematics learning. The **discovery-oriented approach** involves inductive learning, usually with minimal teacher-imposed structure, or through teacher-led discourse and argument, eventuating in "proving" a mathematical process and solution. The **cognitively guided approach** emphasizes the problem-solving aspect of mathematics, focusing on the solution strategies that students use.

The appropriateness of math instruction using primarily the discovery-oriented approach has been called into question relative to many learners with learning difficulties. Harris and Pressley (1989) noted that true discovery is rare, inefficient, and time consuming. Further, it is impossible for students to discover all that they need to know; discovery may be full of errors; some students experience high levels of frustration under discovery approaches, and only a small proportion of students may make most of the discoveries. Characteristics such as distractibility, short-attention spans, difficulties in mastering basic algorithms, difficulties in changing from one topic to another, and difficulties with abstractions point to the need for well-structured, systematically presented instruction (Lloyd & Keller, 1989). While embracing the use of manipulatives and teaching specific strategies, Lloyd and Keller propose that this instruction must be explicit and teacher directed, providing for guided practice and corrective feedback.

Instructional Materials

The mathematics instruction in most classrooms has as its core a basal mathematics series, typically one that has been adopted on a district-wide basis. **Basal programs** include student and teacher materials for sequentially planned instruction in Grades Kindergarten–6. Each of the ten to twelve topical units at each grade focuses on a particular set of related skills such as addition, subtraction, multiplication, and division. Basal series traditionally have taken a spiral approach, repeating (NCTM, 1989, p. 66) "topics, approaches and level of presentation in grade after grade." In practice, this often has resulted in curricular fragmentation as well as boring, unnecessary repetition of many topics and superficial coverage of others. For example, one study found that teachers devote less than 30 minutes in instructional time across the entire year to 70% of the topics they covered (Porter, 1989). In addition to superficial coverage and extensive repetition, other criticisms of basal math series have included inadequate practice and preview, lack of real-life problems, inadequate use of concrete objects, and poorly developed teachers' guides. Current revisions of these basals are attempting to address many of these issues, particularly those having to do with fragmentation of concepts and skills, rote learning, and inadequate real-life practice.

Cawley's (1984) textbook, *Developmental Teaching of Mathematics for the Learning Disabled*, provides further discussion of conceptually oriented, discovery-based approaches to teaching mathematics to students with learning textbook difficulties. Cawley, Fitzmaurice-Hayes, and Shaw's (1988) *Mathematics for the Mildly Handicapped: A Guide to Curriculum and Instruction*, provides additional specific instructional recommendations for using multidimensional problem-solving approaches to math instruction.

Science Research Associates (SRA) has been the key publisher for curriculum materials that provide for direct instructional approaches. A carefully sequenced instructional guide for teachers is the *Direct Instruction Mathematics* (Silbert, Carnine, & Stein, 1990). The most recent developmental SRA series, developed for all students with particular attention to those with special learning needs, is *Connecting Math Concepts* (Englemann & Carnine, 1991). This program emphasizes the connections among math concepts and the higher-order thinking skills associated with math proficiency. Carefully conceptualized and researched, the series organizes lessons by related strands, not single topics; provides both guided and independent practice; emphasizes problem solving; and includes ideas of cooperative learning, using manipulative materials, and expanding on the concepts taught.

In addition to basal or other comprehensive programs, many supplemental mathematics curriculum materials are available. Some are of a remedial nature or designed to provide practice on a specific set of skills. Others are collections of various manipulative materials that can be used effectively to develop conceptual understandings and to encourage experimentation. Examples of the latter include:

- **Cuisenaire rods (Cuisenaire Company of America).** Consisting of 291 wooden rods, with different lengths and colors representing different values. They are useful in teaching readiness skills, and computation of whole numbers and fractions.
- **Developmental Learning Materials for Math (Developing Learning Co.).** Appropriate for use in Grades Kindergarten–6, these materials include manipulatives for readiness development, number lines, balance scales, fraction cards, abacuses, metric materials, and various games to teach concepts and procedures.
- **Montessori materials (Educational Teaching Aids).** Manipulative materials including such items as cylinder blocks, bead frames, number cars, metric number roles, and learn-

ing boards with skittles and pegs for computation. They provide concrete learning experiences for students.

- **Structural Arithmetic (Houghton Mifflin Co.).** Four kits, one each for Grades Kindergarten–3, this program provides concrete materials, student workbooks, and a teacher's guide for conducting math experiments that guide students in making discoveries about mathematical relationships and principles.
- **Unifix materials (Educational Teaching Aids).** The wide variety of materials, including interlocking Unifix cubes, can be used to teach basic arithmetic concepts and skills.

Lesson Delivery

A five-step instructional process has proven effective in teaching math to students with achievement difficulties. These steps include: (1) review, (2) teacher presentation and modeling, (3) high levels of active practice for all students, (4) systematic feedback and correction, and (5) seatwork/homework practice. Table 12.2 presents the guidelines for effective math instruction developed by the Missouri Mathematics Effectiveness Project (Good & Grouws, 1979).

Mathematics class can begin with a warm-up activity involving a word problem to solve, a short writing assignment (e.g., "Give me an example of a fraction and when you might use it."), or a few (perhaps five to ten) basic facts to practice. The purpose of a warm-up is to review prior learning and to get the students involved in thinking about mathematics. Class usually continues with the introduction or further development of a concept, or procedure. The teacher overviews the topic to be presented, and carefully chooses examples with which to model or demonstrate the fact, concept, or procedure. Whenever possible, the modeling should include manipulative materials, real-world objects, pictures, or diagrams. During this step, the teacher can guide students to recognize that the topic can be represented in more than one way. Additional practice on the topic can be provided through small group work involving manipulatives and other models that the teacher introduces. Working in small, heterogeneous groups to explore problem situations can be effective with students of a wide range of ability levels (Cohen, 1986). The group task should require conceptual thinking rather than memorization, rote practice, or simple rule application.

The teacher monitors the small group work by circulating around the room, asking and answering questions, correcting errors, and challenging students to persist in arriving at solutions. Lloyd and Keller (1989, p. 5) have noted that when "students answer questions or perform algorithms incorrectly, they provide one of the most important opportunities to teach." The teacher can analyze mistakes to determine if they are due to mistaken strategies, error in strategy application, failure to recall the basic facts, common computation "bugs," or inadequately developed preskills or conceptual understanding. The teacher can then provide correction in the form of modeling the algorithm and stating the correct fact, or teaching the prerequisite or procedural skills lacking. The teacher simply nodding, saying "yes," or repeating the student's correct answers also serve to reinforce accuracy (Lloyd & Keller, 1989). Students graphing their daily performances can decrease careless errors and increase correct responding (Fink & Carnine, 1975).

Instruction can close with a brief group discussion and search for consensus or generalizations. Seatwork and homework should provide approximately 15 minutes of independent practice to solidify and/or automatize skills already learned in the classroom. This independent practice can include games, work with manipulatives, and real-life tasks (e.g., measuring the floor, writing, making a pattern with silverware, and conducting small surveys), as well as drill and practice. The teacher can use computer software for drill and practice, for reteaching, and for review, and as simulations.

TABLE 12.2   Lesson Delivery Format: Recommendations for Effective Instruction from the Missouri Mathematics Effectiveness Project

Daily review (first 8 minutes except Mondays)
 a. Review the concepts and skills associated with the homework
 b. Collect and deal with homework assignments
 c. Ask several mental computation exercises

Development (about 20 minutes)
 a. Briefly focus on prerequisite skills and concepts
 b. Focus on meaning and promoting student understanding by using lively explanations, demonstrations, process explanations, and illustrations
 c. Assess student comprehension
  1. Using process/product questions (active interaction)
  2. Using controlled practice
 d. Repeat and elaborate on the meaning portion as necessary

Seatwork (about 15 minutes)
 a. Provide uninterrupted successful practice
 b. Momentum—keep the ball rolling—get everyone involved, then sustain involvement
 c. Alerting—let students know their work will be checked at end of period
 d. Accountability—check the students' work

Homework assignment
 a. Assign on a regular basis at the end of each math class except Fridays
 b. Should involve about 15 minutes of work to be done at home
 c. Should include one or two review problems

Special reviews
 a. Weekly review/maintenance
  1. Conduct during the first 20 minutes each Monday
  2. Focus on skills and concepts covered during the previous week
 b. Monthly review/maintenance
  1. Conduct every fourth Monday
  2. Focus on skills and concepts covered since the last monthly review

Source: From "The Missouri mathematics effectiveness project: An experimental study in fourth-grade classrooms" by T. L. Good and D. A. Grouws (1979). *Journal of Educational Psychology, 71*, pp. 355–362. Copyright 1979 by the American Psychological Association. Reprinted by permission.

TEACHING MATHEMATICS CONCEPTS AND PROCEDURES

Students are expected to learn a wide range of declarative and procedural mathematics knowledge. **Declarative knowledge** refers to factual knowledge about numbers and their relations, while **procedural knowledge** refers to knowing how to perform algorithms (e.g., the steps used to solve a mathematical problem). The scope of mathematics knowledge is represented in the NCTM Standards depicted earlier. A list of interrelated mathematical skills, beginning at the earliest stages of development, and continuing through secondary school, is presented as follows:

Prenumber and number concepts
Place value and basic symbols
Basic facts and algorithms
Fractions and decimals
Estimation and mental computation
Measurement

Algebra

Geometry

Real-life math problem solving

Some skill listings include money and time concepts as separate instructional categories; here they are viewed as being integrated into such categories as numeration, basic facts, estimation, fractions and decimals, and so forth. When teaching the skills and concepts related to each category, it is important to keep in mind that learning can occur at concrete, semiconcrete, and abstract levels. For example, at the *concrete level,* actual objects or manipulatives would be used; at the *semiconcrete level,* pictures or illustrations can be used (including slash marks or *x*'s on the chalkboard or paper); at the *abstract level,* numbers are gradually introduced to take the place of the pictures or slash marks.

Prenumber and Number Concepts

Young children need to learn about numbers and other important concepts such as counting, recognizing and writing numerals, and constructing and recognizing sets of various sizes. They also need experience with classification and comparison. All of these skills are important for further work in mathematics and in everyday life. For example, children need to be able to focus on various attributes of objects, such as sizes, colors, and thicknesses, and to make comparisons based on these attributes. Materials that are useful include collections of various everyday objects, such as buttons, bottle caps, and containers, as well as attribute blocks, which are sets of geometric shapes in various shapes, colors, sizes, and thicknesses.

When teaching number concepts, the initial emphasis should be on oral **rote counting,** then on identifying and counting out the correct number of objects, counting backward (a component skill of subtraction), and ordinal counting (e.g., first, second, third . . .). Recognizing and writing numerals comes later. Counting involves two separate skills: (1) knowing the number-word sequences and (2) making one-to-one correspondence between objects being counted and number words. In order to attach meaning to counting,

students must realize that the last number said when counting names the quantity of the set. It can be helpful for children, particularly those with learning difficulties and/or abstract learning problems, to deal with concrete objects when learning to count.

The *equality principle,* in which both sides of an equation depict the same numerical value, is a key concept that is critical for basic arithmetic strategies (e.g., adding and subtracting). The teacher should introduce mathematics vocabulary such as *more/less, next, following, by,* and *in/on.* The teacher can set up demonstrations with real objects during math instruction, lead "Simon says" games, and then emphasize these relationships throughout the day (e.g., "Put you books *on* your desk." "Put the pencil *next* to the paper.").

It is both natural and practical to relate the development of basic money concepts and skills with early number work. When children understand what *four* means, for example, they can count out four pennies as one model for the number. After number meanings to five have been developed, a follow-up might be to teach the equivalence of five pennies and one nickel. Carefully structured, money activities can reinforce number meanings and skills, helping the children see the connection between mathematics and their world. The importance of integrating money concepts throughout mathematics instruction is underscored by Halpern's (1981) estimate that 83% of the math that adults use deals with buying and selling, and that another 11% deals with money in other ways.

Instructional Recommendations: Prenumber and Number Concepts. Children can be taught to categorize similar items using the "I Know" activity. Here, the teacher names objects, shows pictures of objects, or uses real objects that belong together in some way, instructing the students to think about why the items are grouped together. When students figure it out, they should say "I know!" and describe the set named. For example, oranges, hamburgers, carrots, and cereal can be grouped together. They are foods people eat. Autos, buses, boats, and airplanes are all transportation items.

A similar activity is "Odd One Out." Here, the teacher arranges on a table or chalk ledge four items (e.g., pencils, cups, buttons, and hats) that are alike and one that is different. The children take turns finding the item that does not belong.

The One-Difference Game is an excellent way to provide practice in recognizing and classifying items on the basis of differences. The general rules governing the One-Difference Game can be modified to match the developmental level and capabilities of the children involved. They include:

1. Use some means to decide which child goes first. One possibility: the child who first draws a red block from the bag.
2. The first player selects a block from a mixed collection of blocks and places it in the middle of the working area. For example, a child might select a large red triangle.
3. The player to the left of the first player then selects a block which is the same as the one just played, with the exception of one attribute. This piece is then placed next to the first piece in the playing area. For example, a child might select a large red square, which is different from the large red triangle in one way: shape.
4. The next person then selects a block from those not yet played that differs from the last block in exactly one attribute. This piece is then played next to the last piece played. For example, a child might select a large yellow square, which is different from the large red square in one way: color.
5. Play continues with each student earning 1 point for each block correctly played. Any of the players can challenge the play. If a challenge holds, the person playing the challenger receives the point. If the challenge is not correct, the person challenging loses the next turn.

This game can also be played as a Two-Difference or a Three-Difference Game. Each of these is more difficult that the One-Difference Game and should only be played after the students have mastered the One-Difference Game.

Attaining proficiency at rote counting requires considerable practice for some students. Using a model-lead-test procedure, teachers should provide practices in counting, maintaining a lively pace. Distributed practices of 2–3 minutes each several times a day can curtail frustration and inattention, particularly when some of the practice opportunities are real-life trials (e.g., lining up for lunch or recess).

Once students can rote count, they can ten count objects to determine the quantity in the group. Using beads, blocks, or other materials, they can move each object to another part of the table or desk as it is counted, thereby reducing the likelihood of counting objects twice or skipping an object while counting. A container can be used as the "destination" for the counted objects. A piece of paper, a paper plate, or a cup can serve this purpose.

An activity to develop the concept of "one more" requires that the child place a specified number of items on the table, adding one more and counting how many there are now. For example: "Johnny, would you take six red chips from the box and place them on the table for me? . . . Now put just one more chip on the table. How many chips now? Let's count." The teacher can group the objects to form a sight group from which he can count. For instance, grouping the chips by three means that Johnny could count from either the three or the six to reach the correct answer of seven.

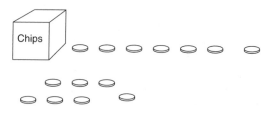

Recognizing and writing numerals can be developed through activities that integrate counting and symbol skills. Silbert, Carnine, and Stein (1990) recommend separating numerals and similar-sounding numbers during initial numeral identification instruction. For example, students may have difficulty visually discriminating between 6 and 9, and auditorily discriminating between "four" and "five." A sequence that separates these numerals would include: 4, 2, 6, 1, 5, 3, 8, 5, 9, 10.

"Feely" numbers can be used to focus student's attention on critical shape features by using large, textured numerals (made out of sandpaper or felt numerals; or those drawn with a broad felt-tipped pen and retraced with glue or covered with dry pasta or beans) that have three-dimensional effects. The teacher introduces a numeral by asking the child to finger-trace its shape and say its name. From the beginning, correct formation is stressed and cues are used to help the child remember the numeral shape: "The 1 is tall and straight. The 2 is a candy cane with a stick on the bottom. The 3 goes round and round like a busy bee. The 4 is tall sticks: down, over down." For children who experience particular difficulty, tracing numerals in sand trays might be helpful. Stencils can also be used to guide the formation of numerals, progressing to writing the numeral without the stencil, with the stenciled numeral serving as a pattern.

Children can use grease pencils to trace over or to finish numerals on laminated boards showing numerals with green dots indicating starting points and arrows indicating the direction to proceed. A variation on this is to place a prepared transparency of a numeral on the overhead so children can trace its image on the wall. After a numeral is traced, children clap as many times as is necessary to represent its value (three claps for the numeral three).

Place Value and Basic Symbols

A working knowledge of the ten concepts is crucial to accurate calculation. Inadequate development of base ten concepts may underlie many of the math deficiencies of students with learning difficulties (Russell & Ginsburg, 1984; Resnick, 1983). One study reported that as many as three-fourths of junior high school students with learning disabilities have significant difficulties with place value (McLeod & Armstrong, 1982). In order to become proficient in math, students must be able to read and write hundreds, thousands, ten thousands, and so forth, translating each digit into a value according to its position or place and then identifying the entire number. Understanding this ten-for-one or one-for-ten relationship is foundational to further work with operations. Students who do not understand this relationship will have difficulty with regrouping (i.e., "borrowing") in subtraction, handling money, and other applications.

Instructional Recommendations: Base Ten Numbers and Place Value. Once students have demonstrated the ability to read and write numbers from 1 to 10, they can be taught to read and write numbers in the teens, hundreds, thousands, and so forth. Carnine and Stein (1981) outlined a sequence for teaching numeration and place value to students with learning difficulties. They must learn the proper names for the numbers between 11 and 20 (e.g., with teens, one says the *ones* number first, e.g., *seventeen,* although this does not hold with irregular numbers, e.g., 12 is not *two*teen and 15 is not *five*teen). Once students can read and write teen numbers with some fluency, they should be taught to count by ones and by tens to 100. They should begin to read these numbers starting with the tens place (e.g., eight tens are 80, and six tens are 60). They also learn the irregular forms, for example, two tens are not "*twoty*" three tens are not "*threety*" and five tens are not "*fivety*." As a part of this instruction, students should be taught to expand numbers into their component parts, utilizing the symbols for addition (+) and equal, (=). For example, 12 = 1 ten + 2 ones and 85 = 8 tens + 5 ones. A place value grid can be helpful in initially teaching this concept:

Tens	Ones
8	5

Similar procedures can be used with numbers over 100. Expanded notation can be used to help students read and write numbers, and as an aid to column alignment. For example, students can learn to rewrite the number 546 into 500 + 40 + 6, or, in its vertical form:

$$
\begin{array}{r}
500 \\
40 \\
+6 \\
\end{array}
$$

Teachers can use manipulatives to help students develop the concepts of a base ten number system and place value. In selecting manipulatives for teaching place value, a critical criterion is the ease with which they show the ten-for-one and one-for-ten trades. Manipulative materials might include individual dry beans for ones and small cups to serve as containers for tens, bean sticks (which consist of individual dry beans for ones and ten beans glued to popsicle sticks for tens). **Base ten blocks** such as **Dienes' blocks** (which include *units* of 1 cubic centimeter, *longs* of 10 × 1 × 1 centimeters, *flats* of 10 × 10 × 1 centimeters or 100 units, and blocks of 10 × 10 × 10 centimeters, or 1000 units) may also be used. Edge and Ashlock (1982) found that it is equally effective to use only one type of manipulative as it is to use a variety.

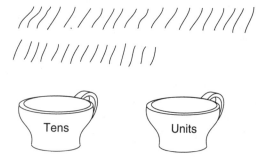

The completed task looks like this:

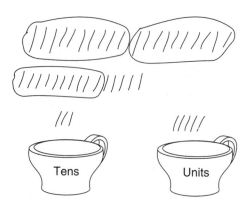

Individual students can use place value manipulatives such as chips or blocks to demonstrate two-digit numbers (e.g., 3 tens, 2 ones, or 4 tens, 6 ones). Provided with worksheets depicting ten spots, children are given sets of chips that they count by placing a chip on each of the spots. When all spots are covered, the children make a stack with their chips (tens unit) and repeat covering spots until they have used all the chips given to them. They then can take turns telling the number of stacks (tens) and leftovers (ones) they have.

2 stacks of 10 plus 6 leftovers = 26

Basic Facts and Algorithms

There are 390 **basic facts:** 100 addition, 100 subtraction, 100 multiplication, and 90 division facts. Math instruction should be designed to help students make connections between words, models, and symbols; to model the various operations with manipulatives; and to use thinking strategies to approach problem situations. Finally, instruction should provide drill-and-practice activities to assist in memorizing the facts.

Whole number addition and subtraction are based on the concept that joining elements to a set increases the number of elements in the set and removing elements decreases the number of elements in the set (Carpenter & Moser, 1984). Prerequisites to basic addition and subtraction include rote and rational counting, equality, numeral identification and writing numbers 0–10, equation reading, and counting from a number. Additional prerequisites for multidigit operations include place value and basic facts; and for subtraction, renaming. Addition and subtraction include join, separate, part-whole, and comparison problems.

In *join* and *separate* problems, action is involved. *Join* problems involve a situation in which a group is being increased. For example, "Maria had three apples. Her mother gave her two more. How many apples does Maria have now?"

Separate problems involve a situation in which a group is being decreased. For example, "Maria had five apples. She ate two apples. How many apples does she have now?"

In *part-whole* problems, no action is involved. Rather, these problems present situations in which a whole consisting of two parts is being described. For example, "Maria has three red apples and two green apples. How many apples does she have in all?"

Comparison addition and subtraction problems involve comparing two situations. The following are examples of comparison problems:

1. Maria has three apples. Tony has two more apples than Maria has. How many apples does Tony have?
2. Tony has five apples. Maria has two less apples than Tony has. How many apples does Maria have?
3. Maria has three apples. Tony has two apples. How many more apples does Maria have than Tony? (or How many less apples does Tony have than Maria?)

Students also need to learn about other laws or properties of arithmetic. The order property of addition, called the *commutative property,* indicates that the sum is the same regardless of the order in which numbers are added (e.g., $5 + 2 = 7$ and $2 + 5 = 7$). The *associative property of addition* states that any method of grouping may be used to obtain the sum of several addends. For example:

$$(2 + 3) + 3 = 8 \text{ or } 2 + (3 + 3) = 8$$
$$5 + 3 = 8; 2 + 6 = 8$$

The *effect of zero* (adding or subtracting zero does not change a number) and the *effect of one* in addition and subtraction problems also are important concepts. Students can explore what happens when the numbers are reversed in addition or subtraction problems, or what happens when a zero is in addition or subtraction problems. Understanding these relationships will facilitate students' later work with basic facts and algorithms.

In **renaming** numbers, students need to learn to convert sums of 10 or more into tens and units groups (e.g., 17 is 10 and 7) so that numbers can be aligned according to place value. This facilitates carrying of partial sums over 10. **Regrouping** is another name for renaming. For example:

$$7 + 4 = 11$$

Addition and Subtraction

According to Carpenter and Moser (1984), children approach addition and subtraction at three levels of abstraction, employing strategies based on: (1) direct modeling with the use of manipulatives, (2) counting sequences, and (3) recall of number facts. These strategies appear to develop universally in children, without explicit instruction. At the first and most basic level is the *Count-*

ing All with Models and involves counting two sets of actual objects, one for each addend. The second level of addition is referred to as *Counting All without Models.* One strategy at this level involves counting in the same manner as with *Counting All with Models* only without physical models. In another strategy, *Counting on from First,* the student states the name of the first addend and then counts on from that number until all counts of the second addend have been included (e.g.; 3 + 5; 3, 4, 5, 6, 7, 8). A similar strategy, *Counting on From Larger* (also known as the Min strategy), is identical except that the student begins counting forward from the larger of the two addends (e.g., 5, 6, 7, 8). After sufficient practice, the student begins to recall the basic number facts from memory.

While subtraction develops at the same three levels (direct modeling, counting, and recall), a more varied set of strategies exists at the direct modeling and counting levels. Children use a *Separate From* strategy to physically remove the objects to be taken away and then counts the objects in the remaining set. A similar approach is the *Counting Down From* strategy wherein the child begins counting backward from the larger given number until all the counts in the smaller set have been included (e.g., 8 − 5 = 8, 7, 6, 5, 4, 3). The last number uttered in the counting sequence is the answer. The *Separating To* strategy involves physically removing from the set enough objects so that the amount remaining is the number being subtracted, and then counting the objects removed.

Another set of subtraction strategies involve the *Adding On* of objects to the smaller set until the larger number is reached, and then counting the number added on. A second basic strategy involves the *Matching* of concrete objects. The third strategy is called *Choice* and involves either the *Counting Down from* and *Counting Up from Given* strategy, depending on which is the most efficient. For example, to find 9 − 3, it would be more efficient to *Count Down from* (8, 7, 6̲), whereas for 9 − 6, it would be more efficient to *Count up* (7, 8, 9).

Multiplication and Division

Multiplication depends on mastering several prerequisite skills in addition to those identified for addition and subtraction. These include skip counting and basic fact memorization at the introductory level and expanded notation; renaming, complex addition facts, and comma usage at the advanced levels. Multiplication concepts include repeated addition, combinations (also called Cartesian products), and area problems. In *repeated addition problems,* the number and size of the groups are given and the task involves finding the whole. For example: Mark has three bags of apples. There are six apples in each bag. How many apples does Mark have altogether?

In *combination problems,* the number of possibilities of each of two quantities are given and the task involves finding the number of possible combinations or pairings. For example, consider the following problem: Mark has three new pairs of slacks and six new shirts. How many outfits can Mark make?

In *area problems,* the number and size of the rows of a rectangular arrangement are given, and the task involves finding the total number. For example: Mark's classroom has three rows. There are six desks in each row. How many desks are in Mark's classroom?

Students also need to learn about the commutative property of multiplication, the effects of zero and one in multiplication problems, and the distributive property of multiplication. For example, students can explore what happens when the

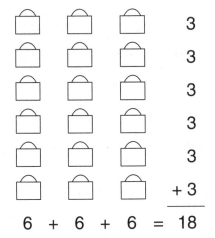

$$6 + 6 + 6 = 18$$

numbers are reversed, when zero or one is in a multiplication problem, or when a quantity in a multiplication problem is broken into two parts.

Multiplication is a prerequisite to simple long division, and developing basic division facts, facts with remainders, subtraction with renaming, and rounding off whole numbers and facility with multidigit multiplication is necessary to perform multidigit division operations. Division concepts include fair sharing or partitioning, and repeated subtraction or measurement. In *fair sharing problems,* also referred to as partitive division, the number of groups is given and the task involves finding the size of the groups. For example: Juan has six apples. He wants to split them equally between two bags. How many apples will be in each bag?

In *measurement division problems,* the size of the groups is given and the task involves finding the number of groups. For example: Anita has six apples. She wants to put two in each bag. How many bags will Anita need?

Students can discuss whether there is an order property for division, as well as the effects of zero and one in situations involving division. They can explore what happens when the numbers are reversed, when zero or one is either the **dividend** (e.g., $0 \div 6$) or the **divisor** (e.g., $6 \div 0$).

Developing Automaticity. Once students have learned the processes involved in each of the

arithmetic operations (adding, subtracting, multiplying, and dividing), they begin to recall basic facts from memory without employing problem-solving strategies. They develop **automaticity** in the recall of basic operations, a critical milestone in mathematics learning. Reliance on less efficient counting strategies can interfere with higher-level math skills such as multiple-digit addition and subtraction, long division, and fractions (Resnick, 1983). The slow execution of operations, or low operational efficiency, may well be the major factor contributing to achievement difficulties in arithmetic (Kirby & Becker, 1988). Not only are simple tasks the components of more complex ones, but the slow execution of simple tasks overloads the working memory and reduces the likelihood that relevant information is active when it is needed (Torgenson, 1986). As basic math facts become committed to memory and their recall becomes automatic, more of the individual's cognitive processing capacity is free to execute higher-level skills.

Students with learning difficulties typically learn math facts more slowly than their age peers (Russell & Ginsburg, 1984). At the middle school/junior high and senior high school levels, as many as 60% of the students may still use finger counting as a major problem-solving strategy (McLeod & Armstrong, 1982). These students may not have learned basic facts at the automatic recall level, or they may not have learned efficient procedural strategies and may still be relying on less efficient and more primitive strategies. In the former instance, drill and practice is called for, while in the latter strategy instruction is needed, coupled with sufficient practice to make using these strategies efficient.

Algorithms and Strategy Training. **Algorithms** are the procedures used in computation. In assisting students in learning algorithms, teachers should de-emphasize rote, meaningless rules and procedures. Rather, instruction should stress main ideas and relate them to concrete models. After students are able to build concrete models, instruction should help them develop computational expertise at more abstract levels by connecting models with symbols and meaningful procedures.

Many mathematics errors that children make are due to incorrect strategies or procedures (Kirby & Becker, 1988). Children may select the wrong operation (e.g., adding instead of subtracting; or taking the wrong number away in subtraction, as in 4 – 7 = 3); they may have place-value difficulties with large numbers in computations; or they may have inadequate knowledge of particular procedures (e.g., borrowing). Frequently, students (both those competent in math as well as those with achievement difficulties) will fail to use the most efficient strategies available. Reliance on these less efficient strategies, such as counting, instead of memory-retrieval strategies to solve basic mathematical facts is a particularly significant problem area for students with learning difficulties.

Instructional Recommendations: Arithmetic Facts and Algorithms. Hasselbring, Goin, and Bransford (1987, p. 31) made several recommendations for developing automaticity, the automatic recall or execution of basic facts, with students with learning difficulties including "assessing current level of automaticity, building on existing knowledge, focusing on a small set of facts, and using 'challenge times.'"

Fact Automaticity. Assessment to determine which facts students already have automatized can be performed using either flashcards or a computer program entitled Chronometric Assessment of Math Strategies (CAMS) (Hasselbring & Goin, 1986). Facts that students recall instantaneously can be considered automatic, while those for which the students take more than 1 or 2 seconds, or obviously are using counting strategies to solve, are scored as nonautomatized. A Fast Facts matrix, such as depicted in Figure 12.2, can then be constructed to represent the facts that have and have not been mastered at an automatic recall level. Teachers can build on these known facts by connecting them with unknown facts using thinking strategies such as counting on

	0	1	2	3	4	5	6	7	8	9
0	0+0	0+1	0+2	0+3	0+4	0+5	0+6	0+7	0+8	0+9
1	1+0	1+1	1+2	1+3	1+4	1+5	1+6	1+7	1+8	1+9
2	2+0	2+1	2+2	2+3	2+4	2+5	2+6	2+7	2+8	2+9
3	3+0	3+1	3+2	3+3	3+4	3+5	3+6	3+7	3+8	3+9
4	4+0	4+1	4+2	4+3	4+4	4+5	4+6	4+7	4+8	4+9
5	5+0	5+1	5+2	5+3	5+4	5+5	5+6	5+7	5+8	5+9
6	6+0	6+1	6+2	6+3	6+4	6+5	6+6	6+7	6+8	6+9
7	7+0	7+1	7+2	7+3	7+4	7+5	7+6	7+7	7+8	7+9
8	8+0	8+1	8+2	8+3	8+4	.8+5	8+6	8+7	8+8	8+9
9	9+0	9+1	9+2	9+3	9+4	9+5	9+6	9+7	0+8	9+9

FIGURE 12.2   Fast Facts Matrix

(e.g., 3 + 2 can be determined by starting at 3 and counting forward two times: "3, 4, 5") and properties such as the commutative property (e.g., 2 + 3 = 5, so 3 + 2 = 5). Teachers should work with only a small set of facts, perhaps only two or three new facts and their commutatives, at a given time (Hasselbring, Goin, & Sherwood, 1986), interspersing these with reviews of previously learned facts. When students can consistently retrieve a fact, even though it make take 3–5 seconds, the teacher can introduce the use of "challenge time" to gradually reduce the latency down to around 1 second. The teacher can use the CAMS program or flash cards for this process.

Another approach to developing automatic recall involves gradual fading of the answers. Here the answers to simple number fact exercises are gradually obscured by covering them with cellophane. With this procedure, students may reach criteria nearly twice as rapidly and making only one-fifth as many errors as with traditional drill-and-practice instruction (Haupt, Van Kirk, and Terraciano, 1975). Constant time-delay procedures can be effective for teaching multiplication facts to middle school students. Research by Mattingly and Bott (1990) utilized one hundred multiplication fact cards, with individual instruction provided on twenty-five facts at a time during two daily 16-minute sessions. The teacher would introduce each fact, obtain the student's attention by saying "Look" and then state: "Read the fact. Say the answer." The teacher would immediately prompt the response, which the student then repeated (e.g., "Six times four equals twenty-four."). All subsequent training on the target set of twenty-five fact cards used a 5-second time delay. The teacher would present the fact card, say: "Read the fact. Say the answer." and then give the student 5 seconds after reading the fact aloud to state the correct product. The 5 seconds constituted a wait period, after which the teacher would provide the answer. When students gave correct responses, the teacher said, "Good," then repeated the fact and the answer and reinforced the student with one token. If the student gave an incorrect response before the 5-second wait time had passed, the teacher would say, "No, wait for me to tell you if you don't know," and then remove the card from the table, and drop her head for 5 seconds as a brief time-out from the teacher's attention before proceeding to the next fact card. This procedure resulted in the students learning nearly errorless multiplication facts.

Calculator use. While it is important for students to master basic computation facts, these basic facts should not be the driving force of the curriculum; nor should they serve as the "gatekeeper," preventing students who have not mastered these facts from proceeding to more advanced topics. Calculator use can circumvent these situations by reducing the need for much of the complex paper-and-pencil proficiency traditionally emphasized in mathematics courses. According to the NCTM (1986), all students should use calculators to:

- Concentrate on the problem-solving process rather than on the calculations associated with problems
- Gain access to mathematics beyond their levels of computational skills
- Explore, develop, and reinforce concepts, including estimation, computation, approximation, and properties
- Experiment with mathematical ideas and discover patterns
- Perform those tedious computations that arise when working with real data in problem-solving situations

Explicit instruction in calculator use should identify the purpose of the various keys, including the "clear" and memory keys. The instruction should also identify the importance of determining the accuracy of a result by either considering its reasonableness (e.g., should the answer to 257 + 745 be around 100 or 1,000?) or by solving the problem a second time and comparing the answers.

Algorithms. Developing declarative knowledge (e.g., information about facts and their relationships) to a level of automaticity lays an important foundation for developing higher-level math skills. Prior to teaching for automaticity, however, it is best to develop the conceptual understanding of these math facts as procedural knowledge.

Students can practice basic algorithms using manipulatives. They can practice number combinations using paper clips or clothespins to illustrate numerals on flashcards. For example, when making the number 6, a child can clip two clothespins on one side of the card and four clothespins on the other, while another child clips three clothespins on each side. The teacher can prompt the students in discussing the equivalency of these combinations: "Do each of these show 6? Does the arrangement matter?"

An important preskill for addition is mastering the plus-1 process wherein students learn that when they add 1, they say the next number. Teachers can begin by presenting series of numbers orally, pausing, and cuing the students to state the next number (4, 5, 6, 7). When students develop proficiency at this, the teacher can shift to saying only one number, and having students name the next one (6, 7). The relationships among facts can be emphasized through series saying, an activity in which the teacher leads the students in saying a consecutively ordered set of fact statements:

$$5 + 3 = 8$$
$$5 + 4 = 9$$
$$5 + 5 = 10$$

A simple game of "doubles race" provides practice with number doubles, the simplest addition algorithm for students to learn. The teacher draws a game track on a file folder, marking each square with numerals 0–9 to connect the "start" point to the "finish." The first student rolls the die and moves a marker as many spaces as indicated on the die, saying the double of the digit indicated in each of the spaces. If a miss is made, the student places the marker beside that space until her next turn. The first student to reach the finish wins. An answer key for the doubles makes this an activity in which pairs of students participate independent of close teacher's supervision.

Beginning practice with two-digit subtraction with renaming can be provided through a simple activity requiring a bank of place value manipulatives (tens and ones) and a deck of laminated two-digit numeral cards such as the following:

Tens	Ones
2	7

Children take turns drawing cards and using the manipulatives to show values. The teacher leads the following discussion: "How many ones make a fair trade?" (10 ones for 1 ten) "Write what you have now." "The bank need another ten. Will you trade one of your tens for ones?"

Multiplication practice can be provided with a simple game requiring a spinner with the digits 2, 3, 4, 5, 6, 7, 8, and 9. Each student spins and then multiplies by a given number (e.g., 9), the number that appears on the spinner. A running total of each student's products is kept, with the winner being the first student to get a total of 300 or more.

Another game using the same spinner provides each player with eight cards, two each of 1, 2, 3, and 4. The student spins the spinner, and then multiples that number by a given value (e.g., 5 times). The card matching the 10 digits of the product is then put in the center of the table (e.g., if the spinner lands on 3, then $3 \times 5 = 15$, and the 1 card matches the 10 digit. The first player to turn in each of the eight cards wins.

Strategy training. Explicit strategy training can be an efficient and effective way of teaching students each of the steps of algorithms. Strategies for straight computation exercises are fairly straightforward but are considerably more complex for story problems. The latter are described elsewhere in this chapter.

In teaching more efficient strategies, the teacher should identify the strategy level at which the student is proficient and then teach each of the intermediary strategies rather than simply skipping on to the most efficient strategy of math-fact recall. Instruction that is complete is more effective than less complete instruction (Lloyd, 1980). In teaching algorithms, the teacher should model the strategy, and provide guided practice and corrective feedback. In a review of research on teaching math strategies to students with learning difficulties, Lloyd and Keller (1989) drew the following conclusions:

1. Strategies for both simple mathematics tasks (e.g., number-numeral equivalences) and more complex tasks (e.g., long division) can be taught to students who are atypical.
2. Greater generalization is attained when the component skills of a strategy are pretaught.
3. Students can learn similar strategies for closely related tasks (e.g., multiplication and division) without confusing them.
4. Teachers' modeling of the strategy steps promotes acquisition by the students.
5. Teachers should prompt each step of the strategies during initial strategy learning, with the prompting faded as students approach mastering the strategies.

Math strategies can be as simple as teaching students to circle and name the operation sign in addition and subtraction in order to cue the procedure. Teaching labels for each step of a problem solution is a form of strategy training. Students with learning difficulties have been shown to solve problems more quickly when they are taught to verbalize the steps as they proceed through the problem solutions (Johnston & Whitman, 1987; Schunk & Cox, 1986: Whitman & Johnston, 1983). As noted by Lloyd and Keller (1989), self-verbalization of strategies often include components of self-monitoring and self-reward as well. Table 12.3 shows an example of using self-verbalization in a solution algorithm for finding equivalent fractions.

Fractions and Decimals

Fractions and decimals have traditionally been difficult for students. Instruction should focus on helping students learn the meaning of the symbolic notations used for fractions and decimals; to develop concepts (such as order and equivalence) that are important in fostering a sense of the relative size of fractions and decimals; and to connect their intuitive understandings and strategies to more general, formal methods.

Topics of instruction include fraction concepts, order, and equivalence, in addition to operations on fractions. Teachers should begin instruction on fractions and decimals by developing understanding of fraction concepts, including partitioning, comparing, and finding equivalent fractions, before proceeding to operations on fractions. *Concept tasks* include partitioning a whole into parts and naming those parts. *Comparison tasks* (also referred to as *ordering*) involve determining the larger or smaller (or largest or smallest) of a collection of fractions or decimals, for example, 1/2 > 1/3. **Equivalence** activities involve generating or recognizing multiple names for the same fraction, for example, 1/2 = 2/4.

Students should learn to identify, read, and write *mixed numbers* (e.g., 1 1/2) and discriminate *proper fractions* (numerator less than denominator) and *improper fractions* (numerator greaterr than denominator). They must learn to write whole numbers as fractions, and translate improper fractions into mixed numbers and mixed numbers into improper fractions. This means that students must identify the *greatest common factor* (e.g., 3 is the greatest common factor of 9/12, 2 is the greatest common factor of 6/8), and the *lowest common denominator* (the lowest common denominator for 1/3 + 1/2 is 6, for 1/4 + 2/5 is 20). They must use these concepts in reducing fractions to their simplest forms (e.g., 12/18 = 2/3) and in performing operations (adding, subtracting, multiplying, and dividing) on them. Students also must learn different forms of rational numbers (e.g., fractions, decimals, ratios, proportions, and percents).

Instructional Recommendations: Fractions and Decimals. Teachers should use manipulatives as well as specific vocabulary in teaching fraction and decimal concepts. Symbols should not be introduced until students are familiar with the concepts and their related vocabulary. Word names (such as "one-half") should be introduced before symbol names (such as 1/2) in initial work with fractions and decimals. Instruction should be geared toward helping students connect word names and symbol names to displays of manipulatives, pictures, diagrams, and real-world objects. Also, teachers should limit the size of denominators in initial concepts, order, and equivalence work to those that children are familiar with and can show with available manipulatives.

The process of each operation on fractions should be demonstrated with manipulatives and pictures before algorithms are taught. Manipulatives can include commercially available items such as pattern blocks, fraction bars, Cuisenaire rods, and base ten blocks. Also useful are teacher-made fraction circles, rectangles, and strips. Beans or other loose objects (colored tiles, lots-of-links, and colored chips) that can be sorted, can help develop students' understanding of the fractional parts as well as the meaning of operations.

TABLE 12.3 Example of a Solution Algorithm for Finding Equivalent Fractions

Step	Description	Action	Computation
1. Read	Pupil reads problem to herself.	"Let's see . . . um, 9/17ths is equal to how many 102nds?"	$\frac{9}{17} = \frac{?}{102}$
2. Plan	Pupil describes general process to herself.	"Okay, I've got to multiple 9/17ths by some fraction that's the same as one, and then I can get the number of 102nds that it equals."	$\frac{9}{17} = \frac{?}{102}$
3. Rewrite	Pupil rewrites problem, providing space for work. Note: This step can be completed while performing Step 2.	"Here's my work-space. . . ."	$\frac{9}{17}(-) = \frac{?}{102}$
4. Identify known part	Pupil identifies part of equivalence for which numbers are known.	"Okay, I've got two out of three numbers here (pointing to denominators), so I can start on that part."	$\frac{9}{17}(-) = \frac{?}{102}$ $\quad 17\overline{)\,102}$ underneath with 5, 95, 17
5. Solve known part	Pupil uses prior knowledge to solve for missing multiplier.	"So, 17 times something equals 102 . . . um . . . I'll just figure that out . . . 17 is almost 20 and 20 goes into 100 five times, so I'll try that . . . nope, 17 leftover, so it's 6 times . . . great! It's even."	$\frac{9}{17}\left(\frac{6}{6}\right) = \frac{?}{102}$
6. Substitute	Pupil uses information derived in Step 5 to complete fraction in equation.	"And that means this (writing) is 6 over 6 . . . which is the same as one, so . . ."	$\frac{9}{17}\left(\frac{6}{6}\right) = \frac{?}{102}$
7. Derive missing numerator	Pupil solves for missing numerator using information from Step 6.	"Now, I can just multiply these 'cause I've got two out of three and . . . 6 times 9 is 54, sooo . . ."	$\frac{9}{17}\left(\frac{6}{6}\right) = \frac{?}{102}$
8. Read	Pupil reads completed problem.	"9/17ths is equal to 54/102nds."	$\frac{9}{17}\left(\frac{6}{6}\right) = \frac{?}{102}$

Source: From "Effective mathematics instruction: Development, instruction, and programs." J.W. Lloyd and C.E. Keller, *Focus on Exceptional Children, 21(7)*, pp. 1–10. March 1989. Reprinted by permission of Love Publishing, Denver.

Through instruction, students learn that it is possible to divide by fractions, for example. They also learn to connect operations on fractions to the real world. For example, determining how many 1/2 cup servings are in an 8-cup container involves dividing by a fraction, in this case, 8 ÷ 1/2.

To practice finding equivalent fractions, each child can be given equivalent-sized sheets of paper or construction paper. First, the students fold sheets of paper in half, then opening their papers and shading one of the halves. After leading a discussion of the fraction, 1/2, the teacher can direct the children to fold the paper again, making sure that all parts are the same size and shape. The teacher asks the students such questions as: "How many parts are now on the sheet of paper?" (four) "How many of them are shaded?" (two) The teacher guides the students in discussing the relationship of the fractions (e.g., 2/4 and 1/2), emphasizing that as the number of pieces in the whole are doubled, the number also is considered doubled. The children can then fold the sheets of paper again, with the teacher again posing questions about the results: "How many parts are now on the sheet of paper?" (eight) "How many of them are shaded?" (four) The new fraction (4/8) is discussed in relation to 1/2 and 2/4.

Identifying the relative sizes of fractions can be practiced in a game format involving two students and requiring a card deck of thirty-six cards with two sets of each of the following fractions:

1/2, 1/3, 2/3, 1/4, 3/4, 1/5, 2/5,
3/5, 4/5, 1/6, 5/6, 1/10, 3/10,
7/10, 9/10, 1/12, 7/12, and 11/12.

Fraction circles for each of these fractions also are needed. The cards are shuffled and dealt out face down among the players. Simultaneously, each player flips over a card and determines which card depicts the greater fraction. Players use the fraction circles to verify their choices. The player who has the fraction card with the greater value says out loud, "1/3 is greater than 1/4," and takes both cards. The player with the most fraction cards after all have been played is the winner.

Real-world examples can be used to demonstrate operations with fractions. For example, "Maria ate 1/4 of the twelve pieces of candy in the bag. How many pieces did she eat?" "Tom asked for 1/6 of half of a cake. He got 1/12 of a whole cake. Did he get what he asked for?" To solve these types of problems, the students can be given sheets of 8 1/2 × 11-inch paper and instructed to fold the paper in half and shade one-half of the paper. Unfold the sheet of paper. They then fold the sheet of paper into thirds and shade two-thirds of the paper with different shading than used before. The teacher guides them by asking: "How many sections are on the sheet of paper?" (six) "How many of those sections are double shaded?" (two out of six sections). "What fraction does that represent? (2/6)." This example illustrates the problem 2/3 of 1/2, or 2/3 × 1/2.

Estimation and Mental Computation

Estimation and mental computation are crucial life skills that people use more frequently than they do actual calculations. Both contribute to number sense, that is, common sense about numbers. **Estimation** enhances concept development, has many real-life applications, and is critical to the effective use of calculators. It entails a process of forming an approximate answer. Such approximations are sufficient for many life-problems. Estimation also is useful in checking exact answers that have been calculated. Effective estimation involves using mental calculations of approximate (rounded off) amounts. For example, in multiplying 29 × 31, rounding off to 30 × 30 suggests that the answer is about 900.

Instruction on estimation and mental calculation has applications to every aspect of mathematics. Initial instruction can involve having students make guesses about the quantity of a group of objects or the measure of an object, such as how much, how many, how far, how long, or what fraction. Students can be taught to round off to the nearest ten, hundred, or thousand, as well as to the nearest whole number.

Mental calculation, on the other hand, is the process of calculating mentally the exact answer in a computation situation. This skill can be facilitated through practice with multiples of 10 and 100: adding and subtracting multiples of 10, multiples of 100, single-digit numbers, and two-digit or three-digit numbers with and without regrouping; to add single-digit numbers; to count by fives, tens, twenty-fives, fifties, and hundreds; to multiply single-digit numbers by multiples of 10 and 100; and to double a number and find half of a number for multiples of 10 and 100.

Instructional Recommendations: Estimation and Mental Calculation. Number lines can be useful in teaching students to round off to the nearest ten, hundred, thousand, and so forth. Students can locate the number 21, for example, and determine whether it is closer to 20 or to 30 on the number line. Base ten blocks also can be used to display a number, such as 318, with the students being asked to determine if the number is closer to 310 or 320 (for rounding off to tens), or closer to 300 or to 400 (for rounding off to the nearest hundred).

Practice in combining numbers to make 100 can improve estimation skills. Cards containing numbers such 82, 73, 48, 47, 86, 37, 27, 53, 18, 63, 52, 14, and so on can be used. The cards are spread out on the table, and each student is asked to select sets of numbers that add up to 100. As a variation, the teacher can orally state a number and have the students choose what can be added to it to make 100.

A functional life activity "How Much Do I Need?" teaches students to estimate grocery prices. A single small group or several simultaneous small groups can engage in this activity. Grocery advertisements from newspapers can be glued to index cards. Each card should contain the name of an item, its picture, and its price. For example, one card might contain the name, the picture, and the price of a box of laundry detergent, while another might contain the picture and the price of a six-pack of soda. Taking turns, one student at a time turns over three cards, with members of the group then estimating the total amount of money needed to purchase these items. Any disagreements among the students are discussed and a tally is kept of the number of times all players agree. If more than one group is involved, each group's tally can be compared with that of the other groups. A variation on this can involve designating an amount of money (e.g., $25.00) that a student has to purchase groceries, and then pointing to a series of item cards and asking the student if there is sufficient money to purchase all these. An additional use of calculators in teaching estimation is to use the calculators to check the responses of team members in estimating the total cost of two or more items. One member from each team of students says one number (two digit or three digit) and then both players silently estimate the sum to the two numbers. After 5 seconds, the players check their estimates using the calculators to determine who was the closest. Correct answers receive 1 point.

Similar exercises can be used to estimate size (e.g., room measurements, height, and length), weight, and other quantities. Students can also be given practice in estimation by deciding whether answers to given problems are *close to* or *far away from* the actual answer (e.g., $84 + 15 = 56$; $58 + 23 = 719$; $44 + 30 = 70$; $434 + 789 = 8,200$).

Students can be encouraged to utilize shortcuts in solving simple problems as another means of developing estimation skills. A variety of math exercises can be written on index cards, which are placed facedown on the table. Sample exercises might be as follows:

$$5 + 7 + 3 + 5 + 8 + 6 + 2 =$$
$$37 + 25 + 63 + 75 =$$
$$2 \times 3 \times 7 \times 5 =$$
$$4 \times 17 \times 250 =$$
$$8 \times 19 \times 14 \times 10 \times 0 \times 2 \times 1 =$$
$$8 \times 19 \times 14 \times 10 \times 0 \times 2 + 1 =$$
$$24 \times 5 =$$
$$24 \times 25 =$$

Each student draws a card and then describes an "easy way" to arrive at the solution. The students explain the shortcuts and/or rules they would use to derive an approximate answer (e.g., anything times 0 = 0; 75 and 25 = 100, then add 37 and 63 = 100 to get 200, and so forth). The students can discuss alternative procedures among themselves and practice independently with cards and worksheets, sharing their answers as they proceed.

Students can use dominoes and calculators, as well as flash cards and software practice programs for practice in estimating multiplication and division. A set of double-nine, large-format dominoes can be used with small groups. The teacher, aide, or a student can hold up a domino for 3 seconds, asking the students to give a "thumbs up" if they believe that the product of the two sides is more than, less than, or equal to a given number. For example, the domino might be:

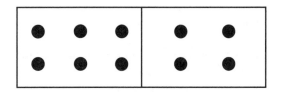

For practice in estimation, the teacher writes a number such as 70 on the chalkboard. The teacher then holds up a domino, gives students 3 seconds to count the number of dots and divide 70 by that number. The students then can signal if the quotient is less than, more than, or equal to a given number, such as "6."

Real objects and pictures of objects can be used as prompts to estimate the fractions or proportions. Students can estimate the proportion of the glass that is filled with water, the fraction of the pie that is left, the proportional relationship of the length of two pencils, the fraction of an hour left, and so forth. Initially, instruction should focus on 1/2, and then "more than one-half" and "less than one-half," gradually moving on to 1/4 and 3/4. Students can estimate the portion of an hour that they spend in daily activities (e.g., eating breakfast, taking a bath, and walking to school), the fraction of quarts of milk that their

families use for dinner, or the percentage of seat-work problems they have left to complete.

Measurement

Measurement is an important tool by which students can learn about the environments in which they live. Common quantitative information derived from measurement includes length, distance, area, volume, mass, temperature, time, and angle. According to Smith (1991), measurement topics of importance to all students include: (1) converting and comparing units of measures; (2) estimating and measuring length; (3) determining perimeter, area, and volume; and (4) using measurement instruments. Measurement requires using appropriate tools, which are selected on a basis of the measures to be made and the uses to which the measures are to be put. Common measuring tools are rulers, meter sticks, tape measures, graduated beakers, measuring cups, measuring spoons, pan balances, bathroom scales, thermometers, timers, and protractors. Students must learn to use these tools and to understand that measurement is approximate because of the limitations of the ability to read a measuring instrument and the precision of the measuring instrument.

Specific vocabulary is required for both metric and nonmetric measures. Students need to be able to use nonstandard, metric, and customary units of measure to estimate and measure length, volume, and weight. They should learn to use digital and traditional clocks to tell time, as well as learn how to read and interpret Celsius and Fahrenheit temperatures on thermometers, choose appropriate units of measure and use a variety of measurement instruments, and to recognize and count money. Students need to become proficient at measuring various figures and deriving the appropriate formulas to find perimeters, areas, and volumes. Finally, they must learn to use estimation to approximate measurements.

Instruction should enable students to make comparisons, such as "Who is the tallest? Shortest?," as well as to measure several objects using different units, such as hand spans, strides, and paper clips, and compare results. Students should have the opportunity to relate measurement to their everyday lives and to use a variety of measurement instruments. They should differentiate between and develop proficiency with the two basic measurement systems: the customary system used in the United States and a few other countries, and the metric system used in most countries of the world as well as in scientific applications.

Instructional Recommendations: Measurement.

Materials necessary for teaching measurement include standard measuring instruments, such as those previously listed; as well as nonstandard units, such as pencils and paper clips; and "junk," such as bottles, tiles, string, containers of various sizes, and old clocks. In addition, geoboards, centimeter cubes and Cuisenaire rods are useful teaching tools.

Instruction should begin with measurement using nonstandard measures prior to introducing standard measures. This instruction will help students form concepts of relative size, appreciate the role of measurement in society, and provide nonthreatening instruction. It is important to remember that measurement should be taught primarily as a "doing" activity; students should actually measure things rather than merely interpret pictures of measurements in books.

Children can compare their relative heights. Three children can stand while a fourth arranges them in order from shortest to tallest. Students can line up for activities from tallest to shortest. They can trace around their feet and compare foot sizes. Two or more objects of different lengths can be presented, with students asked to pick the longer, longest; shorter, shortest. Strips of paper of varying lengths can be placed around the room (e.g., on the wall, or the tagboard), with some hung vertically, some horizontally, and some diagonally. The teacher can identify two strips and have a child choose the longer or shorter of those two strips. This can emphasize that length does not depend on direction.

Graph paper can be used to reinforce the concept of area measurement. The students can lay the graph paper over various regions, trace the regions on the paper, and count the squares. Ceramic tiles that are 1 square centimeter can be used to measure a surface. The students can cover the surface with the squares and them count them to determine the square centimeters of area.

Only after students have had many experiences with basic measurement concepts and relative measures (e.g., bigger, shortest, fastest, slowest, coolest, warmest, more, and less) should the teacher introduce common units for length, weight, and area. It is easiest to begin with metric measures, given the ease with which their base ten feature can be converted. Shaw (1985) recommends beginning with a decimeter length strip of paper or template and using this to measure line segments of 1 decimeter each drawn in horizontal, vertical, and slanting positions. Students can identify various items in the room that are approximately 1 decimeter in length (estimation), such as the width of the light switch cover, the length of a piece of chalk, and so forth. They then can measure items that are not exactly 1 decimeter and round off their results. The use of estimating and rounding suggest the need for more accurate measures, which can lead to introducing the centimeter unit. After working with this measuring tool, students can move on to meters, and then to inches, feet, and yards.

The students can move on to measuring real objects (e.g., each other's height and weight, the size of their desks, and the size of their classroom) using standard measures of inches and feet, pounds and ounces, as well as using metric units. Students can be given problems that require them to convert ounces to pounds, inches to feet, feet to yards, and so forth. A balance scale can be used to demonstrate weight measurement, and varying sizes of containers (cup, pint, quart, and gallon) can be used to demonstrate liquid measurement. Containers of different shapes can be used for practice in conservation (e.g., a pint of liquid in a tall, narrow cylinder is the same as a pint of liquid in a long, flat pan).

Geometry

Geometry is the branch of mathematics concerned with observations, construction, and description of shapes, and with location of points in one-, two-, and three-dimensional space (Schminke, Maeterns, & Arnold, 1978). The concepts and skills related to geometry can promote the development of logical thinking and spatial intuitions.

Real objects and abstract figures have one-, two-, and/or three- dimensional features that can be examined, compared, and analyzed. The specific attributes and properties of geometric figures can be identified, classified, and named. They can be described in terms of their relationships with other figures, including relative size, position, orientation, congruence, and similarity. Relationships within and between geometric figures can be revealed through measuring and looking for patterns. Constant relationships can be expressed as formulas.

An NCTM report in 1981 indicated that all students should be able to identify and define various geometric figures, including measuring areas of these figures and constructing figures. Children need to be able to identify, classify, and describe common two-dimensional figures (such as rectangles, squares, triangles, circles, cubes, spheres, and polygons) as well as three-dimensional geometric figures, (such as cylinders, cones, and rectangular prisms). Students should master the correct vocabulary related to these processes, be able to identify congruence and noncongruence among figures, and to be able to construct models of three-dimensional figures. Students need experiences with symmetry and transformations, such as translations (slides), rotations (turns), reflections (flips), and dilations (stretching and shrinking).

Initial geometric knowledge begins to develop as infants move about in their cribs and then crawl around rooms. They experience the concepts of near and far, discover boundaries, and learn about component parts and sequences. A broad sequence of developmental levels in acquiring geometric concepts and skills include

the following (Cruickshank, & Sheffield, 1988, p. 253):

- **Level 1: Recognition.** Children can recognize various shapes by repeatedly seeing them as separate objects. Children do not notice the less common characteristics of similar figures.
- **Level 2: Description.** Children observe and manipulate figures, thus determining the properties necessary for identifying various shapes. Measuring is one way children learn necessary properties.
- **Level 3: Relation.** Children establish relationships between figures and their properties. Children understand that a square is also a rectangle, a parallelogram, and a quadrilateral. The importance of definitions is recognized.
- **Level 4: Deduction.** Children use deduction while working with postulates, theorems, and proofs.
- **Level 5: Rigor.** Children employ rigorous applications in their study of various geometries.

The concepts upon which geometry is built begin with the simplest abstraction or figure, the point. They then expand to encompass lines, line segments, curves, and two- and three-dimensional figures. Manipulative materials and models play an important role in developing geometric concepts, especially those dealing with three-dimensional objects. Useful materials include geoboards, geometric solids, pattern blocks, protractors, compasses, and Miras (for symmetry).

Instructional Recommendations: Geometry. Young children can learn about their body shapes and space. One activity involves using chalk to trace the body space of individual students as they lie on butcher paper. Students can compare their shapes and sizes. In another activity, the students stand far enough apart so that, with arms outstretched, they cannot reach each other. Using a cube or other solid shape, the students then identify all the space their bodies can reach from the spot on which they are standing—in front, be-hind, and to either side. This is their body space. The teacher can direct the students to dramatize the vocabulary of body to object and other spatial relationships by moving the the cube:

- Right to left and back again (across the body midline)
- Up high and down low
- On, over, and around
- Across, under, near, and far
- Beside and between

Students then can be directed to feel and de-scribe various shapes such as flat faces, straight edges, five corners, and square desk tops. They can construct models of shapes by bending heavy wires or by gluing small doweling to surfaces, differentiating between open spaces and closed spaces. Students can use parquetry blocks to de-velop and construct shape patterns and to practice symmetry. Beginning at the intermediate grade levels, students should be taught to use compasses and straightedges to construct shapes. They can learn to copy line segments and angles, to con-struct circles with a given radii, to perpendicu-larly bisect line segments and to construct triangles of given dimensions.

Tasks that involve displaying several solids of different sizes, colors, and shapes along the chalk tray can provide students with practice classifying solids in different ways. The teacher selects one solid and calls on children individu-ally to find and describe another one which is like (or different from) it in some way. The students can also be directed to match like solids that they identify both inside and outside of school. They should be encouraged to use proper names when identifying the solids (e.g., sphere rather than "ball") and to describe as many properties of each shape as possible.

Teachers can introduce children to angles by taping to the floor a straight walking line that, at some point, changes directions. Children can walk along the line, reach the point of the turn, and point one arm in the direction they have been

going and the other arm in the direction of the change. They can describe the angles made by their arms. Logo, the computer language of turtle graphics, can be used to provide many varied expe-riences in exploring geometric shapes. Through-out geometry instruction, measurement skills and estimation skills can be practiced.

Problem-solving experiences can be intro-duced by having students identify pattern se-quences, providing oral clues for shapes that are to be developed on geoboards, and developing ac-tivities that employ map codes to find routes to familiar places (e.g., school, the zoo, or a friend's house). Activities such as these can assist stu-dents in developing logical thinking and general problem-solving skills, as well as provide a foun-dation for the more formal proof structures that many students will be expected to learn in geome-try classes at the secondary school level.

Problem Solving

The ability to apply mathematics concepts and operations to real-life situations is the goal of mathematics instruction. However, schools have not been particularly successful in developing this ability in most students. Data from the Na-tional Assessment of Educational Progress indi-cate that at ages 9, 13, and 17, most students could solve one-step story problems but experi-enced considerable difficulties with more compli-cated problems, including two-step problems and problems involving multiplicative reasoning (Mullis, Dossey, Owen, & Phillips, 1991). Prob-lems involving addition typically are easier for students to solve than those requiring subtraction (Nesher, 1982).

While all algorithms can be thought of as variations of problem solving, the actual applica-tion of mathematical knowledge to real-world situations involves comprehension of a problem situation (who is doing what to whom), deciding on what the relevant information is and how the relevant quantities associated with the relevant subjects change (Greeno, 1978). Based on this in-formation, the student then selects and executes appropriate problem-solving strategies and evaluates the solution.

According to Polya (1957), an effective model of problem solving includes the following steps:

1. Identify the knowns and the unknowns
2. Identify the relationship among the knowns and the unknowns
3. Define the type of problem it is
4. Plan how to solve the problem
5. Carry out the plan
6. Evaluate the answer in the context of the preceding information.

This model underpins most problem-solving strategies emphasized today. Fleischner, Nuzum and Marzola (1987) described a similar approach, depicted in Table 12.4, for developing a problem-solving curriculum for students with learning disabilities. A prompt card to help students select the correct process is presented in Table 12.5.

Other strategies effective in solving problems include guess and check, draw a picture, identify all relevant data and introduce a suitable notation system, act it out, model with manipulatives, look for a pattern, make a table or chart, make an organized list, work backwards, use logical reasoning, solve a simpler problem, refer to a problem with a similar unknown, and write an equation or open sentence.

The teacher's role in problem-solving instruction is multifaceted. The teacher must guide students to focus attention on the action implied in the problem, on the part-part-whole relationship within the problem, and on the size of the answer (Zweng, Garaghty, & Turner, 1980). In story problem instruction, the teacher should read the problem aloud and then have the students restate the problem in their own words, identifying what is known and what is being asked. While students are solving the problem, the teacher should be an active listener, prepared to give hints rather than answers and to praise for appropriate efforts. After the problem is solved, the teacher should have groups of students share their solution strategies and answers. They can discuss the thinking that went into the selection of proce-

TABLE 12.4   Fleischner's Model of Elements Necessary for Constructing the Problem-Solving Curriculum

1. Knowledge generated from the problem
   - Identification of the question (information wanted)
   - Identification of the given information
   - Interrelationship of the wanted and given
2. Knowledge specific to the task
   - Calculating
   - Recognizing addition problems
   - Discriminating between addition and subtraction problems
   - Identifying two-step problems
   - Identifying problems with extraneous information
3. Procedural knowledge
   - Recognizing the problem statement
   - Setting a plan
   - Generating and testing hypotheses
   - Evaluating

Source: From "Devising an instructional program to teach arithmetic problem-solving skills to students with learning disabilities" by J.E. Fleischner, M.B. Nuzum, and E.S. Marzola, 1987, *Journal of Learning Disabilities, 20(4),* p. 216. Copyright 1987 by PRO-ED, Inc. Reprinted by permission.

TABLE 12.5 Prompt Card

Phase I Final Prompt Card

Type of Prompt	Sample Question
Read	What is the question?
Reread	What is the necessary information?
Think	Putting together? = Add
	Taking apart? = Subtract
	Do I need all the information?
	Is it a two-step problem?
Solve	Write the equation
Check	Recalculate
	Label
	Compare

Source: From "Devising an instructional program to teach arithmetic problem-solving skills to students with learning disabilities" by J.E. Fleischner, M.B. Nuzum, and E.S. Marzola, 1987, *Journal of Learning Disabilities, 20(4),* p. 216. Copyright 1987 by PRO-ED, Inc. Reprinted by permission.

dures, validate or assess their own answers, and make generalizations when appropriate.

Cawley (1985b) has emphasized that much of what is presented as verbal problems in the math instruction are actually only computational exercises embedded in words. They can be solved without understanding actual problem situations and do not require students to analyze, interpret, and make strategy decisions in order to obtain solutions. Frequently, students ignore the verbal information and attend only to the numbers, looking for key words (e.g., *altogether, more, less,* and *into*) that will cue them as to the operation to be performed. They then will rotely apply the computation principle to all numbers.

There are several approaches to making problems more complex. One is using *indirect semantic formats,* where common key words and semantic features do not cue the selection of an operation. Consider, for example, the following two representations of the same problem:

1. **Direct semantic format:** Maria had six cookies and gave two of them to Paula. How many cookies does Maria now have?

2. **Indirect semantic format:** Maria had four cookies after giving two of them to Paula. How many cookies did Maria start with?

Including extraneous or irrelevant information is another approach to making problems more complex, requiring students to differentiate the essential from the nonessential information. Englert et al. (1987) observed that students with learning problems rely on subject information (e.g., "Who are we talking about and how much does that individual have?") as a basis for initially deciding object ownership and identifying nonoverlapping subsets. Students tend to identify and exclude irrelevant subject information with some facility. However, they are less attentive to separate object sets and have difficulties dealing appropriately with numerical distractors. Students tend to enter all numerical information presented in the problem statements, regardless of their relevance, into the problem equations. Using manipulatives in problem solving permits the teacher to more directly observe the processes students use to arrive at solutions and to identify points at which the students fail to comprehend the problem situations.

Instructional Recommendations: Problem Solving. Cawley, Miller, and School (1987) listed considerations for teaching problem-solving skills and strategies to students with learning difficulties. They identified both effective and ineffective practices.

Effective teaching practices:
- Begin problem solving early in the school year (as well as in the early grade levels).
- Make problem solving the focus and reason for computation.
- Solve problems using various modes.
- Have students write or modify problems.
- Distinguish between knowledge and process.
- Present problems involving familiar situations.
- Constantly monitor children's progress.
- Alter problems based on children's abilities and deficits.

Ineffective teaching practices:

- Use key words to signal an operation.
- Teach students incorrect generalizations to help them choose operations (such as, "If there is one big number and one small number, subtract.").
- Do problem solving as the last problem (or bonus problem) of an assignment.
- Mark a child wrong if he makes a computational error when solving a problem by using the correct operation.
- Skip problem solving or do it infrequently.
- Present problems haphazardly.

In addition to employing the effective strategies listed previously, recommendations for improving verbal problem-solving performances include having students orally reread the story problems in order to diminish the "rote computational habit" (Blankenship & Lovitt, 1976) and/or rewrite the problems to make them easier (Cohen & Stover, 1981). Paraphrasing or restating the problems can improve performances as can self-verbalization of the procedural steps and self-reinforcement. Table 12.6 presents strategy that involves many of these steps.

Because students with learning difficulties tend to be slower and less accurate in solving verbal problems, even when they comprehend the problem situations, developing automaticity of math facts and basic algorithms is particularly important. Using calculators for performing specific operations can also be beneficial. Increased fluency in these areas should increase speed, decrease miscalculations, and improve the execution of procedures. While students are developing this fluency, however, educators should provide instruction that reduces the gap between the students' computational skill requirements and problem-solving abilities.

HIGHER MATHEMATICS/ REAL-LIFE MATHEMATICS

At the secondary school level, some students who have learning difficulties will have the mathe-

TABLE 12.6   Steps in Verbal Mathematics Problem Solving Strategy

1. Read the problem aloud
2. Paraphrase
   - Give important information.
   - Repeat the question aloud.
   - What is asked? What am I looking for?
3. Visualize
   - Draw a diagram.
4. State the problem
   - I have . . . I want to find . . .
5. Hypothesize
   - If I . . . then . . .
   - How many steps?
6. Estimate
   - Round the numbers.
7. Calculate
   - Label.
   - Circle.
8. Self-check
   - Check every step.
   - Check calculation.
   - Does the answer make sense?

Source: From "The effect of cognitive strategy training on verbal math problem solving performance of learning disabled adolescents" by M. Montague and C.S. Bos, 1986, *Journal of Learning Disabilities, 19(1),* pp. 26–33. Copyright 1986 by PRO-ED, Inc. Reprinted by permission.

matics proficiency to succeed in higher-level mathematics classes of algebra, geometry, and trigonometry. If needed, special education teachers or other personnel can provide resource support.

Most students with learning difficulties, however, reach high school age having attained mathematics proficiency at only about the fourth-grade level (McLeod & Armstrong, 1982). Because their skill deficits may be of such a magnitude that it is unlikely that they will ever function mathematically at grade level, the instructional focus for some students needs to shift from developmental and remedial mathematics instruction to real-life skills they will need as adults. Halpern (1981) has recommended that functional skills needed for adult living be the focus of all math instruction for students with learning disabilities, infused throughout the math curriculum, beginning in the earliest grades.

Topics that might be included in a functional curriculum are basic operations, consumer skills, telling time and estimating time intervals, general estimation, budgeting and money management, banking skills, calculating simple interest, computing taxes, and evaluating insurance and benefit plans. Table 12.7 provides a listing of recommended functional math skills for students with handicaps.

Math skills required for vocational fields are somewhat broader in scope. Many occupations require skills in calculating areas, volumes, weights, surface areas, and capacities of geometrical shapes and solids. Additional vocational math requirements are solving mixture problems; calculating ratios, percentages, averages, and proportions; and reading meters, bills, and specification reports. Finally, isolating variables and relating variables to understand their mutual effects and individual contribution to problems or solutions are other areas of proficiency that some occupations require. In addition to real-life and vocational math skills, the increased technology and science permeating society means that all citizens need more sophisticated skills than was true 25 years ago. Table 12.8 presents skills and competencies that adults need to function competently in today's society.

SUMMARY

Effective mathematics instruction for all children requires careful consideration of the content to be taught; methods and techniques of teaching that content; and the abilities, understandings, and motivational levels of the students. Mathematics instruction cannot be limited to the topics of addition, subtraction, multiplication, and division. Students must learn to solve real-world problems, estimate, reason, and communicate about mathematics. Developing true understanding should be the goal of mathematics instruction for all students.

TABLE 12.7   Content for Teaching Functional Math Skills

Consumer Skills
Making change
Determining cost of sale items utilizing percentages (e.g., "25% off")
Determining tax amounts
Doing cost comparisons
Buying on "time"
Balancing a checkbook
Determining total cost of purchases

Homemaking Skills
Measuring ingredients
Budgeting for household expenses
Calculating length of cooking and baking time when there are options (e.g., for a cake using two 9-inch round pans vs two 8-inch round pans)
Measuring material for clothing construction
Doing cost comparisons

Health Care
Weighing oneself and others
Calculating caloric intake
Determining when to take medication

Auto Care
Calculating cost of auto parts
Measuring spark plug gaps
Determining if tire pressure is correct
Figuring gas mileage

Home Care
Determining amount of supplies (e.g., paint or rug shampoo) to buy
Determining time needed to do projects
Measuring rods and drapes
Finding cost of supplies
Finding cost of repairs

Vocational Needs
Calculating payroll deductions
Determining money owed
Knowing when to be at work
Doing actual math for various jobs

Source: From "Mathematics for handicapped learners: A functional approach for adolescents" by S.E. Schwartz and D. Budd, *Focus on Exceptional Children 13(7)*, March 1981, pp. 7–8. Reprinted by permission of Love Publishing, Denver.

TABLE 12.8 Real Life Mathematical Concepts

1. Number and numerals
   - Express a rational number using a decimal notation.
   - List the first ten multiples of 2–12.
   - Use the whole numbers (four basic operations) in problem solving.
   - Recognize the digit, its place value, and the number represented through billions.
   - Describe a given positive rational number using decimal, percentage, or fractional notation.
   - Convert to Roman numerals from decimal numerals and conversely (e.g., data translation).
   - Represent very large and very small numbers using scientific notation.
2. Operations and properties
   - Write equivalent fractions for given fractions such as 1/2, 2/3, 3/4, and 7/8.
   - Use the standard algorithms for the operations of arithmetic of positive rational numbers.
   - Solve addition, subtraction, multiplication, and division problems involving fractions.
   - Solve problems involving percentage.
   - Perform arithmetic operations with measures.
   - Estimate results.
   - Judge the reasonableness of answers to computational problems.
3. Mathematical sentences
   - Construct a mathematical sentence from a given verbal problem.
   - Solve simple equations.
4. Geometry and measurement
   - Recognize horizontal lines, vertical lines, parallel lines, perpendicular lines, and intersecting lines.
   - Recognize different shapes.
   - Compute areas, surfaces, volumes, and densities.
   - Understand similarities and congruence.
   - Use measurement devices.
5. Relations and functions
   - Interpret information from a graphical representation.
   - Understand and apply ratio and proportion.
   - Construct scales.
6. Probability and statistics
   - Determine mean, average, mode, and median.
   - Understand simple probability.
7. Mathematical reasoning
   - Produce counterexamples to test invalidity of a statement.
   - Detect and describe flaws and fallacies in advertising and propaganda in which statistical data and inferences are employed.
   - Gather and present data to support an inference or argument.
8. General skills
   - Maintain personal bank records.
   - Plan a budget and keep personal records.
   - Apply a simple interest formula to calculate interest.
   - Estimate the real cost of an item.
   - Compute taxes and investment returns.
   - Appraise insurance and retirement benefits.

Source: M.C. Sharman (1984). "Mathematics in the real world." pp. 227–252. In J.F. Cawley (Ed.). *Developmental Teaching of Mathematics for the Learning Disabled.* Copyright 1984 by PRO-ED, Inc. Reprinted by permission.

This chapter has reviewed key features of the mathematics reform movement, with emphasis on understanding and applying mathematics knowledge to real-life situations. It overviewed key learner characteristics as they relate to math instruction, identifying rate of learning, past learning, memory, verbal and symbol skills, the ability to identify and attend to relevant features of a problem situation, and problem-solving approaches as critical variables. A lesson delivery structure was delineated, and math curricula and instructional aids were reviewed. Instructional topics were described with instructional recommendations presented for the following areas: prenumber and number concepts, place value and basic symbols, basic facts and algorithms, fractions and decimals, estimation and mental computation measurement, and geometry, as well as applications of math concepts and operations to real-life problems. Throughout, the use of manipulatives, concrete experiences, and teacher-guided instruction were emphasized.

CONTENT MASTERY QUESTIONS

1. Discuss the current recommendations for changing the focus of mathematics curricula.

2. Describe the seven student characteristics related to mathematics learning.

3. List and review the appropriateness of the two approaches to mathematics instruction.

4. Critique the use of basal programs, direct instruction materials, and manipulative materials for mathematics instruction.

5. Explain the five-step instructional process for effective lesson delivery to students with achievement difficulties.

6. Name and define the two types of mathematical knowledge.

7. List the ten interrelated concepts within the NCTM mathematical scope of mathematical knowledge.

8. Describe the skills to be learned within the ten concepts on the NCTM scope of sequence.

9. Discuss effective teaching strategies for mathematics instruction for each level of the scope of the sequence.

10. Describe materials and activities for effective teaching of the ten content areas of mathematics instruction.

REFERENCES

Baker, J., & Zigmond, N. (1989. *Snapshots of an elementary school: Are regular education classes equipped to accommodate learning disabled students?* Paper presented at the conferences of the American Educational Research Association, San Francisco, April, 1989.

Bartel, N. (1982). Problems in mathematics achievement. In D. Hammill and N. Bartel. *Teaching children with learning and behavior problems,* (3rd ed). (pp. 27–42). Boston: Allyn and Bacon.

Blankenship, C. S., & Lovitt, T. C. (1976). Story problems: Merely confusing or downright befuddling? *Journal of Research in Mathematics Education, 7,* 290–298.

Capps, L., & Cox, L. S. (1991). Improving the learning of mathematics in our schools. *Focus on Exceptional Children, 23*(9), 1–8.

Carpenter, R. L. (1985). Mathematics instruction in resource rooms: Instruction time and teacher competency. *Learning Disability Quarterly, 8,* 95–100.

Carnine, D., & Stein, M. (1981). Organizational strategies and practice procedures for teaching basic facts. *Journal for Research in Mathematics Education, 12*(1), 65–69.

Carpenter, T. P., & Moser, J. M. (1984). The acquisition of addition and subtraction concepts in grades one through three. *Journal for Research in Mathematics Education, 15,* 179–202.

Cawley, J. F. (1985a). Cognition and the learning disabled. In J. Cawley (Ed.), *Cognitive strategies and mathematics for the learning disabled* (pp. 1–31). Rockville, MD: Aspen Systems Corp.

Cawley, J. F. (1985b). Thinking. In J. Cawley (Ed.), *Cognitive strategies and mathematics for the learning disabled* (pp. 1–31). Rockville, MD: Aspen Systems Corp.

Cawley, J. F. (1984). Selection, adaptation, and development of curricula and instructional materials. In J. F. Cawley (Ed.), *Developmental teaching of mathematics for the learning disabled* (pp. 227–252). Rockville, MD: Aspen Systems Corp.

Cawley, J., Fitzmaurice-Hayes, A., & Shaw, R. A. (1988). *Mathematics for the mildly handicapped: A guide to curriculum and instruction.* Boston: Allyn & Bacon.

Cawley, J. F., Fitzmaurice, A. M., Shaw, R. A., Kahn, H., & Bates, H. (1979). Math word problems: Suggestions for LD students. *Learning Disability Quarterly, 2,* 25–41.

Cawley, J. F., Miller, J. H., & School, B. A. (1987). A brief inquiry of arithmetic word problem-solving among learning disabled secondary students. *Learning Disabilities Focus, 2*(2), 87–93.

Cohen, E. G. (1986) *Designing groupwork: Strategies for the heterogeneous classroom.* New York: Teachers College Press.

Cohen, S. A., & Stover, G. (1981). Effects of teaching sixth-grade students to modify variables of math word problems. *Reading Research Quarterly, 16,* 175–199.

Cruickshank, D. E., & Sheffield, L. J. (1988). *Teaching mathematics to elementary school children: A foundation for the future.* Columbus, OH: Merrill.

Derr, A. M. (1985). Conservation and mathematics in the learning disabled child. *Journal of Learning Disabilities, 18,* 333–336.

Edge, D., & Ashlock, R. B. (1982). Using multiple embodiments of place value concepts. *Alberta Journal of Educational Research, 28,* 276–279.

Englemann, S., & Carnine, D. (1991). *Connecting math concepts.* Chicago, IL: Science Research Associates.

Englert, C. S., Culatta, B. E., & Horn, D. G. (1987). Influence of irrelevant information in addition word problems on problems solving. *Learning Disability Quarterly, 10,* 29–36.

Fink, W. T., & Carnine, D. W. (1975). Control of arithmetic errors using information feedback and graphing. *Journal of Applied Behavioral Analysis, 8,* 461 (Abstract).

Fleischner, J. E., Nuzum, M. B., & Marzola, E. S. (1987). Devising an instructional program to teach arithmetic problem-solving skills to students with learning disabilities. *Journal of Learning Disabilities, 20,* 214–217.

Geary, D.C, Widaman, K. F., Little, T. A.D., & Cormier, P. (1987). Cognitive addition: Comparison of learning disabled and academically normal elementary school children. *Cognitive Development, 2,* 249–269.

Good, T. L., & Grouws, D. A. (1979). The Missouri mathematics effectiveness project: An experimental study in fourth-grade classrooms. *Journal of Educational Psychology, 71,* 355–362.

Goodstein, H. A., Cawley, J., Gordon, S., & Helfgott, J. (1971). Verbal problem-solving among educable mentally retarded children. *American Journal of Mental Deficiency, 76,* 238–241.

Greeno, J. G. (1978). A study of problem-solving. *In* R. Glaser (ed.). *Advances in instructional psychology.* (vol. 1.) Hillsdale, NJ: Lawrence Erlbaum.

Grimes, K. (1981). Learned helplessness and attribution theory: Redefining children's learning problems. *Learning Disability Quarterly, 4,* 238–243.

Halpern, N. (1981). Mathematics for the learning disabled. *Journal of Learning Disabilities, 16,* 616–620.

Harris, K., & Pressley, M. (1989). The nature of cognitive instruction: Interactive strategy construction. *Exceptional Children, 57*(5), 392–404.

Hasselbring, T. S., & Goin, L. I. (1986). *CAMS: Chronometric assessment of math strategies.* Nashville, TN: Expert Systems Software, Inc.

Hasselbring, T. S., & Goin, L. I., & Bransford, J. D. (1987). Developing automaticity. *Teaching Exceptional Children, 19*(3), 30–33.

Hasselbring, T. S., & Goin, L. I., & Sherwood, R. (1987). *The effects of computer-based drill-and-practice on automaticity,* Technical Report. Nashville, TN: Vanderbilt University, Learning Technology Center.

Haupt, E. J., Van Kirk, M. J., & Terraciano, T. (1975). An expensive fading procedure to decrease errors and increase retention of number facts. In E. Ramp and G. Semb (eds.). *Behavior analysis: Areas of research and application.* (pp. 79–92). Englewood Cliffs, NJ: Prentice-Hall.

Johnston, M. B., & Whitman, T. L. (1987). Enhancing math computation through variations in training format and instructional content. *Cognitive Therapy and Research, 11,* 381–397.

Kamii, M. (1982). Children's ideas about written numbers. *Topics in Learning and Learning Disabilities, 1,* 247–251.

Kirby, J. R., & Becker, L. D. (1988). Cognitive components of learning problems in arithmetic. *Remedial and Special Education, 9,* 7–16.

Lloyd, J. W. (1980). Academic instruction and cognitive-behavior modification: The need for attack strategy training. *Exceptional Education Quarterly, 1*(1), 53–63.

Lloyd, J. W., & Keller, C. E. (1989). Effective mathematics instruction: Development, instruction, and programs. *Focus on Exceptional Children, 21,* 1–10.

Mastropieri, M. A., & Scruggs, T. E. (1987). *Effective instruction for special education.* Austin, TX: PRO-ED.

Mathematical Sciences Education Board (1989). *Mathematics education: Wellspring of U.S. industrial strength.* Washington, DC: National Academy Press.

Mattingly, J. C., & Bott, D. A. (1990). Teaching multiplication facts to students with learning problems. *Exceptional Children, 56(5),* 438–449.

McLeod, T., & Armstrong, S. (1982). Learning disabilities in mathematic skill deficits and remedial approaches at the intermediate and secondary grades. *Learning Disability Quarterly, 5,* 305–311.

Montague, M., & Bos, C. S. (1986). The effect of cognitive strategy training on verbal math problem solving performance of learning disabled adolescents. *Journal of Learning Disabilities, 12,* 26–33.

Mullis, I. V.S., Dossey, J. A., Owen, E. H., & Phillips, G. W. (1991). *The STATE of Mathematics Achievement (Executive Summary).* U. S. Department of Education, Report No. 21-ST-03.

National Council of Supervisors of Mathematics (1988). *Essential elements of school mathematics.* Reston, VA: National Council of Teachers of Mathematics.

National Council of Teachers of Mathematics. (1986). *Position statement on calculator usage.* Reston, VA. National Council of Teachers of Mathematics.

National Council of Teachers of Mathematics. (1989). *Curriculum and evaluation standards for school mathematics.* Reston, VA. National Council of Teachers of Mathematics.

Nesher, P. (1982). Levels of description in the analysis of addition and subtraction word problems. In T. P. Carpenter, J. M. Mosher, and T. A. Rosenberg (Eds.), *Addition and subtraction: A cognitive perspective.* (pp. 25–38). Hillsdale, NJ: Lawrence Erlbaum Associates.

Parner, R. S., & Cawley, J. F. (1991). Challenging the routines and passivity that characterize arithmetic instruction for children with mild handicaps. *Remedial and Special Education 12*(5), 22–32, 43.

Peters, E. Lloyd, J., Hasselbring, T., Goin, L., Bransford, J., & Stein, M. (1986). Effective mathematics instruction. *Teaching Exceptional Children, 31,* 30.

Polya, G. (1957). *How to solve it* (2nd ed.). Princeton, NJ: Princeton University Press.

Porter, A. (1989). A curriculum out of balance: The case of elementary school mathematics. *Educational Researcher, 18*(5), 9–15.

Reisman, F. R., & Kauffman, S. H. (1980). *Teaching mathematics to children with special needs.* Columbus, OH: Merrill.

Resnick, L. B. (1983). A developmental theory of number understanding. In H. O. Ginsburg (Ed.). *The development of mathematical thinking.* (pp. 99–151). New York: Academic Press.

Russell, R. L., & Ginsburg, H. P. (1984). Cognitive analysis of children's mathematical difficulties. *Cognition and Instruction, 1,* 217–244.

Schminke, C., Masters, N., & Arnold, W. (1978). *Teaching the child mathematics.* New York: Holt.

Schunk, D. H., & Cox, P. D. (1986). Strategy training and attributional feedback with learning disabled students. *Journal of Educational Psychology, 78,* 201–209.

Schwartz, S. E., & Budd, D. (1981). Mathematics for handicapped learners: A functional approach for adolescents. *Focus on Exceptional Children, 13(7),* 7–8.

Sharman, M. C. (1984). Mathematics in the real world, pp. 227–252. In J. F. Cawley (Ed.), *Developmental teaching of mathematics for the learning disabled.* Austin, TX: PRO-ED.

Shaw, R. A. (1985). Measurement concepts and skills. In J. F. Cawley (Ed.), *Secondary school mathematics for the learning disabled.* Rockville, MD: Aspen Systems Corp.

Silbert, J., Carnine, D., & Stein, M. (1990). *Direct instruction mathematics.* Columbus, OH: Merrill.

Smith, D. D. (1991). *Teaching students with learning and behavior problems,* (2nd ed.) Englewood Cliffs, NJ: Prentice-Hall.

Torgenson, J. K. (1986). Using computers to help learning disabled children practice reading: A research-based perspective. *Learning Disabilities Focus, 1*(2), 72–81.

Whitman, T., & Johnston, M. B. (1983). Teaching addition and subtraction with regrouping to educable mentally retarded children: A group self-instructional training program. *Behavior Therapy, 14,* 127–143.

Zweng, M. J., Garaghty, J., & Turner, J. (1980). *Children's strategies of solving verbal problems. Final Report.* Washington, DC: National Institute of Education.

CHAPTER 13

Promoting Learning in Content Classes

B. KEITH LENZ
JANIS A. BULGREN

CHAPTER OBJECTIVES

At the conclusion of this chapter, the reader will be able to:

1. Describe the factors that contribute to the difficulties low-achieving students experience and the methods the schools use to alleviate these difficulties.
2. Differentiate between internally mediated and externally mediated strategies that can assist students with learning problems to improve learning.
3. Describe teacher-mediated strategies that can be implemented to enhance content.
4. Give examples of content enhancement routines and devices.
5. Describe what a teacher might do when planning, selecting, and implementing content enhancement.
6. Identify ways to help students develop self-responsibility.
7. Discuss the salient features of a cooperative teaching model, describing the roles of both the content teacher and the support teacher.

Many students with learning problems find the transition from elementary to secondary school settings difficult. They are not prepared for the more impersonal and more strongly academic focus of the secondary schools. The core demands of secondary schools emphasize understanding and remembering associated concepts and facts presented in content classes (e.g., social studies, science, and history), and applying these concepts and facts in a manner (usually written) that demonstrates mastery of them (Lenz & Mellard, 1989). Due to academic problems in the elementary grades, the students may not have adequate background knowledge for the more rigorous content-area courses in social studies, science, language arts, mathematics, and vocational education. To further complicate matters, limited mastery of reading, written expression, and study skills may make it difficult for these students to handle the learning tasks presented. Finally, structural features of the secondary schools such as large classes of 50 minutes in length taught by teachers who see 120–150 or more students per day, as well as difficult textbooks that may not be "user friendly" and complex language demands can contribute to achievement problems.

Given their long histories of academic difficulties, students' motivation for content learning may be low. Faced with continued failure, these students are at risk of dropping out of school. These students need special assistance if they are to meet the task-demands of the school environment, learn the skills and content that will prepare them for successful transitions to adulthood, and graduate from high school.

This chapter describes approaches for promoting effective and efficient acquisition of content-area information. It reviews student-mediated approaches and focuses on teacher-mediated approaches. The term *mediators* refers to those techniques or strategies that an individual utilizes for the purpose of improving learning or performance. Mediators assist the individual in translating new information into a form that is meaningful and memorable. Mediators can be either externally generated or internally generated. **Externally generated mediators** include such elements as curriculum materials, texts, graphics, media, and teacher's instruction. **Internally generated mediators** are produced by the learner at her convenience to meet particular learning needs, and include the internal information and cognitive processing of the student.

This chapter extends the discussion presented in Chapter 9 on teaching students learning strategies that can assist them to become independent learners. The chapter reviews applying this approach as the preferred intervention in the secondary schools and overviews the *Strategies Intervention Model* curriculum, a research-based program developed specifically for secondary-age students. The chapter focuses on teacher-mediated strategies that make the content more accessible and meaningful to students. Using audiovisual aides, study guides, and computer-assisted instruction are examples of such strategies.

Throughout, the chapter stresses the teacher's role as a strategist or "good thinker" who integrates what students must learn with information about how students learn in order to select appropriate methods for content delivery. Teachers must identify the parameters of instructional problems, think about their relevant dimensions, select intervention strategies, teach the strategies to students, monitor their effectiveness, and make necessary adaptations and/or changes. Ultimately, they must promote active student learning by emphasizing and using learning cues.

MEETING STUDENTS' NEEDS

Historically, schools have attempted to deal with the challenges of lower-quartile students in a variety of ways. **Tracking** into different ability groups or curricular tracks (special, vocational, or general education; college-prep; or honors track) has sought to reduce the heterogeneity of students in courses, and to adapt course content and instruction to students' ability levels and learning characteristics. In the 70's and 80's, this approach has been criticized as discriminatory to many low-income students from minority groups. Concerns have been raised that tracking may deny students the opportunities to participate in important learning opportunities, restrict their access to content knowledge, and limit their educational progress. The **remedial approach** attempts to help students "catch up" by developing the basic skills they failed to learn at the elementary levels. However, students who have experienced failure in these basic skills for 6–10 years tend to be poorly motivated ("try, try, and try again"). Furthermore, time spent acquiring basic skills curtails the time available for instruction in higher-order skills or for acquiring content knowledge of their courses. The **tutorial approach** provides one-on-one or small group tutoring in the academic content areas. This is teacher intensive, time demanding, and fails to establish the students' independent learning skills.

In the 90's, the focus of programs for students with learning difficulties in the secondary schools has shifted to helping students become strategic learners. As described in Chapter 9, **learning strategies** are "tools" that learners can use to facilitate their analysis of the demands of given problems, guide their completion of the tasks, and help them to monitor their learning along the way. They are student-mediated devices that assist students in becoming more efficient and independent learners. In addition, teachers using the **content enhancement** approaches can facilitate student learning. These teacher-mediated strategies focus students' attention on critical elements of the information to be learned. These include both individual and peer-assisted approaches for orienting students to the material to be learned, manipulating this information, and completing assignments.

INTERNALLY MEDIATED INTERVENTIONS

Many students develop internally generated mediators as outgrowths of their own active learning and content comprehension. For students with difficulties in these areas, various approaches have been developed for assisting them. These approaches have focused on developing study skills and learning strategies.

In the 80's and 90's, study skills instruction has become a popular intervention. Because these skills can be applied across subject areas, they frequently are viewed as a generalized approach to addressing difficulties in content achievement. Traditional study skills programs focus on procedures for taking notes, studying for tests, making outlines, and so forth. In the 80's and 90's, research into study skills instruction has emphasized the importance of teaching students not only how to perform skills or processes, but on how to make decisions relative to using the skills. For example, traditional instruction in outlining presented the various levels of an outline followed by practice in arranging content in the outline form. Newer instructional approaches in outlining also teach students how to decide when and what to outline, and how to determine the relative importance of information that might be included on the outlines.

Learning strategy instruction represents the second broad area of student-mediated interventions. It is concerned first with determining the demands of the content learning environment and then with teaching the students strategies related to meeting those demands. It focuses on the ways in which students think and act when planning, executing, and evaluating performance on a task and its outcomes (Deshler & Lenz, 1989). Through instruction in strategies, students are taught how to learn and to perform in manners that enable them to:

1. Acquire the critical skills and content necessary for success in the secondary school setting and in the community.
2. Acquire the appropriate social skills that will enable them to interact appropriately with others across both in-school and out-of-school situations.
3. Become motivated to set and attain goals related to completing school, and to personal and life tasks.

4. Generalize learned skills and knowledge across settings and situations for both immediate success and success in making a transition to postsecondary life.

Strategies Intervention Model

Researchers at the University of Kansas Institute for Research in Learning Disabilities developed a comprehensive strategies curriculum. This **Strategies Intervention Model (SIM)** is specifically designed to promote content-area learning with students who are low-achieving or have mild disabilities. Strategies for assisting the students to meet the demands of the regular classroom environments have been developed in four areas: (1) learning strategies; (2) social strategies; (3) motivation strategies; and (4) executive strategies. Each intervention consists of strategies linked and organized in a fashion that promotes an effective and efficient approach to tasks associated with success in the mainstream setting. As a result, in one strategy intervention, there may be six or seven cognitive or metacognitive strategies linked together and cued to promote successful task response. Therefore, the focus of the instruction is on whole-to-part learning with sufficient instruction in the parts to enable students' success.

The specific learning strategy interventions included in SIM were based on an analysis of the demands placed on students in regular middle and secondary school settings. These demands include: (1) acquiring information, (2) storing information so that it can be retrieved and used as needed, and (3) expressing and demonstrating information that has been learned in an effective manner (Deshler & Schumaker, 1988). The strategies designed to address each of these learning demands are presented in the following descriptions.

Acquisition Strategies

- *The Word Identification Strategy.* This strategy teaches students a problem-solving procedure for quickly attacking and decoding unknown words when reading passages.

- *The Paraphrasing Strategy.* Using this strategy, students read a limited section of materials, ask themselves the main ideas and the details of the sections, and put that information in their own words. This strategy improves comprehension by focusing attention on the important information in the passages and by stimulating active involvement with the passages.

- *The Self-questioning Strategy.* When students generate questions about key pieces of information in passages and then read to find the answers to these questions, reading comprehension improves.

- *The Visual Imagery Strategy.* Improved students' acquisition, storage, and recall of prose material are the goals of this strategy. Students read short passages and then visualize the scenes they describe, incorporating actors, actions, and details.

- *The Interpreting Visuals Strategy.* This strategy aids students in reading and interpreting visuals such as maps, graphs, pictures, and tables that are commonly found in textbooks.

- *The Multipass Strategy.* When using this strategy, students make three passes through passages to focus their attention on main ideas and key details. They survey chapters or passages to get an overview, size up sections of the chapters by systematically scanning to locate relevant information, and sort out important information in the chapters by locating answers to specific questions.

Storage Strategies

- *The FIRST-Letter Mnemonic Strategy.* By teaching students to design mnemonics or memorization aids from lists of crucial information, this strategy is designed to aid students in memorizing lists of information.

- *The Paired Associates Strategy.* Student memorization of pairs or small groups of information is improved when they learn to match two items through using visual imagery, employing a keyword technique, matching pertinent information with familiar objects, or coding important dates.

- *The Listening and Notetaking Strategy.* This strategy enhances listening competency by teaching students to identify the verbal cues or mannerisms that signal when speakers are about to give important information. This assists students to organize their notes into outlines for future reference or study.

Expression and Demonstration of Competence Strategies

- *The Sentence Writing Strategy.* This strategy is designed to teach students how to recognize and generate four types of sentences: (1) simple, (2) compound, (3) complex, and (4) compound-complex.

- *Paragraph Writing Strategy.* This strategy is designed to teach students how to write well-organized, complete paragraphs by outlining ideas, selecting a point-of-view and tense for the paragraphs, sequencing ideas, and checking their work.

- *The Error Monitoring Strategy.* With this strategy, students learn a process for detecting and correcting errors in their writings, and for producing neater written products. Students learn to locate errors in paragraph organization, sentence structure, capitalization, overall editing and appearance, punctuation, and spelling by asking themselves a series of questions. They correct their errors and rewrite the passages before submitting them to their teachers.

- *The Theme Writing Strategy.* This strategy assists students in writing five-paragraph themes. Students learn how to generate ideas for themes, how to organize those ideas into logical sequences, how to write five-paragraph themes, how to monitor errors, and how to edit and rewrite the themes.

- *The Assignment Completion Strategy.* With this strategy, students learn to monitor assignments from the time they are given until they are completed and turned in to the teacher. Students write down assignments; analyze them; schedule various subtasks; complete the subtasks, and ultimately, the entire task; and finally, submit the completed work.

- *The Test Taking Strategy.* Students use this strategy when taking tests. It teaches them to carefully allocate time, and to carefully read the directions and questions. They learn to either answer questions quickly or abandon them for later consideration. Students then eliminate obviously wrong answers from the abandoned questions and make reasonable guesses at their answers. Finally, they survey their entire tests for unanswered questions.

Because the procedures the SIM researchers developed for training teachers to use these strategies are detailed and specific, instructional information and materials on the strategies are available only through enrollment in training provided by SIM-certified instructors. Therefore, the content of specific strategies is not included in this chapter. The following discussion presents critical features of SIM using examples from *The Paraphrasing Strategy* (Schumaker, Denton, & Deshler, 1984).

Each strategy has a remembering system that is used to promote the strategy learning. Each also includes an instructional process that help students to engage in certain procedural and cognitive activities corresponding to each of the steps in the remembering system. Figure 13.1 illustrates the steps of *The Paraphrasing Strategy* remembering system. Figure 13.2 illustrates several activities that the remembering system is designed to cue.

Each strategy is taught through an eight-stage instructional process designed to promote strategy acquisition and generalization to regular classroom settings. Figure 13.3 presents the stages associated with promoting strategy acquisition and generalization.

Throughout the instructional process the student explores how each strategy can be used in content-area classes. Strategy generalization is promoted through the combined efforts of the stu-

R = Read a paragraph.

A = Ask yourself, "What are the main ideas and details in this paragraph?"

P = Put the main idea and details into your own words.

FIGURE 13.1   The Remembering System of the Paraphrasing Strategy

Source: Reproduced with permission from J.B. Schumaker, P. Denton, and D.D. Deshler (1984). *The Learning Strategies Curriculum: The Paraphrasing Strategy.* Lawrence: The University of Kansas Institute for Research in Learning Disabilities.

dents and the teachers from various courses who prompt strategy usage. The criterion for success of the intervention is based on evaluating of content-area performance.

Promoting Generalization of Strategies

Even after students have demonstrated appropriate mastery levels in specific strategies, **generalization,** that is, the ability to correctly apply what is known in one setting to another, may not automatically occur. The generalization of acquired skills is one of the most difficult challenges that teachers face with low-achieving students. If the student has learned a strategy in a pull-out or special support class program, part of the responsibility for ensuring its generalization rests with the support class teacher, part rests with the student, and part rests with the content-area teacher. The support class teacher must specifically teach generalization skills, the student must engage in the generalization process, and the content-area teacher must facilitate these processes.

If students are to have sufficient opportunities to apply a strategy and to experience success with them, the support teacher and the content-area teachers must engage in **cooperative teaching** in which teaching interventions occur cooperatively across settings in both the support class setting and the content learning setting. The content-area teacher should inform the support class

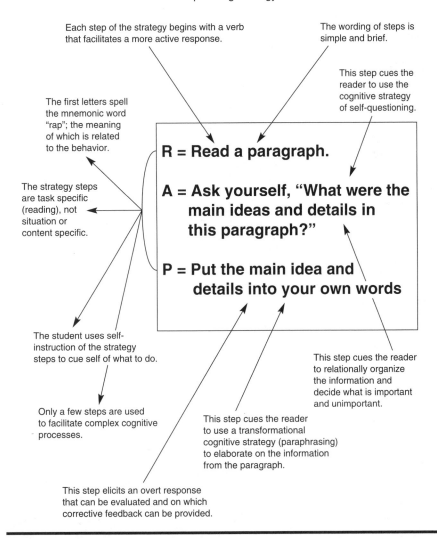

Anatomy of a Learning Strategy

The Remembering System of the
Paraphrasing Strategy

Each step of the strategy begins with a verb that facilitates a more active response.

The wording of steps is simple and brief.

This step cues the reader to use the cognitive strategy of self-questioning.

The first letters spell the mnemonic word "rap"; the meaning of which is related to the behavior.

The strategy steps are task specific (reading), not situation or content specific.

R = Read a paragraph.

A = Ask yourself, "What were the main ideas and details in this paragraph?"

P = Put the main idea and details into your own words

The student uses self-instruction of the strategy steps to cue self of what to do.

This step cues the reader to relationally organize the information and decide what is important and unimportant.

Only a few steps are used to facilitate complex cognitive processes.

This step cues the reader to use a transformational cognitive strategy (paraphrasing) to elaborate on the information from the paragraph.

This step elicits an overt response that can be evaluated and on which corrective feedback can be provided.

FIGURE 13.2   Anatomy of a Learning Strategy for the Remembering System of the Paraphrasing Strategy

Source: Reproduced with permission from Ellis and Lenz (in press).

teacher when a student is having difficulty in a class so that the support teacher can select a strategy and instruct the student in its use. The two teachers should communicate regularly to determine if the strategy is being used successfully. In addition, the support class teacher should communicate with other content-area teachers, provide progress feedback to the student, and help the student plan for long-term application of the strategy across settings. Content-area teachers

Stage 1: Pretest and make commitments
      Phase 1: Orientation and pretest
      Phase 2: Awareness and commitment

Stage 2: Describe the strategy
      Phase 1: Orientation and overview
      Phase 2: Present strategy and remembering system

Stage 3: Model the strategy
      Phase 1: Orientation
      Phase 2: Presentation
      Phase 3: Student enlistment

Stage 4: Verbal elaboration and rehearsal
      Phase 1: Verbal elaboration
      Phase 2: Verbal rehearsal

Stage 5: Controlled practice and feedback
      Phase 1: Orientation and overview
      Phase 2: Guided practice
      Phase 3: Independent practice

Stage 6: Advanced practice and feedback
      Phase 1: Orientation and overview
      Phase 2: Guided practice
      Phase 3: Independent practice

Stage 7: Confirm acquisition and make generalization commitments
      Phase 1: Confirm and celebrate
      Phase 2: Forecast and commit to generalization

Stage 8: Generalization
      Phase 1: Orientation
      Phase 2: Activation
      Phase 3: Adaptation
      Phase 4: Maintenance

FIGURE 13.3   The Stages of Strategy Acquisition and Generalization
Source: From Ellis, Deshler, Lenz, Schumaker & Clark (1991).

should monitor the application of the strategy to the specific content learning demands of the class. This requires that they be familiar with the strategy steps and criteria for successful application, be prepared to cue the student when appropriate, and prompt and lead if necessary. Finally, once the strategy is generalized, content-area teachers can work with the student to attain greater efficiency in using the strategy as a tool for new learning challenges.

One approach to promoting strategy generalization is to give the student a 3 × 5-inch card or bookmark with the remembering system or strategy steps written on it. Placing this cue card in textbooks and notebooks where it can be seen can serve to prompt applying the strategy in appropriate contexts. The content-area teacher can check to see if this cueing system has been implemented, and if it has not, the teacher can prompt the student to design his own cue card.

Sometimes the student will need direct guidance in determining when to use a strategy. Direct ways for cueing strategy use include: (1) discretely telling the student to use a particular strategy,

(2) informing the whole class to use a particular strategy on a routine basis, (3) putting the name of the strategy on the chalkboard or bulletin board, and (4) prompting peers who know the strategy to cue those who do not.

Persistent problems with strategy generalization suggest that the strategy instruction in the support settings is flawed. It may be that the student(s) did not possess the required prerequisite skills when instruction began, or that mastery of the strategy was not obtained before it was applied in the content classroom. Failure to generalize a strategy can also occur if the student was insufficiently motivated to learn the strategy, and therefore is not committed to its application across settings.

It is clear that strategy instruction represents an important approach to promoting the independent success of students in learning content-area subjects. However, student mediation alone cannot ensure academic success. The following section describes externally mediated interventions, particularly those that the teacher does that also facilitate student learning.

EXTERNALLY MEDIATED INTERVENTIONS

Many curriculum materials or instructional methods use externally generated mediators to improve student learning and performance. Examples are inserting questions in text and restructuring text organization (e.g., Armbruster & Anderson, 1985; Kameenui, Simmons & Darch, 1987), using structured study guides (Lovitt, Rudsit, Jenkins, Pious, & Benedetti, 1985), using skill-assisted audiotape recording packages (Schumaker, Denton, & Deshler, 1984), and employing computer assisted instruction (Ellis & Sabornie, 1986). Well-selected external stimuli or cues can lead to more efficient information processing and, therefore, to higher student achievement. In general, the success of these types of mediators appears to depend on the teaching agent's ability to incorporate them into the instructional process in a manner that will have a positive influence on learning.

Teacher-Mediated Approaches

The primary approach for implementing teacher-mediated interventions is to use teaching routines and devices that enhance the meaningfulness of content by promoting student organizing, understanding, and remembering. This process, referred to as *Content Enhancement* (Lenz, Bulgren, & Hudson, 1990; Schumaker, Deshler, & McKnight, in press), requires teachers to carefully select, organize, and manipulate the critical features of the information that students are to learn. Teachers analyze the curriculum to distinguish the important information from the less important information. They decide how to make abstract concepts more concrete, how to reorganize poorly organized information, how to clarify the relationships among information, how to explore important points, how to devise alternate avenues to achieve understanding, and how to embellish potentially meaningless or dull concepts. To facilitate the active involvement of students in mediating their own learning, teachers can explain how specific mediators or teaching strategies promote learning and prompt the students to be as strategic and independent as possible.

Routines for Content Enhancement

Content Enhancement routines attempt to structure the teaching act so as to minimize the learning difficulties of students with achievement difficulties. Sets of integrated instructional procedures that guide the delivery of large chunks of information in a lesson can be thought of as routines that *orient* students to the material to be learned, routines that guide students to *understanding* the material, and as routines that develop *self-responsibility* for learning.

Orientation Routines

Orientation is the process of preparing students for instruction by directing their attention to what they already have learned and its relationship to what is to be learned (Ausubel, 1963; Ausubel,

Novak & Hanesian, 1968). The teacher might think about preparing for the orientation process in the following manner:

> *Okay, tomorrow I need to begin to cover the section of the chapter on reproduction in flowering plants. . . . hmm . . . . . . Let's see, today we finished the section on simple forms of reproduction. . . . I want them to see the relationship between some of the concepts that we learned in the last section and how these concepts apply to reproduction in flowering plants. . . . Okay, tomorrow I will begin by first reviewing the last section. I want to really draw their attention to some of the bridging concepts. . . . hmm. . I think I will write these concepts on the chalkboard and have them define them for me . . . they should know these. . . . Next, I want them to understand the major topics . . . Maybe, I better have these on the chalkboard, too. . . . I should have a list of the vocabulary I want them to know from a study guide I did last year. . . . hmm, here it is . . . Let's see . . . there are quite a few words, I better prepare a handout of the key vocabulary words to give to them right away. If I don't, it will take some of them forever to get these words down. I'll tell them to write the definitions down as as we cover the words in class. Good, that should be a good way to start . . . Let's see, that should take about 5 or 6 minutes. . . . Okay . . . let's look at how I am going to teach this. . . .*

In this way, the teachers review what has been learned, preview what is to be learned, and make decisions about how students can be guided to learn the content. The teachers draw on their knowledge of and previous experiences with the content, their knowledge of the structure of the textbook or materials, and their knowledge of how students are likely to process the information. They also make judgments about the relative importance of the information to which students will be exposed.

This orientation process should occur at each level of information organization (i.e., lesson, chapter, unit, and course). For example, as a student begins a course in biology, the teacher should orient the student to the broad concepts related to biology that will cut across the course as each unit and chapter is covered. The same orientation process should occur as a new unit is begun and as a new chapter is initiated. The orientation process places the current learning goals, at whatever level, in the context of what the student already knows and relates them to expected outcomes.

Throughout the content instruction, teachers continue to orient students to the lessons. Teachers point out instances in which students already have prior knowledge and experience related to specific topics, they orient students as to where they are within the context of the the overall learning task, and, finally, at the close of the lesson, they check to see if students actually have learned the critical information. When this mastery has not occurred, teachers refocus their attention on the most important information or concepts.

Lenz, Ellis and Scanlon (in press) have identified approaches to incorporating organizer components prior to beginning a content lesson, during instruction, and after instruction. While these are conceptualized here as teacher-mediated approaches, over time, students can learn to cue themselves in using organizers (Lenz, Alley & Schumaker, 1987). The three types of organizers include:

1. Advance organizer

- Gain students' attention and tell them that you are going to start with an organizer.
- Review prior learning, eliciting responses related to content that students should have mastered.
- Identify goals for content mastery.
- Define the topics and subtopics that will be covered.
- Personalize the learning, providing specific, short-term, and individualized rationales that show content applications that affect students.
- Identify expectations by specifying those activities in which both the teacher and students will be engaged during the lesson.

2. Lesson organizer

- As the content is presented, cue the structural organization of the information in a manner that is consistent with the structure presented during the advance organizer.
- As the content is presented, cue those features of the content that are central to the learning goals.
- Cue the students on how to integrate concepts, or aspects of concepts, that are being presented, and relate current learning to information that has been mastered in previous lessons.
- Continuously remind students of established expectations and inform them of changes related to activity directions or in learning goals.

3. Post organizer

- Inform students of the close of the lesson and remind them that it is time to begin constructing the review organizer.
- Evaluate content acquisition by eliciting information from students that relates to the learning goals.
- Evaluate the extent to which the students have integrated the concepts from the lesson and integrated them with concepts from previous lessons.
- Promote generalization by pointing out applications of the concepts in future learning or daily living.
- Inform students about how well they have attained the learning goals and prompt them to self-evaluate.
- Inform students of what will be covered in the next lesson.

The Textbook as an Organizer

The primary organizer for most courses is the textbook. Its structure can serve to orient students to the targeted content. Teachers can guide students in surveying the table of contents, chapter or section introductions and summaries, and chapter headings and subheadings. However, when the textbook is poorly organized or when students do not have the necessary reading proficiency to use the text with facility, the teacher must compensate for the shortcomings of the text.

A routine that Schumaker and McKnight (1989) developed can be used to analyze a textbook or chapter for useful organizers or cues. The routine, referred to by the acronym **TRIMS,** focuses attention on the (1) *T*itle, (2) *R*elationships, (3) *I*ntroduction, (4) *M*ain parts, and (5) *S*ummary. If the organizers are not present in the text, the teacher can then use the TRIMS process to enhance the "inconsiderate" text (Armbruster, 1984). The following checklist (Schumaker & McKnight, 1989) guides the teacher through the textbook analysis:

1. Does the title reflect the main idea or topic of the chapter?
2. Does the table of contents show relationships of main ideas between units as well as between chapters within units?
3. Does the introduction identify chapter goals and objectives explicitly, implicitly, or not at all?
4. Does the introduction employ signal words that illustrate the idea relationship structure of the chapter? (For example, cause-and-effect structures may be signaled by the word *consequently*; comparison/contrast structures may be signaled by *however*; and sequence structures may be signaled by *later*.)
5. Do chapter headings and subheadings clearly reflect the main idea structure of information presented?
6. Are new vocabulary words highlighted by using listing, underlining, or italics or boldface print?
7. Does the summary synthesize the chapter information into a single summary statement?
8. Is there an equal balance in review questions between main idea and factual, detail and supporting information questions?
9. Do the chapter review questions focus on the most important information in the chapter?

An example of how a teacher might think through the process of preparing to use the TRIMS routine is as follows:

Let's see now. I am introducing the students to a new chapter on the reconstruction of the South tomorrow. Let me look at the title this author uses. Hmm . . . he calls this chapter "The Union Helps Restore the South." Well, I think we need to paraphrase this title. I will explore with the students what restore *means. Most of them will know it means something like "to rebuild" or "to put back in its original shape." Maybe we can come up with some analogies . . . let me think. I know John is working with his father on restoring a historic old house. Maybe I can get John to contribute something there. Joan is also helping to restore an antique car with her father. These may be good analogies. I will also need to explore extensions of the word* restore *as a synonym for* reconstruction *so that we can begin to use the phrase "reconstruction of the South." This is a common term and I think it will be introduced soon. We can make the text friendlier by introducing it right up front. Also, I will have to go over the concept of the* Union *and to balance it out, the concept of the* Confederacy. *There, I can get a lot out of the title.*

Next, I need to look at the relationships. I think we can build from previous chapters because this text generally has a couple of common structures: cause and effect and temporal sequencing. Let's see . . . students were very good about picking out the temporal sequencing and the cue words for that, but I will need to review the cause-and-effect terminology because it is often embedded or implied. I will signal this format when I talk about taking notes.

Well, now let me look at the introduction. This is one of the weakest areas of this text because instead of an introduction, the authors use a story about a fictional person of the time. I know it's supposed to add interest, and maybe it does, but I still think we need a lot better introduction. I have been teaching the students to look at the summary statement and to review the questions that come after each section. That's been a good plan. We will do that together.

Now let me look at the main parts. This is a good text in that the main headings are clear.

Let's see. This one is "Programs to restore the South." That is pretty clear, and the students will be able to understand that after our initial discussion. However . . . one thing that I know is weak in this text are the subheadings. The author usually starts out right, but puts in something unrelated. So . . . let me look. Yes, just as I suspected. The first subheading is "Lincoln's Program" and the second is "The Wade-Davis Bill." The third, however, is "The Assassination of Lincoln." This is relevant, but certainly does not fit under the heading of "Programs to Restore the South." How will I handle this? I could just point it out, but I think the students should be noticing things like this already. I will try to elicit this structural problem from the class; most of them should have a grasp of this by now.

Finally, we should look at the summary. Yes, I generally like the summary, and this is also a good one. I will continue to break up into small groups for 2 minutes of work on agreeing on a single sentence paraphrase of the summary paragraph. This always generates some good thinking. There! I can give these students a good overview.

After analyzing the relevant chapter(s), the teacher presents the information to the students. As a part of this presentation, the teacher provides advance organizers, describes rationales for using TRIMS, and provides directions related to taking notes from the chapter. The teacher then describes and models the identification of each of the parts of the text that TRIMS addresses, and the teacher elicits student participation in the identification process. After this initial instruction on TRIMS, the teacher should:

1. Distribute to and review with students note-taking guides constructed to match the TRIMS components. (Older students should write the information generated in the discussion on their guides. With younger students, the teacher can write the information on an overhead transparency.)

2. Ask a student to read and paraphrase the title of the chapter.

3. Using the table of contents as a reference, have students identify the relationship be-

tween the previous chapter and the current chapter.

4. Direct a student to read the introduction to the chapter and paraphrase what the introduction says.
5. Ask the students to identify the major topics and subtopics listed in the chapter as the teacher draws a diagram on the chalkboard depicting the organization of these topics.
6. Have students identify important information about each of the topics and subtopics based on textual cues, and place them in the diagram.
7. Direct a student to read the summary of the chapter and paraphrase what it says.

Routines for Understanding

The process of *understanding* is a fundamental and pervasive part of all learning that requires integrating new information with prior knowledge and storing this information in long-term memory. According to cognitive psychology, the process of understanding content requires that the learner identify and organize the relationships in the content, retrieve related knowledge acquired through prior learning, decide on the relevance of that prior knowledge to new information, translate the content into networks of prior knowledge, and make conclusions based on integrating prior knowledge with new information (e.g., Gagné, 1985; Mayer, 1987) As a content-area teacher moves from orientation to understanding, he might prepare to promote understanding in the following manner:

> *Okay, now let me see how I can teach this information about reproduction in flowering plants. The first part of this section covers the parts of a flower, the second part of this section covers fertilization in flowers, the third part covers the development of the seed, the fourth part covers methods of pollination, the fifth part covers functions of fruits, and the sixth part is about the plant life cycle. . . . So, there are some parts that are very descriptive . . . some concepts . . . (and some of the concepts are pretty abstract) . . . the stu-*

> *dents are going to have to understand the process of fertilization. . . . Okay, I am going to start by describing the parts of the flower . . . I will put a picture of a flower on the overhead projector and label each part as I describe it. . . . then I think I will remove my labels and have the class generate the labels . . . I also think I will make copies of the flower and have them label each part as a class activity. . . . let me see there are six main parts to a flower . . . I know that there are some kids who will have a hard time remembering those parts . . . and they need to know the parts in order to understand the process of fertilization and pollination . . . let me see if I can come up with a way to make it easier for them to remember the six parts of a flower. . . .*

As a first step in planning instruction, the teacher has to identify the content learning demands that are placed on students. These may include: (1) learning concepts; (2) applying or generalizing learned concepts to novel situations; (3) comparing and contrasting concepts; (4) learning rules and propositions (which specify the relationship between concepts); (5) learning and integrating main ideas and details; (6) learning procedures, processes, or sequences of actions; (7) learning cause-and-effect relationships; and (8) exploring problems and arriving at solutions. The teacher's role is first to determine if one of these content learning demands is present, induced by either the text or the learning objectives and goals. If so, she must then organize and manipulate the content in a manner that highlights these demands, and promote content acquisition in a manner consistent with the learning goals.

Diagraming Techniques

Diagraming techniques are instructional devices designed to promote teaching and learning specific content learning demands. An example of a diagraming technique is a concept diagram. A **concept diagram,** such as depicted in Figure 13.4, clarifies the characteristics of concrete items such as components of the internal combustion machine, or much more abstract concepts such as democracy by using a graphic organizer. The diagram can be constructed by the teacher and implemented with students using a specific concept teaching routine. To prepare a concept diagram, a teacher may do the following:

1. **Specify the concept name.** A given concept may be designated by a single word such as *stamen,* or more than one word such as *political system.*
2. **Identify the characteristics of the concept.** The potential features, traits, or qualities of a given concept can be categorized into three groups: (1) those that must be present in a concept; (2) those that are sometimes present in a concept; and (3) those that are never present in a concept.
3. **Locate examples and nonexamples of the concept.** *Examples* are cases or illustrations of the concept, while *nonexamples* are cases or illustrations that lack one or more characteristics necessary for membership in the concept class. Well-matched nonexamples and examples can be collected or devised and then arranged into a sequence of example/nonexample pairs. These pairs can then be presented in a sequence progressing from easy to difficult (Merrill & Tennyson, 1977).
4. **Construct a definition.** For diagraming purposes, the concept definition should include the name of a supraordinate concept (e.g., a larger concept into which the concept under consideration fits), a listing of the characteristics that must always be present in the concept, and the identification of the relationships among those characteristics.

After completing a concept diagram, the teacher can then teach the the concept to the class using the following concept teaching routine:

1. **Provide an advance organizer.** An advance organizer sets the stage for instruction. The teacher should explain the use of the concept diagram, emphasize the purpose for learning the concept, and specify what the students need to do to participate in the routine.
2. **Elicit a key word list associated with the concept.** In teaching with the concept diagram, the teacher should determine the relevant knowledge that students already have about the concept. The key word list can be utilized to involve the students in an interactive exchange, with the teacher eliciting from the students those words that they found to be the most important in their assigned readings.
3. **Explain or review symbols on the concept diagram.** Those elements of the concept diagram that are essential for participating actively in the instruction should be reviewed. For example, rectangles always signal the name or definition of the concept, solid lines signal characteristics that are present, broken lines signal characteristics that are never present, solid ovals signal examples, and broken ovals signal nonexamples.
4. **Name and define the concept.** In a lecture-discussion format, the teacher might write the name of the concept at the top of the concept diagram. In a discovery format, the teacher would first present paired examples and nonexamples and the name of the concept would not be discovered until the concept diagram was completed. Teachers often choose to delay constructing the definition until the end of the concept teaching session so that students can draw from a broader, more meaningful information base.
5. **Discuss the characteristics "always present," "sometimes present," And "never present."** The definition of a *concept* is closely tied to its characteristics. Some characteristics must always be present for the item to claim membership in a given class. Other characteristics may sometimes be present (a situation that can stimulate some of the best class discussions regarding which items are true examples of a concept). Finally, some characteristics can never be present if an example is to be classified under a given class. Stressing these three types of

CONCEPT DIAGRAM

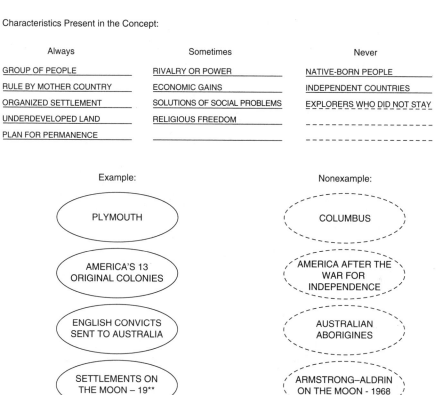

Concept
Name:

COLONIZATION

Definitions:

Colonization is the organized permanent settlement of an
underdeveloped land by a group of people who remain under the
rule of their mother country

Characteristics Present in the Concept:

Always	Sometimes	Never
GROUP OF PEOPLE	RIVALRY OR POWER	NATIVE-BORN PEOPLE
RULE BY MOTHER COUNTRY	ECONOMIC GAINS	INDEPENDENT COUNTRIES
ORGANIZED SETTLEMENT	SOLUTIONS OF SOCIAL PROBLEMS	EXPLORERS WHO DID NOT STAY
UNDERDEVELOPED LAND	RELIGIOUS FREEDOM	
PLAN FOR PERMANENCE		

Example:

PLYMOUTH

AMERICA'S 13
ORIGINAL COLONIES

ENGLISH CONVICTS
SENT TO AUSTRALIA

SETTLEMENTS ON
THE MOON – 19**

Nonexample:

COLUMBUS

AMERICA AFTER THE
WAR FOR
INDEPENDENCE

AUSTRALIAN
ABORIGINES

ARMSTRONG–ALDRIN
ON THE MOON - 1968

FIGURE 13.4   An Example of a Concept Diagram

Source: © Janis Bulgren, University of Kansas Institute for Research in Learning Disabilities.

characteristics can be a useful way to clarify student misunderstanding or faulty prior knowledge.

6. **Provide examples and nonexamples of the concept.** As indicated in Figure 13.4, there are spaces in the concept diagram for writing examples and nonexamples of a concept. As students interact with their teachers in filling out concept diagrams, they can determine whether items are to be placed in the "example" or in the "nonexample" sections. Students then can determine whether that item has all the "always" characteristics and none of the "never" characteristics.

7. **Link examples and nonexamples to characteristics.** Through having students indicate the placement of an item in the "example" or "nonexample" category, the teacher can guarantee students' involvement and interaction. It is helpful for the teacher, with the advice of the students, to draw lines from each proposed example to each characteristic on the diagram. As the teacher checks each characteristic, she places a "+" beside characteristics present in the proposed example and a "0" beside characteristics not present in the proposed example (Figure 13.5). To be a member of the concept class, an item must possess all of the "always" characteristics, but none of the "never" characteristics. The "sometimes" characteristics are, of course, variable and may or may not be present in all of the proposed examples.

8. **Provide a post organizer.** The post organizer restates the findings and allows for review of the concept. This is a good time to check for any misunderstandings about examples and to review the rationale for and process of using the concept diagram.

Mapping Techniques

Mapping is a highly individualized approach that encourages students to relate new vocabulary in a content area to their unique prior knowledge of the words. These **mapping techniques** involve structuring categories of information into a free-form graphic web such as a **semantic map** (Anders & Bos, 1984; Johnson & Pearson, 1984; Johnson, Toms-Bronowski, & Pittelman, 1982) or a **concept web** (Lenz & Bulgren, 1989). To implement this procedure, the teacher selects a key content word that represents a concept or topic and writes it in a central position on the chalkboard. Students are asked to suggest words that they believe are related to the key word. When the goal is to explore or check on the students' prior knowledge, the teacher writes the words on the board in a random order surrounding the name of the targeted concept (Figure 13.6.). When a teacher wants to move from unstructured exploration of students' prior knowledge to more specific discussion of the concept, he draws lines representing the relationships among different concepts, examples of concepts, and characteristics (Figure 13.7). In either case, the active involvement of the students in constructing the map is an important learning activity.

Feature Analysis Techniques

Feature analysis techniques that utilize a table to display relationships among examples of a concept include **semantic feature analysis** and a concept analysis table. (Bos & Anders, 1987; Johnson & Pearson, 1984; Johnson et al., 1982; Lenz & Bulgren, 1989). As depicted in Figure 13.8, words that relate to a designated topic are listed in the column on the left side of the table. In the row along the top of the table, features shared by some of the words are written. Students then place pluses on the table to show positive relationships or minuses to show negative relationships between the words listed in the vertical column and the features listed horizontally. Zeros indicate no relationship and question marks indicate uncertainty. Again, students' discussion and involvement in developing the table are important features of the learning task.

The techniques just described are graphic structures designed for specific instructional goals relating to concept exploration, comprehension, and comparison. The semantic map or a concept web can be used to guide initial exploration of a new topic. By asking students what they associate with selected words, teachers can assess the level of knowledge that they have about a topic or concept. Comprehension of important concepts can be promoted through class discussion using the concept diagram and associated concept teaching routine. Students can analyze a given concept, define it, and then analyze proposed examples to determine if they are members of the concept class under consideration. Finally, com-

CONCEPT DIAGRAM WITH LINKS

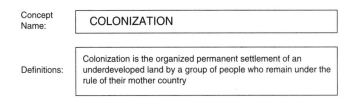

Concept Name:

COLONIZATION

Definitions:

Colonization is the organized permanent settlement of an underdeveloped land by a group of people who remain under the rule of their mother country

Characteristics Present in the Concept:

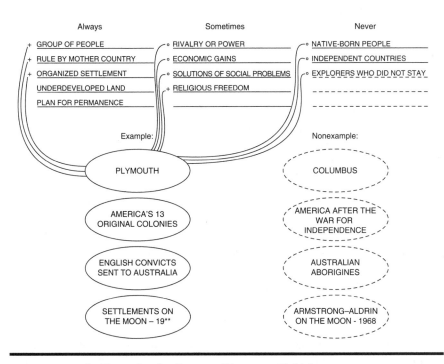

Always	Sometimes	Never
+ GROUP OF PEOPLE	∘ RIVALRY OR POWER	∘ NATIVE-BORN PEOPLE
+ RULE BY MOTHER COUNTRY	∘ ECONOMIC GAINS	∘ INDEPENDENT COUNTRIES
+ ORGANIZED SETTLEMENT	∘ SOLUTIONS OF SOCIAL PROBLEMS	∘ EXPLORERS WHO DID NOT STAY
UNDERDEVELOPED LAND	+ RELIGIOUS FREEDOM	
PLAN FOR PERMANENCE		

Example:

PLYMOUTH

AMERICA'S 13 ORIGINAL COLONIES

ENGLISH CONVICTS SENT TO AUSTRALIA

SETTLEMENTS ON THE MOON – 19**

Nonexample:

COLUMBUS

AMERICA AFTER THE WAR FOR INDEPENDENCE

AUSTRALIAN ABORIGINES

ARMSTRONG–ALDRIN ON THE MOON - 1968

FIGURE 13.5   An Example of a Concept Diagram with Links
Source: © Janis Bulgren, University of Kansas Institute for Research in Learning Disabilities.

paring two or more concepts or several examples of one concept, using the matrix format of the semantic feature analysis or concept analysis table, can expand and deepen concept comprehension.

Routines for Teaching Self-Responsibility

At the secondary school level students are expected to assume primary responsibility for learn-

ing content. They must exercise independence in finding, manipulating, memorizing, and then expressing content information. To facilitate students with learning problems in these activities, the teacher should provide explicit instruction in the elements of assignments and the steps for successful assignment completion. By guiding students to independent performance, providing insights related to task completion, and gradually increasing expectations for independent effort,

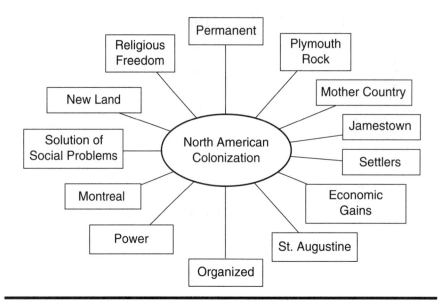

FIGURE 13.6   An Example of Concept Web

Source: © Janis Bulgren, University of Kansas Institute for Research in Learning Disabilities.

teachers can shift responsibility for learning to the students themselves.

Structuring Assignments to Promote Success

Teachers can promote students' independence by carefully developing assignments. They can analyze assignments to identify the most important information to be learned, to determine the types of learning demands represented in the assignments, and to decide if the format of the information presentation should be altered or augmented. Teachers can point out any additional demands to the students and provide information on how to meet them. Otherwise, students who are not skilled in adapting their approach to a task are unlikely to know how to complete the task.

Providing Learning Cues

Teachers need to determine what difficulties students might have in completing assignments and provide cues that will promote successful performance. To accomplish this, teachers can re-

view the target goals for assignments and ask themselves what students will have to do in order to successfully attain the goals. By either visualizing or actually doing the assignments, teachers can identify the task requirements and analyze these components to determine the difficulties that students might have completing the assignments.

Based on this information, the teachers can brainstorm ways to provide cues that will guide students in processing the information. For example, the teachers may direct students to the appropriate context, telling them the portion of the chapter or topic headings for the concepts covered. While the teachers probably would not want to tell students the exact page or paragraph for the information, minimal prompts such as these can get the students going.

Personalizing the Content

Much of what is learned in school, in both the skill and content areas, is soon forgotten. The more personally useful and meaningful the infor-

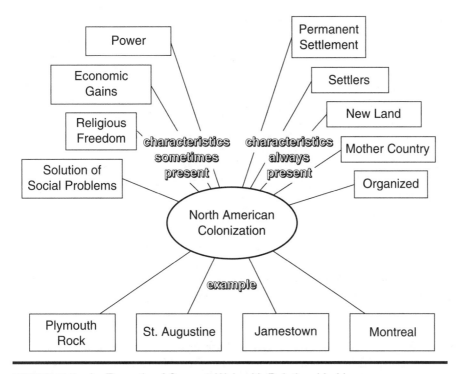

FIGURE 13.7   An Example of Concept Web with Relationship Lines

Source: © Janis Bulgren, University of Kansas Institute for Research in Learning Disabilities.

mation is, the more likely it is to be remembered. Several approaches can be used for personalizing content. These include:

- Allowing students to select assignments that reflect their interests and utilize their strengths.
- Assigning project-type assignments to be completed over a period of time (e.g., designing their own political parties based on personal interests).
- Permitting students to outline chapter portions instead of answering chapter questions.
- Having students reconstruct the content from their own perspectives, rewriting a segment of the content making themselves key agents of the action (e.g., describing what they saw happening as the sixteenth President or describing the growth of a seed as watched through an underground glass window).
- Allowing students to present information about projects in writing, on posters, or in

oral presentations to the class, a small peer group, or privately to the teacher.

- Requiring students to apply concepts from the content to their own experiences and fields of awareness (e.g., the concepts of democracy colonization, discrimination, and heredity applied to family life, moving to a new place, social cliques, and current news headlines).

Completing Assignments

One approach to teaching assignment completion is through separate and direct strategy instruction (discussed previously). As a first step, helping students identify the learning goals associated with the assignment provides an advance organizer. Directing their attention to the structure of the assignment can help them identify any novel or unique elements. Evaluation criteria for the as-

Characteristics

Examples	Settlers	New Land	Mother Country	Power	Economic Gains	Religious Freedom	Solve Social Problems		
Plymouth	X	X	X	?/-/o	X	X	?/-/o		
St. Augustine	X	X	X	X	X	?/-/o	?/-/o		
Jamestown	X	X	X	?/-/o	X	-	?/-/o		
Montreal	X	X	X	X	-	?/-/o	?/-/o		
Georgia	X	X	X	?/-/o	X	?/-/o	X		

FIGURE 13.8   Concept Analysis Table: North American Colonization

Source: © Janis Bulgren, University of Kansas Institute for Research in Learning Disabilities.

signment should be explained and directions for completing the assignment provided. The teacher should describe and model each step for completing the assignment, listing key words related to these steps on the chalkboard. After checking to see if the students understand the process, the teacher then can help them get started by leading the group in doing a portion of the assignment. The teacher should carefully monitor the students' independent work and provide additional teaching and/or assignments as needed. A final review and check can ensure that all students understand the assignment, its various parts, and any specific requirements, criteria, or procedures.

Setting Individual Goals

Another approach to teaching assignment completion is to make each assignment a mini-lesson in completing assignments. Generally, each content class is characterized by specific types of lessons. For example, end-of-chapter questions, vocabulary exercises, study guides, and chapter reports are often given. After an individual or group has completed two or three assignments of

a particular type, the teacher can review with them data on overall assignment completion as well as information on the specific types of problems they are experiencing. Teachers can present averages of group performance to the class and provide each student with individual performance reports. They then can guide students in setting goals related to improving grades on specific types of assignments as well as the rate of assignment completion. Performance toward achieving these goals can be monitored by both the teacher and the student. Self-recording techniques such as described in Chapter 3 and teacher-student contracts such as described in Chapter 5 can be used.

Peer-Assisted Assignment Completion

Research on the effects of students working together indicates that peers can greatly facilitate content learning. Procedures related to peer tutoring, student learning teams, and cooperative learning have been developed to guide teachers in promoting successful learning through these types of arrangements. The goal of these procedures is to transfer the mediational responsibilities of learning from the teacher to the student and the student's peer group.

Cooperative learning approaches vary extensively, running the gamut from high-structured activities with well-specified academic and social outcomes, to less structured, more autonomous student-directed activities. These approaches can involve brief interactions at the beginning or end of instruction, or they can encompass lengthier group tasks. Cooperative learning assignments are not appropriate for introducing new content, but should focus either on exploring content and relationships that the teacher or the textbook already presented, or on extending and expanding relationships that might exist in the content that the teacher or the textbook already presented. Guidelines for structuring and monitoring peer-assisted cooperative learning dyads and groups are described in Chapter 8.

CONTENT ENHANCEMENT DEVICES

The preceding discussion has focused on one element of content enhancement, the content enhancement routines. Examples of orientation routines, understanding routines, and assignment completion routines have been discussed. Another component in the content enhancement process centers around using *content enhancement devices*. Although content enhancement devices are designed to be embedded within a larger teaching routine, they represent an important element of the content enhancement process.

A **content enhancement device** is an instructional procedure or tactic designed to achieve a singular goal. This device is associated with facilitating organizing, understanding, or remembering information. It usually covers a small segment of a lesson and is embedded in a teaching routine for the purpose of helping students memorize features salient to that concept. Such devices make abstract information more concrete and connect new information with content already learned. Content enhancement devices can

highlight relationships and organizational structures of the information presented, and assist students to take notes. The following "teacher talk" demonstrates how the content teaching device can be used:

> *Yes, I think I will be covering the concept of "colonization" tomorrow. . . . Okay, I have generated advance and post organizers, and I have completed a concept diagram for the concept of "colonization" that I will present in a concept teaching routine . . . . We will spend most of the class tomorrow exploring and discussing this concept. . . . hmm, I know that these characteristics always present in colonization are going to be hard for about half of the class to remember. . . . Now, how can I make this easier to remember? . . . . Let's see, the characteristics are: a group of people; ruled by the mother country; with organized settlements; moving to an unsettled or underdeveloped area; with a plan for permanence. If I take the first letter of each of the key words in the five characteristics—G̲roup, R̲uled, O̲rganized, U̲nderdeveloped, and P̲lan—I can create the acronym GROUP. Great! If they have trouble figuring out a way to remember these examples, I am ready with something that might work. . . . Now, can I think of something that will make the entire concept of colonization less abstract? . . . Hmm. . . .*

As illustrated in the previous example, the teaching device is used when specific elements of a lesson appear to present difficult learning demands for the student. As a result, teaching devices can be inserted during any of the instructional routines. During the orientation routine, for example, inserting a graphic may facilitate using organizers. During an understanding routine, analogies may be used to clarify a concept. During an activation routine, a method might be inserted to teach students how to create remembering devices and prompt students to create their own remembering system for a set of information. These instructional devices are categorized into three groupings: (1) organizing devices; (2) understanding devices; and (3) remembering devices.

Organizing Devices

Wherever specific information or the relationship between pieces of information needs to be drawn to the students' attention, teachers can use oral cues, graphic organizers, and study/lecture guides to focus attention on the relationships among bits of information. These **organizing devices** serve the same purpose as the advance and post organizer routines discussed earlier. They build on the advance organizers, reinforce them, and guide the students' attention to the structure of the information. The three primary types of devices for organizing include: (1) illustrators; (2) guides; and (3) cues.

1. **Illustrators.** Illustrators consist of any graphic or visual used to present content material. Time lines, continuum scales, steps in an experiment, or cycles are examples of illustrations useful for describing a sequence of events. Illustrations also can be used to describe the cause and effects of certain events or of problems and solutions. These typically involve an illustration of a situation and the actions that follow.

2. **Guides.** Study guide materials can be used to focus attention, point out important information, and guide closer inspection of material. Bergerud, Lovitt, and Horton (1988) reported two types of guide. One provided graphics or diagrams with parts of the pictures or labels missing so that students could complete the guides. The other provided questions on main concepts and vocabulary words from assigned passages. Both types of organizing guides were found to be more helpful to students than self-study alone. Using graphics was judged to be the most effective.

3. **Cues.** Teachers can use verbal cues to focus students' attention on the organization of information. A strategy being developed at the University of Kansas by Robinson, Deshler, Denton and Schumaker teaches students to develop content outlines from listening to a lecture and identifying verbal cues that the teacher plans to use over and over again. The verbal cues the teacher provides help students to structure their note-taking and organize the lecture information. The lesson organizers presented earlier in the discussion of orientation routines are examples of ways in which to cue organization.

Understanding Devices

Many of the previously described routines for understanding depend on good **understanding devices** to make them effective. The concept diagram and other devices previously described can be effective in helping students understand important concepts. Additional devices for promoting understanding include providing examples, making comparisons, and demonstrating cause and effect. Such understanding devices can be implemented in verbal, concrete, or activity forms in the following ways:

1. **Examples.** When an example is used as a device, the focus is generally upon a single concept (e.g., Plymouth is an example of colonization in North America). It may be as simple as a single word or as complex as a story. Concrete examples include using pictures or actual objects to illustrate the object being discussed. Active examples include simple demonstrations to illustrate single concepts such as cutting an apple to illustrate the concept of *halves* and *quarters* or using a yeast mixture to illustrate the process of *fermentation*.

2. **Comparisons.** Comparisons usually involve exploring the similarities or differences between two or more concepts (e.g., transpiration in plants is similar to perspiration in humans). Comparisons build upon using examples but involve more than one concept. For example, in a verbal comparison, the teacher could use single words that are synonyms and antonyms, or he could utilize more complex comparisons such as similes, metaphors, or analogies. A concrete comparison would involve using samples of sedimentary and metamorphic rocks, in addition to igne-

ous rocks, to show similar and different characteristics. To use comparisons in an active manner, the teacher could set up debates or role play situations in which different opinions, beliefs, or theories could be examined.

3. **Cause and Effect.** When the instruction goal is to help the student understand a relationship, cause-and-effect devices can be helpful. Cause-and-effect devices call for identifying sequences of actions or events (e.g., before Gorbachev was the leader of the former Soviet Union, there were many communist countries; after Gorbachev became president of the former Soviet Union, many of these countries began to move toward democracy). A cause-and-effect relationship can be presented verbally by using terms such as *If . . . then . . .* to draw attention to relationships. Concrete cause-and-effect representations would include pictures of "before, during, and after," or diagrams representing events or processes. An active form of a cause-and-effect explanation could include demonstrations of multiple-step processes.

Each of these understanding devices can be included within a given teaching routine to enhance student mastery of the content. Some could be inserted into teaching routines as short, spontaneous clarifications in response to perceived needs, with others involving longer time periods to enhance student understanding.

Remembering Devices

Teachers construct and use **remembering devices** to assist students in memorizing information, and to compensate for the possibility that many students may have ineffective and inefficient memorization strategies. Creating mental images, making familiar associations, using FIRST-letter mnemonics, or using key word strategies are examples of remembering devices. They also can be inserted at any point in the lesson when the student is expected to memorize factual information.

Although there are many possible remembering devices, a few of the more popular memory devices are described in the following paragraphs.

1. **Picture device.** Mental imagery can facilitate memorizing information presented in classroom lectures (Bulgren, Deshler, & Schumaker, in press). If students must remember three things that contributed to the settling of the West (e.g., the windmill, the steel plow, and barbed wire), the teacher might guide students to evoke a mental image in which a farmer is plowing a field with a steel plow; a barbed wire fence surrounds the field; and beside the fence is a rapidly turning windmill. Students should be encouraged to make the pictures colorful and active to promote remembering.

For information where it would be difficult to create an exact mental representation, some elaboration or change is required. For example, if students were to remember that the Confederacy won the Battle of Bull Run, the teacher could help students to create mental images of the Confederate flag and a scene of a bull running. By combining the two images, the final result might be a mental image of a bull running across a field with a Confederate flag draped over him.

2. **Familiar association device.** This device extends the mental image strategy yet another step. Since some items that students must remember are not easily translated to mental images, the students can be taught to link a target item to something familiar. For example, if students must remember that Sherman was a Confederate general, they might link a friend named Sherman to a Confederate flag. This strategy works well when the name of a friend, or of a familiar person, can be linked with the name of a famous figure that the students must remember. The students can use figures from their own lives, as well as movie and television celebrities, to serve as familiar associations with which to link items to remember.

3. **Keyword device.** The most common version of the keyword method involves constructing interactive visual images. In order to do this, the learner generates an image of the referent as it in-

teracts with a familiar concrete word that resembles a salient part of the unfamiliar vocabulary word. Pressley, Levin, & McDaniel (1987) illustrated this concept with the example that the English word *carlin* means "old woman." Using the keyword *car,* a learner could create a mental image of an old women driving a car. Because of the sound similarity between *car* and *carlin,* the learner can retrieve the meaning through the image. Bulgren and Schumaker (in press) have developed a similar "boxing strategy" in which students are taught to "box" or isolate key syllables that may be suitable to remembering mental images. For example, if students must remember that "Jaruzelski was the leader in Poland," then students can be taught to isolate syllables such as *Jar* and *Pol* and to create mental images of a jar on a pole. This can be made into a distinct memorable image depending upon the student's imagination. Students should be cued that this device is most useful on tests involving multiple choice or matching since they have memorized syllables rather than entire words. Considerable research indicates that students can learn to use the Keyword Mnemonic technique (Mastropieri, Scruggs, Levin, Graffney & McLoone, 1985).

4.   Rhyming device. Bellezza (1981) noted that at times information can be remembered by putting it into the form of a rhyme. Almost every school child has learned rhymes designed to remember dates ("In 1492, Columbus sailed the ocean blue."); rhymes designed to aid in spelling ("*I* before *E* except after *C.*"); or rhymes designed to cue associations ("Thirty days has September, April, June and November."). For classes in which the students are particularly receptive to this technique, the teacher could encourage constructing rhymes designed with the help of class members. For example, a class studying the amendments to the Constitution of the United States might devise a rhyme such as "Amendment number twenty-three means votes for Washington, DC."

5.   FIRST-letter mnemonic device. This strategy, which Nagel, Shumaker, and Deshler (1986) described, requires students to first organize a list of words that must be remembered and write the first letter of each word. These letters are then analyzed to determine if they can be used to form a word. A common example of this mnemonic is the cue of HOMES to remember the Great Lakes: Huron, Ontario, Michigan, Erie, and Superior. If the first letters do not form a word, words can be chosen that start with the same letters to form a memorable sentence or phrase.

There are many examples of devices that may be used to enhance memory. However, while their use is attractive and interesting, the research base is not sufficient to determine which types of devices are most suited to various content areas, which devices are most palatable to students at the upper levels, and which devices fit into common presentation formats in content-area classes. For these reasons, teachers should be cautious about spending time instructing students in their use.

PLANNING TEACHER-MEDIATED INTERVENTIONS

To deliver content instruction effectively, teachers should have not only a sound foundation in the content information itself, but facility with a variety of instructional strategies that can promote students learning that content. Clark and Peterson (1986, p. 262) indicated that "the most obvious function of teacher planning in American schools is to transform and modify curriculum to fit the unique circumstances of each teaching situation." This section overviews the processes, which Lenz and Bulgren (1989) identified, in which teachers might engage while planning, selecting, and implementing instruction that enhances content learning. These are fine steps in planning to implement the content enhancement process.

Identifying Content Drivers

The first step in the content enhancement process is to specify what determines or drives the content that will be taught to students. Unlike the basic academic skill areas, the body of knowledge in many content courses may not be carefully defined, sequenced, or measured. Frequently, the sole content drivers may be the textbooks and the teachers' preferences. Because teachers tend to deviate little from the scope and sequence of the textbooks they use, textbooks must be considered as the major determinant of instructional content. Additional content drivers include state-mandated course competencies in content areas, an outgrowth of the recent educational reform efforts across the nation. Finally, the individual teacher makes decisions about the relative importance of the specified competencies and about possibly including other competencies that are, in the teacher's professional judgment, important to content mastery.

Mapping the Critical Content

The second step of the content enhancement process is to map the critical content. The teacher must organize content information into instructional lessons, typically of 30–50 minutes in length at the middle and secondary school levels. The content map is not the lesson itself; rather, it assists the teacher to construct the lesson by organizing the information and relationships.

Using a content map, teachers can organize the content topic, subtopics, and supporting details into a graphic display. Two approaches to content mapping include: (1) *highlighting a textbook* and (2) *outlining the content* that the textbook publisher provides. The content map presented in Figure 13.9 may be useful to those teachers who have not yet developed their own notational systems for specifying topics and details, or for those who wish to consider alternate forms.

Analyzing Prerequisite Knowledge Requirements

The third step in the content enhancement process is to analyze what the student is expected to know. By identifying the body of background information required to understand new content,

teachers can make quick checks of their students' knowledge bases. They decide how to enhance background knowledge, when necessary, and how to present new knowledge in terms that the students are best able to comprehend. Hansen (1984) pointed out that students with learning problems often suffer either because they do not have as much background knowledge as their peers or because they lack confidence in the knowledge that they do have. Either of these two situations hinders their acquisition to learn new information.

To some degree, most teachers identify background information and deal with the need to expand the students' awareness when preparing a lesson. Such planning is reflected in developing listings of new vocabulary words and their definitions. Teachers also might explore basic concepts and terms covered in previous courses.

Students' knowledge of particular vocabulary should be a key consideration in planning for instruction. Figure 13.10 demonstrates how a content map might be used to identify vocabulary that might be unfamiliar to students.

Reaching Enhancement Decisions

The fourth step in the content enhancement process is to decide how the content will be transformed to promote learning. At this point in the planning process, teachers must decide how to manipulate, enrich, and transform the content in order to promote learning. Then they must identify or develop appropriate instructional materials and activities. The procedures described in the following list can assist teachers in making these content enhancement decisions.

1. **Scan the content map.** Review the words and phrases that have been circled, underlined, and checked, as well as others added to the content map that reflect differing instructional levels. Identify those concepts that must be taught during the lesson.
2. **Construct an advance organizer.** Using an advance organizer during an initial activity

CLASS: *General Biology*   TIME PERIOD: *9/12 - 9/18*

TOPIC	*Sense Organs - Chapter 14*			
SUBTOPIC	*eye*	*tongue & nose*	*ear*	*skin*
DETAILS	*List and describe the four outside parts of the eye and five inside parts of the eye.* *Describe the four steps of how the eye sends messages to the brain through neurons*	*Explain how the tongue and nose work together.* *How do neurons make the tongue work?* *What are the four tastes?* *How do neurons make the nose work?*	*How do air molecules affect hearing?* *Describe the four steps of how the ear sends messages to the brain through neurons.* *What are the parts of the ear?*	*List and describe the four neurons in the skin and the conditions they detect.*

FIGURE 13.9   An Example of a Content Map

Source: From "Content Area Skill Assessment" by B. K. Lenz and D. Mellard, *Assessing Students with Special Needs,* Robert A. Gale and Jo M. Hendrickson (Eds.). Copyright © 1990 by Longman Publishers. Reprinted with permission.

helps the teacher identify structures, relationships, and outcomes.

3. **Prepare the instructional materials.** Design instructional materials to teach the concepts using the procedures described earlier in this chapter for concept teaching.

4. **Identify additional learning demands.** Study the content map for elements that might cause difficulty for students, and construct the appropriate understanding routines and associated materials.

5. **Review the content map and the selected routines.** Identify the need for additional specific devices that might be helpful for promoting understanding, remembering, and organizing.

6. **Identify the outcomes associated with the lesson.** Select and prepare the appropriate materials, devices, and activities.

7. **Construct an advance organizer.** To accomplish this, review all the routines and devices that have been constructed.

8. **Decide how each of the enhancements will be employed.** Analyze the overall lesson to determine the most optimal use of the enhancements.

Teaching Enhanced Content

The fifth step in the content enhancement process is to teach the content in a manner that compensates for a students lack of good learning strategies. For content enhancement processes to be successful, students must be informed of and involved in these processes. They must see the benefits of these processes on their performance. This calls for a true partnership between the students and their teachers, with both knowing their individual roles as well as the roles of others in the classes. Teachers can take an active role in involving the students in the learning process, informing them of teaching techniques, clarifying expectations of students as partners in the learn-

CONTENT MAP

Important Concepts 1.) neurons 2.) organs 3.) molecules

NAME: *General Biology*   TIME PERIOD: *9/12 - 9/18*

TOPIC	*Sense (organs) - Chapter 14*			
SUBTOPIC	*eye*	*tongue & nose*	*ear*	*skin*
DETAILS	*List and describe the four outside parts of the eye and five inside parts of the eye*	*Explain how the tongue and nose work together*	*How do air (molecules) affect hearing?*	*List and describe the four (neurons) in the skin and the conditions they detect.*
	Describe the four steps of how the eye sends messages to the brain through (neurons)	*How do (neurons) make the tongue work?*	*Describe the four steps of how the ear sends messages to the brain through (neurons)*	
		What are the four tastes?		
		How do (neurons) make the nose work?	*What are the parts of the ear?*	

FIGURE 13.10   An Example of a Prior Knowledge Vocabulary Analysis
Source: Lenz & Mellard (1990).

ing process, and holding them accountable for their roles in the learning process.

Students can be taught to promote their own learning. They can learn to: (1) make a commitment to content-area learning; (2) call upon prior knowledge to facilitate learning; (3) share responsibility for both teaching and learning; and (4) develop and apply appropriate learning strategies to promote independent learning. On the simplest level, the student who attends to the instruction the teacher delivers is the "receiver" of knowledge. For meaningful learning to occur, however, students must be involved at higher levels of activity as well. They must become aware that teachers not only impart information, but also provide structures for understanding that information. By explaining instructional methods,

techniques, or routines, teachers can prepare students to participate appropriately in the instruction. Students can approach learning tasks with the expectations that they will link new information with prior knowledge and incorporate new information into familiar frameworks.

Teaching About Enhancement Routines

Teaching students about content enhancements is similar to teaching students a strategy. Teachers need to:

1. Inform students of *how content has previously been presented* and what their *level of performance* has been.

2. *Describe* the enhancement to the students and explain that its use can improve learning.

3. *Model* the enhancement, showing how students should respond, the cues that will be used, and how the use of the enhancement will be evaluated.

4. *Question* students about what each part of the enhancement means to ensure that they understand its value and application. Make sure that the students understand all forms used, such as study guides, graphics, illustrators, and concept diagrams.

5. *Verbally rehearse* the enhancement to encourage memorizing how the enhancement will be used.

6. *Apply* the enhancement as soon as possible after it has been presented, demonstrating to students how the enhancement contributes to learning.

7. *Monitor* the success with which the students use the enhancement.

8. *Decrease* the cuing process, making it less explicit as both the teacher and the student master each enhancement.

9. *Gradually add* other types of enhancements and begin to integrate them into the teaching process while maintaining the use of enhancements that have already been implemented.

Ongoing Delivery of Enhancements

During instruction, teachers should refer to each specific enhancement used by name and review its goal or purpose. Teachers should remind students of how they can use the enhancement to facilitate learning and actively involve students in the enhancement process. Throughout, teachers should emphasize a teacher-learner partnership (e.g., "What would be a good heading for this list, Randy? Okay, the first step is to . . . so what would be the answer to this first part . . . great! Now the second part is . . . " and so forth.). When students have difficulty, teachers should provide explanations (e.g., "Let me explain the steps and

criteria for developing a good heading for a list"). Finally, teachers should elicit correct responses from students who continue to have difficulty (e.g., "Okay, so here is a new list. What would be a good heading for this list, Randy? That's right. You got it!"). Once the enhancement has been accomplished, the teachers should review it, checking to see if students are making the appropriate associations. If students are not using the enhancement information as part of an active response to the demands of content learning, the teachers should review the process, model using the enhancement to facilitate learning, and set goals with the students for better attention to and use of the enhancement.

Teachers must be prepared to abandon specific routines and devices if they do not work, and to implement alternate learning activities. The flexibility during lesson presentation of deciding to abandon a plan and to generate a new routine in order to successfully respond to student's failure is what makes the teaching process dynamic.

Evaluating the Effectiveness of Content Enhancements

The teaching process is not complete until the teachers have ascertained the level of understanding of students in their classes and provided feedback for those in need of further content clarification. Students' attitudes, answers, and nonverbal behaviors can all inform the teachers when mastery problems exist. In addition, frequent progress checks help teachers identify which aspects of the lessons and the content enhancement process are successful and which are not. Regular comprehension checks can consist of informal teacher questioning and feedback, or more formal quizzes or tests. A curriculum-based assessment approach, such as the one Lenz and Mellard (1989) described, can be used to evaluate students' progress in content-area learning that is either student-centered (e.g., application of learning strategies to content-area learning) or teacher-centered (e.g., content enhancements or modifications).

Using these approaches, the teachers can determine which enhancements were and were not successful. When their lessons and the enhancements are successful, this should be noted on the lesson plans and filed for future use. If the lessons or specific enhancements in the the lessons were not successful, the teachers should identify whether the enhancement process or the lesson delivery was at fault.

Re-evaluating Content Drivers

Re-evaluation, the final step in the content enhancement process guides the teacher in planning the next set of lessons. The teacher must assume ongoing responsibility for ensuring that students develop the knowledge base needed for subsequent learning activities. Subsequent lessons must be conceptualized, in part, on the basis of the content that was not successfully presented and learned by students in the previous lesson. Hence, content not learned in current lessons becomes part of the content drivers for subsequent lessons. Planning and implementing the content enhancement process begins again.

TEACHING PARTNERSHIPS

Efforts to promote maximum content learning should benefit all students in the class. The preparing, implementing, and evaluating of interventions that benefit all students must be easily integrated into ongoing instruction time frames. Further, interventions to address the needs of students with learning problems should occur across settings, in both the support class setting and the content learning setting (Deshler & Schumaker, 1988). This underscores the importance of instructional models that promote cooperative teaching, planning, and consulting between the support class teacher and the regular education teacher.

The roles of all those involved in the instructional process (the content-area teacher, the support class teacher, and the student) must be clearly specified and articulated among all instructional staff. Generalization of mediational strategies should be both the ultimate goal and evaluative criteria of the strategy instruction. Additional support systems involving administrators, family members, and other professionals are important for promoting the student's success and adjustment.

A clear understanding of the primary roles for the support class teacher, the content teacher, and the student set the stage for success in mainstream content classes. Deshler and Schumaker (1988) have suggested that the four primary roles of the support class teacher in promoting content-area success include:

1. Teaching specific strategies that will assist the student with learning problems in meeting the demands of the content learning setting.
2. Modeling strategic learning and performance, and creating an environment in which the student is expected and prompted to perform strategically across all tasks.
3. Facilitating the student's independence through communicating high expectations for independent study and assignment completion, and shaping the student's involvement in independent thinking and problem solving.
4. Assuming primary responsibility for managing and implementing the cooperative planning process with content-area teachers.

It is the content teacher's responsibility to deliver content in a manner that all students can understand and remember, and to prompt the generalization and maintenance of strategies learned in the support class. Checking, cueing, prompting, modeling strategy applications, and providing feedback to students on their performance are important components of the content teacher's instruction. The primary roles of students include participating in the decision-making process about the strategies they will learn, mastering the targeted strategies, and generalizing the strategies to content-area learning tasks across settings and over time. Generalization involves a series of metacognitive and cognitive tasks. Students must remember the learned strategies and be alert for cues that suggest their use. They need to maintain a constant awareness of the availability of strategies that can be adapted and modified to meet the unique requirements of mainstream classes. Finally, they should be prepared to fluently integrate several task-specific strategies into a "package" for use in the mainstream class (Deshler & Schumaker, 1988).

SUMMARY

This chapter has touched on the wealth of information available to the teacher to guide the content teaching and learning process. The procedures included are grounded in a growing body of research on information processing by the teacher as well as the student (Joyce, 1978–79; Vygotsky, 1978). The majority of the specific methods, guidelines, and procedures described have been either validated with at risk students or have been derived from an analysis and synthesis of numerous research studies on such students. The content enhancement processes provide a means of orchestrating this research into a meaningful whole.

The chapter divides these processes into two main categories: (1) those that are internally mediated (e.g., by the student) and (2) those that are externally mediated (e.g., curriculum materials, teachers, and media). This chapter overviews learning strategies and outlines Strategies Intervention Model, developed at the University of Kansas. Teacher-mediated approaches include content enhancement routines or procedures and content enhancement devices. Routines for orienting students to the learning (before, during, and after instruction) and for understanding the content (diagraming, mapping, and feature analysis) are described. Teaching routines designed to develop self-responsibility include carefully structuring lessons, providing learning cues, per-

sonalizing the content, and specifically teaching assignment completion. Devices for enhancing content learning include those designed to help organize the content (e.g., illustrations, study guides, and cues), devices to promote understanding (e.g., examples, comparisons, and cause-and-effect relationships), and devices for remembering (e.g., mental imagery, familiar associations, key words and rhymes, and mnemonics).

The processes in which teachers must engage while planning, selecting, and implementing meaningful content instruction are detailed. Teachers must identify the major determinants of the content, map the critical content, and analyze prerequisite skills. They must then decide how to manipulate, enrich, and transform the content to facilitate student learning. A process of evaluating instructional outcomes and incorporating knowledge of students' performance into subsequent lesson planning are final steps in the content enhancement process.

While it might seem that structured routines and devices of the content enhancement could mechanize the teaching process, the opposite is true. The teacher is not a technician who executes performances according to prescriptions that othersdefine; the teacher is a professional similar to a physician, a lawyer or an architect (Clark and Peterson, 1986). By understanding the processes involved in both teaching and learning, and applying these processes to teaching content, the teacher can be free to construct successful learning experiences and enjoy the educational process.

The information included in this chapter should help teachers improve content-area instruction for students with achievement difficulties. Improved content learning is unlikely to occur as the result of casually selecting and implementing these procedures. Rather, success will be attained when the teacher makes a commitment to improve the content learning of all students, and then applies these principles and procedures consistently, systematically, and collaboratively over a period of several years.

CONTENT MASTERY QUESTIONS

1. Discuss the three factors that contribute to the difficulties students with learning problems experience.

2. Describe four methods schools employ to alleviate the difficulties.

3. Outline the progression of study skills instruction to its present form.

4. Describe two learning strategies for each of the four demands in the regular middle and secondary school settings.

5. Describe the critical features of a learning strategy intervention.

6. Discuss the importance of generalization for acquisition level strategies, and describe the roles of the content-area and support class teacher in this process.

7. Discuss the four components of the orientation routines for content enhancement.

8. Describe the three categories of techniques included in the routines for the understanding portion of content enhancement.

9. Describe six strategies employed for facilitating learning assignment completion skills.

10. Define a content enhancement device and discuss its importance in the content enhancement process.

11. Delineate three devices that promote the following: (a) understanding, (b) remembering, and (c) organizing. Provide an example for each device (i.e., nine strategies).

12. Discuss and describe the planning and selection portion of the content enhancement process.

13. Discuss how to successfully implement content enhancement in the classroom.

14. Discuss the importance of evaluating the implementation of content enhancement processes and of re-evaluating content drivers. Provide three methods for evaluating the effectiveness of content enhancement.

15. Describe the importance of a cooperative teaching model for content enhancement and the roles of the three individuals involved in the model.

REFERENCES

Anders, P. L., & Bos, C. S. (1984). In the beginning: Vocabulary instruction in content classrooms. *Topics in Learning and Learning Disabilities, 3*(4), 53–65.

Armbruster, B. B. (1984). The problem of "inconsiderate text." In G. G. Duffy, L. R. Roehler, & J. Mason (Eds.). *Comprehension Instruction: Per-* *spectives and suggestions.* New York: Longman, 202–217.

Armbruster, B. B., & Anderson, T. H. (1985). Frames: Structures for informative text. In D. H. Johnson (Ed). *The technology of text,* (Vol. 2, pp. 90–104). Englewood Cliffs, NJ: Educational Technology Publications.

Ausubel, D. P. (1963). *The psychology of meaningful verbal learning.* NY: Grune & Stratton.

Ausubel, D. P., Novak, J. D., & Hanesian, H. (1968). *Educational psychology: A cognitive view,* (2nd ed.). New York: Holt, Rinehart & Winston.

Bellezza, F. S. (1981). Mnemonic Devices: Classification, characteristics, and criteria. *Review of Educational Research 51*(2), 247–275.

Bergerud, D., Lovitt, T. C., & Horton, S. (1988). The effectiveness of textbook adaptations in life science for high school students with learning disabilities. *Journal of Learning Disabilities, 21*(2), 70–76.

Bos, C. S., & Anders, P. L. (1987). Semantic feature analysis: An interactive teaching strategy for facilitating learning from text. *Learning Disability Focus, 3*(1), 55–59.

Bulgren, J. A., Deshler, D. D., & Schumaker, J. B., (in press). *A training manual for teaching mainstream teachers how to facilitate the remembering of classroom lectures.* (Curriculum material). Lawrence: University of Kansas, Institute for Research in Learning Disabilities.

Bulgren, J. A., & Schumaker, J. B. (in press). *Learning strategies curriculum: The paired-associates strategy.* Lawrence: University of Kansas Institute for Research in Learning Disabilities.

Clark, C. M., & Peterson, P. L. (1986). Research on teaching social studies. In Wittrock, M. C. (Eds.). *Handbook of Research on Teaching,* (3rd.). pp. 942–952.

Deshler, D. D., & Lenz, B. K. (1989) The strategies instructional approach international. *Journal of Disability, Development, and Education, 36*(3), 203–224. New York: Macmillan Publishing Co.

Deshler, D. D., & Schumaker, J. B. (1988). An instructional model for teaching students how to learn. In: J. L. Graden, J. E. Zins, and M. J. Curtis (Eds.). *Alternative educational delivery systems: Enhancing instructional options for all students.* Washington, DC: NASP, 391–411.

Ellis, E. S., Deshler, D. D., Lenz, B. K., Schumaker, J. B., & Clark, F. L. (1991). An instructional model for teaching learning strategies. *Focus on Exceptional Children, 23*(6), 1–24.

Ellis, E. S., & Lenz, B. K. (in press). *Arrive: Creating learning strategy interventions.* Lawrence, KS: Edge Enterprises.

Ellis, E. S., & Sabornie, E. J. (1986). Effective instruction with microcomputers. Promises, practices,

and preliminary findings. *Focus on Exceptional Children, 19,* 1–16.

Gagne, E. D. (1985). *The cognitive psychology of school learning.* Boston: Little, Brown.

Hansen, J. (1984). The role of prior knowledge in content area learning. *Topics in Learning and Learning Disabilities, 3*(4), 66–77.

Johnson, D. D., Toms-Bronowski, S., & Pittelman, S. D. (1982). *An investigation of the effectiveness of semantic mapping and semantic feature analysis with intermediate grade level children.* Program Report 83-3. Madison: University of Wisconsin, Wisconsin Center for Education Research.

Johnson, D. D., & Pearson, P. D. (1984). *Teaching reading vocabulary,* 2nd ed. New York: Holt, Rinehart & Winston.

Joyce, B. R. (1978–1979). Toward a theory of information processing teaching. *Educational Research Quarterly, 3*(4), 66–77.

Kameenui, E. J., Simmons, D. C., & Darch, C. B. (1987). LD children's comprehension of selected textual features: Effects of proximity of information. *Learning Disabilities Quarterly, 10*(3), 237–248.

Lenz, B. K., Alley, G. R., & Schumaker, J. B. (1987). Activating the inactive learner: Advance organizers in the secondary content classroom. *Learning Disability Quarterly, 10*(1), 53–67.

Lenz, B. K., & Bulgren, J. A. (1989). Dimensions of the content enhancement model (Research Report). Lawrence, KS: University of Kansas Institute for Research in Learning Disabilities.

Lenz, B. K., Bulgren, J. A., & Hudson, P. (1990). *Content enhancement: A model for promoting the acquisition of content learning by individuals with learning disabilities.* In T. E. Scruggs & B. Y. L. Wong (Eds.). Intervention research in learning disabilities. New York: Springer–Verlag.

Lenz, B. K., Ellis, E.S, & Scanlan, D. (in press). *Designing effective instruction for adolescents with learning disabilities.* Austin, TX: PRO-ED.

Lenz, B. K., & Mellard, D. F. (1989). Content area skill assessment. In R. A. Gable & J. M. Hendrickson (Eds.). *Error patterns in academics: Identification and remediation.* White Plains, NY: Longman, Inc.

Lovitt, T., Rudisit, J., Jenkins, J., Pious, C., & Benedetti, D. (1985). Two methods of adapting science materials for learning disabled and regular seventh graders. *Learning Disability Quarterly, (8),* 275–285.

Mastropieri, M. A., Scruggs, T. E., Levin, J. R., Gaffney, J., & McLoone, B. (1985). Mnemonic vocabulary instruction for learning disabled students. *Learning Disability Quarterly, 8*(1), 57–64.

Mayer, R. E. (1987). *Educational psychology: A cognitive approach.* Boston: Little, Brown.

Merril, M.D, & Tennyson, R. D. (1977). *Teaching concepts: An instructional design guide.* Englewood Cliffs, NJ: Educational Technology.

Nagle, D. R., Schumaker, J. B., & Deshler, D. D. (1986). *The learning strategies curriculum: The FIRST-letter mnemonic strategy.* Lawrence, KS: Edge Enterprises.

Pressley, M., Levin, J. R., & McDaniel, M. A. (1987). Remembering versus inferring what a word means: Mnemonic and contextual approaches. In M. G. McKeown & M. E. Curtis (Eds.). *In the nature of vocabulary acquisition.* (pp. 107–127). Hillsdale, NJ: Lawrence Erlbaum Associates.

Robinson, S., Deshler, D. D., Denton, P., & Schumaker, J. B. (in prep.) *The learning strategies curriculum: A listening and notetaking strategy.* Lawrence, KS: Edge Enterprises.

Schumaker, J. B., Denton, P. H., & Deshler, D. D. (1984). *The learning strategies curriculum: The paraphrasing strategy.* Lawrence: The University of Kansas, Institute for Research in Learning Disabilities.

Schumaker, J. B., Deshler, D. D., & McKnight, P. (1991). Teaching routines for content areas at the secondary level. In G. Stoner, M. R. Shinn, and H. M. Walker (Eds.). *Interventions for Achievement and Behavior Problems.* (pp. 473–494). Washington, DC: National Association of School Psychologists.

Schumaker, J. B., & McKnight, P. (1989). Teaching routines to enhance the mainstream performance of adolescents with learning disabilities. Final report submitted to the U. S. Department of Education, Special Education Services, Washington, DC.

Vygotsky, L. S. (1978). *Mind in society: The development of higher psychology processes.* Cambridge, MA: Harvard University Press.

CHAPTER 14

Additional Preparation
for Adulthood:
Transition Planning

SUSAN BRODY HASAZI
KATHARINE S. FURNEY
MARC HULL

CHAPTER OBJECTIVES

At the conclusion of this chapter, the reader will be able to:

1. Describe the rationale for and concept of transition planning for secondary level students with disabilities and their families.
2. Describe major pieces of legislation enacted by the U.S. Congress that promote the practice of transition planning.
3. Discuss the process for identifying a transition team and carrying out the transition planning process for students with disabilities and their families.
4. Describe student-centered strategies that have shown promise in preparing students to live, work and participate in the community following graduation from high school.
5. Describe program-centered strategies that foster collaboration, communication, and a team approach to special education services and transition planning efforts, and result in effective programs and positive outcomes for students with disabilities and their families.

PREPARATION FOR ADULTHOOD

Over the past decade, issues related to the transition of students with disabilities from school to adult life have become a major concern to parents, professionals, policymakers, and students themselves (Will, 1984; Clark, 1984; Edgar, 1987). Making the transition from the relatively familiar and secure environment of school, to the complex demands of the adult community is challenging for most students and their families.

In its narrowest sense, *transition* is defined as the process for ensuring that students successfully move from school to the work world (Clark & Kolstoe, 1990). A broader interpretation views transition as a comprehensive process that focuses on improving the quality of a student's employment outcomes, residential options, and interpersonal networks following exit from school (Halpern, 1985). In this chapter, the term *transition* is used to encompass the series of purposeful activities designed to ensure that students have the skills, opportunities, and supports needed to locate and maintain employment, to pursue postsecondary education and training, to participate in the social fabric of the community, and to make decisions about their lives. According to Will (1984, p. 1), transition planning assists persons with disabilities in moving "between the security and structure offered by the school and the opportunities and risks of adult life."

The formal transition planning process should be initiated beginning no later than ninth grade. This process can serve to clarify students' aspirations, goals, and life-style choices relative to future employment, postsecondary education, living environments, and leisure activities. By focusing on these issues at the beginning of high school, they can be addressed while students are still in school. Instructional interventions, critical adult adjustment experiences, and needed supports can be tailored to promote attaining each student's personal transition goals (McDonnell & Hardman, 1985).

The transition planning process links the efforts of schools with those of other entities in preparing students for adult life. Included are potential employers; adult human service agencies; postsecondary education and training institutions; families; and the community, which will ultimately "receive" the students. The resulting individual transition plan (ITP) should ensure that the "hand off" from the school to the postsecondary receiving agencies is a relatively smooth event (Edgar, 1987).

While the focus of this chapter, as well as much of the legislation supporting transition, is on the secondary school, in actual fact, developing critical transition skills starts much earlier. When students at young ages first begin to learn self-control and self-responsibility skills, as well as specific academic and task-oriented behaviors, they are mastering critical transition skills. If elementary and middle school programs fail to address these skills, the task of preparing secondary-age youngsters for transition is almost impossible. Developing transition skills is a continuing and never-ending process of extension and refinement.

This chapter overviews the rationale for transition planning and the legislation supporting this process. It presents program models that are individualized and collaborative, involving partnerships among the school, the community, and the family. This chapter describes transition planning process and activities, and details specific student-centered strategies. It provides a culminating focus for the skills and strategies that have been presented throughout this book.

THE NEED FOR TRANSITION PLANNING

The Tenth Annual Report to Congress (1989) identified vocational training, counseling, and placement services as priority needs. A major impetus for the increased concern about the transition process has been a growing realization that many individuals with disabilities do not achieve their full potential as independent, contributing and participating members of society. A series of follow-up studies conducted with students with disabilities following their exit or graduation

from school underscored this fact (Hasazi, Gordon & Roe, 1985a, 1985b; Mithaug, Horiuchi & Fanning, 1985; Wehman, Kregel & Seyforth, 1985; Wagner, 1989). These studies indicated that: (1) more than 30% of students who received special education services at the secondary level dropped out of school before graduating; (2) fewer than 15% of former special education students who were out of school longer than 1 year participated in postsecondary education and training (Wagner, 1989); (3) 30%–40% of students were unemployed following exit from school, and of those who were employed, only about half were working fulltime; (4) many students with disabilities were not linked up with adult community services and educational agencies prior to graduation; and (5) individuals with disabilities have low rates of employment within the first year of exiting from school; and (6) young women with disabilities were unemployed at rates significantly higher than young men with disabilities or young women without disabilities.

Unemployment, underemployment, sporadic employment, dependency, and various forms of public assistance are too frequently the plight of adults with disabilities. This relatively bleak picture notwithstanding, recent programmatic and research efforts demonstrate that individuals with disabilities have considerable potential for productive employment in integrated, mainstream settings (Mank & Horner, 1988). In an attempt to foster this potential, Congress has enacted several pieces of legislation to provide greater opportunities for adolescents with disabilities. These are described in the following section and are summarized in Table 14.1.

LEGISLATIVE MANDATES

The 1983 Education of the Handicapped Amendments (EHA) (PL 98-199) authorized funding to support model demonstration programs that would strengthen and coordinate the education, training, and related services programs designed to assist youth with disabilities in the transition from school

TABLE 14.1 Key Legislation Affecting Transition

Individuals with Disabilities Education Act, 1990
Education of the Handicapped Amendments (1990)
- Included transition services as a part of special education and related services
- Required inclusion for students with disabilities, no later than 16 years of age, of transition objectives in the Individual Education Program

Americans with Disabilities Act (1990)
- Specified the civil rights protections of individuals with disabilities in private sector employment, public services, transportation, and telecommunications

Carl Perkins Vocational and Applied Technology and Education Act (1990)
- Students with disabilities and their parents must be informed about vocational education opportunities by the time students are 14 years old
- Provided counseling services and adaptive instruction to facilitate transition from school to postschool employment
- Mandated full access by students with disabilities to a full range of local vocational program options

---

to adult life. The 1990 EHA Amendments, referred to as the Individuals with Disabilities Education Act (IDEA), expanded the definition of special education and related services to include the provision of transition services. It defined *transition services* as a "coordinated set of activities for a student, designed within an outcome oriented process, which promotes movement from school to integrated employment (including supported employment), post-secondary education, vocational training, continuing and adult education, adult services, independent living or community participation." In addition to including transition services as a component of special education, Congress mandated that a statement of a student's needed transition services be included in the Individualized Education Program (IEP) by 16 years of age (or earlier if appropriate), and that this statement be reviewed annually until graduation or exit from high school.

According to Halpern (1985), the purpose of transition services, as reflected in the 1990 IDEA, is to provide programs and opportunities that lead to "living successfully in one's community." This perspective highlights the need for students to acquire specific skills and knowledge related to

community living, employment, postsecondary education and training, and decision making (Halpern, 1985; Hasazi & Clark, 1988; Will, 1984;). The 1990 reauthorization of PL 94-142 includes amendments addressing the importance of assistive technology for students in transition from school to postschool settings. Through the provision of special funding, the bill also encouraged developing and using assistive technology services in promoting transition. In acknowledging the value of transition services, the 1990 IDEA reinforced the importance of postschool outcomes in the design, implementation, and evaluation of special education programs for students at the secondary level.

A second important piece of legislation that Congress passed in 1990 was the Americans with Disabilities Act (ADA). Although not specifically targeted at the transition from school to adult life, this legislation had important implications for students with disabilities. According to the Council for Exceptional Children (1990), the ADA provided "civil rights protection to individuals with disabilities in private sector employment, all public services, public accommodations, transportation, and telecommunications." It included a variety of provisions related to ensuring accommodations for, and accessibility to, services and employment opportunities for individuals with disabilities.

Finally, the Carl Perkins Vocational and Applied Technology and Education Act of 1990 included several provisions designed to improve the access to vocational education programs for students with disabilities. For example, the Act specified that prior to the beginning of the ninth grade, all students with disabilities and their parents must be informed of the programs available through vocational education, and their accompanying entry requirements. In addition, the Act provided for counseling services designed to facilitate the transition from school to postschool employment and career opportunities, as well as adaptation of curricula, instruction equipment, and facilities. Finally, the act required that local vocational education programs ensure equal access to the full range of vocational program options and involve special education personnel in planning program modifications for students with disabilities.

PROGRAM ELEMENTS

These initiatives lead to a renewed interest in and examination of the goals and activities associated with existing high school programs for students with disabilities. As a result, new service delivery models have evolved at the state and local levels (Johnson, Bruininks & Thurlow, 1987; Rusch & Phelps, 1987). The primary thrust of these efforts has been improving the postschool outcomes related to employment, independent living, community participation, building friendship networks, and decision making.

Reports on the efficacy of these efforts have identified the following elements of effective transition planning:

1. *The planning process itself,* including a written plan of action that specifies key personnel, activities, and timelines for meeting transition goals.

2. Using *curricula and instructional approaches that include a variety of student-centered strategies and activities,* such as self-advocacy skills, experiences in paid work, vocational training and education, job-seeking skills, and instructional presentation strategies.

3. Program-centered *strategies that promote collaboration and communication* among families, schools, adult human service agencies, and the community-at-large.

Promising practices identified for these three categories are designed to increase the academic and life skills of students, as well as to provide meaningful social interactions in employment, educational, and community environments. The collaborative nature of this process promotes a climate where transition planning is valued and promoted, and where the efforts of teams and individuals are likely to be rewarded with positive outcomes for students and their families. Frequent evaluation of student outcomes provides opportunities to make programmatic adjustments and to determine which student-centered and program-centered strategies are most successful.

TRANSITION PLANNING PROCESS

The transition planning process provides the framework for identifying, planning, and carrying out activities that will help a student make a successful transition to adult life. The planning process is *individualized* in the sense that it focuses on the unique needs of the student, and *collaborative* in that it involves a team of people drawn from different parts of the student's school and community life.

Given the individualized nature of this process, no two transition plans will look alike. However, a generic set of factors can guide the transition planning steps, for example, assembling a team, implementing the planning process, selecting strategies and activities, and following up on identified activities. These guidelines will be discussed in this chapter, along with a case study of the transition planning process and a transition plan format.

Transition planning for high school students with disabilities should be accomplished through the IEP process, as specified in the 1990 IDEA. Because the entitlement to educational services ends, in most states, at 21 years of age, and adult services are not mandatory for all individuals who are in need of services, it is essential that the IEP include components that focus on vocational, postsecondary education, and community participation concerns. To facilitate this, transition planning teams need to include representatives from a variety of disciplines, each of whom may offer different perspectives on objectives, strategies, and resource availability. The composition of a transition team should reflect the individual student's needs. For example, a team for a student interested in attending a postsecondary technical school might be composed of the student, one or more family members, a special education teacher, a vocational education teacher, a representative from the technical school, a representative from a local community agency connected with residential options, and a community member. Other transition planning teams might include representatives from Rehabilitation Services.

The goal of the transition planning process is to ensure that the student has acquired the skills needed to participate fully in the community following graduation from high school. To meet this goal, the process needs to be a cooperative effort focused on the unique aspirations, needs, and goals that each student and his family specify. Both the students and their parents should be taught the mechanics of developing an ITP, as well as information relative to various options and opportunities for youth with disabilities. This can be provided through individual meetings with school and transition agency personnel, and parent-student transition information programs at school.

In developing the plan, the team should consider issues related to employment, residential placement, postsecondary education, recreation and leisure, transportation, medical needs, income and insurance needs, and interpersonal relationships. An assessment should be made of the student's current skills, needs, and opportunities in each of the previously mentioned areas. The student's aspirations for the future need to be identified and clarified with the team, as should parental preferences and support options. Family involvement is a critical element, for research has shown that parents, siblings, and family friends exert a powerful influence on the career attitudes and options of students (Wheeler, 1987), and constitute a key resource in obtaining initial and subsequent jobs (Hasazi, Gordan & Roe, 1985a). This family/friend network can be the critical variable in the transition to successful adult living.

Together, the results of the assessment and the student's vision of the future should guide the team to identify focal issues for transition. The individualized transition plan provides a vehicle for implementing the designated transition services. It specifies annual goals, objectives, activities, timelines, and the assignments for key personnel. The resulting transition plan should be initiated when the student enters high school and revised at least annually as part of the IEP process.

TRANSITION CULMINATION

The culmination stage of transition encompasses the period of time beginning 2 years before the student leaves school and continues for 2 years after. According to the California Department of Education (1987, p. 1), during this time period, "responsibility for transition management shifts from the educational system to the student, the family, and/or the adult service delivery system." The school hands off the students to the receiving environments (Maddox & Edgar, 1985). Involved are the steps for obtaining additional training and services (e.g., filling out applications and eligibility paperwork), doing final student assessments, identifying transitions resources and supports, and assigning responsibilities for implementing the postschool transition services. Students in high school typically have had little contact with adult service agencies and neither they nor their families are prepared for the myriad of complex steps involved in obtaining services from these agencies. The 1990 IDEA therefore requires that a planned and systematic process of referral to adult serve agencies be included in the student's IEP and ITP beginning when the student is 16 years of age. The ultimate goal is for the student to achieve active client status with the adult agency prior to graduation. Final steps in the transition process include follow-up of students as a program evaluation activity that should ultimately inform future program planning efforts.

Parent involvement becomes even more critical at the culmination stage. Schools should provide structured training programs that teach parents the process of adult agency referral, effective strategies for supporting the efforts of a working student, strategies for accessing adult community services, and other information specific to their student's transition from school to the adult community (Berkell, 1988). Parental participation in such training is increased if there is a parent facilitator on the transition team who can visit the family in its home to explain the transition program and the parent involvement opportunities. Additional incentives include transportation assistance, child care relief, stipends, and scheduling convenience (e.g., early evenings instead of daytime).

In much the same vein, active student participation in the transition planning process can be facilitated through teacher planning. Teachers can prepare students to participate more meaningfully in this process, thereby facilitating their becoming more self-determining individuals. For example, teachers can have students practice developing lists of their own transition goals and writing "rough drafts" of their own ITPs.

Case Study

The case study that follows is an example of how the transition planning process outlined previously can be used effectively to help a student with a mild disability focus her high school program to meet her individual academic, voca-

tional, residential, and social needs while moving towards her image of the future. A written transition plan is also included to illustrate how the planning process can be recorded and included as part of an IEP document (Figure 14.1).

Michelle

Michelle is a 16-year old student in the tenth grade who was labeled as learning disabled in elementary school and had a variety of special education services before entering high school. Her teachers and family describe her as a likable young woman who is interested in science- and health-related issues. Michelle wants to do well in school but is sometimes frustrated by the difficulties she encounters in academic areas. This frustration seems to have a negative impact on her self-confidence, and she often appears shy in the presence of peers and adults.

Recent standardized assessments of Michelle's academic skills indicate that she reads at a fourth-grade level, but her teachers note that her reading comprehension improves when she is interested in the subject material. Writing mechanics are difficult for Michelle and she frequently has trouble organizing her thoughts when preparing to write. Her computational mathematics skills, however, are equal to those of her peers.

Michelle is currently enrolled in regular tenth-grade English, mathematics, biology, and living arts classes. Her special education teacher team teaches in Michelle's science class and provides Michelle with individual support during a daily structured study hall period. Outside of school, Michelle enjoys music and family activities such as swimming and bowling. She does not participate in any extracurricular activities at school.

Description of the Transition Planning Process

Prior to Michelle's annual IEP meeting at the beginning of her tenth-grade year, the special education teacher discussed the concept of transition planning with Michelle, and her parents and teachers. Data on Michelle's academic perform-

---

Student: <u>Michelle G</u>

Date of Plan: <u>September 29,1990</u>

Current Classroom Placement: <u>10th Grade</u>

Projected Graduation Date: <u>June 1993</u>

Goal Area: Income

Objectives: By June 1993, Michelle will have a plan in place to support herself while attending technical school.

Activities:
1. Michelle and her guidance counselor will apply for a scholarship to technical school, by January 1993.
2. Michelle and her parents will make an agreement regarding the amount of financial support they will provide while she attends technical school, by June 1993.
3. Michelle and her job training specialist will locate part-time employment to help support Michelle following graduation and during attendance at technical school, by June 1993.

Goal Area: Employment and Training

Objectives: By June 1993, Michelle will complete at least two (2) part-time work experiences in a health-related field.

By June 1993, Michelle will complete a 2-year vocational education program in health occupations.

1. Michelle will work with the job training specialist and vocational coop coordinator to complete a job-seeking skills curricula and related activities necessary for her to locate and obtain at least two (2) work experiences in a health-related field, by June 1993.
2. Michelle will successfully complete the two (2) work experiences identified previously, by June 1993.
3. Michelle will "job-shadow" a student in the health occupations program who is employed in a health-related field, by January 1991.
4. Michelle will successfully complete the vocational education program in health occupations, by June 1993.
5. Michelle will successfully complete required minimum courses in English, biology, and mathematics, with accommodations as necessary, which are needed for her acceptance to technical school and to meet high school graduation requirements, by June 1993.

Goal Area: Postsecondary Education

Objectives: By June 1993, Michelle will be enrolled in the Valley Technical School in the medical technician training program.

Activities:
1. Michelle's special education teacher will contact the Valley Technical school to obtain information on entrance requirements, available programs, and support services available to students with disabilities, by September 1991.
2. Michelle's special education teacher will invite a faculty or staff member of the technical school to act as her "link" and to attend transition meetings, beginning in September 1991.
3. Michelle and her guidance counselor will complete the technical school's application process, by December 1992.

Goal Area: Living Arrangements

Objectives: By June 1993, Michelle will establish a budget for living expenses projected for the following year.

By September 1993, Michelle will live in an apartment with a friend.

Activities: 1. Michelle's IEP will specify her enrollment in English and mathematics classes, which teach skills needed to establish and maintain a budget, manage a checkbook, and respond to classified ads, by September 1991.
2. Michelle, her special education teacher, and her parents will answer classified ads, visit potential apartments, and select an apartment for Michelle to live in, by August 1993.
3. Michelle and her parents will interview potential roommates and identify one to live with her, by September 1993.

Goal Area: Friends/Advocates

Objectives: By June 1991, Michelle will spend at least two (2) evenings per month participating in community- or school-related activities with a friend.

Activities: 1. Michelle's science teacher will use peer partners as a way for students to complete labs and assignments, and involve Michelle in at least five (5) partnership situations, by June 1991.
2. Michelle will participate as a volunteer in the school blood drive, by June 1991.
3. Michelle will identify and join at least one (1) community recreational organization (e.g., bowling league), by June 1991.

Goal Area: Long-Term Planning

Objectives: By June 1995, Michelle will complete a technical school program to prepare her for a career as a medical technician.
By August 1995, Michelle will locate and secure full-time employment as a medical technician, and will be financially able to support herself.
By August 1995, Michelle will live with a friend in an apartment of her choice and participate in a variety of community activities.

Activities: Activities listed in previous sections of the plan will enable Michelle to achieve these objectives. Additional activities may be developed during future transition planning meetings.

FIGURE 14.1   Transition Plan

ance were gathered from a variety of sources, including standardized tests, curriculum-based measures, and current grade averages. Michelle's special education teacher spent time talking with Michelle about her views on her current school program and future goals, where she learned that Michelle's main career interest was to become a medical technician.

Based on the information obtained, it was decided that Michelle's transition planning team at this time should include Michelle, her parents, the special education teacher, a science teacher, the health occupations teacher from a regional vocational center, and a job training specialist. At the first team meeting, team members reviewed relevant assessment data and discussed the nature of the transition process. Michelle and her parents were asked to talk about their aspirations for the future in the areas of employment, community living, and recreation and leisure, while the teachers and vocational specialists were asked to speak about various options that might be available for Michelle.

The result of this first team meeting was an outline of broad goals and activities related to major transition areas. In the area of employment, it was decided that Michelle should enroll in the health occupations program at the vocational center during her junior and senior years. This program would allow her to gain specific training in the health occupations field as well as to become exposed to a variety of job opportunities related to the medical technician position.

The vocational placement would be preceded by several activities during Michelle's tenth-grade year, including a 2-week shadowing experience at the vocational center, in which Michelle would be paired with a student she knew while the student attended her cooperative work experience at a local hospital. The job training specialist agreed to work with Michelle to help her obtain work experience in the medical field, with the goal that Michelle have at least two different paid work experiences by the time she graduated from high school. Michelle's academic program would be designed to include courses pertaining to her chosen field, including biology, math, and English. The team emphasized the importance of providing Michelle's academic coursework through mainstream classes, but made note of accommodations that would be needed both in regular classrooms and at the vocational center. These included provisions for Michelle to take tests orally, organizational strategies such as study guides and homework assignment sheets, and assistance in organizing materials in preparation for writing assignments. Finally, the special educator agreed to contact Michelle's guidance counselor to gather information on 2-year postsecondary programs to train people to work as medical laboratory technicians, including information on programs and support systems available to students

with disabilities at the identified institutions. It was noted that representatives from one or more of the postsecondary institutions would be invited to attend transition meetings during Michelle's senior year.

Next, the team discussed residential options that might be available to Michelle following high school. Michelle's desire was to share an apartment with a friend. The team concurred that this would be an appropriate and reachable goal, provided that Michelle's mathematics and English courses include some practical living skills such as budgeting, keeping a checkbook, and filling out job applications. In addition, the team agreed that, if necessary, appropriate community members could be called upon later to help the team identify potential apartment options.

The final topic for discussion was about social, recreational, and leisure activities. Michelle and her parents and teachers identified this as an area of concern, noting that while Michelle had some classmates whom she considered to be friends, she did not spend time with them outside of school. Michelle's science teacher noted that several of these students were in Michelle's biology class, and that Michelle could be paired with them on an informal basis for in-class assignments and labs. The health occupations teacher suggested that Michelle participate as a student volunteer in an upcoming blood drive at school, both as a way to further her interest in the medical field and to get to know some students better. Michelle and her parents agreed to investigate some organized community recreation activities such as a bowling league for teenagers. Transportation was identified as a stumbling block in allowing Michelle to participate in social activities and Michelle's parents agreed to set aside at least two Friday nights per month when they would be available to transport Michelle and a friend to an activity of their choice.

Follow-up to the Transition Planning Process

At the conclusion of the planning process, Michelle's special education teacher outlined plans for follow-up. Responsibilities and timelines for each team member were reviewed. The special education teacher agreed to coordinate the activities and set a date for a follow-up call with each team member. The team listed the names of other persons who would be invited to attend future meetings. Finally, they established their next meeting date and time, and drafted an agenda for the meeting.

INSTRUCTIONAL RECOMMENDATIONS

An important step in the transition planning process is to provide experiences that meet individual student's needs and ensure that transition goals will be met. These strategies and experiences are the "how-to's" of transition planning in that they provide the vehicle for accomplishing transition goals that a student and her family specify. It is unlikely that a single transition plan would contain all these strategies, but planning teams and students need to be aware of these "promising practices" that may increase students' opportunities and abilities to live, work, and participate in the community.

Experiences and approaches specifically associated with transition include developing self-advocacy skills; participating in paid work experiences, vocational training at community sites, and vocational education and job-seeking skills. Other promising practices such as learning strategies, cooperative group learning, peer tutoring, and peer partnerships are more typically associated with strategies to improve overall classroom instruction. They may be equally important to transition planning, however, because they increase students' opportunities to acquire academic skills and widen their social networks.

In general, the more opportunities a student has in high school to make decisions about the future, engage in paid work experience, and interact with peers and adults in regular classroom environments, at work, and in the community, the more likely it seems that the student will have positive experiences in the transition from school to adult life. A brief description of promising practices in student-centered strategies and their importance to transition planning follows.

Self-Advocacy

There has been a growing concern among individuals connected with transition planning that educators and adult services professionals have assumed too much responsibility for decisions that govern the lives of students and adults with disabilities. The self-advocacy movement is dedicated to the belief that individuals with disabilities have the right to direct their own lives through making choices, speaking for themselves, and reducing dependence on specialized services.

The issue of self-advocacy is critical for any student about to enter into transition from high school to adult life, but it appears especially difficult for students with disabilities. On the one hand, students must make a host of choices about where and how to live, work, and become active members of a complex adult world. On the other hand, students may have few real choices in their communities and little experience in making decisions. Family members, friends, and professionals may be well-meaning, but they may also be prone to making decisions *for,* rather than *with,* students (Gould & McTaggart, 1989).

This pattern may be detrimental for several reasons. First, students who are not involved in making choices and planning their educational programs in high school may not be personally invested in the choices made for them. As a result, otherwise well-designed strategies may fail. Second, students who are not encouraged to make their own decisions may not develop a sense of responsibility for their own actions. Young adults need to be given the "right to fail," since failure is an experience that helps develop both one's sense of abilities and limitations (Ward, 1988). Third, students who are not encouraged to speak for themselves in school will be less likely and perhaps less able to make choices in the adult world. Students who are self-advocates are empowered to make changes in their lives and their communities, and have a chance to break the cycle of dependence and the "eternal child" myth, which so often characterize the lives of individuals with disabilities (Kelley-Laine, 1988).

Attempts to help students build and expand on their roles as self-advocates focus on two aspects: (1) identifying and pursuing one's needs and desires, and (2) joining with others to pursue common interests (Gould, 1985). In order for young people to focus on personal goals and needs, they need opportunities to sample a variety of jobs, and acquire an understanding of the kinds of living situations, activities, and resources that will be available to them in their communities. A high school curriculum that provides a variety of options and experiences (e.g., paid work experiences, community experiences, vocational classes, traditional academic classes, and extracurricular activities), and ensures that students are actively involved in developing their own programs will promote self-advocacy. Instructional strategies such as peer partnerships and cooperative group learning (see the following sections on peer power) indirectly promote self-advocacy by encouraging students to speak for themselves in the context of a group.

Students can learn to advocate for themselves through actively participating in their own transition planning (Gould, 1985). Following is a list of skills to be covered in a self-advocacy curricula (Michaels, 1989):

1. Accepting criticism and changing behavior to reflect input.
2. Dealing with supervisors/managers, including discussing the disability and requesting appropriate accommodations.
3. Evaluating self-performance, monitoring task completion, and providing self-feedback.
4. Goal setting, developing short- and long-term goals, and monitoring self-progress.
5. Participating in developing a vocational plan that includes goals for career advancement and protecting one's own interests.

6. Developing social skills and appropriate behavior/interactions for the job setting.

Some students will require instruction in self-advocacy skills, and may benefit from curricula which assist them in acquiring skills such as communicating with others, defining personal goals, identifying alternative strategies for reaching these goals, decision making, negotiating, problem-solving, and group processing. Examples of curricula incorporating these goals include job-seeking skills curricula (Allen, Patten, Hasazi, & Cobb, 1989; Kimeldorf, 1985; Farr, Faither, & Pickrell, 1983) and self-advocacy curricula (Deschler, 1988, unpublished data; Gould, 1985; Walker, McConnell, Holmes, Todes, Walker, & Golden, 1983).

Finally, IEP and transition planning processes need to ensure that students' needs are recognized and pursued. Planning strategies such as Personal Futures Planning (O'Brien, 1987) and the McGill Action Planning System (Forest & Lusthaus, 1990; O'Brien, Forest, Snow & Hasbury, 1989) make conscious attempts to personalize the planning process and address the self-advocacy issue. They also focus on creative approaches to meeting students' needs, and support students and their families in finding solutions in informal community networks rather than adult human service agencies (Perske & Perske, 1988). For example, students and families seeking appropriate and affordable housing might form cooperatives and use paid and volunteer community members to assist their sons and daughters in living as independently as possible (Carney & Orelove, 1988). This approach carries the notion of self-advocacy one step further because it encourages students and families to join together and speak out as a group to overcome barriers to full community participation.

Paid Work Experience

Students with disabilities who hold paying jobs while in high school are more likely to be employed following graduation than those who do not (Hasazi et al., 1985a and 1985b; Edgar, 1987). These students also are more apt to remain in school, seek postsecondary education opportunities, and become self-supporting adults (Edgar, 1987). However, only about 6% of students with mild disabilities receive community-based instruction (Halpern & Benz, 1987).

Paid work experiences may help students to acquire an understanding of the contingencies associated with earning wages, and learn to observe and collaborate with co-workers. The manner in which these experiences might occur include supervised part-time work after school or on weekends, part-time or full-time summer work, or a combination of these options. Only through actual paid employment experiences will students acquire an appreciation for the social ecology of the work place and the natural consequences inherent in real work. For example, it is essential to learn that break time in a work environment has a beginning and an end, and usually involves some form of social interaction between co-workers. It is also critical to experience the relationship between work accomplishments and tangible rewards such as money and increased participation in leisure activities that require financial resources.

Vocational Training at Employment Sites

In order to prepare students for employment, research has demonstrated that instruction provided in community work settings is an essential component of a vocational program (Cobb, Hasazi, Collins, & Salembier, 1988). The range of potential difficulties that may occur at a work site cannot be anticipated and accommodated in a classroom-based vocational education environment, and, for many students, can best be addressed at the actual work place. Specific vocational skills are more effectively taught in the environments in which skills are naturally utilized and rewarded (Sailor et al., 1986). Vocational training at employment sites can include a variety

of support services. An individual might require short-term intensive training that a job trainer provides, which would include a planned process for fading the training support. Another individual might require only that the trainer provide intermittent follow-up support in order to monitor changes in the work routine by the employer and provide retraining if necessary. Yet another individual might not require direct training or monitoring, but might need support in relationships with co-workers or supervisors.

Participation in Vocational Education Programs

Vocational education at the secondary level is generally provided for half the school day during the junior and senior years. The goals of vocational education are to assist students to acquire: (1) personal skills and attitudes, (2) communication and computational skills and technological literacy, (3) employability skills, (4) broad and specific skills and knowledge, and (5) foundations for career planning and life-long learning (National Commission on Secondary Vocational Education, 1984). Curriculum-based vocational assessment (CBVA) is a recently developed approach that directly measures a student's performance in a vocational program. It can be an integral aspect of all phases of the vocational preparation program (prior to initial placement, during the program, and on-the-job during transition), providing data that guide the transition planning process as well the day-to-day vocational instruction program.

Various social skills have proven to be critical for maintaining employment. These skills may be taught at the high school level in a one-semester course that covers such job-keeping behaviors as dressing appropriately on the job, filling out time cards, getting along with supervisors and co-workers, asking for assistance, giving and accepting praise, interacting with the public, and so forth. In addition, on-the-job teaching of skills, job coaching, crisis intervention, and close employer communication are effective strategies for promoting job maintenance skills.

Vocational education is organized around three major components: (1) in-school vocational skill instruction, (2) out-of-school work experience, and (3) vocational student organizations. Historically, students with disabilities have had difficulty gaining access to regular vocational education, particularly to the work experience and student organization components (Birchenall & Wanat, 1981). However, research has indicated that students with mild disabilities who did gain access to regular in-school vocational instruction were later employed in the jobs that paid higher wages than those students who did not participate in regular vocational education (Hasazi et al., 1985a).

In recent years, vocational educators and special educators have placed greater emphasis on collaborating to provide the supports necessary for students with disabilities to succeed in vocational classes (Hasazi & Clark, 1988). Vocational classes provide a practical "hands on" education for these students, but as society has become more technical, the vocational courses that are in place to train students have also become more technical, requiring more in the way of reading, mathematics, and problem-solving skills (Touzel, 1989). Most vocational centers employ a full-time or part-time vocational resource teacher who works with vocational educators to plan, monitor and/or implement, and evaluate strategies to meet the individual student's needs.

The level of support provided to teachers and students varies according to individual needs and classroom demands. For example, in-service training could be provided to vocational instructors to help make them aware of whole-class, effective teaching strategies such as modeling and questioning for understanding (Christenson, Ysseldyke, Thurlow, 1989; Brookover, Beamer, Eftheim, Hathaway, Lezotte, Miller, Passalacqua, & Tornatzky, 1982). An auto mechanics teacher might find that one student in her class understands the concepts of auto mechanics, but has difficulty memorizing vocabulary words for written tests. This student's needs could be met through a peer partnership program, developed jointly by the vocational class teacher and vocational resource teacher, in which a peer who typically finishes class assignments early is trained to work with the student on vocabulary comprehension. A second student in the class may have difficulties expressing himself in writing; that student could be allowed to take tests orally with the vocational resource teacher. A student experiencing greater difficulties learning the auto mechanics curriculum might require more significant curriculum modifications. In this case, the vocational instructor and vocational resource teacher would consider the student's strengths and learning style in light of curriculum demands, determining which curriculum competencies could be met as written and which would need to be adapted so that the student could realistically attain them (Eddy, Mack, & Ringe, 1989).

Job-Seeking Skills Curricula

A systematic job search curriculum can be a critical component of a secondary transition program. Youth with mild disabilities should be specifically taught those skills associated with successfully seeking employment. These include reading classified ads, identifying locations of job postings and information, filling out job applications, dressing appropriately for job interviews, preparing resumes, and actual job interviewing. A unit of instruction lasting 3–4 weeks should focus on these skills, with students filling out at least six real job applications, participating in role plays, videotaping several simulated interviews, and identifying and obtaining the essential documents (e.g., birth certificates, state identification cards, work permits, and Social Security cards) needed for getting jobs.

Because utilizing the family/friend network appears to be a successful strategy for locating work and the most frequently used (Hasazi et al., 1985a, 1985b), curricula designed to teach students how to use their networks to find jobs seems to be extremely valuable. Many of the job-seeking curricula available (Allen et al., 1989; Kimeldorf, 1985; Farr et al., 1983) have drawn on the work of Nathan Azrin and Victoria Besalel, who developed an approach to job-seeking known as the "job club" (Azrin & Besalel, 1980). Azrin and his colleagues demonstrated positive outcomes for unemployed adults in job clubs in which participants supported one another to gain skills in job hunting, identify potential jobs, and share their knowledge of community resources.

At the secondary level, job club approaches teach students skills related to self-assessment of job-related skills, completing application forms, writing resumes, making telephone contacts, pursuing job leads, participating in interviews, and writing letters to employers. Several key elements characterize these job-seeking approaches. Students are taught to emphasize the self/family/friend network rather than professionals or classified ads in locating job openings. Job-seeking skills that students acquire are put directly to use in an actual job hunt. Self-reliance and self-advocacy are promoted in a supportive atmosphere in which peers have the opportunity to assist one another, locate potential jobs, provide feedback on resources and simulated interviews, and become part of one another's job-seeking "networks." The job-seeking approach allows the student to look for employment without assistance from specialized agencies and provides the student with skills that can be used in future job-seeking efforts

Social-Vocational Skills

One of the major reasons that individuals with disabilities encounter problems in getting and retaining jobs is the lack of appropriate social skills, rather than poor job performance (Chadsey-Rusch et al., 1994). They tend to lose jobs due to behaviors such as the (failure to ask questions, and accept directions, and social awareness difficulties.

Employers value social behaviors that are related to work productivity more highly than gen-

eral personal social behaviors. For example, listening without interrupting, acknowledging comments and directions, and expressing appreciation to co-workers are viewed as important. In jobs carried out in a social context where workers interact frequently with each other and/or customers (such as kitchen helpers and food service workers), social skills are considered more important than in jobs that do not require much social interaction. Critical social skills important to obtaining and maintaining employment are as follows:

1. Asking supervisors for assistance
2. Following directions
3. Responding to criticism
4. Getting information before a job
5. Offering to help co-workers
6. Using social amenities
7. Extending greetings
8. Giving positive comments

The primary goal of social skills training for persons with disabilities is that their employers and co-workers view them as having adequate social competence (Chadsey-Rusch, 1984). Research has demonstrated that social skills training can effectively decrease inappropriate social behaviors (Rusch, Weither, Menchetti, & Schutz, 1980) as well as develop or increase appropriate social behaviors.

Students have been taught skills such as how to interview for jobs, comply with employer directions, increase their frequency of question asking during conversations, handle criticism, take a joke, solicit assistance, and act appropriately during break times. These skills may be taught through a combination of social skills techniques and the use of behavioral techniques.

Community Living Skills

An important component of transition to adulthood, in addition to vocational/employment skills, is the variety of community living skills required to living independently in the community (Clark & Kolstoe, 1990; Halpern, 1985). These include competence in money management; social networking; home maintenance; food management; health care; employment; transportation; leisure pursuits; and accessing/using financial guidance, legal services, and mental health services (Halpern, 1985; Clark and Kolstoe, 1990).

INSTRUCTIONAL APPROACHES

Approaches to teaching vocational and community living skills are essentially the same as those described as effective throughout the book. Direct instructional presentation approaches focus students' attention and move them rapidly through the curriculum. At the same time, instruction in learning strategies can provide tools applicable to successful life-long development and learning. Cooperative or "peer power" approaches can facilitate social and interpersonal skills, and promote the integration of students with disabilities.

Learning Strategies

The learning curriculum Strategies Intervention Model, developed at the University of Kansas Institute for Research in Learning Disabilities (Deshler & Schumaker, 1986), can help students develop skills that will facilitate their transition to adult life. First, students with learning difficulties who successfully use the learning strategies approach experience greater academic success, which in turn may lead to increased self-esteem and social contact with their peers without disabilities. Strong social networks are often associated with greater opportunities to locate and obtain employment. Second, a major focus of the learning strategies approach is on learning to generalize skills to other settings. Students may be provided with specific instruction in how to transfer strategies to the work place, thus increasing the likelihood that they will be able to move beyond unskilled entry-level positions to jobs requiring higher levels of reading and writing skills. Third, the learning strategies approach is important for students who are interested in pursuing postsecondary education and training,

where complex written materials are often used for teaching specific concepts and skills.

Peer Power Approaches

The term *peer power* is used here to describe several strategies that classroom teachers may use as ways of organizing their classrooms to maximize students' learning, and increase interactions between students with and without disabilities. These strategies include peer tutoring, cooperative group learning, and informal peer partner arrangements. The strategies are important for students who are beginning the transition to adult life because they provide them with opportunities for increased integration, improved performance in mainstream academic and vocational classes, and heightened self-esteem (Villa & Thousand, 1990). The strategies increase opportunities for students with and without disabilities to interact in positive ways, offering potential solutions to the challenge of helping students to build social networks that will support them in and beyond high school.

Peer power strategies are appealing to teachers because they may be used in any content area. The more formal approaches, peer tutoring and cooperative learning, require some training on the part of teachers and students, but once learned they become a natural part of the teacher's repertoire of approaches to use with students experiencing difficulty in the classroom. Peer power strategies are *not* just for students with learning difficulties. They have been shown to benefit students of all ability levels. They are a cost-effective way for teachers to provide greater individualized attention to students (Armstrong, Stahlbrand, Conlon, & Pierson, 1979). Teachers who are able to use a variety of peer power strategies find that different strategies work best with different students and instructional tasks. Overall, they make the task of teaching classes of varying ability levels more manageable. A brief description of peer power strategies follows.

Peer tutoring is an instructional approach that has proved effective with high school students with disabilities (Jenkins & Jenkins, 1985; Maher, 1984). In a formal peer-tutoring program, students experiencing difficulty in the classroom are paired with trained peers for one-on-one instruction. This instruction generally focuses on helping students to acquire, maintain, and clarify the skills being taught in the classroom. Daily objectives are specified so that both the tutor and the student being tutored know what is expected of them. A typical use of peer tutoring is shown in the following example:

> *Robert, a student with learning disabilities, is having difficulty in his basic skills math class with the concept and application of percentages. Jake, a student who has been trained as a peer tutor and has a free period during Robert's math class, attends the class and works individually with Robert any time that the teacher assigns individual seat work. Robert also has the option of meeting with Jake for additional help during his study hall time or after school. As a result of Jake's assistance, Robert maintains passing grades in his math class and does not have to resort to switching to a special math class held in the resource room. In addition, he and Jake learn that they have a common interest in music; they plan to get together after school to listen to music and buy compact discs together.*

Cooperative group learning models are another example of a peer power strategy shown to be effective in numerous research studies (Johnson & Johnson, 1987; Slavin, 1984, 1987). In cooperative group learning, students learn how to work in small groups to solve problems and/or complete tasks that the teacher assigns to them. Rather than focusing on individual performance, cooperative group learning emphasizes successful group interactions that lead to a positive group outcome. Cooperative learning models include the following elements: (1) face-to-face interaction among a heterogeneous group of students; (2) positive interdependence (structured through common goals or products, joint rewards, division of labor and roles, division of materials or information); (3) teaching small group interpersonal skills; (4) regular assessment and goal setting regarding the appropriate use of small group and interpersonal skills; and (5) individual accountability for achieving individualized academic and social objectives (Villa & Thousand, 1990).

A vocational teacher in food services might, for example, establish cooperative groups to accomplish the task of putting together a faculty luncheon at a high school. Three or four groups would be responsible for planning, cooking, and serving different parts of the meal, while a fifth group might be in charge of hospitality. A student labeled mildly mentally retarded assigned to the hospitality group might have difficulty writing invitations and menus for the meal, but the group could appoint him to help choose, purchase, and set up decorations. In doing so, the student would help accomplish the assigned group task as well as satisfy some IEP goals in mathematics and social skills.

Cooperative group models challenge teachers and students to be creative in promoting group planning, processing, and problem-solving skills while meeting students' individual academic and social needs. Experiences in working as a group to complete various tasks will be invaluable to students about to enter the work force, or participate in community events and recreational activities.

Peer partnerships are informal arrangements in which a teacher pairs two learners to complete a given activity. Partnerships differ from peer tutoring in that there is not a "tutor/tutee" relationship, no student training is required, partners are usually classmates, the makeup of partnerships may change often, and the partner activities almost always occur within the classroom (unless unfinished work is assigned as homework). The teacher may find it advantageous to pair students with differing abilities for a particular activity, but should emphasize the strengths of each student in the partnership. For example, a student with a writing disability might be paired with a peer without a disability for a newspaper story assignment, capitalizing on the fact that the first student is creative and not afraid to interview people, while the second is good at organizing ideas and the mechanics of writing. In this way, each student's strengths are recognized, and the final product will reflect the combination. This experience is important for both students, and it is a reflection of how people work and relate to one another in the community.

PROGRAM-CENTERED STRATEGIES

In addition to student-centered strategies, issues related to program policies and organizational design have been identified as important to the overall delivery of services that are likely to contribute to a successful transition from school to adult life. These include strong parent/professional partnerships, a team approach to delivering of special education at the secondary level, interagency collaboration, and utilization of community resources. Schools and communities with these strategies in place tend to foster communication and collaboration, making them conducive to transition planning efforts and welcoming to young adults with disabilities. Promising practices relative to programmatic issues are discussed as follows.

Parent/Professional Partnerships

Strong partnerships between parents of students with disabilities and professionals are critical to the success of transition planning efforts. Successful working relationships between parents and professionals are characterized by openness, honesty, and acceptance. Strong parent/professional partnerships are important to the success of program-centered strategies in the same way that self-advocacy among students is important to the success of student-centered strategies. Schools and transition teams may initiate well-meaning programs and plans, but if these lack parent support, they are not likely to succeed. Parents who feel they have true voices in determining their children's futures are more likely to feel connected to their schools and communities, and empowered to influence high school and

adult programs to be more responsive to the needs of students in transition to adult life (Wilcox, 1987).

Approaches to working with families recognize the expert knowledge that parents possess and the ways that parents can enrich the transition planning process (Foster, Berger, & McLean, 1981). These approaches acknowledge that parents know their children and their children's strengths, skills, and preferences better than anyone else. Parents have the greatest vested interest in their children's learning. They often possess unique access to information about their children and communities, and the alternatives available within communities. Parents may have political influences in schools and communities that allow them to make changes and create new opportunities on a systems level (Giangreco, & Cloninger, Mueller, Uyan, & Ashworth, 1990, unpublished data; Villa & Thousand, 1990; Wilcox, 1987).

While it was once assumed that parents would naturally prefer to utilize adult human service agencies in planning their children's futures, professionals now realize that many parents have become frustrated with the lack of available resources, and are willing to look at creative and informal options in the communities to meet their children's needs (Hamre-Nietupski, Krajewski, Nietupski, Ostercamp, Sensor, & Opheim, 1988). Transition teams that value and encourage parent participation are likely to conduct more in-depth and accurate assessments of students, set clearer and more meaningful goals, have a greater likelihood of follow-through, and have a reduced dependency on external sources than are teams that ignore or devalue the contributions of family members.

Unfortunately, some parents have become accustomed to less-than-equal treatment from professionals; therefore, they may need extra support and encouragement if they are to become active participants in the transition process. They may find it helpful to receive training in group processing and advocacy skills, as well as to receive information on available resources and services. Transition teams may also have to deal with conflicts between students and parents regarding dreams and expectations for the future. In these cases, team members outside of the family will need to act as facilitators to help family members resolve their differences while respecting one another's opinions (Forest et al., 1989).

Interagency Collaboration

A secondary level program with employment or further education and training as one of its primary goals requires using resources from both generic and specialized service agencies. An excellent mechanism for identifying human and financial resources is through developing local interagency agreements between vocational education, special education, vocational rehabilitation, and employment and training agencies (Stodden & Boone, 1987). The purpose of these agreements is to minimize service duplication while maximizing the availability and quality of services that different agencies provide.

Increased interagency collaboration has been a federal level priority and has resulted in written joint policy statements between the offices of Special Education Programs and Community Health Services, and between Vocational Education and Vocational Rehabilitation (Schalock, 1985). Federal mandates have encouraged many states to establish local interagency agreements (Johnson, Bruininks, & Thurlow, 1987). Interagency agreements should specify the underlying values and beliefs of service agencies and policies; the services provided by each agency; procedures for identifying the extent and range of needs at the local level; provisions for developing a local plan to meet those needs; procedures for identifying and informing potential consumers of the services available; procedures for monitoring consumer services and programs; provisions for developing and delivering jointly sponsored in-service training for professionals from the various agencies; and procedures for monitoring, evaluating, and revising the local agreement. These procedures need to be clearly articulated in language that avoids agency jargon and demon-

strates the consensus as to the purpose and type of service that each agency provides. In formulating the local agreement, particular attention should be directed toward including generic agencies or programs such as community colleges, area vocational-technical schools, adult education programs, and state employment and training services.

Interagency agreements improve the transition planning process by overcoming expressed barriers to service provision. Barriers that parents and service providers identify include a lack of coordination among services, a lack of information about available services, difficulties interpreting varying bureaucratic procedures (e.g., application procedures, and fiscal cycles), and difficulties assessing available services. Interagency agreements provide transition planning teams with accurate, updated information that has been gathered from a variety of sources and has been coordinated in an understandable way. In the act of producing interagency agreements, local agencies tend to improve their efforts to streamline and coordinate services, thus creating a service system that is easier to access and more capable of meeting the needs of young adults in transition. When one or more transition planning teams identify needed improvements in service provision or coordination, the agreement can be used as a mechanism for systems change. Finally, monitoring and evaluation procedures developed through interagency agreements may be used by transition planning teams who wish to analyze the outcomes and costs and benefits of a particular service (Johnson et al., 1987). While it is acknowledged that many states and regions need to further develop the kinds of agreements specified previously, it seems clear that interagency agreements are critical to the success of transition planning efforts.

Team Approach

Earlier descriptions of the transition planning process discussed the importance of a collaborative team approach to planning and delivering services. A successful transition planning effort requires parents and professionals to be flexible in their roles and responsibilities in planning and delivering services. At one time, the responsibilities of special educators, vocational educators, and vocational rehabilitation counselors were quite separate from one another. Special educators tended to focus on direct instruction in the context of a high school setting, vocational educators were primarily concerned with providing instruction in vocational classes, and rehabilitation counselors dealt with employment issues. Today, educators and adult service providers are faced with the reality and challenge of meeting students' needs in a variety of school, vocational, and community-based settings. Students making the transition from school to adult life are especially likely to participate in activities and programs that cross disciplines and involve adults with a variety of "professional hats." For these reasons, it is important to conceptualize special education services in a holistic way that acknowledges special educators, classroom teachers, vocational educators, rehabilitation counselors, postsecondary educators, employers, parents, and community members as equal partners in the education of students with disabilities. These partnerships must be formed on the basis of collaboration and teamwork, and the educators and other professionals involved in them must be trained in the skills and knowledge to work collaboratively with one another.

Transition services are most likely to be effective if *all* special education services at the secondary level are developed and delivered by a team of educators skilled at identifying and adapting resources available in regular high schools and communities. This team should include at least one special educator, referred to here as a collaborating teacher; a transition specialist; and other regular and special educators as necessary given the specific needs of an individual student.

Team members should bring some common skills to the team, as well as areas of expertise that may be shared in collaborative ways to benefit students. For example, all team members should possess strong interpersonal and communication skills, as well as knowledge and skills related to transition planning, systems change, choice making on the part of students with disabilities, working with families, and the principles of effective instruction. The collaborating teacher's specialty area would most likely include knowledge and skills related to student-centered strategies such as curriculum adaptations, learning strategies, and peer power strategies. In a team approach, this person would collaborate with regular educators to design and prepare curriculum materials, modify and adapt instructional methods, and participate in team teaching activities. The collaborating teacher might also teach learning strategies and study skills to students with and without cognitive disabilities.

The transition specialist should be skilled in student-centered strategies directly connected with students' transition to adult life. This team member would collaborate with vocational educators, vocational rehabilitation counselors, employers and postsecondary education professionals to assist in designing and implementing program options that prepare students for work, independent living, postsecondary education, and utilizing community resources. In order to avoid the proliferation of separate and parallel programs, the transition specialist should use resources and services that already exist for students without disabilities. For example, many schools employ a cooperative education teacher who works with employers to locate training and employment sites for students participating in vocational education programs. The cooperative education teacher and the transition specialist could work together to identify job sites and train students for specific jobs.

Utilizing Community Resources

Given the broad range of skills and opportunities that students will need to make a successful transition from school to adult life, their communities need to be viewed as learning environments in which students may apply the strategies outlined previously. Resources such as institutions of higher education (including community colleges, vocational technical schools, and universities) may provide invaluable exploration experiences for students considering postsecondary schooling, and may assist in identifying and developing the supports that students will need to be successful in these environments. Community organizations and clubs may provide both work experiences and opportunities for socialization that lead to developing long-term social networks. For example, most communities have recreational clubs that encourage noncompetitive leisure activities. Participating in one of these could lead to developing life-long interests in given sports, and encourage stable and valued friendships based on mutual interests. It is essential that students learn about the resources available to them in their communities, for it is only through connections with community members that students with disabilities can gain access to the full range of opportunities available to all citizens.

Organizational Strategies

Schools wishing to foster the transition planning process can create environments that are conducive to collaborative teamwork. To begin with, teachers and administrators must believe in the value of helping students plan for the transition from school to adult life. This ideal is most likely to be realized if it is included in a written school philosophy or statement of purpose, which views the transition to a meaningful life in the community as an important educational goal for all students.

Utilizing the team approach also requires schools to be organized to allow teachers and administrators sufficient planning time and flexibility in their schedules. Master schedules need to be designed so that team members have overlapping planning time, preferably at least two periods per week. Transition specialists responsible for establishing job sites and training students may need to work afternoons and early evenings, or early mornings and afternoons, in cases where stu-

dents' work experiences or jobs do not correspond with traditional school hours. Similarly, many of the social and recreational events offered in the community (e.g., dances, movies, softball leagues, and YWCA activities) occur in the evenings. If teachers are needed to attend meetings, provide transportation, or consult with sponsoring agencies, they must be allowed some flexible scheduling.

If effective transition planning services and student-centered strategies are not already in place, teachers and administrators must be prepared to advocate for systems changes that will lead to their establishment and implementation. Systems change efforts require planners to identify potential barriers to delivering services, set goals for improving service delivery, brainstorm and carry out activities designed to carry out these goals, and evaluate systems change activities and strategies. Examples of systems change strategies that might be used to implement effective transition planning include developing of a school philosophy that includes transition planning as a goal, in-service training in peer power strategies, establishing a work experience program, or restructuring special education service delivery leading to a team approach.

Obtaining and Using Outcome Measures

In order to determine whether or not transition planning efforts have been successful at the program level, schools need to establish evaluation procedures that will yield data on students' success in achieving independence, employment, and community participation. One effective means of doing this is to establish outcome measures in each of these areas and to develop an accompanying questionnaire that can be used to conduct interviews with former students. Interviews should be conducted either on the telephone or in person, 8–12 months following graduation, and reviewed from individual and programmatic perspectives. For example, information regarding a particular youth may indicate that a referral to an appropriate adult services agency is required. In addition, responses across all the interviews need to be analyzed to determine if there are trends that point to effective and less effective programs and services. Although the information acquired through the questionnaires may not be conclusive, it will provide a framework for continuing to examine programs and services as they relate to postschool outcomes.

SUMMARY

The period of transition from school to adult life is challenging for students with disabilities and their families. A transition planning process that addresses students' needs related to employment, postsecondary education, living environments, and leisure activities is critical if young adults are to achieve full community participation. The results of recent model demonstrations and research projects suggest that several factors contribute to a successful effort to help students in transition. These include careful attention to assembling a transition planning team, and a transition planning process that clarifies and acknowledges the goals and aspirations of students and their families.

This chapter delineates instructional considerations that encompass a range of curricula components. Among these are self-advocacy skills, experiences in paid work, vocational education, social skill training, and preparation for community living. Instructional presentation techniques and strategies also are described. In combination, these are designed to increase students' academic, vocational, and life skills, along with opportunities for meaningful social interactions with peers and adults in a variety of school and community settings. Finally, successful transition planning makes use of program-centered strategies that promote a philosophy of community integration for students with disabilities, and create opportunities for collaboration among students, families, school personnel, adult human service providers, and community members. These strategies include efforts to create strong parent/professional partnerships, interagency collaboration, a team approach to delivering special education, utilizing community resources, and organizational patterns that promote teamwork in schools.

The relative success of student-centered and program-centered strategies implemented to improve transition planning efforts should be measured by establishing evaluation procedures that yield data on students' abilities to locate and maintain employment, live as independently as possible, and participate in a variety of community activities. These data will help schools and the community-at-large to analyze their continued and important efforts to support students with disabilities, and their families as they encounter the challenges associated with the transition from school to adulthood.

Successful transition to adulthood is built on the academic, personal/social, community living, and vocational skills that students develop throughout their school careers. The instructional approaches described throughout this book lay the foundation for planning and implementing programs that facilitate the life-long success of students with learning difficulties.

CONTENT MASTERY QUESTIONS _____

1. What factors have led to the increased concern about transition to adulthood for students with disabilities?

2. List and describe the three federal laws that address the transition needs of students with disabilities.

3. List various individuals who might serve on a transition planning team and describe the contributions they may make.

4. Describe the transition planning process.

5. List and briefly describe seven components of a transition curriculum.

6. Discuss considerations relating to self-advocacy, and describe ways of teaching and promoting self-advocacy skills.

7. Describe three peer power approaches to instruction.

8. Discuss the importance of involving parents in the transition planning process.

9. Identify outcome variables of potential interest, and describe ways in which these measures might be obtained and utilized.

REFERENCES

Allen, K., Patten, A., Hasazi, S., & Cobb, B. (1989). The effect of an adapted job club program on job-finding performance of learning disabled youth. In G. F. Elrod (Ed.) *Career education for special needs individuals: Learning, earning, and contributing.* Columbia, SC: Dance Graphics.

Armstrong, S., Stahlbrand, K., Conlon, M., & Pierson, P. (1979). *The cost-effectiveness of peer and cross-age tutoring.* Paper presented at the International Convention of the Council for Exceptional Children. (ERIC Document Reproduction Service No. ED 171 059).

Azrin, N. H., & Besalel, V. A. (1980). *Job club counselor's manual: A behavioral approach to vocational counseling.* Baltimore, MD: University Park Press.

Birchenall, J., & Wanat, J. (1981). Serving the handicapped in vocational student organizations. *Voc Ed, 56,* 51–54.

Brookover, W., Beamer, L., Eftheim, H., Hathaway, D., Lezotte, L., Miller, S., Passalacqua, J., & Tornatzky, L. (1982). *Creating effective schools.* Holmes Beach, FL: Learning Publications.

California Education Transition Center. (1990). *Synthesis of Individual Transition Plans: Format and Process.* Sacramento, CA: California Department of Education.

Carney, I., & Orelove, F. (1988). Implementing transition programs for community participation. In B. L. Ludlow, A. P. Turnbull, and R. Luckasson (Eds.). *Transitions to adult life for people with mental retardation.* (pp. 137–157). Baltimore, MD: Paul H. Brookes Publishing Co.

Chadsey-Rusch, et al. (1984). Teaching conversation skills to adults who are mentally retarded. *Mental Retardation, 22,* 218–225.

Chadsey-Rusch, J. C. (1985). Community integration and mental retardation: The ecobehavioral approach to service provision and assessment. In R. H. Buininks & K. C. Lakin (Eds.), *Living and learning in the least restrictive envvironment* (pp. 245-260). Baltimore: Paul H. Brookes.

Christenson, S., Ysseldyke, J., & Thurlow, M. (1989). Critical instructional factors for students with mild handicaps: An integrative review. *Remedial and Special Education, 10*(5), 21–31.

Clark, G. M. (1984). Issues in teacher education for secondary special education: Time for hindsight and foresight. *Teacher Education and Special Education, 7,* 170–177.

Clark, G. M. (1990). *Career development and transition education for adolescents with disabilities.* Boston, MA: Allyn and Bacon.

Clark, G. M., & Kolstoe, O. P. (1990). *Career development and transition education for adolescents with disabilities.* Boston, MA: Allyn and Bacon.

Cobb, R. B., Hasazi, S. B., Collins, C. M., & Salembier, G. (1988). Preparing school-based employment specialists. *Teacher Education and Special Education, 11*(2), 64–71.

The Council for Exceptional Children (1990). Americans with disabilities act of 1990: What should you know? *Exceptional Children, 57,* precis.

Deshler, D. (1988). *Self-advocacy curriculum.* Unpublished manuscript, Lawrence, KS: University of Kansas.

Deshler, D. D., & Schumaker, J. B. (1986). Learning strategies: An instrumental alternative for low-achieving adolescents. *Exceptional Children, 54*(6), 583–590.

Eddy, J., Mack, K., & Ringe, J. (1989). Vocational outreach services: A joint vocational education/special education program. In G. F. Elrod (Ed.). *Career education for special needs individuals: Learning, earning, and contributing.* Columbia, SC: Dance Graphics.

Edgar, E. (1987). Secondary programs in special education: Are many of them justifiable? *Exceptional Children, 53*(7), 555–561.

Farr, J. M., Faither, R., & Pickrell, R. M. (1983). *The work book: Getting the job you really want.* Bloomington, IL: McKnight Publishing Co.

Forest, M., & Lusthaus, E. (1990). Promoting educational equality for all students: Circles and maps. In S. Stainback, W. Stainback, and M. Forest (Eds.). *Educating all students in the mainstream of regular education.* (pp. 43–57). Baltimore, MD: Paul H. Brookes Publishing Co.

Foster, M., Berger, M., & McLean, M. (1981). Rethinking a good idea: a reassessment of parent involvement. *Topics in Early Childhood Education.* 143–163.

Giangreco, M., Cloniger, C., Mueller, P., Yuan, S., & Ashworth, S. (1990). *A guest to be heard: Perspectives of parents whose children are dual sensory impaired.* Unpublished manuscript).

Goldstein, A. (1980). *Skillstreaming and the adolescent: A structured learning approach to teaching prosocial skills.* Champaign, IL: Research Press.

Gould, M., & McTaggart, N. (1989). Self-advocacy for transition: Indications of student leadership potential today. *American Rehabilitation* Winter, 1988–1989, 6–28.

Halpern, A. (1985). Transition: A look at the foundations. *Exceptional Children, 51*, 479–486.

Halpern, A. S., & Benz, M. R. (1987). A statewide examination of secondary special education for students with mild disabilities: Implications for the high school curriculum. *Exceptional Children, 54*, 122–129.

Hamre-Nietupski, S., Krajewski, L., Nietupski, J., Osterkamp, D., Sensor, K., & Opheim, B. (1988). Parent/professional partnerships in advocacy: Developing integrative options within resistive systems. *Journal of the Association for Persons with Severe Handicaps, 13*(4), 251–259.

Hasazi, S. B., & Clark, G. M. (1988). Vocational preparation for high school students labeled mentally retarded: Employment as a graduation goal. *Mental Retardation, 26*(6), 343–349.

Hasazi, S. B., Gordon, L. R., & Roe, C. A. (1985a). Factors associated with the employment status of handicapped youth exiting high school from 1979 to 1983. *Exceptional Children, 51*(6), 455–496.

Hasazi, S. B., Gordon, L. R., Roe, C. A., Hull, M., Finck, K., & Salembier, G. (1985b). A statewide follow-up on post high school employment and residential status of students labeled "mentally retarded." *Education and Training of the Mentally Retarded, 20*(6), 222–234.

Jenkins, J., & Jenkins, L. (1985). Peer tutoring in elementary and secondary programs. *Focus on Exceptional Children 17*(6), 1–2.

Johnson, D., Bruininks, R., & Thurlow, M. (1987). Meeting the challenge of transition service planning through improved interagency cooperation. *Exceptional Children, 53*(6), 522–530.

Johnson, D., & Johnson, R. (1987). *Learning together and alone: Cooperation, competition, and individualization,* (2nd ed.). Englewood Cliffs, NJ: Prentice-Hall.

Kelley-Laine, K. (1988). *Disabled youth: The right to adult status,* (Report No. 92-64-13132-9) Washington, DC: Office of Special Education and Rehabilitative Services.

Kimeldorf, M. (1985). *Job search education program guide and workbook.* New York, NY: Educational Design.

Maddox, M., & Edgar, E. (1985). Maneuvering through the maze: Transition planning for human service agency clients. In J. Chadsey-Rusch (Eds.), *Enhancing transition from school to the workplace for handicapped youth,* pp. 58–69. Urbana-Champaign: National Network for Professional Development in Vocational Special Education, University of Illinois, Urbana-Champaign.

Maher, C. (1984). Handicapped adolescents as cross-age tutors: Program description and evaluation. *Exceptional Children 51*(1), 56–63.

McDonnell, J., & Hardman, M. (1985). Planning the transition of severely handicapped youth from school to adult services: A framework for high school programs. *Education and Training of the Mentally Retarded, 20*, 275–284.

Mithaug, D. E., Horiuchi, C. N., & Fanning, P. N. (1985). A report on the Colorado statewide follow-up survey of special education students. *Exceptional Children, 51,* 397–404.

O'Brien, J. (1987). A guide to personal futures planning. In G. T. Bellamy and B. Wilcox (eds.). *The activities catalog: A community programming guide for youth and adults with severe disabilities.* Baltimore, MD: Paul H. Brookes Publishing Company.

O'Brien, J., Forest, M., Snow, J., & Hasbury, D. (1989). *Action for inclusion.* Toronto, Ontario: Frontier College Press.

Perske, R., & Perske, M. (1988). *Circles of friends: People with disabilities and their friends enrich the lives of one another.* Nashville, TN: Parthenon Press.

Rusch, F. R., & Phelps, L. A., (1987). Secondary education and transition from school to work: A national priority. *Exceptional Children, 53,* 487–492.

Rusch, F. R., Weithers, J. A., Menchen, B. & Schutz, R. P., (1980). Social validation of a program to reduce topic repetition in a non-sheltered setting. *Education and Training in Mental Retardation, 15* (3), 187-194.

Slavin, R. (1984). Review of cooperative learning research. *Review of Educational Research, 50,* 315–342.

Slavin, R. (1987). Ability grouping and student achievement in elementary school: A best evidence synthesis. *Review of Educational Research, 57,* 293–336.

Stodden, R., & Boone, R. (1987). Assessing transition services for handicapped youth: A cooperative interagency approach. *Exceptional Children, 53*(6), 537–545.

U. S. Department of Education (1988). Tenth annual report to Congress on the Implementation of the Education of the Handicapped Act. Washington, D. C.: U. S. Department of Education.

Villa, R. and Thousand, J. (1990, April). *The power of student collaboration or practicing for life in the 21st century.* Paper presented at the 68th Annual Council for Exceptional Children International Convention, Toronto, Canada.

Wagner, M. (1989). *The transition experience of youths with disabilities: A report from the national longitudinal transition study.* Menlo Park, CA: SRI International.

Walker, H. M., McConnell, S., Holmes, D., Todis, B., Walker, J. & Golden, U. (1983). *The Walker social skills curriculum: The ACCEPTS program.* Austin, TX: PRO. ED.

Ward, H. (1988). The many facets of self-determination. *Transition Summary, 5,* 2–3.

Wehman, P., Kregel, and Seyfarth, J. (1985). Transition from school to work for individuals with severe handicaps: A follow-up study. *Journal of the Association for Persons with Severe Disabilities, 10*(3), 132–139.

Wheeler (1987): *Transitioning persons with moderate and severe disabilities from school to adulthood: what makes it work.* Monominie, WI; University of Wisconsin: Materials Development Center.

Wilcox, B. (1987, September). High school programs for students with disabilities. *The Exceptional Parent,* September, 31–41.

Will, M. (1984, March–April). *Bridges from school to work: Programs for the handicapped.* Washington, DC: Clearinghouse on the Handicapped.

GLOSSARY

AB Design The simplest single-subject design for modifying a behavior with two phases—baseline (A) and intervention (B).

ABAB Design "Involves four steps: (A) collect baseline data, (B) institute the intervention, (C) withdraw the intervention, and (D) reinstate the intervention. It provides research control and serves to validate the interventions.

Accountable Physical evidence of performance

Active participation A presentation skill in which students say, do, or write something several times during each minute of the lesson.

Activity structure The activity structure of collaborative consultation focuses specifically on what is done and by whom, and includes identifying all consultation participants and their specific roles in the process.

ADA Americans with Disabilities Act. An Act passed by Congress in 1990, providing civil rights protections to individual with disabilities in private sector employment, public services, public accommodations, transportation, and telecommunications.

Add-on programs Additional services out of the regular school program are provided.

Addends Numbers that are being added together in an addition problem.

Advance organizer Instructional routine designed to gain students' attention, review prior learning, identify goals, define topics, personalize learning, and identify expectations.

Aim lines Describe the progress required to reach a predetermined criterion.

Algorithms A set of rules or procedures that one can repeat to arrive at an answer. For example, the method referred to as *long division* is an algorithm for solving division problems.

Allocated time Time scheduled in the classroom for instruction.

Antecedents Environmental stimuli or conditions that occur just prior to behavior.

At risk When a student shares with others certain characteristics for which there is a known probability of academic difficulties and/or failure.

Author's chair An occasion for student authors to share what they have written. The author usually sits in a chair, reads his or her story, and then invites the audience to ask questions on or comments about the story.

Automaticity Automatic recall or execution of basic facts.

Basal programs Student's and teacher's materials for sequentially planned instruction in Grades Kindergarten–6.

Base ten blocks Rectangular solids, often made of wood or plastic, in four sizes: 1 cubic centimeter, often referred to as a *unit* or a *one*; often referred to as *long* or a *ten*; $10 \times 10 \times 1$ centimeters, often refer.

Baseline data Three to five observations for academics and five to seven observations for social behaviors.

Basic facts For addition, the one hundred problems using the number 0–9 as addends. For subtraction, the one hundred problems using the number 0–9 as the subtrahend and the difference. For multiplication, the one hundred problems using the number 0–9.

Behavioral consultation One of three most common theoretical approaches to consultation, that focuses on assisting the consultee in introducing specific changes in the students environment to modify the targeted observable and/or measurable problem(s) in a predictable direction.

Body The second component of the lesson design model during which active teaching of the skill occurs through the model, prompt, check model.

Brainstorming A strategy for preparing students to write by retrieving related information about a topic from their background knowledge. Students brainstorm ideas by thinking about personal experiences or prior knowledge of a given topic.

Brophy-Good Teacher-Child Dyadic Interaction System Assessment tool used to assess the quantity and quality of teacher student interactions.

CAPS strategy A story structure and self-questioning strategies designed for students with learning disabilities to increase passage comprehension of narrative materials.

Category systems   One of three dimensions of data collection that is appropriate for large response classes with multiple forms or behaviors.

CBVA   Curriculum based vocational assessment. An assessment system that directly measures a student's performance in a vocational program. Results of the assessment may be used to set goals for daily instruction is a vocational program, as well as long-range transition planning.

Central tendency lines   Horizontal lines drawn through the mean data point for each phase or condition.

Checks   Allowing the student to perform the skill without assistance prior to independent practice.

Close   The final component for the lesson design model during which the skills learned are reviewed, linked to future lessons, and independent work is assigned.

Cognitive Strategy Instruction in Writing (CSIW)   An instructional program that provides direct instruction in metacognitive processes related to planning, organizing, drafting, editing, and revising expository texts.

Cognitively guided approach   Instruction that emphasizes problem solving.

Collaborative consultation model   Resource teachers serve as consultants to regular class teachers.

Collaborative consultation   An interactive process that enables teams of people with diverse expertise to generate creative solutions to mutually defined problems. The outcome is enhanced and altered from the original solutions that any team member would produce independently.

Concept analysis table   A feature analysis technique that utilizes a table to display the relationship between various examples of a concept by identifying characteristics possessed by each example.

Concept diagram   An instructional device in the form of a single-page diagram containing graphic symbols associated with specific meaning designed to promote the understanding of concepts and generalization of knowledge by using interactive decision making between the teacher and the students.

Concept webs   An instructional technique that involves mapping categories information into free-form or structured graphic webs.

Consequences   Events or stimuli that occur just after a behavior.

Constructivist   Implies that learners construct knowledge through self-regulated transformation of old knowledge to new knowledge.

Consultant and consultee problem identification and remediation   One of three consultant relationships in which both the consultee and consultant have joint-ownership of the problem. They are both actively involved in problem identification and in consensus decision making.

Consultant identification of the problem and the consultee teacher's remediation of the problem   One of three consultant relationships in which an experienced teacher (consultee) is having difficulty identifying the problem. The consultant identifies the problem so that the consultee can implement the appropriate intervention procedure.

Consultant   In the triadic model of consultation, the consulting teacher who directly interacts with the mediator.

Consultee problem identification–consultant remediation   One of three consultant relationships in which a teacher (consultee) identifies a problem and requests assistance from a consultant. This relationship does not focus on developing the competencies the consultee needs in order to manage similar problems in the future without assistance from a consultant.

Content enhancement device   An instructional procedure or tactic designed to achieve a singular goal associated with facilitating understanding, remembering, or organizing information. It usually covers a small segment of a lesson and is embedded in a teaching routine.

Content enhancement routine   An instructional procedure designed for content-area instruction that provides a framework for teaching important, but difficult, information through the use of content enhancement devices and student activation.

Content enhancement   Teacher-mediated educational approaches that focus students' attention on critical elements of the information to be learned. May include individual and peer-assisted approaches for orienting students to the material to be learned, manipulating this information, and completing assignments.

Content validity   The extent to which the sample of items included on a test are representative of the entire domain or universe.

Contextual analysis Using surrounding information to decode words.

Contingency contract A formal, written agreement that specifies the relationship of the behaviors of the participating parties. They should be individually negotiated between the student and all involved parties.

Continuous reinforcement When a student receives reinforcement every time she emits a target behavior.

Cooperative Group Learning Models Structured group learning situations in which groups of students of various abilities work together to solve problems and complete tasks.

Cooperative teaching Teaching interventions that occur cooperatively across settings in both the support class setting and the content learning setting.

COPS strategy An error-monitoring strategy designed for students with learning disabilities for proofreading written work.

Criterion-referenced techniques Measurement approaches used to determine whether or not given behaviors are meeting a specific level (criterion).

Criterion-referenced Measurement of specific skills to determine what a person can and cannot do.

Critical level The level of reading comprehension in which readers make judgments and evaluations.

Cuisenaire rods Rectangular solids (rods), often made of wood or plastic, in ten sizes: 1 cubic centimeter, $2 \times 1 \times 1$ centimeters, $3 \times 1 \times 1$ centimeters, $4 \times 1 \times 1$ centimeters, $5 \times 1 \times 1$ centimeters, $6 \times 1 \times 1$ centimeters, $7 \times 1 \times 1$ centimeters, $8 \times 1 \times 1$ centimeters, $9 \times 1 \times 1$ centimeters, and $10 \times 1 \times 1$ centimeters. Each size is a different color; for example, the 1-cubic centimeter rod is white, the $4 \times 1 \times 1$-ccm rod is red, and so forth.

Curriculum-based assessment (CBA) Obtaining direct and frequent measures of a student's performance on a series of sequentially arranged objectives derived from the curriculum used in the classroom.

Data collection Documents the process of a consultative activity.

Declarative knowledge Factual knowledge about numbers and their relations.

Denominator "Bottom part" of a fraction, refers to the number of equal parts into which a whole has been divided.

Diagraming techniques Instructional devices such as the concept diagram designed to promote teaching and learning specific content learning demands.

Dienes' blocks See base ten blocks.

Discovery-oriented approach Instructions that involve inductive learning or teacher-led discourse and argument.

Dividend The number that is being divided into in a division problem for example, in the problem $12/4 = 3$, the dividend is 12.

Divisor The number that is being divided into the dividend in a division problem. For example, in the problem $12/4 = 3$, the divisor is 4.

Drafting The act of transforming brainstormed ideas or tentative plans into written texts.

Drill-and-practice programs Computer software designed to provide follow-up to teacher-direct instruction for high rates of accuracy and fluency.

Duration data Depicting behaviors where the length of the occurrence is important based time.

Editing The third stage of the writing process in which the writer edits, revises, and prepares the text for an audience.

EHA The Education of the Handicapped Act. This Federal legislation, originally passed in 1975, guaranteed that individuals with disabilities would receive a free and appropriate public education. The EHA has been amended several times, including a 1990 amendment which required transition planning to be included in the IEPs of students of 16 years of age and older. At this time the EHAs name was changed to the Individuals with Disabilities Act, or IDEA.

Engaged time Time in which students are actually engaged in the instructional lesson.

Equivalent fractions Fractions that represent the same amount of a whole. For example, 1/2 and 4/8 simplest.

Error drill Providing repeated practice until a student is making the learned response firmly and efficiently.

Estimation Finding an approximation either for a measurement (e.g., About how tall is that man?) or for a computation (e.g., Is 1,002 a reasonable solution to 24 + 78).

Event recording Simple frequency counts or as percentages or rates of occurrence of target behavior.

Expository material Material from a content-area class such as social studies, science, or health.

Externally mediated intervention Elements affecting learning that are under teacher's control such as curriculum materials, texts, graphics, media, and teacher's instruction.

Extinction Refers to the behavioral procedure of withholding reinforcement from a response that previously was reinforced.

Factors Numbers that are being multiplied in a multiplication problem.

Feature analysis techniques Instructional techniques such as semantic feature analysis or concept webs that utilize a table to display the relationship among examples of a concept.

Fixed interval schedule Reinforce the response the first time it occurs after a preset period of time (e.g., 10 minutes).

Fixed rate schedule Reinforce every so many occurrences of the behavior.

Flanders Interaction Analysis Categories Is an assessment tool which can be used to assess the quantity and quality of teacher-student interactions.

Fluency-building drill Providing repeated practice until a student is making the learned response firmly and efficiently.

Formative evaluation Data collected on an ongoing basis to guide activities (e.g., directly observing a student's behavior)

Frequency data The easy data to collect by tallying the occurrence or nonoccurrence of a target behavior.

Generalizable Usable with a larger set of skills or information rather than a specific skill or information.

Generalization Using learned skills in other settings, with new materials, or in novel situations.

Grandma's law Refers to Premack Principle or the statement, "First you can eat your vegetables and then you may have your dessert."

Guided practice Practice that is provided under the direct guidance of the teachers, typically during the *body* of the lesson.

Heterogeneous classrooms Classrooms containing a variety of students with varying needs, abilities, levels of performance, and disabilities.

IDEA PL 94-142 as amended by the Individuals with Disabilities Act. Strong emphasis on preparing students for transition into adulthood and meeting needs of special education students from diverse ethnolinguistic backgrounds.

IDEA Individuals with Disabilities Education Act. In 1990, the EHA was amended to include a provision for transition planning for students with disabilities who are 16 years of age or older. The EHA was re-named as the Individuals with Disabilities Education Act, or IDEA.

IEP Individualized Education Program. A written plan developed by a team that specifies the goals, objectives, activities, timelines, supports, responsible persons, and evaluation criteria to be used in the education of a student with disabilities. As of 1990, the IEP must include goals and objectives outlining a plan for the student's transition from school to adult life.

In-class programs Teacher or instructional aide works directly with student in regularly assigned setting.

Individually referenced strategies Probably the most commonly used qualitative evaluation technique used in consultative activities. They focus on measuring a relative change in the targeted problem area(s) over time, and in comparing past and present levels of performance.

Inert knowledge Knowledge that is possessed by students about a particular topic but which is not activated during writing or reading with a resultant loss in comprehension or communication.

Inferential comprehension The reading comprehension level in which readers go beyond what is explicitly stated in the text to determine implied meanings.

Intermittent reinforcement When reinforcement occurs for only some, but not all, instances of the target behavior.

Internally mediated intervention Techniques or strategies affecting learning that the learner produces at her convenience to meet particular learning needs.

Interval data Data collected at or during set periods of time.

Irregular words Words containing one or more letters not representing its most common sound.

ITP Individual Transition Plan. A written plan included as part of a student's IEP which outlines the goals, objectives, activities, timelines, supports needed to move successfully into adult life.

Learning strategies Task-specific techniques that students can use in responding to classroom tasks.

Lesson organizer Instructional routine designed to cue the structural organization of information, the critical features and concepts, the expectations, and the adjustments in the activities or goals.

Level of accuracy A student's percentage of correct responding.

Line of progress Line drawn on a behavior chart to depict actual progress of student.

Literal comprehension The simplest level of reading comprehension in which readers recognize and understand material explicitly stated in the text.

Mapping techniques Instructional techniques that involve structuring categories of information into a free-form graphic web such as semantic maps of concept webs.

Mediator In the triadic model of consultation, the teacher or other service delivery person who interacts indirectly with the targeted person, and must be the one who sees the need and requests "expert" advice about a particular situation(s).

Mental calculation The process of calculating mentally the exact answer in a computation situation.

Mental health consultation One of three most common theoretical approaches to consultation generally directed toward changing the feelings of clients so that the targeted problems are eliminated or changed in a desired direction.

Metacognition One's awareness, monitoring, and regulating of one's cognitive processes.

Metacognitive strategies Techniques for appraising, managing, and regulating one's performance.

Mnemonics A strategy to aid in memorizing a learning strategy through association with a word or list of letters.

Modeling Providing a visual demonstration of the skill being taught as well as a verbal description of the steps displayed.

Models A person who is an expert in that behavior demonstrating it.

Momentary time sampling Recording behaviors at the beginning or end of a specified interval time.

Movement cycle When the behavior begins and when it ends.

Multiple coding systems One of three dimensions of data collection designed to collect data from settings where some elements of both category and sign systems data may be prevalent. This setting would include large response classes that have specific discrete characteristics. Such consultation situations would include ones in which both the quality or type of instruction provided and the

consequent student responding are both of interest.

Negative reinforcers Consequences that increase the probability of a behavior occurring in the future.

Negative Ripple Effect When a teacher responds to a students behavior in a harsh or angry manner, it may tend to make several students anxious and more disruptive and frequently undermining any positive control that the teacher may have had.

Nonseclusionary time-out procedure Removing the reinforcing consequences for the student.

Norm-referenced techniques These techniques are useful when a valid normative comparison group is available to compare to the targeted student's performance.

On-task Students are engaged with instructional lesson.

One-to-one correspondence Establishing a one-for-one relationship between objects. For example, matching a straw with each glass or a pencil for each child.

Opening The first component of the lesson design model during which attention is gained, prior lessons are reviewed, and the current lesson is previewed.

Operant behaviors Behaviors that are learned or acquired as a function of their consequences.

Operant Behaviors that are controlled by their consequences.

Organizational comprehension The reading comprehension level requiring readers to organize content according to order of importance and text structure.

Organizational developmental consultation One of three most common theoretical approaches to consultation that targets improved client functioning within a complex social system. The emphasis is on assisting targeted persons to better understand the complex social system they live in and thereby become more effective at functioning within that system.

Organizing Devices Instructional techniques designed to prepare students for instructions by directing their attention to what they already have learned and its relationship to what is to be learned.

Partial interval time samples Samples the behavior occurring at some time during the time interval.

Peer conferencing An occasion when an author shares his or her stories with a peer to invite comments or questions that might assist him or her in revising the story.

Peer Power Strategies used by classroom teachers to maximize student learning and increase interactions between students with and without disabilities. These may include peer tutoring, cooperative group learning, and informal peers partnerships.

Peer tutoring An instructional approach which pairs students experiencing difficulties in the classroom with trained peers for one-on-one instruction.

Peer-assisted instruction Lessons in which students work together with a single partner or in a small group.

Percentage data When time periods vary or when opportunities to respond vary.

Permanent products The tangible proctus of task engagement, such as test papers or written projects.

Phonetic spelling The third stage of spelling development in which words are spelled exactly as they sound.

Phonics Pertaining to the relationship between letters and sounds.

PL 94-142 Mandated free, appropriate education for all children with handicapping conditions. Also emphasized nonbiased and broad-based assessment and team planning, parental participation, and placement in the least-restrictive environment.

Planned ignoring Teacher ignores the student for a brief time contingent upon the student emitting a specific target behavior.

PLANS strategy An instructional technique that involves students in setting product goals for what a paper will accomplish and articulating process goals for achieving these goals. The mnemonic PLANS represents four planning sequences: Pick goals, List ways to meet goals, And make Notes, and Sequence the notes.

Polygon A closed *n*-sided plan figure with line segments as sides.

Positive Ripple Effect When a teacher responds to students behavior in a calm, matter-of-fact manner, in addition to altering the behavior of the targeted student, it results in behavioral improvements among the other students in the classroom.

Post organizer Instructional routine designed to inform students of the close of the lesson, to review the content, evaluate learning, promote generalization, give feedback, and inform students about the next lesson.

POWER strategy A writing strategy for expository materials that utilizes specially designed think sheets to guide students in completing the steps of the writing process.

Preliterate spelling The earliest stage of spelling development in which letters and symbols are randomly ordered without regard to letter-sound relationships.

Premack Principle This principle states that when a low probability behavior is followed by a high probability behavior, the likelihood of the low probability behavior occurring again in the future is increased.

Prerequisite skills Component skills essential to the performance of a new task.

Preview Stating the goal of the lesson, providing a rationale for skill to be taught, linking the current lesson to prior learning, and overviewing lesson structure.

Prewriting The processes that students engage in prior to writing their first draft, including, considering their audience and writing purpose, brainstorming, and organizing their ideas.

Primary prevention Refers procedures or processes that are made available to the general student population that will either reduce the rate of occurrence of a particular problem or make its occurrence less likely to happen among students who currently are believed to be at risk but who do not, as yet, manifest the problem.

Problem corroboration The second of five stages of consultation that involves collecting data in a systematic manner to validate the problem identified earlier.

Problem identification stage The first of five stages of consultation, that entails using collaborative efforts between the consultant and the consultee to identify and prioritize the student's problem(s), as well as to establish methodology to confirm the problem(s) and to establish methodology to confirm that the problem(s) exist and its parameters.

Procedural knowledge Knowledge about performing solution algorithms.

Program development The third of five stages of consultation that entails the highest levels of direct contact between consultant and consultee, and is a prerequisite to actually implementing any intervention, or plan or action.

Program evaluation The final of five stages of consultation, typically characterized by the collection and analysis of data upon which to judge the success of the intervention effort.

Program operationalization Encompasses actually implementing the intervention(s) designed to change the targeted problem in a predictable direction. Depending on the problem-solving relationship, this stage will involve varying levels of collaborative efforts.

Prompts Assistance provided before a target response for the purpose of increasing the likelihood of the correct behavior occurring.

Publication The process of publishing a student's written text in a form that can be shared and disseminated with other students in the writing community.

Pull-out programs Student removed from regular classroom to receive special instruction.

Quotient The answer to a division problem. For example, in the problem 12/4 = 3, the quotient is 3.

RAP strategy A verbal rehearsal strategy designed for elementary and middle school students with learning disabilities to increase passage comprehension of expository materials.

Rate data Describes the performance of a behavior in relation to a given time frame. The number of behaviors divided by the amount of time. Rate. Fluency.

RCRC strategy A test preparation strategy for expository content that utilizes verbal rehearsal.

Regrouping Exchanging (or trading) equivalent amounts. For example, ten ones can be regrouped into one ten.

Regular words Those in which each letter represents its most common sound.

Reinforcers Consequences that strengthen the responses.

Reliability Consistency of a measure; agreement from one observation to another.

Remedial approach Instructional approach designed to help students develop the basic skills they failed to learn in previous educational experiences.

Remembering Devices Instructional techniques designed to assist students in remembering information, and to compensate for ineffective and inefficient memorization strategies. Techniques may include creating mental images, making familiar associations, and using acronyms or key word strategies.

Renaming Changing the way a number is symbolized. For example, 17 can be renamed as 10 + 7.

Respondent behaviors Behaviors that are more or less automatic and are considered part of the physiology of the individual.

Respondent Involuntary or reflexive responses.

Response cost Removal or withdrawal of reinforcers contingent on a behavior.

Review: Summary of the critical information presented in the lesson.

Rote counting Repeating a sequence of number words (such as "one, two three, four, . . . ") without making a one-to-one correspondence between the number words and the objects being counted.

Salient Critical for future study in a content area, for functioning in the school environment, or for functioning in adult life.

Schoolwide programs At least 75% of students in school qualify for Chapter 1 services.

SCORER A test-taking strategy for all tests that encourages students to answer easier items, look for clue words in test items, and review all answers.

Seclusion Physically isolating a student with an effective time-out procedure.

Secondary prevention Refers to a targeted select student population that is known to exhibit risk factors whose outcomes are not desirable.

Self-management A generalization strategy that encourages the student to monitor, evaluate, and record his own daily performance of a specified skill.

Semantic feature analysis A feature analysis technique that utilizes a table to display relationships.

Semantic map An instructional technique that involves mapping categories of information into a free-form graphic web.

Semiphonetic spelling The second stage of spelling development in which letters are used to correctly represent some sounds heard in the word.

Shaping Develops a new behavior through differentially reinforcing successive approximations of that behavior.

Sight words Words that the reader automatically recognizes.

Sign strategies One of three dimensions of data collection, used to collect specific or discrete events or behaviors that lend themselves well to time-sampling procedures.

Simultaneous prompting   Guided practice during which the student and teacher both perform the skill and observe each other.

Split-middle trend line   A quarter-intersection line connecting the two points of intersection.

Standard deviation   A measure of central tendency for a group of scores providing an indication of how far from the mean score, or midpoint, a particular score falls.

Stimulus control   When the desired response occurs predictably in the presence of a given stimulus but not in the presence of other stimuli.

Story structure   A text structure that underlies the construction of narrative stories, consisting of setting, initiative event or problem, internal response, overt attempts to solve the problem, outcome of attempts, and story conclusion.

Strategies Intervention Model (SIM)   A research-based program developed specifically to address the needs of secondary-age students in learning situations.

Structural analysis   Applying rules for forming words by adding prefixes, suffixes, or other meaningful word units to a base word.

Student contract   When students experience ongoing behavioral difficulty, the teacher might want to consider individual contracts. A contract is a clearly stated agreement written specify the exact behavior the student will emit as well as the contingencies associated with that behavior.

Study skills   Procedures that can be used across subject areas such as instruction in taking notes, studying for a test, and making outlines.

Summative evaluation   Periodic evaluations of status of the individual relative to the variables measured, (e.g., mathematics skills mastered and general grade level achievement).

Systematic evaluation   Daily or semiweekly tests to measure student's progress.

Systematic review   Consistent review of previously taught skills and concepts to promote retaining these skills and concepts.

Targeted person   In the triadic model of consultation, the student or person with whom the mediator interacts directly.

Teacher conferencing   Teacher meets with a student author on a one-on-one basis to support their writing development. Conferences can focus on various issues related to writing, including the writing processes the author uses, the content of the written stories, writing skills needed by the author, or editorial changes that can improve a particular story.

Teacher-directed instruction   Lessons in which the teacher actively teaches the skill to be learned.

Tertiary prevention   Programs that attempt to deal with students' problems after they have been found to exist. They attempt to both prevent a problem from becoming worse, and also to positively impact on the immediate aspects of the problem as they relate to school.

The Instructional Environment Scale (TIES)   Non-normed instrumentation that uses a qualitative approach to data collection. This scale consists of three components: (1) a classroom observation, (2) a structured student interview, and (3) a structured teacher interview.

The Instructional Environment Scale (TIES)   Is a vehicle for systematically describing qualitative aspects of the learning environment, which includes three components: classroom observation, structured student interview, and structured teacher interview.

Time out   A procedure where, contingent upon a target behavior, there is less reinforcement available to a student.

Title I programs   Attempted to compensate for presumed environmental deficits associated with poverty and help educationally deprived students catch up with their peers.

Token economies   A contingency management systems wherein students can earn tokens for specific appropriate behaviors and can they exchange these tokens at a later time for backup reinforcers.

Topography   The form and content of a response; the observable features of a response.

Tracking   Assigning students to different ability groups or curricular tracks.

Transition   Amount of time between lessons.

Transition   A series of purposeful activities designed to ensure that students have the skills, opportunities, and supports needed to locate and maintain employment, pursue postsecondary education and training, live as independently as possible, participate in their communities, and make decisions about their lives.

Transitional spelling   The stage of spelling development immediately preceding standard spelling in which vowels are used in every syllable and some spelling rules are used.

TREE strategy A writing strategy for students with learning disabilities for producing expository materials

TRIMS An instructional routine designed for use in analyzing a textbook or chapter for useful organizers or cues by focusing on the title, relationships, introduction, main parts, and summary.

Tutorial approach Instructional approach designed to assist students to learn new skills and/or knowledge.

Tutorial programs Structured programs, including print and software programs, designed to introduce a new skill and/or provide guided practice.

Understanding Devices Instructional techniques designed to facilitate integrating new information with prior knowledge and storing this information in long-term memory.

Validity The extent to which data measures what it is intended to measure.

Variable interval schedule Reinforce behavior after a predetermined variable passage of time.

Variable rate schedule Reinforce at a predetermined average rate, such as an average of every six times the response is emitted (FR6).

Wait time Amount of time between teacher's question and student's response.

Whole interval time samples Requires that the behavior take place for the entire duration of the time-sample interval.

Word attack Applying phonic, structural, and/or contextual analysis to decode unknown words.

Word recognition Acquiring sight word vocabulary along with word attack skills necessary for decoding unknown words.

Writing mechanics The skills or conventions that underlie effective writing, such as punctuation, grammar, capitalization, and spelling.

Writing productivity The number or quantity of words in students' papers. Productivity can be measured in terms of the number of words that students write per story or per unit of time (e.g., per minute).

AUTHOR INDEX

SUBJECT INDEX

Medical Terminology

made Incredibly Easy!®

Fourth Edition

Clinical Editor
David W. Woodruff, PhD, APRN, CNE, FNAP
Faculty Development Specialist
Chamberlain University
Downers Grove, Illinois

Wolters Kluwer

Philadelphia · Baltimore · New York · London
Buenos Aires · Hong Kong · Sydney · Tokyo

Executive Editor: Nicole Dernoski
Development Editor: Maria M. McAvey
Editorial Coordinator: David Murphy, Jr.
Production Project Manager: Bridgett Dougherty
Design Coordinator: Elaine Kasmer
Manufacturing Coordinator: Kathleen Brown
Marketing Manager: Linda Wetmore
Prepress Vendor: SPi Global

4th edition

Library of Congress Cataloging-in-Publication Data
Names: Woodruff, David W., editor.
Title: Medical terminology made incredibly easy! / clinical editor, David Woodruff.
Description: 4th edition. | Philadelphia : Wolters Kluwer, [2018] | Includes bibliographical references and index.
Identifiers: LCCN 2017033413 | ISBN 9781496374073
Subjects: | MESH: Terminology as Topic
Classification: LCC R123 | NLM W 15 | DDC 610.1/4—dc23 LC record available at https://lccn.loc.gov/2017033413

Contributors

Cathleen Crowley-Koschnitzki, DNP, FNP-C, WHNP-BC, CNM, CNE
Associate Professor
Chamberlain University
Downers Grove, Illinois

Robin S. Goodrich, EdD, RN
Campus President
Chamberlain College of Nursing
North Brunswick, New Jersey

Lisa Johnson, PhD, RN, CPN
Curriculum Coordinator/Assistant
    Professor
Community College of Philadelphia
Philadelphia, Pennsylvania

Kathryn L. Kay, DNP, RN, PCCN-CMC
Associate Dean of Faculty
Chamberlain College of Nursing
Downers Grove, Illinois

Susan M. McClendon, MSN, CNS
Assistant Professor
Lakeland Community College
Kirtland, Ohio

Diana J. Meeks, PhD, MSN, CS, FNP, CNE, NE-BC
Professor
Chamberlain University
Marietta, Georgia

Elizabeth M. Moots, MSN, RN
Director of the LPN to RN Diploma
    Program
Sandusky Career Center
Sandusky, Ohio

Jennifer Mundine, EdD, MSN, RN, CNE
Assistant Professor
West Coast University
Dallas, Texas

Nancy H. Scroggs, PhD, RN, CNE
Associate Professor
Chamberlain College of Nursing
Moravian Falls, North Carolina

Adele A. Webb, PhD, RN, FNAP, FAAN
Campus President
Chamberlain College of Nursing
Cleveland, Ohio

David Zaworski, MSN, RN
Assistant Professor
Chamberlain College of Nursing
Cleveland, Ohio

Previous Edition Contributors

Helen Christina Ballestas, RN, MSN, CRRN, PhD[C]

Kim Davis, MSN

Vivian C. Gamblian, RN, MSN

Donna Headrick, RN, MSN, FNP

Shelley Huffstutler-Hawkins, DSN, APRN-BC, FNP, GNP, FAANP

Julia Anne Isen, RN, BS, MSN, FNP-C

Hope Siddons Knight, RN, BSN

Megan McClintock, RN, BSN

Aaron Pack, RN, BSN

Noel C. Piano, RN, MS

Angela R. Roughley, RN

Donna Scemons, RN, MSN, FNP-C, CNS, CWOCN

Marilyn D. Sellers, APRN, BC, MSN

Connie K. Smith, RN, MS

Jennifer K. Sofie, APRN, MSN

Benita Walton-Moss, APRN, BC, DNS

Foreword

If you're like me, you're too busy caring for your patients to have the time to wade through a foreword that uses pretentious terms and umpteen dull paragraphs to get to the point. So let's cut right to the chase! Here's why this book is so terrific:

1. It will teach you all the important things you need to know about medical terminology. (And it will leave out all the fluff that wastes your time.)
2. It will help you remember what you've learned.
3. It will make you smile as it enhances your knowledge and skills.
   Don't believe me? Try these recurring logos on for size:

 Pump up your pronunciation—charts at the beginning of each chapter that help you "talk to the walk" by sounding out the most difficult terms

 Anatomically speaking—anatomic images that bring you face to face with the structures you're trying to pronounce

 Beyond the dictionary—sidebars on the origins of words, which can help you remember and dissect their meanings

 The real world—tidbits on more informal terminology that you may hear used in daily practice.

See? I told you! And that's not all. Look for me and my friends in the margins throughout this book. We'll be there to explain key concepts, provide important care reminders, and offer reassurance. Oh, and if you don't mind, we'll be spicing up the pages with a bit of humor along the way, to teach and entertain in a way that no other resource can.

 I hope you find this book helpful. Best of luck throughout your career!

Joy

Contents

Chapter 1

Key concepts of medical terminology

Just the facts

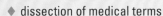

In this chapter, you'll learn:

♦ dissection of medical terms

♦ meaning determination of medical terms using roots, prefixes, and suffixes

♦ examination of tips for pronunciation

♦ exploration of common eponyms used in medicine.

Dissecting medical terms

Because many medical terms derive from Greek and Latin, learning medical terminology is like learning a new language. As you learn about the key elements that combine to form medical terms and practice interpreting them, quick understanding of their total meaning becomes easier.

Take it apart

Learning the meaning of medical terms and how to use them requires knowledge of common medical roots and the prefixes and suffixes used to modify them. Most medical terms are a combination of two or more of these parts. If you can successfully interpret each part, you can usually grasp the essential meaning of the word.

Root it out

In medical terminology, many medical roots signify a disease, procedure, or body part. A root is the essential core component of a word, holds its essential meaning, and cannot stand alone as a complete term. It requires another element, an added modifier, for it to have full meaning. The root can appear at the beginning, middle, or end of a word, depending on its overall meaning. Prefixes and suffixes are modifiers used before or after the root to further describe or define the core word. For example, the root *therm* refers to *temperature* but is not a complete word. If the prefix *hyper-*, which means *above*

Deciphering medical terminology requires deduction, my dear Watson.

1

or beyond, is added at the beginning of the root, *therm*, it becomes *hypertherm*, which further defines temperature and literally means *above temperature*. Clearly though, it needs another element to complete a word that has full meaning. Adding the suffix -ia to the end results in a complete term, *hyperthermia* whose literal meaning is *the condition of above or beyond temperature*. When used in the medical context, it means temperature above or beyond the normal temperature range. Besides using prefixes and suffixes to form a medical term, two or more roots may be combined, as in *cardi-o-pulmonary* and *cardi-o-vascular*. The letter *o* is the vowel most commonly used when combining two roots in medical terminology.

Here are some examples of roots used in different positions:

- a root at the beginning of a word—*angi*oedema (*angi* is a root that means *vessel*)
- a root in the middle of a word—en*cephal*ic (*cephal* is a root that means *head*)
- a root at the end of a word—sclero*derma* (*derm* is a root that means *skin*)
- a combination of roots—*phototherapy* (*photo* is a root that means *light; therapy* is a root that means *treatment*).

Consider the most common word roots used in medical terminology in the following table.

(Text continues on page 6.)

Common root words used in medical terminology

Roots	Meaning	Example
abdomin(o)-	abdomen	abdominopelvic (abdomen and pelvis)
acou-	hearing	acoustics (the science of sounds)
acr(o)-	extremity, peak	acrodermatitis (inflammation of skin of the extremities)
aden(o)-	gland	adenocele (cystic tumor in a gland)
adipo-	fat	adipose (fatty)
alb-	white	albumin (protein found in the blood)
andr(o)-	male	androgen (male sex hormone)
angi(o)-	vessel	angiography (X-ray of a vessel)
ankyl-	crooked, fusion	ankylosis (consolidation of a joint)
bili-	bile	biliary (pertaining to bile or the gallbladder)
blast- or -blast	embryonic state	blastocyte (embryonic cell)
blephar(o)-	eyelid	blepharitis (inflammation of the eyelid)
brachi(o)-	arm	brachial artery (artery of the upper arm)
brady-	slow	bradycardia (slow heart rhythm)

Common root words used in medical terminology (*continued*)

Roots	Meaning	Example
calc-	heel	calcaneus (heel bone)
carcin(o)-	cancer	carcinoma (malignant growth)
cardi(o)-	heart	cardiac muscle (heart muscle)
caud-	tail	caudal (toward the tail)
cephal(o)-	head	cephalalgia (pain in the head)
cerebr(o)-	cerebrum	cerebral embolism (occlusion of a cerebral vessel by a blood clot)
cervic(i)(o)-	neck	cervical plexus (network of cervical nerves)
chol(e)-	bile	cholecystitis (inflammation of the gallbladder)
chondr(o)-	cartilage	chondritis (inflammation of cartilage)
col(i)(o)-	colon	colitis (inflammation of the colon)
cost(o)-	rib	costochondral (relating to a rib and its cartilage)
cut-	skin	cutaneous (relating to skin)
cyan(o)-	blue	cyanotic (blue colored)
cyst(i)(o)-	bladder	cystitis (inflammation of the urinary bladder)
cyt(o)-	cell	cytology (study of cells)
derm- or -derm	skin	dermatitis (skin inflammation)
dors(i)(o)-	back	dorsiflexion (upward bending of hand or foot)
enter(o)-	intestine	enterocolitis (inflammation of the intestines and colon)
erythr(o)-	red	erythrocytes (red blood cells)
fasci-	bundle	fasciae (bundles of muscle fibers)
febri-	fever	febrile (feverish)
fil-	threadlike	filament (fine thread)
galact(o)-	milk	galactose (sugar obtained from milk)
gastro-	stomach	gastritis (inflammation of the stomach)
ger(o)- or geront(o)-	aging	gerontology (study of aging)
gest-	carry	gestation (pregnancy)
gloss(o)-	tongue	glossitis (inflammation of the tongue)
glyc(o)- or gluc(o)-	sweet	glycogen, glucogen (forms of sugar)
gyn(o)-	woman, particularly female reproductive organs	gynecology (study of women's reproductive organs)
heme(a)(o)- or hemato-	blood	hematology (study of blood)
hepat(o)-	liver	hepatitis (inflammation of the liver)

(*continued*)

Common root words used in medical terminology (*continued*)

Roots	Meaning	Example
hist(i)(o)-	tissue	histography (process of describing tissue and cells)
hydro-	water, hydrogen	hydrops (excess watery fluid)
hyster-	uterus	hysterectomy (surgical removal of the uterus)
ile(o)-	ileum	ileostomy (surgical opening in the ileum)
ili(o)-	ilium, flank	iliac muscle (muscle that allows thigh movement)
ischi(o)-	hip	ischiopubic (pertaining to the ischium and pubes)
jejun(o)-	jejunum	jejunectomy (excision of the jejunum)
kerat(o)-	horny tissue, cornea	keratectasia (a thin, scarred cornea)
kine(t)(o)-	movement	kinetic (pertaining to motion)
labio-	lips	labiograph (an instrument that records lip movement)
lact(o)-	milk	lactation (secretion of milk by the breasts)
laryng(o)-	larynx	laryngectomy (surgical removal of the larynx)
latero-	side	lateroflexion (flexion to one side)
leuk(o)-	white	leukocytes (white blood cells)
lip(o)-	fat	lipedema (excess fat and fluid in subcutaneous tissue)
lith(o)-	stone	lithocystotomy (surgical removal of bladder stones)
mamm(o)-	breast	mammogram (breast X-ray)
mast(o)-	breast	mastectomy (surgical removal of breast tissue)
melan(o)-	black	melancholia (depression)
meno-	menses	menostaxis (prolonged menstrual period)
ment-	mind	mental illness (psychiatric disorder)
mio-	less, smaller	miosis (excessive contraction of the pupil)
mito-	threadlike	mitochondria (rod-shaped cellular organelle)
my(o)-	muscle	myocele (hernia of muscle)
myc(o)-	fungus	mycology (study of fungi and fungal diseases)
myel(o)-	marrow, spinal cord	myelalgia (pain in the spinal cord)
myx-	mucus	myxoid (resembling mucus)
nas(o)-	nose	nasolabial (between the nose and lip)
nephr(o)-	kidney	nephritis (kidney inflammation)
ocul(o)-	eye	oculomotor (eye movement)
ophthalm(o)-	eye	ophthalmia (inflammation of the eye)
orchi(o)-	testes	orchitis (inflammation of the testes)
oro-	mouth	oronasal (mouth and nose)
oss- or oste(o)-	bone	osteomyelitis (inflammation of bone and muscle)

Common root words used in medical terminology (*continued*)

Roots	Meaning	Example
ot(o)-	ear	otitis (ear inflammation)
ox(y)-	oxygenation	oxyhemoglobin (hemoglobin combined with molecular oxygen)
path(o)-	disease	pathogen (disease-causing organism)
ped(o)-	child	pediatrics (care of children)
pharmaco-	medicine	pharmacotherapy (treatment with medication)
pharyng(o)-	pharynx	pharyngitis (sore throat)
phleb(o)-	vein	phlebitis (inflammation of a vein)
phot(o)-	light	phototherapy (treatment by exposure to light)
plasm(o)-	liquid part of blood	plasminogen (protein found in tissues and body fluids)
pleur(o)-	pleura, rib, side	pleurisy (inflammation of the pleura)
pneum(o)-	lung	pneumonia (inflammation of the lung)
pod(o)-	foot	podiatry (care of the foot)
proct(o)-	rectum	proctectomy (excision of the rectum)
prote(o)-	protein	proteinemia (excess protein in the blood)
psych(o)-	mind	psychiatry (study and treatment of mental disorders)
pulmo(n)-	lung	pulmoaortic (pertaining to the lungs and aorta)
pyel(o)-	kidney	pyelonephrosis (disease of the kidney and renal pelvis)
pyr(o)-	heat	pyrogen (an agent that causes fever)
ren(o)-	kidney	renography (X-ray of the kidney)
rhin(o)-	nose	rhinitis (inflamed mucous membranes of the nose)
rub(r)-	red	bilirubin (bile pigment)
sangui-	blood	sanguineous drainage (bloody drainage)
sarc(o)-	flesh	sarcoma (a highly malignant tumor made of connective tissue cells)
scler(o)-	hard	sclerosis (hardening of tissue)
scolio-	crooked	scoliosis (curvature of the spine)
sensi-	perception, feeling	sensory (pertaining to the senses)
sep-	decay	sepsis (infection in the bloodstream)
soma- or somat(o)-	body	somatization (psychiatric condition expressed through physical symptoms)
sten(o)-	narrow	stenosis (narrowing of a body passage)
tachy-	rapid, swift	tachycardia (rapid heart beat)
therm(o)-	heat	thermometer (instrument for measuring temperature)
thorac(o)-	chest	thoracotomy (surgical opening of the chest wall)
thromb(o)-	clot	thrombectomy (excision of a clot from a blood vessel)

(*continued*)

Common root words used in medical terminology (*continued*)

Roots	Meaning	Example
toxi(o)-	poison	toxicosis (poisoning)
trache(o)-	trachea	tracheobronchitis (inflammation of the trachea and bronchi)
ur(o)-	urinary, urine	uropoiesis (formation of urine)
vas(o)-	vessel	vasospasm (spasm of a blood vessel)
ven(i)(o)-	vein	venosclerosis (sclerosis or hardening of the veins)
vesic(o)-	bladder	vesicospinal (pertaining to the urinary bladder and spine)

In the beginning: Prefixes

A prefix consists of one or more letters attached to the beginning of a root. Prefixes are used to modify the root to make its meaning clearer or specific. Many prefixes used in forming medical terms are also used in standard English vocabulary. Sometimes, to determine the meaning of a prefix in a medical term, consider a familiar word that begins with the same prefix. For example, the prefix *anti-* has the same meaning—*against*—in both *antislavery* and *antihistamine*, literally *against slavery* and *against histamine* (the compound that produces allergic reactions).

The below table contains prefixes used frequently in forming medical terms.

A suffix is one or more letters attached to the end of a root. When a suffix begins with a consonant, a combining vowel, such as *o*, is placed before the suffix. A common use of suffixes in medical terminology includes adding a *-y* to a word to denote a procedure, such as *gastroscopy*, which means *endoscopic examination of the stomach*. Similarly, adding *-ly* to a word denotes an act or process; for example, *splenomegaly*, which means *the abnormal enlargement of the spleen*.

Prefixes and suffixes are important, but focus on the root of the word to get the meaning quickly.

If you can understand the building blocks, then you'll have the foundation for learning even the most complicated medical terminology.

Break it down; build it up

With a bit of practice, you'll quickly discover how easy it can be to interpret the parts of a medical term and then combine them to identify the term's meaning. For example, in *acrocyanosis*, the root *acr* *(extremities)* and the vowel *o* are combined with the root *cyan* (blue) and the suffix *-osis* (condition) to form a term that means *a condition characterized by blue extremities.* (For another example of how to dissect a medical term to decipher its meaning, see *Dem bones*, page 10.)

(*Text continues on page 9.*)

Common prefixes used in forming medical terminology

Prefixes	Meanings	Examples
a(n)-	absence, without	anuria (lack of urine output)
ab-	away from	abduct (move away from)
ad-	toward	adduct (move toward)
ambi-	both sides	ambidextrous (using both hands)
ante-	before, forward	anterior (front of the body)
anti-	against	antibody (immune response to an organism)
apo-	away from	apophysis (growth or protuberance)
aut(o)-	self	autoanalysis (self-analysis)
bi-	two	bigeminy (occurring in pairs)
diplo-	double	diplopia (double vision)
dys-	difficult, painful	dysuria (painful urination)
ec-	out of	ectopic (out of place)
end(o)-	inward	endoscope (a device used to examine a body cavity)
eu-	normal, health	euthyroid (normal thyroid function)
ex-	outside	exfoliation (peeling of layers)
hetero-	other, different	heterogeneous (different characteristics)
hyper-	above, beyond	hypernatremia (excess sodium)
hypo-	below	hypotension (low blood pressure)
infra-	beneath	infra-axillary (below the axilla)
intra-	within, into	intramuscular (into the muscle)
juxta-	near	juxta-articular (near a joint)
macr(o)-	large, long	macromastia (excessive breast size)
mal-	bad, abnormal	malformation (abnormally formed)
mega-	great, large	megacolon (enlarged colon)
meta-	beyond, change	metaphase (second stage of cell division)
micr(o)-	small	microbe (tiny organism)
mono-	one	monochromatic (having only one color)
morph(o)-	shape	morphology (study of the form and structure of organisms)
multi-	many	multifocal (arising from many locations)
olig(o)-	few, little	oliguria (too little urine)
par(a)-	near, beside, accessory to	paracentesis (puncture of a cavity for aspiration of fluid)
peri-	around	pericecal (around the cecum)
pico-	one-trillionth	picornavirus (extremely small RNA virus)
poly-	much, many	polydipsia (excessive thirst)

(continued)

Common prefixes used in forming medical terminology (*continued*)

Prefixes	Meanings	Examples
post-	behind, after	postoperative (after surgery)
pre-	before, in front	preanesthesia (before anesthetic is given)
pro-	favoring, supporting, substituting for, in front of	procoagulant (promotes coagulation)
pseudo-	false	pseudocyst (a cavity resembling a true cyst)
re-	back, contrary	recurrent fever (fever that returns after a remission)
retr(o)-	backward	retroauricular (behind the auricle)
semi-	half	semiflexion (position of a limb midway between extension and flexion)
sub-	under	subclinical (without symptoms)
super-	above	supercilia (the eyebrow)
supra-	above, upon	supraorbital (above the orbit)
tetra-	four	tetralogy (group of four)
trans-	across, through	transdermal (entering through the skin)

Common suffixes used in forming medical terminology

Suffixes	Meanings	Examples
-algia	pain	neuralgia (nerve pain)
-ectomy	surgical removal	splenectomy (removal of the spleen)
-itis	inflammation	colitis (inflammation of the colon)
-lys(i)(o)	breakdown	fibrinolysis (breakdown of a clot)
-oma	tumor	blastoma (cancer composed of embryonic cells)
-osis	condition	fibrosis (formation of fibrous tissue)
-phobia	abnormal fear	agoraphobia (fear of open spaces)
-plasia	growth	hypoplasia (incomplete development)
-plasty	surgical repair	angioplasty (surgical repair of blood vessels)
-plegia	paralysis	paraplegia (paralysis of lower body)
-pnea	breathing	apnea (absence of breathing)
-poiesis	production	hematopoiesis (production of blood cells)
-praxia	movement	apraxia (inability to perform purposeful movement)
-rrhea	fluid discharge	diarrhea (frequent soft or liquid bowel movements)
-scope	observe	endoscope (tool for observing the interior of body organs)

Common prefixes used in forming medical terminology (*continued*)

Suffixes	Meanings	Examples
-stomy	opening	colostomy (portion of the colon is opened and brought through the abdominal wall)
-taxis	movement	ataxia (uncoordinated movements)
-tomy	incision	thoracotomy (surgical opening of the chest wall)
-tripsy	crushing	lithotripsy (crushing stones in the bladder, kidney, gallbladder, or other organs)
-trophy	growth	hypertrophy (overgrowth)

Forming plural words

The rules for forming plurals of many medical terms are different from routine English words because of their Greek and Latin roots. Plural words in English are usually formed by adding *s* or *es* to the end of a noun. Generally, plural words derived from Greek and Latin are formed by adding or substituting vowels or syllables at the end of the word.

Examples of plurals of medical terms are:

* *maculae* (singular: *macula*)
* *adenomata* (singular: *adenoma*)
* *glomeruli* (singular: *glomerulus*)
* *pelves* (singular: *pelvis*).

Pronouncing medical terms

Medical terms can be difficult to pronounce if you've never heard them spoken. In this book, we'll show you how to pronounce words by placing them in all capital letters, with the syllable receiving the greatest stress appearing in tall capitals and the remaining syllables in smaller capitals. For example, in the word **cancer,** the stress is on the first syllable, so it would appear as follows: CAN-CER.

Here are some additional tips for pronunciation:

* only the *s* sound in *ps* is pronounced, as in *Pseudomonas*
* only the *n* sound in *pn* is pronounced, as in *pneumococcal*
* *g* and *c* assume the soft sounds of *j* and *s,* respectively, when used before *e, i,* and *y;* examples are *gene, gingivitis, cycle,* and *cytology*
* *ph* sounds like *f,* as in *phlegm*
* *x* sounds like *z,* as in *xeroderma* (pronounced ZEE-ROH-DER-MAH)
* *g* and *c* have hard sounds in front of other letters, such as *gangrene, gastritis, cornea,* and *cortex*

Memory jogger

To remember where a prefix goes and where a suffix goes, you can do two things:

1. Think of the word prefix: **Pre-** means before, so a prefix is a word or word component that's "fixed" to the word "before" the root. If the prefix comes before the root, then the suffix comes afterwards.

2. If that doesn't jazz you, just use the alphabet: *P* comes before *S* in the alphabet, so a prefix comes before a suffix—and before a root, for that matter, which starts with *R.* So now you have **PRS** (pretty riveting stuff?).

Beyond the dictionary

'Dem bones

A specialist in **osteopathology** studies bone diseases. The root **oste** is the Greek word for *bone*. A second root, **patho,** is derived from **pathos,** meaning **disease.** The suffix **-logy** is derived from the Greek root **logia,** meaning *the study of.* Put these parts together and you have the definition for **osteopathology**—*the study of bone diseases.*

At the root of disease?
A branch of medicine called **osteopathy** contends that skeletal misalignment impinges on adjacent nerves and blood vessels, causing disease.

Be careful! Words like **ileum** and **ilium** sound the same but have different meanings.

- *ae* and *oe* are pronounced *ee,* as in *fasciae*
- *i* at the end of a word usually denotes a plural and is pronounced *eye,* as in *fasciculi*
- *es* at the end of a word may be pronounced as a separate syllable, as in *nares,* pronounced NEH-REEZ.

  Because phonetic spelling isn't used in medicine, it's important to consult a dictionary when in doubt about pronunciation. Also, some terms sound the same but are spelled differently and refer to different things. For example, *ileum* and *ilium* are pronounced alike, but the first term is part of the intestinal tract and the second one is a pelvic bone.

Understanding eponyms

An eponym is a medical term that's derived from the name of a person, usually the scientist who discovered the corresponding body part or disease. Many procedures and tests are also named after the persons who invented or perfected them.

Name that condition

Examples of eponyms for medical conditions include:
- **Addison's disease,** a syndrome resulting from insufficient production of hormones from the cortex of the adrenal gland
- **Alzheimer's disease,** a type of irreversible dementia
- **Cushing's syndrome,** a syndrome resulting from the production of excess cortisol from the adrenal cortex
- **Parkinson's disease,** a progressive degeneration of the nervous system that causes weakness, rigidity, and tremors
- **Stokes-Adams syndrome,** a heart condition characterized by sudden loss of consciousness.

Famous body parts

Parts of the body named for their discoverers include:
- Bartholin's glands, located in the female perineum
- **Cowper's glands,** located beneath a portion of the male urethra
- Wernicke's center, a speech center in the brain.

Featured procedures

Examples of eponyms for medical procedures include:
- **Allen's test,** a test for occlusion of radial or ulnar arteries
- **Belsey Mark IV operation,** a procedure to correct gastroesophageal reflux
- Heimlich maneuver, a technique for removing foreign objects from the airway of a choking victim.

What's in a name?

Medical devices such as catheters (tubes passed through body channels) are often named for their inventors; for example:
- the Foley catheter is an indwelling urinary catheter
- a **Hickman catheter** is a central venous catheter inserted for long-term use
- a **Malecot catheter** is a tube used for gastrostomy feedings
- a **Swan-Ganz catheter** is threaded into the pulmonary artery.

Prefixes and suffixes are important, but focus on the root of the word to get the meaning quickly.

Vocabulary builders

At a crossroads

Completing this crossword puzzle will help you get to the root of medical vocabulary. Good luck!

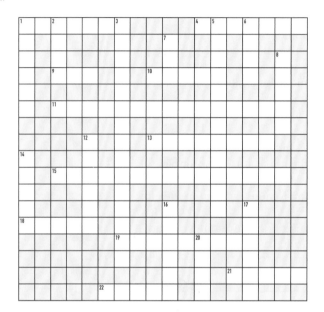

Across

1. Suffix meaning *production*
4. Root for *cancer*
9. Root for *decay*
10. Root for *fat*
11. Suffix in **splenectomy** means this (two words)
13. An eponymic maneuver
15. An eponymic speech center in the brain (two words)
18. Root for *male*
19. Root for *eye*
21. Root for *water*
22. Root for *bone*

Down

1. Syllable attached to the beginning of a word
2. Suffix for **inflammation**
3. **Pro-** means this (two words)
5. **Phobia** is a root meaning this (two words)
6. Second root in **erythrocyte** means this
7. Root of **pediatric**
8. Meaning of root in 7 down
12. Root for *heart*
14. Prefix meaning *upon*
16. Prefix meaning *different*
17. Term for a word derived from a person's name
20. Root for *vessel*

Match game

Match the following roots and prefixes to their correct meanings.

Clues	Choices
1. Super	A. Rapid
2. Tachy	B. Stone
3. Thrombo	C. Above
4. Thermo	D. Large
5. Poly	E. Heat
6. Post	F. After
7. Oxy	G. Clot
8. Mono	H. Oxygen
9. Lith	I. Many
10. Mega	J. One

Finish line

Fill in the blanks below with the words that correctly identify key concepts of medical terminology.

Generally, plural words derived from Latin and Greek are formed by adding or substituting _____ or syllables at the end of the word.
1

A _____ consists of one or more letters attached to the beginning of a root.
2

In the word *oliguria,* the prefix ***olig*** means _____.
3

A _____ is the essential component of a word.
4

The term *Alzheimer's disease* is an example of an _____.
5

A _____ is one or more letters attached to the end of a root.
6

The plural of *pelvis* is_____.
7

Talking in circles

Use the clues below to fill in the blanks with the appropriate word. Then unscramble the circled letters to find the answer to the question posed below.

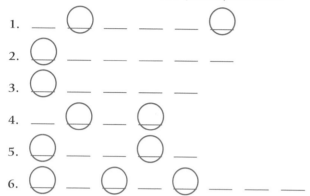

1. This root means *mental health.*
2. This root means *growth.*
3. This prefix means *backward.*
4. This prefix means *against.*
5. *Stone* is the meaning of this root.
6. If your patient has a sore throat, you may have to use this root and the suffix *-itis* to describe the condition.

Answers

At a crossroads

```
 ¹P  O  ²I  E   S   I  ³S   .   .   .  ⁴C  A  ⁵R  ⁶C   I   N   O
  R  T   .  .   S   U   .  ⁷P   .   .   B  E   .   C
  E  I   .  .   B   .   .   E   .   .   N  L   .  ⁸C
  F ⁹S   E  P   S   .  ¹⁰A  D   I   P   O  .   L   H
  I  .   .  .   T   .   .   .   .   R   .   .   I
  X ¹¹S  U  R   G   I   C   A   L   R   E  M   O   V   A   L
  .  .   . ¹²C  T   .  ¹³H   E   I   M   L   I   C   H
 ¹⁴S .   W  A   U   .   E   .   .   F
  U ¹⁵W  E  R   N   I   C   K   E   S   C   E   N   T   E   R
  P  .   D  I   N   .   .   .   A
  R  .   I  G  ¹⁶H   .   R  ¹⁷E
 ¹⁸A N   D  R   O   .   E   .   P
  .  .   . ¹⁹O  P   H   T  ²⁰A   L   M   O
  .  .   .  R   .   E   .   N   .   O
  .  .   .  R   .   G  ²¹H   Y   D   R   O
  .  .  ²²O S   T   E   O   .   I   .   M
```

Match game

Answers: 1. C; 2. A; 3. G; 4. E; 5. I; 6. F; 7. H; 8. J; 9. B; 10. D

Finish line

Answers: 1. Vowels; 2. Prefix; 3. Little; 4. Root; 5. Eponym; 6. Suffix; 7. Pelves.

Talking in circles

Answers: 1. Psycho; 2. Trophy; 3. Retro; 4. Anti; 5. Litho; 6. Pharyngo

Answer to puzzle—Rhinoplasty

Suggested references

Nielsen-Bohlman, L. (2004). *Health literacy. [electronic resource]: A prescription to end confusion.* Washington, DC: National Academies Press.

Pieterse, A. H., Jager, N. A., Smets, E. A., & Henselmans, I. (2013). Lay understanding of common medical terminology in oncology. *Psycho-Oncology, 22*(5), 1186–1191. doi:10.1002/pon.3096

Selekman, J. (2014). It's not called that anymore: Changes in medical terminology. *NASN School Nurse (Print), 29*(1), 43, 44.

Chapter 2

Body structure

Just the facts

In this chapter, you will learn:

◆ terminology related to cells, organs, and tissues

◆ terminology related to the systems of the body

◆ terminology related to the directions, regions, and positions of the body.

Cells: Nature's building blocks

The cell is the body's basic building block and the smallest living component of an organism. In the late 1600s, British physicist Robert Hooke first observed plant cells with a crude microscope. He decided that the structures reminded him of tiny prison cells—hence the name **cell**. (See *Pronouncing key terms related to the cell*, page 17.)

Specialized units

The human body contains millions of cells grouped into highly specialized units that function together. Large groups of individual cells form tissues, such as muscle, blood, and bone. Tissues in turn form organs, such as the brain, heart, and liver. Organs and tissues are integrated into body systems—such as the central nervous system, cardiovascular system, and digestive system.

Cells like me are the basic building blocks of the body.

A peek inside the cell

Cells are composed of many structures, or **organelles**, that each have a specific function. The word **organelles** is from the neo-Latin word *organella*, an altered form of *organum*, which means *organ*. (See *Just your average cell*, Page 18.)

Pump up your pronunciation

Pronouncing key terms related to the cell

Below is a list of key terms, along with the correct way to pronounce them.

Adenosine	UH-**DEEN**-OH-SEEN
Cytokinesis	**SEYE**-TOE-KUH-**NEE**-SIS
Epithelial	EH-PEH-**THEE**-LEE-UL
Golgi (as in Golgi apparatus)	**GAWL**-JEE
Meiosis	MEYE-**OH**-SIS
Mitochondria	**MEYE**-TOE-**KAHN**-DREE-UH
Ribonucleic acid	REYE-BOH-NOO-**KLAY**-IK **AS**-ID
Squamous	**SKWAY**-MUHS

Cyto surroundings

Organelles live in **cytoplasm**—an aqueous mass that's surrounded by the cell membrane. *Cyto-* is from the Greek root *kytos*, which means *container* or *body*; it denotes a relationship to a cell. The **cell membrane**, also called the **plasma membrane**, encloses the cytoplasm and forms the outer boundary of each cell.

Nuclear power

The largest organelle is the **nucleus**, a word derived from the Latin word *nuculeus*, which means *kernel*. The nucleus is the control center of the cell. It stores deoxyribonucleic acid (DNA), which carries genetic material and is responsible for cellular reproduction or division.

The typical animal cell is characterized by several additional elements:

- **Adenosine triphosphate**, the energy that fuels cellular activity, is made in the **mitochondria**, the cell's power plant.
- **Ribosomes** and the **endoplasmic reticulum** synthesize proteins and metabolize fat within the cell.
- The **Golgi apparatus** holds enzyme systems that assist in completing the cell's metabolic functions.
- **Lysosomes** contain enzymes that allow cytoplasmic digestion. (See *Why call it a lysosome?*, page 19.)

Just your average cell

The illustration below shows the components and structures of a cell. Each part has a function in maintaining the cell's life and homeostasis.

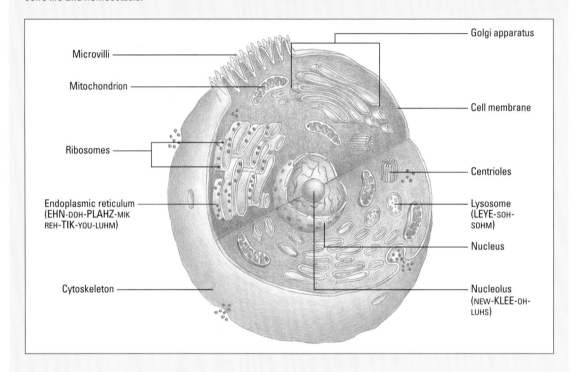

Cell division and reproduction

Individual cells are subject to wear and tear and must reproduce quickly to replace themselves. Genetic information passes from one generation of cells to the next in an intricate process that is vital to survival. Mistakes here can lead to lethal genetic disorders, cancer, and other conditions.

Mitosis

All cells except gametes (ova and spermatozoa) reproduce through a process called **mitosis** (from the Greek root *mitos*, which means *thread*, with the suffix *-osis*, which denotes *an action or state*). During mitosis, the nucleus and genetic material of the cell divide, resulting in the formation of two separate daughter cells. The process is completed when the cell body completes its division (called **cytokinesis**, from the Greek root *kytos* and the Greek word *kinesis*, which means *movement*). (See *Divide and conquer: Five stages of mitosis.*)

Ready? Set? Divide

Cell division consists of one inactive phase and four active phases. Before a cell can divide, it must double in mass and content. This begins during the inactive growth phase of mitosis, called **interphase**. At this phase, **chromatin** (the network of small, slender rods in the nucleus that give it its glandular appearance) begins to form.

Replication and duplication of DNA occur during the four active phases of mitosis:

1. prophase
2. metaphase
3. anaphase
4. telophase.

Prophase

During **prophase**, the chromosomes coil and shorten and the nuclear membrane dissolves. Each chromosome is made up of a pair of strands, called **chromatids**. Chromatids are connected by a spindle of fibers called a **centromere.**

Metaphase

During **metaphase**, chromosomes line up in the center of the cell. The centromeres then replicate.

Anaphase

At the onset of **anaphase**, centromeres begin to separate and pull the newly replicated chromosomes toward opposite sides of the cell. The centromere of each chromosome splits to form two new chromosomes, each consisting of a single DNA molecule. By the end of anaphase, 46 chromosomes are present on each side of the cell.

Telophase

In the final step of mitosis—**telophase**—a new membrane forms around each set of 46 chromosomes. The spindle fibers disappear and the cytoplasm divides, producing two new identical "daughter" cells.

Why call it a lysosome?

The term **lysosome** comes from the Greek word *lysis*, which means *dissolution*. In plain terms, *lysis* means *destruction by enzymatic digestion*.

Memory jogger

As a way to remember the processes of mitosis, think of the phrase "I pulled my act together":

Interphase

Prophase

Metaphase

Anaphase

Telophase.

Divide and conquer: Five stages of mitosis

Through the process of mitosis, the nuclear content of all body cells (except gametes) reproduces and divides. The result is the formation of two new daughter cells.

Interphase

During *interphase*, the nucleus and nuclear membrane are well defined, and the nucleolus is visible. As chromosomes replicate, each forms a double strand that remains attached at the center by a centromere.

Centrioles

Nucleolus

Prophase

In *prophase*, the nucleolus disappears and the chromosomes become distinct. *Chromatids*, halves of each duplicated chromosome, remain attached by the centromere. Centrioles move to opposite sides of the cell and radiate spindle fibers.

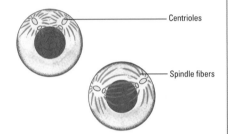

Centrioles

Spindle fibers

Metaphase

Metaphase occurs when chromosomes line up randomly in the center of the cell between the spindles, along the *metaphase plate*. The centromere of each chromosome then replicates.

Centromere

Metaphase plate

Anaphase

Anaphase is characterized by centromeres moving apart, pulling the separate chromatids (now called *chromosomes*) to opposite ends of the cell. The number of chromosomes at each end of the cell equals the original number.

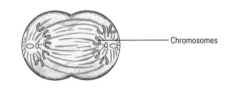

Chromosomes

Telophase

During *telophase*, the final stage of mitosis, a nuclear membrane forms around each end of the cell and spindle fibers disappear. The cytoplasm compresses and divides the cell in half. Each new cell contains the diploid (46) number of chromosomes.

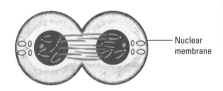

Nuclear membrane

Each of these cells can grow and develop, perhaps becoming a mother to new cells. (See *Tell me about telophase.*)

Meiosis

Gametes (**ova** and **spermatozoa**) reproduce through a process called *meiosis* (Greek, meaning *lessening*). The word **gamete** comes from the Greek root *gamet*, which means either *wife (gamete)* or *husband (gametes)* depending on its ending. **Ova** is the plural form of **ovum**, which means *egg*; both words come directly from Latin without change. **Spermatozoa** is the plural form of **spermatozoon**, formed from the Greek *spermat*, meaning *seed*, and the Greek root *zôion*, meaning *animal*.

In meiosis, genetic material between similarly structured chromosomes is intermixed and the number of chromosomes in the four daughter cells diminishes by half. Meiosis consists of two divisions separated by a resting phase.

Beyond the dictionary

Tell me about telophase

The prefix **telo-** in **telophase** is derived from the Greek word **telos**, which means *an ultimate end*. Telophase marks the end of mitosis, yielding two daughter cells.

Fluid movement

A cell must move various molecules in and out through the plasma membrane and between compartments inside the cell. There are several different ways fluids and **solutes** (dissolved substances) move through membranes at the cellular level.

Going with the flow

In **diffusion**, solutes move from an area of higher concentration to an area of lower concentration. This movement eventually results in an equal distribution of solutes within the two areas. Diffusion is known as **passive transport** because no energy is needed to make it happen. Like fish traveling downstream, solutes involved in diffusion just go with the flow.

Letting fluids through

Osmosis (from the Greek root *osm*, meaning *to push*, and the Greek suffix *-sis*, which is used to form a noun from a word that was originally a verb) is another passive transport method. Unlike diffusion, osmosis involves the movement of a water (solvent) molecule across the cell membrane from a dilute solution, one with a high concentration of water molecules, to a concentrated one, one with a lower concentration of water.

Osmosis is influenced by the **osmotic pressure** of a solution. Osmotic pressure reflects the water-attracting property of a solute. It's determined by the number of dissolved particles in a given volume of solution.

Energy required

Unlike passive transport, **active transport** requires energy. Usually, this mechanism moves a substance from an area of lower concentration to an area of higher concentration. Think of this as swimming upstream. When a fish swims upstream, it uses energy.

Against the grain

The energy required for a solute to move against a concentration gradient comes from a substance produced and stored within the cell, **adenosine triphosphate**, or **ATP**. ATP supplies the energy for solute movement in and out of cells. Some solutes, such as sodium and potassium, use ATP to move in and out of cells in a form of active transport called the **sodium-potassium pump**. Other solutes that require active transport to cross cell membranes include calcium ions, hydrogen ions, amino acids, and certain sugars.

Sometimes you need to work at it. Active transport requires energy, like swimming upstream.

Body tissues: Holding it all together

Tissues are groups of similar cells that perform the same role; each tissue has at least one unique function. Tissues are classified by structure and function and are divided into four types: epithelial, connective, muscle, and nervous.

Epithelial tissue

Epithelial **tissue** (the **epithelium**) is a continuous cellular sheet that covers the body's surface, lines body cavities, and forms certain glands. It contains at least two types of epithelial cells.

Endothelium and mesothelium

Epithelial tissue with a single layer of squamous cells attached to a basement membrane is called **endothelium**. Such tissue lines the heart, lymphatic vessels, and blood vessels. Tissue that lines the surface of serous membranes, such as the pleura, pericardium, and peritoneum, is called **mesothelium**. Epithelial tissue is classified by the number of cell layers it has and the shape of the cells on its surface.

Layer upon layer

Depending on the number of cell layers, epithelial tissue may be simple or stratified:
- **Simple** epithelial tissue contains one layer of cells.
- **Stratified** epithelial tissue has three or more layers.

Classified by shape

Based on the shape of its surface cells, epithelial tissue may be characterized as squamous, columnar, cuboidal, transitional, or pseudostratified columnar:
- **Squamous** epithelial tissue has flat surface cells.
- **Columnar** epithelial tissue has tall, cylindrical, prism-shaped surface cells.
- Cuboidal epithelial tissue has cube-shaped surface cells.
- **Transitional** epithelial tissue has a unique arrangement of cell shapes in a stratified (layered) sheet. This type of tissue can stretch, such as the bladder does when it's full.
- **Pseudostratified columnar** epithelial tissue has one layer of oddly shaped columnar cells.

I swear it's true. The prefix *pseudo-* means false.

Connective tissue

Connective tissue is classified by structure into one of the following four categories: fibrous, bone, cartilage, or blood. Connective tissue is found in or around almost every organ of the body. Its function is to support, connect, and transport.

Fibrous

Fibrous tissue can be dense, loose, or adipose.

Cut loose

Loose connective tissue has large spaces that separate the fibers and cells. It contains much intercellular fluid.

Dense support

Dense connective tissue provides structural support. It has a greater fiber concentration.

Who are you calling fat?

Adipose tissue (fat) is a specialized type of loose connective tissue in which a single fat droplet occupies most of the cell. It cushions

Beyond the dictionary

Where *adipose* comes from

Adipose tissue is sometimes referred to as fat. The word **adipose** is derived from ***adiposus***, a word with Greek and Latin origins: the Latin prefix ***adip-*** and the Greek root ***aleipha***, which mean *fat* or *oil*.

internal organs and acts as a reserve supply of energy. (See *Where adipose comes from.*)

Bone

Bone is hard, dense tissue with a calcified matrix.

Cartilage

Cartilage is a flexible matrix with a gristle-like gel.

Blood

Blood is a liquid matrix that contains red and white blood cells.

Muscle tissue

The three basic types of **muscle tissue** are striated, cardiac, and smooth.

Striated muscle tissue

Striated muscle tissue gets its name from the striped, or striated, appearance it has when viewed under a microscope. All striated muscle tissue capable of voluntary contraction is called **skeletal muscle tissue.**

Cardiac and smooth muscle tissue

Cardiac muscle tissue is striated, but it contracts involuntarily. **Smooth** muscle tissue lacks the striped pattern of striated tissue; it consists of long, spindle-shaped cells. Its activity is stimulated by the autonomic nervous system and isn't under voluntary control. Smooth muscle tissue lines the wall of many internal organs and other structures, such as the walls of arteries and veins.

Nervous tissue

The main function of **nervous tissue** is communication. Its primary properties are **irritability** (the capacity to react to various physical and chemical agents) and **conductivity** (the ability to transmit the resulting reaction from one point to another). Nervous tissue cells may be neurons or neuroglia.

Neurons consist of three parts: dendrites, the cell body, and axons. Like tiny antennas, dendrites receive impulses and conduct them into the cell body. **Axons** carry impulses away from the cell body.

Check out my dendrites. They receive and conduct impulses.

Neuroglia form the support structure of nervous tissue, insulating and protecting neurons. They're found only in the central nervous system.

Organs and systems: The specialists

When a group of tissues handles a more complicated task than any one tissue could perform alone, they're called **organs.**

Organs combine to form **systems,** which perform a more complex function than any one organ can manage on its own. The body depends on these systems in the following ways:

- The **immune system** protects the body from disease and invading organisms.
- The **nervous system** and **sensory system** process incoming information and allow the body to respond.
- The **genitourinary system** manages reproduction and urine excretion.
- The **gastrointestinal system** digests and absorbs food and excretes waste products.
- The **cardiovascular system** transports blood.
- The **respiratory system** maintains the exchange of oxygen and carbon dioxide in the lungs and tissues and regulates acid-base balance.
- The **integumentary system**—which includes skin, hair, nails, and sweat glands—protects the body and helps regulate body temperature. (See *Why call it* integumentary?)
- The **muscular system** allows the body to move.
- The **skeletal system** supports the body and gives muscles a place to attach.
- The **endocrine system** consists of glands that secrete regulating chemicals called **hormones.**
- The **circulatory system** consists of the heart and blood vessels. Oxygen and other nutrients are transported throughout the body via this system.
- The **reproductive system** includes the organs of reproduction, such as the gonads (testes in the male and ovaries in the female), which produce germ cells and manufacture hormones.

Beyond the dictionary

Why call it *integumentary?*

It's easy to see why **integumentary** is the term for a body system that includes the hair, skin, nails, and sweat glands. The origin of this word is the Latin word *integumentum*, which means *to cover.*

Directions, regions, and positions

Determining directions within the body is essential to accurately pinpoint the locations of structures. Terms that describe body planes, cavities, and regions are also useful.

Giving directions

Specific terms are used to define the relationship between body areas and the locations of structures. These terms describe the body in anatomic **position**—standing erect with arms hanging to the side and palms facing forward:

- **Superior** means *above*; for example, the knees are superior to the ankles.
- **Inferior** means *below*; for example, the feet are inferior to the ankles.
- **Anterior** means *front* or *in front of*; for example, the sternum is an anterior structure. **Ventral** is sometimes used instead of anterior.
- **Posterior** means *back* or *in back of*; for example, the spine is a posterior structure. **Dorsal** may be used instead of posterior.
- **Medial** (midline) means *toward the center*.
- **Central** means *in the center*.
- **Peripheral** means *away from the center*.
- **Lateral** refers to the sides, or *away from the midline*.
- **Proximal** means *nearest to*.
- **Distal** describes a point farthest from the point of origin.
- **Superficial** describes a point nearest the body surface.
- **Deep** means *away from the surface*.

Body planes and sections

The body is theoretically divided into three areas called the sagittal, the frontal (coronal), and the transverse planes. (See *Body reference planes.*)

Sagittal plane

The **sagittal plane** runs lengthwise from front to back and divides the body into right and left sides. A **median sagittal** cut produces two equal halves, each containing an arm and a leg. (Don't try this at home!)

Frontal plane

The **frontal plane** runs lengthwise from side to side, dividing the body into **ventral** and **dorsal** (front and back) sections.

Transverse plane

The **transverse plane**, also called the **horizontal plane**, cuts the body into upper and lower parts. These are known as the **cranial** (head) and the **caudal** (tail) portions.

Plainly speaking, the body is divided into three planes: sagittal, frontal, and transverse.

Body cavities

A **cavity** is a hollow space within the body that usually houses vital organs. The two major cavities are the ventral cavity and the dorsal cavity. They are divided into smaller spaces for the internal organs. (See *Locating body cavities*, page 29.)

Ventral cavity

The **ventral cavity** contains the thoracic (chest) cavity and the abdominopelvic cavity. The **thoracic cavity**, located above the diaphragm, contains the heart, lungs, and large blood vessels that join the heart. The **abdominopelvic cavity**, located below the diaphragm, consists of the **abdominal cavity** (stomach, most of the intestines, kidneys, liver, gallbladder, pancreas, and spleen) and the **pelvic cavity** (urinary bladder, rectum, and internal parts of the reproductive system).

Body reference planes

Body reference planes are used to indicate the locations of body structures. Here are the median sagittal, the frontal, and the transverse planes, which lie at right angles to one another.

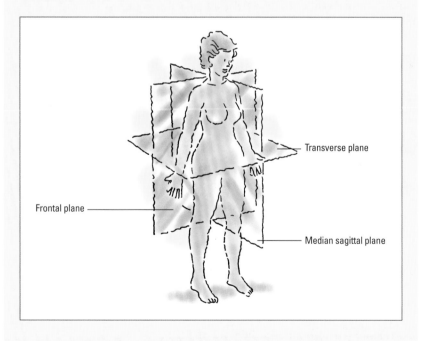

Transverse plane

Frontal plane

Median sagittal plane

Dorsal cavity

The **dorsal cavity** includes both the cranial and spinal cavities:
- The **cranial cavity** is relatively small; it houses and protects the brain.
- The **spinal cavity** contains the spinal column and spinal cord.

Abdominal regions

So many organs and structures lie inside the abdominal and pelvic cavities that special terms are used to pinpoint different areas. Nine regions are identified from right to left and top to bottom:
- The **right** hypochondriac **region** contains the right side of the liver, the right kidney, and a portion of the diaphragm.
- The epigastric **region** contains the pancreas and portions of the stomach, liver, inferior vena cava, abdominal aorta, and duodenum.
- The **left hypochondriac region** contains a portion of the diaphragm, the spleen, the stomach, the left kidney, and part of the pancreas.
- The **right lumbar region** contains portions of the large intestines and the right kidney.
- The umbilical **region** contains sections of the small and large intestines and a portion of the left kidney.
- The **left lumbar region** contains portions of the small and large intestines and a portion of the left kidney.
- The **right iliac (inguinal) region** includes portions of the small and large intestines.
- The **hypogastric region's** prominent structures include a portion of the sigmoid colon, the urinary bladder and ureters, and portions of the small intestine.
- The **left iliac (inguinal) region** contains portions of the small and large intestines. (See *Anterior view of the abdominal regions*, page 30.)

Positions

Patients may be placed in several positions for examination, testing, and treatment. (See *Picturing positions*, page 31.) These positions are described by many terms. The most frequently used include:
- **Fowler's**—head of bed raised 45 to 60 degrees, with knees slightly flexed
- **lateral recumbent**, or **Sims'**—lying on the left side with the right thigh and knee drawn up

Locating body cavities

The dorsal cavity, in the posterior region of the body, is divided into the cranial and vertebral cavities. The ventral cavity, in the anterior region, is divided into the thoracic and abdominopelvic cavities.

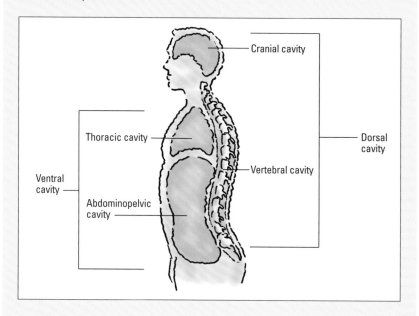

- lithotomy—lying on the back with the hips and knees flexed and the thighs abducted and externally rotated
- **supine**—lying flat on the back
- **prone**—lying face down
- **Trendelenburg's**—lying flat with the head lower than the body and legs
- **knee-chest**—on knees with the chest resting on the bed.

The prone position is the perfect position for a back massage.

(Text continues on page 32.)

Anterior view of the abdominal regions

This illustration shows the abdominal regions from the front.

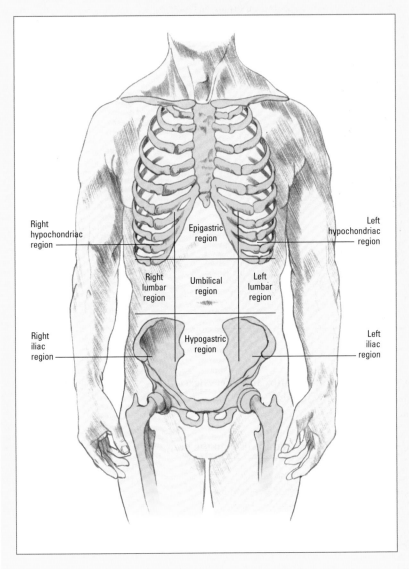

Right
hypochondriac
region

Epigastric
region

Left
hypochondriac
region

Right
lumbar
region

Umbilical
region

Left
lumbar
region

Right
iliac
region

Hypogastric
region

Left
iliac
region

The abdomen is divided like a tic-tac-toe board into nine distinct regions.

Picturing positions

The illustrations below depict the various positions that the patient may be placed in for examinations, testing, and treatments.

Supine

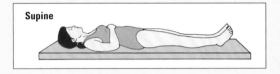

Sims'

Knee-chest

Lithotomy

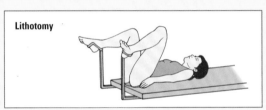

Prone

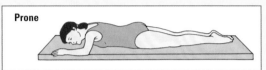

Fowler's

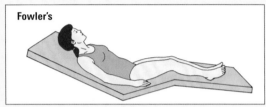

Trendelenburg's

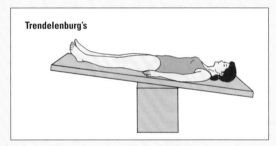

Keep in mind that you should only place your patient in positions that her condition allows.

Vocabulary builders

At a crossroads

Completing this crossword puzzle will help build your medical vocabulary. Good luck!

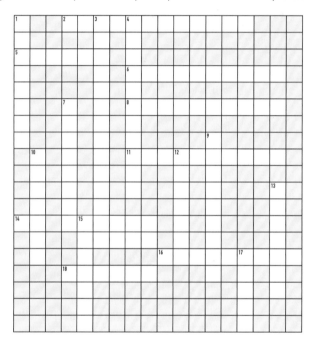

Across

2. Site of adenosine triphosphate production
5. Only type of cell that undergoes meiosis
6. Name for the structures of a cell
8. Growth phase of mitosis
11. Type of epithelial tissue that has three or more layers
14. Support structure of nervous tissue
16. The final step of mitosis
18. Eponym for a position in which the head of the bed is raised and the patient's knees are slightly flexed

Down

1. One of three body reference planes
3. Eponym for a position in which the patient's head is lower than his body or legs
4. Cell movement
7. Word that means *in front of*
9. When solutes move from an area of higher concentration to an area of lower concentration
10. Largest organelle
12. Type of tissue in which a fat droplet occupies most of the cell
13. Process of cell division from the Greek word for *thread*
15. Passive transport method whose root comes from the Greek word meaning *to push*
17. Physicist to first coin the term *cell*

Match game

Tissues are groups of similar cells that perform the same role. Each tissue also has at least one unique function. Match each clue to the correct type of tissue.

Clues	Choices
1. Tissue that lines the surface of serous membranes, such as the pleura, pericardium, and peritoneum	A. Loose connective
2. Epithelial tissue that has only one layer of cells but appears to have more	B. Mesothelium
3. Tissue that has cube-shaped surface cells	C. Neurons
4. Tissue that has large spaces that separate the fibers and cells and contains a lot of intercellular fluid	D. Pseudostratified
5. Tissue with a striped appearance	E. Cuboidal
6. Nervous tissue that consists of three parts: dendrites, cell body, and axons	F. Striated muscle

Knowing the different tissue types brings you one step closer to mastering anatomy.

O see, can you say?

Sound out each group of pictures and symbols below to reveal a term that was reviewed in the chapter.

1.

2.

3.

This is easy! Even long, medical words are simply a sum of their parts.

Talking in circles

Use the clues below to fill in the blanks with the appropriate word. Then, unscramble the circled letters to find the answer to the question posed below.

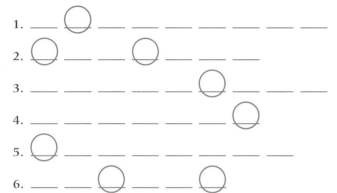

1. __ ◯ __ __ __ __ __ __ __

2. ◯ __ __ ◯ __ __ __

3. __ __ __ __ __ ◯ __ __ __

4. __ __ __ __ __ __ ◯

5. ◯ __ __ __ __ __ __ __

6. __ __ ◯ __ __ ◯

1. This is an aqueous mass that is surrounded by the cell membrane.
2. Only gametes (ova and spermatozoa) undergo this type of reproduction.
3. Particles or solutes move from an area of higher concentration to an area of lower concentration in this type of movement.
4. The cavity that houses and protects the brain.
5. This plane runs lengthwise front to back and divides the body into right and left sides.
6. This prefix means *false*.

I'm hungry ... and I need something other than a knife and fork! Which organelle is responsible for helping me digest foreign material?

Answers

At a crossroads

		²M	I	T	O	⁴C	H	O	N	D	R	I	A		
¹S															
A		R		Y											
⁵G	A	M	E	T	E			T							
I				N		⁶O	R	G	A	N	E	L	L	E	S
T				D		K									
T		⁷A		E		⁸I	N	T	E	R	P	H	A	S	E
A		N		L		N									
L		T		E		E			⁹D						
¹⁰N	E		N		¹¹S	T	R	¹²A	T	I	F	I	E	D	
U		R		B			I		D		F				
C		I		U			S		I		F		¹³M		
L		O		R					P		U		I		
¹⁴N	E	U	R	¹⁵O	G	L	I	A		O		S		T	
U				S					S		I		O		
S				M			¹⁶T	E	L	O	P	¹⁷H	A	S	E
			¹⁸F	O	W	L	E	R		N		O		I	
				S								O		S	
				I								K			
				S								E			

Match game

Answers: 1. B; 2. D; 3. E; 4. A; 5. F; 6. C

O see, can you say?

Answers: 1. Mitochondria; 2. Cytokinesis; 3. Meiosis

Talking in circles

Answers: 1. Cytoplasm; 2. Meiosis; 3. Diffusion; 4. Cranial;
5. Sagittal; 6. Pseudo

Answer to Puzzle—Lysosome

Suggested references

D'Amico, D., & Barbarito, C. (2012). *Health & physical assessment in nursing* (2nd ed.). Boston: Pearson.

Huether, S., & McCance, K. (2012). *Understanding pathophysiology* (5th ed.). St. Louis, MO: Mosby/Elsevier.

Jarvis, C. (2016). *Physical examination & health assessment* (7th ed.). St. Louis, MO: Elsevier.

Lewis, S. L., Bucher, L., Heitkemper, M. M., & Ruff-Dirksen, S. (2013). *Medical-surgical nursing: Assessment and management of clinical problems* (9th ed.). St. Louis, MO: Elsevier.

Marieb, E. N., & Hoehn, K. (2013). *Human anatomy & physiology.* Boston, MA: Pearson.

Potter, P. A., Perry, A. G., Stockert, P., & Hall, A. (2017). *Fundamentals of nursing* (9th ed.). St. Louis, MO: Elsevier.

Chapter 3

Skeletal system

Just the facts

In this chapter, you'll learn:

♦ terminology related to the anatomy of the skeletal system

♦ terminology needed for physical examination of the skeletal system

♦ tests that help diagnose skeletal system disorders

♦ disorders of the skeletal system and their treatments.

Anatomy of the skeleton

The 206 bones of the adult skeletal system carry out six important anatomic and physiologic functions:

1. They protect internal tissues and organs; for example, the 33 vertebrae surround and protect the spinal cord.
2. They stabilize and support the body.
3. They provide surfaces for muscle, ligament, and tendon attachment.
4. They act as lever arms when muscles contract.
5. They produce red blood cells (RBCs) in the bone marrow (a process called **hematopoiesis**, from the Greek *haima*, or blood, and *poiesis*, meaning *making* or *forming*).
6. They store mineral salts; for example, approximately 99% of the body's calcium. (See *Pronouncing key skeletal terms*, page 39.)

Bones-r-us

The skeleton is divided into two parts: the **axial** (from the Latin *axis*, meaning *axle* or *wheel*) and **appendicular** (from the Latin *appendare*, meaning to *add* or *append*). The **axial skeleton** forms the body's vertical axis and contains a total of 80 bones: 74 bones in the head and torso, and it includes 6 bones of the middle ear. The **appendicular skeleton** contains 126 bones and includes the body's **appendages**, or upper and lower extremities. (See *The body's bones*, page 40.)

Pump up your pronunciation

Pronouncing key skeletal terms

Below is a list of key terms, along with the correct way to pronounce them.

Acetabulum	AS-UH-TAH-BYOU-LUHM
Arthrocentesis	AR-THROH-SEN-TEE-SIS
Arthrodesis	AR-THROD-UH-SIS
Astragalus	AS-TRAG-UH-LUHS
Calcaneus	KAL-KAY-NEE-UHS
Canaliculi	KAN-UH-LIK-YOU-LEYE
Cartilaginous	KAR-TUH-LAJ-UH-NUHS
Coccyx	KOK-SIKS
Costochondritis	KOS-TOH-KON-DREYE-TIS
Hematopoiesis	HEE-MUH-TOE-POY-EE-SIS
Hyaline	HEYE-UH-LIN
Kyphosis	KEYE-FOH-SIS
Lambdoid	LAM-DOYD
Malleolus	MAH-LEE-OH-LUHS
Medullary	MED-UH-LAIR-EE
Occipital	OK-SIP-UH-TUHL
Periosteum	PER-EE-OS-TEE-UHM
Xiphoid process	ZEYE-FOYD PRAH-SESS

The axial skeleton

The axial skeleton forms the long axis of the body and includes bones of the skull, vertebral column, and rib cage.

The skull

The **skull** contains 28 irregular-shaped bones in two major areas: the brain case, or **cranium** (from the Greek *kranion*, meaning *upper part of the head*), and the **face**. Eight bones form the **cranium**, 14 bones make up the face, and 6 **ossicles** (from the Latin *ossiculum*, meaning *bone*) or 3 small bones make up each ear. The jaw bone, or **mandible** (from the Latin *mandibula*, meaning *jaw*), is the only movable bone in the skull. (See *Bones of the skull*, page 42.)

The body's bones

The human skeleton contains 206 bones; 80 form the axial skeleton and 126 form the appendicular skeleton. The illustrations below show some of the major bones and bone groups.

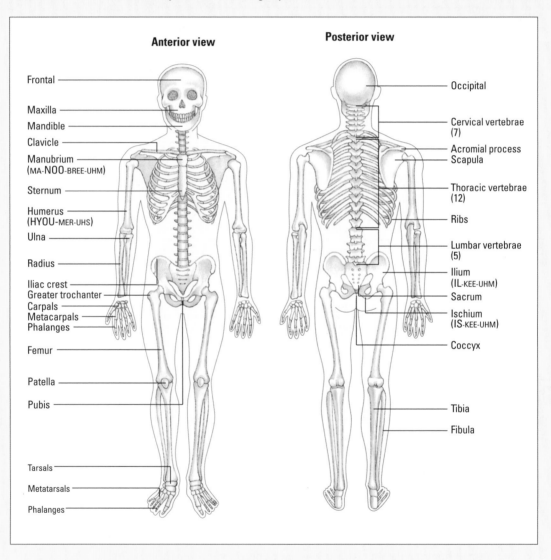

Anterior view

Frontal

Maxilla
Mandible
Clavicle
Manubrium
(MA-NOO-BREE-UHM)

Sternum

Humerus
(HYOU-MER-UHS)
Ulna

Radius

Iliac crest
Greater trochanter
Carpals
Metacarpals
Phalanges

Femur

Patella

Pubis

Tarsals

Metatarsals

Phalanges

Posterior view

Occipital

Cervical vertebrae
(7)
Acromial process
Scapula

Thoracic vertebrae
(12)

Ribs

Lumbar vertebrae
(5)
Ilium
(IL-KEE-UHM)
Sacrum

Ischium
(IS-KEE-UHM)

Coccyx

Tibia

Fibula

Getting it together

Sutures are immobile joints that hold the skull bones together. The **coronal suture** unites the frontal bone and the two parietal bones. In infants, this suture isn't closed immediately after birth, leaving a diamond-shaped area (called the **anterior** fontanel), which is covered only by a membrane. This soft spot closes between ages 10 and 18 months. At the back of the head of infants, the **posterior fontanel** closes by age 2 months. (See *Little fountain.*)

An airhead

Sinuses are air-filled spaces within the skull that lessen the bone weight, moisten incoming air, and act as resonating chambers for the voice.

Up front

The sinuses, the forehead, and the area directly behind these areas are part of the **frontal bone.** This bone also forms the **orbits** (eye sockets) and the front part of the cranial floor.

Take it from the top

The main part of the skull consists of a number of bones sutured together:
- The **coronal suture** connects the frontal bone with the parietal bones.
- Two **parietal bones** crown the head, forming the roof and the upper part of each side of the skull.
- The **squamous suture** connects the parietal bones with the temporal bones.
- **Temporal bones** form the lower part of the sides of the skull and part of its floor. They contain structures of the middle and inner ear and the **mastoid sinuses.**
- The **lambdoid suture** connects the parietal bones to the occipital bone.
- The **occipital bone** forms the rear portion and the base of the skull and forms a movable joint with the first cervical vertebra.
- A large opening at the base of the occipital bone, called the **foramen magnum** (meaning *large hole*), allows the spinal cord to pass from the encephalon into the spine.

A bat in the belfry

The **sphenoid bone** looks like a bat with outstretched wings and legs. Located in the cranial floor, this bone is an anchor for the frontal, parietal, occipital, and ethmoid bones. It also supports part of the eye sockets and forms the lateral walls of the skull. The **sphenoid sinuses** are large air-filled spaces within the sphenoid bone.

Little fountain

Fontanel, also spelled *fontanelle,* derives from French and means *little fountain.* It can also refer to any membrane covered area between two bones.

Bones of the skull

The skull is a complex bony structure. It's formed by two sets of bones, the cranial bones and the facial bones.

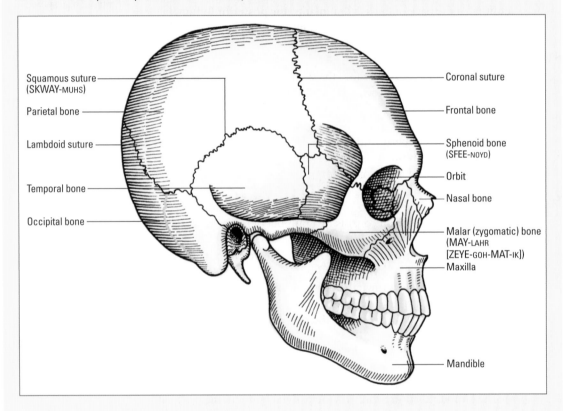

Squamous suture (SKWAY-MUHS)

Parietal bone

Lambdoid suture

Temporal bone

Occipital bone

Coronal suture

Frontal bone

Sphenoid bone (SFEE-NOYD)

Orbit

Nasal bone

Malar (zygomatic) bone (MAY-LAHR [ZEYE-GOH-MAT-IK])

Maxilla

Mandible

Facial bones

The bones of the face include:

- two **maxillary bones** that form the upper jaw, nose, orbits, and roof of the mouth as well as the **maxillary sinuses**
- the cheekbones, called zygomatic or **malar bones**, that attach to chewing muscles
- two **nasal bones** that form the upper part of the bridge of the nose (**cartilage** forms the lower part)
- the **mandible** that forms the lower jaw
- two **lacrimal bones** that contain the lacrimal bag (part of the conduit through which tears drain in the nasal cannula)
- the vomer that's part of the nasal septum

- two palatine **bones** that form the posterior portion of the hard palate, lateral side of the nasal cavity, and small part of the orbit.

The spinal column

The flexible spinal column contains 24 **vertebrae** (plural of **vertebra**), the **sacrum**, and the coccyx. (See *Some thorny words of the spine.*)

Joints between the vertebrae allow forward, backward, and sideways movement. The spinal column supports the head while suspending the ribs and organs in front. It also anchors the pelvic girdle and provides attachment points for many important muscles. The spinal column contains:

- 7 **cervical** (neck) vertebrae, which support the skull and rotate
- 12 **thoracic** (chest) vertebrae, which attach to the ribs
- 5 **lumbar** (lower back) vertebrae, which support the small of the back
- the **sacrum**, a single bone that results from the fusion of 5 vertebrae and attaches to the pelvic girdle
- the **coccyx**, or tailbone, which is located at the bottom tip of the spinal column and is a single bone formed from the fusion of 4 or 5 vertebrae.

The spinal column is curved to increase its strength and make balance possible in an upright position. The vertebrae are cushioned by intervertebral disks composed of cartilage. (See *A look at the spinal column*, page 44.)

Memory jogger

As a way to remember the bones of the skull, use your head and think "part of man":

PARietal

Temporal

Occipital

Frontal

MAlar

Nasal

Beyond the dictionary

Some thorny words of the spine

Spine comes from the Latin word *spina*, which means *thorn*, and is related to **spike** as well. Latin writers likened the thorn to the prickly bones in animals and fish and, thus, the word also became the designation for the vertebral column.

Vertebra and spondylo

Also from Latin, *vertebra* derives from a verb meaning *to turn*. Therefore, it formerly connoted any joint—not just those of the spine. A Greek word, *spondylos*, has the same meaning as **vertebra**. It shows up in words like **spondylitis,** which is an inflammation of the vertebrae.

Sacrum and coccyx bringing up the rear

The **sacrum** was formerly known as the **os sacrum**, literally the *holy bone*, so called because it was thought to be offered to the gods in sacrifice. The **coccyx** derives its name from the Greek word for the cuckoo, *kokkyx*. The Greek anatomist Galen thought this triangular bone resembled the shape of the bird's bill.

Note: Joints between the vertebrae allow forward, backward, and sideways movement. Not all at once, though!

A look at the spinal column

The 33 vertebrae of the spinal column surround and protect the spinal cord. They're divided into five sections: cervical vertebrae, thoracic vertebrae, lumbar vertebrae, sacrum, and coccyx.

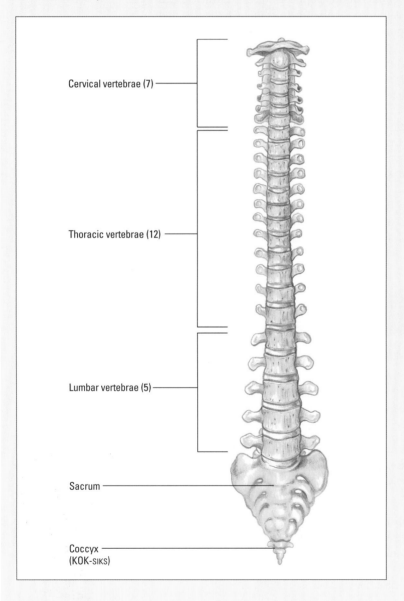

Cervical vertebrae (7)

Thoracic vertebrae (12)

Lumbar vertebrae (5)

Sacrum

Coccyx
(KOK-SIKS)

Yep. I have 33 vertebrae—and they're all perfect specimens, if I do say so myself.

Sternum

Located in the center of the chest, the **sternum** is a flat, sword-shaped bone that's attached to the **clavicles** (collarbones) and the innermost part of the first two pairs of ribs.

Caged in

The sternum, ribs, and thoracic vertebrae form a protective enclosure around the vital organs. Known as the **thoracic cage**, or **thorax**, this flexible structure protects the heart and lungs and allows the lungs to expand during respiration.

Ribs

The flat, curved bones attached to the thoracic portion of the spinal column are called **ribs**.

Ribs—true or false?

The term **costal** refers to ribs. The first seven pairs of ribs are attached to the sternum by **costal cartilage**; they're called **true ribs**. The remaining five pairs of ribs are called **false ribs** because they aren't attached directly to the sternum. All ribs are independently attached to the spinal column.

Appendicular skeleton

The appendicular skeleton includes the upper and lower extremities.

The upper extremities

The **clavicles**, or collarbones, are two flat bones attached to the sternum on their anterior side and to the scapulae (shoulder blades) laterally. This forms the **sternoclavicular joint**.

The scapulae are a pair of large, triangular bones that are located at the back of the thorax. These bones, plus the clavicles, form the shoulder girdles.

Armed and dangerous

The **humerus**, or upper arm bone, is a long bone with a shaft and two bulbous ends. The two long bones of the lower arm are the **ulna**, located on the little finger side of the humerus, and the **radius**, on the thumb side. These bones articulate with the humerus to form the elbow joint.

The **wrists** are composed of eight small, irregular **carpal** bones aligned in two rows and bind together by ligaments.

A handful of terms

The bones of the hand are comprised of metacarpal bones and phalanges. (See *Bones of the hand*.)

The ulna and the radius articulate with the humerus to form the elbow joint.

Bones of the hand

A view of the right hand, illustrating the positions of the carpals, metacarpals, and phalanges.

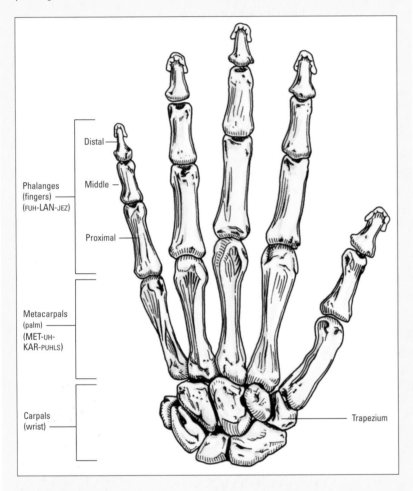

The way these bones come together enables movement of the hand:

- Five small, long **metacarpal** bones attach to the carpals and form the palm of the hand.
- **Phalanges,** or finger bones, are miniature, long bones. Each finger has three phalanges, while the thumb has two. (See *A phalanx of phalanges.*)

- The thumb **metacarpal** has a freely movable joint, allowing a wide range of movement between the thumb metacarpal and the **trapezium**, the carpal at the base of the thumb.

Lower extremities

The lower extremities contain bones of the hip, thigh, leg, ankle, and foot.

Girdle words

Three pairs of bones fuse during childhood to form the **pelvic girdle**, the broadest bone in the body. This bone supports the trunk, protects the abdominal organs within its basin, and attaches the lower extremities to the body. The three pairs of fused bones include the **ilium**, which is the largest and uppermost of the three; the **ischium**, the lower and strongest set of bones; and the **pubis**, a pair of anterior bones that meet at the **symphysis pubis**—a cartilaginous joint.

Give 'em a leg up

The two **femurs**, or upper leg bones, are the longest and heaviest bones in the body. They connect at the proximal end with the hip, articulating with the **acetabulum**, or hip socket. The femurs connect with the **tibia** at the distal end. The kneecap, or **patella**, is a small, flat bone that protects the knee joint and overlaps the distal end of the femur and the proximal end of the tibia.

Below the knee

The **tibia**, sometimes called the **shinbone**, is the largest and strongest of the lower leg bones. It articulates with the femur at the proximal end and meets the fibula and the talus at the distal end. The **fibula** connects with the tibia at its proximal and distal ends. The fibula's distal end also articulates with the talus. The articulation of the fibula, tibia, and talus bones creates the bony prominence on the outside of the ankle, called the **lateral malleolus**.

Now, fleetly, to the foot

The foot bones form a strong, stable arch with lengthwise and crosswise support. Strong ligaments and tendons of the leg muscles help the foot bones maintain their arched position:

- Seven short **tarsal bones** structurally resemble the wrist, and they articulate with the tibia and fibula:
  ○ The **talus bone (astragalus)** forms part of the ankle joint.
  ○ The heel, called the **calcaneus**, is the largest tarsal bone.
  ○ The **scaphoid bone** is also called the **navicular** because of its boat shape.
  ○ The **cuneiforms** (the **lateral**, **intermediate**, and **medial**) are three wedge-shaped bones that form the arch of the foot.

Beyond the dictionary

A phalanx of phalanges

Phalanges is the plural of the Greek word *phalange*, or *phalanx*. The latter term was applied to Greek and Roman army troop formations, noted for their closely joined and unified maneuvers.

The word **patella**, for kneecap, is a Latin word that means a small, flat dish—just what the kneecap looks like.

- The cuboid **bone** articulates in the front with the metatarsal bones.
- Five **metatarsal bones** form the foot and articulate with the tarsal bone and the phalanges.
- The fourteen **phalanges** (toes) are similar to fingers, with three bones in each toe except the great toe, which, like the thumb, contains only two bones.

Anatomy of bones

Bones are classified according to their shape:
- **Long bones** are the main bones of the limbs, except the patella, and those of the wrists and ankles.
- **Short bones** are the bones of the wrists and ankles.
- **Flat bones** include the sternum, scapulae, and cranium, among others.
- **Irregular bones** include the vertebrae and hip bones.

Boning up on bone material

All bones consist of two types of bone material: an outer layer of dense, smooth **compact bone** and an inner layer of spongy, **cancellous** (porous) bone. Compact bone is found in the shaft of long bones and in the outer layers of short, flat, and irregular bones. Cancellous bone fills the central regions of the epiphysis (the end of a long bone where bone formation takes place) and the inner portions of short, flat, and irregular bones.

Along the long bones

Long bones contain a number of visible, common structures:
- diaphyses (singular: diaphysis)—the long, narrow shaft of the bone contains the bone marrow and has two irregular ends
- epiphyses (singular: epiphysis)—the bulbous ends of long bones that provide a large surface for muscle attachment and give stability to joints
- articular cartilage—a thin layer of hyaline cartilage that covers and cushions the articular (joint) surfaces of the epiphyses
- periosteum—a dense membrane that covers the shafts of long bones; it consists of two layers: a fibrous outer layer and a bone-forming inner layer containing osteoblasts (bone-producing cells) and osteoclasts (bone-destroying cells)
- medullary cavity—a cavity filled with bone marrow
- endosteum—a thin membrane that lines the medullary cavity and contains osteoblasts and osteoclasts.

Feeding the long bones

Within compact bone are **haversian systems**. (See *Haversian diversion*.) The haversian systems are made up of the following structures:

- lamellae—thin layers of ground substance
- lacunae—small hollow spaces that contain osteocytes
- canaliculi—small canals
- **haversian canals**—central canals that contain blood and lymph vessels, nerves, and, sometimes, marrow.

Blood reaches bone by arterioles in haversian canals; by vessels in Volkmann's canals (which connect one haversian canal to another and to the outer bone); and by vessels in the bone ends and within the marrow. (See *Two views of a long bone*.)

Beyond the dictionary

Haversian diversion

The **haversian systems** were named in honor of the 17th century British doctor and anatomist Clopton Havers, who discovered them.

 Anatomically speaking

Two views of a long bone

Here's a look at a long bone from interior and cross-section views.
Internal view of long bone

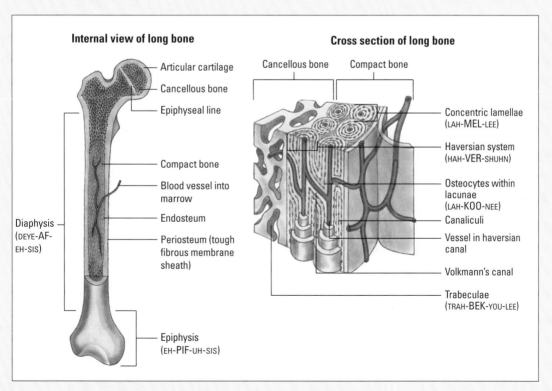

Internal view of long bone

- Articular cartilage
- Cancellous bone
- Epiphyseal line
- Compact bone
- Blood vessel into marrow
- Endosteum
- Periosteum (tough fibrous membrane sheath)

Diaphysis (DEYE-AF-EH-SIS)

Epiphysis (EH-PIF-UH-SIS)

Cross section of long bone

Cancellous bone   Compact bone

- Concentric lamellae (LAH-MEL-LEE)
- Haversian system (HAH-VER-SHUHN)
- Osteocytes within lacunae (LAH-KOO-NEE)
- Canaliculi
- Vessel in haversian canal
- Volkmann's canal
- Trabeculae (TRAH-BEK-YOU-LEE)

To marrow, and to marrow, and to marrow . . .

In a child's body, nearly all the bones contain **red bone marrow**. In an adult, red bone marrow is found in the femur, ribs, vertebrae, and the ends of the humerus in the upper arm. Red bone marrow performs **hematopoiesis or** makes new red blood cells for the body.

Bone growth and resorption

Bones grow both in length and in thickness. At the epiphyses, they grow longer; and at the diaphyses, they grow in diameter through the activity of osteoblasts in the periosteum. A hormone secreted by the anterior lobe of the pituitary gland controls bone growth. (See *Bone up on* osteo- *and* oss-.)

As osteoblasts add new tissue to the outside of a bone, large phagocytic cells called **osteoclasts** eat away bony tissue in the medullary cavity to keep the bone from becoming too thick. A healthy bone is constantly broken down, resorbed, and repaired long after it stops growing in size. During adulthood, bone formation (or **ossification**) and bone **resorption** balance one another so that each bone remains a constant size. During childhood and adolescence, ossification is faster than resorption and bones grow larger.

Cartilage

Bones and joints need support as well as shock absorption. **Cartilage** is a dense connective tissue and consists of fibers embedded in a strong, gel-like substance with shock absorption capabilities. Unlike rigid bone, cartilage has the flexibility of firm plastic.

Beyond the dictionary

Bone up on *osteo*- and *oss*-

Osteon, Greek for *bone*, provides a key word-forming root for medical terms relating to bones, *oste-* or *osteo-*. **Osteoblast** is a compound of *osteo-* and *-blast*; the latter is another common medical root derived from a Greek word that means a *bud* or a *shoot of a developing organism*. An **osteoblast** is thus *a cell that buds forth new bone tissue*. The Greek word *clast*, on the other hand, means *to break* or *fragment*. Therefore, an **osteoclast** is *a cell that breaks down bone*.

The Romans had a name for it

Another very common root for forming words is the Latin word *os*, or *oss-*, also meaning *bone*. This root is contained in words like ossify, meaning *to change* or *to become bone*, and **ossification**, *the process of becoming bone*.

Cartilage supports and shapes various structures, such as the auditory canal and the intervertebral disks. It also cushions and absorbs shock. However, cartilage has no blood or nerve supply.

Types of cartilage

Cartilage types may be fibrous, hyaline, or elastic:
- **Fibrous cartilage** forms at the meniscus and the intervertebral disks.
- Hyaline **cartilage** covers articular bone surfaces (where one or more bones meet at a joint), connects the ribs and sternum, and appears in the trachea, bronchi, and nasal septum.
- **Elastic cartilage** is located in the auditory canal, external ear, and epiglottis.

Bone movement

Bones are rigid structures that can't bend without being damaged, so individual bones move at joint sites, or **articulations.** Every bone in the body except the hyoid bone, which anchors the tongue, is connected to another bone by flexible connective tissue.

Classifying joints

Joints can be classified by the type of movement they allow and by their structure.

How does it move?

The three classes of joints identified by the range of movement they allow are:
- synarthrosis—immovable
- amphiarthrosis—slightly movable
- diarthrosis—freely movable.

What is it made of?

By structure, a joint may be classified as fibrous, cartilaginous, or synovial. In **fibrous joints**, the articular surfaces of the two bones are bound closely by fibrous connective tissue and little movement is possible. The cranial sutures are examples of fibrous joints.

In **cartilaginous joints**, cartilage connects one bone to another; these joints allow slight movement. An example is the symphysis pubis (the junction of the pelvic bones).

Body surfaces in the **synovial joints** are covered by articular cartilage and joined by **ligaments** (dense, strong, flexible bands of fibrous connective tissue that bind bones to other bones) lined with synovial membrane. Freely movable, synovial joints include most joints of the

Our joints move freely! It must be the diarthrosis.

arms and legs. Synovial joints also include an **articular capsule**—a saclike envelope, whose outer layer is lined with a vascular synovial membrane. This membrane contains synovial fluid—a viscid fluid, produced by the synovial membrane that lubricates the joint.

Small bursae (singular: bursa) are synovial fluid sacs located at friction points of all types of joints as well as between tendons, ligaments, and bones. Bursae cushion these structures and decrease stress on adjacent ones. (See *The bag for bones*.)

Synovial subdivisions—joints in the neighborhood

Based on their structure and the type of movement, synovial joints fall into various subdivisions:
- **Gliding joints**, such as the wrists and ankles, allow adjacent bone surfaces to move against one another.
- **Hinge joints**, such as the elbows and knees, permit movement in only one direction.
- **Pivot joints** (also called **rotary joints** or **trochoid joints**), such as the neck and elbows, allow a movable bone to pivot around a stationary bone.

Knuckleheads

- **Condylar**, or **knuckle joints**, contain an oval head of one bone that fits into a shallow depression in a second bone. The union between the radius (arm bone) and the carpal bones of the hand is an example of a condylar joint.
- **Saddle joints** resemble condylar joints but allow greater freedom of movement. The only saddle joints in the body are the carpometacarpal joints of the thumb.
- **Ball-and-socket joints (spheroid joints)** get their name from the way their bones connect—the spherical head of one bone fits into a socket of another bone. The hip and shoulder joints are the only ball-and-socket joints in the body.

Beyond the dictionary

The bag for bones

You may notice that the word **bursa** sounds a bit like the word **purse**. That's more than a coincidence. Both words come from the Latin word *bursa*, which means *a small bag or sac*.

In the body, bursae are sacs of synovial fluid that cushion skeletal structures, such as tendons, ligaments, and bones.

Physical examination terms

When a patient seeks medical help for a skeletal problem, it's usually because of a physical mishap. Here are some terms related to examination of the skeletal system that you'll need to know:
- **angular**—at an angle
- **circular**—circle like or round
- **crepitus**—a cracking noise or the sensation that's commonly felt when the hand is placed over a fracture site and the broken bone ends are moved
- **posture**—the position of the limbs or the body as a whole
- **range of motion**—the total degree of motion or joint movement
- **symmetry**—equality of two sides of the body.

Movement and range of motion

Common terms used to describe movement and range of motion in joints include:
- **abduction**—moving away from the midline of the body
- **adduction**—moving toward the midline of the body
- **circumduction**—moving in a circular manner
- **extension**—straightening or increasing the joint angle
- **flexion**—bending or decreasing the joint angle
- **pronation**—turning downward
- **internal rotation**—turning toward midline of the body
- **external rotation**—turning away from midline of the body
- **supination**—turning upward.

Common complaints

Patients with joint injuries usually complain of pain, swelling, or stiffness, and they may have noticeable deformities. A deformity can also occur with a bone fracture, which causes sharp pain when the patient moves the affected area.

Common terms used to describe patient complaints include:
- **arthralgia**—pain in a joint
- **arthredema**—joint swelling
- **arthropyosis**—pus formation in a joint cavity
- **bursitis**—inflammation of a bursa, the fluid-filled sac that prevents friction within a joint
- chondralgia—pain originating in the cartilage
- **chondritis**—inflammation of the cartilage
- chondromalacia—abnormal softening of the cartilage
- coxitis—inflammation of the hip joint
- epiphysitis—inflammation of the epiphysis of a bone
- hemarthrosis—blood in a joint cavity
- hydrarthrosis—accumulation of watery fluid in a joint cavity
- kyphosis—the Greek word for *hunchback,* an abnormally increased convexity in the curvature of the thoracic spine
- **lordosis**—forward curvature of the lumbar spine; also known as **sway back**
- **lumbago**—pain in the lower back (lumbar) region
- ostealgia—bone pain
- osteitis—inflammation of bone
- osteochondritis—inflammation of bone and cartilage
- osteolysis—degeneration of bone from calcium loss.

Remembering what arthralgia is can be easy when you break it apart: **arthr-** is the root for *joint*; **-algia** is the suffix for *pain.*

SNAP

Diagnostic tests

Tests to determine bone and joint diseases or injuries include blood tests, aspiration tests, and radiologic tests.

Blood tests

Several blood tests can help determine bone and joint disorders:

- **Alkaline phosphatase (ALP)** is an enzyme produced by the bones and liver. Because blood concentrations of ALP rise with increased activity of bone cells, high ALP levels help diagnose bone disorders.
- **Erythrocyte sedimentation rate (ESR)** is the rate at which RBCs settle in a tube of unclotted blood. An elevated ESR indicates inflammation.
- **Rheumatoid factor (RF)** is a blood test used to distinguish rheumatoid arthritis from other disorders.
- **Serum calcium** measures the amount of calcium in the blood. Abnormally high levels are present with Paget's disease and other diseases of the bone.

Aspiration tests

Aspiration tests use fluid withdrawn by a suction device, usually a needle:

- In **arthrocentesis**, a joint is surgically punctured with a needle to aspirate synovial fluid for analysis or to remove accumulated fluid. (See *Simplifying* arthrocentesis.)
- In **bone marrow aspiration**, a needle is forced through the outer cortex of a flat bone—such as the sternum or iliac crest—and bone marrow is aspirated for analysis.
- In **lumbar puncture**, a needle is inserted into the subarachnoid space surrounding the spinal cord to remove a sample of cerebrospinal fluid.

Radiologic tests

- **Bone X-ray**, the simplest radiologic procedure, is used to examine a bone for disease or fracture.
- **Computed tomography (CT) scan**, or **computerized tomography scan**, is a series of X-ray photographs that represent cross-sectional images of the bone. These images are translated by a computer and displayed on an oscilloscope. (See *Cat's tale*.)

Beyond the dictionary

Simplifying *arthrocentesis*

Arthrocentesis becomes a simple compound word when its components are understood. **Arthro-** comes from the Greek word **arthron**, which means *joint*, and **-centesis** derives from the Greek word **kentesis**, which means *puncture*. So **arthrocentesis** must be *a joint puncture*.

The real world

Cat's tale

You may hear a computed axial tomography or referred to as a **CAT scan**.

- **Arthrography** employs contrast dye to observe the interior of a joint, such as the knee, shoulder, ankle, or elbow. Dye is injected into the joint space, and a CT scan records images of the joint.
- **Bone densitometry** is a noninvasive technique in which X-rays are used to measure bone mineral density and identify the risk of osteoporosis. The results are analyzed by a computer to determine bone mineral status.
- **Bone scan** helps detect bony metastasis, benign disease, fractures, avascular necrosis, and infection. After I.V. administration of a radioactive material, a counter detects the gamma rays, indicating areas of increased uptake, suggesting an abnormality.
- **Myelography** is a radiographic examination of the spinal cord following injection of a contrast medium.

Procedures

- **Arthroscopy** is also used to observe the interior of a joint—most commonly the knee. A fiberoptic viewing tube is inserted directly into the joint, allowing a doctor to examine its interior.
- **Bone marrow biopsy** removes a piece of bone containing intact marrow.
- **Magnetic resonance imaging** (MRI) uses an electromagnetic field and radio waves to transfer visual images of soft tissue, such as tendons, to a computer screen.

Disorders

Disorders of the skeletal system include fractures, dislocations, herniations, cancer, and other diseases.

Fractures and other injuries

Fractures, traumatic injuries or breaks in bone tissue, most commonly occur in the long bones of the arms and legs. They can occur in all age-groups in any portion of the skeletal system. Fractures can be caused by direct injury or can occur spontaneously when bone is weakened by disease; the latter is called a **pathologic fracture. A closed** or simple **fracture** is seen when the broken bone doesn't protrude through the skin. **An open** or compound **fracture** occurs when the bone breaks through the skin, causing tissue damage.

Fracture features

Fractures can be classified according to the bone fragment position or by the fracture line:

- Colles' fracture—a fracture of the radius at the lower end of the wrist in which the bone fragment is displaced backward
- **linear fracture**—a fracture that runs along the long axis of a bone
- **comminuted fracture**—a bone is broken into two or more fragments
- **greenstick fracture**—involves a break in only one part of the bone thickness
- **transverse fracture**—the fracture line is perpendicular to a bone's long axis
- **spiral fracture**—the fracture line goes around, or spirals, the bone.

It's simple. A closed fracture occurs when the bone doesn't break through the skin.

Bone away from home

A **dislocation** is the displacement of a bone from its normal position within the joint. It can occur at birth, called a **congenital dislocation**, or may be caused by a disease or trauma. With a dislocation, joint tissue is generally torn and stretched, possibly rupturing blood vessels. Subluxation, or a partial dislocation that separates the joint's movable surfaces, occurs most commonly in the shoulder, hip, and knee.

Don't play this disk

A **herniated disk**, a ruptured area in the cartilage that cushions the intervertebral disks of the spinal column, is a painful condition. The soft, central cartilage balloons out from the disk and puts pressure on the nerve roots. Herniation can happen suddenly with lifting or twisting or may result from degenerative joint disease and other chronic conditions.

Don't be callous about bunions

Here are some other injuries related to the skeletal system that you may encounter:
- **Bunions** are localized areas of swelling that occur on the foot near the joint of the big toe, caused by inflammation and fibrosis of the bursae.
- **Calluses** are hard bone formations that may occur at the site of bone fractures. Calluses also occur due to thickening of the skin and often occur on parts of the feet or fingers.

Diseases

Some of the most common diseases of the skeletal system and terms to describe skeletal disorders are presented here:
- **Ankylosing spondylitis** is a slow, progressive inflammatory disease of the spine, the **sacroiliac** joint, and the larger joints of the extremities (hips, knees, and shoulders) that leads to a fibrous or bony ankylosis (immobility) and deformity.

- **Osteoarthritis**, also known as **degenerative arthritis**, affects the joints of the hand, knee, hip, and vertebrae. It can be a major cause of disability.
- **Osteomalacia** is softening of the bones that is characterized by inadequate mineralization of newly formed bone matrix due to vitamin D deficiency. It is the adult form of rickets.
- **Osteomyelitis** is an inflammation of the bone, bone marrow, and surrounding soft tissue that's caused by **pyogenic** (pus-producing) bacteria.
- **Osteoporosis** is a disorder in which bone mass is reduced, leading to enhanced bone fragility and an increased fracture risk.
- **Rickets** is a condition of abnormal bone growth in children caused by insufficient vitamin D, calcium, and phosphorus.
- **Rheumatoid arthritis** is a chronic autoimmune disorder that affects the synovial membranes. Painful inflammation of the joints may lead to crippling deformities and affect many organ systems.
- **Scurvy** is a condition caused by lack of vitamin C in the diet, which results in abnormal bones and teeth.

Osteomyelitis is an inflammation of the bone, bone marrow, or soft tissue that's caused by bacteria.

Bone tumors

Bone tumors can be **benign** (noncancerous) or **malignant** (cancerous). Here are some tumor types:
- **Osteochondroma** is a common tumor that causes **projections** (spurs) at the end of long bones, especially the knees, ankles, hips, shoulders, and elbows. (See *Tumor terminology*)
- **Osteosarcoma** is a fast-growing malignant tumor of skeletal tissue with a high mortality rate. Common sites of involvement are the tibia, femur, and humerus. This tumor commonly metastasizes to the lungs.
- **Chondrosarcoma** is a large, slow-growing malignant tumor that affects the hyaline cartilage. It occurs most often in the femur, spine, pelvis, ribs, or scapulae.

Beyond the dictionary

Tumor terminology

The word for a bone tumor begins with the common root *osteo-*, meaning *bone*. *Chondr-* is a root meaning *cartilage*, and *-oma* is a suffix meaning *tumor*. **Osteochondroma** is thus *a tumor of the bone and cartilage.*

Treatments

Noninvasive treatment options for bone and joint injuries includes:
- a **splint**, which is a removable appliance that immobilizes, restrains, and supports the injured or displaced body part
- a **cast**, which is a rigid dressing that's placed around an injured body part to support, immobilize, and protect it and promote healing
- a **closed reduction**, which is a manual alignment of a fracture and may precede the application of a cast

- **traction**, which may use a system of weights and pulleys to immobilize and relieve pressure on a fractured bone to maintain proper position and to facilitate healing.

Bones—a fixation on bones

Some fractures require **internal fixation** devices, such as pins, plates, screws, wires, and surgical cement, to stabilize the bone fragments. An **open reduction with internal fixation** is a surgical procedure that allows the surgeon to directly align the fractured bone and apply internal fixation devices. (See *Let's reduce that reduction.*)

Cut to the bone

These terms relate to invasive treatment of joints and bones:
- **Arthrectomy** is the excision of a joint.
- In arthrodesis, a bone graft (typically from the patient's iliac crest) is used to fuse joint surfaces; it's called **spondylosyndesis** when this procedure is applied to the vertebrae. (See *Spelling out* spondylosyndesis.)
- **Arthroplasty** surgically reconstructs a joint.
- **Bone marrow transplant** involves I.V. administration of marrow aspirated from the donor's bones to a recipient.
- Chemonucleolysis is when a drug is injected into a herniated disk that dissolves the **nucleus pulposus**, the pulpy, semifluid center of the disk.
- Costectomy is the surgical excision of a rib.
- Diskectomy is the excision of an intervertebral disk.
- **Hip replacement** is when a diseased hip joint is replaced with a **prosthesis** (artificial substitute for a missing body part).
- **Laminectomy** is the surgical excision of the lamina.
- **Laminotomy** is the transection of a vertebral lamina.
- Ostectomy is the excision of a bone or part of a bone.
- **Osteotomy** is an incision or transection of a bone.
- **Sternotomy** is a cut made through the sternum.

The real world

Let's reduce that reduction

In the real world, you may hear people refer to open reduction with internal fixation as an "ORIF."

Beyond the dictionary

Spelling out *spondylosyndesis*

Spondylo- comes from the Greek word ***spondylos***, which means *vertebra*; ***syndesis*** is the Greek word that means *binding together*. Therefore, **spondylosyndesis** is the *binding together of the spine*, or *spinal fusion*.

Vocabulary builders

At a crossroads

Completing this crossword puzzle will help you bone up on your medical vocabulary. Good luck!

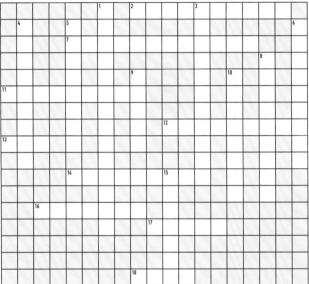

Across

2. Bone's membrane
7. Another name for a joint
11. Dense connective tissue
12. Collarbones
13. Color of marrow that makes blood cells
14. Ends of a long bone
16. Mineral found in bones
17. Bag of synovial fluid
18. Rigid dressing on an extremity

Down

1. Degenerative joint disease
3. Immature bone cells
4. Fingers and toes
5. Jaw bone
6. Main shaft of a long bone
8. Bone cavity
9. Upper leg bone
10. Two bones at top of the head
15. Immovable joints

Finish line

The root **osteo-**, meaning *bone*, forms many words related to bone disorders and diseases. Complete the sentences below by filling in each blank with the appropriate word that begins with **osteo-**.

1. Osteo _____ is a disorder in which bone mass is reduced.
2. A generalized infection of the bone marrow is called osteo _____.
3. A term used to describe the cutting of a bone is osteo _____.
4. A cell that destroys bone tissue is an osteo _____.
5. Osteo _____ is a common tumor that causes spurs at the end of long bones.

Match game

Match each of the musculoskeletal system terms below with its definition.

Terms	Definitions
1. Sternum	A. Production of red blood cells in the bone marrow
2. Tibia	B. Jaw bone
3. Hematopoiesis	C. Tailbone
4. Coccyx	D. Flat, sword-shaped bone that's attached to the collarbones
5. Epiphyses	E. Upper arm bone
6. Humerus	F. Finger or toe bones
7. Femur	G. The largest and strongest of the lower leg bones
8. Osteochondritis	H. The longest and heaviest bone in the body
9. Phalanges	I. Bulbous ends of long bones that provide a large surface for muscle attachment and give stability to joints
10. Mandible	J. Inflammation of bone and cartilage

Talking in circles

Use the clues below to fill in the blanks with the appropriate word. Then unscramble the circled letters to find the answer to the question posed below.

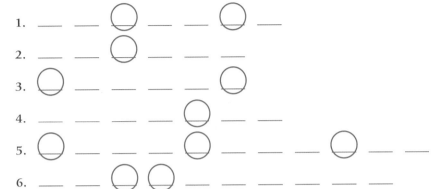

1. ___ ___ ◯ ___ ___ ◯ ___

2. ___ ___ ◯ ___ ___ ___

3. ◯ ___ ___ ___ ___ ◯

4. ___ ___ ___ ___ ◯ ___ ___

5. ◯ ___ ___ ___ ◯ ___ ___ ___ ◯ ___ ___

6. ___ ___ ◯ ◯ ___ ___ ___ ___ ___ ___

1. This is the suture that connects the frontal bone with the parietal bones.
2. This is the cartilage that attaches the sternum to the ribs.
3. This is what the lower arm bone on the thumb side is called.
4. This is the type of joint in the wrists and ankles.
5. This is the term for displacement of a bone from its normal position.
6. This is the term for joint swelling.

Our bones really move freely in this joint. What makes this possible?

Answers

At a crossroads

				¹O	²P	E	R	I	³O	S	T	E	U	M	
	⁴P		⁵M	S											⁶D
	H		⁷A	R	T	I	C	U	L	A	T	I	O	N	I
	A		N	E				E		⁸M					A
	L		D	O	⁹F			O		¹⁰P	E				P
¹¹C	A	R	T	I	L	A	G	E		B	A				H
	N		B	R	M			L		R	U				Y
	G		L	T	U		¹²C	L	A	V	I	C	L	E	S
¹³R	E	D	E	H	R			S		E	L				I
	S			T				T		A					S
			¹⁴E	P	I	P	H	Y	¹⁵S	E	S		A		R
			T					U					L		Y
		¹⁶C	A	L	C	I	U	M		T					
			S			¹⁷B	U	R	S	A					
						R									
						E									
			¹⁸C	A	S	T									

Finish line

Answers: 1. Porosis; 2. Myelitis; 3. Tomy; 4. Clast; 5. Chondroma

Match game

Answers: 1. D; 2. G; 3. A; 4. C; 5. I; 6. E; 7. H; 8. J; 9. F; 10. B

Talking in circles

Answers: 1. Coronal; 2. Costal; 3. Radius; 4. Gliding; 5. Dislocation; 6. Arthredema

Answer to puzzle—Diarthrosis

Suggested references

Renowden, S. A. (2012). Normal anatomy of the spinal cord. *Practical Neurology, 12*(6), 367–370. doi:10.1136/practneurol-2012-000247

Standring, S. A. (2016). *Gray's anatomy: The anatomical basis of clinical practice.* Ipswich, MA: Elsevier Health Sciences.

Chapter 4

Muscular system

Just the facts

In this chapter, you'll learn:

♦ terminology related to the structure and function of the muscular system

♦ terminology needed for physical examination of the muscular system

♦ tests that help diagnose muscular disorders

♦ disorders of the muscular system and their treatments.

Muscle structure and function

A key to learning terminology related to the muscular system is knowing the medical prefix for muscle, *my(o)-*, from the Greek word for muscle, *mys*. Combined with other words, this prefix forms such terms as **myology** (the study of muscles), **myocardium** (heart muscle), and **myositis** (inflammation of voluntary muscle tissues). (See *A close look at* myocardium and *Pronouncing key muscular system terms.*)

More than just heavy lifting

Muscles have three functions:
1. They support the body.
2. They permit movement.
3. They produce body heat.
   They're also an integral part of internal organs, such as the heart, lungs, uterus, and intestines.

Tissue issue

The three major types of muscle in the human body are classified by the tissue they contain:
• **Skeletal** muscles are **voluntary** (controlled by will) muscles that attach to the skeleton and consist of **striated** (in thin bands) tissue. They move body parts and the body as a whole, maintain posture, and implement voluntary and reflex movements. Skeletal muscles also generate body heat. (See *a close look at skeletal muscles,* page 65.)

Beyond the dictionary

A close look at *myocardium*

The Greek word for *muscle* is *myos,* and *cardiac* is the Greek word for *heart.* Therefore, **myocardium** means *heart muscle.*

Pronouncing key muscular system terms

Below is a list of key terms, along with the correct way to pronounce them.

Aspartate aminotransferase	AHS-PAR-TAYT AH-MEE-NOH-TRANS-FUHR-RAYS
Buccinator	BUHK-SUH-NAY-TUHR
Creatine kinase	KREE-UH-TEEN KEYE-NAYS
Dystonia	DIS-TOH-NEE-UH
Epimysium	EP-UH-MISS-EE-UHM
Fasciorrhaphy	FASH-EE-OR -EH-FEE
Gastrocnemius	GAS-TROK-NEE-MEE-UHS
Leiomyosarcoma	LEYE-OH-MEYE-OH-SAR-KOH-MUH
Myasthenia gravis	MEYE-AHS-THEE-NEE-UH GRAH-VUHS
Myokinesimeter	MEYE-OH-KIN-UH-SIM-UH-TER
Myositis purulenta	MEYE-OH-SEYE-TIS PER-UH-LENT-UH
Sarcolemma	SAR-KOH-LEM-UH
Torticollis	TOR-TUH-KOL-LIS
Trapezius	TRAH-PEE-ZEE-UHS

- **Visceral** muscles are **involuntary** (not controlled by will) muscles that contain smooth-muscle tissue. They're found in such organs as the stomach and intestines. (See *Gut reaction.*)
- **Cardiac** muscle is made up of involuntary, striated tissue. It's controlled by the autonomic nervous system and specialized **neuromuscular** (meaning both nerve and muscle) tissue located within the right atrium.

The muscles' makeup

Muscle tissue cells perform specialized activities and vary greatly in size and length. Because they're usually long and slender with a threadlike shape, muscle cells are called fibers.

Connective tissue holds muscle fibers together. Bundles of muscle fibers are enclosed by a fibrous membrane sheath called fascia.

Although muscle cells have the same parts as other cells, several of their structures have special names. A muscle fiber's plasma membrane is called a sarcolemma, and its cytoplasm is called sarcoplasm. (See *Origins of* sarcolemma *and* sarcoplasm.)

Gut reaction

The word **visceral** is derived from the Latin word **viscera**, meaning *internal organs*. **Visceral** also means *intensely emotional* or *instinctive*. Think of a "gut reaction."

Anatomically speaking

A close look at skeletal muscles

Each muscle is classified by the movement it permits. For example, flexors permit the bending of joints, or flexion; abductors permit shortening so that joints can be straightened, or abducted. The illustrations below show some of the body's major muscles.

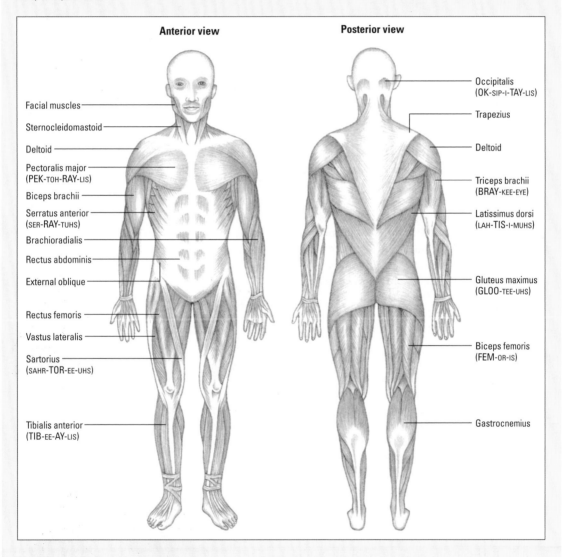

Anterior view

Facial muscles
Sternocleidomastoid
Deltoid
Pectoralis major
(PEK-TOH-RAY-LIS)
Biceps brachii
Serratus anterior
(SER-RAY-TUHS)
Brachioradialis
Rectus abdominis
External oblique
Rectus femoris
Vastus lateralis
Sartorius
(SAHR-TOR-EE-UHS)
Tibialis anterior
(TIB-EE-AY-LIS)

Posterior view

Occipitalis
(OK-SIP-I-TAY-LIS)
Trapezius
Deltoid
Triceps brachii
(BRAY-KEE-EYE)
Latissimus dorsi
(LAH-TIS-I-MUHS)
Gluteus maximus
(GLOO-TEE-UHS)
Biceps femoris
(FEM-OR-IS)
Gastrocnemius

Beyond the dictionary

Origins of *sarcolemma* and *sarcoplasm*

A muscle fiber's plasma membrane is called a **sarcolemma**, and its cytoplasm is called **sarcoplasm**. In Latin, *sarco* means *flesh*. Both **sarcolemma** and **sarcoplasm** share this Latin root.

The word **ligament** comes from the Latin *ligare*, which means to tie or bind—and that is exactly what ligaments do to your bones.

The ties that bind us

Tendons are bands of fibrous connective tissue that attach muscles to the **periosteum**, a fibrous membrane that covers the bone. Tendons enable bones to move when skeletal muscles contract, creating energy through the release of the enzyme **adenosine triphosphate** from the cells.

Ligaments are dense, strong, flexible bands of fibrous connective tissue that bind bones to other bones. Ligaments in the skeletal muscle system connect the **articular** (relating to a joint) ends of bones. They provide stability and can either limit or facilitate movement. Deeper inside the body, ligaments support the organs.

Most skeletal muscles are attached to bones either directly or indirectly. In a direct attachment, the **epimysium** (fibrous sheath around a muscle) of the muscle fuses to the **periosteum** of the bone. In an indirect attachment, the fascia extends past the muscle as a tendon or **aponeurosis** (deeply set fascia), which in turn attaches to the bone. In the human body, indirect attachments outnumber direct attachments.

Remember: An **antagonist** is one who opposes another...

Putting it in motion

Muscles depend on one another for movement; a muscle rarely acts on its own. **Prime movers** are muscles that actively produce a movement. **Antagonists** are muscles that oppose the prime movers and relax as the prime movers contract. **Synergists** contract along with the prime movers and help execute the movement or provide stability.

During contraction, one of the bones to which the muscle is attached stays stationary while the other is pulled in the opposite direction. The point where the muscle attaches to the stationary bone is called the **origin**; the point where it attaches to the more moveable bone, the **insertion**. The origin usually lies on the **proximal** (nearest to) end of the bone; the insertion, on the **distal** (farthest away) end.

...and **synergy** means working together.

Key muscles

The name of a skeletal muscle may come from its location, action, size, shape, attachment points, number of divisions, or direction of fibers. (See *Muscle structure*, below.)

Anatomically speaking

Muscle structure

Each muscle contains cell groups called *muscle fibers* that extend the length of the muscle. A sheath of connective tissues—called the **perimysium**—binds the fibers into a bundle, or **fasciculus**.

A strong sheath

A stronger sheath, the **epimysium**, binds the fasciculi together to form the fleshy part of the muscle. Beyond the muscle, the epimysium becomes a tendon.

Fine fibers

Each muscle fiber is surrounded by a plasma membrane called the **sarcolemma**. Within the **sarcoplasm** (or cytoplasm) of the muscle fiber lie tiny myofibrils. Arranged lengthwise, myofibrils contain still finer fibers, called *thick fibers* and *thin fibers*.

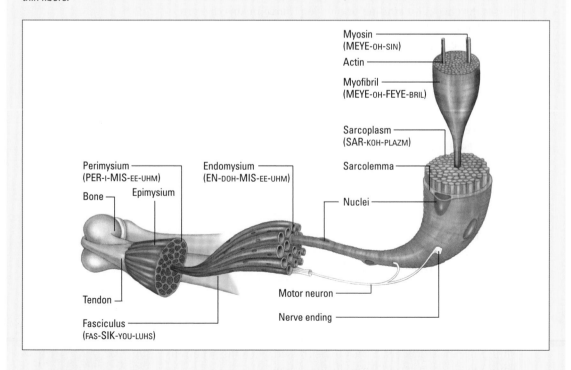

Scalp muscles

The top of the head contains no muscles but has a broad, flat tendon called the **epicranial aponeurosis** that connects to three nearby muscle groups. (See *Dissecting* epicranial aponeurosis.)

- The **occipitofrontal group** houses both the **occipitalis** muscle, which pulls the scalp backward, and the frontalis muscle, which pulls it forward. Raising the eyebrows and wrinkling the forehead use the frontalis muscle.
- The **temporoparietal group** includes the **temporalis** muscle, which tightens the scalp and moves the ears forward.
- The **auricular group** contains three muscles (the **anterior**, **superior**, and **posterior**), which move the ear forward, upward, and backward.

Facial muscles

Facial expressions, such as a smile, frown, or look of surprise, depend on specialized muscles.

Smile later, buccinator

The **buccinator** muscle, also called the **trumpeter** muscle, compresses the cheeks for smiling or blowing (*bucca* means *cheek* in Latin). The corrugator **supercilii** draws the eyebrows together in a frown (*corrugatus* means *wrinkled*, as in a corrugated box). When the eyes widen in surprise, the **orbicularis oculi** (*orbit* means *around* and *ocul* means *eye*) moves the eyelids.

Chew on this

The **masseters** are the chewing muscles (*masticate* means *chew*), and the pterygoids open and close the mouth. The prefix *pteryx-* means *wing* and describes the shape of these muscles. (See *Saying* pterygoid isn't p-terribly difficult, page 69.)

Neck and shoulder muscles

Sternocleidomastoid **muscles** are paired muscles on either side of the neck that allow the head to move. This name combines the muscles' origins in the **sternum** and **clavicle** with their insertion point in the **mastoid process** of the temporal bone.

No shrugging it off

The **trapezius** muscle on the back of the neck raises and lowers (shrugging) the shoulders. Arms can be crossed when the **pectoralis major** muscle adducts and flexes the upper arm.

Beyond the dictionary

Dissecting epicranial aponeurosis

Epicranial aponeurosis looks intimidating until you break it down. In Greek, *epi* means *upon*, *kranion* means *skull*, *apo* means *away*, and *neuron* means *tendon*. Epicranial aponeurosis is a fibrous membrane that covers the **cranium**, or skull, between the occipital and frontal muscles of the scalp.

When you see my cheeks (or *buccae*, in Latin) go up in a smile, you know I'm using my buccinator muscles!

Beyond the dictionary

Saying *pterygoid* isn't p-terribly difficult

English doesn't have a sound for the consonant cluster **pt** at the beginning of a word. **Pterygoid** is derived from the Greek word for *wing*, **pteryx**. When **pt** is pronounced in English, the **p** is simply silent, as it is when you say the name of the "winged" dinosaur, the pterodactyl. Therefore, **pterygoid** is pronounced TEHR-ɪн-ɢoʏᴅ.

Thorax muscles

The **diaphragm**, a dome-shaped muscle located in the chest, flattens during inspiration to increase the size and volume of the thoracic cavity. This allows air to enter the lungs.

Now for a little ribbing

The **external intercostal** (*costa* means *rib* in Latin) muscles lift the ribs during breathing, and the **internal intercostals** lower them. The use of these muscles is most noticeable when a person is out of breath.

Abdominal muscles

Muscles in the abdominal cavity form three layers, the **external oblique** (the outermost), the **internal oblique** (the middle), and the **transversus abdominis** (the innermost), with fibers running in different directions.

A muscular girdle

The three layers form a strong "girdle" of muscle that protects and supports the internal organs. These muscles contract during childbirth, defecation, coughing, and sneezing. The **rectus abdominis** muscle runs down the midline of the abdomen and helps flex the spinal column as well as support the abdomen.

Arm and hand muscles

Several important muscles contribute to the movement of the arms and hands:
- **triceps brachii**, which extends the lower arm
- **brachialis**, which flexes the lower arm

The diaphragm flattens during inspiration to increase the size and volume of the thoracic cavity.

The prefix **brachi-** comes from the Latin word that means *arm*, **brachium**, from which we also get the word *embrace*!

- **biceps brachii**, which flexes the lower arm and **supinates** (turns upward) it along with the hand
- **pronator teres**, which flexes and pronates (rotates the forearm so that the palm of the hand faces downward) the lower arm.

It's all in the wrist

Many small muscles work together to flex and extend the wrists, hands, and fingers. Here are a few examples:
- **Flexor** muscles bend the fingers.
- **Lumbrical** muscles allow fine movements of the hands.
- The **flexor carpi radialis** and the **flexor carpi ulnaris** both flex and adduct the wrist joints.

Pelvic floor muscles

A muscular "floor" called the **perineum** supports the pelvic organs and protects the diamond-shaped pelvic opening. The perineum occupies the space between the anus and vagina in females and the anus and scrotum in males.

The **levator ani** muscle and the **ischiococcygeus** and **sacrococcygeus** muscles support the pelvic organs and assist with childbirth and defecation. (See *How do I say coccygeus?*.) The **sphincter ani** muscle keeps the anus closed.

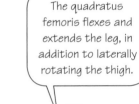

The quadratus femoris flexes and extends the leg, in addition to laterally rotating the thigh.

Thigh and upper leg muscles

Three groups of muscles affect movement in the thigh and upper leg area.

The first group includes those that cross the front of the hip:
- The **internal obturator** laterally rotates the thigh and extends and abducts the thigh when it's flexed.
- The **external obturator**, along with both the **superior** and **inferior gemellus**, laterally rotates the thigh as well.

Pump up your pronunciation

How do I say *coccygeus?*

Coccygeus is pronounced COCK-SIHJ-EE-UHS. It's derived from *coccyx*, the Greek name for the *cuckoo*, whose bill was thought to have a similar shape to the small bone (henceforth termed the **coccyx**) at the base of the spinal cord in the human body.

- The **piriformis** laterally abducts, rotates, and extends the thigh.
- The **quadratus femoris** flexes and extends the leg in addition to laterally rotating the thigh.

Bringing up the rear

The second group consists of the gluteals (from the Greek word *gloutos*, which means *buttocks*). The **gluteus minimus** and **medius** abduct and rotate the thigh while the **gluteus maximus** extends and rotates the thigh.

Adduction is the function

The third group, the **adductors**, includes the powerful **longus**, **brevis**, and **magnus** muscles, which draw back the thigh after abduction. The gracilis flexes and adducts the leg and also adducts the thigh.

The **sartorius muscle** gets its name from the Latin word **sartor**, which means *tailor*.

Lower leg muscles

Two groups of muscles move the lower leg. The first, the **quadriceps femoris**, includes the **vastus lateralis**, **medialis**, and **intermedius**—all of which work to extend the leg—and the **rectus femoris**, which flexes the thigh and extends the leg. (See *Quads*.)

The second group of muscles passes behind the thigh, and their tendons form the **hamstrings**, from which the group takes its name. The **semimembranosus** and **semitendinosus** extend the thigh, and the **biceps femoris** helps to both extend the thigh and flex the leg.

Tailor made

Other lower leg muscles include the **gastrocnemius** and the sartorius. The gastrocnemius flexes the leg and extends the foot. It's commonly called the **calf muscle** (the **Achilles tendon** attaches to this muscle). The sartorius flexes and adducts the leg into the "tailor" position.

The real world

Quads

While working out in the gym, you often hear the word **quads** applied to the thigh muscles as a whole. In medical terminology, it's important to know the four muscles that make up the **quadriceps femoris**—the **rectus femoris**, **vastus lateralis**, **vastus medialis**, and **vastus intermedius**.

Foot muscles

Extrinsic foot muscles are located in the leg but pull on tendons that move bones in the ankle and foot. These muscles allow **dorsiflexion** (upward turning of the foot or toes), **plantar flexion** (movement toward the toes), **inversion** (turning inward movement), and **eversion** (turning outward movement) of the foot.

Intrinsic foot muscles are located within the foot and produce flexion, extension, abduction, and adduction of the toes. The most important muscles of the foot include:

- **soleus**, which extends and rotates the foot (the Latin word for *sun* is *sol*; just as the sun causes the earth to rotate, this muscle causes the foot to rotate)
- **tibialis anterior**, which elevates and flexes the foot
- **tibialis posterior**, which extends the foot and turns it inward
- **peroneus longus**, which extends and abducts the foot and turns it outward
- **peroneus brevis**, which extends and abducts the foot
- **peroneus tertius**, which flexes the foot and turns it outward.

Memory jogger

The acronym **TIPS** will keep you on your toes and help you remember the muscles of the foot:

TIbialis anterior and posterior

Peroneus longus, brevis, and tertius

Soleus.

Physical examination terms

When a patient seeks medical help for a muscular problem, it's usually because of a physical mishap or a chronic ache.

Common complaints

The term myopathy refers to any disease of the skeletal muscles. Below are other terms you may need to know when examining a patient with a myopathic condition or other muscular complaints:

- Myalgia is muscle pain or tenderness. For instance, an athlete with a patient with a sore pitching shoulder might have myalgia.
- **Myoclonus** is a spasm of a muscle.
- Myotasis is a continual stretching of a muscle, commonly referred to as a **pulled muscle.**
- Myotonia is chronic muscle contraction or irritability. Myotonia may be confirmed if there's isometric **contraction**—the muscle length remains the same as the tension on it increases.
- Tenalgia is a pain in the tendon, such as tennis elbow.
- **Tetany** is hyperexcitability of nerves and muscles, which results from lessened concentration of extracellular ionized calcium.
- A **tic** is a small muscle spasm.

The suffix *-algia* comes from the Greek and means *pain*. So **tenalgia** means *pain in the tendon*. I could tell you that!

Common observations

Below are some terms that are useful while performing a physical examination:

- Myelomalacia is muscle softening, which may indicate myoatrophy (muscle wasting) or **myonecrosis** (death of muscle tissue fibers).
- **Myosclerosis** is muscle hardening.

Action reaction

- Myobradia is the term used to describe the slow reaction of a muscle to prodding. It may be caused by tissue wasting or death.
- **Myospasm** is the term used to describe muscle convulsions that occur with prodding. It may signal an inflammation of the voluntary muscle tissue, or myositis.

Diagnostic tests

Three types of samples—blood, urine, and tissue—may be taken to diagnose muscle disorders. Scanners and other equipment are commonly necessary as well. Below are some of the terms, tests, and tools that may be used.

Physical tests

Three tests are commonly used to assess a patient for carpal tunnel syndrome.

Tingle is the signal

Tinel's sign—a tingling over the median nerve on light percussion—is seen in cases of carpal tunnel syndrome.

Flex test

Phalen's maneuver is used to reproduce the symptoms of carpal tunnel syndrome. In this test, the patient extends his forearms horizontally while completely flexing the wrists for 1 minute. If the patient experiences tingling, numbness, or pain, carpal tunnel syndrome may be present.

> If Phalen's maneuver produces pain, carpal tunnel syndrome is present.

Compression impression

A **compression test** can be used to support a diagnosis of carpal tunnel syndrome. A blood pressure cuff is placed on the forearm and inflated above the patient's systolic blood pressure for 1 to 2 minutes.

If carpal tunnel syndrome is present, this intervention produces paresthesia along the distribution of the median nerve.

The presence of myoglobin in a urine sample indicates extensive muscle damage.

Blood tests

Enzyme levels or the presence of acids in the bloodstream can help diagnose muscular disease. Blood tests are named after the enzyme or acid they're designed to detect:
- Elevated levels of **alanine aminotransferase**, a skeletal enzyme, may indicate muscle tissue damage.
- Elevated levels of **aspartate aminotransferase**, another skeletal muscle enzyme, may indicate muscle damage from muscle trauma or muscular dystrophy.
- **Creatine** kinase, an isoenzyme found in both skeletal and cardiac muscle, may indicate damage from muscle trauma, I.M. injections, myocardial infarction, or muscular dystrophy.

Urine tests

A **myoglobin** urine test is used to detect the presence of myoglobin in urine. Myoglobin is normally found in the heart and skeletal muscle and, when found in the urine, indicates extensive muscle damage.

Muscle biopsy

In **muscle biopsy**, a needle or incision biopsy is used to extract a specimen of muscle tissue for examination. This microscopic evaluation of muscle tissue samples is commonly required for an accurate diagnosis of muscular disorders.

Tools of the trade

An accurate "image" of the myopathy, which is possible with the use of various types of equipment, may aid in diagnosis.

The equipment

In **computed tomography scanning**, multiple X-ray beams pass through the body at different angles, striking radiation detectors that produce electrical impulses. A computer converts the impulses into digital information that detects tumors in muscle tissue. (See *CAT scan*.)

The real world

CAT scan

The **computed tomography scan** was originally known as the **computerized axial tomography scan**. That's why in practice you'll still hear this test referred to as a **CAT scan**.

An **electromyogram** records the electrical activity of skeletal muscles through surface or needle electrodes. It's used to diagnose neuromuscular disorders and pinpoint motor nerve lesions.

In **magnetic resonance imaging**, a powerful magnetic field and radiofrequency energy are used to produce images based on the hydrogen content of body tissues. Also called **nuclear magnetic resonance**, it's used to diagnose muscle disease.

A **myokinesimeter** measures the muscular contractions that result from stimulating the muscles with electrical current.

Disorders

A wide range of factors, including trauma, heredity, autoimmunity, and the normal aging process, can lead to muscle disorders. This section covers terms associated with muscular disorders.

Muscle conditions

Below are terms for common muscle conditions:
- **Atrophy** is the wasting of muscle.
- **Contractures**, the abnormal flexion and fixation of joints, are typically caused by muscle atrophy and may be permanent.
- **Footdrop** is the inability to maintain the foot in a normal, flexed position (dragging of the foot). This complication is commonly associated with trauma or paralysis.
- A **shin splint** is a strain of the long flexor muscle of the toes that's caused by strenuous athletic activity.
- **Spastic paralysis** is the involuntary contraction of a muscle with an associated loss of function.
- A **sprain** is a complete or incomplete tear in the supporting ligaments surrounding a joint.
- A **strain** is an injury to a muscle or tendinous attachment.

Tumors and lesions

Below are terms for muscle tumors and lesions:
- A **fibroid tumor**, or **leiomyoma**, is a **benign** (noncancerous) tumor found in smooth muscle. It's most common in the uterus.
- A **leiomyosarcoma** is a malignant tumor of smooth muscle that's usually found in the uterus.

- A **myoblastoma** is a benign lesion of soft tissue.
- A **myofibroma** is a benign tumor containing muscular and fibrous tissue.
- A **myosarcoma** is a malignant tumor derived from muscle tissue.
- A **rhabdomyoma** is a benign tumor of striated muscle.
- A **rhabdomyosarcoma** is a highly malignant tumor that originates from striated muscle cells.

Infection and inflammation

Listed here are terms for muscular infection and inflammation:
- **Bursitis** is a painful inflammation of one or more of the **bursae**, closed sacs that cushion muscles and tendons over bony prominences such as the knee.
- **Dermatomyositis** is a connective tissue disease that's marked by itching and skin inflammation in addition to tenderness and weakness of muscles.
- **Epicondylitis**, also known as **tennis elbow**, is an inflammation of tendons in the forearm at their attachment to the humerus.
- **Fasciitis** is inflammation of the fasciae.
- **Myocellulitis** is inflammation of the cellular tissue within a muscle.
- **Myofibrosis** is an overgrowth of fibrous tissue that replaces muscle tissue.
- **Myositis purulenta** is any bacterial infection of the muscle tissue that may result in pus formation and, ultimately, gangrene.
- **Tendinitis**, a painful inflammation of tendons and their muscle attachments to bone, is commonly caused by trauma, congenital defects, or rheumatic diseases. (See *Understanding the suffix* -itis.)

Epicondylitis anyone?

Beyond the dictionary

Understanding the suffix *-itis*

The suffix *-itis* is derived from Greek and means *the inflammation of*. Anyone who has suffered the burning pain of **tendinitis** (inflammation of the tendons and their attachments to the bone) can confirm the accuracy of this suffix.

Syndromes and diseases

Below are terms for muscular syndromes and diseases:

- An **Achilles tendon contracture** is a shortening of the Achilles tendon. It can cause pain and reduced dorsiflexion.
- **Carpal tunnel syndrome** is a painful disorder of the wrist and hand that results from rapid, repetitive flexion and extension of the wrist.
- **Dupuytren's contracture** is a progressive, painless contracture of the palmar fasciae. It causes the last two fingers to contract toward the palm. (See *Dupuytren's contracture*.)
- **Fibromyalgia syndrome**, the cause of which is unknown, is a chronic disorder that produces pain in the muscles, bones, or joints.
- **Muscular dystrophy** is a group of degenerative genetic diseases characterized by weakness and progressive atrophy of skeletal muscles, with no evidence of involvement of the nervous system.
- Myasthenia **gravis** is an abnormal weakness and fatigability, especially in the muscles of the throat and face. It results from a defect in the conduction of nerve impulses at the myoneural junction.
- **Torticollis** is a neck deformity in which the neck muscles are spastic and shortened, causing the head to bend toward the affected side and the chin to rotate toward the unaffected side.

People who do a lot of typing commonly suffer from carpal tunnel syndrome.

Treatments

Rest is commonly all that's needed to treat muscle conditions. Other common options include immobilizing the muscle with a **sling** (a bandage that supports an injured body part), **splint** (an orthopedic appliance that immobilizes and supports an injured body part), or **cast** (a rigid dressing that's placed around an extremity); undergoing physical therapy; applying cold or hot **compresses** (wet or dry cloths); and medicating with prescription drugs.

Douse the flame

Drug therapy includes nonsteroidal anti-inflammatory drugs to decrease inflammation, muscle relaxants to combat spasticity and relax muscles, and corticosteroids to combat inflammation.

Drain the pain

When inflammation is the problem, as in such conditions as tendinitis and bursitis, fluid is sometimes removed from the joint with a hollow needle. The term for this procedure is **aspiration.**

Free at last

When a muscle compresses a nerve, as in carpal tunnel syndrome, surgery may be required if more conservative treatments fail. In carpal tunnel syndrome, **neurolysis,** the freeing of the nerve fibers, is used to remove the entire carpal tunnel ligament so there's more space for the median nerve to pass through the carpal tunnel.

Heat wave

Short-wave diathermy, in which a current is used to generate heat within the muscle, is used to control pain and decrease muscle spasm.

Rubout

Massage is the methodical use of manipulation, pressure, friction, and kneading to promote circulation, relieve pain, and reduce tension. Massage is used for patients who have restricted movement.

Beyond the dictionary

Dupuytren's contracture

Guillaume Dupuytren (DOO-PWEE-TRAH) (1777 to 1835) was a French surgeon and clinical teacher. He became intrigued by a peculiar form of contracture (the permanent **contraction** of a muscle) that caused the fingers to curl in the hand. After dissection, he discovered the problem was centered in the palmar fasciae.

Vocabulary builders

At a crossroads

Here's a little crossword puzzle to help pump up your mental muscle. Good luck!

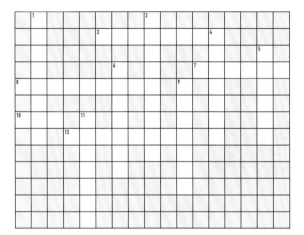

If you've got any muscles left over, pass 'em along.

Across

3. Floor of the pelvis
7. Fibrous membrane sheath
8. Critical for breathing
10. A muscle twitch
12. Muscles composed of thin bands

Down

1. Inflamed bursae
2. Responsible for attaching bones to each other
4. Muscle pain or tenderness
5. Muscle cell groups
6. Adjective for heart muscles
9. Attaches muscles to the periosteum
11. Reduction in the size of muscles

Finish line

The suffix **-itis** comes from the Greek and means *the inflammation of.* Fill in the blanks below to form the correct muscle disorder.

1. Painful inflammation of tendons is called _____ itis.
2. Painful inflammation of one or more bursae is called _____ itis.
3. Inflammation of the fasciae is called _____ itis.
4. Inflammation of cellular tissue within a muscle is called _____ itis.
5. Inflammation of connective tissue and weakness of muscle is called _____ itis.

O see, can you say?

Sound out each group of pictures and symbols below to reveal a term that was reviewed in the chapter.

1.

2.

3.

4.

Talking in circles

Use the clues below to fill in the blanks with the appropriate word. Then unscramble the circled letters to find the answer to the question posed below.

1. ___ ___ ◯ ___ ___ ___ ___ ___ ___

2. ___ ___ ___ ___ ___ ___ ___ ◯

3. ___ ___ ___ ___ ◯ ___ ___ ___ ___

4. ___ ___ ___ ___ ◯ ___ ___

5. ___ ___ ___ ◯ ___ ___ ___ ___

6. ___ ◯ ___ ___ ___ ___

1. The point where a muscle attaches to a more moveable bone
2. The muscle that creates horizontal wrinkles on the forehead
3. The group of muscles that wiggle the ears
4. The muscle that flexes the lower arm
5. The muscle that allows the leg to cross in the tailor position
6. A paroxysmal muscle spasm

Answers

At a crossroads

	[1]B							[2]L							
	U				[3]P	E	R	I	N	E	U	[4]M			
	R							G				Y	[5]F		
	S					[6]C		A	[7]F	A	S	C	I	A	
[8]D	I	A	P	H	R	A	G	M		[9]T	L		B		
	T					R		E		E		G	E		
[10]T	I	C		[11]A		D		N		N		I	R		
	S		[12]S	T	R	I	A	T	E	D		A	S		
				R		A		S		O					
				O		C				N					
				P						S					
				H											
				Y											

Finish line

Answers: 1. Tendin; 2. Burs; 3. Fasci; 4. Myocellul; 5. Dermatomyos

O see, can you say?

Answers: 1. Trapezius; 2. Gastrocnemius; 3. Buccinator;
4. Leiomyosarcoma

Talking in circles

Answers: 1. Insertion; 2. Frontalis; 3. Auricular; 4. Brachialis;
5. Sartorius; 6. Tetany

Answer to puzzle—Soleus

Suggested references

Netter, F. H. (2014). *Atlas of human anatomy*, Professional edition. Philadelphia, PA: Elsevier Health Sciences.

Standring, S. A. (2016). *Gray's anatomy: The anatomical basis of clinical practice*. Ipswich, MA: Elsevier Health Sciences.

Chapter 5

Integumentary system

Just the facts

In this chapter, you'll learn:

♦ terminology related to the structure and function of the integumentary system

♦ terminology needed for physical examination of the integumentary system

♦ tests that help diagnose disorders of the integumentary system

♦ disorders of the integumentary system and their treatments.

Skin structure and function

The largest body system, the integumentary system includes the skin, or **integument** (from the Latin word *integumentum*, which means *covering*), and its appendages—hair, nails, and certain glands. It covers an area that measures 10 ¾ to 21 ½ ft² and accounts for about 15% of body weight. (See *Pronouncing key integumentary system terms.*)

Skin layers

Two distinct layers of skin, the **epidermis** and **dermis**, lie above a third layer of subcutaneous **fat**.

On the face of it

The outermost layer, the **epidermis**, varies in thickness from less than 0.1 mm on the eyelids to more than 1 mm on the palms and soles. It's composed of **avascular** (without a direct blood supply), **squamous** tissue that's **stratified** (arranged in multiple layers). (See *Squamous tissue revealed*, page 85.)

The **stratum corneum**, the outermost part of the epidermis, consists of cellular membranes and **keratin**, a protein. Langerhans' cells are interspersed among the keratinized cells below the stratum corneum. Epidermal cells are usually shed from the surface as **epidermal dust**.

Dermatology, the study of skin, comes from the Greek words *derma*, which means skin, and *logos*, which means science.

Pronouncing key integumentary system terms

Below is a list of key terms, along with the correct way to pronounce them.

Aphthous stomatitis	AF-THUHS STOH-MUH-TEYE-TIS
Ecchymosis	EK-EE-MO-SIS
Eczema	EK-ZEH-MUH
Erythema	ER-EH-THEE-MUH
Onychomycosis	ON-EH-KOH-MEYE-KOH-SIS
Petechia	PEH-TEE-KEE-UH
Phthirus pubis	THEYE-RUHS PYOU-BIS
Rosacea	ROH-ZAY-SHEE-UH
Sebaceous	SEE-BAY-SHUHS
Subcutaneous	SUHB-KYOU-TAY-NEE-UHS
Telangiectasis	TEL-AN-JEE-EK-TAY-SIS
Verrucae	VEH-ROO-KEE
Vitiligo	VIT-IH-LEYE-GOH

The word **stratum** comes from the Latin **sternere,** which means to spread out.

Stratum basale, also called the **basal** or **base layer**, produces new cells to replace superficial keratinized cells that are continuously shed or worn away. It also contains specialized skin cells called **melanocytes** that protect the skin by producing and dispersing **melanin** to surrounding epithelial cells. Melanin is a brown pigment that helps filter ultraviolet light. (See *Close-up view of the skin.*)

Digging beneath the surface

The skin's second layer, the **dermis**, also called the **corium**, is an elastic system that contains and supports blood vessels, lymphatic vessels, nerves, and epidermal appendages.

Most of the dermis is made up of extracellular material called **matrix**. Matrix contains connective tissue fibers, including **collagen**, a protein that gives strength to the dermis; **elastin**, which makes the skin pliable; and **reticular fibers**, which bind the collagen and elastin fibers together. These fibers are produced by **dermal fibroblasts**, spindle-shaped connective tissue cells.

Anatomically speaking

Close-up view of the skin

The illustration below can help you visualize the major components of the skin.

Beyond the dictionary

Uncovering the panniculus adiposus

The **panniculus adiposus** is a specialized skin layer that's primarily composed of fat cells. In fact, ***panniculus*** is a Latin term that means *a small piece of cloth or covering,* or *a layer.* **Adipose** means *fat.*

Beyond the dictionary

Squamous tissue revealed

Squamous is derived from the Latin term for the scale of a fish or serpent, ***squama.*** It's used in anatomy to describe thin, flat platelike or scalelike structures—in this case, squamous tissue.

The dermis has two layers:

1. The **papillary dermis** has fingerlike projections (papillae) that nourish epidermal cells. The epidermis lies over these papillae and bulges downward to fill the spaces. A collagenous membrane known as the **basement membrane** separates the epidermis and dermis and holds them together.
2. The **reticular dermis** covers a layer of subcutaneous tissue, the **adipose** or panniculus **adiposus**, that's primarily composed of fat cells. In addition to insulating the body, the reticular dermis provides energy and absorbs mechanical shock. (See *Uncovering the panniculus adiposus.*)

Epidermal appendages

Numerous epidermal appendages occur throughout the skin. They include the hair, nails, sebaceous **glands**, and two types of sweat glands—eccrine and apocrine.

Hair

Hairs are long, slender shafts composed of keratin. At the expanded lower end of each hair is a bulb or root. On its undersurface, the root is indented by a **hair papilla**, a cluster of connective tissue and blood vessels.

A hair-raising experience

Each hair lies within an epithelial-lined sheath called a **hair follicle**. A bundle of smooth-muscle fibers, the **arrector pili**, extends through the dermis and attaches to the base of the follicle. When these muscles contract, hair stands on end.

Nails

Situated over the distal surface of the end of each finger and toe, nails are specialized types of keratin. The **nail plate**, surrounded on three sides by the **nail folds** (or **cuticles**), lies on the **nail bed**. The nail

Put the emphasis on the **p**. The **p**apillary dermis has **p**rojections that **p**ush into and nourish the epidermal cells above it.

plate is formed by the **nail matrix**, which extends proximally about ¼″ (5 mm) beneath the nail fold.

Under the keratin moon

The distal portion of the matrix shows through the nail as a pale crescent-moon-shaped area, called the **lunula**. The translucent nail plate distal to the lunula exposes the nail bed. The **vascular bed** imparts the characteristic pink appearance under the nails. (See *Lunar expedition*.)

The sebaceous glands

Sebaceous glands occur on all parts of the skin except the palms and soles. They are most prominent on the scalp, face, upper torso, and genitalia.

Nature's conditioner

Sebaceous glands produce **sebum**, an oily, lipid substance that helps protect hair and skin. Sebaceous glands secrete sebum into hair follicles via the sebaceous ducts. Sebum then exits through the hair follicles' openings to reach the skin's surface.

The sweat glands

Widely distributed throughout the body, **eccrine glands** produce an odorless, watery fluid with a sodium concentration equal to that of plasma. A duct (pore) from the coiled secretory portion passes through the dermis and epidermis, opening onto the skin surface.

Located chiefly in the axillary and anogenital areas, the **apocrine glands** have a coiled secretory portion that lies deeper in the dermis than that of the eccrine glands. Ducts connect the apocrine glands to the upper portions of the hair follicles.

A puddle under pressure

Eccrine glands in the palms and soles secrete fluid, mainly in response to emotional stress. The other three million eccrine glands respond primarily to thermal stress, effectively regulating temperature.

Apocrine glands begin to function at puberty. They have no known biological function but may be involved with sexual olfactory messages. As bacteria decompose the fluids that these glands produce, body odor occurs.

Function

The integumentary system performs many vital functions, including protection of inner body structures, sensory perception, and regulation of body temperature and blood pressure.

Lunar expedition

The **lunula** gets its name from its crescent-moon shape. *Luna* is the Latin word for *moon*, and the suffix *-ula* indicates *small*. Another word that shares this root is **lunacy**—literally, *moon-sickness*.

Calling Doctor Langerhans

Many medical terms are named after the doctors who first brought attention to them.

Paul Langerhans (1847 to 1888), a German doctor, anatomist, and pathologist, is best known for his research on clusters of pancreatic cells, now known as the **islets of Langerhans**. However, he also identified **Langerhans' cells**, which are specialized cells in the skin that help enhance the body's immune system.

More than just a pretty face

The top layer of the skin protects the body against traumatic injury, noxious chemicals, and bacterial and microorganismal invasion. Langerhans' cells, specialized cells in this layer, enhance the body's immune response by helping process antigens that enter the skin. (See *Calling Doctor Langerhans.*)

Keeping you in touch

Sensory nerve fibers originate in the nerve roots along the spine and terminate in segmental areas of the skin known as **dermatomes**. These nerve fibers carry impulses from the skin to the central nervous system.

An all-weather covering

Abundant nerves, blood vessels, and eccrine glands within the skin's deeper layer aid **thermoregulation**, or control of body temperature. When the skin is too cold, blood vessels constrict, leading to a decrease in blood flow through the skin and conservation of body heat.

When the skin is too hot, small arteries in the second skin layer dilate, increasing blood flow and reducing body heat. If this doesn't adequately lower temperature, the eccrine glands act to increase sweat production, and subsequent evaporation cools the skin.

Pressure cooker

Dermal blood vessels also aid regulation of systemic blood pressure through vasoconstriction.

Other odd jobs

When stimulated by ultraviolet light, the skin synthesizes vitamin D_3 (cholecalciferol). It also excretes sweat through the sweat glands. Sweat contains water, electrolytes, urea, and lactic acid.

Memory jogger

To remember the functions of the skin, think **PPR**:

Perception (sensory)

Protection (of the body)

Regulation (of body temperature and blood pressure).

Physical examination terms

The skin can provide useful information about the body's overall condition. Below are terms associated with a complete skin examination.

Skin color

Decreased hemoglobin level and oxygen in the blood cause changes in skin color. Skin color also responds to changes in the quality and amount of blood circulating through superficial blood vessels.

Blue in the face

Cyanosis is a bluish skin color that's caused by an excess of oxygen-starved hemoglobin molecules in the blood. Pale skin is called **pallor**, and pale, cyanotic skin around the lips is known as **circumoral pallor**.

Seeing red

Ecchymosis is a reddish purple skin discoloration that's caused by hemorrhages in the dermal or intradermal spaces. **Erythema** refers to redness or inflammation of the skin resulting from congestion of the superficial capillaries.

Purpura is purple-red or brown-red discoloration on the skin due to hemorrhage in the tissues. Small (pinpoint) discolored areas are called **petechiae**, whereas large ones are called **ecchymoses**.

Feeling yellow—not mellow

Yellowing of the skin, known as **jaundice**, is caused by elevated bilirubin levels.

Carotenemia is a yellow-orange skin discoloration that's caused by excess levels of **carotene** in the bloodstream.

Cyanosis is Greek to me no longer. **Cyan-** *comes from the Greek word* **kuanos**, *meaning dark blue.*

Skin turgor

Turgor is a condition of normal tension in the skin and reflects the skin's elasticity.

Keeping its shape

Turgor is assessed by gently grasping and pulling up a fold of skin. Normal skin returns to its flat shape within 3 seconds. Abnormal (slow) turgor may be a sign of dehydration or connective tissue disorders. (See Turgor *and its Latin root.*)

Carotene is an enzyme that's also found in carrots. When a person has **carotenemia**, *an excess of carotene in the bloodstream, he turns orange like a carrot.*

Lesions

Allergens, weather, injury, and various diseases can produce **lesions**, or abnormal changes in the skin. Types of lesions include wounds, sores, tumors, and rashes.

First signs of trouble

Primary lesions are the first lesions of an onsetting disease. Below are examples:

- A **bulla** is a fluid-filled lesion, also called a **blister** or **bleb**.
- A **cyst** is a semisolid encapsulated mass that extends deep into the dermis.
- A **macule** is a flat, pigmented area that's less than ⅜″ in diameter; a **freckle** is an example of a macule.

- A **papule** is a firm, raised lesion up to ¼″ in diameter that may be the same color as the skin or may be pigmented.
- A **plaque** is a flat, raised patch on the skin.
- A **pustule** is a lesion that contains pus, which gives it a yellow-white color.
- A **tumor** is an elevated solid lesion larger than ¾″ that extends into the dermal and subcutaneous layers.
- A **vesicle** is a raised, fluid-filled lesion that's less than ¼″ in diameter. Chickenpox produces vesicles.
- A **wheal** is a raised, firm lesion with intense, usually temporary, swelling around the area. **Urticaria**, or hives, are a type of wheal.

As if that wasn't bad enough

A **secondary** lesion results when changes occur in a primary lesion. Below are examples:

- **Atrophy** is thinning of the skin surface that may be caused by a disorder or aging.
- **Crust** is dried **exudate** (drainage) covering an eroded or weeping area of skin.
- An **erosion** is a lesion that's caused by loss of the epidermis.
- **Excoriation** is a linearly scratched or abraded area.
- Fissures are linear cracks in the skin that extend into the dermal layer. Chapped skin causes fissures.
- A **keloid** is a hypertrophied scar.
- **Lichenification** is characterized by thick, roughened skin with exaggerated skin lines.
- **Scales** are thin, dry flakes of shedding skin.
- **Scars** are fibrous tissue caused by trauma, deep inflammation, or a surgical incision.
- An **ulcer** is an epidermal and dermal destruction that may extend into the subcutaneous tissue.

Turgor and its Latin root

Turgid and **turgor** come from the Latin word **turgidus**, which means *swollen*. However, **turgor** refers to the normal tension of the skin, or the lack of excessive swelling.

Urtica is the Latin word for the nettle plant. **Urticaria**, or hives, are temporary lesions that are similar to the ones you get when you accidentally rub up against a nettle.

Diagnostic tests

Many skin conditions are diagnosed on sight, but several studies are used to diagnose skin disorders and systemic problems.

Allergy testing

The **patch test** identifies allergies to such substances as dust, mold, and foods. During this test, paper or gauze that has been saturated with a possible **allergen** (a substance capable of producing an allergic reaction) is applied to the skin. The test result is positive if redness or swelling develops.

Scratching the surface

Another method for detecting allergies is the **scratch test**. This test involves inserting small amounts of possible allergens into scratches on the skin surface and watching for a sensitivity reaction.

Cultures

Gram stains rapidly provide diagnostic information about which organism is causing an infection. A Gram stain separates bacteria into two categories based on cell wall composition. **Gram-positive** organisms retain crystal violet stain after decoloration. **Gram-negative** organisms lose the violet stain but stain red with safranin.

The **Tzanck test** requires smearing vesicular fluid or drainage from an ulcer on a glass slide and then staining the slide with several chemicals. Herpes virus infection is confirmed by examining the fluid under a microscope. (See *How do I say* Tzanck?)

A sensitive matter

A **culture** is used to isolate and identify an infectious agent. In a culture, a sample of tissue or fluid is placed in a jellylike medium that provides nutrients for microorganisms. If an organism is present, it may multiply rapidly or may take several weeks to grow.

A **sensitivity** test determines the drug that will best treat an infection. Drugs are added to a cultured sample to see which ones kill the offending organism.

The scratch test involves inserting small amounts of possible allergens into scratches on the skin surface and watching for a sensitivity reaction.

Biopsies and smear tests

A **biopsy** is the removal of tissue for microscopic examination. Below are types of biopsies used for skin disorders:
- A **skin biopsy** is used to test a small piece of tissue from a lesion suspected of malignancy or other disorder.

Pump up your pronunciation

How do I say *Tzanck?*

Named after Arnault Tzanck (1886 to 1954), a Russian dermatologist who worked in Paris, the **Tzanck test** requires smearing vesicular fluid or drainage from an ulcer on a glass slide and then staining the slide with several chemicals. The *t* sound in **Tzanck** is silent as is the *t* sound in **tsar**. Therefore, **Tzanck** is pronounced ZANK.

- In a **shave biopsy**, the lesion is shaved above the skin line, leaving the lower layers of dermis intact.
- In a **punch biopsy**, an oval plug is removed from the center of a lesion.
- An **excision biopsy** may be used to remove an entire lesion, if it's small enough.

A smear campaign

A somewhat less invasive method than biopsy is the **smear test**, in which cells are spread on a slide and studied under a microscope. In the **buccal smear** test, cells are scraped from the inner surface of the cheek to detect hereditary abnormalities.

Tools of the trade

During **phototesting**, small areas of skin are exposed to ultraviolet light to detect photosensitivity (acute sensitivity to light). A **Wood's light** is an ultraviolet light that's used to diagnose **tinea capitis**. Hairs infected by this fungus appear fluorescent under a Wood's light.

Disorders

Skin forms a barrier against the environment and also reflects problems within the body, so it's an easy target for infection, injury, and infestation.

Bacterial infections

Below are some common bacterial infections:

- **Impetigo** is a contagious, superficial skin infection that's usually caused by *Staphylococcus aureus*. Impetigo lesions start as macules and then develop into vesicles that become pustular with a honey-colored crust. When the vesicle breaks, a thick yellow crust forms from the exudate.
- **Cellulitis** is an inflammation of subcutaneous and dermal tissues caused by a bacterial infection. It often appears around a break in the skin, such as an insect bite or a puncture wound. The affected area is red, swollen, and warm. Fever, chills, headache, and tiredness commonly accompany cellulitis.
- **Folliculitis** is a bacterial infection of the hair follicles that's usually caused by *S. aureus*. A **furuncle**, or **boil**, begins deep in the hair follicles. When a boil spreads to surrounding tissue and produces a cluster of furuncles, it's called a **carbuncle**.
- A **stye** is an abscess in the eyelash follicle that's caused by a staphylococcal infection.

Carbuncle means a small live coal in Latin. The burning and glowing of hot coals is an apt image for a carbuncle, which is a cluster of angry, painful boils.

Viral infections

Two common manifestations of viral infections are the sores associated with different types of **herpes** and **warts**.

A not-so-simple(x) infection

The word **herpes**, often used as a singular word, actually refers to a variety of viruses. Below are some common types of herpes:

- **Herpes simplex virus type 1** causes painful cold sores and fever blisters on the skin and mucous membranes. After initial infection, patients are susceptible to recurrent bouts with the virus. Outbreaks are accompanied by burning pain, swelling, redness, and fatigue.
- **Herpes simplex virus type 2**, also known as **genital herpes**, produces lesions in the genital area. Patients complain of flulike signs and symptoms, including headache, fatigue, muscle pain, fever, and loss of appetite. Both herpes simplex types 1 and 2 are caused by contact with an infected lesion.
- **Herpes zoster**, also known as **shingles**, is caused by **varicella-zoster**, the chickenpox virus. Lesions called **spinal ganglia** appear along spinal nerve fibers outside the central nervous system. The virus is dormant until the patient's resistance is low, and then a row of vesicular skin lesions erupts along a spinal nerve pathway, accompanied by severe pain, fever, and weakness. (See *A creeping virus.*)

As common as a toad

Verrucae **(warts)** are common, harmless infections of the skin and mucous membranes. They're caused by the human **papillomavirus** and can be transmitted by direct contact. Diagnosed by their appearance, warts are divided into the following categories:

- **common** (also called **verruca vulgaris**)—rough, elevated wart appearing most commonly on extremities, especially hands and fingers
- **filiform**—stalklike, horny projection commonly occurring around the face and neck
- **flat**—multiple groupings of up to several hundred slightly raised lesions with smooth, flat, or slightly rounded tops
- **genital** (also called **condyloma acuminatum**)—sexually transmitted infection appearing on the penis, scrotum, vulva, and anus
- **periungual**—rough wart appearing around the edges of fingernails and toenails
- **plantar**—appearing as a singular lesion or in large clusters, primarily at pressure points of the feet, with lesions that are slightly elevated or flat.

Beyond the dictionary

A creeping virus

Hippocrates used the term *herpes*, the Greek word for *creeping*, to describe a spreading cutaneous infection. Galen later revived the term during the 2nd century and diagnosed three types of the infection. Until the 18th century, the term was used for a number of conditions, including varieties of eczema and psoriasis. Around this time, English doctor Robert Willan restricted its use to the definition used today.

Parasitic infections

Pediculosis results from the infestation of bloodsucking lice. These lice feed on human blood and lay their eggs, or **nits**, in body hair or clothing fibers. When a louse bites, it injects a toxin into the skin that produces mild irritation and a reddened spot. Repeated bites can lead to serious inflammation. Three types of lice attack humans:

- *Pediculus humanus capitis*, or head louse
- *Pediculus humanus corporis*, or body louse
- *Phthirus pubis*, or pubic louse (see *Crabs*).

The nesting instinct

Scabies, another common parasitic infection, is caused by a female mite that penetrates and burrows into the skin. Under the skin, the mite lays eggs that mature and rise to the surface. A scabies infestation produces intense itching and secondary infections from the excoriation caused by scratching. Wavy, brown, threadlike lines appear on the hands, arms, body folds, and genitals.

Fungal infections

Dermatophytosis is the general name for a fungal infection. Mushrooms, molds, and yeasts are common **fungi** (plural of **fungus**). Fungi are present in the air, soil, and water, but only a few species of fungi cause disease.

One of the most common fungal disorders is **tinea**, or **ringworm**. Each type of tinea is named according to the body part it affects:

- **Tinea barbae** affects the bearded area of the face and neck. This infection produces raised areas that have marked crusting.
- **Tinea capitis** is characterized by small, spreading papules on the scalp that cause patchy hair loss with scaling.
- **Tinea corporis** affects the body and produces lesions with a ring-shaped appearance.
- **Tinea cruris**, commonly called **jock itch**, produces red, raised itchy lesions on the groin and surrounding areas.
- **Tinea pedis** is also called **athlete's foot**. This infection causes scaling and maceration between the toes, severe itching, and pain.
- **Tinea unguium**, also called **onychomycosis**, usually starts at the tip of one or more toenails and produces gradual thickening, discoloration, and crumbling of the nail.

The real world

Crabs

In nonmedical settings, you'll often hear pubic lice called **crabs**. This makes sense figuratively because pubic lice move in a crablike manner. Thus, the term **crabs** has become common slang for cases of sexually transmitted pubic lice.

The red on a baby's bottom

Candidiasis, also called **moniliasis**, is a mild, superficial fungal infection of the skin, nails, or mucous membranes. The patient develops a scaly, reddened papular rash with severe itching and burning. This fungus is often the culprit in diaper rash and vaginal infections. It's diagnosed through skin scrapings.

The white on another set of cheeks

Thrush is a fungal infection of the oral mucous membranes caused by *Candida albicans*. This infection develops most commonly in patients whose defenses are weakened by illness, malnutrition, infection, or prolonged treatment with antibiotics. White patches develop on a red, moist, inflamed surface inside the mouth, usually the inner cheeks. Thrush is accompanied by pain and fever.

Remember to break down seemingly difficult words such as **dermatophytosis**. In Greek, **derma** means skin, **phyto** means plant, and **osis** means disease.

Inflammatory disorders

Different types of dermatitis make up the most common inflammatory skin disorders.

Dermatitis

Superficial skin infections are known as **dermatitis**. Dermatitis can be caused by numerous things, including drugs, plants, chemicals, and food.

Hands off!

Contact dermatitis occurs when direct contact with an irritant causes the epidermis to become inflamed and damaged. Touching such substances as poison ivy, poison oak, detergents, and industrial chemicals can lead to pain, burning, itching, and swelling—signs and symptoms of dermatitis.

Other types of dermatitis include:

- **atopic dermatitis**—a chronic inflammatory response. **Atopic** refers to a tendency to develop allergies, and **dermatitis** is an inflammation of the skin. The most common symptoms are dry, itchy (pruritic) skin and rashes on the face, inside the elbows, on the hands and feet, and behind the knees. Atopic dermatitis is often called **eczema**.
- **exfoliative dermatitis**—a severe chronic inflammation characterized by peeling of the skin
- **localized dermatitis**—a superficial inflammation characterized by redness and widespread erythema and scaling

- **nummular dermatitis**—a chronic form of dermatitis characterized by coin-shaped, pruritic, crusted scales
- **seborrheic dermatitis**—an acute or subacute skin disease that primarily affects the scalp and face and is characterized by dry or moist greasy scales and yellowish crusts
- **stasis dermatitis**—fragility with fibrous changes of the skin that are accompanied by tan pigmentation, patchy redness, and petechiae; typically caused by swelling from impaired venous circulation.

Other inflammatory disorders

Here are some other inflammatory skin disorders, including allergies.

Don't eat that!

Angioedema is characterized by urticaria and edema that occur as an allergic reaction, usually to a certain food. It occurs in the subcutaneous tissues of isolated areas, such as the eyelids, hands, feet, tongue, larynx, GI tract, or lips.

Silvery scales

Psoriasis is a chronic skin disorder, commonly with unknown causes, that's characterized by periods of remission and worsening. Psoriasis usually starts between ages 25 and 30. Lesions appear as reddened papules and plaques covered with silvery scales; they vary widely in severity and location.

To pronounce **psoriasis**, think of the word "sore." The **p** is silent.

Skin tumors

Most skin tumors are **benign** (noncancerous), but they can be a starting point for skin cancer.

An **angioma** is formed by a group of blood vessels that dilate and form a tumorlike mass. A port-wine birthmark is a typical angioma. **Spider angiomas**, also called **telangiectases**, are made up of tiny, dilated veins that spread outward with a spiderlike appearance. (See *Caught in a web*.)

Not so benign...

Basal cell carcinoma is a type of skin cancer arising in the basal cell layer of the epidermis. Commonly found on the face and upper trunk, these tumors are painless and may go unnoticed by the patient.

Squamous cell carcinoma, another form of skin cancer, begins in the epidermis and produces a firm, **nodular** (knot-like) lesion covered with a crust or a central ulceration.

Beyond the dictionary

Caught in a web

The word **telangiectases** derives from Greek. **Tela** is the Greek term for *weblike*, **angi-** is a Greek affix for *vessels*, and **ectasia** is the Greek word for *distended*. Put them all together and you have a good description of **telangiectases**—distended weblike veins.

...and malignant

In **malignant melanoma**, cancer arises from the **melanocytes** (pigment cells) of the skin and its underlying structures. There are three types of malignant melanoma, which are categorized by location and description:

- **Superficial spreading melanoma** arises from an area of chronic irritation and is characterized by irregular colors and margins.
- **Nodular melanoma** grows vertically, invading the dermis and metastasizing early.
- Lentigo **maligna melanoma** arises from a lentigo maligna on an exposed skin surface and features a large lesion with scattered black nodules.

Cutaneous ulcers

An **ulcer** is an open sore. Ulcers on the skin are usually caused by a lack of circulation to a vulnerable area. Ulcers may be **superficial**, caused by local skin irritation, or **deep**, originating in the underlying tissue.

Under pressure

Pressure ulcers are localized areas of cellular death that occur most commonly in the skin and subcutaneous tissue over bony prominences. Increased pressure impairs circulation.

Not in a good flow

Stasis ulcers are caused by chronic **venous stasis** (poor blood flow) due to inefficient or obstructed veins. Prolonged standing in one position and obesity are predisposing factors for stasis ulcers.

> Remember, *ulcer* comes from the Latin word *ulcus*, which means sore.

Burns and cold injury

The skin is an effective protective covering. It can, however, be severely damaged when it comes in contact with excessive heat or cold.

Too hot

A burn is an injury to tissue caused by contact with dry heat (fire), moist heat (steam), electricity, chemicals, lightning, or radiation. Categorized according to depth, burns are referred to as **superficial**, **partial-thickness**, or **full-thickness**. When named according to severity, burns are called **first**, **second**, **third**, or **fourth degree**. (See *Assessing burns.*)

Assessing burns

Assessing a burn means determining the depth of skin and tissue damage. It's traditional to describe burn depth by degrees, although most burns are a combination of different degrees and thickness.

First-degree, or superficial, burn
In a first-degree burn, damage is limited to the epidermis, causing redness and pain. The skin is dry, with no blisters or drainage. A sunburn is a type of first-degree burn.

Second-degree, or partial-thickness, burn
In a second-degree burn, the epidermis and part of the dermis are damaged, producing blisters and mild-to-moderate edema and pain. Large, moist blisters may occur, and the skin is mottled with dull white, tan, pink, or cherry-red areas. Spilling a hot cup of coffee on the skin could produce a second-degree burn.

Third-degree, or full-thickness, burn
In a third-degree burn, the dermis and epidermis are damaged. No blisters appear, but white, brown, or black leathery tissue and thrombosed vessels are visible. Little or no pain accompanies this burn because the nerves are damaged. The skin doesn't blanche with pressure. Contact with hot liquids, flames, chemical, or electricity may cause a third-degree burn.

Fourth-degree burn
In a fourth-degree burn, damage extends through deeply charred subcutaneous tissue to muscle and bone.

Too cold

Cold injury, or **frostbite**, results from overexposure to cold air or water. Upon returning to a warm place, a person with superficial frostbite experiences burning, tingling, numbness, swelling, and a mottled, blue-gray skin color. Deep frostbite causes pain, blisters, tissue death, and gangrene. The skin appears white until it thaws and then appears purplish blue.

Chilblain is a combination of the English word **chill** and the Old English word for *sore*, **blain**.

Other skin disorders

Here are some other common skin disorders:
- **acne**—an inflammatory skin eruption caused by plugged sebaceous glands, resulting in papules and pustules
- **albinism**—an inherited condition of defective melanin production, causing lack of pigmentation to the skin
- **alopecia**—hair loss
- **aphthous stomatitis (canker sores)**—recurring ulcers on the mucous membrane of the mouth, with small, white lesions

Chilblain is a combination of the English word *chill* and the Old English word for *sore*, **blain**.
- **chigger**—the larvae of a mite, which attach to the host's skin, causing severe itching and dermatitis
- **chilblain**—redness, burning, and swelling of the skin caused by exposure to cold, damp conditions

- nevus—a benign birthmark
- rosacea—a chronic skin disease that causes dilated and inflamed surface blood vessels and reddening of the nose and adjoining areas; commonly is accompanied by acne **(acne rosacea)**.
- vitiligo—irregularly shaped patches of lighter or white skin caused by the loss of pigment-producing cells.

Treatments

Treating skin disorders is an example of hands-on health care. Most medicines are applied **topically** (to the affected area only). Surgery is typically performed with only a local anesthetic, and monitoring depends mostly on simple observation.

Drug therapy

Drugs used to treat skin disorders include **local anti-infectives** to treat infection, **topical corticosteroids** to reduce inflammation, **protectants** to prevent skin breakdown, **keratolytics** to loosen thickened layers of skin, **astringents** to shrink tissues, and **emollients** and **demulcents** to soothe the skin.

Laser surgery

The word **laser** stands for "light amplification by the stimulated emission of radiation." The highly focused and intense light of **lasers** is used to treat many types of skin lesions. Performed on an outpatient basis, laser surgery typically spares normal tissue (with the exception of carbon dioxide [CO_2] lasers), promotes healing, and helps prevent postsurgical infection.

Set your lasers on...

Three types of lasers are used in dermatology:

- The blue-green light of **argon lasers** is absorbed by the red pigment in hemoglobin. It coagulates small blood vessels and treats superficial vascular lesions.
- The **CO_2 laser** emits an invisible beam in the far-infrared wavelength; water absorbs this wavelength and converts it to heat energy. This laser helps treat warts and malignancies.
- The **tunable dye laser** is also absorbed by hemoglobin and has successfully treated port-wine stains.

Other surgery

Cryosurgery causes epidermal-dermal separation above the basement membranes, which prevents scarring. In this common dermatologic procedure, the application of extreme cold leads to tissue destruction. It can be performed simply by applying liquid nitrogen to the skin with a cotton-tipped applicator or may involve a complex cryosurgical unit.

Mohs' micrograph surgery involves excising (cutting out) the smallest possible amount of cancerous tissue in a step-by-step manner to determine whether all cancer cells have been removed. This procedure helps prevent cancer recurrence by removing all malignant tissue.

No more childhood scars

Dermabrasion is the removal of superficial scars on the skin using revolving wire brushes or sandpaper. Dermabrasion is typically used to reduce facial scars caused by acne.

I don't know why I'm crying. **Cryosurgery** may sound complicated but it's often just liquid nitrogen applied to the skin with a cotton-tipped applicator.

Skin grafts

Skin grafts cover defects caused by burns, trauma, or surgery. They're used when primary closure of the skin isn't possible or cosmetically acceptable, when the defect is on a weight-bearing surface, when primary closure would interfere with functioning, and when a skin tumor is **excised**.

Types of skin grafts include:
- **split-thickness grafts**, which consist of the epidermis and a small portion of dermis
- **full-thickness grafts**, which include all of the dermis as well as the epidermis
- **composite grafts**, which also include underlying tissues, such as muscle, cartilage, and bone.

The gift of the graft

An **autologous graft**, or **autograft** (*auto-* means *self*), is taken from the patient's own body and is the most successful type of skin graft. A graft from a genetically similar person, such as a twin, is an **isologous graft**, or **isograft** (*iso-* means *alike*).

Patching it up

Biological dressings function like skin grafts to ease pain and prevent infection and fluid loss. However, they're only temporary; eventually, the body rejects them. If the underlying wound hasn't healed, these dressings must be replaced with an autologous graft.

Debridement is borrowed from the French and means *to unbridle*. Originally a medical term, it was first used to describe the cutting of constricting bands—similar to a horse's bridle.

There are four types of biological dressings:

- **Homografts (allografts)**, which are harvested from cadavers, are rejected in 7 to 10 days. They're used to debride wounds, protect new tissue growth, serve as test grafts before skin grafting, and temporarily cover burns. (*Allo* is Greek for *deviating from normal* and *homo* refers to *human beings.*)
- **Heterografts (xenografts)**, grafts harvested from animals (usually pigs), are also rejected after 7 to 10 days. They're used for the same purposes as homografts and are also used to cover exposed tendons and burns that are only slightly contaminated.
- **Amnion**, made from the amnion and chorion membranes (fetal membranes), is used to protect burns and temporarily cover new tissue while awaiting an autograft.
- **Biosynthetic grafts**, which are woven from manmade fibers, are used to cover donor graft sites, protect wounds awaiting autografts, and cover meshed autografts.

Debridement

Debridement is the use of mechanical, chemical, or surgical techniques to remove **necrotic** (dead) tissue from a wound. Although it can be extremely painful, debridement is necessary to prevent infection and promote healing of burns and skin ulcers.

There are three types of debridement:

- **Chemical debridement** involves special wound-cleaning beads or topical medications, which absorb drainage and debris from a wound. These agents also absorb bacteria, reducing the risk of infection.
- **Mechanical debridement** may involve dressings, irrigation, **hydrotherapy** (whirlpool baths), or bedside removal of necrotic tissue. During bedside debridement, dead tissue is scraped off or cut away with a scalpel or scissors.
- **Surgical debridement** requires anesthesia and is usually reserved for burn patients or those with extremely deep or large ulcers.

Therapeutic baths

Also known as **balneotherapy**, baths are used to treat many skin conditions, including psoriasis, eczema, exfoliative dermatitis, and bullous diseases that cause blisters.

The four types of baths commonly used are **antibacterial**, **colloidal**, **emollient**, and **tar**. In addition to promoting relaxation, these baths permit treatment of large areas. Therapeutic baths are limited to 30 minutes because they can cause dry skin, itching, scaling, and fissures. (See *The baths.*)

The baths

There are four types of therapeutic baths:

- **Antibacterial baths** are used to treat infected eczema, dirty ulcerations, and furunculosis. Acetic acid, hexachlorophene, potassium permanganate, and povidone-iodine are commonly used.
- **Colloidal baths** relieve itching and soothe irritated skin. They're indicated for any irritating or oozing skin condition, such as atopic eczema. Oatmeal, starch, and baking soda are used for colloidal baths.
- In **emollient baths**, bath oils and mineral oil are used to clean and hydrate the skin. They're helpful for any dry skin condition.
- In **tar baths**, special bath oils are used with tar or coal tar concentrate to treat scaly skin disorders. This bath loosens scales and relieves itching.

Phototherapy

Used to treat skin conditions such as psoriasis by exposure to ultra-violet radiation, **phototherapy** slows the growth of epidermal cells, most likely by inhibiting the synthesis of deoxyribonucleic acid. Two different ultraviolet light wavelengths are used: ultraviolet A (UVA) is the component of sunlight that tans skin and ultraviolet B is the component that causes sunburn.

Light plus drugs equals...

Photochemotherapy is a treatment in which a drug called **psoralen** is given to the patient to make his skin more sensitive to UVA light. The combination of psoralen with UVA is also known as **PUVA therapy**.

Vocabulary builders

At a crossroads

Hopefully, this is a crossword puzzle that won't get under your skin. Good luck!

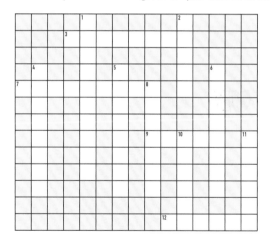

Get ready to toughen up! These puzzles are pretty difficult.

Across

3. An excess of this enzyme turns the skin yellow-orange
7. The outermost layer of skin
9. A fluid-filled lesion
12. Word that describes pale skin

Down

1. The specialized cells in the skin layer that enhance the immune system are named after this doctor
2. The Greek word for *skin*
4. Glands that begin to function at puberty
5. A contagious, superficial skin infection
6. A protein that gives strength to the dermis
8. Caused by female mites
10. Crescent-moon–shaped area on the nail
11. Condition of normal tension in the skin

Finish line

One of the most common fungal disorders is tinea. Each specific type of tinea is named according to the body part it affects. Fill in the blanks to complete each type of this fungal disorder.

1. Tinea _____ affects the bearded area of the face and neck.
2. Tinea _____ produces raised itchy lesions in the groin area.
3. Tinea _____ is also called *athlete's foot.*
4. Tinea _____ usually starts at the tip of one or more of the toenails.
5. Tinea _____ affects the body.
6. Tinea _____ is characterized by small papules on the scalp.

O see, can you say?

Sound out each group of pictures and symbols below to reveal a term that was reviewed in the chapter.

1.

2.

3.

Talking in circles

Use the clues below to fill in the blanks with the appropriate word. Then, unscramble the circled letters to find the answer to the question posed below.

1. ___ ___ ___ ___ ◯ ___ ___ ___ ___ ___

2. ___ ___ ◯ ___ ___ ___ ___ ___

3. ___ ___ ◯ ___ ___ ___ ___ ___ ___ ___

4. ___ ◯ ___ ___ ___ ___ ___

5. ___ ___ ___ ◯ ___ ___ ___ ___ ___

1. Areas of nerve fibers
2. From the Latin, meaning *scalelike*
3. The term used to describe the removal of dead tissue from a wound
4. Hair loss
5. A word from the English word for *chill* and the Old English word for *sore*

You're working at a "blistering" pace. What skin lesion are you likely to get?

Answers

At a crossroads

			¹L				²D			
		³C	A	R	O	T	E	N	E	
			N				R			
	⁴A		G		⁵I		M		⁶C	
⁷E	P	I	D	E	R	M	I	⁸S	A	O
	O		R		P		C		A		L
	C		H		E		A		L	
	R		A		T		⁹B	U	¹⁰L	L	A	¹¹T
	I		N		I		I		U		G		U
	N		S		G		E		N		E		R
	E				O		S		U		N		G
									L				O
								¹²P	A	L	L	O	R

Finish line

Answers: 1. Barbae; 2. Cruris; 3. Pedis; 4. Unguium; 5. Corporis; 6. Capitis

O see, can you say?

Answers: 1. Sebaceous; 2. Verrucae; 3. Petechia

Talking in circles

Answers: 1. Dermatomes; 2. Squamous; 3. Debridement; 4. Alopecia; 5. Chilblain

Answer to puzzle—Bulla

Good goin'. Let's move on to the cardiovascular system without skipping a beat.

Suggested references

Al-Mousawi, A., Suman, O., & Herndon, D. (2012). Teamwork for total burn care: Burn centers and multidisciplinary burn teams. In D. Herndon (Ed.), *Total burn care* (pp. 9–15). Beijing, China: Saunders Elsevier.

Castelluccio, D. (2012). Implementing AORN recommended practices for laser safety. *AORN Journal, 95*(5), 612–627. doi:10.1016/j.aorn.2012.03.001.

Cohen, B., & DePetris, A. (2014). *Medical terminology: An illustrated guide.* Philadelphia, PA: Lippincott, Williams & Wilkins.

Ehrlich, A., & Schroeder, C. (2013). *Medical terminology for health professions.* Clifton Park, NY: Delmar Cengage Learning.

Gylys, B. A., & Maters, R. M. (2010). *Medical terminology simplified: A programmed learning approach by body system* (4th Ed.). Philadelphia, PA: F. A. Davis.

Hutton, A. (2016). *An introduction to medical terminology for health care* (5th ed.). London: Churchill Livingstone.

National Pressure Ulcer Advisory Panel & European Pressure Ulcer Advisory Panel. (2009). Pressure ulcer treatment recommendations. In *Prevention and treatment of pressure ulcers: Clinical practice guideline* (pp. 51–120). Washington, DC: National Pressure Ulcer Advisory Panel.

Stanfield, P., Hui, Y., & Cross, N. (2015). *Essential medical terminology.* Burlington, ON: Jones Bartlett.

Chapter 6

Cardiovascular system

Just the facts

In this chapter, you'll learn:

◆ terminology related to the structure and function of the cardiovascular system

◆ terminology needed for physical examination of the cardiovascular system

◆ tests that help diagnose cardiovascular disorders

◆ disorders of the cardiovascular system and their treatments.

Heart structure and function

A key to learning terminology related to the cardiovascular system is knowing the medical word for *heart:* it's the Latin word ***cardium,*** borrowed from the Greek word ***kardia.*** Cardium is often combined with other words in the forms ***cardi*** or ***cardio.*** Some examples include *cardiology, electrocardiogram, cardiogenic,* and *tachycardia.* (See Cardiac *versus* heart and *Pronouncing key cardiovascular system terms.*)

The heart's protector

The heart is protected by a thin sac called the pericardium. *Peri-* is a Greek prefix that means *around.* The pericardium has an inner, or **visceral,** layer that forms the epicardium and an outer, or **parietal,** layer.

A three-layered heart

The heart wall is composed of three layers. The outer layer is the **epicardium.** *Epi-* is a Greek prefix that means *on or above.* The myocardium is the heart muscle itself, and the endocardium is the innermost layer, which lines the heart's chambers and covers its valves. *Endo-* is a Greek prefix that means *within.*

Beyond the dictionary

Cardiac versus *heart*

The word **cardiac** is nearly as familiar to most English-speaking people as the word **heart.** Because Greek and Latin were the primary languages of universities up until the 1900s, terms from those languages were adopted for scientific use. Some of those terms, like **cardiac,** have migrated into ordinary English speech as well.

Pronouncing key cardiovascular system terms

Below is a list of key terms, along with the correct ways to pronounce them.

Aneurysm	AN-you-RIZM
Angina	AN-JEYE-NUH
Arrhythmia	AH-RITH-MEE-UH
Arteriosclerosis	AR-TEER-EE-OH-SKLER-OH-SIS
Coarctation	KOH-ARK-TAY-SHUHN
Defibrillation	DEE-FIB-RUH-LAY-SHUHN
Diuretic	DEYE-YUH-REH-TIK
Electrophysiologic	E-LEK-TROH-FIZZ-EE-OH-LOJ-IK
Ischemia	IS-KEE-MEE-UH
Paroxysmal atrial tachycardia	PAR-OK-SIZZ-MUHL AY-TREE-UHL TAK-EH-KAR-DEE-UH
Pericardiocentesis	PER-UH-KAR-DEE-OH-SEN-TEE-SIS
Prinzmetal's angina	PRINTS-MET-UHL AN-JEYE-NUH
Sphygmomanometer	SFIG-MOH-MAHN-OM-UH-TER
Thrombophlebitis	THROM-BOH-FLEH-BEYE-TIS

Welcome to my chambers

The heart consists of four chambers. Each of the two upper chambers is called an **atrium** (plural: **atria**). The atria are thin-walled chambers that serve as reservoirs for blood. Each atrium is connected by its own valve to a chamber below it. The two lower chambers are called **ventricles** (also called **ventriculi**). The ventricles have thick walls and are responsible for pumping blood throughout the body. (See *Why the atria are called* atria.)

Blood's path

Blood is carried into the heart through several major vessels, all of which empty into either the **superior vena cava** or **inferior vena cava** (plural: **venae cavae**). The superior vena cava carries blood from the upper body to the right atrium; it's called **superior** because that

Why the atria are called *atria*

It's fitting that the upper chambers of the heart are called **atria** because, in a Roman house, the atrium was an entrance where a person was greeted before moving into other rooms, also referred to as a central court. The atria are the first chambers in the heart to receive blood before it empties into the ventricles and is pumped throughout the body.

And those ventricles?
The word **ventricle** derives from the Latin word *ventriculus*, which means *little stomach* and refers to any small cavity of the body. The hollow part of the ventricle allows for blood to fill the chamber and then be pumped to the lungs or the rest of the body. There are two ventricles in the heart and four in the brain, each with their own specific functions.

How do I say *vena cava?*

In the term **vena cava,** the first word looks like the word **vein,** and that's exactly what it means. It's pronounced VEE-NAH. The second word is pronounced with a long first *a* and *a* short final *a* sound, CAY-VAH. The plural **venae cavae,** pronounced VEE-NAY KAH-VAY, refers to both veins.

Why call it the aorta?

Aorta means *that which is hung.* Because of the arching curve in the aorta as it exits the heart and its subsequent descent into the body, it looks something like a modern clothes hanger. Apparently, Aristotle had a similar notion; he was the first to apply the name to this artery.

means *near the top.* **Inferior** means *situated below,* and the inferior vena cava carries blood from the lower body to the right atrium. (See *How do I say* vena cava?)

Through the pulmonary artery and into the lungs

Blood in the right atrium empties into the right ventricle mostly by gravity. When the ventricle contracts, the blood is ejected into the **pulmonary artery** (called such because *pulmon* is the Latin word for *lung*). The blood is pushed through the pulmonary arteries to the lungs. When comparing arteries and veins, veins return blood to the heart, and arteries carry blood away from the heart. The pulmonary arteries are the only arteries to carry deoxygenated blood away to the lungs.

The final trip

From the lungs, blood travels to the left atrium through the **pulmonary veins,** as veins return blood to the heart. The left atrium empties blood into the left ventricle. The left ventricle pumps the blood into the **aorta** and, from there, it travels throughout the body. (See *Why call it the* aorta?)

The heart's valves

The heart contains two **atrioventricular (AV)** valves (the tricuspid and mitral) and two **semilunar** valves (the pulmonic and aortic). The tricuspid valve separates the right atrium from the right ventricle. It has three flaps or cusps.

The **pulmonic** valve separates the right ventricle from the pulmonary artery.

The **mitral** valve separates the left atrium from the left ventricle. It has two flaps or cusps and is also known as the **bicuspid** valve. (See *Inside the heart.*)

Inside the heart

This illustration shows a cross-sectional view of the structures and blood flow of the heart and major blood vessels.

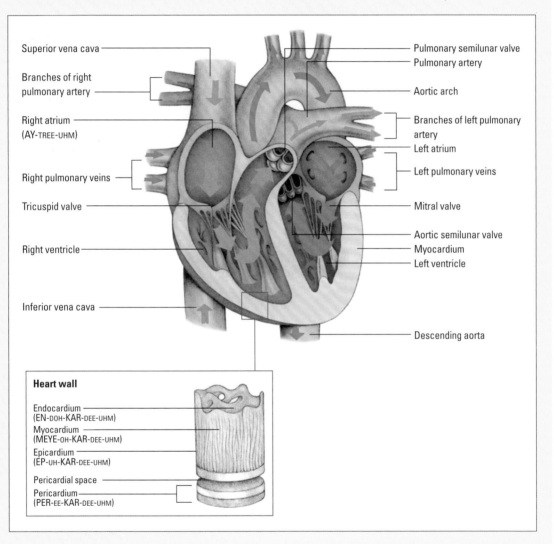

Superior vena cava

Branches of right pulmonary artery

Right atrium (AY-TREE-UHM)

Right pulmonary veins

Tricuspid valve

Right ventricle

Inferior vena cava

Pulmonary semilunar valve

Pulmonary artery

Aortic arch

Branches of left pulmonary artery

Left atrium

Left pulmonary veins

Mitral valve

Aortic semilunar valve

Myocardium

Left ventricle

Descending aorta

Heart wall

Endocardium (EN-DOH-KAR-DEE-UHM)

Myocardium (MEYE-OH-KAR-DEE-UHM)

Epicardium (EP-UH-KAR-DEE-UHM)

Pericardial space

Pericardium (PER-EE-KAR-DEE-UHM)

The heart's rhythm

Contractions of the heart occur in a rhythm—the cardiac cycle—and are regulated by impulses that normally begin at the **sinoatrial (SA) node,** the heart's pacemaker. The impulses are conducted from there through the **AV node,** down through the **AV bundle,** or the **bundle of His** (pronounced HIHS), and through the **Purkinje fibers,** where the impulse stimulates ventricular contraction. (See *What's a Purkinje?*)

For every opposite action

The autonomic nervous system has two divisions that have opposite actions on the heart. The **parasympathetic** division acts on the SA and AV nodes. This division slows heart rate, reduces impulse conduction, and dilates coronary arteries.

The **sympathetic** division also acts on the SA and AV nodes but with an opposite effect. This division increases heart rate and impulse conduction and constricts and dilates the coronary arteries.

The mitral valve looks like a bishop's miter—hence the name **mitral valve.**

Cardiac cycle

No discussion of heart functions would be complete without an explanation of the **cardiac cycle,** the period from the beginning of one heartbeat to the beginning of the next. During this cycle, electrical and mechanical events must occur in the proper sequence and to the proper degree to provide adequate blood flow to all body parts. (See *Cardiac conduction route.*)

The two phases

The cardiac cycle has two phases: systole and diastole. **Systole** is the period when the ventricles contract and send blood on an outward journey to the aorta or the pulmonary artery. **Diastole** is when the heart relaxes and fills with blood. Diastole is about twice as long as systole, to allow for adequate filling of the ventricles. During diastole, the mitral and tricuspid valves are open, and the aortic and pulmonic valves are closed. (See *Systole and diastole.*)

Diastole—Passive, then active

Diastole consists of two parts, **ventricular filling** and **atrial contraction.** During the first part of diastole, 70% of the blood in the atria drains into the ventricles as a result of gravity, a passive action.

The active period of diastole, atrial contraction (also called **atrial kick**), accounts for the remaining 30% of blood that passes into the ventricles. Diastole is also the period in which the heart muscle receives its own supply of blood, which is transported there by the **coronary arteries.**

Beyond the dictionary

What's a Purkinje?

The Purkinje (PUHR-KIN-JEE) fibers are microscopic muscles first distinguished from ordinary heart muscle tissue by the Czech physiologist Jan Purkinje (1787–1869), who also originated the analysis and classification of fingerprints.

Cardiac conduction route

Specialized fibers propagate electrical impulses throughout the heart's cells, causing the heart to contract. This illustration shows the elements of the cardiac conduction system.

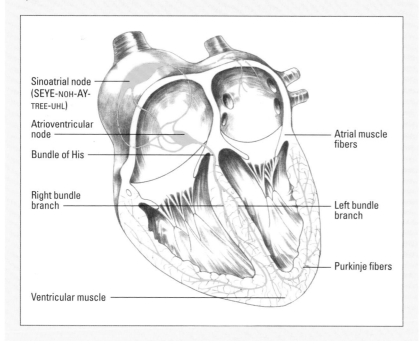

Sinoatrial node
(SEYE-NOH-AY-TREE-UHL)

Atrioventricular node

Bundle of His

Right bundle branch

Ventricular muscle

Atrial muscle fibers

Left bundle branch

Purkinje fibers

Systole and diastole

Systole (pronounced SIS-TOH-LEE) and *diastole* (pronounced DEYE-AH-STOH-LEE) have the same Greek root, *stole*, which means *to send*.

Apart or together?
The prefixes are the keys to these words. The prefix *dia-* means *apart;* and *sy-*, a contraction of *syn-*, means *together.* If you think about the relaxation of the muscle and the walls moving apart, you'll remember **diastole.** If you think about the interior wall of the ventricles contracting, coming closer together, you'll remember **systole.**

Lub...

Systole is the period of ventricular contraction. As pressure within the ventricles rises, the mitral and tricuspid valves snap closed. This closure leads to the first heart sound, S_1 (the *lub* of *lub-dub*).

When the pressure in the ventricles rises above the pressure in the aorta and pulmonary artery, the aortic and pulmonic valves open. Blood then surges from the ventricles into the pulmonary artery to the lungs and into the aorta to the rest of the body.

...then *dub*

At the end of ventricular contraction, pressure in the ventricles drops below the pressure in the aorta and the pulmonary artery. That pressure difference forces blood to back up toward the ventricles and causes the aortic and pulmonic valves to snap shut, which produces the second heart sound, S_2 (the *dub* of *lub-dub*). As the valves shut, the atria fill with blood in preparation for the next period of diastolic filling, and the cycle begins again.

Pumping it out

Cardiac output refers to the amount of blood pumped out by the heart in 1 minute and is determined by the **stroke volume,** the amount of blood ejected with each heartbeat multiplied by the number of beats per minute. Stroke volume, in turn, depends on three factors:

- **Contractility** refers to the ability of the myocardium to contract normally.
- **Preload** is the stretching of muscle fibers in the ventricles. This stretching results from the volume of blood in the ventricles at the end of diastole. The more muscles stretch, the more forcefully they contract during systole.
- **Afterload** refers to the pressure the ventricular muscles must generate to overcome the higher pressure in the aorta.

Coronary **arteries** got their name because they encircle the heart like a crown. The word **coronary** comes from the Greek **koron,** which means crown.

Vascular network

The peripheral vascular system consists of a network of arteries, arterioles, capillaries, venules, and veins.

Keep air in there

Artery comes from the Greek words *aer,* which means *air,* and *terein,* which means *to keep* because the ancients believed that arteries contained air. Arteries carry blood away from the heart. Nearly all arteries carry oxygen-rich blood from the heart to the rest of the body. The only exception is the pulmonary artery, which carries oxygen-depleted blood to the lungs.

Smaller and smaller

The exchange of fluid, nutrients, and metabolic wastes between blood and cells occurs in the **capillaries.** Capillaries are connected to arteries and veins through intermediary vessels called **arterioles** and **venules,** respectively. (See *Call it a capillary.*)

You're so vein

Veins carry blood toward the heart. Nearly all veins carry oxygen-depleted blood. The sole exception to this is the pulmonary vein, which carries oxygen-rich blood from the lungs to the heart.

Beyond the dictionary

Call it a capillary

Capillary is a Latin word that means *hairlike.* It refers to the minute size of these vessels.

Physical examination terms

This section introduces terms associated with examination of the heart and abnormalities an examination might reveal.

Vital signs

The physiologic condition of a patient is reflected in his vital signs. The vital signs that are directly related to the cardiovascular system are pulse and blood pressure, and in some cases, pulse oximetry, respiratory rate, and pain.

Stay on the beat

A patient's **pulse** is the expansion and contraction of an artery in a regular, rhythmic pattern; this happens when the left ventricle of the heart ejects blood into the aorta as it contracts, causing waves of pressure.

We thrive on pressure

A person's **blood pressure** is maintained by the complex interaction of the homeostatic mechanisms of the body and is influenced by the volume of blood, the lumen of the arteries and arterioles, and the force of the cardiac contraction.

When you take a blood pressure, you're measuring the pressure exerted by the circulating volume of blood on the walls of the arteries, the veins, and the chambers of the heart.

Systole and diastole again

A typical blood pressure reading consists of systolic blood pressure and diastolic blood pressure; pulse pressure is a third measurement that depends on the other two pressures. Here's a description of each:

- **Systolic blood pressure** is the blood pressure caused by the contraction phase, or systole, of the left ventricle of the heart. It's the top number given in a blood pressure measurement. For example, the systolic blood pressure in a measurement of 120/80 mm Hg is 120.
- **Diastolic blood pressure** is the pressure during the heart's relaxation phase, or diastole. It's the bottom number given in a blood pressure measurement. For example, the diastolic blood pressure in a measurement of 120/80 mm Hg is 80.
- **Pulse pressure** is the numerical difference between the systolic and diastolic blood pressures. For example, if the patient's blood pressure reading is 120/80 mm Hg, the pulse pressure is 40 mm Hg.

Tools of the trade

To take a blood pressure, you use a **sphygmomanometer,** an instrument that consists of an inflatable cuff, an inflatable bulb, and a gauge, which is designed to measure arterial blood pressure.

You also listen to the sound of flowing blood with a **stethoscope.** The word **stethoscope** comes from the Greek words *stethos,* which means *chest,* and **skopein,** which means *to examine.* A stethoscope is an instrument used for auscultation of respiratory, cardiac, intestinal, uterine, fetal, arterial, and venous sounds; it consists of two earpieces that are connected by flexible tubing to a diaphragm, which is placed against the patient's body.

Sphygmoma-....
What? Oh, it's just a jazzed-up name for a blood pressure cuff.

What you hear

In determining blood pressure, you should listen for **Korotkoff's sounds,** which are the first faint sounds heard as the pressure in the cuff is released and blood begins to flow, and the last sound heard before silence as blood flows. These two points correspond to the systolic and diastolic pressures, respectively.

Abnormalities in the physical examination

Auscultation may reveal a murmur, a soft blowing or fluttering sound of cardiac or vascular origin, or a **bruit,** an abnormal sound heard over arteries that indicates turbulent blood flow. (See *What's all the bruit about?*)

Color matters, too

Other signs of cardiovascular problems include **cyanosis,** a bluish discoloration of the skin and mucous membranes that results from an excessive amount of deoxygenated hemoglobin in the blood or a structural defect in the hemoglobin molecule. The word **cyanosis** comes from the Greek word *cyanos,* which means *dark blue.* You may also encounter patients with **pallor.** Pallor is a fancy term for paleness or a decrease or absence of color in the skin. Assessing the patient's conjunctiva may also be helpful in patients with cyanosis or pallor. A normal conjunctiva should be pink, a pale color could indicate lack of oxygenated blood flow.

Too much liquid

The examination can also reveal **edema,** the accumulation of abnormal amounts of fluid in the intercellular tissues, pericardial sac, pleural cavity, peritoneal cavity, or joint capsules. Any of these conditions

Pump up your pronunciation

What's all the bruit about?

It's easy to mispronounce **bruit** because it's a French word. It means *noise, din,* or *racket.* It's pronounced BROOEE; the *t* sound is dropped.

may be accompanied by **diaphoresis,** profuse perspiration associated with an elevated body temperature, physical exertion, heat exposure, and mental or emotional stress. (See *Edema! That's just swell!*)

Too much pain

Angina, also called **angina pectoris,** is chest pain that lasts several minutes and results from an inadequate supply of oxygen and blood flow to the heart muscle.

Diagnostic tests

No single test can help diagnose cardiovascular disease. Therefore, your patient will undergo more than one—sometimes several—tests if a cardiovascular disease or disorder is suspected. These tests are described here.

Blood tests

Three important blood tests may be used to help diagnose cardiovascular problems.

Clotting by the clock

Activated partial thromboplastin time, the test to measure the time required for formation of a fibrin clot requires a blood sample to evaluate all the clotting factors (except platelets) of the intrinsic pathway.

Any damage here?

The **cardiac enzyme** test is used to determine if cardiac tissue has been damaged. Normally present in high concentrations within the heart muscle, cardiac enzymes are released into the bloodstream from their normal intracellular area during cardiac trauma and create an elevation of the serum cardiac enzyme levels. Elevated levels of the enzyme creatine kinase (CK) and the isoenzyme CK-MB over a 72-hour period usually confirm a myocardial infarction (MI) but cannot be used exclusively to determine if a myocardial infarction took place.

Did I have an MI?

In the **cardiac troponin** test, a blood sample is used to measure the cardiac protein called **troponin.** This specific lab test is the most precise way to diagnose an MI.

Beyond the dictionary

Edema! That's just swell!

The word **edema** is a recent borrowing from Greek. It means *swelling*.

Radiologic tests

Here are some terms for common radiologic tests:

- **Cardiac catheterization** is a diagnostic procedure in which a catheter is inserted into a large artery or vein (usually in an arm or the groin) and then threaded through the vessel to the patient's heart. After injection of a radiopaque contrast medium, X-rays are taken to detect heart anomalies.
- **Angiocardiography** creates an X-ray of the heart and great vessels after injection of contrast medium into a blood vessel or one of the heart chambers. (See *Angiocardiography*.)
- **Angiography** produces an X-ray of the blood vessels after injection of a radiopaque contrast medium.

I know I'm good-looking, but a little contrast medium and an X-ray really show me off!

Let's see what's going on in there

A radionuclide **scan** is a test that helps to measure heart function and damage. During this test, a mildly radioactive material is injected into the patient's bloodstream. Computer-generated pictures are used to locate the radioactive element in the heart.

Running hot and cold

The thallium **stress test** helps diagnose coronary artery disease. For this test, the patient is given a thallium isotope I.V. after a treadmill stress test. The isotope doesn't collect in areas of poor blood flow and damaged cells, so these areas show up as "cold spots" on a scanner.

Other invasive tests

Electrophysiologic studies are invasive tests that help diagnose conduction system disease and serious heart rhythm disturbances. The **cardiologist,** or electrical physiologist (heart specialist), induces a rhythm disturbance by using different medications or procedures. After identifying the source of the rhythm disturbance, the cardiologist either administers medications to terminate the disturbance or eliminates the abnormal pathway in the heart by treatment with high-frequency waves.

Pericardiocentesis is a surgical procedure in which the pericardium cavity is punctured for the aspiration of fluid from the pericardial sac. This procedure can be performed for both diagnosis and treatment of some cardiac disorders.

Transesophageal echocardiography is a technique in which a probe is passed through the mouth and down the esophagus to study

Beyond the dictionary

Angiocardiography

The word **angiocardiography** looks overwhelming, but it becomes easier if you break it down. **Angio-** comes from the Greek word for *vessel*, **cardi-** means *heart,* and **-graphy** comes from the Greek word **graphein,** which means *to write.*

Two troublesome terms

Pericardiocentesis and **transesophageal** look like hard words, but they're easy to understand if broken apart.

Around the heart + puncture
Pericardiocentesis comes from the Greek word ***kentesis***, which means *to puncture*. The prefix ***peri-*** means *around*, and the root ***cardio-*** means *heart.* Put it all together and you have the meaning—*a procedure that requires puncturing the sac around the heart.*

Through the esophagus
The first part of **transesophageal, *trans-,*** means *through;* therefore, **transesophageal** means *through* the *esophagus.* Transesophageal echocardiography is an echocardiogram performed through the esophagus.

the structure and motion of the heart using an echo obtained from beams of ultrasonic waves directed through the esophagus. (See *Two troublesome terms.*)

Noninvasive tests

An **electrocardiogram** (ECG) is a graphic record that's produced by an electrocardiograph and shows variations in electrical potential, as detected at the body surface, resulting from excitation of the heart muscle. An ECG displays a wave that represents phases of the cardiac cycle. (See *Electrocardiogram.*)

In a normal rhythm, the P wave is the first wave seen in the cardiac cycle. Atrial depolarization is represented on the ECG by the P wave. After atrial depolarization, electrical activity is absent for a brief period. This is known as the PR interval.

Next, ventricular depolarization is represented on the ECG by a waveform configuration known as the QRS complex. With the QRS complex representing ventricular contraction, it is demonstrated as a larger wave form than the P wave, which demonstrates atrial contraction. After ventricular activation, ventricular repolarization begins. The ST segment represents the actual recovery or repolarization of the ventricular muscle. The T wave represents the actual recovery.

Let me sound you out

Transthoracic echocardiography is a diagnostic technique that's used to study the structure and motion of the heart by the echo obtained from beams of ultrasonic waves directed through the chest wall. (See *Did you hear an echo?*)

Electrocardiogram

The prefix ***electro-*** comes from the Greek word ***elektron,*** which refers to the semiprecious stone amber. (Rubbing amber produces an electric charge.)
Cardiogram comes from the Latin word ***cardium,*** which means *heart,* and the Greek term ***gramma,*** which means *mark.*

Disorders

Some cardiovascular problems occur suddenly and without warning, whereas others are long-term problems. Either way, when the heart is sick, the entire body is affected. Many types of injury or illness cause problems for the heart, resulting in serious cardiac complications. (See *Cardiac complications.*)

Types of cardiac disorders include:

* cardiac arrhythmias
* congenital heart defects
* degenerative disorders
* inflammatory heart disease
* vascular disorders
* valvular heart disease.

Cardiac arrhythmias

Arrhythmia means the lack of normal heart rhythm (indicated by the prefix *a-*). A more accurate term to describe what are commonly referred to as arrhythmias is **dysrhythmia,** which means an abnormality in rhythm. However, these terms are used interchangeably.

There are a number of different arrhythmias:

* **Atrial flutter** is an arrhythmia in which atrial rhythm is regular, but the rate is 250 to 400 beats/minute. The flutter waves that result have a sawtooth appearance.
* **Bradycardia** is a slow heartbeat, usually less than 60 beats/minute.
* **Fibrillation** refers to an uncoordinated, irregular contraction of the heart muscle, which may originate in the atria (atrial fibrillation) or in the ventricles (ventricular fibrillation). If left untreated, ventricular fibrillation can result in cardiac arrest.
* **Heart block** describes an impaired conduction of the heart's electrical impulses at the AV node, which commonly leads to a slow heartbeat.
* **Paroxysmal atrial tachycardia** is an arrhythmia in which the atrial and ventricular rates are regular and exceed 160 beats/minute. This arrhythmia is typically characterized by a sudden onset and termination.
* **Premature atrial contraction** is an arrhythmia characterized by premature abnormal-looking P waves that differ in configuration from normal P waves followed by normal QRS complexes.
* In **premature ventricular contraction (PVC),** the QRS complex is premature, wide, and distorted. PVCs occur singly, in pairs, or in larger groups and alternate with normal beats. They may originate from one or more sites in the ventricles.

The real world

Did you hear an echo?

In practice, you'll commonly hear **echocardiography** referred to as an **echo.** You'll also hear **cardiac catheterization** referred to as **cath.** For example, you might hear someone say, "Mrs. Heartman is scheduled for her **echo** today."

Cardiac complications

Here's a list of cardiac complications you may encounter:
- **Aortic aneurysm,** is an outpouching, stretching, or bulging section in the wall of the aorta
- **Cardiac arrest** is when the heart stops abruptly with an absence of blood pressure or pulse.
- In **cardiac tamponade,** blood or fluid fills the pericardial space and presses against the heart, compressing the heart chambers and obstructing venous return to the heart.
- **Cardiogenic shock,** also called *pump failure,* results when more than 40% of the heart muscle is damaged by a myocardial infarction. As a result, the heart can't pump effectively and body tissues don't receive the necessary amounts of oxygen and nutrients. The ventricular rate is variable.
- **Hypotension** refers to blood pressure that's below normal values.
- **Hypovolemic shock** occurs when reduced intravascular blood volume causes circulatory dysfunction and inadequate blood flow to tissues.
- **Pulmonary edema** is an accumulation of excess fluid in the lungs.
- **Ventricular aneurysm** is an outpouching of the ventricular wall that's most commonly seen in the left ventricle.

- **Tachycardia** refers to a resting heartbeat greater than 100 beats/minute.
- **Ventricular tachycardia** is a potentially deadly arrhythmia in which QRS complexes are wide and bizarre and originate in the ventricles.

Congenital heart defects

Congenital means *present at birth.* Infants with congenital heart problems have structural defects of the heart or its **blood vessels.** The term **blue baby** describes cyanosis that's caused by several of these congenital defects:
- **Atrial septal defect** is an opening between the two atria. Because left atrial pressure is slightly higher than right atrial pressure, blood shunts from left to right. This shunting causes an overload on the right side of the heart, which enlarges to accommodate the increased volume.
- **Coarctation of the aorta** is narrowing of the **lumen** (opening of the aorta), which results in high pressure above and low pressure below the stricture.
- **Patent ductus arteriosus** occurs when the **ductus arteriosus,** a passage between the aorta and pulmonary artery that normally closes at birth, remains open, sending oxygenated blood back through the lungs.
- The **tetralogy of Fallot** got its name because it involves four (hence *tetra-*) major defects of the heart and great vessels and was first described by the French doctor Etienne Fallot (1850 to 1911).

Memory jogger

To distinguish **bra**dy-cardia from **ta**chycardia, think of an airplane either **bra**king (slowing down) or **ta**king off (speeding up) on the runway.

- In **ventricular septal defect,** an opening between the two ventricles allows blood to shunt between them. Depending on the anomaly's size, spontaneous closure may occur (if small); if closure doesn't occur, right- and left-sided heart failure and cyanosis occur.

It seems like so many things can go wrong. It just breaks my heart to think about it!

Degenerative heart conditions

Degenerative heart disease is a progressive deterioration of heart structures, tissue, and function. Some forms of degenerative heart disease are listed here:

- **Coronary artery disease (CAD)** occurs when the arteries that serve the heart are obstructed or narrowed. The most common cause of CAD is **atherosclerosis** (deposits of plaque inside the arteries). In addition to slowing blood flow, atherosclerosis damages and deforms the muscular arterial walls, increasing the risk of aneurysm. (See *Atherosclerosis: The hard facts.*)
- In **dilated cardiomyopathy,** the heart dilates and takes on a round shape as a result of extensively damaged heart muscle fibers.
- **Heart failure** develops when the heart can't effectively pump blood and becomes congested with extra fluid.
- **Hypertension** refers to blood pressure that's above normal values, typically greater than 140/90 mm Hg (or 130/80 mm Hg in patients with diabetes or chronic kidney failure). A patient with a systolic blood pressure of 120 to 139 and a diastolic pressure of 80 to 89 is considered **pre-hypertensive.**
- **Hypertrophic cardiomyopathy** is a primary disease of cardiac muscle that's characterized by disproportionate thickening of the interventricular septum and ventricular walls.
- In an **MI,** commonly called a **heart attack,** reduced blood flow through one of the coronary arteries results in myocardial ischemia (lack of blood supply) and necrosis (tissue death).
- **Restrictive cardiomyopathy** is characterized by restricted ventricular filling (the result of left ventricular hypertrophy) and endocardial fibrosis.

Beyond the dictionary

Atherosclerosis: The hard facts

Breaking apart the word **atherosclerosis** is easy. The Greek word ***athere*** means *soft, fatty,* and *gruel-like,* and ***scler-*** means *hard.* Put them together, and these terms accurately describe the material deposited on the inner lining of an artery that causes atherosclerosis.

Inflammatory heart disease

Types of heart inflammation, caused by injury or tissue destruction, are described below:

- **Endocarditis** is a bacterial or fungal infection of the heart valves or endocardium.
- **Myocarditis** is an inflammation of the heart muscle that can be acute or long term.

- **Pericarditis** is an inflammation of the pericardium, the protective sac that encloses the heart. In constrictive pericarditis, the pericardium thickens and constricts the heart's ability to pump, causing heart failure.
- **Rheumatic fever** is a childhood disease caused by streptococcal bacteria.

Inflammation can be pretty serious business.

Vascular disorders

The following terms are associated with disorders of the vascular system:

- **Arterial occlusive disease** is caused by obstruction of the lumen of the arteries, causing **ischemia** (decreased blood flow and tissue hypoxia), most commonly to the legs and feet.
- **Raynaud's disease** is an arteriospastic disease characterized by episodic vasospasm in the arteries or arterioles that's precipitated by cold or stress.
- **Thrombophlebitis** is an acute condition characterized by inflammation and thrombus formation. Thrombophlebitis may occur in deep (intramuscular) or superficial (subcutaneous) veins. Deep vein thrombophlebitis can affect small veins, such as the soleal venus sinuses, or large veins such as the venae cavae.

Weak walls

An aneurysm (a weakening of the walls of a vessel) occurs most commonly in the aorta but can happen in any vessel and can take some different forms:

- **Abdominal aortic aneurysm,** an abnormal dilation in the arterial wall, most commonly occurs in the aorta below the renal arteries and above the iliac branches.
- **Aortic dissection** is usually caused by high blood pressure that forces the layers of the aortic walls to separate, creating a false lumen. Acute aortic dissection is characterized by sharp, tearing pain in the chest or back.
- **Thoracic aortic aneurysm** is an abnormal widening of the ascending, transcending, or descending part of the aorta above the diaphragm.

  Aneurysms may be **saccular** (unilateral pouchlike bulge with a narrow neck), **fusiform** (spindle-shaped bulge encompassing the entire diameter of the vessel), or **false** (a pulsating hematoma resulting from trauma and often mistaken for an abdominal aneurysm).

Valvular disorders

When a valve fails, several different disorders can result, including stenosis and cardiac insufficiency.

The thick of it

Stenosis, a thickening of valvular tissue that results in narrow valve openings, can occur as one of three types:
- **Aortic stenosis,** or narrowing of the aortic valve, creates elevated pressure in the left ventricle.
- **Mitral stenosis,** or narrowing of the mitral valve, obstructs blood flow from the left atrium to the left ventricle, causing enlargement of the left atrium as a form of compensation.
- **Tricuspid stenosis** obstructs blood flow from the right atrium to the right ventricle, causing the right atrium to enlarge.

Insufficient funds

Four types of **coronary insufficiency,** the incomplete closure of a valve, may also result in the following:
- **Aortic insufficiency** occurs when blood leaks back into the left ventricle during the diastolic phase of the heartbeat, when the ventricles rest. The left ventricle enlarges and fluid builds up in the left atrium and the pulmonary system, leading to left-sided heart failure and pulmonary edema.
- **Mitral valve insufficiency** occurs when blood from the left ventricle flows back into the left atrium, causing the left atrium and ventricle to enlarge as compensation for the heart's decreased efficiency.
- **Pulmonary valve insufficiency** allows blood from the pulmonary artery to flow back into the right ventricle during diastole.
- In **tricuspid insufficiency,** blood flows back into the right atrium as the ventricles contract during systole. This reduces blood flow to the lungs and the left side of the heart and also decreases cardiac output.

Valves can be tricky!

Treatments

Cardiovascular disorders can be treated with drug therapy and surgery. Here's a list of treatments and surgical interventions.

Drug therapy

These drugs may be used alone or in combination to treat cardiovascular disorders:
- **Adrenergics** help treat serious hypotension.
- **Angiotensin-converting enzyme inhibitors** are used to treat hypertension and heart failure. They're also used to prevent future heart attacks.
- **Antianginal** drugs treat or prevent cardiac pain.
- **Antiarrhythmics** can prevent or treat arrhythmias.

- **Antihypertensives** reduce cardiac output or decrease peripheral vascular resistance to lower blood pressure.
- **Beta-adrenergic blockers** are used to treat hypertension, angina, and heart failure.
- **Calcium channel blockers** lower blood pressure and reduce the workload of the heart.
- **Cardiac glycosides** are used to manage heart failure and certain types of arrhythmias.
- **Diuretics** treat edema and hypertension by reducing circulating fluid volume.
- **Thrombolytic therapy** is used to dissolve clots.

Surgery and procedural interventions

Here are some common surgical and procedural interventions used to correct functional or structural heart problems:
- **Ablation** is a procedure in which small, selected areas of the heart are destroyed to treat refractive tachycardia.
- **Cardiac conduction surgery** is done to treat atrial and ventricular tachycardias that can't be controlled by drug therapy or pacing.
- **Coronary artery bypass graft (CABG)** surgery restores circulation when occluded coronary arteries prevent normal blood flow to the heart muscle. Occluded arteries are replaced with segments (grafts) from other vessels, most commonly the saphenous veins in the leg. This can also be accomplished using a less invasive procedure called **minimally invasive surgery.** (See *Cabbage is slang for CABG.*)
- **Heart transplantation** is a complex procedure that involves replacing a diseased heart with the healthy heart of a brain-dead donor.

Other treatments

- **Advanced cardiac life support** involves the recognition and treatment of acute cardiac emergencies, such as cardiac arrest, MI, and lethal arrhythmias.
- **Cardiopulmonary resuscitation** is a basic life support procedure performed on victims with cardiac arrest.
- In **defibrillation,** an electric shock is used to terminate tachyarrhythmias and ventricular fibrillation.
- An **implantable cardioverter-defibrillator** is an implanted device that senses an arrhythmia and delivers an electric shock to the myocardium, terminating the arrhythmia.
- In **intra-aortic balloon counterpulsation,** a device is inserted through the femoral artery and used to temporarily reduce the left ventricle's workload. This is an inflatable balloon that works as a pump that inflates the balloon while the ventricle rests and

The real world

Cabbage is slang for CABG

You may hear **coronary artery bypass surgery** referred to as **cabbage. Cabbage** is slang for CABG, the abbreviation for coronary artery bypass graft. A **triple cabbage** is a three-vessel bypass procedure.

Profiling PTCA

The term **percutaneous transluminal coronary angioplasty** is abbreviated **PTCA.**

First half
The first component of the term, **per-**, means *through* and **cutaneous** means *the skin*—so *through the skin*. The prefix **trans-** means *through*; **luminal** refers to *a blood vessel*.

Second half
Coronary refers to the two arteries and their branches that stem from the aorta, which supply the heart tissue with blood. **Angio-** also means *blood vessel*, and **plasty** is a suffix that means *the repair of.*

All together
So PTCA really means *repair of a coronary blood vessel by way of the skin and another blood vessel.*

deflates it at the start of each ventricular contraction. The inflated balloon forces blood into the major arteries and reduces the heart's workload during contraction.

- During **laser-enhanced angioplasty,** a doctor threads a laser-con-taining catheter into the diseased artery. Rapid laser pulses destroy the occlusion, and balloon angioplasty is performed later.
- **Pacemakers** use electrical impulses to regulate cardiac rhythm. Pacemakers can be permanent, transvenous, or transcutaneous.
- **Percutaneous transluminal coronary angioplasty (PTCA)** is a nonsurgical alternative to CABG surgery. During this procedure, a guide catheter is threaded into the coronary artery and positioned at the site of an stenosis or occlusion. A doctor then inserts a small balloon catheter through the guide catheter and positions the balloon inside the stenosis or occlusion. When the balloon is inflated, the coronary artery dilates and blood flow improves. (See *Profiling PTCA.*)
- In some cases, a **stent** (tube or coil) is placed inside the artery to support it and prevent reocclusion.
- **Synchronized cardioversion** delivers an electric charge to the myocardium at the peak of the R wave on the ECG. This electrical charge stops the arrhythmia and allows the SA node to resume control.
- **Valve replacement surgery** is used to replace faulty valves in patients with severe symptoms who don't respond to more conservative approaches. Both mechanical and biological prosthetic valves are com-monly used.
- A **ventricular assist device** is a temporary, life-sustain-ing treatment that diverts systemic blood flow from a diseased ventricle into a centrifugal pump.

There sure are a lot of ways to get me back in the game.

Vocabulary builders

At a crossroads

Here's a puzzle that's sure to tug at your heartstrings. Good luck!

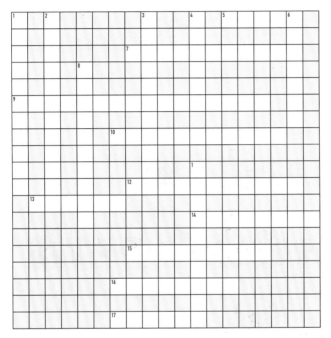

This type of exercise is hard work, but mental exercise can be pretty tough, too!

Across
5. Return blood to the heart
7. Smallest blood vessels
9. Hardening of the arteries
10. Thin sac that protects the heart
12. Rapid heartbeat
13. Chest pain
14. Blue-colored skin
15. Lower chamber of the heart
16. Carry blood away from the heart
17. Upper chamber of the heart

Down
1. Lining of the heart's chambers
2. High blood pressure
3. Slow heartbeat
4. Word for *abnormal paleness*
6. When the heart contracts
8. Deviation from normal rhythm
11. Heart muscle

Finish line

The Latin word **cardium,** which means *heart,* appears in almost all medical terminology relating to that structure. Fill in each of the blanks below with the prefix, suffix, or root that finishes the heart-related term.

1. A heart doctor specializing in dysrhythmias is an electrical _____.
2. A patient with _____ cardia has a fast heartbeat.
3. Another name for the condition of an enlarged heart is cardio _____.
4. Inflammation of the heart muscles due to infection is called card _____.
5. The _____ cardio _____ is a device for recording the electrical activity of the myocardium.

O see, can you say?

Sound out each group of pictures and symbols below to reveal a term that was reviewed in the chapter.

1.

2.

3.

Match game

Match the choices below to the appropriate answers.

Clues

1. Add the prefix that means rapid to the correct form of the root **cardium.** _____

2. Add the prefix that means *around* and the affix that means *to puncture* to the correct form of the root **cardium.** _____

3. Add the prefix that means *muscle* to the correct form of the root **cardium.**
_____

4. Add the suffix that refers to the *lungs* to the correct form of the root **cardium.**
_____

5. Add the prefix that means *within* to the correct form of the root **cardium.**
_____

6. Add the prefix that means *on* to the correct form of the root **cardium.** _____

7. Add the prefix that means *vessel* and the suffix that means *to write* to the correct form of the root **cardium.** _____

Choices

A. Pericardiocentesis

B. Tachycardia

C. Cardiopulmonary

D. Myocardial

E. Epicardium

F. Angiocardiography

G. Endocardium

Add muscle to cardium? You've got it!

Talking in circles

Use the clues below to fill in the blanks with the appropriate word. Then unscramble the circled letters to find the answer to the question posed below.

1. ◯ ___ ___ ___ ◯ ___ ___ ___ ___ ___ ___ ___

2. ___ ___ ___ ___ ___ ___ ◯ ___ ◯ ___

3. ◯ ___ ___ ___ ___ ___ ___ ___ ___

4. ___ ___ ___ ◯ ___ ◯ ___ ___ ___

5. ___ ___ ___ ___ ◯ ___

1. Heart doctor
2. An artery to the lungs
3. Means *near the top*
4. Consists of ventricular filling and atrial contraction
5. Pain resulting from an inadequate supply of oxygen

What's it called when a person has the "blues?"

Answers

At a crossroads

¹E	²H				³B		⁴P	⁵V	E	I	N	⁶S	
N	Y				R		A					Y	
D	P			⁷C	A	P	I	L	L	A	R	I	E	S
O	E		⁸A		D		L					T	
C	R		R		Y		O					O	
⁹A	R	T	E	R	I	O	S	C	L	E	R	O	S	I	S
R	E		H		A							L	
D	N		Y	¹⁰P	E	R	I	C	A	R	D	I	U	M
I	S		T		D								
U	I		H		I		¹¹M						
M	O		M		¹²T	A	C	H	Y	C	A	R	D	I	A
	¹³A	N	G	I	N	A		O					
			A				¹⁴C	Y	A	N	O	S	I	S
							A						
				¹⁵V	E	N	T	R	I	C	L	E	
							D						
			¹⁶A	R	T	E	R	I	E	S			
							U						
			¹⁷A	T	R	I	U	M					

Finish line

Answers: 1. Physiologist; 2. Tachy; 3. Megaly; 4. Itis;
5. Electro, graph

O see, can you say?

Answers: 1. Diuretic; 2. Thrombophlebitis; 3. Sinoatrial

Match game

Answers: 1. B; 2. A; 3. D; 4. C; 5. G; 6. E; 7. F

Talking in circles

Answers: 1. Cardiologist; 2. Pulmonary; 3. Superior;
4. Diastole; 5. Angina

Answer to puzzle—Cyanosis

WOW!
That wasn't
easy!

Suggested references

Diagnostics: An A-to-Z guide to laboratory tests & diagnostic procedures. Springhouse, PA: Springhouse Corp., 2001.

Katrukha, I. A. (2013). Human cardiac troponin complex. Structure and functions. *Biochemistry, 78*(13), 1447–1465.

Shen, X., Fang, Z., Hu, X., Liu, Q., Zhou, T., Tang, J., & Lu, X. (2011). Cardiac perforation and tamponade in percutaneous cardiac intervention. *Zhong Nan Da Xue Xue Bao Yi Xue Ban, 36*(1), 74–79.

Sole, M. L., Klein, D. G., & Mosely, M. J. (2013). *Introduction to critical care nursing* (6th ed.). St. Louis, MO: Elsevier.

To, A. C. Y., Schoenhagen, P., & Desai, M. Y. (2013). Role of tomographic imaging in preoperative planning and postoperative assessment in cardiovascular surgery. *Heart, 99*(14), 1048.

Chapter 7

Respiratory system

Just the facts

In this chapter, you'll learn:

♦ terminology related to the structure and function of the respiratory system

♦ terminology needed for physical examination of the respiratory system

♦ tests that help diagnose respiratory disorders

♦ common respiratory system disorders and their treatments.

Respiratory structure and function

The **respiratory system** consists of the upper and lower respiratory tracts and the thoracic cage. In addition to maintaining the exchange of oxygen (O_2) and carbon dioxide (CO_2) in the lungs and tissues, the respiratory system helps regulate the body's acid-base balance. (See *Pronouncing key respiratory system terms.*)

Upper respiratory tract

The **upper respiratory tract** consists primarily of the nose, mouth, nasopharynx, oropharynx, laryngopharynx, and larynx. Besides warming and humidifying inhaled air, these structures enable taste, smell, and the chewing and swallowing of food. (See *Structures of the respiratory system*, page 133.)

Nose

Air enters the respiratory tract through the mouth and **nares** (nostrils). In the nares, small hairs filter out dust and large foreign particles. Air then passes into the two **nasal passages**, which are

Pronouncing key respiratory system terms

Below is a list of key terms related to the respiratory system, along with the correct ways to pronounce them.

Alveoli	AL-**VEE**-OH-LEYE
Atelectasis	AHT-UH-**LEHK**-TAY-SIS
Bronchioles	**BRONG**-KEE-OHLZ
Conchae	**KON**-KEE
Cor pulmonale	**KOR**-PULL-MAH-**NAL**-LEE
Oropharynx	OR-OH-**FAR**-INKS
Sarcoidosis	SAHR-KOY-**DOH**-SIS

separated by the **septum**. **Cartilage** forms the anterior walls of the nasal passages.

Humidifiers

Bony structures, conchae (singular: concha), form the posterior walls of the nasal passages. The conchae warm and humidify air before it passes into the pharynx (plural: **pharynges**) or **throat**, which serves as a passageway for the digestive and respiratory tracts.

Pharynx

The pharynx consists of three sections:
1. The nasopharynx extends from the posterior nares to the soft palate.
2. The oropharynx extends from the soft palate to the upper portion of the epiglottis.
3. The laryngopharynx extends to the esophagus and larynx. (See *The three pharynges.*)

Larynx

The larynx, which contains the **vocal cords**, connects the pharynx with the trachea. (See *Learn to say* larynx.)

Beyond the dictionary

The three pharynges

Notice that the words for the three parts of the pharynx are all connected by the common root *pharynx*, which is Greek for *throat*. **Nasopharynx** uses the word for *nose*, *naso*, and the root *pharynx* to describe the upper portion of the pharynx. **Oropharynx** uses the Latin word for *mouth*, *or*, from which we also get *orifice*. **Laryngopharynx** adds **laryngo**, a form of **larynx** that's used when it's combined with another word.

Structures of the respiratory system

This illustration shows the structures of the respiratory system, which include the organs responsible for external respiration.

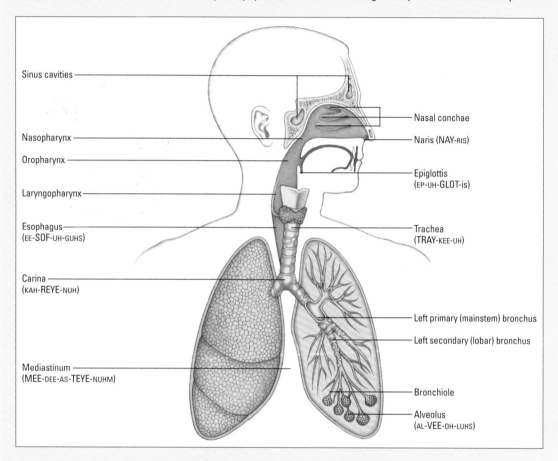

Sinus cavities

Nasopharynx

Oropharynx

Laryngopharynx

Esophagus
(EE-SOF-UH-GUHS)

Carina
(KAH-REYE-NUH)

Mediastinum
(MEE-DEE-AS-TEYE-NUHM)

Nasal conchae

Naris (NAY-RIS)

Epiglottis
(EP-UH-GLOT-is)

Trachea
(TRAY-KEE-UH)

Left primary (mainstem) bronchus

Left secondary (lobar) bronchus

Bronchiole

Alveolus
(AL-VEE-OH-LUHS)

Learn to say *larynx*

It's likely you'll hear **larynx** (LAHR-INKS) pronounced LAHR-NIKS, with the sounds of the L and the N reversed. Although this reversal of sounds, called **metathesis**, is a common mix-up in all languages, you may save yourself some embarrassment if you say LAHR-inks.

Speaking of the voice box

The larynx is also called the **voice box**. It's the main organ of speech. Air passing through the glottis—a slitlike opening between the vocal cords—causes vibration of the cords during expiration, creating the sound of the voice. The larynx is protected during swallowing by the epiglottis, a flexible cartilage that bends reflexively to close the larynx to swallowed substances.

> Epiglottis ... let's see. The prefix **epi-** comes from Greek, meaning upon. **Glottis** comes from the Greek word **glossa**, which means tongue.

Lower respiratory tract

The **lower respiratory tract** is contained within the **thoracic cavity** and consists of the trachea, **bronchi**, and **lungs**. This space within the chest wall is bounded below by the diaphragm, above by the scalene muscles and fasciae of the neck, and around the circumference by the ribs, intercostal muscles, vertebrae, sternum, and ligaments.

Trachea

The tubular **trachea**, also called the **windpipe**, lies half in the neck and half in the thorax. C-shaped cartilage rings reinforce and protect the trachea, preventing its collapse. The trachea is lined with a mucous membrane covered with small hairlike projections called cilia. The cilia continuously sweep foreign material out of the breathing passages toward the mouth.

Bronchi

The trachea branches at the carina (also known as the **tracheal bifurcation**) into two smaller airways, the left and right **mainstem bronchi** (primary bronchi). (See *Careening with the carina*.)

The right mainstem bronchus—shorter, wider, and more vertical than the left—supplies air to the right lung; the left mainstem bronchus delivers air to the left lung.

A way in

The mainstem bronchi—along with blood vessels, nerves, and lymphatics—enter the **pleural cavity** (the space between the visceral and parietal pleurae) at the hilum. Located behind the heart, the **hilum** is a slit on the lungs' medial surface where nerves, lymphatic ducts, and blood vessels enter and leave the lungs. In the lung, the mainstem bronchi divide into five **lobar bronchi** (secondary bronchi), so called because they enter into the **lobes** of the lung, one for each of the three lobes of the right lung and two for the left.

First branches, now twigs

The lobar bronchi divide into smaller and smaller branches, until they become **bronchioles**. Each bronchiole branches into a **lobule**. The lobule includes **terminal bronchioles** and the **acinus**—the chief respiratory unit for gas exchange. (See *Looking at a lobule*.)

Careening with the carina

It's more accurate to say the *carina of the trachea* because a **carina** (KAH-REYE-NAH) can be any keel-shaped or ridge-shaped anatomic part. The word derives from Latin, meaning *hull* or *keel of a ship*, and was pronounced KAH-REE-NAH. This is still the word **carina's** secondary pronunciation, and it's the pronunciation for the verb ***careen***, which is also derived from **carina**.

Looking at a lobule

As illustrated below, each lobule contains terminal bronchioles and the acinus, which consists of respiratory bronchioles and alveolar sacs.

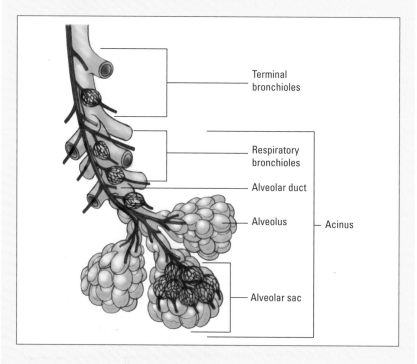

Ducts and sacs

Within the acinus, terminal bronchioles branch into yet smaller **respiratory bronchioles**. The respiratory bronchioles feed directly into alveoli at sites along their walls. The respiratory bronchioles eventually become alveolar **ducts**, which terminate in clusters of capillary-swathed alveoli called **alveolar sacs**.

Fruit of the vine

The walls of the ducts contain **alveoli** (singular: **alveolus**), grapelike clusters where O_2 is exchanged for CO_2.

Capillary network

Surrounded by networks of tiny blood vessels called **capillaries**, alveoli have thin walls through which gas exchange occurs. The average pair of lungs has about 300 million alveoli.

Lungs

The cone-shaped lungs differ slightly from one another. The right lung is shorter, broader, and larger than the left. The right lung has three lobes and handles 55% of gas exchange. The left lung has only two lobes; it shares the left side of the thoracic cavity with the heart. Each lung's concave base rests on the **diaphragm**. The **apex** (extreme top) of each lung extends about ⅓″ (1 cm) above the first rib. (See *Studying the lungs*.)

Remember the membrane

The **pleura** is the membrane that totally encloses the lungs. It's composed of a visceral layer and parietal layer. The **visceral pleura** hugs the entire lung surface, including the areas between the lobes. The **parietal pleura** extends from the roots of the lungs and covers the sides of the pericardium to the chest wall and backward to the spine.

Fluid space

The **pleural cavity**—the tiny area between the visceral and parietal pleural layers—contains a thin film of **serous fluid**. This fluid has two functions:
1. It lubricates the pleural surfaces so that they slide smoothly against each other during respiration.
2. It creates a bond between the layers that causes the lungs to move within the chest wall during breathing.

In the middle

The mediastinum (the space between the lungs) contains the:
* heart and pericardium
* thoracic aorta

Beyond the dictionary

Studying the lungs

Pulmonology, which comes from the Latin word **pulmo**, meaning *lung*, and the suffix **-ology**, meaning *the study of*, is the science that studies the lungs.

See the space between my lobes? It's called the **mediastinum**.

- pulmonary artery and veins
- venae cavae and azygos veins
- thymus, lymph nodes, and lymphatic vessels
- trachea, esophagus, and thoracic duct
- vagus, cardiac, and phrenic nerves.

Thoracic cage

Several structures support and protect the lungs and aid in respiration. Composed of bone and cartilage, the **thoracic cage** supports and protects the lungs and permits them to expand and contract. The anterior portion of the thoracic cage consists of the manubrium, **sternum**, xiphoid **process**, and 10 pairs of **ribs**. The posterior portion of the thoracic cage consists of the vertebral **column**, the same 10 pairs of ribs, and 2 pairs of floating ribs.

Respiration

Effective respiration consists of a gas exchange in the lungs, called **external respiration**, and a gas exchange in the tissues, called **internal respiration**. External respiration occurs through three processes:

1. **diffusion**—gas movement through a semipermeable membrane from an area of greater concentration to one of lesser concentration (internal respiration occurs only through diffusion)
2. **pulmonary perfusion**—blood flow from the right side of the heart, through the pulmonary circulation, and into the left side of the heart
3. **ventilation**—gas distribution into and out of the pulmonary airways.

Air supply

Adequate ventilation depends on the proper working of the nervous, musculoskeletal, and respiratory systems to accomplish the necessary changes in lung pressure. (See *Ventilation and perfusion.*)

At the base

The most important muscle for respiration is the **diaphragm**, a dome-shaped organ composed of muscle and membrane separating the thoracic and abdominal cavities. During inspiration, the diaphragm moves down and expands the volume of the thoracic cavity; during expiration, it moves up, reducing the volume.

Adequate ventilation depends on the proper working of the nervous, musculoskeletal, and respiratory systems.

Ventilation and perfusion

Effective gas exchange depends on a stable relationship between ventilation and perfusion. You'll see this called the **$\dot{V}/\dot{Q}$ ratio**. A **$\dot{V}/\dot{Q}$ mismatch** accounts for many respiratory disorders and can affect all body systems. The following types of mismatch can occur.

Need more oxygen
Inadequate ventilation, also called a **shunt**, occurs when pulmonary circulation is adequate but not enough oxygen (O_2) is available in the lungs. As a result, a portion of the blood flowing through the pulmonary capillaries doesn't receive O_2. Perfusion without ventilation usually results from airway obstruction, particularly that caused by acute diseases, such as atelectasis and pneumonia, which produce a low $\dot{V}/\dot{Q}$ ratio.

Need more blood
Inadequate perfusion, also called **dead-space ventilation**, produces a high $\dot{V}/\dot{Q}$ ratio. Ventilation is normal, but blood flow in the pulmonary capillaries isn't adequate. Narrowed capillaries, decreased cardiac output, and pulmonary emboli (blood clots) commonly cause this condition.

Need both!
Inadequate ventilation and perfusion, also referred to as a **silent unit**, describes a lack of O_2 in the lungs (ventilation) and in the pulmonary circulation (perfusion). When entire sections of the lung become "silent," the body compensates by delivering blood flow to better ventilated lung areas. Chronic alveolar collapse and pulmonary emboli can create silent units.

Respiration chemistry

The body depends on a delicate balance between acids and bases to sustain life. The lungs help maintain this balance by altering the rate and depth of respiration in response to changes in blood pH.

Acids and bases

To understand acid-base balance, you need to know three important terms:
- **acids**, which are substances that dissociate (become *fragmented*, or *separate*) in solution, releasing hydrogen ions (carbonic acid is an example of an acid found in the body)

- **bases**, such as bicarbonate, which are substances that dissociate to yield hydroxide ions in aqueous solutions
- **pH**, which represents the relative concentration of hydrogen ions in a solution compared to the hydrogen ion concentration of a standard solution (normally, blood pH level measures 7.35 to 7.45).

A solution with more base than acid contains fewer hydrogen ions, resulting in a higher pH. A solution that contains more acid than base has more hydrogen ions, resulting in a lower pH.

Think of it this way. More base elevates the pH.

Staying in balance

A deviation in pH level can compromise essential body functions, including electrolyte balance, the activity of critical enzymes, muscle contraction, and basic cellular function. The body normally maintains a pH level within a narrow range by carefully balancing acidic and alkaline elements. When one aspect of that balancing act breaks down, the body can't maintain a healthy pH level as easily, and problems arise.

Regulating method

The lungs use **hyperventilation** (increased ventilation) or **hypoventilation** (decreased ventilation) to regulate blood levels of CO_2, a gas that combines with water to form **carbonic acid**. Increased carbonic acid levels lead to a decrease in pH level.

Eliminate CO_2, increase pH

Chemoreceptors in the brain sense pH changes and vary the rate and depth of breathing to compensate. Breathing faster or more deeply eliminates more CO_2 from the lungs. The more CO_2 is expelled, the less carbonic acid is made and, as a result, the pH level rises. (See *CO_2 and hyperventilation*.)

Increase CO_2, reduce pH

The body normalizes such a change in pH by slowing the rate or decreasing the depth of breathing, thus reducing CO_2 excretion. CO_2 and pH move in opposite directions. If pH rises, CO_2 falls, and vice versa.

CO$_2$ and hyperventilation

When a patient's respiratory rate increases, carbon dioxide (CO$_2$) is "blown off" and the CO$_2$ level drops.

Respiratory rate

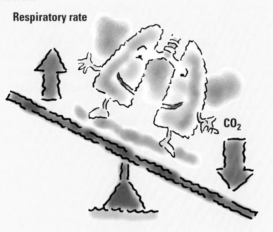

Physical examination terms

Examining a patient's respiratory status requires observation, palpation, and the ability to identify breath sounds. (See *Name that breath sound.*) Before you can perform a complete physical examination, you need to understand these essential respiratory terms:

- anoxia—absence or near absence of O$_2$ in inhaled air, body tissues, or arterial blood
- auscultation—assessment step; listening, either directly or with a stethoscope, for sounds within the body
- bronchospasm—sudden, forceful, involuntary contraction of the smooth muscle of the bronchi, causing narrowing and obstruction of the airway
- chest retraction—visible depression of soft tissues of the chest between and around the cartilaginous and bony ribs, occurring with increased inspiratory effort
- clubbing—enlargement of the soft tissues of the distal phalanges that occurs in children with congenital heart disease and in older children and adults with long-standing pulmonary disease
- cyanosis—bluish discoloration of the skin and mucous membranes resulting from an excessive amount of deoxygenated hemoglobin in the blood
- dyspnea—shortness of breath, difficulty breathing, or labored breathing

Name that breath sound

Listed below are normal and abnormal breath sounds, including their characteristics and where they're heard.

Normal sounds

Normal breath sounds reflect air movement through the tracheobronchial tree. Normal breath sounds are described below:

- **Tracheal** breath sounds are harsh, discontinuous sounds heard over the trachea. They occur when a patient inhales or exhales.
- **Bronchial** breath sounds are loud, high-pitched sounds normally heard below the trachea at the manubrium. They're discontinuous and loudest when the patient exhales.
- **Vesicular** breath sounds are heard in front of the chest, on both sides, and in back. They're longer and louder during inspiration than expiration and can be heard in the peripheral lung fields.
- **Bronchovesicular** breath sounds can be auscultated over the mainstem bronchi and between the shoulder blades. They have a soft, medium-pitched, breezy sound. They're lower pitched than bronchial sounds, but higher pitched than vesicular sounds.

Abnormal sounds

Abnormal breath sounds, also called **adventitious sounds**, help diagnose many respiratory disorders.

- **Crackles** are crackling sounds, like hairs being rubbed together, usually heard first over the lung bases during inspiration. Crackles are further classified by pitch as **high (fine)**, **medium**, or **low (coarse)**. Crackles are sometimes called **rales**.
- **Rhonchi** are loud, coarse, low-pitched bubbling sounds heard primarily when a patient exhales, although they may also be heard when the patient inhales. Rhonchi are sometimes called **sonorous wheezes**. You'll auscultate rhonchi over the central airways.
- **Wheezes** are high-pitched, musical sounds that may occur during inspiration but occur predominantly during expiration. Wheezes are heard over the large bronchi.
- **Pleural friction rubs** are coarse, low-pitched abnormal breath sounds heard at the anterolateral chest wall (in front, near the ribs) during inspiration and expiration. A friction rub sounds like pieces of sandpaper being rubbed together.
- **Grunting** respirations refer to a coarse, grunting noise heard during expiration.
- **Stridor** is a crowing sound heard during inspiration that is caused by air whistling as it passes through swollen upper airways.
- **Decreased breath sounds** describes abnormally diminished sounds in areas of the lung.
- **Absent breath sounds** refers to a lack of sound over areas of the lungs that normally have breath sounds.

Abnormal breath sounds are also called **adventitious** sounds. It may help you to think of the word **adventure**, because these sounds are out of the ordinary.

The real world

Three-pillow orthopnea

You may hear the term **three-pillow orthopnea** used to describe a patient's sleeping habits. This means the patient requires three pillows to breathe comfortably while sleeping.

- **expectoration**—ejection of mucus from the trachea and lungs by coughing and spitting
- **expiration**—act of exhaling air
- hemoptysis—coughing or spitting up blood
- **inspiration**—act of inhaling air
- orthopnea—discomfort in breathing except in an upright position (see *Three-pillow orthopnea*)
- **palpation**—assessment step; feeling the body surface with the hand
- **percussion**—assessment step; striking a part of the body with short, sharp blows of the fingers to detect changes in sound or mobilize lung secretions
- **respiratory rate**—number of breaths per minute
- **shunting**—condition in which blood moves from the venous circulation to the arterial circulation without participating in gas exchange, leading to hypoxemia
- **subcutaneous crepitus**—soft, popping sound produced by palpation or stroking of the skin; caused by bubbles of air or other gases such as CO_2 trapped in the subcutaneous tissue; may occur with pneumothorax
- tactile fremitus—vibration in the chest wall that may be felt when a hand is applied to the thorax while the patient is speaking.

Beyond the dictionary

Cheyne-Stokes

Cheyne-Stokes respirations were named after John Cheyne, a Scottish doctor, and William Stokes, an Irish doctor.

Respiratory patterns

The following terms describe different respiratory patterns:
- apnea—absence of breathing (may be periodic)
- apneustic **breathing**—prolonged, gasping inspirations followed by extremely short, inefficient expirations
- **Biot's respirations**—irregular periods of apnea alternating with periods of four or five breaths having the same depth
- bradypnea—unusually slow, regular respirations
- Cheyne-Stokes respirations—alternating periods of apnea and deep, rapid breathing (see *Cheyne-Stokes*)
- **eupnea**—normal respiratory rate and rhythm
- Kussmaul's respirations—faster and deeper respirations than normal, without pauses
- **tachypnea**—abnormally rapid respiratory rate.

Diagnostic tests

Below are the names of some diagnostic tests for the respiratory system and its associated disorders.

Ventilation tests

Ventilation tests, also called **pulmonary function tests**, include a series of measurements that evaluate the lungs' ventilatory function:

- **diffusing capacity for carbon monoxide (DLCO)**—amount of carbon monoxide diffused per minute across the alveolar membrane
- **expiratory reserve volume (ERV)**—volume of air that can be exhaled after normal expiration is completed
- **forced expiratory volume (FEV)**—volume of air expired in the first, second, and third seconds of the forced vital capacity test
- **forced vital capacity (FVC)**—volume of air that can be exhaled after maximum inspiration
- **functional residual capacity (FRC)**—volume of air remaining in the lungs after normal expiration
- **inspiratory capacity (IC)**—volume of air that can be inhaled after normal expiration
- **inspiratory reserve volume (IRV)**—maximum volume of air that can be inspired after normal inspiration is complete
- **maximum voluntary ventilation (MVV)**—the greatest volume of air breathed per unit of time
- **minute volume (V_E)**—volume of air breathed per minute, calculated from the tidal volume
- **residual volume (RV)**—volume of air that is *always* in the lungs and can't be exhaled (must be measured indirectly)
- **tidal volume (V_T)**—volume of air inhaled or exhaled during normal breathing
- **total lung capacity (TLC)**—volume of the lungs at peak inspiration
- **vital capacity (VC)**—maximum volume of air that can be exhaled after maximum inspiration.

Radiologic tests

Radiologic tests, which use X-rays or electromagnetic waves to create images of interior structures, can be used to diagnose respiratory problems:

- **Chest radiography**, commonly known as chest **X-ray**, creates an image of the thorax to reveal abnormalities.
- **Magnetic resonance imaging (MRI)** is a procedure in which the patient is placed in a magnetic field into which a radiofrequency beam is introduced. Resulting energy changes are measured and computed, generating images on a monitor. Cross-sectional images of the anatomy can be viewed in multiple planes.

- **Pulmonary angiography**, also called **pulmonary arteriography**, is the radiographic examination of the pulmonary circulation after injection of a radiopaque contrast dye into the pulmonary artery or one of its branches.
- **Thoracic computed tomography (CT) scan** provides cross-sectional views of the chest by passing an X-ray beam from a computerized scanner through the body at different angles. CT scanning may be done with or without an injected contrast dye.
- **Ventilation-perfusion scan** combines two procedures to evaluate the lungs' ventilation and perfusion. The ventilation scan is performed after the patient inhales a mixture of air and radioactive gas that delineates areas of the lung ventilated during respiration. The perfusion scan produces an image of pulmonary blood flow after I.V. injection of a radioactive dye.

I could paint you a picture but radiologic tests help you get a good look at me.

Other tests

Here are other tests used to diagnose respiratory system disorders:
- **Arterial blood gas measurement** provides levels of O_2 and CO_2 in arterial blood to evaluate acid-base balance and to assess and monitor a patient's ventilation and oxygenation status. (See *What a gas!* and *What arterial blood gases reveal.*)
- **Bronchoscopy** allows visual inspection of the tracheobronchial tree. (See *Understanding bronchoscopy.*)
- **Capnography** is a noninvasive procedure used to measure the amount of exhaled carbon dioxide through a device similar to a nasal cannula.
- **Culture and sensitivity tests** help identify the causative organism in bacterial, viral, or fungal infections. This is typically completed on sputum.
- **Lung biopsy** is an invasive procedure to collect a sample of lung tissue to test for culture or histologic analysis.
- **Pulse oximetry** is a continuous noninvasive study of arterial blood oxygen saturation using a probe or clip attached to a sensor site, typically completed with vital signs.
- **Sputum analysis** is the examination of a sample of expectorated material from the patient's lungs.
- In **thoracentesis**, a needle is used to puncture the chest and aspirate fluid from the parietal cavity for diagnostic or therapeutic purposes.

The real world

What a gas!

In practice, you'll commonly hear **arterial blood gases** referred to as *ABGs*, *blood gases*, or simply *gases*—as in "Let's draw some gases."

Understanding bronchoscopy

In **bronchoscopy**, a bronchoscope is used to examine the bronchi. This procedure is also used to obtain specimens or to remove foreign bodies.

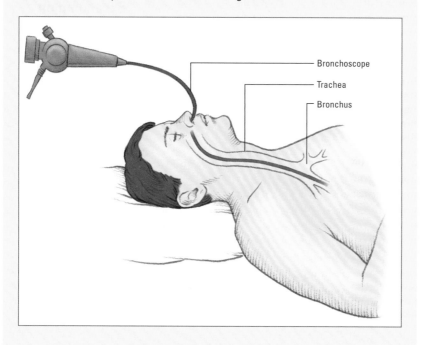

Bronchoscope

Trachea

Bronchus

Disorders

The respiratory system is such a complex network that many things can go wrong. Here's is a list of major respiratory disorders:

- **Acute bronchitis** is an inflammation of the bronchi accompanied by mucus production and subsequent obstruction of airflow. Infectious agents, such as influenza virus, streptococci, pneumococci, staphylococci, and *Haemophilus* organisms, can cause acute bronchitis.
- **Acute respiratory failure (ARF)** is caused by the cardiac and pulmonary systems inadequately exchanging O_2 and CO_2 in the lungs.
- **Acute respiratory distress syndrome (ARDS)** is a form of pulmonary edema that can quickly lead to acute respiratory failure.
- **Asbestosis** is caused by prolonged inhalation of asbestos fibers, which become encased in the bronchioles and alveolar walls in a proteinlike sheath.

What arterial blood gases reveal

Arterial blood gas analysis helps to diagnose the following disorders:
- **respiratory acidosis**, or excess carbon dioxide (CO_2) retention, which is typically caused by hypoventilation
- **respiratory alkalosis**, which occurs when too much CO_2 is excreted (hyperventilation is the primary cause)
- **metabolic acidosis**, which reflects elevated acid levels and may be caused by loss of bicarbonate, excess acid production, or a combination of both
- **metabolic alkalosis**, which reflects elevated bicarbonate levels, decreased acid levels, or both (prolonged vomiting and loss of potassium can deplete the body's acid stores; overuse of alkaline medications such as antacids can produce elevated bicarbonate levels).

- Atelectasis is the collapse of lung tissue or incomplete expansion of a lung caused by the absence of air in a portion of the lung or the entire lung. (See *Expanding on atelectasis*.)
- **Bronchiectasis** is a condition marked by chronic abnormal dilation of bronchi and destruction of bronchial walls.
- **Chronic obstructive pulmonary disease (COPD)** refers to a group of long-term pulmonary disorders marked by resistance to air flow (hence the term **obstructive**). Types of COPD include:
  - ○ **asthma**—episodic airway obstruction caused by bronchospasm, increased mucus secretion, and mucosal edema; may be either **extrinsic (atopic)**, a reaction to specific external allergens, or **intrinsic**, a reaction to internal, nonallergenic factors
  - ○ **chronic bronchitis**—characterized by excessive mucus production with productive cough lasting at least 3 months per year for 2 successive years; usually caused by prolonged exposure to bronchial irritants such as smoking, secondhand smoke, air pollution, dust, and toxic fumes
  - ○ **emphysema**—abnormal, permanent enlargement of the acini that's accompanied by destruction of the alveolar walls. It occurs when alveolar gas is trapped and gas exchange is compromised.
- **Cor pulmonale** is a heart condition in which hypertension of the pulmonary circulation leads to enlargement of the right ventricle.
- **Croup** is a severe inflammation and obstruction of the upper airway that usually follows an upper respiratory tract infection. It's a childhood disease characterized by a sharp barklike cough.
- **Cystic fibrosis** is a multisystem genetic disorder, a defect of the exocrine glands, causing tenacious mucus in the lungs.
- **Empyema** is a form of pleural effusion in which the fluid in the pleural space contains pus.
- **Epiglottiditis** is an acute inflammation of the epiglottis that tends to cause airway obstruction.
- **Hemothorax** is a collection of blood in the pleural cavity.
- **Hypercarbia** is the retention of carbon dioxide.
- **Hypoxemia** is a deficiency of O_2 in the arterial blood but isn't as severe as anoxia.
- **Hypoxia** is a deficiency of O_2 at a cellular level.
- **Legionnaires' disease** is an acute, noncommunicable bronchopneumonia caused by an airborne bacillus.
- **Lung abscess** is a lung infection accompanied by pus accumulation and tissue destruction.

Beyond the dictionary

Expanding on atelectasis

Atelectasis derives from the Greek terms **ateles**, meaning *imperfect*, and **ektasis**, meaning *expansion*. It refers to the collapse of lung tissue or incomplete expansion of a lung.

- **Obstructive sleep apnea** is an obstruction of the upper airway during sleep causing periods of apnea.
- **Pleural effusion** is accumulation of fluid in the interstitial and air spaces of the lung.
- **Pleurisy** is an inflammation of the pleurae characterized by dyspnea and stabbing pain, leading to restriction of breathing.
- **Pneumonia** is an acute infection of lung parenchyma commonly impairing gas exchange.
- **Pneumothorax** is a collection of air in the pleural cavity that leads to partial or complete lung collapse. (See *Pneuma: A breath of air.*) Different types of pneumothorax include:
  - ○ **closed pneumothorax**—condition in which air enters the pleural space from within the lungs
  - ○ **open pneumothorax**—condition in which atmospheric air flows directly into the pleural cavity
  - ○ **tension pneumothorax**—condition in which air in the pleural space compresses the thoracic organs, possibly causing **mediastinal shift** of organs and blood vessels, thus reducing blood flow to and from the heart.
- **Pulmonary edema** is a common complication of cardiac disorders in which extravascular fluid accumulates in the lung tissues and alveoli.
- **Pulmonary embolism** occurs when a clot or foreign substance lodges in a pulmonary artery.
- **Pulmonary fibrosis** is scar tissue formation in the connective tissue of the lungs.
- **Pulmonary hypertension** is any condition that increases resistance to blood flow in the pulmonary vessels. The most common cause is COPD.
- **Pulmonary infarction** occurs when lung tissue is denied blood flow and dies.
- **Respiratory distress syndrome**, also called **hyaline membrane disease**, is the most common cause of neonatal mortality. In respiratory distress syndrome, the premature infant develops widespread alveolar collapse.
- **Sarcoidosis** is a multisystem, granulomatous disorder that characteristically produces enlarged lymph nodes, pulmonary infiltration, and skeletal, liver, eye, or skin lesions.
- **Silicosis** is a progressive disease characterized by nodular lesions that commonly progress to fibrosis.
- **Sudden infant death syndrome (SIDS)**, also known as **crib death**, is the unexplained sudden death of a healthy infant (younger than 1 year) during sleep. Although the cause is unknown, placing the infant on his back to sleep has been shown to significantly decrease the incidence of SIDS.

Don't let the name fool you. **Tension pneumothorax** doesn't result from stress. Instead, it occurs when air in the pleural space compresses the thoracic organs.

Beyond the dictionary

Pneuma: A breath of air

In English, the **Pn-** combination always indicates a word of Greek origin, and the **p** isn't pronounced. **Pneuma**, the Greek word for *breath*, *spirit*, or *wind*, has given rise to a number of words. In medical terminology, it means *air* or *lung*. **Thorax** is a Greek word that means *chest*. It makes sense then that a **pneumothorax** is a collection of air in the chest.

- Tuberculosis is an infectious disease in which pulmonary infiltrates accumulate in the lungs, cavities develop, and masses of granulated tissue form. It may also infect other body organs and tissues.

Treatments

In this section, you'll learn the devices, surgical interventions, and other treatments used to improve oxygenation.

Tools of the trade

These are names of medical devices used to treat respiratory disorders:

- **bronchoscope**—used therapeutically to remove foreign bodies and tenacious secretions from the trachea and bronchi and to visualize the tissues
- **chest tube**—a tube inserted through a thoracostomy into the pleural space and used to remove blood, fluid, or air in cases of hemothorax, pleural effusion, pneumothorax, or acute empyema
- **endotracheal (ET) tube**—a flexible catheter inserted into the trachea via the mouth or nose and used to deliver O_2 into the lungs and maintain a patent airway
- **nasal cannula**—small tubes that deliver a variable, low-flow O_2 supply through the nasal passages (see *A look at a nasal cannula*)
- **nebulizer**—a device that delivers a fine spray for inhalation of moisture or drug therapy
- **resuscitation bag**—an inflatable device that can be attached to a facemask or directly to an ET or tracheostomy tube that's designed to manually deliver O_2 or room air into the lungs
- **stethoscope**—an instrument used for auscultation of respiratory, cardiac, arterial, and venous sounds consisting of two earpieces connected by flexible tubing to a diaphragm, which is placed against the patient's body
- **tracheostomy tube**—a tube inserted into the surgical opening through the neck into the trachea, which is used to relieve upper airway obstruction and aid breathing; may be used with a mechanical ventilator. (See *A look at a tracheostomy tube.*) The tracheostomy may be permanent or temporary, depending on the patient condition.
- **Venturi mask**—a device designed to deliver a high-flow, precise O_2 mixture. (See *A look at a Venturi mask.*)

A look at a nasal cannula

A *nasal cannula* delivers a low-flow oxygen supply to the nasal passages through small, plastic tubes, as shown in the illustration below.

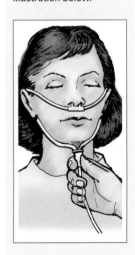

A look at a tracheostomy tube

A *tracheostomy tube* is used to relieve upper airway obstruction and to aid breathing. The tube can be made of plastic or metal and comes in three varieties: uncuffed, cuffed, and fenestrated. A plastic-cuffed tracheostomy tube is shown here. Tracheostomy tubes can be reusable or disposable according to the manufacturer.

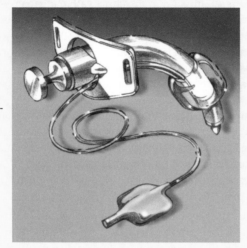

Surgery

Here are the names of surgical procedures used to treat respiratory disorders:

- **pneumonectomy**—surgical removal of the lung
- **thoracentesis**—a needle puncture of the chest performed to drain fluid from the parietal cavity; it may be performed at the bedside or as an outpatient procedure

A look at a Venturi mask

A *Venturi mask* is a device designed to deliver a high-flow, precise mixture of oxygen and air.

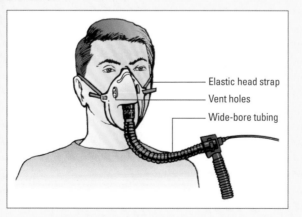

Elastic head strap

Vent holes

Wide-bore tubing

- thoracostomy—the surgical creation of an opening in the chest wall for the purpose of drainage
- thoracotomy—a surgical incision in the chest wall made to excise a lung or portions of it; thoracotomy can be further classified in three ways:
  - ○ lobectomy—the surgical excision of a lobe of a lung
  - ○ **segmental resection**—surgical removal of one or more of the lung's segments (removes more functional tissue than a lobectomy)
  - ○ **wedge resection**—the surgical removal of a triangular section of lung tissue
- tracheotomy—a surgical opening in the trachea that provides an airway for intubated patients who need prolonged mechanical ventilation; also used to help remove lung secretions and bypass upper airway obstruction.

Ventilation therapies

Ventilation therapy moves air in and out of a patient's lungs, but it doesn't ensure adequate gas exchange.

Manual ventilation

In **manual ventilation**, a handheld resuscitation bag is used to deliver room air or O_2 to the lungs of a patient who can't breathe spontaneously. (See *Vent 'em, bag 'em.*)

Noninvasive Ventilation

Noninvasive positive pressure ventilation (NPPV) uses a tight-fighting mask and seal with the ability to improve gas exchange without the need for intubation. Examples include CPAP (continuous flow of oxygen) and BiPAP (provides positive pressure on inhalation and exhalation).

Mechanical ventilation

Mechanical ventilators may supply negative or positive pressure. Negative pressure on the chest and lungs expands them during inspiration and is used to treat neuromuscular disorders. Positive pressure, the most commonly used mechanical ventilation system, is used to treat respiratory disorders.

Be positive

The **positive-pressure system** exerts positive pressure on the airway to inflate alveoli during inspiration. The inspiratory cycles of these

The real world

Vent 'em, bag 'em

The handheld resuscitation bag is commonly referred to as an **Ambu bag**. You may hear people refer to the process of using this device as *bagging the patient.* For example, "Disconnect him from the ventilator and bag him." If a patient requires a mechanical ventilator to assist with breathing, you may hear people say that the patient is *on a vent.*

ventilators may vary in volume, pressure, or time. There are three inspiratory cycle types:

- **Pressure-cycled** ventilation provides a continuous flow of O_2 until a preset pressure is reached.
- **Time-cycled** ventilation provides flow for a preset amount of time.
- **Volume-cycled** ventilation delivers a preset volume of air.

In the mode

Ventilation is provided through several ventilator modes:

- **Control mode** completely controls the patient's respiration, delivering a set tidal volume at a prescribed rate.
- **Assist mode** allows the patient to initiate a breath and receive a tidal volume from the machine.
- **Assist-control mode** allows the patient to initiate breathing, but a backup control delivers a preset number of breaths at a set volume.
- **Continuous positive airway pressure (CPAP)** maintains positive pressure in the airways throughout the entire respiratory cycle.
- In the **positive end-expiratory pressure (PEEP) mode**, positive pressure is applied during expiration.
- **Pressure support ventilation** augments the patient's spontaneous breath with a preset pressure. It doesn't provide the entire volume. The rate isn't set by the machine; it's set by the patient's spontaneous efforts.
- In **synchronized intermittent mandatory ventilation (SIMV)**, a machine delivers a set number of specific-volume breaths. The patient can breathe on his or her own between SIMV breaths at volumes that differ from those on the machine. SIMV is commonly used as a weaning tool, conditioning the patient's respiratory muscles.

Drug therapy

Drug therapy for respiratory disorders includes:

- **antitussives** to suppress cough
- **antihistamines** to manage seasonal allergies and allergic reactions
- **bronchodilators** to relax smooth muscle and dilate constricted airways, increasing airflow
- **corticosteroids** to reduce inflammation and bronchoconstricting agents
- **decongestants** to relieve swelling and inflammation in nasal passages
- **expectorants**, which liquefy secretions to help remove mucus
- **methylxanthine agents** to relax bronchial smooth muscle in patients with asthma and to stimulate respiratory drive in patients with bronchitis, emphysema, and apnea
- **mucolytics** to enhance mucus removal.

Memory jogger

In this case, mad is good! To remember the essentials of drug therapy for respiratory disorders, think "B-CAME MAD":

Bronchodilator

Corticosteroids

Antihistamines

Methylxanthine agents

Expectorants

Mucolytics

Antitussives

Decongestants.

Other therapies

Here are other therapies to treat respiratory disorders:
- **Aerosol treatments** deliver drugs by way of a nebulizer, which turns liquid into a spray the patient breathes.
- **Deep breathing** loosens secretions and opens airways.
- **Oxygen therapy** is delivered by a nasal cannula, catheter, mask, or transtracheal catheter; it prevents hypoxemia and eases the patient's breathing.
- **Postural drainage** uses gravity to help move secretions from the lungs and bronchi into the trachea to be coughed up.
- **Percussion** involves cupping hands and fingers together and clapping them alternately over the patient's lung fields to loosen secretions for expectoration.
- An **ultrasonic nebulizer** mobilizes thick secretions and promotes a productive cough.

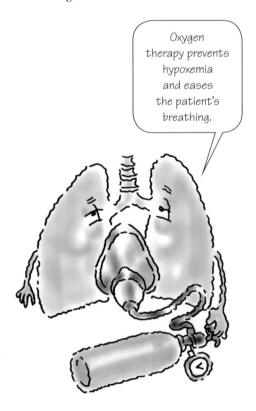

Vocabulary builders

At a crossroads

Completing this crossword puzzle will help you breathe more easily about respiratory system terms. Good luck!

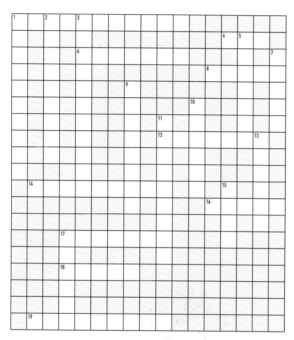

No need to hyperventilate. This is just a game.

Across

1. Space between the lungs
4. Acronym for volume of air that can be exhaled after maximum inspiration
6. Another word for **windpipe**
8. Absence of breathing
12. Deficiency of O_2 at a cellular level
14. Surgical excision of a lung lobe
16. Slit on the lungs' medial surface
17. Bony structures that form the posterior walls of the nasal passages
18. The lung that's shorter, broader, and larger than the other
19. Unusually slow, regular respirations

Down

1. Type of ventilation that uses a positive-pressure system
2. Most important muscle for respiration
3. Drug type that acts to suppress cough
5. Eponym for a mask designed to deliver a high-flow, precise O_2 mixture
7. Another word for **nostrils**
9. Another word for **larynx**
10. The respiratory system structure that separates the nasal passages
11. Plural form of **pharynx**
13. Chief respiratory unit for gas exchange
15. Eponym for respirations characterized by irregular periods of apnea alternating with four or five breaths of the same depth
17. Another word for **tracheal bifurcation**

Match game

When assessing a patient's respiratory system, it's important to know the terms for different breath sounds. Match the description of each breath sound below to its name.

Clues

Choices

Normal sounds

1. Loud, high-pitched sounds that are heard at the manubrium and are loudest on expiration ____

A. Absent

B. Bronchial

2. Sounds heard in the lung's periphery, in front of the chest, on both sides, and in the back that are longer and louder during inspiration than expiration ____

C. Bronchovesicular

D. Crackles

E. Decreased

3. Soft, medium-pitched, breezy sounds that are lower pitched than bronchial sounds but higher pitched than vesicular sounds ____

F. Pleural friction rubs

G. Rhonchi

H. Stridor

Abnormal sounds

4. Sounds like hairs being rubbed together, usually heard first over the lung bases ____

I. Vesicular

J. Wheezes

5. Loud, coarse, low-pitched bubbling sounds heard primarily during expiration ____

6. High-pitched, musical sounds that may occur during both inspiration and expiration but predominantly during expiration ____

7. Coarse, low-pitched sounds heard at the anterolateral chest wall (in front, near the ribs) during inspiration and expiration that sound like pieces of sandpaper being rubbed together ____

8. Crowing sound heard during inspiration, caused by air whistling as it passes through swollen upper airways ____

9. Abnormally diminished breath sounds in areas of the lung ____

10. Lack of sound over areas of the lungs that normally have breath sounds ____

Talking in circles

Use the clues below to fill in the blanks with the appropriate word. Then unscramble the circled letters to find the answer to the question posed below.

1. __ __ __ ◯ __ __

2. __ __ __ __ __ __ __ __ __ __ __ ◯

3. __ __ __ ◯ __

4. __ __ ◯ __ __

5. __ ◯ __ __ __ __

1. The Greek word for *breath*, *spirit*, or *wind*
2. Sudden, forceful, involuntary contraction of the smooth muscle of the bronchi
3. Small, hairlike projections in the trachea
4. The Latin word for *lung*
5. The Greek word for *throat*

You probably enter a house through a door, but my friends—the lungs—admit my blood vessels and the mainstem bronchi through what structure?

O see, can you say?

Sound out each group of pictures and symbols below to reveal a term that was reviewed in the chapter.

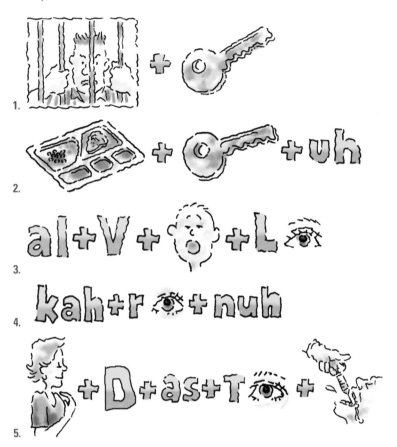

1.

2.

3.

4.

5.

Answers

At a crossroads

¹M	E	²D	³A	S	T	I	N	U	M					
E		I	N							⁴F	⁵V	C		
C		A	⁶T	R	A	C	H	E	A		E	⁷N		
H		P	I					⁸A	P	N	E	A		
A		H	T	⁹V					T		R			
N		R	U	O		¹⁰S			R		E			
I		A	S	I	¹¹P	E			U		S			
C		G	S	C	¹²H	Y	P	O	X	I	¹³A			
A		M	I	E	A	T					C			
L			V	B	R	U			¹⁵B		I			
¹⁴L	O	B	E	C	T	O	M	Y		M	N			
				X	N				¹⁶H	I	L	U	M	
				G					O		S			
		¹⁷C	O	N	C	H	A	E	T					
		A					S							
		¹⁸R	I	G	H	T								
		I												
		N												
¹⁹B	R	A	D	Y	P	N	E	A						

Match game

Answers: 1. B; 2. I; 3. C; 4. D; 5. G; 6. J; 7. F; 8. H; 9. E; 10. A

Talking in circles

Answers: 1. Pneuma; 2. Bronchospasm; 3. Cilia; 4. Pulmo;
5. Pharynx

Answer to puzzle—Hilum

O see, can you say?

Answers: 1. Conchae; 2. Trachea; 3. Alveoli; 4. Carina;
5. Mediastinum

Suggested references

Cooper, K., & Gosnell, L. (2015). *Foundations for adult health nursing* (7th ed.). St. Louis, MO: Elsevier.

Haines, L. E. (2017). Continuous wave-form capnography: A crucial tool for ED clinicians. *American Nurse Today, 12*(1), 6–8.

Ignatavicius, D. D., & Workman, M. L. (2016). *Medical-surgical nursing: Patient centered collaborative care* (8th ed.). St. Louis, MO: Elsevier.

Lilley, L. L., Collins, S. R., & Snyder, J. S. (2017). *Pharmacology and the nursing process* (8th ed.). St. Louis, MO: Elsevier.

Patton, K. T., & Thibodeau, G. A. (2014). *The human body in health & disease* (6th ed.). St. Louis, MO: Elsevier.

Sole, M. L., Klein, D. L., & Moseley, M. J. (2017). *Introduction to critical care nursing* (7th ed.). St. Louis, MO: Elsevier.

Urden, L. D., Stacy, K. M., & Lough, M. E. (2016). *Priorities in critical care nursing* (7th ed.). St. Louis, MO: Elsevier.

Chapter 8

Gastrointestinal system

Just the facts

In this chapter, you'll learn:

♦ terminology related to the structure and function of the GI system

♦ terminology needed for physical examination of the GI system

♦ tests that help diagnose GI disorders

♦ common GI disorders and their treatments.

GI structure and function

This chapter introduces terms associated with the GI system, the system responsible for digestion and elimination. The first part of the word **gastrointestinal**, *gastro-*, is a Greek word that means *stomach*; it's used in many medical terms. The second part of the word refers, of course, to the intestines. But the GI system includes more than just the stomach and the intestines. (See *Pronouncing key GI system terms*.)

Two parts

The GI system has two major components:

- **alimentary canal** (also called the **GI tract**)—the mouth, pharynx, esophagus, stomach, intestines, rectum, and anus
- **accessory GI organs**—the liver, gallbladder, biliary duct system, and pancreas.

Two functions

Together, the alimentary canal and the accessory organs serve two major functions:

- **digestion**—the breakdown of food and fluid into simple chemicals that can be absorbed into the bloodstream and transported throughout the body

Let's see. **Gastro** means *stomach*; **entero** means *intestine*; and **-ology** means *study*. Seems simple— **gastroenterology** is the study of the stomach and intestines.

Pronouncing key GI system terms

Below is a list of key terms related to the GI system, along with the correct ways to pronounce them

Anastomosis	UH-NAS-TUH-MOH-SIS
Cachexia	KUH-KEK-SEE-UH
Cholangiogram	KOH-LAN-JEE-OH-GRAM
Diverticulosis	DEYE-VER-TIK-YOO-LOH-SIS
Gastroenteritis	GAS-TROH-EN-TER-EYE-TIS
Submandibular	SUHB-MAN-DIHB-YOU-LUHR
Tunica adventitia	TOO-NIK-UH AD-VEN-TI-SHUH

- **elimination**—the expulsion of waste products from the body through excretion of feces.

Alimentary canal

Here are the terms and descriptions of structures of the alimentary canal.

Mouth

Also called the **buccal cavity** or **oral cavity**, the mouth is bounded by the lips, cheeks, **palate** (the roof of the mouth), and tongue. It also contains the teeth. The mouth initiates the mechanical breakdown of food. Ducts connect the mouth with three major pairs of **salivary glands**, which secrete **saliva** to moisten food during chewing and convert starch into maltose. The three pairs are:

- **parotid**—located at the side of the neck in front of and below the external ear
- **submandibular**—located, as the name indicates, beneath the mandible, or lower jaw
- **sublingual**—located, as the name indicates, under the tongue. (See *Structures of the GI system.*)

The breakdown of food begins in the **oral cavity**—that's the mouth.

Structures of the GI system

The GI system includes the alimentary canal (the pharynx, esophagus, stomach, and small and large intestines) and the accessory organs (the liver, biliary duct system, and pancreas). These structures are shown below.

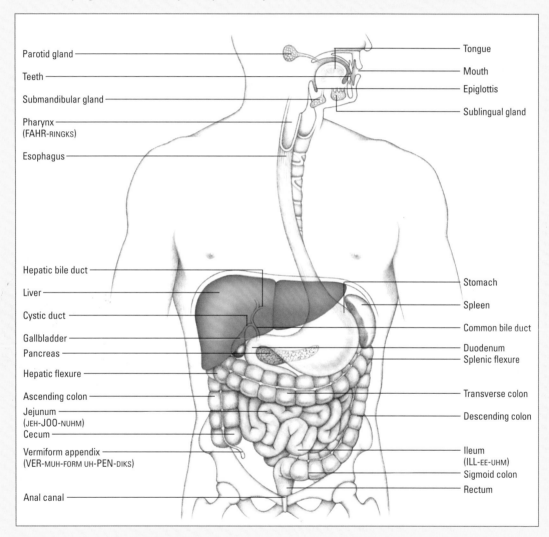

Pharynx
(FAHR-RINGKS)

Jejunum
(JEH-JOO-NUHM)

Vermiform appendix
(VER-MUH-FORM UH-PEN-DIKS)

Ileum
(ILL-EE-UHM)

Parotid gland — Teeth — Submandibular gland — Pharynx — Esophagus — Hepatic bile duct — Liver — Cystic duct — Gallbladder — Pancreas — Hepatic flexure — Ascending colon — Cecum — Anal canal — Tongue — Mouth — Epiglottis — Sublingual gland — Stomach — Spleen — Common bile duct — Duodenum — Splenic flexure — Transverse colon — Descending colon — Sigmoid colon — Rectum

Pharynx

The **pharynx**, or throat, a cavity extending from the base of the skull to the esophagus, aids swallowing by peristalsis propelling it toward the esophagus.

Esophagus

The **esophagus** is a hollow, muscular tube that extends from the pharynx through the mediastinum to the stomach. The **esophageal sphincter** (a sphincter at the upper border of the esophagus) must relax for food to enter the esophagus. **Peristalsis** (the rhythmic contraction and relaxation of smooth muscle) propels liquids and solids through the esophagus into the stomach.

Stomach

The **stomach** is a collapsible, pouchlike structure in the upper left part of the abdominal cavity, just below the diaphragm. Its upper border attaches to the lower end of the esophagus. The **cardiac sphincter** guards the opening to the stomach and opens as food approaches. It also prevents stomach contents from reentering the esophagus (reflux). The lateral surface of the stomach is called the **greater curvature**, and the medial surface, the **lesser curvature**.

The stomach serves as a temporary storage space for food and also begins digestion. It has four main regions:

1. The **cardia** lies near the junction of the stomach and esophagus.
2. The **fundus** is the enlarged portion above and to the left of the esophageal opening into the stomach.
3. The **body** is the middle portion of the stomach.
4. The **pylorus** is the lower portion, lying near the junction of the stomach and the duodenum.

Stomach's the name. Temporary food storage is my game.

Intestines

After mixing food with gastric secretions, the stomach breaks it down into chyme, a semifluid substance, and then moves the gastric contents into the intestines, which consist of the small intestine and the large intestine.

Small but really lo-o-o-o-n-n-g

Although it's called "small," the narrow tube called the **small intestine** is actually about 20′ (6.1 m) long and is composed of three major divisions:

- The **duodenum** is the most superior division and most active in digestion.
- The **jejunum** is the middle portion.
- The **ileum** is the most inferior portion.

The small intestine completes food digestion. Food molecules are absorbed through its wall into the circulatory system, from which they're delivered to body cells.

Now LARGE

The **large intestine** extends from the **ileocecal valve** (the valve between the ileum of the small intestine and the first segment of the large intestine) to the **anus**. The large intestine absorbs water, secretes mucus, and eliminates digestive wastes. It has six segments:

- The **cecum**, a saclike structure, makes up the first few inches of the large intestine, beginning just below the ileocecal valve.
- The **ascending colon** rises on the right posterior abdominal wall and then turns sharply under the liver at the hepatic flexure.
- The **transverse colon**, situated above the small intestine, passes horizontally across the abdomen and below the liver, stomach, and spleen. At the left splenic flexure, it turns downward.
- The **descending colon** starts near the spleen and extends down the left side of the abdomen into the pelvic cavity.
- The **sigmoid colon** descends through the pelvic cavity, where it becomes the rectum. (See *Sigmoid has an "S" shape.*)
- The **rectum**, the last few inches of the large intestine, terminates at the **anus**.

Inner lining

The wall of the GI tract consists of several layers. The innermost layer, the **mucosa** (also called the **tunica mucosa**), consists of epithelial and surface cells and loose connective tissue. The **submucosa** (also called the **tunica submucosa**) encircles the mucosa. It's composed of loose connective tissue, blood and lymphatic vessels, and a nerve network.

Around the submucosa lies the **tunica muscularis**, which is composed of skeletal muscle in the mouth, pharynx, and upper esophagus and longitudinal and circular smooth muscle fibers elsewhere in the tract.

Outer covering

The **visceral peritoneum** is the GI tract's outer covering. In the esophagus and rectum, it's also called the **tunica adventitia**; elsewhere in the GI tract, it's called the **tunica serosa**.

The visceral peritoneum covers most of the abdominal organs and lies next to an identical layer, the **parietal peritoneum**, which lines the abdominal cavity.

Vital accessories

Accessory organs—the liver, the biliary duct system, and pancreas—contribute hormones, enzymes, and bile, which are vital to digestion. They deliver their secretions to the duodenum through the **hepato-pancreatic ampulla**, also called the **ampulla of Vater** (named after Abraham Vater, a German anatomist). (See *The little jug.*)

Memory jogger

No pussyfooting around this tip. To remember the structures of the large intestine, think "CAT DESIRE":

Cecum

Ascending colon

Transverse colon

DEscending colon

SIgmoid colon

Rectum.

Beyond the dictionary

Sigmoid has an "S" shape

The term **sigmoid** derives from the Greek word *sigma*, the name of the eighteenth letter of the Greek alphabet. In Greek, the letter is represented like this: ς, a kind of truncated *s*, which pretty closely resembles the shape of the sigmoid colon.

The entry of bile and pancreatic juice is controlled by a muscular valve called the **hepatopancreatic sphincter**, or **Oddi's sphincter** (named after Ruggero Oddi, an Italian doctor).

Liver and lobule

The **liver's** digestive function is to produce bile for export to the duodenum. The **liver's** functional unit, the **lobule**, consists of a plate of hepatic cells, or **hepatocytes**, that encircle a central vein and radiate outward.

Caps off to sinusoids

Separating the hepatocyte plates from each other are sinusoids, the liver's capillary system.

Toxic cleanup

Kupffer's cells, which line the sinusoids, remove bacteria and toxins that have entered the blood through the intestinal capillaries. (Kupffer's cells are named after Karl Wilhelm von Kupffer, a German anatomist.)

Beyond the dictionary

The little jug

Who could resist breaking down **hepatopancreatic ampulla?**

Easy ones first
Hepato- comes from the Greek word for the liver, *hepatikos.*
Pancreatic originated from the Latin term *pancreaticus*, which means *pertaining to the pancreas.*

Now for the hard part
Ampulla is a Latin term that means *little jug* or, in medical terms, a flasklike dilation of a tubular structure.

All together now
When these terms are put together, they describe a structure in which the ducts that deliver bile and pancreatic juice from the liver (**hepato**) and pancreas (**pancreatic**) unite at a flasklike (**ampulla**) junction called the **hepatopancreatic ampulla.**

He's the **hepato** part. I'm the **pancreatic** part!

Ducts

Bile, recycled from bile salts in the blood, leaves through biliary ducts that merge into the right and left hepatic ducts to form the **common hepatic duct.** This duct joins the **cystic duct** from the gallbladder to form the **common bile duct**, which leads to the duodenum.

Bully for bile

A yellow-greenish liquid composed of water, cholesterol, bile salts, electrolytes, and phospholipids, **bile** breaks down fats and neutralizes gastric secretions in chyme. Bile prevents jaundice by assisting with excretion of **conjugated bilirubin**, an end product of normal hemoglobin breakdown.

Gallbladder

The **gallbladder** is a pear-shaped organ that's nestled under the liver and joined to the larger organ by the cystic duct. The gallbladder's job is to store and concentrate bile produced by the liver. (See *Why not bilebladder?*)

I'm very proud of my three ducts.

Common Hepatic Duct
Cystic Duct
Common Bile Duct

Of all the gall!

When stimulated by a hormone called **cholecystokinin**, the gallbladder contracts, the hepatopancreatic ampulla relaxes, and bile is released into the common bile duct for delivery to the duodenum. (See *Bile, bladder, and protein,* page 167.)

Pancreas

The **pancreas** lies behind the stomach, with its head and neck extending into the curve of the duodenum and its tail lying against the spleen. The pancreas contains two cell types:
*   **endocrine cells**, from which hormones are secreted into the blood
*   **exocrine cells**, from which enzymes are secreted through ducts to the digestive system.

In the islets of Langerhans

The pancreas's endocrine function involves the **islets of Langerhans**, named for Paul Langerhans (1847–1888), the German doctor who discovered them. These microscopic structures—over 1 million of them—are scattered throughout the pancreas and house two cell types:
*   **alpha cells**, which secrete **glucagon**, a hormone that stimulates the breakdown of glycogen to glucose in the liver—a process referred to as **glycogenolysis**
*   **beta cells**, which secrete **insulin** to promote carbohydrate metabolism.

Physical examination terms

Before you can perform a complete examination of the GI tract, you need to understand the associated terminology:

- **Aaron's sign**, named for American physician Charles Aaron (1866–1951), refers to pain in the chest or abdominal area that's elicited by applying gentle but steadily increasing pressure over McBurney's point (2' [5.1 cm] below the right anterior superior spine of the ilium, on a line between that spine and the umbilicus). A positive sign indicates appendicitis.
- **Abdominal distention** refers to increased abdominal girth—the result of increased intra-abdominal pressure forcing the abdominal wall outward.
- **Anorexia** is a loss of appetite.
- **Ascites** refers to the abnormal accumulation of serous fluid in the peritoneal cavity.
- **Auscultation** is an assessment method; it means to listen carefully, usually with a stethoscope.
- **Ballottement**, lightly tapping or bouncing fingertips against the abdominal wall, elicits abdominal muscle resistance or guarding.
- **Bowel sounds** are auscultated with a stethoscope and provide information about **bowel motility** (movement) and the underlying vessels and organs. Normally, air and fluid moving through the bowel create soft, bubbling sounds, which are often mixed with soft clicks and gurgles, that occur every 5 to 15 seconds. Bowel sounds are described using the following terms:
  - ○ **absent** bowel sounds, when no bowel sounds are heard
  - ○ **borborygmi**, the familiar "growling stomach" of a hungry patient
  - ○ **hyperactive**, which describes rapid, high-pitched, loud gurgling sounds
  - ○ **hypoactive**, which occur at a rate no greater than one per minute.
- **Cachexia** is a profound state of overall ill health and malnutrition characterized by weakness and emaciation.
- **Colic** is acute abdominal pain.
- **Constipation** refers to a decreased passage of stools. A constipated stool is characteristically hard and dry.
- **Cullen's sign** refers to irregular, bluish hemorrhagic patches on the skin around the umbilicus and occasionally around abdominal scars. Cullen's sign indicates massive hemorrhage.
- **Diarrhea** is rapid movement of fecal material through the intestines that causes poor absorption of water and nutrients. Diarrhea stools are watery and frequent.

Beyond the dictionary

Why not bilebladder?

We might just as well call the gallbladder a **bilebladder** because the two words, **gall** and **bile**, refer to the same thing. **Gall** appears in Old English as early as the year 825 in a translation of the Psalms. The word **gall** actually refers to the yellowish color of bile. The word **bile**, on the other hand, is a relatively recent borrowing from Latin by way of French; this word doesn't show up in English until the 17th century.

- Dyspepsia is gastric discomfort, such as fullness, heartburn, bloating, and nausea, that occurs after eating.
- Dysphagia is difficult or painful swallowing.
- **Emesis**, from Greek, is an expulsion of the stomach contents by vomiting.
- Epigastrium refers to the upper and middle regions of the abdomen.
- Fecal **impaction** is an accumulation of hardened feces in the rectum or sigmoid colon that can't be evacuated.
- Fecal **incontinence** refers to an inability to prevent the discharge of feces.
- **Flatulence** refers to a sensation of gaseous abdominal fullness.
- **Grey Turner's sign** is characterized by a bruiselike discoloration of the skin of the flanks that appears 6 to 24 hours after the onset of retroperitoneal hemorrhage in acute pancreatitis.
- **Guarding** is moving away or flinching when a tender area of the abdomen is touched.
- **Heartburn**, also referred to as pyrosis, is a burning sensation in the esophagus or below the sternum in the region of the heart.
- **Hematemesis** is vomiting blood.
- **Hematochezia** is fresh, bright red blood passed from the rectum.
- **Hemoperitoneum** refers to a leakage of blood into the peritoneal cavity.
- Hepatomegaly is an enlarged liver.
- Hypogastrium is the lowest, middle abdominal region.
- Ileus is a mechanical intestinal obstruction.
- **Jaundice** is a yellow appearance of the skin, mucous membranes, and sclerae of the eyes, resulting from elevated serum bilirubin levels.
- **Meconium** is the substance that fills the entire intestine before birth. A neonate's first stool is called a **meconium stool.**
- Melena is black, tarry stools—a common sign of upper GI bleeding.
- **Murphy's sign** refers to pain on deep inspiration that occurs when an inflamed gallbladder is palpated by pressing the fingers under the rib cage. Hepatitis may also produce a positive Murphy's sign.
- **Nausea** is an unpleasant feeling that typically precedes vomiting.
- **Occult blood** is an amount of blood so small that it can be seen or detected only by a chemical test or microscopic examination.
- **Odynophagia** is painful swallowing.
- Pica refers to the craving and ingestion of normally inedible substances, such as plaster, charcoal, clay, wool, ashes, paint, and dirt.
- Polyphagia is consuming abnormally large amounts of food.
- Polydipsia is chronic, excessive thirst.

Beyond the dictionary

Bile, bladder, and protein

Cholecystokinin is easy to dissect:
Chole- is Greek for bile.
Cysto- comes from the Greek word *kystis*, meaning *bladder.*
Kinin is a general term for plasma proteins—like this hormone.

Borborygmi is the familiar "growling stomach" of a hungry patient.

- **Rebound tenderness**, also referred to as **Blumberg's sign**, is pain that occurs when a hand pressing on the abdomen is suddenly released.
- **Rectal tenesmus** is a spasmodic contraction of the anal sphincter with a persistent urge to defecate and involuntary, ineffective straining. This occurs in inflammatory bowel disorders, such as ulcerative colitis and Crohn's disease, and in rectal tumors.
- **Regurgitation** is the backflowing or return of food and fluids into the mouth without nausea or belching.
- **Rigidity** describes a stiff abdominal wall, sometimes called a *boardlike abdomen.*
- **Rovsing's sign**, named after the Copenhagen surgeon Niels Rovsing (1862–1927), who first described this symptom, occurs in acute appendicitis. Pressure on the left lower quadrant of the abdomen will cause pain in the right lower quadrant.
- **Steatorrhea** is excessive fat in the feces that floats and is frothy and foul smelling.
- **Tympany** is a clear, hollow, drumlike sound heard when palpating the abdomen.
- **Vomiting** is forcibly expelling the contents of the stomach through the mouth. Vomiting can be described as:
  - **cyclic** (recurring attacks of vomiting)
  - **dry** (attempt to vomit without emesis)
  - **projectile** (ejected with great force).

Occult blood refers to minute amounts of blood that can be seen or detected only by a chemical test or microscopic examination.

Diagnostic tests

This section covers diagnostic tests used to identify GI disorders.

Blood tests

Serum studies of enzymes, proteins, and formed elements are used to investigate disorders involving the liver, pancreas, gallbladder, and intestinal tract. You'll see the following tests ordered most often:

- The **alkaline phosphatase test** measures the enzyme activity of several alkaline phosphatase isoenzymes found in the liver, bone, kidneys, intestines, and biliary system.
- The *Helicobacter pylori* **antibodies test** checks for the presence of *H. pylori*, which are associated with chronic gastritis and idiopathic chronic duodenal ulceration.
- The **serum amylase test** measures the level of the pancreatic enzyme alpha-amylase, which is active in the digestion of starch and glycogen. Amylase is released with pancreatic damage.

- The **serum bilirubin test** measures serum levels of bilirubin, the main pigment in bile and the major product of hemoglobin breakdown.
- The **serum lipase test** measures the amount of lipase in the blood; large amounts indicate pancreatic damage.
- The **total cholesterol test** measures the circulating levels of free cholesterol and cholesterol esters.

The different serum tests examine the levels of substances in the blood. For example, a serum bilirubin test measures bilirubin level.

Radiologic and imaging tests

Tests that use X-rays, electromagnetic waves, and sound waves to create images of internal structures of the GI system and its function include the following:

- **Abdominal X-ray**, also called a **flat plate** (or **flat and erect plates) of the abdomen**, helps visualize the position, size, and structure of abdominal contents.
- **Barium enema** is the radiographic examination of the large intestine after rectal instillation of barium, a radiopaque contrast medium.
- **Barium swallow** is the radiographic examination of the throat and esophagus after ingestion of a radiopaque contrast medium.
- Cholangiogram is an X-ray of the gallbladder and biliary duct system that's obtained by injecting a radiopaque contrast medium.
- **Computerized tomography (CT) scan** translates the action of multiple X-ray beams into three-dimensional images.
- **Contrast radiography** is a general term that describes several procedures that use a radiopaque contrast medium to accentuate differences among densities of fat, air, soft tissue, and bone.
- **Endoscopic retrograde cholangiopancreatography (ERCP)** is a radiographic examination of the pancreatic ducts and hepatobiliary tree after injection of a contrast medium into the **duodenal papilla** (small nipplelike elevation). This test is done by use of an **endoscope** guided by the use of fluoroscopy. (See *I'd rather say ERCP.*)
- **Esophagogastroduodenoscopy (EGD)** allows visual examination of the esophagus, stomach, and duodenum using a fiberoptic endoscope.
- **Liver-spleen scan** uses a gamma-ray camera to record the distribution of radioactivity within the liver and spleen after injection of a radioactive colloid.
- **Magnetic resonance cholangiopancreatography** is used in much the same way as ERCP but isn't as invasive. It creates images using electromagnetic waves and helps to visualize the biliary structures, bile ducts, pancreatic ducts, and gallbladder.

- **Magnetic resonance imaging (MRI)** creates images by computer analysis of electromagnetic waves directed into the tissues.
- In **percutaneous transhepatic** cholangiography, a radiopaque contrast medium is introduced through a catheter inserted through the skin into the liver to allow examination of the biliary system.
- **Ultrasonography** creates images of deep structures of the body by computer analysis of ultrasonic (high-frequency sound) waves directed into and reflected from tissues.
- **Upper GI and small bowel series** involves the fluoroscopic examination of the esophagus, stomach, and small intestine after the patient ingests a contrast medium.

Other tests

Other tests used to diagnose abnormalities of the GI system include the following:
- **Basal gastric secretion test** measures basal acid secretion during fasting by aspirating stomach contents through a nasogastric (NG) tube.
- **Breath hydrogen analysis** is a simple method of detecting lactose intolerance.
- Colonoscopy is an endoscopic examination of the colon.
- **Endoscopy** is a visual inspection of a body cavity using an optical instrument called an endoscope.
- **Esophageal acidity test** evaluates the competence of the lower esophageal sphincter—the major barrier to reflux—by measuring the pH within the esophagus with an electrode that is attached to a special catheter.
- Fecal **lipids test** is used to detect excessive excretion of lipids in patients with signs of malabsorption.
- **Gastric acid stimulation test** measures the secretion of gastric acid for 1 hour after subcutaneous injection of a drug that stimulates gastric acid output.
- **Gastric emptying study** is used to diagnose impaired gastric motility.
- **Laparoscopy** is an endoscopic examination of the interior of the peritoneal cavity.
- **Manometry** is the use of water-filled catheters connected to pressure transducers in different parts of the GI system to evaluate contractility.
- **Percutaneous liver biopsy** involves aspiration of a core of liver tissue for analysis.
- **Peritoneal fluid analysis** examines a specimen of peritoneal fluid obtained by paracentesis for appearance, red blood cell and white

I'd rather say ERCP

Endoscopic retrograde cholangiopancreatography (ERCP) is a real mouthful, but this word is easy to dissect: **endoscopic** refers to the optical instrument used in the procedure. **Retrograde** means *moving against the usual flow* and refers to dye injected the wrong way in the ampulla of Vater. **Cholangio-** refers to the biliary tract, **pancrea-** means *pancreas*, and **-graphy** is a recording. Therefore, ERCP is a recording of the function of the biliary tract and pancreas.

blood cell counts, cytologic studies, microbiologic studies for bacteria and fungi, and determinations of protein, glucose, amylase, ammonia, and alkaline phosphatase levels.
- **Sigmoidoscopy** is an endoscopic examination of the sigmoid colon.
- **Stool culture** is a bacteriologic examination of feces.
- **Urine bilirubin test** detects abnormally high urine concentrations of direct bilirubin, possibly indicating liver disease.
- **Urine urobilinogen test** detects impaired liver function by measuring urine levels of urobilinogen, which results from the reduction of bilirubin by intestinal bacteria.

Here's a little tune I like to call "Getting to know me."

Disorders

Here are descriptions of disorders of the organs of the GI system.

Mouth and esophagus

The following are important terms used to describe disorders of the upper alimentary canal:
- **Achalasia** is an esophageal motility disorder resulting from neural dysfunction and lower esophageal sphincter dysfunction.
- **Cleft lip** and **cleft palate** are developmental anomalies present at birth. These congenital disabilities typically require surgical repair.
- **Esophageal atresia** refers to a closed esophagus.
- **Esophageal diverticula** are hollowed outpouchings in the esophageal wall.
- **Esophageal stricture** is a narrowing of the esophagus.
- **Esophageal varices** are enlarged, torturous veins in the lower esophagus that are caused by portal hypertension.
- **Erythroplakia** is a red, velvety mucosal lesion on the surface of the oral mucosa.
- **Esophagitis** is the inflammation of the mucous membrane that lines the esophagus.
- **Gastroesophageal reflux** refers to the backflow of gastric or duodenal contents into the esophagus. Severe reflux disease is called **gastroesophageal reflux disease (GERD)**.
- **Gingivitis** is an inflammation of the gums.
- **Glossitis** is an inflammation of the tongue.
- **Hiatal hernia** is the protrusion of the stomach through a structural defect in the diaphragm at the esophageal opening.
- **Kaposi's sarcoma** is a cancer associated with acquired immunodeficiency syndrome. Lesions occur in the skin, lymph nodes, and viscera.

Sigmoidoscopy is an endoscopic examination of the sigmoid colon.

- **Leukoplakia** are firmly attached white patches on the oral mucosa.
- **Mallory-Weiss syndrome** refers to lacerations in the mucous membrane at the esophagogastric junction that result in massive bleeding. The syndrome is typically preceded by vomiting.
- Periodontitis refers to progression of gingivitis involving an inflammation of the oral mucosa.
- **Pyloric stenosis** is an obstruction of the pyloric sphincter caused by hypertrophy of the sphincter muscle. It's most commonly seen in boys between ages 1 and 6 months.
- Stomatitis is an inflammation of the mouth.
- **Tracheoesophageal fistula** is an abnormal connection between the trachea and the esophagus.
- **Vincent's stomatitis**, also known as **trench mouth**, is a severe form of gingivitis that causes necrosis and ulceration of the gums.

Esophageal atresia means the esophagus is closed.

Stomach and intestines

Here are terms that relate to diseases and abnormalities of the stomach and intestines:
- **Ascites** is the accumulation of fluid in the peritoneal cavity.
- **Celiac disease** is a chronic disease in which an individual can't tolerate foods containing gluten (usually found in wheat, rye, barley, and oats).
- Crohn's disease is a chronic inflammatory bowel disease that usually involves the proximal portion of the colon and, less commonly, the terminal ileum. It's named after the American surgeon Burrill Crohn (1884–1983), who first described it in 1932.
- **Curling ulcer** is a stress ulcer of the duodenum that results from burn injuries.
- **Cushing's ulcer** is a stress ulcer of the duodenum associated with severe head trauma or brain surgery.
- Diverticular disease refers to bulging pouches **(diverticula)** in the GI wall—typically in the sigmoid colon—that push the mucosal lining through the surrounding muscle. (See *A diversion on diverticulum.*) Diverticular disease has two clinical forms:
  - ○ Diverticulitis is the inflammation of one or more diverticula.
  - ○ Diverticulosis is the presence of diverticula without accompanying inflammation.
- Gastritis refers to inflammation of the stomach and stomach lining.
- **Gastroenteritis** is inflammation of the lining of the stomach and intestines that accompanies numerous GI disorders.
- **Hirschsprung's disease**, also called **congenital megacolon**, is a congenital disorder of the large intestine characterized by the

absence or marked reduction of nerve cells in the colorectal wall, which results in impaired intestinal motility and constipation.

- **Inactive colon** is a state of chronic constipation that, if left untreated, may lead to fecal impaction.
- **Inguinal hernia** is protrusion of the large or small intestine, omentum, or bladder into the inguinal canal resulting from weakened abdominal muscles, traumatic injury, or aging. The hernia is:
  - ○ **reducible** if it can be moved back into place easily
  - ○ **incarcerated** if it can't be reduced
  - ○ **strangulated** if a portion of the herniated intestine becomes twisted or swollen so that blood flow is impaired.
- **Intestinal obstruction** occurs when the **lumen** (opening) of the bowel is partly or fully blocked. Obstruction is classified as mechanical or nonmechanical:
  - ○ **Mechanical obstruction** results from foreign bodies or compression of the bowel wall.
  - ○ **Nonmechanical obstruction** results from physiologic disturbances, such as paralytic ileus, electrolyte imbalance, and blood clots that cause ischemia of the mesenteric vessels.
- **Intussusception** refers to a telescoping of a portion of bowel into an adjacent distal portion.
- **Irritable bowel syndrome** is a condition characterized by diarrhea, resulting from increased bowel motility, alternating with constipation.
- **Lactose intolerance** is the inability to digest milk sugar.
- **Necrotizing enterocolitis** is an inflammatory disease characterized by diffuse or patchy intestinal necrosis and is accompanied by infection in about one-third of cases. It mostly affects premature infants.
- **Paralytic ileus** is a physiologic form of intestinal obstruction that usually develops in the small bowel after abdominal surgery.
- **Peptic ulcer** is a disruption in the gastric or duodenal lining that occurs when normal defense mechanisms are overwhelmed or impaired by acid or pepsin. An acute form of peptic ulcer is called a **stress ulcer**.
- **Peritonitis** is an acute or chronic inflammation of the **peritoneum** (the membrane that lines the abdominal cavity and covers visceral organs).
- **Pseudomembranous enterocolitis** is an acute inflammation and necrosis (tissue death) of the small and large intestines, usually affecting only the mucosa.
- **Ulcerative colitis** is a chronic, inflammatory disease that affects the mucosa of the colon and produces edema and ulcerations. It typically begins in the rectum and sigmoid colon and may extend upward into the entire colon. It rarely affects the small intestine.
- **Volvulus** is a twisting of intestine at least 180 degrees on its mesentery, resulting in blood vessel compression and ischemia.

Curling's ulcer gets its name from an English surgeon, Thomas Curling, who lived from 1811 to 1888 and was the first person to describe this condition.

Beyond the dictionary

A diversion on diverticulum

A **diverticulum** is, in fact, a *diversion*. The small pouches divert contents of the GI tract; this action gives the structures their name.

Anus and rectum

Disorders of the anus and rectum include the following:
- **Anal fissure** is a laceration or crack in the lining of the anus.
- Anorectal **abscess** is a localized collection of pus due to inflammation of the soft tissue near the rectum or anus.
- **Anorectal fistula** is an abnormal opening in the anal skin that may communicate with the rectum. Inflammation caused by an anorectal abscess may cause the fistula to form.
- **Anorectal stenosis** is narrowing of the anorectal sphincter.
- **Anorectal stricture** occurs when the anorectal lumen size decreases.
- Hemorrhoids are varicosities in the veins of the rectum or anus that result in swelling and pain.
- Pilonidal **cyst** is a hair-containing dermoid cyst that forms in the midline gluteal fold.
- Proctitis is an acute or chronic inflammation of the rectal mucosa.
- Pruritus **ani** is perianal itching, irritation, or superficial burning.
- **Rectal polyps** are masses of tissue that rise above the mucosal membrane and protrude into the GI tract.
- **Rectal prolapse** is the circumferential protrusion of one or more layers of the mucous membrane through the anus.

Got milk? Not if you're lactose intolerant, you don't.

Accessory organs

Disorders of the appendix, liver, gallbladder, and pancreas include the following:
- Appendicitis is an inflammation of the vermiform appendix due to an obstruction.
- Cholecystitis is acute or chronic inflammation of the gallbladder, typically caused by gallstones.
- Cholelithiasis is the presence of gallstones in the gallbladder. (See *Lithos = stone.*)
- Choledocholithiasis occurs when gallstones pass from the gallbladder and lodge in the common bile duct, causing complete or partial obstruction.
- Cirrhosis refers to a chronic, degenerative liver disease in which the lobes are covered with fibrous tissue, the liver parenchyma degenerates, and the lobules are infiltrated with fat.
- **Fatty liver**, also known as **steatosis**, is the accumulation of triglycerides and other fats in liver cells.
- **Hepatic coma** is a neurologic syndrome that develops as a complication of hepatic encephalopathy.

Proctitis is an acute or chronic inflammation of the rectal mucosa.

- **Hepatic encephalopathy** is a degenerative brain condition caused by advanced liver disease.
- **Hepatitis** occurs in two forms, nonviral and viral:
  - ○ **Nonviral hepatitis** is usually caused by exposure to toxins or drugs.
  - ○ **Viral hepatitis** is an acute inflammation of the liver marked by liver cell destruction, necrosis, and **autolysis** (destruction of tissue by enzymes).

  Assessment findings are similar for the different types of hepatitis. The six forms of viral hepatitis are:
  - ○ **type A**, which is spread by direct contact through the oral-fecal route
  - ○ **type B**, which is transmitted by contaminated serum through blood transfusion, needles, I.V. drug use, and direct contact with body fluids
  - ○ **type C**, which is spread through needlesticks, blood transfusion, and I.V. drug use
  - ○ **type D**, which is found only in patients with acute or chronic episodes of hepatitis B and requires the presence of hepatitis B surface antigen (hepatitis D is rare, except among I.V. drug users)
  - ○ **type E**, which is transmitted by the oral-fecal and waterborne routes, much like type A (because this virus is inconsistently shed in the feces, detection is difficult)
  - ○ **type G**, which is transmitted by parenteral and sexual means, has been discovered most recently.
- **Hepatocellular carcinoma (hepatocarcinoma)** is cancer of the liver.
- **Pancreatitis** is an acute or chronic inflammation of the pancreas.
- **Portal hypertension** is increased pressure in the portal vein as a result of obstruction of blood flow through the liver.
- **Wilson's disease** is a rare inherited metabolic disorder characterized by excessive copper retention in the liver, brain, kidneys, and corneas. These deposits of copper eventually lead to hepatic failure.

Beyond the dictionary

Lithos = stone

Cholecystitis is a combination of Greek terms: *chole* means *bile*, *cyst* means *bladder*, and *-itis* means *inflammation*. It makes sense that cholecystitis is *inflammation of the gallbladder*.

Now take it one step further. *Lithos* is the Greek term for *stone*, so it makes sense that **cholelithiasis** is the term for *gallstones*.

Many words associated with me begin with **hepa-**, from the Greek word for *liver*.

Treatments

Here are terms identifying surgical procedures and other treatments to correct GI disorders.

GI tubes

Here are terms related to GI tubes used to treat patients with GI disorders:

- **Gastric lavage** is irrigation or washing of the stomach with sterile water or saline solution using an NG tube.
- **Gavage** is feeding a patient through a stomach tube.
- **Intestinal decompression** removes fluids and gas from the intestine by the insertion of one of several types of tubes:
  - The **Miller-Abbott tube** is a double-lumen tube in which one lumen contains a weighted balloon to ease passage and the other lumen facilitates drainage.
  - The **Harris tube**, used for gastric and intestinal decompression, is a mercury-weighted single-lumen tube that's inserted through the nose and carried through the digestive tract by gravity.
  - The **Cantor tube**, used to relieve obstruction in the small intestine, is a double-lumen nasoenteric tube. One lumen is used to inflate the distal balloon with air, and the other, to instill mercury to weight the tube. The tube also allows for aspiration of intestinal contents.
- **Nasogastric intubation** is insertion of a tube into the stomach through the nose.
- **Sengstaken-Blakemore intubation** is insertion of a triple-lumen catheter used to stop hemorrhaging from esophageal varices. Two lumens end in balloons; one is inflated in the stomach to hold the catheter in place and compress the vessels around the cardia, and the other is inflated in the esophagus to exert pressure against varices in the wall of the esophagus. The third lumen is used to **aspirate** (withdraw) stomach contents.

Lavage and *gavage* are two similar sounding words that can be easily confused. Just remember, **lavage** means the stomach is being laundered; **gavage** means you're giving food to the stomach.

Pharyngeal and esophageal surgeries

Surgical procedures performed on the esophagus include:
- **cricopharyngeal myotomy**—a partial or total incision of the cricopharyngeal muscle that relieves diverticula or severe cricopharyngeal muscle spasm
- **esophagectomy**—removal of part of the esophagus
- **esophagogastrectomy**—removal of all or part of the stomach and esophagus
- **esophagogastrostomy**—removal of a portion of the esophagus and then connecting the remaining healthy portion to the stomach
- **esophagojejunostomy**—attachment of the jejunum to the esophagus to provide a bypass for food for patients with esophageal stricture.

Remember, the suffix *-ectomy* means removal of, and the suffix *-ostomy* means creation of an opening.

Gastric and abdominal surgeries

Surgical procedures on the stomach are explained below:
- **Antrectomy** is the removal of the **antrum**, the lower part of the stomach, which produces gastric acid.
- **Billroth I** is a partial removal of the distal portion of the stomach; the remaining stomach is connected to the duodenum.
- **Billroth II** is a surgical excision of a portion of the stomach with connection of the remaining portion to the jejunum.
- **Gastric bypass surgery (Roux-en-y)** is a weight-loss (bariatric) procedure in which a small pouch is created at the top of the stomach and a bypass is created to a portion of the small intestine.
- **Gastrostomy** is the creation of a hole into the stomach through the abdominal wall to insert an feeding tube.
- **Laparotomy** is a surgical opening of the abdomen. (*See Gastric lingo.*)
- **Pyloroplasty** is surgical enlargement of the pylorus to improve drainage of gastric contents into the small bowel.
- **Total gastrectomy** is removal of the entire stomach.

The Austrian surgeon Christian Albert Theodore Billroth gave his name to two surgeries. Both involve removing a portion of the stomach. I'll keep all my portions, thank you.

Bowel surgery

Listed below are important surgical terms concerning the small intestine, large intestine, and colon:
- **Abdominal perineal resection** is a procedure in which a colostomy is created and the distal sigmoid colon, rectum, and anus are removed.
- **Anastomosis** is a surgical procedure in which two blood vessels, ducts, or other tubelike structures are joined to allow the flow of substances between them.
- **Colectomy** is excision of a portion of the colon.
- **Hemicolectomy** is the removal of one-half or less of the colon.
- Hemorrhoidectomy is the surgical excision of a hemorrhoid.
- **Ileostomy** is the creation of an opening between the ileum and the abdominal wall through which fecal matter is expelled.
- An **ostomy** is an artificial opening or stoma created in the GI or urinary canal or in the trachea.

Colostomy

A **colostomy**, bowel surgery that creates an opening between the colon and the abdominal wall through which feces are expelled, may be created in different portions of the intestine and structured several ways.

Different locations

Named according to their location in the colon, colostomies can be:
- **ascending**—located on the ascending portion of the colon
- **transverse**—located on the transverse portion of the colon
- **descending**—located on the descending portion of the colon
- **sigmoid**—located on the sigmoid colon.

Different structures

These are the main types of colostomy construction:
- A **double-barrel colostomy** creates two separate stomas—usually temporarily—on the abdominal wall. The proximal stoma is the functioning end and is continuous with the upper GI tract. The distal stoma, also referred to as a **mucous fistula**, opens into the nonfunctioning section of the colon that's continuous with the rectum.
- An **end colostomy** creates a single stoma on the abdomen created from the end of the colon, which is brought out through an opening in the abdominal wall.
- A **loop colostomy** involves bringing a loop of bowel through an incision in the abdominal wall.

The real world

Gastric lingo

Let's run another lap.
In practice, people commonly refer to an **exploratory laparotomy** as an *exploratory lap* or *exlap*. So you might hear someone say, "We need to take this patient for an exploratory lap."

NG tube

Rarely will you hear someone refer to a **nasogastric tube** by its full name. In practice, it's simply referred to as an *NG tube*.

Liver surgery

Important terms concerning liver surgery are listed below:
- **Hepatic lobectomy** is removal of a lobe of the liver.
- **Liver resection** is removal of a portion of the diseased or damaged liver tissue.
- **Liver transplant** is reserved for patients with a life-threatening liver disorder that doesn't respond to other treatment.
- **Partial hepatectomy** is excision of a portion of the liver.
- **Transjugular intrahepatic portosystemic shunt** is a procedure in which the radiologist cannulates (creates a tunnel) in the right internal jugular vein and then inserts a metallic, flexible stent into a new pathway created by balloon dilation of the tissue between the hepatic and portal veins in the liver. This artificial shunt creates a new pathway for blood flow and reduces portal hypertension.

> Let me help with **transjugular intrahepatic portosystemic shunt. Transjugular** means the catheter is *inserted through the jugular*; **intrahepatic** means it goes through the hepatic vein; **porto** means it then goes *through the portal vein*; **systemic** means it then shunts blood into *systemic circulation.*

Gallbladder and appendix surgery

Surgical procedures performed on the gallbladder and appendix are explained below:
- **Appendectomy** is the removal of the vermiform appendix.
- **Cholecystectomy** is removal of the gallbladder. (See *Open chole.*)

- Cholecystoduodenostomy is anastomosis of the gallbladder and duodenum.
- Choledochojejunostomy is anastomosis of the common bile duct to the jejunum of the small intestine.

Vocabulary builders

At a crossroads

Completing this crossword puzzle will help you digest GI system terms. Good luck!

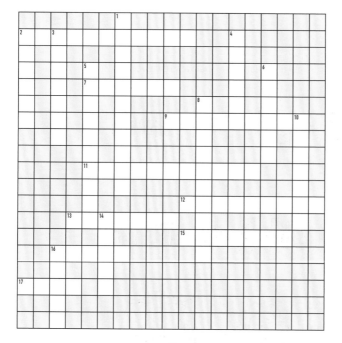

The real world

Open chole

You may hear a conventional **cholecystectomy** be referred to as an *open chole*, pronounced KOH-LEE. This means an open abdominal incision was required to remove the gallbladder, as opposed to **laparoscopic surgery**, which doesn't require an abdominal incision.

Eating helps me think.

Across

2. Rhythmic contraction and relaxation of smooth muscle in the alimentary canal
7. Liver's functional unit
9. Inflammation of the tongue
11. Another name for **Vincent's stomatitis** (two words)
12. Difficult or painful swallowing
13. Clear, hollow, drumlike sound heard on abdominal palpation
15. Greek word that means *little jug*
16. Saclike structure that makes up the first few inches of the large intestine
17. Yellow-green liquid that breaks down fats and neutralizes gastric secretions

Down

1. Pear-shaped organ nestled under the liver
2. Roof of the mouth
3. Eponym for diagnostic sign of appendicitis
4. Enlarged portion of the stomach above and to the left of the esophageal opening
5. Canal also called the GI tract
6. Root from Greek that means *stomach*
8. Growling sound in the stomach that indicates hunger
10. Part of the colon named after a Greek letter
14. Also called the buccal cavity
16. Acute abdominal pain

Match game

Eponyms can be confusing. There are lots of eponyms for GI structures, disorders, and tests. See if you can match each person to his or her discovery.

Clues

1. _____ sphincter

2. Ampulla of _____

3. _____ cells

4. Islets of _____

5. _____'s disease

6. _____'s sign

Choices

A. Karl Wilhelm von Kupffer, German anatomist

B. Paul Langerhans, German doctor

C. Ruggero Oddi, Italian doctor

D. Charles Aaron, American physician

E. Abraham Vater, German anatomist

F. Burnil Crohn, American surgeon

O see, can you say?

Sound out each group of pictures and symbols below to reveal a term that was reviewed in the chapter.

1.

2.

3.

Answers

At a crossroads

					¹G								
²P	E	³R	I	S	T	A	L	S	I	S		⁴F	
A		O			L							U	
L		V	⁵A		L					⁶G		N	
A		S	⁷L	O	B	U	L	E		A		D	
T		I	I		L		⁸B		U	S			
E		N	M		A	⁹G	L	O	S	S	I	T	I	¹⁰S
		G	E	D		R		S		R		I	
			N	D		B		O		G			
		¹¹T	R	E	N	C	H	M	O	U	T	H		M
		A		R		R				M			
		R				¹²D	Y	S	P	H	A	G	I	A
	¹³T	Y	¹⁴M	P	A	N	Y	G				D	
			O			¹⁵A	M	P	U	L	L	A	
	¹⁶C	E	C	U	M		I						
	O		T										
¹⁷B	I	L	E	H									
	I												
	C												

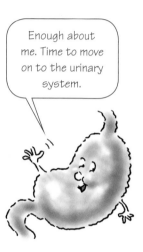

Enough about me. Time to move on to the urinary system.

Match game

Answers: 1. C; 2. E; 3. A; 4. B; 5. F; 6, D

O see, can you say?

Answers: 1. Tunica adventitia; 2. Submandibular; 3. Cholangiogram

---

Suggested references

Drossman, D. A. (2016). Functional gastrointestinal disorders: History, pathophysiology, clinical features, and Rome IV. *Gastroenterology, 150*(6), 1262–1279.

Standring, S. A. (2016). *Gray's anatomy: The anatomical basis of clinical practice.* Ipswich, MA: Elsevier Health Sciences.

Van Oudenhove, L., Levy, R. L., Crowell, M. D., Drossman, D. A., Halpert, A. D., Keefer, L., Lackner, J.M.,… Naliboff, B. D. (2016). Biopsychosocial aspects of functional gastrointestinal disorders: How central and environmental processes contribute to the development and expression of functional gastrointestinal disorders. *Gastroenterology, 150*(6), 1355–1367.

Chapter 9

Urinary system

Just the facts

In this chapter, you'll learn:

♦ terminology related to the structure and function of the urinary system

♦ terminology needed for physical examination of the urinary system

♦ tests that help diagnose urinary system disorders

♦ common urinary system disorders and their treatments.

Urinary structure and function

The **urinary tract** is the body's water treatment plant. It filters the blood and collects and expels the resulting liquid waste products as urine. To help you understand many of the terms relating to this waste control system, three key root words deserve special attention.

In the key of pee

The first key root is the syllable *ur-* or its other forms, ***urin-*** or ***uro-***. This term derives from the Greek verb ***ourein,*** which means *to urinate*. Appropriately, the study of the urinary system is called **urology**.

Two keys to the kidneys

The second and third key terms refer to the kidneys. The second is the adjective **renal.** This word derives from ***ren,*** the Latin word for *kidney*. The kidneys are the filter of our bodies' water treatment plant and perform a number of other vital functions, including:

• regulating acid-base balance
• regulating electrolyte balance
• regulating blood pressure
• aiding in red blood cell (RBC) formation.
  The word **renal** can show up in various medical contexts.
  A medical subspecialization within urology focuses on just the renal system. The name of this specialization, **nephrology,** employs

Pump up your pronunciation

Pronouncing key urinary system terms

Below is a list of key terms related to the urinary system, along with the correct ways to pronounce them.

Azotemia	AZ-OH-TEE-MEE-UH
Creatinine	KREE-AT-IH-NIN
Cystourethroscopy	SIS-TOH-YOU-REE-THROHS-KUH-PEE
Glomerulonephritis	GLAW-MER-YUH-LOH-NEF-REYE-TIS
Nephrotic syndrome	NEH-FROT-IK SIN-DROHM
Prostatitis	PROS-TUH-TEYE-TIS
Pyuria	PYE-YOU-REE-UH

the Greek word for *kidney,* **nephros,** instead of the Latin **ren. Nephro-,** or *nephr-,* our third key term, is identical in meaning with **ren,** and you'll find many words containing these two roots side by side. (See *Pronouncing key urinary system terms.*)

Kidneys

The **kidneys** are bean-shaped, highly vascular organs located at the small of the back on either side of the vertebral column between the 12th thoracic and 3rd lumbar vertebrae. The right kidney, crowded by the liver, is positioned slightly lower than the left. Although each kidney is only about 4″ (10 cm) long, these organs are complicated structures with many functioning units. They receive about 20% of the blood pumped by the heart each minute.

Adrenal gland influence

Atop each kidney lies an **adrenal gland.** These glands affect the renal system by influencing blood pressure and sodium and water retention by the kidneys.

Checking in and checking out

The kidneys receive waste-filled blood from the **renal artery,** a large branch of the abdominal **aorta.** After passing through a complicated network of smaller blood vessels and filtering structures within

Memory jogger

By thinking "BARE," you'll remember that the kidneys affect four main functions of the body:

Blood pressure

Acid-base balance

Red blood cell formation

Electrolyte balance.

the kidneys, the filtered blood returns to the circulation by way of the **renal vein,** which empties into the **inferior vena cava,** the major ascending vein of the lower body. (See *Major structures of the kidney.*)

A tri-umph of organ-ization

Each kidney has three regions. The **renal cortex,** or outer region, contains blood filtering mechanisms. The **renal medulla,** or middle region, contains 8 to 12 renal **pyramids,** which are striated wedges composed of tubular structures.

The tapered portion of each pyramid, called the **apex,** empties into a cuplike **calyx** (plural: **calyces**). The calyces channel urine from the renal pyramids into the **renal pelvis,** which is an expansion of the upper end of the ureters.

Getting to know the nephron

The **nephron** is the functional and structural unit of the kidney; each kidney contains about 1.25 million nephrons. The nephron has two main activities:
- selective resorption and secretion of ions
- mechanical filtration of fluids, wastes, electrolytes, and acids and bases.

Glom on the glomerulus

Three processes—glomerular **filtration, tubular reabsorption,** and **tubular secretion**—take place in the nephrons, ultimately leading to urine formation. Each nephron consists of a long tubular system with a closed, bulbous end called the **glomerular capsule,** or **Bowman's capsule.** Within the capsule are a cluster of capillaries called the glomerulus (plural: **glomeruli**). The glomerulus acts as a filter and passes protein-free and RBC-free filtrate into the tubular system of the nephron. (See *A look at a nephron,* page 186.)

A tireless inner tube

This tubular system has three parts through which the filtrate passes in succession:
- The **proximal convoluted tubules,** along with glomeruli, are located in the cortex of the kidney. This part of the nephron has freely permeable cell membranes that allow glucose, amino acids, metabolites, and electrolytes from the filtrate to pass into nearby capillaries and back into the circulatory system.
- The **loop of Henle,** which forms the renal pyramid in the medulla, is a U-shaped continuation of the renal tubule. In the

---

My three regions

- The *renal cortex* (outer region) contains about 1.25 million renal tubules.
- The *renal medulla* (middle region) functions as my collecting chamber.
- The *renal pelvis* (inner region) receives urine through the major calyces.

Major structures of the kidney

The illustration below shows the structures of the kidney, which plays a major role in the elimination of wastes and excess ions (in urine); blood filtration; acid-base, electrolyte, and blood pressure regulation; and blood cell formation.

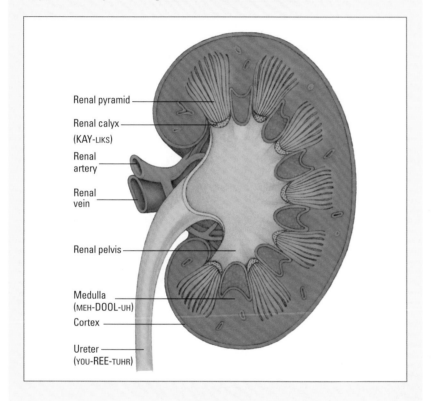

descending loop more water is removed from the filtrate; in the ascending part, sodium and chloride are removed to maintain osmolality.

- The **distal convoluted tubule,** like the proximal tubule, is located in the cortex. In the distal tubule, more sodium and water are removed as potassium and hydrogen ions and ammonia are introduced.

The distal end joins the distal end of other nephrons. Their concentrated filtrate, now urine, flows into larger collecting tubules. These tubules arch back into the medulla as part of the renal pyramids and empty the urine into the calyces.

(Text continues on page 187.)

A look at a nephron

The illustration below shows the structures of the nephron, which performs resorption and secretion of ions and mechanical filtration.

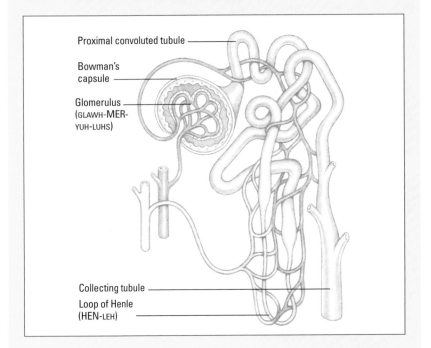

Proximal convoluted tubule

Bowman's capsule

Glomerulus (GLAWH-MER-YUH-LUHS)

Collecting tubule

Loop of Henle (HEN-LEH)

My job is really draining.

Two -*in* words

The words **renin** and **angiotensin** both end with the suffix -**in,** which derives from Latin and means *of* or *belonging to.*

Ren- and *angiotens-*
As in the word renal, the *ren-* in **renin** indicates the kidneys; the word literally means *related to the kidneys. Angio-* derives from Greek and means *blood vessel;* **tens** comes from Latin *tensum,* meaning *stretched.* The word **angiotensin** thus means *relating to the stretching (or tension) imposed on blood vessels,* which is measured as blood pressure.

It's a hormone thing

Hormones help regulate tubular reabsorption and secretion. For example, **antidiuretic hormone (ADH)** acts in the distal tubule and collecting ducts to increase water reabsorption and urine concentration.

Remember renin

By secreting the enzyme **renin**, the kidneys play a crucial role in regulating sodium retention and, therefore, blood pressure and fluid volume. This regulation takes place mostly through a complicated cascade of events in the **renin-angiotensin system.** (See *Two -in words.*)

In the liver, renin converts the substance **angiotensinogen** to **angiotensin I**. Traveling to the lungs, angiotensin I is converted to **angiotensin II**, a potent vasoconstrictor that acts on the adrenal cortex to stimulate the production of the hormone aldosterone.

Retention regulation

Aldosterone affects tubular reabsorption by regulating sodium retention and helping control potassium secretion in the tubules. When serum potassium levels rise, the adrenal cortex responds by increasing aldosterone secretion. Increased aldosterone levels increase sodium and water retention and depress the formation of more renin.

RBC production

Low levels of oxygen in the arterial blood (hypoxemia) tell the kidneys that the body needs more RBCs to deliver oxygen to the tissues. In response, the kidneys secrete a hormone called **erythropoietin**, which travels to the bone marrow and stimulates increased RBC production.

Get ready for reabsorption!

Okay!

Bladder

Each kidney has a **ureter**, a tube that carries urine by peristalsis from the kidney to the **bladder**, a hollow, sphere-shaped, muscular organ in the pelvis that stores urine. Urination results from **involuntary** (reflex) and **voluntary** (learned or intentional) processes. When urine fills the bladder, parasympathetic nerve fibers in the bladder wall cause the bladder to contract and the **internal sphincter** to relax.

You can relax now

This parasympathetic response is called the **micturition reflex**. The cerebrum then stimulates voluntary relaxation and contraction of the **external sphincter** of the bladder, causing urine to pass into the urethra for elimination from the body.

Urethra

The **urethra** is a small duct that channels urine outside the body from the bladder. (See *The urinary tract.*)

Females

In the female, the urethra is embedded in the anterior wall of the vagina behind the **symphysis pubis** (the bony prominence under the pubic hair). The urethra connects the bladder with an external opening called the **urethral meatus**, located anterior to the vaginal opening.

Males

In the male, the urethra passes vertically through the **prostate gland** and then extends through the **urogenital diaphragm** (a triangular ligament) and the **penis**. The male urethra serves as a passageway for semen as well as urine.

Anatomically speaking

The urinary tract

The illustration below shows the structures of the urinary tract.

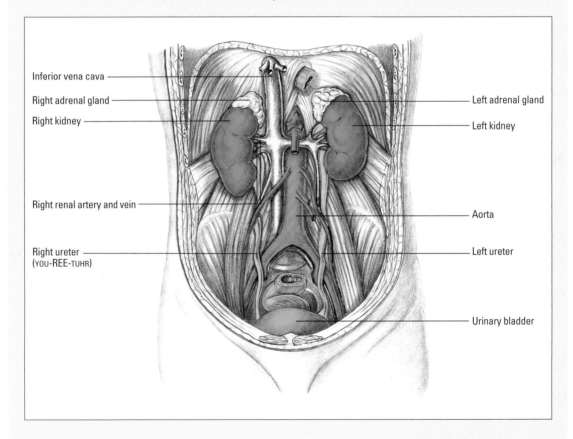

Inferior vena cava

Right adrenal gland

Right kidney

Right renal artery and vein

Right ureter
(YOU-REE-TUHR)

Left adrenal gland

Left kidney

Aorta

Left ureter

Urinary bladder

Physical examination terms

Examining a patient's urinary system requires observation, palpation, and keen interviewing skills. Before you can perform a complete physical examination, you must know these essential urinary system terms:

- Anuria is the absence of urine production. Anuria may also refer to absence of urine output (the body produces urine but can't eliminate it).
- Azotemia, or uremia, refers to accumulation of excess amounts of nitrogenous bodies, particularly **urea**, in the blood.
- Dysuria is painful or difficult urination.
- Enuresis refers to nighttime urinary incontinence in a girl older than age 5 or boy older than age 6.
- Glycosuria is the abnormal presence of glucose in the urine.
- Hematuria is the presence of blood in the urine.
- Nocturia refers to excessive urination at night.
- Oliguria is diminished urine production in relation to fluid intake, usually less than 400 ml in 24 hours.
- Polyuria is excessive production of urine.
- **Proteinuria** refers to the presence of protein in the urine.
- Pyuria is pus in the urine.
- **Renal colic** is sharp, severe pain occurring in the lower back, radiating forward into the area of the groin caused by kidney stones.
- **Thornton's sign** is severe flank pain resulting from kidney stones.
- **Urinary hesitancy** is difficulty beginning urination and subsequent decreased urine flow.
- **Urinary incontinence** refers to a loss of control over bladder and urethral sphincters, resulting in involuntary leakage of urine.
- **Urinary tenesmus** is persistent, ineffective, painful straining to empty the bladder.
- **Urine retention** is retaining urine in the bladder.

Look! Many of these words have a common root—*uria*. It comes from the Greek word *ouron*, which means urine.

Diagnostic tests

Here are common diagnostic tests for patients with urinary system disorders.

Urine and bladder tests

The following urine and bladder tests provide the most direct assessment of urinary function:

- **Cystometry** assesses the bladder's neuromuscular function, including bladder sensation, capacity, and the presence or absence of detrusor muscle contractions. A **cystometer** is the instrument used to measure the amount, flow, and time of voiding.
- **External sphincter electromyography** evaluates urinary incontinence by measuring electrical activity of the urinary sphincter muscle.
- A **24-hour urine specimen** collects urine over a 24-hour period to determine levels of the following:
  - ○ **creatinine,** a nitrogenous waste product produced by working muscle tissue and normally excreted in the urine
  - ○ **protein,** normally absent from urine
  - ○ **uric acid,** an end product of protein metabolism normally excreted in the urine.
- **Urea clearance** measures urine levels of **urea,** the chief end product of protein metabolism. This test measures **glomerular filtration rate (GFR)** an acceptable surrogate for creatinine clearance, but is less accurate than the creatinine clearance, especially when assessing renal function for drug dosing.
- **Urinalysis** tests the urine for color, turbidity, specific gravity, pH, protein, glucose, and ketone bodies. This test also examines sediment for blood cells, casts, and crystals.
- **Urine culture** checks for bacterial growth in the urine, which indicates urinary tract infection (urine is normally sterile).
- **Urine** myoglobin detects the presence of **myoglobin,** a red pigment found in the cytoplasm of cardiac and skeletal muscle that is excreted in the urine as a result of muscle injury.
- **Urine** osmolality is the concentration or osmotic pressure of urine expressed in milliosmols per kilogram of water.
- **Uroflowmetry** measures the volume of urine expelled from the urethra in milliliters per second **(urine flow rate)** and also determines the urine flow pattern. Abnormal results can indicate obstruction of the urethra.

The **glom-** of **glomerular** derives from the Latin word **glomus,** meaning ball, and is akin to the Latin **globus,** meaning globe.

Blood studies

Here are several blood tests used to diagnose urinary disease and evaluate kidney function:

- **Anion gap** is the measurement of the total concentrations of anions and cations in the blood. An increased anion gap is present with renal failure.

- **Blood urea nitrogen** level measures the amount of serum nitrogenous urea. Levels are elevated with kidney failure and dehydration.
- **Calcium and phosphorus levels** indicate the kidney's efficient conversion of vitamin D to a metabolite essential for calcium absorption in the intestines.
- **Chloride tests** measure serum levels of chloride, which helps regulate blood pressure and acid-base balance and is excreted by the kidneys.
- **Creatinine clearance** assesses the GFR by measuring how well the kidneys remove creatinine from the blood over a 24-hour period. This test is an excellent indicator of renal function because it requires blood and urine specimens.
- **Serum creatinine** measures blood levels of creatinine. Creatinine levels are elevated with renal damage.
- **Serum osmolality** tests the concentration of serum expressed in milliosmols per kilogram of water.
- **Serum potassium levels** measure blood potassium, essential for proper renal functioning.
- **Serum sodium levels** are evaluated in relation to the amount of water in the body. Abnormal ratios may indicate renal disease.
- **Serum uric acid levels** measure uric acid, a normal by-product of metabolism that's excreted by the kidneys. Levels may be abnormally high with gout or impaired renal function. Below-normal levels may indicate problems with renal tubular absorption.

Radiologic and imaging tests

Here are the names of radiologic, tomographic, sonographic, and endoscopic diagnostic procedures:
- **Computerized tomography (CT) scan** generates a three-dimensional, computerized image of the kidneys. This test is useful in detecting kidney stones.
- **Cystourethroscopy** uses an endoscopic instrument to examine the bladder, bladder neck, and urethra. (See *Show me a cystoscope.*)
- **Excretory urography**, also known as **I.V. pyelography,** injects a radiopaque contrast medium to visualize renal structures, ureter, bladder, and the urethra. (See *IVP in action.*)
- **Kidney-ureter-bladder (KUB) X-ray** is just that, an X-ray of the kidneys, ureter, and bladder.

The real world

IVP in action

In practice, you'll hear **excretory urography** referred to as an **IVP**, an abbreviation for an older name of the test, intravenous pyelography. For example, you might hear someone say, "We need to take the patient for an IVP to check for an obstruction in the ureter."

Show me a cystoscope

This illustration shows a cystoscope being inserted through the male urethra into the bladder. A cystoscope can be used for visual examination of the bladder or to remove tumors.

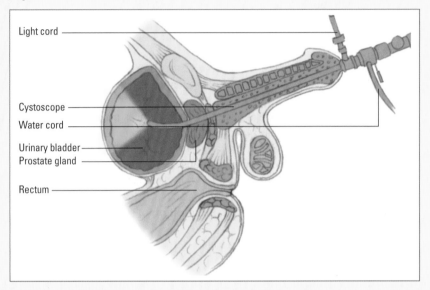

Light cord

Cystoscope

Water cord

Urinary bladder

Prostate gland

Rectum

- **Magnetic resonance imaging (MRI)** creates precise three-dimensional (tomographic) images of tissue by passing magnetic energy through the body.
- **Nephrotomography** creates a tomogram of the kidneys after I.V. injection of a contrast medium.
- **Radionuclide renal scan** requires injecting a **radionuclide** (radioactive material) before **scintigraphy**, which records the relative distribution of radioactivity in the tissues and, therefore, proper functioning of those tissues.
- **Renal angiography** creates X-ray images of renal arterial circulation after the injection of a contrast medium into the aorta and renal arteries.
- **Renal venography** creates X-ray images of the kidneys by injecting a contrast medium into a vein.
- **Retrograde cystography** instills a contrast medium into the bladder, followed by radiographic examination.
- **Ultrasonography** visualizes the urinary system by measuring and recording the reflection of pulses of ultrasonic waves directed into the tissue.
- **Voiding** cystourethrography demonstrates the efficiency of bladder filling and excretion by instilling a contrast medium into the patient's bladder through a urinary catheter. Radiographs are then taken before, during, and after voiding. (See *Cystourethrography.*)

Beyond the dictionary

Cystourethrography

In **cystourethrography** the prefix **cysto-** is the Greek word element for **bladder. Urethro** refers to the urethra and **-graphy** is a method of recording. Thus, cystourethrography is a procedure that records (through radiography) bladder and urethra function.

Disorders

This section covers disorders of the urinary system, including varieties of acute renal failure and other disorders.

Acute renal failure

Acute renal failure is the sudden interruption of renal function, caused by obstruction, poor circulation, or kidney disease. Types of this potentially life-threatening condition are classified by the cause of onset:

- **Intrarenal failure,** also called **intrinsic** or **parenchymal renal failure,** results from damage to the kidneys' filtering structures.
- **Postrenal failure** results from obstruction of urine outflow.
- **Prerenal failure** is caused by any condition that reduces blood flow to the kidneys **(hypoperfusion).**

I can't work without a blood supply.

Stages of acute renal failure

Each type of acute renal failure has three distinct phases:

- The **oliguric phase** is marked by decreased urine output (less than 400 ml in 24 hours).
- The **diuretic phase** occurs when the kidneys produce a high volume of urine.
- The **recovery phase** occurs when the cause of diuresis is corrected, azotemia gradually disappears, and the patient begins to improve.

Other disorders

- **Acute poststreptococcal glomerulonephritis** is a relatively common inflammation of the glomeruli after a streptococcal infection of the respiratory tract.
- **Acute pyelonephritis** is a sudden inflammation of the kidney and its pelvis caused by bacteria.
- **Acute tubular necrosis (ATN),** also called **acute tubulointerstitial nephritis,** destroys the tubular segment of the nephron, leading to renal failure and uremia.
- **Alport's syndrome** is a hereditary kidney inflammation in which the patient may have recurrent gross or microscopic hematuria.
- **Benign prostatic hyperplasia** occurs when the prostate gland enlarges enough to compress the urethra, causing urinary obstruction.

- **Chronic glomerulonephritis** is an inflammation of the glomerulus of the kidney characterized by decreased urine production, blood and protein in the urine, and edema.
- **Chronic renal failure** is the typically slow, progressive loss of kidney function and glomerular filtration.
- **Cystitis** refers to inflammation of the bladder, usually caused by an ascending infection.
- **Cystocele** is a herniation of the urinary bladder through the vaginal wall. (See *Cystocele is all Greek*.)
- **Fanconi's syndrome** is a kidney disorder that produces malfunctions of the proximal renal tubules, leading to elevated potassium levels, elevated sodium levels, glucose in the urine, and, eventually, rickets and retarded growth and development.
- **Hydronephrosis** refers to a distention of the kidneys by urine that's caused by obstruction of the ureter.
- **Hypospadias** is a condition in which the urethra opening is on the ventral surface of the penis. This condition rarely occurs in females, where the opening occurs within the vagina.
- **Nephrotic syndrome** is a condition marked by proteinuria, low blood albumin levels, and edema.
- **Neurogenic bladder** refers to any dysfunction of the nerves that control the bladder. The patient's bladder becomes spastic or flaccid, and urinary incontinence results.
- **Polycystic kidney disease** is characterized by multiple cysts of the kidney.
- **Prostatitis**, an inflammation of the prostate gland, may be acute or chronic.
- **Renal calculi** are **kidney stones** that form from minerals normally dissolved in the urine, such as calcium or magnesium.
- **Renovascular hypertension** is hypertension that occurs as a result of partial blockage of one or both renal arteries. An excessive release of the enzyme renin occurs, which ultimately produces vasoconstriction and hypertension.
- **Renal infarction** occurs when a thrombus or embolus causes ischemia of a kidney.
- **Renal vein thrombosis** is clotting in the renal vein that results in renal congestion, engorgement, and, possibly, infarction.
- **Ureterostenosis** is a ureteral stricture.
- **Urethritis** is inflammation of the urethra.
- **Vesicoureteral reflux** is a condition in which urine flows from the bladder back into the ureters and eventually into the renal pelvis or the parenchyma.

Beyond the dictionary

Cystocele is all Greek

Cystocele is an easy word. **Cysto-** comes from the Greek word *kystis*, which means *bladder* or *pouch*. **Cele-** is also derived from a Greek word, *kele*, which means *hernia*.

Skipping stones. Great! Having stones inside me. Ouch!

Treatments

Noninvasive procedures, dialysis, and surgeries that treat disorders of the urinary and renal systems are described here.

Lithotripsy

There are two procedures that use a process called **lithotripsy** to reduce the size of renal calculi:

- **Extracorporeal shock wave lithotripsy (ESWL)** is a noninvasive treatment that breaks up calculi with high-energy shock waves to allow their passage out of the body.
- **Percutaneous ultrasonic lithotripsy** uses an ultrasonic probe inserted through a nephrostomy tube into the renal pelvis. The probe generates ultrahigh-frequency sound waves that shatter calculi and continuous suctioning removes the fragments.

Catheters

Catheters are used in several ways to treat urinary system disorders:

- **An external catheter,** also called a **Texas** or **condom catheter**, is a urine collection device that fits over the penis and resembles a condom.
- An **indwelling urinary catheter** is a urinary catheter with a balloon end designed to remain in the urinary bladder for a prolonged time. (See *Don't fool with my Foley.*)
- An **intermittent catheterization** is a procedure that drains urine remaining in the bladder after each voiding or as needed for those who can't void.

Dialysis

Dialysis is a technique for removing waste products from the body when the kidneys fail. Several types of dialysis are explained here:

- **Continuous ambulatory peritoneal dialysis (CAPD)** is a form of peritoneal dialysis that allows the patient to continue daily activities.
- **Continuous arteriovenous hemofiltration (CAVH)** filters toxic wastes from the patient's blood and infuses a replacement solution such as lactated Ringer's solution.
- **Continuous arteriovenous ultrafiltration (CAVU)** uses equipment similar to that in CAVH but removes fluid from the patient's blood at a slower rate.
- **Continuous cycling peritoneal dialysis (CCPD)** uses a machine to perform dialysis at night while the patient sleeps, and the patient performs CAPD in the daytime.

The real world

Don't fool with my Foley

You may hear an indwelling urinary catheter referred to as a *Foley*, named after Dr. Frederick Foley, the American doctor who designed the device.

- Hemodialysis filters toxic wastes and other impurities directly from the blood of a patient with renal failure. Blood is pumped through a **dialyzing unit** to remove toxins and is then returned to the body.
- **Peritoneal dialysis** removes toxins from the patient's blood by using the peritoneal membrane surrounding the abdominal cavity as a **semipermeable dialyzing membrane.** In this technique, a dialyzing solution (**dialysate**) is instilled through a catheter inserted into the peritoneal cavity. By diffusion, the dialysate draws excessive concentrations of electrolytes and toxins through the peritoneal membrane. Next, excess water is drawn through the membrane. After an appropriate dwelling time, the dialysate is drained, taking toxins and wastes with it.

Dialysis *derives from a Greek word meaning separation. The medical process separates toxins from the blood.*

Surgery

Common surgical procedures to correct urinary system disorders include the following:

- **Cystectomy** is the partial or total removal of the urinary bladder and surrounding structures. Cystectomy may be partial, simple, or radical:
  - A **partial cystectomy,** also called **segmental cystectomy,** involves **resection** (removal) of only cancerous tissue within the bladder. The patient's bladder function is usually preserved.
  - A **simple,** or **total, cystectomy** involves resection of the entire bladder, but surrounding structures aren't removed.
  - A **radical cystectomy** removes the bladder, prostate, and seminal vesicles in men. The bladder, urethra, uterus, fallopian tubes, ovaries, and a segment of the vaginal wall are removed in women.
- **Cystotomy** uses a catheter, which is inserted through the patient's suprapubic area into the bladder to temporarily divert urine away from the urethra and into a closed collection chamber.
- **Kidney transplantation** is one of the most common and successful organ transplant surgeries. This treatment is an alternative to dialysis for patients with end-stage renal disease.
- **Marshall-Marchetti-Krantz operation** helps correct urinary incontinence in female patients by restoring a weakened urinary sphincter.
- **Prostatectomy** is surgical removal of the prostate gland to remove diseased or obstructive tissue and restore urine flow through the urethra. One of four approaches is used:
  - **Radical perineal prostatectomy** approaches the prostate through an incision in the perineum between the scrotum and the rectum.
  - **Retropubic prostatectomy** uses a low abdominal incision to approach the prostate without opening the patient's bladder.
  - **Suprapubic prostatectomy** uses an abdominal approach to open the bladder and remove the prostate gland.

I spy two more words derived from the Greek word for bladder: cystectomy and cystotomy!

- ○ Transurethral **prostatectomy** approaches the prostate gland through the penis and bladder, using a surgical instrument called a **resectoscope.** The scope has an electric cutting wire to remove tissue. This procedure is also called a **transurethral resection of the prostate (TURP).**
- **Transurethral resection of the bladder (TURB)** is a relatively simple procedure that uses a cystoscope to remove small lesions from the bladder.
- **Urinary diversion** is a procedure that provides an alternative route for urine excretion when the normal channels are damaged or defective. Several types of urinary diversion surgery are performed. (See *Two types of urinary diversion.*)
  - ○ The **ileal conduit** diverts urine through a segment of the small bowel **(ileum),** which is removed for this purpose. A stoma formed on the abdominal wall continually empties urine into a collection bag.
  - ○ A **continent** vesicostomy allows urine to be diverted to a reservoir constructed from a portion of the bladder wall. A stoma is formed, and accumulated urine can be drained by inserting a catheter into the stoma.
  - ○ In a **ureterostomy,** one or both ureters are dissected from the bladder and brought to the skin surface to form one or two stomas that continuously drain urine.

Two types of urinary diversion

Cystostomy
A *cystostomy* is a urinary diversion created when a catheter is inserted through the suprapubic area into the bladder. Urine is diverted away from the urethra.

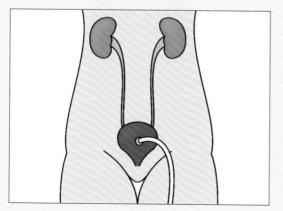

Nephrostomy
A *nephrostomy* is a urinary diversion created when a catheter is inserted through the flank and into the renal pelvis. Urine is diverted away from the bladder.

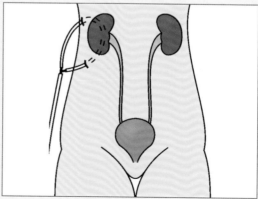

Vocabulary builders

At a crossroads

Completing this crossword puzzle will help you filter through urinary system terms. Good luck!

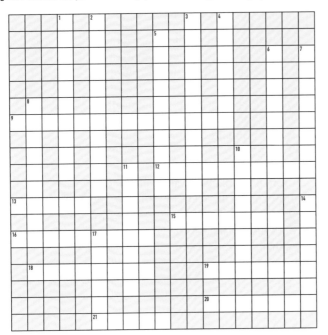

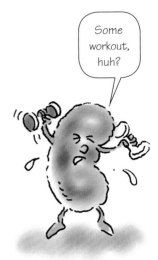

Some workout, huh?

Across

9. Bacterial kidney infection
12. Analysis of urine
13. Artery that brings blood to the kidney
15. Kidney stones
16. Blood in the urine
18. Phase of renal failure when kidneys produce high volume of urine
19. Structure that collects and holds urine
20. Structure through which urine exits the body
21. Hormone involved with blood pressure

Down

1. Study of the renal system
2. Protein in the urine
3. Inflammation of the prostate gland
4. Syndrome resulting from a hereditary kidney inflammation
5. Network of capillaries
6. Striated wedges in the renal medulla
7. Technique for removing waste products when kidneys fail
8. Herniation of the bladder
10. Scant urine output
11. Bladder infection
14. Difficult urination
17. Structure that carries urine from kidney to bladder

Match game

Match each of the urinary system terms below with its definition.

Clues	Choices
1. Catheter that's left in place _____	A. Dialysate
2. External catheter _____	B. Ureterostomy
3. Used for bladder training _____	C. Peritoneal dialysis
4. Uses the peritoneal membrane _____	D. Cystectomy
5. Uses blood _____	E. Indwelling catheter
6. Dialyzing solution _____	F. Strengthening exercises
7. Surgical removal of the prostate gland _____	G. Ileal conduit
8. Bladder surgery _____	H. Condom catheter
9. Ureters brought to the skin surface _____	I. Prostatectomy
10. Diverts urine through small bowel _____	J. Hemodialysis

Match the words to their definitions up top, and fill in the blanks down below.

Finish line

Fill in the blanks below with the word that correctly matches the definition for each urinary system disorder, treatment, or test.

1. Inflammation of the bladder is called _____.

2. Inflammation of the renal glomeruli without infection is called _____.

3. The severe pain caused by kidney stones is called renal _____.

4. Kidney stones are also called renal _____.

5. A coagulated, necrotic area in the kidney caused by occlusion of blood vessels is called renal _____.

6. The phase of acute renal failure marked by decreased urine output is the _____ phase.

7. The phase of acute renal failure marked by excess urine output is called the _____ phase.

8. The initials IVP stand for _____.

O see, can you say?

Sound out each group of pictures and symbols below to reveal a term that was reviewed in the chapter.

1.

2.

3.

4.

Got it!

SNAP

Answers

At a crossroads

			^{1}N	^{2}P				^{3}P	^{4}A					
			E	R		^{5}G	R	L						
			P	O		L	O	P		^{6}P	^{7}D			
			H	T		O	S	O		Y	I			
			R	E		M	T	R		R	A			
	^{8}C		O	I		E	A	T		A	L			
^{9}P	Y	E	L	O	N	E	O	H	R	I	T	O	S	
	S	O	U			L	U	I			M	I	Y	
	T	G	R			L	T		^{10}O	D	I	S	
	O	Y	I	^{11}C	^{12}U	R	I	N	A	L	Y	S	I	S
	C		A	Y	S	S		I					
^{13}R	E	N	A	L	S				G		^{14}D		
	L			T		^{15}C	A	L	C	U	L	I	Y	
^{16}H	E	M	A	T	^{17}U	R	I	A		R		I	S	
				R	T				I		U		
^{18}D	I	U	R	E	T	I	C		^{19}B	L	A	D	D	E	R
				T	S							I	
				E				^{20}U	R	E	T	H	R	A
			^{21}R	E	N	I	N						

Match game

Answers: 1. E; 2. H; 3. F; 4. C; 5. J; 6. A; 7. I; 8. D; 9. B; 10. G

Finish line

Answers: 1. Cystitis; 2. Glomerulonephritis; 3. Colic; 4. Calculi; 5. Infarction; 6. Oliguric; 7. Diuretic; 8. Intravenous pyelography

O see, can you say?

Answers: 1. Pyuria; 2. Cystourethroscopy; 3. Calyx; 4. Henle

Suggested references

Kasper, D., Fauci, A., Hauser, S., Longo, D., Jameson, J., & Loscalzo, J. (2015). *Harrison's principles of internal medicine.* (19th ed.). New York, NY: Mcgraw-hill.

McLafferty, E., Johnstone, C., Hendry, C., & Farley, A. (2014). The urinary system. *Nursing Standard, 28*(27), 42–49. doi:10.7748/ns2014.03.28.27.43.e7283

Standring, S. A. (2016). *Gray's anatomy: The anatomical basis of clinical practice.* Ipswich, MA: Elsevier Health Sciences.

Chapter 10

Reproductive system

Just the facts

In this chapter, you'll learn:

◆ terminology related to the structure and function of the reproductive system

◆ terminology needed for physical examination

◆ tests that help diagnose common reproductive disorders

◆ reproductive system disorders and their treatments.

Reproductive structure and function

Essential terminology related to the structure and normal function of the male and female reproductive systems and associated organs is presented here. A clear understanding of these systems will help you remember the terminology. (See *Pronouncing key reproductive system terms.*)

The male reproductive system produces sperm and some male sex hormones.

Male reproductive system

The male reproductive system consists of the organs that produce, transfer, and introduce mature sperm into the female reproductive tract, where **fertilization** occurs. In addition to producing male sex cells, the male reproductive system secretes some of the male sex hormones. The male reproductive organs include the penis, scrotum and testes, duct system, and accessory reproductive glands.

Penis

The **penis** deposits **sperm** (mature male germ cells) into the female reproductive tract through copulation and acts as the terminal duct for the urinary tract.

Column³

The cylindrical penile shaft contains three columns of spongy vascular tissue that respond to sexual stimulation by becoming engorged with blood. Two of the three columns of this erectile tissue are bound

Pronouncing key reproductive system terms

Below is a list of key terms related to the reproductive systems along with the correct ways to pronounce them.

Adnexa	ADD-NEK -SUH
Ballottement	BAHL-OT-MAW
Dyspareunia	DIS-PEH-ROO-NEE-UH
Epididymis	EP-UH-DID-UH-MISS
Gonadotropin	GOH-NEH-DOH-TROH-PIN
Leydig's cells	LAY-DIGZ SELLZ
Oophorectomy	OH-OFF-UH-REK-TOH-MEE
Symphysis pubis	SIM-FUH-SIS PYOU-BIS

together by heavy fibrous tissue and form the **corpora cavernosa**, the major part of the penis. The third column, on the underside of the shaft, is called the **corpus spongiosum**. It encases the urethra. (See *Caves and sponges.*)

So sensitive

The **glans penis**, at the distal end of the shaft, is a cone-shaped structure formed from the corpus spongiosum. Its lateral margin forms a ridge of tissue known as the corona. The glans is highly sensitive to sexual stimulation.

Caves and sponges

The terms **corpora cavernosa** and **corpus spongiosum** describe the columns of spongy vascular tissue in the penile shaft that respond to sexual stimulation.

Latin roots

Corpora is simply the plural of ***corpus***, a Latin word for the main part of a bodily structure. ***Cavernosa*** is a *cave* or *cavity*. ***Spongiosum*** relates to a sponge, which is made up of little cavities.

Nearest exit

Thin, loose skin covers the penile shaft. The **urethral meatus** opens through the glans to allow urination and ejaculation. (See *Structures of the male reproductive system.*)

Scrotum and testes

The **scrotum**, meaning *pouch*, contains the primary male sex organs and joins with the penis at the **penoscrotal junction**. A thin layer of

Anatomically speaking

Structures of the male reproductive system

The male reproductive system consists of the penis, the scrotum and its contents, the prostate gland, and the inguinal structures. These structures are illustrated below.

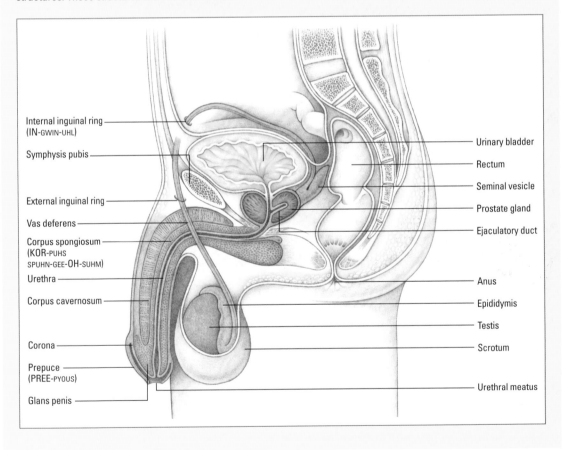

Internal inguinal ring
(IN-GWIN-UHL)

Symphysis pubis

External inguinal ring

Vas deferens

Corpus spongiosum
(KOR-PUHS
SPUHN-GEE-OH-SUHM)

Urethra

Corpus cavernosum

Corona

Prepuce
(PREE-PYOUS)

Glans penis

Urinary bladder

Rectum

Seminal vesicle

Prostate gland

Ejaculatory duct

Anus

Epididymis

Testis

Scrotum

Urethral meatus

skin covers the scrotum, overlying a tighter, muscular layer. Within the scrotum are two sacs that each contain a testis, an epididymis, and a spermatic cord. The seam where the two sacs join is called the **median raphe** and is visible on the exterior of the scrotum. (See *The rap on the median raphe.*)

Totally tubular

The **testes,** also called the **testicles,** are two egg-shaped glands within the scrotum. Enclosed in a fibrous white capsule, each testicle is divided into numerous compartments, or **lobules.** The lobules contain **seminiferous tubules,** where **spermatogenesis** (sperm formation) takes place. This begins when a male reaches puberty and continues throughout life. Stimulated by male sex hormones, sperm continuously form within these tubules.

Duct system

The male reproductive system includes a complicated duct system that delivers sperm from the testes to the ejaculatory ducts near the bladder. This system consists of the epididymides, the vas deferens, and the ejaculatory ducts.

Riding the epididymides

The **epididymides** (singular: **epididymis**) are coiled, tubular reservoirs that store sperm before ejaculation, secrete some of the seminal fluid, and serve as passageways for sperm. One epididymis is located along the border of each testicle.

Bundle of nerves

Mature sperm travel from the epididymis to the **vas deferens,** or **ductus deferens.** These two tubes begin at the epididymides, pass through the **inguinal canal** (formed by the pelvic girdle), and enter the ejaculatory duct inside the prostate gland. Each vas deferens is enclosed by a **spermatic cord,** a compact bundle of vessels, nerves, and muscle fibers.

Ready for discharge

The **ejaculatory ducts** are two short tubes formed by the vas deferens and the ducts of the seminal vesicles. They pass through the prostate gland and enter the urethra. The **seminal vesicles,** two pouches located along the bladder's lower edge, produce most of the liquid part of semen (the thick, whitish secretion that is discharged during ejaculation). The seminal vesicles also produce **prostaglandins,** potent hormonelike fatty acids.

Beyond the dictionary

The rap on the median raphe

The seam where the two scrotal sacs join, called the **median raphe**, is visible on the exterior of the scrotum. **Median** comes from the Latin term *medianus*, meaning *in the midline of a structure.* *Raphe* is the Greek word for *seam.*

How did **prostaglandin** get its name? Prostaglandins were discovered in human semen in 1935 by the Swedish physiologist Ulf von Euler, who named them, thinking that they were secreted by the prostate gland (Utiger, 2009).

Prostate gland

The walnut-sized **prostate gland** is located under the bladder and surrounds the urethra. It consists of three lobules: the left and right lateral lobes and the median (middle) lobe. These lobules continuously secrete **prostatic fluid**—a thin, milky substance that constitutes about one-third of the semen volume and activates the sperm.

Hormones

Male sex hormones, called androgens, are produced in the testes and adrenal glands.

It takes testosterone

Interstitial cells, called Leydig's cells, are found in tissue between the **seminiferous tubules** (the tubules that produce and conduct sperm). Leydig's cells secrete **testosterone,** the most important male sex hormone. A man's body needs testosterone for development of the sex organs, secondary sex characteristics (such as facial hair), and sperm formation.

Two other hormones—**luteinizing hormone (LH),** also known as interstitial **cell–stimulating hormone,** and **follicle-stimulating hormone (FSH)**—directly affect testosterone secretion.

Doctors used to think it was produced in the **prostate gland**. Think *prosta + gland + in*.

Female reproductive system

The **ovaries** are the basic organs of female reproduction. Internal and external female reproductive organs include the fallopian tubes, uterus, vagina, and mammary glands.

External structures

As in males, the **mons pubis** in females is a triangular pad of tissue that's covered by skin and pubic hair and is located over the symphysis pubis, the joint formed by the union of the pubic bones.

Just for her

The external female genitals, sometimes referred to as the pudendum, are contained in the region called the **vulva.** (See *Addendum on the pudendum.*)

Two **labia majora** form the sides of the vulva. The **labia minora,** two moist mucosal folds, lie within and alongside the labia majora.

The perineum consists of muscles, fasciae, and ligaments between the anus and vulva. (See *External structures of the female reproductive system.*)

Beyond the dictionary

Addendum on the pudendum

The term **pudendum** derives from the Latin word *pudendus*. This means, literally, *that of which one is to be ashamed.* In late classical and Latin and early Christian writings, the word came to refer to the external genitalia of both sexes. Now, it more commonly refers to just female genitalia.

Small, but important

The **clitoris** is a small, erectile organ located at the anterior of the vulva. Less visible are the multiple openings of **Skene's glands,** mucus-producing glands found on both sides of the **urethral meatus. Bartholin's glands,** other mucus-producing glands, are located on each side of and behind the vaginal opening. The **hymen,** a tissue membrane varying in size and thickness, can sometimes completely cover the vaginal opening.

Anatomically speaking

External structures of the female reproductive system

This illustration shows the structures of the female reproductive system that are visible externally.

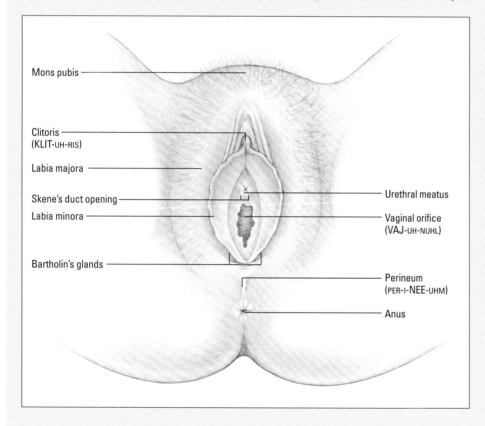

Mons pubis

Clitoris
(KLIT-UH-RIS)

Labia majora

Skene's duct opening

Labia minora

Bartholin's glands

Urethral meatus

Vaginal orifice
(VAJ-UH-NUHL)

Perineum
(PER-I-NEE-UHM)

Anus

Internal organs

The vagina is a highly elastic muscular tube located between the urethra and the rectum. A mucous membrane lining lubricates the vagina during sexual activity. **Rugae,** folds of tissue in the vaginal walls, allow the vagina to stretch. (See *Internal structures of the female reproductive system.*)

Anatomically speaking

Internal structures of the female reproductive system

These illustrations provide a lateral and anterior cross-sectional view of the internal structures of the female reproductive system.

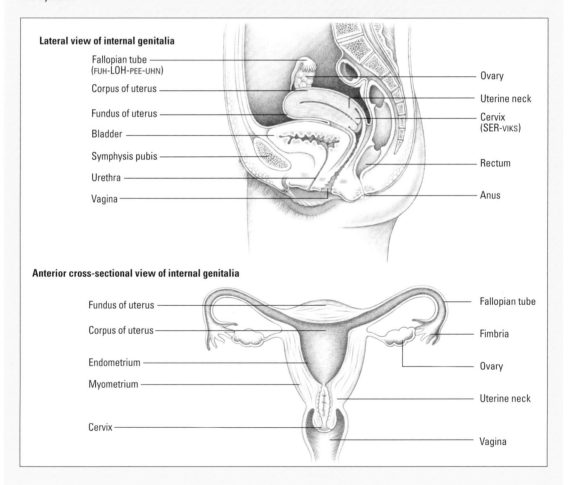

Lateral view of internal genitalia

- Fallopian tube (FUH-LOH-PEE-UHN)
- Corpus of uterus
- Fundus of uterus
- Bladder
- Symphysis pubis
- Urethra
- Vagina

- Ovary
- Uterine neck
- Cervix (SER-VIKS)
- Rectum
- Anus

Anterior cross-sectional view of internal genitalia

- Fundus of uterus
- Corpus of uterus
- Endometrium
- Myometrium
- Cervix

- Fallopian tube
- Fimbria
- Ovary
- Uterine neck
- Vagina

The pear-fect uterus

The vagina leads to the **uterus**, a small, firm, pear-shaped muscular organ resting between the bladder and rectum. The uterus usually lies at a 90-degree angle to the vagina. The mucous membrane that lines the uterus is called the **endometrium**. The muscular layer is called the **myometrium**. (See *Metrium matters*.)

The uterine neck, or isthmus, joins the upper uterus, or fundus, to the **cervix**, the part of the uterus that extends into the vagina. The fundus and isthmus make up the **corpus**, or main body of the uterus.

Certainly the cervix

The mouth of the cervix is called the *os*, a Latin term for a body orifice. The **internal** os opens from the cervix into the cervical canal, and the **external** os leads from the cervical canal to the vagina. A mucous membrane called the **endocervix** lines the cervical canal.

Fundamentally fallopian

The **fallopian tubes** are a pair of ducts attached to the uterus at the upper angles of the fundus. These long, narrow, muscular tubes have fingerlike projections, called **fimbriae** (pronounced: FIHM-BREE-EE), on their free ends that partially surround the ovaries. (See *Fallopian facts*.)

Fertilization of the **ovum** (egg), or female sex cell, usually occurs in the outer third of the fallopian tube.

Obviously ovarian

The **ovaries** are two almond-shaped organs. One ovary is located on each side of the pelvis and is connected to the uterus by a ligament. The main function of the ovaries is to produce mature ova.

At birth, each ovary contains approximately 50,000 graafian follicles, mature ovarian vesicles that each contain an ovum. During childbearing years, one of these graafian follicles produces a mature ovum during the first half of each menstrual cycle.

Metrium matters

The mucous membrane that lines the uterus is called the **endometrium**. The muscular layer is called the **myometrium**. The root of these words, **metrium**, refers to the uterus. It comes from the Greek word **meter**, which is related to and has the same meaning as the English word *mother*.

Beyond the dictionary

Fallopian facts

Although the correct function of the fallopian tubes had been known for more than 2,000 years, these structures received their name from Gabrielle Fallopio, a 16th-century Italian surgeon. He described and named the tubes in his book *Observationes Anatomicae* (published in 1562), which corrected a number of widely held false ideas about anatomy.

Her hormones

At puberty, the ovaries release progesterone and the female sex hormone estrogen. They also release a mature egg during the menstrual cycle. When expelled from the ovary, ova are caught by the fimbriated ends of the fallopian tubes.

The ovarian cycle

The Latin word *menstrualis* means *monthly.* The average **menstrual cycle** occurs over 28 days, roughly 1 month. Regulated by fluctuating, reciprocating hormones, this monthly cycle is divided into three phases: menstrual, proliferative, and luteal.

Phase I—Stimulate

The **menstrual,** or **preovulatory,** phase begins on the first day of menstruation. As the cycle begins, low estrogen and progesterone levels in the bloodstream stimulate the hypothalamus to secrete gonadotropin-**releasing hormone.** In turn, this substance stimulates the anterior pituitary gland to secrete follicle-stimulating hormone (FSH) and luteinizing hormone (LH). When FSH level rises, LH output increases.

Phase II—Proliferate and ovulate

The **proliferative,** or **follicular,** phase lasts from day 6 to day 14. During this time, LH and FSH act on the ovarian follicle containing the ovum and stimulate estrogen secretion. After 14 days, estrogen production decreases, the follicle matures, and ovulation occurs. Normally, one follicle matures and is released from the ovary during each cycle.

Luteal phase—Going down

During the luteal **phase,** which lasts about 14 days, FSH and LH levels drop. Estrogen levels decline at first. After the follicle ruptures and produces progesterone, the yellow structure called the *corpus luteum* (Latin for *yellow body*) begins to function, and estrogen and progesterone levels rise.

Mensis is the Latin word for *month.* It's closely related to the English word **moon,** which has a monthly cycle, too.

During this phase, the endometrium responds to progesterone by becoming thicker and preparing to nourish a fertilized ovum. About 10 to 12 days after ovulation, the corpus luteum diminishes as progesterone and estrogen levels drop. When a fertilized ovum isn't present and hormone levels can't sustain the thickened endometrium, the lining is shed. The process of shedding the lining is known as menses.

Breasts

The **mammary glands**, or **breasts**, are milk-producing structures. Breast development is controlled by estrogen and progesterone, hormones secreted by the ovaries. Each breast contains ducts surrounded by acini (milk-secreting cells). Individual ducts join with others to form larger ducts, which encircle the nipple and end in tiny openings on the **nipple** surface. The anterior lobe of the pituitary gland produces a lactogenic hormone called **prolactin** to stimulate **lactogenesis** (milk production).

The areola is the pigmented area (in Latin, the word means *a little open space*) around the nipple. (See *The female breast.*)

Lactos is Latin for milk. *Genesis* is a Greek word that means creation. Put it together, and you can tell that **lactogenesis** means milk production.

Menopause

Most women cease menstruation between ages 40 and 55. The term menopause applies if a menstrual period hasn't occurred for 1 year. Climacteric refers to a woman's transition from reproductive fertility to infertility. This transitional phase can occur over a period of several years and is also referred to as **perimenopause.**

At the onset of menopause, estrogen and progesterone levels begin to decrease and testosterone secretion increases. The body compensates for estrogen deficiency by producing **estrone**, a weaker form of estrogen.

The female breast

Here's a closer look at terms related to the female breast.

Structures of the female breast

The **areola**—the pigmented area in the center of the breast—contains the nipple. Pigmented erectile tissue in the **nipple** responds to cold, friction, and sexual stimulation. The interior of each breast is composed of glandular and fibrous tissues. Glandular tissue contains 15 to 20 lobes made up of clustered acini, tiny saclike duct terminals that secrete milk. Fibrous **Cooper's ligaments** support the breasts.

Milk production and drainage

Acini draw the ingredients needed to make milk from the blood in surrounding capillaries.

Lactiferous ducts and **sinuses** store milk during lactation, conveying it to and through the nipples.

Glands on the areolar surface, called **Montgomery's tubercles**, produce sebum that lubricates the areola and nipple during breast-feeding.

Lateral cross section

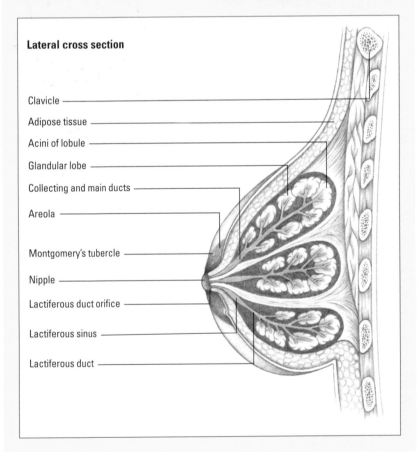

Lateral cross section

Clavicle

Adipose tissue

Acini of lobule

Glandular lobe

Collecting and main ducts

Areola

Montgomery's tubercle

Nipple

Lactiferous duct orifice

Lactiferous sinus

Lactiferous duct

Take a closer look at the body's milk-producing system.

Physical examination terms

Here are terms associated with physical examination of the male and female reproductive systems:

- **Anorchism** is the absence of one or two testes.
- **Anovulation** is the absence of ovulation.
- **Azoospermia** is semen without live sperm.
- **Ballottement** is a physical examination hand maneuver used to evaluate the shape and size of a deep structure or organ.
- **Bimanual examination** is the palpation of the uterus and ovaries using gloved fingers inside the vagina and the other hand outside of the body on the pelvic area.
- **Coitus** is sexual union.
- **Detumescence** is the subsiding of blood-engorged tissue after orgasm.
- **Digital rectal exam** is the examination of the prostate using a gloved finger inserted into the rectum.
- **Dysmenorrhea** refers to painful menstruation. This occurs at least occasionally in nearly all women. (See *Dissecting* dysmenorrhea *and more.*)
- **Dyspareunia** is a condition in women in which sexual intercourse is difficult or painful.
- **Frigidity** is the lack of sexual response.
- **Gynecology** is the branch of medicine concerned with the health care of women, including sexual and reproductive functions and diseases of the reproductive organs.

Beyond the dictionary

Dissecting *dysmenorrhea* and more

Dysmenorrhea means *painful menstruation.* The term is easier to remember if you dissect it. ***Dys-*** means *difficult or painful.* **Meno** literally means *monthly* and refers to menstruation. The third element, ***-rrhea,*** another common Greek word element, means **flow.** So, **dysmenorrhea** is painful menstrual flow.

One root, many terms

Add a few different letters to ***meno*** and you can describe other types of menstrual flow, such as:

- **amenorrhea** (a- means *absence;* amenorrhea is, thus, an *absence of menstrual flow*)
- **menorrhagia** (***-rhagia*** derives from a Greek verb meaning *to burst out* and describes an excessive flow; menorrhagia is, thus, *profuse menstruation*)
- **menostasis** (-stasis means *stoppage,* so this word has the same meaning as amenorrhea)
- **oligomenorrhea** (***oligo-*** means *scant* or *little,* so oligomenorrhea is *scant menstrual flow* or *scant menstruation*).

- **Gynecomastia** is abnormal enlargement or development of the male breast.
- **Hypospadias** is the opening of the male urethra on the underside of the penis.
- **Infertile** means a diminished capacity to produce offspring. An infertile man or woman isn't necessarily sterile.
- **Introitus** is the entrance into a canal such as the vagina.
- **Leukorrhea** is a white or yellowish discharge from the vagina.
- **Libido** is sexual desire.
- **Lithotomy position** is a supine position with the hips and knees fully flexed. It's used to perform female internal pelvic examinations.
- **Mastalgia** is pain in the breast.
- **Menarche** is the time when the first menstrual cycle begins.
- **Metrorrhagia** is abnormal uterine bleeding, especially between menstrual periods.
- **Orgasm** is the climax of sexual excitement.
- **Priapism** is a persistent, abnormal erection of the penis that isn't accompanied by sexual desire.
- **Rectovaginal palpation** is the examination of the posterior portion of the uterus and pelvic cavity by simultaneously inserting a gloved finger into the rectum and vagina.
- **Speculum** is an instrument used to enlarge the vaginal canal opening during a female pelvic examination.
- **Sterile** means that the patient is unable to reproduce due to an abnormality, such as the absence of spermatogenesis in a man or fallopian tube blockage in a woman.
- **Supernumerary nipples** are extra nipples that usually occur in a line below the normal nipples (Medlineplus.gov, 2016).

Leukorrhea is a white discharge—that makes sense. **Leuk** is Greek for white and **-rrhea** means flow.

Diagnostic tests

Diagnostic tests associated with the reproductive system include blood and fluid tests as well as radiologic and other imaging procedures.

Blood and fluid tests

Here are some common blood and fluid tests associated with the reproductive system:

- **Darkfield examination** is a microscopic test of fluid taken from a lesion in suspected primary syphilis. A special microscope makes the syphilis organism appear bright against a dark background (therefore, the term **darkfield**).
- **Papanicolaou (Pap) smear** is widely used for early detection of cervical cancer and inflammatory tissue changes. (See *Pap smear.*)
- **Prostate-specific antigen (PSA)** blood test is used to detect increases in PSA, a normally occurring substance that can indicate prostate disease.
- **Prostatic acid phosphatase test** measures the level of phosphatase enzymes, usually found in the prostate. Above-normal levels are suspicious for prostate cancer.
- **Semen analysis** is an examination of seminal fluid to evaluate male fertility. The procedure includes measuring the volume of seminal fluid, counting sperm, and performing microscopic examination.
- **Serum alpha-fetoprotein (AFP)** study measures the glycoprotein AFP. An above-normal level may indicate testicular cancer. In a fetus, an above-normal level may indicate a neural tube defect.
- In a **urine culture**, a common culture medium is used to detect infectious microorganisms in urine.
- **Venereal Disease Research Laboratory (VDRL)** test confirms a diagnosis of syphilis.

The real world

Pap smear

What everyone commonly refers to as a **Pap smear** or **Pap test** is formally called a **Papanicolaou test.**

It was named after George Papanicolaou (1883 to 1962), a Greek physician who immigrated to the United States and developed the test.

Radiologic and other imaging procedures

Here are some common radiologic and other imaging procedures associated with the reproductive system:

- During **colposcopy,** the examiner studies the vulva, cervix, and vagina with a **colposcope,** an instrument containing a magnifying lens and light.
- **Hysterosalpingography** allows visualization of the uterine cavity, the fallopian tubes, and the peritubal area. (See *Making sense of hysterosalpingography.*)
- **Laparoscopy** allows visual inspection of organs in the peritoneal cavity by inserting a fiberoptic telescope **(laparoscope)** through the abdominal wall.
- **Mammogram** uses low-dose X-rays to detect breast malignancies and evaluate masses.
- **Pelvic ultrasound** passes sound waves through the pelvic area, creating electronic images of internal structures. This test can help to diagnose pelvic disease or examine a developing fetus.

Beyond the dictionary

Making sense of *hysterosalpingography*

The Greek word ***hystero*** means *uterus*. ***Salpingo*** is the Greek term for *fallopian tube,* and ***-graphy*** is the term for *a recording*. So, **hysterosalpingography** means *examination of the uterus and fallopian tubes.*

Sometimes the Greeks got it wrong
Hysteros, the Greek word for the *uterus* or *womb,* also provided the root for another Greek word: ***hysteria***. It seems the ancient Greeks had the notion that only women became extremely emotionally upset. They attributed this perceived difference from men to the presence of the uterus.

- **Sentinel node biopsy** uses radionuclide imaging to identify the first lymph node to receive drainage from a tumor. It is used in breast tumors and melanoma.
- **Transrectal ultrasound** of the prostate is a scan of the prostate performed by placing an ultrasound transducer into the rectum and imaging through the rectal wall. It may also be used to guide a biopsy of the prostate.
- **Urethrogram** is an X-ray of the prostate and urethra.

Disorders

Common disorders associated with the reproductive system are usually gender specific. Sexually transmitted diseases (STDs), however, can affect either gender.

Female reproductive disorders

Here are some common disorders associated with the female reproductive system:
- **Dermoid cysts** are generally benign ovarian cysts consisting of displaced embryonic tissue.
- **Endometriosis** refers to a condition in which endometrial tissue appears outside the lining of the uterine cavity.
- **Oligo-ovulation** is irregular ovulation.
- **Ovarian cysts** are noncancerous sacs containing fluid or semisolid material.
- **Pelvic inflammatory disease (PID)** is an infection of the oviducts and ovaries.
- **Polycystic ovarian syndrome (PCOS)** is a condition in which a woman's levels of estrogen and progesterone are out of balance.

This can cause problems with a women's menstrual cycle, fertility, cardiac function, and appearance (Herndon, 2015).

- **Premenstrual syndrome (PMS)** is characterized by varying symptoms appearing 7 to 10 days before menses and usually subsiding with its onset. The effects of PMS range from minimal discomfort to severe disruptive symptoms that can include nervousness, irritability, depression, and multiple somatic complaints.
- **Rectovaginal fistula** is an abnormal communication (passage) between the vagina and the rectum.
- **Salpingitis** is inflammation of a fallopian tube.
- **Uterine** leiomyomas, also called **myomas, fibromyomas,** or **fibroids,** are the most common **neoplasms** (tumors) occurring among women. They're usually found in the uterus or cervix.
- **Vaginismus** is an involuntary, spastic constriction of the lower vaginal muscles.
- **Vesicovaginal fistula** is an abnormal communication between the vagina and the bladder.

Male reproductive disorders

Here are some common disorders associated with the male reproductive system:

- **Cryptorchidism** is a condition in which one or both testes fail to descend into the scrotum and remain in the abdomen, in the inguinal canal, or at the external inguinal ring.
- **Epididymitis** is inflammation of the epididymis.
- **Peyronie disease** is the buildup of fibrous tissue in the corpus cavernosum that causes a curvature of the penis and pain that worsens with erection.
- **Premature ejaculation** refers to a man's inability to control the ejaculatory reflex during intercourse, resulting in persistently early ejaculation.
- **Prostatitis** refers to a chronic inflammation of the prostate gland, usually from infection.

Impotence

Impotence is also known as **erectile dysfunction.** A man with this problem can't attain or maintain sufficient penile erection to complete intercourse. There are two types of impotence:

- **primary impotence,** in which the patient has never been able to achieve a sufficient erection to complete intercourse
- **secondary impotence,** in which the patient has succeeded in completing intercourse in the past.

Testicular torsion

Testicular torsion is abnormal twisting of the spermatic cord that's caused by rotation of the testis. Two types of testicular torsion are as follows:

- **Extravaginal torsion is** caused by loose attachment of the tunica to the scrotal lining, which in turn causes spermatic cord rotation above the testis.
- **Intravaginal torsion** results from an abnormal tunica or from narrowing of the muscular support. Normally, the tunica vaginalis envelops the testis and attaches to the epididymis and spermatic cord; in intravaginal torsion, testicular twisting may result from an anomaly of the tunica in which the testis is abnormally positioned or from narrowing of the muscular support.

Testicular torsion is abnormal twisting of the spermatic cord that's caused by rotation of the testes.

Other reproductive disorders

Here are some other common reproductive disorders:

- Adenomyosis **of the uterus** is a condition in which endometrial tissue invades the muscular layer of the uterus.
- **Benign prostatic hyperplasia** refers to an enlargement of the prostate gland.
- In **hematocele**, blood collects in a body cavity, such as the scrotum, testis, or pelvis.
- **Hydrocele** is a collection of clear fluid in a testis.
- **Hyperplasia of the endometrium** is the overdevelopment of the uterine lining.
- **Mastitis** is an inflammation of the mammary glands that commonly occurs with breast-feeding.
- **Oligospermia** is a condition in which the amount of sperm in semen is low.
- **Phimosis** is a constriction of the foreskin over the penis that makes it unable to be drawn back over the glans.
- **Precocious puberty** is the early onset of pubertal changes, such as breast development and menstruation before age 9 (in females). Males with the disorder begin to sexually mature before age 10.
- **Prolapse of the uterus** is the protrusion of the uterus thought the vaginal opening.
- **Pruritus vulvae** is intense itching of the vulva.
- **Salpingocele** is a hernial protrusion of the fallopian tube. (See *Salpingocele story*.)
- **Spermatocele** is a cyst containing sperm cells that occurs near the epididymis.
- **Varicocele** is an abnormal condition characterized by dilation of the veins of the spermatic cord.

Beyond the dictionary

Salpingocele story

Salpingocele is a herniation of the fallopian tube. The Greek word *salpinex*, for *trumpet* (a tubular instrument), gives us *salpingo-*, which refers to the fallopian tubes. The *-cele* means *cavity* and, thus, refers to a hernia.

Sexually transmitted diseases

Here are the names of some common STDs and conditions that accompany them:

- Chancroid, also called **soft chancre**, is a venereal disorder marked by painful genital ulcers and inguinal lymph node inflammation.
- Chlamydia is the most common STD in the United States. This group of infections—which includes **urethritis** (inflammation of the urethra) in men and urethritis and **cervicitis** (cervical inflammation) in women—is linked to the *Chlamydia trachomatis* organism.
- **Genital herpes**, also known as **herpes simplex virus, herpes type 2,** or **venereal herpes**, is an acute, inflammatory infection that causes fluid-filled vesicles on the genitalia. The vesicles rupture and develop into shallow, painful ulcers.
- **Genital warts**, also called **condylomata acuminata,** consist of painless **papillomas** (noncancerous skin tumors) with fibrous tissue overgrowth that commonly have a cauliflowerlike appearance.
- Gonorrhea is a common disease caused by the *Neisseria gonorrhoeae* organism. This STD typically affects the urethra and cervix.
- **Syphilis** is a chronic, infectious STD that begins in the mucous membranes and quickly moves through the body by spreading to nearby lymph nodes and the bloodstream. The untreated disease process has four stages:
  1. **Primary syphilis** occurs within 3 weeks of original contact. Patients may develop lymph node tenderness and chancres (small sores) on the body.
  2. **Secondary syphilis** occurs from a few days to 8 weeks after the appearance of sores. Patients develop a rash, white lesions, and flulike symptoms.
  3. **Latent syphilis** is characterized by an absence of symptoms.
  4. **Late syphilis**, also called **tertiary syphilis**, involves other organs, such as those in the cardiovascular and central nervous systems.
- Trichomoniasis is a protozoal infection of the lower urinary tract and reproductive system.

It seems a bit ironic that STDs were once called **venereal** after Venus, the goddess of love.

Treatments and procedures

Here are terms related to surgeries and other treatments of the male and female reproductive systems:

- **Artificial insemination** is the placement of seminal fluid into the patient's vaginal canal or cervix. The procedure is coordinated with ovulation.
- Cervicectomy is removal of the cervix.
- **Circumcision** is the removal of all or part of the **prepuce** (foreskin) of the glans penis.

The real world

Just say "D&C"

In the "real world," **dilation** of the uterine cervix and **curettage** of the endometrium is known as a "D and C." A **dilation and evacuation,** in which suction is used to remove the uterine contents, is referred to as a "D and E."

- In **dilation and curettage (D&C),** a doctor dilates (expands) the cervix to access the endocervix and uterus. A **curette** (an instrument with sharp edges) is used to scrape away endometrial tissue. (See *Just say "D&C."*)
- In **dilation and evacuation**, suction is used to remove the uterine contents. This procedure is typically used to perform elective abortions.
- With **in vitro fertilization,** an ovum is removed from the body and fertilized with sperm in a laboratory culture medium. The resulting embryo is then transferred into the woman's uterus.
- **Kegel exercises** are performed by contracting and relaxing the perineal muscles in order to strengthen the pelvic floor muscles. Kegel exercises are helpful in treating female urinary incontinence.
- During a **laparoscopy**, surgical instruments are inserted through a laparoscope to remove small lesions or perform other diagnostic and therapeutic procedures.
- **Laparotomy** is a surgical incision through the abdomen made to provide access to the peritoneal cavity.
- **Oophorectomy** is excision of one or both ovaries. Bilateral oophorectomy results in surgically induced menopause in women who are still in the reproductive phase of life.
- **Orchiectomy** is removal of one of the testes.
- **Orchiopexy** is the fixation of an undescended testis in the scrotum.
- **Penile prosthesis** is an implanted device used to provide penile erection.
- **Tubal ligation** is the interruption of both fallopian tubes to prevent conception.
- **Vasectomy** is excision of the vas deferens. When done bilaterally, this results in sterility.
- **Vasovasostomy** is the restoration of the vas deferens after a vasectomy in order to regain fertility.

Hysterectomy

Hysterectomy is removal of the uterus. There are four types:
- **Total hysterectomy,** also called a **panhysterectomy,** is removal of all female reproductive organs, including the uterus, cervix, fallopian tubes, and ovaries. It's called a panhysterectomy because a rectangular "pan" is used during surgery to collect all the excised organs.
- **Subtotal hysterectomy** is removal of only part of the uterus. The cervix is left intact.
- **Radical hysterectomy** is removal of all of the reproductive organs and supporting structures.
- **Vaginal hysterectomy** is excision of the uterus through the vagina.

Memory jogger

Both "laparoscopy" and "laparotomy" are surgical procedures, but to help distinguish their meanings remember that laparo**scopy** involves using a "scope" (laparoscope) and laparo**tomy** involves a surgical incision through the "tummy."

Remember, the word **hystero**- means uterus and **-ectomy** means surgical removal. Therefore, a **hysterectomy** is removal of the uterus.

Vocabulary builders

At a crossroads

Completing this crossword puzzle will help you produce the correct terms for the reproductive system. Good luck!

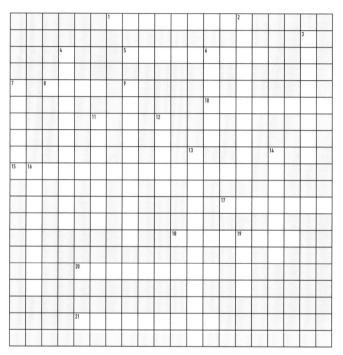

Across

1. Erectile dysfunction
5. Lactogenic hormone
8. Abbreviation for a venereal disease test
10. Visible female genitals
15. Sperm formation
17. Hormone produced after menopause
18. Female sex hormone
20. Two egg-shaped glands within the scrotum
21. Male sex hormones

Down

2. A duct system in the testes
3. An instrument used to enlarge the vaginal canal opening during a female pelvic examination
4. Lining of the uterus
6. Main body of the uterus
7. Upper uterus
9. The abnormal dilation of the veins of the spermatic cord
11. Mammary glands
12. Tissue covering the vaginal opening
13. Male sex hormone
14. Two almond-shaped female organs
16. Area between the anus and the vulva
19. Female sex cell

Match game

Match each description of a reproductive disorder or condition to its name.

Clues	Choices
1. Testicular torsion _____	A. Constriction of the foreskin
2. Endometriosis _____	B. Enlargement of the male breast
3. Leiomyoma _____	C. Fibroid tumor
4. Trichomoniasis _____	D. Ectopic uterine tissue
5. Papillomas _____	E. Genital warts
6. Gynecomastia _____	F. Twisting of the spermatic cord
7. Phimosis _____	G. Protozoal infection

Finish line

Fill in the blanks below with the appropriate word(s).
1. Each _____ _____ is enclosed by a spermatic cord.
2. _____ stimulates milk production.
3. Surgical removal of the uterus is called a _____.
4. A procedure to visualize pelvic organs is called a _____.
5. The process of uniting a sperm and an egg in a culture dish is known as _____ fertilization.
6. The process of instilling seminal fluid into a patient's vaginal canal is called _____ insemination.
7. An _____ is surgical removal of one of the testes.

Answers

At a crossroads

```
            ¹I  M  P  O  T  E  N  C ²E
                                    P              ³S
         ⁴E          ⁵P  R  O  L  A ⁶C  T  I  D     P
          N                         O     D        E
 ⁷F  ⁸V  D  R  L  ⁹V                 R     I        C
  U     O           A            ¹⁰P  U  D  E  N  D  U  M
  N     M  ¹¹B     R     ¹²H        U     Y           L
  D     E  R     I     Y        S     M           U
  U     T  E  C  M  ¹³Y        I        ¹⁴O        M
¹⁵S ¹⁶P  E  R  M  A  T  O  G  E  N  E  S  I  S     V
  E     I  S  C  N     S                 A
  R     U  T  E           T  ¹⁷E  S  T  R  O  N  E
  I     M  S  L           O                 I
  N        E     ¹⁸E  S  T  R ¹⁹O  G  E  N
  E        T           V  S
  U     ²⁰T  E  S  T  I  C  L  E  S  U
  M           R                 M
              O
           ²¹A  N  D  R  O  G  E  N  S
              E
```

Match game

Answers: 1. F; 2. D; 3. C; 4. G; 5. E; 6. B; 7. A

Finish line

Answers: 1. Vas deferens; 2. Prolactin; 3. Hysterectomy; 4. Laparoscopy; 5. In vitro; 6. Artificial; 7. Orchiectomy

Suggested references

Herndon, J. (2015). Polycystic ovarian syndrome. In *Healthline*. Retrieved on November 24, 2016 from http://www.healthline.com/health/polycystic-ovary-disease#Overview1

Utiger, R. (2009). Prostaglandin. In *Encyclopedia Britannica*. Retrieved on November 24, 2016 from https://www.britannica.com/science/prostaglandin

Supernumerary nipple. (2016). Retrieved on November 24, 2016 from https://medlineplus.gov/ency/article/003110.htm

Chapter 11

Maternal health

Just the facts

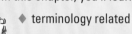

In this chapter, you'll learn:

♦ terminology related to pregnancy and fetal development

♦ terminology needed for physical examination of the pregnant woman and fetus

♦ tests that help diagnose common pregnancy-related problems

♦ pregnancy-related disorders and their treatments.

Pregnancy-related structures and functions

Pregnancy results when a female's egg and a male's sperm unite. This chapter focuses on the terminology associated with pregnancy. (See *Pronouncing key maternal health terms.*)

Conception

Pregnancy begins with **conception**, also called **fertilization**. Conception occurs when an ovum in the fallopian tube is penetrated by a spermatozoon (sperm cell). The **spermatozoon** and the ovum unite to form a single new cell.

Only the strong survive

Although a single ejaculation deposits several hundred million spermatozoa, many are destroyed by acidic vaginal secretions. However, when spermatozoa enter the cervical canal they are able to survive because cervical mucus protects them. Spermatozoa are typically viable (able to fertilize the ovum) for up to 2 days after ejaculation, but they can survive in the reproductive tract for up to 4 days.

Movin' right along

Spermatozoa travel through the female reproductive tract by means of **flagellar** movements (whiplike movements of the tail). After

Pronouncing key maternal health terms

Below is a list of key terms related to maternal health along with the correct way to pronounce them.

Abruptio placentae	UHB-RUHP-SHEE-OH PLAH-SEN-TAY
Amenorrhea	AH-MEN-OR-REE-UH
Ballottement	BAHL-OT-MAW
Conception	KON-CEP-SHUHN
Epididymis	EP-UH-DID-UH-MISS
Fertilization	FER-TIL-UH-ZAY-SHUHN
Gestation	JES-TAY-SHUHN
Lochia	LOH-KEE-AH
Placenta	PLAH-SEN-TAH
Zygote	ZIGH-GOTE

spermatozoa pass through the cervical mucus, however, the female reproductive system assists them on their journey with rhythmic uterine contractions that help them penetrate the fallopian tubes.

> You'll always know your pal if you've ever navigated the cervical canal.

Break on through to the other side

Before a spermatozoon can penetrate the ovum, it must disperse the ovum's granulosa cells (estrogen-producing cells) and penetrate the **zona pellucida**, the thick, transparent layer surrounding the incompletely developed ovum. Enzymes in the spermatozoon's **acrosome** (head cap) permit this penetration.

Divide and fuse

After penetration, the ovum completes its second meiotic division and the zona pellucida prevents penetration by other spermatozoa. The spermatozoon's head then fuses with the ovum nucleus, creating a cell nucleus with 46 chromosomes. (See *How fertilization occurs*, page 227.)

Plant me and watch me grow

The fertilized ovum, or zygote, immediately forms a rounded mass of cells and travels from the fallopian tube to the uterus. In the uterus, it implants itself in the uterine lining and begins growing.

Gestation

Gestation, or the period of pregnancy that begins with conception and ends with childbirth, typically lasts 38 to 40 weeks. During this time, the zygote divides continuously, and a complex sequence of pre-embryonic, embryonic, and fetal developments transforms the zygote into a full-term fetus.

Sizing it up

Because the uterus grows throughout pregnancy, uterine size serves as a rough estimate of gestation. However, the expected delivery date is typically calculated from the beginning of the pregnant woman's last menses using **Nägele's rule:**

First day of the last menstrual period – 3 months + 7 days = estimated date of birth.

Because the fertilization date is rarely known, a woman's expected delivery date is typically calculated using **Nägele's rule.**

Fetal development

During pregnancy, the fetus undergoes three major stages of development:
1. **pre-embryonic period** (the first 3 weeks after fertilization)
2. **embryonic period** (weeks 2 to 8)
3. **fetal period** (end of week 8 through birth).

Pre-embryonic period

The pre-embryonic period starts with ovum fertilization and lasts about 3 weeks. As the zygote passes through the fallopian tube, it undergoes a series of mitotic divisions, or **cleavage**. (See *Pre-embryonic development*, page 228.)

Embryonic period

During the **embryonic period** (beginning at the end of the 2nd week through the 8th week of gestation), the developing zygote starts to take on a human shape and is now called an **embryo**. The growing embryo floats within the **amnion**, a thin, clear sac filled with **amniotic** fluid. Early in this period, the **chorion**, or outer cells of the rounded cell mass, joins with the endometrium to form the **placenta**.

(Text continues on page 230.)

How did I get my start? Well, it all began in the preembryonic period …

How fertilization occurs

Fertilization begins when the spermatozoon is activated upon contact with the ovum. Here's what happens.

The **spermatozoon**, which has a covering called the **acrosome**, approaches the **ovum.**

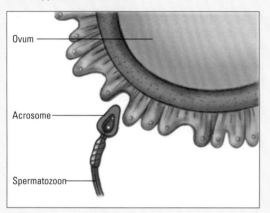

Ovum

Acrosome

Spermatozoon

The acrosome develops small perforations through which it releases enzymes necessary for the sperm to penetrate the protective layers of the ovum before fertilization.

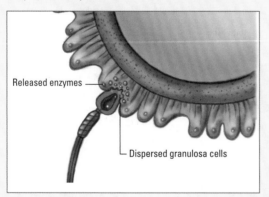

Released enzymes

Dispersed granulosa cells

The spermatozoon then penetrates the **zona pellucida** (the inner membrane of the ovum). This movement triggers the ovum's second meiotic division (following meiosis), making the zona pellucida impenetrable to other spermatozoa.

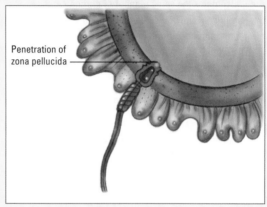

Penetration of zona pellucida

After the spermatozoon penetrates the ovum, its nucleus is released into the ovum, its tail degenerates, and its head enlarges and fuses with the ovum's nucleus. This fusion provides the fertilized ovum, called a **zygote**, with 46 chromosomes.

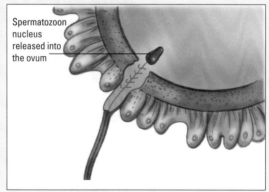

Spermatozoon nucleus released into the ovum

Pre-embryonic development

The pre-embryonic period lasts from conception until about the end of the 3rd week of development.

Zygote formation ...
As the fertilized ovum advances through the fallopian tube toward the uterus, it undergoes mitotic division, forming daughter cells, initially called **blastomeres**. Each blastomere contains the same number of chromosomes as the parent cell. The first cell division ends about 30 hours after fertilization; subsequent divisions occur rapidly.

The **zygote**, as it's now called, develops into a small mass of cells called a **morula**, which reaches the uterus at about the 3rd day after fertilization. Fluid that amasses in the center of the morula forms a central cavity.

...into blastocyst
The structure is now called a **blastocyst**. The blastocyst consists of a thin trophoblast layer, which includes the blastocyst cavity, and the inner cell mass. The trophoblast develops into fetal membranes and the placenta.

The inner cell mass later forms the embryo **(late blastocyst)**.

Getting attached: Blastocyst and endometrium
During the next phase, the blastocyst stays within the zona pellucida, unattached to the uterus. The zona pellucida degenerates, and by the end of the first week after fertilization, the blastocyst attaches to the endometrium. The part of the blastocyst adjacent to the inner cell mass is the first part to become attached.

The trophoblast, in contact with the endometrial lining, proliferates and invades the underlying endometrium by separating and dissolving endometrial cells.

Letting it all sink in
During the next week, the invading blastocyst sinks below the endometrium's surface. The penetration site seals, restoring the continuity of the endometrial surface.

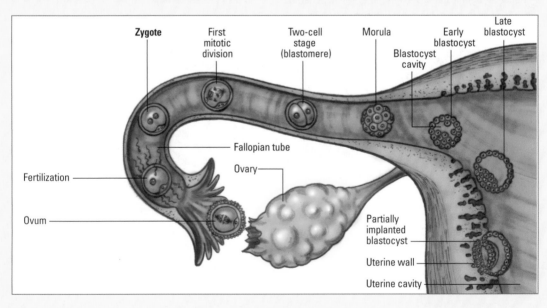

Embryonic development

Each of the three germ layers—ectoderm, mesoderm, and endoderm—forms specific tissues and organs in the developing embryo.

Endoderm
The endoderm, the inner-most layer, becomes the epithelial lining of the:
* pharynx and trachea
* auditory canal
* alimentary canal
* liver
* pancreas
* bladder and urethra
* prostate.

Mesoderm
The mesoderm, the middle layer, develops into:
* connective and supporting tissue
* the blood and vascular system
* musculature
* teeth (except enamel)
* the mesothelial lining of pericardial, pleural, and peritoneal cavities
* the kidneys and ureters.

Ectoderm
The ectoderm, the outer-most layer, develops into the:
* epidermis
* nervous system
* pituitary gland
* tooth enamel
* salivary glands
* optic lens
* lining of lower portion of anal canal
* hair.

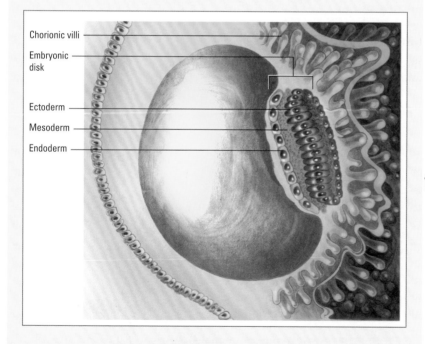

Chorionic villi

Embryonic disk

Ectoderm

Mesoderm

Endoderm

During the embryonic period, three germ layers develop— the *ectoderm*, *mesoderm*, and *endoderm.*

This vital structure provides nutrients for and removes wastes from the embryo via the chorion and the embryo's **umbilical cord.**

Layer up

During the embryonic period, three germ layers develop. Each germ layer—the **ectoderm, mesoderm,** and **endoderm**—eventually forms specific tissues in the embryo. (See *Embryonic development.*)

All systems go!

Organ systems form during the embryonic period. During this time, the embryo is particularly vulnerable to injury from such factors as maternal drug use and certain maternal infections.

Fetal period

The fetal period lasts from the end of the 8th week until birth. During this period, the embryo enlarges, grows heavier, and becomes known as a **fetus.** The fetus's head is disproportionately large compared to its body at this time. (This feature changes after birth as the neonate grows.) The fetus also lacks subcutaneous fat. (Fat starts to accumulate shortly after birth.)

Structural changes related to pregnancy

Pregnancy changes the usual development of the corpus luteum and results in the development of these structures:
- decidua
- amniotic sac and fluid
- yolk sac
- placenta.

Decidua

The **decidua** is the endometrial lining of the uterus that undergoes hormone-induced changes during pregnancy. Decidual cells secrete these substances:
- the hormone **prolactin,** which promotes **lactation** (breast-feeding)
- a peptide hormone called **relaxin,** which induces relaxation of the connective tissue of the symphysis pubis and pelvic ligaments and promotes cervical dilation
- a potent hormonelike fatty acid, **prostaglandin,** which mediates several physiologic functions. (See *Development of the decidua and fetal membranes.*)

The **decidua** is the endometrial lining of the uterus that undergoes hormone-induced changes during pregnancy.

Anatomically speaking

Development of the decidua and fetal membranes

Specialized tissues support, protect, and nurture the embryo and fetus throughout its development. Among these tissues are the decidua and fetal membranes, which begin to develop shortly after conception.

Decidua

During pregnancy, the endometrial lining is called the **decidua**. It provides a nesting place for the developing ovum and has some endocrine functions.

Based primarily on its position relative to the embryo, the decidua may be known as the **decidua basalis**, which lies beneath the chorionic vesicle; the **decidua capsularis**, which stretches over the vesicle; or the **decidua parietalis**, which lines the remainder of the endometrial cavity.

Fetal membranes

The **chorion** is a membrane that forms the outer wall of the blastocyst. Vascular projections, called **chorionic villi**, arise from its periphery. As the chorionic vesicle enlarges, villi arising from the superficial portion of the chorion, called the **chorion laeve**, atrophy, leaving this surface smooth. Villi arising from the deeper part of the chorion, called the **chorion frondosum**, proliferate, projecting into the large blood vessels within the decidua basalis through which the maternal blood flows.

Blood vessels that form within the growing villi become connected with blood vessels that form in the chorion, in the body stalk, and within the body of the embryo. Blood begins to flow through this developing network of vessels as soon as the embryo's heart starts to beat.

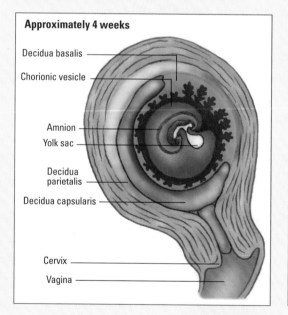

Approximately 4 weeks

- Decidua basalis
- Chorionic vesicle
- Amnion
- Yolk sac
- Decidua parietalis
- Decidua capsularis
- Cervix
- Vagina

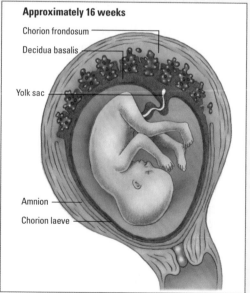

Approximately 16 weeks

- Chorion frondosum
- Decidua basalis
- Yolk sac
- Amnion
- Chorion laeve

Amniotic sac and fluid

The **amniotic sac**, enclosed within the chorion, gradually grows and surrounds the embryo. As it enlarges, the amniotic sac expands into the chorionic cavity, eventually filling the cavity and fusing with the chorion by the 8th week of gestation.

Fluid facts

Amniotic fluid comes from maternal and fetal sources. The amount of fluid in the amniotic sac is usually balanced with the amount lost through the fetal GI tract. The fluid is absorbed into the fetal circulation from the fetal GI tract; some of it is transferred from the fetal circulation to the maternal circulation and excreted in maternal urine.

Amniotic fluid serves the fetus in two ways. During gestation, the fluid gives the fetus a buoyant, temperature-controlled environment. Later, amniotic fluid serves as a fluid wedge that helps to open the cervix during birth.

Ah! This is the life! This amniotic fluid is keeping me warm and buoyant. I may never want to leave!

Yolk sac

The **yolk sac** forms next to the endoderm. A portion of this sac incorporates into the developing embryo and forms the GI tract. Another portion of it develops into primitive germ cells, which travel to the developing gonads and eventually form **oocytes** (the precursor of the ovum) or **spermatocytes** (the precursor of the spermatozoon) after gender has been determined. Early in embryonic development, the yolk sac also forms blood cells. Eventually, this sac atrophies and disintegrates.

Placenta

The **placenta** is a flattened, disk-shaped structure that uses the umbilical cord as a conduit to provide nutrients to and remove wastes from the fetus from the 3rd month of pregnancy until birth. The placenta is formed from the chorion, its chorionic villi, and the adjacent decidua basalis. It plays a key role in producing such hormones as estrogen, progesterone, and human placental lactogen during pregnancy.

The placenta plays a key role in hormone production during pregnancy.

Talkin' about two circulations

The placenta is a highly vascular organ and contains two specialized circulatory systems:

- The **uteroplacental circulation** carries oxygenated arterial blood from the maternal circulation to the **intervillous spaces** (large spaces separating chorionic villi in the placenta).

- The **fetoplacental circulation** transports oxygen-depleted blood from the fetus to the chorionic villi by the umbilical arteries and returns oxygenated blood to the fetus through the umbilical vein.

Labor and birth

Labor is the process by which birth of the fetus is achieved. During this time, the cervix **dilates** and the uterus **contracts** to expel the fetus from the uterus.

Stages of labor

Labor is typically divided into four stages. The first stage, when **effacement** (thinning and shortening of the cervix) and dilation occur, begins with the onset of true uterine contractions and ends when the cervix is fully dilated. This stage may be further divided into three phases:

- **latent** phase, which begins with the onset of regular contractions; the cervix dilates from 0 to 3 cm and becomes fully effaced
- **active** phase, which is characterized by strong, regular, recurrent contractions, cervical dilation from 4 to 7 cm, and fetal descent through the pelvis
- **transition** phase, which is characterized by maximally intense uterine contractions, cervical dilation from 8 to 10 cm, and complete cervical effacement.

The stage is set

The other stages of labor are:

- second stage, which encompasses the actual birth; it begins when the cervix is fully dilated and ends with the birth of the **neonate**
- third stage, also called the **placental** stage, which begins immediately after the birth of the neonate and ends when the placenta is delivered
- fourth stage, which begins after delivery of the placenta; during this stage, homeostasis is reestablished.

The **transition** phase is characterized by maximally intense uterine contractions, cervical dilation from 8 to 10 cm, and complete cervical effacement. Talk about hard work!

Cardinal movements of labor

With labor, the fetus must pass through the birth canal. To do so, the fetus must change position through various movements because of the size of the fetal head in relation to the irregularly shaped maternal

pelvis. Specific, deliberate, and precise, the various movements allow the smallest diameter of the fetal head to pass through the corresponding diameter of the woman's pelvis. These movements include:

- **descent,** the downward movement of the fetus to reach the posterior vaginal floor
- **flexion,** the bending forward of the head so that the chin is pressed to the chest that occurs as a result of the resistance of the fetal head against the pelvic floor
- **internal rotation,** the movement of the head to a transverse (right to left) position
- **extension,** the movement of the head as it passes through the pelvis, with the **occiput** (back part of the head) emerging from the vagina and the back of the neck under the symphysis pubis
- **external rotation** (also called **restitution**), the movement of the head to face one of the mother's inner thighs
- **expulsion,** the birth of the remainder of the fetus's body.

The cardinal movements of labor allow the smallest diameter of the fetal head to pass through the corresponding diameter of the woman's pelvis.

Postpartum period

The time frame after the birth of the neonate is called the **postpartum period.** During this period, the mother's reproductive tract begins to return to its former condition through a process called **involution.** The uterus shrinks quickly during the first 2 weeks after childbirth. As the uterus contracts, the woman may experience pain, commonly referred to as **afterpains.**

Discharge after being discharged

Postpartum vaginal discharge, called **lochia,** persists for several weeks. The color and consistency of the lochia changes.

- **Lochia rubra** is a bloody discharge that appears 1 to 4 days after childbirth.
- **Lochia serosa** is a pinkish brown serous discharge that appears 5 to 7 days after childbirth.
- **Lochia alba** is a grayish white or colorless discharge that appears 1 to 3 weeks after childbirth.

Mama's milk

A postpartum woman's breasts undergo changes in preparation for breast-feeding. If the woman chooses to breast-feed, the first milk produced is called colostrum. It's a thick, sticky, golden yellow, easy-to-digest fluid that contains protein, sugar, fat, water, minerals, vitamins, and maternal antibodies. Colostrum is replaced by mature breast milk by about the second to fourth postpartum day.

Physical examination terms

Here are terms associated with physical examination of the maternal patient:

- **Ballottement** is passive fetal movement that occurs in response to pushing against the lower portion of the uterus. (See *Ball toss.*)
- **Bloody show** refers to the vaginal discharge that occurs as the cervix thins and begins to dilate, allowing passage of the mucus plug that seals the cervical canal during pregnancy.
- **Braxton Hicks** contractions are episodes of light, painless, irregular tightening of the uterus during pregnancy. They may occur during the first trimester and increase in duration and intensity by the third trimester.
- **Chadwick's sign** is a bluish coloration of the vulva and vagina that may occur after the 6th week of pregnancy as a result of local venous congestion.
- **Engorgement** is the feeling of tightness, fullness, and tenderness in the postpartum woman's breasts most likely resulting from venous and lymphatic stasis and accumulation of milk in the breast alveoli.
- **Goodell's sign**, softening of the cervix, is an indication of probable pregnancy.
- **Gravida** refers to a pregnant female. A woman is called gravida 1 during the first pregnancy, gravida 2 in the second pregnancy, and so on.
- **Hegar's sign**, softening of the lower portion of the uterus, occurs around the 7th week of pregnancy. It's considered a sign of possible pregnancy.
- **Lightening** is a subjective sensation reported by some women as the fetus descends into the pelvic inlet and changes the shape and position of the uterus near term.
- **Linea nigra** is a line of dark pigment that appears on a pregnant woman's abdomen.
- **Melasma** refers to the darkened areas that may appear on the face, especially on the cheeks and across the nose; it's also known as **chloasma** or the mask of pregnancy.
- **Obstetrics** is the branch of surgical medicine involving pregnancy and childbirth. It includes care of the mother and fetus throughout pregnancy, childbirth, and the postpartum period.
- **Para** refers to a mother who has produced viable—but not necessarily living—offspring. The numerals used after the term (for example, para 1 or para 2) indicate the number of pregnancies that have produced viable offspring.

Ball toss

Ballottement is the passive fetal movement that occurs in response to pushing against the lower portion of the uterus. It's a combination of the French word *ballotter,* meaning *to toss about,* and the Italian word *ballotta,* meaning *ball.*

Melasma, also known as *chloasma,* refers to the darkened areas that may appear on a pregnant woman's face, especially on the cheeks and across the nose.

- **Primigravida** refers to a woman who's pregnant for the first time (also called gravida 1).
- **Primipara** refers to a woman who has had one pregnancy that resulted in a viable offspring or a woman who's pregnant for the first time (also called para 1).
- **Quickening** refers to the first noticeable fetal movement in utero. It usually occurs at 16 to 20 weeks' gestation.
- **Ripening** refers to the process in which the cervix softens to prepare for dilation and effacement.
- **Striae gravidarum**, also called **stretch marks**, are red streaks that appear on a pregnant woman's abdomen.
- **True** labor is characterized by the uterine contractions that lead to cervical effacement and dilation, bloody show, and rupture of the membranes.

Striae gravidarum, also called **stretch marks,** are red streaks that appear on a pregnant woman's abdomen.

The fetal picture

Here are some terms associated with the physical examination involving the fetus:

- **Attitude** is the degree of flexion and the relationship of the fetal body parts to one another.
- **Breech presentation** indicates that the fetus is in a head-up position with the buttocks (frank breech), feet (incomplete or footling breech), or buttocks and feet (complete breech) as the presenting parts.
- **Cephalic presentation** indicates that the fetal head is the first part to contact the cervix and be expelled from the uterus during birth.
- **Engagement** occurs when the presenting part of the fetus passes into the pelvis to the point where the presenting part is at the level of the ischial spines. (See *Fetal engagement and station.*)
- **Lie** refers to the relationship of the fetal spine to the maternal spine.
- **Position** is the relationship of the presenting part of the fetus to a specific quadrant of the mother's pelvis. It's designated using three letters: The first letter denotes whether the presenting part is facing the woman's right or left side (R or L). The second letter denotes the presenting part as occiput (O); mentum, or chin (M); sacrum (Sa); or shoulder (A). The third letter denotes whether the presenting part points to the anterior (A), posterior (P), or transverse section of the mother's pelvis (T).
- **Presentation** is the portion of the fetus that first enters the birth canal.
- **Station** is the relationship of the presenting part of the fetus to the mother's ischial spines.

Anatomically speaking

Fetal engagement and station

The extent of the fetal presenting part into the pelvis is referred to as **fetal engagement. Station** refers to where the fetal presenting part lies in relation to the maternal ischial spines. Station grades range from −3 (3 cm above the maternal ischial spines) to +4 (4 cm below the maternal ischial spines, causing the perineum to bulge). A zero station indicates that the presenting part lies level with the ischial spines.

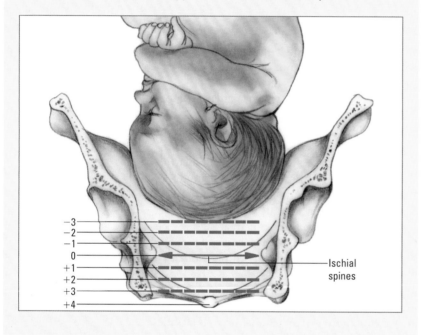

Diagnostic tests

Diagnostic tests associated with maternal health include blood and fluid tests as well as imaging and other tests.

Blood and fluid tests

Here are some common blood and fluid tests associated with maternal and fetal health:

- **Amniocentesis** involves the withdrawal of a sample of amniotic fluid by transabdominal puncture and needle aspiration. (See *Quite a bowlful.*)

Quite a bowlful

The term **amniocentesis** derives from two Greek words: *amnion* and *kentsis*. *Amnion* means *bowl* and *kentsis* means *the act of pricking*. The "bowl" refers to the membrane that envelops the fetus. Put it all together, and *amniocentesis* means the withdrawal of a sample of amniotic fluid from the amniotic sac by transabdominal puncture and needle aspiration.

- **Chorionic villus sampling** is a biopsy in which a minute amount of the chorionic villi (fingerlike projections of the chorion that attach to maternal endometrial tissues) is removed.
- **Indirect Coombs' test** is a blood test that screens maternal blood for red blood cell antibodies.
- **Percutaneous umbilical blood sampling** is an invasive procedure that involves insertion of a spinal needle into the umbilical cord to obtain a fetal blood sample or to transfuse the fetus in utero.
- **Serum alpha-fetoprotein** (AFP) measures the glycoprotein AFP. An above-normal level in an adult may indicate testicular cancer. In a fetus, an above-normal level may indicate a neural tube defect.
- **Triple screen** is a blood test performed between 15 and 20 weeks' gestation to determine whether a fetus is at increased risk for Down's syndrome, a neural tube defect, or other chromosomal abnormalities.
- **Quadruple screen** includes the triple screen blood test as well as an inhibin A test to more accurately predict the likelihood of Down's syndrome. This test, however, isn't available in all facilities.

*Screens aren't just for football, ya know. A **triple screen** is a blood test that determines whether a fetus is at increased risk for Down's syndrome, a neural tube defect, or other chromosomal abnormalities.*

Imaging and other diagnostic tests

Here are some common imaging and other diagnostic tests associated with maternal and fetal health:

- **Amniography** is an X-ray of a pregnant woman's uterus. A contrast medium is injected into the amniotic sac to visualize its contents.
- **External electronic monitoring** is an indirect, noninvasive procedure using two devices that are placed on the pregnant abdomen—an ultrasound transducer that detects the baby's heart rate and a tocotransducer that records the pressure of uterine contractions. Together, they help to evaluate fetal well-being and uterine contractions during labor.

- **Internal electronic monitoring,** also called **direct monitoring,** is an invasive procedure that uses a spiral electrode attached to the presenting fetal part to detect fetal heartbeat and convert it to a fetal electrocardiogram waveform.
- The **nonstress test** is a noninvasive test used to detect fetal heart accelerations in response to fetal movement.
- The **oxytocin challenge test** evaluates the fetus's ability to withstand an oxytocin-induced contraction. The test requires nipple stimulation or intravenous (I.V.) administration of oxytocin in increasing doses until three high-quality uterine contractions occur within a 10-minute period.
- **Pelvic ultrasound** passes sound waves through the pelvic area, creating electronic images of internal structures. This test is used to examine a developing fetus.
- **Vibroacoustic stimulation** test is a noninvasive test using 1 to 5 seconds of vibration and sound to induce fetal reactivity during a nonstress test. Vibration is produced by an artificial larynx or fetal acoustic stimulator that's placed above the head of the fetus.

I'm feeling those good vibrations! The **vibroacoustic stimulation** test is a noninvasive test that uses vibration and sound to induce fetal reactivity during a nonstress test.

Disorders associated with pregnancy, labor, and birth

- **Abruptio placentae** is the premature separation of a normally positioned placenta in a pregnancy of at least 20 weeks' gestation. This separation may occur before or during labor but always occurs before delivery. The classic symptom is painful "rupturing" accompanied by bleeding.
- **Battledore placenta** occurs when the umbilical cord attaches to the placenta marginally rather than centrally.
- **Cephalopelvic disproportion** is a disproportion between the size of the fetal head and the maternal pelvic diameters, usually due to a narrowing or contraction of the birth canal, resulting in a failure to progress in labor.

Pump up your pronunciation

How do I say *dystocia*?

The term describing the failure or inability to progress through the stages of labor—dystocia—is pronounced DIS-TOH-SHUH. The three parts of the word are all derived from Greek terms. **Dys** means *bad;* **toc** (from the word ***tokos***) means *childbirth;* and **ia** means a state or condition.

- **Dystocia** involves the failure or inability to progress through the stages of labor. (See *How do I say* dystocia?)
- **Eclampsia** refers to the development of seizures in a woman with gestational hypertension.
- **Ectopic pregnancy** is the implantation of a fertilized ovum outside the uterine cavity, usually in a fallopian tube.
- **Gestational diabetes** refers to diabetes that emerges during pregnancy and may lead to the birth of a large fetus, possibly weighing more than 10 lb (4.5 kg).
- **Gestational hypertension** is hypertension that usually develops after the 20th week of pregnancy and isn't accompanied by protein in the urine.
- **Hydatidiform** mole is an uncommon chorionic tumor of the placenta. Women with this type of tumor have a good chance of developing cancer later in life. It's also called **gestational trophoblastic disease** or **molar pregnancy**.
- **Hydramnios** refers to an excess amount of amniotic fluid.
- **Hydrorrhea gravidarum** is the discharge of thin, watery fluid from the uterus during pregnancy.
- **Hyperemesis gravidarum** is severe and unremitting nausea and vomiting after the first 12 weeks of pregnancy.
- **Isoimmunization**, also called Rh incompatibility, refers to a condition in which the pregnant woman is Rh negative but the fetus is Rh positive. If this condition is left untreated, the neonate can develop hemolytic disease.
- **Oligohydramnios** is a condition in which a less-than-normal amount of amniotic fluid is present in the amnion during pregnancy. (See *Taking apart* oligohydramnios.)
- **Perineum** is the tissue between the vaginal opening and the anus ("Episiotomy: When It's Needed..." 2015).
- **Placenta previa** is a placenta that develops in the lower segment of the uterus. It's characterized by painless bleeding, which differentiates this disorder from abruptio placentae.
- **Precipitous labor** occurs when uterine contractions are so strong that the woman gives birth with only a few rapidly occurring contractions. It's commonly defined as labor lasting less than 3 hours.
- **Preeclampsia** refers to the nonconvulsive form of hypertension, manifested by the development of hypertension after the 20th week of gestation and accompanied by protein in the urine. It may progress to eclampsia.
- **Premature labor**, also called **preterm labor**, is the onset of rhythmic uterine contractions that produce cervical changes after fetal viability but before fetal maturity (usually between 20 and 37 weeks' gestation).

Hyperemesis gravidarum is severe and unremitting nausea and vomiting after the first 12 weeks of pregnancy.

Beyond the dictionary

Taking apart oligohydramnios

Oligohydramnios is a less-than-normal amount of amniotic fluid. The word *oligo-* means *few* or *scanty*. *Hydro-* means *water* or *fluid*, and *-amnios* refers to the amnion. Thus, **oligohydramnios** means *little fluid in the amnion.*

- **Premature rupture of membranes (PROM)** is a spontaneous break or tear in the amniotic sac before the onset of regular contractions.
- **Spontaneous abortion** is the premature expulsion of an embryo or nonviable fetus from the uterus.
- **Umbilical cord prolapse** occurs when a loop of the umbilical cord slips down in front of the fetal presenting part. It may occur at any time after the membranes rupture, especially if the presenting part isn't fitted firmly into the cervix.

PROM is a spontaneous break or tear in the amniotic sac before the onset of regular contractions.

Treatments and procedures

Here are terms related to treatments and procedures associated with pregnancy, labor, and birth.

- **Abortion** is the termination of a pregnancy. It can be spontaneous (from natural causes), elective (performed as a result of a choice to terminate the pregnancy), or therapeutic (performed to preserve the woman's life or when serious birth defects are expected). Controversial partial birth abortions are those performed late in pregnancy.
- **Amniotomy** requires the use of an instrument such as an amniohook to mechanically rupture the membranes.
- **Artificial insemination** is the placement of seminal fluid into the patient's vaginal canal or cervix. The procedure is coordinated with ovulation.
- **Cervical suturing,** also called **cerclage,** is the use of a purse-string suture to reinforce the cervix.
- **Cesarean birth** involves an incision made through the abdominal and uterine walls to deliver a neonate.
- In **dilation and evacuation,** suction is used to remove the uterine contents. This procedure is typically used to perform elective abortions.
- **Episiotomy** is an incision made at the perineum to prevent tearing during birth of a neonate.
- **Gamete intrafallopian transfer** is a reproductive technology that involves placing ova collected from the ovaries transvaginally into a catheter filled with sperm. The contents of the catheter are injected into the end of the fallopian tube via a laparoscope. This technique allows fertilization and implantation to occur naturally.
- With **in vitro fertilization,** an ovum is removed from the woman's body and fertilized with sperm in a laboratory culture medium. The resulting embryo is then transferred into the woman's uterus.

- **Labor induction** involves stimulating the onset of uterine contractions by medical or surgical methods before the woman begins labor spontaneously.
- **RhoGAM administration** is the administration of Rh_o (D) immune globulin containing Rh_o (D) antibodies to a woman who is Rh negative. This procedure keeps the mother from producing active antibody responses and forming anti-Rh_o (D) to Rh-positive fetal blood cells.
- **Tocolytic therapy** involves using medications to quiet the contracting uterus when preterm labor occurs.
- **Zygote intrafallopian tube transfer** is a reproductive technology that involves fertilization of the ovum outside the mother's body followed by reimplantation of the zygote into the fallopian tube via laparoscopy.

Vocabulary builders

At a crossroads

Test your maternal instincts by completing this crossword puzzle of maternal health terms.

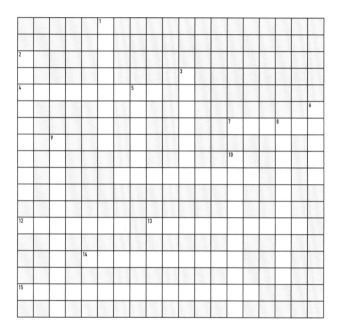

Across

4. Breast-feeding
7. Postpartum vaginal discharge
11. Period of pregnancy that begins with conception and ends with childbirth
12. A pregnant female
13. The first noticeable fetal movement in utero
14. Thinning and shortening of the cervix
15. Rh incompatibility

Down

1. The termination of a pregnancy
2. First milk produced after childbirth
3. Endometrial lining of the uterus
5. Precursor of the ovum
6. Process by which birth of the fetus is achieved
8. An excessive amount of amniotic fluid
9. Cells that move by means of flagellar movements
10. Also called fertilization

Finish line

Fill in the blanks with the appropriate terms.

1. _____ contractions are episodes of light, painless, irregular uterine tightening during pregnancy.

2. The degree of flexion and the relationship of the fetal body parts to one another is called _____.

3. _____ involves the withdrawal of a sample of amniotic fluid by transabdominal puncture and needle aspiration.

4. The implantation of a fertilized ovum outside the uterine cavity, usually in a fallopian tube, is called an _____ pregnancy.

5. _____ involves using medications to quiet the contracting uterus when pre-term labor occurs.

Match game

Match each description of a disorder, condition, or treatment to its name.

Clues	Choices
1. Occurs when a loop of the umbilical cord slips down in front of the fetal presenting part _____	A. Abruptio placentae
2. An incision made in the vulva to prevent tearing during birth of a neonate _____	B. Hydatidiform mole
3. The use of suction to remove the uterine contents _____	C. Umbilical cord prolapse
4. Premature separation of a normally positioned placenta in a pregnancy of at least 20 weeks' gestation _____	D. Cervical suturing
5. The use of an instrument to mechanically rupture the membranes _____	E. Dilation and evacuation
6. An uncommon chorionic tumor of the placenta _____	F. Episiotomy
7. The use of a purse-string suture to reinforce the cervix _____	G. Amniotomy

Answers

At a crossroads

Crossword grid solution:

Down 1: ABORTION
Across 2: C (start of COLOSTRUM going down)
Across 4: LACTATION
Down 5: OOCYTE
Down 3: DECIDUA
Across 7: HOCHIA
Down 6: LABOR
Down 8: HYDRAMNIOS
Down 9: SPERM
Down 10: CONCEPTION
Across 11: GESTATION
Across 12: GRAVIDA
Across 13: QUICKENING
Across 14: EFFACEMENT
Across 15: ISOIMMUNIZATION
Down 12: GRAVIDA (GESTATIOZA column letters G R A V ... O T O Z I S A)

Finish line

Answers: 1. Braxton Hicks; 2. Attitude; 3. Amniocentesis; 4. Ectopic; 5. Tocolytic therapy

Match game

Answers: 1. C; 2. F; 3. E; 4. A; 5. G; 6. B; 7. D

Suggested reference

Episiotomy: When it's needed, when it's not. (2015, July 30). Retrieved on November 25, 2016 from http://www.mayoclinic.org/healthy-lifestyle/labor-and-delivery/in-depth/episiotomy/art-20047282

Chapter 12

Neurologic system

Just the facts

In this chapter, you'll learn:

◆ terminology related to the structure and function of the neurologic system

◆ terminology needed for physical examination of the neurologic system

◆ tests that help diagnose common neurologic disorders

◆ neurologic system disorders and their treatments.

Neurologic structure and function

The neurologic system, also called the nervous system, coordinates all body functions, enabling a person to adapt to changes in internal and external environments. It has two main types of cells (neurons and neuroglia) and two main divisions (the **central nervous system [CNS] and peripheral nervous system**). (See *Pronouncing key neurologic system terms*.)

Cells of the nervous system

The nervous system is packed with intertwined cells.

Neurons—the naked truth

Neurons, the primary functional unit of the nervous system, respond to stimuli and transmit responses by means of electromechanical messages.

The main parts of a neuron are the **cell body** (which contains the nucleus [plural: **nuclei**]) and the **cytoplasm**. This is the metabolic center of the neuron.

One **axon** and several **dendrites** project from each cell body. (See *Parts of a neuron*.) In a typical neuron, one axon and many dendrites extend from the cell body.

Pump up your pronunciation

Pronouncing key neurologic system terms

Below is a list of key terms related to the neurologic system along with the correct ways to pronounce them.

Choroid plexus	KOR-OYD PLEK-SEHS
Echoencephalography	EK-OH-EN-SEF-UH-LAWG-RUH-FEE
Guillain-Barré syndrome	GEE-LAYN BAHR-RAY SIN-DROHM
Gyri	JEYE-REYE
Neuroglia	NEW-ROG-GLEE-UH
Sulci	SUHL-KEYE
Trigeminal neuralgia	TREYE-JEM-UH-NUHL NEW-RAL-JEE-UH
Ventriculoperitoneal shunt	VEN-TRIK-YOU-LOH-PER-UH-TOH-NEE-UHL SHUHNT

Shipping and receiving

Axons conduct nerve impulses away from the cell body. **Dendrites** conduct impulses toward the cell body.

The main function of the axon is to send or transmit signals to other cells. The highly specialized neuron cells can't replace themselves but will attempt to repair themselves if damage is limited to the axon.

Axons can vary in length from quite short to very long—up to 3¼′ (1 m). A typical axon has **terminal branches** and is wrapped in a white, fatty, segmented covering called a myelin sheath. The **myelin sheath** is produced by **Schwann cells**, made up of **phagocytic cells** (cells capable of engulfing and digesting microorganisms and cellular debris) separated by gaps called **nodes of Ranvier.** (See *Schwann and Ranvier*, page 249.)

Dendrites are short, thick, diffusely branched extensions that receive impulses arriving at the neuron from other cells.

Being impulsive

The purpose of a neuron is to initiate, receive, and process messages through electrochemical conduction of impulses, also known as **neurotransmission.** Neuron activity can be provoked by mechanical stimuli, such as touch and pressure; by thermal stimuli, such as heat and cold; and by chemical stimuli, such as external chemicals and chemicals released by the body, such as histamine.

Anatomically speaking

Parts of a neuron

A typical neuron, such as the one shown here, has one axon and many dendrites. A myelin sheath encloses the axon.

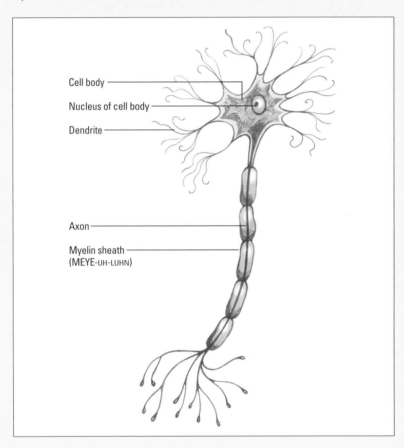

Cell body

Nucleus of cell body

Dendrite

Axon

Myelin sheath
(MEYE-UH-LUHN)

Neurons respond to stimuli and transmit responses by means of electromechanical messages.

Neuro-glue

The supportive structures of the nervous system, neuroglia, are also called glial **cells. Glial** is derived from the Greek word for *glue*; these cells hold the neurons together and form roughly 40% of the brain's bulk. In addition, glial cells nourish and protect the neurons. Four types of neuroglia exist:

1. Astroglia, or **astrocytes**, exist throughout the nervous system. They supply nutrients to neurons and help them maintain their

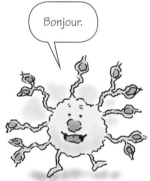

electrical potential. Astrocytes also form part of the **blood-brain barrier** that separates CNS tissue from the bloodstream and guards against invasion by disease-causing organisms and other harmful substances.

2. **Ependymal cells** line the **ventricles**, four small cavities in the brain, as well as the **choroid plexuses**, vascular structures that form a network in the pia mater of the brain and project into the third, lateral, and fourth ventricles. These cells help produce **cerebrospinal fluid (CSF)**.

3. **Microglia** are phagocytic cells that ingest and digest microorganisms and waste products from injured neurons, giving them an important role in host defense.

4. **Oligodendroglia** support and electrically insulate CNS axons by forming protective myelin sheaths.

Brain

The CNS includes the spinal cord and the brain. The brain consists of the **cerebrum**, **cerebellum**, brain stem, and primitive structures that lie below the cerebrum—the **diencephalon**, limbic system, and reticular activating system. (See *Major structures in the brain*, page 251.)

You're so cerebral

The cerebrum has right and left hemispheres. The **corpus callosum**—a mass of nerve fibers—bridges the hemispheres, allowing communication between corresponding centers in each. The rolling surface of the cerebrum is made up of **gyri** (convolutions) and **sulci** (creases or fissures). The thin surface layer, the **cerebral cortex**, consists of **gray matter** (unmyelinated nerve fibers). Within the cerebrum lie **white matter** (myelinated nerve fibers) and islands of internal gray matter.

Name that lobe

Each cerebral hemisphere is divided into four lobes, based on anatomic landmarks and functional differences. The lobes are named for the cranial bones that lie over them—frontal, temporal, parietal, and occipital:

- The **frontal lobe** influences personality, judgment, abstract reasoning, social behavior, language expression, and movement.
- The **temporal lobe** controls hearing, language comprehension, and storage and recall of memories (although memories are stored throughout the entire brain).
- The **parietal lobe** interprets and integrates sensations, including pain, temperature, and touch. It also interprets size, shape, distance, and texture. The parietal lobe of the nondominant hemisphere is especially important for awareness of one's own body shape.
- The **occipital lobe** functions primarily to interpret visual stimuli.

Let's talk about communication.

*Okay. The **corpus callosum** bridges my right and left hemispheres, allowing communication between them.*

Celebrating the cerebellum

The cerebellum, the second largest brain region, lies posterior and inferior to the cerebrum. Like the cerebrum, it has two hemispheres, an outer cortex of gray matter and an inner core of white matter. The cerebellum functions to maintain muscle tone, coordinate muscle movement, and control balance.

Brain stem

The **brain stem** lies immediately inferior to the cerebrum, just anterior to the cerebellum. It's continuous with the cerebrum superiorly and with the spinal cord inferiorly.

Composed of the midbrain, pons, and medulla oblongata, the brain stem relays messages between the parts of the nervous system. It has three main functions:

1. It produces the rigid autonomic behaviors necessary for survival, such as increasing heart rate and respiratory rate and stimulating the adrenal medulla to produce epinephrine.
2. It provides pathways for nerve fibers between higher and lower neural centers.
3. It serves as the origin for 10 of the 12 pairs of cranial nerves.

The **reticular activating system (RAS)**, a diffuse network of hyperexcitable neurons, fans out from the brain stem through the cerebral cortex. After screening all incoming sensory information,

Memory jogger

To distinguish the locations of the "cerebrum" and the "cerebellum," look at the "BR" in "cereBRum" and think "BRow," meaning that the cerebrum is the top (the outermost) part of the brain.

For "cerebellum," look at the "BEL" in "cereBELlum" and think "BELow" because the cerebellum is below and behind the cerebrum.

Anatomically speaking

Major structures in the brain

These illustrations show the two largest structures of the brain—the cerebrum and cerebellum. Also note the locations of the four cerebral lobes, the sensory cortex, and the motor cortex. The bottom illustration shows a cross section of the brain, from its outermost portion (cerebrum) to its innermost (diencephalon).

My lobes are named for the cranial bones that lie over them—frontal, temporal, parietal, and occipital.

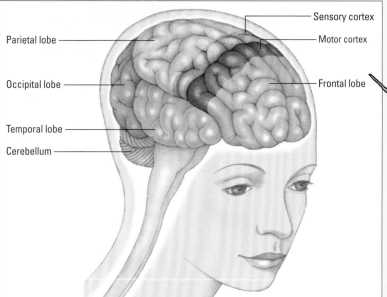

Parietal lobe

Occipital lobe

Temporal lobe

Cerebellum

Sensory cortex

Motor cortex

Frontal lobe

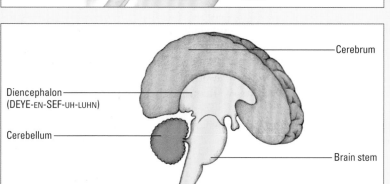

Diencephalon
(DEYE-EN-SEF-UH-LUHN)

Cerebellum

Cerebrum

Brain stem

the RAS channels it to appropriate areas of the brain for interpretation. RAS activity also stimulates wakefulness or arousal of consciousness.

Where nerves volunteer

The **midbrain** connects dorsally with the cerebellum and extends from the pons to the hypothalamus. It contains large voluntary motor nerve tracts running between the brain and spinal cord.

It makes perfect sense. The **pons** acts as a pathway, and **pons** is the Latin term for bridge.

The pons pathway

The **pons** connects the cerebellum with the cerebrum and links the midbrain to the medulla oblongata. It houses two of the brain's respiratory centers that work with those in the medulla to produce a normal breathing rhythm. The pons also acts as a pathway between brain centers and the spinal cord and serves as the exit point for cranial nerves V, VI, and VII.

Inferior, not unimportant

The **medulla** oblongata, the most inferior portion of the brain stem, is a small, cone-shaped structure. It joins the spinal cord at the level of the **foramen magnum**, an opening in the occipital portion of the skull. The medulla oblongata serves as an autonomic reflex center to maintain homeostasis, regulating respiratory, vasomotor, and cardiac functions.

Note to hypothalamus: Please adjust your thermostat!

Primitive structures

The **diencephalon** consists of the thalamus and hypothalamus, which lie beneath the surface of the cerebral hemispheres. The **thalamus** relays all sensory stimuli (except olfactory) as they ascend to the cerebral cortex. Its functions include primitive awareness of pain, screening of incoming stimuli, and focusing of attention. The **hypothalamus** controls or affects body temperature, appetite, water balance, pituitary secretions, emotions, and autonomic functions (including sleep and wake cycles).

Limbo with the limbic system

The **limbic system** is a primitive brain area deep within the temporal lobe. In addition to initiating basic drives, such as hunger, aggression, and emotional and sexual arousal, the limbic system screens all sensory messages traveling to the cerebral cortex. (See *Limbic system and brain stem.*)

Spinal cord

A cylindrical structure in the vertebral canal, the **spinal cord** extends from the foramen magnum at the base of the skull to the upper lumbar region of the vertebral column. The spinal nerves arise from the cord. At the cord's inferior end, nerve roots cluster in the **cauda equina**.

Horn of sensation, horn of activity

Within the spinal cord, the H-shaped mass of gray matter is divided into horns, which consist mainly of neuron cell bodies. Cell bodies in the **posterior horn** primarily relay sensations; those in the **anterior horn** play a part in voluntary and involuntary (reflex) motor activity. White matter surrounding the outer part of these horns consists of myelinated nerve fibers grouped functionally in vertical columns, or **tracts**.

Impulse conductor

The spinal cord conducts sensory nerve impulses to the brain and conducts motor impulses from the brain. It also controls reflexes, including the knee-jerk (patellar) reaction to a reflex hammer.

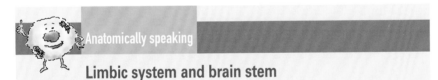

Anatomically speaking

Limbic system and brain stem

The major structures of the limbic system and brain stem, shown here, are associated with emotions and responses such as anger, fear, and sexual arousal.

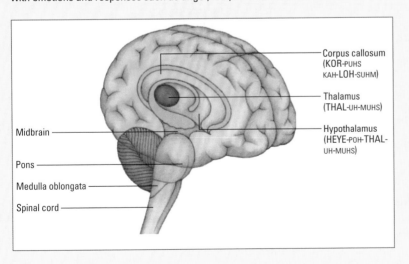

Corpus callosum
(KOR-PUHS
KAH-LOH-SUHM)

Thalamus
(THAL-UH-MUHS)

Hypothalamus
(HEYE-POH-THAL-
UH-MUHS)

Midbrain

Pons

Medulla oblongata

Spinal cord

Pathways in the brain

Nerve impulses to the brain follow sensory pathways. Nerve impulses from the brain—those that control body function and movement—follow motor pathways.

Sensory pathways

Sensory impulses travel via the **afferent**, or **ascending**, neural pathways to the brain's sensory cortex in the parietal lobe, where they're interpreted. These impulses use two major pathways.

Ouch!

Pain and temperature sensations enter the spinal cord through the dorsal horn. After immediately crossing over to the opposite side of the cord, these stimuli then travel to the thalamus via the **spinothalamic tract**.

Touchy-feely with the ganglia

Tactile, pressure, and vibration sensations enter the spinal cord via relay stations called **ganglia** (knotlike masses of nerve cell bodies on the dorsal roots of spinal nerves). These stimuli then travel up the spinal cord in the dorsal column to the medulla, where they cross to the opposite side and enter the thalamus. The thalamus relays all incoming sensory impulses (except olfactory impulses) to the sensory cortex for interpretation.

Motor pathways

Motor impulses travel from the brain to the muscles via **efferent**, or **descending**, pathways. Originating in the motor cortex of the frontal lobe, these impulses reach the lower motor neurons of the peripheral nervous system via **upper motor neurons**. Upper motor neurons originate in the brain and form two major systems:

Just an impulse

- The pyramidal **system**, also called the **corticospinal tract**, is responsible for fine motor movements of skeletal muscle. Impulses in this system travel from the motor cortex, through the internal capsule, and to the medulla, where they cross to the opposite side and continue down the spinal cord.
- The extrapyramidal **system**, or **extracorticospinal tract**, controls gross motor movements. Impulses originate in the premotor area of the frontal lobe and travel to the pons, where they cross to the opposite side. Then the impulses travel down the spinal cord to the anterior horn, where they're relayed to the lower motor neurons. These neurons, in turn, carry the impulses to the muscles.

Ouch! I shouldn't have touched that hot pan! Better alert the spinothalamic tract.

It's all automatic

Reflex responses occur automatically, without any brain involvement, to protect the body. Spinal nerves, which have both sensory
and motor portions, mediate **deep tendon reflexes**—involuntary
contractions of a muscle after brief stretching caused by tendon
percussion—and **superficial reflexes**—withdrawal reflexes elicited
by noxious or tactile stimulation of the skin, cornea, or mucous
membranes.

A simple reflex, such as the **knee-jerk reflex**, requires an **afferent** (sensory) neuron and an **efferent** (motor) neuron. (See *Patellar
reflex arc.*)

Patellar reflex arc

Spinal nerves—which have sensory and motor
portions—control deep tendon and superficial reflexes.
A simple reflex arc requires a sensory (or afferent)
neuron and a motor (or efferent) neuron. The knee-jerk,
or patellar, reflex illustrates the sequence of events in a
normal reflex arc.

First, a sensory receptor detects the mechanical
stimulus produced by the reflex hammer striking the
patellar tendon. Then the sensory neuron carries the

impulse along its axon by way of the spinal nerve to the
dorsal root, where it enters the spinal column.

Next, in the anterior horn of the spinal cord, shown
below, the sensory neuron joins with a motor neuron,
which carries the impulse along its axon by way of the
spinal nerve to the muscle. The motor neuron transmits
the impulse to muscle fibers through stimulation of the
motor end plate. This triggers the muscle to contract and
the leg to extend.

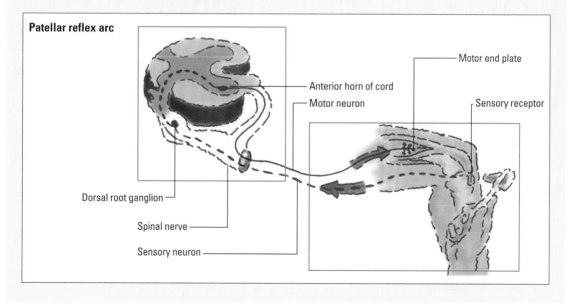

Patellar reflex arc

- Motor end plate
- Anterior horn of cord
- Motor neuron
- Sensory receptor
- Dorsal root ganglion
- Spinal nerve
- Sensory neuron

Protective structures of the CNS

The brain and spinal cord are protected from shock and infection by bones, the meninges, several additional cushioning layers, and CSF.

> Guess what, little one. **Pia mater** is the Latin term for gentle mother. **Dura mater** is Latin for tough mother.

Bones

The **skull**, formed of cranial bones, completely surrounds the brain. It opens at the foramen magnum, where the spinal cord exits.

The **vertebral column** protects the spinal cord. Its 30 vertebrae are separated from one another by an intervertebral disk that allows flexibility.

Meninges

The **meninges** cover and protect the cerebral cortex and spinal column. They consist of three layers of connective tissue: the dura mater, arachnoid membrane, and pia mater. (See *Protective membranes of the CNS.*)

The dura mater truly matters

The **dura mater** is a fibrous membrane that lines the skull and forms reflections, or folds, that descend into the brain's fissures and provide stability. The dural folds include:
- the falx **cerebri**, which lies in the longitudinal fissure and separates the cerebral hemispheres
- the **tentorium cerebelli**, which separates the cerebrum from the cerebellum
- the falx **cerebelli**, which separates the two lobes of the cerebellum.

The **arachnoid villi**, projections of the dura mater into the superior sagittal and transverse sinuses, serve as the exit points for CSF drainage into the venous circulation.

Arachnoid phobia?

A fragile, fibrous layer of moderate vascularity, the **arachnoid membrane** lies between the dura mater and pia mater.

Thin and rich

The extremely thin **pia mater**, the innermost layer, has a rich blood supply. It adheres to the brain's surface and extends into its fissures.

Anatomically speaking

Protective membranes of the CNS

Three membranes—the dura mater, arachnoid membrane, and pia mater—help protect the central nervous system (CNS). The arachnoid villi project from the arachnoid membrane into the superior sagittal and transverse sinuses. The subarachnoid space, filled with cerebrospinal fluid, separates the arachnoid membrane from the pia mater.

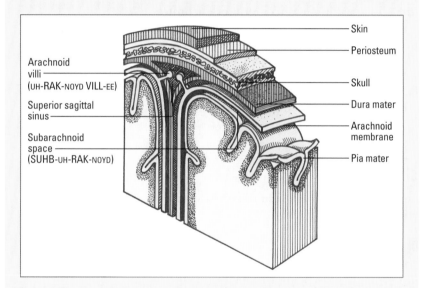

Arachnoid villi (UH-RAK-NOYD VILL-EE)

Superior sagittal sinus

Subarachnoid space (SUHB-UH-RAK-NOYD)

Skin

Periosteum

Skull

Dura mater

Arachnoid membrane

Pia mater

Cushioning layers

Three layers of space further cushion the brain and spinal cord against injury. The **epidural space** (actually, a potential space) lies over the dura mater. The **subdural space** is situated between the dura mater and arachnoid membrane. This closed area—typically the site of hemorrhage after head trauma—offers no escape route for accumulated blood. The **subarachnoid space**, filled with CSF, separates the arachnoid membrane and pia mater.

Cerebrospinal fluid

CSF is a colorless fluid that arises from blood plasma and has a similar composition. It cushions the brain and spinal cord, nourishes cells, and transports metabolic waste.

The epidural space, subdural space, and subarachnoid space protect me against injury.

Fluid factory

CSF forms continuously in clusters of capillaries called the **choroid plexuses**, located in the roof of each ventricle. The choroid plexuses produce approximately 500 mL of CSF each day.

Open to flow

From the lateral ventricles, CSF flows through the **interventricular foramen**, commonly known as the **foramen of Monro**, to the third ventricle of the brain. **Foramen** is a term used to describe a natural opening or passage. The foramen of Monro is named after the man who first described it: Alexander Monro II, a professor of anatomy at the University of Edinburgh. (See *Three men of Monro*.)

From there, it reaches the subarachnoid space and then passes under the base of the brain, upward over the brain's upper surfaces, and down around the spinal cord. Eventually, it reaches the arachnoid villi, where it's reabsorbed into venous blood at the venous sinuses on top of the brain.

Beyond the dictionary

Three men of Monro

The foramen of Monro is named after Alexander Monro II (1733 to 1817), the man who first described it. Monro was the second professor of anatomy at the University of Edinburgh (and the second named Alexander Monro). He succeeded his father in this position and was succeeded by his own son, Alex III.

Peripheral nervous system

The peripheral nervous system consists of the cranial nerves, spinal nerves, and **autonomic nervous system (ANS)**.

Message lines: Neck and above

The 12 pairs of **cranial nerves** transmit motor or sensory messages, or both, primarily between the brain or brain stem and the head and neck. All cranial nerves, except the olfactory and optic nerves, exit from the midbrain, pons, or medulla oblongata of the brain stem. (See *A look at the 12 cranial nerves*.)

Can you hear me now?

The 31 pairs of **spinal nerves** are named for the vertebra immediately below each nerve's exit point from the spinal cord; thus, they're designated from top to bottom as C1 through S5 and the coccygeal nerve. Each spinal nerve consists of afferent and efferent neurons, which carry messages to and from particular body regions called **dermatomes**.

Autonomic nervous system

The vast ANS innervates all internal organs. Sometimes known as **visceral efferent nerves**, the nerves of the ANS carry messages to the viscera from the brain stem and neuroendocrine regulatory centers.

A look at the 12 cranial nerves

As this illustration reveals, 10 of the 12 pairs of cranial nerves (CNs) exit from the brain stem. The remaining two pairs—the olfactory and optic nerves—exit from the forebrain.

It says here that most of the cranial nerves transmit either **motor** or **sensory** information. A few, such as the **vagus nerve**, do both.

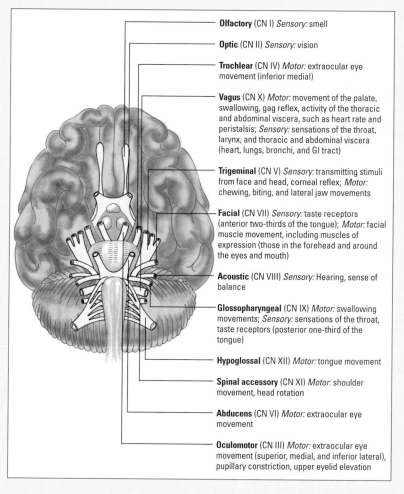

Olfactory (CN I) *Sensory:* smell

Optic (CN II) *Sensory:* vision

Trochlear (CN IV) *Motor:* extraocular eye movement (inferior medial)

Vagus (CN X) *Motor:* movement of the palate, swallowing, gag reflex, activity of the thoracic and abdominal viscera, such as heart rate and peristalsis; *Sensory:* sensations of the throat, larynx, and thoracic and abdominal viscera (heart, lungs, bronchi, and GI tract)

Trigeminal (CN V) *Sensory:* transmitting stimuli from face and head, corneal reflex; *Motor:* chewing, biting, and lateral jaw movements

Facial (CN VII) *Sensory:* taste receptors (anterior two-thirds of the tongue); *Motor:* facial muscle movement, including muscles of expression (those in the forehead and around the eyes and mouth)

Acoustic (CN VIII) *Sensory:* Hearing, sense of balance

Glossopharyngeal (CN IX) *Motor:* swallowing movements; *Sensory:* sensations of the throat, taste receptors (posterior one-third of the tongue)

Hypoglossal (CN XII) *Motor:* tongue movement

Spinal accessory (CN XI) *Motor:* shoulder movement, head rotation

Abducens (CN VI) *Motor:* extraocular eye movement

Oculomotor (CN III) *Motor:* extraocular eye movement (superior, medial, and inferior lateral), pupillary constriction, upper eyelid elevation

The ANS has two major subdivisions: the **sympathetic (thoracolumbar)** nervous system and the **parasympathetic (craniosacral)** nervous system. (See *On autonomic pilot.*)

System response: General

Sympathetic nerves called **preganglionic neurons** exit the spinal cord between the levels of the first thoracic and second lumbar vertebrae.

After they leave the spinal cord, these nerves enter small ganglia near the spinal cord. The ganglia form a chain that spreads the impulse to **postganglionic neurons**, which reach many organs and glands and can produce widespread, generalized physiologic responses.

System response: Specific

Fibers of the parasympathetic nervous system leave the CNS by way of the cranial nerves from the midbrain and medulla and the spinal nerves between the second and fourth sacral vertebrae (S2 to S4).

After leaving the CNS, the long preganglionic fiber of each parasympathetic nerve travels to a ganglion near a particular organ or gland; the short postganglionic fiber enters the organ or gland. This creates a more specific response, involving only one organ or gland.

Physical examination terms

Here are terms associated with procedures and observations one might encounter in a physical examination relating to the neurologic system:

- **Absence seizure** (also known as a **petit mal seizure**) is marked by a sudden, momentary loss of consciousness, typically accompanied by loss of muscle control or spasms, and a vacant facial expression. The patient may experience many seizures per day.
- **Aphasia** is loss or impairment of the ability to communicate through speech, written language, or signs. It typically results from brain disease or trauma.
- **Aphonia** is loss of the ability to speak.
- **Apraxia** is complete or partial inability to perform purposeful movements in the absence of sensory or motor impairment.
- **Ataxia** is impairment of the ability to coordinate voluntary muscle movement.
- **Ataxic speech** is characterized by faulty formation of sounds. It's typically caused by neuromuscular disease.
- **Athetosis** is a condition characterized by constant, slow, writhing, involuntary movements of the extremities, especially the hands.
- **Aura** is the word for the sensations that occur before a paroxysmal attack, such as a seizure or migraine headache.
- **Battle's sign** is discoloration of the skin behind the ear following the fracture of a bone in the lower skull.

Beyond the dictionary

On autonomic pilot

The autonomic nervous system innervates all internal organs. **Autonomic** comes from two Greek words: *auto*, meaning *self*, and *nomos*, meaning *law*. So, this nervous system operates according to its own law, or without conscious control.

Think of the autonomic nervous system as being on autopilot.

- **Biot's respiration** is an abnormal, unpredictable breathing pattern characterized by irregular periods of apnea alternating with periods of four or five breaths of the same depth. Biot's respiration indicates meningitis, a lesion in the medulla, or increased intracranial pressure.
- **Bradylalia** refers to abnormally slow speech, caused by a brain lesion.
- **Brudzinski's sign** is flexion of the hips and knees in response to passive flexion of the neck. A positive Brudzinski's sign signals meningeal irritation.
- **Coma** is a state of unconsciousness from which the patient can't be aroused.
- **Decerebrate posturing** is associated with a lesion of the upper brain stem or severe bilateral lesions in the cerebrum. The patient typically lies with legs extended, head retracted, arms adducted and extended, wrists pronated, and the fingers, ankles, and toes flexed.
- **Decorticate posturing** is associated with a lesion of the frontal lobes, cerebral peduncles, or internal capsule. The patient lies with arms adducted and flexed, wrists and fingers flexed on the chest, legs stiffly extended and internally rotated, and feet plantar flexed.
- **Delirium** is an acute disorientation to time and place; the patient may also experience illusions and hallucinations.
- **Dementia** is an organic mental syndrome marked by general loss of intellectual abilities, with chronic personality disintegration, confusion, disorientation, and stupor. It doesn't include states of impaired intellectual functioning resulting from delirium or depression.
- **Dysphagia** is difficulty swallowing.
- **Dysphasia** is impairment of speech involving failure to arrange words in their proper order, usually resulting from injury to the speech area in the cerebral cortex.
- **Dyspraxia** is a partial loss of the ability to perform coordinated movements, with no associated defect in motor or sensory functions.
- **A generalized tonic-clonic (grand mal) seizure** is an **epileptic seizure** that may be preceded by an aura. This type of seizure is characterized by loss of consciousness and muscle spasms (tonic phase), followed by convulsive movement of the limbs (clonic phase).
- The **Glasgow Coma Scale** is commonly used to assess a patient's level of consciousness (LOC). It was designed to help determine a patient's chances for survival and recovery after a head injury. The scale scores three observations—eye opening response, best

Biot's respiration, pronounced BEE-Oнz, is named after Camille Biot, a 19th-century French doctor.

Dysphasia failure words is proper order in arrange to.

motor response, and best verbal response. Each response receives a point value. If a patient is alert, can follow simple commands, and is well oriented, his score will total 15 points. If the patient is comatose, his score will be 7 or less. The lowest possible score, 3, indicates deep coma and a poor prognosis.

The **Glasgow Coma Scale** was designed to help determine a patient's chances for survival and recovery after a head injury.

- **Headache** is diffuse pain that occurs in different portions of the head and is not confined to any nerve distribution area.
- **Hemiparesis** refers to paralysis or muscular weakness affecting only one side of the body.
- **Hemiplegia** is paralysis of one side of the body.
- **Intracranial pressure (ICP)** is the pressure created by CSF in the subarachnoid space between the skull and brain. ICP may increase as a result of head trauma, brain tumor, stroke, or infection in the brain.
- **Kernig's sign** refers to resistance and hamstring muscle pain that occur when an examiner attempts to extend a patient's knee while the hip and knee are both flexed 90 degrees. This sign is usually present in a patient with meningitis or subarachnoid hemorrhage.
- **Neuralgia** is severe pain in a nerve or nerves.

Reflexes

Reflexes, involuntary responses to stimuli, are discussed here:
- **Achilles tendon reflex** produces plantar flexion when the Achilles tendon is tapped.
- **Babinski's reflex** is dorsiflexion of the big toe in response to scraping the sole of the foot.
- **Biceps reflex** causes contraction of the biceps muscles when the tendon is tapped.

Sorry!

- **Brachioradialis reflex** is flexion and supination of the elbow or visible contraction of the brachioradialis muscle when the radius is tapped 1⅛″ to 2″ (3 to 5 cm) above the wrist while the arm is relaxed.
- **Corneal reflex** is closure of the eyelids when the cornea is touched.
- A negative **oculocephalic reflex**, also known as an absent **doll's eye sign**, is an indicator of brain stem dysfunction. The absence of the doll's eye sign is detected by rapid, but gentle, turning of the patient's head from side to side. The eyes remain fixed in an abnormal straight-ahead position instead of moving in the direction opposite to which the head is turned.

- **Gag reflex** is elicited by touching the soft palate or the back of the pharynx. The normal response is elevation of the palate, retraction of the tongue, and contraction of the constrictor muscle of the pharynx.
- **Knee-jerk reflex** is a kick reflex produced by sharply tapping the patellar ligament. It's also known as the **patellar reflex.**
- **Pupillary reflex** is contraction of the pupils in response to light.
- **Triceps reflex** is visible contraction of the triceps or extension of the arm when the triceps tendon is tapped above the elbow while the arm is flexed.

Diagnostic tests

Diagnostic tests associated with the neurologic system include radiographic and imaging studies, electrophysiologic studies, and CSF and blood tests.

Radiographic and imaging studies

Here are some common radiographic and imaging studies:
- **Cerebral angiography** is a radiographic procedure in which radiopaque contrast is injected into blood vessels to allow visualization of the vascular system of the brain.
- **Computed tomography (CT)** combines radiography and computer analysis of tissue density. When used to diagnose neurologic disorders, it produces images of the structures inside the skull and spinal cord.
- **Digital subtraction angiography (DSA)** traces the cerebral vessels by means of a type of computerized fluoroscopy. The technician takes an image of the area being studied and stores it in the computer's memory. Additional images are taken after the patient receives a contrast medium. By subtracting the original picture from the later images, the computer produces high-resolution images for interpretation.
- **Echoencephalography** is a diagnostic technique that involves the use of ultrasound waves to study structures within the brain.
- **Magnetic resonance angiography (MRA)** is a noninvasive method of scanning that allows visualization of blood flowing through the cerebral vessels.
- **Magnetic resonance imaging (MRI)**, also called **nuclear magnetic resonance**, is a noninvasive method of scanning with an electromagnetic field and radio waves. It provides visual images of structures on a computer screen.

The root **echo** in **echoencephalography** tells you that this test uses sound waves.

Beyond the dictionary

Getting around PEG

Pneumoencephalography is a long word, but it can easily be broken down.
  Pneumo- means *air.* The prefix **en-** means *within*, and **-cephal-** is a Greek term for *head.* So **-encephal-** literally means *within the head* and thus refers to the brain. The suffix **-graphy** refers to a method of recording, in this case X-ray photography. So, the term means *X-ray photography of air (or gas) in the brain.*

- In **myelography**, dye or air is injected into the patient's subarachnoid space after lumbar puncture. X-rays are then taken.
- **Pneumoencephalography (PEG)** enables visualization the fluid-filled structures of the brain after CSF is intermittently withdrawn through lumbar puncture and replaced by air, oxygen, or helium. (See *Getting around PEG.*)
- A **positron emission tomography (PET)** scan is used to determine the brain's metabolic activity after the infusion of radioactive materials.
- **Positron emission tomography-computed tomography (PET/CT)** uses radioactive materials called radiotracers, special X-ray equipment, and a computer to help evaluate brain abnormalities, such as tumors, memory disorders, seizures, and other central nervous system disorders.
- **Skull X-rays** are high-energy radiography used to detect fractures, bony tumors, or vascular abnormalities. They're typically taken from two angles: **anteroposterior** and **lateral**. **Waters' projection** is used to examine the frontal and maxillary sinuses, facial bones, and eye orbits. **Towne's projection** is used to examine the occipital bone.
- **Spinal X-rays** are obtained to detect spinal fractures, displacement of the spine, destructive lesions, structural abnormalities, and other conditions.
- **Stereotaxic neuroradiography** is an X-ray procedure used during neurosurgery to guide a needle or electrodes into a specific area of the brain. (See *Understanding stereotaxic neuroradiography.*)

Electrophysiologic studies

Here are some common electrophysiologic studies associated with the neurologic system:

- **Electroencephalography**, also called **EEG**, records the brain's continuous electrical activity.
- **Evoked potential testing** evaluates the integrity of visual, somatosensory, and auditory nerve pathways by measuring evoked potentials—the brain's electrical response to stimulation of the sensory organs or peripheral nerves. This type of testing is used to detect neurologic lesions and to evaluate multiple sclerosis as well as various vision and hearing disorders.
- **Magnetoencephalography** is a noninvasive test that directly measures the magnetic fields produced by electrical currents in the brain.

Beyond the dictionary

Understanding stereotaxic neuroradiography

Stereotaxic neuroradiography is easy to understand when you break it down into its components. *Stereo-* is a familiar term from the Greek language that refers to something that's *solid*, meaning it has three dimensions. **Taxic** refers to *movement in response to a stimulus*. **Neuro-** refers to the nervous system. **Radiography** is *an X-ray study*. Thus, **stereotaxic neuroradiography** involves movement (of a needle or electrode) in three dimensions accompanied by X-ray photography of the brain.

CSF and blood tests

CSF analysis is performed on CSF that's removed during a lumbar puncture (aspiration of CSF by insertion of a needle into the L3-L4 or L4-L5 interspace). Three common tests of CSF and blood are described here:

- The **amyloid beta-protein precursor test** checks CSF for levels of a substance that produces the protein plaques seen in the brains of patients with Alzheimer's disease.
- Coccidioidomycosis **antibodies** is a blood test to identify a fungal infection that affects CNS and other areas of the body.
- **CSF analysis** of physical characteristics combined with chemical and cellular examination is used to detect the presence of blood, infection, and other abnormalities.

Disorders

This section discusses brain and spinal cord disorders, cranial nerve disorders, degenerative disorders, head trauma, vascular disorders, and miscellaneous neurologic disorders.

Brain and spinal cord disorders

Here are some common brain and spinal cord disorders, including CNS infections and neural tube defects:

- **Cerebral palsy** is a chronic disorder of motor function resulting from nonprogressive brain damage or a brain lesion.
- **Epilepsy** refers to a group of neurologic disorders marked by uncontrolled electrical discharge from the cerebral cortex and typically manifested by seizures with clouding of consciousness. **Status epilepticus** describes a continuous seizure state, which is life-threatening.
- Hydrocephalus is a condition marked by excess CSF within the brain's ventricles. Two types exist; they're named according to their causes. **Noncommunicating hydrocephalus** results from obstruction of CSF flow. **Communicating hydrocephalus** is caused by faulty reabsorption of CSF. (See *Too much water*.)
- **Migraine headache** is a very painful, throbbing headache commonly associated with sensitivity to light and sound. In some people, the headache is preceded by an aura.
- **Subarachnoid hemorrhage** is an intracranial hemorrhage into the subarachnoid space.
- **Subdural hematoma** is accumulation of blood in the subdural space.

Beyond the dictionary

Too much water

Hydrocephalus is a condition marked by excess cerebrospinal fluid within the brain's ventricles. The term **hydrocephalus** originates from the Greek words **hydro**, meaning *water* or *fluid*, and **kephale**, meaning *head*.

CNS infections

CNS infections include encephalitis, meningitis, rabies, and others:
- **Brain abscess**, also known as an **intracranial abscess**, is a free or encapsulated collection of pus, usually found in the temporal lobe, cerebellum, or frontal lobe.
- Encephalitis is an inflammatory disorder of the brain that's commonly caused by the bite of an infected mosquito.
- **Meningitis** refers to the inflammation of the meninges of the brain and spinal cord caused by bacterial, viral, or fungal infection.
- **Myelitis** is an inflammation of the spinal cord.
- **Poliomyelitis** is an acute viral infection and inflammation of the gray matter of the spine, usually caused by poliovirus.
- **Rabies** is an acute, usually fatal CNS disease spread by animals to people through contaminated saliva, blood, or tissue. (See *Afraid of the water.*)

Beyond the dictionary

Afraid of the water

Rabies is also called **hydrophobia**—meaning *fear of water*—because this condition produces muscle spasms in the throat when the patient drinks water.

Neural tube defects

Neural tube defects are serious birth defects involving the spine or brain. They result from failure of the neural tube to close approximately 28 days after conception.

The most common forms of neural tube defects are spina bifida, anencephaly, and encephalocele:
- In **anencephaly**, part of the top of the skull and all or part of the brain are missing.
- In encephalocele, a saclike portion of the meninges and brain protrudes through a defective opening in the skull.
- **Spina bifida cystica** is incomplete closure of one or more vertebrae, which causes spinal contents to protrude in an external sac. The spinal cord is usually normal.
- **Spina bifida with** meningocele is a form of spina bifida in which the sac contains meninges and CSF.
- **Spina bifida with** myelomeningocele (**meningomyelocele**) is a form of spina bifida in which the sac contains meninges, CSF, and a portion of the spinal cord or nerve roots.

Remember, **-itis** refers to inflammation. So **meningitis** is an inflammation of the meninges.

Cranial nerve disorders

Cranial nerve disorders include Bell's palsy and trigeminal neuralgia:
- **Bell's palsy** is a unilateral facial paralysis of sudden onset, attributable to a lesion of the facial nerve. It's generally not permanent.
- **Trigeminal neuralgia**, also called tic douloureux, is a painful disorder affecting one or more branches of the fifth cranial (trigeminal) nerve. With stimulation of a trigger zone, the patient experiences paroxysmal attacks of excruciating facial pain.

Degenerative disorders

Degenerative disorders of the brain include Alzheimer's disease, multiple sclerosis, Parkinson's disease, and others:

- **Alzheimer's disease** produces three hallmark features in the brain: neurofibrillary tangles, neuritic plaques, and granulovascular degeneration. Early signs progress to severe deterioration in memory, language, and motor function.
- **Amyotrophic lateral sclerosis**, also called **Lou Gehrig disease**, is an incurable disease affecting the spinal cord and the medulla and cortex of the brain. It's characterized by progressive degeneration of motor neurons. This degeneration leads to weakness and wasting of the muscles, increased reflexes, and severe muscle spasms. Death typically occurs within 2 to 5 years.
- **Huntington's disease**, also called **Huntington's chorea**, is a hereditary disorder that causes degeneration in the cerebral cortex and basal ganglia. Degeneration leads to chronic, progressive **chorea** (rapid, jerky movements) and mental deterioration and ends with dementia and death.
- **Multiple sclerosis** is a progressive demyelination of the white matter of the brain and spinal cord that results in weakness, incoordination, paresthesia, speech disturbances, and visual complaints.
- **Myasthenia gravis** is abnormal muscle weakness and fatigability, especially in the muscles of the face and throat, resulting from a defect in the conduction of nerve impulses at the myoneural junction.
- **Parkinson's disease** is a slow-progressing, degenerative neurologic disorder that produces muscle rigidity, akinesia, and involuntary tremor.

Asthenia is the Greek word for weakness. **Myasthenia gravis** is abnormal muscle weakness, particularly in the face and throat.

Head trauma

Head trauma can range from concussion to tentorial herniation:

- **Cerebral contusion** is a bruising of the brain tissue as a result of a severe blow to the head. More severe than a concussion, a contusion disrupts normal nerve function in the bruised area and may cause loss of consciousness, hemorrhage, edema, and even death.
- **Concussion**, the most common head injury, results from a blow to the head that's hard enough to jostle the brain and cause it to strike the skull. This causes temporary neural dysfunction and a change in LOC.

- An **epidural hematoma** is the rapid accumulation of blood between the skull and dura mater.
- **Tentorial herniation** occurs when injured brain tissue swells and squeezes through the tentorial notch (an area that contains the midbrain), constricting the brain stem.

Vascular disorders

Vascular disorders include cerebral aneurysm, cerebrovascular accident, and others:

- **Arteriovenous malformation (AVM)** is a congenital malformation characterized by a tangled mass of dilated cerebral vessels that form an abnormal communication between the arterial and venous systems.
- A **cerebral aneurysm** is a localized dilation (ballooning) of a cerebral artery caused by weakness in the arterial wall.
- **Cerebrovascular accident (CVA)** is a condition of sudden onset in which a cerebral blood vessel is occluded by an embolus or cerebrovascular hemorrhage. The resulting ischemia of brain tissue normally perfused by the affected vessel may lead to permanent neurologic damage. (See *CVA substitutes.*)
- A **transient ischemic attack (TIA)** is a recurrent neurologic episode lasting less than 1 hour. It doesn't cause permanent or long-lasting neurologic deficit but is usually considered a warning sign of an impending stroke.

The real world

CVA substitutes

A **cerebrovascular accident (CVA)** is rarely referred to by its proper name in the real world. Rather, it's referred to as a "stroke" or "brain attack."

Miscellaneous neurologic disorders

Other neurologic disorders include Reye's syndrome, tetanus, and Tourette's syndrome:

- **Guillain-Barré syndrome** is an acute, febrile polyneuritis that sometimes occurs after a viral infection. It's marked by rapidly ascending paralysis that begins as weakness and paresthesia of the legs.
- **Neurofibromatosis** is a genetic trait characterized by the presence of multiple neurofibromas (fibrous tumors of peripheral nerves, resulting from abnormal proliferation of Schwann cells) of the nerves and skin, café-au-lait (light, coffee-colored) spots on the skin, and, sometimes, developmental anomalies of the muscles, bones, and visceral tissue.
- **Reye's syndrome** is usually an acute childhood illness that causes fatty infiltration of the liver with concurrent elevated blood ammonia levels, encephalopathy, and increased ICP. Although a definitive cause hasn't been determined, it's associated with the use of aspirin-containing medications in the treatment of viral illnesses.

- **Tetanus** is an acute, commonly fatal infection caused by the anaerobic bacillus *Clostridium tetani,* which usually enters the body through a contaminated puncture wound.
- **Tetany** is hyperexcitability of nerves and prolonged contraction of muscles caused by low calcium levels.
- **Tourette's syndrome** is a condition characterized by facial and vocal tics, generalized lack of coordination, and rarely **coprolalia** (an uncontrollable urge to utter obscenities).

Treatments

The terminology discussed here describes treatments (including surgeries) that may be employed when caring for a patient with a neurologic disorder.

Brain treatments and monitoring tools

Treatments include craniotomy, lobotomy, placement of a ventriculoperitoneal shunt, and different methods of ICP monitoring:

- **Cerebellar stimulator implantation** involves the surgical implantation of electrodes into a patient's brain to regulate uncoordinated neuromuscular activity using electrical impulses. This treatment has also been used to prevent seizures.
- **Craniectomy** is removal of a part of the skull.
- A **craniotomy** is the creation of a surgical incision into the skull to expose the brain for treatment.
- **Hemicraniectomy** is the removal of the skull to expose half of the brain in preparation for surgery.
- **Intracranial hematoma aspiration** is performed to reduce high ICP caused by a collection of blood around the surface of the brain. A craniotomy must be performed to access the brain.
- **Lobectomy** is removal of a lobe of the brain.
- **Lobotomy** is incision into the frontal lobe of the brain to sever connections in the brain's prefrontal lobe through holes drilled into the skull.
- **Stereotactic surgery** provides three-dimensional images that guide the surgeon in removal of small brain tumors and abscesses drainage of hematomas, repair of AVMs, and ablation for Parkinson's disease.
- A **ventriculoperitoneal shunt** is a surgical treatment for hydrocephalus in which a catheter drains CSF from the ventricular system for absorption. The shunt extends from the cerebral ventricle to the scalp, where it's tunneled under the skin and drains into the peritoneal cavity. Shunting lowers ICP and prevents brain damage by draining excess CSF or relieving blockage.

Lobectomy or lobotomy? I'm confused.

In a **lobectomy**, a lobe of the brain is **exc**ised. **Lobotomy** involves incision, not excision.

- In **volumetric interstitial** brachytherapy, radioactive materials are implanted into the skull and left in place for several days to deliver radiation to a brain tumor.

Intracranial pressure monitoring

ICP monitoring is an important part of neurologic treatment because increased ICP can lead to fatal brain herniation. Invasive ICP monitoring is accomplished in one of several ways:
- An **epidural probe** is a tiny fiberoptic sensor inserted in the brain's epidural space through a burr hole (a hole drilled into the skull).
- A **subarachnoid screw** is a small, hollow, steel screw with a sensor tip that's inserted through a burr hole. It's used to monitor pressure in the subarachnoid space.
- A **ventricular catheter**, consisting of a small polyethylene cannula and an external drainage and collection system, is inserted through a burr hole into a lateral ventricle.

Spinal and nerve surgery

Here are some common surgeries performed on the spine or spinal nerves:
- **Chordotomy** is any operation on the spinal cord.
- **Gamma knife surgery** is a noninvasive procedure that uses beams of gamma radiation to precisely target and treat brain lesions such as brain tumors, vascular malformations, and functional disorders such as trigeminal neuralgia.
- **Myelomeningocele repair** is performed to correct a congenital spinal defect as a means of preventing infection. The surgeon isolates neural tissue from the rest of the myelomeningocele sac and fashions a flap from surrounding tissue.
- **Neurectomy** is removal of part of a nerve.
- **Neuroplasty** is surgical repair of a nerve.
- In **sympathectomy**, a surgeon resects a sympathetic nerve or ganglion.
- **Vagotomy** is transection of the vagus nerve.

Other neurologic treatments

Here are some other common neurologic treatments:
- **AVM embolization** is a minimally invasive technique that's used to treat AVMs when surgery isn't an option. To lower the risk of rupture and hemorrhage, a flexible catheter is threaded into the

AVM site, and small, heat-resistant silicon beads or a rapid-setting plastic polymer is inserted. The beads or polymer lodge in the feeder artery and occlude blood flow to the AVM.

- An induced **barbiturate coma** is a treatment of last resort for a patient experiencing sustained or acute episodes of high ICP. The patient receives large doses of a short-acting barbiturate, such as pentobarbital, to induce a coma. The drug reduces the metabolic rate and cerebral blood volume, possibly reducing ICP and protecting cerebral tissue.

- **Drug therapy** for neurologic disorders includes the use of **anticonvulsants** to control seizures, **corticosteroids** to decrease inflammation and edema, **osmotic diuretics** to promote diuresis and reduce cerebral edema, and **antibiotics** to treat infection.

- **Plasmapheresis** is a process by which the blood is cleansed of harmful substances. In this procedure, plasma is removed from withdrawn blood, and the formed blood elements are reinfused after being mixed with a plasma replacement solution. In some methods, the plasma is filtered to remove a specific disease mediator and is then returned to the patient. Plasmapheresis is used to treat Guillain-Barré syndrome, multiple sclerosis, and myasthenia gravis.

Okay, listen up. You anticonvulsants, corticosteroids, osmotic diuretics, and antibiotics may be needed to treat neurologic disorders.

Vocabulary builders

At a crossroads

Completing this crossword puzzle will help test your nerve with the nervous system. Good luck!

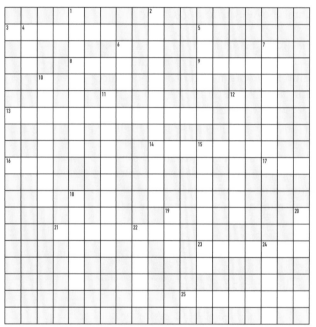

Across

3. Neurons outside the brain
8. Carries impulses away from the cell
9. Plural of **nucleus**
13. "Water on the brain"
14. Another name for **sensory neurons**
16. Acronym for the medical term for *stroke*
17. Records the brain's electrical activity
21. Membranes enclosing the CNS
23. Basic cells of the nervous system
25. Type of headache preceded by an aura

Down

1. First cranial nerve
2. Controls body temperature
4. **Arteriovenous malformation** abbreviation
5. Serves as a bridge
6. **Central nervous system** abbreviation
7. Carries impulses to the cell
10. Another name for **mesencephalon**
11. Infection of the meninges
12. Largest part of the brain
15. Another name for **motor neurons**
18. Sheath covering nerve cells
19. **Cerebrospinal fluid** abbreviation
20. The brain's switchboard
22. Gluelike cells
24. Second cranial nerve

Finish line

Fill in the blanks below with the appropriate word(s).

1. The most common head injury is a _____.
2. A patient who loses the ability to speak or write has _____.
3. Patients commonly experience an _____ just before a migraine headache.
4. Creation of a surgical incision into the skull is a _____.
5. Holes drilled into the skull are known as _____ holes.
6. A subarachnoid screw is used to monitor a patient's _____ _____.
7. _____ _____ is the surgical treatment of hydrocephalus.
8. Plasmapheresis is the therapeutic removal of _____ from the patient's body.

Talking in circles

Use the clues below to fill in the blanks with the appropriate word. Then unscramble the circled letters to find the answer to the question posed at left.

1. __ __ __ __ __ ◯

2. __ __ __ ◯ __ __

__ __ __ __ ◯ __ __ __

3. __ __ ◯ __ __ __ __

4. __ __ ◯ __ __ __ __ __ __ ◯ __

5. ◯ __ __ __ __ __

6. ◯ __ __ __ __ __ ◯ __ __ __ __

I get a lot of support, nourishment, and protein from my nonneuronal buddy cells. Do you know which ones I mean?

1. Highly specialized cell that detects and transmits stimuli electromechanically
2. Autonomic reflex center that maintains homeostasis, regulating respiratory, vasomotor, and cardiac functions
3. Cover and protect the cerebral cortex and spinal column
4. Controls or affects body temperature, appetite, water balance, pituitary secretions, and emotions
5. Acute, usually fatal CNS disease spread by animals to people through contaminated saliva, blood, or tissue
6. An inflammatory disorder of the brain commonly caused by the bite of an infected mosquito

Answers

At a crossroads

My brain got a great workout from this chapter!

Finish line

Answers: 1. Concussion; 2. Aphasia; 3. Aura; 4. Craniotomy; 5. Burr; 6. Intracranial pressure; 7. Ventricular shunting; 8. Plasma

Talking in circles

Answers: 1. Neuron; 2. Medulla oblongata; 3. Meninges; 4. Hypothalamus; 5. Rabies; 6. Encephalitis

Answer to puzzle—Neuroglia

Suggested references

Aminoff, M. J., Greenberg, D. A., & Simon, R. P. (2015). *Clinical neurology* (9th ed.). New York, NY: McGraw-Hill Professional.

Grubenhoff, J. A., & Provance, A. (2012). Physical and neurological exam. In M. W. Kirkwood & K. O. Yeates (Eds.), *Mild traumatic brain injury in children and adolescents: From basic science to clinical management.* New York, NY: Guilford Press.

Huether, S., & McCance, K. (2012). *Understanding pathophysiology* (5th ed.). St. Louis, MO: Mosby/Elsevier.

Jarvis, C. (2016). *Physical examination & health assessment* (5th ed.). St. Louis, MO: Elsevier.

Lewis, S. L., Bucher, L., Heitkemper, M. M., & Ruff-Dirksen, S. (2013). *Medical-surgical nursing: Assessment and management of clinical problems* (9th ed.). St. Louis, MO: Elsevier.

Mosby, Inc. (2009). *Mosby's dictionary of medicine, nursing & health professions.* St. Louis, MO: Mosby/Elsevier.

Selim, M. H., & Edlow, J. A. (2011). *Neurology emergencies.* Oxford: Oxford University Press.

Chapter 13

Endocrine system

Just the facts

In this chapter, you'll learn:

◆ terminology related to the structure and function of the endocrine system

◆ terminology needed for physical examination

◆ tests that help diagnose common endocrine disorders

◆ endocrine system disorders and their treatments.

Endocrine structure and function

The endocrine system (endo = innermost, within; crin = secrete) controls complicated body activities by secreting chemical substances into the circulatory system. The major components of the endocrine system are **glands** (specialized cell clusters or organs) and **hormones** (chemical substances secreted by the glands in response to stimulation). (See *Pronouncing key endocrine system terms*.)

Glands *in a* major key

The major glands of the endocrine system are the:
- pituitary gland
- thyroid gland
- parathyroid glands
- adrenal glands
- pancreas
- pineal body
- thymus. (See *Endocrine system structures*, page 278.)

Pituitary gland

The **pituitary gland**, also known as the **hypophysis**, is no larger than a pea and lies at the base of the brain in a depression of the sphenoid bone called the **sella turcica**.

Memory jogger

Repeating this silly phrase—"Your pit-pat is a pip"—can help you remember the major glands of the endocrine system:

PItuitary

Thyroid

Parathyroid

Adrenal

Thymus

PIneal body

Pancreas.

Pronouncing key endocrine system terms

Below is a list of key terms related to the endocrine system along with the correct ways to pronounce them.

Acromegaly	ACK-roh-MEG-uh-lee
Adenohypophysis	ADD-eh-noh-heye-PAHF-ih-sis
Hyperaldosteronism	HEYE-per-al-DOS-ter-ohn-izm
Luteinizing hormone	LOO-tee-i-neye-zing HOR-mohn
Oxytocin	OCH-see-TOE-sin
Radioimmunoassay	RAY-dee-oh-IM-you-noh-AHS-say
Thymopoietin	THEYE-moh-POY-eh-tin
Thyrotoxicosis factitia	THEYE-roh-TOK-si-KOH-sis fak-TISH-shuh
Triiodothyronine	TREYE-EYE-o-doh-THEYE-roh-neen

Cover and connection

The **pituitary diaphragm**, an extension of the dura mater (the membrane covering the brain), extends over the pituitary gland and protects it. The **pituitary stalk**, a stemlike structure, provides a connection to the hypothalamus.

Master gland

The pituitary gland is also called the "master gland" because it controls all the other glands. It's divided into two regions: the anterior pituitary lobe and the posterior pituitary lobe.

Courtesy of the anterior pituitary

The largest region of the pituitary gland, the **anterior pituitary lobe** (adenohypophysis) produces at least seven hormones. (See *The history of* pituitary, page 279.) These are as follows:

- **Growth hormone (GH)**, or somatotropin, promotes the growth of bony and soft tissues.
- **Thyrotropin**, or **thyroid-stimulating hormone (TSH)**, influences secretion of thyroid hormone (T3 and T4).
- **Corticotropin** stimulates the adrenal cortex to produce cortisol. (See *Turning on to* tropins.)

Hypo- means beneath; *-physis* means to grow.

So ... the **hypophysis** (pituitary gland) "grows" beneath me?

Endocrine system structures

Endocrine glands secrete hormones directly into the bloodstream to regulate body function. This illustration shows the locations of most of the major endocrine glands.

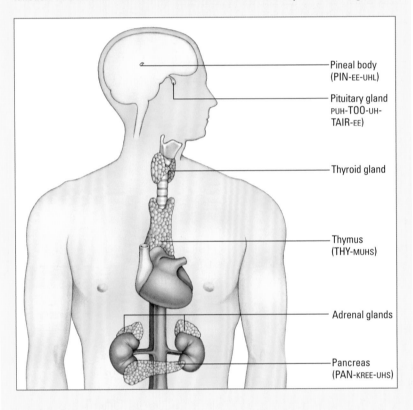

- **Follicle-stimulating hormone (FSH)** stimulates the growth of graafian follicles. It also stimulates estrogen secretion in females and the development of sperm cells in males.
- **Luteinizing hormone (LH)** stimulates maturation of the ovarian follicle and the ovum and ovulation in females. It stimulates production and secretion of testosterone in males.
- **Prolactin (PRL)**, or mammotropin, stimulates breast development during pregnancy and is responsible for the production of milk.
- **Melanocyte-stimulating hormone** is responsible for the formation of melanin pigment in the skin and protection from UV rays.

The history of *pituitary*

The word **pituitary** derives from the Latin word *pituita*, which means *phlegm (mucus)*, and was based on the belief that phlegm was produced by this gland. In the "Doctrine of the Four Humors," a theory of physiology and psychology commonly held during the 17th century, too much of the humor phlegm in one's body resulted in a listless, cold, apathetic personality—in other words, a **phlegmatic** individual.

Thyroid literally means shield-shaped and refers to the shields that ancient Greek soldiers carried.

The posterior plays its part

The **posterior pituitary lobe (neurohypophysis)** makes up about 25% of the gland. It stores and releases **antidiuretic hormone (ADH)** and oxytocin after they're produced by the hypothalamus. ADH, also called vasopressin, stimulates water resorption by the kidneys to limit the production of large volumes of urine. **Oxytocin** stimulates the ejection of breast milk into the mammary ducts. It also stimulates contraction of the uterus during labor.

Thyroid gland

The **thyroid gland** lies directly below the larynx and partially in front of the trachea. Its two lobes are joined by a narrow tissue bridge called the **isthmus**, which gives the thyroid its butterfly shape.

Two lobes as one

The lobes function as one unit to produce the thyroid hormones **thyroxine (T_4), triiodothyronine (T_3),** and **thyrocalcitonin (calcitonin)**. T_3 and T_4 are collectively known as **thyroid hormones**. They influence many metabolic processes, including cellular heat production, protein synthesis, and carbohydrate metabolism. Calcitonin lowers blood calcium and phosphate levels by blocking the resorption of bone, where calcium and phosphate are stored.

Too much of a good thing

Iodine is an essential element of thyroid hormones; many thyroid disorders are caused by overproduction of thyroid hormones and the iodine-containing substances they contain. The iodine within thyroid hormones combines with a protein in the blood to form **protein-bound iodine**. The components separate, however, when the hormone enters the tissues.

Parathyroid glands

Four parathyroid glands lie on the posterior surface of the thyroid, one on each corner. (*Para*- means *alongside*.)

Checking calcium

Like the thyroid lobes, the parathyroid glands work together as a single unit, **producing parathyroid** hormone (**PTH**). This hormone regulates the calcium and phosphorus content of the blood and bones. PTH increases blood calcium and phosphate levels through bone resorption. It antagonizes (works against) the hormone calcitonin. Together, these two hormones maintain calcium balance in the blood.

Adrenal glands

The two **adrenal glands** sit on top of the two kidneys. Each gland contains two distinct structures that function as separate endocrine glands. These include the medulla and the cortex.

Mandatory medulla

The inner portion, or **medulla**, produces the catecholamines **epinephrine** and **norepinephrine.** Because these hormones are vital to the autonomic nervous system, the **adrenal medulla** is also considered a neuroendocrine structure. The adrenal medulla is essential to life, but the **cortex**, the much larger outer layer, isn't.

Zoning in

The cortex has three zones and produces hormones called **corticoids:**
- The outermost zone is the **zona glomerulosa**, which produces mineralocorticoid hormones, primarily aldosterone.
- The **zona fasciculata**, the middle and largest zone, produces glucocorticoids and small amounts of the sex hormones estrogen and androgen.
- The inner zone, the **zona reticularis**, produces mainly glucocorticoids as well as some sex hormones.

Classifying corticoids

The corticoid hormones are classified into three groups:
- **Glucocorticoids** are secreted mainly by the zona fasciculata and include **cortisol (hydrocortisone)** and **corticosterone.** These hormones affect all cells in the body but specialize in controlling the metabolism of carbohydrates, fats, and proteins; stress resistance; antibody formation; lymphatic functions; and recovery from injury and inflammation.

Beyond the dictionary

Turning on to *tropins*

The word **tropin**, or **trophin**, appears in the names of a number of hormones produced by the pituitary gland (for example, *somatotropin* and *mammotropin*). The word derives from a Greek word meaning *to turn*. In reference to a hormone, the sense is that a tropin turns or changes something.

Get me some glucocorticoids. They specialize in helping me recover from injury.

- **Mineralocorticoids** are secreted by the cortex and control the regulation and secretion of sodium and potassium. **Aldosterone** is the principal mineralocorticoid and is responsible for electrolyte and water balance.
- **Sex hormones** are secreted by the zona reticularis and the zona fasciculata. They include small amounts of the male hormone androgen (also present in smaller amounts in females), which promotes such secondary sex characteristics as facial hair and a low-pitched voice.

No corticotropin? Can't secrete.

The adrenal cortex can't secrete androgens and cortisol without the pituitary hormone corticotropin.

The islets of Langerhans are named for Paul Langerhans, the German pathologist who first described these structures in 1869.

Pancreas

The **pancreas** lies along the posterior of the abdominal wall in the upper left quadrant behind the stomach. The **islets of** Langerhans, which perform the endocrine functions of this gland, contain specialized cells that secrete hormones.

Products of the pancreas

Pancreatic hormones include:
- **insulin**, the hormone responsible for the storage and use of carbohydrates and for decreasing the body's blood glucose levels; it's produced by **beta cells** in the pancreas
- **glucagon**, which increases blood glucose levels and is produced by **alpha cells** in the pancreas
- **somatostatin**, a neurotransmitter released by **delta cells** in the pancreas that inhibits the release of glucagon and insulin.

Pineal body

The tiny **pineal body** lies at the back of the third ventricle of the brain and is a neuroendocrine gland. (See *Pining away for the pineal body.*)

Makin' melatonin

This gland produces the hormone **melatonin**, which is involved in the reproductive system and the body's **circadian** (24-hour) rhythms.

Thymus

Located below the sternum, the **thymus** contains lymphatic tissue.

Beyond the dictionary

Pining away for the pineal body

The name **pineal** is derived from the structure's resemblance to a pine cone.

Extra! Extra! Get your T cells here

Although the thymus produces the hormones **thymosin** and **thymo-poietin**, its major role involves the immune system. T cells, important in cell-mediated immunity, are created within the thymus.

Physical examination terms

These physical findings are significant in the diagnosis of endocrine disorders:

- **Buffalo hump** is an accumulation of **cervicodorsal fat** (fat in the neck and back). The condition may indicate hypercortisolism or Cushing's syndrome.
- **Exophthalmos** is the abnormal protrusion of one or both eyeballs. The condition is sometimes the result of thyrotoxicosis (hyperthyroidism).
- A **goiter** is an enlarged thyroid gland, usually evident as swelling in the front of the neck.
- **Hirsutism** is an excessive growth of dark hair. Its occurrence on a woman's body results from excessive androgen production.
- **Moon face**, usually caused by hypercortisolism, results in marked roundness of the face, double chin, and a fullness in the upper lip.
- **Polydipsia** is excessive thirst, a symptom of diabetes mellitus.
- **Polyphagia** is excessive hunger, also a symptom of diabetes mellitus.
- **Polyuria** is the increased excretion of urine by the kidneys; it's a sign of diabetes mellitus and diabetes insipidus.

> Ack!
> Polydipsia
> is excessive
> thirst.

Diagnostic tests

Many diagnostic tests and studies are available to assess the function of the endocrine system and to detect related disorders. These tests include serum studies, urine studies, and radiologic and other imaging tests.

Serum studies

Specific tests are used to measure the blood levels of hormones and other substances and to monitor the function of endocrine glands:

- A **fasting plasma glucose** test is used to measure plasma glucose levels after a 12-hour fast. This test is commonly used to screen for diabetes mellitus.

- **Glycosylated hemoglobin** monitoring provides information about the average blood glucose level during the preceding 2 to 3 months. This test requires one venipuncture every 3 to 6 months to evaluate long-term effectiveness of diabetes therapy. This test is also known as **hemoglobin A_{1C}**, or **HbA_{1C}**.
- The **oral glucose tolerance test** measures plasma and urine glucose levels hourly for 3 hours after ingestion of glucose. This test assesses insulin secretion and the body's ability to metabolize glucose.
- Quantitative analysis of **plasma catecholamines** is used to test for adrenal dysfunction.
- Quantitative analysis of **plasma cortisol** levels is used to test for pheochromocytoma or adrenal medullary tumors.
- The **plasma LH** test, typically ordered for anovulation and infertility studies in women, is a quantitative analysis of plasma LH.
- **Provocative testing** stimulates an underactive gland or suppresses an overactive gland, depending on the patient's suspected disorder. A hormone level that doesn't increase despite stimulation confirms primary hypofunction. Hormone secretion that continues after suppression confirms hyperfunction.
- **Radioimmunoassay (RIA)** is the technique used to determine most hormone levels. In this test, blood or urine (or a urine extract) is incubated with the hormone's antibody and a radiolabeled hormone tracer (antigen). Antibody-tracer complexes can then be measured. (See *Dissecting* radioimmunoassay.)
- **Serum calcium** analysis measures blood levels of calcium to detect bone and parathyroid disorders.
- **Serum FSH** analysis measures gonadal function, especially in women.
- The **serum human growth hormone (hGH)** test is a quantitative analysis of plasma hGH levels that detects hyposecretion or hypersecretion of this hormone.
- **Serum phosphate** analysis measures serum levels of phosphate, the primary anion in intracellular fluid.
- **Serum PTH** measurement evaluates parathyroid hormone function.
- **Serum TSH** levels are measured by RIA, which can detect primary hypothyroidism and determine whether the hypothyroidism results from thyroid gland failure or from pituitary or hypothalamic dysfunction.
- T_3 measurement determines total serum content of T_3 to investigate thyroid dysfunction.
- T_4 measurement determines the total circulating T_4 level, which helps diagnose thyroid disorders.

Indirect tests measure the substance a particular hormone controls, rather than the hormone itself.

Get this man some water. He's scheduled for a catecholamine analysis.

Urine studies

These tests are used to analyze urine samples for evidence of endocrine dysfunction:

- Catecholamine analysis utilizes a 24-hour urine specimen to measure levels of the major catecholamines—epinephrine, norepinephrine, and dopamine—to assess adrenal medulla function.
- **17-hydroxycorticosteroid (17-OHCS)** tests measure urine levels of 17-OHCS—metabolites of the hormones that regulate glyconeogenesis.
- **17-ketosteroid (17-KS)** assays determine urine levels of 17-KS. This test is used to diagnose adrenal dysfunction.

Radiologic and other imaging tests

These tests are used to create images of body structure and assess function:

- **Computed tomography (CT) scanning** provides high-resolution, three-dimensional images of a gland's structure by registering radiation levels absorbed by tissues.
- **Magnetic resonance imaging (MRI)** uses magnetic and radio-frequency waves. The deflection of the waves is interpreted by a computer to provide detailed, three-dimensional images of soft tissues.
- A **radioactive iodine uptake** test evaluates thyroid function by measuring the amount of orally ingested iodine isotope that accumulates in the thyroid.
- In **radionuclide thyroid imaging**, the thyroid is studied with a gamma camera after the patient receives a radioisotope.
- **Thyroid ultrasonography** is a noninvasive procedure used to detect cysts and tumors of the thyroid by directing ultrasonic waves at the gland.

Disorders

Endocrine problems are caused by **hyperfunction**, resulting in excess hormone effects, or **hypofunction**, resulting in hormone deficiency. **Primary dysfunction** is caused by disease within an endocrine gland. **Secondary dysfunction** occurs when endocrine tissue is affected by dysfunction of a nonendocrine organ. **Functional hyperfunction** or **functional hypofunction** results from disease in a nonendocrine tissue or organ.

Pituitary disorders

Here are some of the terms used to describe pituitary dysfunction:

- **Adiposogenital dystrophy** is marked by increased body fat and underdevelopment of secondary sex characteristics in males. This disorder is caused by damage to the hypothalamus, which causes decreased secretion of gonadotropic hormones from the anterior pituitary gland.
- **Diabetes insipidus** is caused by deficiency of circulating ADH, or vasopressin. ADH deficiency leads to extreme polyuria. Patients can urinate up to 30 L of dilute urine per day because the kidneys can't concentrate urine.
- **Syndrome of inappropriate ADH** (SIADH) is a hypersecretion of ADH. Elevated ADH levels cause excess amounts of water to move into the blood and diluted sodium levels.
- **Hypopituitarism** may cause dwarfism as a result of decreased levels of GH when it begins in childhood. It's a complex syndrome that leads to metabolic problems, sexual immaturity, and growth retardation. These complications are caused by a deficiency of hormones secreted by the anterior pituitary gland.
- **Hyperpituitarism** is hypersecretion of one or all of the hormones secreted by the anterior pituitary gland. It is typically caused by a benign tumor in this gland.
- **Panhypopituitarism** refers to a generalized condition caused by partial or total failure of all six of the pituitary gland's vital hormones: corticotropin, TSH, LH, FSH, GH, and PRL.

Here's the long and short of it—a malfunctioning pituitary gland can lead to dwarfism or gigantism.

Gonadotrophic hormone excess

Gonadotrophic hormone excess is a chronic, progressive disease marked by excess GH, tissue overgrowth, and hyperpituitarism. It appears in two forms:

- **Gigantism** begins while the bones are still growing and causes proportional overgrowth of all body tissues.

- Acromegaly occurs after bone growth is complete, causing bones and organs to thicken. Bones of the face, jaw, and extremities gradually enlarge in a patient with this condition.

Thyroid disorders

Two types of thyroid dysfunction, hyperthyroidism and hypothyroidism, are described here.

Hyperthyroidism

Hyperthyroidism results from excess thyroid hormone. The most common cause is **Graves' disease**, which increases T_4 production, enlarges the thyroid gland **(goiter)**, and causes metabolic changes.

Stormy forecast

Forms of hyperthyroidism include:
- **functioning metastatic thyroid carcinoma**, a rare disease that causes excess production of thyroid hormone
- **silent thyroiditis**, a self-limiting form of hyperthyroidism with no inflammatory symptoms
- **subacute thyroiditis**, a viral inflammation of the thyroid gland, which produces short-term hyperthyroidism associated with flu-like symptoms
- **thyroid storm**, an acute exacerbation of hyperthyroidism that's a medical emergency and may lead to cardiac failure
- **thyrotoxicosis factitia**, which results from chronic ingestion of thyroid hormone, sometimes by a person who's trying to lose weight
- **toxic adenoma**, a small, benign nodule in the thyroid gland that secretes thyroid hormone
- **TSH-secreting pituitary tumor**, which causes overproduction of thyroid hormone.

Hypothyroidism

Hypothyroidism results from low serum thyroid hormone or cellular resistance to thyroid hormone. It's caused by insufficiency of the hypothalamus, pituitary gland, or thyroid gland. Here are two related terms:
- **Hashimoto's thyroiditis** is an inflammation of the thyroid gland caused by antibodies to thyroid antigens in the blood. It causes inflammation and lymphocytic infiltration of the thyroid, leading to thyroid tissue destruction and hypothyroidism.
- **Myxedema coma** is a life-threatening complication of hypothyroidism marked by depressed respirations, decreased cardiac output, and hypotension.

Parathyroid disorders

Here's a list of parathyroid disorders:

- **Hypoparathyroidism** is caused by PTH deficiency or decreased effectiveness of PTH on target tissues. Because PTH regulates calcium balance, PTH deficiency causes **hypocalcemia** (low blood levels of calcium), which leads to neuromuscular symptoms, such as **paresthesia** (tingling of the extremities) and **tetany** (muscle rigidity).
- **Hyperparathyroidism**, overactivity of one or more of the parathyroid glands and production of excess PTH, promotes bone resorption, which leads to **hypercalcemia. Hypophosphatemia** results from increased kidney excretion of phosphate. With **primary hyperparathyroidism**, the glands enlarge. In **secondary hyperparathyroidism**, the glands produce excessive PTH to compensate for low calcium levels in the blood caused by some other abnormality.

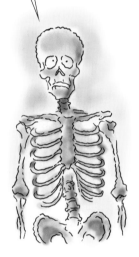

I think I may be in trouble. *Hyperparathyroidism* promotes bone resorption, which leads to hypercalcemia.

Pancreatic disorders

These diseases are associated with the pancreas:

- **Diabetes mellitus** is a chronic insulin deficiency or resistance to insulin by the cells. This form of diabetes causes problems with carbohydrate, protein, and fat metabolism. Diabetes mellitus is classified as type 1 (insulin dependent) or type 2 (non–insulin dependent). Type 2 diabetes is the more prevalent form. (See *Distinguishing mellitus from insipidus.*)
- **Gestational diabetes** is a form of diabetes mellitus that occurs during pregnancy. Usually, the patient's condition returns to normal after delivery, but she may have an increased risk of developing type 2 diabetes later in life.

Beyond the dictionary

Distinguishing mellitus from insipidus

Diabetes mellitus and **diabetes insipidus** are two distinct diseases with similar symptoms, including especially profuse urine excretion. The word ***mellitus*** derives from the Latin word for *honey*; diabetes mellitus refers to the sweet smell of a patient's urine due to excess amounts of glucose. Diabetes insipidus produces no such sweetness and is therefore called **insipidus**, meaning *bland*.

When diabetes gets complicated

A number of complications can occur with diabetes:

- **Diabetic ketoacidosis** is a life-threatening form of metabolic acidosis that can arise as a complication of uncontrolled diabetes mellitus. Due to a lack of available insulin, accumulation of ketone bodies leads to urinary loss of water, potassium, ammonium, and sodium, resulting in hypovolemia, electrolyte imbalances, an extremely high blood glucose level, and, commonly, coma.
- **Hyperosmolar hyperglycemic nonketotic syndrome (HHNS)** is a complication of diabetes mellitus in which the level of blood glucose is increased but, because some insulin is present, ketosis doesn't occur. Coma results when the high concentration of blood glucose causes dehydration of brain tissues.
- **Hypoglycemia** is characterized by an abnormally low blood glucose level. This condition occurs when glucose is utilized too rapidly, when the rate of glucose release falls behind demand, or when excess insulin enters the bloodstream.

> Gestational diabetes is a form of diabetes mellitus that occurs during pregnancy.

Adrenal disorders

Here are names of important adrenal gland disorders:

- **Addisonian** crisis, an acute adrenal crisis, occurs when the body's stores of glucocorticoids and mineralocorticoids are exhausted, leading to hypotension, hypoglycemia, electrolyte imbalances, cardiac arrhythmias, and, ultimately, death.
- **Adrenal hyperfunction**, also called **Cushing's syndrome**, results from excessive levels of adrenocortical hormones, especially cortisol. This condition can be caused by hypersecretion of corticotropin by the pituitary gland, a corticotropin-secreting tumor of another organ, or the use of glucocorticoid medications.
- **Adrenal hypofunction**, also called **Addison's disease**, is the most common sign of adrenal insufficiency, seen when 90% of the gland is destroyed. In this autoimmune process, circulating antibodies react against adrenal tissue, leading to decreased secretion of androgens, glucocorticoids, and mineralocorticoids. (See *Addison and Cushing*.)
- **Hyperaldosteronism** results when the adrenal cortex secretes excess amounts of aldosterone. It can be a primary disease of the adrenal cortex or a response to other disorders. Excessive aldosterone in the bloodstream prompts the kidneys to reabsorb too much sodium and water, excreting too much potassium. The fluid

Beyond the dictionary

Addison and Cushing

Addison's disease is named after the British doctor Thomas Addison (1793 to 1860), who described this form of adrenal insufficiency in 1849. Harvey Cushing (1869 to 1939), an American physiologist, was the first to note the changes in body appearance—development of fat deposits on the face, neck, and trunk and purple striae (streaks) on the skin—associated with pituitary tumors (**Cushing's syndrome**).

retention and hypokalemia caused by this disorder lead to hypertension, decreased hematocrit, muscle weakness, tetany, excess thirst, and many other symptoms.

- **Hypoaldosteronism** results from hyposecretion of aldosterone. It causes a low level of sodium in the blood and decreased blood pressure.
- Pheochromocytoma refers to a vascular tumor of the chromaffin tissue found in the adrenal medulla. This condition is characterized by secretion of epinephrine and norepinephrine, causing hypertension associated with attacks of palpitations, nausea, headache, dyspnea, anxiety, pallor, and profuse sweating. (See *Focus on* pheochromocytoma.)

Treatments

Treatments for endocrine disorders include surgery, radiation therapy, and drug therapy.

Beyond the dictionary

Focus on *pheochromocytoma*

Pheochromocytoma is a vascular tumor of the chromaffin tissue found in the adrenal medulla. To better understand pheochromocytoma, break down the word:

- **pheo-** means *dusky*
- **-chromo-** means *color*
- **-cyt-** refers to *cell*
- **-oma** is a suffix that means *tumor.*

Thus, **pheochromocytoma** is *a tumor of the dusky-colored cells of the adrenal glands.*

Surgery

Surgeries to correct diseases affecting the endocrine systems are described here:

- **Adrenalectomy** is a resection or removal of one or both adrenal glands.
- **Hypophysectomy** is the surgical removal of the pituitary gland. In a procedure called **transsphenoidal hypophysectomy**, the gland is removed by entering the inner aspect of the upper lip through the sphenoid sinus.
- **Pancreatectomy** is removal of the pancreas. This procedure is performed only after more conservative treatment measures have failed.
- **Parathyroidectomy** is the surgical removal of one or more of the four parathyroid glands. It's used to treat hyperparathyroidism. The number of glands removed depends on the underlying cause of the excessive hormone secretion.
- A **subtotal thyroidectomy** is surgical removal of a portion of the thyroid gland.
- **Total bilateral adrenalectomy**, excision of both adrenal glands, eliminates the body's reserve of corticosteroids (which are synthesized in the adrenal cortex). Adrenalectomy is performed only when treatment of the pituitary gland is impossible.
- **Total parathyroidectomy** is removal of all of the parathyroid glands. In such cases, the patient requires lifelong treatment for hypoparathyroidism.
- In **total thyroidectomy**, the entire thyroid gland is removed.

Out I go. **Pancreatectomy** is removal of the pancreas, which is done only after more conservative measures have failed.

Radiation therapy

There are two types of radiation treatment for endocrine disorders:

- **^{131}I administration** uses an isotope of iodine to treat hyperthyroidism or thyroid cancer. It shrinks functioning thyroid tissue, decreases levels of thyroid hormone in the body, and destroys malignant cells.
- **Pituitary radiation** controls the growth of a pituitary tumor or relieves its signs and symptoms.

Get ready for some fun and games!

Drug therapy

Here are some common drug therapies for endocrine disorders:

- **Corticosteroids** and **hormone replacements** are administered to combat hormone deficiencies.
- **Insulin** or **oral antidiabetic agents** may be administered to control glucose levels.

Vocabulary builders

At a crossroads

Completing this crossword puzzle will help stimulate your excretion of correct endocrine system terms. Good luck!

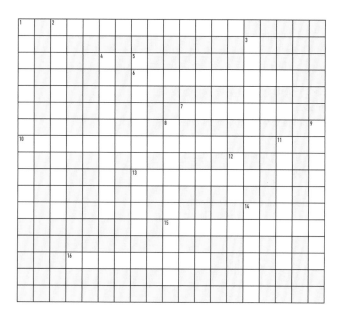

Across

2. Enlarged spleen
6. Also known as the **pituitary gland**
7. Inner portion of the adrenal gland
10. Stimulates the adrenal cortex
13. Stimulates the ejection of breast milk into the mammary ducts
15. Excessive hunger
16. Proportional overgrowth of body tissues

Down

1. Condition characterized by abnormally low blood glucose level
2. Promotes the growth of bony and soft tissues
3. Hormone that decreases blood glucose levels
4. Hormones produced by the adrenal cortex
5. Influences secretion of thyroid hormone
8. Excessive thirst (a sign of diabetes mellitus)
9. Organ that lies along the posterior surface of the abdominal wall behind the stomach
11. Hormone that increases blood glucose levels
12. Abbreviation for **radioimmunoassay**
14. Gland located below the sternum

Match game

As with many medical terms, some endocrine terms go by more than one name. Match each hormone or organ below with its alternate name.

Clues

1. Pituitary gland _____

2. Growth hormone _____

3. Antidiuretic hormone _____

4. Mammotropin _____

Choices

A. Somatotropin

B. Prolactin

C. Hypophysis

D. Vasopressin

Finish line

Fill in the blanks below with the appropriate treatment or surgical intervention.

1. Removal of the entire thyroid gland is known as _____ _____.

2. _____ is a surgery that's used to remove the pancreas after more conservative treatment measures have failed.

3. The resection or removal of one or both adrenal glands is known as _____.

4. _____ _____ controls the growth of a pituitary tumor or relieves its signs and symptoms.

5. When only a portion of the thyroid gland is surgically removed it's called a _____ _____.

6. The surgical removal of the pituitary gland is known as _____.

Answers

At a crossroads

1	2	3	4	5	6	7	8	9	10	11	12	13	14	15	16
¹H	²S	P	L	E	N	O	M	E	G	A	L	Y			
Y	O												³I		
P	M		⁴C	⁵T									N		
O	A		O	⁶H	Y	P	O	P	H	Y	S	I	S		
G	T		R	Y									U		
L	O		T	R	⁷M	E	D	U	L	L	A		L		
Y	T		I	O		⁸P							I		⁹P
¹⁰C	O	R	T	I	C	O	T	R	O	P	I	N	N	¹¹G	A
E	O		O	D		L				¹²R				L	N
M	P		I	¹³O	X	Y	T	O	C	I	N			U	C
I	I		D	P		D				A				C	R
A	N		S	I		I				¹⁴T				A	E
						¹⁵P	O	L	Y	P	H	A	G	I	A
						S	Y	O						O	N
¹⁶G	I	G	A	N	T	I	S	M					M	N	
						A							U		
						S							S		

Match game

Answers: 1. C; 2. A; 3. D; 4. B

Finish line

Answers: 1. Total thyroidectomy; 2. Pancreatectomy;
3. Adrenalectomy; 4. Pituitary radiation; 5. Subtotal thyroidectomy;
6. Hypophysectomy

I've heard the next chapter is a real eye opener.

Suggested references

American Diabetes Association. (2015). Classification and diagnosis of diabetes. *Diabetes Care, 38*(Suppl 1), S8–S16. doi:http://dx.doi.org/10.2337/dc15-S005

American Thyroid Association. (2016). *Iodine deficiency*. Retrieved from http://www.thyroid.org/iodine-deficiency/

Felicilda-Reynaldo, R. F. D., & Kenneally, M. (2016). Antithyroid drugs for hypothyroidism. *MedSurg Nursing, 25*, 50–54.

Leung, A. M., & Braverman, L. E. (2014). Consequences of excess iodine. *Nature Reviews Endocrinology, 10*, 136–142. doi:10.1038/nrendo.2013.251

Hormone Health Network. (2016). What are hormones and what do they do? Retrieved from http://www.hormone.org/hormones-and-health/what-do-hormones-do

Turley, S. M. (2017). *Medical language* (4th Ed.). Boston, MA: Pearson.

Chapter 14

Blood and lymphatic system

Just the facts

In this chapter, you'll learn:

◆ terminology related to the structure and function of the blood and the lymphatic system

◆ terminology needed for physical examination of the blood and lymphatic system

◆ tests that help diagnose blood and lymphatic system disorders

◆ common blood and lymphatic system disorders and their treatments.

Blood and lymphatic structure and function

The circulatory system consists of blood, which is pumped through blood vessels by the heart, and lymphatic fluid, which moves through lymph channels and tissues passively. Blood and the lymphatic system are interconnected. Lymph fluid passes into the veins through the lymphatic and thoracic ducts. (See *Pronouncing key blood and lymphatic system terms*.)

Fancy fluids

The liquid portion of blood is called **plasma**. In the lymphatic system, the liquid portion is called **lymph fluid**. Both fluid types are high in water content, but they differ in their distribution of fats and proteins.

Shared traits

Blood and the lymphatic system share some similar functions. For example, both collect and transport vital substances and both are involved in protecting and healing the body.

They're special, so special

Blood and the lymphatic system each contain specialized cells suspended in fluid. Most of these cells are produced by the bone marrow. The specialized cells help the body protect itself, working as part of the immune system.

Did you know that the average person has 5 to 6 L of circulating blood, which makes up about 5% to 7% of the body's weight?

Pronouncing key blood and lymphatic system terms

Here's a list of key terms related to blood and the lymphatic system, along with the correct ways to pronounce them.

Hemolysis	HEE-MAHL-EH-SIS
Hemorrhage	HEM-EH-REHJ
Immunoelectrophoresis	IM-YOU-NOH-EE-LEK-TROH-FOH-REE-SI
Lymphadenopathy	LIM-FAD-UH-NOP-UH-THEE
Phagocytosis	FAG-OH-SEYE-TOH-SIS
Splenomegaly	SPLEE-NO-MEG-UH-LEE
Thymus	THEYE-MUHS
Trabeculae	TRAH-BEK-YOU-LEE

Cells

Cells specific to the blood and lymphatic system include erythrocytes (also known as **red blood cells** [RBCs]), leukocytes (also known as **white blood cells** [WBCs]), **thrombocytes** (also known as **platelets**), and **pluripotential stem cells** (can grow into different kinds of cells).

Seeing red

RBCs account for 99% of the circulating elements in blood and transport oxygen and carbon dioxide. The average RBC lives about 120 days and then is **phagocytized** (destroyed and digested) by cells in the spleen and liver. Iron from the hemoglobin on the RBCs is recovered and recycled.

The ABCs of WBCs

WBCs are active in the immune system. The various types of WBCs are classified into two categories according to how they appear when stained and viewed under a microscope:
* **granular leukocytes** (having a grainlike appearance)
* **nongranular leukocytes** (having few or no granular particles).
   Although some WBCs constantly circulate, others remain in the tissues of the lymph system, bone marrow, spleen, and other organs.

Breaking down blood formation

Hematopoiesis may seem like a difficult word at first glance, but break it down and the difficulty disappears.
   In Greek, **hematos** is the word for *blood* and **poiesis** means *formation.* Together, they form the word for *blood formation*—**hematopoiesis.**

First responders

Platelets are small cell fragments that circulate in blood and respond to injuries by starting the clotting process and providing **hemostasis** (stoppage of bleeding).

To stem cells and beyond!

Pluripotential stem cells are located in the bone marrow. They develop into various types of blood cells through a process called **hematopoiesis**. (See *Breaking down blood formation.*)

Some stem cells destined to become **lymphocytes** (a type of WBC), whereas others develop into **phagocytes** (cells that engulf and digest microorganisms and cellular debris). Those that become lymphocytes are differentiated to become either B cells (which mature in the bone marrow) or T cells (which travel to the thymus and mature there).

B cells and T cells are distributed throughout the **lymphoid** organs, especially the lymph nodes and spleen. When exposed to antigens (foreign substances such as bacteria or toxins that induce antibody formation), B cells work with T cells to produce antigen-specific antibodies (Huether & McCance, 2016).

I'm a pluripotential stem cell. That means I have the potential to take many (pluri-) forms.

Basic T-cell training

In the **thymus** (a lymph structure located in the mediastinum), T cells undergo a process called **T-cell education**, in which the cells are "trained" to recognize other cells from the same body **(self cells)** and distinguish them from all other cells **(nonself cells).**

Organs and tissues of blood and the lymphatic system

Bone marrow

Bone marrow is found in the cranial bones, vertebrae, ribs, pelvis, sternum, and femurs. It's the site of a process called **hematopoiesis**. **Erythropoiesis** (production of RBCs) occurs when erythropoietin (a potent hormone secreted by the kidneys) stimulates the bone marrow. Platelets and WBCs also originate from stem cells in the bone marrow.

I'm a **T cell** and this is my friend, a **B cell.** We're both lymphocytes, but I grew up in the **t**hymus…

…and I grew up in the bone marrow—that's how we got our names.

Lymphoid

The term lymphoid is used to refer to organs and tissues of the lymphatic system because they're all involved in some way in the growth, development, and dissemination of lymphocytes. (See *How* nymph *became* lymph.)

Lymph nodes

The small, kidney-shaped **lymph nodes** contain **lymphatic tissue** and are located along a network of lymphatic channels. They release lymphocytes, the primary cells of the immune system, and help remove and destroy antigens circulating in the blood and lymphatic vessels. Each lymph node is surrounded by a fibrous capsule that extends trabeculae (bands of connective tissue) into the node.

Function is an emphatic issue for lymphatic tissue

The organs and tissues of the blood and lymphatic systems contribute to the immune system. When lymph fluid enters the node, it's filtered through sinuses before draining into the single exit vessel. The filtration process removes bacteria and other foreign bodies or particles, including malignant cells.

Another function of lymph nodes is **phagocytosis**, the destruction of invading cells or particles. Lymphatic tissue is also the site of final maturation for lymphocytes that migrate from the bone marrow.

Location, location, location

Lymph nodes are classified according to their locations, including:
- **axillary**—underarm and upper chest
- **cervical**—neck
- **inguinal**—groin area
- **popliteal**—behind the knee
- **submandibular**—floor of the mouth and lower jaw.

Lymphatic fluid

Lymphatic fluid (also **lymph fluid** or **lymph**) is a transparent, usually slightly yellow liquid found within the lymphatic vessels. It's collected from all parts of the body and returned to the blood after filtration in the lymph nodes.

Lymphatic vessels

Lymphatic vessels intertwine with blood vessels and distribute lymphatic fluid throughout the body. They remove proteins and water from the interstitial spaces (spaces between cells and outside the blood vessels) and return them to the bloodstream.

Lymphatic vessels located in the small intestine are called lacteals. They absorb fats and other nutrients, producing a milky lymph fluid called **chyle** (from the Greek word *chylos*, or *juice*).

Spleen

The **spleen** is a lymphoid organ located in the left upper quadrant of the abdomen beneath the diaphragm. The largest structure of the

Beyond the dictionary

How *nymph* became *lymph*

Lymph fluid is a clear, transparent liquid that's found in the **lymphatic vessels**, which take their name from this substance. In Greek, *nymph* was the name for a goddess of lower rank usually associated with a river or lake. In turn, the Greeks applied the term to young women, "pure as a virgin river," of marriageable age. Latin borrowed the term, but the *n* mutated to an *l* and it became applied to a fluid thought to be as pure and clear as the nymphs of long ago.

lymphatic system, the spleen initiates an immune response, filters and removes bacteria and other foreign substances from the bloodstream, destroys worn-out blood cells (**hemolysis**), and serves as a blood reservoir. (See *History of* spleen.)

Accessory lymphoid organs and tissues

The tonsils, adenoids, appendix, thymus, and Peyer's patches remove foreign debris in much the same way lymph nodes do. They're located in food and air passages—areas where microbial access is more likely to occur.

Immunity

Immunity is the body's capacity to resist invading organisms and toxins, thereby preventing tissue and organ damage. The immune system's cells and organs are designed to recognize, respond to, and eliminate foreign substances, including bacteria, viruses, and parasites. The immune system also preserves the body's internal environment by scavenging dead or damaged cells and by patrolling antigens.

Getting specific

All foreign substances elicit the same response in general host defenses. In contrast, particular microorganisms or molecules activate specific immune responses and initially can involve specialized sets of immune cells. Such specific responses, classified as either humoral immunity or cell-mediated immunity, are produced by lymphocytes (B cells and T cells).

Humoral immunity

In **humoral immunity**, an invading antigen causes B cells to divide and differentiate into plasma cells. Each plasma cell, in turn, produces and secretes large amounts of antibodies (immunoglobulin molecules that interact with a specific antigen) into the bloodstream. Antibodies destroy bacteria and viruses, thereby preventing them from entering host cells.

Five major classes of immunoglobulin exist:

- **Immunoglobulin (Ig) G** makes up 80% of plasma antibodies. It appears in all body fluids and is the major antibacterial and antiviral antibody.
- **IgM** is the first immunoglobulin produced during an immune response. It's too large to easily cross membrane barriers and is usually present only in the vascular system.
- **IgA** is found mainly in body secretions, such as saliva, sweat, tears, mucus, bile, and colostrum. It defends against pathogens on body surfaces, especially those that enter the respiratory and GI tracts.

The word **lacteal** probably reminds you of the word **lactate**, which means *to produce milk.* Lacteals produce a "milky" lymph fluid.

- **IgD** is present in plasma and is easily broken down. It's the predominant antibody on the surface of B cells and is mainly an antigen receptor.
- **IgE** is the antibody involved in immediate hypersensitivity reactions (or allergic reactions) that develop within minutes of exposure to an antigen. IgE stimulates the release of mast cell granules, which contain histamine and heparin.

Another part of humoral immunity, the **complement system**, is a major mediator of the inflammatory response. It consists of a large number of proteins circulating as functionally inactive molecules. In most cases, an antigen-antibody reaction is necessary for the complement system to activate to destroy invading cells.

Cell-mediated immunity

In **cell-mediated immunity**, T cells respond directly to antigens. This response involves destruction of target cells—such as virus-infected cells and cancer cells—through the secretion of lymphokines (lymph proteins). Organ rejection is an example of cell-mediated immunity.

Acquired immunity

The body readily develops long-term immunity to specific antigens, including pollen, dust, mold, and invading organisms. There are four types of acquired immunity:

1. **Natural, active immunity** occurs when the immune system responds to a harmful agent and develops long-term immunity. This type of immunity is the most effective and longest lasting. For example, people develop immunity to measles after having the disease once.
2. **Natural, passive immunity** is the transfer of antibodies from a mother to a fetus (through the placenta) or to a breast-fed infant. This type of transmission provides temporary, partial immunity.
3. **Artificial, active immunity** is obtained by vaccination with weakened or dead infectious agents introduced into the body to alert the immune system.
4. **Artificial, passive immunity** is provided by substances that offer immediate but temporary immunity, such as antibiotics, gamma globulin, and interferon.

Physical examination terms

The following conditions may be encountered when performing a physical examination of blood and the lymphatic system:

- **Angioedema** is a subcutaneous and dermal eruption that produces deep, large, raised sections of skin (usually on the hands, feet, lips,

Beyond the dictionary

History of *spleen*

Since ancient times, the word **spleen** has been used to designate the largest lymphatic organ. The word probably first appeared in its modern form between 1250 and 1300, having been derived from the Latin word *splen*. The origins of the word go back even further, to the ancient Sanskrit *plihan*.

Spleen: Cheerful or gloomy?
The spleen was considered to be the seat of various emotions or attributes. Some were positive, linking the spleen with cheerfulness, courage, and spirit. At other times, the spleen was thought to be the site of negative attributes, such as a bad temper and a spiteful or gloomy nature.

I'm a natural, thanks to passive immunity!

genitals, and eyelids) and diffuse swelling of the subcutaneous tissue.

- **Butterfly rash** is a classic sign of **systemic lupus erythematosus.** Lesions appear on the cheeks and bridge of the nose, creating a characteristic butterfly-shaped pattern.
- **Chills** (also called **rigors**) are extreme, involuntary muscle contractions with characteristic paroxysms of violent shivering and tooth chattering.
- **Cyanosis** is a blue to purple color of the skin, nail bed, and lips due to a lack of oxygen.
- **Ecchymosis** is another name for a bruise.
- **Embolus** is a mass that travels through the bloodstream and is capable of blocking a vessel.
- **Epistaxis** is a profuse nosebleed.
- **Hematemesis** is vomiting blood.
- **Hematochezia** is the passing of bloody stools.
- **Hemoptysis** is bleeding from the lungs or bronchial tubes.
- **Hemorrhage** refers to uncontrolled bleeding.
- **Lymphadenopathy** is enlarged lymph nodes.
- **Lymphangioma** is a benign tumor caused by congenital malformation of the lymphatic system.
- **Pruritus** is also known as itching.
- **Splenomegaly** is an enlarged spleen.
- **Thrombosis** is the formation of a blood clot inside a blood vessel.
- **Urticaria** is a skin condition that's more commonly known as hives.

Thrombosis is the formation of a blood clot inside a blood vessel.

Diagnostic tests

Most tests use a combination of techniques to evaluate the body's immune response and break down the individual components of blood and the lymphatic system.

Laboratory tests

Here are some common laboratory tests:

- **ABO blood typing** classifies blood according to the presence of major antigens A and B on RBC surfaces and according to serum antibodies anti-A and anti-B. ABO blood typing is required before transfusion to prevent a lethal reaction.
- **Antinuclear antibody (ANA)** measures the levels of a group of antibodies that cause tissue death associated with autoimmune diseases.

- **Complete blood count (CBC)** measures the number of blood elements in a blood sample.
- **Crossmatching** is an antibody detection test that establishes the compatibility of a donor's and recipient's blood.
- A **direct antiglobulin test (direct Coombs' test)** demonstrates the presence of antibodies (such as antibodies to the Rh factor) or complement on circulating RBCs.
- **Enzyme-linked immunosorbent assay (ELISA)** identifies antibodies to bacteria, viruses, deoxyribonucleic acid, allergens, and substances such as immunoglobulins.
- **Erythrocyte sedimentation rate (ESR)** is the degree of erythrocyte settling in a blood sample during a specified period. It signifies inflammatory activity in the body.
- **Hematocrit** measures the percentage of RBCs in a blood sample.
- **Hemoglobin (Hb)** is the measure of the amount of hemoglobin in a volume of blood.
- **Human leukocyte antigen test (HLA)** identifies a group of antigens that are present on the surfaces of all nucleated cells but most easily detected on lymphocytes. These antigens are essential to immunity and determine the degree of histocompatibility between transplant recipients and donors.
- **Immunoelectrophoresis** identifies immunoglobulins in a serum sample. It evaluates the effectiveness of radiation therapy or chemotherapy and detects **hypogammaglobulinemias** (abnormally low levels of gamma globulins causing increased susceptibility to infection).
- The **platelet count** indicates the number of platelets in a microliter of blood.
- **Prothrombin time (PT)** and **international ratio (INR)** are commonly used to evaluate clotting in patients receiving oral anticoagulant therapy.
- **Rheumatoid factor** measures presence of IgG and IgM in diagnosis of autoimmune disorders.
- **Rh typing** classifies blood by the presence or absence of the $Rh_o(D)$ antigen on the surface of RBCs. In this test, a patient's RBCs are mixed with serum containing anti-$Rh_o(D)$ antibodies and are observed for clamping together of antigen-bearing particles of similar size in a solution.
- **Shilling test** determines a patient's ability to absorb vitamin B_{12}, which is necessary for erythropoiesis.
- **WBC count**, also called a *leukocyte count*, is part of a complete blood count. It indicates the number of WBCs in a microliter of whole blood.
- The **WBC differential** evaluates the type, number, and condition of WBCs present in the blood. WBCs are classified as one of five

major types of leukocytes—neutrophils, eosinophils, basophils, lymphocytes, and monocytes—and the percentage of each type is determined in this test.

• **Western blot test** detects the presence of specific viral proteins.

Patch and scratch allergy tests

Patch and scratch allergy tests evaluate the immune system's ability to respond to known allergens, which are applied to hairless areas of the patient's body.

Patch work

In **patch testing**, a dilute solution of each allergen is placed directly on the skin and covered with gauze. In 48 to 72 hours, the appearance of redness, vesicles, itching, or swelling shows a positive reaction.

Scratching the surface

Scratch tests introduce allergens into a scratched area on the patient's skin with a special tool or needle. Test sites are examined 30 to 40 minutes later and compared with a control site; redness, itching, and swelling are considered positive reactions.

Under your skin

Intradermal skin tests evaluate the patient's immune system by injecting **recall antigens** (antigens to which the patient may have been previously sensitized) into the superficial skin layer with a needle and syringe or a sterile four-pronged lancet.

A patch test shows results in 2 to 3 days. A scratch test works more quickly; results show in 30 to 40 minutes.

Bone marrow aspiration

In a **bone marrow aspiration** or biopsy, a small amount of bone marrow is removed (usually from the pelvic bones), and the blood elements and their precursors are evaluated. The specimen is also checked for the presence of abnormal or malignant cells.

Disorders

Bone marrow cells reproduce rapidly and are vulnerable to genetic or environmental conditions that influence cell function or the body's ability to make cells. For example, heredity may cause genetic defects in the type or amount of cells or the ability of cells to function. Environmental factors, such as nutrition, medications, radiation, and toxins, may affect bone marrow's ability to make normal cells.

Additionally, the complex processes involved in host defense and immune response may malfunction. When the body's defenses are exaggerated, misdirected, absent, or depressed, a hypersensitivity disorder, autoimmunity, or immunodeficiency may result.

This section provides terminology associated with blood and lymphatic system disorders.

Blood disorders

Blood disorders may be quantitative or qualitative. Quantitative blood disorders involve abnormalities in the number of cells. These disorders may result from the bone marrow producing too few or too many cells or from processes that destroy cells. Quantitative blood disorders include certain types of anemias, such as these:

- **Aplastic anemia** results from injury to the stem cells in the bone marrow, which causes decreased production of RBCs, WBCs, and platelets.
- **Pernicious anemia** is caused by a deficiency in the absorption of vitamin B_{12} (folic acid) due to a lack of hydrochloric acid in the stomach. (Vitamin B_{12} is essential for the production of RBCs.)
- **Myeloproliferative disorders** occur when the bone marrow produces too many cells, although an excess of RBCs is rare.
- **Erythroblastosis fetalis**, also known as **Rh factor incompatibility** between a mother and her fetus, occurs when antibodies in the mother's blood destroy the fetus's RBCs, resulting in fetal anemia. Intrauterine transfusions can save about 40% of the fetuses affected.
- **Posthemorrhagic anemia** is the result of acute or chronic blood loss.

Quality counts

Qualitative blood disorders involve abnormalities within the cells or plasma components. Here are some examples:

- **Sickle cell anemia** is a hereditary disease in which RBCs are abnormally "sickle" shaped and can't easily travel through the blood vessels.
- **Thalassemia** is a hereditary type of anemia in which Hb isn't produced properly.

Blood disorders may result from abnormalities in the quantity or quality of cells.

Blood-clotting disorders

Blood-clotting or hemorrhagic disorders result from cellular abnormalities in the clotting cycle or problems with clotting factors in the plasma. They may be hereditary or acquired.

Here's a list of some blood-clotting disorders:

- **Disseminated intravascular coagulation (DIC)** is a life-threatening disease in which the patient may suffer severe hemorrhage. It occurs when other conditions cause the circulating clotting factors and platelets to deplete, leaving the patient prone to bleeding.
- **Factor V Leiden mutation** is a relatively common inherited mutation in the factor V gene that may cause the development of inappropriate blood clots and, in young people, an increased risk of stroke.
- **Hemophilias** are a group of hereditary bleeding disorders in which there are deficiencies in the clotting factors necessary for coagulation.
- **Inherited thrombophilias** are diseases in which abnormal clotting factor traits are inherited, causing clots to form in the blood vessels inappropriately.
- **Idiopathic thrombocytopenic purpura** is caused by an abnormal immune response that destroys platelets. It may be acute and follow a viral infection. Patients usually recover without treatment.
- **Thrombocytopenias** are the most common of the blood-clotting disorders and result from deficiencies in the number of circulating platelets.

Hypersensitivity disorders

An exaggerated or inappropriate immune response may lead to various **hypersensitivity** disorders, such as asthma, allergic rhinitis, anaphylaxis, atopic dermatitis, latex allergy, and blood transfusion reactions.

Asthma

Asthma is a chronic, reactive airway disorder leading to episodes of airway obstruction with bronchospasms, increased mucus secretion, and mucosal swelling. (See *How do I [pant] say* asthma?)

Take a deep breath

Here are a few types of asthma:

- **Acute asthma** is an attack that can begin either dramatically with severe symptoms or slowly with gradual symptoms.
- **Extrinsic asthma** results from sensitivity to pollen, animal dander, mold, or other sensitizing substances.
- **Intrinsic asthma** is diagnosed when no extrinsic allergen can be identified.
- **Status asthmaticus** is a persistent, intractable asthma attack that can lead to acute respiratory failure.

Hyperreactivity and **hypersensitivity** share a prefix. *Hyper-* comes from Greek and means *in excess of.* These are disorders that cause an excessive reaction or sensitivity in the immune system.

Allergic rhinitis

Allergic rhinitis is a reaction to airborne (inhaled) allergens. The resulting runny nose, itching, nasal obstruction, and congestion can be seasonal, as in **hay fever**, or year-round, as in **perennial allergic rhinitis**.

Anaphylaxis

Anaphylaxis is a dramatic, acute reaction marked by the sudden onset of rapidly progressive hives and respiratory distress. It can be a life-threatening situation if treatment isn't initiated immediately.

Atopic dermatitis

Atopic dermatitis is a chronic skin disorder characterized by superficial skin inflammation and intense itching.

Latex allergy

Latex allergy is a hypersensitivity reaction to products that contain natural latex, which is derived from the sap of a rubber tree. Hypersensitivity reactions to latex range from local dermatitis to life-threatening anaphylactic reaction.

Blood transfusion reactions

Mediated by immune or nonimmune factors, a **transfusion reaction** happens during or after the administration of blood components. Symptoms can be mild (fever and chills) or severe (acute renal failure or complete vascular collapse and death), depending on the amount of blood transfused, the type of reaction, and the patient's general health.

Poorly made matches

Hemolytic reactions follow transfusions of mismatched blood. When this occurs, RBCs clump together and break down, leading to kidney damage.

Less worrisome

Allergic reactions to transfused blood are fairly common and only occasionally serious. Patients may experience transient hives, itching, chills, and fever. Symptoms resolve quickly when the transfusion is stopped.

Pump up your pronunciation

How do I (pant) say *asthma*?

Asthma derives from Greek and means *gasping* or *panting*. The grouping of consonants in its middle makes it look more difficult to pronounce than it actually is. The *th* is silent, making the word easily pronounceable: AZ-MAH.

Hypersensitivity reactions to latex range from local dermatitis to life-threatening anaphylactic reaction.

More common

Febrile nonhemolytic reactions, the most common type of reaction, develop when antibodies in the patient's plasma attack antigens on lymphocytes, granulocytes, or plasma cells of the transfused blood.

Autoimmune disorders

Autoimmune disorders occur when a misdirected immune response causes the body's defenses to become self-destructive. Here are some types of autoimmune disorders:

- **Ankylosing spondylitis** is a chronic, usually progressive, inflammatory disease that primarily affects the sacroiliac, apophyseal, and costovertebral joints and adjacent soft tissue.
- **Rheumatoid arthritis** is a chronic, systemic inflammatory disease that primarily attacks peripheral joints and surrounding muscles, tendons, ligaments, and blood vessels.
- **Scleroderma** is a diffuse connective tissue disease characterized by fibrotic, degenerative, and occasionally inflammatory changes in the skin, blood vessels, synovial membranes, skeletal muscles, and internal organs.
- **Sjögren's syndrome**, the second most common rheumatoid disorder, is marked by decreased secretions from the lacrimal and salivary glands.
- **Systemic lupus erythematosus (SLE)** is a chronic inflammatory disorder of the connective tissue. It affects multiple organ systems, is characterized by remissions and exacerbations, and can be fatal.
- **Vasculitis** includes a broad spectrum of disorders characterized by inflammation and necrosis of blood vessels.

Immunodeficiency disorders

In immunodeficiency, the immune system is absent or depressed, resulting in increased susceptibility to infection.

Opportunity knocks

Also known as **AIDS, acquired immunodeficiency syndrome** causes progressive damage to the body's immune response and gradual destruction of cells—including T cells. The retrovirus **human immunodeficiency virus (HIV)** causes AIDS.

Major immunity missing

DiGeorge syndrome is a congenital aplasia or hypoplasia of the thymus that's caused by a missing gene on chromosome 22. This abnormality leads to a deficiency of T lymphocytes and compromises cell-mediated immunity.

Chemo complication

Iatrogenic immunodeficiency is a deficiency in the immune response that occurs as a complication of chemotherapy and other medical treatment.

Lupus is Latin for wolf. It was first used as a medical term because disorders such as **systemic lupus erythematosus** were thought to devour the body like a hungry wolf.

Treatments

Various methods are used to combat disorders of blood and the lymphatic system, including drug therapy, radiation therapy, surgery, and bone marrow transplantation.

Drug therapy

Here's a list of drugs commonly used to treat blood and lymphatic system disorders:

- **Anticoagulants** are drugs given to prevent blood clotting.
- **Antihistamines** are medications that block histamine, which is a trigger of allergy symptoms.
- **Antilymphocyte serum**, or **antithymocyte globulin**, is an anti-T-cell antibody that reduces the number and function of T cells. This suppresses cell-mediated immunity. The drug is used to prevent rejection of tissue grafts or transplants.
- **Corticosteroids** are adrenocortical hormones widely used to treat immune disorders because of their anti-inflammatory and immunosuppressant effects. These drugs stabilize the vascular membrane, blocking tissue infiltration by neutrophils and monocytes and thus inhibiting inflammation.
- **Cytotoxic drugs** kill cells while they're replicating. However, most cytotoxic drugs aren't selective and, therefore, interfere with all rapidly growing cells. As a result, they reduce the number of lymphocytes as well as phagocytes.
- **Cyclosporine** is an immunosuppressant drug that selectively suppresses T-helper cells, resulting in depressed immunity. It's used to prevent organ rejection in kidney, liver, bone marrow, and heart transplants.
- **Thrombolytic drugs** are given to break apart blood clots.
- **Iron supplements** may be given to patients with anemia after the cause of the anemia is determined.

Drugs are one way to treat blood and lymphatic system disorders.

Radiation therapy

Radiation therapy is the use of a radioactive substance to treat a disease. Radiation therapy of all major lymph node areas—known as **total nodal radiation**—is used to treat certain disorders, such as Hodgkin's disease.

Surgery

Surgeries for lymphatic and immune system disorders include the removal of a lymph node, a lymph vessel, the spleen, or the thymus:

* **Lymphadenectomy** is surgical removal of a lymph node.
* **Lymphangiectomy** is surgical removal of a lymph vessel.
* **Splenectomy**, or removal of the spleen, causes an increased risk of infection, especially from such bacteria as *Streptococcus pneumoniae*.
* **Thymectomy** is surgical removal of the thymus.

Bone marrow transplantation

Bone marrow transplantation begins with the collection of marrow cells from a donor. The cells are then transferred to an immunosuppressed patient. There are four types of bone marrow transplant:

* **Allogeneic transplant** uses bone marrow from a compatible donor, usually a sibling.
* **Autologous transplant** uses marrow tissue that's harvested from the patient before he receives chemotherapy and radiation therapy, or while he's in remission, and is frozen for later use.
* **Stem cell transplant** involves the transfusion of stem cells, which can develop into RBCs, WBCs, and platelets. Stem cells are typically donated by the patient before chemotherapy.
* **Syngeneic transplant** refers to the transplantation of marrow between identical twins.

Memory jogger

To remember the difference between an "allogeneic" transplant and "autologous" transplant, visualize the "gene" in allo**ge**neic and think "the gene pool that's your family." For **auto**logous, remember that "auto" = self, meaning you can donate blood to yourself.

Blood transfusions

A **blood transfusion** is a procedure in which blood or blood products (platelets, fresh frozen plasma, cryoprecipitate, and clotting factors) are introduced into the patient's bloodstream. Here are two types of blood transfusions:

* **Autologous transfusion** involves a patient donating blood so it can be stored for his own later use.
* **Homologous transfusion** is when blood is voluntarily donated by one person and given to a compatible recipient.

Vocabulary builders

At a crossroads

Completing this crossword puzzle will help you ward off an attack by incorrect blood and lymphatic system terms. Good luck!

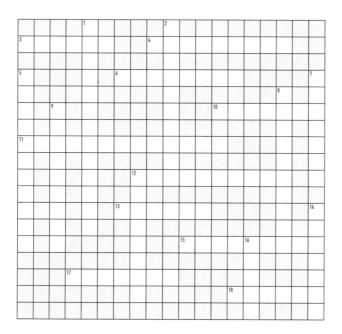

Across

3. The largest structure of the lymphatic system
4. Term indicating *location behind the knee*
6. Term used to refer to immune system organs and tissues
10. Eponym for the second most common auto-immune rheumatoid disorder
11. Process by which stem cells develop into blood cells or immune system cells
12. Immunodeficiency introduced by a medical treatment
13. Response activated by microorganisms
15. The type of transplant of marrow between identical twins
17. Tests that introduce allergens to the skin using a special tool, with results examined 30 to 40 minutes later
18. A chronic, reactive airway disorder

Down

1. The "S" in **ESR**
2. A group of 20 protein compounds that activate to destroy invading cells
5. Exaggerated systemic reaction of the immune system
7. Masses of lymphatic tissue located at the back of the mouth and throat
8. Bands of connective tissue
9. Reactions that follow transfusion of mismatched blood
12. The body's capacity to resist invading organisms and toxins
14. Lymphatic vessel located in the small intestine
16. Acronym for test that identifies antibodies to bacteria, among others

Match game

The long-term immunity the body develops to specific antigens is called *acquired immunity.*
Match the following types of acquired immunity to their definitions.

Clues	Choices
1. Natural, passive _____	A. When the immune system responds to a harmful agent and develops long-term resistance
2. Artificial, active _____	B. The transfer of antibodies from a mother to her fetus or breast-fed infant, providing temporary, partial resistance
3. Natural, active _____	C. Obtained by vaccination with weakened or dead infectious agents
4. Artificial, passive _____	D. Provided by substances that give immediate but temporary immunity, such as antibiotics, gamma globulin, and interferon

Which specialized cell originates as a stem cell in the bone marrow and helps provide the body with immunity?

Talking in circles

Use the clues below to fill in the blanks with the appropriate word. Then unscramble the circled letters to find the answer to the question posed at left.

1. ___ ___ ___ ___ ⭕ ___ ___ ___ ___

2. ___ ___ ___ ⭕ ___ ___ ___ ___ ___

3. ___ ___ ___ ___ ⭕ ___ ___ ___ ___ ___
   ___ ___ ___ ___

4. ⭕ ___ ___ ___ ___

5. ___ ⭕ ___ ___ ___ ___ ___ ___ ___ ___

1. A protein produced in response to specific antigens
2. A lymph node found in the underarm or upper chest
3. The classic sign of SLE
4. A milky lymph fluid produced by lacteals
5. A type of transplant that uses bone marrow from a compatible donor

Answers

At a crossroads

			¹S				²C							
³S	P	L	E	E	N		⁴P	O	P	L	I	T	E	A	L
			D				M							
⁵A			I		⁶L	Y	M	P	H	O	I	D			⁷T
N			M				L				⁸T		O
A		⁹H	E				E		¹⁰S	J	O	G	R	E	N
P		E	N				M				A		S
¹¹H	E	M	A	T	O	P	O	I	E	S	I	S		B		I
Y		O	A				N				E		L
L		L	T		¹²I	A	T	R	O	G	E	N	I	C	S
A		Y	I		M						C		
X		T	O	¹³I	M	M	U	N	E			U		¹⁴L
I		I	N		U						L		A
S		C			N		¹⁵S	Y	N	G	¹⁶E	N	E	I	C
					I					L		T
	¹⁷S	C	R	A	T	C	H			I		E
		Y						¹⁸A	S	T	H	M	A
									A			L

I sense the next chapter will be of great interest!

Match game

Answers: 1. B; 2. C; 3. A; 4. D

Talking in circles

Answers: 1. Antibody; 2. Axillary; 3. Butterfly rash; 4. Chyle; 5. Allogeneic

Solution to puzzle—B cell

Suggested references

Netter, F. H. (2014). *Atlas of human anatomy* (Professional edition). Philadelphia, PA: Elsevier Health Sciences.

Heuther, S. E. & McCance, K. L. (2016). *Understanding pathophysiology*. St. Louis, MO: Elsevier.

Standring, S. A. (2016). *Gray's anatomy: The anatomical basis of clinical practice*. Ipswich, MA: Elsevier Health Sciences.

Chapter 15

Sensory system

Just the facts

In this chapter, you'll learn:

◆ terminology related to the structure and function of the sensory system

◆ terminology needed for physical examination of the sensory system

◆ tests that help diagnose common sensory system disorders

◆ common sensory system disorders and their treatments.

Sensory structure and function

Sensory stimulation allows the body to interact with the environment. The brain receives stimulation from the sense organs—the eyes, the ears, and the **gustatory** (taste) and **olfactory** (smell) organs located in the nose and mouth. (See *Pronouncing key sensory system terms.*)

Vision

The eye is the sensory organ of sight and transmits visual images to the brain for interpretation. The eyeball occupies the **bony orbit**, a skull cavity formed by bones of the face. The term **optic**, as well as the prefixes *oculo-* and *ophthalmo-*, refer to the eye. (See *Eye terms.*)

The outer eye

Six cranial nerves serve the eye, the ocular muscles, and the **lacrimal apparatus**. The coordinated action of six muscles controls eye movement. Extraocular structures—the **eyelids, conjunctivae**, and lacrimal apparatus—protect and lubricate the eye.

Pronouncing key sensory system terms

Here's a list of key terms related to the sensory system, along with the correct ways to pronounce them.

Auricle	AW-RIH-KUHL
Choanae	KOH-**AY**-NEE
Cilia	SILL-EE-AH
Eustachian	YOU-**STAY**-SHEE-UHN
Optesthesia	AHP-TEHS-**THEE**-ZYUH
Tinnitus	TIHN-IH-TEHS OR TIH-**NEYE**-TEHS

Eye protectors

The **eyelids**, also called **palpebrae**, are loose folds of skin covering the front of the eye. They provide protection from foreign bodies, regulate the entrance of light, and distribute tears over the eye by blinking. The lid margins contain hair follicles, which in turn contain eyelashes (**cilia**) and sebaceous glands.

Conjunctivae are transparent mucous membranes that protect the eye from foreign bodies. The **palpebral conjunctiva** lines the eyelids and appears shiny and pinkish red. The **bulbar conjunctiva** joins the palpebral portion and covers the sclera up to the limbus. A small, fleshy elevation called the **caruncle** sits at the nasal aspect of the conjunctivae.

These crying eyes

The **lacrimal apparatus** lubricates and protects the eye with tears produced by **lacrimal glands**. After washing across the eyeball, tears drain through the **punctum**, a tiny opening at the junction of the upper and lower eyelids. From there, tears flow through **lacrimal canals** into the **lacrimal sac**. They then drain through the nasolacrimal duct and into the nose.

The inner eye

The sclera is the white part of the eyeball. Composed of fibrous tissue and fine elastic fibers, it's covered by the conjunctiva and bathed by tears from the lacrimal glands.

Eye terms

Many eye terms are derived from Greek or Latin roots. Recognizing these roots will help you quickly understand many eye terms.

Eye know Greek

The term **optic** means *pertaining to the eye or sight* and derives from the Greek word of the same meaning, *optikos*. The **optic disk**, therefore, is a round area within the eye. The *opt-* of "optic" is used as a prefix to form other terms pertaining to the eye, such as **optometry**, *the science of treating the human eye.*

Ophthalmo-, from the Greek word for eye, *ophthalmos*, also forms "eye words" such as **ophthalmoscope**, *an instrument used for examining the inner eye.*

Eye know Latin

The root *oculo-*, from the Latin word for eye, *oculus*, is also used to form many terms that refer to the eye; for example, **intraocular**, which means *within the eyeball*—as in **intraocular structures**.

The light of the eye

The **cornea** is a smooth, transparent portion of the eyeball through which light enters the eye. It bulges slightly with a domelike protrusion and lacks blood vessels. The cornea is very sensitive to touch.

Looking straight in the eye

The **iris** is a circular disk in the center of the eye with the ability to contract. The **anterior** and **posterior chambers** of the iris are filled with a clear watery fluid called **aqueous humor**. This fluid drains through the trabecular meshwork into Schlemm's canal (a sinus at the junction of the cornea and the iris). **Intraocular pressure (IOP)** is the balance of pressure between secretion and removal of fluid.

Lacrimal comes from the Latin word for a teardrop, *lacrima*.

Focus on this

The **pupil**, or central opening of the iris, is black in color. By expanding and contracting, it regulates the amount of light admitted to the **lens**. Enclosed in an elastic capsule directly behind the iris, the lens acts like a camera lens, refracting and focusing light onto the retina.

The reception area

The **retina** receives visual stimuli and sends them to the brain.

Optical equipment

The **optic disk** is a well-defined, round, yellow to pink disk within the nasal portion of the retina. It allows the optic nerve to enter the retina at the nerve head.

Photoreceptors called **rods** and **cones**, named for their shape, are the visual receptors of the retina and are responsible for vision. The rods, located toward the outside of the retina, respond to low-intensity light and shades of gray. The cones are concentrated in the center and respond to bright light and color.

The lens of a camera takes its name from the lens in our eyes. They perform the same function: refracting and focusing light.

It's all clear here

Located to the side of the optic disk is the macula, which is slightly darker than the rest of the retina. A region in the macula called the fovea centralis is the site of clearest vision, where cones are most concentrated and no rods are found. Because the fovea centralis contains the heaviest concentration of cones, it's a main receiver of vision and color.

Focusing on convergence

The process called **accommodation** allows the eyes to focus on light rays that are close or far away. The eyeballs are **converged** (move together) by muscles attached to the eyeball and the bones of the orbit.

Hearing

The ear is a sensory organ that enables hearing and maintains equilibrium. It's conveniently divided into the **external**, **middle**, and **inner ear**.

The external ear

The **auricle**, or **pinna** (pinna means *wing*), is the cartilage-based outer part of the ear. The **external auditory meatus** (opening) is the short passage leading into the ear. Earwax, also called **cerumen**, lines this canal, which ends at the tympanic membrane.

Drum roll, please…

The **tympanic membrane** separates the external ear from the middle ear. Also called the **eardrum**, it picks up sound waves and transmits them to the auditory nerve in the brain.

The middle ear

The **middle** ear is located in a small, air-filled cavity in the temporal bone called the **tympanic cavity**. It lies between the tympanic membrane and the inner ear and communicates with the throat by way of the **eustachian tube**, which keeps air pressure equal on both sides of the eardrum. The tympanic membrane is so sensitive to air pressure that rapid changes in altitude can produce pain, feelings of pressure, and ringing in the ears **(tinnitus)**.

A hammer, anvil, and stirrup

The middle ear contains three small bones named for their shapes—the **malleus** (hammer), **incus** (anvil), and **stapes** (stirrup). Connected by joints, their mechanical activity transmits sound waves to the inner ear. The three bones together are called the **auditory ossicles** (bones). The stapes sits in an opening called the **oval window** (**fenestra ovalis**), through which sound vibrations travel to the inner ear.

The inner ear

A bony labyrinth and a membrane-covered labyrinth combine to form the inner ear. It consists of the **vestibule**, a small space at the beginning of a canal, and two systems of canals, the **cochlea** and the **semicircular**.

Why is the **tympanic membrane** called the eardrum? For starters, the term comes from the Greek word for kettle drum, **tympanon**, and most importantly, it acts like a drum when struck by sound vibrations.

Otoliths are made up of tiny particles of calcium carbonate and a gelatinous mixture found in the vestibule of the inner ear. They help with maintaining balance and equilibrium.

Ear-y canals

Sensory tissue in the semicircular canals maintains the body's sense of position and equilibrium. The **cochlea** (which means *spiral* or *shell shaped*) contains three canals separated from one another by thin membranes:

- The **vestibular canal** connects with the oval window that leads to the middle ear.
- The **tympanic canal** is connected to the **round window**, which also leads to the middle ear. Both of these canals are bony and contain **perilymph fluid**.
- The **cochlear canal** is membranous and filled with **endolymph fluid**.

Located in the cochlear canal is the **organ of Corti**, a spiral-shaped membrane made up of cells with projecting hairs that transmit sound to the cochlear branch of the acoustic nerve.

Listen up

For hearing to occur, sound waves travel through the ear by two pathways:

1. **Air conduction** occurs when sound waves travel in the air through the external and middle ear to the inner ear.
2. **Bone conduction** occurs when sound waves travel through bone to the inner ear.

For me to hear what Polly is saying, the sound of her voice has to travel to my inner ear through **air conduction, bone conduction,** or both!

Smell

The sensory organ for smell, the **nose**, also warms, filters, and humidifies inhaled air. The word elements *naso-* and *rhino-* and the term **olfactory** refer to the nose, including the external parts and internal cavities.

The nose knows

The **olfactory epithelium** within the nose is the actual organ of smell, perceiving odors when its cells are stimulated. **Olfactory receptors** are located in a narrow shelf formed by the **superior nasal concha**, the upper part of the septum, and—bordering the **nostrils** on the lower part of each side—the winglike **alae**. Smells received by the olfactory epithelium are transmitted to the **olfactory bulb** and continue from there to olfactory centers in the brain. (See *Not that kind of factory*.)

Beyond the dictionary

Not that kind of factory

When studying the sense of smell and the nose, the term **olfactory** comes up often, as in **olfactory epithelium**, the actual organ of smell. Although the term **olfactory** suggests *a smell factory*, the term actually derives from the Latin word for *smell*, **olfactus**.

Nosing around the inside of the nose

The upper third of the nose consists of bone, and the lower two-thirds is made of cartilage. **Cilia**, tiny hairs that filter inhaled air, line the **vestibule**, the area inside the nostrils. The **nasal septum** separates the nostrils. Grooves called **meatuses** separate the three curved, bony structures called **turbinates (superior, middle, and inferior)**, which aid breathing by warming, filtering, and humidifying inhaled air. Posterior air passages known as **choanae** lead to the oropharynx (throat).

And right out in front of your nose

The upper, narrow end of the nose is called the **root**. The **bridge** extends from the root to the **tip**. The **external nares** are the two outer openings, separated by the **nasal septum**. The **alae** flare out from either side of the nares.

The nose can identify about 10,000 odors— but all result from combinations of the six basic odors: flowery, fruity, spicy, resinous, burned, and putrid. Phew!

Touch

The **skin** is the organ of touch, able to receive sensations of pressure, heat, cold, and pain. Touch, or light pressure perception, occurs when **dendrites** (free sensory nerve endings in the skin) are stimulated.

A light touch

Merkel's disks are **tactile corpuscles** in the epidermis that relay light touch and superficial pressure. **Meissner's corpuscles** (in the corium below the epidermis) receive light pressure sensation. Heavy pressure is transmitted by **Pacini's corpuscles**, layered sensory nerve tissues in the skin's subcutaneous layer.

Touchy to temperature changes

The skin reacts to temperature changes of even a few degrees. Although the mechanism is unknown, skin capillaries, free nerve endings, and **Ruffini's corpuscles** (in the corium) help send temperature information to the brain.

Beyond the dictionary

A tasteful history

The term **gustatory** pertains to the sense of taste and derives from the Latin word **gustare**, *to taste*. Another "tasteful" English word, or rather "distasteful," that is derived from that same Latin root is **disgust**, which literally means *to cause nausea*.

Taste

The **taste buds** are the receptors for the taste nerve fibers located in the **papillae** (small projections on the tongue). A few taste buds are found in the mucous membranes of the soft palate, the opening from the mouth to the throat, and the epiglottis. (See *A tasteful history*.)

Physical examination terms

This section will provide terms you may need to know for physical examination of the sensory system.

In the term **blepharospasm,** *blepharo* comes from the Greek word **blepharon,** which means *eyelid.*

Examining vision

An **ophthalmoscope**, which contains a light, a mirror with a single hole, and several lenses, is used for examining the interior structures of the eye. This instrument is also called a **funduscope**. These terms are used in physical examination of the sense of vision:

- **anisopia**—unequal vision in two eyes
- **astigmatism**—impairment in vision due to an irregularity in the curvature of the cornea or lens
- **blepharospasm**—spasms or constant blinking of the eyelid
- **diplopia**—double vision
- **exophthalmos**—unilateral or bilateral bulging or protrusion of the eyeballs
- **floaters**—tiny clumps of vitreous gel appearing to float in the visual field (see *Keeping it simple*)
- **monochromatism**—total color blindness
- **myopia**—nearsightedness
- **nyctalopia**—night blindness
- **optic neuritis**—inflammation of the optic nerve
- **presbyopia**—inability to focus on small print due to loss of elasticity of the lens (a normal sign of aging)
- **ptosis**—drooping of the eyelid
- **strabismus**—absence of coordinated eye movement, leading to misalignment of the eyes
- **uveitis**—inflammation of the uvea, including the iris, ciliary body, and choroid.

Examining hearing

An **otoscope** is a device for examining the ear, including the external ear, eardrum, and ossicles. This instrument includes a device for **insufflation** (blowing vapor or powder into a cavity), a light, and a magnifying glass. Here are terms involved with physical examination of the ear:

- **otorrhagia**—bleeding from the ear
- **otorrhea**—discharge from the ear
- **ototoxic**—a substance toxic to the eighth cranial nerve or the organs of balance and hearing

The real world

Keeping it simple

Not all medical terms are derived from Greek and Latin and contain many syllables. Sometimes, a simple word best describes a medical phenomenon. Take, for example, the term **floaters**, a coined term for the tiny clumps of vitreous gel that appear to "float" in the eyes.

- **tinnitus**—ringing in one or both ears
- **vertigo**—a sensation of movement in which the patient feels himself revolving in space or surroundings revolving about him (may result from inner ear disease).

Examining sense of smell

The following terms are used in the physical examination of the sense of smell:
- **anosmia**—absence of the sense of smell
- **dysosmia**—a defect in or impairment of the sense of smell
- **hyperosmia**—abnormal sensitivity to odors
- **osmesthesia**—inability to perceive and distinguish odors
- **osmodysphoria**—abnormal dislike of certain odors.

Examining sense of taste

The following terms are used in the physical examination of the sense of taste:
- **ageusia**—an impaired or absent sense of taste
- **dysgeusia**—abnormal or distorted sense of taste
- **hypergeusia**—unusual acuteness of taste
- **hypogeusia**—impaired sense of taste.

Diagnostic tests

Many methods are used to diagnose the origins of sensory diseases or conditions. Some tests measure an individual component's level of function in the sensory system, while others examine each component for injury. This section reviews diagnostic test terms for the sensory system.

Eye tests

Eye tests can be conducted either under direct evaluation or with radiologic and imaging equipment.

Direct evaluation

In direct evaluation, tests are applied directly to the eye by the examiner with the aid of various pieces of equipment.

Memory jogger

Here's the near and far, so to speak, of two vision examination terms:

- **myopia** (nearsightedness), vision is better for near rather than far objects.

- **hyperopia** (farsightedness), vision is better for far rather than near objects.

Look into the light

Refraction is an examination to determine and correct refractive eye errors. The **ophthalmologist** usually performs a refraction with a **retinoscope**. In this test, the examiner uses the retinoscope to shine a light into the patient's eye. The examiner then notes the reflexive movements of the fundus.

In the spotlight

Slit-lamp examination gets its name from the piece of equipment used, an instrument equipped with a special lighting system and a binocular microscope that allows the examiner to view details of the eye, including the eyelids, eyelashes, conjunctiva, and cornea.

Eye know IOP

Tonometry permits indirect measurement of IOP.

Radiologic and imaging studies

Radiologic and imaging equipment can make the inner eye visible for closer study.

Most enlightening! In **refraction**, the examiner uses the retinoscope to shine a light into the patient's eye. The examiner then notes the reflexive movements of the fundus.

Shutter bug

Fluorescein **angiography** records the appearance of blood vessels inside the eye through rapid-sequence photographs of the fundus. The photographs follow the I.V. injection of **sodium fluorescein**, a contrast medium.

Sounding it out

Ocular ultrasonography transmits high-frequency sound waves through the eye and measures their reflection from ocular structures.

Eye of the storm

Other eye examinations and terms include the following:
- **Orbital computed tomography (CT)** reveals abnormalities that can't be seen with standard X-rays. The orbital CT scan is a series of tomograms reconstructed by a computer and displayed as anatomic slices on a screen.
- **Orbital radiography** examines the orbit (the deep-set cavity housing the eye), lacrimal gland, blood vessels, nerves, muscles, and fat.
- A **scanning laser ophthalmoscope** is a laser device used to detect abnormal retinal secretions.

Visual acuity tests

A **Snellen eye chart** is the standard chart used in eye examinations, containing block letters of decreasing size read by the patient from a distance.

Visual field tests determine the extent of the retinal area through which the patient can perceive visual stimuli.

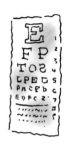

Testing the ears

When performing diagnostic tests on the sense of hearing, the examiner generally needs the participation of the patient. After all, only the individual being tested can tell the examiner whether she heard something.

First look

Otoscopy is the direct visualization of the external auditory canal and the tympanic membrane through an instrument called an **otoscope**.

Tuning fork tests

Tuning fork tests such as Weber's test and Rinne's test are quick screening tools for detecting hearing loss.

Good vibrations

Weber's test evaluates bone conduction by placing a vibrating tuning fork on top of the patient's head at the midline or in the middle of the patient's forehead. The patient should perceive the sound equally in both ears.

Rinne's test compares bone conduction to air conduction in both ears by placing the base of a vibrating tuning fork on the mastoid process and noting how many seconds pass before the patient can no longer hear it.

Audiometric tests

Audiometric tests are performed by **audiologists** to confirm hearing loss. **Audiometry** is the evaluation of hearing using an **audiometer**, a device that measures perception of tones at various frequencies. (See *I hear*.)

Reaching the threshold

Pure-tone audiometry provides a record of the **thresholds**—the lowest intensity levels—at which a patient can hear a set of test tones

Beyond the dictionary

I hear

You're probably familiar with the word audio. You own **audio** equipment (such as a radio) and maybe even consider yourself an **audiophile** *(one devoted to high-quality sound equipment)*. But did you know that *audio* is the Latin word for *I hear?* Therefore, it makes sense that tests that examine your ability to hear are called **audiometrie**.

through earphones or a bone conduction (sound) vibrator. The **test tones** are concentrated at certain frequencies labeled bone conduction thresholds and air conduction thresholds. In **Békésy audiometry**, a patient pushes a button to indicate that a tone was heard.

Going with the flow

Acoustic admittance tests evaluate middle ear function by measuring sound energy's flow into the ear (admittance) and the opposition to that flow (impedance). Two tests are used to measure admittance:
- Tympanometry measures middle ear admittance in response to air pressure changes in the ear canal.
- The **acoustic reflex test** measures the change in admittance produced by contraction of the stapedius muscle as it responds to an intense sound.

Electrocochleography

Electrocochleography measures the electrical current generated in the inner ear after sound stimulation. The current is measured by an electrode in the external acoustic canal. (See *Isn't there an abbreviation?*)

Electronystagmography

In electronystagmography, eye movements in response to specific stimuli are recorded on graph paper and used to evaluate the interactions of the vestibular system and the muscles controlling eye movement in what is known as the **vestibulo-ocular reflex**.

Tests for smell

The **Proetz test** measures the acuity of smell, using different concentrations of substances with recognizable odors.

Do you smell something?

The lowest concentration at which the patient recognizes an odor is called the **olfactory coefficient**, or **minimal identifiable odor**.

Disorders

The sensory system is a complex system with even more complicated components. This section provides terminology related to disorders of the sensory system.

Pump up your pronunciation

Isn't there an abbreviation?

Generally, tests with long, hard-to-pronounce names like **electrocochleography** are referred to by an abbreviation. In this case, maybe ECG would be appropriate; however, that abbreviation is for the term **electrocardiogram**. What do you do then? Take a deep breath and sound it out: EH-**LECK**-TROH-KAWK-LEE-AWG-RAH-FEE.

Eye disorders

Eye disorders can range from common irritation in and around the eyes to impaired vision. Various types of eye disorders are discussed here.

The Proetz (pronounced PRHOTS) test measures the acuity of smell, using different concentrations of substances with recognizable odors.

Common inflammations and infections

- **Blepharitis** is a common inflammatory condition of the eyelids, lash follicles, and glands of the eyelids, characterized by swelling, redness, and crusts of dried mucus on the eyelids.
- **Conjunctivitis** is an inflammation or infection of the conjunctiva, sometimes called **pinkeye**. (See *Is pinkeye pink?*)
- **Dacryocystitis** is a common infection of the lacrimal sac caused by an obstruction (**dacryostenosis**) of the nasolacrimal duct or by trauma.
- **Keratitis** is an inflammation of the cornea, usually confined to one eye, and it may be acute or chronic, superficial or deep.

Other eye disorders

One common cause of vision loss, a **cataract** is a gradually developing opacity of the lens or lens capsule of the eye.

Here are some other eye disorders:

- **Corneal abrasion**, a scratch on the surface epithelium of the cornea, is often caused by a foreign body.
- **Macular degeneration**, the atrophy or degeneration of the macular disk, is the most common cause of blindness in adults.
- **Nystagmus** is recurring, involuntary eyeball movement that produces blurred vision and difficulty in focusing. The movement may be horizontal, vertical, rotating, or mixed.

Too much pressure

Glaucoma is a group of disorders characterized by an abnormally high IOP, which can damage the optic nerve. Left untreated, it can cause blindness. Glaucoma occurs in several forms:

- **Chronic open-angle glaucoma** results from overproduction of aqueous humor.
- **Acute angle-closure glaucoma** results from obstruction to the outflow of aqueous humor.
- **Secondary glaucoma** can result from uveitis, trauma, or drugs such as steroids.

Looking to the retina

In **retinal detachment**, the retinal layers split and create a subretinal space, which fills with fluid (called **subretinal fluid**).

Beyond the dictionary

Is pinkeye pink?

The inflammation caused by **pinkeye** may strike some as pink in color and therefore explain the origin of its use, but the term probably derives from the Middle English word ***pinken***, which means *to prick*.

Pinkeye originally was used to indicate *half-shut*, or what your eye would look like after it was pricked or poked, and what it may look like if you're suffering from pinkeye.

A genetically transmitted disorder, **retinitis pigmentosa** causes progressive destruction of the retinal rods and leads to eventual blindness.

Noninflammatory retinal disorders, called **vascular retinopathies**, result from disruption of the eye's blood supply. The two types of this condition are:

- **Hypertensive** retinopathy results from prolonged hypertensive disease, which produces retinal vasospasm and consequently damages and narrows the arteriolar opening.
- **Diabetic retinopathy** is retinopathy that results as a complication of diabetes.

Ear disorders

Ear disorders can range from common irritation to serious hearing loss.

Hearing loss

Hearing loss (deafness) results from a dysfunction in the mechanical or nervous system that disrupts transmission of sound waves. It's classified as:

- **conductive loss**—interrupted transmission of sound impulses from the external ear to the junction of the stapes and oval window
- **mixed hearing loss**—combined conductive and sensorineural dysfunctions
- **otosclerosis**—slow growth of a spongy bone in the otic capsule, particularly at the oval window (the most common cause of progressive conductive hearing loss)
- **sensorineural loss**—impaired cochlear or acoustic nerve function that prevents transmission of sound impulses within the inner ear or brain.

The older we get

Presbycusis, an effect of aging, results from the loss of hair cells in the organ of Corti. This disorder causes sensorineural hearing loss, usually of high-frequency tones.

Ear disorders without chronic hearing loss

Here are some common disorders of the ear that generally have no long-term effect on hearing:

- **Infectious myringitis** is characterized by inflammation, hemorrhage, and effusion of fluid into the tissue and at the end of the external ear canal and tympanic membrane.
- **Labyrinthitis**, an inflammation of the labyrinth of the inner ear, frequently causes severe vertigo.
- **Mastoiditis** is a bacterial infection and inflammation of the mastoid antrum air cells and is commonly a complication of chronic or acute otitis media.
- **Ménière's disease**, also called **endolymphatic hydrops**, is a labyrinthine dysfunction known to cause violent attacks of severe vertigo lasting from 10 minutes to several hours.
- **Otitis externa** is an inflammation of the external ear canal, which may be acute or chronic.
- **Otitis media** is an inflammation of the middle ear.

I said, *"Presbycusis* comes from the Greek words *presbys*, meaning old man, and *akouein*, which means *to hear."*

Treatments

Treatment options for sensory system disorders include drug therapy, surgery, and, in some cases, a transplant replacing a damaged component.

Eye treatments

Drug therapy is a common treatment for eye disorders.

Drug therapy

The most frequently used drugs include:
- **Anti-infectives**, such as bacitracin and erythromycin, are used to treat infection.
- **Anti-inflammatory agents**, such a dexamethasone, are used to treat inflammatory conditions of the eye.
- **Artificial tears** provide moisture for the eyes when insufficient tear production is a problem.
- **Miotics** are agents that cause constriction of the pupil.
- **Mydriatics** are agents that dilate the pupil of the eye.
- **Ophthalmic anesthetics** prepare the eye for procedures, such as tonometry, suture removal from the cornea, or removal of foreign bodies.

Ménière's disease can cause violent attacks of severe vertigo resulting in dizziness, nausea, and vomiting.

Eye surgery

Surgery may involve the repair, removal, or transplant of a failing component of the eye. Surgeons often employ **laser surgery**, using a laser that generates focused, or monochromatic, light waves; it then magnifies their power by deflecting them off a series of mirrors. The result is a finely focused, high-energy beam.

- **Cataracts** are removed by one of two methods. In **intracapsular cataract extraction**, the entire lens is removed, most often with a **cryoprobe**, a surgical instrument that freezes and adheres to the lens, making the lens easier to remove. **Extracapsular cataract extraction** removes the patient's anterior capsule, cortex, and nucleus, leaving the posterior capsule intact. This technique uses irrigation and aspiration or **phacoemulsification**. Phacoemulsification uses an ultrasonic probe to break the lens into minute particles and aspirate them. (See *How do I say phacoemulsification?*)
- Performed by laser or standard surgery, an **iridectomy** reduces IOP by improving the drainage of aqueous humor. The procedure makes a hole in the iris, creating an opening though which the aqueous humor can flow to bypass the pupil.
- **Radial** keratotomy is a treatment for myopia (nearsightedness) that involves the creation of small radial incisions in the cornea. These incisions flatten the cornea and help properly focus light on the retina.
- **Sclerectomy** is excision of part of the sclera.
- **Scleral buckling** is surgical repair of a detached retina, in which indentations of the sclera are made over the retinal tears to promote retinal adherence to the choroid.
- **Trabeculectomy** is a surgical filtering procedure that removes part of the trabecular meshwork, allowing aqueous humor to bypass blocked channels. This procedure creates a filtering bleb or opening under the conjunctiva.
- A microsurgical procedure, **vitrectomy** removes part or all of the vitreous humor—the transparent gelatinous substance that fills the cavity behind the lens. It's also used for removal of foreign bodies and infection within the eye.

Restoring clarity

In a **corneal transplant**, healthy corneal tissue from a human donor replaces a damaged part of the cornea. The transplant can take one of two forms:

1. **Full-thickness penetrating keratoplasty** involves excision and replacement of the entire cornea.
2. **Lamellar keratoplasty** removes and replaces a superficial layer of corneal tissue.
3. **Lasik surgery** (laser-assisted in situ keratomileusis) uses a laser to reshape the cornea and correct vision.

Pump up your pronunciation

How do I say phacoemulsification?

Phacoemulsification is the process by which an ultrasonic device disintegrates a cataract. *Phakos* is the Greek term for *lens*, and *emulsification* is the process by which something is *emulsified* or *broken down*. This word becomes easier to pronounce when you break it down phonetically: FACK-OH-EE-MULL-SIH-FIH-KAY-SHUN.

In corneal transplantation, corneal tissue from a human donor replaces a damaged part of the cornea.

Ear treatments

Treatments for ear disorders range from drug therapy to surgical intervention.

Drug therapy

The following drugs are used to treat otic disorders:
- **Acetic acid**, or **Domeboro's solution**, treats ear canal infections (and prevents "swimmer's ear").
- **Anesthetics** treat pain from otitis media and assist with removal of cerumen.
- **Antibiotics** treat external ear canal infection.
- **Cerumeolytics** help remove impacted cerumen.
- **Corticosteroids**, such as hydrocortisone, treat inflammation of the external ear canal.

Ear surgery

Surgical procedures can either repair or remove a failing component.

Drum repair

Myringotomy is a surgical incision into the tympanic membrane to relieve pain and drain pus or fluid from the middle ear. Myringoplasty is performed to repair a ruptured tympanic membrane. The surgeon approximates the edges of the membrane or applies a graft taken from the temporalis muscle.

Taking off the stirrups

Stapedectomy removes all or part of the stapes. A **total stapedectomy** involves removal of the entire bone, followed by insertion of a graft and prosthesis to bridge the gap between the incus and the inner ear.

In a **partial stapedectomy**, the surgeon removes part of the bone and rebuilds what's left with a prosthesis. **Laser stapedectomy**, a relatively new technique, is easier to perform but carries a risk of the laser beam penetrating the bone.

Vocabulary builders

At a crossroads

Completing this crossword puzzle will help you come to your senses about correct sensory system terms. Good luck!

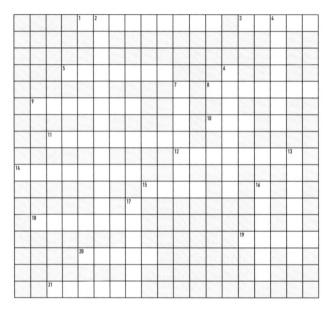

Across

1. Another name for **eyelids**
3. Eponym for the spiral-shaped membrane that transmits sound to the cochlear branch
5. Absence of the sense of smell
8. Latin term for *teardrop*
9. Term for *earwax*
10. Number of basic odors
11. Free sensory nerve endings
12. Particles of calcium carbonate in the small sacs of the vestibule
14. Ringing in the ears
15. Organ of touch
18. Air passages from the nose that lead to the throat
19. This test evaluates bone conduction
20. The eyeball occupies the bony
21. The white part of the eyeball

Down

2. Process that allows eyes to focus on light rays that are close or far away
4. Eponym for corpuscles that are involved in sending temperature information to the brain
6. Location of taste buds
7. Unequal vision in the two eyes
13. Name that lends itself to the standard eye chart
16. Test that measures the acuity of smell
17. Part of the eye that receives visual stimuli

Finish line

Tears protect and lubricate the eye. **Lacrimal** pertains to tears and comes from the Latin word *lacrima*, which means *tear*. Fill in the blanks for the eye structures involved in tear production.

1. The **lacrimal** _____ lubricates and protects the eye with tears.
2. The **lacrimal** _____ produce tears.
3. The **lacrimal** _____ are where tears flow after draining through the punctum.
4. The **lacrimal** _____ is where the tears then collect.
5. The _____-**lacrimal** _____ is where tears drain through into the nose.

Talking in circles

Use the clues below to fill in the blanks with the appropriate word. Then unscramble the circled letters to find the answer to the question posed at left.

1. ___ ___ ___ ___ ◯ ___ ___

2. ◯ ___ ___ ___ ___ ___ ___

3. ___ ◯ ___ ___ ___ ___ ___ ___

4. ◯ ___ ___ ___ ___ ___ ___ ___ ___ ___

5. ___ ___ ___ ___ ◯ ___

6. ___ ◯ ___ ___ ___ ___ ___ ___ ___

7. ___ ___ ___ ___ ◯ ___ ___

I am one of three small bones in the middle ear that hammers away at sound waves. Which bone am I?

1. Contains three canals within the ear and means *shell shaped*
2. The standard chart used in eye examinations
3. A gradually developing opacity of the lens of the eye
4. A surgical incision into the tympanic membrane to relieve pain
5. The central opening of the iris, which is black in color
6. Means *pertaining to the sense of taste*
7. Disks in the epidermis that relay light touch and superficial pressure

Answers

At a crossroads

```
      ¹P  ²A  L   P   E   B   R   A   E       ³C  O  ⁴R  T   I
          C                                       U
          C                                       F
      ⁵A  N   O   S   M   I   A       ⁶P          F
          M               ⁷A  ⁸L  A   C   R   I   M   A
      ⁹C  E   R   U   M   E   N       N       P       N
          O               I       ¹⁰S  I   X       I
      ¹¹D  E   N   D   R   I   T   E   S       L
          A               ¹²O  T   O   L   I   T   H  ¹³S
      ¹⁴T  I   N   N   I   T   U   S       P       A       N
          I           ¹⁵S  K   I   N       E   ¹⁶P       E
          O       ¹⁷R          A       R       L
      ¹⁸C  H   O   A   N   A   E               O       L
          T                           ¹⁹W  E   B   E   R
      ²⁰O  R   B   I   T                       T       N
          N                                   Z
      ²¹S  C   L   E   R   A
```

Finish line

Answers: 1. Apparatus; 2. Glands; 3. Canals; 4. Sac; 5. Naso-, Duct

Talking in circles

Answers: 1. Cochlea; 2. Snellen; 3. Cataract; 4. Myringotomy; 5. Pupil; 6. Gustatory; 7. Merkel's

Solution to puzzle—Malleus

I can sense without even looking that you've done a great job with this chapter.

Suggested references

Gould, B. E., & Dyer, R. (2014). *Pathophysiology for the health professions-E-Book*. St. Louis, MO: Elsevier Health Sciences.

Patel, N., Jankovic, J., & Hallett, M. (2014). Sensory aspects of movement disorders. *The Lancet Neurology, 13*(1), 100–112.

Standring, S. A. (2016). *Gray's anatomy: The anatomical basis of clinical practice*. Ipswich, MA: Elsevier Health Sciences.

Chapter 16

Pharmacology

Just the facts

In this chapter, you'll learn:

♦ terminology related to the fundamentals of clinical pharmacology

♦ terminology associated with drug administration

♦ medications that affect each body system.

Pharmacology basics

Pharmacology is the scientific study of the origin, nature, chemistry, effects, and uses of medications. The term **pharmacology** originated from the Greek root *pharmako*, which means *medicine*. (See *Pronouncing key pharmacology terms*.)

Pharmacology contains three main branches:

1. **Pharmacokinetics** refers to the absorption, distribution, metabolism, and excretion of a drug in a living organism.
2. **Pharmacodynamics** is the study of the biochemical and physical effects of drugs and the mechanisms of drug actions in living organisms.
3. **Pharmacotherapeutics** refers to the use of drugs to prevent and treat diseases.

Pharmacokinetics

The term **kinetics** means *movement*; therefore, **pharmacokinetics** refers to a drug's movement through the body, including how the drug is:

- absorbed
- distributed
- metabolized
- excreted.

There's a lot to know when it comes to pharmacology.

Pronouncing key pharmacology terms

Here's a list of key pharmacology terms, along with the correct ways to pronounce them.

Antiemetics	AN-TEE-EH-MET-IKS
Bioavailability	BEYE-OH-EH-VAYL-EH-BIHL-IH-TEE
Catecholamines	KAT-UH-KOH-LAH-MEENZ
Iatrogenic effects	EYE-AT-ROH-JEN-IK EH-FEKS
Lipodystrophy	LIHP-OH-DIHS-TROH-FEE
Palliative therapy	PAL-EE-AY-TIV THER-UH-PEE
Parasympathomimetic	PAR-UH-SIM-PUH-THOH-MI-MEH-TIK
Pharmacodynamics	FAR-MAH-KOH-DEYE-NAM-IKS
Pharmacogenetics	FAR-MAH-KOH-JEH-NEHT-IKS
Pharmacokinetics	FAR-MAH-KOH-KUH-NET-IKS
Pharmacotherapeutics	FAR-MAH-KOH-THER-UH-PYOU-TIKS

Absorption

The process of drug **absorption** covers the progress of a drug from the time it's administered, through the time it passes to the tissues, until it becomes available for use by the body. On a cellular level, drugs are primarily absorbed through passive or active transport.

No energy required

Passive transport requires no cellular energy because the drug moves from an area of higher concentration to one of lower concentration. It occurs when small molecules diffuse across membranes. **Diffusion** (movement from a higher concentration to a lower concentration) stops when drug concentration on both sides of the membrane equalizes.

Energy required

Active transport requires cellular energy to move the drug from an area of lower concentration to one of higher concentration. Active transport is used to absorb electrolytes, such as sodium and potassium.

In passive transport, a drug moves from an area of higher concentration to one of lower concentration.

Active transport requires energy.

Distribution

Drug **distribution** is the process by which a drug is delivered to the tissues and fluids of the body. Distribution of an absorbed drug within the body depends on blood flow, solubility, and protein binding.

Go with the flow

After a drug reaches the bloodstream, its distribution in the body depends on blood flow. The drug is quickly distributed to organs with a large supply of blood, such as the heart, liver, and kidneys.

Drug crossing

The ability of a drug to cross a cell membrane depends on whether the drug is water soluble or lipid soluble. **Lipid-soluble** drugs (those capable of dissolving in fat) easily cross through cell membranes, while **water-soluble** drugs (those capable of dissolving in water) can't.

Ties that bind

As a drug travels through the body, it comes in contact with proteins such as the plasma protein albumin. The drug can either remain free or bind to the protein. The portion of a drug that's **protein bound** is inactive and can't produce a therapeutic effect. Only the free (or unbound) portion remains active.

Metabolism

Drug metabolism, also known as **biotransformation**, refers to the body's ability to change a drug from its dosage form to a more water-soluble form that can later be excreted.

Excretion

Drug **excretion** refers to the elimination of a drug from the body. Most drugs are excreted by the kidneys and leave the body through urine. However, drugs can also be excreted through the lungs, exocrine glands (sweat, salivary, or mammary glands), skin, and intestinal tract.

Half and half

The **half-life** of a drug refers to the time it takes for half of the drug to be eliminated by the body. Knowing how long a drug remains in the body helps determine how frequently a drug should be administered.

The **half-life** of a drug refers to the time it takes for half of the drug to be eliminated by the body.

Onset, peak, and duration

In addition to absorption, distribution, metabolism, and excretion, three other factors play important roles in a drug's pharmacokinetics:
- onset of action
- peak concentration
- duration of action.

Lights, camera ... action!

Onset of action refers to the time interval that starts when the drug is administered and ends when the therapeutic effect actually begins. Rate of onset varies depending on the route of administration and other pharmacokinetic properties.

Peak performance

As the body absorbs more of a drug, blood concentration levels of that drug rise. The **peak concentration** level is reached when the absorption rate equals the elimination rate.

Total effect

The **duration of action** is the total length of time the drug produces its therapeutic effect.

Pharmacodynamics is the study of drug mechanisms that produce biochemical or physiologic changes in the body.

Pharmacodynamics

Pharmacodynamics is the study of drug mechanisms that produce biochemical or physiologic changes in the body. Interaction at the cellular level represents **drug action**. The response resulting from this drug action is referred to as the **drug effect.**

That's stimulating

Many drugs work by stimulating or blocking drug **receptors** (a specialized location on a cell membrane or inside a cell). A drug that's attracted to a receptor displays an affinity—or attraction—for that receptor. When a drug displays an affinity for a receptor and stimulates it, the drug acts as an **agonist.** The drug's ability to initiate a response after binding with the receptor is referred to as intrinsic activity.

Response buster

If a drug has an affinity for a receptor but displays no intrinsic activity (in other words, it doesn't stimulate the receptor), it's called an **antagonist.** The antagonist prevents a response from occurring.

On-site competition

Antagonists can be competitive or noncompetitive. A **competitive antagonist** competes with the agonist for receptor sites. Because this type of receptor binds reversibly to the receptor site, increased doses of an agonist can overcome the antagonist's effects. A **noncompetitive antagonist** binds to receptor sites and blocks the effects of the agonist.

Any one will do

If a drug acts on a variety of receptors, it's said to be **nonselective** and can cause multiple and widespread effects. Some receptors are further classified by their specific effects. For example, **beta receptors** typically produce increased heart rate and bronchial relaxation as well as other systemic effects.

It's got the power

Drug potency refers to the relative amount of a drug required to produce a desired response. Drug potency is also used to compare two drugs.

Safety margin

Most drugs produce a range of multiple effects. The relationship between a drug's desired therapeutic effect and its adverse effect is called the drug's **therapeutic index.**

Memory jogger

Here's a tip for remembering the difference between **agonist** and **antagonist**: "Agonists are **a go**," meaning that they give the go-ahead for a drug to stimulate a receptor.

Pharmacotherapeutics

Pharmacotherapeutics is the use of drugs to treat disease. When choosing a drug to treat a particular condition, health care providers consider the drug's effectiveness along with other factors, such as the type and duration of therapy the patient will receive.

Therapy, not always the same

The type of therapy a patient receives depends on the severity, urgency, and prognosis of the patient's condition. A patient may receive:
- **acute therapy,** which is used for those who are symptomatically ill and require therapy to correct an underlying condition
- **empiric therapy,** which is based on practical experience rather than on pure scientific data
- **maintenance therapy,** which is used to treat chronic conditions that can't be cured
- **supplemental** or **replacement therapy,** in order to replenish or substitute missing substances, such as enzymes or hormones, in the body

- **supportive therapy,** which doesn't effectively treat the cause of the disease but maintains other threatened body systems until a patient's condition improves or resolves
- **palliative therapy,** which is used to treat end-stage or terminal diseases to make the patient as comfortable as possible.

Different reactions

Certain drugs have a tendency to create drug tolerance and drug dependence. **Drug tolerance** occurs when a patient shows a decreased response to a particular drug over time. The patient then requires larger doses of that drug to produce the same response.

Drug tolerance differs from **drug dependence,** in which a patient displays a physical or psychological need for the drug. **Physical dependence** produces withdrawal symptoms when the drug is stopped, while **psychological dependence** causes drug-seeking behaviors.

> In **drug dependence,** a patient displays physical or psychological need for the drug.

> **Drug tolerance** occurs when a patient shows a decreased response to a particular drug over time.

Drug interactions

Drug interactions can occur between drugs or between drugs and foods. Interactions may impede the results of a laboratory test or produce physical or chemical incompatibilities. The risk of drug interactions increases in relation to the amount of drugs a patient receives. Potential drug interactions include:
- additive effects
- synergistic effects
- antagonistic effects.

Two drugs are better than one

An **additive effect** can occur when two drugs with similar actions are administered to a patient. The effects are equivalent to the sum of the effects of either drug administered alone in higher doses.

> Drugs can interact with other drugs or with food.

Teamwork

A synergistic **effect,** also called **potentiation,** occurs when two drugs that produce the same effect are given together and one drug potentiates (enhances the effect of) the other drug. The combined effect is greater than either drug can produce when taken alone—for example, the effect produced by taking fentanyl (Sublimaze) and midazolam (Versed) concomitantly.

Duking it out

An **antagonistic effect** occurs when the combined response of two drugs is less than the response produced by either drug alone.

Adverse drug reactions

An **adverse drug reaction** (also called a **side effect** or **adverse effect**) is a harmful, undesirable response to a drug. Adverse reactions can range from mild ones that disappear when the drug is discontinued to debilitating diseases that become chronic. Adverse drug reactions are classified as dose related or patient sensitivity related. Dose-related reactions include:

- secondary effects
- hypersusceptibility
- overdose
- iatrogenic effects.

*An **overdose** occurs when an excessive dose of a drug is taken either intentionally or by accident, so don't abuse me!*

Special effects

In addition to its major therapeutic effect, a drug typically produces additional **secondary effects** that are either beneficial or adverse. For example, morphine used to relieve pain may cause respiratory depression as an undesirable secondary effect. Diphenhydramine used as an antihistamine may produce the adverse effect of drowsiness; therefore, it's sometimes prescribed as a sleep aid.

Hyped-up action

Even when the correct therapeutic dose is determined, a patient may experience an excessive therapeutic response called **hypersusceptibility**. Hypersusceptibility typically results from altered pharmacokinetics leading to higher-than-expected blood concentration levels.

Over the top

An **overdose** occurs when an excessive dose of a drug is taken either intentionally or by accident. The result is an exaggerated response (or **toxic reaction)** to the drug that causes transient changes or more serious reactions, such as cardiovascular collapse, respiratory depression, or death.

Simon says

Some adverse reactions, known as **iatrogenic effects,** can mimic pathologic disorders. For example, propranolol can induce asthma.

Too sensitive

Patient sensitivity–related reactions aren't as common as are dose-related reactions. Sensitivity-related reactions result from a patient's unusual and extreme sensitivity to a drug. These adverse reactions arise from a unique tissue response rather than from an exaggerated pharmacologic action. Extreme patient sensitivity can occur as a drug allergy.

A **drug allergy** occurs when a patient's immune system identifies a drug, a drug metabolite, or a drug contaminant as a dangerous foreign substance that must be neutralized or destroyed. Previous exposure to the drug or to one with a similar chemical characteristic sensitizes the patient's immune system, and subsequent exposure causes an **allergic reaction** (hypersensitivity) to occur.

Silent but deadly

The allergic reaction can vary in intensity from an immediate life-threatening **anaphylactic reaction** (a dramatic, acute reaction marked by sudden onset of rapidly progressive hives and respiratory distress) to a mild rash and itching. (See *What's behind an anaphylactic reaction.*)

Beyond the dictionary

What's behind an anaphylactic reaction

An anaphylactic reaction is characterized by a sudden onset of progressive hives and respiratory distress in response to a drug. *Ana-* comes from the Greek words *an-*, meaning *not*, and *phylaxis*, meaning *protection*.

Drug administration

Because prescribing and administering drugs is a critical responsibility for health care providers, it's important to understand the terminology associated with drug administration.

Drug orders

In an outpatient setting, a doctor or health care provider who's licensed to prescribe drugs writes an order on a special pad and gives it directly to the patient. This is known as a **prescription.**

Drug orders in the inpatient setting differ. The following drug orders are used in inpatient settings:

- **Standard written orders** are written by the health care provider and apply indefinitely until another order is written to discontinue or alter the first one.
- **One-time orders** are orders written for a medication that's given only once.
- **Stat orders** are written for medications that must be administered immediately to treat an urgent patient problem.

Beyond the dictionary

As needed

The abbreviation **p.r.n.** is derived from the Latin phrase **pro re nata**, meaning *as the occasion arises*. Prescribers write p.r.n. orders for medications that are to be given when needed.

- Prescribers write **p.r.n. orders** for drugs that are to be given as needed. (See *As needed.*)
- **Standing orders**, also known as **protocol orders**, establish guidelines for treating a particular disease or set of symptoms.
- **Verbal orders** are medication orders that are given in urgent situations.
- **Telephone orders** are verbal orders prescribed over the telephone. This type of drug order is usually only given in urgent situations and must be repeated back to the prescriber for verification.

Drug forms

Drugs are manufactured in many different forms, such as solids, liquids, suppositories, injectables, and inhalants. Other drug forms include sprays, which are used with several administration routes; creams, lotions, and patches, which are administered topically; and lozenges, which are used to treat local effects.

> A tablet is a drug that's been compressed into a certain shape. Tablets come in different forms.

Solidifying solids

Solid drug forms include capsules and tablets. **Capsules** are hard or soft gelatin shells that contain the drug in a powder, in sustained-release beads, or in a liquid form.

A **tablet** is a drug that's been compressed to form a certain shape. Some tablets are uncoated, while others differ in composition:

- **Enteric-coated tablets** have a thin coating that allows the tablet to pass through the stomach and disintegrate or dissolve in the small intestine, where the drug is absorbed.
- Osmotic **pump tablets** release the drug through a single tiny hole in the tablet.
- **Wax matrix tablets** distribute the drug through a honeycomb-like material made of wax.

Liquefying liquids

Liquid medications are usually given orally or parenterally. Orally administered liquids contain the drug mixed with some type of fluid and are classified as:

- **syrups**—drugs mixed in a sugar-water solution
- **suspensions**—finely divided drug particles suspended in a suitable liquid medium
- **tinctures**—hydroalcoholic drug solutions
- **elixirs**—hydroalcoholic solutions that contain glycerin, sorbitol, or other sweeteners.

Packaging parenterals

Parenteral is a term that literally means *outside the intestines.* Drugs given parenterally are administered outside the GI tract, through injection, and are available in three package styles:

- **vials**—bottles sealed with a rubber diaphragm that contain a single dose or several doses
- **ampules**—glass containers with a thin neck that's typically scored so it can be snapped off easily
- **prefilled system**—a single dose of a drug contained in a plastic bag or a prefilled syringe.

Supposing suppositories

Suppositories deliver medications in a solid base that will melt at body temperature. They can be administered rectally or vaginally.

Inhaling inhalants

Inhalants are drugs that are administered in powdered or liquid form using the respiratory route. Inhalants are absorbed by the rich supply of capillaries in the lungs.

Routes of administration

The GI tract provides a fairly safe (but relatively slow-acting) site for drug absorption. When a drug is administered using the GI tract, it's called **enteral administration**. A drug administered by injectable route is referred to as **parenteral administration.** Other routes that bypass the GI tract and are not injectable are referred to as nonparenteral administration.

There are many ways to take drugs. Inhalants are administered via the respiratory system.

Enteral administration

Oral, sublingual, buccal, and rectal preparations are administered by the GI tract:

- Drugs administered by the **oral route** are placed in the patient's mouth and swallowed. Tablets, capsules, liquids, and lozenges are administered this way.
- The **sublingual route** involves placing an uncoated tablet under the tongue, where it disintegrates and dissolves.
- A drug administered by the buccal **route** is placed between the cheek and gum, where it disintegrates and dissolves.
- Suppositories and **enemas** (a solution introduced into the rectum or colon) are administered by the **rectal route**. This route is commonly used when the oral route is prohibited, such as in a patient with nausea or vomiting.

Parenteral administration

Drugs may be administered parenterally through four types of direct injections:

- **intradermal**—injected directly into the skin
- **subcutaneous**—injected into the subcutaneous tissue
- **intramuscular**—injected directly into a muscle
- **intravenous**—injected into a vein.

Under my skin ...

Intradermal **(I.D.) injections** are used for skin tests such as tuberculin. The **ventral** (anterior portion) forearm is the site of choice for I.D. injections.

Simplifying subcutaneous

Subcutaneous **injections** (Subq) provide a slow, sustained release of medication and a longer duration of action. Subcutaneous injections are used when the total volume injected is less than 1 mL of liquid. Drugs commonly administered by the subcutaneous route include insulin, heparin, and epinephrine. (See *Subq injections.*)

Subcutaneous injection sites include the area over the scapula, the lateral aspects of the upper arm and thigh, and the abdomen.

Mr. Muscle

Intramuscular **(I.M.) injections** are given when rapid absorption of medication is desired. The onset of action usually occurs within 10 to 15 minutes after the I.M. injection. A larger amount of fluid (between 2 and 5 mL, depending on the site) can be administered using I.M. rather than S.C. injections.

Commonly used I.M. injection sites include the **dorsogluteal muscle** (in the back of the buttocks), **ventrogluteal muscle** (in the anterior portion of the buttocks), **vastus lateralis muscle** (in the lateral thigh), **rectus femoris muscle** (in the upper thigh), and **deltoid muscle** (the upper arm muscle that covers the shoulder prominence).

I.V. intro

Medications are administered by the **intravenous (I.V.) route** to obtain an immediate onset of action, to attain the highest possible blood concentration level of a drug, or to treat conditions that require constant **titration** (increase or decrease of dosage according to the patient's response).

I.V. medications can be administered by several methods:

- **direct bolus and I.V. push**—the medication is injected directly into the I.V. catheter over a recommended time interval

The real world

Subq injections

In practice, you may hear a subcutaneous injection referred to as a **subq** injection—for example, "Administer this dose of insulin **subq.**"

- **intermittent infusion or I.V. piggyback**—the medication is infused through an I.V. catheter at various time intervals
- **continuous infusion**—the medication is infused through an I.V. catheter for a prolonged period.

I.V. meds pack a punch!

Nonparenteral routes

Other routes that are used for medication administration include the intrathecal, epidural, intra-articular, dermal, ophthalmic, otic, nasal, sinus, and respiratory routes.

Into the great intrathecal space

Intrathecal **administration** involves introducing a catheter into the intrathecal space of the spinal canal for drug administration. Drugs are delivered by bolus or continuous infusion. Chemotherapeutic agents are sometimes administered by this route.

Epidural space travel

Epidural administration occurs when a catheter is introduced into the epidural space of the spinal column for drug administration. Drugs are delivered by bolus or continuous infusion. Pain medications are commonly administered by this route.

Joint relief

Intra-articular administration is characterized by injecting a drug directly into a joint. Patients with severe joint inflammation sometimes receive intra-articular injections of steroids.

Over the top

Medications given by **dermal** or **topical administration** are applied directly to the skin. Medications administered by this route include creams, lotions, ointments, powders, and patches.

Eye it up

Ophthalmic **administration** involves instilling liquid or ointment medications topically into the eye.

Friends, Romans… lend me your ear

Medications given by **otic administration** are administered into the ear canal.

Nosing around

Nasal or **sinus administration** refers to the administration of liquid or powdered forms of the drug into the patient's nose and sinuses by instillation or by an atomizer (a device that changes a jet of liquid into a spray).

On the fast tract

Respiratory administration refers to the delivery of medications directly into the respiratory tract. Almost all of the drugs administered by this route have a **systemic effect,** which means that they affect the entire body because of the rich blood supply in the lungs. The drug forms commonly administered by this route are gas and liquid.

Nebulization is one method commonly used to administer drugs by the respiratory route. There are three types of nebulizers:

- The **ultrasonic nebulizer** uses a small volume of medication combined with normal saline solution. Air forced into the nebulizer delivers the medication in a fine mist.
- A **metered-dose inhaler** requires a nebulizer that's prefilled by the manufacturer with several doses of the drug.
- A **dry-powder inhaler** is similar to a metered-dose inhaler. It's activated by an inhaled breath, and a precise amount of medication is then delivered.

Drug classifications

Drugs that share similar characteristics are grouped together as a pharmacologic class or family. Terminology associated with drugs in each pharmacologic class is broken down according to the body system that's affected.

Nervous system drugs

Many drugs affect the nervous system. They include cholinergic drugs, cholinergic blocking drugs, adrenergic drugs, adrenergic blocking drugs, skeletal muscle relaxants, neuromuscular blocking drugs, and anticonvulsant drugs.

Copycats

Cholinergic drugs promote the action of **acetylcholine** (a neurotransmitter). These drugs are also called **parasympathomimetic drugs** because they produce effects that mimic parasympathetic nerve stimulation.

There are two major classes of cholinergic drugs:

- **Cholinergic agonists** mimic the action of the neurotransmitter acetylcholine.
- **Anticholinesterase drugs** block the action of the enzyme acetylcholinesterase (which breaks down acetylcholine) at cholinergic receptor sites, preventing the breakdown of acetylcholine.

Cholinergic busters

Cholinergic blocking drugs interrupt parasympathetic nerve impulses in the central and autonomic nervous systems. These drugs are also referred to as **anticholinergic drugs** because they prevent acetylcholine from stimulating cholinergic receptors.

Similar to the sympathetic

Adrenergic drugs are also called sympathomimetic **drugs** because they create effects similar to those produced by the sympathetic nervous system. Adrenergic drugs are classified into two groups based on their chemical structure: catecholamines (which stimulate the nervous system, constrict peripheral blood vessels, increase heart rate, and dilate the bronchi) and **noncatecholamines** (which have many effects on the body, including local or system constriction of blood vessels, nasal and eye decongestion, bronchiole dilation, and smooth muscle relaxation).

Adrenergic drugs are also divided by their mechanism of action:

- **Direct-acting adrenergics** act directly on the organ or tissue that's **innervated** (supplied with nerves or nerve impulses) by the sympathetic nervous system.
- **Indirect-acting adrenergics** trigger the release of a neurotransmitter, typically norepinephrine.
- **Dual-acting adrenergics** have both direct and indirect actions.

> Adrenergic drugs are also called **sympathomimetic drugs** because they create effects similar to those produced by the sympathetic nervous system.

The road to disruption

Adrenergic blocking drugs (also called sympatholytic drugs) are used to disrupt the function of the sympathetic nervous system. These drugs work by blocking impulse transmission at adrenergic receptor sites.

Adrenergic blocking drugs are classified according to their site of action:

- **Alpha-adrenergic blockers** work by interrupting the actions of the catecholamines epinephrine and norepinephrine at alpha receptor sites.
- **Beta-adrenergic blockers** prevent stimulation of the sympathetic nervous system by inhibiting the action of catecholamines at beta-adrenergic receptors. (See *Taking out the* adrenergic.)

Muscle R and R

Skeletal muscle relaxants are used to relax skeletal muscles and treat acute pain or muscle spasticity associated with multiple sclerosis.

The real world

Taking out the *adrenergic*

In practice, the most widely used adrenergic blockers are beta-adrenergic blockers, simply referred to as **beta-blockers.**

Motor end plate stopper

Neuromuscular blocking drugs relax skeletal muscles by disrupting the transmission of nerve impulses at the motor end plate (the branching terminals of a motor nerve axon).

Seizure silencers

Anticonvulsants, also known as **antiseizure drugs,** inhibit neuromuscular transmission in order to prevent seizure activity.

Pain medications

Drugs used to control pain range from mild, over-the-counter preparations, such as acetaminophen, to potent general anesthetics. Here's a list of drugs commonly used to treat pain:

- **Nonopioid analgesics** are drugs that don't contain opioids but that still control pain. Some of these drugs also exhibit an **antipyretic** action, which means they control fever.
- **Nonsteroidal anti-inflammatory drugs (NSAIDs)** control pain by combating inflammation.
- **Opioid agonists** are opium derivatives and synthetic drugs with similar properties used to relieve or decrease pain without causing the person to lose consciousness.
- **Opioid antagonists** block the effects produced by opioid agonists to reverse adverse drug reactions.
- **Anesthetic drugs** depress the central nervous system (CNS) and produce loss of consciousness, loss of responsiveness to sensory stimulation (including pain), and muscle relaxation.

Antiarrhythmic drugs help me keep my rhythm.

Cardiovascular system drugs

Types of drugs used to improve cardiovascular function include cardiac glycosides and **phosphodiesterase** (PDE) inhibitors, antiarrhythmics, and antianginal drugs.

Cardiac glycosides and PDE inhibitors

Cardiac glycosides and **PDE inhibitors** increase the force of the heart's contractions. This is known as a positive **inotropic effect** (affecting the force or energy of muscular contractions).

Changing the rhythm

Antiarrhythmic drugs are used to treat **arrhythmias** (disturbances in normal heart rhythm).

Stopping heart pain

Antianginal drugs are used to treat angina (chest pain) by reducing the amount of oxygen the heart needs to do its work, increasing the supply of oxygen to the heart, or both.

There are three commonly used classes of antianginal drugs:

1. **Nitrates** are the drugs of choice for relieving acute anginal pain. Nitrates cause smooth muscles of the veins and arteries to relax and dilate. When the vessels dilate, blood flow to the myocardium increases, which relieves the pain.
2. **Beta-adrenergic blockers** are drugs used for long-term prevention of angina. Beta-adrenergic blockers decrease blood pressure and block beta-adrenergic receptor sites in the heart muscle and conduction system. They work by decreasing heart rate and reducing the force of the heart's contractions, which results in a lower demand for oxygen.
3. **Calcium channel blockers** are used only for long-term prevention of angina. They prevent the passage of calcium ions across the myocardial cell membrane and vascular smooth muscle cells. This causes dilation of the coronary and peripheral arteries, which decreases the force of the heart's contractions and reduces the workload of the heart.

Pressure droppers

Antihypertensive drugs act to reduce blood pressure. Three types of commonly used antihypertensive drugs include:

- **sympatholytic drugs**—which reduce blood pressure by inhibiting or blocking the sympathetic nervous system
- **vasodilating drugs**—which relax peripheral vascular smooth muscle, causing vessels to dilate, thereby lowering blood pressure
- **angiotensin-converting enzyme (ACE) inhibitors**—which reduce blood pressure by interrupting the renin-angiotensin-aldosterone system.

Antihypertensive drugs can help bring a patient's blood pressure down.

Water works

Diuretics are used to promote the excretion of water and electrolytes by the kidneys. Major diuretics include thiazide and thiazide-like diuretics, loop diuretics, and potassium-sparing diuretics:

- **Thiazide** and **thiazide-like diuretics** work by preventing sodium resorption in the kidneys.
- **Loop diuretics** act primarily on the loop of Henle to increase the secretion of sodium, chloride, and water.
- **Potassium-sparing diuretics** conserve potassium and exert weaker diuretic and antihypertensive effects.

Lower lipid levels

Antilipemic drugs lower abnormally high blood levels of lipids, such as cholesterol, triglycerides, and phospholipids.

Clot stoppers

Anticoagulant drugs are used to reduce the ability of the blood to clot. **Antiplatelet drugs** are administered to prevent arterial thromboembolism, particularly in patients at risk for myocardial infarction, stroke, and arteriosclerosis (hardening of the arteries). **Antithrombolytic drugs** are used to dissolve a preexisting clot or thrombus, commonly in an acute or emergency situation.

Respiratory system drugs

Drugs used to improve respiratory function include methylxanthines, expectorants, antitussives, mucolytics, beta-adrenergic agonists, and decongestants.

Breathing gone awry

Methylxanthines are used to treat breathing disorders. They work by decreasing airway reactivity and relieving bronchospasm by relaxing the bronchial smooth muscle.

Thinner and smoother

Expectorants thin mucus so it can be cleared more easily out of airways. They also soothe mucous membranes in the respiratory tract.

Suppress and inhibit

Antitussive drugs suppress or inhibit coughing.

Mucus movers

Mucolytics act directly on mucus, breaking down sticky, thick secretions to make them easier to eliminate.

Oh, what a relief

Decongestants relieve the symptoms of swollen nasal membranes resulting from hay fever, allergic rhinitis, sinusitis, and the common cold.

H_2-receptor antagonists block histamine from stimulating acid secretion.

GI system drugs

Some classes of drugs that are used to improve GI function include histamine-2 (H_2)-receptor antagonists, proton pump inhibitors, antiemetics, and emetics.

Histamine halters

H₂-receptor antagonists are commonly prescribed as antiulcer drugs. They block histamine from stimulating the acid-secreting parietal cells of the stomach.

Chemical disruption

Protein pump inhibitors disrupt chemical binding in stomach cells to reduce acid production, lessening irritation and allowing peptic ulcers to heal.

Opposites don't always attract

Antiemetics and **emetics** represent two groups of drugs with opposing actions. Antiemetic drugs decrease nausea, reducing the urge to vomit. Emetic drugs do just the opposite—they produce vomiting.

Reproductive system drugs

Various drugs may be used to address sexual dysfunction, fertility, and contraception.

When ED comes to visit

Phosphodiesterase type 5 inhibitors such as sildenafil (Viagra) are used to treat penile erectile dysfunction (ED). These drugs increase smooth muscle relaxation, promoting the flow of blood into the corpus cavernosum of the penis.

A helping hand for women

Here are some examples of drugs that help women with fertility and its associated conditions:

- Danazol (Danocrine), a **synthetic steroid,** is used to treat endometriosis, a condition that may decrease fertility. The drug suppresses the hormonal cycle and decreases the inflammation associated with endometriosis.
- **Chlorotrianisene derivatives** such as clomiphene citrate (Clomid) are used to stimulate ovulation.
- **Progestins** such as progesterone gel (Prochieve) improve fertility by supplementing progesterone and improving the cervical mucus environment.

There's nothing wrong with a little improvement. Men with hypogonadism may need drugs such as HCG to improve sperm quality.

A helping hand for men

For men with hypogonadism secondary to pituitary or hypothalamic failure, treatment to improve sperm quality may include administering **human menopausal gonadotropins (hMGs), human** chorionic gonadotropin (HCG), or **pulsatile gonadotropin-releasing hormone (Gn-RH)**.

Preventive medicine

Contraceptives are hormonal drugs consisting of synthetic estrogen and progesterone that are used to prevent conception or impregnation. The estrogen suppresses production of follicle-stimulating hormone and luteinizing hormone, which then acts to suppress ovulation. Contraceptives may be administered orally or I.M. or through transdermal patches, subdermal implants, and vaginal rings.

Spermicides are inserted into the vagina to kill the sperm before they enter the cervix. Spermicides are available as gels, creams, films, and suppositories.

Maternal health drugs

Several drugs may be used to treat complications of pregnancy and labor. Drugs that are known to cause fetal anomalies are called teratogens. These drugs should be avoided unless the benefits of the drug outweigh the risks. (See *Tackling* teratogen.)

Here are some common maternal health drugs:
- **Folic acid** is a B vitamin that is essential for RBC formation and DNA synthesis. Adequate intake of folic acid during pregnancy has been shown to reduce the incidence of fetal neural tube defects.
- **Tocolytic drugs** are used to manage labor or prevent preterm labor by decreasing uterine muscle contractions.
- **Uterotropic drugs** improve uterine contractions by stimulating the smooth muscle of the uterus.

Anti-infective drugs

Anti-infective drugs are chosen after the infective organism is identified. Anti-infective agents are effective only against specific organisms. Anti-infective drugs include:
- **antibacterial drugs**—used mainly to treat systemic bacterial infections
- **antiviral drugs**—used to prevent or treat viral infections
- **antitubercular drugs**—used to treat tuberculosis
- **antimycotic drugs**—used to treat fungal infections.

Beyond the dictionary

Tackling *teratogen*

A **teratogen** is anything (such as a drug, an infection, or an environmental factor) that interferes with normal fetal growth, causing abnormal prenatal development. It comes from the Greek words *teras*, which means *monster*, and *genes*, which means *born* or *producing*.

Immune system drugs

Immune and inflammatory responses protect the body from invasive foreign substances. These responses can be modified by certain classes of drugs:

- **Antihistamines** block the effects of histamine on target tissues.
- **Corticosteroids** suppress immune responses and reduce inflammation.
- **Noncorticosteroid immunosuppressants** prevent rejection from transplanted organs and can be used to treat autoimmune disease.
- **Uricosurics** prevent or control the frequency of gouty arthritis attacks.

Sedatives can be used to induce sleep.

Psychiatric drugs

Various drugs are used to treat sleep and other psychogenic disorders, such as anxiety, depression, and psychotic disorders.

You're getting sleepy

Sedatives reduce anxiety or excitement. Some degree of drowsiness commonly accompanies sedative use. When given in large doses, sedatives are considered **hypnotics,** which induce a state that resembles natural sleep. The three main classes of synthetic drugs used as sedatives and hypnotics are:

1. benzodiazepines, which work on receptors in the reticular activating system of the brain (the portion associated with wakefulness and attention)
2. barbiturates, which depress the sensory cortex of the brain, decrease motor activity, alter cerebral function, and produce drowsiness, sedation, and hypnosis
3. **nonbenzodiazepine-nonbarbiturate drugs,** which act as hypnotics for short-term treatment of simple insomnia.

Mood modifiers

Antidepressants and antimanic drugs are used to treat affective disorders—such as mood disturbances—that are typically characterized by intense episodes of depression and elation.

Three drug classes are commonly used to treat affective disorders:

- **Monoamine oxidase inhibitors (MAOIs)** relieve the symptoms of depression by inhibiting the enzyme monoamine oxidase.

- **Tricyclic antidepressants (TCAs)** effectively treat episodes of major depression by increasing the amount of chemicals in the brain.
- **Selective serotonin reuptake inhibitors (SSRIs)** are used to treat major depressive episodes by inhibiting the neuronal reuptake of the neurotransmitter serotonin.

Anxiety critic

Anxiolytics, also called **antianxiety drugs,** are used primarily to treat anxiety disorders. Two of the main types are benzodiazepines and barbiturates.

Symptoms under wrap

Antipsychotic drugs control psychotic symptoms—such as delusions, hallucinations, and thought disorders—that sometimes occur with schizophrenia, mania, and other psychoses.

Benzodiazepines and barbiturates are the two main types of anxiolytics.

Endocrine system drugs

Together with the CNS, the endocrine system regulates and integrates the body's metabolic activities and maintains homeostasis.

Too little? Too much?

Patients who produce too little thyroid hormone (as in hypothyroidism) may need supplements such as levothyroxine. Patients who produce too much thyroid hormone (as in hyperthyroidism) may be given drugs such as propylthiouracil (PTU) to suppress thyroid function.

Sugar up... sugar down

Insulin, a pancreatic hormone, and **oral antidiabetic drugs** are classified as **hypoglycemic drugs** because they lower blood glucose levels. **Glucagon,** another pancreatic hormone, is classified as a **hyperglycemic drug** because it raises blood glucose levels.

Vocabulary builders

At a crossroads

Don't get caught up in the conundrum of medication administration terms. Complete this puzzle to prove that you've received the correct dose of clinical pharmacology terminology.

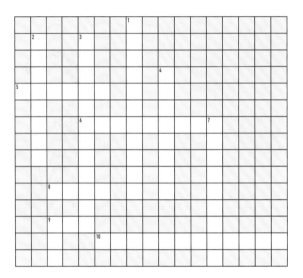

Across

5. A drug that's compressed to form a shape
6. Decreased response to a drug over time
8. Type of drug that's administered directly into the ear
9. Type of order that allows drugs to be given as needed
10. Study of drugs

Down

1. Drug that promotes the action of acetylcholine
2. Drug administered via the respiratory route
3. Drug interaction in which one drug enhances the effect of the other drug
4. Increase or decrease of drug dosage according to the patient's response
7. Process by which a drug is eliminated by the body
9. Type of inhibitor that increases the force of the heart's contractions

Match game

For some types of drug administration, the location of administration is self-explanatory; for example, **intrathecal administration** refers to drug administration into the intrathecal space of the spinal canal. However, other terms used to describe administration routes aren't so apparent. Match the drug administration route below with its correct definition.

Clues

1. Intra-articular _____
2. Dermal _____
3. Buccal _____
4. Ophthalmic _____
5. Intradermal _____
6. Otic _____
7. Sublingual _____
8. Intravenous _____

Choices

A. Into the skin
B. Under the tongue
C. Into a vein
D. In the ear
E. Between the cheek and gum
F. Into a joint
H. Onto the skin
I. Into the eye

Finish line

The Greek root **_pharmako_** indicates that a word has to do with drugs. Fill in the blanks below to complete the drug-related terms.

1. **Pharmaco** _____ is the use of drugs to prevent or treat diseases.

2. **Pharmaco** _____ is the study of the origin, nature, chemistry, effects, and uses of drugs.

3. **Pharmaco** _____ is the study of the biochemical and physical effects of drugs and the mechanisms of drug actions in living organisms.

4. **Pharmaco** _____ is how drugs are absorbed, distributed, metabolized, and excreted in a living organism.

Answers

At a crossroads

						¹C							
	²I		³P		H								
	N		O		O	⁴T							
	H		T		L	I							
⁵T	A	B	L	E	T	I	T						
	L		N		N	R							
	A		⁶T	O	L	E	R	A	N	C	⁷E		
	N		I		R	T				X			
	T		A		G	I				C			
			T		I	O				R			
	⁸O	T	I	C	C	N				E			
			O							T			
	⁹P	R	N							I			
	D			¹⁰P	H	A	R	M	A	C	O	L	O	G	Y
	E									N			

Match game

Answers: 1. F; 2. H; 3. E; 4. I; 5. A; 6. D; 7. B; 8. C

Finish line

Answers: 1. Therapeutics; 2. Logy; 3. Dynamics; 4. Kinetics

Suggested references

ATI Nursing Education. (2016). Medication routes: Accepted practice. Retrieved from http://www.atitesting.com/ati_next_gen/skillsmodules/content/medication-administration-1/equipment/routes.html

Duell, D. J., Martin, B. C., & Smith, S. F. (2004). *Clinical nursing skills: Basic to advanced skills* (6th ed., p. 517). Upper Saddle River, NJ: Pearson Education, Inc.

Perry, A. G., & Potter, P. A. (2006). *Clinical nursing skills and techniques* (6th ed., p. 622). St. Louis, MO: Elsevier Mosby.

The Joint Commission. (2007). Patient safety goal: Improve the effectiveness of communication among caregivers. Retrieved from https://www.jointcommission.org/assets/1/18/improving_health_literacy.pdf

Chapter 17

Mental health

Just the facts

In this chapter, you'll learn:

◆ terminology related to the definition and assessment of mental health disorders

◆ terminology needed for examination of patients with mental health disorders

◆ tests that help diagnose mental health disorders

◆ terminology related to the types of mental health disorders

◆ mental health disorders and their treatments.

Mental health overview

From teenage depression and suicide to increased substance abuse and elderly depression, the risk of mental disorders is on the rise. This chapter introduces terms associated with the diagnosis and treatment of mental health disorders. (See *Pronouncing key mental health terms*.)

The emphasis in mental health diagnoses is on observable data rather than subjective and theoretical impressions.

DSM–5. Say what?

The American Psychiatric Association's *Diagnostic and Statistical Manual of Mental Disorders*, **Fifth Edition**, provides a unified system of classifying mental disorders. Diagnostic criteria, followed by a detailed description, are provided for each mental disorder. This approach makes psychiatric diagnoses more reliable and has led to improvements in treating and managing mental health disorders.

Defining mental disorders

The *DSM-5* defines a mental disorder as "a syndrome characterized by clinically significant disturbance in an individual's cognition, emotion regulation, or behavior that reflects a dysfunction in the psychological, biological, or developmental processes underlying mental functioning" (APA, 2015).

355

Pronouncing key mental health terms

Below is a list of key terms related to mental health, along with the correct way to pronounce them.

Cyclothymia	SIGH-KLOH-THIGH-MEE-UH
Echolalia	EK-OH-LAY-LEE-UH
Narcissism	NAR-SIH-SISM
Schizoid	SKIT-SOYD
Tardive dyskinesia	TAR-DIV DIS-KIH-NEE-ZHUH
Tourette's syndrome	TOO-RET SIN-DROHM
Wernicke-Korsakoff syndrome	VER-NIH-KUH KOR-SEH-KOFF SIN-DROHM

And now, for the diagnosis

The DSM-5 guides clinicians to identify disorders through identification of the most prominent symptoms. Research has shown that many symptoms can relate to more than one disorder, or change a diagnosis over time. The clear descriptors of each disorder allows for more accurate diagnosis because of the explicit diagnostic criteria.

Psychological examination terms

Here are some important terms to understand when examining a patient with mental health issues.

Assessment terms

- **Attention level** refers to the ability to concentrate on a task for an appropriate length of time.
- **Behavior** includes the patient's demeanor and overall attitude, mannerisms (such as nail biting, fidgeting, or pacing), tics or tremors, and how the patient responds to the interviewer (for example, cooperative, friendly, hostile, or indifferent).
- **Chief complaint** is the main reason the patient has sought help and includes when symptoms began, whether symptoms are abrupt or gradual, the severity of symptoms, how long symptoms last, and how symptoms affect the patient's level of functioning.

- **Cultural and religious beliefs** include the patient's cultural background and values and how these factors affect the patient's response to illness and adaptation to hospital care. Keep in mind that certain questions or behaviors considered inappropriate in one culture may be acceptable in another.
- **Current symptoms** are the subjective and objective symptoms that are currently affecting the patient, including their severity and persistence and whether they occurred abruptly or gradually.
- **Demographic data** include the patient's age, sex, ethnic origin, primary language, birthplace, religion, and marital status.
- **General appearance of the patient** helps determine the patient's emotional and mental status. When evaluating a patient's appearance, include information about dress, grooming, posture, gait, and facial expression.
- **Medication history** includes information about what drugs (including over-the-counter and herbal supplements) the patient has taken in the past and what he or she is currently taking. This information is important to collect because certain drugs can cause symptoms of mental illness. If the patient is taking an antipsychotic, antidepressant, anxiolytic, or antimanic drug, include information about whether symptoms have improved or adverse reactions have occurred.
- **Mood** refers to the internal emotional state and physical expressions of an individual's current feelings (for example, depression, crying, sweating, breathing heavily, or trembling).
- **Nonverbal communication** (body language) consists of eye contact, posture, facial expression, gestures, clothing, affect, and silence (which can convey a powerful message). In addition to observing the patient's nonverbal communication during the assessment process, you'll need to be aware of your own.
- **Patient history** helps establish a baseline for future assessments. It includes the chief complaint, current symptoms, psychiatric history, demographic and socioeconomic data, cultural and religious beliefs, medication history, and history of physical illnesses that may cause disorientation, distorted thought processes, depression, or other symptoms of mental illness.
- **Psychiatric assessment** is the process of identifying a patient's psychosocial problems, strengths, and concerns.
- **Psychiatric history** includes information about past psychiatric disturbances, such as episodes of delusions, hallucinations, violence, attempted suicide, drug or alcohol abuse, or depression, and previous psychiatric treatment.
- **Socioeconomic data** refer to the patient's economic and personal situation and how it impacts current psychological status. Information may include educational level, housing conditions, income, and current employment status.

Gathering demographic, socioeconomic, and cultural data is an important part of diagnosing mental health problems.

During a mental health assessment, be aware of your nonverbal communication as well as the patient's.

- **Therapeutic relationship** is a relationship between the patient and the health care provider that's based on trust. The health care provider's words and actions must communicate to the patient that his or her thoughts and behaviors are important.
- **Thought processes and cognitive function** are assessed based on orientation to time, place, and person and the presence of confusion or disorientation. Speech characteristics that may indicate altered thought processes include minimal monosyllabic responses, irrelevant or illogical replies to questions, convoluted or excessively detailed speech, repetitive speech patterns, a flight of ideas, and sudden silence without an obvious reason.

Acting out involves repeating certain actions to ward off anxiety without weighing the possible consequences of those actions.

Signs and symptoms

- **Acting out** involves repeating certain actions to ward off anxiety without weighing the possible consequences of those actions.
- **Compensation** (also called **substitution**) refers to an individual's attempt to make up for feelings of inadequacy or frustration in one area by excelling or overindulging in another area.
- **Compulsion** is a ritualistic, repetitive, and involuntary defensive behavior that's performed to reduce anxiety, which increases the likelihood that the behavior will recur.
- **Coping mechanisms** (also called **defense mechanisms**) are behaviors that operate on an unconscious level to protect the ego.
- **Delusions** are false ideas or beliefs accepted as real by the patient. Delusions of grandeur, persecution, and reference are common in schizophrenia.
- **Denial** is a way of protecting oneself from unpleasant aspects of life by refusing to perceive, acknowledge, or deal with them.
- **Displacement** refers to misdirecting pent-up feelings toward something or someone that's less threatening than what triggered the response.
- **Fantasy** is the creation of unrealistic or improbable images to escape from daily pressures and responsibilities.
- **Hallucinations** are false sensory perceptions with no basis in reality. Usually visual or auditory, hallucinations also may be olfactory or tactile.
- **Identification** involves unconsciously adopting the personality characteristics, attitudes, values, and behavior of someone else as a way to alleviate anxiety
- **Intellectualization** (also called **isolation**) refers to an individual removing self from emotional events. The patient may discuss painful events in a detached, impersonal way because describing true feelings is too difficult.

Excessive hand washing in a ritualistic, involuntary manner is an example of a compulsion.

- **Introjection** refers to an individual adopting someone else's values and standards without exploring whether they're appropriate for him or her.
- **Obsession** is an intrusive or inappropriate recurrent idea, thought, image, or impulse that causes marked anxiety or distress.
- **Projection** is the displacement of negative feelings onto another person.
- **Rationalization** is substituting acceptable reasons for the real or actual reasons that are motivating the patient's behavior
- **Reaction formation** refers to the display of behavior that's opposite of the individual's true feelings.
- **Regression** occurs when an individual returns to an earlier developmental stage.
- **Repression** refers to unconsciously blocking out painful or unacceptable thoughts and feelings, leaving the feelings to operate in the subconscious.
- **Self-destructive behavior** is death-seeking behavior, including suicidal tendencies.
- **Sublimation** is transforming unacceptable needs into acceptable ambitions and actions. For example, a person with highly aggressive tendencies may study and excel in the martial arts.
- **Undoing** refers to an individual trying to undo the harm the individual feels he or she has done to others.
- **Withdrawal** refers to growing emotionally uninvolved by retreating and becoming passive.

> *Regression* occurs when a patient returns to an earlier developmental stage.

Diagnostic tests

Various laboratory tests and psychological and mental status tests provide information about the patient's mental status and possible physical causes of signs and symptoms.

> *Toxicologic studies* are blood and urine tests that can detect the presence of many drugs.

Laboratory tests

- **Toxicologic studies** are blood and urine tests that can detect the presence of many drugs and quantify the blood levels of these drugs. Patients undergoing treatment with psychotherapeutic drugs may need routine toxicology screening to ensure that they aren't receiving a toxic dose.

Psychological and mental status tests

Here are some examples of tests that evaluate the patient's mood, personality, and mental status:

- **Beck Depression Inventory** helps diagnose depression and determine its severity. This test may provide objective evidence of the need for treatment. It's also used to monitor the patient's response during treatment.
- **Cognitive Assessment Scale** measures orientation, general knowledge, mental ability, and psychomotor function.
- **Cognitive Capacity Screening Examination** measures orientation, memory, calculation, and language.
- **Eating Attitudes Test** detects patterns that suggest an eating disorder.
- **Edinburg Postnatal Depression Scale (EPDS)** screens for signs of postnatal depression and can be used through the postnatal year.
- **Functional Dementia Scale** measures orientation, affect, and the ability to perform activities of daily living.
- **Global Deterioration Scale** assesses and stages primary degenerative dementia based on orientation, memory, and neurologic function.
- **Minnesota Multiphasic Personality Inventory** helps assess personality traits and ego function in adolescents and adults. Test results provide information on coping strategies, defenses, strengths, gender identification, and self-esteem. The test pattern may strongly suggest a diagnostic category, point to a suicide risk, or indicate the potential for violence.
- **Mini-Mental Status Examination** measures orientation, registration (the ability of a patient to name three objects previously mentioned by the examiner), recall, calculation, language, and graphomotor (the movements required in writing) function.

The **Minnesota Multiphasic Personality Inventory** helps assess personality traits and ego function in adolescents and adults.

Disorders

This section provides terminology related to mental health disorders, which can affect any age group.

Disorders of infancy, childhood, and adolescence

Here are some examples of disorders of infancy, childhood, and adolescence:

- **Anorexia nervosa** is self-imposed starvation resulting from a distorted body image and an intense and irrational fear of gaining weight, even when obviously emaciated. It mainly affects adolescents.

- **Attention deficit hyperactivity disorder** is a disorder in which the child has difficulty focusing the attention, engaging in quiet passive activities, or both. This condition is usually diagnosed after age 4 or 5.
- **Autistic disorder** is a severe, pervasive developmental disorder marked by unresponsiveness to social contact, gross deficits in cognitive and language development, ritualistic and compulsive behaviors, restricted capacity for developmentally appropriate activities and interests, and bizarre responses to the environment. Autistic disorder usually becomes apparent before age 3.
- **Bulimia nervosa** is a disorder marked by eating binges followed by feelings of guilt, humiliation, and self-deprecation. These feelings precipitate self-induced vomiting, use of laxatives or diuretics, or strict dieting or fasting to overcome the effects of the binges. As with anorexia nervosa, this condition usually affects adolescents.
- **Conduct disorder** is characterized by aggressive behavior. A child with this disorder fights, bullies, intimidates, and assaults others physically or sexually and is truant from school at an early age.
- **Down syndrome** (also known as **mongolism** and **trisomy 21 syndrome**) is a disorder attributed to a chromosomal aberration and characteristically produces mental retardation, abnormal facial features, and other distinctive physical abnormalities.
- **Mental retardation**, as defined by the American Association on Mental Retardation, is "significantly subaverage general intellectual function existing concurrently with deficits in adaptive behavior manifesting itself during the developmental period" (before age 18). This disorder is transmitted genetically.
- **Tic disorders** are a group of three disorders that include Tourette's syndrome, chronic motor or vocal tic disorder, and transient tic disorder. They involve involuntary, spasmodic, recurrent, and purposeless motor movements or vocalizations. These disorders tend to appear before age 21.

Anorexia nervosa is self-imposed starvation resulting from a distorted body image and an intense and irrational fear of gaining weight.

Substance-related disorders

Substance-related disorders include alcoholism and drug abuse and dependence, which affect the central nervous system, causing physical and mental harm.

- **Alcoholism** is a chronic disorder most commonly described as the uncontrolled intake of alcoholic beverages that interferes with physical and mental health, social and familial relationships, and occupational responsibilities.
- **Drug abuse** is defined by the National Institute on Drug Abuse as the use of a legal or an illegal drug that causes physical, mental, emotional, or social harm.

Psychotic disorders

Characterized by disordered thinking, psychotic disorders include delusional disorders and schizophrenia.

- According to the *DSM-5*, **delusional disorders** are characterized by false beliefs despite contradictory information. Delusional disorders are known to involve erotomanic, grandiose, jealous, or somatic themes as well as persecutory delusions. For example, an individual may believe a sexual partner is being unfaithful without any factual information to support the belief.
- **Schizophrenia** is characterized by disturbances in thought content and form, perception, affect, language, social activity, sense of self, volition, interpersonal relationships, and psychomotor behavior.

Mood disorders

A mood disorder involves disturbances in the regulation of a person's mood, behavior, and affect. With these disorders, a person's mood becomes so intense and persistent that it interferes with social and psychological function.

- **Bipolar disorder** is an affective disorder marked by severe pathologic mood swings from hyperactivity and euphoria to sadness and depression. Some patients suffer from acute attacks of mania only.
- **Cyclothymia** is a variant of bipolar disorder in which numerous episodes of hypomania and depressive symptoms are too mild to meet the criteria for major depression or bipolar illness. (See *How do I say* cyclothymia?)
- **Major depression** is defined as a depressed mood on a daily basis for 2 weeks or longer. It's a syndrome of persistent sad, dysphoric mood accompanied by disturbances in sleep and appetite, lethargy, and an inability to experience pleasure (anhedonia).

Anxiety disorders

Anxiety disorders are characterized by apprehension, feelings of tension, and avoidant behavior. Here's a list of major anxiety disorders:

- **Generalized anxiety disorder** is characterized by a feeling of apprehension caused by a threat to a person or his or her values.
- **Obsessive-compulsive disorder** is characterized by obsessive thoughts and compulsive behaviors that represent recurring efforts to control overwhelming anxiety, guilt, or unacceptable impulses that persistently enter the consciousness.

Pump up your pronunciation

How do I say *cyclothymia?*

Cyclothymia—a mild form of bipolar disorder—is pronounced SIGH-KLOH-THIGH-MEE-UH. It's a combination of two Greek words, ***kyklos***, meaning *circle* or *recurring*, and ***thymos***, meaning *mind*. A patient with this disorder alternates between episodes of hypomania and depression.

Major depression is defined as a depressed mood on a daily basis for 2 weeks or longer.

- **Panic disorder** is characterized by recurrent and unpredictable episodes of intense apprehension, terror, and impending doom. Panic disorder involves anxiety in its most severe form.
- A **phobia** is a persistent and irrational fear of a specific object, activity, or situation that results in anxiety. A phobia causes a compelling desire to avoid the perceived hazard. Panic attacks can be triggered by the phobia. Examples of phobias include:
  - **agoraphobia** (fear of leaving familiar settings or of open space)
  - **social phobia** (fear of embarrassing oneself in public)
  - **pharmacophobia** (fear of drugs)
  - **triskaidekaphobia** *(fear of the number 13). (See Taking apart triskaidekaphobia.)*
- **Posttraumatic stress disorder** refers to a persistent psychological disturbance that occurs following a traumatic event.

Beyond the dictionary

Taking apart triskaidekaphobia

Triskaidekaphobia is an illogical or irrational fear of the number thirteen. Its roots are from the Greek words ***treis***, meaning *three*; ***deka***, meaning *ten*; and ***phobos***, meaning *fear* or *having an aversion to*.

Somatoform disorders

The patient with a **somatoform disorder** complains of physical signs and symptoms and typically travels from doctor to doctor in search of treatment. Physical examinations and laboratory tests fail to uncover an organic basis for the patient's signs and symptoms, and the somatic symptoms aren't due to the effects of alcohol or recreational or prescription drugs. Here's a list of major somatoform disorders:

- **Body dysmorphic disorder** involves a preoccupation with an imagined (or, if present, slight) defect in physical appearance.
- **Conversion disorder** (previously called **hysterical neurosis, conversion type**) allows a patient to resolve a psychological conflict through the loss of a specific physical function, for example, through paralysis, blindness, or the inability to swallow.
- **Hypochondriasis** (previously referred to as **hypochondriacal neurosis**) is an unrealistic misinterpretation of the severity and significance of physical signs or sensations. This condition leads to a preoccupation with having a serious disease. This fear persists despite medical reassurance to the contrary. (See *Feeling ill?*)
- **Pain disorder** is a persistent complaint of pain. The pain is severe enough to warrant clinical attention, and significantly impairs social, occupational, or other important areas of functioning.
- In **somatization disorder**, which primarily affects females, the patient has multiple unintentional physical complaints from different systems. The patient's complaints are typically dramatic but inconsistent. Mood changes and anxiety are common and may be the result of drug interactions.

Beyond the dictionary

Feeling ill?

Hypochondriasis is a chronic and abnormal anxiety about imaginary symptoms and ailments. The ancients thought that this condition was caused by the disturbed function of the *hypochondria*, another name for the upper abdominal regions.

Dissociative disorders

Dissociation refers to an unconscious defense mechanism that keeps troubling thoughts out of a person's awareness. The patient with a **dissociative disorder** experiences temporary changes in consciousness, identity, and motor function.

- **Depersonalization disorder** is characterized by persistent or recurrent episodes of detachment. During these episodes, self-awareness is temporarily altered or lost; the patient typically perceives this alteration in consciousness as a barrier between self and the outside world.
- **Dissociative amnesia** is a sudden inability to recall important personal information that can't be explained by ordinary forgetfulness.
- **Dissociative identity disorder** is a complex disturbance of identity and memory characterized by the existence of two or more distinct, fully integrated personalities in the same person.

The patient with **dissociative disorder** experiences temporary changes in consciousness, identity, and motor function.

Personality disorders

The patient with a **personality disorder** possesses chronic, inflexible, and maladaptive patterns of behavior that cause social discomfort and impair social and occupational functioning. Here's a list of major personality disorders:

- **Histrionic disorder** applies to an individual who's excessively emotional and constantly seeking attention.
- **Schizoid disorder** is characterized by emotional detachment from other people. The patient is emotionally cold and distant and has a limited range of emotional expressions.
- **Antisocial disorder** is marked by the disregard for social norms. Patients commonly display deceitful behavior and don't show remorse or take responsibility for their actions.

Sexual disorders

These disorders affect a person's sexual ability or response, gender identity, or sexual behavior:

- **Arousal disorder** is the inability to experience sexual pleasure. It's one of the most severe forms of female sexual dysfunction.
- **Exhibitionism** is marked by sexual fantasies, urges, or behaviors involving surprise exposure of the genitals to strangers.
- **Fetishism** is characterized by sexual fantasies, urges, or behaviors that involve the use of a fetish—a nonhuman object or a nonsexual part of the body—to produce or enhance sexual arousal.

- **Frotteurism** is sexual arousal from touching or rubbing against a nonconsenting person.
- **Gender identity disorder** produces persistent feelings of gender discomfort and dissatisfaction.
- **Orgasmic disorder**, the most common type of female sexual dysfunction, is an inability to achieve orgasm. The patient may desire sexual activity and become aroused but feels inhibited as she approaches orgasm.
- **Paraphilias** are complex psychosexual disorders and are characterized by a dependence on unusual behaviors or fantasies to achieve sexual excitement. The imagery or acts may involve the use of inanimate objects (especially clothing), repetitive sexual activity that includes suffering or humiliation, or sexual behavior with nonconsenting partners.
- **Pedophilia** is marked by sexual fantasies, urges, or activity involving a child, usually age 13 or younger.
- **Sexual masochism** is sexual gratification from being physically or sexually abused.
- **Sexual sadism** is achieving sexual gratification by inflicting pain, cruelty, or emotional abuse on others.
- **Transvestic fetishism** involves a heterosexual male dressing in female clothes to produce or enhance sexual arousal.
- **Voyeurism** involves deriving sexual pleasure from looking at sexual objects or sexually arousing situations such as an unsuspecting couple engaged in sex.

> *Other possible sexual disorders include* **dyspareunia**, *or painful intercourse, and* **vaginismus**, *the involuntary spastic constriction of the lower vaginal muscles. Both can lead to a woman's lack of interest in intercourse.*

Treatments

Here's a list of common psychiatric treatments:
- **Assertiveness training** uses positive reinforcement, **shaping** (modifying existing behavior into desired behavior), and **modeling** (demonstrating desired behavior) to reduce anxiety. It teaches the patient ways to express feeling, ideas, and wishes without feeling guilty or demeaning others.
- **Aversion therapy** uses a painful stimulus to create an aversion to the obsession underlying the patient's undesirable behavior.
- **Behavior therapy** assumes that problematic behaviors are learned and, through special training, these behaviors can be unlearned and replaced by acceptable behaviors. Behavior therapy may be used with an individual or with a group and may include treatments such as assertiveness training, aversion therapy, desensitization, flooding, positive conditions, response prevention, thought stopping, thought switching, and token economy.

> **Assertiveness training** *uses positive reinforcement, shaping, and modeling to reduce anxiety.*

- According to cognitive theory, depression stems from low self-esteem and belief that the future is hopeless. **Cognitive therapy** helps identify and change the patient's negative generalizations and expectations and thereby reduces depression, distress, and other emotional problems.
- **Crisis intervention** seeks to help the patient develop adequate coping skills to resolve an immediate problem. Therapy focuses on helping the patients resume their precrisis functional level. Therapy may include family members.
- **Desensitization** slowly exposes the patient to something he or she fears.
- **Detoxification** programs offer a relatively safe alternative to self-withdrawal after prolonged dependence on alcohol or drugs. They provide symptomatic treatment as well as counseling or psychotherapy on an individual, group, or family basis.
- **Drug therapy** includes the use of antidepressants, antianxiety agents, and antipsychotics. This therapy requires careful monitoring and possible dosage changes.
- **Electroconvulsive therapy (ECT)** is used for major depression. After the patient is anesthetized, a tiny electric current is sent to the brain for 1 second through electrodes placed above the temples. The current produces a seizure, which lasts 30 seconds to 1 minute. The prevailing theory is that ECT temporarily alters some of the brain's electrochemical processes.
- **Family therapy** aims to alter relationships within a family and change the problematic behavior of one or more of its members.
- **Flooding** (also called **implosion therapy**) involves direct exposure to an anxiety-producing situation. It also uses the idea that confrontation helps the patient overcome fear.
- **Group therapy**, guided by a psychotherapist, involves a group of people (ideally 4 to 10) who are experiencing similar emotional problems meeting to discuss their concerns.
- **Individual therapy** involves a series of therapy sessions that promote personality growth and development. It may be short or long term.
- **Milieu therapy** uses the patient's environment as a tool for treating mental and emotional disorders. The patient's surroundings become a therapeutic community, and the patient shares responsibility for establishing group rules and policies.
- **Positive conditioning** attempts to gradually instill a positive or neutral attitude toward a phobia. A pleasurable stimulus is introduced along with the phobic stimulus.
- **Psychotherapy** involves a range of approaches—from in-depth psychoanalysis to 1-day crisis counseling—that aims to change a

Drugs used to treat mental health disorders include antidepressants, antianxiety agents, and antipsychotics.

patient's attitudes, feeling, or behavior. Types of psychotherapy include individual therapy, group therapy, cognitive therapy, family therapy, and crisis intervention.

- **Response prevention** seeks to prevent compulsive behavior through distraction, persuasion, or redirection of activity.
- **Thought stopping** helps break the habit of fear-inducing anticipatory thoughts by focusing attention on calmness and muscle relaxation.
- **Thought switching** teaches the patient to replace fear-inducing self-instructions with competent self-instructions.
- **In token economy**, the therapist rewards acceptable behavior by giving out tokens, which the patient uses to "buy" a privilege or object.

Vocabulary builders

At a crossroads

Completing this crossword puzzle will help you wrap your head around mental health terms.

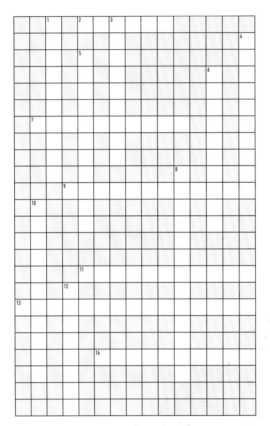

Across

2. A persistent and irrational fear of a specific object, activity, or situation
7. An involuntary spastic constriction of the lower vaginal muscles
9. An unconscious defense mechanism that keeps troubling thoughts out of an individual's awareness
11. A dependence on unusual behaviors or fantasies to achieve sexual excitement
13. The process of slowly exposing the patient to something he or she fears
14. Uncontrolled intake of alcohol

Down

1. Growing emotionally uninvolved by pulling back and being passive
3. An intense preoccupation that interferes with daily living
4. Returning to an earlier developmental stage
5. Transforming unacceptable needs into acceptable ambitions and actions
6. Displacement of negative feelings onto another person
8. A false sensory perception with no basis in reality
10. Pain associated with intercourse
12. A false idea or belief that's accepted as real

Match game

Match each description of a disorder to its name.

Clues

Choices

1. Characterized by disturbances in thought content and form, perception, affect, language, social activity, sense of self, volition, interpersonal relationships, and psychomotor behavior _____

A. Anorexia nervosa

2. An uncontrolled intake of alcoholic beverages that interferes with physical and mental health, social and familial relationships, and occupational responsibilities _____

B. Conduct disorder

3. Self-imposed starvation resulting from a distorted body image and an intense and irrational fear of gaining weight _____

C. Tic disorders

4. Involuntary, spasmodic, recurrent, and purposeless motor movements or vocalizations _____

D. Schizophrenia

5. Characteristically produces mental retardation, abnormal facial features, and other distinctive physical abnormalities _____

E. Panic disorder

6. Characterized by recurrent and unpredictable episodes of intense apprehension, terror, and impending doom _____

F. Conversion disorder

7. Characterized by aggressive behavior _____

G. Alcoholism

8. Allows a patient to resolve a psychological conflict through the loss of a specific physical function _____

H. Down's syndrome

Finish line

Fill in the blanks below with the appropriate word(s).

1. _____ includes emotional and physical expressions of current feelings, such as depression, crying, sweating, breathing heavily, or trembling.

2. Repeating certain actions to ward off anxiety without weighing the possible consequences of those actions is called _____ _____.

3. An _____ is an intense preoccupation that interferes with daily living.

4. Transforming unacceptable needs into acceptable ambitions and actions is called _____.

5. _____ is returning to an earlier developmental stage.

Done! Done! Done! I'm really in the mood to celebrate!

Answers

At a crossroads

W	P	H	O	B	I	A								
I			B								R			
T	S		S								E			
H	U		E							P	G			
D	B		S							R	R			
R	L		S							O	E			
V	A	G	I	N	I	S	M	U	S	J	S			
W	M		O							E	S			
A	A		N							C	I			
L	T							H		T	O			
	D	I	S	S	O	C	I	A	T	I	O	N		
D			O					L		O				
Y			N					L		N				
S								U						
P								C						
A		P	A	R	A	P	H	I	L	I	A	S		
R	D									N				
D	E	S	E	N	S	I	T	I	Z	A	T	I	O	N
U	L									T				
N	U									I				
I	S		A	L	C	O	H	O	L	I	S	M		
A	I									N				
	O													
	N													

Match game

Answers: 1. D; 2. G; 3. A; 4. C; 5. H; 6. E; 7. B; 8. F

Finish line

Answers: 1. Mood; 2. Acting out; 3. Obsession; 4. Sublimation; 5. Regression

---

Suggested reference

American Psychiatric Association. (2013) Diagnostic and statistical manual of mental disorders (DSM V). Retrieved from http://dx.doi.org/10.1176/appi. books.9780890425596

Index

Note: Page numbers followed by "i" indicate figures and those followed by "t" indicate tables.

Note: Page numbers followed by "i" indicate figures and those followed by "t" indicate tables.

Note: Page numbers followed by "i" indicate figures and those followed by "t" indicate tables.

Note: Page numbers followed by "i" indicate figures and those followed by "t" indicate tables.

Note: Page numbers followed by "i" indicate figures and those followed by "t" indicate tables.

Note: Page numbers followed by "i" indicate figures and those followed by "t" indicate tables.

Note: Page numbers followed by "i" indicate figures and those followed by "t" indicate tables.

Note: Page numbers followed by "i" indicate figures and those followed by "t" indicate tables.

Note: Page numbers followed by "i" indicate figures and those followed by "t" indicate tables.

Note: Page numbers followed by "i" indicate figures and those followed by "t" indicate tables.

Note: Page numbers followed by "i" indicate figures and those followed by "t" indicate tables.

Note: Page numbers followed by "i" indicate figures and those followed by "t" indicate tables.

Note: Page numbers followed by "i" indicate figures and those followed by "t" indicate tables.

Note: Page numbers followed by "i" indicate figures and those followed by "t" indicate tables.

Note: Page numbers followed by "i" indicate figures and those followed by "t" indicate tables.

Note: Page numbers followed by "i" indicate figures and those followed by "t" indicate tables.

Note: Page numbers followed by "i" indicate figures and those followed by "t" indicate tables.